The Little, Brown Handbook

Instructor's Annotated Edition

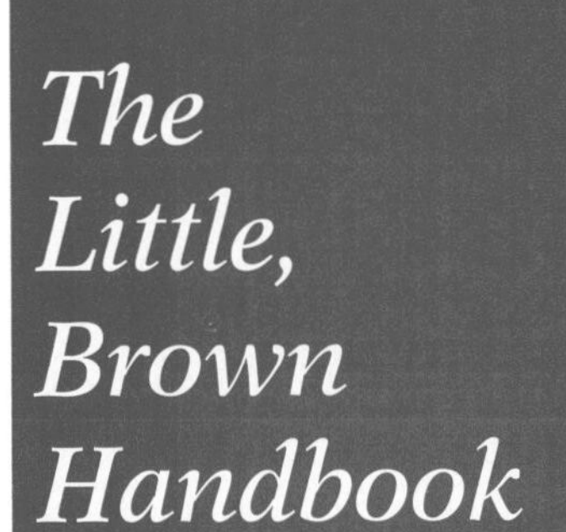

The Little, Brown Handbook

Seventh Edition

Instructor's Annotated Edition

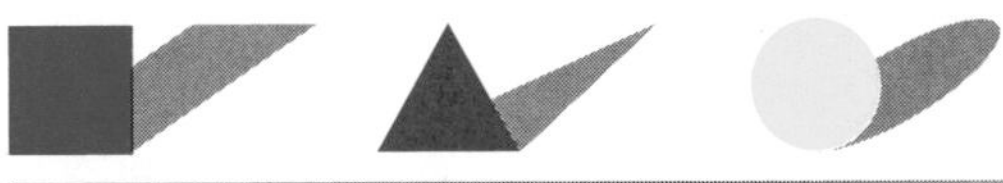

H. Ramsey Fowler *University of Memphis*
Jane E. Aaron *New York University*
Rebecca Brittenham *Rutgers University*

LONGMAN

An imprint of Addison Wesley Longman, Inc.

New York • Reading, Massachusetts • Menlo Park, California • Harlow, England
Don Mills, Ontario • Sydney • Mexico City • Madrid • Amsterdam

Senior Editor: Patricia Rossi
Development Editor: Thomas Maeglin
Supplements Editor: Donna Campion
Project Editorial Manager: Robert Ginsberg
Design Manager: John Callahan
Cover Designer: Kay Petronio
Production Manager: Valerie A. Sawyer
Desktop Administrator: Jim Sullivan
Manufacturing Manager: Hilda Koparanian
Electronic Page Makeup: Dorothy Bungert/*EriBen Graphics,* Carole Desnoes, and York Production Services
Printer and Binder: RR Donnelley & Sons Company
Cover Printer: The Lehigh Press, Inc.

The authors and publisher are grateful to the many students who allowed their work to be reprinted here and to the copyright holders who are listed on pages 837–38. Those pages are hereby made an extension of this copyright page.

ISBN 0-321-01216-X (student edition)
ISBN 0-321-40262-6 (instructor's edition)

12345678910—DOC—00999897

Contents

Designing and Teaching Composition Courses

These chapters appear only in this *Instructor's Annotated Edition.*

Brief Contents of the Student Edition

The complete student edition of *The Little, Brown Handbook,* Seventh Edition, with its detailed table of contents, follows the six chapters appearing only in this instructor's edition. The annotations in the margins of this instructor's edition—which include answers to the exercises and tips for presenting the material—do not appear in the student edition.

The Little, Brown Handbook

Instructor's Annotated Edition

Designing and Teaching Composition Courses

Chapter 1 Teaching Writing as a Process

Writing as a how

Drawing on the results of three decades of research into the composing processes of writers, most writing instructors now emphasize the *how* of writing. While theorists such as Lester Faigley and Susan Miller have pointed out the limitations of trying to define systematically what happens when a writer sits down to compose a work, most writing teachers and their students have effectively adapted a focus on the processes through which students generate and revise their writing, rather than focusing solely on a final product. This book is designed to support that focus on the "hows" of writing.

Most writers agree that at least three components contribute to the processes they use most of the time: *prewriting,* the finding and exploring of ideas and the construction of plans for expressing them (in classical terminology, *invention*); *drafting,* getting the ideas down on paper and generating sentences about them; and *revising,* reconsidering the ideas, the treatment they receive, the plans for expressing them, and the ways they are expressed (in classical terminology, *arrangement, style,* and to some extent, *delivery*).

Theories about the writing process have focused on the ways in which writers:

- perceive and explore themselves and their worlds through the medium of language;
- consider their subject matter as the occasion for interpretive analysis and as the testing ground for ideas and hypotheses;
- respond to, understand, and to some degree, invent their audiences; and
- position themselves in relation to writerly conventions, institutional restraints, and to communities within and outside of the classroom.

These assumptions are based on the theories outlined below.

Writing as an expressive process

Many theories of the writing process from the 1960s and 1970s focused on its expressive content, the attempts of writers to use language to capture and articulate the unique vision of the writer. For instance, D. Gordon Rohman and Albert O. Wlecke argue that techniques such as meditative exercises, journal keeping, and the composition of analogies (called "existential sentences") help writers find a personal truth in even the most abstract of subjects. They argue that such "prewriting" techniques lead in a smooth and linear fashion to drafting and revision as writers refine the expression of the truth they tell. This privileging of self-discovery, what is sometimes called the *expressionistic* or *romantic* view of composing, is also held by Peter Elbow, Ken Macrorie, William Coles, and Donald Murray, to name a few of its most influential proponents. Elbow argues for the efficacy of freewriting and drafting in helping writers explore ideas before worrying about structure and presentation. Macrorie encourages students to use "case histories" of past experiences and to work from direct observation in order to go beyond the obvious clichés, which he calls "Engfish" (because they stink of insincerity). Coles values prewriting because it allows students to explore multiple relationships to readers and subjects (what he calls "plural I's"). Murray emphasizes aspects of prewriting that cultivate surprise, originality, and new combinations of ideas which lead to personal discovery.

The expressionistic theory gives discovery of ideas primacy in the writing process and sees the writer's personal vision as more important than conventions and codes; its emphasis on pre- and freewriting is an attempt to give writers the power to control or even exploit conventions and expectations in the interests of conveying an original vision. These beliefs have thus attracted criticism from those who believe that the teacher's responsibility is to show writers how to become part of a community, not how to put themselves outside it. However, the expressionists' contributions to our understanding of the formative stages of prewriting and drafting and their respect for students as writing colleagues have benefited many teachers and theorists. Ann Berthoff's work is an interesting example of that influence; she draws on the expressionistic emphasis by stressing the power of the imagination to create relationships between ideas, but in "Recognition, Representation and Revision" she also develops an understanding of revision as a nonlinear part of the composing process, an ongoing reconsideration of those relationships. Where many expressionists might insist that prewriting generates the ideas, that revision is the process of getting them right, and that editing is the radically separate task of adjusting the etiquette of presentation (spelling, punctuation, and the like), Berthoff and others view revision as a recursive process, as the meaningful reconsideration and development of ideas articulated through the grammar of the paragraph and the sentence.

Writing as a cognitive process

A second school of theories about the writing process is deeply rooted in psychology, particularly in studies of cognition. For such *cognitive* theorists, "protocols" (detailed descriptions of how a document is produced) and draft analyses play a key role. One of the earliest such cognitive studies is Janet Emig's. In *The Composing Process of Twelfth Graders* (1971), she studies writing behaviors: how student writers find and develop their ideas. Drawing on James Britton's terminology, she finds that these processes differ with the audience: if students write for themselves (expressively), they are concerned with the presentation of ideas, but if students write for teachers (transactionally), they are concerned (even obsessed) with mechanical correctness. Emig's technique of asking writers to compose out loud has also been used by Sondra Perl in her studies of unskilled writers and by Carol Berkenkotter in her study of a professional writer's composing processes. Nancy Sommers's comparisons of student and experienced adult writers show that experienced writers come to value the development of ideas far more than mechanical correctness, whereas student writers' concern with correctness and with the demands of the writing situation often impedes the development of ideas.

Richard Young, Alton Becker, and Kenneth Pike also developed a cognitive theory of the writing process; however, theirs depends on the writer's knowledge not of the audience but of the subject. Their "tagmemics" theory models cognitive efforts to know a subject; it focuses on how writers perceive a subject's individuality, variability, and place in a larger system. These cognitive efforts should help writers find and develop new combinations of ideas. Like the romantic theories, tagmemics emphasizes prewriting and only discusses drafting or revision as it manifests writers' developing understanding of their subject matter.

The cognitivist position has been most fully expanded by Linda Flower, John Hayes, and their graduate students and colleagues at Carnegie-Mellon University. They view the composing process as a series of decision-making strategies: planning texts, translating those plans into sentences, and revising the texts produced to bring them in line with the original (or reshaped) plans. Although Emig first suggested it, Flower and Hayes and their collaborators have done most to demonstrate the recursive and hierarchical levels of writing processes, especially in the planning and revising stages of writing activities.

Cognitivists find linear expressionist models too simplistic; they argue that writers continually move back and forth between stages to adjust their plans. Like the expressionists, the cognitivists value personal expression highly, claiming it represents most validly an individual's way of thinking. Cognitivists spend little time discussing the finished forms writing may take; it's rare to see an entire piece of discourse reproduced in their discussions. More recently, they have been giving slightly more emphasis to the audience's role in the cognitive workings of writers. But for cognitivists, the writer's "brain work" and reflections on it remain paramount. This position has been challenged as an attempt to systematize the complex cognitive processes of writers and their varying situations.

However, cognitive studies have arguably helped teachers to become more attentive to the varied composing processes of individuals and better able to respond to the particular challenges faced by student writers.

Writing as a social process

Most recently, as theorists have focused on the social functions of, and constraints on, writing, studies of the writing process have broadened to examine the contexts in which writing occurs, to define the discourse communities in which particular writing processes participate. This broadening has also been influenced by the changing demographics of college populations. As more and more nontraditional students—nonyoung, non-upper/middle class, of non-European origin—have entered the academy, teachers have been forced to change their expectations about the kinds of knowledge students bring with them. No longer can a teacher take for granted that students know what an essay looks like, or what "thesis and support" are, or how academics think. (Indeed, research conducted by Robert Connors and Andrea Lunsford suggests that an unfamiliarity with the look of the printed page may be responsible for many student "errors.")

Because of the traditional link between writing programs and English departments, one response to this situation has been to teach students the kinds of discourse that scholars trained in literature and its criticism value: journals, poetry, fiction, and literary analysis. But the "social-epistemic" theorists, as James Berlin called them, have argued that the role of writing programs is to prepare students to read and respond to the various specialized languages—academic, legal, governmental—they might encounter.

Such social theories of the writing process have two current focuses. According to the political focus, represented by David Bartholomae and Anthony Petrosky, Patricia Bizzell, and others influenced to some extent by the Brazilian theorist Paolo Freire, awareness of the constraints of a discourse community is politically liberating, potentially enabling, and revolutionary. If students can understand the constraints of that community and master them, they can come to control and change the community through their own discourse. For theorists who believe this, discovery of the contexts in which students write and the constraints that govern those contexts comes before any other part of the writing process. In terms of classroom practice such theories emphasize a problem-solving format in which students often work with discursive academic prose in peer-group settings and use revision and rereading to establish articulate positions within and against those discourses. A number of contemporary writing texts now employ this multicultural and overtly political approach to collegiate writing.

Another socially focused theory sees writing as a fundamental tool for learning in all communities and at all curricular levels and attempts to foster the teaching of writing beyond the limits of traditional writing programs. In particular, this focus is apparent in "writing-across-the-curriculum," and "writing-across-the-disciplines" movements, which have achieved increasing success in the colleges where they have been implemented. Toby Fulwiler and Barbara Walvoord, two noted proponents of the movement, have both argued convincingly for the benefits of writing instruction beyond the first-year courses. Related "social construction" theories make the case that knowledge is achieved as a consensus among communities rather than as a hierarchical transfer of information from teacher to student. In *Collaborative Learning: Higher Education, Interdependence, and the Authority of Knowledge,* Kenneth Bruffee argues for collaborative student learning as the process through which students become members in their college communities and in communities of knowledge. While social constructionism has been critiqued for its goal of consensus on the grounds that it erases vital differences and competing discourses within communities, collaborative work has become an invaluable part of most classrooms (see for instance the criticisms of Stewart and the recent review by Sullivan).

Ultimately, most teachers adapt the theories and methods that make the most sense given the needs of their students and the shape of their institutional setting. The key effort of this book is to support a range of pedagogical emphases on the composing processes of writers and to help students understand rhetorical forms as flexible frameworks rather than as rigid formulas—as essential parts of a creative composing process.

Resources for teaching writing

Bartholomae, David. "A Conversation with Peter Elbow." *College Composition and Communication* 46(1995): 62–71.

———. "Inventing the University." In *When a Writer Can't Write: Studies in Writer's Block and Other Composing Process Problems.* Ed. Mike Rose. New York: Guilford, 1985. 134–65.

Beach, Richard, and Lillian S. Bridwell, eds. *New Directions in Composition Research.* New York: Guilford, 1984.

Berlin, James. "Rhetoric and Ideology in the Writing Class." *College English.* 50 (1988): 477–94.

Berthoff, Ann. *The Making of Meaning: Metaphors, Models, and Maxims for Writing Teachers.* Upper Montclair: Boynton/Cook, 1981.

———. *Reclaiming the Imagination: Philosophical Perspectives for Writers and Teachers of Writing.* Upper Montclair: Boynton/Cook, 1984.

———. "Recognition, Representation and Revision." *Rhetoric and Composition.* Ed. Richard L. Graves. Upper Montclair: Boynton/Cook, 1984.

Bizzell, Patricia. *Academic Discourse and Critical Consciousness.* Pittsburgh: U Pittsburgh P, 1992.

Bloom, Lynn Z., Donald A. Daiker, and Edward M. White, eds. *Composition in the Twenty-First Century: Crisis and Change.* Carbondale: Southern Illinois UP, 1996.

Britton, James. "Theories of the Disciplines and a Learning Theory." *Writing, Teaching, and Learning in the Disciplines.* Ed. Anne Herrington and Charles Moran. New York: MLA, 1992. 47–60.

Bruffee, Kenneth. *Collaborative Learning: Higher Education, Interdependence, and the Authority of Knowledge.* Baltimore: Johns Hopkins UP, 1993.

Clifford, John, and John Schilb, eds. *Writing Theory and Critical Theory: Research and Scholarship in Composition.* New York: MLA, 1994.

Coles, William E., Jr. *The Plural I: The Teaching of Writing.* New York: Holt, 1978.

Connors, Robert J., and Andrea A. Lunsford. "Frequency of Formal Errors in Current College Writing, or Ma and Pa Kettle Do Research." *College Composition and Communication* 39 (1988): 395–409.

Elbow, Peter. "Reflections on Academic Discourse: How It Relates to Freshmen and Colleagues." *College English* 53 (1991): 135–55.

Emig, Janet. *The Composing Processes of Twelfth Graders.* Urbana: NCTE, 1971.

———. *The Web of Meaning.* Upper Montclair: Boynton/Cook, 1983.

Faigley, Lester. *Fragments of Rationality: Postmodernity and the Subject of Composition.* Pittsburgh: U of Pittsburgh P, 1992.

Flower, Linda. *The Construction of Negotiated Meaning: A Social Cognitive Theory of Writing.* Carbondale: Southern Illinois UP, 1994.

Flower, Linda, and John R. Hayes. "A Cognitive Process Theory of Writing." *College Composition and Communication* 32 (1981): 365–87.

———. "The Construction of Purpose in Writing and Reading." *College English* 50 (1988): 528–50.

Fulwiler, Toby, and Art Young, eds. *Language Connections: Writing and Reading Across the Curriculum.* Urbana: NCTE, 1978.

———. *Programs that Work: Models and Methods for Writing Across the Curriculum.* Portsmouth, NH: Boynton/Cook Heineman, 1990.

Hairston, Maxine. "The Winds of Change: Thomas Kuhn and the Revolution in the Teaching of Writing." *College Composition and Communication* 33 (1982): 76–88.

———. "Different Products, Different Processes: A Theory About Writing." *College Composition and Communication* 37 (1986): 442–52.

Hayes, John R., and Linda S. Flower. "Writing Research and the Writer." *American Psychologist* 41:10 (1986): 1106–13.

Macrorie, Ken. *Searching Writing.* Upper Montclair: Boynton/Cook, 1980.

Miller, Susan. *Textual Carnivals: The Politics of Composition.* Carbondale: Southern Illinois UP, 1991.

———. "Writing Theory: Theory Writing." In *Methods and Methodology in Composition Research.* Gesa Kirsch, and Patrick A. Sullivan, eds. Carbondale: Southern Illinois UP, 1992: 62–83.

Moffett, James. *Teaching the Universe of Discourse.* Boston: Houghton, 1968.

Murray, Donald M. *The Craft of Revision.* New York: Harcourt Brace, 1991.

———. *Expecting the Unexpected: Teaching Myself—and Others—to Read and Write.* Portsmouth, NH: Heinemann, 1989.

North, Steven. *The Making of Knowing in Composition: Portrayal of an Emerging Field.* Portsmouth, NH: Heineman, 1987.

Odell, Lee, ed. *Theory and Practice in the Teaching of Writing: Rethinking the Discipline.* Carbondale: Southern Illinois UP, 1993.

Pemberton, Michael A. "Modeling Theory and Composing Process Models." *College Composition and Communication* 44:1 (1993): 40–58.

Perl, Sondra. "The Composing Process of Unskilled College Writers." *College Composition and Communication* 31 (1980): 389–401.

Perelman, Les. "The Context of Classroom Writing." *College English* 48 (1986): 471–79.

Reither, James A. "Writing and Knowing: Toward Redefining the Writing Process." *College English* 47 (1985): 620–28.

Robinson, Jay L. "Literacy in the Department of English." *College English* 47 (1985): 482–98.

Rohman, D. Gordon, and Alberto O. Wlecke. *Pre-Writing: The Construction and Application of Models for Concept-Formation in Writing.* USOE Cooperative Research Project No. 2174. East Lansing: Michigan State UP, 1964.

Rose, Mike. "Rigid Rules, Inflexible Plans, and the Stifling of Language: A Cognitivist Analysis of Writer's Block." *College Composition and Communication* 31 (1980): 389–401.

Russell, David P. *Writing in the Academic Disciplines: A Curricular History.* Carbondale: Southern Illinois UP, 1991.

Sommers, Nancy. "Revision Strategies of Student Writers and Experienced Adult Writers." *College Composition and Communication* 31 (1980): 378–88.

Stewart, Donald. "Collaborative Learning and Composition: Boon or Bane?" *Rhetoric Review* 7 (1988): 58–85.

Sullivan, Patricia A. "Social Constructionism and Literacy Studies." *College English* 57 (1995): 950–959.

Walvoord, Barbara E. "The Future of WAC." *College English* 58.1 (1996): 58–79.

Chapter 2

Using The Little, Brown Handbook

In many writing courses, the writing done by the students in that class serves as the core. The text or texts the instructor chooses should serve as resources to encourage and improve that writing. And the instructor's choice should be based on a clear understanding of the assumptions on which each text is founded.

Assumptions shaping *The Little, Brown Handbook*

It would be foolish to suggest that all composition instructors who emphasize the composing process are in agreement over specific teaching strategies—or that they ought to be. Two teachers who share a belief in the importance of revision or who encourage students to discover ideas and information through freewriting may also disagree strongly about the purposes for writing. Yet it is possible to identify some generally agreed-upon elements of a process paradigm.

The process paradigm of *The Little, Brown Handbook* is based on the following assumptions:

- Writing consists of a variety of activities including *developing* (exploring, gathering, focusing, organizing); *drafting* (finding and expressing meaning, establishing relationships); and *revising* (rethinking, rewriting, editing, proofreading).
- The activities that make up the writing process are recursive, not fixed in order. For example, revising often includes the discovery of fresh insights, and the drafting of one part of a paper may occur at the same time the writer is gathering materials for another part.
- Writing often is a process of discovering ideas, arriving at knowledge of the self, and selecting effective ways to present concepts and information.

- Knowledge of the conventions of expression and of stylistic options is an important part of the writer's repertoire, but a premature striving for correctness and for grace and clarity often can impede the free flow of ideas and the discovery of appropriate form. Thus, activities such as editing and proofreading, which pay considerable attention to style, grammar, and mechanics, are generally best left until relatively late in the composing of an essay.
- Skilled writers (in contrast to unskilled writers) are characterized by the range of strategies they know and employ in developing, drafting, and revising—strategies that can be both taught and learned.
- Effective writing is the product of interaction among the four elements of the writing situation: author, subject, language, and audience.

These assumptions shape the advice offered throughout *The Little, Brown Handbook,* not only in the Introduction on critical thinking, reading, and writing and discussions of the writing process and the whole paper (Part I), but also in treatments of the research paper, writing about literature, and writing in the disciplines (Part VIII) and in the treatment of strategies for clear and effective sentences (Parts III and IV). Even the discussions of grammatical sentences (Part II), punctuation (Part V), and mechanics (Part VI) mix firm and relatively conservative advice with an awareness of the demands of various audiences and of the difference between an early draft and a final, carefully edited draft.

At the same time, however, discussions in the handbook point out that different writing situations may call for different composing processes and that the knowledge of forms for expression—the *what* of writing—is an important companion to an awareness of the *how.* In this, the handbook agrees with the work of theorists and teachers such as Maxine Hairston, James Reither, Patricia Bizzell, and Arthur Applebee. These writers share a belief that the process paradigm needs to be augmented by

- an awareness of the ways the writing process varies according to the writer's purpose and the social context;
- a recognition of the important roles knowledge of form and convention can play in guiding the composing process; and
- an acknowledgment of the extent to which communities of readers and writers are bound together by specific expectations governing the form and content of discourse.

The handbook recognizes that the processes of composing are "strategies that writers employ for particular purposes" (Applebee 106) and emphasizes this perspective in

- critical thinking, reading, and writing (Introduction);
- the initial treatment of composing (Chapters 1 and 2); and
- the discussions of commonly used rhetorical patterns and specialized forms of writing:

  Paragraphing (Chapter 3)
  Argument (Chapter 4)

The research paper (Chapters 35–38)
Writing about literature (Chapter 39)
Writing in the academic disciplines (Chapter 40)
Writing essay exams (Chapter 41)
Writing business letters and memoranda (Chapter 42)

The emphasis throughout is on seeing the forms as the shared expectations of readers and writers and using these expectations to guide the discovery and expression of ideas so as not to constrain creativity.

Familiarizing students with the handbook

Many students have little experience with a comprehensive handbook like *The Little, Brown Handbook,* so it is well worth your time and theirs to review where they can find material, how the book is organized, and how they might use it. Encourage students to personalize the book by marking sections that are particularly useful to them and by keeping an ongoing list of the sections they find themselves returning to for reference or that correspond to their identified patterns of error. The new Editing Checklist (pp. 74–75) is a useful place to begin discussions about recognizing common errors and also provides a touchstone for your responses to student papers. It is equally important to make handbook usage part of the continuing conversation of the classroom, with frequent, in-class index and content searches, so that the handbook becomes a familiar resource. Such exercises can be a useful accompaniment to group or class-wide revision work on student papers.

Several users of previous editions of this handbook have successfully used a quiz as a means of orienting students to the material it contains. We offer this one with thanks to George Meese of Eckerd College, Florida.

QUIZ FOR HANDBOOK USERS

Your goal is to show me that you can find answers to common writing questions by using your handbook. For instance, if the question is how to paraphrase material from a book in your research paper, you would need to turn to Chapter 36b (pp. 569–78). For each question below, list the page or section you would consult to answer this question. For extra credit, answer the question itself.

1. You need to cite an article in the *New York Times* using the MLA system of citations.
2. You can't decide whether to use *that* or *which* in a sentence.
3. You need pointers for writing the introduction for your essay.
4. You can't decide whether to use *rise* or *raise* as the verb in your sentence.
5. You need to know how to type a business letter.
6. You're confused about the difference between *affect* and *effect.*
7. You need to know whether to put a comma before *and* in the phrase *environment, politics and society.*

8. You need to know if the period goes before or after the quotation marks at the end of a direct quote.
9. You have trouble narrowing the topic for your essay.
10. You need to know how to fix a comma splice in your essay.

Organizing a composition course

Organizing a composition course means choosing to emphasize those aspects of writing or kinds of texts that the instructor or the department considers most important and that meet the students' needs. Each institution will set its own goals and standards for what students are expected to achieve in a required writing course, and your class must help students meet those goals. This discussion may be particularly useful for inexperienced teachers who are planning a course for the first time.

In recent years, composition teaching has followed several general patterns for organizing a course, including emphasis on

- patterns of expression and thought,
- the writing process,
- content and ideas, and
- academic writing (writing across the curriculum).

Each approach can be successful if it meets the needs of a particular group of students and if the instructor pays some attention to all aspects of composing.

Emphasis on patterns of expression and thought

Many instructors believe that a composition course ought to give students a chance to understand and practice basic patterns of expression and thought. Such courses may vary widely in the patterns they emphasize:

- rhetorical and logical patterns, such as classification, comparison-contrast, and deduction;
- general essay structures, such as thesis and support or general to specific;
- types of essays, such as informative and argumentative;
- patterns of paragraph development;
- sentence patterns.

Courses designed in this fashion are often used as basic writing courses, designed to meet the needs of students who enter college with limited experience in reading and writing. These courses emphasize the writing skills and patterns of thought essential to success in college courses. Although courses of this kind have their roots in "current-traditional rhetoric," an approach that tended to emphasize product over process, they can be adapted to take students' composing processes into consideration. The course might begin with sentence and paragraph construction, moving to longer essay forms as students become more comfortable with different kinds of paragraphs. A process approach would vary the focus from sentence-level constructions to considerations of the student's overall project in the paragraph and in the essay in order to emphasize their interrelated functions.

Organizing the course

In organizing a skills course, you might begin with a unit on sentence structure, drawing on Chapters 5–9 of the handbook ("Grammatical Sentences"), and you might stress an understanding of phrases, clauses, basic sentence types, and verb forms and tenses. Along with this, you might require paragraph-length writing that helps students to understand the functions of those sentence structures, and make use of the extensive discussion in Chapter 3 ("Paragraphs"). Paragraph- and essay-length writing can continue through the semester, accompanied by work in Chapters 10–15 ("Clear Sentences") and 16–19 ("Effective Sentences"). Chapters on punctuation, mechanics, diction, and usage can be assigned whenever they meet the needs of the class or of individual students. Students might also use the Editing Checklist to keep track of the patterns of error that recur in their writing. In-class sessions can reinforce this practice by focusing on identifying errors in order to create meaningful revisions.

Teaching suggestions

Start paragraphs as early in the semester as possible to give students a sense of accomplishment and a chance to put into practice what they are learning in the sentence units. Also early on, you can incorporate essay-length writings into the course by requiring students to keep a writing journal with a specific number of pages to be devoted to a single topic at least once a week. You can integrate the journals into the class work by having them serve as topics for the students' paragraph and sentence constructions. This helps students to understand the relationship between the function of individual sentences and paragraphs and the overall purpose of an essay.

Other considerations

Although an effective basic course, often planned for developmental students, can focus on sentence, paragraph, and essay patterns, it also needs to pay attention to the writing process and to audience (see Chapters 1 and 2 in the handbook). Students who have trouble mastering the basic forms of expression are also likely to underestimate the importance of planning and revising and to have difficulty shaping their writing to the needs of an audience. Collaborative revision work can help by providing students with immediate feedback from an identified audience of their peers. These matters can also be reinforced throughout the course with assignments that require planning, drafting, and revising and also create realistic audiences and situations for students to address in their writing. For example, the exercises in Chapter 1c and 1d on purpose and audience can be developed into group projects on which students work collaboratively to create directed appeals to the campus newspaper, to local government, or to a defined public organization.

Emphasis on patterns of development

Rhetorically oriented courses use standard essay types or patterns of development (for instance, comparison-contrast or process analysis) as a means of probing subjects and developing and organizing essays. Instructors who use such approaches share the belief that helping students understand these patterns and practice them in their writing will enable them to use the patterns in a variety of writing tasks. Most of these instructors would also agree that each pattern of development directs attention to a different aspect of a subject and thus the patterns can be seen as shaping the way we think about a subject and as affecting a reader's attitudes. Instructors of rhetorically oriented courses often rely on a reader or rhetoric to provide examples of essay types and patterns of development.

Organizing the course

If you wish to give your course a rhetorical orientation, you may want to begin with Chapters 1–4 of the handbook ("The Whole Paper and Paragraphs") as a way of showing students how to develop, write, revise, and edit an essay and to adapt it to an audience. Later in the course, you may want to return to this material to remind students how important the stages of the writing process are, particularly planning and revising. You can also point out that Chapters 1 and 3 treat the rhetorical patterns as answers to questions about aspects of a topic, as well as ways of organizing and developing essays and paragraphs. The main portion of the course might consist of a review of essay types or patterns of essay and paragraph development (Chapters 1–3) with assignments that give students a chance to use the forms. The chapters on coordination and subordination, parallelism, sentence emphasis, and variety (Chapters 16–19, "Effective Sentences") can be introduced later in the course to add variety and style to students' writing. The Editing Checklist and the chapters on common sentence errors, punctuation, mechanics, diction, and usage can be assigned according to the needs of individuals or of the class and may also be used for reference. The course might culminate in a research paper (Chapters 35–38) or essay questions and business writing (Chapters 41–42).

Teaching suggestions

The risk in a rhetorically oriented course is that students will come to regard the various forms as ends in themselves and ignore the role they play in viewing experience and in shaping communication to an audience or situation. For this reason, many instructors emphasize throughout the course the process of exploring subjects and revising the plan for an essay, and they encourage students to create specific audiences and situations to address in their writing. Collaborative work in which students debate topics in class and/or through a Web site can be enormously useful in helping students to work toward particular audiences and purposes. Students also become aware that the forum of the computer link, the face-to-face discussion, and the revised results (which can be "published" for the class) powerfully affects the choices they make as writers.

Emphasis on the writing process

Some instructors choose to orient their courses around an exploration of the writing process, so that students become aware of the range of strategies and choices available to them as writers and become confident in their ability to respond to future writing tasks. In such courses,

- students are taught to respond to writing situations with a full awareness of the importance of discovering, focusing, planning, drafting, revising, and editing;
- students are given the opportunity to adapt the process to the demands of different kinds of writing;
- forms of expression are presented as strategies best learned in the context of a particular writing task; and
- grammar, punctuation, and mechanics are introduced when necessary for effective communication in an essay.

Organizing the course

In organizing a course that emphasizes the writing process, you might begin by having students look over the discussion of the process in the handbook (Introduction, "Critical Thinking, Reading, and Writing," and Chapters 1 and 2, "Developing an Essay" and "Drafting and Revising the Essay"). You will have to review briefly the writing process as part of each assignment, both to remind students that each of the elements of composing is important and to show how the kinds of planning and revising a writer must do will vary slightly depending on the subject, the aim of the writing task, and the audience for the essay. You may wish to include personal writing as a way to enhance students' awareness of the range of approaches and personas available to them as writers. When you move to more public kinds of writing, however, Chapter 4 (section e, "Reaching Your Readers") will help alert students to the need to take their readers into account as they shape what they have to say and decide how to say it.

Teaching suggestions

Assignments in a process-oriented course should stress planning and revising in all writing tasks and also suggest a range of writing strategies that students can use to deal with a subject and meet the needs of a reader.

If the assigned essay requires particular attention to paragraphing—a persuasive paper, for example—then students might be required to look at Chapter 3 ("Writing and Revising Paragraphs"). Chapters 16–19 ("Effective Sentences") will also help introduce students to useful strategies and Chapters 35–40 ("Research

Writing") and Chapters 41–42 ("Special Writing Situations") can be good resources when students are asked to write academic papers or memos directed at a business or professional audience. Coverage of matters of grammar, punctuation, diction, and usage will depend on the needs of the class and of individual students.

Since many problems in student writing stem from a lack of effective planning or revising, a composition course that emphasizes process can have a significant effect on student writing. But students need to be aware that word choice, sentence structure, paragraph development, and essay organization also contribute to the effectiveness of writing. Therefore a course that emphasizes the writing process needs to introduce students to the options made possible by formal proficiency (the flexibility that semicolon usage can add to a writer's repertoire, for example—see Chapter 22). Collaborative peer-group revision work supported by the handbook can help student writers to understand the usefulness of formal strategies in communicating the purpose of an essay to an audience.

Emphasis on content and ideas (thematic courses)

In some writing courses, the writing grows out of the students' strong need to communicate about significant ideas and issues. Such courses focus on ideas and issues, whether personal (family life, education, social relationships) or public policy (pornography, the American legal system). The source for content may be an anthology, a lecture series, films, or the students' own research and experience. Although the handbook uses many examples that are thematically organized around the subject of the environment, students working with this or any other thematic content could be encouraged to draw examples from their own writing to consider in conjunction with those offered by the handbook. Instructors looking for a theme around which to organize their own courses may wish to add to the environment-oriented examples in the handbook with a supplemental collection of readings on the environment, or with other locally available material, so that students get more exposure to extended pieces of discourse on this topic. Because students may be unused to working interpretively with discursive prose, exercises that encourage them to practice responding to quotes, individually and in groups, will be particularly useful. See Chapter 36, especially sections b and c, for exercises that help students to position themselves in relation to the other authors they are using. Depending on the kinds of material that students are reading, Chapter 39 ("Reading and Writing About Literature") and Chapter 40 ("Writing in Other Disciplines") encourage students to recognize relationships between formal, discipline-based strategies and thematic content.

Organizing the course

Since instructors who teach such courses generally value the content of a piece of writing most, they cover the forms of writing and the writing process primarily to help students communicate ideas and feelings clearly and effectively. If you choose to emphasize the content of essays in your composition course, you may wish to begin by introducing students to the writing process and the basic forms of the essay with Chapters 1–4 ("The Whole Paper and Paragraphs"). These chapters suggest ways students can develop their ideas and organize them into paragraphs and whole essays. The Introduction on "Critical Thinking, Reading, Writing" can also help students to analyze the strategies of the writers they are reading and to respond effectively.

Teaching suggestions

As students struggle to express their ideas, you may wish to assign Chapters 31–34 ("Effective Words") to help them communicate more precisely and Chapters 16–19 ("Effective Sentences") to help them add variety, clarity, and style to their writing. The Editing Checklist can be a useful touchstone in helping students to identify patterns of error that recur in their work; students can often use the recognized error (such as comma splices, fused sentences, ambiguous pronoun references) as the occasion for substantive revision. Chapters on punctuation, mechanics, grammar, and usage can be assigned to the class or to individual students according to need. Whether or not students are required to use research in their writing, this discussion of differences among summary, paraphrase, and analysis in Chapters 35–40 ("Research Writing") can help students to work effectively with their quoted sources.

Emphasis on writing about literature

Writing about literature in a writing course

In a writing class that includes literature, many sections of *The Little, Brown Handbook* will be relevant. Students can begin by reviewing the Introduction on critical thinking, reading, and writing and the material in section I about beginning a writing project, and then move on to Chapter 39, "Reading and Writing About Literature," which shows how those general skills translate into questions and strategies for reading and writing about fiction, poetry, and drama. Thorough coverage of MLA documentation in Chapter 37 and 38 will also be useful, as will the strategies for conducting research in Chapter 35. And the high standards of editing usually found in literary texts can profitably be tied to the discussions of sentence construction problems in Chapters 10–15 and to matters of punctuation in Chapters 20–25.

Writing about literature in literature courses

Many college and university literature courses now stress writing as well as reading, and *The Little, Brown Handbook* can play a vital role in such courses. The guide to writing about literature in Chapter 39 stresses the interplay of critical thinking, reading, and writing first discussed in the Introduction and shows students how to transfer those skills to the literature classroom. The thorough coverage of style (Chapters 16–19 on fluid and effective sentences, Chapters 31–33 on diction and word choice) can be used not only to help students analyze the works of literature they read but also to help them write more effectively about those works. And the material in Chapter 39 on drafting, writing, and revising a literary analysis, along with the sample student paper and thorough coverage of MLA documentation, will prove invaluable to students and teachers in any literature course.

Teaching suggestions

Because of the pressure to cover content issues, many literature classes underemphasize the role of drafting and revision. Assignments that foreground these processes, such as prewriting in response to quotes, in-class work with student drafts, and group revisions of selected paragraphs and single sentences by student writers, will help students to develop and gain confidence in their writing skills.

Emphasis on academic writing

Writing across the curriculum in a writing course

Chapter 40 of the handbook, "Writing in Other Disciplines," covers much of the territory appropriate for a course emphasizing writing across the curriculum. Such a course may ask students to write papers in each of the areas covered by the chapter—the humanities, the social sciences, and the natural and applied sciences—and may ask students to become acquainted with the research tools in each area (also discussed in detail in Chapter 40). The treatment of the writing process in Chapters 1 and 2, of paragraphing in Chapter 3, of critical thinking and writing in the Introduction, and of the functions of sentence structure in Chapters 16–19 can also be important elements of a course built around the varieties of academic writing.

Writing across the curriculum in the disciplines

In many writing-across-the-curriculum programs, writing instruction is part of content courses, employed both as a tool for learning and as a way of sharing knowledge in forms appropriate to a discipline. Because it is designed as a reference tool and therefore does not impose a particular design on a course, the handbook can be a useful resource for content courses emphasizing writing. It provides discussions of the writing process and of research and documentation in specific disciplines as well as resources for editing style, grammar, and mechanics. Whatever the particular uses of writing in a course, the handbook's advice about the process of writing (Chapters 1 and 2) is likely to prove valuable.

Using the handbook with other texts

Although the handbook can be used as the only text in a course, many instructors also adopt a reader, a rhetoric, or a workbook such as *The Little, Brown*

Workbook. Each kind of text enables you to emphasize different elements of the course and also provides activities to help students develop their writing.

Readers

Readers are generally of three kinds: rhetorical, thematic, or cross-curricular.

Rhetorical readers

Rhetorical readers illustrate different aims and patterns of writing with selections by professional authors and sometimes by students. Readers of this type frequently begin with writing patterns that students find most accessible—narration, description, exemplification—and move on to patterns that students find more difficult to use—classification, comparison-contrast, inductive and deductive argument. Many readers provide extensive introductions to the rhetorical patterns, discussing their uses in writing and the aspects of a subject that they focus on. Some recent rhetorical readers go beyond the basic rhetorical patterns to discuss common forms of nonfiction writing—such as the problem-solution report, the personal essay, the evaluation, and the proposal—that combine the basic patterns in a number of ways. The questions accompanying the essays in most rhetorical readers direct students' attention to the most important features of the models and suggest ways students can incorporate such features in their own writing.

Thematic readers

Thematic readers illustrate and explore a number of themes, such as the stages of personal growth or family relationships, or topics of general interest, such as capital punishment or the impact of technology. The readings may include fiction or poetry as well as essays. If the main purpose for using the reader is to provide subject matter for essays, a thematic reader may be preferable because, as a rule, readers of this type provide several perspectives on a subject and more background information to get class discussion started and give students material to use in their writing.

Some readers are both rhetorical and thematic in organization and coverage, providing a table of contents for each emphasis. Both types of readers can be used to generate class discussion and topics for student writing. Some readers even provide questions to stimulate discussion and include lists of possible topics for papers, as well as bibliographies for further reading and research.

Cross-curricular readers

Cross-curricular readers typically provide examples of writing in a variety of disciplines and cover a range of topics. Some include essays directed to general readers as well as specialists. Others focus on the kinds of writing expected from students or professionals in a discipline. Readers of this kind often emphasize writing as a social process and are designed to help students participate actively within specialized discourse communities. While the primary aim of readers of this type is to provide models of academic and professional prose, some also arrange readings in thematic clusters designed to encourage discussion and suggest subjects for students to pursue in their own writing. Instructors often choose a problem-posing approach to the readings by encouraging students to work on an essay individually and in groups, identifying difficult passages and terms and creating interpretive responses. Classroom practice focuses on student responses to texts, and particularly on the revision process as the means to create meaningful positions in relation to those readings.

Integrating *The Little, Brown Handbook* with a reader

Instructors who adopt a reader typically make discussion of its essays a major activity in the course, yet they also tend to make significant use of a handbook. If the reader chosen for a course does not provide a rhetorical framework for students' essays or a thorough coverage of writing and reasoning processes, instructors using *The Little, Brown Handbook* may wish to direct students to the coverage of these matters in Chapters 1, 2, and 4. As students begin working with quotations and citation, the Introduction on critical reading and Chapter 35 can become useful resources, even outside of the research context. The handbook provides explanations and examples of other matters frequently not covered in readers, such as the Editing Checklist, paragraphing (Chapter 3); sentence structure, grammar, and style (Chapters 5–19); diction and usage (Chapter 31 and Glossary of Usage); the research paper (Chapters 35–38); and writing in the disciplines (Chapters 39–40). In addition, the handbook can be used as a reference guide for punctuation and mechanics, as an aid in marking student papers, and as a guide for revision. Some instructors who use a reader like to devote one period each week to subjects covered in the handbook; others like to set aside part of each day.

Rhetorics

Rhetorics and handbooks

Rhetorics cover many of the same topics as handbooks—discovering, planning, drafting, revising, rhetorical patterns, and paragraphing—but do so in greater depth, at the same time giving less coverage to grammar, punctuation, mechanics, and usage. A rhetoric usually embodies a particular perspective toward writing and the teaching of writing—a theoretical bias, perhaps, or an emphasis on thesis-and-support essays, personal writing, academic writing, argumentation, critical thinking, or tone and style. Since a rhetoric helps determine the emphasis within a course, it provides less flexibility for the teacher than the handbook does, especially if the rhetoric has been chosen by a department rather than by the instructor.

Integrating *The Little, Brown Handbook* with a rhetoric

Because rhetorics provide full coverage in some areas at the expense of others, instructors frequently adopt a handbook as a supplement. Used in this way,

The Little, Brown Handbook can provide treatment of sentence style (Chapters 16–19), the research paper (Chapter 35–38), and writing in the disciplines (Chapters 39–40) for rhetorics that give only brief attention to these matters. It can also provide discussion and exercises for sentence structure and grammar (Chapters 5–15), punctuation and mechanics (Chapters 20–30), and diction and usage (Chapter 31 and Glossary of Usage). The discussions of critical thinking, the writing process, paragraphs, and argument (Introduction and Chapters 1–4) can supplement the material in a rhetoric and provide useful exercises.

When the handbook is used with a rhetoric, instructors often assign its chapters and exercises along with those in the rhetoric, and they devote class time to discussing both texts and reviewing the exercises. They also use the handbook as a reference for students, as an aid to grading papers, and as a guide for revision.

The handbook's ancillary publications

When combined with its ancillary publications—*The Little, Brown Workbook,* Seventh Edition; *The ESL Worksheets;* Competency, Sample CLAST, and Sample TASP Test; the *Student Manual for Peer Evaluation; Researching Online and Off* to accompany *The Little, Brown Handbook; Teaching Online: Internet Research, Conversation, and Composition;* a portable correction chart; transparency masters; and several other learning aids, including heuristic writing software, *The Writer's Workshop*—the handbook is the center of an instructional package that will meet the needs of many classes.

The *Little, Brown Workbook* is designed to give students more extensive practice with fundamentals than the handbook alone can provide. Since each section of the workbook includes a brief, simplified version of the discussion in the handbook, the workbook can be used on its own. Yet because each section corresponds to the treatment of the same subject in the handbook, the workbook can be a source of individual and class activities to complement the primary text. Answers for exercises in the handbook and the workbook are published as separate booklets that instructors can order, free, for their students.

The ESL Worksheets provide opportunities for students to practice using English grammar that ESL students find particularly troublesome.

Longman's new *Teaching Online: Internet Research, Conversation, and Composition,* prepared by Daniel Anderson, Bret Benjamin, Chris Busiel, and Bill Paredes-Holt, provides a range of ideas for using Internet resources in the writing classroom. Instructors with little or no on-line experience will find basic definitions, numerous examples, and detailed information about finding and using Internet resources in each chapter. Those more familiar with on-line resources will find additional information about: using e-mail and Listservs to foster a workshop atmosphere in the classroom; Usenet newsgroups to emphasize critical thinking; MOO and IRC to link conversation and composition; Gopher and the World Wide Web to begin a research project and learn how to evaluate sources; and HTML to expand audience, publish Web pages, and use graphics and imagemaps. Chapter-end case studies and a sample research paper show numerous applications of on-line composition, conversation, and research.

A new guide, *Researching Online and Off* to accompany *The Little, Brown Handbook* replaces the familiar *Documentation Guide*. This booklet still offers up-to-date documentation guidelines for MLA, ACW, CMS, APA, and CBE styles, as they are presented in *The Little, Brown Handbook*. It also guides students in using electronic research resources found on the Internet and through the library.

The new *Student Manual for Peer Evaluation* by Tori Haring-Smith guides students in reading and evaluating the work of their peers. It offers question sets on forms tailored to a variety of editing and writing purposes. Questions help students focus their attention at various stages of revision on the aspects of others' writing as their instructor desires. Each form is generalized to work in any classroom and can easily be adapted as the instructor sees fit.

In addition to these ancillary publications, the marginal notes in this *Instructor's Annotated Edition* describe many activities appropriate for collaborative group work, for computer classrooms, and for ESL writers. The chapter "Using Collaborative Learning with the Handbook" on pages IAE-49–IAE-62 of the *Instructor's Annotated Edition* discusses how the handbook may be used in courses emphasizing collaborative learning and includes advice on adapting particular handbook exercises for small-group work. Susan Lang's essay on using the handbook with computers (pp. IAE-63–IAE-77) identifies ways in which the resources of an electronic age can be integrated with students' composing processes and become the basis for classroom activities. The essay on "Teaching Writing to ESL Students" (pp. IAE-79–IAE-90) emphasizes the handbook exercises that are keyed to the particular needs of second-language speakers.

Sentence combining with the handbook

During the past decade, extensive research has shown that having students work with the elements of sentences—manipulating, combining, and altering—leads not only to a greater understanding of sentence structure but also to a greater willingness to experiment stylistically, leading to more flexible, expressive syntax characteristic of mature writing. However, teachers and students can get carried away with sentence combining. Doing exercises with someone else's prose can be fun; students seem to enjoy the activities, but they are no substitute for the students writing their own sentences and applying the techniques to their own sentences as part of a larger writing assignment.

What sentence combining is

Sentence combining arose from applications of transformational-generative grammar principles to classroom practices. Researchers such as Kellogg Hunt and Frank O'Hare determined that encouraging students to expand sentences by coordinating (adding on), deleting (eliminating repeated words), and embedding (inserting new information into a main clause) enables them to write complex, fluent sentences without having to master elaborate grammatical terminology. The practice they recommend is to give students a base sentence and several other sentences of information to incorporate in the base sentence then have students experiment with various ways to combine the information.

In most sentence-combining instruction, students learn various kinds of combinations, starting with relatively simple coordination and subordination using conjunctions. Then they progress to removing repeated elements and embedding information such as adjectives and phrases, culminating in "advanced" structures such as adverbials and absolutes. After they control the structures, they are introduced to the punctuation conventions the new sentences require. Students are encouraged to practice not only on the words of other writers but on their own sentences in their drafts as they master new stylistic patterns.

Sentence Combining and the Teaching of Writing, an anthology compiled by Donald Daiker, Andrew Kerek, and Max Morenberg, is the most extensive review of this practice. Stephen Witte's review of this book makes some wise suggestions about how the method might be used more productively in classes.

A sequence for sentence combining

Chapter 5 introduces students to basic sentence structures, and Chapters 14 and 21 introduce modifying clauses and phrases along with their primary focus on grammar and punctuation. Chapters 21 and 22 present strategies of coordination as well as of punctuation, and Chapters 16 and 17 introduce progressively more sophisticated sentence strategies. In Chapters 18 and 19 students encounter sentence patterns characteristic of mature writing, and in Chapter 3 they get a chance to combine all the strategies in paragraphs.

The handbook exercises you might stress in teaching sentence combining are these:

Chapter 3, Exercises 4, 11
Chapter 5, Exercises 3, 5, 8, 10, 12, 13, 15–17, 21
Chapter 6, Exercise 4
Chapter 11, Exercise 3
Chapter 14, Exercise 7
Chapter 16, Exercises 1, 3, 7
Chapter 17, Exercises 2, 3
Chapter 18, Exercises 1, 5
Chapter 19, Exercises 1, 3, 6
Chapter 21, Exercises 2, 4, 6
Chapter 22, Exercises 2, 4

Tutoring with the handbook

Writing centers and tutoring programs can make good use of the handbook to set common goals and to develop a common language that will sustain the diverse relationships among students, tutors, and teachers. For example, the handbook provides a reference point for teachers' responses to student papers, which can then become the basis for tutoring sessions on the identified points of difficulty in student work: paragraphing, interpretive work with quotes, particular patterns of error. Students are also able to refer to explanations and exercises in the tutor's absence, to keep a journal of their error patterns and sample revisions, and to refer back to the handbook to reinforce what they have learned in tutoring sessions. The handbook can also become a primary reference for the tutoring center or lab, by providing advice and practice exercises for targeted areas. Tutors should encourage students to bring the handbook along with their work-in-progress. Once tutor and student together have identified revision areas or targeted patterns of error, they might review the relevant sections of the handbook together; the tutor might then give the student a chance to revise a targeted area on his or her own. As a resource tool for the lab or tutoring center, the handbook can help resolve conflicts over points of grammar and usage, becoming a primary reference or arbiter in debates. It can be a training manual for new tutors, providing simple and clear explanations of problems they will encounter every day. In particular, the revision worksheets included in the essay on collaborative learning (pp. IAE-53–IAE-59) can be used as the basis for tutorial sessions. And the handbook can be a reference for students who are working on a paper in the writing center without direct supervision by a tutor.

The *Little, Brown Workbook* and the *ESL Worksheets* can provide the "raw material" of tutoring—sample sentences, exercises, and brief explanations—to be used in discussion with the student or for independent work. The workbook can be particularly effective for tutoring if students are taking a composition course that uses the handbook, because the language, rules, and exercises encountered in tutoring will be consistent with those encountered in the classroom.

Sample syllabi

Syllabus for a ten-week course with four graded papers

Week	Goals
1	Introduction and course description; diagnostic writing sample; critical thinking, reading, and writing (Introduction). Begin discussion of essay development (Chapter 1); assign first essay.
2	Drafting and revising essays (Chapter 2); first peer response workshop. Preparing a manuscript (Appendix A).
3	Writing and revising paragraphs (Chapter 3); conferences with students to discuss drafts and journals. Review common errors seen in drafts (Parts III–VII).
4	First essay due. Assign second essay. Repeat emphasis on prewriting (Chapter 1); discuss correction symbols and grading.
5	Return first essay; discuss clear sentences (Part III). Peer response workshop for second paper.
6	Effective words (Part VII); conferences to discuss drafts and journals. If needed, discuss with the class common errors or problems.

7	Second essay due; assign third essay. Work on invention strategies in small groups.
8	Return second essay; peer group workshop in class; work on effective sentences (Part IV). Introduce basics of argument (Chapter 4).
9	Third essay due; assign last essay, which may be a revision of an earlier piece of writing, an essay from another course, or an essay exam. Peer-group activities. If students are keeping portfolios (see p. IAE-43), final copies of first two papers are due this week. Journals due.
10	Return third essay. Final essay due; individual conferences and course evaluations; last two papers for portfolio due.

Syllabus for a fifteen-week course with five graded papers, including a research paper

Week	Goals
1	Course introduction and requirements; writing sample. Discuss Chapter 1. Introduce journals.
2	Assign first paper. Begin draft work. Review Appendix B if relevant. Discuss Chapter 2 and Part III.
3	Chapter 3. Conferences about drafts. Discuss Chapter 3.
4	Take up journals. Second peer-response session for first paper. Review Appendix A. Discuss Chapters 21 and 22.
5	First paper due. Assign second paper. Discuss Chapter 2 again; discuss Chapters 16 and 17.
6	Return first paper. Discuss evaluation criteria and correction symbols. If appropriate, discuss Chapter 41. Draft work on second paper. Peer-group critique of second paper.
7	Discuss Chapter 31. Discuss Chapters 18 and 19. Second peer critique for second paper.
8	Second paper due. Assign third paper. Take up journals. Re-emphasize developing the essay (Chapter 1) and conduct microclinics on problem areas with small groups of students. Conferences to discuss drafts and journals.
9	Return second paper. Assign fourth paper (research paper). Discuss Chapter 35. Peer response for third paper. Assign each student an appropriate section from Chapter 40.
10	Research week. Library tour (if available). Chapter 36a–36e.
11	Third paper returned. Documentation week. Chapters 36, 37, and appropriate sections of 40. Miniconferences to address specific problems.
12	Fourth paper due. Discuss Chapter 38 and appropriate sections of Chapter 40. Discuss Appendix A.

13	Fourth paper returned. Assign fifth paper. Discuss Chapter 4. Journals due.
14	Draft work for fifth paper. If students are keeping portfolios (p. IAE-43), edited copies of first four papers are submitted this week.
15	Finished copy of fifth paper due. Individual conferences and course evaluations.

Resources for designing a writing course

Applebee, Arthur N. "Problems in Process Approaches: Toward a Reconceptualization of Process Instruction." In *The Teaching of Writing.* Chicago: National Society for the Study of Education, 1986. 95–113.

Bartholomae, David, and Anthony Petrosky. *Facts, Counterfacts, Artifacts: Theory and Method for a Reading and Writing Course.* Upper Montclair: Boynton/Cook, 1986.

Daiker, Donald, Andrew Kerek, and Max Morenberg, eds. *Sentence Combining and the Teaching of Writing.* Conway: L & S Books, 1979.

Dawkins, John. "Teaching Punctuation as a Rhetorical Tool." *College Composition and Communication* 46:4 (1995): 533–48.

Eble, Kenneth E. *The Craft of Teaching: A Guide to Mastering the Professor's Art.* 2nd ed. San Francisco: Jossey-Bass, 1988.

Enos, Theresa, ed. *A Sourcebook for Basic Writing Teachers.* New York: Random, 1987.

Farber, Jerry. "Learning to Teach: A Progress Report." *College English* 52 (1990): 135–41.

Foster, David. *A Primer for Writing Teachers: Theories, Theorists, Issues, Problems.* Upper Montclair: Boynton/Cook, 1983.

Gebhardt, Richard C. "Unifying Diversity in the Training of Writing Teachers." In *Training the New Teacher of College Composition,* ed. Charles W. Bridges. Urbana: NCTE, 1986. 1–12.

George, Diana. "Who Teaches the Teacher? A Note on the Craft of Teaching College Composition." *College English* 51 (1989): 418–23.

Graves, Richard L., ed. *Rhetoric and Composition: A Sourcebook for Teachers and Writers.* Upper Montclair: Boynton/Cook, 1st ed. 1976; 2nd ed. 1983; 3rd ed. 1990.

Hashimoto, Irvin Y. *Thirteen Weeks: A Guide to Teaching College Writing.* Portsmouth NH: Boynton/Cook, 1991.

Herzberg, Bruce. "Composition and the Politics of the Curriculum." *The Politics of Writing Instruction: Postsecondary.* Ed. Richard Bullock and John Trimbur. Portsmouth NH: Boynton/Cook (Heineman) 1991.

Hoffman, Eleanor M., and John P. Schifsky. "Designing Writing Assignments." *English Journal* 66 (1977): 41–45.

Hunt, Kellogg. *Grammatical Structures Written at Three Grade Levels.* Urbana: NCTE, 1965.

Irmscher, William. *Teaching Expository Writing.* New York: Holt, 1979.

Lindemann, Erika. *A Rhetoric for Writing Teachers,* 2nd ed. New York: Oxford UP, 1987.

———. "Teaching as a Rhetorical Art," *CEA Forum* 15:2 (1985): 9–12.

Lindemann, Erika, and Gary Tate, eds. *An Introduction to Composition Studies.* New York: Oxford UP, 1991.

O'Hare, Frank. *Sentence Combining: Improving Student Writing Without Formal Grammar Instruction.* Urbana: NCTE, 1973.

Passmore, John. *The Philosophy of Teaching.* London: Duckworth, 1980.

Ponsot, Marie, and Rosemary Deen. *Beat Not the Poor Desk! Writing: What to Teach, How to Teach It, and Why.* Upper Montclair: Boynton/Cook, 1982.

Rankin, Elizabeth. "From Simple to Complex: Ideas of Order in Assignment Sequences." *Journal of Advanced Composition* 10:1 (1990): 126–35.

Scott, Patrick, and Bruce Castner. "Reference Sources for Composition Research: A Practical Survey." *College English* 45 (1983): 756–68.

Shaughnessy, Mina. *Errors and Expectations: A Guide for the Teacher of Basic Writing.* New York: Oxford UP, 1977.

Tarvers, Josephine Koster. *Teaching Writing: Theories and Practices.* 4th ed. New York: HarperCollins, 1993.

Tobin, Lad. "Reading Students, Reading Ourselves: Revising the Teacher's Role in the Writing Class." *College English* 53 (1991): 333–48.

Witte, Stephen. Review of *Sentence Combining and the Teaching of Writing,* ed. Donald Daiker et al. *College Composition and Communication* 31 (1980): 433–37.

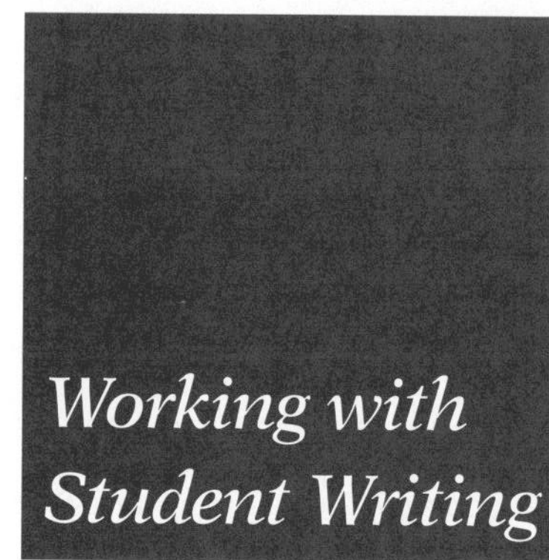

Chapter 3 Working with Student Writing

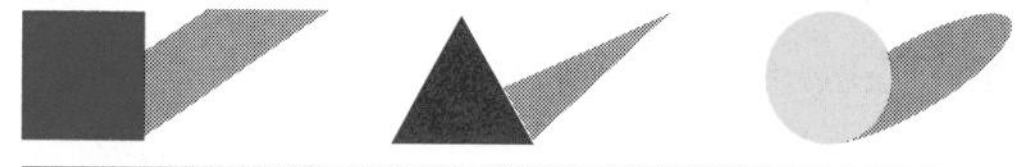

Nothing we do as composition teachers—not lecturing, setting up peer critique groups, leading discussions, or preparing activities—has as much potential for helping students improve their writing as do our efforts to respond as sensitive and thorough readers. Moreover, as readers we can play several roles, some of them simultaneously. We can respond to a work in progress, acting as editors and critics with suggestions for revision or as ordinary readers whose reactions students can take into account as they shape the final product. Or we can be judges of a finished work, justifying a grade (as evaluators) or pointing out strengths and weaknesses (as teachers), encouraging students to build on one and avoid the other.

At some time, of course, all the work that you and students put into the course has to be judged—and in the final analysis, you'll be the one who has to make the judgments and assign the grade. This is one of the hardest parts of your job as a writing teacher, but it's also one of the most essential. But you needn't go it alone; students can collaboratively do a good deal of the preliminary work for you and set standards that enable you and your students to agree upon grades.

The roles of response

It takes more than an efficient correction system to bring about improvement in writing. How we respond and when are most important. In addition, the correction system we choose needs to be consistent with our purposes for responding and the roles we play as readers.

Responses to papers in progress

Responses directed toward a paper in progress often need to focus as much on the way the writer approaches the task as on the evolving text. On the one hand, it makes little sense to comment on detailed matters of punctuation in a draft full of helter-skelter ideas, thereby drawing attention away from advice about strategies the writer can employ to develop focus and discover purpose. On the other hand, helpful comments on agreement or mechanics coming at later stages in the writing of an essay can enable students to understand the importance of editing and can provide knowledge for later use.

Responses to a paper in progress ought to focus to a considerable extent on the writer's behaviors. Novice writers generally need to pay as much attention to learning how to discover ideas or draft an entire paper as to using topic sentences and effective patterns of paragraph development. Much of the advice in the handbook, especially in Chapters 1 and 2, is directed toward strategies for writing. Other discussions, such as the treatment of paragraphs in Chapter 3, pay more attention to the specific features of essays, though they do not ignore the process of composition.

In commenting on drafts of an essay, we can assume the role of a general reader, noting points of interest or confusion, expressing an interest in more information or requesting stronger support, sharing feelings of pleasure and surprise—but always recognizing that at this point a paper belongs primarily to the writer, not yet to the reader. When a draft of an essay has a clear purpose and structure, however, we can read as editors or critics, identifying particular options for paragraphing or expression the writer might consider during revision or suggesting areas of grammar and style that need attention.

Responses to final drafts

Response to a final draft ought to provide a clear evaluation and the justification for it yet at the same time look toward future efforts. Student writers need to recognize and consolidate their successes; they need as well to understand what steps they can take in later essays. The essentially supportive tone of explanations in the handbook can help create this kind of understanding even when comments or the number-and-letter codes are used to identify outright errors.

When as evaluators we comment on a graded final draft, we need to provide a clear justification for the judgment on one or more of the following grounds:

- the paper's success in achieving its goals
- the requirements set by the assignment
- the standards established for the course

Comments that refer students to a particular section of the handbook, perhaps to specific sets of exercises, can provide a bridge to future writing efforts.

Composing comments

Most students will give you an honest effort. They will use the strategies they know to complete an assignment well and to win your approval in the form of a high grade. But effort notwithstanding, students will have differing degrees of success with an assignment. And your reactions will have to differ accordingly.

Any writing effort will have strengths, even if they are few and sometimes hard to find. It's essential to identify these; not only do they show what goals have been attained, but they also help the students see which competencies they can apply to different situations. Even if you praise a very minor feature or an insight that could be developed more, the positive reinforcement may encourage the student: she has something to start from in a revision or in the next paper. And, of course, the strengths often outweigh the weaknesses; then the only problem is deciding what to praise. No matter what the level of skill in the paper however, your goal is to help each student recognize and learn to capitalize on his strengths in future papers. The role of encouragement is often underestimated, seen as the "positive spin" tacked onto the "real" message of critique; instead, it should be viewed as a powerful tool for improvement. Students need to know when they have revised (even one paragraph) effectively, when they have gained control over a single pattern of error, when they have successfully used a quotation, even if their overall argument fell apart in the process.

But what about the weaknesses? These, of course, are what most of us first see when we read a student paper. We feel compelled to alert our students to these problems so that their writing can improve. But the method of identifying such weaknesses must be constructive and goal-oriented. Ideally, students will be able to read our responses and focus on the one substantive issue or skill that will move their writing forward. As Nancy Sommers discovered in her research on teachers' responses, many teachers try to mark every error (often idiosyncratically and elliptically), leaving students with the confused sense that the paper is "all wrong" but with no sense of revision priorities. The effect of such comments is to superimpose the grid of an "ideal" paper against the actual project that the student writer was trying to accomplish. Sommers proposes instead a carefully selected and focused comment that enters into the student's own project and suggests a way to move it forward. The teacher might also identify a single pattern of error, mark several instances, ask the student to find several more instances and then to hand in revised versions of all those sentences. In some cases, the pattern of error and the substantive comment are linked, as for example a pattern of fused sentences manifesting the writer's tendency to rush cryptically through ideas rather than slowing down to think them through. In those cases, recognition of the error can lead the student to the points in the paper that are most rushed and become the basis for an effective revision (see Richard Straub's useful review article for a discussion of Sommers, Brannon/Knoblauch, and styles of teacher response).

Mina Shaughnessy, in her book *Errors and Expectations,* did all of us a great service by reminding us that the intentionality of student texts is quite different from that of literary works. In a literary work the writer is in control; he or she adheres to or violates conventions based on deliberate decisions. But when students violate the etiquette of syntax or spelling or punctuation, Shaughnessy reminds us, we assume that they did so with the same kind of artistic control experience that writers wield (or with a studied carelessness). And this is not the case. Students rarely if ever make deliberate errors; they are trying to succeed. Often, however, they attempt syntactic structures or make linguistic choices over which they have imperfect control. They approximate control of discourse structures and vocabulary that they have not yet mastered fully. And so we must not regard their errors and weaknesses as intentions to fail; rather, we must determine at what they were trying to succeed. We must not just identify and criticize their errors; we must analyze them and try to help students fulfill their true intentions.

David Bartholomae, applying some of Shaughnessy's observations to basic writers, argues that such error analysis can be a valuable diagnostic technique for instructors. "By investigating and interpreting the patterns of error in [students'] writing, we can help them begin to see those errors as evidence of hypotheses or strategies they have formed and, as a consequence, put them in a position to change, experiment, imagine other strategies. Studying their own writing puts students in a position to see themselves as language users, rather than as victims of a language that uses them" (258).

Many times, in fact, errors and weaknesses signal growth. Often student papers submitted after sentence-combining practices are plagued with comma splices, as students struggle to master new syntactic patterns. The students are courageously trying new techniques; penalizing them for failing on the first try to master the punctuation etiquette required may defeat your attempts to help them grow. Sometimes, of course, there will be careless errors: a word transposed or omitted in copying, the phonetic mis-hearing of a term (such as Freud's "edible complex"), an embarrassing or amusing typo (such as "Shakespeare's play of love and punishment, *Romeo and Joliet*"). These represent failures of editing skills, language performance rather than language competence, and can be treated as such.

Commenting on papers

Composition instructors have developed innovative and useful ways of evaluating student writing, including conferences, tape-recorded commentary, and peer evaluation. The handbook can be a useful aid for all these approaches, particularly peer evaluation (see "Using Collaborative Learning with the Handbook," pp. IAE-49–IAE-62). Many teachers, however, still prefer to respond to student essays through marginal and summary comments. These responses take three general forms: a correction code, correction symbols, and written comments. Each method has advantages and disadvantages; some teachers choose to combine them to draw on the strengths of each while others feel that correction codes and symbols undercut students' individualized projects. Some teachers use a correction code method accompanied by student conferences in which they give more personalized feedback; other teachers use written comments and establish feedback sessions, during which students respond to those comments and outline a revision plan or a goal for the next paper. The important thing is that your students understand your method and are able to work productively from your comments.

Using the correction code

To use the correction code, an instructor simply writes in the margin of a paper the number and letter of the section of the handbook a student should consult for help with a particular problem or error, for example, 8b (pronoun and antecedent agreement), 11a (comma splice), or 1f (problem with thesis). The code for each section of the handbook is listed inside the front cover; after a short time, most instructors find they have memorized the codes for common problems and seldom have to consult the list.

Here is a section of a student paper marked using the correction code:

> Parents have become more lenient with regard to television watching. For example, allowing their children to watch cartoon in the early morning before school. As soon as they come home from school they sit before the set again, completely ingrossed with a soap opera or a talk show. Some parents actually allow their children to watch television while they are at the supper table. Of course, the latter part of the evening, the prime time, is solely set aside for the purpose of watching a special show or a favorite series. In some ways, parents are using the television as a substitute for personal communication with the child. The days then, remain a never ending chain of program after program.

When students get their graded papers back, they need only turn to the front of the handbook to understand what the instructor's notations mean and then refer to the appropriate section of the text for a full explanation (the code for each section appears in colored boxes at the sides of the pages). Students, too, quickly learn to recognize the notations for common errors and problems. An important follow-up to this method is to ask students to identify several more instances of one kind of error, and revise those sentences using the handbook. The goal is to help students identify the kinds of errors that commonly occur in their writing so that they can look for those errors on the next draft. As a helpful accompaniment to this method you might ask students to keep a list or journal of the errors that you have marked and that they have revised as a resource for future revisions. That journal can also become the basis for an individual conference, in which you and the student discuss a pattern of error and its significance for revision (a pattern of vague pronoun references that manifests the student's difficulty in defining and working with key terms, for instance).

Using the correction symbols

Correction symbols work in much the same way as the number-and-letter code. An instructor locates the appropriate symbol in the list inside the back cover of the handbook (e.g., *dev, log, agr, coh*) and writes it in the margin of the essay, often drawing a line to indicate the location and extent of the problem. Students reverse the procedure, looking up symbols on the list, which also gives the name of the problem and a reference to the appropriate section of the text: for example, *dm*—Dangling modifier, 14f. Here is the passage from above marked in this way:

> Parents have become more lenient with regard to television watching. For example, allowing their children to watch cartoons in the early morning before school. As soon as they come home from school, they sit before the set again, completely ingrossed with a soap opera or a talk show. Some parents actually allow their children to watch television while they are at the supper table. Of course, the latter part of the evening, the prime time, is solely set aside for the purpose of watching a special show or a favorite series. In some ways, parents are using the television as a substitute for personal communication with the child. The days, then, remain a never ending chain of program after program.
>
> [Marginal marks: frag, rep, p, ww, sp, ref, mm, p, hyph]

Because correction symbols are easier to remember than the number-and-letter code, both students and teachers can spend less time turning away from a paper to consult the list of symbols than they might do with the code. Yet symbols are less specific than the code; *shift,* for instance, covers a variety of problems—13a (person and number), 13b (tense and mood), and 13c (subject and voice). Moreover, instead of being able to turn directly from the paper to a discussion in the handbook, students may need to consult the list of symbols to find the appropriate section of the text. Most of the symbols, however, also appear in the colored boxes in the margins of the pages. It becomes increasingly important, then, to augment the symbol method with comments or conferences that help students create revision priorities. For instance, you might write a marginal comment next to the first instance of a sentence fragment, then put the symbol (*frag*) next to three other occasions of the same error. An end comment or conference would direct the student to Chapter 10 of the handbook, would ask the student to locate several more instances of the error in their paper, and would ask for revisions. Once students understand that the fragment is often an undeveloped thought they are able to use their recognition of the error to create substantive revisions, not only of sentences but of paragraphs and papers as well.

Using written comments

Written comments can appear in two places: in the margins or at the paper's end. Each does a different job, and students need to learn what those jobs are. Marginal comments generally note specific areas of strength or weakness in student papers. As Nancy Sommers reminds us, marginal comments focus a student's attention on a particular draft, often causing the student to ignore the possibilities of revision and moving on in new drafts. Students sometimes become so overwhelmed by marginal comments that they want only to "fix" what's "wrong" with a particular draft. Sparing use of marginal comments may make students look to the end comments for your directions. Carefully phrased marginal comments can also direct students to revise. Often in such a system, the marginal comments that identify weaknesses are questions or statements that lead students to examine the text more carefully: "Can you give a more precise description of the hotel than 'nice' and 'rad'?" "What's your evidence for this claim?" "Does your reader know what a 'buydown mortgage' is?" Or they can describe your reaction as a reader ("I can't see the connection between these two ideas. Did you leave a step out?") Occasionally you may want to refer the student to a particular reference source ("Your citations should be in MLA form; see Chapter 37 of the handbook").

Checks in the margin can direct a student's attention to mechanical, grammatical, or stylistic weaknesses. Such individual problems should be summed up as part of your end comment: "Often you provide a quotation to support your assertions, but you rarely analyze the quotations to show how they fit into your argument. Where you do this, as on p. 3, it really strengthens your argument. Where you leave it out, your argument is less persuasive—you make your readers guess the connections you see." "A lot of the check marks have to do with where commas go in complex sentences. Review Chapter 21 to correct these problems."

The second kind of comment, usually at the end of the paper, should direct students to new writing goals. Whether you rely on a single method or a combination of methods to mark students' papers, it is usually important to provide students with a comment at the end of their papers to explain the grade and to tie together the marginal commentary, emphasizing the key points. This is also a good place to assign exercises in the handbook and to remind students what they need to do in future essays. The discussion "Evaluating Essays for a Grade" later in this chapter contains several examples of summary comments. Your end comments need to give clear rhetorical response and guidance to your students: "Your careful examination of King's religious language gives your paper a great deal of credibility. In your subsequent papers you can use this sensitivity to language to support you own assertions." Every writer likes to know he or she has succeeded; tell your students what competencies they show, and give them goals to strive for. Your end comment needs a context just like the student papers do; don't neglect it.

Establishing priorities for the students

When commenting on students' papers, try to be selective about the issues you address. Two, or at most three, weaknesses are enough for a student to focus on for the next paper. Focus on the largest issues first; if the writer can't address an audience or formulate a thesis, spelling and colon placement are trivial problems. And often, as in the cases discussed above, the weaknesses are signs of growth. Even if a student has not yet learned to analyze evidence, he's learned to provide it; even if a student continues to make comma splices, she's learning to write more complex sentences. Your comments can be phrased to reflect these tentative steps of growth: "I'm glad you tried some of the sentences combining we practiced. Now that you've learned the patterns, take a close look at where the punctuation goes so that you can use those elaborate sentences to their best effect." "You've picked really sharp quotations to back up your points. Next time follow up each of those quotes with a sentence or two of comment to help your audience see how they fit into your argument."

Finally, your response should help the writer set and reach new goals. These will usually involve mastering skills that were not used effectively in the current text or moving on to apply those skills in new contexts. Here is where the critical teaching in comments takes place: you want the student to move to a new level of achievement. The goals should be clearly expressed: "Now that you've mastered simple and compound sentences, it's time to move to complex ones." "It's clear you can persuade an audience that basically agrees with you. Next time why don't you aim to persuade a mildly hostile audience?" And your comments should suggest clear strategies for achieving those goals: "Try brainstorming and using the journalist's questions to generate more details about your subject. Then you can choose which ones you want to use." "Write down all the arguments opposed to your position that you can think of, and try to find reasonable answers to those objections." You may even need to offer a small reward to encourage timorous students to take risks: "Try to write some different kinds of sentence patterns; I won't 'mark off' if you don't quite master the punctuation next time." Your response can also encourage students to reconsider their writing processes: "The drafts of this paper show you just changed a few words; you didn't revise much. Next time, once you've got your ideas down, allow yourself to move paragraphs around, change sentences, scratch out! Revision is the chance to improve the problems mentioned above; make your organization clearer, smooth sentences, add details. Let your drafts be messy."

In sum, your end comments should encourage the student not only to go back into this paper but to move forward to the next. If you keep the tripartite structure in mind—praise strengths, identify weaknesses, set goals—you'll find it relatively easy to write a coherent, goal-oriented end comment. Encourage students to discuss those comments with you before they submit their next paper;

often a word or two of reinforcement or clarification can lead to quantum leaps in writing performance.

Making sure students understand your comments

Dealing with codes and symbols

Perhaps the most common reason students fail to understand our comments is that they do not understand the symbols or terms we use. If you were to ask a class what a fused sentence is, some students might answer in this vein: "a sentence where everything seems to run together and gets confused or awkward." Such terms as *reference, development,* and *parallelism* are also likely to draw puzzled or incorrect responses, though a few students might be able to give general explanations. Asking students the meaning of such common symbols as *pass, cs, dm,* and [*dv*] will produce similar results.

Telling students to look up correction marks on the front or back endpapers of the handbook can help, as can alerting them to the Glossary of Grammatical Terms or handing out a list of terms you plan to use in written comments. A lot of students, however, are likely to put off learning the symbols or terms until they absolutely have to, perhaps several papers into the semester, when they realize how much help they need to improve their writing. One technique that can speed the process is to foreground student papers in group work and in revision exercises with the entire class. For example, you might hand out a paper that has two sentence fragments and a comma splice in a key paragraph. After asking students to use the Editing Checklist and the relevant sections from the handbook to identify and "correct" the errors, have them work in groups to revise the errors substantively and in doing so to develop the content of the paragraph. In a follow-up class you might hand out the revised paragraphs created in the groups and ask students to compare the different analytical and grammatical choices that were made. Such exercises help students to understand the reasons for seemingly arbitrary codes.

Discussing a graded paper

Another good way to help students understand your comments is to discuss a graded paper with them. As noted earlier, Chapter 2 of the handbook (pp. 77–79) contains an example of a marked paper that you may wish to use as the basis of class discussion. In addition, the paragraphs presented earlier in this chapter contain many errors of the kind likely to turn up on student papers. The paragraphs can be distributed in class with either or both of the marking systems or with some other system you prefer. If you choose to distribute the paragraphs without markings, you can ask the students to work with you in identifying errors and choosing appropriate symbols or comments.

Evaluating essays for a grade

A grade can carry several messages: it can describe the overall quality of a paper; it can indicate how close the essay comes to achieving the goals for writing set forth in the course; and it can help tell a student writer what elements to work on in the next assignment. But unless grading standards are clear, the grades we assign will have little value for teaching beyond establishing a final grade for the course.

To help establish clear evaluation standards, many instructors discuss grading criteria with students and distribute sample papers, either already graded or to be graded in class. Another method is to attach to each paper a comment sheet reflecting the goals for the assignment. Preparing a comment sheet for each assignment can be taxing, however, and so many instructors prepare a sheet that can be used for all assignments. Here are two samples, each of which uses different grading criteria:

These are the areas in which your paper is

strong		weak
	thesis	
	development	
	paragraphs	
	sentences	
	word choice	
	punctuation	
	style	

Comment/grade:

If you do not like to use comment sheets, you may prefer to hand out grading criteria at the beginning of the course. Sometimes a department or program provides its own set of criteria for grading papers; if yours does not, you may wish to adapt for your own use the following set that reflects the major areas of emphasis in the handbook:

Thesis:

Organization:

Development:

Grammar and punctuation:

Style:

Comment/grade:

- *A* (superior). An *A* paper meets the standards in all these areas and excels in one or more of them:

  The *paper as a whole* presents a fresh subject or main idea or treats it in an interesting or original manner, displaying unusual insight and taking appropriate account of the audience. The *paragraphs* are fully developed with detail that supports the main idea; sentences within the paragraphs are clearly linked, forming an appropriate pattern; transitions are effective. *Sentences* are varied and imaginative in style, concise and creative in wording. The paper contains few errors in *grammar and punctuation* or errors only in sophisticated matters, and few *spelling* errors.
- *B* (strong). A *B* paper meets the standards in all these areas:

  The *paper as a whole* presents an interesting subject or main idea and approaches it in a consistent and careful manner, displaying good insight, though without the freshness or originality characteristic of the *A* paper. The writing makes use of consistent rhetorical strategies and a tone appropriate to the audience. *Paragraphs* are, with only a few exceptions, adequately developed and generally successful in supporting the main idea; transitions are clear, and sentences within the paragraphs are, for the most part, clearly related. *Sentences* are generally clear and correct in structure and style and are not excessively wordy. Word choice is usually appropriate. *Grammar, punctuation,* and *spelling* follow accepted conventions, except for a few minor errors.
- *C* (adequate). A *C* paper is seriously deficient in one of these areas:

  The *paper as a whole* presents a clearly defined subject or main idea, but the treatment may be trivial, uninteresting, or too general and the insight adequate but not marked by independent thought. The plan and purpose are clear but inconsistently or incompletely carried out; tone may be inconsistent. Some paragraphs may lack adequate supporting detail or may be only loosely linked to the main idea. Sentences within paragraphs may be only loosely related, and some transitions may be missing. *Sentences* are generally correct in structure but may be excessively wordy, vague, or, at times, even incorrect. Style and word choice may be flat, inconsistent, or not entirely appropriate to the audience. The paper may display isolated serious errors in *grammar and punctuation* or frequent minor errors that do not interfere substantially with meaning or that do not greatly distract the reader; the paper may contain occasional *misspellings*.

- *D* (weak). A *D* paper is seriously deficient in any one of these areas:

  The *paper as a whole* presents a poorly defined or inconsistently treated subject or central idea and displays little insight or development. The tone is inappropriate to the audience. *Paragraphs* contain little supporting detail. Sentences within paragraphs are often unrelated to the main idea and transitions are lacking. *Sentences* are frequently incorrect in structure, vague, wordy, and distracting. Style and word choice are inappropriate, incorrect, or inconsistent. The paper may contain serious and distracting errors in *grammar and punctuation* as well as numerous irritating minor errors and frequent *misspellings*.

- *F* (unacceptable/no credit). An *F* paper is unacceptable in any one of these areas:

  The *paper as a whole* does not have a clear subject or main idea and has no apparent purpose or plan; or the subject and main idea are defined and treated in a way that clearly does not meet the requirements of the assignment. *Paragraphs* are not related to the main idea; sentences within paragraphs are unrelated, and transitions are missing. *Sentences* are so faulty in structure and style that the essay is not readable. Frequent serious errors in *grammar, punctuation,* and *spelling* indicate an inability to handle the written conventions; there are excessive minor errors or misspellings.

These criteria need to be adapted to the level of students in a particular course or institution and to the goals set for the course. For example, admirable organization or style may differ markedly for a student in a two-year technical program and a student in a four-year school that stresses the arts and humanities.

Evaluating for revision

Revision in composition teaching

In recent years the process of revision has come to be viewed as increasingly important in composition instruction. Instructors who make revision a regular part of their composition classes argue that writers should be judged not (or not only) on the early version of an essay but on what they are able to make of the essay after they have had a chance to revise it and, perhaps, to take into account the comments of readers.

Composition instructors have long viewed revision as an important process for student writers to learn. What is new is the extent to which revision is being made a regular part of instruction, an emphasis reflected in the extensive treatment of both revision and editing in Chapter 2 of the handbook. In addition, many instructors have begun structuring their classes around collaborative learning groups that provide audiences for papers in progress and advice for revision. This method is reinforced in the handbook's Chapter 2, which contains checklists for students' giving and receiving criticism. The chapter "Using Collaborative Learning with the Handbook," which follows this discussion, contains suggestions for handouts to help students analyze their peers' work. Furthermore, students' increasing access to computers and the availability of computer classrooms have made possible a range of new approaches to the revision process (see Susan Lang's essay on pp. IAE-63–IAE-76).

Commenting on drafts for revision

The distinction made in Chapter 2 of the handbook between revision and editing is important for instructors to keep in mind when responding to a student paper in progress. For essays whose perspective, form, and content are well enough developed to require only editing, your role may be simply to call attention to errors or to suggest ways to polish sentences and paragraphs. Many of the techniques already discussed for commenting on papers can be used to aid editing, particularly those that refer students to sections of the handbook for advice on improving a passage or correcting a problem. In addition, you may wish to refer students to the Editing Checklist in Chapter 2 (pp. 74–75).

Evaluation for revision, however, is more likely to suggest extensive changes in a paper, often encouraging the writer to adopt a different perspective on a topic. Since revision may and often should involve substantial changes in the direction of an essay, you should be wary, however, of comments that impose your view of what a paper should do or how it should be accomplished. Instead, try to identify a problem clearly and offer some possible solutions but at the same time leave the student writers free to make their own choices. Such comments as "Your thesis statement needs to focus more sharply on the specific government toxic-waste regulations to which you object" may be helpful in cases where the student's intentions and the direction of a paper are quite clear. But when a writer is still struggling with subject and intention, such statements may limit the process of revision rather than encourage it. A comment like the following, however, leaves the eventual direction of the essay up to the student:

> I'm not sure which specific regulations you object to most. Is this a place in the essay where you want to focus your concerns sharply for readers? From the detailed evidence you present later about the struggles of small businesses to pay for state-of-the-art pollution equipment, I suspect that one of your main purposes is to have readers understand the hard times these ordinary people are facing. What do you care most about in this subject, and what do you most want your audience to understand and feel?

In commenting on papers for revision, you should call attention to any serious errors. At the same time, however, keep in mind this maxim: "Don't spend time improving a sentence that ought to be dropped from the paper." Remember, too, that awkward and confused sentences are often signs of confusion about the overall direction of an essay, and problems at the sentence level may disappear as the writer resolves the larger problems.

> You shift pronouns often in this passage, sometimes addressing the reader as "you," sometimes using "one" or "we." I think the root of the problem is that you are not sure of your relation to your readers. Since you are talking about a situation that you face along with most readers, you might choose "we" and stick to it.

In addition, most students need more than advice about what sections of a paper need to be revised; they need advice about the process of revision itself. By focusing your comments on how to go about revising rather than solely on the direction of possible changes, you can avoid doing the students' work for them and can instead help them develop an effective writing/revising process.

Coping with the paper load

At this point, you may well be asking "How am I supposed to do all these things—run groups, intervene in processes, hold conferences, analyze errors, write long comments—and remain sane?" That's a good question—and probably the most vexing one writing teachers face. You can't avoid it: grading papers takes time, lots of it, time that you'd often rather spend reading or working on your own scholarship or having a personal life or just enjoying fresh air and natural light. The best way to speed up the grading process, then, is to reduce the amount of grading you have to do. Several techniques will help you achieve this goal.

Grading the paper

Evaluating student papers can be time-consuming: instructors often report spending fifteen to twenty minutes on each paper, making marginal notes, writing summary comments, and deciding on a grade. Many set aside hours of office time for individual conferences. To help make the job of marking papers somewhat easier and quicker, *The Little, Brown Handbook* provides a number of aids:

- a list of correction symbols keyed to discussions in the text;
- a number-and-letter correction code that refers students to appropriate sections of the handbook; and
- a thorough index and glossary of terms directing students to explanations of grammatical and rhetorical terms used in an instructor's written comments.

Some practical tips will help you speed the grading process:

1. Start with carefully designed assignments and give the students enough time to complete the assignment successfully. The clearer the assignment, the

fewer variables are left for you to cope with; the more adequate the time, the fewer hasty or careless errors you (should) have to contend with.

2. Be realistic when telling students when they'll get papers back. Many authorities insist that teachers return papers at the first class meeting after the assignments are submitted. Two class meetings—or a week—is more realistic. The students also need at least one class meeting to review your comments and suggestions on one paper before submitting their next effort—and more time is helpful if they need a conference to discuss those comments with you. Schedule papers far enough apart to let you grade them carefully, and don't make promises you can't keep.

3. Not all papers must be new assignments. Students often profit from revising and reshaping an earlier paper, either one of their own choosing or one that you suggest they revise. Such assignments teach students the crucial importance of revising while giving you time to hold conferences, attend to individual problems, and design subsequent assignments.

4. Set a schedule for your grading and keep it. If you must grade fifty papers in five days, that's ten a day. At half an hour for each paper (a good beginner's rate), that's five hours of grading a day (you'll need a break or two to maintain your concentration).

5. Set reasonable time limits. Buy a timer and be ruthless about paying attention to it. Allow yourself a maximum time per paper—as a beginner, twenty-five or thirty minutes for an average (500–700 word) paper; as you get more experienced, fifteen to twenty minutes. Read the paper through once in its entirety before you mark anything, even minor mechanical errors. This allows you to assess the biggest strengths and weaknesses, to target your attention. Reread the paper, making your minimal marks and marginal comments. Then skim it one more time and compose your end comments. Sometimes the end comments written by beginning teachers are a page or longer; you'll learn to control this with experience. Again, using the three-part formula—strengths, a few weaknesses, and goals and strategies—can help you compose a response quickly.

Although you may find yourself calling on stock phrases to compose your end comments, it will help to refer back to specific marginal comments and moments in the paper as well. For example, you might say "One of the strongest things about this paper is your use of quotations to support your opinions. On p. 2, for example, I've noted a particularly well-chosen quote and suggested ways that you might further develop your response to it." The relationship that you develop between your marginal comments and your end comment can be particularly helpful in guiding students from their global priorities for revision to local examples of where they might begin (or may already have begun) to develop the paper further.

6. Write a good end comment. If you have clear grading standards, put a letter grade on the paper after you've written your end comment; if not, sort all the papers into roughly defined piles—the good ones, the okay ones, the problem ones—and go back to assign grades later. If your time runs out, finish your note immediately and move on; you're probably asking the student to address too many issues. If you finish early, take a quick stretch and keep going; you'll want

that time later. If a paper is very weak, set it aside; you'll want time to write a thoughtful note later. Don't turn the end comment into a justification or apology for a low grade; use it as a chance to teach the student ways to improve. If you think that assigning a very low grade would be detrimental to the student's progress, you can always mark the paper "No grade pending conference," discuss the paper with the student, and grade it after the student has revised it further. This solution works best when used sparingly and privately; otherwise you'll have B+ students clamoring for a chance to rewrite papers to get an A. (You can choose to allow such students to do so, of course, but be prepared to fight accusations of grade inflation.)

7. Keep good records. Don't just put the grade on the paper; record it in your grade book or progress folder immediately. If you're keeping a progress chart in the student's folder, make a few sketchy notes now; you can go back and elaborate later if necessary. If you forget to record grades now, you'll eventually find yourself in the position of returning a set of papers without having recorded the grades; then you have to go through all sorts of contortions to get the papers back to record the grades. Such a time-consuming annoyance can be avoided by keeping records carefully from the beginning.

Portfolios

You can reduce the number of assignments you actually give letter grades by allowing students to select some of their papers to submit as a portfolio for the class. Usually students submit drafts at an early point in the semester for your comments, then revise them and choose which ones to submit for their final grade in the course. Such an approach grants them more autonomy and may heighten their desire to achieve. Portfolios also encourage students to see writing as a process, enabling their growth as writers; for this reason, many colleges and universities are using portfolios not only in first-year writing but throughout a student's academic career; these portfolios become substantially more than just an evaluation method.

The problems with portfolios chiefly involve quantity and quality; rather than mark 25 papers nine times a semester, you'll have to mark 225 per class at one time. If you teach multiple sections, the problem will mushroom. You can lessen the burden by requiring that two papers be chosen for the portfolio by midsemester and the others at the end of term or by otherwise adjusting the due dates to meet your own—and the class's—needs. You'll still need to provide students with feedback on the individual papers, so they know what points to work on and which papers to revise as their "best."

Portfolio grading, at its best, empowers students and spurs revision; thus, it has drawn a great deal of attention in recent years as programs struggle with the whole question of evaluation. Several fine collections of perspectives on the portfolio question have appeared in recent years, including *Portfolios: Process and Product,* edited by Pat Belanoff and Marcia Dickson; *Portfolios and Beyond: Collaborative Assessment in Reading and Writing* by Susan Mandel Glazer and Carol Smullen Brown; *Process and Portfolios in Writing Instruction,* edited by

Ken Gill and the Committee on Classroom Practices; and *Portfolio Resource Guide: Creating and Using Portfolios in the Classroom* by Judith C. Gilbert. However, some studies (particularly in Vermont) have questioned how well portfolios function in measuring students' writing ability over time. Others have pointed to the fact that while many people claim portfolios' virtues, very few studies have demonstrated either the practical use of handling them in the classroom or their effectiveness in helping students become better writers over the course of their college careers. Portfolio theory is still in its infancy, and much research remains to be done to understand how portfolios can best be used. Thus, this method will certainly continue to draw critical scrutiny.

Conference

You can also work individually with students on the development of their papers, looking at rough drafts of either portions or complete versions of their texts. You could "evaluate" some papers in one-to-one conferences, assigning verbal grades of "excellent," "very good," "fair," and the like. Since these grades will likely be high, reflecting your evaluation of the project at many stages, you might then assign letter grades only to papers students produce independently, alternating conference and independent papers. This strategy reduces by half the number of written comments you must produce; its drawback is the amount of time such conference teaching requires. Some teachers address the time issue by meeting with selected groups of students for intensive revision discussions focused on those students' particular needs. An additional advantage of conferences is that you can work through relevant sections of the handbook with students, so that they have specific places to look for information as they revise their papers. A good rule of thumb in planning conferences is to set a defined agenda in advance so that students come to the conference with a particular piece of writing, a list of questions, or a revision plan, and with a mutually understood goal for the session.

Collaborating

A different kind of workload reduction can be achieved by letting your students do some of the work for you collaboratively. When students work effectively in small and large groups, they can identify writing problems at the draft stage and help their fellow students remedy weaknesses. Group proofreading sessions likewise can find and solve many mechanical problems before they reach your desk. If you train the groups to look for the kinds of problems students are having, they can do a great deal of the diagnostic work for each other. You'll occasionally have to correct a faulty diagnosis but you will save yourself a little time while promoting students' independent revision and editing skills. If all students have access to computer facilities, you can encourage them to use spelling checker programs, and perhaps to create networked revision groups or e-mail chat groups to support each other's editing processes. See the essay on "Collaborative Learning" (on pp. IAE-49–IAE-62).

Student-set standards

You can also encourage students to set the standard for achievement in the class, perhaps using a model such as the description of letter grades given above. Or, using that model as a general criterion, you might ask students to derive a more specific set of criteria from a particular assignment. Such an exercise might ask: "What kinds of things does this assignment ask for? What might be a minimal (*C*-level) response to this assignment? What kinds of strategies might an excellent (*B*- to *A*-level paper) adopt in responding to this assignment?" Or, early in the semester, you can have students develop sets of criteria that characterize above-average, average, and below-average writing; then hold them to these criteria in assigning grades. Duplicate the criteria and distribute them to the class members; use them to develop goals in assignments, to develop heuristics for group work, and to support your comments. A good example of student-set standards is included in Josephine Koster Tarvers's *Teaching Writing: Theories and Practices,* 4th ed., pages 115–16.

Evaluation *can*'s and *can't*'s

Some teachers, particularly beginning ones, have an extremely idealistic view of evaluation. They see it as a cure-all for all the writer's problems. To gain these results, they write comments that may approach (or exceed) the original paper in length. The overwhelmed student may try to respond but is usually daunted by all the advice and suggestions—and subsequent papers sometimes are disasters. It's particularly crucial to remember that students can rarely learn a new skill or learn to recognize and correct even a single pattern of error overnight. It takes an enormous amount of practice and consideration for a student to locate sentence fragments in his or her own writing—about as much time as it takes to create well-developed paragraphs. Although it can be frustrating to see recurring errors of exactly the same type that you have carefully marked in previous papers, those errors are rarely a sign of carelessness; more often they suggest that the student needs more personalized support (a conference, a tutoring session, an assigned task using the handbook).

Evaluating individual written products is a matter of seeing how well students have reached intermediate goals in the course. It can't be done on the bell curve; writing progress is too individual a process for that. While you'll want to apply the same standards to all students, you'll probably have to allow some leeway in measuring achievement. Students who quickly master narrow competencies (such as mechanics or syntactic variety) should receive credit for these successes but should probably be judged more on how well they master more open matters—audience manipulation, voice, development, and so on. Students who have a great deal of difficulty mastering the narrow skills—those who come from particularly weak backgrounds or who have dialect interference problems, for example—may have excellent ideas but difficulty in presenting them. They should be rewarded for the content of their papers but encouraged to master the conventions of academic discourse as well. Make it clear to students that you're not evaluating how well they compete against other students—or against your ideals—but how much progress they're making in achieving the goals set for all students.

Likewise, you may be tempted to reward a student's effort on a paper rather than the product he or she actually produces ("This just doesn't hold together, but he worked so hard; look at all these drafts!"); such sympathy may be human, but it's not going to help the student. Giving good grades for effort rather than for results provides students with false assessments of their achievements. It's dishonest. Better in such cases to withhold a grade pending a conference and revision than to inflate students' expectations artificially.

Resources for response and evaluation

Bartholomae, David. "The Study of Error." *College Composition and Communication* 31 (1980): 253–69.

———. "Released into Error: Errors, Expectations and the Legacy of Mina Shaughnessy." In *The Territory of Language,* Donald A. McQuade, ed. Carbondale: Southern Illinois UP, 1986.

Belanoff, Pat, and Marcia Dickson, eds. *Portfolios: Process and Product.* Portsmouth: Boynton/Cook, 1991.

Boynton, Victoria. "Collaborative Power Sharing." *Composition Chronicle* 6:1 (February 1993): 6–8.

Brannon, Lil, and C. H. Knoblauch. "On Students' Rights to Their Own Texts: A Model of Teacher Response." *College Composition and Communication* 33 (1982): 157–66.

Conners, Robert J., and Andrea Lunsford. "Teachers Rhetorical Comments on Student Papers." *College Composition and Communication* 44:2 (May 1993): 200–233.

Cooper, Charles R., and Lee Odell, eds. *Evaluating Writing: Describing, Measuring, Judging.* Urbana: NCTE, 1977.

Faigley, Lester. "Judging Writing, Judging Selves." *College Composition and Communication* 40 (1989): 395–412.

Ford, James E., and Gregory Larkin. "The Portfolio System: An End to Backsliding Writing Standards." *College English* 39 (1978): 950–55.

Freedman, Sarah Warshauer. *Responses to Student Writing.* Urbana: NCTE, 1987.

———, and Melanie Sperling. "Teacher–Student Interaction in the Writing Conference: Response and Teaching." In *The Acquisition of Written Language: Response and Revision.* Ed. Sarah Warshauer Freedman. Norwood: Ablex, 1985.

Garrison, Roger. *One-to-One: Making Writing Instruction Effective.* Instructor's Manual to Accompany Garrison's *How a Writer Works.* New York: Harper & Row, 1981.

———. "One-to-One: Tutorial Instruction in Freshman Composition." *New Directions for Community Colleges* 2 (Spring 1974): 55–84.

Gere, Ann Ruggles, and Robert Stevens. "The Language of Writing Groups: How Oral Response Shapes Revision." In *The Acquisition of Written Language: Response and Revision.* Ed. Sarah Warshauer Freedman. Norwood: Ablex, 1985. 85–105.

Gilbert, Judith C. *Portfolio Resource Guide: Creating and Using Portfolios in the Classroom.* Ottawa, KS: The Writing Conference, 1993.

Gill, Ken, and the Committee on Classroom Practices, eds. *Process and Portfolios in Writing Instruction.* Urbana: NCTE, 1993.

Glazer, Susan Mandel, and Carol Smullen Brown. *Portfolios and Beyond: Collaborative Assessments in Reading and Writing.* Norwood: Christopher-Gordon, 1993.

Hamp-Lyons, Liz. "Uncovering Possibilities for a Constructivist Paradigm for Writing Assessment." Review in *College Composition and Communication* 46:3 (Oct. 1995): 446–55.

Hillocks, George. "The Interaction of Instruction, Teacher Comment, and Revision in Teaching the Composing Process." *Research in the Teaching of English* 16 (1982): 261–78.

Hunter, Susan, and Ray Wallace. *The Place of Grammar in Writing Instruction, Past, Present, Future.* Portsmouth, NH: Boynton/Cook, 1995.

Larson, Bruce, Susan Stern Ryan, and Ross Winterowd, eds. *Encountering Student Texts: Interpretive Issues in Reading Student Writing.* Urbana: NCTE, 1990.

McDonald, W. U. Jr. "The Revising Process and the Marking of Student Papers." *College Composition and Communication* 29 (1978): 167–70.

Miller, Linda P. "A Conference Methodology for Freshman Composition." *Teaching English in the Two-Year College* 7 (1980): 23–26.

Noguchi, Rei R. *Grammar and the Teaching of Writing: Limits and Possibilities.* Urbana: NCTE, 1991.

Olsen, Gary A. "Beyond Evaluation: The Recorded Response to Essays." *Teaching English in the Two-Year College* 8 (1982): 121–23.

Purves, Alan. "The Teacher as Reader: An Anatomy." *College English* 46 (1984): 259–65.

Schiff, Peter. "Responding to Writing: Peer Critiques, Teacher-Student Conferences, and Essay Evaluations." In *Language Connections: Writing and Reading Across the Curriculum.* Urbana: NCTE, 1982. 153–65.

Shaughnessy, Mina. *Errors and Expectations: A Guide for the Teacher of Basic Writing.* New York: Oxford UP, 1977.

Shaw, Margaret L. "What Students Don't Say: An Approach to the Student Text." *College Composition and Communication* 42 (1991): 45–54.

Sommers, Nancy. "Responding to Student Writing." *College Composition and Communication* 33 (1982): 148–56.

Stanford, Gene, Ed. *How to Handle the Paper Load.* Urbana: NCTE, 1978.

Straub, Richard. "The Concept of Control in Teacher Response: Defining the Varieties of "Directive" and "Facilitative" Commentary." *College Composition and Communication* 47:2 (May 1996): 223–51.

Tarvers, Josephine Koster. *Teaching Writing: Theories and Practices.* 4th ed. New York: HarperCollins, 1993.

Yancey, Katherine Blake, ed. *Portfolios in the Writing Classroom: An Introduction.* Urbana: NCTE, 1992.

Chapter 4

Using Collaborative Learning with the Handbook

Collaborative learning activities have become a widely accepted practice. Small group collaborations provide effective ways to get students writing to a tangible audience of their peers, to practice their revision skills in a supportive, nonintimidating environment, and to experience the reality of alternative perspectives and approaches to writing and to the course readings. Group work also shifts classroom learning to an ongoing conversation between students rather than as a constant deferral to the teacher's greater authority. Kenneth Bruffee, a key proponent of collaborative learning, argues that because knowledge itself is the result of consensus among members of a community, and is produced by collaborative activity, "interdependent" student groups offer the ideal learning tool (Bruffee 3). They become "transition communities or support groups that students can rely on as they go through the risky process of becoming new members of the knowledge communities" (Bruffee 4). While Bruffee argues for a long history of informal cooperation and support systems among students as the natural basis for collaborative classroom assignments, others have pointed to the difficulty of grafting collaborative procedures into institutions that base their standards on individual performance and reward individual excellence (Gergits and Schramer). Still others have countered Bruffee's model of consensus as one that overlooks or erases the powerful differences between groups and individuals, differences that are the basis for continual collaborative negotiation (Trimbur and Spellmeyer, for example).

As these theoretical models suggest, it is important to be aware of potentially contradictory messages when setting up collaborative activities. For instance, students may not readily embrace a collaborative revision exercise if the grading system for the class, the teacher's responses on papers, and other classroom practices are all focused on individual performance. Conversely, the more collaborative work that students do, and the more that work is supported by surrounding classroom practices, the more students will understand the goals of group activities and feel confident in negotiating group dynamics. It also helps to remember that collaborative groups are part of a complex social process; as students work to overcome the social awkwardness of organizing and starting the task, they are also finding some common ground, finding ways to communicate across (sometimes) enormous ideological and conceptual differences (see *Singular Texts/Plural Authors,* Andrea Lunsford and Lisa Ede).

Inexperienced teachers who are considering collaborative activities may find the following suggestions useful. Collaborative groups can vary in size and configuration depending on the activity—from pairs to groups of four or five. For example, if the task is to choose a passage from the reading and come up with an interpretive response to present to the class, a larger group is useful in producing energetic debates (especially if each student is responsible for presenting some of the material). If you are having students work with the handbook to identify and revise particular patterns of error, groups of three allow for both a range of grammatical skills and attention to individual difficulties. Students might begin with the Editing Checklist (pp. 74–75) to identify the recurrent patterns of error in other's work, then revise those errors using the relevant sections from the handbook (see Chapters 20–25 in particular). If your revision groups of three or four are becoming careless in their suggestions for each other's papers, you might pair students in groups of two and ask them to respond in writing and at length to another student's paper.

Some teachers always allow students to choose their own groups; the advantage here is that students generally establish a working dynamic and continue to choose the same group throughout the course. Other teachers select groups in order to mix or isolate skill levels or to create productive environments for silent or outspoken students. Again, you might make this decision based on the particular task and on group dynamics. If the task you have assigned is to revise a sentence or a paragraph in a student essay you might streamline the process by asking students to work with the person next to them. If you notice a larger revision group veering into discussions of movies or a sociology exam, you might sit in with them for that session to listen to the group dynamic, then make an effort to reorganize groups for the next session (see Brook, Mirtz, et al. for further discussion of small group dynamics).

One way to reinforce collaborative goals in a course in which grades depend upon individual performance is to incorporate peer-review suggestions into your final graded comments on each student's paper. After reading the student's paper and scanning the peer-review worksheets or marked drafts, you might say, for example, "You have effectively made use of Jeffrey D.'s suggestion about developing paragraphs 5–8. Audrey F.'s question about your transitions on pages 4 and 5 might have led you to strengthen your argument—look out for those transitional movements next time!" Another way to reinforce those goals is to assign one or two collaboratively written and graded projects.

Many instructors assign students in pairs or small teams to collaborate on papers; for certain kinds of writing, especially research writing, such strategies can be very effective and will prepare students well for the kinds of writing they may do in their careers. Many of the exercises in Chapters 35 and 36 can be adapted for collaborative projects (see annotations in each chapter). Collaborative projects can be combined with individually produced and evaluated papers as well. For example, you might have students work in pairs to write out the different sides of a debate, then ask each student to produce an individually written paper that takes the other student's perspective into account. Highlighted "Collaborative Learning" exercises in Chapter 4 suggest various ways for students to produce arguments and to analyze each other's claims.

As with any other process, collaborative work is a slowly developed skill. New teachers will sometimes report that they tried it once and it "didn't work" so they're hesitant to try it again. Remember that groups might not seem highly productive at first; students can be unsure of their revision skills, hesitant about showing their work, and dependent on the teacher's greater authority. One way to make group work more productive from the start is to give students shorter, highly directed tasks at first; for example, each group might read and discuss Chapter 3, section c on developing paragraphs, then work together to revise a student writer's paragraph. It also helps to model the assigned activity within the class as a whole before moving to smaller groups. For example, you might bring in a sample student paper, have each student come up with a revision suggestion or practice revising a sample sentence, then share the results with the class. Then, when students undertake a similar activity in smaller groups, you can refer back to the previous class-wide activity. Also, in many cases in which group work appears to "fail," students are simply confused about the assigned activity. It helps to be extremely clear about what you want each group to accomplish—even provide a written handout or worksheet (sample worksheets follow this discussion). It's also important that students recognize the relationship between the group activity and their personal goals as writers; many teachers preface group work with a discussion of those goals in relation to the group task.

The crucial thing to remember is that working in revision or writing groups is as much a skill to be demonstrated and learned as any other. In working with a sample paper, for example, you might start with some basic questions that help students to look globally at pieces of discourse as a teacher (evaluator) looks at it. "What's the point of this paper? Who are the readers supposed to be? What are some things this writer does well?" Then you might ask students to look more specifically at the construction of the paper: the places where assertions are backed up by evidence and the places where more evidence is needed; the indications of strong organizational control and the places where the text seems choppy and disorganized; the clear definition with supporting examples and the terms of the essay that need further clarification and development. The sample worksheets that accompany this chapter can be modified to guide students through particular tasks. For example, you might ask each student writer to create a self-evaluation of the paper (Form G) then compare it to their group's suggestions (Form A, B, or C). If students seem to be supplying vague responses to larger questions about audience and argument, Forms D, E, and F suggest ways to focus the groups on extremely specific areas of the essay.

In addition to identifying strengths and problem areas, collaborative groups can go on to help each writer begin the work of revision. If, for instance, the text seems choppy or disorganized, they can experiment with rearranged paragraphs (using Exercise 20 in Chapter 1d for example) or look for transition problems (using Exercise 29, Chapter 3b). If the thesis is underdeveloped, they might apply the questions in Chapter 4g, Exercise 12 to suggest places where new examples or analysis would help. Or, if the essay seems to lack a directed purpose, Exercises 8 and 10 in Chapter 1d offer specific and effective ways for students to think about audience. Many of the other exercises in *The Little, Brown Handbook* are well suited to such collaborative work; a list of them is provided below.

Many teachers like to modify the worksheets and exercises for the uses of a particular class. For instance, worksheet questions can be adapted to focus on a particular reading or essay assignment. Some teachers begin the course with detailed revision worksheets then gradually taper off as group members become familiar with each other and confident about their revision skills. Teachers working in a computer classroom can supplement these exercises by creating networked revision groups, e-mail chat groups, and virtual-reality publications that help students experience various audience responses to their work (see Barrett for example and Susan Lang's essay on pp. IAE-63–IAE-77).

While some teachers are active participants in group activities, other teachers try not to intervene directly in groups unless students have questions or have ceased to address the task (for more on this topic see Bosworth and Hamilton and "A Conversation About Small Groups" in Brook et al.). The teacher's primary role in a collaborative classroom is to plan group tasks that are effectively designed and that take the varying needs of students into account. For example, highly skilled students may not always trust their peers to give them revision advice. For those students it is important to emphasize that in learning to critique another writer's work in a way that encourages a productive revision they are honing their own revision skills as well. Conversely, less-skilled writers occasionally feel overwhelmed by the group's advice and may seek to deflect attention from the paper by protesting that it's not a real draft or that it's not ready to be read. Here it helps to emphasize that active revision can begin from a sketchy paragraph or from notes. In some cases, the most effective task for a group might be to help the writer pinpoint useful passages in the readings, or ask the writer to describe verbally where he or she intends to go with the project. In this sense, collaborative work can be flexibly attuned to the needs of various writers at different stages of a project. In a process-oriented class, this emphasis on the way different writers work can be a useful focus for class-wide discussions—and a way to encourage students to take themselves and each other seriously as writers.

Since students may profit from having specific guidelines for collaboration, we've prepared the following worksheets that will help you guide collaborative activities in your classroom.

Worksheets for collaborative activities

FORM A

General Guidelines for Peer Readers Commenting Directly on a Writer's Work

Author: Reader:

As a reader, you are going to comment directly on a photocopy of a classmate's paper. Read the paper through carefully before making any comments. Then follow the guidelines below. If the writer has submitted a self-evaluation sheet, read it after answering question 1.

1. Consider the thesis, purpose, and audience for the paper. Are they indicated clearly? Are they consistent? If not, ask the writer questions to help clarify these essential elements of writing.

2. Skim the paper to see how it is organized. Are there any breaks in the organization? If so, try to explain why you feel that a gap exists. Whenever possible, phrase your comments as questions, not judgments. If you think that the organization needs to be revised significantly, skip to question 7 after answering this question.

3. Now go back and look at each paragraph. Is it unified, coherent, and developed? If not, ask the writer a question to help focus or complete the paragraph.

4. Are the paragraphs connected to one another smoothly and logically? If there are any logical gaps between the paragraphs, ask the writer how one paragraph is linked to the next. If you think that most of the paragraphs need to be revised significantly, skip to question 7 after answering this question.

5. Now look at sentences. Do any sentences confuse you? If so, try to describe your confusion or ask the writer a question about the sentence.

6. Are there any mechanical or grammatical problems in the paper? If so, point them out to the writer, but do not correct them.

7. Decide what the paper's two most important strengths are. Point these out to the writer.

FORM B

Reader Response Sheet for a Descriptive Critique

Author: Reader:

Answer the questions below, being as specific as possible.

1. Read the first paragraph and then pause. Write down what you expect will be the topic, purpose, and audience of the paper.

2. Now finish reading the paper. Were your expectations for the paper's topic, purpose, and audience fulfilled? If not, what do you now think the topic, purpose, and audience are?

3. What do you think the main idea, or thesis, of the paper is?

4. What sort of evidence is used to develop or support this main idea?

5. Summarize the paper, devoting one sentence to each paragraph.

FORM C

Reader Response Sheet for an Evaluative Critique

Author: Reader:

Answer the questions below, being as specific as possible. If the author has included a self-evaluation sheet, do not read it until you have answered questions 1 through 6.

1. Read the first paragraph and then pause. Write down what you expect will be the topic, purpose, and audience of the paper.

2. Now finish reading the paper. Were your expectations for the paper's topic, purpose, and audience fulfilled? If not, what do you now think the topic, purpose, and audience are?

3. What do you think the main idea, or thesis, of the paper is?

4. What sort of evidence is used to develop or support this main idea?

5. Summarize the paper, devoting one sentence to each paragraph.

6. What did you like best about the paper?

7. Did anything in the paper surprise you?

8. What two features of the paper most need improvement?

9. Please respond to the author's questions on the back of this sheet.

To the author: Before giving this sheet to your reader, list below the three questions that you would like your reader to answer about this paper.

FORM D

Reader Response Sheet for a Thorough Critique

Author: Reader:

Answer the questions below, being as specific as possible. If the author has included a self-evaluation sheet, do not read it until you have answered questions 1 through 3.

1. Read the first paragraph and then pause. Write down what you expect will be the topic, purpose, and audience of the paper.

2. Now finish reading the paper. Were your expectations for the paper's topic, purpose, and audience fulfilled? If not, what do you now think the topic, purpose, and audience are?

3. Summarize the paper, devoting one sentence to each paragraph.

4. What do you think the main idea, or thesis, of the paper is? Do you agree with this thesis? Why or why not? What is your position on this topic?

5. What sort of evidence is used to develop or support this main idea? Is this evidence appropriate? Is there sufficient evidence? If not, what sort of evidence should the writer consider?

6. Does the author take into account different points of view about the thesis of the paper? Does the author consider counterarguments?

7. Are there any counterarguments that the author does not consider, but should?

8. What did you like best about this paper?

9. What two features of the paper most need improvement?

10. Please respond to the author's questions on the back of this sheet.

To the author: Before giving this sheet to your reader, list below the three questions that you would like your reader to answer about this paper.

FORM E

Author's and Reader's Responses in the Second Round of a Thorough Critique

Author: Reader:

Author's section. Please attach a revision of your original paper to this form and answer the following questions.

1. What do you think is your reader's point of view on this subject? Do you share that point of view?

2. What assumptions does your reader make about the topic? Do you agree with these assumptions? Why or why not?

3. What two comments by the reader were the most useful? Why were they helpful?

4. What are the two most important changes that you have made in this revision?

5. What do you like best about the essay?

6. What two questions would you like your reader to answer about this revision?

Reader's section. Please respond to the questions below.

1. Please summarize the author's revision, devoting one sentence to each paragraph.

2. How do you think that the author has improved the essay?

3. Has the author changed your feeling about the topic?

4. What is the strongest argument against the revised essay?

5. What two features most need improvement?

6. Respond to the author's questions.

FORM F

Reader Response Sheet for an Essay Assignment Stressing Paragraphing (Handbook, Chapter 3)

Author: Reader:

Answer the questions below, being as specific as possible. If the author has included a self-evaluation sheet, do not read it until you have answered questions 1 through 6.

1. Read the first paragraph and then pause. Write down what you expect will be the topic, purpose, and audience of the paper.

2. Now finish reading the paper. Were your expectations for the paper's topic, purpose, and audience fulfilled? If not, what do you now think the topic, purpose, and audience are?

3. What do you think the main idea, or thesis, of the paper is?

4. What sort of evidence is used to develop or support this main idea?

5. Next, number the paragraphs. Are the author's paragraphs unified, coherent, and developed? If so, note them. Also indicate any that confuse you, and explain why.

6. Do the paragraphs follow a logical order? Describe how the argument does or does not flow from the first to the second, from the second to the third, and so on.

7. What did you like best about the paper?

8. What two features of the paper most need improvement?

FORM G

Self-Evaluation Sheet to Accompany an Essay for Peer Response or Instructor's Evaluation

Author: In order to help your instructor or peer reader evaluate this essay, you should explain where you are in the writing process. Be as specific as possible in answering the following questions.

1. What are you trying to say in this paper? What is your main idea?

2. Who might be interested in reading this paper?

3. What do you like best in the paper?

4. What do you like least in the paper?

5. What would you work on if you had twenty-four hours more to spend on the project?

6. What three questions would you like to ask your reader? How can your reader help you develop the paper further?

Exercises for collaborative work

The annotations in this *Instructor's Annotated Edition* also contain a number of collaborative activities you can use.

Introduction: Exercises 1–6
Chapter 1: Exercises 2, 4, 5, 8, 10, 11, 17–19
Chapter 2: Exercises 1, 2, 4, 6–8, 10–12
Chapter 3: Exercises 1, 2, 6, 9, 11–16, 19, 20
Chapter 4: Exercises 1, 2, 4–13
Chapter 5: Exercises 7, 11, 12–15, 17, 20, 21
Chapter 6: Exercises 3, 4
Chapter 7: Exercises 8–10, 13
Chapter 8: Exercises 1–4
Chapter 9: Exercises 2, 3, 5, 6
Exercise on Chapters 6–9 (following Chapter 9)
Chapter 10: Exercises 1–3
Chapter 11: Exercises 1–4
Chapter 12: Exercises 2, 3
Chapter 13: Exercise 4
Chapter 14: Exercises 2, 3, 7
Chapter 15: Exercises 1, 3–5
Exercise on Chapters 10–15 (following Chapter 15)
Chapter 16: Exercises 1–7
Chapter 17: Exercises 1–4
Chapter 18: Exercises 1–5
Chapter 19: Exercises 1–7
Exercise on Chapters 16–19 (following Chapter 19)
Chapter 20: Exercise 4
Chapter 21: Exercises 2–6, 11–13
Chapter 22: Exercises 2–4, 6, 7
Chapter 23: Exercise 6
Chapter 24: Exercises 3, 4
Chapter 25: Exercise 5
Exercise on Chapters 20–25 (following Chapter 25)
Exercise on Chapters 26–30 (following Chapter 30)
Chapter 31: Exercises 1–5; 7–11, 13
Chapter 33: Exercises 1, 2, 4
Chapter 35: Exercises 1, 2, 4
Chapter 36: Exercises 1, 4–6, 10–12
Chapter 37: Exercises 2, 3

Resources for collaborative learning and peer criticism

Arkin, Marian, and Barbara Shollar. *The Writing Tutor.* New York: Longman, 1982.

Barrett, Edward. "Collaboration in the Electronic Classroom." *Technology Review* 96:2 (Feb./March 1993): 51–55.

Bishop, Wendy. "Helping Peer Writing Groups Succeed." *Teaching English in the Two-Year College* 15 (1988): 120–25.

Bizzaro, Patrick, and Stuart Werner. "Collaboration of Teacher and Counselor in Basic Writing." *College Composition and Communication 38* (1987): 397–425.

Bormann, Ernest. *Small-Group Communication: Theory and Practice.* New York: Harper, 1990.

Brook, Robert, Ruth Mirtz, and Rick Evans, eds. *Small Groups in Writing Workshops.* Urbana: NCTE, 1994.

Bruffee, Kenneth. *Collaborative Learning: Higher Education, Interdependence, and the Authority of Knowledge.* Baltimore: Johns Hopkins UP, 1993.

Clark, Beverly Lyon. *Talking About Writing: A Guide for Tutor and Teacher Conferences.* Ann Arbor: U of Michigan P, 1985.

Clarke, Irene L. "Portfolio Evaluations, Collaboration, and Writing Centers." *College Composition and Communication* 44:4 (Dec. 1993): 515–24.

Corder, Jim W. "Tribes and Displaced Persons: Some Observations on Collaboration." In *Theory and Practice in the Teaching of Writing: Rethinking the Discipline.* Ed. Lee Odell. Carbondale: Southern Illinois UP, 1993. 271–88.

Elbow, Peter. "Reflecting on Academic Discourse: How It Relates to Freshmen and Colleagues." *College English* 53 (Feb. 1991): 135–55.

Fontaine, Sheryl L. "The Unfinished Story of the Interpretative Community." *Rhetoric Review* 7 (1988): 86–96.

Forman, Janis, ed. *New Visions of Collaborative Writing.* Portsmouth, NH: Cook/Boynton, 1992.

Fraser, Scott C., et al. "Two, Three, or Four Heads Are Better Than One: Modification of College Performance by Peer Monitoring." *Journal of Educational Psychology* 69 (1977–78): 101–08.

Gebhardt, Richard. "Team Work and Feedback: Broadening the Base of Collaborative Writing." *College English* 42 (1980): 69–74.

Gergits, Julia M., and James J. Schramer. "The Collaborative Classroom as the Site of Difference." *Journal of Advance Composition* 14:1 (Winter 1994): 187–202.

George, Diana. "Working with Peer Groups in the Composition Classroom." *College Composition and Communication* 35 (1984): 320–26.

Gere, Anne Ruggles. *Writing Groups: History, Theory, and Implications.* Carbondale: Southern Illinois UP, 1987.

———, and Robert D. Abbott. "Talking About Writing: The Language of Writing Groups." *Research in the Teaching of English* 19 (1985): 362–86.

———, and Ralph Stevens. "The Language of Writing Groups: How Oral Response Shapes Revision." In *The Acquisition of Written Language: Response and Revision.* Ed. Sarah Warshauer Freedman. Norwood: Ablex, 1985. 85–105.

Golub, Jeff, and the Committee on Classroom Practices, eds. *Focus on Collaborative Learning.* Urbana: NCTE, 1988.

Harris, Joseph. "The Idea of Community in the Study of Writing." *College Composition and Communication* 40 (1989): 11–22.

Harris, Muriel. "Peer Tutoring: How Tutors Learn." *Teaching English in the Two-Year College* 15 (1988): 28–33.

Hillocks, George. "Environments for Active Learning." In *Theory and Practice in the Teaching of Writing: Rethinking the Discipline.* Ed. Lee Odell. Carbondale: Southern Illinois UP, 1993. 244–70.

Kail, Harvey. "Collaborative Learning in Context: The Problem with Peer Tutoring." *College English* 45 (1983): 817–23.

Knox-Zuinn, Carolyn. "Collaboration in the Writing Classroom: An Interview with Ken Kesey." *College Composition and Communication* 41 (1990): 309–17.

Lunsford, Andrea, and Lisa Ede. "Rhetoric in a New Key: Women and Collaboration." *Rhetoric Review* 8 (1990): 234–41.

———. *Singular texts/Plural Authors: Perspectives on Collaborative Writing.* Carbondale: Southern Illinois UP, 1992.

Lyon, Arabella. "Re-presenting Communities: Teaching Turbulence." *Rhetoric Review* 10 (1992): 279–90.

Madden-Simpson, Janet. "A Collaborative Approach to the Research Paper." *Teaching English in the Two-Year College* 16 (1989): 113–15.

Reither, James A., and Douglas Vipond. "Writing as Collaboration." *College English* 51 (1989): 855–67.

Smit, David W. "Some Difficulties with Collaborative Learning." *Journal of Advanced Composition* 9 (1989): 45–58.

Spear, Karen. *Sharing Writing: Peer Response Groups in English Classes.* Portsmouth: Heinemann, 1988.

Spellmeyer, Kurt. "On Conventions and Collaboration: The Open Road and the Iron Cage." In *Writing Theory and Critical Theory.* Ed. John Clifford and John Schilb. New York: MLA, 1994.

Stewart, Donald. "Collaborative Learning and Composition: Boon or Bane?" *Rhetoric Review* 7 (1988): 58–85.

Teich, Nathaniel, ed. *Rogerian Perspectives: Collaborative Rhetoric for Oral and Written Communication.* Norwood: Ablex, 1992.

Trimbur, John. "Collaborative Learning and Teaching Writing." In *Perspectives on Research and Scholarship in Composition.* Ed. Ben W. McClelland and Timothy R. Donovan. New York: MLA, 1985. 87–109.

———. "Consensus and Difference in Collaborative Learning." *College English* 51 (1989): 602–16.

Tobin, Lad. *Writing Relationships: What Really Happens in the Composition Class.* Portsmouth: Boynton/Cook, 1993.

Wiener, Harvey S. "Collaborative Learning in the Classroom: A Guide to Evaluation." *College English* 48 (1986): 52–61.

By Susan Lang

Chapter 5

Using Computers to Teach Writing

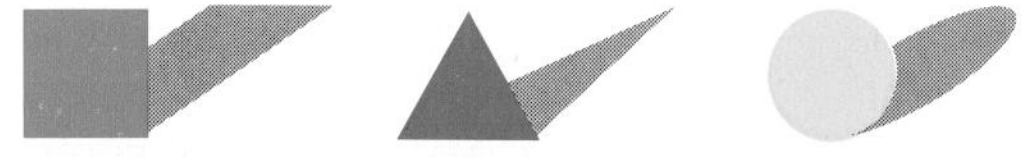

An uneven process of integration of computers into writing classrooms and curriculum has produced a variety of situations for instructors. Some instructors have lobbied long and hard to obtain computer access for their students and have developed ways to teach in a computer classroom. Others, though, find themselves placed into computer classrooms as part of a larger institutional mandate without having time to prepare themselves or their course materials adequately. This chapter is directed primarily toward the concerns of that second group. It aims to acquaint readers with the benefits and problems of teaching writing in a computer-equipped classroom and point out how *The Little, Brown Handbook,* its ancillaries, and other resources can help. (If you need brief definitions and descriptions of terms used in the chapter, you may wish to refer to Appendix B of the student text for basic computing operations and Chapter 35 for various Internet tools.)

Working in the wired classroom

Computers are especially suited to classrooms in which process and collaboration are stressed. Instructors who have access to computers in their classrooms can provide students with more opportunities to write in class. Either stand-alone or networked computers can assist an instructor in enhancing the composition classroom's workshoplike atmosphere. For example, rather than spend most class sessions discussing writing (or the topics for individual assignments) as a large group while leaving the actual composing for outside of class, students can generate ideas on screen even as they talk aloud with each other and then break out for a short individual composing session prior to the conclusion of the class. Conversely, the instructor may choose to get students focused quickly at the beginning of the class by having them write to answer a short discussion prompt, then use the responses as a way to begin class discussion. The instructor then may conclude class by asking the students to return to their original responses and start to revise them. These responses may either be e-mailed to the instructor or saved by the student for later work.

Working with computers can help students to focus more on the specific aspects of revision rather than worrying about "getting the paper typed." The fluidity of words on the screen makes tinkering with text easy; on screen, students can arrange and rearrange lists or preliminary outlines at will. They can also take a set of ideas and supporting evidence and create drafts that appeal to different audiences or attempt to fulfill different purposes without having to retype entire drafts. This elimination of the "busy work" of retyping parts of a text that are not being changed does much to make a student more receptive to experimentation with various revision strategies. The ability to print out clean copies of their work will also help many students in editing, since they will no longer need to read through a marked-up and often illegible draft of their text as they type or write the final copy.

Networked computers add even more to a process-based pedagogy. E-mail, class Listservs, or chat rooms can facilitate student-student and student-instructor communication in a number of ways. For instance, by allowing all students and the instructor to view a text, discuss options for developing or revising that text, make various changes, and analyze the results, e-mail or synchronous chat applications can enable in-class modeling of composing, revising, and editing strategies.

In collaborative composing or revising/reviewing situations, students can distribute texts over a network for peer-review sessions. Many find that they focus more closely on the text online without the anxious author watching over their shoulder as they read and critique.

Networked computers can also ease the "paper flow" problem between students and instructor and between students. Instructors who have limited use of a copier can distribute copies of revision or editing activities online to their students, who can complete the activities and either print them out or save the changes and return them to the instructor on disk or via a classroom server. Furthermore, computers can provide a way for students to keep their writing for a class more easily organized/filed—although keeping a backup disk is essential.

Computers can also help instructors break down the boundaries of the traditional classroom. If, for example, both classroom and school library are networked, the instructor can demonstrate library research strategies to the class, and students may design and implement searches for their research projects during class without having to move physically to the library. Your students may also use e-mail and Listservs for collaboration with other class members or with students at other schools who are using common texts or working on similar projects. (The Listservs listed on p. IAE-77 can help you locate a potential collaborating class.) Students who are reluctant or unable to meet in person may use e-mail as a means for communicating with instructors about assignments or other class activities.

While many writing instructors are already using the computer to enhance existing pedagogical strategies, some are beginning to offer their students an alternative to the conventional essay in the form of electronic hypertext. Students and instructors can easily and economically produce hypertext documents using only a simple text editor (such as *Notepad,* found on all IBM compatible computers running *Windows,* and *TeachText* or *SimpleText* for Macintosh) and a Web browser (such as *Netscape* or *Mosaic*). The uses of hypertext are still developing. While this makes incorporating hypertext into the classroom a challenge, instructors are finding that students who may show little enthusiasm for conventional essay assignments often view hypertextual assignments differently. Some instructors currently use hypertextual authoring activities to give students a new way of seeing their conventionally structured texts. By asking students to transfer their word processed essays into an electronic hypertext, instructors may call attention to features of internal structure and organization that students otherwise tend to overlook. Interactive hypertexts on the World Wide Web can also provide students with models of texts in flux—as ongoing, yet readable processes rather than static products.

Given the advantages that teaching writing with computers presents, not to mention the national call for increased computer literacy among students, one might wonder why so many instructors are just beginning to explore the possibilities of teaching in a networked classroom. Gaining access to suitable equipment is often the first problem a writing instructor faces. Even if a school has made a commitment to increasing the presence of computers in the educational process, the space designated as a writing classroom may not contain more than some older, stand-alone computers and a printer or two. Such machines may not be able to run current software applications nor be easily upgraded to include networking capabilities which are essential for using the technology to its fullest capabilities. Many teachers are able to work with such limited technology by creating hybrid classrooms, in which students work on computer-based activities alone or in pairs, then reconvene for class discussion or to work on hard copy.

Expanding or upgrading existing facilities may be left up to the instructor who takes the initiative for doing so. Sometimes, though not often, this may be as simple as writing a memo to your writing program director, or other appropriate individuals, in which you demonstrate a need for a particular product or service. It may be very worthwhile to meet with a school administrator to express interest in obtaining funding for additional classrooms. Such meetings often prove more productive if you can provide the administrator with several examples of ways in which you use computers in your classroom and what the benefits have been. An old syllabus of a course not taught in a computer classroom can illustrate how classroom activities and dynamics have changed by integrating the computer.

Even if suitable physical facilities are available to writing instructors, a number of other issues can make teaching in a computer classroom difficult. Instructors who are planning to teach in a computer classroom for the first time may find that their class preparation time doubles. Why (and what can you do about it)?

- The instructor may be unfamiliar with the hardware and software of the facilities. You should make a dry run of the activities that you are planning to use in class to locate and clear up possible problems before your students encounter them.
- A significant portion of a syllabus may need restructuring to take full advantage of the available facilities. Expect to make some changes in your class activities each semester, but don't try to overhaul your syllabus completely when you first enter a computer classroom. It usually works best for both you and your students to focus on just a few uses of computers (involving only two or three types of applications) while you are still becoming familiar with the technology.
- Instructors may find themselves inundated with e-mail. Students may enjoy having the opportunity to contact their instructor via e-mail and it can take some time to reply to all the messages. One way to deal with this is by setting up a class listserv and encouraging students to address each others' concerns on it. Doing so often fosters a sense of shared authority and responsibility for the class.
- Many instructors find themselves generating a larger volume of comments on student texts when they compose their comments online. Creating macros that will allow you to insert frequently used comments with a few keystrokes may help you comment more efficiently. Also, you may have previously developed your own system of codes for marking student work or you may use the coding systems present in *The Little, Brown Handbook* (see pp. IAE-32–IAE-33); experiment with ways to use those systems when grading online.

Familiarizing students with the software and hardware used in the classroom can present a problem, since most instructors wish to spend as little time as possible teaching students the fundamentals of using word processing or other applications. Some instructors supply their students with handouts that cover the "basics" for word processing or e-mail. Other instructors send students to introductory workshops offered by their college's computing services. It is a good idea to talk with the people giving these workshops or attend one yourself to be sure that students will be covering the needed material. Especially for teachers who have less experience teaching in the computer classroom, it can be helpful to have someone from academic computing introduce your students to the lab's hardware and software. However, it is important to work closely with academic computing to ensure that the presentation is tailored to your students' needs and leaves plenty of time for hands-on exercises and for students' questions. Other instructors introduce their students to the hardware and software with assignments that have students writing their own basic users' guide to the class computers. They may later use the texts as a way to introduce concepts of audience and purpose as well as essential computing operations. (See, for example, Exercises 8–10 on p. 35–36 that address particular audiences.)

Perhaps the most vexing issue facing instructors when learning to teach in an electronic environment is the lack of support from their colleagues and their institutions. Departmental colleagues, whether in composition or literature, may not see the importance of bringing computers into the classroom, even if they find them valuable for their own work. They may suspect that in a computerized classroom "teaching technology" takes precedence over teaching writing, or they may simply feel too unfamiliar with or intimidated by the machines to want to deal with them in a classroom setting. Some instructors may also believe that their pedagogical strategies are inappropriate for use in a computer classroom. Whatever their reasons, their attitudes toward the computer classrooms too often manifest themselves as a lack of support for the instructors who do want to teach in the new classroom environment. If you find yourself isolated in your efforts, remember that many instructors who teach in computer classrooms participate in discussion groups, MOO sessions, (text-based, virtual meeting places where users can interact with each other in real time), and other online activities. The resource section beginning on page IAE-75 lists several "virtual spaces" (that is, meeting places that are only found online) where instructors gather to share ideas, discuss problems, and offer encouragement.

Keep in mind that you can minimize most of the difficulties instructors encounter by making sure that you are reasonably familiar with the machines that your students will use. Find out what the capabilities of the lab are. What types of computers, printers, networking facilities, and software will be available for classroom use? What facilities do students have access to outside of class? You will also want to know who is responsible for the maintenance of the facility. Will there be someone available to take care of details like refilling printers with paper, replacing toner cartridges, booting up an uncooperative hard drive, or will the instructor be responsible for taking care of these things during class? Is there a system for reporting technical glitches? Find out who your technical support people are and make sure that you make time to meet with the person(s) responsible for your classroom prior to an emergency. Build a rapport with those responsible for maintaining classroom computers. They may be able to offer tips on how new software and hardware upgrades can assist you in the classroom.

It can also help to find out how many of your students have their own computers or have easy access to labs on campus as you design out-of-class assignments. If you sense that compatibility issues will be a factor, try to limit outside activities to those that aren't platform-specific (usually e-mail and individual drafting activities).

The page meets the screen: Incorporating *The Little, Brown Handbook* into the wired classroom

Using *The Little, Brown Handbook* in a computer classroom

Many instructors wonder how textbooks fit into the environment of the computer classroom. At present, it is impossible to predict how soon, or if, the dominant medium for instructional publishing will shift from the bound book to CD-ROM, Web site, or other medium. Remembering that access to computer classrooms many vary greatly from instructor to instructor, the seventh edition of *The Little, Brown Handbook* and its ancillaries provide resources for teaching all phases of the writing process for instructors working in both electronic and traditional classroom environments. Additionally, the book design facilitates quick reference while working online through checklists and other emphasized material set aside in quickly identifiable yellow boxes, a list of which appears in the endpapers. Chapters 1–4 of the handbook now include suggestions and strategies for using computers as students draft and revise texts and includes the computer as a composing option for all phases of composing.

Prewriting

Online ideas for prewriting are specifically mentioned in Exercises 1 and 13 in Chapter 1; instructors may also ask students to use a computer to complete the writing tasks required by any of the other exercises in the first chapter. Composing these shorter assignments online may help students who have little computer experience become less apprehensive about using the machines to complete longer assignments. Instructors should encourage students to make use of their word processor's cut-and-paste features to experiment with different arrangements of ideas in their outlines and other preliminary writing. The *Writer's Workshop* software (described on page IAE-21) offers a number of prewriting prompts that students may respond to online and then save their responses for integration into a draft.

Drafting and revising

One of the first items noted in Chapter 2 of the handbook is how the computer can help break down the boundaries between prewriting and drafting. The rest of the chapter expands on this notion, explaining how the boundaries between individual drafts can also vanish, and provide several suggestions to students for keeping drafts distinct, if you require submission of multiple drafts. Students are also cautioned against falling prey to editing "screen by screen" and encouraged to examine connections among parts of an entire essay and the essay as a whole.

You may find it particularly helpful to have students work online while completing many of the exercises in Chapter 3. The exercises in the text may be extended and reinforced by giving students other paragraphs (perhaps some culled from previous student papers) to manipulate in a variety of ways. For example, you may ask students to use a variety of fonts or textual formats to identify topic sentences, transitions, phrases indicating types of organization, and various types of supporting evidence. If you have a network file server available to you, students may access the material directly from the server; if not, you may be able to send these and other assignments to the students via e-mail.

The discussion in Chapter 4 of ways to develop arguments may also be augmented by having students work online. One useful activity for either stand-alone or networked computers is to have students practice arguing a variety of perspectives on an issue by writing a paragraph to introduce an argument, and then either moving to another computer (stand-alone) or e-mailing their text to another student (network). As students move to another machine or receive an e-mail message with the first paragraph, you may ask them to expand the argument of the first paragraph or provide a counterargument. You can repeat this exercise as many times as you wish. Students often gain a sense of what level of detail is needed to maintain an argument, since some of the more sketchily developed paragraphs (or those containing logical fallacies) make it difficult for other writers to further the argument.

Editing and other sentence-level activities

Teaching grammar, mechanics, punctuation, and other sentence-level concerns with computers can require some extra creativity. Instructors who have students submit work on disk or via e-mail or file server drop boxes can also create customized exercises for their students by extracting examples of particular problems from current and past students' work. Students may be asked to identify various sentence structures or problems by underlining or boldfacing text, or reconstructing problem sentences. (If students need additional practice using a word processor, many of the exercises presented in Chapters 5–30 can also be completed online.) Students could also use the Error Checklist and other appropriate sections of the handbook to identify and revise common errors in their own writing. Students can compile those examples from their own work along with personalized revision advice into an auxiliary resource, which can be "published" via the file server (preferable if you ask students to add to it throughout the course) or in hard copy. You may also have students keep a file in which they record their common grammatical and mechanical errors; have them copy and paste problem sentences into this file and then create a revised version below the original. This file should be kept on the student's course disk. Students will then have examples of their most common errors and a strategy for fixing them at their fingertips when writing. Students should also be aware that selections from the handbook may be accessed online via the *Writer's Workshop* software, and the *SuperShell* software provides students with additional online grammar tutorials that have the benefit of immediate feedback.

Research-based writing

Chapter 35, "Beginning a Research Project," has added material to reflect the integration of computers into the research process. Since computing facilities differ from school to school, the text first provides students with questions that they should ask to become familiar with the resources available on their own campus. The chapter then guides students through the steps they will need to perform in order to find both print and electronic sources in an institution's library. The chapter also contains material on locating sources available via the Internet and World Wide Web, as well as explanations of some of the basic search tools available via the Internet. The *Writer's Workshop*'s annotated bibliography function can assist students in creating bibliographies in either MLA or APA formats. Students may also add annotations of up to 300 words per source. Chapter 36, "Working with Sources and Writing the Paper," considers how students should evaluate sources obtained via the Internet, while Chapter 37 includes coverage of the Alliance for Computers and Writing (ACW) documentation format for citing electronic sources as well as electronic formats for MLA, APA, and CBE styles.

Hypertextual composing

Appendix B provides information for students with various levels of expertise and interest in writing with a computer. The first section discusses some basic terminology and operations; the second section focuses on the many uses of computers as tools for collaborative writing. The third section treats the creation of hypertext documents, concentrating on the building of simple documents using a text editing program and a Web browser. It also provides suggestions for critically evaluating the texts students find on the World Wide Web.

Ancillaries to *The Little, Brown Handbook*

For more ideas on using Internet resources in the writing classroom, Longman offers *Teaching On-Line: Internet Research, Conversation, and Composition* prepared by Daniel Anderson, Bret Benjamin, Chris Busiel, and Bill Paredes-Holt, all of the University of Texas at Austin. Instructors with little or no online experience will find basic definitions, numerous examples, and detailed information about finding and using Internet resources in each chapter. Those more familiar with online resources can learn more about using e-mail and Listservs to foster a workshop atmosphere in the classroom; Usenet newsgroups to emphasize critical reading; MOO and IRC (Internet Relay Chat) to link conversation and composition; Gopher and the World Wide Web to begin a research project and learn how to evaluate sources; and HTML (hypertext markup language) to expand audience, publish Web pages, and use graphics and image maps. Chapter-end case studies and a sample research paper show numerous applications of online composition, conversation, and research.

Two software programs that accompany the handbook can assist the student with various aspects of the composing process. The *Writer's Workshop* has three parts: an electronic version of the student handbook; a variety of prewriting and revision prompts that students may respond to and then save their responses for later use; and "Documentor," a bibliography feature that helps students produce bibliographies (with optional annotations of up to 300 words) in either MLA or APA formats. IBM-compatible *SuperShell II* provides students with self-paced diagnostic testing and tutorials in grammar, punctuation, and mechanics.

Other software programs: Whole process environments

Although you can set up and run a classroom that asks students to draft, revise, and collaborate on both essays and hypertextual documents with only a word processor, e-mail program, and web browser or file server, most instructors teaching in a computer classroom for the first time find an additional framework helpful. Several software applications have been developed for use in a writing classroom (such as *Aspects Collaborative Writing Software* and *DIWE*—the *Daedalus Integrated Writing Environment*). These applications can assist instructors in structuring classroom activities and assignments and provide students and instructors with the opportunity to combine individual writing assignments with collaboration at any point of the writing process.

Generally, integrated classroom applications include a synchronous (real-time) discussion function; facilitation for groups to view and comment upon a common text simultaneously; and a custom-designed word processor as well as compatibility with outside word processing applications. They may also include such features as local area e-mail capabilities (especially useful if your classroom has no Internet connection); the ability to distribute and collect assignments across a network; prepared prompts for prewriting and evaluating texts; a function for instructors to create custom sets of questions and guidelines for students; text annotation capabilities; and ways to store source information and generate formatted bibliographies.

The type of classroom software you can use may depend on the platform of the computers in your facilities. Some applications—but not all—are available for both Macintosh and IBM and compatible computers.

If your course incorporates a substantial research component, consider *Take Note!*, software designed to help students organize research projects. *Take Note!* includes note-taking and categorizing capabilities, an outlining component, and a bibliographic database that helps students record and format source information. If your classroom has Internet capabilities, you can take advantage of *Take Note!*'s Web research and composing features that allow students to bookmark important sites and also compose their projects for publication on a Web site.

Other software programs: Dictionaries, thesauruses, style checkers, and grammar tutorials

If your classroom has Internet capabilities, your students can access a variety of dictionaries and thesauruses, in addition to those included with word processing applications. Applications devoted to issues of grammar, mechanics, and punctuation generally fall into one of two categories—tutorials or style checkers. Tutorials contain sets of questions (multiple choice, true/false, or short answer) on various topics. They may also contain various levels of description and explanation of the topics covered, as well as diagnostic or proficiency tests. Tutorials currently available on the market include *Grammar-ROM, Grammar Tutor, The Grammar Tree, The Grammar Key,* and *Easy English Grammar,* the last designed for ESL and EFL students. Style checkers examine writing for potential grammatical problems. Microsoft Word and WordPerfect now include style checkers, and others available include *Grammar Slammer, Collexion Grammar Checker, Proper Grammar, Correct Grammar,* and *Grammatik.* Though occasionally useful in helping students spot specific flaws in their work, these applications should never be viewed as a substitute for careful and thorough editing.

Using the internet to teach writing

Currently, most writing instructors use the Internet for two purposes—online research and collaboration. Students can currently access library catalogs, databases, full text archives of previously printed material, online editions of current newspapers and magazines, reference materials, and countless other resources. They can also locate and participate in various discourse communities by examining the thousands of special interest discussion groups and newsgroups on the Internet. While students must be cautioned to evaluate their Internet sources with at least the same critical examination that they give printed texts (see page 566 in the student text for suggested guidelines for evaluation), the Internet can provide current information and sources that would be difficult, if not impossible, for students to obtain otherwise.

You may also choose to have your students collaborate on writing projects with those at other schools via e-mail, Listserv discussions, or MOO sessions. Such collaboration can be as informal as having students assemble in a MOO or post ideas about possible writing topics to a Listserv or the collaboration can take place over a longer period of time and produce a collaboratively authored text or texts. Such collaborations, especially if they can take place between people who cannot meet face to face, make students focus on making themselves understood via their writing instead of relying on spoken explanations to clarify their work.

But the Internet can also assist you as you discuss the process of writing with your students. The World Wide Web represents an enormous collection of writing, and a significant portion of the Web has been created by nonprofessional writers. The fact that one can use the Web to prove to students that people do write outside of writing courses (often for the sheer pleasure of it) more than compensates for the uneven quality of portions of the Web. Examining individuals' homepages on the World Wide Web is an excellent way to open a discussion of why people write, and for whom they write. For example, you might ask your students to spend some time searching the Web for examples of sites with clearly defined audiences and sites that seem less thoughtfully developed. You might also direct students to find examples of sites that invite readers back to see "future developments" and have them keep track of whether or not these sites do evolve and how they are revised or expanded. Such an activity may be used in conjunction with class discussions of revising texts, just as an examination of sites that invite user feedback can help launch conversations about the types of comments most useful in peer review activities. You can even base discussions of effective grammar, mechanics, and writing styles on the results of student Web explorations. Ask students to find examples of pages that suffer, in their opinions, because of the style of the writing used at the site. Vary the task by asking them to find pages that effectively serve their purpose despite their violation (or perhaps because of their violation) of prose conventions. Use the subsequent discussion to direct students' attention to relationships between writing styles and purposes. If you have students composing both conventional essays and electronic hypertexts, these conversations can be used in conjunction with the material in Appendix B to help students develop their own guidelines for composing hypertexts. When developing course assignments involving the Internet, be creative and remember that you have an endless supply of texts available for analysis and comment.

Sample schedule for a first-year composition course

The following schedule represents one possible way of structuring a composition course using *The Little, Brown Handbook* and teaching in a computer classroom. The schedule assumes that you meet in a computer classroom during all class sessions; alterations to accommodate courses that only meet part-time in a computer classroom are labeled "CC:" and placed in parentheses. Students will complete four major projects during the course; these may either be graded individually or collectively in a portfolio, depending on your institution's requirements.

In the objectives-and-requirements portion of your syllabus, be sure to explain fully any requirements involving technology as you would any others. For example:

- Require that students purchase at least two floppy disks for the course and that they back up all their work. Make it known that technical difficulties such as lost or damaged disks are unacceptable excuses for not turning in assignments.
- Clarify participation requirements in class Listservs or other online discussions, while taking into account that some students may need to participate as "lurkers" for a week or two before involving themselves in conversations. In the following schedule, students will use word processing, e-mail, a Web browser, the *Writer's Workshop (WW)* ancillary and some type of synchronous discussion software such as *DIWE* or *Aspects*.
- If you expect students to attend computer-related workshops or complete computer-related tasks such as obtaining e-mail accounts outside of class, provide them with handouts and schedules that will help them do so.

Week one

General course introduction, including objectives; discussion of requirements—assignments, participation, attendance. Complete writing sample, if desired. Assign handbook Introduction. (CC: introduction to computers on campus—including options for using computers outside of class time. If students are not assigned e-mail accounts automatically, provide directions on how to obtain these.)

Week two

Discussions of purpose and audience in writing, using various examples from online and printed sources. Assign first essay and Chapters 1 and 2. Discuss invention techniques and have students apply to first assignment. (CC: Have students engage in blind freewriting or other brainstorming activities using *DIWE* or *WW*.)

Week three

Draft of first essay due. Discuss and model peer response techniques with a common paper downloaded from file server or e-mailed to all students. Have students review each others' work, via e-mail or synchronous discussion. Review drafts yourself, focusing on scope and suitability to objectives of the assignment. In your comments, suggest appropriate sections of Chapters 2, 3, or 4, as necessary. (CC: Use class to model effective and ineffective peer review strategies on one or two sample papers; have students practice responding to sample texts via e-mail or synchronous chat.)

Week four

Discuss problem areas individually or in small groups with students, or e-mail suggestions on drafts, referring students to appropriate chapters in Parts II, V, or VI as needed; final revisions on first essay, which is due at the end of the week. (CC: discuss and model revision strategies via e-mail or synchronous chat.)

Week five

Assign second essay. Repeat invention strategies for first essay; have students (in groups of three or four) exchange e-mail that explores possible ways of developing their topics in discussion. Begin drafting essays. (CC: Collaborative brainstorming using synchronous chat or e-mail.)

Week six

Online peer review of drafts; assign and discuss Chapter 3, and sections from Parts III and IV, as appropriate. Revise drafts. (CC: Online peer review—save and print transcripts of peer review discussions for subsequent class.)

Week seven

Second essay due. Assign third essay (research-based). Assign Chapter 35. In-class introduction to research techniques. (CC: In-class demonstration of online library catalog and databases, as appropriate and if available; or else discussion of computer as research tool.)

Week eight

Online discussions of research projects; work in class to compile working bibliography of online and print sources. Individual conferences with students about progress of research. (CC: Model Net Search strategies; discuss bibliographic features of *WW* and/or *DIWE*.)

Week nine

Working bibliographies due. Assign Chapter 36–37. Discuss evaluating sources, integration of quotations, and paraphrase and summary. Begin drafting essay. (CC: Class discussion on evaluation of online sources, using specific sources found by students in their searches.)

Week ten

Individual conferences during class with students on their projects. Other students should use class time to draft, revise as needed. (CC: Online evaluation of model research projects.)

Week eleven

Peer response to research projects. Final revisions. Research projects due. (CC: Online peer review—save and print transcripts as before for reference/evaluation.)

Week twelve

Assign fourth project—a hypertextual version of the student's research project or a collaborative essay. Introduction to basic HTML coding or principles of writing collaboratively. Assign appropriate sections of Appendix B. (CC: Students should engage in collaborative brainstorming or receive an introduction to HTML coding.)

Week thirteen

Workshop in class, either on hypertext or collaborative essay. Individual or group discussions as needed. (CC: Practice drafting collaboratively or use time to answer questions about HTML.)

Week fourteen

Drafts due. Peer review (in the case of collaborative essays, have groups exchange texts). Individual and small group discussions as necessary. Begin final editing. (CC: Peer review of essays/hypertexts.)

Week fifteen

In-class editing. Final drafts due. Course evaluations. (CC: Course evaluations.)

Resources for using computers to teach writing

Books and articles

Bolter, Jay David. *Writing Space: The Computer, Hypertext, and the History of Writing.* Hillsdale, NJ: Erlbaum, 1991.

Bridwell-Bowles, Lillian. "Designing Reseach on Computer-Assisted Writing." *Computers and Composition* 7 (1988): 79–91.

Bruce, Bertram C., Joy Kreeft Peyton, and Trent Batson. *Network-Based Classrooms: Promises and Realities.* New York: Cambridge UP, 1993.

Christina Haas. *Writing Technology: Studies on the Materiality of Literacy.* Mahwah, NJ: Erlbaum, 1996.

Cochran-Smith, Marilyn, Cynthia L. Paris, and Jessica L. Kahn. *Learning to Write Differently.* Norwood, NJ: Ablex, 1991.

Crump, Eric, and Nick Carbone. *The English Student's Guide to the Internet.* New York: Houghton, 1996.

Halpern, Jeanne W., and Sarah Liggett. *Computers and Composing: How the New Technologies Are Changing Writing.* Carbondale: Southern Illinois UP, 1984.

Haas, Christina. "Composing in Technological Contexts: A Study of Note-Making." *Written Communication* 7 (1990): 512–47.

Handa, Carolyn, ed. *Computers and Community: Teaching Composition in the Twenty-first Century.* Portsmouth, NH: Boynton/Cook, 1990.

Hawisher, Gail E., and Cynthia Selfe, eds. *Evolving Perspectives on Computers and Composition Studies: Questions for the 1990s.* Urbana, IL: NCTE, 1991.

Hawisher, Gail E., and Paul LeBlanc, eds. *Re-Imagining Computers and Composition: Teaching and Research in the Virtual Age.* Portsmouth, NH: Heinemann, 1992.

Holdstein, Deborah H., and Cynthia Selfe, eds. *Computers and Writing: Theory, Research, Practice.* New York: MLA, 1990.

Jonassen, David H., and Heinz Mandl, eds. *Designing Hypertext/Hypermedia for Learning.* Heidelberg: Springer-Verlag, 1990.

Landow, George P. *Hypertext: The Convergence of Contemporary Critical Theory and Technology.* Baltimore: Johns Hopkins UP, 1992.

Lanham, Richard A. *The Electronic Word: Democracy, Technology, and the Arts.* Chicago: U of Chicago P, 1993.

Myers, Linda. *Approaches to Computer Writing Classrooms: Learning from Practical Experience.* Albany, NY: SUNY Press, 1993.

Selfe, Cynthia L., and Susan Hilligoss. *Literacy and Computers: The Complications of Teaching and Learning with Technology.* New York: MLA, 1994.

Selfe, Cynthia, Gail Hawisher, Charles Moran, and Paul Leblanc. *Computers and the Teaching of Writing in American Postsecondary Education, 1979–1994: A History.* Norwood, NJ: Ablex, 1996.

Tuman, Myron C., ed. *Literacy Online: The Promise (and Peril) of Reading and Writing with Computers.* Pittsburgh: U of Pittsburgh P, 1992.

Journals

Computers and Composition

Kairos: A Journal For Teachers of Writing in Webbed Environments

College English

CCC

Computer Assisted Composition Journal

Listservs devoted to some aspect of the teaching of writing

ACW-L (sponsored by the Alliance for Computers and Writing). listproc@listserv.ttu.edu

MBU-L (teaching composition with computers). listproc@ttu.edu

RHETNT-L (an electronic journal on rhetoric and writing). listserv@mizzou1.missouri.edu

TCC-L (teaching in community colleges). listserv@uhccvm.uhcc.hawaii.edu

TESL-L (teaching English as a second language). listserv@cunyvm.cuny.edu

WPA-L (writing program administration). listserv@asuacad.bitnet

MOOs

A selection of MUDs (Multi User Domains) and MOOs (MUD Object Oriented) with rooms/spaces dedicated to rhetoric and composition:

DaedalusMOO.logos.daedalus.com 7777

Diversity University.moo.du.org 8888

MediaMOO (MIT).mediamoo.media.mit.edu 8888

Web sites

MOO Central.http://www.pitt.edu/~jrgst>/MOO central.html

Alliance for Computers and Writing. http://prairie_island.ttu.edu/acw/ acw.html

Computer-Mediated Communication Magazine.http://www.rpi.edu/~decemj/cmc/mag/current/toc.html

University of Texas Computer Writing and Research Lab. http://www.en. utexas.edu

Language & Literature (many useful links to other WWW services). http:// galaxy.einet.net/galaxy/Arts-and-Humanities/Language-and-Literature.html

Michigan Techical University class resources. gopher://gilligan.hu.mtu.edu/11/dept/class

Rhetnet: A CyberJournal for Rhetoric and Writing. http://www.missouri.edu/~wleric/rhetnet/rhetnet.html

Salt Lake Community College (comp & rhet), especially in 2-year colleges. http://pc10-l1-englab.slcc.edu/welcome.htm

By Jocelyn Steer

Chapter 6

Teaching Writing to ESL Students

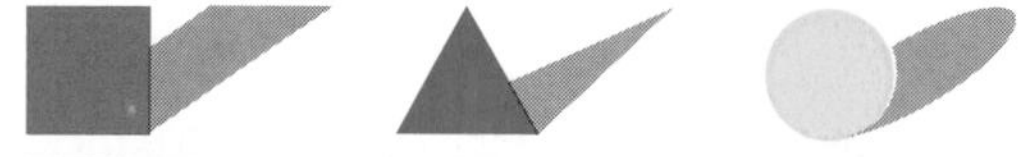

The composition instructor's reaction to having ESL students in a class of native speakers can be a mixture of pleasure and apprehension. On the one hand, students using English as a second language can introduce a fresh perspective to class discussions and in their written work. Competing with this positive response to the richness of cultural diversity, however, may be a feeling of trepidation at entering into the syntactical and lexical labyrinth of the ESL student's written world. There is no question about it: ESL writers struggle with a number of language problems that do not beset native speakers and for which writing instructors may not have quick solutions. However, encouraging ESL writers to become outspoken members of the class and shaping the overall goals of the class to include ESL needs provides benefits for native and nonnative speakers alike.

This chapter is intended to help instructors to find their way within that ESL labyrinth. It presents a profile of ESL students, an overview of how culture shapes their notions about learning and composing, a description of effective approaches to teaching writing to ESL students, and some guidelines for evaluating their writing. A cursory look at the most common grammatical errors found in ESL writing is also included.

Profile of ESL students

The "ESL" label indicates that a student's first language is not English, but it says nothing about the student's country of origin or reasons for being at college and very little about specific language problems. In fact, ESL students are a remarkably heterogeneous group, about which it is often difficult to make any generalizations. One of the first and most important distinctions to make is between international and permanent resident students.

Generally speaking, international students (also referred to as foreign students) reside permanently in another country and obtain student (F-1) visas in order to study in a school in the United States. Their stay in the United States is usually funded by their parents, their place of employment, their government, or their own savings. Their countries of origin vary; they come to the United States in waves, affected by global political and economic events.

Most likely these international students have had previous formal English language instruction in their home country or in the United States. Students trained in their home countries have probably had heavy doses of grammar, vocabulary, and reading, with some translation. Although they will be proficient readers with good command of grammar, they may lack ease and confidence in speaking up in class. Their written work may be mechanically accurate but lack fluency and appropriate organization. International students who have learned English at a language institute in this country will have a higher degree of oral fluency and some basic notions about the conventions of higher education in the United States.

Unlike international students, permanent residents usually do not plan to return to their home country. Their reasons for staying in the United States are varied and include the need for political asylum, economic advancement, and family ties.

Most students admitted to the United States with refugee status have come for political, and not economic, reasons. Refugee students have come from places such as Cambodia, Vietnam, Laos, Eastern Europe, El Salvador, Haiti, Ethiopia, and Somalia. Many came to the United States as children and went through the public school system here; others are adults who have decided to return to school to get a better job. Students who graduate from a high school in the United States and who are permanent residents are usually admitted to universities and colleges without submitting a Test of English as a Foreign Language (TOEFL) score, which is required of international students.

Not all permanent residents are refugees seeking political asylum. Many have come to the United States for family or employment reasons. Immigrants are given a resident alien card (a "green card"), which does not grant them citizenship but does allow them to reside permanently in the United States and to work here legally. After a number of years, green card holders may apply for citizenship and become naturalized citizens. Immigrants are given permanent resident status for many reasons; for example, they may have married a U.S. citizen or have been sponsored by a family member. Immigrant students usually acquire English informally, so their spoken English is quite fluent, but their written English requires more formal instruction to achieve the same fluency and accuracy.

Obviously, ESL students have varying degrees of language ability in speaking, reading, and writing. You can also expect to see wide gaps in socioeconomic status among ESL students in the same class, even among those from the same country, and such differences may create friction. ESL students may also hold varying attitudes toward the United States, ranging from open anti-American hostility to a Pollyanna-like view of the United States as the epitome of freedom and opportunity. This range of attitudes can provide an interesting basis for in-class discussions by including a variety of perspectives and by stimulating native speakers to rethink their cultural assumptions.

Cross-cultural issues

Some ESL students will freely admit to being in a mild state of confusion much of the time during their academic experience. Clearly, a large portion of this confusion may be attributed to having to read and write at a very sophisticated level in a language that they have not yet mastered. There are also cultural factors less visible to the student and the instructor: the unwritten, but well-entrenched, conventions of the academy. These range from the acceptable forms of compiling a research paper to the appropriate ways of addressing an instructor. Because of their prior experience and training, native speakers may be somewhat familiar with these academic conventions, while ESL students may not even know that they exist. However, one advantage in having ESL writers as active participants in a class is that their questions can propel the class as a whole to discover the reasons for conventions that often seem puzzlingly arbitrary. In some cases while working through sentence-level revisions I have found that the ESL students know the "rules" of grammar far better than the native speakers and can called upon to share that expert knowledge.

Ideas about learning

ESL students may approach the learning situation from a schema formed largely by their experiences in their first culture. For example, many Latin cultures foster more cooperative learning, whereas Japan adheres to a hierarchical, teacher-dominated model. While these cultural generalities cannot be presumed to apply to individual students they can be useful in sensitizing us to our own cultural assumptions. The situation in a college classroom may well shock ESL students—the informality of instructors who sit on the desk, classmates who openly disagree with or interrupt their professors. Such students are not comfortable with the open discussion format in which American students feel free to express their opinions, whether or not those opinions align with the professor's. Instructors may view their more quiet ESL students as resistant or unprepared, when in fact these students are showing respect by remaining silent.

In some cultures, professors are expected to mentor and guide students to a greater extent than they do in the United States. Thus, many ESL students may feel that their professors do not do enough for them. It is not unusual for an ESL student to bring in a piece of writing for another class and ask the composition instructor to correct it. Or some students may attempt to negotiate grades because they "need" that grade for a scholarship or admission to a school, and they may be visibly disappointed when an instructor refuses to change a grade. While a teacher in the United States may interpret such behavior as impertinent, the student may view it as a chance for the instructor to use his or her power to further the student's career. And while ESL students may find the informality of the classroom surprising, many find constant testing, penalties for absences, and general surveillance of the instructor to be offensive to their sense of maturity. Many ESL students have attended foreign universities that do not monitor student behavior so closely.

Cross-cultural discussions in which students trace how basic assumptions result in varying styles of learning behavior may be useful for both ESL and native-speaking students. Many ESL students benefit from such discussions because they wish to conform to the conventions of their school in order to enjoy academic success. Similarly, such explorations can help native speakers develop sensitivity to these cross-cultural issues.

Contrastive rhetoric

Cross-cultural analyses of ESL student writing can also be fruitful. Cultures express ideas using different organizational patterns and types of support, and the written and unwritten rules governing what is considered appropriate writing in the culture are transmitted to children in school. It is not surprising, therefore, that ESL students use these first-language writing strategies when they compose in English. The result is often a grammatically correct piece of writing with an idiosyncratic development.

Instructors need to apply the principles of contrastive rhetoric cautiously. Although it is not necessary to undertake an extensive study of the rhetorics of all languages, it is important to recognize how a culture shapes its members' expectations of good writing. An instructional approach that places too much emphasis on contrastive rhetoric, on the other hand, is reductionistic. Such an approach would fail to account for a specific writer's process, potentially misinterpreting a writer's lack of experience as interference from first-language writing strategies. (For a detailed discussion of contrastive rhetoric, consult Ilona Leki's *Understanding ESL Writers: A Guide for Teachers.*)

Levels of support and specificity

One important feature of ESL writing that varies among cultures is the level of support and specificity required for assertions. It is not always obvious to ESL writers that facts and statistics are usually considered to be the strongest method of support in English and that if a student makes an assertion, that assertion must be supported with specific examples or quantifiable measures. Other cultures may rely on the hierarchical, rather than the scientific, model of proof. It is not unusual, for example, to have ESL students use quotes from the Koran or statements made by a political leader as evidence for their assertions. Students will need practice in identifying and supplying the kinds of support expected in academic writing in English.

Another central issue in cross-cultural analyses of texts is the level of explicitness expected in academic writing. English is a "writer-responsible" language: the onus is on the writer to present ideas clearly and succinctly. If the reader has difficulty with a text, the blame usually rests with the writer and not the reader. We expect to have the main points stated directly and clearly in a piece of writing, which may help to explain some of our frustration at reading a piece of writing by an ESL student who does not share the same expectation.

This distinction is especially pertinent to native writers of Japanese and Chinese, which are "reader-responsible" languages. Japanese and Chinese readers do not expect the writer to link information and draw conclusions; they expect to do that as readers. A Japanese student explained this when I asked her why she used transitions so sparingly and never seemed to tie up her examples with a general statement: she said that doing so would be insulting to Japanese readers, who are expected to be informed and sensitive enough to be able to make those inferences on their own.

Attitudes toward plagiarism

American students who commit plagiarism have a sense that it is an academic offense. ESL students, however, may come from countries where plagiarism, although not completely ethical, is more easily overlooked or accepted. Research and writing in the United States is prized for its originality, but this is not the case in all cultures. Some ESL students may have been taught to incorporate great writing from their culture into their own work out of respect for those scholars. Other students may be too modest to believe that they can paraphrase the writing of a respected author.

Of course, there are many ESL students who copy for the same reasons American students do—because it's easier, faster, and sure to be more fluent. Whether or not your students are "guilty," they need to be warned that plagiarism is unacceptable in a college in the United States. Be sure to discuss the issue of plagiarism early in the semester and invite students to share their understanding of the differences between quoting, paraphrasing, and plagiarizing. Chapter 36c can be particularly useful here in showing students examples of unacceptable writing with plagiarized sections.

Topic selection

Topics that seem to be extremely pertinent to the lives of your native speakers may be inappropriate or difficult for ESL writers. An essay on breaking away from family or living on one's own, for example, may have no meaning for those ESL students who expect to live with their families until they get married. In fact, you may find that your ESL students are more comfortable writing about impersonal subjects than those designed to facilitate self-discovery. Other topics may offend certain groups of students due to their religious beliefs—living together before marriage, gay rights, evolution. I once used what seemed to me to be an innocuous topic—"superstitions in my culture"—only to find out that the

Islamic religion does not tolerate superstitions. At the same time, some topics will be more appealing to ESL students, who are often better informed about and more interested in topics dealing with global issues than American students.

Issues in working with ESL writing

The above discussion of cross-cultural differences in organization, style, and topic selection underscores the need to provide ESL students with guidelines and models of academic writing so that they can function smoothly and successfully in the college culture. Yet there is a danger—as there is in any acculturation process—of placing too great a value on the expected and accepted form of the writing and too little value on the writer's discovery of voice.

Process versus product approach to writing

This dilemma between emphasizing the product over the process of writing is not a new one but one that takes on a slightly different slant when applied to teaching writing to ESL students. An approach that emphasizes the conventions of academic discourse provides ESL students with models of discipline-specific writing that they can emulate, along with guidelines for operating within that discipline. It has been my experience that ESL students welcome this type of instruction. Since they lack the cultural and linguistic schema of native speakers, they benefit from explicit instruction in how to complete academic tasks. Essay-test prompts are an excellent example of this: native speakers have a better notion than ESL students of what is meant by "discuss," for example. By the same token, when ESL students feel free to raise questions about the wording of assignments, the whole class often benefits from the discussion. Assignments that allow students to practice writing essay exams, critical reviews, laboratory reports, case reports, and so on will also help to equip students with the necessary tools for their academic careers.

The danger in such an approach is that students may begin to rely more on the imposed model of academic communication than on their own voice and expression. Zamel cautions against accepting "reductionist, narrowly conceptualized, and exclusionary notions of academic discourse" (*Questioning* 35). The result may be mimicry rather than inspiration. This is especially true for ESL students who enter the writing process haltingly. An approach that emphasizes the process of brainstorming, sharing ideas, and collaborating on a topic nurtures ESL students' wavering self-confidence as writers in a second language. By engaging students in the discovery of ideas, this approach also distracts them from ruminating over potential surface errors.

Since a process approach to writing does not outline a single "accepted" product, it encourages students to identify their own personal style first before reconciling that with the models of writing endorsed by the academic community. Yet we would be remiss if we failed to provide our ESL students with those models. Clearly, a combination of the two approaches, without overreliance on product or neglect of process, will serve your ESL students best. As with any student it is important to focus on the strengths of an ESL writer's work and to suggest one or two issues for revision rather than to view the paper as a minefield of errors.

Attitudes toward errors

While research indicates that ESL students need more work with actual composing than with language development (Zamel, *Composing*), it may be difficult persuading your ESL students of this. They may believe that good writing means producing grammatically correct sentences. They see errors as obstacles to good writing, and unlike many native speakers, they do not perceive them as symbols of personal failure. They expect to make mistakes since they are learning a second language, and they expect those errors to be corrected. Leki's survey on student perceptions of teacher feedback supports what any ESL teacher might have predicted: students believe that error correction is important. Out of 100 ESL college students surveyed, 91 percent believed that it was very important to have as few errors as possible in their writing, and 93 percent stated that it was important to have the teachers correct the errors.

It was once thought that errors in a second language were the result of interference from the first language. For example, if writers had problems with word order in English, this was because they were applying first-language rules of word order to the second language. Now, however, it is largely believed that most ESL errors are the result of an "interlanguage," a system for communicating in the second language that the student has developed based on what he or she knows about the second language.

Theoretically, this interlanguage is constantly changing as the learner mentally reorganizes what is known about the language. This is an important point and a distinction between the native English and ESL writers. During the course of a semester, your ESL students will probably make a great deal of progress in English because their language-acquisition process is still activated. Their improvement will result not only from your class but also from exposure to other sources of language input.

Viewing ESL errors as temporary edifices supporting an ESL writer's ideas lends credence to the argument against correcting every single error in an ESL composition. These errors will disappear as students gain more control over the second language. Errors that seem to be careless mistakes to the reader may not be that at all. They may be the student's individual system for organizing English structure, which will change as the student acquires more language. Nor is it uncommon for advanced ESL students to regress temporarily in their language accuracy as they struggle with new forms and constructions.

You may have some students in your class who have been in the United States for quite some time and who for some reason may have reached a plateau; second-language researchers say that these students' errors are "fossilized." It is not clear why fossilization occurs, but it is clear that working with fossilized errors can be difficult. Distinguishing between errors that occur as the result of fossilization and those that occur due to interlanguage is important; unlike interlanguage errors, which remit spontaneously with increased exposure to the language, fossilized errors require more explicit and direct treatment.

Techniques for responding to ESL writing

As an experienced composition instructor, you have probably developed a variety of techniques and strategies for providing effective feedback to your students. (Chapter 3 in the *Instructor's Annotated Edition,* "Working with Student Writing," provides guidelines for responding to student work.) Below are some suggested techniques and strategies that may be especially helpful in providing feedback to your ESL students.

In general, it is best to provide feedback on grammar, punctuation, and spelling in earlier drafts so that students can incorporate those corrections into subsequent drafts. Students are not as likely to benefit from feedback that is offered on a final draft; they will often look at the grade, read the comments quickly, and file the paper away. However, you can encourage attention to final drafts by asking for localized revisions of a particular pattern of error or of a paragraph. Students can also be encouraged to make note of their common patterns of error and to keep revised examples as a resource for the next paper.

There is no one method for drawing students' attention to sentence-level errors, but generally it is best to locate the error for the student and have the student correct the error on a subsequent draft. Leki's survey found that students like to be given a clue regarding the nature of the error. A numbering system for the most basic errors (for example, verb tense, number agreement, word order, spelling, punctuation, and word form) works well because students seem to respond better to numbers than to abbreviations or words (for example, *sp, awk*), and they become familiar with the errors they tend to make often. The correction code in the handbook is easy to use; it includes a number-and-letter system that directs students to the appropriate section in the handbook that deals with the error. (See p. IAE-32 for a more detailed description of the correction code.) It is most useful to identify one or two significant patterns of error (subject-verb problems and misused articles, for example) rather than correcting every example of error.

Some errors—often those pertaining to sentence boundaries, clause structure, and choice of words—cannot be identified by circling and numbering. When the writer's meaning is unclear, avoid the temptation to rewrite the sentence for the student. On many occasions I have found my interpretation to be quite different from what the student intended. It's best to ask the student to rewrite the passage.

A concern that continues to surface when dealing with ESL writing is knowing what and how much to correct. As noted earlier, students make many errors; some of these may be careless mistakes, but more likely, the sentences were carefully constructed using the students' still-developing knowledge of English structure and vocabulary. Correcting ESL work seems to be more of an art than a science, because the instructor needs to gauge the particular student's threshold for error correction and identify the errors that the student will benefit from knowing about.

I have also found that students are very receptive to and benefit a great deal from immediate, oral feedback, especially when they solicit it. Students often ask for help with grammar and vocabulary during in-class writing, and they almost always incorporate those revisions into their writing.

Some teachers and students find it helpful to keep track of repeated errors. Using a numbering system such as the one mentioned above can facilitate this process. (See Chapter 2 in the handbook for a model that can be used to track errors.) In any case, it is very important to recommend or require that students consult the handbook. Not only will it help clarify a confusing grammatical point, but it will also teach students to edit their work independently, an extremely important skill for the ESL student.

Evaluation

The question of evaluation is a thorny one in composition classes comprising both native and nonnative speakers. Some of the questions that come up are: How do I compare the two? Will I need to lower my standards? Should I expect error-free writing from my ESL students? Should I give a grade to each draft? How many revisions should I allow before assigning a grade?

Keep a few points in mind when deciding how to evaluate ESL writers. First, the ESL student is writing in a second (or third or fourth) language. It is next to impossible to achieve native fluency and accuracy in a second language, especially when the learner began acquisition as an adult. Thus, we need to consider whether it is realistic to expect ESL students to produce error-free writing.

Research (Santos) has indicated that college professors in disciplines other than English tend to be more forgiving of ESL-type errors than of native speakers' errors, which they regard as careless. In addition, although ESL students may not always produce fluent English, their prior training and knowledge in their field of study may far exceed that of their native-speaking classmates. Professors may be delighted to have their input, both in writing and in class discussions, because of the value of their comments and diverse points of view for the class. In such cases, the standards of these professors and their discipline may be less stringent than those maintained in the composition class.

When assigning grades to ESL students, there are a few guidelines that may make the situation more equitable for ESL writers. If at all possible, allow students the opportunity to write multiple drafts that are not graded. This will permit ESL writers the opportunity to refine a piece of writing to their satisfaction. A split grade for the content (for example, organization, development, exemplification) and form (for example, the grammar, spelling, and punctuation) sometimes proves beneficial, especially when ESL students have many good ideas but still struggle with expression. Other solutions include assigning a satisfactory/unsatisfactory grade for work done during the semester and requiring a portfolio of the student's best work at the end of the class. (See p. IAE-43 for a discussion of portfolios.) The final grade is based on the final portfolio and not the individual assignments.

A final, very important consideration is the time it takes for ESL students to complete written work. It may seem obvious that ESL writers need more time to complete their assignments, but even after many years of teaching ESL students, I am still surprised at the amount of time they actually do need. All writers need help getting started, but ESL writers seem more frightened of that first sentence than native speakers do. It's almost as if they believe that once they put that first sentence down, they are wed to it forever. As Ann Raimes has said, "The first sentence restricts them before they have begun to develop their ideas" (261). If at all possible, allow students a flexible schedules of deadlines.

Sentence-level errors in ESL writing

English composition instructors know a great deal about grammar and punctuation, but many who have not worked extensively with ESL students are puzzled by the errors such students make. Below are a few areas of grammar that are especially troublesome to many ESL students. All these trouble spots are discussed and illustrated in *The Little, Brown Handbook.* For more detailed explanations, consult Maria Celce-Murcia and Diane Larsen-Freeman's *Grammar Book,* a specialized ESL reference grammar for the instructor, or Jocelyn Steer and Karen Carlisi's *Advanced Grammar Book,* an ESL grammar textbook for the student.

Verb tenses

ESL students have difficulty with verb tenses and forms of helping verbs. Some tenses in English are straightforward and usually have a direct translation in most languages. These include the past tense, the future tense, and in some cases the present tense. However, other tenses (for example, present progressive and the present perfect) do not have equivalent forms in some languages. (See handbook section 7e.)

Helping verbs

Students often have difficulty choosing the appropriate form of the helping verb in a sentence. You may encounter sentences like *He should has been gone* rather than *He should have gone.* (See handbook section 7d.)

Verb endings

ESL students often leave off the *-ed* endings on verbs used in the passive (*It was return*) and in the past perfect tense (*I had return it*). One explanation may be that they do not hear the *-ed* ending in spoken English. (See handbook sections 7c and 7d-2.) They also often forget to add the *-s* or *-es* ending on present-tense verbs in the third-person singular (*He go; it don't work*) but can correct this error immediately when it is pointed out. It's a good idea to have your ESL students check their papers for subject-verb agreement before handing them in to you. (See handbook section 8a.)

Verbs with gerunds or infinitives

One particularly difficult area for ESL students to master is the use of a gerund or an infinitive after a verb. Some English verbs may be followed by a gerund (*He recommended going*). Others may be followed by an infinitive (*I want to go*). Some may be followed by either a gerund or an infinitive with no change in meaning (*I continued eating; I continued to eat*). Finally, some verbs may be followed by either form, but with a change in meaning (*I stopped smoking yesterday; I stopped to smoke*). (See handbook section 7i.)

Count and noncount nouns

The distinction between count and noncount nouns in English is especially troublesome for ESL students, because correct choice of article or quantifier and agreement with the verb depend on the differences. When ESL students first learn about count and noncount nouns, they are told that count nouns (*book/books; girl/girls*) are easily divided and counted, whereas noncount nouns are not. This rule is fine for the clear-cut examples such as *water, cheese,* or *love.* However, when students learn that money is a noncount noun, the rule seems to fall apart: who hasn't counted money easily and successfully? (See handbook section 9i.)

Articles

Choosing an appropriate article is extremely trying for ESL students, especially students whose native language (e.g., Japanese, Chinese) does not have articles. It is equally trying for ESL teachers to explain why a definite article is used instead of an indefinite one. Once again, students learn rules to guide them in their choices. (See handbook section 9i.)

Verbs with particles

Students often complain about prepositions in English. These combinations of verbs and so-called particles (some of them adverbs) are particularly confusing: what may seem to be a simple construction of two (or three) words has a specific meaning that cannot be discerned from the meanings of the specific verb and preposition. There are literally hundreds of these idiomatic constructions. (See handbook section 7j.)

Conclusion

Initially, you may feel overwhelmed by the number of errors your ESL students make, and you may even harbor some resentment that you have to spend so much time correcting them. In such cases, it's important to remember that these students are still learning the language as well as writing skills. Don't feel compelled to correct every single mistake. Help students instead to develop and organize their ideas. And keep in mind that it may take your ESL students a long time before they write without making a lot of errors.

As you can see, ESL students—regardless of the cultural or socioeconomic group they may be from—confront a number of obstacles in their daily college lives. Most of these students spend an enormous amount of energy simply listening to lectures and trying to understand the language and the cultural content of what the instructor is saying. Anyone who has lived in a foreign country and listened to a foreign language continuously knows how exhausting negotiating simple tasks in the foreign culture can be. As their instructor, you have a chance to assist your students in this process of acculturation to the academic community and to give them the encouragement they need to succeed in their academic endeavors.

Resources for teaching ESL students

Arnaudet, Martin L., and Mary Ellen Barrett. *Academic Approaches to Reading and Writing.* Englewood Cliffs: Prentice-Hall, 1985. An excellent source for the ESL writer—includes chapters on reading textbooks, writing research papers, and writing critical reviews.

Auerbach, Elsa Roberts. "The Politics of the ESL Classroom: Issues of Power in Pedagogical Choices." In *Power and Inequality in Language Education.* Ed. James Tollefson. Cambridge: Cambridge UP, 1995. 9–33.

Celce-Murcia, Maria, and Diane Larsen-Freeman. *The Grammar Book.* Boston: Heinle, 1983. An excellent reference book on ESL grammar for instructors.

Kroll, Barbara, ed. *Second Language Writing: Research Insights for the Classroom.* New York: Cambridge UP, 1990. This collection of articles by distinguished researchers in second-language writing is very interesting and provides some of the most recent findings.

Leki, Ilona. "The Preferences of ESL Students for Error Correction in College-Level Writing Classes." *Foreign Language Annals* 24 (1991): 203–14.

———. *Understanding ESL Writers: A Guide for Teachers.* Portsmouth, NH: Boynton/Cook, 1992.

Raimes, Ann. "Anguish as a Second Language? Remedies for Composition Teachers." *Composing in a Second Language.* Ed. Sandra McKay. Rowley: Newbury, 1984.

———. "Out of the Woods: Emerging Traditions in the Teaching of Writing." *TESOL Quarterly* 25 (1991): 407–30.

Santos, Tony. "Professors' Reactions to the Academic Writing of Nonnative-Speaking Students." *TESOL Quarterly* 22 (1988): 69–90.

Steer, Jocelyn, and Karen Carlisi. *The Advanced Grammar Book.* Boston: Heinle, 1991. An ESL grammar textbook with oral and written exercises.

Zamel, Vivian. "The Composing Process of Advanced ESL Students: Six Case Studies." *TESOL Quarterly* 17 (1983): 165–87.

———. "Questioning Academic Discourse." *College ESL* 3:1 (1993): 28–39.

The Little, Brown Handbook

Seventh Edition

The Little, Brown Handbook

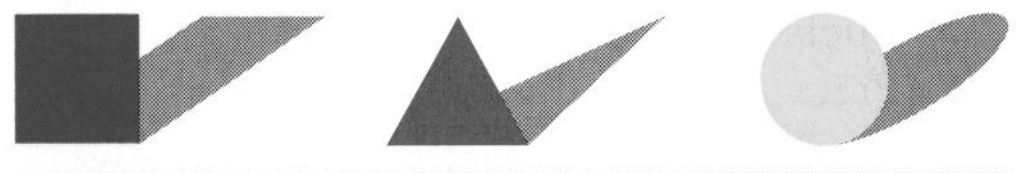

H. Ramsey Fowler *University of Memphis*
Jane E. Aaron *New York University*

An imprint of Addison Wesley Longman, Inc.

New York • Reading, Massachusetts • Menlo Park, California • Harlow, England
Don Mills, Ontario • Sydney • Mexico City • Madrid • Amsterdam

Senior Editor: Patricia Rossi
Development Editor: Thomas Maeglin
Supplements Editor: Donna Campion
Project Editorial Manager: Robert Ginsberg
Design Manager: John Callahan
Cover Designer: Kay Petronio
Text Designer: Dorothy Bungert/*EriBen Graphics*
Art: Dorothy Bungert/*EriBen Graphics*
Production Manager: Valerie A. Sawyer
Desktop Administrator: Jim Sullivan
Manufacturing Manager: Hilda Koparanian
Electronic Page Makeup: Dorothy Bungert/*EriBen Graphics* and Carole Desnoes
Printer and Binder: RR Donnelley & Sons Company
Cover Printer: The Lehigh Press, Inc.

The authors and publisher are grateful to the many students who allowed their work to be reprinted here and to the copyright holders who are listed on pages 837–38. Those pages are hereby made an extension of this copyright page.

Library of Congress Cataloging-in-Publication Data

Fowler, H. Ramsey (Henry Ramsey)
The Little, Brown handbook / H. Ramsey Fowler, Jane E. Aaron.—7th ed.
p. cm.
Includes index.
ISBN 0-321-01216-X
1. English language—Grammer—Handbooks, manuals, etc. 2. English language—Rhetoric—Handbooks, manuals, etc. I. Aaron, Jane E. II. Title.
PE1112.F64 1997
808'.042—dc21 97–12644
CIP

ISBN 0-321-01216-X

12345678910—DOC—00999897

This seventh edition of *The Little, Brown Handbook* appears amid a sea change in writing instruction caused by computers. Electronic media are transforming classrooms, research methods, forms of presentation, even the writing process itself. Revising *The Little, Brown Handbook,* we faced a dual challenge: to revamp the book so that it serves computer-using students and teachers and yet to retain the handbook's strengths as a comprehensive, clear, and accessible reference guide and classroom text.

The list of changes in the seventh edition could run even more pages than it does. Here we hit the highlights.

Computers in writing and research

We have woven computers into the cloth of the handbook:

- **Tips for computer use** appear throughout the chapters on thinking, writing, and research writing. Always signaled in the margin by the computer image shown here, these tips range from journal keeping to revising on a word processor to downloading sources. (See pp. 38, 67, and 576 for examples.)
- **Electronic research** is the focus of the book's most substantial additions. We provide extensive guidance on conducting electronic searches (p. 522), including discovering what's available, searching productively and efficiently, and evaluating a search. We also provide a thorough introduction to electronic sources, especially those available over the Internet (p. 535). The discussion ranges from electronic addresses to Web search engines to synchronous communication, and screen shots illustrate a student's Internet search.

- A new section on **evaluating electronic sources** gives students concrete, usable advice for separating the worthy from the worthless (p. 566).
- **Documenting electronic sources** receives special attention with each documentation style covered: MLA (p. 619), Chicago (p. 701), APA (p. 716), and CBE (p. 732). We supplement the MLA models with those endorsed by the Alliance for Computers and Writing (p. 622).
- A new **sample MLA paper,** "The Information Superhighway: Toll Road or Public Way?" (p. 632), not only addresses a computer issue but also illustrates electronic research: 60 percent of its works cited are electronic sources (p. 658). The paper builds from examples of the student's work (for instance, pp. 520, 542) and includes detailed facing-page annotations (pp. 639, 659).
- New material on **document design** includes advice about typefaces, illustrations, color, and other elements (p. 765). Examples include a report and a newsletter.
- For **computers in business writing,** we offer a contemporary résumé (p. 754) and extensive discussion of electronic mail (p. 757).
- A new appendix provides basic tips for **word processing** (p. 773), guidelines for **writing collaboratively on computers** (p. 775), and suggestions for **creating hypertext documents** (p. 778).

English as a second language

As before, the material for nonnative English speakers is thoroughly integrated into the main text, so that students do not have to distinguish between ESL problems and those they share with native speakers. At the same time, a small color block (ESL) highlights the material so that it can be easily consulted or easily skipped. (See pp. 243 and 259 for examples.)

Much ESL material is new to this edition:

- An **ESL guide** inside the back cover provides a ready reference to all the ESL material so that it can be taught or consulted as a unit.
- **Forty-two new ESL notes** (for a total of fifty-five) deal with issues of process and rhetoric as well as grammar. For instance, see the notes on thesis sentences (p. 48), transitional expressions (p. 101), subordinating conjunctions (p. 183), and originality in research writing (p. 563).
- **Three new sections** (for a total of fourteen) treat ESL grammar issues in detail. See, for instance, modal verbs (p. 216) and adverb placement (p. 301).

Critical thinking and the writing process

The book's Introduction and Chapters 1–2 have seen important additions besides those dealing with computers:

- The Introduction, "Critical Thinking, Reading, and Writing," includes a new discussion and illustration of a **reading journal** (pp. 4, 7); a new **text for critical reading,** Thomas Sowell's essay "Student Loans" (p. 8); and a new **annotated student critique** of Sowell's essay (p. 19).
- A much longer section on **journals** details the uses of a journal, offers encouragement, and provides four examples (p. 37).
- New material on the **thesis sentence** (p. 48) and **organization** (p. 52) makes these key topics more accessible and practical for students.
- A new **checklist for revision** (p. 69) stresses key concerns (purpose, thesis, and so on), and a new **checklist for editing** (p. 74) highlights the most common errors.
- A new section on **writing portfolios** discusses the purposes of a portfolio and offers tips for preparing one (p. 82).
- Throughout the discussion of the writing process, we continue to show a student's **work in progress,** signaled by the notebook image shown here.

Research writing

In addition to the changes addressing electronic research, the chapters on research writing have been strengthened in several ways:

- **Evaluating and synthesizing sources** receive more attention (p. 563), including a procedure for synthesis (p. 567) and, as mentioned earlier, tips for evaluating electronic sources (p. 566).
- The expanded discussion of **integrating quotations,** with additional examples, now focuses more on alterations in quotations and placement of signal phrases (p. 591).
- A new **general introduction to documenting sources** discusses academic standards and styles (p. 598).
- Besides a thorough treatment of electronic sources, coverage of **MLA documentation** includes new models of in-text citations (p. 600), an expanded discussion of placing in-text citations (p. 605), and new models of works-cited entries (p. 607).
- For **other disciplines,** the expansions are similar. The handbook adds new documentation models and sample page formats for all three styles (Chicago, p. 696; APA, p. 707; CBE, p. 729). Further, each style has its own colored page borders for easy reference.

Other additions

Several further improvements increase the handbook's usefulness for students both in and out of English courses:

- The chapter on **writing about literature,** contributed by Sylvan Barnet, now includes a discussion of critical approaches to literature (p. 673) and a new student paper on drama (p. 687) to complement the papers on fiction and poetry.
- The chapter on **essay exams** includes two annotated sample essays on the same question, one a successful answer and one not (p. 742).
- A new appendix on **oral presentations** offers advice for preparing and delivering a talk or speech (p. 784).
- We have added or expanded discussions of many key topics, such as **transitions** (pp. 99, 123, 373), **comma splices** (p. 274), **shifts** in form of quotation and question (p. 294), misuse of a **comma after a conjunction** (p. 384), and the trickier uses of the **ellipsis mark** (p. 424).
- We have greatly expanded the coverage of **biased language** to emphasize not just sexist language but also stereotypes of race, age, religion, and other characteristics (p. 459).

Continuing features

We want to put in a word for what has *not* changed in this seventh edition:

- Text **explanations** are clear and practical, assuming little or no knowledge of terms and concepts and emphasizing the essentials of writing.
- **Examples** represent subjects from across the curriculum, reflect students' diverse backgrounds, and, above all, illustrate concepts clearly. **Annotations** on the examples demonstrate concepts with more immediacy than do text explanations (pp. 111, 243).
- Plentiful **exercises** encourage students to tackle writing from many angles. Sentence exercises are always in **connected discourse** so that students work at the level of the paragraph rather than the isolated sentence (pp. 245, 250). **End-of-part revision exercises** ask students to revise brief essays containing a range of errors, not just one type (pp. 264, 316).
- *The Little, Brown Handbook* is **accessible. Endpapers** provide a complete contents (front), an ESL guide (back left), a list of editing symbols (back right), and an index of useful lists and summaries (just before the back endpapers). The uncluttered **design** invites students in and clarifies the relationship of elements. More than 140 **boxes** highlight important information (pp. 139, 579). **Cross-references** give page numbers, not code numbers (pp. 266, 365). Two extensive **glossaries** before the index answer usage questions and define terms (pp. 793, 812).

And the **index** itself is the most comprehensive available, listing not only terms but problem expressions (p. 839).

Supplements

An extensive package of supplements accompanies *The Little, Brown Handbook,* some for instructors and some for students. An asterisk (*) precedes any item or items that are complimentary to qualified adopters of the handbook.

For instructors

- *The **Instructor's Annotated Edition,** revised and updated by Rebecca Brittenham, Rutgers University, combines essays and annotations for instructors with the text of the student edition in one convenient volume. This edition includes "Using Computers to Teach Writing," an essay by Susan Lang of Southern Illinois University, which describes how computers can enrich the composition classroom and details how *The Little, Brown Handbook* supports the uses of computers for teaching writing. This edition also annotates the student text's exercises with ideas for completing them collaboratively or with computers. As before, the IAE contains answers to all exercises (adjacent to the exercises), scores of classroom discussion topics and activities, extensive reading suggestions, and helpful essays for both new and experienced teachers.
- *Several supplements reproduce parts of the text or IAE for classroom use or portability: a set of **transparency masters** with key boxes and lists from the text; a separate **answer key** containing all exercise answers; and a **correction chart** duplicating the book's endpapers.
- ***Teaching Online: Internet Research, Conversation, and Composition*** is an accessible introduction to Internet resources for teaching writing. Written by Daniel Anderson, Bret Benjamin, Chris Busiel, and Bill Paredes-Holt of the University of Texas at Austin, the book offers basic definitions and information on Internet access and shows how to integrate a variety of Internet tools in writing courses.
- *An extensive **assessment package** includes diagnostic tests and TASP and CLAST exams. All tests are keyed to the handbook, and all are available both in print and on computer software. In addition, the software versions can be customized and used on a network for online testing.
- *Two books contain photo-reproducible material that can be distributed to students: ***Eighty Practices,*** a collection of grammar and usage exercises, and ***Model Research Papers from***

Across the Disciplines, a collection of student papers in the humanities, social sciences, and natural sciences.

- *The series **Longman Resources for Instructors** includes five valuable works: *Teaching in Progress: Theories, Practices, and Scenarios,* by Josephine Koster Tarvers; *Teaching Writing to the Non-Native Speaker,* by Jocelyn Steer; the videos *Writing, Teaching, and Learning,* by David Jolliffe, and *Writing Across the Curriculum: Making It Work,* produced by Robert Morris College and the Public Broadcasting System.

For students

- ***The Little, Brown Workbook,*** Seventh Edition, by Donna Gorrell, St. Cloud University, parallels the handbook's organization but provides briefer text and many more exercises. This edition includes a new sample research paper.
- ***ESL Worksheets,*** by Jocelyn Steer, provides nonnative speakers with extra practice in the areas that tend to be most troublesome for them.
- *A new guide for students, ***Researching Online and Off,*** combines research and documentation information from *The Little, Brown Handbook* with information on Internet access and resources from *Teaching Online* in a handy format.
- *****The Writer's Workshop,*** keyed to the handbook, is a heuristics program that helps students explore, form, and express their ideas while writing arguments, research papers, and literary analyses. A new feature, Paper-in-Progress, follows one paper through successive stages to show how one student drafted and revised in response to peer and instructor comments. Also included is a tool for formatting source citations (MLA or APA documentation style) and an online version of *The Little, Brown Handbook,* Seventh Edition. (IBM and Macintosh.)
- A CD-ROM, ***Electric Library,*** co-produced by Longman and Infonautics, gives access to full-text electronic sources from a large collection of newspapers, magazines, and books available online through Prodigy. This powerful and easy-to-use researching tool allows keyword searching on the daily-updated database. With the purchase of *Electric Library* comes one free month of Prodigy.
- *****Supershell*** provides a self-paced grammar and usage tutorial for IBM-compatible computers.
- *****Reading Critically: Text, Charts, and Graphs,*** Second Edition, by Judith Olson-Fallon, complements the handbook's Introduction. It provides a framework for developing critical reading questions and gives detailed information on preparing reading notes, study summaries, and graphic organizers.

- *Two guides to **collaborative learning,** both by Tori Haring-Smith, help students work together in groups: *Learning Together* discusses the advantages and varieties of collaborative work; and *Student Manual for Peer Evaluation,* with a new introduction by Helon Raines, contains forms to guide students' peer editing.
- ***Eighty Readings,*** Second Edition, is a versatile collection of professional and student essays organized thematically, with an alternate rhetorical table of contents. The new edition raises the issues that confront today's students.
- A **dictionary** can be packaged with the handbook: *The New American Webster Handy Dictionary,* Third Edition.
- Two guides to **writing with a word processor,** *Using WordPerfect in Composition* and *Using Microsoft Word in Composition,* help students master word-processing functions while they develop their own writing processes.

Acknowledgments

Over the life of *The Little, Brown Handbook,* thousands of teachers have talked with sales representatives and editors, answered questionnaires, participated in focus groups, sent us personal notes, and written detailed reviews. The handbook remains fresh and useful because of this communication, and we are grateful for it.

For the seventh edition, the following instructors offered welcome insights from their rich experience with students: Joseph A. Alvarez, Central Piedmont Community College; Crystal Bacon, Gloucester County College; Cynthia Bates, University of California, Davis; Russell Bignano, Pennsylvania State University, Beaver; Nancy Blattner, Southeast Missouri State University; Kay Bosgraaf, Montgomery College; Phyllis Brotemarkle, Frostburg State University; Larry Brunner, Hardin-Simmons University; Ellen Burke, Casper College; Terrence Burke, Cuyahoga Community College; Peggy Cole, Arapahoe Community College; Geraldine DeLuca, Brooklyn College; Nancy Enright, Seton Hall University; Tom Ezzy, Dawson College; Richard Fabrizio, Pace University; Stuart Foreman, Millersville University; Rob Friedman, New Jersey Institute of Technology; Judith Gallagher, Tarrant County Junior College; Barbara Granger, Thomas Nelson Community College; Ida Hagman, College of DuPage; Marcia Halio, University of Delaware; Carol Hammond, Yavapai College; Judy Hemmington, San Joaquin Delta College; Maurice Hunt, Baylor University; Peggy Jolly, University of Alabama, Birmingham; Michael Keller, South Dakota State University; Malcolm Kiniry, Rutgers University, Newark; James Scott King, Delaware State University; Paul Kleinpoppen, Florida Community College at Jacksonville, South Campus; Richard N. Lewis,

Jr., Sandhills Community College; Rob Little, Rend Lake College; Dara Llewellyn, Florida Atlantic University; Mike Matthews, Tarrant County Junior College; Patricia M. Medeiros, Scottsdale Community College; Troy D. Nordman, Butler County Community College; George Redman, Benedict College; Ken Risdon, University of Minnesota, Duluth; Joan K. Robertson, North Central Technical College; Jan Schmidt, SUNY, New Paltz; Jeff Schonberg, Hardin-Simmons University; Marilyn Schultz, Lincoln University; Eileen Schwartz, Purdue University, Calumet; Richard Sisk, Mount San Jacinto College; Paul Sladky, Augusta College; Frances Smith, Grand Canyon University; Linda Tappmeyer, Southwest Baptist University; Patricia Terry, Gonzaga University; Donald Tighe, Valencia Community College; Warren Westcott, Francis Marion University; Sherri Winans, Whatcom Community College.

A number of instructors also gave very useful comments on the Instructor's Annotated Edition: Jane Allwardt, North Central Technical College; Jan Anderson, Clackamas Community College; Jerrie Callan, Baylor University; Susan Lang, Southern Illinois University; Lynn Langer Meeks, Utah State University; Leonard Sanazaro, City College of San Francisco; Bruce W. Speck, University of Memphis; Alison Warriner, Sacred Heart University.

In addition to these thoughtful critics, a group of creative people helped substantially with parts of the book. Andrew Christensen, David Gibbs, and Deborah A. Person contributed ideas and research support. Isa Engleberg, Prince George's Community College, offered advice for oral presentations, drawing on her text *The Principles of Public Presentation*. Kathleen Shine Cain, Merrimack College, provided crucial material for the research-writing chapters. Susan Lang, Southern Illinois University, advised us on electronic composition and research. And Sylvan Barnet, Tufts University, helped us revise his chapter, "Reading and Writing About Literature," adapted from his *Short Guide to Writing About Literature* and *Introduction to Literature* (with Morton Berman, William Burto, and William E. Cain). We are grateful to all these contributors.

From Longman, the publisher, we had not only support but camaraderie. Patricia Rossi, the editor and captain, was, as always, clever, patient, and true. Her assistant, Lynne Cattafi, apparently found no request too urgent or tiresome. Thomas Maeglin, assisted by Reka Simonsen, led the authors through development with keen intelligence and gentle strength. Robert Ginsberg deftly managed the myriad details and challenges of production. Kathryn Graehl copyedited with precision and tact. And Dorothy Bungert yet again provided creative solutions in design and page make-up. To all, our deep thanks.

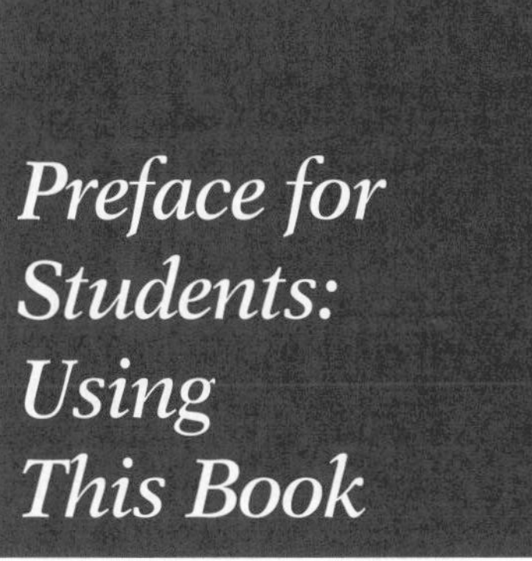

Preface for Students: Using This Book

The Little, Brown Handbook is a basic resource that will answer almost any question you have about writing. Here you can find out how to get ideas, punctuate quotations, search the Internet, cite sources, or write a résumé. The handbook can help you not only in writing courses but in other courses and beyond school.

Don't let the size of the handbook put you off. You need not read the whole book to get something out of it, and no one expects you to know everything included. Primarily a reference tool, the handbook is written and arranged to help you find the answers you need when you need them, quickly and easily.

Using this book will not by itself make you a good writer; for that, you need to care about your work at every level, from finding a subject to spelling words. But learning how to use the handbook and the information in it can give you the means to write *what* you want in the *way* you want.

Organization and content

An overview of the handbook appears inside the front cover. Briefly, the book divides into the following sections:

- The Introduction lays a foundation with the essential skills of critical thinking, reading, and writing.
- Chapters 1–4 deal with the big picture: the writing process, paragraphs, and argument.
- Chapters 5–19 cover sentence basics: the system of English grammar and its conventions, errors that affect clarity, and techniques of effective sentences.

- Chapters 20–30 treat two technical elements of sentences and words: punctuation and mechanics (meaning capital letters, underlining, and the like).
- Chapters 31–34 move to words—how to choose them, look them up, learn them, spell them.
- Chapters 35–38 cover research writing from planning through revising, with a complete guide to citing sources.
- Chapters 39 and 40 introduce writing about literature and writing in the other academic disciplines.
- Chapters 41 and 42 contain practical information on taking essay exams and writing business letters and job applications.
- Appendixes A, B, and C provide information on formatting and designing documents, writing with a computer (word processing, collaborating, and creating hypertext documents), and making oral presentations.
- Two glossaries—one of problem words and expressions, the other of terms—and a detailed index finish the book.

Finding information

How you use the handbook will depend on your instructor's wishes and your own inclinations. Your instructor may assign whole sections of the book and discuss them in class or may use comments on your papers to direct you to particular sections. He or she will certainly encourage you to look things up on your own whenever you have a question. To help you do that, the handbook provides many ways of finding information quickly. Some of these surround the main text:

- The **Plan of the Book,** inside the front cover, displays the book's entire contents in abbreviated form. This plan also shows the system of coded headings (explained opposite).
- The **Contents,** immediately after this preface, gives a more detailed version of the book's plan.
- The **ESL Guide,** inside the back cover, indexes the book's topics for students using English as a second language.
- The list of **Editing Symbols,** also inside the back cover, gives the abbreviations often used to mark papers (see p. xvi).
- The list of **Useful Lists and Summaries,** just before the back endpapers, indexes topics that students frequently ask about.
- The **Index,** on the last pages of the book, lists every term and concept and every problem word or expression mentioned in the book. It is very detailed so that you can locate the precise point you seek and the page number where the point is discussed.

Many of the handbook's reference and learning aids appear on the text pages themselves, as illustrated by the reduced samples opposite. On these pages notice especially the heading code in

❶ Running head (header): the topic being discussed on this page.

❷ Section heading in blue-green. The boxed code (**8b**) consists of the chapter number (**8**) and section letter (**b**).

❸ Page tab in blue-green, containing the nearest section code (**8b**) and the editing symbol for the topic being discussed (**agr**).

❹ Examples, always indented, often showing revision.

❺ Box in pale yellow, containing a summary or checklist.

❻ Pointer for students using English as a second language, flagged with a small yellow box.

❼ Subsection heading in red, with heading number in triangle.

❽ Exercise with yellow vertical line.

❶

246 Agreement

❷ **8b** **Make pronouns and their antecedents agree in person, number, and gender.**

❸ agr 8b

The **antecedent** of a pronoun is the noun or other pronoun it refers to.

Homeowners fret over *their* tax bills.
❹ antecedent pronoun

Its constant increases make the tax *bill* a dreaded document.
pronoun antecedent

Since a pronoun derives its meaning from its antecedent, the two must agree in person, number, and gender.

Person, number, and gender in pronoun-antecedent agreement

❺

PERSON	NUMBER *Singular*	*Plural*
First	*I*	*we*
Second	*you*	*you*
Third	*he, she, it* indefinite pronouns singular nouns	*they* plural nouns
GENDER		
Masculine	*he,* nouns naming males	
Feminine	*she,* nouns naming females	
Neuter	*it,* all other nouns	

❻ ESL The gender of a pronoun should match its antecedent, not a noun that the pronoun may modify: *President Clinton appointed his* [not *her*] *wife to redesign health care.* Also, nouns in English have only neuter gender unless they specifically refer to males or females. Thus nouns such as *book, table, sun,* and *earth* take the pronoun *it.*

❼ 1 **Antecedents joined by *and* usually take plural pronouns.**

Two or more antecedents joined by *and* usually take a plural

The old group have gone *their* separate ways.

In the last example, note that the verb and pronoun are consistent in number (see also p. 243).

❹ INCONSISTENT The old group *has* gone *their* separate ways.
CONSISTENT The old group *have* gone *their* separate ways.

❽ Exercise 2
Revising: Pronoun-antecedent agreement

Revise the following sentences so that pronouns and their antecedents agree in person and number. Some items have more than one possible answer. Try to avoid the generic *he* (see the previous page). If you change the subject of a sentence, be sure to change verbs as necessary for agreement. If the sentence is already correct as given, circle the number preceding it.

Example:
Each of the Boudreaus' children brought their laundry home at Thanksgiving.
Each of the Boudreaus' children brought *his or her* laundry home at Thanksgiving. *Or: All* of the Boudreaus' children brought *their* laundry home at Thanksgiving.

1. Each girl raised in a Mexican American family in the Rio Grande Valley of Texas hopes that one day they will be given a *quinceañera* party for their fifteenth birthday.

both blue-green boxes (**8b** in the samples) and the symbol in the marginal box (**agr** in the samples). Your instructor may use either or both of these to mark specific weaknesses in your papers—for instance, either **8b** or **agr** on your paper would indicate an agreement problem. To discover just what the problem is and how to revise it, you can consult the plan of the book or the list of editing symbols, or you can thumb the book. (A sample student paper marked by an instructor with some codes and symbols appears on pp. 77–79.)

The handbook's reference aids are meant to speed your work, but you need not use any or all of them. You may of course browse or read this book like any other, with no particular goal in mind but seeing what you can learn.

Special symbols

Frequently throughout the handbook, you'll see the following symbols:

- The computer shown here signals tips for using computers productively for all kinds of writing activity, from discovering ideas through citing sources.

- The notebook shown here marks examples from students' work-in-progress, applications of the text's principles in specific writing situations.
- The symbol ESL flags material for students using English as a second language, which is integrated throughout the handbook. A guide to the ESL topics appears inside the back cover.

Recommended usage

The conventions described and illustrated in this handbook are those of standard written English—the label given the language of business and the professions. (See also p. 454.) Written English is more conservative than spoken English in matters of grammar and usage, and a great many words and constructions that are widely spoken remain unaccepted in careful writing.

When clear distinctions exist between the language of conversation and that of careful writing, the handbook provides examples of each and labels them *spoken* and *written*. When usage in writing itself varies with the level of formality intended, the handbook labels examples *formal* and *informal*. When usage is mixed or currently changing, the handbook recommends that you choose the more conservative usage because it will be acceptable to all readers.

Contents

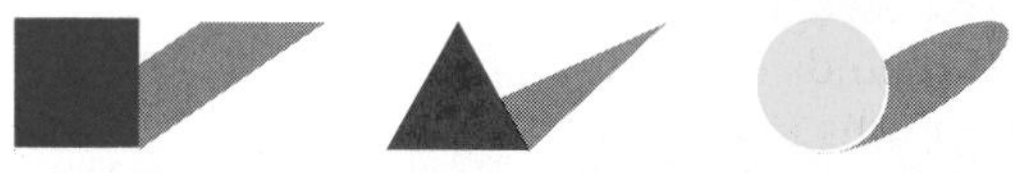

Part III
Clear Sentences *265*

The Little, Brown Handbook

Introduction

Critical Thinking, Reading, and Writing

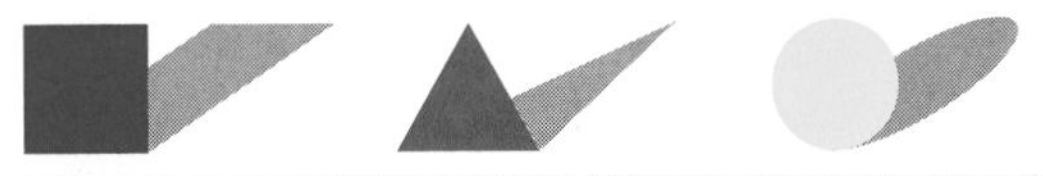

Why does a book on writing begin with an introduction to thinking and reading as well as writing? The answer is that the three can't be separated: thinking underlies reading and writing; writing demands reading; reading and writing clarify and toughen thinking. To get the most out of this book—and your education—you will need to be adept at all three skills.

This Introduction serves as a foundation for several assignments you may encounter in college: writing essays (Chapters 1–2), reading and writing arguments (Chapter 4), writing research papers (Chapters 35–38), reading and writing about literature (Chapter 39), and writing in other disciplines (Chapter 40). All of these assignments require that you foster a critical perspective (section I1), develop a process of critical thinking and reading (I2), and learn to write critically (I3).

I1 Fostering a critical perspective

The kind of thinking, reading, and writing we're concerned with here goes beyond obvious meanings and easy answers. It is called **critical,** meaning "skeptical," "exacting," "creative." When you operate critically, you question, test, and build on what others say and what you yourself think. The word *critical* does not mean "negative" in this context. It comes from Greek words meaning "to separate" and "to discern": a critical thinker, reader, or writer separates a subject into its parts, discerns how the parts work together

HIGHLIGHTS

Some high school seniors write few texts longer than a paragraph in length, and others only complete fill-in or multiple-choice tests on reading comprehension. So becoming explicitly aware of their critical powers, and then learning to use them, may seem overwhelming to students trying to cope with all the changes the first year of college brings.

The chapter starts with the sometimes challenging concept of being critical without being negative. The example of a popular and non-threatening magazine, *People,* helps students feel at ease, and the example of Thomas Sowell's provocative essay, "Student Loans," wakes them up and models truly academic critical reading. Both examples pop up in the chapter's coverage of active reading, summarizing, and constructing a critical response with the use of analysis, interpretation, synthesis, and evaluation.

Finally, the chapter focuses on communicating the results of critical thinking and reading to an audience through critical writing. An annotated student paper responding to Sowell's essay helps students learn to shape and produce a coherent critical response and ushers them into the development and refinement of their writing skills explained in the next sections of this handbook.

RESOURCES AND IDEAS

Many fine studies exist on critical thinking, reading, and writing, including the following:

Anson, Chris M. ed. *Writing and Response: Theory, Practice, and Research.* Urbana: NCTE, 1989. A collection of essays that explore the practical and theoretical issues involved in reading and commenting on student texts.

Carter, Duncan. "Critical Thinking for Writers: Transferable Skills or Discipline-Specific Strategies?" *Composition Studies: Freshman English News* 21 (1993): 86–93. Carter explores the question of whether critical thinking skills are transferable across discourse communities.

Emig, Janet. "Writing as a Mode of Learning." *College Composition and Communication* 28 (1977): 122–28. A seminal analysis of the ways in which writing facilitates mental processes like intuition, reformulation, and the construction of meaningful relationships between ideas.

Marzano, Robert J. *Cultivating Thinking in English: The Language Arts.* Urbana: NCTE, 1991. Marzano explores strategies for enhancing student learning, emphasizing ways in which students can analyze their own values and responses to class texts and discussions.

Odell, Lee. "*Strategy* and *Surprise* in the Making of Meaning." In *Theory and Practice in the Teaching of Writing: Rethinking the Discipline.* Ed. Lee Odell. Carbondale: Southern Illinois UP, 1993. 213–243. This essay explores the debates over fostering spontaneity and intuitive insights in the teaching of writing as opposed to teaching conscious control, and identifies several approaches that work to do both.

Salvatori, Mariolina. "Conversations with Texts: Reading in the Teaching of Composition." *College English* 58 (1996): 440–54. Salvatori examines the theoretical basis for the argument that critical reading and writing are linked learning activities.

Shaughnessy, Mina. *Errors and Expectations: A Guide for the Teacher of Basic Writing.* New York: Oxford UP, 1977. This pathbreaking study of the challenges faced by basic writers reveals the connections between student error and issues of critical thinking.

Toulmin, Stephen, Richard Rieke, and Allan Janik. *An Introduction to Reasoning,* 2nd ed. New York: Macmillan, 1984. Toulmin et al. detail the reasoning processes involved in making claims, supplying evidential backing, and preparing for rebuttal.

The meaning of *critical*

One of the greatest difficulties in teaching critical strategies is the problems students have with the negative connotations of the word *critical.* Brainstorm all the meanings and uses of the word they know; beyond those implying value judgments, some students will come up with "critical temperature," "critical mass," "critical condition," "critical point of the game," and so on. By showing how these terms connect to discernment, or important stages of development, you can demonstrate that the word need not always have negative overtones and thus help students to study these techniques with a better attitude.

Challenging texts (ESL)

Critical activities may provide an additional hurdle for students from other countries. In

and how the subject relates to other subjects, and (often) judges the subject's quality and value.

You already operate critically every day of your life, as when you probe a friendship ("What did she mean by that?") or when you discuss a movie you just saw ("Don't you think the villain was too obvious?"). Such questioning helps you figure out why things happen to you or what your experiences mean.

Operating critically in other spheres—school courses, career, our democratic society—expands the subjects and the benefits.

- Critical thinking, reading, and writing improve your ability to learn and to perform as a student and a worker. Your teachers and employers in every field, from the arts to zoology, will expect you to assess what you read and hear and to make a good case for your own ideas.
- Operating critically helps you understand your own actions and ideas, weigh them against opposing views, and persuasively articulate your reasoning and motivations.
- Your very independence and freedom depend on your ability to think, read, and write critically. An open democracy like ours allows as much play for stupid and false claims as for sound ones, and the ones that seem sound often conflict with each other. Whether you are watching the evening news, reading an advertisement, or voting, critical thinking empowers you to decide for yourself what's useful, fair, and wise—and what's not.

There's no denying that critical thinking, reading, and writing require discipline and hard work. Besides channeling your curiosity, paying attention, and probing, you will often need to consult experts, interpreting and evaluating their ideas. Such an approach also requires a healthy tolerance for doubt or uncertainty—that feeling you may have had when the old rules don't seem to apply or when a change is frightening but still attractive. Out of uncertainty, though, comes creativity—the capacity to organize and generate knowledge, to explain, resolve, illuminate, play. Compared to passive, rote learning, creative work is more involving, more productive, and more enjoyable.

I2 Thinking and reading critically

You can think critically about almost anything: an argument you overhear on a bus, a new CD by your favorite solo musician, your roommate's ideas about baseball, even a dog-food commercial. By "separating" and "discerning" any of these, you would be able to understand it better, see its relations to other events or things, and evaluate it.

Of course, in college much of your critical thinking will focus on written texts, such as a short story, an Internet posting, or a journal article. Like all subjects worthy of critical consideration, written texts operate on at least three levels: (1) what the author actually says, (2) what the author does not say but builds into the text (intentionally or not), and (3) what you think. Discovering the text at each level involves a number of techniques.

Techniques of critical reading

- **Writing:** making notes on your reading throughout the process (p. 4)
- **Previewing:** getting background; skimming (p. 5)
- **Reading:** interacting with and absorbing the text (p. 6)
- **Summarizing:** distilling and understanding content (p. 10)
- **Forming your critical response** (p. 11)

  Analyzing: separating into parts
  Interpreting: inferring meaning and assumptions
  Synthesizing: reassembling parts; making connections
  Evaluating: judging quality and value

Keep in mind that these are techniques, not steps in a firm sequence. You will not use all of them for all the reading you do. On some occasions, even when a close, critical reading is required, you may simply lack the time to preview, read, and reread. (But if your reading time is continually squeezed by your schedule, you may need to rethink your schedule.) On other occasions your reason for reading (your purpose) will determine which techniques you use. For instance, let's say you're reading *People* magazine.

Purpose	Learn some gossip while filling time in the dentist's office.
Kind of reading	Quick, uncritical
Purpose	Examine *People* as an artifact of our popular culture that reflects and perhaps even molds contemporary values.
Kind of reading	Close, critical

Course assignments, too, differ in their requirements. A book report may require writing, previewing, reading, and summarizing but not intense critical reading. An evaluation of a journal article, in contrast, requires all the techniques listed.

ESL The idea of reading critically may require you to make some adjustments if readers in your native culture tend to seek understanding or agreement more than engagement from what they read. As noted above, readers of English read for all kinds of rea-

many cultures, students are taught not to challenge ideas in print; such questions may be considered disrespectful by some who see print as an indication of authority and value. (This is especially true if the text refers to religious beliefs.) Other students, especially those who grew up in nondemocratic societies, may know from experience how dangerous it can be to challenge the

TRANSPARENCY MASTER I.1

"party line" espoused in school. And depending on the area of the United States you teach in, you may find students who believe in the "inerrancy of the word," even if the text is not biblical. Discuss the students' right to ask questions about, respond to, and challenge printed works, whether in published texts or in personal manuscripts.

Matthieson's mistake

One good anecdote to share with students concerns F. O. Matthieson's classic work of literary criticism, *American Renaissance.* When it first appeared in 1941, it contained a passage praising the irony in Herman Melville's metaphor "the soiled fish of the sea" (describing an eel). When readers rushed to read the Melville passage in question, however, they found that "soiled" was actually a typographical error; the correct reading was "coiled." Matthieson's brilliant critique of Melville's irony was founded on a typesetter's mistake. Students find it comforting to know that great critics can make mistakes, too; you can point out that it was, in fact, people employing critical reading who found Matthieson's misreading!

RESOURCES AND IDEAS

Brookfield, Stephen D. *Developing Critical Thinkers.* San Francisco: Jossey-Bass, 1987. Brookfield encourages connections between critical skills developed in school and their applications in daily life.

Elbow, Peter. "Ranking, Evaluating, and Liking: Sorting Out Three Forms of Judgment." *College English* 55 (1993): 187–206. Elbow's essay is largely concerned with these three activities as part of teacher assessment of student writing, but it gives many ideas that can be translated into classroom practice.

Fiske, John. *Introduction to Communication Studies.* New York: Routledge, 1990. Fiske provides a general overview (for students and teachers) of the methods of cultural criticism, with explicit connections to the teaching of writing.

Golub, Jeff, and the NCTE Committee on Classroom Practices, eds. *Activities to Promote Critical Thinking*. Urbana: NCTE, 1986. The authors have compiled a collection of essays focusing on practical advice and teaching strategies.

Greene, Stuart, and John M. Ackerman. "Expanding the Constructivist Metaphor: A Rhetorical Perspective on Literary Research and Practice." *Review of Educational Research* 65 (Winter 1995): 383–420. This review essay evaluates a number of constructivist explanations of the relationship between reading and writing as a learning model.

Jones, Libby Falk. "Exploring Beliefs Through Dialectical Thinking." *The Critical Writing Workshop: Designing Writing Assignments to Foster Critical Thinking*. Ed. Toni-lee Capossella. Portsmouth, NH: Boynton, 1993. 17–34. This essay and the collection as a whole offer general discussion and practical examples of how to structure thought-provoking assignments.

Killingsworth, M. Jimmie. "Discourse Communities—Global and Local." *Rhetoric Review* 11 (Fall 1992): 110–22. Killingsworth makes readers aware that they are members of both kinds of communities, and he suggests ways to negotiate the bridge(s) between the two.

McLeod, Susan H. "Cultural Literacy, Curricular Reform, and Freshman Composition." *Rhetoric Review* 8 (1990): 270–78. McLeod argues that students can move beyond personal experience in writing essays by reading scholarly materials and responding to them.

Mirskin, Jerry. "Writing as a Process of Valuing." *College Composition and Communication* 46 (1995): 387–410. Mirskin argues that because values shape meaning, teachers must learn to recognize students' systems of value in order to best help them make meaningful connections within an academic environment.

Qualley, Donna. "Using Reading in the Writing Classroom." In *Nuts and Bolts: A Practical Guide to Teaching College Composition*. Ed. Thomas Newkirk. Portsmouth, NH: Boynton, 1993. Qualley lays out strategies for integrating critical reading and writing using journals, reading conferences, and small group discussions.

sons, including pleasure, reinforcement, information, and many others. But they also read skeptically, critically, to see the author's motives, test their own ideas, and arrive at new knowledge.

Writing while reading

There are two good reasons to write while you read: to record information and ideas for future use, and to get more out of the text. The first is discussed in detail as part of research writing (see pp. 517–18). The second has more to do with critical reading.

Critical reading is *active* reading. You interact with the text, getting involved with it, bringing to it *your* experiences, ideas, and questions. When you use a pen or pencil or keyboard while reading, you create writing in response to writing. In this way you "translate" the text into your own words and reconstruct it for yourself.

Many readers keep a **reading journal**, a notebook or computer file in which they regularly work out questions and thoughts about what they read. One technique for keeping such a journal is to divide a page or computer screen into two vertical columns, the left side for the text itself, such as summary and questions, and the right side for what the text makes you think, such as agreements or doubts based on your own experiences, comparisons with other texts, and ideas for writing. A two-column journal can encourage you to go beyond summarizing what you read to interacting critically with it because the blank right column will beckon you to respond. See pages 7–8 for an example of this technique. And see pages 37–38 for more on journal keeping.

If you don't keep a regular reading journal, you can still benefit from writing while reading in other ways.

- If you're reading a printed text that you own, you may opt to write directly on the pages as you read them (an illustration of this method appears on p. 7).
- If you don't own the material, make your notes on a separate sheet or in a computer file or, if the material is brief enough, on a photocopy of it.
- If you're reading a page on the World Wide Web or another online source, you can open your word-processing program at the same time, adjust the sizes of the Web page and the word-processing document so that both fit on the screen, and make notes in the word-processing document. Or compose electronic mail while you're reading and then send it to yourself. You may also be able to download the online material directly into your word-processing program and annotate it there. (But be cautious. Check the copyright notice at the source to see whether downloading is restricted in any way. Most source authors allow

students to download material and use it as long as the source is fully acknowledged. See p. 576 for more on downloading sources and p. 582 for more on acknowledging sources.)

Note Whenever you download a document or take notes separately from the text you're reading, be sure to record all necessary information about the text's location so that you can find it again and cite it fully if you use it. See page 560 for a list of information to record.

b Previewing the material

When you're reading a work of literature, such as a story or a poem, it's often best just to plunge right in. But for critical reading of other texts, it's worthwhile to form some expectations about the text and even some preliminary questions before you start reading word for word. Your reading will be more informed and fruitful.

One way to preview a text is to **skim** it: go quickly through it looking for clues about its content, its author, and how you will interact with it. Not the same as idly turning pages or scrolling through screens, skimming is a focused, concentrated activity in which you seek information. Use the questions below as a guide. In your journal write down any impressions that you may want to return to later.

Questions for previewing a text

- **Length:** Is the material brief enough to read in one sitting, or do you need more time? (It can be difficult to gauge the length of an online source such as a site on the World Wide Web. Try scrolling through the text and following a couple of links to estimate the source's complexity and length.)
- **Facts of publication:** Does the date of publication suggest currency or datedness? Does the publisher or publication specialize in a particular kind of material—scholarly articles, say, or popular books? For an online source, what does the address indicate about origin? For instance, *edu* in the address indicates an academic institution, whereas *gov* indicates a government agency. (See p. 536 for more about electronic addresses.)
- **Content cues:** What do the title, summary or abstract, headings, illustrations, and other features tell you? What questions do they raise in your mind?
- **Author:** What does the biographical information tell you about the author's publications, interests, biases, and reputation in the field?
- **Yourself:** Do you anticipate particular difficulties with the content? What biases of your own may influence your response to the text—for instance, anxiety, curiosity, boredom, or an outlook similar or opposed to that of the author?

Robertson, Julie Fisher, and Donna Rane Szotstak. "Using Dialogues to Develop Critical Thinking Skills: A Practical Approach." *Journal of Adolescent and Adult Literacy* 39 (April 1996): 552–56. Robertson and Szotstak describe how students can write, analyze, and perform dialogues in order to develop critical thinking skills.

Shor, Ira. *Empowering Education: Critical Teaching for Social Change.* Chicago: U of Chicago P, 1992. Shor promotes critical thinking as a part of a pedagogy designed to empower students and citizens.

Walsh, John A. "Circle Diagrams for Narrative Essays." *Journal of Reading* 32 (1989): 366–68. Use of a graphic technique of concentric circles (similar to Venn diagrams) helps students comprehend and analyze narrative events, relationships, and significance.

Wiley, Mark. "How to Read a Book: Reflections on the Ethics of Book Reviewing." *Journal of Advanced Composition* 13 (1993): 477–92. Wiley discusses communities of inquiry and why we grant some readers more authority over texts than others.

TRANSPARENCY MASTER I.2

COLLABORATIVE LEARNING

Even after they work through the materials in this chapter, students will need to practice critical reading until it becomes a familiar process. Having students work in groups to answer previewing questions or to create questions for rereading can make the critical approach to reading more accessible, and will result in a broader range of interpretive responses.

RESOURCES AND IDEAS

More information about keeping journals is found in the annotations for 1e.

Berrent, Howard I. "Open to Suggestion: OH RATS—A Note-taking Technique." *Journal of Reading* 27 (1984): 548–50. This essay outlines a useful note-taking strategy to complement critical reading.

Berthoff, Ann E. "A Curious Triangle and the Double-Entry Notebook: Or, How Theory

Can Help Us Teach Reading and Writing." *The Making of Meaning: Metaphors, Models, and Maxims for Writing Teachers.* Upper Montclair: Boynton/Cook, 1981. Berthoff shows how use of a double-entry journal can help students improve critical reading skills.

Chambers, Marilyn J. "Text Cues and Strategies Successful Readers Use to Construct the Gist of Lengthy Written Arguments." *Reading Research Quarterly* 30 (1995): 778–807. Chambers examines students' strategies for identifying argument structure, claim, and evidence in lengthy texts.

Jenseth, Richard. "Understanding Hiroshima: An Assignment Sequence for Freshman English." *College Composition and Communication* 40 (1989): 215–19. Jenseth describes a course wherein students focus on one work (or theme) for an entire semester, considering and reconsidering issues from various critical perspectives.

Kline, Nancy. "Intertextual Trips: Teaching the Essay in the Composition Class." *Journal of Teaching Writing* 8 (1989): 15–37. Kline describes an "active and playful" strategy used by writers of essays and suggests ways to help students detect and appreciate it.

Matthews, Mitford M. "The Freshman and His Dictionary." *About Language.* Ed. William H. Roberts and Gregoire Turgeon. Boston: Houghton, 1986. Matthews outlines three categories of information students can find in dictionaries; useful on inference.

Price, Gayle B. "A Case for a Modern Commonplace Book." *College Composition and Communication* 31 (1980): 175–82. Price suggests using classic techniques for commonplace books in conjunction with other journal activities.

Tierney, Robert J., John E. Readence, and Ernest K. Dishner, eds. *Reading Strategies and Practices: A Compendium,* 3rd ed. Boston: Allyn and Bacon, 1990. This textbook approach to reading offers a number of exercises and worksheets that help to focus students on particular aspects of the reading process.

Zeller, Robert. "Developing the Inferential Reasoning of Basic Writers." *College Composition and Communication* 38 (1987): 343–46. Zeller suggests that asking students to make connections between visual prompts like photographs and writing helps their critical thinking skills.

Reading

Reading is itself more than a one-step process. Your primary goal is to understand the first level on which the text operates—what the author actually says.

First reading

The first time through new material, read as steadily and smoothly as possible, trying to get the gist of what the author is saying and a sense of his or her tone.

- To help your concentration, read in a quiet place away from distractions such as music or talking.
- Give yourself time. Rushing yourself or worrying about something else you have to do will prevent you from grasping what you read.
- Try to enjoy the work. Seek connections between it and what you already know. Appreciate new information, interesting relationships, forceful writing, humor, good examples.
- Make notes sparingly during this reading. Mark major stumbling blocks—such as a paragraph you don't understand—so that you can try to resolve them before rereading. If you're reading a Web site with a lot of links to other sites, jot down the links you follow as you read so that you can recall them or explore new ones later. But otherwise resist any urge to make frequent or extensive notes until your next pass.

ESL On your first reading, don't stop and look up every unfamiliar word. You will lose more in concentration than you gain in understanding. Instead, try to guess the meanings of words from their contexts (see p. 496), or circle unfamiliar words and look them up later.

Rereadings

After the first reading, plan on at least one other. This time read *slowly.* Your main concern should be to grasp the content and how it is constructed. That means rereading a paragraph if you didn't get the point, or looking up key words in a dictionary, or following more links at a Web site.

Use your pen, pencil, or keyboard freely to annotate the text or make separate notes.

- If you can't write directly on the material (because you don't own it or it's online), make separate notes as suggested on page 4.
- If you're reading an online source that you can download into your word processor, highlight text you have questions or comments on, and insert your own comments in bold or italic type.

- If you can write directly on the material, use any system of annotations that works for you—perhaps "?" in the margin next to passages you don't understand, circles around unfamiliar words, underlining or brackets for main points, "*" for passages you agree with, "!" for those you find startling, "So what?" for those you can't see the point of.

Following are examples of active reading from a student, Charlene Robinson. She was responding to Thomas Sowell's "Student Loans," an essay reprinted on pages 8–10. First Robinson annotated a photocopy of the essay (the first four paragraphs appear below).

> The first lesson of economics is scarcity: There is never enough of anything to fully satisfy all those who want it.
>
> The first lesson of politics is to disregard the first lesson of economics. When politicians discover some group that is being vocal about not having as much as they want, the "solution" is to give them more. Where do politicians get this "more"? They rob Peter to pay Paul.
>
> After a while, of course, they discover that Peter doesn't have enough. Bursting with compassion, politicians rush to the rescue. Needless to say, they do not admit that robbing Peter to pay Paul was a dumb idea in the first place. On the contrary, they now rob Tom, Dick, and Harry to help Peter.
>
> The latest chapter in this long-running saga is that politicians have now suddenly discovered that many college students graduate heavily in debt. To politicians it follows, as the night follows the day, that the government should come to their rescue with the taxpayers' money.

Basic contradiction between economics and politics

biblical reference?

ironic and dismissive language

politicians = fools? or irresponsible?

After reading the text, Robinson wrote about it in the journal she kept on her computer. She divided the journal into two columns, one each for the text and her responses. Here is the portion pertaining to the paragraphs above:

Text	**Responses**
Economics teaches lessons (1), and politics (politicians) and economics are at odds	Is economics truer or more reliable than politics? More scientific?
Politicians don't accept econ. limits--always trying to satisfy "vocal" voters by giving them what they want (2)	Politicians do spend a lot of our money. Is that what they're elected to do, or do they go too far?
"Robbing Peter to pay Paul" (2)--from the Bible (the Apostles)?	

COLLABORATIVE LEARNING

Choose a relatively complex essay from your reader or another published collection. Ask students to work through various sections of the essay in small groups, then present their findings to the class. After those presentations, students might reread the essay and write an interpretive response to a short passage from the essay, which they again can share and critique in groups. Students can also use the essay as the basis for the appropriate exercises in this chapter. This will give them further confidence in their critical skills.

A READING STRATEGY (ESL)

Even advanced ESL students may read too slowly to process the main points and connections between ideas. Encourage students on the first reading to read just a bit faster than is comfortable for them. While students certainly need to acquire dictionary skills, the first reading is not the time to practice those skills. Suggest that students put question marks in the margin next to lines containing unfamiliar words. This system allows them to continue reading without breaking their concentration unnecessarily.

Text	Responses
Politicians support student loan program with taxpayer funds bec. of "vocal" voters (2-4): another ex. of not accepting econ. limits	I support the loan program, too. Are politicians being irresponsible when they do? (Dismissive language underlined on copy.)

You should try to answer the questions about meaning that you raise in your annotations and your journal, and that may take another reading or some digging in other sources, such as dictionaries and encyclopedias. Recording in your journal what you think the author means will help you build an understanding of the text, and a focused attempt to summarize will help even more (see p. 10). Such efforts will resolve any confusion you feel, or they will give you the confidence to say that your confusion is the fault of the author, not the reader.

ANSWERS: EXERCISE 1

Individual response.

COLLABORATIVE LEARNING

Since students in your class will have different abilities as well as different levels of experience with texts like this, their responses may be widely different. Having students discuss their responses in small groups lets them see a variety of reading and understanding strategies at work; students who had difficulty with the passage should be encouraged to talk about the part(s) that gave them trouble and ask for suggestions on how to tackle similar readings in the future. You might ask each group to create a list of key quotes, questions, and comments, which they can later summarize for the class.

If possible, avoid giving students a "correct" response (usually one you've written) to this exercise and the other exercises in this chapter, since it subconsciously but powerfully reinforces the mistaken stereotype that there is one right way to read an essay—the teacher's.

Exercise 1
Reading

Reprinted below is an essay by Thomas Sowell on the federal government's student loan program. A respected conservative economist, Sowell is also a newspaper columnist and the author of many books on economics, politics, and education. This essay appeared in Sowell's collection *Is Reality Optional?*

Read this essay at least twice, until you think you understand what the author is saying. Either separately or on these pages, note your questions and reactions in writing. Look up any words you don't know, and try to arrive at answers to your questions. (It may help to discuss the selection with classmates.)

Student Loans

The first lesson of economics is scarcity: There is never enough of anything to fully satisfy all those who want it. 1

The first lesson of politics is to disregard the first lesson of economics. When politicians discover some group that is being vocal about not having as much as they want, the "solution" is to give them more. Where do politicians get this "more"? They rob Peter to pay Paul. 2

After a while, of course, they discover that Peter doesn't have enough. Bursting with compassion, politicians rush to the rescue. Needless to say, they do not admit that robbing Peter to pay Paul was a dumb idea in the first place. On the contrary, they now rob Tom, Dick, and Harry to help Peter. 3

The latest chapter in this long-running saga is that politicians have now suddenly discovered that many college students graduate heavily in debt. To politicians it follows, as the night follows the day, that the government should come to their rescue with the taxpayers' money. 4

How big is this crushing burden of college students' debt that 5 we hear so much about from politicians and media deep thinkers? For those students who graduate from public colleges owing money, the debt averages a little under $7,000. For those who graduate from private colleges owing money, the average debt is a little under $9,000.

Buying a very modestly priced automobile involves more debt 6
than that. And a car loan has to be paid off faster than the ten years that college graduates get to repay their student loans. Moreover, you have to keep buying cars every several years, while one college education lasts a lifetime.

College graduates of course earn higher incomes than other 7
people. Why, then, should we panic at the thought that they have to repay loans for the education which gave them their opportunities? Even graduates with relatively modest incomes pay less than 10 percent of their annual salary on the loan the first year—with declining percentages in future years, as their pay increases.

Political hysteria and media hype may focus on the low- 8
income student with a huge debt. That is where you get your heart-rending stories—even if they are not at all typical. In reality, the soaring student loans of the past decade have resulted from allowing high-income people to borrow under government programs.

Before 1978, college loans were available through government 9
programs only to students whose family income was below some cut-off level. That cut-off level was about double the national average income, but at least it kept out the Rockefellers and the Vanderbilts. But, in an era of "compassion," Congress took off even those limits.

That opened the floodgates. No matter how rich you were, it 10
still paid to borrow money through the government at low interest rates. The money you had set aside for your children's education could be invested somewhere else, at higher interest rates. Then, when the student loan became due, parents could pay it off with the money they had set aside—pocketing the difference in interest rates.

To politicians and the media, however, the rapidly growing 11
loans showed what a great "need" there was. The fact that many students welshed when time came to repay their loans showed how "crushing" their burden of debt must be. In reality, those who welsh typically have smaller loans, but have dropped out of college before finishing. People who are irresponsible in one way are often irresponsible in other ways.

No small amount of the deterioration of college standards has 12
been due to the increasingly easy availability of college to people who are not very serious about getting an education. College is not a bad place to hang out for a few years, if you have nothing better to do, and if someone else is paying for it. Its costs are staggering, but the taxpayers carry much of that burden, not only for state universities and city colleges, but also to an increasing extent even for "private" institutions.

Numerous government subsidies and loan programs make it 13
possible for many people to use vast amounts of society's resources

at low cost to themselves. Whether in money terms or in real terms, federal aid to higher education has increased several hundred percent since 1970. That has enabled colleges to raise their tuition by leaps and bounds and enabled professors to be paid more and more for doing less and less teaching.

Naturally all these beneficiaries are going to create hype and hysteria to keep more of the taxpayers' money coming in. But we would be fools to keep on writing blank checks for them. 14

When you weigh the cost of things, in economics that's called "trade-offs." In politics, it's called "mean-spirited." Apparently, if we just took a different attitude, scarcity would go away. 15

—THOMAS SOWELL

RESOURCES AND IDEAS

Lambert, Judith R. "Summaries: A Focus for Basic Writers." *Journal of Developmental Education* 8 (1984): 10+. Lambert reviews advantages of teaching students to summarize.

Sherrard, Carol. "Summary Writing: A Topographical Study." *Written Communication* 3 (1986): 324–43. Sherrard shows that assigning longer summaries forces students to use their own words instead of copying from the source.

WRITING SUMMARIES (ESL)

While ESL students may find synonyms for some key words in the sentences that express the main points of a source, they may feel insecure about using other sentence structures. Encourage students to change the sentence structure as well as the vocabulary of the original in writing summaries. Working collaboratively on summaries helps students see alternative ways to express ideas; in addition, stronger students (and native speakers) can help the weaker students and, in so doing, reinforce their own writing skills. Alice Oshima and Ann Hogue, in Chapter 9 of *Writing Academic English* (2nd ed., New York: Addison-Wesley, 1991), include useful exercises for students who need additional practice in summarizing.

COLLABORATIVE LEARNING

Comparing summaries

Ask students to compare their summaries in groups and list points that are similar and different among the summaries in their group. Then, as a way of deciding how much information is

d Summarizing

Before you can see what is beneath the surface of a text and figure out what you think of it, you need to understand exactly what the author is actually saying. A good way to master the content of a text and see its strengths and weaknesses is to **summarize** it: distill it to its main points, in your own words.

Some assignments call for brief summaries, as when you summarize the plot in a critical essay about a novel (p. 680). Summary is also an essential tool in research papers and other writing that draws on sources (p. 572). Here, though, we're concerned with summarizing for yourself—for your own enlightenment.

A summary should state in as few words as possible the main ideas of a passage. When you need to summarize a few paragraphs or a brief article, your summary should not exceed one-fifth the length of the original. For longer works, such as chapters of books or whole books, your summary should be quite a bit shorter in proportion to the original. A procedure for drafting a summary appears in the box below. (You've seen the beginning of this process in Charlene Robinson's journal on pp. 7–8.)

Writing a summary

- Look up words or concepts you don't know so that you understand the author's sentences and how they relate to each other.
- Work through the text to identify its sections—single paragraphs or groups of paragraphs focused on a single topic, related links in a page on the World Wide Web. To understand how parts of work relate to each other, try drawing a tree diagram or creating an outline (p. 55). Although both tools work well for straight text, the tree diagram may work better for nonlinear material such as a Web site.
- Write a one- or two-sentence summary of each section you identify. Focus on the main point of the section, omitting examples, facts, and other supporting evidence.

- Write a sentence or two stating the author's central idea.
- Write a full paragraph (or more, if needed) that begins with the central idea and supports it with the sentences that summarize sections of the work. The paragraph should concisely and accurately state the thrust of the entire work.
- *Use your own words.* By writing, you re-create the meaning of the work in a way that makes sense for you.

Capturing the essence of even a single paragraph can be tricky. Here is one attempt to summarize paragraphs 1–4 of Thomas Sowell's "Student Loans" (p. 8):

Draft summary

As much as politicians would like to satisfy voters by giving them everything they ask for, the government cannot afford a student loan program.

This sentence "misreads" the four paragraphs because it asserts that the government cannot afford student loans. Sowell's point is more complicated than that. This accurate summary captures it:

Revised summary

As their support of the government's student loan program illustrates, politicians ignore the economic reality that using resources to benefit one group (students in debt) involves taking the resources from another group (taxpayers).

Note When you write a summary, using your own words will ensure that you avoid plagiarism. Even when the summary is in your own words, if you use it in something written for others you must cite the source of the ideas. See pages 578–82.

Exercise 2
Summarizing

Start where the preceding summary of Thomas Sowell's essay ends (at paragraph 5) to distill the entire selection reprinted on pages 8–10. Your summary, in your own words, should not exceed one paragraph.

e Forming your critical response

Once you've grasped the content of what you're reading—what the author says—then you can turn to understanding what the author does not say outright but suggests or implies or even lets slip. At this stage you are concerned with the purpose or intention of the author and with how he or she carries it out. Depending on what you are reading and why, you may examine evidence, organization, attitude, use of language, and other elements of the text.

needed to create an effective summary, have each student defend the places where his or her summary differs from the group consensus.

Movie critic exercise

To help students understand the concept of "misreading," try the "movie critic" exercise: a movie critic writes that a film is "one of the really great awful films of the decade." An ad for the film that claims "Critic So-and-So calls this 'one of the really great . . . films of the decade'" is a deliberate misreading. Ask students to construct deliberate misreadings of reviews or critiques as a way of teaching them what not to do in their own summaries.

COLLABORATIVE LEARNING

Make Exercise 2 collaborative by asking each group of students to write a collective summary; then switch summaries among groups and have the readers decide how effective the other group's effort is in conveying the essential information in Sowell.

ANSWERS: EXERCISE 2

Possible answer

As their support of the government's student loan program illustrates, politicians ignore the economic reality that using resources to benefit one group (students in debt) involves taking the resources from another group (taxpayers). Students' average debt is not even that high, and college graduates can afford to pay it off. The greatest attention is paid to the graduate with a large debt, but the law also allows affluent students to borrow, even if their parents profit and they drop out of school or waste time there. Funded by taxpayers, the loan program has contributed to declining educational standards, rising tuitions, and rising professors' salaries. Taxpayers should balk at funding the program further.

RESOURCES AND IDEAS

Carella, Michael J. "Philosophy as Literacy: Teaching College Students to Read Critically and Write Cogently." *College Composition and Communication* 34 (1983): 57–61. Carella argues that students can be taught not only to summarize complex arguments but to respond critically to them.

Nelson, Jennie. "Reading Classrooms as Text: Exploring Student Writers' Interpretive Practices." *College Composition and Communication* 46 (1995): 411–429. Nelson examines four case studies to show students' strategies for reading and responding to assignments, grading practices, and teacher comments.

Tripp, Ellen L. "Speak, Listen, Analyze, Respond: Problem-Solving Conferences." *Teaching English in the Two-Year College* 17 (1990): 183–86. Tripp suggests collaborative and individual activities to be completed before students write final papers proposing solutions.

COLLABORATIVE LEARNING

Encourage students to bring magazines of various kinds to class. Have students work in groups to brainstorm lists similar to the one shown here for each magazine they collected. Each group might present their most surprising or revealing findings to the class.

Critical thinking and reading consist of four operations: analyzing, interpreting, synthesizing, and (often) evaluating. Although we'll look at them one by one, these operations interrelate and overlap. Indeed, the first three are often combined under the general label *analysis,* and evaluation is sometimes taken for granted as a result of the process.

Analyzing

Analysis is the separation of something into its parts or elements, the better to understand it. To see these elements in what you are reading, begin with a question that reflects your purpose in analyzing the text: why you are curious about it or what you're trying to make out of it. This question will serve as a kind of lens that highlights some features and not others. Here, for example, are some questions you might ask about *People* magazine, listed along with the elements of the magazine that each question highlights:

Question for analysis	Elements
Does *People* challenge or perpetuate stereotypes?	Stereotypes: explicit and implicit stereotypes or challenges in the magazine
Does the magazine offer positive role models for its readers?	Role models: text and photographs presenting positive or negative role models
Does the magazine's editorial material (articles and accompanying photographs) encourage readers to consume goods and entertainment?	Encouragement of consumption: references to goods and entertainment, focus on consumers, equation of consumption with happiness or success

A question for analysis concentrates your attention on relevant features and eliminates irrelevant features. To answer the last question above, you would focus on items that feature consumption and the products consumed: for instance, photographs of designer clothes and celebrities' well-appointed homes, articles on the authors of best-selling books and the stars of new movies. At the same time, you would skip over items that have little or no relevance to consumption, such as uplifting stories about families or the physically challenged.

Analyzing Thomas Sowell's essay "Student Loans" (pp. 8–10), you might ask, for example, what Sowell's attitude is toward politicians. That question would lead you to examine Sowell's references to politicians—the content of what he says, his words, his tone. Or you might ask how Sowell supports his assertions about the loan program's costs or recipients. Then you would focus on evidence, such as statistics and examples.

A difference in the kinds of questions asked is a key distinction among academic disciplines. A sociologist neatly outlined three disciplines' approaches to poverty:

> Political science does a wonderful job looking at poverty as a policy issue. Economics does an equally wonderful job looking at it from an income-distribution perspective. But sociology asks how people in poverty live and what they aspire to.

Even within disciplines, approaches may differ. The sociologist quoted above may focus on how people in poverty live, but another might be more interested in the effects of poverty on cities or the changes in the poor population over the last fifty years. (See Chapters 39 and 40 for more on the disciplines' analytical questions.)

Interpreting

Identifying the elements of something is of course only the beginning: you also need to interpret the meaning or significance of the elements and of the whole. Interpretation usually requires you to infer the author's **assumptions,** opinions or beliefs about what is or what could or should be. (**Infer** means to draw a conclusion based on evidence.)

The word *assumption* here has a more specific meaning than it does in everyday usage, where it may stand for expectation ("I assume you'll pay"), speculation ("It was a mere assumption"), or error ("The report was riddled with assumptions"). Defined more strictly as what a person *supposes* to be true, assumptions are unavoidable. We all adhere to certain values and beliefs; we all form opinions. We live our lives by such assumptions.

Though pervasive, assumptions are not always stated outright. Speakers and writers may judge that their audience already understands and accepts their assumptions; they may not even be aware of their assumptions; or they may deliberately refrain from stating their assumptions for fear that the audience will disagree. That is why your job as a critical thinker is to interpret what the assumptions are.

Like an author deciding what to say in an article, the publishers of *People* magazine make assumptions that guide their selection of content for the magazine. One set of assumptions, perhaps the most important, concerns what readers want to see: as a for-profit enterprise, the magazine naturally aims to maintain and even expand its readership (currently about 3.5 million each week). If your analysis of the magazine's editorial material reveals that much of it features consumer products, you might infer the following:

Reasonable The publishers of *People* assume that the magazine's readers are consumers who want to see and hear about goods and entertainment.

TEACHING TIP

See the many references and suggestions in the annotations to Chapter 4 for further help in teaching students to understand assumptions and inferences.

COLLABORATIVE LEARNING

COMPUTER EXERCISE

Having students summarize and draw inferences from one another's work can be a useful exercise for both reader and writer. Have students work in pairs (either on the computer or on printed copy) to summarize, then practice reasonable and deliberately faulty inferences of passages from each other's work. In each case, the writer of the passage can argue for his or her intention in writing the passage and evaluate the effectiveness of the summary, while the reader can point to evidence or lack of evidence for the inference. Particularly in a networked classroom, each student pair can send two passages with attached summary and inferences to another group for evaluation, and/or the instructor can post one or two examples for the entire class. See Rick Monroe's *Writing and Thinking with Computers: A Practical and Progressive Approach* (Urbana: NCTE, 1993). Monroe lays out the nuts and bolts of establishing a networked computer lab and of rethinking classroom practice in relation to computer use. For further sources on working in a networked classroom see Susan Lang's essay on "Using Computers to Teach Writing" on pages IAE-63–IAE-77.

Nowhere in *People* will you find a statement of this assumption, but the evidence implies it.

Similarly, Thomas Sowell's "Student Loans" (pp. 8–10) is based on certain assumptions, some obvious, some not so obvious. If you were analyzing Sowell's attitude toward politicians, as suggested earlier, you would focus on his statements about them. Sowell says that they "disregard the first lesson of economics" (paragraph 2), which implies that they ignore important principles (knowing that Sowell is an economist himself makes this a reasonable assumption on your part). Sowell also says that politicians "rob Peter to pay Paul," are "[b]ursting with compassion," do not admit to a "dumb idea," are characters in a "long-running saga," and arrive at the solution of spending taxes "as the night follows the day"—that is, inevitably (paragraphs 2–4). From these statements and others, you can infer the following:

Reasonable Sowell assumes that politicians become compassionate when a cause is loud and popular, not necessarily just, and they act irresponsibly by trying to solve the problem with other people's (taxpayers') money.

Interpreting assumptions in this way gives you greater insight into an author's intentions. But it's crucial that inferences fit the evidence of the text, as those above about *People* and Sowell's essay do. Sometimes it's tempting to read too much into the text:

Faulty *People*'s publishers deliberately skew the magazine's editorial material to promote products on which they receive kickbacks. [The inference is far-fetched, even absurd. It would be reasonable only if there were hard evidence of kickbacks.]

TRANSPARENCY MASTER I.3

TEACHING TIP

Students may need help in applying these broad guidelines for analysis, interpretation, and synthesis to specific readings. Ask students to work individually or in pairs to choose a key passage from the reading and then to use the guidelines to compose a list of specific questions about the elements of that passage.

Guidelines for analysis, interpretation, and synthesis

- What is the purpose of your reading?
- What questions do you have about the work? Which question interests you the most or opens up the most possibilities? What elements does the question highlight for examination? What elements can be ignored as a result?
- How do you interpret the meaning and significance of the elements, both individually and in relation to the whole text? What are your assumptions about the text? What do you infer about the author's assumptions?
- What patterns can you see in (or synthesize from) the elements? How do the elements relate? How does this whole text relate to other texts?
- What do you conclude about the text? What does this conclusion add to the text?

Faulty Sowell thinks that politicians should not be entrusted with running the country. [The inference misreads Sowell. Although he does not outline a solution for politicians' irresponsibility, there's no evidence that he would overhaul our democratic political system.]

Faulty inferences like those above are often based on the reader's *own* assumptions about the text or its subject. When thinking and reading critically, you need to look hard at *your* ideas, too.

Synthesizing

If you stopped at analysis and interpretation, critical thinking and reading might leave you with a pile of elements and possible meanings but no vision of the whole. With **synthesis** you make connections among parts *or* among wholes. You create a new whole by drawing conclusions about relationships and implications.

The following conclusion about Thomas Sowell's essay "Student Loans" connects his assumptions about politicians (see opposite) to a larger idea also implied by the essay:

Conclusion Sowell's view that politicians are irresponsible with taxpayers' money reflects his overall opinion that the laws of economics, not politics, should drive government.

The next statement pulls together the analysis of *People* magazine's editorial content (p. 12) and the interpretation of the publishers' assumptions about readers (p. 13).

Conclusion *People* magazine appeals to its readers' urge to consume by displaying, discussing, and glamorizing consumer goods.

You can also synthesize your critical readings of a number of sources, again drawing your own conclusions:

Conclusion In *People, Us, Vanity Fair,* and other magazines aimed at consumers, the line between advertising and editorial material is sometimes almost invisible.

(Synthesizing several sources is important in research writing. See pp. 567–68.)

To create your own links between experiences, ideas, and entire sources, it helps (again) to write while reading and thinking. The active reading recommended earlier (p. 6) is the place to start, as you note your questions and opinions about the text. You can also create connections with a combination of writing and drawing: start with your notes, or write your ideas out fresh, and draw connections between related thoughts with lines and arrows. (On a

computer you can underline or boldface related ideas or use the an-

notation feature on your word processor to signal connections.) You want to open up your thinking, so experiment freely.

With synthesis, you create something different from what you started with. To the supermarket shopper reading *People* while standing in line, the magazine may be entertaining and inconsequential. To you—after a critical reading in which you analyze, interpret, and synthesize—the magazine is (at least in part) a significant vehicle of our consumer culture. The difference depends entirely on the critical reading.

Evaluating

Many critical reading and writing assignments end at analysis, interpretation, and synthesis: you explain your understanding of what the author says and doesn't say. Only if you are expected to **evaluate** the work will you state and defend the judgments you've made about its quality and its significance. You'll inevitably form such judgments while reading the work: "What a striking series of images," or "That just isn't enough evidence." In evaluating, you collect your judgments, determine that they are generally applicable and are themselves not trivial, and turn them into assertions: "The poet creates fresh, intensely vivid images"; "The author does

Guidelines for evaluation

- What are your reactions to the text? What in the text are you responding to?
- Is the work sound in its general idea? In its details and other evidence?
- Has the author achieved his or her purpose? Is the purpose worthwhile?
- Does the author seem authoritative? Trustworthy? Sincere?
- Is the work unified, with all the parts pertaining to a central idea? Is it coherent, with the parts relating clearly to each other? (If the material is from an online source such as a site on the World Wide Web, these ideals of unity and coherence might be given a backseat in favor of expansive and varied lines of thought connected to the site by links. Then ask what the purpose of the links is and whether they provide worthwhile insight into the subject.)
- If the work includes color, graphics, or (online) sound or video, do these elements contribute meaning to the work or merely dress it up?
- What is the overall quality of the work? What is its value or significance in the larger scheme of things?
- Do you agree or disagree with the work? Can you support, refute, or extend it?

ANSWERS: EXERCISE 3

Possible answers

1. *Analysis:* What is the author's position on violence in movies? Key words reveal this position: *should, prevent, from seeing and being harmed.*

Interpretation: Should be rated means the author holds this opinion; *to prevent* indicates a cause/effect relationship; *being harmed* reveals the possible effect of violent movies on children. Author's assumptions: Children should be protected from harm. Violent movies harm the children who see them in some way. An effective, enforceable rating system exists. Violence merits an R rating.

Synthesis: The author believes that violent movies harm children in some way and that outside regulation (in the form of ratings) is needed to control who sees such films.

Evaluation: This is a biased statement against violent movies and in favor of rating such movies to prevent children from seeing them. But do ratings work? Don't parents and caretakers have primary responsibility to choose what their children see? Why should ushers or film raters do parents' work for them? What about when these movies appear at home, on videos or TV? What proof is there that movie violence harms children? Who will rate the movies? What constitutes violence?

2. *Analysis:* What is the basis for the author's comparison of print and televised journalism? The key words are *demand reading, not just viewing.*

Interpretation: Are better . . . than implies a value judgment. *Demand reading, not just viewing* reveals the author's assumption that viewing is somehow less worthy than reading, perhaps because viewing is more passive.

Synthesis: This author prefers print journalism and disparages television journalism because

not summon the evidence to support his case." And you support these statements with citations from the text.

Evaluation takes a certain amount of confidence. You may feel that you lack the expertise to cast judgment on another's writing, especially if the text is difficult or the author well known. True, the more informed you are, the better a critical reader you are. But conscientious reading and analysis will give you the internal authority to judge a work *as it stands* and *as it seems to you,* against your own unique bundle of experiences, observations, and attitudes. The box opposite gives questions that may help you evaluate many kinds of texts. (For arguments and in academic disciplines, you'll require additional, more specific criteria. See Chapters 4, 39, and 40.)

Exercise 3
Thinking critically

Following are some statements about the communications media. Use systematic critical thinking to understand not only what the statement says but why its author might have said it. As in the example, do your thinking in writing: the act of writing will help you think, and your notes will help you discuss your ideas with your classmates. (Additional exercises in critical reading appear on pp. 568–69.)

Example:

Statement: Every year sees the disappearance of more book publishers because the larger companies gobble up the smaller ones.

Analysis: Why did the author make this statement? Certain words reveal the author's purpose: *disappearance of more book publishers; because; larger companies gobble up smaller ones.*

Interpretation: More book publishers means others have disappeared. *Because* specifies cause. *Gobble up* implies consumption, predator to prey. Author's assumptions: Large publishers behave like predators. The predatory behavior of large companies causes the disappearance of small companies. The more publishing companies there are, the better.

Synthesis: The author objects to the predatory behavior of large publishing companies, which he or she holds responsible for eliminating small companies and reducing the total number of companies.

Evaluation: This biased statement against large publishers holds them responsible for the shrinking numbers of book publishers. But are the large companies solely responsible? And why is the shrinking necessarily bad?

1. Violent movies should be rated R to prevent children from seeing and being harmed by them.

of the different activities needed to partake of them.

Evaluation: This statement shows the author's bias in favor of written news and implies some contempt for TV news. The author's reasons for preferring reading over viewing are not evident and require explanation. Some other questions: Are people who get their news from TV less well-informed than those who get it from reading? Even if television news is inferior, isn't it better than no news at all (for those who won't or can't read)? Might television news be preferable for its immediacy?

3. *Analysis:* What is the author's purpose? The key words are *true, democratic, giving voice to,* and *Americans of all persuasions.*

Interpretation: Democratic means "of or for the people." *True democratic forum* means that there are competing, perhaps misleading, forums. *Giving voice to Americans* appeals to a sense of fair play and belief in free speech, while *all persuasions* implies open-mindedness. The author assumes that Americans need a public forum where they can voice their opinions. Because it is immediate, radio gives people the freedom to say what they want. Other forums may censor or restrict who can say what.

Synthesis: The writer values radio call-in shows for affording all kinds of people a chance to express themselves without censorship.

Evaluation: This writer evidently believes that radio is somehow freer than other places for people to speak their minds. What other forums for free speech are there? Does radio censor or alter the opinions expressed? (What about the time delays for objectionable language?) Are "Americans of all persuasions" really calling such shows, or just some kinds of Americans? Are unedited, inexpert opinions a democratic necessity?

COLLABORATIVE LEARNING

When students have completed Exercises 3 and 4 individually, it is beneficial to have them share their analyses in small groups, so that they are able to note and discuss the differing conclusions that each student may have reached.

ANSWERS: EXERCISE 4

Individual response.

Put the elements in the third sentence of the instruction on an overhead transparency or write them on the board to focus student attention on the elements that might be identified and interpreted in Sowell's essay.

COLLABORATIVE LEARNING

Students might want to begin their essays in their journals, then shape their final products as letters to a classmate or the class as a whole detailing what they've found. If you use this strategy, allow time for the recipients to respond. The exchange of letters encourages not only dialogue but further critical penetration into the text.

ANSWERS: EXERCISE 5

Individual response.

RESOURCES AND IDEAS

Langer, Judith A. "Learning Through Writing: Study Skills in the Content Area." *Journal of Reading* 29 (1986): 400–06. Langer contends that students learn more effectively by writing full essays about their reading than by just taking notes or answering questions.

Lent, Robin. "'I Can Relate to That . . .': Reading and Responding in the Writing Classroom." *College Composition and Communication* 44 (1993): 232–40. Lent demonstrates how using short, informal response papers can deepen students' interpretations of assigned readings.

Morris, Barbara S. *Disciplinary Perspectives on Thinking and Writing.* Ann Arbor: U of Michigan English Composition Board, 1989. This essay collection demonstrates different modes of inquiry and acceptable responses among various disciplines.

Williams, James D., David Huntley, and Christine Hanks. *The Interdisciplinary Reader: A Collection of Student Writing.* New York: HarperCollins, 1992. The editors provide a collection of student essays from various dis-

2. Newspapers and newsmagazines are better news sources than television because they demand reading, not just viewing.
3. Radio call-in shows are the true democratic forum, giving voice to Americans of all persuasions.

Exercise 4
Reading critically

Reread Thomas Sowell's "Student Loans" (pp. 8–10) in order to form your own critical response to it. Follow the guidelines for analysis, interpretation, synthesis, and evaluation in the boxes on pages 14 and 16. Focus on any elements suggested by your question about the text: possibilities are assumptions, evidence, organization, use of language, tone, authority, vision of education or students. Be sure to write while reading and thinking; your notes will help your analysis and enhance your creativity, and they will be essential for writing about the selection (Exercise 7, p. 21).

Exercise 5
Reading critically

Do your own critical reading of *People* or another magazine. What do you see beyond the obvious? What questions does your reading raise? Let the guidelines on pages 14 and 16 direct your response, and do your work in writing. (A writing suggestion based on this exercise appears on p. 21.)

13 Writing critically

Like critical reading, critical writing is largely influenced by its purpose and by the discipline or profession in which it occurs. Thus the topic is covered more extensively in Chapters 4 (argument), 39 (literature), and 40 (other disciplines), and an example using sources appears in Chapter 38 on research writing. In this introduction we'll look at some fundamentals and an illustration.

It is no doubt obvious by now that critical writing is *not* summarizing. You may write a summary to clarify for yourself what the author says (pp. 10–11) and may briefly summarize a work in your own larger piece of writing. But your job in critical writing is not just to report what a text says; it is to transmit your analysis, interpretation, synthesis, and perhaps evaluation of the text.

The following essay by Charlene Robinson, a student, is a response to Thomas Sowell's "Student Loans" (pp. 8–10). Robinson arrived at this response through the process of critical reading outlined in this chapter and then by gathering and organizing her ideas, developing her own central idea (or thesis sentence) about Sowell's text, and drafting and revising until she believed she had supported her central idea. Robinson does not assume that her readers see the same things in Sowell's essay or share her views, so she offers evidence of Sowell's ideas in the form of direct quotations, summaries, and paraphrases (restatements in her own words). (See pp. 572–76 for more on these techniques.) Robinson then documents these borrowings from Sowell using the style of the Modern Language Association (MLA): the numbers in parentheses are page numbers in the book containing Sowell's essay, listed at the end as a "work cited." (See pp. 599–627 for more on MLA style.)

ciplines, accompanied by critiques of their effectiveness in writing critically for particular discourse communities.

Weighing the Costs

In his essay "Student Loans," the economist Thomas Sowell challenges the US government's student loan program for several reasons: a scarce resource (taxpayers' money) goes to many undeserving students, a high number of recipients fail to repay their loans, and the easy availability of money has led to both lower academic standards and higher college tuitions. Sowell wants his readers to "weigh the costs of things" (133) in order to see, as he does, that the loan program should not receive so much government funding. But does he provide the evidence of cost and other problems to lead the reader to agree with him? The answer is no, because hard evidence is less common than debatable and unsupported assumptions about students, scarcity, and the value of education.

Introduction:

1. Summary of Sowell's essay

2. Robinson's critical question

3. Thesis sentence

Sowell's portrait of student loan recipients is questionable. It is based on averages, some statistical and some not, but averages are often deceptive. For example, Sowell cites college graduates' low average debt of $7,000 to $9,000 (131) without acknowledging the fact that many students' debt is much higher or giving the full range of statistics. Similarly, Sowell dismisses "heart-rending stories" of "the low-income student with a huge debt" as "not at all typical" (132), yet he invents his own exaggerated version of the typical loan recipient: an affluent slacker ("Rockefellers" and "Vanderbilts") for whom college is a place to "hang out for a few years" sponging off the government, while his or her parents clear a profit from making use of the loan program (132). While such students (and parents) may well exist, are they really typical? Sowell does not offer any data one way or the other—for instance, how many loan recipients come from each income group, what percentage of loan funds go to each group, how many loan recipients receive significant help from their parents, and how many receive none.

First main point

Evidence for first point:

1. Paraphrases and quotations from Sowell's text (with source citations in MLA style)

2. Sowell's omissions

Another set of assumptions in the essay has to do with "scarcity": "There is never enough of anything to fully satisfy all those who want it," Sowell says (131). This statement appeals to readers' common sense, but does the "lesson" of scarcity necessarily apply to the student loan program? Sowell omits many important figures needed to prove that the nation's resources are too scarce to support the program, such as the total cost of the program, its percentage of the total education budget and the total federal budget, and its cost compared to the cost of defense, Medicare, and other expensive programs. Moreover, Sowell does not mention the interest paid by loan recipients, even though the interest must offset some of the costs of running the program and covering unpaid loans.

Transition to second main point

Second point

Evidence for second point: Sowell's omissions

The most fundamental and most debatable assumption underlying Sowell's essay is that higher education is a kind of commodity that not everyone is entitled to. In order to diminish the importance of graduates' average debt from education loans, Sowell claims that a car loan will probably be higher (131). This comparison between education and an automobile implies that the two are somehow equal as products and that an affordable higher education is no more a right than a new car is. Sowell also condemns the "irresponsible" students who drop out of school and "the increasingly easy availability of college to people who are not very serious about getting an education" (132). But he overlooks the value of encouraging education, including education of those who don't finish college or who aren't scholars. For many Americans, education has a greater value than that of a mere commodity like a car. And even from an economic perspective such as Sowell's, the cost to society of an uneducated public needs to be taken into account.

Third main point

Evidence for third point: paraphrases and quotations of Sowell's text (with source citations in MLA style)

Sowell writes with conviction, and his concerns are valid: high taxes, waste, unfairness, declining educational standards, obtrusive government. However, the essay's flaws make it unlikely that Sowell could convince readers who do not already agree with him. He does not support his portrait of the typical loan recipient, he fails to demonstrate a lack of resources for the loan program, and he neglects the special nature of education compared to other services and products. Sowell may have the evidence to back up his assumptions, but by omitting it he himself does not truly weigh the costs of the loan program.

Conclusion:

1. Acknowledgment of Sowell's concerns

2. Summary of three main points

3. Return to theme of introduction: weighing costs

Work Cited

Sowell, Thomas. "Student Loans." Is Reality Optional? and Other Essays. Stanford: Hoover, 1993. 131–33.

Reference to complete source for Sowell's essay (in MLA style)

—Charlene Robinson

Exercise 6
Responding to critical writing

Read Charlene Robinson's essay carefully. What is her critical question about Sowell's essay? How does it relate to her thesis sentence? What assumptions does she identify in Sowell's essay? What conclusions does she reach about the essay? Do you think her response is accurate and fair? Is it perceptive? Does Robinson provide enough evidence from Sowell's essay to convince you of her points? Does she miss anything you would have mentioned? Write your responses in a brief essay.

Exercise 7
Writing critically

Write an essay based on your own critical reading of Thomas Sowell's essay (Exercise 4, p. 18). Your critique may be entirely different from Charlene Robinson's, or you may have developed some of the same points. If there are similarities, they should be expressed and supported in your own way, in the context of your own approach.

Exercise 8
Writing critically

Write an essay based on your critical response to *People* magazine or another magazine (Exercise 5, p. 18). Follow the guidelines on pages 18–19 for developing and organizing your essay.

COLLABORATIVE LEARNING/ COMPUTER EXERCISE

Have students form a networked chatgroup (or work in small groups) to discuss the questions for Exercise 6 and come up with a number of responses to each question. Then ask each student to revise those responses individually into a brief essay. When students exchange the completed essays in their group they are often surprised by the varying interpretations developed by the individual essays.

Alternatively, have students start their responses in their journals and convert the finished copy into a review or letter addressed to you or to their classmates.

If time and your classroom situation permit, you might put students into groups to compare their answers to these questions, and post the group's consensus on the network or write it on overhead transparencies or large sheets of paper so that students can compare their responses with those of their classmates. Encourage students to focus not only on points on which they agree but on their disagreements. Such differences of opinion indicate where their analytical frameworks and assumptions vary, even though they may consider themselves all part of the same "audience."

ANSWERS: EXERCISE 6

Individual response.

ANSWERS: EXERCISE 7

Individual response.

ANSWERS: EXERCISE 8

Individual response.

Part I

The Whole Paper and Paragraphs

HIGHLIGHTS

Why write? Many students are likely to have this question in mind when they first open *The Little, Brown Handbook* or even when they first register for a composition course or sit listening to the instructor on the first day of the class.

This chapter begins by addressing the question directly and recognizing the difficulties faced by all writers—experienced or inexperienced. Next, the chapter alerts students to the various elements of the writing situation and the writing process and discusses ways to discover subjects and purposes for writing. The concluding sections explore flexible strategies for considering audience, developing and grouping ideas, focusing on a thesis, and creating a plan for the initial draft.

Exploratory strategies discussed are journal writing, observing, freewriting, listing, clustering, reading, questioning, and using patterns of development. Strategies for developing and planning include using thesis sentences, tree diagrams, and outlines. Two special features of this chapter are the attention paid to the role of audience throughout the composing process and the list of "Questions About Audience" (page 33).

Though Chapter 1 looks at activities typical of the early stages of composing and Chapter 2 treats drafting and revising, the text does not endorse a strictly linear view of the composing process. Instead, both chapters emphasize the writer's many options and the flexibility of the composing process. They point out that writing is a way of thinking and discovering: that in the middle of drafting an essay a writer may recognize the need to develop new supporting ideas, to make major changes in the organization, or to shift the purpose of the essay and modify the thesis.

A WRITER'S PERSPECTIVE

I've decided that if you wait for the perfect time to write, you'll never write.

—Margaret Atwood

You get all your best ideas in the shower.

—Clint Eastwood

AT EASE

Students often bring their apprehensions about writing (and writing instructors) with them to class. To create a positive atmosphere for your course, you may wish to establish a set-

Chapter 1 Developing an Essay

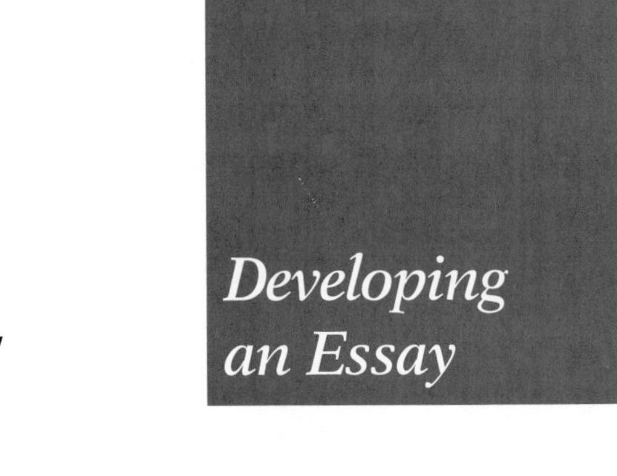

"Writing is easy," snarled the late sportswriter Red Smith. "All you have to do is sit down at the typewriter and open a vein." Most writers would smile in agreement, and so might you. Like anything worthwhile, writing well takes hard work. This chapter and the next will show you some techniques that successful writers use to minimize the discomfort of writing and turn it into gain.

Before you start on these chapters, clear your head of a very common misconception that may be lurking there: *writing is not only, or even mainly, a matter of correctness.* True, any written message will find a more receptive audience if it is correct in grammar, spelling, and similar matters. But these concerns should come late in the process, after you've allowed yourself to discover what you want to say, freeing yourself to make mistakes along the way. As one writer put it, you need to get the clay on the potter's wheel before you can shape it into a bowl, and you need to shape the bowl before you can perfect it. So get your clay on the wheel, and work with it until it looks like a bowl. Then worry about correctness.

1a The writing situation and the writing process

All writing occurs in a context that simultaneously limits and clarifies the writer's choices. Most obviously, context includes the nature of the assignment, the assigned length, and the deadline. But context can also be seen as the **writing situation,** in which you aim to communicate something you think about a subject to a particular audience of readers. For each writing task, considering the following questions can help you define and make choices:

- What is your subject?
- Who is your audience?
- What is your purpose?
- How can you present yourself and your subject to that audience in order to achieve your purpose?

Understanding the writing situation is an important part of the **writing process**—the term for all the activities, mental and physical, that go into writing what eventually becomes a finished piece of work. Even for experienced writers the process is usually messy, which is one reason that it is sometimes difficult. Though we may get a sense of ease and orderliness from a well-crafted magazine article, we can safely assume that the writer had to work hard to achieve those qualities, struggling to express half-formed thoughts, shaping and reshaping paragraphs to make a point convincingly.

There is no *one* writing process: no two writers proceed in the same way, and even an individual writer adapts his or her process to the task at hand. Still, most experienced writers pass through certain stages that overlap and circle back on each other.

- *Developing or planning:* discovering a subject, gathering information, focusing on a central theme, and organizing material.
- *Drafting:* expressing and connecting ideas.
- *Revising:* rethinking and improving structure, content, style, and presentation.

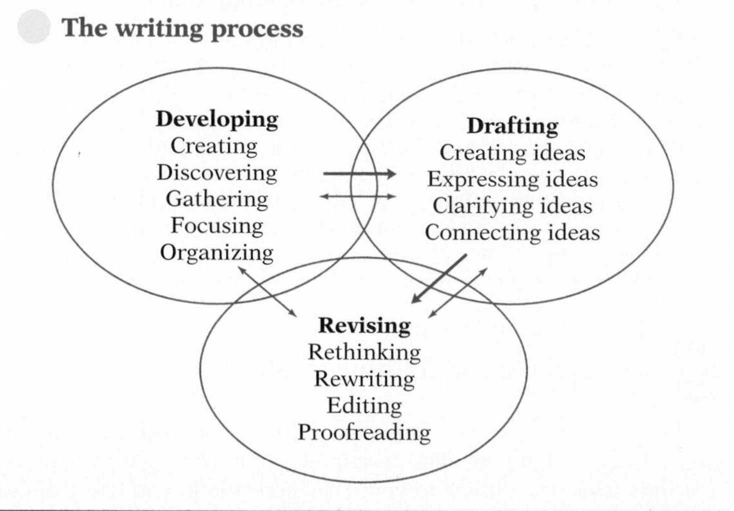

ting in which students feel at ease about acknowledging and sharing their apprehensions. One way to do this is to ask them to *list* what they dislike (and like) about writing without worrying about the form or correctness of entries in their lists. Voluntary sharing of the entries can help reduce the isolation many students feel and help you (and them) set priorities for instruction.

RESOURCES AND IDEAS

The writing situation

Brady, Laura. "Overcoming Resistance: Computers in the Writing Classroom." *Computers and Composition* 7:2 (1990): 21–33. Brady found that word processing in the first-year composition classroom increased the volume of student writing, prompted new ways of thinking about topics, encouraged collaboration, and fostered a positive workshop atmosphere.

Brooke, Rupert, Ruth Mirtz, and Rick Evans, eds. *Small Groups in Writing Workshops: Invitations to a Writer's Life.* Urbana: NCTE, 1994. This collection of essays offers many strategies for using collaborative group work to create an active learning situation.

Flower, Linda S., and John R. Hayes. "The Cognition of Discovery: Defining a Rhetorical Problem." *College Composition and Communication* 31 (1980): 21–32. This article reports

TRANSPARENCY MASTER 1.1

on a detailed study of how good writers and poor writers conceive of writing tasks as they begin to compose.

Golub, Jeff. *Activities for an Interactive Classroom.* Urbana: NCTE, 1994. Golub provides a number of hands-on suggestions for creating an effective workshop environment.

Hillocks, George Jr. "Environments for Active Learning." In *Theory and Practice in the Teaching of Writing: Rethinking the Discipline.* Ed. Lee Odell. Carbondale: Southern Illinois UP, 1993. 244–70. Hillocks' essay is part case study and part analysis of a classroom structure based on student interactions with each other and with texts.

Summerfield, Judith. "Is There a Life in This Text? Reimagining Narrative." In *Writing*

Theory and Critical Theory: Research and Scholarship in Composition. Ed. John Clifford and John Schilb. NY: MLA, 1994. 179–194. Summerfield examines the role of student narratives in the composition class, especially the extent to which they can provoke and sustain students' "authentic" voices.

Tedlock, David. "The Case Approach to Composition." *College Composition and Communication* 32 (1981): 253–61. Tedlock argues for the use of cases—detailed, self-contained descriptions of a writing situation—as a basis for assignments and instructions.

The writing process

Bartholomae, David. "Inventing the University." In *When a Writer Can't Write: Studies in Writer's Block and Other Composing Process Problems.* Ed. Mike Rose. New York: Guilford, 1985. 134–65. Bartholomae argues persuasively that many student writers, especially those with little writing experience, need to be taught explicitly the discourse standards of an academic community in order to write successfully for it.

Berlin, James A. "Contemporary Composition: The Major Pedagogical Theories." *College English* 44 (1982): 765–77. Berlin points out that various process approaches have consequences instructors must consider.

Flower, Linda, and John R. Hayes. "A Cognitive Process Theory of Writing." *College Composition and Communication* 32 (1981): 365–87. This classic article contains what is probably the best-known and most widely accepted discussion of the components of the writing process, though its model is more theoretical than practical.

Lindemann, Erika. "Three Views of English 101." *College English* 57 (1995): 287–302. This article lays out the opposing claims and assumptions of the "process," "product," and "system of social action" approaches to the writing classroom.

Sherman, Linda K., and Beverly Wall. "The Things that Go Without Saying in Composition Studies: A Colloquy." *Journal of Advanced Composition* 15 (1995): 281–320. The authors assemble a many-voiced critique of some of the current assumptions of composition pedagogy, including the process paradigm.

Tobin, Lad, and Thomas Newkirk, eds. *Taking Stock: The Writing Process Movement in the*

You, too, will experience these stages as you write. At various points, you will need to take stock of these elements:

Your topic (section 1b)
Your purpose (1c)
Your audience (1d)

And you will probably find it helpful to experiment with some techniques that have worked for experienced writers:

Developing a topic (1e)	Revising (2b)
Developing a thesis (1f)	Editing (2c)
Organizing (1g)	Proofreading (2d)
Drafting (2a)	Receiving comments (2e)

With experience, as you complete varied assignments and try varied techniques, you will develop your own basic writing process.

Exercise 1
Starting a writing journal

Recall several writing experiences that you have had—a letter you had difficulty with, an essay you enjoyed, an all-nighter spent happily or miserably on a term paper, a posting to an online newsgroup that received a surprising response. What do these experiences reveal to you about writing, particularly your successes and problems with it? For instance:

Do you like to experiment with language?
Are some kinds of writing easier than others?
Do you have trouble getting ideas or expressing them?
Do you worry about grammar and spelling?
Do your readers usually understand what you mean?

Record these thoughts as part of continuing journal entries that track your experiences as a writer. (See pp. 37–39 on keeping a journal.) Specific suggestions for considering your past work appear in Exercises 3, 6, 9, 11, 16, and 20 in Chapter 1; Exercises 2, 5, and 7 in Chapter 2; and Exercises 3, 10, 15, 18, and 20 in Chapter 3. As you complete writing assignments for your composition course and other courses, keep adding to the journal, noting especially which procedures seem most helpful to you. Your aim is to discover your feelings about writing so that you can develop a dependable writing process of your own.

1b Discovering and limiting a subject

For most college and business writing, you will write in response to an assignment. The assignment may specify your subject, or it may leave the choice to you. (If you're stuck, you can use the discovery techniques on pp. 36–46 to think of subjects.) Whether the subject is assigned or not, it will probably need some thought if it is to achieve these aims:

- The subject should be suitable for the assignment.
- It should be neither too general nor too limited for the length of project and deadline assigned.
- It should be something you care about.

1 Pursuing your interests and experiences

Some assignments, such as a physics lab report or a business case study, leave you little room to express yourself. But even these assignments provide some leeway—for instance, in how you conduct and write your research. And many other subjects that may seem inflexible actually allow you considerable freedom. If you are assigned a comparison-and-contrast essay on two people you know, the choice of people and the way you compare them could make the difference for you between simply enduring the writing process or enjoying and learning from it.

When no subject is assigned, find one in your experiences, interests, or curiosities.

- What subject do you already know something about or have you been wondering about? Athletic scholarships? Unemployment in your town?
- Have you recently participated in a lively discussion about a controversial topic? About an event in your family's history? About a change in relations between men and women?
- What have you read or seen lately? A shocking book? A violent or funny movie? An effective television commercial?
- What topic in the reading or class discussion for a course has intrigued you or seemed especially relevant to your own experiences? An economic issue such as taxes? A psychological problem such as depression?
- What makes you especially happy or especially angry? A hobby? The behavior of your neighbors?
- Which of your own or others' dislikes and preferences would you like to understand better? A demand for gas-guzzling cars? A taste for raw fish?

2 Matching subject and assignment

When you receive an assignment, consider the following questions to guide your choice of subject:

- What's wanted from you? Many writing assignments contain words such as *describe, analyze, report, interpret, explain, define, argue,* or *evaluate.* These words specify the way you are to

'90's. Portsmouth, NH: Boynton, 1994. This collection of essays analyzes the goals of the writing process movement, its application in particular institutions, and the ways in which a focus on the writing process can be adapted for the classrooms of the future.

ANSWERS: EXERCISE 1

Individual response

More information about journals is found on page 37.

RESOURCES AND IDEAS

Guiher-Huff, Susan. "Involvement in a Current Problem as a Basis for Writing." *Teaching English in the Two-Year College* 17 (1990): 187–88. Guiher-Huff describes how students used a range of essay formats, made a cause-and-effect oral presentation, and wrote persuasive letters around the topic of pollution. The sustained topic seemed to make the writing meaningful for the students.

Schreffler, Peter H. "'Where All the Children Are Above Average': Garrison Keillor as a Model for Personal Narrative Assignments." *College Composition and Communication* 40 (1989): 82–85. Schreffler discusses the delightful experience personal narrative writing can be as students delve into themselves as well as into the world around them.

Seabury, Marcia Bundy. "The Abstraction Ladder in Freshman Composition." *College Composition and Communication* 40 (1989): 89–92. Seabury has found that teaching S. I. Hayakawa's abstraction ladder can benefit first-year composition students in their thinking through and writing about their topics.

Wallace, David. "From Intention to Text: Articulating Initial Intentions for Writing." *Research in the Teaching of English* 30 (1996): 182–219. This essay explores the relationship between the planning and composing stages of writing. Wallace's study found that students who were most able to articulate their initial intentions for a writing task were also most able to complete the task effectively.

TRANSPARENCY MASTER 1.2

TEACHING TIP

Other good subject areas that give students practice in narrowing topics are movies, cars, television programs, and academic fields (for example, sociology, geology).

COMPUTER EXERCISE

If your classroom is linked to the Internet, ask your students to do a subject search on a broad topic, like the "environment," and to note the successive points at which they will be able to narrow the topic by choosing among lists of subheadings. At a later stage you might ask students to create their own hypertext document in which a broad subject heading leads the user to information on more specific topics. *Teaching Online: Internet Research, Conversation, and Composition,* 2nd ed., by Daniel Anderson, Bret Benjamin, Christopher Busiel, and Bill Paredes-Holt offers useful advice on browsing the Web and on creating hypertext (New York: Longman, 1996).

RESOURCES AND IDEAS

Coe, Richard M. "If Not to Narrow, Then How to Focus: Two Techniques for Focusing." *College Composition and Communication* 32 (1981): 272–77. Coe describes ways to get students to focus on a particular aspect of a topic as an alternative to the usual approach of narrowing a topic.

Tucker, Amy. *Decoding ESL: International Students in the American College Classroom.* Portsmouth, NH: Boynton, 1995. This book explores the larger issues of how to read and respond to ESL writers, and includes (particularly in Chapter 8) strategies for using readings as the prompts for writing assignments.

NARROWING SUBJECTS TO TOPICS

Clustering (1e-5) and asking the journalist's questions (1e-6) can also help narrow subjects to topics. For example, the broad subject "Federal Aid to College Students" can be the center point of a cluster, and students can write related topic ideas such as "types of aid," "why students should receive aid," or "information about aid" in branches radiating from the center. "Federal aid to college students" can also be narrowed by

approach your subject, what kind of critical thinking is expected of you, and what your broad purpose is. (See the book's Introduction and pp. 30–31.)

- For whom are you writing? Some assignments will specify your readers, but usually you will have to figure out for yourself whether your audience is the general reading public, your classmates, your boss, the college community, your instructor, or some other group or individual. (For more on analyzing your audience, see pp. 31–35.)
- What kind of research is required? Sometimes an assignment specifies the kinds of sources you are expected to consult, and you can use such information to choose your subject. (If you are unsure whether research is required, check with your instructor.)
- What is the length of the paper, and how far away is the deadline? Having a week to write 750 words or three weeks to write 2,000 words can make a big difference in the subject you select (see "Limiting the Subject," below).

3 Limiting the subject

Because most assignments leave some room for you to shape the subject, they are usually quite general. The same may be true of your first attempts to make the assigned subject your own or to invent a subject. Lincoln's weaknesses as President, federal aid to college students, corporate support for the arts, summer jobs—all these cover broad areas that whole books might be written about. For a brief paper, you'd need a topic much narrower, much more specific, so that you could provide the facts, examples, and other details that make writing significant and interesting.

The following examples illustrate how broad subjects can be scaled down to one of several manageable **topics**—limited, specific essay subjects.

Broad subjects	Specific topics
Lincoln's weaknesses as President	Lincoln's most significant error as commander-in-chief of the Union army Lincoln's delay in emancipating the slaves Lincoln's difficulties in controlling his cabinet
Summer jobs	Kinds of summer jobs for unskilled workers How to find a summer job What a summer job can teach
Federal aid to college students	Which students should be entitled to federal aid Kinds of federal aid available to college students Why the federal government should (or should not) aid college students

Here are some guidelines for narrowing subjects to topics:

- Again, pursue your interests, and consider what the assignment tells you about purpose, audience, sources, length, and deadline (see pp. 27–28).
- Break your subject into as many topics as you can think of. Make a list.
- For the topic that interests you most and fits the assignment, roughly sketch out the main ideas and consider how many paragraphs or pages of specific facts, examples, and other details you would need to pin those ideas down. This thinking should give you at least a vague idea of how much work you'd have to do and how long the resulting paper might be.
- If an interesting and appropriate topic is still too broad, break it down further and repeat the previous step.

Don't be discouraged if the perfect topic does not leap into your head. You may find that you need to do some planning and writing, exploring different facets of the general subject and pursuing your specific interests, before you hit on the best topic. And the topic you select may require further narrowing or may shift subtly or even dramatically as you move through the writing process.

asking such questions as "*Who* should receive federal aid?," "*What* types of federal aid are available?," "*Why* should the government aid college students?," "*How* can the government aid students?," "*How* can students obtain federal aid?," and "*Where* can students obtain information about federal aid?"

Exercise 2
Working with assignments

Following are some general writing assignments. Use the given information and your own interests to find specific topics for three of these assignments.

1. For a letter to the editor of the town newspaper, describe the effects of immigration on your community. Length: two pages. Deadline: unspecified.
2. For a course in environmental science, research and evaluate the federal government's policies for an environmental hazard. Length: five pages. Deadline: three weeks.
3. For a writing course, explain some aspect of campus employment. Length: three pages. Deadline: one week.
4. For the school newspaper, report on an issue in sports. Length: four pages. Deadline: two weeks.
5. For a course in sociology, research and analyze the dynamics of a particular group of people. Length: unspecified. Deadline: four weeks.
6. For a writing course, read and respond to an essay in a text you are using. Length: three pages. Deadline: two weeks.
7. For a government course, consider possible restrictions on legislators. Length: five pages. Deadline: two weeks.

Exercise 3
Considering your past work: Discovering and limiting a subject

Think of something you've recently written—perhaps an application essay, a business report, or a term paper. How did your subject

COLLABORATIVE LEARNING

Have students work in groups to find specific topics for the assignments in Exercise 2, and then share their conclusions with the class. Students benefit from realizing the numerous and varied options for narrowing a broad subject.

ANSWERS: EXERCISE 2

Possible answers

1. The positive effects of immigration on food choices.
2. The policy for ocean dumping of shipboard waste.
3. How to get a campus job.
4. The gambling rules in professional ice hockey.
5. How slang binds members of the college community.
6. How X's point about math anxiety applies to me.
7. Why legislators should not be limited to a certain number of terms.

ANSWERS: EXERCISE 3

Individual response.

COLLABORATIVE LEARNING

As part of the process of developing their topics for Exercise 4, have students verbally articulate their ideas in small groups and receive suggestions for further development and focus.

ANSWERS: EXERCISE 4

Individual response.

IDENTIFYING PURPOSE

Use paragraphs drawn from magazine articles, essays in a reader, or student papers as the basis for class discussion of the purposes of writing. You may ask students to work individually or in groups to compare the aims of individual paragraphs with the overall purpose of the essay from which they are taken and to decide what role the paragraphs play within the essay.

RESOURCES AND IDEAS

Ede, Lisa, and Andrea Lunsford. "Audience Addressed/Audience Invoked: The Role of Audience in Composition Theory and Pedagogy." *College Composition and Communication* 35 (1984): 155–71. The authors suggest a negotiated balance between the writer's desires and the audience's needs. See also their "Representing Audience: 'Successful' Discourse and Disciplinary Critique" in *College Composition and Communication* 47 (1996): 167–179.

Kirsch, Gesa, and Duane H. Roen. *A Sense of Audience in Written Communication.* Newbury Park: Sage, 1990. Sixteen interdisciplinary essays on audience treat the subject from a number of critical perspectives.

Park, Douglas B. "Analyzing Audiences." *College Composition and Communication* 37 (1986): 478–88. Understanding the social context of a writing act helps students define their audiences.

Roth, Robert G. "'The Evolving Audience': Alternatives to Audience Accommodation." *College Composition and Communication* 38 (1987): 47–55. Roth argues that student writers should focus more on how to claim an audience's attention than on heuristics defining the audience.

Rieff, Mary Jo. "Rereading 'Invoked' and 'Addressed' Readers Through a Social Lens: To-

evolve from beginning to end? In retrospect, was it appropriate for your writing situation? How, if at all, might it have been modified?

Exercise 4
Finding a topic for your essay

As the first step in developing a three- to four-page essay for your writing course, choose one of the topics you arrived at in Exercise 2 or some other topic you like. Use the guidelines in the previous section to come up with a topic that is suitably interesting, appropriate, and narrow.

1c Defining your purpose

When you write, your **purpose** is your chief reason for communicating something about a topic to a particular audience. Purpose thus includes all three elements of the writing situation: you the writer, your topic, and your audience. It ties together both the specific context in which you are working and the goal you hope to achieve.

The purposes for writing

- To entertain readers
- To express your feelings or ideas
- To explain something to readers (exposition)
- To persuade readers to accept or act on your opinion (argument)

Most college and business writing has the primary purpose of explaining or persuading.

- Writing that is mainly explanatory is often called **exposition** (from a Latin word meaning "to explain or set forth"). Almost any topic is suitable for exposition: how to pitch a knuckleball, why you want to major in business, the implications of a new discovery in computer science, the interpretation of a short story, the causes of an economic slump. Exposition is the kind of writing encountered most often in newspapers, magazines, and textbooks.
- Writing that is primarily persuasive is often called **argument.** A newspaper editorial favoring city council reform, a business proposal for a new personnel policy, a student paper recommending more required courses or defending a theory about human psychological development—all these are arguments. (Chapter 4 discusses argument in some detail and provides illustrative essays.)

Often a writing assignment will specify or imply your purpose: when assigned a report on a physics experiment, for instance, you know the purpose is to explain; when assigned an editorial presenting a case for or against expanding your school's health facilities, you know the purpose is to persuade. If the assignment leaves your purpose up to you, then try to define it soon after you have your topic, to give yourself some direction. Don't despair if you aren't successful, though. Sometimes you may not discover your purpose until you begin drafting, or you may find that your initial sense of purpose changes as you move through the writing process.

Exercise 5
Finding purpose in assignments

For each of your narrowed topics in Exercise 2 (p. 29), suggest a likely purpose (entertainment, self-expression, explanation, persuasion).

Exercise 6
Considering your past work: Defining a purpose

Look over two or three things you've written in the past year or so. What was your purpose in each one? How did that purpose influence your writing? Did you achieve your purpose?

Exercise 7
Defining a purpose for your essay

To begin developing a brief essay of your own, select a topic that has particular interest for you. (The topic may come from your answer to Exercise 4, opposite.) Define a purpose for your essay.

1d Considering your audience

Who are your readers? Why are they reading your writing? What do they need and expect from you? These questions are central to the writing process and will crop up again and again because (except in writing only for yourself) you are always trying to communicate something to readers.

Like purpose, audience is often specified or implied in a writing assignment. When you write an editorial for the student newspaper favoring expansion of the college health facilities, your audience is fellow students, who will be reading the paper for information of general and personal interest. When you write a report on a physics experiment, your audience is your physics instructor, who will be reading to evaluate your competence and see if you need help. If no particular audience is specified or implied, then, as with purpose, you are free to decide whom you want to address:

wards a Recognition of Multiple Audiences." *Journal of Advanced Composition* 16 (1996): 407–24. Reiff reviews ways in which the term *audience* has been evoked by composition theorists and examines ways that writing teachers and students can take multiple audience perspectives into account.

Wells, Susan. "Rogue Cops and Health Care: What Do We Want from Public Writing?" *College Composition and Communication* 47 (1996): 325–41. Wells explores the problems of addressing a "general public" audience in student assignments.

Willey, R. J. "Audience Awareness: Methods and Madness." *Freshman English News* 18:2 (1990): 20+. Willey found that when rhetorical, informational, and social perspectives on audience awareness were considered in the composition classroom, the social perspective was the most productive because of its transactional nature.

COLLABORATIVE LEARNING

Ask students to develop their responses to Exercise 5 in groups, paying particular attention to places where the purposes of a given topic could differ. This discussion will help students to explore ways in which a topic might lend itself to various purposes.

ANSWERS: EXERCISE 5

Possible answers

1. Effects of immigration: explanation.
2. Government policies for an environmental hazard: explanation or persuasion.
3. Campus employment: explanation.
4. An issue in sports: explanation.
5. Dynamics of a group of people: explanation.
6. Response to an essay: self-expression or persuasion.
7. Restrictions on legislators: explanation or persuasion.

ANSWERS: EXERCISE 6

Individual response.

your classmates? your boss and others at work? those who drive cars? Whatever the audience, it can help you decide what to say about your topic and how to say it.

ESL If English is not your native language, you may not be accustomed to appealing to your readers when you write. In some cultures, readers may accept a writer's statements with little or no questioning. Readers of English, however, expect the writer to reach out to them by being accurate, fair, interesting, and clear.

ANSWERS: EXERCISE 7

Individual response.

COLLABORATIVE LEARNING

Sharing past work can help students connect the writing they are doing in your class to their broader experience as writers, a connection that helps them to gain greater awareness of their own progress as writers. Have students bring in a piece of previous work and present it to their group, describing the context in which that piece was written, their purpose in writing it, what they learned from writing it, and how it differs from other kinds of writing they have done. Ask groups to report on the interesting or unexpected moments that occurred in the group presentations.

TRANSPARENCY MASTER 1.3

Knowing what readers need

As a reader yourself, you know what readers need:

- *Context:* a link between what they read and their own knowledge and experiences.
- *Predictability:* an understanding of the writer's purpose and how it is being achieved.
- *Information:* the specific facts, examples, and other details that make the subject clear, concrete, interesting, and convincing.
- *Respect:* a sense that the writer respects their values and beliefs, their background, and their intelligence.
- *Voice:* a sense that the writer is a real person.
- *Clarity and correctness:* writing free of unnecessary stumbling blocks and mistakes.

For much academic and business writing, the needs and expectations of readers are specifically prescribed; thus Chapters 39, 40, and 42 discuss the special concerns of writing in various disciplines and in business. But even in these areas, you must make many choices based on audience. In other areas where the conventions of structure and presentation are vaguer, the choices are even more numerous. The box opposite contains questions that can help you define and make these choices.

If you write on a computer, you can store these questions in a file or a macro (a repeatable sequence of actions). Then, for each assignment, you can call up the file or macro and insert appropriate answers between the questions. Save the answers, and print a copy for reference while you draft your paper.

RESOURCES AND IDEAS

Ong, Walter J., S. J. "The Writer's Audience Is Always a Fiction," *PMLA* 90 (1975): 9–21. Ong argues that writers must construct audiences in their imaginations as an essential part of the act of writing and that readers must play the role defined for them by the writer's act of imag-

Writing for a specific audience

Your sense of your audience will influence three key elements of what you write:

- The specific information you use to gain and keep the attention of readers and to guide them to accept your conclusions. This

Questions about audience

- Who *are* my readers?
- Why are readers going to read my writing? What will they expect?
- What do I want readers to know or do after reading my work, and how should I make that clear to them?
- What characteristic(s) of readers are relevant for my topic and purpose? For instance:

  Age or sex
  Occupation: students, professional colleagues, etc.
  Social or economic role: adult children, car buyers, potential employers, etc.
  Economic or educational background
  Ethnic background
  Political, religious, or moral beliefs and values
  Hobbies or activities

- How will the characteristic(s) of readers influence their attitudes toward my topic?
- What do readers already know and *not* know about my topic? How much do I have to tell them?
- If my topic involves specialized language, how much should I use and define?
- What ideas, arguments, or information might surprise readers? excite them? offend them? How should I handle these points?
- What misconceptions might readers have of my topic and/or my approach to the topic? How can I dispel these misconceptions?
- What is my relationship to my readers? What role and tone should I assume?
- What will readers do with my writing? Should I expect them to read every word from the top, to scan for information, to look for conclusions? Can I help with a summary, headings, or other aids? (See pp. 759–72 on document format.)

information may consist of concrete details, facts, examples, or any other evidence that makes your ideas clear, supports your assertions, and suits your readers' background, biases, and special interests.

- The role you choose to play in relation to your readers. Depending on your purpose and your attitude toward your topic, you will want readers to perceive you and your attitude in a certain way. The possible roles are many and varied—for instance, portrait painter, storyteller, lecturer, guide, reporter, advocate, inspirer.
- The tone you use. **Tone** in writing is like tone of voice in speaking: words and sentence structures on the page convey some of the same information as pitch and volume in the voice. Your

TRANSPARENCY MASTER 1.4

ination. Of course, students are probably aware that in many writing circumstances, such as writing for a professor or a manager at work, the audience is real, not fictional. It's worth discussing how a writer's task can be shaped by his or her knowledge of actual readers.

Vandenberg, Peter. "Pick Up This Cross and Follow: (Ir)responsibility and the Teaching of 'Writing for Audience.'" *Composition Studies: Freshman English News* 20 (Fall 1992): 84–97. Vandenberg reviews debates over the changing concept of audience and pinpoints some of the contradictions that students face as they try to write for particular audiences.

AUDIENCE INVENTORY

Ask students to choose a possible topic for an essay and to list the kinds of people who might be interested in the topic. Tell students that if they wish they may employ the "Questions About Audience" on this page. (In theory, the lists might be very long. In practice, students soon run out of ideas, but not until they have begun to visualize the audience for their essays.) To extend the exercise, ask students what part of the potential audience they would most like to address or what kinds of people would be most interested in the topic. Then ask them to list either (1) what the restricted audience probably already knows about the topic and what it needs to know or (2) what its attitudes are and what kinds of arguments will be needed to change them.

COLLABORATIVE LEARNING

Ask students to compare the lists they developed for the audience inventory and suggest changes, additions, or deletions.

RESOURCES AND IDEAS

Rose, Shirley K. "The Voice of Authority: Developing a Fully Rhetorical Definition of Voice in Writing." *Writing Instructor* 8 (1989): 111–18. Rose argues that voice, or authority, over one's texts is a measure of effective writing and shows how this quality can be developed in students' writing in a fifteen-week time period.

COLLABORATIVE LEARNING

DISCOVERING SOMEONE ELSE'S AUDIENCE

Distribute to your class an article from a special-interest magazine, a newspaper feature or editorial, or another brief essay whose appeal to a particular audience students will be able to recognize fairly easily. Ask students to read the essay and then to work together to identify the characteristics and attitudes of the intended audience as they think the author viewed it. Ask them also to identify the tone of the essay and to decide whether or not it is appropriate to the subject, the intended audience, and the publication in which the essay appeared. Tell them to be ready to point out what evidence in the essay they used to identify the intended audience and the tone.

Rather than bring articles to class yourself, ask students either individually or as teams to bring in a variety of essays or writings aimed at particular audiences. Some target audiences you might pick are consumers, sports fans, parents, businesspeople, patients, or health-care workers.

tone will say a lot about your attitude, whether forceful, calm, warm, irritated, or bored.

To see how these three elements may change for different audiences, consider the following two memos. Both are by a student who works part-time in a small company and wants to get the company to conserve paper. The first is addressed to his fellow clerical workers, the second to the managers of the company.

> Ever notice how much paper collects in your trash basket every day? Well, most of it can be recycled with little effort, I promise. Basically, all you need to do is set a bag or box near your desk and deposit wastepaper in it. I know, space is cramped in these little cubicles. But what's a little more crowding when the earth's at stake? . . .

Information: how employees could handle recycling; no mention of costs

Role: cheerful, equally harried colleague

Tone: informal, personal (*Ever notice; you; what's; Well; I know, space is cramped*)

> In my four months here, I have observed that all of us throw out baskets of potentially recyclable paper every day. Considering the drain on our forest resources and the pressure on landfills that paper causes, we could make a valuable contribution to the environmental movement by helping to recycle the paper we use. At the company where I worked before, the employees separate clean wastepaper from other trash at their desks. The maintenance staff collects trash in two receptacles, and the trash hauler (the same one we use here) makes separate pickups. I do not know what the hauler charges for handling recyclable material. . . .

Information: specific reasons; view of company as a whole; reference to another company; problem of cost

Role: serious, thoughtful, responsible employee

Tone: formal, serious (*Considering the drain; forest resources; valuable contribution;* no *you* or contractions)

Typically for business reports and memos, the information grows more specific and the tone more formal as the rank and number of readers rises.

These days you may "publish" some of your writing online—for instance, via electronic mail, an Internet newsgroup, or a network linking your class members and instructor. If you are addressing readers who haven't met you or to whom you are anonymous (as sometimes occurs with an online writing workshop), you can't assume that your readers will draw the conclusions you wish or give you the benefit of the doubt because they know how you usually write. In such a situation, then, your words alone represent you, and you need to take special care with your tone and your evidence.

Of course, much of your college writing will have only one reader besides you: the instructor of the course you are writing for. Whether this person knows you well or not, he or she will take a certain approach to your work. In a composition course your instructor is likely to read your work as a representative of a general audience and respond to it in the additional role of helpful critic (see p. 80). That means you should not assume specialized interest in or knowledge of your topic, nor should you expect the patience of a doting parent who fills in what his or her child can't (or won't) express. If something about your topic would need to be said to a classmate or a reader of your local newspaper, say it clearly and carefully.

In academic courses such as literature, psychology, management, and chemistry, your writing will be addressed to a specialized audience of practitioners of the discipline, represented by your instructor. If you are writing a paper on the economic background of the War of 1812 for an American history course, you may assume your instructor's familiarity with the key events, players, and published interpretations. Your job is to show your own command of them and their relevance to your topic while assuming an appropriate academic role and tone.

- Present yourself as a serious and competent student of the subject you are writing in.
- Demonstrate that you have at least a basic understanding of the discipline's research methods, vocabulary, and principles.
- Be specific.
- Write clearly and concisely.
- Avoid undue informality.

These requirements allow considerable room for your own voice, as these two passages on the same topic prove:

> One technique for heightening the emotional appeal of advertisements is "color engineering." Adding color to a product or the surrounding advertisement can increase sales despite the fact that the color serves no practical purpose. For example, until the 1920s fountain pens were made of hard black rubber. When colorful pens were suddenly introduced, sales rose dramatically.
>
> "Color engineering" can intensify the emotional appeal of advertisements. New color in a product or the surrounding ad can boost sales even when the color serves no other use. In the 1920s, for example, fountain pens that had been hard black rubber suddenly became colorful, and sales shot up.

As you gain experience with academic writing, you will develop the flexibility to write in your voice while also respecting the conventions of the various disciplines.

Exercise 8
Considering audience

Choose one of the following topics and, for each audience specified, ask the questions on page 33. Decide on four points you

Have students work in groups to critique and revise one of their paragraph-length responses to Exercise 8. In networked classrooms, students can "publish" the revised paragraphs for the class.

ANSWERS: EXERCISE 8

Possible answers

1. *For elementary school students:* physical effects in simple terms; statistics in simple figures; difficulty of quitting once addicted; importance of resisting peer pressure.
   Role: combined teacher and parent. Tone: warm, slightly admonitory.

For adult smokers: graphic depiction of physical effects; detailed statistics; influence on children; effect on smoker's appearance, odor, breath.
Role: combined friend and lecturer. Tone: no-nonsense.

2. *For someone who is on welfare:* help for children; need to seek work, while receiving benefits in order to become self-supporting; need for bureaucracy to manage system; need for periodic checks to protect against cheating by a few recipients.
Role: caring observer. Tone: sympathetic.
For someone who opposes welfare: need to provide for people who can't work; need to provide for children; low cost relative to other budget expenditures; low incidence of cheating.
Role: fellow citizen. Tone: reasonable, appealing to shared values.
3. *For your neighbors:* feelings of neighborhood residents; dangers to children and pets; lowered property values; threat of petition to zoning board.
Role: peer. Tone: direct, a bit angry.
For the zoning board: violation of zoning regulations; length of time the wrecked truck has been present; number of unsuccessful appeals to neighbors; dangers to children and pets.
Role: plaintiff. Tone: serious, reasonable.

ANSWERS: EXERCISE 9

Individual response.

ANSWERS: EXERCISE 10

Individual response.

COLLABORATIVE LEARNING

Ask students to bring in journal or newspaper articles on controversial topics, and work individually or in groups to compose letters of response "to the editor." Students should consult with their groups to determine the appropriate tone and implied journal or newspaper audience for each response.

would make, the role you would assume, and the tone you would adopt for each audience. Then write a paragraph for each based on your decisions.

1. The effects of smoking: for elementary school students and for adult smokers
2. Your opinion of welfare: for someone who is on welfare and for someone who is not and who opposes it
3. Why your neighbors should remove the wrecked truck from their yard: for your neighbors and for your town zoning board

Exercise 9
Considering your past work: Writing for a specific audience

How did audience figure in a piece of writing you've done in the recent past—perhaps an essay for an application or a paper for a course? Who were your readers? How did your awareness of them influence your choice of information, your role, and your tone? At what point in the writing process did you find it most productive to consider your readers consciously?

Exercise 10
Analyzing the audience for your essay

Use the questions on page 33 to determine as much as you can about the probable readers of your essay-in-progress (see Exercise 7). What does your analysis reveal about the specific information your readers need? What role do you want to assume, and what tone will best convey your attitude toward your topic?

1e Developing your topic

To develop your topic means to generate the ideas and information that will help you achieve your purpose. Sometimes ideas will tumble forth on paper or screen, especially if your topic is very familiar or personal. But when they do not, you shouldn't wait around for inspiration to strike. Instead, use a technique for freeing ideas. Anything that gets your mind working is appropriate: if you like to make drawings or take pictures, for instance, then try it.

The following pages describe some strategies for generating ideas. These strategies are to be selected from, not followed in sequence: some may help you during early stages of the writing process, even before you're sure of your topic; others may help you later on; and one or two may not help at all. Experiment to discover which strategies work best for you.

NOTE *Whatever strategy or strategies you use, do your work in writing, not just in your head.* Your work will be retrievable, and the act of writing will help you concentrate and lead you to fresh, sometimes surprising, insights.

Techniques for developing a topic

- Keep a journal (below).
- Observe your surroundings (p. 39).
- Freewrite (p. 38).
- Make a list or brainstorm (p. 41).
- Cluster (p. 42).
- Ask the journalist's questions (p. 43).
- Use the patterns of development (p. 44).
- Read (p. 45).
- Think critically (p. 46).

ESL The discovery process encouraged here rewards rapid writing without a lot of thinking beforehand about what you will write or how. If you are not comfortable or fluent in English, you may find it helpful initially to do this exploratory writing in your native language and then to translate the worthwhile material for use in your drafts.

Keeping a journal

A place to record thoughts and observations, a **journal** can be a good source of ideas for writing. It is a kind of diary, but one more concerned with ideas than with day-to-day events. *Journal* comes from the Latin for "daily," and many journal keepers do write faithfully every day; others make entries less regularly, when the mood strikes or an insight occurs or they have a problem to work out.

Advantages of a journal

Writing in a journal, you are writing to yourself. That means you don't have to worry about main ideas, organization, correct grammar and spelling, or any of the requirements of public writing. You can work out your ideas and feelings without the pressure of an audience "out there" who will evaluate your thinking and expression. The freedom and flexibility of a journal can be liberating. Like many others, you may find writing easier, more fun, and more rewarding than you thought possible.

You can keep a journal either on paper (such as a notebook) or on a computer. If you write in the journal every day, or almost, even just for a few minutes, the routine will loosen up your writing muscles and improve your confidence. Indeed, journal keepers often become dependent on the process for the writing practice it gives them, the concentrated thought it encourages, and the connection it fosters between personal, private experience and public information and events.

COLLABORATIVE LEARNING

Students can often experience difficulty in identifying the implied readers of their own work. Have students work in small groups to compare their responses to Exercise 10, to help one another identify the probable readers of their essays-in-progress, and to note places in each essay where too much or too little information is supplied.

RESOURCES AND IDEAS

Flower, Linda S., and John R. Hayes. "Problem-Solving Strategies and the Writing Process." *College English* 39 (1977): 449–61. Flower and Hayes describe techniques for discovering and developing ideas, including cue words, nutshelling, idea trees, role playing, and brainstorming.

Hunter, Susan. "Oral Negotiations in a Textual Community: A Case for Pedagogy and Theory." *Writing Instructor* 8 (1989): 105–10. Hunter states that validating oral communication during the composing process is theoretically sound and helpful in generalizing successful oral communication to successful written communication.

Keeping journals

Students may have mixed feelings about journal keeping, so it's important to explain to them why writers find keeping journals so valuable. Make clear how journals differ from diaries and how many (and what kind of) entries you expect per week or term. Giving some guidelines or prompts for students to follow helps them get started. Students can also add clippings, photocopies, pictures, and cartoons and even use tapes and videos in their journals as a way of expanding their horizons. (These other media will have to be submitted separately if you have students hand their journals in.)

It's important to make the journal a productive tool, not just make-work. Encourage students to plumb their journals for essay topics and samples of strategies they might use in more formal pieces of writing. You can also make journals productive by encouraging students to write journal entries as letters to you or classmates, then incorporate your or their classmates' answers into the journal as well.

Most instructors react to issues raised or comment on attempts to try new strategies without

dev 1e

actually grading the journal. Students will often include very personal material in their journals, so they should be encouraged to fold over, staple, or secure (but not remove) personal material before they show it to you; and they must trust that you will respect their confidentiality.

RESOURCES AND IDEAS

Fulwiler, Toby, ed. *The Journal Book.* Portsmouth: Boynton/Cook, 1987. The essays in this collection describe the uses of journals for discovering and exploring ideas and as an important strategy for writing and learning in various subject areas.

Gannett, Cinthia. *Gender and the Journal: Diaries and Academic Discourse.* Albany: State U of New York P, 1992. Gannett discusses the development of the genre and how it has been "feminized," with consideration of the pedagogical implications of this history.

White, Fred D. "Releasing the Self: Teaching Journal-Writing to Freshmen." *The Writing Instructor* 1 (1982): 147–54. White offers practical advice on the use of journals: kinds of journals and entries, professional samples, exercises, and a summary of supporting research.

Whitehill, Sharon. "Using the Journal for Discovery: Two Devices." *College Composition and Communication* 38 (1987): 472–74. Whitehill argues that journal assignments calling for lists and for imaginary dialogues can help generate ideas and alleviate writing blocks, and she provides detailed examples of each strategy.

ACTIVITIES THAT SUGGEST TOPICS AND IDEAS

1. Ask students to take a notebook with them to some place likely to be filled with activity and vivid sense impressions—a laundromat, the center of the campus, a busy restaurant. They can record their impressions of the scene in the notebook, later turning those impressions into a structured description or using the material in some other form of writing.
2. Ask students to look at a variety of magazines and to bring in a list of the topics covered in the articles. These topics may in turn suggest topics for student essays. The exercise can be extended by asking students

Usually for the same reasons, teachers of writing and other subjects sometimes require students to keep journals. The teachers may even collect students' journals to monitor progress, but they read the journals with an understanding of purpose (in other words, they do not evaluate work that was not written to be evaluated), and they usually just credit rather than grade the work.

ESL A journal can be especially helpful if you're writing in English as a second language. You can practice writing to improve your fluency, try out sentence patterns, and experiment with vocabulary words. Equally important, you can experiment with applying what you know from experience to what you read and observe.

Uses of a journal

Two uses of a journal are discussed elsewhere in this book: a reading journal, in which you think critically (in writing) about what you read (pp. 4, 669), and a research journal, in which you record your activities and ideas while you pursue a research project (p. 517). But you can use a journal for other purposes as well. Here are just a few:

- Confide your hopes.
- Write about your own history: an event in your family's past, a troubling incident in your life, a change you've seen.
- Analyze a relationship that troubles you.
- Explore your reactions to movies, television, and music as well as to your reading.
- Practice various forms or styles of writing—poems or songs, for instance, or reviews of movies or reports for TV news.
- Pursue ideas—maybe a theory about human psychology or business management that came up in a class, or a social concern like nursing-home care that's in the news.
- Build ideas for specific writing assignments.

The writing you produce in your journal will help you learn and grow, and even the personal and seemingly nonacademic entries can supply ideas when you are seeking a subject to write about or are developing an essay. A thought you recorded months ago about a chemistry lab may provide direction for a research paper on the history of science. Two entries about arguments with your brother may suggest what you need to anchor a psychology paper on sibling relations. (If you keep your journal on a computer, you can even move passages from it directly into your drafts.)

The following student samples give a taste of journal writing for different purposes. In the first, Charlie Gabnes tries to work out a personal problem with his child:

> Will's tantrums are getting worse—more often, more intense. Beginning to realize it's affecting my feelings for him. I feel resent-

ment sometimes, and it's not as easy for me to cool off afterward as for him. Also I'm afraid of him sometimes for fear a tantrum will start, so treat him with kid gloves. How do we break this cycle?

In the next example Megan Polanyis ponders something she learned from her biology textbook:

> *Ecology* and *economics* have the same root—Greek word for house. Economy = management of the house. Ecology = study of the house. In ecology the house is all of nature, ourselves, the other animals, the plants, the earth, the air, the whole environment. Ecology has a lot to do with economy: study the house in order to manage it.

In the next example Terry Perez responds to the day's news. (We'll follow Perez's writing process in this chapter and the next. The notebook symbol in the margin signals stages in that process.)

> The paper today was full of bad news. Does it only seem this way, or do newspapers and TV really play up conflicts between racial and ethnic groups? Here at school there are some conflicts, sure. But it's more interesting how many different types of people from different backgrounds manage to live together and learn from each other. Isn't that true elsewhere?

2 Observing your surroundings

Sometimes you can find a good subject or good ideas by looking around you, not in the half-conscious way most of us move from place to place in our daily lives but deliberately, all senses alert. On a bus, for instance, are there certain types of passengers? What seems to be on the driver's mind? On campus, which buildings stand out? Are bicyclists and pedestrians at peace with each other?

To get the most from observation, you should have a tablet and pen or pencil handy for notes and sketches. If you have a camera, you may find that the lens sees things your unaided eyes do not notice. (When observing or photographing people, though, keep some distance, take photographs quickly, and avoid staring. Otherwise, your subjects will feel uneasy.) Back at your desk, study your notes, sketches, or photographs for oddities or patterns that you'd like to explore further.

3 Freewriting

Another way to find a subject is to write your way into it: write without stopping for a certain amount of time (say, ten minutes) or to a certain length (say, one page). The goal of this **freewriting** is to generate ideas and information from *within* yourself by going around the part of your mind that doesn't want to write or can't think of anything to write. You let words themselves suggest other

to summarize the contents of one or more of the articles and to indicate how the content might appeal to a particular audience.

3. Check with your audiovisual center or a film rental service for short films that deal with values or controversies. The films or the ensuing discussions can become the basis of student papers.
4. Set up class presentations or debates on an issue in order to provide information and sharpen the focus for papers dealing with the issue or related topics.

dev 1e

RESOURCES AND IDEAS

Lackey, Kris. "Amongst the Awful Subtexts: Scholes, The *Daily Planet*, and Freshman Composition." *College Composition and Communication* 38 (1987): 88–93. In this thought-provoking piece, Lackey suggests encouraging and enabling students to tease out the binary oppositions in texts as a way of discovering various subtexts that suggest topics for students' own writing.

PLACES TO WRITE

To help students discover interesting topics and ideas through freewriting, you might give them some places to begin. For essays focusing on events:

> sports, contests, camping, accidents, storms, childhood experiences, giving a speech, getting lost in a department store, robberies, fires

For writing about a scene or character:

> outdoors—woods, seashore, mountains, fields, city streets, parks
> indoors—dorm rooms, laundromats
> scenes—family gatherings, football games, funerals, a snowy morning
> people—parents, grandparents, uncles, aunts, childhood friends, people in a public place, teachers, unpleasant people, cartoon characters

For informative or explanatory writing:

> hobbies, jobs, investments, fields of study, recent scientific discoveries, places to visit, ways to save money, fishing, gardening, study habits, car repairing, canoeing, audio equipment, magazines

dev 1e

For persuasive writing:

campus issues, environmental concerns, automobile or airline safety, support for education, cost of medical care, regulation of new drugs, specialized education versus liberal arts education, rights of minorities and women, gun control, divorce and child rearing, school prayer, censorship, proposals to improve campus or local services, ways of dealing with a social problem

COLLABORATIVE LEARNING

Teamed freewriting

A good variation on freewriting is to make it collaborative: have students write freely for five or ten minutes, then pass their freewriting to the students sitting next to them. Students should read the freewriting, then reflect on it in another freewriting session. This encourages not only more perspectives on a topic but the notion that writing is a dialogue between writer and reader—and it teaches the value of feedback and audience awareness in writing as well.

COMPUTER EXERCISE

Have students freewrite on the computer using the "invisible writing" technique if desired. During the next class period ask students to revise their freewriting into a paragraph, then e-mail that paragraph to another student in the class for a further critique and for revision suggestions. After a final revision, students might "publish" the resulting paragraphs on the network or hand them in for the teacher's evaluation. For further suggestions on using the computer to help students generate material and collaborate on the revision process see Susan Lang's essay on "Using Computers to Teach Writing" on pp. IAE-63–IAE-77.

RESOURCES AND IDEAS

Elbow, Peter. *Writing Without Teachers.* New York: Oxford UP, 1973. In this classic work, Elbow discusses freewriting and other techniques for tapping imagination and creativity during the writing process.

words. *What* you write is not important; that you *keep* writing is. Don't stop, even if that means repeating the same words until new words come. Don't go back to reread, don't censor ideas that seem dumb or repetitious, and above all don't stop to edit: grammar, punctuation, spelling, and the like are irrelevant at this stage.

If you write on a computer, you can ensure that your freewriting keeps moving forward by turning off your computer's monitor or turning its brightness control all the way down so that the screen is dark. The computer will record what you type but keep it from you and thus prevent you from tinkering with your prose. This **invisible writing** may feel uncomfortable at first, but it can free the mind for very creative results. When you've finished freewriting, simply turn the monitor on or turn up the brightness control to read what you've written, and then save or revise it as appropriate. Later, you can transfer some of your freewriting into your draft.

ESL Invisible writing can be especially helpful if English is a second language for you and you tend to worry about errors while writing. The blank computer screen leaves you no choice but to explore ideas without regard for their expression.

The physical act of freewriting may give you access to ideas you were unaware of. For example, the following freewriting by a student, Robert Benday, gave him the subject of writing as a disguise:

> Write to write. Seems pretty obvious, also weird. What to gain by writing? never anything before. Writing seems always—always—Getting corrected for trying too hard to please the teacher, getting corrected for not trying hard enuf. Frustration, nail biting, sometimes getting carried away making sentences to tell stories, not even true stories, *esp.* not true stories, *that* feels like creating something. Writing just pulls the story out of me. The story lets me be someone else, gives me a disguise.

(A later phase of Benday's writing appears on p. 43.)

Focused freewriting is more concentrated: you start with your topic and write about it without stopping for, say, fifteen minutes or one full page. As in all freewriting, you push to bypass mental blocks and self-consciousness, not debating what to say or editing what you've written. With focused freewriting, though, you let the physical act of writing take you into and around your subject.

An example of focused freewriting can be found in the work of Terry Perez, whose journal entry appears on page 39. In a composition course, Perez and her classmates read and discussed an essay titled "America: The Multinational Society," by Ishmael Reed. Their instructor then gave them the following assignment:

> Respond to Reed's essay with a limited and well-supported opinion of your own about cultural diversity in the United States. Your paper should be 500–750 words. The first draft is due Friday for discussion in class.

Reed's essay argues that the United States is a "multinational society," consisting of many different cultural groups with their own customs, beliefs, and languages, and that the country is stronger for its diversity. Perez agreed with Reed but saw little point in just saying so. She reread Reed's essay for passages that might spark ideas of her own. Several did, but Perez was especially struck by Reed's point that conflict among different people "is played up and often encouraged by the media." It was a thought Perez herself had recorded in her journal, and it prompted the following freewriting:

> Cultural diversity in the media? The media has a one track mind, cultural diversity is bad. Like Reed says the media makes a big deal of conflict between racial and ethnic groups, it's almost constant in the papers, on TV. TV especially—the news vs. all the white bread programs, the sitcoms and ads. That's a whole other view—no conflict, no tension. No diversity. So we have all people the same except when they're not, then they're at war. Two unreal pictures.

With this freewriting, Perez discovered some interesting complexity in her topic that she had originally missed: the media do overplay cultural conflict, she thought, but they also downplay cultural diversity by portraying people as basically similar.

4 Making a list

Like focused freewriting, list making requires opening yourself to everything that seems even remotely connected to your topic, without concern for order or repetition or form of expression. You can let your topic percolate for a day or more, recording thoughts on it whenever they occur. (For this approach to work, you need to keep paper or a computer with you at all times.) Or, in a method more akin to freewriting, you can **brainstorm** about the topic—that is, focus intently on the topic for a fixed amount of time (say, fifteen minutes), pushing yourself to list every idea and detail that comes to mind.

Like freewriting, brainstorming requires turning off your internal editor so that you keep moving ahead instead of looping back over what you have already written to correct it. It makes no difference whether the ideas and details are expressed in phrases or complete sentences. It makes no difference if they seem silly or irrelevant. Just keep pushing. (The technique of invisible writing on a computer, described opposite, can help you move forward.)

Here is an example of brainstorming by a student, Johanna Abrams, on what a summer job can teach:

summer work teaches—

how to look busy while doing nothing
how to avoid the sun in summer
seriously: discipline, budgeting money, value of money

Price, Gayle B. "A Case for a Modern Commonplace Book." *College Composition and Communication* 31 (1980): 175–82. This article reviews freewriting and other techniques for helping students generate ideas and tells how students can use a notebook to record ideas.

Reynolds, Mark. "Make Free Writing More Productive." *College Composition and Communication* 39 (1988): 81–82. Reynolds offers twenty "questions, activities, and guidelines" for drawing useful ideas and promising topics from the often jumbled material provided by freewriting.

which job? Burger King cashier? baby sitter? mail-room clerk?
mail room: how to sort mail into boxes: this is learning??
how to survive getting fired—humiliation, outrage
Mrs. King! the mail-room queen as learning experience
the shock of getting fired: what to tell parents, friends?
Mrs. K was so rigid—dumb procedures
Mrs. K's anger, resentment: the disadvantages of being smarter than your boss
The odd thing about working in an office: a world with its own rules for how to act
what Mr. D said about the pecking order—big chick (Mrs. K) pecks on little chick (me)
probably lots of Mrs. Ks in offices all over—offices are all barnyards
Mrs. K a sad person, really—just trying to hold on to her job, preserve her self-esteem
a job can beat you down—destroy self-esteem, make you desperate enough to be mean to other people
how to preserve/gain self-esteem from work??
if I'd known about the pecking order, I would have been less show-offy, not so arrogant

(A later phase of Abrams's writing appears on p. 55.)

When you think you've exhausted the ideas on your topic, edit and shape the list into a preliminary outline of your paper (see pp. 52–58).  Working on a computer makes this step fairly easy: you can delete weak ideas, expand strong ones, and rearrange items with a few keystrokes. You can also freewrite from the list if you think some items are especially promising and deserve more thought.

 5 Clustering

Like freewriting and list making, **clustering** draws on free association and rapid, unedited work. But it also emphasizes the *relations* between ideas by combining writing and nonlinear drawing. When clustering, you radiate outward from a center point—your topic. When an idea occurs, you pursue related ideas in a branching structure until they seem exhausted. Then you do the same with other ideas, staying open to connections, continuously branching out or drawing arrows.

The example of clustering opposite shows how Robert Benday used the technique for ten minutes to expand on the topic of creative writing as a means of disguise, an idea he arrived at through freewriting (see p. 40). Though he ventured into several dead ends, Benday also came to the interesting possibility (at the bottom) that the fiction writer is like a god who forgives himself by creating characters that represent his good and bad qualities.

TOPIC CLUSTERS

The topic clusters we show are very well developed; students need to know it's acceptable to develop smaller or more messy clusters. You might ask students to work on topic clusters in groups. If your classroom permits, you might also want to try doing clusters on overhead transparencies or the blackboard, so that students can add to and change their contents more easily.

RESOURCES AND IDEAS

Frye, Bob. "Artful Compositions, Corder's 'Laws of Composition,' and the Weekly Letter: Two Approaches to Teaching Invention and Arrangement in Freshman English." *Journal of Teaching Writing* 8 (1989): 1–14. Frye argues that having students write replies to the instructor's weekly letters allows them to ex-

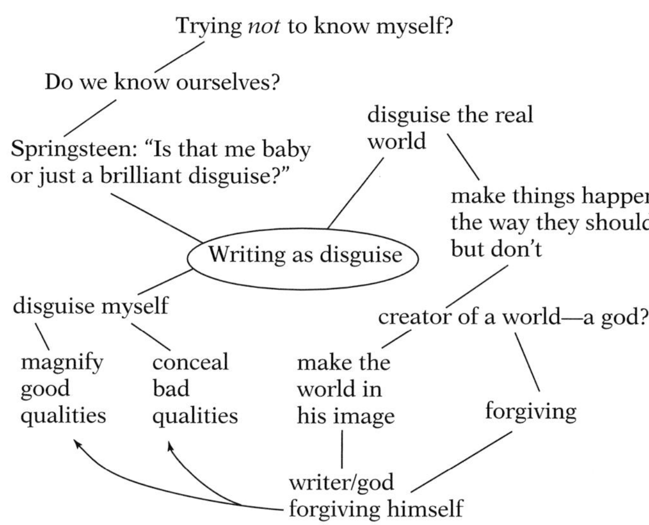

 6 Using the journalist's questions

Asking yourself a set of questions about your topic—and writing out the answers—can help you look at the topic objectively and see fresh possibilities in it. Asking questions can also provide some structure to the development of ideas.

One such set of questions is that posed by a journalist with a story to report:

Who was involved?
What happened and what were the results?
When did it happen?
Where did it happen?
Why did it happen?
How did it happen?

These questions can also be useful in probing an essay topic, especially if you are telling a story or examining causes and effects. (See also the next page.)

If you write on a computer, you can create a form for the journalist's questions to use for different writing projects. Simply type the list, save it in a file, and then duplicate it for each project, inserting answers between questions. Print your answers so they're handy while you draft, or split your computer screen horizontally so that it shows the answers above while you draft below. You may even be able to import passages from the answers into your draft.

perience genuine rhetorical invention rather than experiencing closure, often the product of structure.

Rico, Gabriele Lusser. *Writing the Natural Way.* Los Angeles: Tarcher, 1983. Rico draws on research about brain functions as the basis for advice about strategies—especially clustering—that encourage creativity in expression.

TEACHING TIP

Students often don't know how to respond to readings; role-playing exercises that ask them to pose as book reviewers or discussants on a political talk show may help them find an "angle" to start responding to a reading.

RESOURCES AND IDEAS

Kneupper, Charles W. "Revising the Tagmemic Heuristic: Theoretical and Pedagogical Considerations." *College Composition and Communication* 31 (1980): 160–68. Kneupper offers a simplified version of the powerful question system introduced by Young, Becker, and Pike in their text, *Rhetoric: Discovery and Change* (New York: Harcourt, 1970).

Washington, Eugene. "WH-Questions in Teaching Composition." *College Composition and Communication* 28 (1977): 54–56. Washington suggests using what, why, where, and how questions to increase density of information in essays and clarify structure.

 COMPUTER EXERCISE

As an ongoing exercise, have students generate electronic worksheets on which they adjust or add to these journalist's questions to fit the needs of particular assignments.

Using the patterns of development

The **patterns of development**—such as narration, definition, and comparison and contrast—are ways we think about and understand a vast range of subjects, from our own daily experiences to the most complex scientific theories. They also serve as strategies for writing about these subjects, as illustrated by the discussions and paragraph-length examples on pages 106–14.

To see your topic from many angles and open up ideas about it, you can ask the following questions based on the patterns of development. (On a computer you can create a form as suggested on the previous page for the journalist's questions and reuse the form for different writing projects.) Not all these questions will be productive, but at least a few should open up new possibilities.

How did it happen?

In **narration** you develop the topic as a story, with important events usually arranged chronologically (as they occurred in time): for instance, an exciting basketball game or the steps leading to a war.

How does it look, sound, feel, smell, taste?

In **description** you use sensory details to give a clear impression of a person, place, thing, or feeling, such as a friend, a favorite room, a building, or an experience.

What are examples of it or reasons for it?

The pattern of **illustration** or **support** suggests development with one or more examples of the topic (one couple's efforts to adopt a child, say, or three television soap operas) or with the reasons for believing or doing something (three reasons for majoring in English, four reasons for driving defensively).

What is it? What does it encompass, and what does it exclude?

These questions lead to **definition:** specifying what the topic is and is not to give a precise sense of its meaning. Abstract terms—such as *justice, friendship,* and *art*—especially need defining. (See p. 129.)

What are its parts or characteristics?

Using the pattern of **division** or **analysis,** you separate a subject into its elements and examine the relations between elements. The first step in critical thinking, analysis is also discussed on page 46.

What groups or categories can it be sorted into?

Classification involves separating a large group (such as cars) into smaller groups (subcompact, compact, and so on) based on the

USING QUESTIONS AND PATTERNS

To help students discover the power of sets of questions or the patterns of development for exploring topics, begin by giving them a list of general subjects—music, sports, guns, the environment—and then ask them to explore each, looking for limited aspects that might make good topics for essays. Do not encourage students to use either the questions or the patterns in probing the topics. Class discussion can focus on how to limit the topics and can indicate how an audience might respond to them.

Following the discussion, ask students to explore the same topics using either the journalist's questions (1e7) or the patterns of development as described in 1e8. Ask students to direct their attention to as many different aspects of the topic as they can and at the same time to suggest ways of developing it and organizing an essay around it. Discussion should focus on differences between the "guided" and "unguided" approaches to developing a topic.

RESOURCES AND IDEAS

D'Angelo, Frank J. *A Conceptual Theory of Rhetoric.* Cambridge: Winthrop, 1975. D'Angelo argues that rhetorical patterns of organization (e.g., analysis, classification, and description) are also patterns of thought and invention and can be used to probe experience as part of the composing process. See also D'Angelo's "Topoi and Form in Composition," *The Territory of Language.* Ed. Donald A. McQuade. Carbondale: Southern Illinois UP, 1986. 114–22.

Dean, Terry. "Casual, Not Casual: An Advance Organizer for Cause-and-Effect Composition." In *Structuring for Success in the English Classroom.* Ed. Candy Carter. Urbana: NCTE, 1982. 92–97. Dean describes exercises to make students aware of casual relationships and to provide a basis for writing.

Podis, Leonard A. "Teaching Arrangement: Defining a More Practical Approach." *College Composition and Communication* 31 (1980): 197–204. Podis describes a teaching sequence designed to make students aware of the basic principles of organization, and he reviews some standard patterns of arrangement useful for academic and professional writing.

characteristics of the individual items (the sizes of the cars). Another example: academic, business, personal, literary, and other types of writing.

How is it like, or different from, other things?

With **comparison and contrast** you point out the similarities and differences between ideas, objects, people, places, and so on: the differences between two similar computer systems, for instance, or the similarities between two opposing political candidates.

Is it comparable to something that is in a different class but more familiar to readers?

This question leads to **analogy,** an extended comparison of unlike subjects. Analogy is often used to explain a topic that may be unfamiliar to readers (for instance, the structure of a government) by reference to a familiar topic (the structure of a family).

Why did it happen, or what results did it have?

With **cause-and-effect analysis,** you explain why something happened or what its consequences were or will be, or both: the causes of cerebral palsy, the effects of a Supreme Court decision, the causes and effects of a gradual change in the climate.

How do you do it, or how does it work?

In **process analysis** you explain how the topic is accomplished (how to write an essay) or how it happens (how a plant grows, how a robot works).

As you can see on pages 106–14, the patterns of development also provide a means of introducing information in paragraphs. Further discussion of how the patterns may combine in an essay appears on pages 123–25.

Reading

Many assignments require reading. To respond to Ishmael Reed's essay on cultural diversity, for instance, Terry Perez had to digest Reed's work. And essays on literary works as well as research papers demand reading. But even when reading is not required by an assignment, it can help you locate or develop your topic by introducing you to ideas you didn't know or expanding on what you do know.

Say you were writing in favor of amateur athletics, a subject you had given a lot of thought to. You might be inclined to proceed entirely on your own, drawing on facts, examples, and opinions already in your head. But a little digging in sources might open up more. For instance, an article in *Time* magazine could introduce

Wilcox, Lance. "Time Lines in the Composing of Narratives: A Graphic Aid to Organization." *The Writing Instructor* 6 (1987): 162–73. Wilcox describes in detail the use of time lines to help develop and organize narrative essays.

you to an old rule for amateur status, or a posting to an online newsgroup could suggest a pro-amateurism argument that hadn't occurred to you. (See pp. 522–58 for techniques of library and computer research that you can use to locate sources on a topic.)

People often read passively, absorbing content like blotters, not interacting with it. To read for ideas, you need to be more active, probing text and illustrations with your mind, nurturing any sparks they set off. Always write while you read so that you can keep notes on content and—just as important—on what the content makes you *think*. If you haven't done so already, consult this book's Introduction, especially pages 6–8, which discuss the process of active reading in some detail.

Note Whenever you use the information or ideas of others in your writing, you must acknowledge your sources in order to avoid the serious offense of plagiarism. (See p. 578.)

9 Thinking critically

Even if you do not read for information and ideas on your topic, you can still think critically about it. Critical thinking (discussed on pp. 1–17) can produce creative ideas by leading you to see what is not obvious. It can also lead you systematically to conclusions about your topic.

Terry Perez, writing about the media and cultural diversity, used the operations of critical thinking to explore her topic.

- **Analysis:** What are the subject's elements or characteristics? Perez looked at the media's images of cultural diversity and its opposite, cultural sameness.
- **Interpretation:** What is the meaning or significance of the elements? Perez saw images in which culturally diverse groups were in conflict and images in which cultural diversity was not apparent at all.
- **Synthesis:** How do the elements relate to each other, or how does this subject relate to another one? Perez concluded that the media tend to present cultural diversity in only one way, as a source of tension and conflict. Otherwise, she concluded, cultural diversity barely exists in the media's world.
- **Evaluation:** What is the value or significance of the subject? Perez judged that the media fail in their responsibility to represent their audience accurately.

ANSWERS: EXERCISE 11

Individual response.

Exercise 11
Considering your past work: Developing a topic

In the past how have you generated the ideas for writing? Have you used any of the techniques described on the preceding pages (perhaps not called by the same names)? Have you found the process of generating ideas to be especially enjoyable or difficult? If some writing tasks have been easier than others, what do you think made the difference?

Exercise 12
Keeping a journal

If you haven't already started a journal on your own or in response to Exercise 1, try to do so now. Every day for at least a week, write for at least fifteen minutes about whatever comes into your mind—or consult the list on page 38 for ideas of what to write about. At the end of the week, review and write about your experience and your journal entries. What did you like about journal writing? What didn't you like? What did you learn about yourself or the world from the writing? What use can you put this knowledge to?

Exercise 13
Using freewriting, brainstorming, or clustering

If you haven't tried any of them before, experiment with freewriting (p. 39), brainstorming (p. 41), or clustering (p. 42). Continue with the topic you selected in Exercise 4 (p. 30), or begin with a new topic. Write or draw for at least ten minutes without stopping to reread and edit. (Try using invisible writing as described on p. 40 if you're freewriting or brainstorming on a computer.) When you finish your experiment, examine what you have written for ideas and relationships that could help you develop the topic. What do you think of the technique you tried? Did one or another help you loosen up and generate ideas?

Exercise 14
Developing your topic

Use at least two of the discovery techniques discussed on the preceding pages to develop the topic you selected in Exercise 4 (p. 30). (If you completed Exercise 13, then use one additional technique.) Later exercises for your essay-in-progress will be based on the ideas you generate in this exercise.

ANSWERS: EXERCISE 12

Individual response.

 **COMPUTER EXERCISE**

Exercise 13 can be readily transferred to the computer classroom to encourage students to practice generating material on the computer. At the end of the exercise you might ask students to read through their material to develop ideas and to highlight ideas for future revision, but to avoid deleting material. As a take-home assignment or in the following class, students can revise and delete more extensively; they might then present the resulting material to their groups.

ANSWERS: EXERCISE 13

Individual response.

ANSWERS: EXERCISE 14

Individual response.

1f Developing your thesis

Your readers will expect an essay you write to be focused on a central idea, or **thesis,** to which all the essay's paragraphs, all its general statements and specific information, relate. The thesis is the controlling idea, the main point, the conclusion you have drawn about the evidence you have accumulated. (Even if you create a hypertext document, such as a site on the World Wide Web, you'll have a core idea that governs the links among pages and sites.)

RESOURCES AND IDEAS

Liszka, Thomas R. "Formulating a Thesis for Essays Employing Comparison." *College Composition and Communication* 38 (1987): 474–77. Liszka offers a method that helps students to generate theses and guides them in organizing and developing their essays; the method appears to be adaptable to various kinds of essays.

dev
1f

The thesis will not usually leap fully formed into your head. Even when you begin with an idea you want to communicate, you will need to refine that idea to fit the realities of the paper you write. And often you will have to write and rewrite before you come to a conclusion about what you have. Still, it's wise to try to pin down your thesis when you have a fairly good stock of ideas. Then it can help you start drafting, help keep you focused, and serve as a point of reference when changes inevitably occur.

1 Conceiving your thesis sentence

A good way to develop your thesis is to frame it in a **thesis sentence.** The thesis sentence gives you a vehicle for expressing your thesis at an early stage, and eventually it or (more likely) a revised version may be placed in the introduction of your final essay as a promise to readers of what they can expect.

ESL In some cultures it is considered rude or unnecessary for a writer to state his or her main idea outright or to state it near the beginning. But readers of English usually expect a clear and early idea of what a writer has to say.

As an expression of the thesis, the thesis sentence serves two crucial functions and one optional one:

Functions of the thesis sentence

- It narrows the topic to a single, central idea that you want readers to gain from your essay.
- It names the topic and asserts something specific and significant about it.
- It often provides a concise preview of how you will arrange your ideas in the essay.

Here are some examples of topics and corresponding thesis sentences (with the topic and assertion highlighted in brackets):

Topic	Thesis sentence
1. The pecking order in an office	Two months working in a large government agency taught me that an office's pecking order should be respected. [*Topic:* office's pecking order. *Assertion:* should be respected.]
2. The dynamics of single-parent families	In families consisting of a single parent and a single child, the boundaries between parent and child may disappear so that the two interact like siblings or like a married couple. [*Topic:* boundaries between parent and child. *Assertion:* may disappear.]

TRANSPARENCY MASTER 1.5

IMPLIED VERSUS EXPLICIT THESIS

Students need to understand that all good writing has a controlling idea (an implied thesis) but that some good writing doesn't have an explicit thesis. Asking students to look for theses in various kinds of writing (from textbooks to novels to travel articles to junk mail) is one way of showing them that a writer must decide whether to use an explicit thesis based on his or her purpose and audience.

ORAL PROGRESS REPORTS

Have students report orally to the class or to their peer writing groups on topics and thesis statements for a coming paper. Giving an oral presentation forces students to focus their ideas and adopt a stance. As they speak, moreover, students may sense difficulties with the topic or thesis. Comments from classmates can help identify strengths and weaknesses and suggest an appropriate tone for the essay.

3. What public relations does	Although most of us are unaware of the public relations campaigns directed at us, they can significantly affect the way we think and live. [*Topic:* public relations campaigns. *Assertion:* affect the way we think and live.]
4. Preventing juvenile crime	Juveniles can be diverted from crime by active learning programs, full-time sports, and intervention by mentors and role models. [*Topic:* juveniles. *Assertion:* can be diverted from crime in three ways.]
5. Abraham Lincoln's delay in emancipating the slaves	Lincoln delayed emancipating any slaves until 1863 because his primary goal was to restore and preserve the Union, with or without slavery. [*Topic:* Lincoln's delay. *Assertion:* was caused by his goal of preserving the Union.]
6. Federal aid to college students	To compete well in the global economy, the United States must make higher education affordable for any student who qualifies academically. [*Topic:* United States. *Assertion:* must make higher education affordable.]
7. The effects of strip-mining	Strip-mining should be tightly controlled in this region to reduce its pollution of water resources, its destruction of the land, and its devastating effects on people's lives. [*Topic:* strip-mining. *Assertion:* should be tightly controlled for three reasons.]

Notice that sentences 4 and 7 clearly predict the organization of the essay that will follow. Notice, too, that every sentence conveys the purpose of its writer. Sentences 1–5 announce that the writers mainly want to explain something to readers: office pecking order, family dynamics, public relations, and so on. Sentences 6 and 7 announce that the authors mainly want to convince readers of something: the federal government should aid college students; strip-mining should be controlled.

 Drafting and revising your thesis sentence

To draft a thesis sentence, ask these questions:

- What conclusion can I draw from the work I have done so far?
- How can I express that idea by naming the topic and making an assertion about it?
- How can I convey my purpose in that assertion?

TEACHING TIP

Often the exercise of condensing the main ideas of a paper in a separate forum can help writers recognize and articulate their thesis. Ask students to set their paper-in-progress aside and write a short (three sentence to one paragraph) abstract summarizing its central argument.

STUDENT MODELS

You may wish to copy effective thesis statements from student papers to use in class discussion or small-group work. The statements will provide positive models and may suggest topics for future essays. You can vary this exercise by copying ineffective statements and discussing how they may be revised. Be sure to keep the discussion of ineffective statements positive in tone, however.

To answer these questions, you may need to write one or more drafts of your essay. And you may need multiple drafts of the thesis sentence itself.

Terry Perez went through a common procedure in writing and revising her thesis sentence on cultural diversity in the media. After gathering her thoughts into a conclusion, she then stated her topic and commented on it:

> Television, newspapers, and magazines present contrasting views of the United States.

This sentence focused on Perez's topic but did not specify what the contrasting views are. Nor did it convey Perez's purpose in writing. Realizing as much, Perez rewrote the sentence:

> The media image of the United States is unrealistic, and people are depicted as being either in ethnic conflict or blissfully all the same.

This sentence solved the problems with the previous try: Perez clearly wanted to explain a media image that she disputed (she found it *unrealistic*). But Perez now needed to make a unified statement by pulling together the two halves that were separated by *and:*

> The media project unrealistic images of the United States as a nation of either constant ethnic conflict or untroubled homogeneity.

In this sentence Perez succeeded in stating her topic (*the media*) and making a specific, significant assertion about the topic (*project unrealistic images*). (Notice that she substituted the word *homogeneity,* which she learned from her sociology textbook, for the phrase *all the same. Homogeneity* means "similarity in kind.") In specifying the contrasting false images, Perez also forecast the organization of her essay.

When you are writing and revising your thesis sentence, check it against the following questions:

Checklist for revising the thesis sentence

- Does the sentence make an *assertion* about your topic?
- Is the assertion *limited* to only one idea?
- Is the assertion *specific* and *significant?*
- Does the sentence convey your *purpose?*
- Is the sentence *unified* so that the parts relate to each other?

Here are other examples of thesis sentences revised to meet these requirements:

SUPPLYING AN OMITTED THESIS STATEMENT

Ask students to read their papers to the class or to a peer group, deliberately leaving out the thesis statement. Ask the other students to supply a thesis for the essay. If the original thesis and the one supplied by the students match, fine. If not, the thesis a student has chosen may be inappropriate for the paper and the discussion that follows can suggest possible revisions.

COLLABORATIVE LEARNING

ASKING READERS TO AGREE ON THE THESIS

Ask students to read an essay from a collection or a fellow student's paper and then to state

FAULTY ORIGINAL	REVISED
This new product brought in over $300,000 last year. [A statement of fact, not an assertion: what is significant about the product's success?]	This new product succeeded because of its innovative marketing campaign, including widespread press coverage, in-store entertainment, and a consumer newsletter.
People should not go on fad diets. [A vague statement that needs limiting with one or more reasons: what's wrong with fad diets?]	Fad diets can be dangerous when they deprive the body of essential nutrients or rely on excessive quantities of potentially harmful foods.
Televised sports are different from live sports. [A general statement: how are they different, and why is the difference significant?]	Although television cannot transmit all the excitement of a live game, its close-ups and slow-motion replays more than compensate.
Seat belts can save lives, but now carmakers are installing air bags. [Not unified: how do the two parts of the sentence relate?]	If drivers had used lifesaving seat belts more often, carmakers might not have needed to install air bags.

Exercise 15
Evaluating thesis sentences

Evaluate the following thesis sentences, considering whether each one is sufficiently limited, specific, and unified. Rewrite the sentences as necessary to meet these goals.

1. Aggression usually leads to violence, injury, and even death, and we should use it constructively.
2. Gun control is essential.
3. One evening of a radio talk show amply illustrates both the appeal of such shows and their silliness.
4. Good manners make our society work.
5. The poem is about motherhood.

Exercise 16
Considering your past work: Developing a thesis

Have you been aware in the past of focusing your essays on a central idea, or thesis? Have you found it more efficient to try to pin down your idea early or to let it evolve during drafting? To what extent has a thesis helped or hindered you in shaping your draft?

Exercise 17
Drafting and revising your own thesis sentence

Continuing from Exercise 14 (p. 47), write a limited, specific, and unified thesis sentence for your essay-in-progress.

its thesis in their own words. If students are working in groups, ask the group members whether they can agree on the thesis. Next have the students try to identify a thesis statement in the essay. If the essay has an explicit thesis statement, ask if they consider it effective or if the thesis statement they produced would be more effective. If the thesis is implicit, ask students whether or not the essay would benefit from an explicit thesis statement.

ANSWERS: EXERCISE 15

1. The sentence lacks unity because the two halves do not seem to relate to each other.
   Possible revision: We should channel our natural feelings of aggression toward constructive rather than destructive ends.
2. Both halves of the sentence need to be more specific: What kind of gun control? Essential for what end?
   Possible revision: To curb the rising rate of murder with handguns, restrictions on the sale of handguns should be legislated and strictly enforced.
3. Good thesis sentence: limited, specific, and unified.
4. Both *good manners* and *make our society work* need to be more specific.
   Possible revision: Courtesy between people makes human interaction smoother and more efficient.
5. The sentence simply states a fact.
   Possible revision: The poem makes motherhood seem a saintly calling.

ANSWERS: EXERCISE 16

Individual response.

COLLABORATIVE LEARNING

In preparation for Exercise 17 have students work in small groups to discuss and expand on the topic ideas generated in Exercise 14.

ANSWERS: EXERCISE 17

Individual response.

WRITING PATTERNS (ESL)

In some cultures, expository writing patterns are circular rather than linear: students will repeat or restate the topic sentence before going on to the next topic. As a result, students seem to be "writing in circles" when they are simply following the pattern they have been taught. Explain to students that in American expository writing development is linear; that transitions, not restated topics, link ideas together in a paper; and that the conclusion is the point at which ideas are restated or summarized.

- I. Introduction with thesis
  - A. Idea 1
    - 1. Support
  - B. Idea 2 (with transition)
    - 1. Support
- II. Conclusion
  - A. Summarize ideas
  - B. Restate thesis in a fresh way

RESOURCES AND IDEAS

Lotto, Edward. "Utterance and Text in Freshman English." *College English* 51 (1989): 677–87. Lotto analyzes the differences between spoken and written language as they relate to the difficulties students have in supporting generalizations with concrete examples. He makes suggestions for helping students become aware of text and concrete expression.

Perdue, Virginia. "The Politics of Teaching Detail." *Rhetoric Review* 8 (1990): 280–88. Perdue provides methods for using detail to arrive at broader thoughts in the composing process.

Walvoord, Barbara, Virginia Johnson Anderson, John R. Breihan, Lucille Parkinson McCarthy, Susan Miller Robinson, and A. Kimbrough Sherman. "Functions of Outlining Among College Students in Four Disciplines." *Research in the Teaching of English* 29 (1995): 390–421. The authors demonstrate the varying functions served by outlining across the disciplines and explore the strategies that students use in different situations.

1g Organizing your ideas

An effective essay has a recognizable shape—an arrangement of parts that guides readers, helping them see how ideas and details relate to each other and contribute to the whole. You may sometimes let an effective organization emerge over one or more drafts. But many writers find that organizing ideas to some extent before drafting can provide a helpful sense of direction, as a map can help a driver negotiate a half-familiar system of roads. If you feel uncertain about the course your essay should follow or have a complicated topic with many parts, devising a shape for your material can clarify your options.

Before you begin organizing your material, look over all the writing you've done so far—freewriting, notes from reading, lists, whatever. Either on paper or on a computer, pull together a master list of all the ideas and details you think you may want to include. Leave wide margins for additions that will occur to you as you think about shape.

1 Distinguishing the general and the specific

To organize material for an essay, you need to distinguish general and specific ideas and see the relations between ideas. **General** and **specific** refer to the number of instances or objects included in a group signified by a word. The following "ladder" illustrates a general-to-specific hierarchy.

MOST GENERAL
↑ life form
plant
flowering plant
rose
American Beauty rose
↓ Uncle Dan's prize-winning American Beauty rose
MOST SPECIFIC

Here are some tips for arranging your ideas:

- Underline, boldface, or circle the most general ideas. These are the ideas that offer the main support for your thesis sentence. They will be more general than the evidence that in turn supports them.
- Make connections between each general idea and the more specific details that support it. On paper, start with a fresh sheet, write each general idea down with space beneath it, and add specific information in the appropriate spaces. On a computer, rearrange supporting information under more general

points. You can also use the annotation feature on many word-processing programs to add notes about connections.

- As you sort ideas, respect their meanings. Otherwise, your hierarchies could become jumbled, with *rose* illogically subordinated to *animal*, or *life form* somehow subordinated to *rose*.
- Once you have sorted out general ideas and specific supporting information, delete information that has no place, or fill in holes where support is skimpy.
- Experiment with various arrangements of your general ideas and their supporting information, seeking an order that presents your material clearly and logically. This experiment is easy to do on a computer: save the master list, duplicate it, and then use the computer's copy and paste functions to move material around. You can also experiment on paper by cutting the master list apart, allotting one general idea to each slip of paper, and arranging the slips in different orders.

2 Choosing an organizing tool

Some writers view outlines as chores and straitjackets, but they need not be dull or confining. There are many different kinds of outlines, some more flexible than others. All of them can enlarge and clarify your thinking, showing you patterns of general and specific, suggesting proportions, highlighting gaps or overlaps in coverage. The outlining function of most word-processing programs simplifies the construction and revision of an outline with automatic indentions, numbering, and other features.

Many writers use outlines not only before but also after drafting—to check the underlying structure of the draft when revising it (see p. 68). No matter when it's made, though, an outline can change to reflect changes in your thinking. You should view any outline you make as a tentative sketch, not as a fixed paint-by-numbers diagram.

Using a scratch or informal outline

For many essays, especially those with a fairly straightforward structure, a simple listing of ideas and perhaps their support may provide adequate direction for your writing. A **scratch outline** lists the key points of the paper in the order they will be covered.

Here is Terry Perez's scratch outline for her essay on diversity in the media:

THESIS SENTENCE

The media project unrealistic images of the United States as a nation of either constant ethnic conflict or untroubled homogeneity.

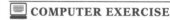

COMPUTER EXERCISE

Ask students to use the bold function or particular fonts to highlight general ideas and distinguish them from specific ideas.

PURPOSE OUTLINES

Some students have trouble maintaining unity of purpose and coherent organization even after they have outlined an essay because the outline describes the content of the essay but does not indicate the function of each part. To help students overcome this problem, ask them to add a statement of purpose to each major section of their outlines and to indicate how the section will carry out the purpose of the paper, as in this example:

> In this section I plan to explain how much money industries lose by failing to treat industrial waste to recover precious metals like chromium, gold,

silver, and platinum. This will be the second of the three little-known costs of pollution that my thesis statement promises the paper will discuss.

Statements of purpose can alert students to potential problems in the organization or unity of an essay, and they can provide instructors with a quick way to spot the problems. Some instructors even ask students to submit "purpose outlines" in place of formal outlines:

> In this section of the paper, I plan to show that there is a real need for this university to provide more funds for the library. To support my point, I plan to explore three serious effects of underfunding—lack of basic reference materials, lack of staff to shelve books properly and check for missing volumes, and poor maintenance of the library building.

USING VISUAL CUES

Some students find it handy to write their purpose statement or thesis on squares of stick-on paper and post these on their drafts, over their desks, or on the monitor of their word processors, in order to keep these ideas clearly in mind.

Scratch outline

Media images—
  Ethnic conflict
    —news stories—examples
    —the real story—examples
  Sameness—homogeneity
    —TV sitcoms and ads: the happy (white) family
    —the real story—examples

Perez put more into this outline than its simplicity might indicate. She worked out the order in which she would cover the media's contradictory images. And under each type of image she established a pattern of contrasting examples from the media and from real life. Perez might have begun drafting from this outline, but she opted to expand it first into a detailed formal outline (see p. 56).

An **informal outline** is usually more detailed than a scratch outline, including key general points and the specific evidence for them. Here is a student's informal outline:

Thesis sentence

The main street of my neighborhood contains enough variety to make almost any city dweller feel at home.

Informal outline

The beginning of the street
  high-rise condominium occupied by well-to-do people
  ground floor of building: an art gallery
  across the street: a delicatessen
  above the delicatessen: a tailor's shop, a camera-repair shop, a lawyer's office
The middle of the street
  four-story brick apartment buildings on both sides
  at ground level: an Italian bakery and a Spanish bodega
  people sitting on steps
  children playing
The end of the street
  a halfway house for drug addicts
  a boarding house for retired men
  a discount drugstore
  an expensive department store
  a wine shop
  another high-rise condominium

Using a tree diagram

In a **tree diagram** ideas and details branch out in increasing specificity. Like any outline, the diagram can warn of gaps, overlaps, and digressions. But unlike more linear outlines, it can be supplemented and extended indefinitely, so it is easy to alter for new ideas and arrangements discovered during drafting and revision.

Following is Johanna Abrams's tree diagram, based on her earlier list of ideas on a summer job (pp. 41–42). Each main part of the four-part diagram represents a different general idea about the summer-job experience. Within each part, information grows more specific as it branches downward.

Thesis sentence

Two months working in a large government agency taught me that an office's pecking order should be respected.

Tree diagram

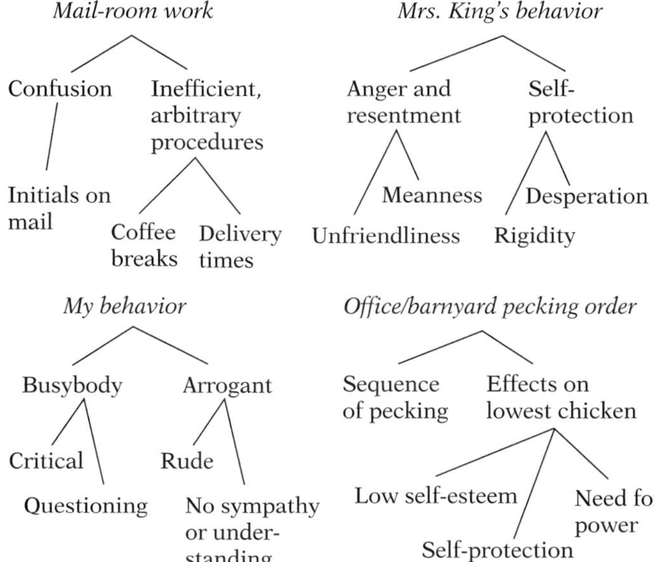

Using a formal outline

For complex topics requiring complex arrangements of ideas and support, you may want or be required to construct a **formal outline.** More rigidly arranged and more detailed than other outlines, a formal outline not only lays out main ideas and their support but also shows the relative importance of all the essay's elements and how they connect with each other.

Note Because of its structure, a formal outline can be an excellent tool for checking a draft before revising it. See page 68.

On the basis of her scratch outline (p. 54), Terry Perez prepared this formal outline for her essay on cultural diversity in the media:

COLLABORATIVE LEARNING

PRACTICING OUTLINING STRATEGIES

Ask each group of students to outline the same essay. Then have the entire class compare the outlines—where they agree and where they differ. This exercise helps students see how different readers perceive different kinds of organizational cues and react to them.

Thesis sentence

The media project unrealistic images of the United States as a nation of either constant ethnic conflict or untroubled homogeneity.

Formal outline

I. Images of ethnic conflict, not coexistence
  A. News stories
    1. Ethnic gang wars
    2. Defaced Jewish synagogues and cemeteries
    3. Korean and non-Korean disputes
    4. Burned African American churches
  B. The real story
    1. No war among groups
    2. Coexistence among groups
II. Images of untroubled homogeneity, not diversity
  A. People pictured in TV shows and ads
    1. Mainly white people
    2. Mainly middle-class people
    3. Mainly attractive people
  B. People missing from TV shows and ads
    1. Ethnic groups
    2. Poor people
    3. Other groups

Perez's outline illustrates several principles of outlining that can help ensure completeness, balance, and clear relationships. (These principles largely depend on distinguishing between the general and the specific. See p. 52.)

- All the outline's parts are systematically indented and labeled: Roman numerals (I, II) for primary divisions of the essay; indented capital letters (A, B) for secondary divisions; further indented Arabic numerals (1, 2) for principal supporting examples. A level of detail below the Arabic numbers would be indented further still and labeled with small letters (a, b). Each succeeding level contains more specific information than the one before it.
- The outline divides the material into several groups. An uninterrupted listing of ideas like the one following would indicate a need for tighter, more logical relationships among ideas. (Compare this example with part II of Perez's actual outline.)

II. Images of untroubled homogeneity, not diversity
  A. Mainly white people
  B. Mainly middle-class people
  C. Mainly attractive people
  D. No ethnic groups
  E. No poor people
  F. Other groups also missing

Principles of the formal outline

- Labels and indentions indicate order and relative importance.
- Sections and subsections reflect logical relationships.
- Topics of equal generality appear in parallel headings.
- Each subdivision has at least two parts.
- Headings are expressed in parallel grammatical form.
- The introduction and conclusion may be omitted (though not, of course, from the essay).

- Within each part of the outline, distinct topics of equal generality appear in parallel headings (with the same indention and numbering or lettering). In the following example points C and D are more specific than point B, not equally general, so they should be subheadings 1 and 2 under it. (See section IB of Perez's outline.)

    B. The real story
    C. No war among groups
    D. Coexistence among groups

- All subdivided headings in the outline break into at least two parts because a topic cannot logically be divided into only one part. The following example violates this principle.

    B. The real story: no war among groups
        1. Coexistence among groups

  Any single subdivision should be matched with another subdivision (as in section IB of Perez's outline), combined with the heading above it, or rechecked for its relevance to the heading above it.
- All headings are expressed in parallel grammatical form. Perez's is a topic outline, in which each heading consists of a noun plus modifiers. In a sentence outline all headings are expressed as full sentences, as in this rewrite of part I of Perez's outline.

    I. The media project images of ethnic conflict, not coexistence.
        A. News stories emphasize incidents of conflict.
            1. Some gang wars occurred between ethnic groups.
            2. Some Jewish synagogues and cemeteries were defaced.
            3. Some Korean shopkeepers got into disputes with non-Korean customers.
            4. Some African American churches were burned by white teenagers.
        B. The real story is quite different.
            1. Groups are not at war with each other.
            2. Groups coexist with each other.

- The outline covers only the body of the essay, omitting the introduction and the conclusion (see "Choosing a Structure," below). The beginning and the ending are important in the essay itself, but you need not include them in the outline unless you are required to do so or anticipate special problems with their organization.

3 Choosing a structure

Most essays share a basic shape consisting of an introduction, a body, and a conclusion.

- The **introduction,** usually a paragraph or two, draws readers into the world of the essay, stating the topic and often the thesis sentence. It makes a commitment that the rest of the essay delivers on. (See pp. 117–19.)
- The **body** of the essay is its long center, the part that develops the thesis and thus fulfills the commitment of the introduction. The paragraphs in the body develop the general points that support the thesis—the items that would be labeled with Roman numerals and capital letters in a formal outline like the one on page 56. These general points are like the legs of a table supporting the top, the thesis. Each general point may take a paragraph or more, with the bulk of the content providing the details, examples, and reasons (the wood of the table) to support the general point and thus the thesis.
- The **conclusion** generally gives readers something to take away from the essay—a summary of ideas, for instance, or a suggested course of action. (See pp. 120–21.)

In almost any writing situation, at least one of the schemes listed below will be appropriate for organizing the body of your essay. These schemes are so familiar that readers expect them and look for them. Thus the schemes both help you arrange your material and help readers follow you.

Schemes for organizing ideas in an essay

- Space
- Time
- Emphasis

General to specific	Increasing importance
Specific to general	Decreasing familiarity
Problem-solution	Increasing complexity

Organizing by space or time

Two organizational schemes—spatial and chronological—grow naturally out of the topic. A **spatial organization** is especially appropriate for essays that describe a place, an object, or a person. Following the way people normally survey something, you move through space from a chosen starting point to other features of the subject. Describing a friend, for instance, you might begin with his shoes and move upward or begin with his face and move downward. The informal outline on page 54 illustrates a spatial organization, moving from one end of the street to the other.

A **chronological organization** reports events as they occurred in time, usually from first to last. This pattern, like spatial organization, corresponds to readers' own experiences and expectations. It suits an essay in which you do one of the following:

- Tell a story about yourself or someone else.
- Explain a process from beginning to end—for instance, how to run a marathon or how a tree converts carbon dioxide to oxygen.
- Recount a sequence of events, such as a championship baseball game or the Battle of Gettysburg.
- Explain the causes that led to an effect, such as a bill passed by the legislature or a car model's design. Alternatively, explain how a cause, such as a flood or a book, had multiple effects.
- Provide the background to a situation—for instance, the separate lives of a group of friends who gather to help in a soup kitchen or the making of a movie that turned out to be a hit.

A chronological organization structures the essay on pages 83–84.

Organizing for emphasis

Some organizational schemes must be imposed on ideas and information to aid readers' understanding and achieve a desired emphasis. Two of these depend on the distinction between the general and the specific, discussed on page 52. The **general-to-specific scheme** is common in expository and argumentative essays that start with a general discussion of the main points and then proceed to specific examples, facts, or other evidence. The following thesis sentence forecasts a general-to-specific organization:

> To compete well in the global economy, the United States must make higher education affordable for any student who qualifies academically.

The body of the essay might first elaborate on the basic argument and then provide the supporting data.

In some expository or argumentative essays, a **specific-to-general scheme** can arouse readers' interest in specific examples or other evidence, letting the evidence build to more general ideas. The following thesis sentence could be developed in this way:

> Although most of us are unaware of the public relations campaigns directed at us, they can significantly affect the way we think and live.

The writer might devote most of the essay to a single specific example of a public relations campaign and then explain more generally how the example typifies public relations campaigns.

Many argumentative essays use a **problem-solution scheme:** first outline a problem that needs solving; then propose a solution. (If the solution involves steps toward a goal, it may be arranged chronologically.) The following thesis sentence announces a problem-solution paper:

> To improve work flow and quality, the data-processing department should add one part-time staffer and retrain three others in the new systems.

A complete problem-solution paper appears on pages 157–60.

A common scheme in both explanations and arguments is the **climactic organization,** in which ideas unfold in order of increasing drama or importance to a climax. For example, the following thesis sentence lists three effects of strip-mining in order of their increasing severity, and the essay would cover them in the same order:

> Strip-mining should be tightly controlled in this region to reduce its pollution of water resources, its destruction of the land, and its devastating effects on people's lives.

As this example suggests, the climactic organization works well in arguments because it leaves readers with the most important point freshest in their minds. In exposition such an arrangement can create suspense and thus hold readers' attention.

Expository essays can also be arranged in variations of the climactic pattern. An essay on the effects of air pollution might proceed from **most familiar to least familiar**—from effects readers are likely to know to ones they may not know. Similarly, an essay on various computer languages might proceed from **simplest to most complex,** so that the explanation of each language provides a basis for readers to understand the more difficult one following.

RESOURCES AND IDEAS

Suggest that students also read 3b for more suggestions on improving the links within and between paragraphs.

 4 Checking for unity and coherence

In conceiving your organization and writing your essay, you should be aware of two qualities of effective writing that relate to organization: unity and coherence. When you perceive that someone's writing "flows well," you are probably appreciating these two qualities. An essay has **unity** if all its parts relate to and support the thesis sentence. Check for unity with these questions:

- Is each main section relevant to the main idea (thesis) of the essay?
- Within main sections of the outline, does each example or detail support the principal idea of that section?

An essay has **coherence** if readers can see the relations among parts and move easily from one thought to the next. Check for coherence with these questions:

- Do the ideas follow in a clear sequence?
- Are the parts of the essay logically connected?
- Are the connections clear and smooth?

A unified and coherent outline will not necessarily guide you to a unified and coherent essay, because so much can change during drafting. Thus you shouldn't be too hard on your outline, in case a seemingly wayward idea proves useful. But do cut obvious digressions and rearrange material that clearly needs moving.

The unity and coherence of an essay begin in its paragraphs, so these two concepts are treated in greater detail in Chapter 3. You may want to consult several sections in particular before you begin drafting:

- The topic sentence and unity (pp. 87–90).
- Transitions and coherence (pp. 92–102, 122).
- Linking paragraphs in the essay (pp. 123–25).

Note Unity and coherence may seem unimportant with electronic hypertext, such as a site on the World Wide Web, in which entire documents are linked to each other so that it's easy to move among them. True, an effective hypertext document may not flow in the way we expect from conventional nonfiction, and following links may require seemingly abrupt changes of course. But the notions of unity and coherence still apply: Are all the links clearly related to the central idea of the main document? Do the links extend or support the central idea (instead of merely decorating it)? Does each link have a clear point of its own?

Exercise 18
Organizing ideas

The following list of ideas was extracted by a student from freewriting he did for a brief paper on soccer in the United States. Using his thesis sentence as a guide, pick out the general ideas and

Sloan, Gary. "The Frequency of Transitional Markers in Discursive Prose." *College English* 46 (1984): 158–79. Sloan shows how infrequently explicit transition markers are used by either professional or student writers.

Smith, Rochelle. "Paragraphing for Coherence: Writing as Implied Dialogue." *College English* 46 (1984): 8–21. Smith uses reader-response theory and the notion of author-reader dialogue to improve paragraph cohesion.

Witte, Stephen P., and Lester Faigley. "Coherence, Cohesion, and Writing Quality." *College Composition and Communication* 32 (1981): 189–204. Students need to learn the features of coherence that extend across sentence boundaries; the article stresses ways to make them aware of coherence strategies.

ANSWERS: EXERCISES 18 AND 19

Possible answer

I. Fans resist [new general idea].
  A. Sports seasons are already too crowded for fans.
    1. Baseball, football, hockey, and basketball seasons already overlap.
    2. Fans have limited time to watch.
    3. Fans have limited money to pay for sports.

dev 1g

B. Soccer is unfamiliar [new general idea].
   1. A lot of kids play soccer in school, but the game is still "foreign."
   2. Soccer rules are unfamiliar.

II. Backers resist [new general idea].
   A. Sports money goes where the money is.
      1. Soccer fans couldn't fill huge stadiums.
      2. Backers are concerned with TV contracts.
      3. TV contracts almost matter more than live audiences.
      4. American soccer fans are too few for TV interest.
   B. Backers are wary of losing money on new ventures.
      1. Failure of the U.S. Football League was costly.
      2. Previous attempts to start a pro soccer league failed.

COLLABORATIVE LEARNING

Ask students to compare their responses to Exercise 18 and then to work in pairs to create the formal outline described in Exercise 19. The discussions necessitated by this collaborative project encourage students to think through and articulate an organizational logic.

COMPUTER EXERCISE

The flexibility of the computer software's cut-and-paste or block-and-move features allows students to arrange ideas in various orders and then to consider the result. As a follow-up to Exercise 18 and 19, pose a thesis statement (such as one of the revised examples from Exercise 15), then have students brainstorm on the computer to come up with a related list of ideas and organize them into several possible outlines.

ANSWERS: EXERCISE 20

Individual response.

ANSWERS: EXERCISE 21

Individual response.

arrange the relevant specific points under them. In some cases you may have to infer general ideas to cover specific points in the list.

Thesis sentence

Despite the 1994 World Cup competition held in the United States, soccer may never be the sport here that it is elsewhere because both the potential fans and the potential backers resist it.

List of ideas

Sports seasons are already too crowded for fans.
Soccer rules are confusing to Americans.
A lot of kids play soccer in school, but the game is still "foreign."
Sports money goes where the money is.
Backers are wary of losing money on new ventures.
Fans have limited time to watch.
Fans have limited money to pay for sports.
Backers are concerned with TV contracts.
Previous attempts to start a pro soccer league failed.
TV contracts almost matter more than live audiences.
Failure of the US Football League was costly.
Baseball, football, hockey, and basketball seasons already overlap.
Soccer fans couldn't fill huge stadiums.
American soccer fans are too few for TV interest.

Exercise 19
Creating a formal outline

Use your arrangement of general ideas and specific points from Exercise 18 as the basis for a formal topic or sentence outline. Follow the principles given on pages 56–58.

Exercise 20
Considering your past work: Organizing ideas

What has been your experience with organizing your writing? Many writers find it difficult. If you do, too, can you say why? What kinds of outlines or other organizing tools have you used? Which have been helpful and which not?

Exercise 21
Organizing your own essay

Continuing from Exercise 17 (p. 51), choose an appropriate organization for your essay-in-progress. Then, experiment with organizing tools by preparing a tree diagram or a scratch, informal, or formal outline.

Chapter 2

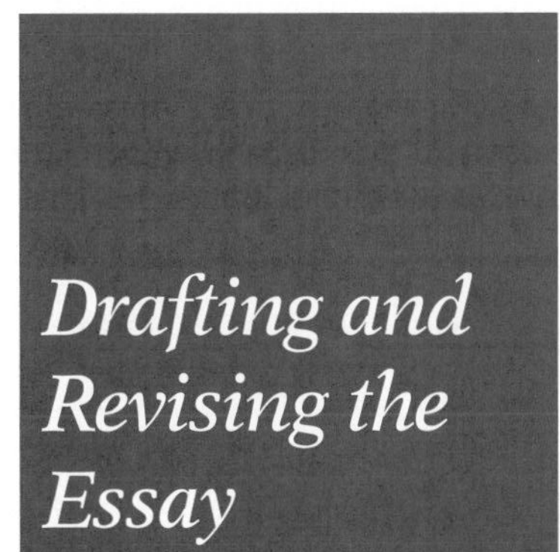

Drafting and Revising the Essay

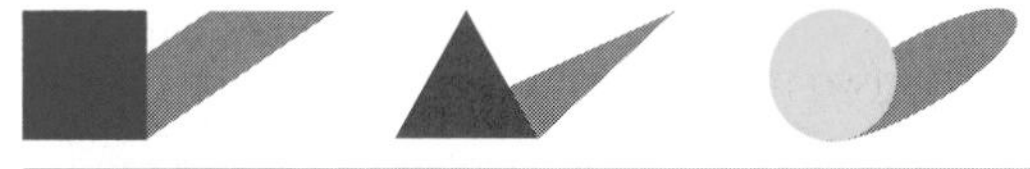

The separation of drafting and revising from the planning activities discussed in Chapter 1 is somewhat artificial because the stages almost always overlap during the writing process. Indeed, if you compose on a computer, you may not experience any boundaries between stages at all. Still, your primary goal during the writing process will usually shift from planning to forming connected sentences and paragraphs in a draft and then restructuring and rewriting the draft.

2a Writing the first draft

The only correct drafting style is the one that works for you. Generally, though, the freer and more fluid you are, the better. Some writers draft and revise at the same time, but most let themselves go during drafting and *especially* do not worry about errors. Drafting is the occasion to find and convey meaning through the act of writing. If you fear making mistakes while drafting, that fear will choke your ideas. You draft only for yourself, so errors do not matter. Write freely until you have worked out what you want to say; *then* focus on any mistakes you may have made.

Starting to draft sometimes takes courage, even for seasoned professionals. Students and pros alike find elaborate ways to procrastinate—rearranging shelves, napping, lunching with friends. Such procrastination may actually help you if you let ideas for writing simmer at the same time. At some point, though, enough is

HIGHLIGHTS

This chapter continues the exploration, begun in Chapter 1, of writing as a flexible process and looks in detail at strategies for drafting, revising, editing, and proofreading. The journey from initial draft to finished essay may involve many decisions and changes of direction for which there are no firm rules. To alert student writers to the options available to them, the chapter provides lists of strategies for drafting an essay and checklists for revising and editing. It also provides concrete advice for the stages of composing that many writers find the most difficult: getting started and completing the initial draft.

Students who view revising as an expendable stage in the writing process may benefit from following, draft by draft, the development of Terry Perez's essay (begun in Chapter 1) on media diversity in the portrayal of ethnic groups. Like most initial efforts, Perez's early draft can benefit from revisions in organization, content, tone, and approach to clarify the essay's purpose and the relationships among its ideas and also to make it easier for readers to share Perez's perspective. The revised draft, in turn, needs editing for clarity, style, and correction of errors in grammar, usage, punctuation, and spelling—changes that appear in the final version of the essay, along with the instructor's corrections and comments.

Teachers who draw on the handbook in correcting and commenting on student papers may wish to direct students' attention to the instructor's corrections on Terry Perez's full essay (pages 77–79); these corrections use a combination of the number-and-letter codes, symbols, and written comments. To familiarize students with use of the handbook, you can assign Exercise 10, which asks them to revise Perez's essay by making use of the instructor's comments. The additional student paper at the end of the chapter (Exercise 12) is also appropriate for class discussion and criticism. Both papers can provide material for small-group discussion and evaluation, and the section on benefiting from criticism (2e) can help students learn to work effectively in peer critique groups. "Commenting on others' writing" and "Benefiting from comments on your writing" on pages 80 and 81 clarify peer review in a helpful list format.

A WRITER'S PERSPECTIVE

I've never thought of myself as a good writer; anyone who wants reassurance of that should read one of my first drafts. But I'm one of the world's great rewriters.

—JAMES MICHENER

How can I know what I think until I see what I say?

—E. M. FORSTER

OVERCOMING WRITING BLOCKS

Many students have a hard time writing first drafts because they try to get everything right the first time. They end up writing sentences and then crossing out what they have written so often that they have no time left to revise their thoughts in a second draft. Sometimes the pressure of perfection is so great that students become blocked writers, unable to finish even a single draft before the deadline. Here are four ways to help students get started and to help them develop flexibility and self-confidence in their approach to the task:

1. Show them copies of your own first and final drafts to indicate that you were not afraid to make mistakes in the initial draft because you had a chance to correct them in the later versions.
2. Give students a time limit for the first draft, perhaps an hour and a half or two hours, depending on the length of the assignment. Require them to hand in the draft with the final paper so that you can see how they approached the task of writing.
3. Have students start writing in class, where you can encourage them to get ideas down on paper before they try to perfect the wording.
4. Require students to spend some time either jotting down ideas and phrases or freewriting so that they will be loosened up before tackling the initial draft.

TEACHING TIP

Writers can often become anxious about adding in or losing track of ideas that don't seem

enough: the deadline looms; you've got to get started. If the blankness still stares back at you, then try one of the following techniques for unblocking.

Ways to start drafting

- Read over what you've already written—notes, outlines, and so on—and immediately start your draft with whatever comes to mind.
- Freewrite (see p. 39).
- Write scribbles or type nonsense until words you can use start coming.
- Pretend you're writing to a friend about your topic.
- Conjure up an image that represents your topic—a physical object, a facial expression, two people arguing over something, a giant machine gouging the earth for a mine, whatever. Describe that image.
- Write a paragraph on what you think your essay will be about when you finish it.
- Skip the opening and start in the middle. Or write the conclusion.
- Using your outline, divide your essay into chunks—say, one for the introduction, another for the first point, and so on. Start writing the chunk that seems most eager to be written, the one you understand best or feel most strongly about.

You should find some momentum once you've started writing. If not, however, or if your energy flags, try one or more of the following techniques to keep moving ahead.

Ways to *keep* drafting

- Set aside enough time for yourself. (For a brief essay, a first draft is likely to take at least an hour or two.)
- Work in a place where you won't be interrupted.
- Make yourself comfortable.
- If you must stop working, leave a note with the draft about what you expect to do next. Then you can pick up where you stopped with minimal disruption.
- Be as fluid as possible, and don't worry about mistakes. Spontaneity will allow your attitudes toward your subject to surface naturally in your sentences, and it will also make you receptive to ideas and relations you haven't seen before. Mistakes will be easier to find and correct later, when you're not also trying to create.
- Keep going. Skip over sticky spots; leave a blank if you can't find the right word; put alternative ideas or phrasings in brackets so that you can consider them later without bogging down. If an

idea pops out of nowhere but doesn't seem to fit in, quickly jot it down on a separate sheet, or write it into the draft and bracket or boldface it for later attention. You can use an asterisk (*) or some other symbol to mark places where you feel blocked or uncertain. On a computer you can find these places later using the search command to locate the symbol.

- Resist self-criticism. Don't worry about your style, grammar, spelling, punctuation, and the like. Don't worry about what your readers will think. These are very important matters, but save them for revision. If you can't seem to resist self-criticism and you're using a computer, try invisible writing as described on page 40.
- Use your thesis sentence and outline to remind you of your planned purpose, organization, and content.
- But don't feel constrained by your thesis and outline. If your writing leads you in a more interesting direction, follow.

If you write on a computer, frequently save the text you're drafting—at least every twenty minutes or every couple of pages and every time you leave the computer. In addition, back up your drafts on a separate disk, and perhaps even print paper copies (so-called hard copy) in case anything happens to your disks.

Whether you compose on paper or on a computer, you may find it difficult to tell whether a first draft is finished. The distinction between drafts can be significant because creating text is different from rethinking it (see p. 67) and because your instructor may ask you and your classmates to submit your drafts, either on paper or over a computer network, so that others can give you feedback on them (see p. 80). For your own revision or others' feedback, you might consider a draft finished for any number of reasons: perhaps you've reached the assigned length and have run out of ideas; perhaps you find yourself writing the conclusion; perhaps you've stopped adding content and are just tinkering with words.

Terry Perez's first draft on diversity in the media appears below. (Her earlier work appears on pp. 39, 41, 50, 53–54, and 56.)

First draft

Title?

In "America: The Multinational Society," Ishmael Reed mentions that the communications media sensationalizes the "conflict between people of different backgrounds." Either that, or it depicts Americans as homogeneous. The media projects unrealistic images of the US as a nation either of constant ethnic conflict or untroubled homogeneity.

It is easy to find examples of the emphasizing of conflict among

to fit as they write out a rough draft. Students who are composing on the computer might keep a notebook nearby to scrawl down extra ideas that occur as they write. If your students' computer programs have a second document feature, you can also encourage students to shift quickly to a second document to note ideas that don't seem to fit into the document they're composing.

RESOURCES AND IDEAS

Bartholomae, David. "Inventing the University." In *When a Writer Can't Write: Studies in Writer's Block and Other Composing Process Problems*. Ed. Mike Rose. New York: Guilford, 1985. 134–65. Bartholomae points out that one of the factors causing blocks or writing anxiety may be an unfamiliarity with the community for which the writer is writing, and he suggests ways to familiarize writers with the discourse expectations of academic writing.

Bloom, Lynn Z. "Research on Writing Blocks, Writing Anxiety, and Writing Apprehension." In *Research in Composition and Rhetoric*. Ed. Michael G. Moran and Ronald F. Lunsford. Westport: Greenwood, 1984. 71–91. Bloom surveys research on the fears and blocks that many writers encounter and examines strategies, similar to those presented in this chapter, for overcoming the difficulties.

Rose, Mike. *Writer's Block: The Cognitive Dimension*. Carbondale: Southern Illinois UP, 1984. The case studies of student writers that Rose discusses demonstrate that blocked writers often follow rigid, absolute rules about the forms and process of writing, whereas fluent writers use flexible, enabling strategies.

ethnic groups. The news is full of stories of Hispanic gangs fighting African American gangs, Korean shopkeepers pitted against non-Korean customers, African American churches are burned by white teenagers. In fact, New York City, with its dense and ethnically diverse population, regularly supplies stories for other cities' news media when they run out of local stories of hate and mayhem. My brother who lives in San Francisco is always complaining about all the New York stories in the news. What he doesn't realize is that it's not New York's fault, it's the media's for always playing up the bad news. Bad news is what the media specializes in--as everyone is always complaining. When it comes to ethnic relations, this is certainly the case. All sorts of different people mingle together peacefully, but not in the media.

There the only peace belongs to a very narrow band of people. Especially in television fiction and advertising. They have usual characteristics: they are white, married or expecting to be someday, unethnic, white collar, well-to-do, settled, materialistic, good looking, and thin. Many, many groups are excluded from this TV type, such as ethnic groups, poor people, and the disabled. A certain commercial is typical of TV with the happy prosperous nuclear family enjoying breakfast together.

The problem with this media image, with its extremes of peace and conflict, is that it is untrue. It caters to the ones who feel that the US should be a "monoculture" and would be. If only we could battle down the ones who don't belong or won't. A different picture is possible, but we aren't getting it.

Exercise 1
Analyzing a first draft

Compare Perez's draft with the previous step in her planning (her formal outline) on page 56. List the places in the draft where the act of drafting led Perez to rearrange her information, add or delete material, or explore new ideas.

Exercise 2
Considering your past work: Drafting

Think back over a recent writing experience. At what point in the writing process did you begin drafting? How did drafting go—

ANSWERS: EXERCISE 1

Possible answers

Some significant differences between Perez's outline and her first draft:

In paragraph 2 Perez followed a thread about the media and New York City.

In paragraph 3 she expanded the description of the typical media presentation and added an example.

In paragraph 4 she broached the idea of a "different picture" the media could be presenting.

COLLABORATIVE LEARNING

Ask students to work in groups to complete Exercise 1, and to use that exercise as the occasion to discuss their own drafting processes (Exercise 2). Students can benefit a great deal both from articulating their habits, choices, and difficulties throughout the writing process and hearing how other writers work.

ANSWERS: EXERCISE 2

Individual response.

smoothly, haltingly, painfully, painlessly? If you had difficulties, what were they? If you didn't, why not?

Exercise 3
Drafting your own essay

Prepare a draft of the essay you began in Chapter 1. Use your thesis sentence and your outline as guides, but don't be unduly constrained by them. Concentrate on opening up options, not on closing them down. Do not, above all, worry about mistakes.

2b Revising the first draft

Revision literally means "re-seeing"—looking anew at ideas and details, their relationships and arrangement, the degree to which they work or don't work for the thesis. While drafting, you focus inwardly, concentrating on pulling your topic out of yourself. In revising, you look out to your readers, trying to anticipate how they will see your work. You adopt a critical perspective toward your work (see p. 1), examining your draft as a pole-vaulter or dancer would examine a videotape of his or her performance. (As noted below, writing teachers often ask students to read each other's drafts partly to train the students in using and benefiting from this critical perspective. See p. 80.)

Computerized word processing has removed the mechanical drudgery of revision. With a few keystrokes you can add, delete, and move words, lines, or whole passages. Writers disagree, though, over whether it's better to consider revisions on paper or on screen.

- Paper copy allows you to see the whole draft at once and may be easier to read accurately, but if your work is stored on a computer you then have to key in your changes.
- Working on a computer allows you to see changes as you make them and to experiment with different versions of the same passage, but it can prevent you from seeing your work as a whole.

Whatever your own preference, do take a couple of precautions: save successive drafts under their own file names in case you need to consult them for ideas or phrasings, and work on a duplicate of any draft you're revising so that the original remains intact until you're truly finished with it.

Reading your own work critically requires that you create some distance between it and yourself—not always an easy task. The following techniques may help.

ANSWERS: EXERCISE 3

Individual response.

RESOURCES AND IDEAS

Many writers find that the computer facilitates their composing and revision processes without realizing the extent to which the medium has changed the way we think and write. In "The Metaphor of Collage: Beyond Computer Composition," Russel Wiebe and Robert S. Dornsife Jr. argue that computers are not simply an addition to the classroom; rather, they revolutionize the way we and our students write and think about texts. The authors use the metaphor of a multimedia collage to describe the best pedagogical approach to these changes (*Journal of Advanced Composition* 15 (1995): 131–37). See also, Cynthia Selfe and Susan Hilligoss, *Literacy and Computers: the Complications of Teaching and Learning with Technology* (New York: MLA, 1994).

REVISION ACTIVITIES

Here are a few revision activities for students working on their own or in groups:

Making out an inventory. After students have written an initial draft, ask them to complete a brief version of the audience inventory described in Chapter 1 (p. 33). Their completed inventory can help guide the choices they make during revision. Students may wish to share drafts and inventories with other students.

Using dialogue. For narrative writing, ask students to circle every use of "He said that" and "She thought that" or similar phrases in their own or someone else's paper. Then ask them to consider replacing the indirect discourse with dialogue and direct quotations to make the writing more vivid and realistic.

Using the senses. For narrative and descriptive writing, ask students to check how many of the senses they have drawn on: then ask them to consider making use of the other senses.

Adding other arguments. For argumentative essays, have students list all the arguments they could use but have not yet included in the paper; they may wish to turn to other students for advice about including these arguments.

rev
2b

TRANSPARENCY MASTER 2.1

Soliciting class suggestions. For argumentative essays, ask students to summarize their theses and supporting arguments for their classmates. Then ask the other students to suggest more supporting arguments and opposing arguments the writer might consider during revision.

Answering more questions. For expository essays, ask students to answer these questions for their own or someone else's paper: What five things do you know about this topic that are not included in the draft? Which ones could be put into the essay without harming its unity or coherence? What three things are readers most likely to find interesting, useful, or surprising about this topic? Could these three things be given more emphasis without disrupting the organization or clarity of the essay?

RESOURCES AND IDEAS

Elbow, Peter. *Writing with Power: Techniques for Mastering the Writing Process.* New York: Oxford UP, 1981. Elbow's book offers detailed, practical, and often innovative advice on drafting, revising, shaping for an audience, and making use of feedback, including several chapters on revising ("Quick Revising," "Thorough Revising," "Revising with Feedback," and "Cut and Paste Revising and the Collage").

Rose, Mike. "Writing Around Rules." *Patterns in Action,* 2nd ed. Ed. Robert A. Schwegler. Glenview: Scott, 1988. 473–80. As an illustration of the kinds of rules that block writing and the kinds of strategies that enable it, Rose tells of the difficulties he encountered in titling a poem.

Sommers, Nancy. "Revision Strategies of Student Writers and Experienced Adult Writers." *College Composition and Communication* 31 (1980): 378–88. According to Sommers, students see revision as changes in small units—words and sentences. Experienced writers see it as a recursive process directed at larger units of the text and the meaning it conveys.

Sperling, Melanie. "Constructing the Perspective of Teacher as Reader: A Framework for Studying Response to Student Writing." *Re-*

Ways to gain distance from your work

- Take a break after finishing the draft to pursue some other activity. A few hours may be enough; a whole night or day is preferable. The break will clear your mind, relax you, and give you some objectivity.
- Ask someone to read and react to your draft. Many writing instructors ask their students to submit their first drafts so that the instructor and, often, the other members of the class can serve as an actual audience to help guide revision. (See also pp. 80–81 on receiving and benefiting from comments.)
- If you compose your draft in handwriting, retype it on a typewriter or computer before revising it. The act of transcription can reveal gaps in content or problems in structure.
- If you compose on a computer, print your draft on paper. You'll be able to view all pages of the draft at once, and the different medium can reveal weaknesses you didn't see on screen.
- Outline your draft. While reading it, highlight the main points supporting the thesis. Write these sentences down separately in outline form. (If you're working on a computer, you can copy and paste these sentences.) Then examine the outline you've made for logical order, gaps, and digressions. A formal outline can be especially illuminating because of its careful structure. (See pp. 52–58 for a discussion of outlining.)
- Listen to your draft: read it out loud, read it into a tape recorder and play the tape, or have someone read the draft to you. Experiencing your words with ears instead of eyes can alter your perceptions.
- Ease the pressure. Don't try to re-see everything in your draft at once. Use a checklist like the one opposite, making a separate pass through the draft for each item.

Strictly speaking, revision includes editing—refining the manner of expression to improve clarity or style or to correct errors. In this chapter, though, revision and editing are treated separately to stress their differences: in revision you deal with the underlying meaning and structure of your essay; in editing you deal with its surface. You can avoid the temptation to substitute editing for revision and prevent them from interfering with each other by making at least two separate drafts beyond the first: a revised one and then an edited one (p. 73).

This two-step approach can also save you from a common trap of computerized word processing: letting the ease of changing copy lure you into obsessive rewriting, a kind of wheel spinning in which changes cease to have any marked effect on meaning or clarity and may in fact sap the writing of energy. Planning to revise and then to edit encourages you to look beyond the confines of the screen so that deeper issues of meaning and structure aren't lost to surface matters such as word choice and sentence arrangement.

Set aside at least as much time to revise your essay as you took to draft it. Plan on going through the draft several times to answer the questions in the checklist below and to resolve any problems. (If you need additional information on any of the topics in the checklist, refer to the page numbers given in parentheses.) Note that the checklist can also help you if you have been asked to comment on another writer's draft (see p. 80).

Checklist for revision

See also specific revision checklists for arguments (p. 157), research papers (p. 596), and literary analyses (pp. 679–80).

- **Purpose:** What is the essay's purpose? Does that purpose conform to the assignment? Is it consistent throughout the paper? (See pp. 30–31.)
- **Thesis:** What is the thesis of the essay? Where does it become clear? How well do thesis and paper match: Does the paper stray from the thesis? Does it fulfill the commitment of the thesis? (See pp. 47–51.)
- **Structure:** What are the main points of the paper? (List them.) How well does each support the thesis? How effective is their arrangement for the paper's purpose? (See pp. 58–60.)
- **Development:** How well do details, examples, and other evidence support each main point? Where, if at all, might readers find support skimpy or have trouble understanding the content? (See pp. 31–35, 104–15.)
- **Tone:** What is the tone of the paper? How do particular words and sentence structures create the tone? How appropriate is it for the purpose, topic, and intended readers? Where is it most or least successful? (See pp. 33–34.)
- **Unity:** What does each sentence and paragraph contribute to the thesis? Where, if at all, do digressions occur? Should these be cut, or can they be rewritten to support the thesis? (See pp. 60–61, 87–90.)
- **Coherence:** How clearly and smoothly does the paper flow? Where does it seem rough or awkward? Can any transitions be improved? (See pp. 60–61, 92–102.)
- **Title, introduction, conclusion:** How accurately and interestingly does the title reflect the essay's content? (See p. 70.) How well does the introduction engage and focus readers' attention? (See pp. 117–19.) How effective is the conclusion in providing a sense of completion? (See pp. 120–21.)

search in the Teaching of English 28 (1994): 175–223. This article studies one teacher's responses to student papers in order to evaluate the impact of teacher comments on student writing.

QUESTIONING TABOOS

A good way to emphasize the distinction between revising and editing is to ask students to brainstorm a list of the taboos they've been taught about writing: "Don't begin sentences with I"; "Don't end sentences with prepositions"; "Never use contractions"; and so on. Then discuss the possible reasons for these rules and the occasions when they would apply. Once students understand the reasons for the rules they are much more able to check for usage errors in the editing process and to avoid allowing such taboos to hamper their revision processes.

COLLABORATIVE LEARNING

The revision checklist (p. 75) provides an effective worksheet for collaborative revision groups. If groups have trouble working through the entire checklist in one class session, you might have students begin by looking at each other's work for thesis, structure, and paragraph development, then have them read for additional elements like overall coherence, organization, introduction, title, and conclusion in a later session.

COLLABORATIVE LEARNING

Ask students to work with their revision group to create several possible titles for each other's revised drafts. This kind of discussion often helps the writer of each paper to reconsider and articulate the central aims of the piece.

RESOURCES AND IDEAS

Collaborative revision

Peer editing and collaborative learning have become regular features of many composition courses over the past decade, and these approaches are particularly well suited to drafting and revising activities. Section 2e coaches students in giving and receiving criticism. And the essay "Using Collaborative Learning with the Handbook" on pages IAE-49–IAE-62 offers detailed advice about designing collaborative activities and preparing students to work in groups. It also provides sample reader response forms, which you may wish to copy and use in your class.

Much has been written recently about collaborative learning and peer writing groups. See, for example, the *Journal of Advanced Composition* 14:1 (1994); the entire issue is devoted to issues of collaboration. The following two works offer good starting points for someone interested in examining both the opportunities offered by this approach and the controversies that it has created:

Gere, Anne Ruggles. *Writing Groups: History, Theory, and Implications*. Carbondale: Southern Illinois UP, 1987. Gere reviews the history, theory, and practice of writing groups and collaborative learning; she also provides a useful annotated bibliography of research and pedagogy.

Trimbur, John. "Collaborative Learning and Teaching Writing." In *Perspectives on Research and Scholarship in Composition*. Ed. Ben W. McClelland and Timothy R. Donovan. New York: MLA, 1985. 87–109. Trimbur offers a compact survey of the history and theories behind collaborative learning and raises important questions about the roles of response and evaluation in a student- (rather than teacher-) centered classroom.

A note on titling your essay

The revision stage is a good time to consider a title. After drafting, you have a clearer sense of your direction, and the attempt to sum up your essay in a title phrase can help you focus sharply on your topic, purpose, and audience.

Here are some suggestions for titling an essay:

- A **descriptive title** is almost always appropriate and is often expected for academic writing. It announces the topic clearly, accurately, and as briefly as possible. The title Terry Perez finally chose, "America's Media Image," is an example. Other examples are "Images of Lost Identity in *North by Northwest*"; "An Experiment in Small-Group Dynamics"; "Why Lincoln Delayed Emancipating the Slaves."
- A **suggestive title**—the kind often found in popular magazines—may be appropriate for more informal writing. Examples include "Making Peace" (for an essay on the Peace Corps) and "Royal Pain" (for an essay on Prince Charles of England). For a more suggestive title, Perez might have chosen something like "Distorted Pictures." Such a title conveys the writer's attitudes and main concerns but not the precise topic, thereby pulling readers into the essay to learn more. A source for such a title may be a familiar phrase, a fresh image, or a significant expression from the essay itself.
- A title tells readers how big the topic is. For Perez's essay, the title "Watching the Media" or "Cultural Diversity in American Society" would have been too broad, whereas "The Media and Cultural Conflict" or "Exclusion in the Media" would have been too narrow.
- A title should not restate the assignment or the thesis sentence, as in "What Ishmael Reed Means by Cultural Diversity" or "How I Feel About Cultural Diversity."

For more information on essay titles, see pages 286 (avoiding reference to the title in the opening of the paper), 431 (capitalizing words in a title), and 761 (the format of a title in the final paper).

In revising her first draft, Terry Perez had the help of her instructor and several of her classmates, to whom she showed the draft as part of her assignment. (See p. 80 for more on this kind of collaboration.) Based on the revision checklist, she felt that she wanted to stick with her initial purpose and thesis sentence and that they had held up well in the draft. But she also knew without being told that her introduction was too hurried and that the body of the essay was thin: she hadn't supplied enough details to support her ideas and convince her readers.

Perez's readers confirmed her self-criticism: some were confused by the introduction; others were unconvinced by her essay; everyone asked for more examples. And among other comments, her readers raised additional points that she had not considered. They are reflected in this comment by a classmate:

> I tend to agree with you about the media, but I'd be more willing to go along if you admitted somewhere that ethnic conflict *does* exist (TV and the papers don't just make it up!). Also, what about exceptions to the "TV type"—what about Bill Cosby or Roseanne? Finally, I don't see the point you're trying to make about New York, and your brother doesn't seem relevant at all. How does this relate to your thesis?

For her revision, Perez printed out a paper copy and then made changes directly on the draft. The revision begins on the next page. The principal changes are explained below and keyed to the revision by numbers (some numbers are used more than once).

1. With a fairly descriptive title, Perez intended to give readers a sense of her topic and also remind them that the media create an image for the nation as well as for politicians and movie stars.
2. Perez rewrote and expanded the previous abrupt introduction to give more of a sense of Reed's essay and to make a clearer transition to her additional point about the media (the new sentence beginning *Another false media picture*).
3. Perez's instructor and one of her classmates pointed out that *media* is a plural noun (*medium* is the singular) and thus takes a plural verb. Hence Perez's changes to *media sensationalize* and *media project.*
4. At these points Perez added examples and other details to support her general statements. This and the following category of changes occupied most of Perez's attention during revision.
5. In response to her classmates, Perez added several concessions and exceptions. As soon as she had written these passages, she saw that they strengthened her essay by balancing it.
6. Perez cut a digression that her readers had found distracting and irrelevant.
7. Her conclusion had received few comments in class, but Perez thought that it, too, needed revision. She concentrated on clarifying the opening of the paragraph and adding details about her own "picture" to the end.

RESOURCES AND IDEAS

Independent revision

Even though you encourage students to revise and offer them detailed advice about what and when to revise, you may still find that their revisions are limited to superficial changes. Part of the problem may be that students have not yet become good enough readers of their own texts to identify features that might be altered or dropped and to identify places where something might be added. Here are some resources for helping students to become active readers and writers, aware of what they have written and how it might be changed:

Beck, James P. "Asking Students to Annotate Their Own Papers." *College Composition and Communication* 33 (1982): 322–26. Beck asks students to identify specific techniques they have used in their writing (including features of structure, detail, argument, and style) and to evaluate how well they have used those techniques.

Sommers, Jeffrey. "The Effects of Tape-Recorded Commentary on Student Revision: A Case Study," *Journal of Teaching Writing* 8 (1989): 49–75. Sommers argues that students can misunderstand instructor response to their writing and demonstrates how tape-recorded responses led one student through a series of successive revisions.

Straub, Richard. "The Concept of Control in Teacher Response: Defining the Varieties of 'Directive' and 'Facilitative' Commentary." *College Composition and Communication* 47 (1996): 223–51. Straub reviews the influential studies on teacher response in an effort to identify the kinds of comments that encourage students to produce effective independent revisions.

ENCOURAGING REVISION

The only way to get students to revise regularly is to require it. You may need some ingenuity; one strategy that works is to require students to revise each graded essay and return it to you. Only when the essay is revised do you formally record a grade. Then students who don't revise won't get credit for their papers. Another method rev 2b

for encouraging revision efforts is to focus your written comments on the areas that students have revised effectively or failed to revise. Later in the semester it can also be useful to ask students to choose one of their own earlier papers to revise in the light of further reading or increased skills. This practice helps students to gain confidence in their own revision skills.

Revised first draft

~~Title?~~ America's Media Image 1

Is the United States a "monoculture," a unified homogeneous society? Many 2
Americans would like it to be or they think that it is now. But the writer
Ishmael Reed says no. His essay is titled "America: The Multinational
Society." In it he speaks out for cultural diversity. He thinks it makes the
nation stronger. In passing he

~~In "America: The Multinational Society," Ishmael Reed~~ mentions
that the communications media sensationalize~~s~~ the "conflict between 3
Another false media picture of America can be added to Reed's
people of different backgrounds." ~~Either that, or it depicts Americans~~
point. The picture of Americans as socially, economically, and ethnically similar.
~~as homogeneous~~. The media project~~s~~ unrealistic images of the US as a
nation either of constant ethnic conflict or untroubled homogeneity.

It is easy to find examples of the emphasizing of conflict among
ethnic groups. The news is full of stories of Hispanic gangs fighting
swastikas are painted on Jewish synagogues and cemeteries,
African American gangs, Korean shopkeepers pitted against non- 4
Haitians battle Cubans,
Korean customers, African American churches are burned by white
These are real stories, and all-too-real ethnic conflict should not be
teenagers. ~~In fact, New York City, with its dense and ethnically diverse~~ 5
covered up. However, these stories are blown out of proportion.
~~population, regularly supplies stories for other cities' news media~~ 6
~~when they run out of local stories of hate and mayhem. My brother~~
~~who lives in San Francisco is always complaining about all the New~~
~~York stories in the news. What he doesn't realize is that it's not New~~
~~York's fault, it's the media's for always playing up the bad news. Bad~~
~~news is what the media specializes in—as~~ Everyone is always complain~~-~~
that the media never present enough good news.
~~ing~~. When it comes to ethnic relations, this is certainly the case. ~~All~~
~~sorts of different people mingle together peacefully, but not in the~~
~~media~~.

Pakistanis, Russians, Mexicans, Chinese, Mayflower descendants, great-grand 4
children of African slaves. All these and more mingle on the nation's streets,
attend school together, work together. Integration is very far from complete, 5
severe inequality persists. Real conflict exists. But for the most part, cultural
groups are not at war.

However, in the media
~~There~~ the only peace belongs to a very narrow band of people.
Especially in television fiction and advertising. They have usual characteristics: they are white, married or expecting to be someday, unethnic, white collar, well-to-do, settled, materialistic, good looking,
These are but a few of the groups excluded from this TV type: Polish
and thin. ~~Many, many groups are excluded from this TV type, such~~ 4
Americans, homeless families, homosexuals, Lebanese immigrants, unmarried couples
~~as ethnic groups, poor people, and the disabled. A certain commercial~~

(heterosexual and homosexual), stay-at-home fathers, transients, disabled people,
~~is typical of TV with the happy prosperous nuclear family enjoying~~
elderly, homely people, fat people, small people. Exceptions come and go, such 5
~~breakfast together~~. *as the working-class and overweight Roseanne and her*
husband, the Cosbys, and more recent African American sitcoms and dramas.
However, the norm is easy to recognize. For example, a cereal commercial that 4
features a mother who is overseeing her husband's and children's breakfasts. The
kitchen is full of the latest appliances and decorations. Everyone is white. Every-
one is fit and cute, beautiful, or handsome. All well dressed and cheerful.
The media's two extremes of peace and conflict create a composite picture 7
of a nation where
~~The problem with this media image, with its extremes of peace~~
and ~~conflict, is that it is untrue. It caters to the ones who feel that the~~
is desirable and all but achieved.
~~US should be~~ a "monoculture" ~~and would be~~. If only we could battle
Imagine a *though.*
down the ones who don't belong or won't. A different picture ~~is possi-~~
In this one people coexist, who have diverse backgrounds, interests, incomes, 4
~~ble, but we aren't getting it.~~
living arrangements, and appearances. Sometimes they stay apart, sometimes they
blend. Sometimes they clash or prey on each other, sometimes they laugh
together. It all happens now and we could be watching.

Exercise 4
Analyzing a revised draft
Compare Perez's revised draft with her first draft on pages 65–66. Based on the discussion of her intentions for revision (pp. 70–71), can you see the reasons for most of her changes? Where would you suggest further revisions, and why?

Exercise 5
Considering your past work: Revising
In the past, have you usually revised your drafts extensively? Do you think your writing would benefit from more revision of the sort described in this chapter? Why or why not? Many students who don't revise much explain that they lack the time. Is time a problem for you? Can you think of ways to resolve the problem?

Exercise 6
Revising your own draft
Revise your own first draft from Exercise 3 (p. 67). Use the checklist for revision on page 69 as a guide. Concentrate on purpose, content, and organization, leaving smaller problems for the next draft.

COLLABORATIVE LEARNING

Exercise 4 works well as a small-group project. Encourage students to discuss their differing ideas for further revisions and then have each group present their conclusions to the class.

ANSWERS: EXERCISE 4

Answers will vary.

ANSWERS: EXERCISE 5

Individual response.

ANSWERS: EXERCISE 6

Individual response.

2c Editing the revised draft

Editing for style, clarity, and correctness may come second to more fundamental revision, but it is still very important. A carefully developed essay will fall flat with readers if you overlook awkwardness and errors.

When you have revised your first draft, try the following approaches to editing.

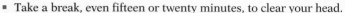

Ways to find what needs editing

- Take a break, even fifteen or twenty minutes, to clear your head.
- If possible, work on a paper copy, even if you compose and revise on a computer. Most people find it much harder to spot errors on a computer screen than on paper. (Print your draft double-spaced so you have room for changes.)

- Read the draft *slowly,* and read what you *actually see.* Otherwise, you're likely to read what you intended to write but didn't.
- As you read the draft, imagine yourself encountering it for the first time, as a reader will.
- Have a friend or relative read your work. (If your native language is not English, you may find it especially helpful to have a native speaker read your revised drafts.) When you share your work in class, listen to the responses of your classmates or instructor. (See p. 80.)
- As when revising, read the draft aloud, preferably into a tape recorder, listening for awkward rhythms, repetitive sentence patterns, and missing or clumsy transitions.
- Learn from your own experience. Keep a record of the problems that others have pointed out in your writing. (See p. 82 for a suggested format.) When editing, check your work against this record.

In your editing, work for clarity and a smooth movement among sentences and for correctness. Use the questions in the checklist below to guide your editing. (Chapter and page numbers in parentheses indicate where you can look in the handbook for more information.) Note that the checklist may also serve as a guide if you are commenting on another writer's paper (see p. 80).

Checklist for editing

- **Clarity:** How well do words and sentences convey their intended meanings? Which if any words and sentences are confusing? See Chapters 10–15. Check the paper especially for these:

  Exact words (pp. 463–72)
  Parallelism (pp. 331–34)
  Clear modifiers (pp. 297–305)
  Clear reference of pronouns (pp. 282–88)

TRANSPARENCY MASTER 2.2

TEACHING TIP

Since most students' work demonstrates patterns of repeated error, have them keep ongoing lists of their recurring editing errors and stylistic problems. Ask them to bring their lists to class for in-class revision and editing sessions and to have their revision group help them look particularly for those errors.

Complete sentences (pp. 266–72)
Sentences separated correctly (pp. 274–80)

- **Effectiveness:** How well do words and sentences engage and direct readers' attention? Where, if at all, does the writing seem wordy, choppy, or dull? See Chapters 16–19 and 31. Check the paper especially for these:

  Smooth and informative transitions (pp. 99–102)
  Variety in sentence length and structure (pp. 347–54)
  Appropriate words (pp. 454–62)
  Concise sentences (pp. 473–80)
  Consistent, appropriate tone (pp. 33–35)

- **Correctness:** How little or how much do surface errors interfere with clarity and effectiveness? See Chapters 6–9, 20–30, and 34. Check the paper especially for these:

  Spelling (pp. 499–511)
  Pronoun forms (pp. 198–205)
  Verb forms, especially *-s* and *-ed* endings and correct forms of irregular verbs (pp. 207–14)
  Verb tenses, especially consistency (pp. 219–20, 292–93)
  Agreement between subjects and verbs, especially when words come between them or the subject is *each, everyone,* or a similar word (pp. 239–45)
  Agreement between pronouns and antecedents, especially when the antecedent contains *or* or it is *each, everyone,* or a similar word (pp. 246–50)
  Commas, especially with *and* or *but* (pp. 365–66), with introductory elements (368–69), with nonrestrictive elements (370–74), and with series (pp. 376–77)
  Apostrophes in possessives but not plural nouns (*Dave's/witches,* pp. 397–401) and in contractions but not possessive personal pronouns (*it's/its,* pp. 401–02)

Editing on a computer presents distinct advantages and disadvantages, whether you edit on screen or work on printed copy and transfer corrections onto the computer.

- If you edit printed copy, the search command can help you find the passages to change on the computer copy.
- If you're aware of mistakes or stylistic problems that tend to crop up in your writing—certain misspellings, overuse of *there is,* wordy phrases such as *the fact that,* and so on—you can use the search command to find and correct them.
- The ease of editing on a computer can lead to overediting and steal the life from your prose. Resist any temptation to rewrite sentences over and over.

- Inserting or deleting text on a computer requires special care not to omit needed words or leave in unneeded words.
- A computer printout may look perfect just because it's clean. To make sure it's perfect, read the printout carefully. (See the suggestions on pp. 74 and 77.)
- Computer programs such as spelling checkers and grammar and style checkers are severely limited and cannot substitute for your own care and attention. Spelling checkers can't distinguish a misuse of a correctly spelled word, such as *their* for *there* or *not* for *now*. Grammar and style checkers often misidentify errors and ignore errors they're not capable of spotting. Use such programs only as a starting point. Check for spelling, grammar, and style problems yourself. (For more on optional word-processing programs, see pp. 774–75.)

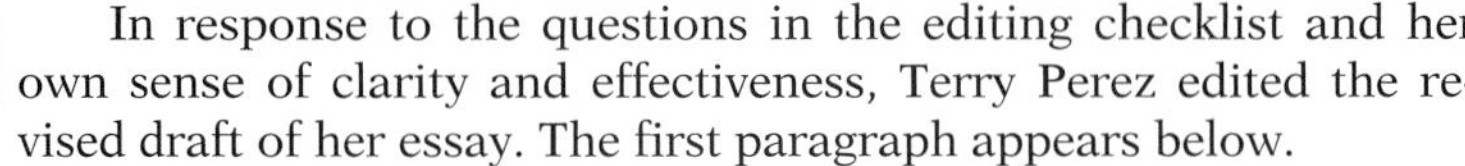

In response to the questions in the editing checklist and her own sense of clarity and effectiveness, Terry Perez edited the revised draft of her essay. The first paragraph appears below.

Edited draft (excerpt)

Is the United States a "monoculture," a unified, homogeneous society? Many Americans ~~would like it to be or they think that it is now.~~ think that it is or should be. But the writer Ishmael Reed says no. ~~His essay is titled~~ In "America: The Multinational Society/," ~~In it he~~ Reed speaks out for cultural diversity. He thinks it makes the nation stronger. In passing he mentions that the communications media sensationalize the "conflict between people of different backgrounds." ~~Another false media picture of America can be added to Reed's point.~~ To Reed's point can be added the media's other false picture of America, ~~T~~the picture of Americans as socially, economically, and ethnically similar. The media project unrealistic images of the ~~US~~ United States as a nation either of constant ethnic conflict or untroubled homogeneity.

Exercise 7
Considering your past work: Editing

How do you find what needs editing in your drafts? What kinds of changes do you make most often? Have you tried focusing on particular kinds of changes, such as correcting mistakes you made in previous writing? If your readers often comment on editing concerns in your work, what can you do to reduce such comments?

Exercise 8
Editing your own draft

Use the checklist for editing (pp. 74–75) and your own sense of your essay's needs to edit the revised draft of your essay-in-progress.

COLLABORATIVE LEARNING

Have students respond individually to the questions in Exercise 7 and then return to those questions as they work through drafts in their revision groups. Especially if students are working regularly with a particular group, they can be extremely helpful in pointing to one another's recurring strengths and problems.

ANSWERS: EXERCISE 7

Individual response.

ANSWERS: EXERCISE 8

Individual response.

2d Proofreading and submitting the final draft

After editing your essay, recopy, retype, or print it once more for submission to your instructor. Follow the guidelines in Appendix A or the wishes of your instructor for an appropriate document format. Be sure to proofread the final essay several times to spot and correct errors. To increase the accuracy of your proofreading, you may need to experiment with ways to keep yourself from relaxing into the rhythm and the content of your prose. The box below gives a few tricks, including some used by professional proofreaders.

Techniques for proofreading

- Read printed copy, even if you will eventually submit the paper electronically. Most people proofread more accurately when reading type on paper than when reading it on a computer screen. (At the same time, don't view the printed copy as necessarily error-free just because it's clean. Clean-looking copy may still harbor errors.)
- Read the paper aloud, very slowly, and distinctly pronounce exactly what you see.
- Place a ruler under each line as you read it.
- Read "against copy," comparing your final draft one sentence at a time against the edited draft you copied it from.
- Take steps to keep the content of your writing from distracting you while you proofread. Read the essay backward, end to beginning, examining each sentence as a separate unit. Or, taking advantage of a computer, isolate each paragraph from its context by printing it on a separate page. (Of course, reassemble the paragraphs before submitting the paper.)

Terry Perez's final essay, along with her instructor's comments, follows. The instructor pointed out the strengths he saw in the essay as well as the flaws remaining in it. He used a combination of written comments, correction symbols (from inside the back cover of this handbook), and correction codes (from inside the front cover).

Final draft with instructor's comments

America's Media Image

Is the United States a "monoculture," a unified, homogeneous society? Many Americans think that it is or should be. But the writer Ishmael Reed says no. In "America: The Multinational Society," Reed speaks out for cultural diversity. He thinks it makes the nation

RESOURCES AND IDEAS

Harris, Jeanette. "Proofreading: A Reading/Writing Skill." *College Composition and Communication* 38 (1987): 464–66. Harris argues that proofreading is a reading skill, a process of looking at each word and punctuation mark rather than of paying attention to the meaning of the text; and she suggests teaching students strategies like those outlined in this chapter—using a pointer (finger, pencil), reading aloud, reading in reverse order, and letting time elapse between writing and proofreading—in order to develop the specialized skill of proofreading.

Harrington, Jane. "Editing: the Last Step in the Process." In *Nuts and Bolts: a Practical Guide to Teaching*. Ed. Thomas Newkirk. Portsmouth, NH: Boynton, 1993. 151–178. Harrington defines the editing process and provides practical suggestions for making editing a familiar part of classroom practice.

Horner, Bruce. "Rethinking the 'Sociality' of Error: Teaching Editing as Negotiation." *Rhetoric Review* 11 (1992): 172–99. Horner argues for a consideration of editing as a process of social exchange best supported by peer groups and one-on-one conferences.

stronger. In passing he mentions that the communications media sen- *nice sentence except for repetition*

the picture of Americans as socially, economically, and ethnically similar. The media project unrealistic images of the United States as a nation of either constant ethnic conflict or untroubled homogeneity. *strong, clear thesis*

It is easy to find examples of the emphasizing of conflict among *awk* ethnic groups. The news is full of stories of Hispanic gangs fighting African American gangs, swastikas are painted on Jewish synagogues and cemeteries, Korean shopkeepers are pitted against non-Korean customers, Haitians battle Cubans, or African American churches are burned by white teenagers. *//* It's not that these aren't real stories, or that all-too-real ethnic conflict should be covered up; it's just that these *CS* stories are blown out of proportion.

Everyone complains that the news media never present enough good news. When it comes to ethnic relations, this is certainly the case. Pakistanis, Russians, Mexicans, Chinese, Mayflower descendants, *frag* great-grandchildren of African slaves. All these and more mingle on the nation's streets, attend school together, work together. Granted, integration is very far from complete; severe inequality persists. *CS* Real conflict exists. But for the most part, cultural groups are not at war.

In the media, though, especially television fiction and advertising, the only peace belongs to a very narrow band of people. They are usually white, married or expecting to be someday, unethnic, white collar, well-to-do, settled, materialistic, good looking, and thin. These are but a few of the groups excluded from this TV type (some overlap): Polish Americans, homeless families, homosexuals, factory workers, *this list may be a bit overdone* Lebanese immigrants, teenage mothers, amputees, Japanese Americans, unmarried couples (heterosexual or homosexual), loners, stay-at-home fathers, transients, disabled people, elderly pensioners, homely people, fat people, small people. ¶ Exceptions come and go, of course, *Break this very long ¶* such as the working-class and overweight Roseanne and her husband, the Cosbys, and more recent African American situation comedies and dramas. However, the norm is easy to recognize. For example, in a cereal commercial they feature a mother who is overseeing her hus- *see 12d* band's and children's breakfasts. The kitchen is full of the latest appli-

TEACHING TIP

Students often struggle to recognize common proofreading errors in their own work. Ask students to keep an ongoing list of the misspellings, typos, and minor grammatical errors that occur frequently in their own work and use that list for proofreading.

ANSWERS: EXERCISE 9

An environmental group, National Resources Defense Council, has estimated that 5500 to 6200 children who are in preschool today may contract cancer during their lives because of the pesticides they consume in their food. In addition, these children will be at greater risk for kidney damage, problems with immunity, and other serious impairments. The government bases its pesticide-safety standards on adults, but children consume much more of the fruits and fruit products likely to contain pesticides.

ANSWERS: EXERCISE 10

Possible revisions

Paragraph 1

Sentence 4: . . . *Reed speaks out for cultural diversity. He thinks it makes the nation stronger.*

ances and decorations. Everyone is white. Everyone is fit and cute, beautiful, or handsome. Everyone is well dressed and cheerful.

The media's two extremes of peace and conflict create a composite picture of a nation where a "monoculture" is desirable and all but achieved. If only we could battle down the ones who don't belong or won't belong. Imagine a different picture, though. In this one people coexist who have diverse backgrounds, interests, incomes, living arrangements, and appearances. Sometimes they stay apart, sometimes they blend. Sometimes they clash or prey on each other, sometimes they laugh together. It all happens now and we could be watching.

frag—attach to previous sentence for clarity *21b* *21j-4* *CS* *CS* *21a*

You did a fine job of adding details and acknowledging exceptions and actual problems. Your introduction and conclusion are also much stronger than in your first draft. This is a solid, convincing essay.

In future work, pay attention to your use (and misuse) of commas. A number of comma splices and other comma errors mar the clarity and effectiveness of your paper. I suggest you read and do the exercises in Chapters 11 (splices) and 21 (commas).

Exercise 9
Proofreading

Proofread the following passage, using any of the techniques listed on page 77 to bring errors into the foreground. There are thirteen errors in the passage: missing and misspelled words, typographical errors, and the like. If you are in doubt about any spellings, consult a dictionary.

An envirnmental group, National Resources Defense Council, has estimated that 5,500 to 6,200 children who are preschool today may contract cancer durng there lives becuase of the pesticides they consume in there food In addition, these children will be at greater risk for kidney damage, problems with immunity, and other serious imparments. The government bases it's pesticide-safety standards on adults, but childen consume much more the fruits and fruit products likely too contain pestcides.

Exercise 10
Revising an essay

To become familiar with the symbols and codes of this handbook, revise Perez's essay wherever her instructor has used a symbol or code to mark a problem.

Exercise 11
Preparing your final draft

Prepare the final draft of the essay you have been working on throughout Chapters 1 and 2. Proofread carefully and correct all errors before submitting your essay for review.

Sentence 6: *To Reed's point can be added the media's other false picture of Americans as socially, economically, and ethnically similar.*

Paragraph 2

Sentence 1: *It is easy to find examples of exaggerated conflict among ethnic groups.* Or: *Examples of exaggerated ethnic conflict are easy to find.*

Sentence 2: *The news is full of stories of Hispanic gangs fighting . . . , swastikas painted . . . , Haitians battling . . . , shopkeepers pitted . . . , churches burned. . . .*

Sentence 3: *It's not that . . . all-too-real ethnic conflict should be covered up. It's just that these stories are blown out of proportion.*

Paragraph 3

Sentences 3–4: *Pakistanis, Russians, . . . slaves—all these and more mingle . . . .*

Sentence 5: *Granted, integration is very far from complete. Severe inequality exists.*

Paragraph 4

Sentence 6: *For example, a cereal commercial features a mother . . . .*

Paragraph 5

Sentences 1–2: *. . . is desirable and all but achieved, if only we could . . . .*

Sentence 4: *In this one, people coexist who have diverse backgrounds . . . .*

Sentence 5: *Sometimes they stay apart; sometimes they blend.*

Sentence 6: *Sometimes they clash or prey on each other; sometimes they laugh together.*

Sentence 7: *It all happens now, and we could be watching.*

COLLABORATIVE LEARNING

Exercises 10 and 11 are productive collaborative projects. Ask students to use the symbols and codes to revise Perez's essay and then to practice using those symbols and codes to proofread each other's work.

ANSWERS: EXERCISE 11

Individual response.

RESOURCES AND IDEAS

Gilliam, Alice M. "Returning Students' Ways of Writing: Implications for First-Year College Composition." *Journal of Teaching Writing* 10:1 (1991): 1–20. Gilliam discusses the stresses and constraints returning students face and suggests ways to help such students succeed in the classroom.

Greenwood, Claudia M. "'It's Scary at First': Reentry Women in College Composition Classes." *Teaching English in the Two-Year College* 17 (1990): 133–42. Greenwood identifies several constant negative internal factors—feelings of guilt, inferiority, doubt, of being out of place—among women reentering higher education, but she finds that the positive internal factors outweigh the negative.

Grimm, Nancy. "Constructing Ideas of the Social Self." *Journal of Teaching Writing* 8 (Spring 1989): 11–20. Social pressures, social rules, and social values are at work in the composition classroom and may interfere in collaborative learning, particularly in classes made up of a culturally diverse student population. The classroom composition must be considered when instructors expect students to think critically and to question dominant cultural values.

McKendy, Thomas F. "Legitimizing Peer Response: A Recycling Project for Placement Essays." *College Composition and Communication* 41 (1990): 89–91. McKendy found that

TRANSPARENCY MASTER 2.3

when students in a remedial writing course holistically scored placement essays, their scoring correlated closely with that of trained readers. This exercise led to the students being more accepting of their placement in the course and more trusting of each others' responses to their writing.

O'Hearn, Carolyn. "Recognizing the Learning-Disabled College Writer." *College English* 51 (1989): 294–304. O'Hearn offers diagnostic techniques and strategies for helping such students survive in a mainstreamed classroom.

TEACHING TIP

Students sometimes initially think of "criticizing" as a negative activity rather than a sup-

2e Giving and receiving comments

Almost all the writing you do in college will generate responses from an instructor. In writing courses you may submit early drafts as well as your final paper, and your readers may include your classmates as well as your instructor. Like Terry Perez's, many writing courses feature **collaborative learning,** in which students work together on writing, from completing exercises to commenting on each other's work to producing whole papers. (At more and more schools this group work occurs over a computer network.)

Whether you participate as a writer or as a writing "coach," collaboration can give you experience in reading written work and in reaching readers through writing. You may at first be anxious about criticizing others' work or sharing your own rough drafts, but you'll soon grow to appreciate the interaction and the confidence it gives you in your own reading and writing.

ESL Collaboration may be uncomfortable if you come from a culture in which writers do not expect criticism from readers or readers do not expect to think and speak critically about what they read. Writers in English often consider a draft or even a final paper to be more an exploration of ideas than the last word on a subject. They usually welcome questions and suggestions from readers. Readers of English, in turn, often approach a text in a skeptical frame of mind. Their tactful questions and suggestions are usually considered appropriate.

If you are the reader of someone else's writing, keep the following principles in mind.

Commenting on others' writing

- Be sure you know what the writer is saying. If necessary, summarize the paper to understand its content. (See pp. 10–11.)
- Read closely and critically. (See pp. 2–17.)
- Unless you have other instructions, address only your most significant concerns with the work. If you point out every flaw you detect, the writer may have trouble sorting out the important from the unimportant. (Use the revision checklist on p. 69 as a guide to what is significant in a piece of writing.)
- Be specific. If something confuses you, say *why*. If you disagree with a conclusion, say *why*.
- While reading, make your comments in writing, even if you'll be discussing the paper with its writer later on. Then you'll be able to recall what you thought. If you are reading the paper on a computer, not in print, be sure to specify what part of the paper each of your comments relates to. (See pp. 775–78 for more on collaboration on computers.)

- Remember that you are the reader, not the writer. Resist the temptation to edit sentences, add details, or otherwise assume responsibility for the paper.
- Word your comments supportively. Question the writer in a way that emphasizes the effect of the work on *you*, the reader ("I find this paragraph confusing"), and avoid measuring the work against a set of external standards ("This essay is poorly organized"; "Your thesis sentence is inadequate").
- Be positive as well as honest. Instead of saying "This paragraph doesn't interest me," say "You have a really interesting detail here that seems buried in the rest of the paragraph." And tell the writer what you like about the paper.

When you *receive* the comments of others, whether your classmates or your instructor, you will get more out of the process if you follow the guidelines below.

Benefiting from comments on your writing

- Think of your readers as counselors or coaches who will help you see the virtues and flaws in your work and sharpen your awareness of readers' needs.
- Read or listen to comments closely.
- Make sure you know what the critic is saying. If you need more information, ask for it, or consult the appropriate section of this handbook. (See "Preface for Students: Using This Book," p. xiii, for a guide to the handbook.)
- Don't become defensive. Letting comments offend you will only erect a barrier to improvement in your writing. As one writing teacher advises, "Leave your ego at the door."
- When comments seem appropriate, revise your work in response to them, whether or not you are required to do so. You will learn more from the act of revision than from just thinking about changes.
- Though you should be open to suggestions, you are the final authority on your paper. You are free to decline advice when you think it is inappropriate.
- Keep track of both the strengths and the weaknesses others identify. Then in following assignments you can build on your successes and give special attention to problem areas.

As the last item above indicates, you'll gain the most from collaboration if you carry your learning from one assignment into the next. You can record things to work on in a chart like the one on the next page, with a vertical column for each assignment (or draft) and a horizontal row for each weakness. The handbook section is noted for each problem, and check marks indicate how often

portive practice. These "suggestions for commenting" on each other's writing can help set a supportive tone for collaborative revision groups. Criticism that is given in a helpful and careful manner is perhaps the easiest kind of criticism to benefit from. You can also encourage student writers to take an active role by bringing in questions and concerns about their own papers and by probing their peers' comments for specific examples and explanations: "Can you show me the places where my organization starts to break down?" See the chapter "Using Collaborative Learning with the Handbook" on pages IAE-49–IAE-62 for a detailed discussion on preparing students to provide and receive peer criticism. You may wish to draw on this discussion as a way of helping your students learn how to benefit from criticism and learn how to offer

TRANSPARENCY MASTER 2.4

their classmates advice that can lead to real improvements in expression.

ELECTRONIC COLLABORATION

If students have easy access to e-mail, it's possible to post drafts or sample essays on a bulletin board or class account to receive comments and feedback. See Susan Lang's essay on "Using Computers to Teach Writing" on pages IAE-63–IAE-77 for more information on working in a computer classroom.

RESOURCES AND IDEAS

Curtis, Marcia S. "Windows on Composing: Teaching Revision on Word Processors." *College Composition and Communication* 39 (1988): 337–44. Curtis reviews what research has so far shown (and not shown) about the computer's role in revision.

Harris, Muriel. "Composing Behaviors of One- and Multi-Draft Writers." *College English* 51 (1989): 174–91. Harris emphasizes the differences in revision techniques and success of student writers.

Laib, Nevin. "Conciseness and Amplification." *College Composition and Communication* 41 (1990): 443–59. Laib argues for a balance between brevity and abbreviation.

rev 2f

Schwartz, Mimi. "Revision Profiles: Patterns and Implications." *College English* 45 (1983): 549–58. Schwartz maintains that revisers can be grouped by the revision strategies they use.

Sirc, Geoffrey, and Tom Reynolds. "The Face of Collaboration in the Networked Writing Classroom." *Computers and Composition* 7 (1990): 53–70. Sirc and Reynolds discuss the use of networked classrooms in peer response to compositions.

Weissberg, Bob. "Speaking of Writing: Some Functions of Talk in the ESL Composition Class." *Journal of Second Language Writing* 3 (1994): 1121–39. This essay examines class discussion and peer input as learning factors, particularly in the ESL context.

COLLABORATIVE LEARNING

Ask students to prepare to hand in their portfolios by orally presenting some of their chosen work to their regular revision group. Each student can briefly describe the pieces they have chosen and describe how each piece has contributed to that student's progress. Revision group members can often remind writers of noticeable overall strengths that they might have overlooked.

the problem occurs in each essay. The chart also provides a convenient place to keep track of words you misspell so that you can master their spellings.

	Assignment			
Weaknesses	**1**	**2**	**3**	
not enough details for readers (1d)	✓	✓	✓	
unity—wanders away from thesis (1g)	✓			
parallelism (17)	✓✓	✓	✓	
agreement (8a)	✓		✓	
comma splice (11)	✓✓	✓	✓	
misspellings	among deceive	rebel seize	omission cruelty	

2f Preparing a writing portfolio

Your writing teacher may ask you to assemble samples of your writing into a portfolio, or folder, once or more during the course. Such a portfolio gives you a chance to consider all your writing over a period and showcase your best work.

Teachers' requirements for portfolios vary. For instance, some teachers ask students to choose their five or so best papers and to submit final drafts only. Others ask for final papers illustrating certain kinds of writing—say, one narrative, one critique, one argument, one research paper, and so on. Still others ask for notes and drafts along with selected papers.

Just as teachers' requirements differ, so do their purposes. But most are looking for a range of writing that demonstrates your progress and strengths as a writer. You, in turn, see how you have advanced from one assignment to the next, as you've had time for new knowledge to sink in and time for practice. Teachers often allow students to revise papers before placing them in the portfolio, even if the papers have already been submitted earlier. In that case, every paper in the portfolio can benefit from all your learning.

An assignment to assemble a writing portfolio will probably also provide guidelines for what to include, how the portfolio will be evaluated, and how (or whether) it will be weighted for a grade. Be sure you understand the purpose of the portfolio and who will read it. For instance, if your composition teacher will be the only reader and her guidelines urge you to show evidence of progress, you might include a paper that took big risks but never entirely succeeded. In contrast, if a committee of teachers will read your work and the guidelines urge you to demonstrate your competence as a writer, you might include only papers that did succeed.

Unless the guidelines specify otherwise, provide error-free copies of your final drafts, label all your samples with your name, and assemble them all in a folder. Add a cover letter or memo that lists the samples and explains why you've included each one. The self-evaluation involved should be a learning experience for you and will help your teacher assess your development as a writer.

Exercise 12
Analyzing an essay

Carefully read the essay below by Johanna Abrams. (Abrams's earlier work on this essay appears on pp. 41–42 and 55.) Answer the following questions about the essay:

1. What is Abrams's purpose?
2. Who do you think constitutes Abrams's intended audience? What role does she seem to be assuming? What does the tone reveal about her attitude toward the topic?
3. How well does the thesis sentence convey Abrams's purpose and attitude? What assertion does the thesis sentence make? How specific is the sentence? How well does it preview Abrams's ideas and organization?
4. What organization does Abrams use? Is it clear throughout the essay?
5. What details, examples, and reasons does Abrams use to support her ideas? Where is supporting evidence skimpy?
6. How successful is Abrams in making you care about the topic and her views of it?

Working in the Barnyard

Until two months ago I thought summer jobs occupied time and helped pay the next year's tuition but otherwise provided no useful training. Then I took a temporary job in a large government agency. Two months there taught me the very valuable lesson that the hierarchy of supervisor to employee should be respected.

Last May I was hired by the personnel department of the agency to fill in for vacationing workers in the mail room. I had seven coworkers and a boss, Mrs. King. Our job was to sort the huge morning and afternoon mail shipments into four hundred slots, one for every employee in the agency. Then we delivered the sorted mail out of grocery carts that we wheeled from office to office along assigned corridors, picking up outgoing mail as we went along. Each mail delivery took an entire half-day to sort and deliver.

COLLABORATIVE LEARNING

Ask students to work together to answer each question for Exercise 12 and then have groups present their various conclusions to the class.

ANSWERS: EXERCISE 12

Possible answers

The numbers below match the question numbers in the exercise instruction. (Note that the ways of linking paragraphs in the essay are analyzed in the answer to Chapter 3, Exercise 19.)

"Working in the Barnyard"

1. The writer's purpose is primarily self-expression but also explanation.

2. The writer seems to conceive of her readers as other inexperienced workers like herself. She assumes the role of a confider, sharing a difficult experience. Her tone is straightforward yet strangely subdued when she tells of Mrs. King's tyranny. We sense from the beginning that the writer was humbled by her experience, and the last paragraph is genuinely humble in tone.

3. The thesis sentence (the last sentence of paragraph 1) clearly and specifically states the writer's topic (a work experience) and perspective on that topic (learning something valuable).

4. The essay's organization is clearly chronological. The writer adheres to the organization throughout, providing ample signals to help the reader follow the narrative (e.g., *Last May, then, as soon as I arrived*).

5. This otherwise competent essay is marred by omissions of concrete details and examples that would give the reader a sense of actually sharing the experience instead of rushing through it. Paragraph 2: What did Mrs. King look like? How huge were the mail shipments? Paragraph 3: What were some of the actual words spoken by the writer and Mrs. King? Paragraph 4: What was inefficient about delivery routes and times for coffee breaks? What exactly did Mrs. King do or say in reacting to the writer's questions? Paragraph 5: In what specific ways did the writer pester Mrs. King? How were the efforts fruitless? How counterproductive? What snide names did Mrs. King use? How did she pick on the writer's work? What reprimands did she issue?

6. Answers will vary.

My troubles began almost as soon as I arrived. Hundreds of pieces of mail were dumped on a shallow table against a wall of mail slots. I was horrified to see that the slots were labeled not with people's names but with their initials—whereas the incoming letters, of course, contained full names. Without thinking, I asked why this was a good idea, only to receive a sharp glance from Mrs. King. So I repeated the question. This time Mrs. King told me not to question what I didn't understand. It was the first of many such exchanges, and I hadn't been on the job a half-hour.

I mastered the initials and the sorting and delivery procedures after about a week. But the longer I worked at the job, the more I saw how inefficient all the procedures were, from delivery routes to times for coffee breaks. When I asked Mrs. King about the procedures, however, she always reacted the same way: it was none of my business.

I pestered Mrs. King more and more over the next seven weeks, but my efforts were fruitless, even counterproductive. Mrs. King began calling me snide names. Then she began picking on my work and singling me out for reprimands, even though I did my best and worked faster than most of the others.

Two months after I had started work, the personnel manager called me in and fired me. I objected, of course, calling up all the deficiencies I had seen in Mrs. King and her systems. The manager interrupted to ask if I had ever heard of the barnyard pecking order: the top chicken pecks on the one below it, the second pecks on the third, and so on all the way down the line to the lowliest chicken, whose life is a constant misery. Mrs. King, the manager said, was that lowliest chicken at the bottom of the pecking order in the agency's management. With little education, she had spent her entire adult life building up her small domain, and she had to protect it from everyone, especially the people who worked for her. The arbitrariness of her systems was an assertion of her power, for no one should doubt for a moment that she ruled her roost.

I had a month before school began again to think about my adventure. At first it irritated me that I should be humiliated while Mrs. King continued on as before. But eventually I saw how arrogant, and how unsympathetic, my behavior had been. In my next job, I'll learn the pecking order before I become a crusader, *if* I do.

—Johanna Abrams

Chapter 3

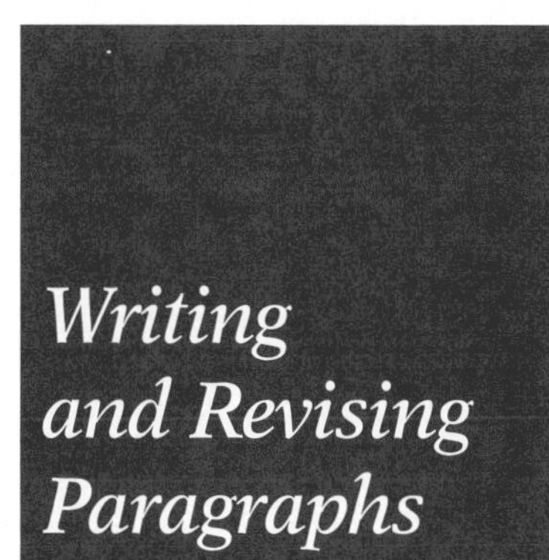

A **paragraph** is a group of related sentences set off by a beginning indention or, sometimes, by extra space. For you and your readers, paragraphs provide breathers from long stretches of text and indicate key changes in the development of your thesis. They help to organize and clarify ideas.

In the body of your essay, you may use paragraphs for any of these purposes:

- To introduce one of the main points supporting your essay's central idea (its thesis) and to develop the point with examples, facts, or other supporting evidence. (See pp. 47–51 for a discussion of an essay's thesis.)
- Within a group of paragraphs centering on one main point, to introduce and develop a key example or other important evidence.
- To shift approach—for instance, from pros to cons, from problem to solution, from questions to answers.
- To mark movement in a sequence, such as from one reason or step to another.

In addition, you will sometimes use paragraphs for special purposes:

- To introduce or to conclude an essay. (See pp. 117 and 120.)
- Occasionally, to give strong emphasis to an important point or mark a significant transition from one point to another. (See p. 121.)
- In dialogue, to indicate that a new person has begun speaking. (See p. 122.)

HIGHLIGHTS

The writing some American high school students do is no more than a paragraph in length, so learning to think of paragraphs as units in larger pieces of discourse may be a challenge for your students. If they have written longer essays, these probably have been in the familiar "five-paragraph theme" pattern of introduction, three paragraphs of development, and conclusion. Don't be surprised, then, if learning to use paragraphs in different ways presents a challenge for your students.

Here we present a strategy of developing paragraphs as mini-essays, each with a generalization (topic sentence) supported by limitations and evidence. Practicing these essays-in-miniature can help students develop longer essays as they gain more skill. Of course, not all paragraphs in professional writing conform in length, structure, or purpose to the models this chapter provides.

The chapter reviews strategies for improving paragraph unity, achieving paragraph coherence, developing paragraph content, and writing special-purpose paragraphs. It concludes by showing how paragraphs can be linked within the larger context of the essay. Helping students learn and practice the standard paragraphing strategies elaborated in this chapter can be a good way to help them improve their writing. The annotations provided for sample paragraphs help students see the strategies explained in the chapter "in practice."

RESOURCES AND IDEAS

Rhetorical scholarship is split on a number of the "givens" of paragraphing: whether paragraphs are self-contained units or building blocks of larger discourses, whether topic sentences are needed, and so on. These references offer you a fairly mainstream view of research into paragraphing.

Knoblauch, C.H. "The Rhetoric of the Paragraph." *Journal of Advanced Composition* 2 (1981): 53–61.

Stern, Arthur A. "When Is a Paragraph?" *College Composition and Communication* 27 (1976): 253–57. Stern argues for the rhetorical flexibility of paragraphs as development devices.

¶ un
3a

The following paragraph illustrates simply how an effective body paragraph works to help both writer and reader. The thesis of the essay in which this paragraph appears is that a Texas chili championship gives undue attention to an unpleasant food.

> Some people really like chili, apparently, but nobody can agree how the stuff should be made. C. V. Wood, twice winner at Terlingua, uses flank steak, pork chops, chicken, and green chilis. My friend Hughes Rudd of CBS News, who imported five hundred pounds of chili powder into Russia as a condition of accepting employment as Moscow correspondent, favors coarse-ground beef. Isadore Bleckman, the cameraman I must live with on the road, insists upon one-inch cubes of stew beef and puts garlic in his chili, an Illinois affectation. An Indian of my acquaintance, Mr. Fulton Batisse, who eats chili for breakfast when he can, uses buffalo meat and plays an Indian drum while it's cooking. I ask you.
>
> —CHARLES KURALT, *Dateline America*

General statement relating to thesis: announces topic of paragraph

Four specific examples, all providing evidence for general statement

While you are drafting, conscious attention to the requirements of the paragraph may sometimes help pull ideas out of you or help you forge relationships. But don't expect effective paragraphs like Kuralt's to flow from your fingertips while you are grappling with what you want to say. Instead, use the following checklist to guide your revision of paragraphs so that they work to your and your readers' advantage.

Checklist for revising paragraphs

- Is the paragraph **unified?** Does it adhere to one general idea that is either stated in a **topic sentence** or otherwise apparent? (See opposite.)
- Is the paragraph **coherent?** Do the sentences follow a clear sequence (p. 94)? Are the sentences linked as needed by parallelism (p. 97), repetition or restatement (p. 98), pronouns (p. 98), consistency (p. 99), and transitional expressions (p. 99)?
- Is the paragraph **developed?** Is the general idea of the paragraph well supported with specific evidence such as details, facts, examples, and reasons? (See p. 104.)

ESL The conventions of paragraphing described here are not common to all languages. If your native language is not English and you have difficulty with paragraphs, don't worry about paragraphing during drafting. Instead, during a separate step of revi-

TRANSPARENCY MASTER 3.1

HIGHLIGHTS

Section 3a of this chapter addresses the need for a paragraph to focus on a topic and to make the focus clear to the reader through an explicit statement in the form of a topic sentence. It introduces the basic form of the expository paragraph—topic sentence, illustrations, and details—and indicates how this pattern can be varied to suit a writer's purpose and to fit within the context created by the surrounding paragraphs.

The concept of a clearly stated and variously placed topic sentence that controls the shape of a paragraph is an oversimplification. But it appears to help students a great deal to think of the paragraph as a unit dominated and controlled by an expressly stated generalization. Students can see the topic sentence as a commitment they

sion, divide your text into parts that develop your main points. Mark those parts with indentions.

3a Maintaining paragraph unity

Readers generally expect a paragraph to explore one idea. They will be alert for that idea and will patiently follow its development. In other words, they will seek and appreciate paragraph **unity,** clear identification and clear elaboration of one idea and of that idea only.

In an essay the thesis sentence often asserts the main idea as a commitment to readers (see p. 47). In a paragraph a **topic sentence** often alerts readers to the essence of the paragraph by asserting the central idea and expressing the writer's attitude toward it. In a brief essay each body paragraph will likely treat one main point supporting the essay's thesis sentence; the topic sentences simply elaborate on parts of the thesis. In longer essays paragraphs tend to work in groups, each group treating one main point. Then the topic sentences will tie into that main point, and all the points together will support the thesis.

 Focusing on the central idea

Like the thesis sentence, the topic sentence is a commitment to readers, and the rest of the paragraph delivers on that commitment. Look again at Kuralt's paragraph on chili (opposite page): the opening statement conveys the author's promise that he will describe various ways to make chili, and the following sentences keep the promise. But what if Kuralt had written this paragraph instead?

> Some people really like chili, apparently, but nobody can agree how the stuff should be [Topic sentence: general statement] made. C. V. Wood, twice winner at Terlingua, uses flank steak, pork chops, chicken, and green chilis. My friend Hughes Rudd, who imported five hundred pounds of chili powder into Russia as a condition of accepting employment as Moscow correspondent, favors [Two examples supporting statement] coarse-ground beef. He had some trouble finding the beef in Moscow, though. He sometimes had to scour all the markets and wait in long lines. For any American used to overstocked supermarkets and department stores, Russia can be quite a shock. [Digression]

By wandering off from chili to consumer deprivation in Russia, the paragraph fails to deliver on the commitment of its thesis sentence.

make to the reader, with the rest of the paragraph following through on the commitment. Seeing the obvious parallel between the paragraph's topic sentence and the essay's thesis statement is also helpful to many students. Finally, stating a central point in a single sentence and marshaling support for it enables students to see more clearly what is required for unity.

The exercises for this section ask students to identify the central idea in unified paragraphs, to revise paragraphs, to build a paragraph by combining and revising kernel sentences, and to write their own paragraphs. These exercises can be easily adapted to small-group work: in coming to understand how others view paragraphs, students may more readily understand the influence of paragraph structure and unity on readers.

RESOURCES AND IDEAS

Becker, A. L. "A Tagmemic Approach to Paragraph Analysis." *College Composition and Communication* 16 (1965): 237–42. Becker observes that expository paragraphs generally follow a variation of one of two patterns: topic-restriction-illustration (TRI) or problem-solution (PS).

Wiener, Harvey S. "The Single Narrative Paragraph and College Remediation." *College English* 33 (1972): 660–69. Wiener suggests using paragraph-length narrative themes to help students develop both paragraph and essay skills.

COLLABORATIVE LEARNING

USING STUDENT WRITING

Ask students to choose key paragraphs from their work-in-progress and read them aloud to their groups. The listeners should take notes on the effectiveness of the various unity strategies they hear in each paragraph. If students have trouble responding without seeing a written text, you can have them work in pairs to critique and revise the unity of each other's paragraphs.

COLORING PARAGRAPHS

Bring in copies of sample paragraphs and felt-tipped pens or pencils in two colors. Split the class into groups and ask each group to underline topic sentences in one color and examples and details in another color. Students should then be able to discover the arrangement of each paragraph, the placement of the topic sentence, and the way the parts fit together to form a unified whole. Students working in a computer classroom can use the bold feature and designated fonts instead of pens to identify each of these elements.

COLLABORATIVE LEARNING

USING STUDENT WRITING

Ask students to bring in paragraphs from writings in other classes or other disciplines to use in the "coloring paragraphs" activity. They will find it instructive to note how different writers decide to place, emphasize, or omit topic sentences. They can also perform this exercise on the paragraphs in their drafts.

SEEING PARAGRAPHS

Visually, students may find it easier to understand topic sentence placement and paragraph arrangement by using these diagrams as guides:

Topic sentence at the beginning:	△
Topic sentence at the beginning and in the middle:	△ △
Topic sentence at the end:	▽
Topic sentence at the beginning and the end:	◇

You should expect digressions while you are drafting: if you allow yourself to explore ideas, as you should, then of course every paragraph will not be tightly woven, perfectly unified. But spare your readers the challenge and frustration of repeatedly shifting focus to follow your rough explorations: revise each paragraph so that it develops a single idea.

2 Placing the topic sentence

The topic sentence of a paragraph and its supporting details may be arranged variously, depending on how you want to direct readers' attention and how complex your central idea is. In the most common arrangements, the topic sentence comes at the beginning of the paragraph, comes at the end, or is not stated at all but is nonetheless apparent. The advantages of each approach are described below. If you write on a computer, you can easily experiment with different positions by moving the topic sentence around (or deleting it) to see the effect. (The sentence will probably take some editing to work smoothly into various positions.)

Topic sentence at the beginning

When the topic sentence appears first in a paragraph, it can help you select the details that follow. For readers, the topic-first model establishes an initial context in which all the supporting details can be understood. Look again at Kuralt's paragraph on page 86 to see how easily we readers relate each detail or example back to the point made in the first sentence.

The topic-first model is common not only in expository paragraphs, such as Kuralt's, but also in argument paragraphs, such as the one following:

> It is a misunderstanding of the American retail store to think we go there necessarily to buy. Some of us shop. There's a difference. Shopping has many purposes, the least interesting of which is to acquire new articles. We shop to cheer ourselves up. We shop to practice decision-making. We shop to be useful and productive members of our class and society. We shop to remind ourselves how much is available to us. We shop to remind ourselves how much is to be striven for. We shop to assert our superiority to the material objects that spread themselves before us.
>
> —PHYLLIS ROSE, "Shopping and Other Spiritual Adventures"

Topic sentence: statement of misconception

Correction of misconception

Topic sentence at the end

In some paragraphs the central idea may be stated at the end, after supporting sentences have made a case for the general statement. Since this model leads the reader to a conclusion by presenting all the evidence first, it can prove effective in argument. And because the point of the paragraph is withheld until the end, this model can be dramatic in exposition too, as illustrated by the following example. In the sentence before the paragraph, the author says that the television game show *Wheel of Fortune* provides a "scenario" of material success.

> The terminology of the rules of the game are consistent with the scenario being played out. A contestant "*earns* the right to buy a prize" by solving a puzzle and accumulating money by spinning The Wheel. If you win the game, you take the money you have accumulated and then go shopping, at the "actual retail prices," for the prizes offered until you have exhausted your account. You can also elect to bank your money, hoping that you can solve another puzzle without hitting "bankrupt," which wipes out all you've earned but not your merchandise, "because once you buy a prize, it's yours to keep." So whether you can spend only $200 for a framed print or $15,000 for a Mustang convertible depends upon a combination of common sense, basic literacy and luck. It is, plain and simple, a microcosm of the mechanisms operating in the American ideology of an open society and the work ethic.
>
> —Gloria Naylor, "Sexual Equality in a TV Fantasy"

[Margin annotations: Transition from preceding paragraph; Information supporting and building to topic sentence; Topic sentence]

Expressing the central idea at the end of the paragraph does not eliminate the need to unify the paragraph. The idea in the topic sentence must still govern the selection of all the preceding details.

Central idea not stated

Occasionally, a paragraph's central idea will be stated in the previous paragraph or will be so obvious that it need not be stated at all. The following is from an essay on the actor Humphrey Bogart:

> Usually he wore the trench coat unbuttoned, just tied with the belt, and a slouch hat, rarely tilted. Sometimes it was a captain's cap and a yachting jacket. Almost al-

COMPUTER EXERCISE

REORGANIZING PARAGRAPHS

For students working on computers, the reorganization of paragraphs is particularly easy. Encourage students to select one or two paragraphs from their drafts and reorganize them with the controlling idea at the end, as Naylor does. Then ask them to judge whether they gain any rhetorical advantage from such a rearrangement. Leonard A. Podis suggests some other exercises of this nature in "Teaching Arrangement: Defining a More Practical Approach," *College Composition and Communication* 31 (1980): 197–204, and JoAnne M. Podis and Leonard A. Podis present more exercises in "Identifying and Teaching Rhetorical Plans for Arrangement," *College Composition and Communication* 41 (1990): 430–42.

COLLABORATIVE LEARNING

Some research suggests that the necessity of a topic sentence is determined by the author's relation to his or her readers; a writer writing to less expert or more expert readers is more likely to use a topic sentence than one writing for peers, for instance. Ask students to work in groups to collect examples of topic sentence use and omission, then analyze the different author-reader relationships implied in each example. Encourage students to collect samples from their own journals and papers, but also from various kinds of published writing, to get the best results from this survey.

ways his trousers were held up by a cowboy belt. You know the kind: one an Easterner waiting for a plane out of Phoenix buys just as a joke and then takes a liking to. Occasionally, he'd hitch up his slacks with it, and he often jabbed his thumbs behind it, his hands ready for a fight or a dame.

—PETER BOGDANOVICH, "Bogie in Excelsis"

Details adding up to the unstated idea that Bogart's character could be seen in the details of his clothing

Paragraphs in descriptive writing (like the one above) and in narrative writing (relating a sequence of events) often lack stated topic sentences. But a paragraph without a topic sentence still should have a central idea, and its details should develop that idea.

COLLABORATIVE LEARNING

Exercise 1 works well as a group project. Ask each group to discuss what effect the particular placement of each topic sentence has, and then to report back to the class on the sentences that best express the central idea of each paragraph.

ANSWERS: EXERCISE 1

1. The central idea is sentence 8: The black bourgeoisie feel a sense of shame about their own identity.
2. The central idea is sentence 1: Scientists know something about the song of the humpback whale.

Exercise 1
Finding the central idea

What is the central idea of each paragraph below? In what sentence or sentences is it expressed?

1. Today many black Americans enjoy a measure of economic 1
security beyond any we have known in the history of black America. But if they remain in a nasty blue funk, it's because their very 2
existence seems an affront to the swelling ranks of the poor. Nor 3
have black intellectuals ever quite made peace with the concept of
the black bourgeoisie, a group that is typically seen as devoid of
cultural authenticity, doomed to mimicry and pallid assimilation.
I once gave a talk before an audience of black academics and edu- 4
cators, in the course of which I referred to black middle-class culture. Afterward, one of the academics in the audience, deeply af- 5
fronted, had a question for me. "Professor Gates," he asked rhe- 6
torically, his voice dripping with sarcasm, "what *is* black middle-
class culture?" I suggested that if he really wanted to know, he 7
need only look around the room. But perhaps I should just have 8
handed him a mirror: for just as nothing is more American than
anti-Americanism, nothing is more characteristic of the black
bourgeoisie than the sense of shame and denial that the identity
inspires. —HENRY LOUIS GATES, JR., "Two Nations . . . Both Black"

2. Though they do not know why the humpback whale sings, sci- 1
entists do know something about the song itself. They have mea- 2
sured the length of a whale's song: from a few minutes to over half
an hour. They have recorded and studied the variety and complex 3
arrangements of low moans, high squeaks, and sliding squeals that
make up the song. And they have learned that each whale sings in its 4
own unique pattern. —JANET LIEBER (student), "Whales' Songs"

COLLABORATIVE LEARNING

Have students work in groups to complete Exercise 2, then ask groups to consider how they might revise and expand the deleted material to include it in a follow-up paragraph.

ANSWERS: EXERCISE 2

The topic sentence is sentence 1. Unrelated are sentences 4 and 7.

Exercise 2
Revising a paragraph for unity

The following paragraph contains ideas or details that do not support its central idea. Identify the topic sentence in the paragraph and delete the unrelated material.

In the southern part of the state, some people still live much 1
as they did a century ago. They use coal- or wood-burning stoves 2
for heating and cooking. Their homes do not have electricity or in- 3
door bathrooms or running water. The towns can't afford to put in 4
sewers or power lines, because they don't receive adequate funding
from the state and federal governments. Beside most homes there 5
is a garden where fresh vegetables are gathered for canning. Small 6
pastures nearby support livestock, including cattle, pigs, horses,
and chickens. Most of the people have cars or trucks, but the vehi- 7
cles are old and beat-up from traveling on unpaved roads.

Exercise 3
Considering your past work: Paragraph unity

For a continuing exercise in this chapter, choose a paper you've written in the past year. Examine the body paragraphs for unity. Do they have clear topic sentences? If not, are the paragraphs' central ideas still clear? Are the paragraphs unified around their central ideas? Should any details be deleted for unity? Should other, more relevant details be added in their stead?

ANSWERS: EXERCISE 3

Individual response.

Exercise 4
Writing a unified paragraph

Develop the following topic sentence into a unified paragraph by using the relevant information in the statements below it. Delete each statement that does not relate directly to the topic, and then rewrite and combine sentences as appropriate. Place the topic sentence in the position that seems most effective to you.

Topic sentence

Mozart's accomplishments in music seem remarkable even today.

Supporting information

Wolfgang Amadeus Mozart was born in 1756 in Salzburg, Austria.
He began composing music at the age of five.
He lived most of his life in Salzburg and Vienna.
His first concert tour of Europe was at the age of six.
On his first tour he played harpsichord, organ, and violin.
He published numerous compositions before reaching adolescence.
He married in 1782.
Mozart and his wife were both poor managers of money.
They were plagued by debts.
Mozart composed over six hundred musical compositions.
His most notable works are his operas, symphonies, quartets, and piano concertos.
He died at the age of thirty-five.

ANSWERS: EXERCISE 4

Delete statements not pertaining to Mozart's accomplishments: when he was born, where he lived, when he married, his debts. Possible paragraph:

> Mozart's accomplishments in music seem remarkable even today. At the age of six he made his first concert tour of Europe, playing harpsichord, organ, and violin. He had begun composing music at the age of five, and by adolescence he had published numerous musical compositions. When he died at thirty-five, his work included over six hundred compositions, most notably operas, symphonies, quartets, and piano concertos.

COMPUTER EXERCISE

Exercises 4 and 5 work well in a computer classroom because students have the flexibility to rearrange sentences multiple times without retyping them. Students can print out the results in order to compare their differing responses in groups. In a networked classroom you might ask students to e-mail their responses to a partner in the class, or you could post several volunteer responses on the network for the whole class to read and discuss.

Exercise 5
Turning topic sentences into unified paragraphs

Develop three of the following topic sentences into detailed and unified paragraphs.

ANSWERS: EXERCISE 5

Individual response.

1. Men and women are different in at least one important respect.
2. AIDS should be everybody's concern.
3. Fans of country music [or rock music, classical music, jazz] come in [*number*] varieties.
4. Professional sports have [or have not] been helped by extending the regular season with championship play-offs.
5. Working for good grades can interfere with learning.

HIGHLIGHTS

This section of the chapter (3b) deals with paragraph coherence, addressing it from the reader's perspective as well as the writer's. Students are shown how the devices they use to achieve paragraph coherence help readers to follow the arguments or information being presented.

TRANSPARENCY MASTER 3.2

The discussion emphasizes the need to maintain a clear organizational pattern as one of the principal ways to ensure coherence, and it presents examples of two basic ways of organizing paragraphs: organizing by space or time and organizing for emphasis. Students who have difficulty organizing their own writing can usually see the pattern of organization in a well-made example from another writer's work.

Following the discussion of patterns, the section takes up and illustrates other methods of achieving coherence: parallelism; repetition of words; careful use of pronouns; consistency in person, tense, and number; and transitional expressions. Analysis of paragraphs can help students understand these explicit and implicit means by which individual sentences are held together so that the reader effortlessly follows the flow of ideas and information. As in the preceding section, the exercises move from analysis to revision to production and are useful in small-group activities as well as individual work.

RESOURCES AND IDEAS

These two sources draw on current linguistic and rhetorical theory to provide frameworks for describing patterns of coherence and development in paragraphs.

3b Achieving paragraph coherence

A paragraph is unified if it holds together—if all its details and examples support the central idea. A paragraph is **coherent** if readers can see *how* the paragraph holds together—how the sentences relate to each other—without having to stop and reread. Coherent paragraphs convey relations in the ways summarized below.

Ways to achieve paragraph coherence

- Organize effectively (p. 94).
- Use parallel structures (p. 97).
- Repeat or restate words and word groups (p. 98).
- Use pronouns (p. 98).
- Be consistent in nouns, pronouns, and verbs (p. 99).
- Use transitional expressions (p. 99).

Incoherence gives readers the feeling of being yanked around, as the following example shows:

> The ancient Egyptians were masters of preserving dead people's bodies by making mummies of them. Mummies several thousand years old have been discovered nearly intact. The skin, hair, teeth, finger- and toenails, and facial features of the mummies were evident. It is possible to diagnose the diseases they suffered in life, such as smallpox, arthritis, and nutritional deficiencies. The process was remarkably effective. Sometimes apparent were the fatal afflictions of the dead people: a middle-aged king died from a blow on the head, and polio killed a child king. Mummification consisted of removing the internal organs, applying natural preservatives inside and out, and then wrapping the body in layers of bandages.

[Annotations: "Topic sentence" (first sentence); "Sentences related to topic sentence but disconnected from each other" (remaining sentences)]

The paragraph as it was actually written is much clearer. The writer organized information and linked sentences to help readers move easily from one sentence to the next.

> The ancient Egyptians were masters of preserving dead people's bodies by making mummies of them. Basically, mummification consisted of removing the internal organs, applying natural preservatives inside and out, and then wrapping the body in layers of bandages. And the process was remarkably effective. Indeed, mummies several thousand years old have been discovered nearly intact. Their skin, hair, teeth, finger- and toenails, and facial features are still evident. Their diseases in life, such as smallpox, arthritis, and nutritional deficiencies, are still diagnosable. Even their fatal afflictions are still apparent: a middle-aged king died from a blow on the head; a child king died from polio.
>
> —Mitchell Rosenbaum (student), "Lost Arts of the Egyptians"

Here is the same paragraph annotated to show its shape and its connections:

> The ancient Egyptians were masters of preserving dead people's bodies by making mummies of them. Basically, mummification consisted of removing the internal organs, applying natural preservatives inside and out, and then wrapping the body in layers of bandages. And the process was remarkably effective. Indeed, mummies several thousand years old have been discovered nearly intact. Their skin, hair, teeth, finger- and toenails, and facial features are still evident. Their diseases in life, such as smallpox, arthritis, and nutritional deficiencies, are still diagnosable. Even their fatal afflictions are still apparent: a middle-aged king died from a blow on the head; a child king died from polio.

Topic sentence

Circled words: pronouns; repeated or restated key terms

Boxed words: links between sentences

Point 1: what mummification is

Point 2: why the Egyptians were masters

Specific examples of point 2

Underlined phrases: parallel form for parallel content

Though some of the connections in this paragraph were added in revision, the writer attended to them while drafting as well. Not only superficial coherence but also an underlying clarity of relationships can be achieved by tying each sentence to the one before—generalizing from it, clarifying it, qualifying it, adding to it, illustrating it. Each sentence in a paragraph creates an expectation

Coe, Richard M. *Toward a Grammar of Passages.* Carbondale: Southern Illinois UP, 1988.

Markels, Robin Bell. *A New Perspective on Cohesion in Expository Paragraphs.* Carbondale: Southern Illinois UP, 1984.

Other good readings on paragraph coherence include the following:

Sloan, Gary. "The Frequency of Transitional Markers in Discursive Prose." *College English* 46 (1984): 158–79. Sloan shows how infrequently explicit transition markers are used by either professional or student writers.

Smith, Rochelle. "Paragraphing for Coherence: Writing as Implied Dialogue." *College English* 46 (1984): 8–21. Smith uses reader-response theory and the notion of author-reader dialogue to improve paragraph cohesion.

Witte, Stephen, and Lester Faigley. "Coherence, Cohesion, and Writing Quality." *College Composition and Communication* 32 (1981): 189–204. Students need to learn the features of coherence that extend across sentence boundaries; the article stresses ways to make them aware of coherence strategies.

of some sort in the mind of the reader, a question such as "How was a mummy made?" or "How intact are the mummies?" or "What's another example?" When you recognize these expectations and try to fulfill them, readers are likely to understand relationships without struggle.

1 Organizing the paragraph

The paragraphs on mummies illustrate an essential element of coherence: information must be arranged in an order that readers can follow easily and that corresponds to their expectations. The common organizations for paragraphs correspond to those for entire essays (see pp. 58–60): by space, by time, and for emphasis. (In addition, the patterns of development also suggest certain arrangements. See pp. 106–14.)

If you want to try rearranging a paragraph to achieve different emphases, you can easily do so on a computer by moving sentences around. To evaluate the versions, however, you need to edit each one so that the sentences flow smoothly, attending to parallelism, repetition, transitions, and the other techniques discussed in this section.

PICTURING THE PARAGRAPH

A good metaphor to use with students is that of cinematography and film. Remind them how in movies the camera can give wide shots, pan in for close-ups, or sweep across a scene for effect. A writer chooses similar "shots" (i.e., positions from which to view the material) in order to organize paragraphs.

Organizing by space or time

A paragraph organized **spatially** focuses readers' attention on one point and scans a person, object, or scene from that point. The movement usually parallels the way people actually look at things, from top to bottom, from side to side, from near to far. Virginia Woolf follows the last pattern in this paragraph:

> The sun struck straight upon the house, making the white walls glare between the dark windows. Their panes, woven thickly with green branches, held circles of impenetrable darkness. Sharp-edged wedges of light lay upon the window-sill and showed inside the room plates with blue rings, cups with curved handles, the bulge of a great bowl, the criss-cross pattern in the rug, and the formidable corners and lines of cabinets and bookcases. Behind their conglomeration hung a zone of shadow in which might be a further shape to be disencumbered of shadow or still denser depths of darkness.
>
> —Virginia Woolf, *The Waves*

Description moving from outside (closer) to inside (farther)

Central idea implied: sunlight barely penetrated the house's secrets

Another familiar way of organizing the elements of a paragraph is **chronologically**—that is, in order of their occurrence in time. In a chronological paragraph, as in experience, the earliest events come first, followed by more recent ones.

> Nor can a tree live without soil. A hurricane-born mangrove island may bring its own soil to the sea. But other mangrove trees make their own soil—and their own islands—from scratch. These are the ones which interest me. The seeds germinate in the fruit on the tree. The germinated embryo can drop anywhere—say, onto a dab of floating muck. The heavy root end sinks; a leafy plumule unfurls. The tiny seedling, afloat, is on its way. Soon aerial roots shooting out in all directions trap debris. The sapling's networks twine, the interstices narrow, and water calms in the lee. Bacteria thrive on organic broth; amphipods swarm. These creatures grow and die at the tree's wet feet. The soil thickens, accumulating rainwater, leaf rot, seashells, and guano; the island spreads.
>
> —ANNIE DILLARD, "Sojourner"

Topic sentence

Details in order of their occurrence

Organizing for emphasis

Some organizational schemes are imposed on paragraphs to achieve a certain emphasis. In the **general-to-specific** scheme, the topic sentence generally comes first and then the following sentences become increasingly specific. The paragraph on mummies (p. 93) illustrates this organization: each sentence is either more specific than the one before it or at the same level of generality. Here is another illustration:

> Perhaps the simplest fact about sleep is that individual needs for it vary widely. Most adults sleep between seven and nine hours, but occasionally people turn up who need twelve hours or so, while some rare types can get by on three or four. Rarest of all are those legendary types who require almost no sleep at all; respected researchers have recently studied three such people. One of them—a healthy, happy woman in her seventies—sleeps about an hour every two or three days. The other two are men in early middle age, who get by on a few minutes a night. One of them complains about the daily fifteen minutes or so he's forced to "waste" in sleeping.
>
> —LAWRENCE A. MAYER, "The Confounding Enemy of Sleep"

Topic sentence

Supporting examples, increasingly specific

In the **specific-to-general** organization, the elements of the paragraph build to a general conclusion.

PARAGRAPH PATTERNS I

Give students a topic sentence and a set of assertions, facts, and details in undeveloped form. Tell them to use the material to write a coherent paragraph, following one of the patterns described in the handbook: spatial, chronological, general-to-specific, specific-to-general, problem-solution, climatic, most familiar to least familiar, or simplest to most complex. Students can manipulate the material however they wish to achieve an effect that is appropriate to the pattern. You may want to ask for several paragraphs, each using the same content but a different pattern.

PARAGRAPH PATTERNS II

As a quiz or an in-class exercise, ask students to write a paragraph following one of the basic organizational schemes discussed in 3b-1. Leave the subject and content of the paragraph up to the individual student. If they wish, students may make up information, as long as they keep it plausible. Students can compare results in group, then work together to revise one of those responses into a paragraph to be "published" on the class computer network or printed out and distributed.

¶ coh
3b

EXTRA EXAMPLES

The following examples illustrate the specific-to-general pattern in a sentence and may be extended to short sample paragraphs:

(specific) + good study habits
(specific) + consistent effort
(specific) + curiosity
(general) = good grades

Good study habits, consistent effort, and intellectual curiosity will result in good grades.

(specific) + seeds
(specific) + soil
(specific) + sunlight
(specific) + water
(general) = good vegetable crop

A combination of fresh seeds, well-balanced soil, and adequate sunlight and water results in a good vegetable crop.

DRAMATIC EXAMPLES

Climatic order is a form of structuring that moves from least to most important. To help explain this strategy you may wish to draw examples from drama, particularly from the structure

It's disconcerting that so many college women, when asked how their children will be cared for if they themselves work, refer with vague confidence to "the day care center" as though there were some great amorphous kiddie watcher out there that the state [Common belief] provides. But such places, adequately funded, well run, and available to all, are still scarce in this country, particularly for middle-class women. And figures show that when she takes time off for family-connected reasons (births, child care), a woman's chances for career advancement plummet. In a job market that's steadily tightening and getting more competitive, these obstacles bode the kind of danger ahead that can shatter not only professions, [Actual situation] but egos. A hard reality is that there's not much more support for our daughters who have family-plus-career goals than there was for us; there's simply a great deal more self and societal pressure. [General conclusion: topic sentence]

—JUDITH WAX, *Starting in the Middle*

As its name implies, the **problem-solution** arrangement introduces a problem and then proposes or explains a solution. This paragraph explains how the Gopher program helps computer users navigate the Internet:

As the Internet has grown, users have run into two related problems: so much information is available that nobody can find it all, and umpteen different ways exist to get to different resources. Gopher solves these [Topic sentence: statement of the problem] problems quite well by reducing nearly everything to menus. You pick an item, and it shows you another menu. After a certain amount of wandering from menu to menu, you get menus with actual, useful stuff. Gopher gets much of its power from the fact that any item in any menu can reside on any host in Gopherspace. Gopher automatically takes care of finding whatever data you want, no matter where they are. [Solution to the problem]

—Adapted from JOHN R. LEVINE and CAROL BAROUDI, *The Internet for Dummies*

When your details vary in significance, you can arrange them in a **climactic** order, from least to most important or dramatic.

Nature has put many strange tongues into the heads of her creatures. There is the [Topic sentence]

frog's tongue, rooted at the front of the mouth so it can be protruded an extra distance for nabbing prey. There is the gecko lizard's tongue, so long and agile that the lizard uses it to wash its eyes. But the ultimate lingual whopper has been achieved in the anteater. The anteater's head, long as it is, is not long enough to contain the tremendous tongue which licks deep into anthills. Its tongue is not rooted in the mouth or throat: it is fastened to the breastbone.

—ALAN DEVOE, "Nature's Utmost"

Least dramatic example

Most dramatic example

In other organizations, you can arrange details according to how you think readers are likely to understand them. In discussing the virtues of public television, for instance, you might proceed from **most familiar to least familiar,** from a well-known program your readers have probably seen to less well-known programs they may not have seen. Or in defending the right of government employees to strike, you might arrange your reasons from **simplest to most complex,** from the employees' need to be able to redress grievances to more subtle consequences for relations between employers and employees.

2 Using parallel structures

Another way to achieve coherence, although not necessarily in every paragraph, is through **parallelism**—the use of similar grammatical structures for similar elements of meaning within a sentence or among sentences. (See Chapter 17 for a detailed discussion of parallelism.) Parallel structures help tie together the last three sentences in the paragraph on mummies (p. 93). In the following paragraph, underlining highlights the parallel structures linking sentences. Aphra Behn (lived 1640–89) was the first Englishwoman to write professionally.

> In addition to her busy career as a writer, Aphra Behn also found time to briefly marry and spend a little while in debtor's prison. She found time to take up a career as a spy for the Eng lish in their war against the Dutch. She made the long and difficult voyage to Suriname [in South America] and became involved in a slave rebellion there. She plunged into political debate at Will's Coffee House and defended her position from the stage of the Drury Lane Theater. She actively argued for women's rights to be educated and to marry whom they pleased, or not at all. She defied the seventeenth-century dictum that ladies must be "modest" and wrote freely about sex.
>
> —ANGELINE GOREAU, "Aphra Behn"

of tragedy. Othello provides an obvious example of structuring that moves from least dramatic/tension-filled to most dramatic/tension-filled.

Least dramatic—Othello marries Desdemona
More dramatic—Othello suspects Desdemona of infidelity
More dramatic—Desdemona defends her chastity and argues for her life
Most dramatic (climax)—Othello kills Desdemona and then realizes that she has been faithful to him

RESOURCES AND IDEAS

Brostoff, Anita. "Coherence: 'Next to' Is Not 'Connected to.'" *College Composition and Communication* 32 (1981): 278–94. Brostoff discusses the causes of lack of coherence in writing and describes a program for helping students achieve coherence.

Christensen, Francis. "A Generative Rhetoric of the Paragraph." In *Notes Toward a New Rhetoric: Nine Essays for Teachers,* 2nd ed. Ed. Francis Christensen and Bonniejean Christensen. New York: Harper & Row, 1978. 74–103. Christensen views paragraphs as a series of statements on differing levels of generality, often moving from more general toward the specific.

Winterowd, W. Ross. "The Grammar of Coherence." *College English* 31 (1971): 828–35. This article describes the kinds of relations that link sentence to sentence and paragraph to paragraph.

LISTENING TO THE MUSIC

To recognize the power of repetition, students need only turn to rock music. Have them begin by listing the titles of popular songs whose lyrics they know by heart. Then ask them to identify words and phrases that they remember best from the songs or that they learned first. Chances are that they will identify the chorus because it is the element of the song most often repeated. You might point out that choruses help unify songs. Students may also note that the considerable amount of repetition in many songs makes them easy to remember and helps create a unified effect. This exercise may also be used to point out the difference between effective use of repetition and overuse.

HE'S ON SECOND

To illustrate the importance of clear pronoun reference in paragraphs, try to locate a recording or transcript of the famous Abbott and Costello skit, "Who's on First." While humorous, this skit demonstrates the frustration a reader can feel when encountering a series of pronouns with unclear antecedents. Keep in mind that students' use of unclear pronoun antecedents may signal a larger difficulty in defining or expanding on their subject matter.

3 Repeating or restating words and word groups

Repeating or restating key words or word groups is an important means of achieving paragraph coherence and of reminding your readers what the topic is. In the next example, notice how the circled words tie the sentences together and stress the important ideas of the paragraph:

> Having listened to both Chinese and English, I also tend to be suspicious of any comparisons between the two languages. Typically, one language—that of the person doing the comparing—is often used as the standard, the benchmark for a logical form of expression. And so the language being compared is always in danger of being judged deficient or superfluous, simplistic or unnecessarily complex, melodious or cacophonous. English speakers point out that Chinese is extremely difficult because it relies on variations in tone barely discernible to the human ear. By the same token, Chinese speakers tell me English is extremely difficult because it is inconsistent, a language of too many broken rules, of Mickey Mice and Donald Ducks. —AMY TAN, "The Language of Discretion"

NOTE Though planned repetition can be effective, careless or excessive repetition weakens prose (see p. 476).

4 Using pronouns

Pronouns, such as *she, he, it, they,* and *who,* refer to and function as nouns (see p. 165). Thus pronouns naturally help relate sentences to one another. In the following paragraph the pronouns and the nouns they refer to are circled:

> After dark, on the warrenlike streets of Brooklyn where I live, I often see women who fear the worst from me. They seem to have set their faces on neutral, and with their purse straps strung across their chests bandolier-style, they forge ahead as though bracing themselves against being tackled. I understand, of course, that the danger they perceive is not a hallucination. Women are particularly vulnerable to street violence, and young black males are drastically overrepresented among the perpetrators of that violence. Yet these truths are no solace against the kind of alienation that

comes of being ever the suspect, a fearsome entity with whom pedestrians avoid making eye contact.

—BRENT STAPLES, "Black Men and Public Space"

5 Being consistent

Being consistent is the most subtle way to achieve paragraph coherence because readers are aware of consistency only when it is absent. Consistency (or the lack of it) occurs primarily in the tense of verbs and the number and person of nouns and pronouns (see Chapter 13). Although some shifts will be necessary because of meaning, inappropriate shifts, as in the following passages, will interfere with a reader's ability to follow the development of ideas.

SHIFTS IN TENSE

In the Hopi religion, water *is* the driving force. Since the Hopi *lived* in the Arizona desert, they *needed* water urgently for drinking, cooking, and irrigating crops. Their complex beliefs *are* focused in part on gaining the assistance of supernatural forces in obtaining water. Many of the Hopi kachinas, or spirit essences, *were* directly concerned with clouds, rain, and snow.

SHIFTS IN NUMBER

Kachinas represent spiritually the things and events of the real world, such as cumulus clouds, mischief, cornmeal, and even death. A *kachina* is not worshipped as a god but regarded as an interested friend. *They* visit the Hopi from December through July in the form of men who dress in kachina costumes and perform dances and other rituals.

SHIFTS IN PERSON

Unlike the man, the Hopi *woman* does not keep contact with kachinas through costumes and dancing. Instead, *one* receives a tihu, or small effigy, of a kachina from the man impersonating the kachina. *You* are more likely to receive a tihu as a girl approaching marriage, though a child or older woman sometimes receives one, too.

6 Using transitional expressions

Specific words and word groups, called **transitional expressions,** can connect sentences whose relationships may not be instantly clear to readers. Notice the difference in these two versions of the same paragraph:

Medical science has succeeded in identifying the hundreds of viruses that can cause the common cold. It has discovered the most effective means of prevention. One person

Paragraph is choppy and hard to follow

READING ALOUD

Often students can spot a lack of transitions in their own writing if they read their papers aloud. If you ask students to read one another's papers aloud, the student writers will often be able to recognize missing or unclear transitions at those points where the readers stumble over a passage or have to stop to puzzle out the meaning.

¶ coh
3b

HIGHLIGHTING TRANSITIONS

Encourage students to use highlighting pens or the highlighting feature on a word processor to mark where transitional expressions appear in their texts; if they think too few "highlights" show up, students can add more.

PARAGRAPH SCRAMBLES

These activities are suitable for students working individually; when assigned to small groups, however, the activities work even better by encouraging considerable discussion and discovery.

1. Take a good paragraph, by either a student or a professional, and rearrange the sentences. Then ask students to unscramble the sentences and make a clear, coherent paragraph. This exercise will make students aware of the flow of a coherent paragraph and will alert them to the number of examples and details found in a well-developed paragraph.
2. Choose a paragraph that lacks coherence and rearrange the sentences. Tell students to unscramble the sentences to form a coherent paragraph. Indicate that students are free to add any transitions, sentences, illustrations, or details they feel are necessary to make the paragraph both coherent and well developed. Students will quickly spot any coherence problems in the original paragraph, and unless the topic of the paragraph is quite unusual, they will be able to add any necessary content.

COLLABORATIVE LEARNING

Ask students to work in groups to analyze what happens when they substitute another transition from the same group into one of the sentences from Kathleen LaFrank's paragraph. How can a transitional word affect the meaning of that sentence and of the relationships between sentences?

transmits the cold viruses to another most often by hand. An infected person covers his mouth to cough. He picks up the telephone. His daughter picks up the telephone. She rubs her eyes. She has a cold. It spreads. To avoid colds, people should wash their hands often and keep their hands away from their faces.

Medical science has thus succeeded in identifying the hundreds of viruses that can cause the common cold. It has also discovered the most effective means of prevention. One person transmits the cold viruses to another most often by hand. For instance, an infected person covers his mouth to cough. Then he picks up the telephone. Half an hour later, his daughter picks up the same telephone. Immediately afterward, she rubs her eyes. Within a few days, she, too, has a cold. And thus it spreads. To avoid colds, therefore, people should wash their hands often and keep their hands away from their faces.

Transitional expressions (boxed) remove choppiness and spell out relationships

—Kathleen LaFrank (student), "Colds: Myth and Science"

To see where transitional expressions might be needed in your paragraphs, examine the movement from each sentence to the next. (On a computer or on paper, you can highlight the transitional expressions already present and check the sentences without them.) Abrupt changes are most likely to need a transition: a shift from cause to effect, a contradiction, a contrast. But you can also smooth and clarify other kinds of transitions, such as those in the headings of the box below. (You can smooth and clarify transitions *between* paragraphs, too. See pp. 122 and 123–25.)

Transitional expressions

To add or show sequence

again, also, and, and then, besides, equally important, finally, first, further, furthermore, in addition, in the first place, last, moreover, next, second, still, too

To compare
also, in the same way, likewise, similarly

To contrast
although, and yet, but, but at the same time, despite, even so, even though, for all that, however, in contrast, in spite of, nevertheless, notwithstanding, on the contrary, on the other hand, regardless, still, though, yet

To give examples or intensify
after all, an illustration of, even, for example, for instance, indeed, in fact, it is true, of course, specifically, that is, to illustrate, truly

To indicate place
above, adjacent to, below, elsewhere, farther on, here, near, nearby, on the other side, opposite to, there, to the east, to the left

To indicate time
after a while, afterward, as long as, as soon as, at last, at length, at that time, before, earlier, formerly, immediately, in the meantime, in the past, lately, later, meanwhile, now, presently, shortly, simultaneously, since, so far, soon, subsequently, then, thereafter, until, when

To repeat, summarize, or conclude
all in all, altogether, as has been said, in brief, in conclusion, in other words, in particular, in short, in simpler terms, in summary, on the whole, that is, therefore, to put it differently, to summarize

To show cause or effect
accordingly, as a result, because, consequently, for this purpose, hence, otherwise, since, then, therefore, thereupon, thus, to this end, with this object

---

Note Draw carefully on this list of transitional expressions because the ones in each group are not interchangeable. For instance, *besides, finally,* and *second* may all be used to add information, but each has its own distinct meaning.

ESL If you are writing in English as a second language, you may be tempted to add transitional expressions at the beginnings of most sentences. But such explicit transitions aren't needed everywhere, and in fact too many can be intrusive and awkward. When inserting transitional expressions, consider the reader's need for a signal: often the connection from sentence to sentence is already clear from the context, or it can be made clear by relating the content of sentences more closely (see p. 98). When you do need transitional expressions, try varying their positions in your sentences in the beginning, sometimes in the middle, even sometimes at the end. The sample paragraph on the preceding page illustrates such variety.

Punctuating transitional expressions

A transitional expression is usually set off by a comma or commas from the rest of the sentence:

> *Immediately afterward*, she rubs her eyes. *Within a few days*, she, *too*, has a cold.

See page 373 for more on this convention and its exceptions.

7 Combining devices to achieve coherence

The devices we have examined for achieving coherence rarely appear in isolation in effective paragraphs. As any example in this chapter shows, writers usually combine sensible organization, parallelism, repetition, pronouns, consistency, and transitional expressions to help readers follow the development of ideas. And the devices also figure, naturally, in the whole essay (see pp. 123–25 for an example of paragraphs linked in an essay).

Exercise 6
Analyzing paragraphs for coherence

Study the paragraphs by Janet Lieber (p. 90), Hillary Begas (p. 106), and Freeman Dyson (p. 108) for the authors' use of various devices to achieve coherence. Look especially for organization, parallel structures and ideas, repetition and restatement, pronouns, and transitional expressions.

Exercise 7
Arranging sentences coherently

After the topic sentence (sentence 1), the sentences in the student paragraph below have been deliberately scrambled to make the paragraph incoherent. Using the topic sentence and other clues as guides, rearrange the sentences in the paragraph to form a well-organized, coherent unit.

We hear complaints about the Postal Service all the time, but 1
we should not forget what it does *right*. The total volume of mail 2
delivered by the Postal Service each year makes up almost half
the total delivered in all the world. Its 70,000 employees handle 3
140,000,000,000 pieces of mail each year. And when was the last 4
time they failed to deliver yours? In fact, on any given day the Postal 5
Service delivers almost as much mail as the rest of the world combined. That huge number means over 2,000,000 pieces per employee 6
and over 560 pieces per man, woman, and child in the country.

Exercise 8
Eliminating inconsistencies

The following paragraph is incoherent because of inconsistencies in person, number, or tense. Identify the inconsistencies and revise

COLLABORATIVE LEARNING

Exercise 6 works well as a group exercise because students have more opportunity to debate and explore options. Have each group report back to the class on the different methods each writer uses to achieve coherence.

ANSWERS: EXERCISE 6

1. *Lieber paragraph* (p. 90): Organization: general to specific. Parallelism after first sentence: *They have measured . . . recorded and studied . . . learned.* Repetition: *whale, sings, song.* Pronoun: *they.* Transitional expression: *And.*
2. *Begas paragraph* (p. 106): Organization: chronological. Parallelism: *They persuaded . . . they deprived; Jill became . . . she dropped out.* Repetition: *lonely, college/school.* Pronouns: *Jill/she; men and women/they.* Transitional expressions: *Between . . . , increasingly, Before long, too.*
3. *Dyson paragraph* (p. 108): Organization: climatic. Parallelism and repetition: *reason is the need . . . reason is the need . . . reason is our spiritual need.* Further repetition: *space, earth/this planet.* Pronouns: *we, our, us.* Transitional expressions: *first, second, third.*

COMPUTER EXERCISE

The computer makes scrambling exercises particularly viable. Ask each student to scramble the sentence order deliberately in one of their own paragraphs and then present that exercise in "unscrambling" to their group. It can be very useful for each writer to hear their own coherence "clues" being analyzed and debated.

the paragraph to give it coherence. (For further exercises in eliminating inconsistencies, see pp. 292, 293, and 296.)

The Hopi tihu, or kachina effigy, is often called a "doll," but its owner, usually a girl or woman, does not regard them as a plaything. Instead, you treated them as a valued possession and hung them out of the way on a wall. For its owner the tihu represents a connection with the kachina's spirit. They are considered part of the kachina, carrying a portion of the kachina's power.

Exercise 9
Using transitional expressions

Transitional expressions have been removed from the following paragraph at the numbered blanks. Fill in each blank with an appropriate transitional expression (1) to contrast, (2) to intensify, and (3) to show effect. Consult the list on page 100 if necessary.

All over the country, people are swimming, jogging, weightlifting, dancing, walking, playing tennis—doing anything to keep fit. ___(1)___ this school has consistently refused to construct and equip a fitness center. The school has ___(2)___ refused to open existing athletic facilities to all students, not just those playing organized sports. ___(3)___ students have no place to exercise except in their rooms and on dangerous public roads.

Exercise 10
Considering your past work: Paragraph coherence

Continuing from Exercise 3 (p. 91), examine the body paragraphs of your essay to see how coherent they are and how their coherence could be improved. Do the paragraphs have a clear organization? Do you use parallelism, repetition and restatement, pronouns, and transitional expressions to signal relationships? Are the paragraphs consistent in person, number, and tense? Revise two or three paragraphs in ways you think will improve their coherence.

Exercise 11
Writing a coherent paragraph

Write a coherent paragraph from the following information, combining and rewriting sentences as necessary. First, begin the paragraph with the topic sentence given and arrange the supporting sentences in a climactic order. Then combine and rewrite the supporting sentences, helping the reader see connections by introducing parallelism, repetition and restatement, pronouns, consistency, and transitional expressions.

Topic sentence

Hypnosis is far superior to drugs for relieving tension.

Supporting information

Hypnosis has none of the dangerous side effects of the drugs that relieve tension.

ANSWERS: EXERCISE 7

Possible answer

The coherent order would be 1, 2, 5, 3, 6, 4.

ANSWERS: EXERCISE 8

The Hopi tihu, or kachina effigy, is often called a "doll," but its owner, usually a girl or woman, does not regard <u>it</u> as a plaything. Instead, <u>she treats it</u> as a valued possession and <u>hangs it</u> out of the way on a wall. For its owner<u>,</u> the tihu represents a connection with the kachina's spirit. <u>It is</u> considered part of the kachina, carrying a portion of the kachina's power.

ANSWERS: EXERCISE 9

Possible answers

1. *Yet, However, Even so,* or *Nevertheless*
2. *even, also,* or *further*
3. *As a result, Consequently,* or *Therefore*

COLLABORATIVE LEARNING

Ask students to compare answers to Exercise 9 and discuss the effects of each student's choices on the meaning of the sentences and of the paragraph.

ANSWERS: EXERCISE 10

Individual response.

ANSWERS: EXERCISE 11

Possible paragraph

Hypnosis is far superior to drugs for relieving tension. It is inexpensive even for people who have not mastered self-hypnosis, whereas drugs are expensive. It is nonaddictive, whereas drugs foster addiction. And most important, hypnosis has none of the dangerous side effects of drugs, such as weight loss or gain, illness, or even death.

COMPUTER EXERCISE

Exercise 11 is particularly feasible on the computer since students can rearrange the information in multiple ways without retyping.

COLLABORATIVE LEARNING

The kind of the coherence achieved in Exercises 11 and 12 will depend a great deal on each individual's choice of connective strategies. When students compare their responses to Exercises 11 and 12 in groups it is beneficial for them to note the results of other writers' differing choices.

ANSWERS: EXERCISE 12

Individual response.

Tension-relieving drugs can cause weight loss or gain, illness, or even death.
Hypnosis is nonaddicting.
Most of the drugs that relieve tension do foster addiction.
Tension-relieving drugs are expensive.
Hypnosis is inexpensive even for people who have not mastered self-hypnosis.

Exercise 12
Turning topic sentences into coherent paragraphs

Develop three of the following topic sentences into coherent paragraphs. Organize your information by space, by time, or for emphasis, as seems most appropriate. Use parallelism, repetition and restatement, pronouns, consistency, and transitional expressions to link sentences.

1. The most interesting character in the book [or movie] was ________.
2. Of all my courses, ________ is the one that I think will serve me best throughout life.
3. Although we Americans face many problems, the one we should concentrate on solving first is ________.
4. The most dramatic building in town is the ________.
5. Children should not have to worry about the future.

HIGHLIGHTS

This section (3c) looks at ways to convey the central idea of a paragraph fully and convincingly to the reader. Developing paragraphs and essays fully is often difficult for students. One of the important differences between casual conversation and formal writing is the degree to which ideas must be concretely developed in writing. Because students are more experienced in conversation than in writing, they find generalizations much easier to come by than the details, examples, and reasons to support them.

All of us must grapple with the student essay or single paragraph that is largely a succession of generalizations without support or explanation. Part of the solution to such problem paragraphs is to make students aware of readers as a special kind of audience for ideas. Another part is to make them aware of different strategies for developing paragraphs or essays.

The ways to develop ideas are infinite, but this section focuses on a limited number. The initial emphasis falls on the use of details, examples, and reasons, which are essential to any

3c Developing the paragraph

In an essay that's understandable and interesting to readers, you will provide plenty of solid information to support your general statements. You work that information into the essay through the paragraph, as you build up each point relating to the thesis.

A paragraph may be unified and coherent but still be inadequate if you skimp on details. Take this example:

> Despite complaints from viewers, television commercials aren't getting any more realistic. Their makers still present idealized people in unreal situations. And the advertisers also persist in showing a version of male-female relationships that can't exist in more than two households. What do the advertisers know about us, or about how we see ourselves, that makes them continue to plunge millions of dollars into these kinds of commercials?

General statements needing examples to be convincing

This paragraph lacks **development,** completeness. It does not provide enough information for us to evaluate or even care about the writer's assertions.

 Using specific information

If they are sound, the general statements you make in any writing will be based on what you have experienced, observed, read, and thought. Readers will assume as much and will expect you to provide the evidence for your statements—sensory details, facts, statistics, examples, quotations, reasons. Whatever helps you form your views you need, in turn, to share with readers.

Here is the actual version of the preceding sample paragraph. With examples, the paragraph is interesting and convincing.

> Despite complaints from viewers, television commercials aren't getting any more realistic. Their makers still present idealized people in unreal situations. Friendly shopkeepers stock only their favorite brand of toothpaste or coffee or soup. A mother cleans and buffs her kitchen floor to a mirror finish so her baby can play on it. A rosy-cheeked pregnant woman uses two babies, two packaged diapers neatly dissected, and two ink blotters to demonstrate one diaper's superior absorbency to her equally rosy-cheeked and pregnant friend. The advertisers also persist in showing a version of male-female relationships that can't exist in more than two households. The wife panics because a meddlesome neighbor points out that her husband's shirt is dirty. Or she fears for her marriage because her finicky husband doesn't like her coffee. What do the advertisers know about us, or about how we see ourselves, that makes them continue to plunge millions of dollars into these kinds of commercials?
>
> —KELLY PHELPS (student), "Television Advertising"

Examples supporting general statements about idealized people and false relationships

If your readers often comment that your writing needs more specifics, you should focus on that improvement in your revisions. Try listing the general statements of each paragraph on lines by themselves with space underneath. Then use one of the discovery techniques discussed on pages 38–45 (freewriting, brainstorming, and so on) to find the details to support each sentence. Write these into your draft. (If you write on a computer, you can do this revision directly on your draft. Working on a copy, separate the sentences and explore their support. Then rewrite the details into sentences, reassemble the paragraph, and edit it for coherence.)

more specific method of development. Students are encouraged to follow the standard methods or patterns of development by posing questions about an idea, event, or object in order to uncover concrete information about it.

You may wish to ask students to spend time in class or in groups working with sample topics to discover how the methods of development can be used to probe a topic and how the questions reveal different aspects of a topic. This discussion may help students see how the process of development can be an act of discovery. You will probably want to stress, however, that the methods of development covered in the handbook are not the only ones writers can use and that most paragraphs use more than a single method.

The exercises for this section range from analyzing paragraphs to producing them, and whether used in groups or by students working individually, they encourage students to treat the patterns of development as different ways of viewing a topic.

¶ dev
3c

RESOURCES AND IDEAS

Cohan, Carol. "Writing Effective Paragraphs." *College Composition and Communication* 27 (1976): 363–65. Cohan suggests encouraging paragraph development by treating topic sentences as questions to be answered by the paragraph that follows.

THE SUBJECTIVE-OBJECTIVE BOUNDARY

Students may find that the subjective-objective boundary is sometimes fuzzy. Even the objective paragraph has judgmental language like "piercing" in it. Perhaps a way of solving this dilemma is to say that in *subjective* description, the writer's intention is to interpret experience for readers, while in *objective* description, the writer's intention is to allow the audience to interpret the reported experiences themselves.

2 Using a pattern of development

If you have difficulty developing an idea or shaping your information, then try using one of the patterns of development. (They correspond to the patterns of essay development discussed on pp. 44–45.) Ask yourself a series of questions about an idea.

How did it happen? (Narration)

Narration retells a significant sequence of events, usually in the order of their occurrence (that is, chronologically):

> Jill's story is typical for "recruits" to religious cults. She was very lonely in college and appreciated the attention of the nice young men and women who lived in a house near campus. They persuaded her to share their meals and then to move in with them. Between intense bombardments of "love," they deprived her of sleep and sometimes threatened to throw her out. Jill became increasingly confused and dependent, losing touch with any reality besides the one in the group. She dropped out of school and refused to see or communicate with her family. Before long she, too, was preying on lonely college students.
>
> —HILLARY BEGAS (student), "The Love Bombers"

Important events in chronological order

As this paragraph illustrates, a narrator is concerned not just with the sequence of events but also with their consequence, their importance to the whole. Thus a narrative rarely corresponds to real time; instead, it collapses transitional or background events and focuses on events of particular interest. In addition, writers often rearrange events, as when they simulate the workings of memory by flashing back to an earlier time.

How does it look, sound, feel, smell, taste? (Description)

Description details the sensory qualities of a person, place, thing, or feeling. You use concrete and specific words to convey a dominant mood, to illustrate an idea, or to achieve some other purpose. Some description is **subjective:** the writer filters the subject through his or her biases and emotions. In Woolf's subjective description on page 94, the *glare* of the white walls, the *impenetrable darkness,* the *bulge of a great bowl,* and the *formidable corners and lines* all indicate Woolf's feelings about what she describes.

In contrast to subjective description, journalists and scientists often favor description that is **objective,** conveying the subject without bias or emotion:

The two toddlers, both boys, sat together for half an hour in a ten-foot-square room with yellow walls (one with a two-way mirror for observation) and a brown carpet. The room was unfurnished except for two small chairs and about two dozen toys. The boys' interaction was generally tense. They often struggled physically and verbally over several toys, especially a large red beach ball and a small wooden fire engine. The larger of the two boys often pushed the smaller away or pried his hands from the desired object. This larger boy never spoke, but he did make grunting sounds when he was engaging the other. In turn, the smaller boy twice uttered piercing screams of "No!" and once shouted "Stop that!" When he was left alone, he hummed and muttered to himself.

—RAY MATTISON (student), "Case Study: Play Patterns of Toddlers"

Objective description: specific record of sensory data without interpretation

What are examples of it or reasons for it? (Illustration or support)

Some ideas can be developed simply by **illustration or support**—supplying detailed examples or reasons. The writer of the paragraph on television commercials (p. 105) developed her idea with several specific examples of each general statement. You can also supply a single extended example:

The language problem that I was attacking loomed larger and larger as I began to learn more. When I would describe in English certain concepts and objects enmeshed in Korean emotion and imagination, I became slowly aware of nuances, of differences between two languages even in simple expression. The remark "Kim entered the house" seems to be simple enough, yet, unless a reader has a clear visual image of a Korean house, his understanding of the sentence is not complete. When a Korean says he is "in the house," he may be in his courtyard, or on his porch, or in his small room! If I wanted to give a specific picture of entering the house in the Western sense, I had to say "room" instead of house—sometimes. I say "sometimes" because many Koreans entertain their guests on their porches and still are considered to be hospitable, and in the Korean

Topic sentence (assertion to be illustrated)

Single detailed example

CROSS-CULTURAL COMMUNICATION (ESL)

This pan-cultural example lends itself to collaborative discussion; students might collect and discuss examples of mistranslations from other languages to English or from English to other languages. For instance, the Chevy Nova was a failure when it was introduced in Puerto Rico because *No va* means "It doesn't run" in Spanish. Students for whom English is a second language can contribute many examples of idioms that give them trouble.

¶ dev
3c

> sense, going into the "room" may be a more intimate act than it would be in the English sense. Such problems!
>
> —KIM YONG IK, "A Book-Writing Venture"

Sometimes you can develop a paragraph by providing your reasons for stating a general idea:

> There are three reasons, quite apart from scientific considerations, that mankind needs to travel in space. The first reason is the need for garbage disposal: we need to transfer industrial processes into space, so that the earth may remain a green and pleasant place for our grandchildren to live in. The second reason is the need to escape material impoverishment: the resources of this planet are finite, and we shall not forgo forever the abundant solar energy and minerals and living space that are spread out all around us. The third reason is our spiritual need for an open frontier: the ultimate purpose of space travel is to bring to humanity not only scientific discoveries and an occasional spectacular show on television but a real expansion of our spirit.
>
> —FREEMAN DYSON, "Disturbing the Universe"

Topic sentence

Three reasons arranged in order of increasing drama and importance

What is it? What does it encompass, and what does it exclude? (Definition)

A **definition** says what something is and is not, specifying the characteristics that distinguish the subject from the other members of its class. You can easily define concrete, noncontroversial terms in a single sentence: *A knife is a cutting instrument* (its class) *with a sharp blade set in a handle* (the characteristics that set it off from, say, scissors or a razor blade). But defining a complicated or controversial topic often requires extended explanation, and you may need to devote a whole paragraph or even an essay to it. Such a definition may provide examples to identify the subject's characteristics. It may also involve other methods of development discussed below, such as classification or comparison and contrast.

The following definition of the word *quality* comes from an essay asserting that "quality in product and effort has become a vanishing element of current civilization":

> In the hope of possibly reducing the hail of censure which is certain to greet this essay (I am thinking of going to Alaska or possibly Patagonia in the week it is published), let me say that quality, as I understand it, means

investment of the best skill and effort possible to produce the finest and most admirable result possible. Its presence or absence in some degree characterizes every man-made object, service, skilled or unskilled labor—laying bricks, painting a picture, ironing shirts, practicing medicine, shoemaking, scholarship, writing a book. You do it well or you do it half-well. Materials are sound and durable or they are sleazy; method is painstaking or whatever is easiest. Quality is achieving or reaching for the highest standard as against being satisfied with the sloppy or fraudulent. It is honesty of purpose as against catering to cheap or sensational sentiment. It does not allow compromise with the second-rate.

—BARBARA TUCHMAN, "The Decline of Quality"

General definition

Activities in which quality may figure

Contrast between quality and non-quality

What are its parts or characteristics? (Division or analysis)

Division and **analysis** both involve separating something into its elements, the better to understand it. Here is a simple example:

A typical daily newspaper compresses considerable information into the top of the first page, above the headlines. The most prominent feature of this space, the newspaper's name, is called the *logo* or *nameplate.* Under the logo and set off by rules is a line of small type called the *folio line,* which contains the date of the issue, the volume and issue numbers, copyright information, and the price. To the right of the logo is a block of small type called a *weather ear,* a summary of the day's forecast. And above the logo is a *skyline,* a kind of advertisement in which the paper's editors highlight a special feature of the issue.

—KANSHA STONE (student), "Anatomy of a Paper"

The subject being divided

Elements of the subject, arranged spatially

Generally, analysis goes beyond simply identifying elements. Often used as a synonym for *critical thinking,* analysis also involves interpreting the elements' meaning, significance, and relationships. You identify and interpret elements according to your particular interest in the subject. (See pp. 10–17 for more on critical thinking and analysis.)

The following paragraph comes from an essay about soap operas. The analytical focus of the whole essay is the way soap operas provide viewers with a sense of community missing from their own lives. The paragraph itself has a narrower focus related to the broader one.

EXTRA EXAMPLES

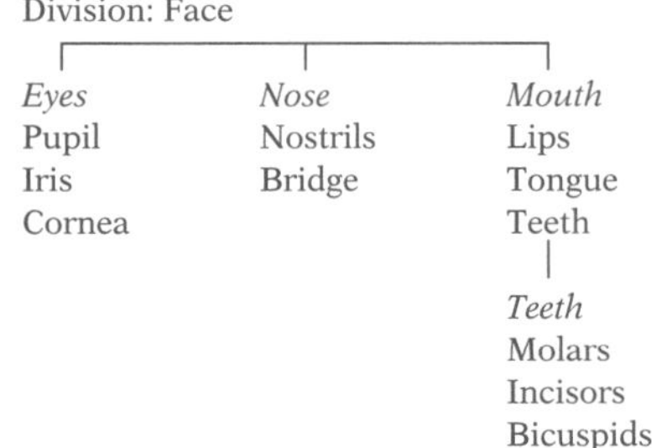

The surface realism of the soap opera conjures up an illusion of "liveness." The domestic settings and easygoing rhythms encourage the viewer to believe that the drama, however ridiculous, is simply an extension of daily life. The conversation is so slow that some have called it "radio with pictures." (Advertisers have always assumed that busy housewives would listen, rather than watch.) Conversation is casual and colloquial, as though one were eavesdropping on neighbors. There is plenty of time to "read" the character's face; close-ups establish intimacy. The sets are comfortably familiar: well-lit interiors of living rooms, restaurants, offices, and hospitals. Daytime soaps have little of the glamour of their prime-time relations. The viewer easily imagines that the conversation is taking place in real time.

—Ruth Rosen, "Search for Yesterday"

Topic and focus: how "liveness" seems an extension of daily life

Elements:
Slow conversation
Casual conversation
Intimate close-ups
Familiar sets
Absence of glamour
Appearance of real time

What groups or categories can it be sorted into? (Classification)

Classification involves sorting many things into groups based on their similarities. Using the pattern, we scan a large group composed of many members that share at least one characteristic—office workers, say—and we assign the members to smaller groups on the basis of some principle—salary, perhaps, or dependence on computers. Here is an example:

In my experience, the parents who hire daytime sitters for their school-age children tend to fall into one of three groups. The first group includes parents who work and want someone to be at home when the children return from school. These parents are looking for an extension of themselves, someone who will give the care they would give if they were at home. The second group includes parents who may be home all day themselves but are too disorganized or too frazzled by their children's demands to handle child care alone. They are looking for an organizer and helpmate. The third and final group includes parents who do not want to be bothered by their children, whether they are home all day or not. Unlike the parents in the first two groups, who care for their children whenever and however they can, these parents are looking for a permanent substitute for themselves.

—Nancy Whittle (student), "Modern Parenting"

Topic sentence

Three groups:
Alike in one way (all hire sitters)
No overlap in groups (each has a different attitude)

Classes arranged in order of increasing drama

CLASSIFICATION PRACTICE

Other topics to be classified might include car models, job categories, types of music, and local restaurants. (You might want to bring in the Yellow Pages for the last topic.)

EXTRA EXAMPLES

Classification:

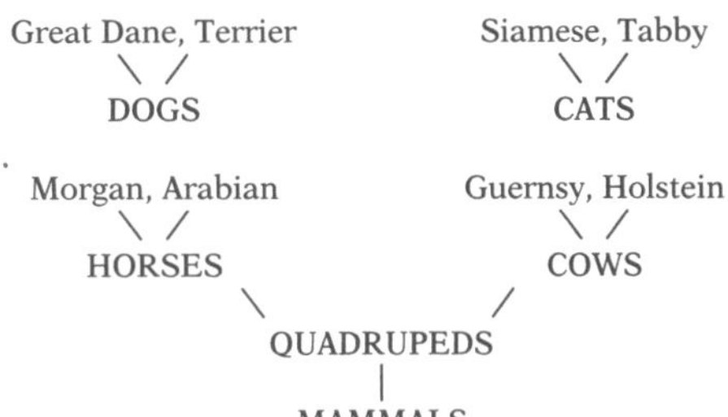

IMITATING PARAGRAPHS

Choose a successful paragraph (student or professional) with a clear pattern, and discuss it in class. Then ask students to write paragraphs imitating the pattern but not the content of the model paragraph.

How is it like, or different from, other things? (Comparison and contrast)

Asking about similarities and differences leads to **comparison and contrast:** comparison focuses on similarities, whereas contrast focuses on differences. The two may be used separately or together to develop an idea or to relate two or more things. Commonly, comparisons are organized in one of two ways. In the first, **subject by subject,** the two subjects are discussed separately, one at a time:

> Consider the differences also in the behavior of rock and classical music audiences. At a rock concert, the audience members yell, whistle, sing along, and stamp their feet. They may even stand during the entire performance. The better the music, the more active they'll be. At a classical concert, in contrast, the better the performance, the more *still* the audience is. Members of the classical audience are so highly disciplined that they refrain from even clearing their throats or coughing. No matter what effect the powerful music has on their intellects and feelings, they sit on their hands.
>
> —Tony Nahm (student), "Rock and Roll Is Here to Stay"

Subjects: rock and classical audiences

Rock audience

Classical audience

In the second comparative organization, **point by point,** the two subjects are discussed side by side and matched feature for feature:

> The first electronic computer, ENIAC, went into operation not even fifty years ago, yet the differences between it and today's home computer are enormous. ENIAC was enormous itself, consisting of forty panels, each two feet wide and four feet deep. Today's PC or Macintosh, by contrast, can fit easily on one's desk. ENIAC had to be configured by hand, with its programmers taking up to two days to reset switches and cables. Today, the average home user can change programs in an instant. And for all its size and inconvenience, ENIAC was also slow. In its time, its operating speed of 100,000 pulses per second seemed amazingly fast. However, today's home machine can operate at 4 million pulses per second or faster.
>
> —Shirley Kajiwara (student), "The Computers We Deserve"

Subjects: ENIAC and home computer

Size: ENIAC, home computer

Ease of programming: ENIAC, home computer

Speed: ENIAC, home computer

The following examples show the two organizing schemes in outline form. The one on the left corresponds to the point-by-point

COLLABORATIVE LEARNING

Team classification

Ask teams of students to compile the group of sentences or facts from an area they know well (for instance, sports, business, entertainment, social groups, or activities). Have the groups exchange sets of sentences and then attempt to assemble them into paragraphs. When the paragraphs are written, the "expert" collectors should critique the perspective each offers.

paragraph about computers. The one on the right uses the same information but reorganizes it to cover the two subjects separately, first one, then the other.

POINT BY POINT	SUBJECT BY SUBJECT
I. Size	I. ENIAC
A. ENIAC	A. Size
B. Home computer	B. Ease of programming
II. Ease of programming	C. Speed
A. ENIAC	II. Home computer
B. Home computer	A. Size
III. Speed	B. Ease of programming
A. ENIAC	C. Speed
B. Home computer	

Is it comparable to something that is in a different class but more familiar to readers? (Analogy)

Whereas we draw comparisons and contrasts between elements in the same general class (audiences, computers), we link elements in different classes with a special kind of comparison called **analogy.** Most often in analogy we illuminate or explain an unfamiliar, abstract class of things with a familiar and concrete class of things:

> We might eventually obtain some sort of bedrock understanding of cosmic structure, but we will never understand the universe in detail; it is just too big and varied for that. If we possessed an atlas of our galaxy that devoted but a single page to each star system in the Milky Way (so that the sun and all its planets were crammed on one page), that atlas would run to more than ten million volumes of ten thousand pages each. It would take a library the size of Harvard's to house the atlas, and merely to flip through it, at the rate of a page per second, would require over ten thousand years.
>
> —TIMOTHY FERRIS, *Coming of Age in the Milky Way*

Abstract subject: the universe, specifically the Milky Way

Concrete subject: an atlas

Why did it happen, or what results did it have? (Cause-and-effect analysis)

When you use analysis to explain why something happened or what is likely to happen, then you are determining causes and effects. **Cause-and-effect analysis** is especially useful in writing about social, economic, or political events or problems. In the next paragraph the author looks at the causes of Japanese collectivism, which he elsewhere contrasts with American individualism:

> The *shinkansen* or "bullet train" speeds across the rural areas of Japan giving a quick

COMBINING FOR EMPHASIS

Put together a group of sentences or bits of information about a topic, perhaps drawing the material from an essay in a reader or a magazine article. Ask students, working individually or in groups, to combine the material into a paragraph that has a distinct point of view. You might, for example, provide information about a recent controversial incident and ask for a paragraph emphasizing one perspective toward the incident or one perspective on its causes and effects.

> view of cluster after cluster of farmhouses surrounded by rice paddies. This particular pattern did not develop purely by chance, but as a consequence of the technology peculiar to the growing of rice, the staple of the Japanese diet. The growing of rice requires the construction and maintenance of an irrigation system, something that takes many hands to build. More importantly, the planting and the harvesting of rice can only be done efficiently with the cooperation of twenty or more people. The "bottom line" is that a single family working alone cannot produce enough rice to survive, but a dozen families working together can produce a surplus. Thus the Japanese have had to develop the capacity to work together in harmony, no matter what the forces of disagreement or social disintegration, in order to survive.
>
> —WILLIAM OUCHI, *Theory Z: How American Business Can Meet the Japanese Challenge*

Effect: pattern of Japanese farming

Causes: Japanese dependence on rice, which requires collective effort

Effect: working in harmony

Cause-and-effect paragraphs tend to focus either on causes, as Ouchi's does, or on effects, as this paragraph does:

> At each step, with every graduation from one level of education to the next, the refrain from bystanders was strangely the same: "Your parents must be so proud of you." I suppose that my parents were proud, although I suspect, too, that they felt more than pride alone as they watched me advance through my education. They seemed to know that my education was separating us from one another, making it difficult to resume familiar intimacies. Mixed with the instincts of parental pride, a certain hurt also communicated itself—too private ever to be adequately expressed in words, but real nonetheless.
>
> —RICHARD RODRIGUEZ, "Going Home Again"

Cause: education

Effects:
Pride
Separation
Loss of intimacies
Hurt

How does one do it, or how does it work? (Process analysis)

When you analyze how to do something or how something works, you explain the steps in a **process.** Paragraphs developed by process analysis are usually organized chronologically, as the steps in the process occur. Some process analyses tell the reader how to do a task:

> As a car owner, you waste money when you pay a mechanic to change the engine oil. The job is not difficult, even if you know little about cars. All you need is a wrench to remove

Process: changing oil

COLLABORATIVE LEARNING

PRACTICAL INSTRUCTIONS

The most hilarious process exercise is one of the oldest: bring the ingredients for peanut butter and jelly sandwiches to class. Have each group write instructions for making a peanut butter and jelly sandwich. Then have the groups exchange instructions and make the sandwich exactly according to instructions they receive. (Typically, students' instructions will omit using a knife to spread the fillings, or putting together the sides with fillings.) The results are usually hilarious—and messy—but prove the point that process paragraphs must be complete to be effective.

DEVELOPING PARAGRAPHS

Take underdeveloped paragraphs on subjects likely to be familiar to students and ask them to develop the paragraphs fully by drawing on their own knowledge. Student paragraphs often provide good material for this exercise. Students can work collaboratively in groups of two or three to develop each person's paragraph. Alternatively, groups can supply a list of questions for each paragraph based on the questions provided in this chapter. Then each student can brainstorm responses to the questions and use that material to revise his or her own paragraph.

PARAGRAPH COHERENCE

Students sometimes have the idea that "next to" means "connected to" as far as coherence goes; this is emphatically not the case. Take a paragraph like this one and have students mark the coherence devices used; or sabotage a paragraph by removing or disguising the coherence devices, and ask students to put them back in.

A WRITER'S PERSPECTIVE

The purpose of paragraphing is to give the reader a rest. The writer is saying . . . : "Have you got that? If so, I'll go on."

—H. W. FOWLER

RESOURCES AND IDEAS

Eden, Rick, and Ruth Mitchell. "Paragraphing for the Reader." *College Composition and Communication* 37 (1986): 416–30. The authors suggest that judgments about length and paragraph decisions should be made with the readers in mind.

Lanham, Richard. *Analyzing Prose.* New York: Scribner's, 1983. Lanham offers extensive advice on revising paragraphs for stylistic effect.

Witte, Stephen, and Lester Faigley. "Coherence, Cohesion, and Writing Quality." *College Composition and Communication* 32 (1981): 189–204. Students need to learn the features

the drain plug, a large, flat pan to collect the draining oil, plastic bottles to dispose of the used oil, and fresh oil. First, warm up the car's engine so that the oil will flow more easily. When the engine is warm, shut it off and remove its oil-filler cap (the owner's manual shows where this cap is). Then locate the drain plug under the engine (again consulting the owner's manual for its location) and place the flat pan under the plug. Remove the plug with the wrench, letting the oil flow into the pan. When the oil stops flowing, replace the plug and, at the engine's filler hole, add the amount and kind of fresh oil specified by the owner's manual. Pour the used oil into the plastic bottles and take it to a waste-oil collector, which any garage mechanic can recommend.

[Margin annotations: Equipment needed; Steps in process]

—ANTHONY ANDREAS (student), "Do-It-Yourself Car Care"

Other process analyses explain how processes are done or how they work in nature. Annie Dillard's paragraph on mangrove islands (p. 95) is one example. Here is another:

What used to be called "laying on of hands" is now practiced seriously by nurses and doctors. Studies have shown that therapeutic touch, as it is now known, can aid relaxation and ease pain, two effects that may in turn cause physiological healing. A "healer" must first concentrate on helping the patient. Then, hands held a few inches from the patient's body, the healer moves from head to foot. The state of concentration allows the healer to detect energy disturbances in the patient that indicate localized tension, pain, or sickness. With further hand movements, the healer can redirect the energy. Patients report feeling heat from the healer's hands, perhaps indicating an energy transfer between healer and patient.

[Margin annotations: Process: therapeutic touch; Benefits; Steps in process; How process works]

—LISA KUKLINSKI (student), "Old Ways to Noninvasive Medicine"

Combining patterns of development

Whatever pattern you choose as the basis for developing a paragraph, other patterns may also prove helpful. We have seen combined patterns often in this section: Dyson analyzes causes and effects in presenting reasons (p. 108); Tuchman uses contrast to define *quality* (pp. 108–09); Nahm uses description to compare (p. 111); Ouchi uses process analysis to explain causes (pp. 112–13).

As you will see on pages 123–25, the paragraphs within an essay inevitably will be developed with a variety of patterns, even when one controlling pattern develops and structures the entire essay.

of coherence that extend across sentence boundaries; the article stresses ways to make them aware of coherence strategies.

 Checking length

The average paragraph contains between 100 and 150 words, or between four and eight sentences. The actual length of a paragraph depends on its topic, the role it plays in developing the thesis of the essay, and its position in the essay. Nevertheless, very short paragraphs are often inadequately developed; they may leave readers with a sense of incompleteness. And very long paragraphs often contain irrelevant details or develop two or more topics; readers may have difficulty sorting out or remembering ideas.

When you are revising your essay, reread the paragraphs that seem very long or very short, checking them especially for unity and adequate development. If the paragraph wanders, cut everything from it that does not support your main idea (such as sentences that you might begin with *By the way*). If it is underdeveloped, supply the specific details, examples, or reasons needed, or try one of the methods of development we have discussed here.

Exercise 13
Analyzing paragraph development

Examine the paragraphs by Gloria Naylor (p. 89), Henry Louis Gates, Jr. (p. 90), and Judith Wax (p. 96) to discover how the authors achieve paragraph development. What pattern or patterns of development does each author use? Where does each author support general statements with specific evidence?

Exercise 14
Analyzing and revising skimpy paragraphs

The following paragraphs are not well developed. Analyze them, looking especially for general statements that lack support or leave questions in your mind. Then rewrite one into a well-developed paragraph, supplying your own concrete details or examples.

1. One big difference between successful and unsuccessful teachers is the quality of communication. A successful teacher is sensitive to students' needs and excited by the course subject. In contrast, an unsuccessful teacher seems uninterested in students and bored by the subject.

2. Gestures are one of our most important means of communication. We use them instead of speech. We use them to supplement the words we speak. And we use them to communicate some feelings or meanings that words cannot adequately express.

3. Children who have been disciplined too much are often easy to spot. Their behavior toward adults may reflect the harsh treat-

ANSWERS: EXERCISE 13

1. *Naylor paragraph* (p. 89): Pattern of development: process analysis. Supporting information: all sentences except the first and the last.
2. *Gates paragraph* (p. 90): Patterns of development: cause-and-effect analysis and illustration. Supporting information: mainly the example in sentences 4–8.
3. *Wax paragraph* (p. 96): Pattern of development: cause-and-effect analysis. Supporting information: first three sentences.

COLLABORATIVE LEARNING

When students work together to analyze the paragraphs in Exercise 13 they benefit by discovering a broader range of interpretive responses. Those discoveries can be put to work in revising the under-developed paragraphs in Exercise 14 either individually or in groups.

ANSWERS: EXERCISE 14

Possible answers

1. Sentence 1 requires some expansion to explain *quality of communication.* Each of the next

two sentences needs to be supported with specific examples of the two qualities named.

2. Sentences 2, 3, and 4 should each be followed by at least two specific examples of gestures to make the writer's meaning concrete.

3. Sentences 2 and 3 require specific support, perhaps both citations of studies that have demonstrated the effects mentioned and examples of children's behavior.

ANSWERS: EXERCISE 15

Individual response.

COLLABORATIVE LEARNING

In exercises like 15 and 16, where students may find it difficult to develop their own paragraphs, they can work initially with their revision groups to pinpoint unsupported statements, highlight unclear claims, and to create a list of specific questions to aid each writer in a further revision.

ANSWERS: EXERCISE 16

Individual response.

COMPUTER EXERCISE

In a networked classroom, students might complete the draft of their paragraphs then e-mail them to a revision partner for comments and suggestions before reworking them. It is important for students to recognize that a well-developed paragraph generally emerges from successive drafts. You can dramatize this process by posting student paragraphs at various stages of revision on the class network and holding discussions about strategies for developing each example further.

USING JOURNALS

Encourage students to ransack their journals for topics to use in Exercise 16.

ment they have received from adults. And their behavior toward other children may be uncontrolled.

Exercise 15
Considering your past work: Paragraph development

Continuing from Exercises 3 (p. 91) and 10 (p. 103), examine the development of the body paragraphs in your writing. Where does specific information seem adequate to support your general statements? Where does support seem skimpy? Revise the paragraphs as necessary so that readers will understand and appreciate your ideas. It may help you to pose the questions on pages 106–13.

Exercise 16
Writing with the patterns of development

Write at least three unified, coherent, and well-developed paragraphs, each one developed with a different pattern. Draw on the topics provided here, or choose your own topics.

1. *Narration*
   An experience of public speaking
   A disappointment
   Leaving home
   Waking up
2. *Description (objective or subjective)*
   Your room
   A crowded or deserted place
   A food
   An intimidating person
3. *Illustration or support*
   Why study
   Having a headache
   The best sports event
   Usefulness (or uselessness) of a self-help book
4. *Definition*
   Humor
   An adult
   Fear
   Authority
5. *Division or analysis*
   A television news show
   A barn
   A set for a movie or play
   A piece of music
6. *Classification*
   Factions in a campus controversy
   Styles of playing poker
   Types of street people
   Kinds of teachers
7. *Comparison and contrast*
   Driving a friend's car and driving your own car
   AM and FM radio announcers
   High school and college football
   Movies on TV and in a theater
8. *Analogy*
   Paying taxes and giving blood
   The US Constitution and a building's foundation
   Graduating from high school and being released from prison
9. *Cause-and-effect analysis*
   Connection between tension and anger
   Causes of failing a course
   Connection between credit cards and debt
   Causes of a serious accident
10. *Process analysis*
   Preparing for a job interview
   Making a cabinet
   Protecting your home from burglars
   Making a jump shot

3d Writing special kinds of paragraphs

Several kinds of paragraphs do not always follow the guidelines for unity, coherence, development, and length because they serve special functions. These are the essay introduction, the essay conclusion, the transitional or emphatic paragraph, and the paragraph of spoken dialogue.

1 Opening an essay

Most of your essays will open with a paragraph that draws readers from their world into your world. A good opening paragraph usually satisfies several requirements:

- It focuses readers' attention on your subject and arouses their curiosity about what you have to say.
- It specifies what your topic is and implies your attitude.
- Often it states your thesis sentence.
- It is concise and sincere.

To grab readers' attention, you have a number of options:

Some strategies for opening paragraphs

- Ask a question.
- Relate an incident.
- Use a vivid quotation.
- Offer a surprising statistic or other fact.
- State an opinion related to your thesis.
- Outline the argument your thesis refutes.
- Provide background.
- Create a visual image that represents your subject.
- Make a historical comparison or contrast.
- Outline a problem or dilemma.
- Define a word central to your subject.
- In some business or technical writing, summarize your paper.

ESL These options for an introduction may not coincide with what you are used to if your native language is not English. In other cultures, readers may seek familiarity or reassurance from an author's introduction, or they may prefer an indirect approach to the subject. In English, however, writers and readers prefer originality and concise, direct expression.

One reliably effective introduction forms a kind of funnel: it starts generally with a statement or question about the subject, clarifies or narrows the subject in one or more sentences, and then, in the thesis sentence, asserts the central idea of the essay (see pp. 46–51). Here are two examples:

HIGHLIGHTS

This section addresses introductory and concluding paragraphs, the occasionally useful transitional and short emphatic paragraphs, and the conventions of paragraphing in dialogue. The emphasis you give to introductory and concluding paragraphs may vary with the experience of your students. For some, writing a straightforward introductory paragraph that simply sets the stage for the essay and presents a thesis statement will be an accomplishment. Others will benefit from experimenting with some of the variations illustrated. Most, however, will appreciate the list of *don't*'s for introductory paragraphs.

Because concluding paragraphs often present a special problem, you may wish to highlight the common inept endings that trap students and then suggest satisfactory alternatives.

USING JOURNALS

Encourage students to collect a repertoire of introduction strategies in their journals. They can draw these strategies from class readings, other courses, and their outside reading. They might also make a log of the ways television news or tabloid shows introduce various subjects and add them to this repertoire. This strategy can also be applied to conclusions.

TRANSPARENCY MASTER 3.3

MAGAZINE MODELS

Magazines like *Time, Glamour, Outdoor Life,* and *Self* contain a variety of informative articles. The authors of these articles and students writing expository essays face a similar problem—how to get readers interested enough to keep reading. Have students collect effective openings and bring them to class for discussion. Students can also comb editorials and magazine articles for openings of argumentative essays.

LEARNING STRATEGIES

To help students learn effective strategies for writing opening paragraphs, give the class outlines of well-known essays and ask students to construct opening paragraphs based on the in-

¶ 3d

formation provided. Compare students' opening paragraphs with those of the essays. This exercise will expose students to the numerous possibilities for creating good opening paragraphs and will promote discussion of the relative merits of different techniques for a specific subject, essay, or audience.

RESOURCES AND IDEAS

McClish, Glen. "Of Attention-Getting Openers and Contracts: A Reassessment of an Introductory Dilemma." *Journal of Teaching Writing* 13: 1 (1996): 197–207. McClish discusses the metaphor of the "contract" as a way to teach students about the rhetorical impact of introductions without prompting clichés.

We Americans are a clean people. We bathe or shower regularly and spend billions of dollars each year on soaps and deodorants to wash away or disguise our dirt and odor. Yet cleanliness is a relatively recent habit with us. From the time of the Puritans until the turn of the twentieth century, bathing in the United States was rare and sometimes even illegal.

—AMANDA HARRIS (student), "The Cleaning of America"

Subject related to reader's experience

Narrowing of subject: bridge to thesis sentence

Thesis sentence

Can your home or office computer make you sterile? Can it strike you blind or dumb? The answer is: probably not. Nevertheless, reports of side effects relating to computer use should be examined, especially in the area of birth defects, eye complaints, and postural difficulties. Although little conclusive evidence exists to establish a causal link between computer use and problems of this sort, the circumstantial evidence can be disturbing.

—THOMAS HARTMANN, "How Dangerous Is Your Computer?"

Subject related to reader's experience

Clarification of subject: bridge to thesis sentence

Thesis sentence

Several other types of introduction can be equally effective, though they are sometimes harder to invent and control. You can begin with a quotation that leads into the thesis sentence:

> "It is difficult to speak adequately or justly of London," wrote Henry James in 1881. "It is not a pleasant place; it is not agreeable, or cheerful, or easy, or exempt from reproach. It is only magnificent." Were he alive today, James, a connoisseur of cities, might easily say the same thing about New York or Paris or Tokyo, for the great city is one of the paradoxes of history. In countless different ways, it has almost always been an unpleasant, disagreeable, cheerless, uneasy and reproachful place; in the end, it can only be described as magnificent.
>
> —*Time*

You can relate an incident or convey a visual image that sets the stage for the thesis:

> Canada is pink. I knew that from the map I owned when I was six. On it, New York was green and brown, which was true as far as I could see, so there was no reason to distrust the map maker's portrayal of Canada. When my parents took me across the border and we entered the immigration booth, I looked excitedly for the pink earth. Slowly it dawned on me; this foreign, "different" place was not so different. I discovered that the world in my head and the world at my feet were not the same.
>
> —ROBERT ORNSTEIN, *Human Nature*

You can open with a startling question or opinion:

Caesar was right. Thin people need watching. I've been watching them for most of my adult life, and I don't like what I see. When these narrow fellows spring at me, I quiver to my toes. Thin people come in all personalities, most of them menacing. You've got your "together" thin person, your mechanical thin person, your condescending thin person, your tsk-tsk thin person. All of them are dangerous. —SUZANNE BRITT, "That Lean and Hungry Look"

When some background to the essay is useful, you can begin with a historical comparison or contrast:

Throughout the first half of this century, the American Medical Association, the largest and most powerful medical organization in the world, battled relentlessly to rid the country of quack potions and cure-alls; and it is the AMA that is generally credited with being the single most powerful force behind the enactment of the early pure food and drug laws. Today, however, medicine's guardian seems to have done a complete about-face and become one of the pharmaceutical industry's staunchest allies—often at the public's peril and expense. —MAC JEFFERY, "Does Rx Spell Rip-off?"

An effective introductory paragraph need not be long, as the following opener shows:

I've often wondered what goes into a hot dog. Now I know and I wish I didn't. —WILLIAM ZINSSER, *The Lunacy Boom*

When writing and revising an introductory paragraph, avoid the following approaches that are likely to bore readers or make them question your sincerity or control:

Openings to avoid

- Don't reach back too far with vague generalities or truths, such as those beginning "Throughout human history . . ." or "In today's world. . . ." You may have needed a warm-up paragraph to start drafting, but your readers can do without it.
- Don't start with "The purpose of this essay is . . . ," "In this essay I will . . . ," or any similar flat announcement of your intention or topic.
- Don't refer to the title of the essay in the first sentence—for example, "This is my favorite activity" or "This is a big problem."
- Don't start with "According to Webster . . ." or a similar phrase leading to a dictionary definition. A definition can be an effective springboard to an essay, but this kind of lead-in has become dull with overuse.
- Don't apologize for your opinion or for inadequate knowledge with "I'm not sure if I'm right, but I think . . . ," "I don't know much about this, but . . . ," or a similar line.

¶ 3d

COMPARING CLOSINGS

Using the same essays gathered for the preceding activity, ask students to read all but the conclusions. Then have them underline the thesis statement and the main ideas of each paragraph. Finally, have students write their own conclusions. This exercise will help students to recognize the structure, effectiveness, and importance of concluding paragraphs and will provide diverse examples of how key information may be arranged for variety and emphasis.

TRANSPARENCY MASTER 3.4

IMITATING OPENINGS AND CLOSINGS

When experienced writers have trouble beginning or ending essays, they usually turn to strategies that have been successful on other occasions. To help student writers develop similar resources, distribute opening and closing paragraphs that demonstrate particularly effective strategies and ask students to write their own paragraphs using the same strategies but containing different content.

 Closing an essay

Most of your essays will end with a closing statement or conclusion, a signal to readers that you have not simply stopped writing but have actually finished. The conclusion completes the essay, bringing it to a climax while assuring readers that they have understood your intention. Usually set off in its own paragraph, the conclusion may consist of a single sentence or a group of sentences. It may take one or more of the approaches below.

Some strategies for closing paragraphs

- Strike a note of hope or despair.
- Give a symbolic or powerful fact or other detail.
- Give an especially compelling example.
- Create a visual image that represents your subject.
- Use a quotation.
- Recommend a course of action.
- Summarize the paper.
- Echo the approach of the introduction.
- Restate your thesis and reflect on its implications.

The following paragraph concludes the essay on bathing habits whose introduction is on page 118:

> Thus changed attitudes and advances in plumbing finally freed us to bathe whenever we want. [Summary] Perhaps partly to make up for our ancestors' bad habits, we have transformed that freedom into a national obsession. [Link between past and today]
>
> —Amanda Harris (student), "The Cleaning of America"

Maxine Hong Kingston uses a different technique—a vivid image—to conclude an essay on her aunt, a suicide by drowning:

> My aunt haunts me—her ghost drawn to me because now, after fifty years of neglect, I alone devote pages of paper to her, though not origamied into houses and clothes. I do not think she always means me well. I am telling on her, and she was a spite suicide, drowning herself in the drinking water. [Summary] The Chinese are always very frightened of the drowned one, whose weeping ghost, wet hair hanging and skin bloated, waits silently by the water to pull down a substitute. [Image]
>
> —Maxine Hong Kingston, "No Name Woman"

In the next paragraph the author concludes an essay on environmental protection with a call for action.

> Until we get the answers, I think we had better keep on building power plants and growing food with the help of fertilizers and such insect-controlling chemicals as we now have. The risks are well known, thanks to the environmentalists. If they had not created a widespread public awareness of the ecological crisis, we wouldn't stand a chance. But such awareness by itself is not enough. Flaming manifestos and prophecies of doom are no longer much help, and a search for scapegoats can only make matters worse. The time for sensations and manifestos is about over. Now we need rigorous analysis, united effort and very hard work.
>
> —PETER F. DRUCKER, "How Best to Protect the Environment"

Summary and opinion

Call for action

These three paragraphs illustrate ways of avoiding several pitfalls of conclusions:

Closings to avoid

- Don't simply restate your introduction—statement of subject, thesis sentence, and all. Presumably the paragraphs in the body of your essay have contributed something to the opening statements, and it's that something you want to capture in your conclusion.
- Don't start off in a new direction, with a subject different from the one your essay has been about. If you arrive at a new idea, this may be a signal to start fresh with that idea as your thesis.
- Don't conclude more than you reasonably can from the evidence you have presented. If your essay is about your frustrating experience trying to clear a parking ticket, you cannot reasonably conclude that *all* local police forces are tied up in red tape.
- Don't apologize for your essay or otherwise cast doubt on it. Don't say, "Even though I'm no expert," or "This may not be convincing, but I believe it's true," or anything similar. Rather, to win your readers' confidence, display confidence.

TRANSPARENCY MASTER 3.5

3 Using short emphatic or transitional paragraphs

A short emphatic paragraph can give unusual stress to an important idea, in effect asking the reader to pause and consider before moving on.

PAIRS OF IDEAS

Students may hone their skills with transitional paragraphs by being given pairs of seemingly unrelated ideas and being asked to link them. For example, using the topic of capital punishment, have students create a transitional paragraph linking the discussion of legal implications to the discussion of moral implications.

ONE-SENTENCE PARAGRAPHS

Students may be confused about the use of one-sentence paragraphs. Take time to discuss publicly the uses of such paragraphs and to make them aware of any taboos or restrictions you place on such paragraphs; this will save you and your students time and grief later.

> In short, all those who might have taken responsibility ducked it, and catastrophe was inevitable.

A transitional paragraph, because it is longer than a word or phrase and set off by itself, moves a discussion from one point to another more slowly or more completely than does a single transitional expression or even a transitional sentence attached to a larger paragraph.

> These, then, are the causes of the current contraction in hospital facilities. But how does this contraction affect the medical costs of the government, private insurers, and individuals?
>
> So the debates were noisy and emotion-packed. But what did they accomplish? Historians agree on at least three direct results.

Use transitional paragraphs only to shift readers' attention when your essay makes a significant turn. A paragraph like the following one betrays a writer who is stalling.

> Now that we have examined these facts, we can look at some others that are equally central to an examination of this important issue.

Writing dialogue

When recording a conversation between two or more people, start a new paragraph for each person's speech. The paragraphing establishes for the reader the point at which one speaker stops talking and another begins.

> The dark shape was indistinguishable. But once I'd flooded him with light, there he stood, blinking.
>
> "Well," he said eventually, "you're a sight for sore eyes. Should I stand here or are you going to let me in?"
>
> "Come in," I said. And in he came.
>
> —Louise Erdrich, *The Beet Queen*

Though dialogue appears most often in fictional writing (the source of the preceding example), it may occasionally freshen or enliven narrative or expository essays. (For guidance in using quotation marks and other punctuation in passages of dialogue, see pp. 380–81 and 408–09.)

COLLABORATIVE LEARNING

Students can work together effectively to analyze the introductory and concluding paragraphs of the student essay in Chapter 2, the openings and closings of published essays, and the opening and closing paragraphs from their own pa-

Exercise 17
Analyzing an introduction and conclusion

Analyze the introductory and concluding paragraphs in the first and final drafts of the student essay in Chapter 2, pages 65–66 and 77–79. What is wrong with the first-draft paragraphs? Why are the final-draft paragraphs better? Could they be improved still further?

Exercise 18

Considering your past work: Introductions and conclusions

Most writers struggle over introductions and conclusions. Have you devised any strategies that help you with these paragraphs? If you have problems with them, what are the difficulties?

Examine the opening and closing paragraphs of the essay you've been analyzing in Exercises 3, 10, and 15. Do the paragraphs fulfill the requirements and avoid the pitfalls outlined on pages 117–21? Revise them as needed for clarity, conciseness, focus, and interest.

3e Linking paragraphs in the essay

Your paragraphs do not stand alone: each one is a key unit of a larger piece of writing. Though you may draft paragraphs or groups of paragraphs almost as mini-essays, you will eventually need to stitch them together into a unified, coherent, well-developed whole. The techniques parallel those for linking sentences in paragraphs:

- Make sure each paragraph contributes to your thesis.
- You will probably use varied patterns of development for individual paragraphs, even when the whole essay is developed and structured by some other pattern. Just be sure to follow through on your overall pattern.
- Arrange the paragraphs in a clear, logical order. See pages 58–61 for advice on essay organization.
- Create links between paragraphs. Use repetition and restatement to stress and connect key terms, and use transitional expressions and transitional sentences to indicate sequence, direction, contrast, and other relationships.

The following essay illustrates the way effective paragraphs can build an effective essay. The overall pattern of development is analysis. The overall organization is climactic. Sentences and paragraphs are linked by repetition and restatement (circled words), transitional expressions (boxed words), and transitional sentences, pronouns, and parallelism (all noted in annotations).

A Picture of Hyperactivity

A hyperactive committee member can contribute to efficiency. A hyperactive salesperson can contribute to profits. When a child is hyperactive, though, people—even parents—may wish he had never been born. A collage of those who must cope with hyperactivity in children is a dark picture of frustration, anger, and loss.

Thesis sentence

pers. Ask each group of students to create their own list of effective opening and concluding strategies accompanied by quoted examples from these various readings.

ANSWERS: EXERCISE 17

Possible answers

The introduction in the first draft rushes to Reed's essay without first securing the reader's interest. Reed's essay is also given short shrift—the author's point of view is not explained. And the other false picture is introduced abruptly (*Either that, or . . .*). In contrast, the final introduction approaches readers with a question of general interest, concisely but fully explains Reed's point, and moves deliberately to the other picture.

The conclusion in the first draft does not bring the *extremes of peace and conflict* together into one image and does not describe the *different picture* that we're not getting from the media. The final conclusion solves these problems, ending strongly with an affirmative but not unrealistic picture.

ANSWERS: EXERCISE 18

Individual response.

¶
3e

The first part of the collage is the doctors. In their terminology the word *hyperactivity* is short for H-LD, a hyperkinesis-learning disability syndrome. They apply the word to children who are "abnormally or excessively busy." But doctors do not fully understand the problem and thus differ over how to treat it. For example, some recommend a special diet; others, behavior-modifying drugs; and still others, who do not consider hyperactivity to be a medical problem, a psychiatrist for the entire family. The result is a merry-go-round of tests, confusion, and frustration for the parents and the child.

Transitional topic sentence

Pronouns

Paragraph developed by definition, example, and cause-and-effect analysis

As the parent of a hyperactive child, I can say what the word *hyperactivity* means to the parents who form the second part of the collage. It means a worry that is deep and enduring. It means a despair that is a companion on dark and sleepless nights. It means a fear that is heart twisting and constant, for the hyperactive child is most destructive toward himself. It means a mixture of frustration, guilt, and anger. And finally, since there are times when that anger goes out of control and the child is in danger from the parent, it means self-loathing.

Transitional topic sentence

Pronouns and parallelism

Paragraph developed by definition and cause-and-effect analysis

The weight of hyperactivity, however, rests not on the doctors or the parents but on the child. For him is reserved the final and darkest part of the collage because he is most affected. From early childhood he is dragged from doctor to doctor, is attached to strange and frightening machines, and is tested or discussed by physicians, parents, neighbors, teachers, peers. His playmates dislike him because of his temper and his unwillingness to follow rules; and even his pets fear and mistrust him, for he treats them erratically, often hurting them without meaning to. As time goes on, he sees his parents more and more often in tears and anger,

Transitional sentence

Topic sentence

Pronouns

Paragraph developed by narration and cause-and-effect analysis and he knows that he is the cause. Though he is highly intelligent, he does poorly when he enters school because of his short attention span. He is fond of sports and games but never joins the other children on the playground because he has an uncontrollable temper and poor coordination. By the time he reaches age seven or eight, he is obsessed with one thought: "Mama," my son asks me repeatedly, "why do I have to be hyperactive?"

At last the collage is completed, and it is dark and somber. *Hyperactivity,* as applied to children, is a word with uncertain, unattractive, and bitter associations. But the picture does have a bright spot, for inside every hyperactive child is a loving, trustful, calm person waiting to be recognized.

Transitional sentence

—LINDA DEVEREAUX (student)

Exercise 19
Analyzing paragraphs in essays

Analyze the ways in which paragraphs combine in the two student essays in Chapter 2, pages 77 and 83. With what techniques, if any, does each writer link paragraphs to the thesis sentence and to each other? Where, if at all, does the writer seem to stray from the thesis or fail to show how paragraphs relate to it? How would you revise the essays to solve any problems they exhibit?

Exercise 20
Considering your past work: Paragraphs in the essay

Examine the overall effect of the essay you've been analyzing in Exercises 3, 10, 15, and 18. Do all the paragraphs relate to your thesis? Are they arranged clearly and logically? How do repetition and restatement, transitional expressions, or transitional sentences connect the paragraphs? Can you see ways to improve the essay's unity, coherence, and development?

ANSWERS: EXERCISE 19

Possible answers

1. Essay on page 77 ("America's Media Image"): Every paragraph after the first is linked to the thesis sentence with the words *conflict, ethnic, media,* or *peace,* so that it is immediately apparent how the paragraph will relate to the thesis. Within paragraphs, too, these key words are repeated and restated so that connections remain clear. In addition, the author uses a transitional expression at the start of paragraph 4 (*though*) to signal a shift. (Further analysis of this essay appears in Chapter 2 of the handbook and in the answer to Exercise 17 here in Chapter 3.)

2. Essay on page 83 ("Working in the Barnyard"): The paragraphs in this narrative essay relate clearly to the thesis and proceed smoothly from one incident to the next. Transitions are provided primarily by time markers such as *Last May* (paragraph 2), *as soon as I arrived* (paragraph 3), *after about a week* (paragraph 4), *over the next seven weeks* (paragraph 5), *Two months after I had started work* (paragraph 6), and *a month before school began* (paragraph 7). (Further analysis of this essay appears in the answer to Chapter 2, Exercise 12.)

COLLABORATIVE LEARNING

Ask students to work in groups to complete Exercise 19 and then to translate that same analytical approach to one sample of each student's work as specified in Exercise 20.

ANSWERS: EXERCISE 20

Individual response.

Chapter 4

Reading and Writing Arguments

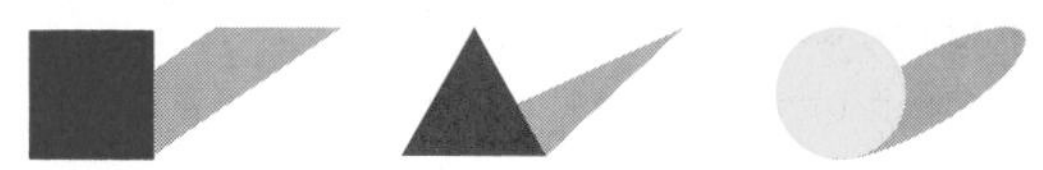

Argument is writing that attempts to change readers' minds or move readers to action. A good argument is neither a cold exercise in logic nor an attempt to beat others into submission. It is a work of negotiation and problem solving in which both writer and reader search for the knowledge that will create common ground between them.

Of course, not all arguments are "good." Whether deliberately or not, some are unclear, incomplete, misleading, or downright false. The negotiation fails; the problem remains unsolved. This chapter will help you recognize good arguments when you read them (4a–4b) and write good arguments when you need to (4b–4g).

ESL The ways of reading and writing arguments described in this chapter may be initially uncomfortable to you if your native culture approaches such writing differently. In some cultures, for example, a writer is expected to begin indirectly, to avoid asserting his or her opinion outright, to rely for evidence on appeals to tradition, or to establish a compromise rather than argue a position. Writers of English, as this chapter explains, are expected to take a position, gather evidence from many sources, and argue the position directly and concisely.

4a Reading arguments critically

Few arguments are an easy read. Most demand the attentive critical reading discussed in this book's Introduction. (If you haven't read pp. 1–17, you should do so before continuing.) As a

HIGHLIGHTS

This chapter presents a discussion of reading arguments critically: assertions, evidence, and assumptions are presented, followed by techniques for testing assertions; for identifying fact, opinion, belief, and prejudice; and for looking at a writer's definition of terms, use of evidence, and appeals to beliefs or needs (4a). The two essays in Exercise 1 are used as a basis for discussion throughout the rest of the chapter. Students are instructed to examine the reliability of evidence as it works to connect assumptions to assertions, to listen for tone, and to question whether a writer is reasonable. Ways for students to recognize logical fallacies—evasions, oversimplifications—comprise the final section on reading critically.

Students are then introduced to conceiving their own written arguments: the topic, thesis, purpose, and audience are considered before the students are introduced to the concepts of arguing inductively and deductively. As they construct their arguments students will consider their own use of evidence, the most effective appeal to their readers, how to deal with opposing view, organizing their argument, and revising their argument. A helpful checklist for revising an argument is given on page 157. The chapter concludes with an annotated sample argument.

This chapter assumes that students have read the Introduction, "Critical Thinking, Reading, and Writing," and are familiar with its terminology and research.

RESOURCES AND IDEAS

Bator, Paul. "Aristotelian and Rogerian Rhetoric." *College Composition and Communication* 31 (1980): 427–32. Bator describes the differences between the two schools of argument and helps students understand when each strategy is most appropriate.

Brent, Doug. "Young, Becker, and Pike's 'Rogerian' Rhetoric: A Twenty-Year Reassessment." *College English* 53 (1991): 452–66. Brent reassesses the usefulness of argument based on common views and values in a culturally diverse world.

Ferris, Dana R. "Rhetorical Strategies in Student Persuasive Writing: Differences Between Native and Non-native Speakers." *Research in the Teaching of English* 28 (1994): 45–65. Ferris analyzes sixty persuasive essays by first-year composition students to show the

reader of argument, your purpose will almost always be the same: you'll want to know whether you should be convinced by the argument. This purpose focuses your attention on the elements that make an argument convincing, or not.

In one simple scheme an argument has three parts:

1. **Assertions:** positive statements that require support. In an argument the central assertion is stated outright as the **thesis** (see p. 47): it is what the argument is about. For instance:

   The college needs a new chemistry laboratory to replace the existing outdated lab.

   Several minor assertions, such as that the present equipment is inadequate, will contribute to the central assertion.
2. **Evidence:** the facts, examples, expert opinions, and other information that support the assertions. Evidence to support the preceding assertion might include the following:

   The present lab's age
   An inventory of equipment
   The testimony of chemistry professors

   Like the assertions, the evidence is always stated outright.
3. **Assumptions:** opinions or beliefs held by the writer that tie the evidence to the assertions. For instance, the following assumption might connect the evidence of professors' testimony with the assertion that a new lab is needed:

   Chemistry professors are the most capable of evaluating the present lab's quality.

In the following pages, we'll examine each of these elements and the ways they are put together.

Questions for critically reading an argument

- What kind of **assertions** does the writer make? (p. 128)
- What kind and quality of **evidence** does the writer use? (p. 130)
- What **assumptions** is the writer making? (p. 133)
- What is the writer's **tone?** How does the writer use **language?** (p. 134)
- Is the writer **reasonable?** (p. 135)
- Is the argument logical? Has the writer committed any **fallacies?** (p. 138)
- Are you convinced? Why or why not?

Note The student paper in the book's Introduction, Charlene Robinson's "Weighing the Costs" (pp. 19–21), provides a good ex-

particular difficulties that nonnative speakers can encounter in formulating claims, using data, and anticipating counterarguments.

Katula, Richard A., and Richard W. Roth. "A Stock-Issues Approach to Writing Arguments." *College Composition and Communication* 31 (1980): 183–96. The authors use problem-solving strategies as ways to build arguments.

Maxley, John M. "Reinventing the Wheel or Teaching the Basics: College Writers' Knowledge of Argumentation." *Composition Studies: Freshman English News* 21 (1993): 3–15. Maxley reviews various approaches to teaching argument, including the "Toulmin model" in an effort to identify the most effective strategies.

Rapkins, Angela A. "The Uses of Logic in the College Freshman English Classroom." *Activities to Promote Critical Thinking: Classroom Practices in Teaching English.* Urbana: NCTE, 1986. Rapkins argues that students should be introduced to logic early in the semester, even if writing arguments comes later.

Toulmin, Stephen, Richard Rieke, and Allan Janik. *An Introduction to Reasoning.* New York: Macmillan, 1979. This is a classic textbook exposition of reasoning.

A WRITER'S PERSPECTIVE

A great many people think they are thinking when they are merely rearranging their prejudices.

—William James

TRANSPARENCY MASTER 4.1

DEFINING ARGUMENT

Some students may need instruction on the technical meaning of argument, since their view of this rhetorical mode may include only vehement disagreement. Ask students to look up *argument* in various dictionaries and bring a number of definitions of this word to share with their group. Have them discuss how all come into play in persuasive writing.

RESOURCES AND IDEAS

Winder, Barbara E. "The Delineation of Values in Persuasive Writing." *College Composition and Communication* 29 (1978): 55–58. Winder asks writers to spell out both sides of an argument to make them sensitive to their own values and those of their readers.

COLLABORATIVE LEARNING

CUT AND PASTE

Ask groups of students to identify an issue, collect newspaper or magazine articles on it, and bring the articles to class (in photocopied form, if possible). Then ask them to work in groups to identify what the articles say on the different sides of the issue and to cut out the assertions and paste them in columns (or simply write them out) according to the particular perspective on the argument they represent.

ANALYZING ISSUES

Have students, in groups, discuss a campus issue like residential policies, parking arrangements, or library or computer services, trying to identify the assertions and supporting evidence on each side of the argument. As each group reports back on their findings, list the assertions and evidence on the board so that students can distinguish fact from opinion and identify terms that need defining. If students know enough about issues of public policy (such as gun control, capital punishment, or nuclear disarmament), these topics, too, can be used for discussion.

ample of critically reading an argument for its assertions, evidence, and assumptions.

1 Testing assertions

The assertions in an argument carry specific burdens: they should state arguable opinions, and they should define their terms.

Fact, opinion, belief, and prejudice

Most statements we hear, read, or make in speaking and writing are assertions of fact, opinion, belief, or prejudice. In an argument the acceptability of an assertion depends partly on which of these categories it falls into.

A **fact** is verifiable—that is, one can determine whether it is true. It may involve numbers or dates:

> World War II ended in 1945.
> The football field is 100 yards long.

The numbers may be implied:

> The earth is closer to the sun than Saturn is.
> The cost of medical care is rising.

Or the fact may involve no numbers at all:

> The city council adjourned without taking a vote.
> The President vetoed the bill.

Facts provide crucial evidence for the assertions of an argument, and as evidence they may be problematic because they can be misinterpreted or distorted (see p. 132). But they are ultimately verifiable, so they do not make worthwhile arguments by themselves.

An **opinion** is a judgment *based* on facts, an honest attempt to draw a reasonable conclusion from evidence. For example:

> Mandatory drug testing in workplaces is essential to increase employees' productivity.
>
> Mandatory drug testing in workplaces does not substantially increase employees' productivity.
>
> Mandatory drug testing in workplaces violates constitutional freedoms.

All three of these opinions share certain features:

- They express viewpoints based on an interpretation of facts.
- They are arguable. Indeed, they argue with each other, though each writer had access to the same facts.
- They are potentially changeable. With more evidence the writers might alter their opinions partly or wholly.

The main assertion, or thesis, of an argument is always an opinion. Other, more specific assertions of opinion generally form the backbone of the argument supporting the thesis. By themselves, however, opinions do not make arguments. As a critical reader, you must satisfy yourself that the writer has specified the evidence and that the assumptions linking assertions and evidence are clear and believable.

An opinion is not the same as a **belief,** a conviction based on cultural or personal faith, morality, or values:

> Abortion is legalized murder.
>
> Capital punishment is legalized murder.
>
> The primary goal of government should be to provide equality of opportunity for all.

Such statements are often called opinions because they express viewpoints, but they are not based on facts and other evidence. Since they cannot be disproved by facts or even contested on the basis of facts, they cannot serve as the central assertion of an argument. (Statements of belief do figure in argument, however: they can serve as a kind of evidence, and they often form the assumptions linking assertions and evidence. See pp. 131 and 133.)

One kind of assertion that has no place in argument is **prejudice,** an opinion based on insufficient or unexamined evidence:

> Women are bad drivers.
> Fat people are jolly.
> Teenagers are irresponsible.

Unlike a belief, a prejudice is testable: it can be contested and disproved on the basis of facts. Very often, however, we form prejudices or accept them from others—parents, friends, the communications media—without questioning their meaning or testing their truth. Writers who display prejudice do not deserve the confidence and agreement of readers. Readers who accept prejudice are not thinking critically.

Defined terms

In any argument, but especially in arguments about abstract ideas, clear and consistent definition of terms is essential. In the following assertion the writer is not clear about what she means by the crucial term *justice:*

> Over the past few decades, justice has deteriorated so badly that it almost does not exist anymore.

The word *justice* is **abstract:** it does not refer to anything specific or concrete and in fact has varied meanings. (The seven definitions in *The American Heritage Dictionary* include "the principle of moral rightness" and "the administration and procedure of law.") When the writer specifies her meaning, her assertion is much clearer:

> If by *justice* we mean treating people fairly, punishing those who commit crimes, and protecting the victims of those crimes, then justice has deteriorated badly over the past few decades.

Writers who use highly abstract words such as *justice, equality, success,* and *maturity* have a responsibility to define them. If the word is important to the argument, such a definition may take an entire paragraph. As a reader you have the obligation to evaluate the writer's definitions before you accept his or her assertions. (See Chapter 3, pp. 108–09, for more on definition and a paragraph defining the abstract word *quality.*)

 2 Weighing evidence

In argument, evidence demonstrates the validity of the writer's assertions. If the evidence is inadequate or questionable, the assertions are at best doubtful.

Kinds of evidence

Writers draw on several kinds of evidence to support their assertions:

Evidence for argument

- **Facts:** verifiable statements
- **Statistics:** facts expressed in numbers
- **Examples:** specific cases
- **Expert opinions:** the judgments of authorities
- **Appeals to readers' beliefs or needs**

Facts are statements whose truth can be verified by observation or research (see p. 128):

> Poland is slightly smaller than New Mexico.
> Insanity is grounds for divorce in a majority of the states.

Facts employing numbers are **statistics:**

> Of those polled, 62 percent stated a preference for a flat tax.
>
> In 1988 there were 2,138,000 men and women in the US armed forces.
>
> The average American household consists of 2.64 persons.

Examples are specific instances of the point being made, including historical precedents and personal experiences. The pas-

COLLABORATIVE LEARNING

EVIDENCE IN EDITORIALS

Distribute copies of newspaper editorials, and ask students, in groups, to examine the evidence the editorials contain in order to (1) identify facts, statistics, examples, and expert opinions and (2) evaluate the evidence for accuracy, relevance, representativeness, adequacy, and reliability. Then ask the groups to compare the results of their analysis and evaluation.

This activity can be made more collaborative by asking students to supply the materials used, assigning each group a genre or audience to survey for materials. Students should also be encouraged to plumb their journals for materials for this exercise.

TRANSPARENCY MASTER 4.2

COLLABORATIVE LEARNING

SURVEYING PERSUASION

Assign students to keep track of all the persuasive attempts they are exposed to in the course of one day and to share that list with their groups. (Attempts may include advertisements, conversations, television programs, junk mail, songs on the radio, and so on.) Then ask each group to classify and weigh the kinds of evidence used to support each of these persuasive appeals. Which kinds are used most and least often?

sage below uses a personal narrative as partial support for the assertion in the first sentence:

> Besides broadening students' knowledge, required courses can also introduce students to possible careers that they otherwise would have known nothing about. Somewhat reluctantly, I enrolled in a psychology course to satisfy the social science requirement. But what I learned in the course about human behavior has led me to consider becoming a clinical psychologist instead of an engineer.

Expert opinions are the judgments formed by authorities on the basis of their own examination of the facts. In the following passage the writer cites the opinion of an expert to support the assertion in the first sentence.

> Despite the fact that affirmative action places some individuals at a disadvantage, it remains necessary to right the wrongs inflicted historically on whole groups of people. Howard Glickstein, a past director of the US Commission on Civil Rights, maintains that "it simply is not possible to achieve equality and fairness" unless the previous grounds for discrimination (such as sex, race, and national origin) are now considered as grounds for admission to schools and jobs (26).

As this passage illustrates, a citation of expert opinion should always refer the reader to the source, here indicated by the page number in parentheses, "(26)." Such a citation is also generally accompanied by a reference to the expert's credentials. See pages 594 and 599–600.

ESL In some cultures a person with high standing in politics, society, or organized religion may be considered an authority on many different subjects. For native English speakers, authority tends to reflect study, learning, and experience: the more someone knows about a subject, the more authority he or she has.

An **appeal to beliefs or needs,** a fourth kind of evidence, asks readers to accept an assertion in part because they already accept it as true without evidence or because it coincides with their needs. Each of the following examples combines such an appeal (second sentence) with a summary of factual evidence (first sentence).

> Thus the chemistry laboratory is outdated in its equipment. In addition, its shabby, antiquated appearance shames the school, making it seem a second-rate institution. [Appeals to readers' belief that their school is or should be first-rate.]

> That police foot patrollers reduce crime has already been demonstrated. Such officers might also restore our sense that our neighborhoods are orderly, stable places. [Appeals to readers' need for order and stability.]

RESOURCES AND IDEAS

Chambers, Marilyn J. "Text Cues and Strategies Successful Readers Use to Construct the Gist of Lengthy Written Arguments." *Reading Research Quarterly* 30 (1995): 778–807. Chambers examines students' strategies for comprehending the argument structure, claims, and evidence in lengthy texts.

McCormick, Kathleen. "Teaching Critical Thinking and Writing." *The Writing Instructor* 2 (1983): 137–44. McCormick suggests having students develop critical and analytical skills by critiquing flawed essays, and she describes several units in a course employing this strategy.

EXPERT OPINIONS?

A common variation of the expert opinion is a celebrity endorsement. Students should be asked to decide what various celebrities' credentials are for offering their opinions and why the persuaders thought celebrities were the best people to endorse their respective products.

(For more on beliefs, see p. 129. For more on appeals to emotion, see pp. 152–53.)

The reliability of evidence

To support assertions and convince readers, evidence must be reliable. The tests of reliability for appeals to readers' beliefs and needs are specific to the situation: whether they are appropriate for the argument and correctly gauge how readers actually feel (see p. 153). With the other kinds of evidence, the standards are more general, applying to any argument.

Accurate evidence is true:

- It is drawn from trustworthy sources.
- It is quoted exactly.
- It is presented with the original meaning undistorted.

In an essay favoring gun control, the writer should not rely exclusively on procontrol sources, which are undoubtedly biased. Instead, the writer should also cite anticontrol sources (representing the opposite bias) and neutral sources (attempting to be unbiased). If the writer quotes an expert, the quotation should present the expert's true meaning, not just a few words that happen to support the writer's argument. (As a reader you may have difficulty judging the accuracy of quotations if you are not familiar with the expert's opinions.)

Not just opinions but also facts and examples may be misinterpreted or distorted. Suppose you were reading an argument for extending a three-year-old law allowing the police to stop vehicles randomly as a means of apprehending drunk drivers. If the author cited statistics showing that the number of drunk-driving accidents dropped in the first two years of the law, but failed to note that the number rose back to the previous level in the third year, then the evidence would be distorted and thus inaccurate. You or any reader would be justified in questioning the entire argument, no matter how accurate the rest seemed.

Relevant evidence pertains to the argument:

- It comes from sources with authority on the subject.
- It relates directly to the point the writer is making.
- It is current.

In an argument against a method of hazardous-waste disposal, a writer should not offer his aunt's opinion as evidence unless she is an authority on the subject and her expertise is up to date. If she is an authority on Method A and not Method B, the writer should not use her opinion as evidence against Method B. Similarly, the writer's own experience of living near a hazardous-waste site may be relevant evidence *if* it pertains to his thesis. His authority in this case is that of a close observer and a citizen.

TRANSPARENCY MASTER 4.3

Criteria for weighing evidence

- Is it **accurate:** trustworthy, exact, undistorted?
- Is it **relevant:** authoritative, pertinent, current?
- Is it **representative:** true to context?
- Is it **adequate:** plentiful, specific?

Representative evidence is true to its context:

- It reflects the full range of the sample from which it is said to be drawn.
- It does not overrepresent any element of the sample.

In an essay arguing that dormitories should stay open during school holidays, a writer might say that "the majority of the school's students favor leaving the dormitories open." But that writer would mislead you and other readers if the statement were based only on a poll of her roommates and dormitory neighbors. A few dormitory residents could not be said to represent the entire student body, particularly the nonresident students. To be representative, the poll would have to take in many more students in proportions that reflect the numbers of resident and nonresident students on campus.

Adequate evidence is sufficient:

- It is plentiful enough to support the writer's assertions.
- It is specific enough to support the writer's assertions.

A writer arguing against animal abuse cannot hope to win over readers solely with statements about her personal experiences and assertions of her opinions. Her experience may indeed be relevant evidence if, say, she has worked with animals or witnessed animal abuse. And her opinions are indeed important to the argument, to let readers know what she thinks. But even together these are not adequate evidence: they cannot substitute entirely for facts, nonpersonal examples, and the opinions of experts to demonstrate abuse and describe the scope of the problem.

3 Discovering assumptions

Assumptions connect evidence to assertions: they are the opinions or beliefs that explain why a particular piece of evidence is relevant to a particular assertion. As noted in the book's Introduction on critical thinking (pp. 13–15), assumptions are not flaws in arguments but necessities: we all acquire beliefs and opinions that shape our view of the world. Here are some examples that you, or people you know, may hold:

Criminals should be punished.
Hard work is virtuous.
Teachers' salaries are too low.

Assumptions are inevitable in argument, but they aren't neutral. For one thing, an assumption can weaken an argument. Say that a writer claims that real estate development should be prevented in your town. As evidence for this assertion, the writer offers facts about past developments that have replaced older buildings. But the evidence is relevant to the assertion only if you accept the writer's extreme assumptions that old buildings are always worthy and new development is always bad.

In such a case, the writer's bias may not even be stated. Hence a second problem: in arguments both sound and unsound, assumptions are not always explicit. Here, for example, is a summary of a reasonable argument. What is the unstated assumption?

Assertion

The town should create a plan to manage building preservation and new development.

Evidence

Examples of how such plans work; expert opinions on how and why both preservation and development are needed.

In this instance the assumption is that neither uncontrolled development nor zero development is healthy for the town. If you can accept this assumption, you should be able to accept the writer's claim (though you might still disagree over particulars).

Here are some tips for dealing with assumptions:

TRANSPARENCY MASTER 4.4

Guidelines for analyzing assumptions

- What are the assumptions underlying the argument? How does the writer connect assertions with evidence?
- Are the assumptions believable? Do they express your values? Do they seem true in your experience?
- Are the assumptions consistent with each other? Is the argument's foundation solid, not slippery?

JUNK MAIL

Studying junk mail is an excellent way to evaluate the use of tone. How does each solicitor try to persuade the reader to buy/use/subscribe to his or her product? Likewise, advertisements in magazines are often full of subtle and not-so-subtle examples of tone.

Watching language, hearing tone

Tone is the expression of the writer's attitudes toward himself or herself, toward the subject, and toward the reader (see p. 33 for a discussion). Tone can tell you quite a bit about the writer's intentions, biases, and trustworthiness. For example:

> Some women cite personal growth as a reason for pursuing careers while raising children. Of course, they are equally concerned with the personal growth of the children they relegate to "child-care specialists" while they work.

In the second sentence this writer is being **ironic,** saying one thing while meaning another. The word *relegate* and the quotation marks with *child-care specialists* betray the writer's belief that working mothers may selfishly neglect their children for their own needs. Irony can sometimes be effective in argument, but here it marks the author as insincere in dealing with the complex issues of working parents and child care.

When reading arguments, you should be alert for the author's language. Look for words that **connote,** or suggest, certain attitudes and evoke certain responses in readers. Connotative language is no failure in argument; indeed, the strongest arguments use it skillfully to appeal to readers' hearts as well as their minds (see pp. 152–53). But be suspicious if the language runs counter to the substance of the argument.

Look also for evasive words. **Euphemisms,** such as *attack of a partly sexual nature* for "rape" or *peace-keeping force* for a war-making army, are supposedly inoffensive substitutes for words that may frighten or offend readers (see pp. 458–59). In argument, though, they are sometimes used to hide or twist the truth. An honest, forthright arguer will avoid them.

Finally, watch carefully for sexist, racist, and other biased language that reveals deep ignorance or, worse, entrenched prejudice on the part of the writer. Obvious examples are *broad* for woman and *fag* for homosexual. (See pp. 459–62 for more on such language.)

5 Judging reasonableness

The **reasonableness** of an argument is the sense you get as reader that the author is fair and sincere. The reasonable writer does not conceal or distort facts, hide prejudices, mask belief as opinion, manipulate you with language, or resort to any of dozens of devices used unconsciously by those who don't know better and deliberately by those who do.

Reasonableness involves all the elements of argument examined so far: assertions, evidence, assumptions, and language. In addition, the fair, sincere argument always avoids so-called fallacies (covered in the next section), and it acknowledges the opposition.

Judging whether a writer deals adequately with his or her opposition is a fairly simple matter for the reader of argument. By definition, an arguable issue has more than one side. Even if you have no preconceptions about a subject, you will know that another side exists. If the writer pretends otherwise, or dismisses the opposition too quickly, you are justified in questioning the honesty and fairness of the argument. (For the more complicated business of *writing* an acknowledgment of the opposition, see p. 154.)

COLLABORATIVE LEARNING

Students will benefit from working together on Exercise 1. In discussing possible responses and debating the evidence for each response they will learn even more about how each argument is crafted and its effects on different readers. Since the skill of analyzing arguments in these terms is a crucial and challenging one, you might expand on Exercise 1 by bringing in other examples of persuasive argumentation and ask students to analyze further examples using these terms.

ANSWERS: EXERCISE 1

Possible answers

Sale essay

Assertions: Thesis (paragraph 5): Individuals' conservation efforts do not raise the consciousness necessary to solve the ecological crisis. Supporting assertions: Individuals' conservation does not make a significant dent in energy consumption dominated by industry and government (1, 2). The ecological crisis requires a *drastic overhaul of this civilization,* not individual *life-style solutions* (3). Such solutions divert individuals from *the hard truths and hard choices* of truly changing consciousness (4).

Evidence: Statistics and other facts: 2–5. Examples: 1, 3–5. Appeals to beliefs or needs: mainly, we should do what's necessary to solve the ecological crisis (throughout).

Assumptions: Notably: There is an environmental crisis. It must be solved. Ozone depletion and rain forest destruction are *corporate crimes* (2). Industry and government are powerful and self-protective. They will not respond appropriately to the ecological crisis unless forced to do so by the people. The people are unwilling to make more than life-style changes to solve the crisis.

Tone: No-nonsense (*I don't . . . believe that I am saving the planet*), unrestrained (*patently corporate crimes; truly pernicious*), sardonic (*"all of us"; "our" control; life-style solutions; write-your-congressperson solutions*).

Exercise 1
Reading arguments critically

Following are two brief arguments. Though not directly opposed, the two arguments do represent different stances on environmental issues. Read each argument critically, following the process outlined in the Introduction (pp. 2–17) and answering the questions in the box on page 127 (questions about assertions, evidence, assumptions, and the other elements of argument). Develop your responses in writing so that you can refer to them for later exercises and class discussion.

The Environmental Crisis Is Not Our Fault

I am as responsible as most eco-citizens: I bike everywhere; I don't own a car; I recycle newspapers, bottles, cans, and plastics; I have a vegetable garden in the summer; I buy organic products; and I put all vegetable waste into my backyard compost bin, probably the only one in all of Greenwich Village. But I don't at the same time believe that I am saving the planet, or in fact doing anything of much consequence about the various eco-crises around us. What's more, I don't even believe that if "all of us" as individuals started doing the same it would make any but the slightest difference. 1

Leave aside ozone depletion and rain forest destruction—those are patently corporate crimes that no individual actions can remedy to any degree. Take, instead, energy consumption in this country. In 1987 (the most recent figures) residential consumption was 7.2 percent of the total, commercial 5.5 percent, and industrial 23.3 percent; of the remainder, 27.8 percent was transportation (about one-third of it by private car) and 36.3 percent was electric generation (about one-third for residential use). Individual energy use, in sum, was something like 28 percent of total consumption. Although you and I cutting down on energy consumption would have some small effect (and should be done), it is surely the energy consumption of industry and other large institutions such as government and agribusiness that needs to be addressed first. And it is industry and government that must be forced to explain what their consumption is for, what is produced by it, how necessary it is, and how it can be drastically reduced. 2

The point is that the ecological crisis is essentially beyond "our" control, as citizens or householders or consumers or even voters. It is not something that can be halted by recycling or double-pane insulation. It is the inevitable by-product of our modern industrial civilization, dominated by capitalist production and consumption and serviced and protected by various institutions of government, federal to local. It cannot possibly be altered or reversed by simple individual actions, even by the actions of the mil- 3 lions who took part in Earth Day—and even if they all went home and fixed their refrigerators and from then on walked to work. Nothing less than a drastic overhaul of this civilization and an abandonment of its ingrained gods—progress, growth, exploitation, technology, materialism, anthropocentricity, and power—will do anything substantial to halt our path to environmental destruction, and it's hard to see how life-style solutions will have an effect on that.

4 What I find truly pernicious about such solutions is that they get people thinking they are actually making a difference and doing their part to halt the destruction of the earth: "There, I've taken all the bottles to the recycling center and used my string bag at the grocery store; I guess that'll take care of global warming." It is the kind of thing that diverts people from the hard truths and hard choices and hard actions, from the recognition that they have to take on the larger forces of society—corporate and governmental—where true power, and true destructiveness, lie.

5 And to the argument that, well, you have to start somewhere to raise people's consciousness, I would reply that this individualistic approach does not in fact raise consciousness. It does not move people beyond their old familiar liberal perceptions of the world, it does nothing to challenge the belief in technofix or write-your-Congressperson solutions, and it does not begin to provide them with the new vocabulary and modes of thought necessary for a true change of consciousness. We need, for example, to think of recycling centers not as the answer to our waste problems, but as a confession that the system of packaging and production in this society is out of control. Recycling centers are like hospitals; they are the institutions at the end of the cycle that take care of problems that would never exist if ecological criteria had operated at the beginning of the cycle. Until we have those kinds of understandings, we will not do anything with consciousness except reinforce it with the same misguided ideas that created the crisis.

—KIRKPATRICK SALE

Myths We Wouldn't Miss

1 There are tall tales and legends. There are fables and apocryphal stories. And there are myths—a number of which we would like to see disappear. Here are some myths that would not be missed:

2 MYTH: Offshore drilling would be an ecological disaster.

3 Truth is, there hasn't been a serious spill in US waters resulting from offshore drilling operations in more than twenty years—and even that one, in Santa Barbara Channel in 1969, caused no permanent damage to the environment.

4 This is why we always have such a problem with the reasoning of those who call for moratoriums or outright bans on such activity while the nation continues to import foreign oil. The fact is, oil industry offshore drilling operations cause less pollution than urban runoff, atmospheric phenomena, municipal discharges or natural seeps.

Reasonableness: Sale is obviously biased, so his reasonableness will probably reside in the eye of the beholder. He does offer evidence for his key assertion about the environmental responsibility of industry and government, and his examples show him to be familiar with the mentality of most recyclers (a group he even includes himself in). He acknowledges the opposition most clearly in paragraph 5, where he rebuts the claim that the individualistic approach is at least a start on consciousness raising.

Fallacies: See the answer to Exercise 4.

Evaluation: Answers will vary.

Mobil advertisement

Assertions: Thesis (paragraphs 2, 6, 10, 13): Myths about oil exploration, waste, and conservation do not address America's true energy needs. Supporting assertions: Offshore drilling is necessary and does not unduly pollute (4). Though heavy, America's energy use is appropriate for the nation's size and productivity (7, 9). Favoring conservation over exploration would increase oil imports or stop economic growth (12).

Evidence: Statistics and other facts: 3–4, 7–9, 12. Examples: 3. Appeals to beliefs or needs: Mainly, America is a strong country whose economic health is crucial for all (throughout).

Assumptions: Notably: Policy needs to be guided by truths, not myths. Importing foreign oil is undesirable. Some pollution is inevitable and acceptable. America is justified in using energy proportionate to its size and productivity. Conservation is desirable. Economic growth is essential.

Tone: Sincere (*a mystery we hope puzzles others as much as it does us; We probably can—and should—do more*), candid (*Truth is; The fact is; In fact; Let's face it; No doubt about it*), perplexed (*We always have such a problem; where is the waste*).

Reasonableness: Like Sale's essay, Mobil's ad is strongly biased, but the statistics and other facts and the sincere tone contribute to a sense of reasonableness. So do the several bows to the opposition, including the statements of the objectionable myths themselves and the support for conservation.

Fallacies: See the answer to Exercise 4.

Evaluation: Answers will vary.

Why this nation would choose *not* to drill for oil and *not* to 5
provide the jobs, profits and taxes such activity would mean for the American economy when there are no better alternatives is a mystery we hope puzzles others as much as it does us.

MYTH: America is a profligate waster of energy. 6

The myth makers like to throw around numbers that read like 7
this: with only 5 percent of the world's population, the US uses about 25 percent of the world's energy. But ours is a big country—three thousand miles from one ocean to the next. Transportation accounts for more than 60 percent of US oil use. We could probably cut down if we moved everybody into one corner of the country, but where is the waste?

It certainly isn't the automobiles that are inefficient. They are 8
twice as efficient as the ones we used twenty years ago. If American drivers use more gasoline than their counterparts in Europe and Japan, it may just have something to do with the country's size.

In fact, proof of the country's size may be in our economic 9
output—and may also hold a clue as to why we use the energy we do. Despite having only 5 percent of the world's population, America may indeed use 25 percent of the world's energy. However, according to the latest statistics, we also produce about 25 percent of the world's goods and services. Again, where's the waste?. . .

MYTH: Conservation is *the answer* to America's energy problems. 10

No doubt about it, we all need to be careful of the amount of 11
energy we use. But as long as this nation's economy needs to grow, we are going to need energy to fuel that growth.

For the foreseeable future, there are no viable alternatives to 12
petroleum as the major source of energy, especially for transportation fuels. Let's face it. Over the past twenty years we *have* learned to conserve—in our factories, our homes, our cars. We probably can—and should—do more. But conservation and new exploration should not be mutually exclusive, because even without an increase in energy consumption, we are using up domestic reserves of oil and gas and must replace them. For the good of the economy, those reserves should be replaced with new domestic production, to the extent economically possible. Otherwise, the only solutions would be additional imports or no growth. And stifling growth would be a gross disservice to the people for whom such growth would provide the opportunity for a better life.

Simply put, America is going to need more energy for all its 13
people.

And that is no myth. 14

—MOBIL CORPORATION ADVERTISEMENT

4b Recognizing fallacies

This section falls between reading and writing arguments because you'll need to know **fallacies**—errors in argument—as both a reader (to spot them) and a writer (to avoid them). The many common fallacies fall into two groups. Some evade the issue of the argument. Others treat the argument as if it were much simpler than it is.

Checklist of fallacies

Evasions

- **Begging the question:** treating an opinion that is open to question as if it were already proved or disproved.
- **Non sequitur** ("it does not follow"): drawing a conclusion from irrelevant evidence.
- **Red herring:** introducing an irrelevant issue to distract readers.
- **Inappropriate appeals:**

  Appealing to readers' fear or pity.
  Snob appeal: appealing to readers' wish to be like those who are more intelligent, famous, rich, and so on.
  Bandwagon: appealing to readers' wish to be part of the group.
  Flattery: appealing to readers' intelligence, taste, and so on.
  Argument ad populum ("to the people"): appealing to readers' general values, such as patriotism or love of family.
  Argument ad hominem ("to the man"): attacking the opponent rather than the opponent's argument.

Oversimplifications

- **Hasty generalization (jumping to a conclusion):** asserting an opinion based on too little evidence. **Absolute statements** and **stereotypes** are variations.
- **Reductive fallacy:** generally, oversimplifying causes and effects.
- **Post hoc fallacy:** assuming that *A* caused *B* because *A* preceded *B*.
- **Either/or fallacy (false dilemma):** reducing a complicated question to two alternatives.
- **False analogy:** exaggerating the similarities in an analogy or ignoring key differences.

1 Recognizing evasions

The central assertion of an argument defines an issue or question: Should real estate development be controlled? Should drug testing be mandatory in the workplace? An effective argument faces the central issue squarely with relevant opinions, beliefs, and evidence. An ineffective argument dodges the issue.

Begging the question

A writer **begs the question** by treating an opinion that is open to question as if it were already proved or disproved. (In essence, the writer begs readers to accept his or her ideas from the start.)

TRANSPARENCY MASTER 4.5

NAMING FALLACIES

Many students are put off by the terminology used to classify fallacies. Let them know that the fallacies sometimes overlap and that it is more important for them to recognize and avoid oversimplifications and evasions than to know the correct terms for them.

RESOURCES AND IDEAS

Moore, Vincent. "Using Role Playing in Argument Papers to Deconstruct Stereotypes." *Teaching English in the Two-Year College* 22 (1995): 190–96. Moore argues for the efficacy of role-playing to help students gain flexibility in seeing multiple perspectives when developing an argument.

Rapkins, Angela A. "The Uses of Logic in the College Freshman English Curriculum." In *Activities to Promote Critical Thinking.* Ed. Jeff Golub. Urbana: NCTE, 1986. 130–35. Rapkins suggests emphasizing logic in all the papers in a course and describes in detail the use of ads in a final argumentation unit, a strategy that expands awareness of the logical fallacies students have been developing throughout the course.

COLLABORATIVE LEARNING

FALLACY HUNTING

To sharpen student sensitivity to fallacies, assign teams to go "fallacy hunting." Each team should try to collect at least one example of each fallacy in the checklist. If students compile the fallacies on a computer disk or on overhead transparencies, it will be relatively easy for you to prepare a "dictionary of fallacies" to distribute for your students' reference through the network or in printed form.

> The college library's expenses should be reduced by cutting subscriptions to useless periodicals. [Begged questions: Are some of the library's periodicals useless? Useless to whom?]
>
> The fact is that the welfare system is too corrupt to be reformed. [Begged questions: How corrupt is the welfare system? Does corruption, even if extensive, put the system beyond reform?]

Non sequitur

A **non sequitur** occurs when no logical relation exists between two or more connected ideas. In Latin *non sequitur* means "it does not follow." In the sentences below, the second thought does not follow from the first.

> If high school English were easier, fewer students would have trouble with the college English requirement. [Presumably, if high school English were easier, students would have *more* trouble.]
>
> Kathleen Newsome has my vote for mayor because she has the best-run campaign organization. [Shouldn't one's vote be based on the candidate's qualities, not the campaign organization's?]

Red herring

A **red herring** is literally a kind of fish that might be drawn across a path to distract a bloodhound from a scent it's following. In argument, a red herring is an irrelevant issue intended to distract readers from the relevant issues. The writer changes the subject rather than pursue the argument.

> A campus speech code is essential to protect students, who already have enough problems coping with rising tuition. [Tuition costs and speech codes are different subjects. What protections do students need that a speech code will provide?]
>
> Instead of developing a campus speech code that will infringe on students' First Amendment rights, administrators should be figuring out how to prevent another tuition increase. [Again, tuition costs and speech codes are different subjects. How would the code infringe on rights?]

Inappropriate appeals

Appeals to readers' emotions are common in effective arguments. But such appeals must be relevant and must supplement rather than substitute for facts, examples, and other evidence.

Writers sometimes ignore the question with **appeals to readers' fear or pity.**

> By electing Susan Clark to the city council, you will prevent the city's economic collapse. [Trades on people's fears. Can Clark single-handedly prevent economic collapse?]

She should not have to pay taxes because she is an aged widow with no friends or relatives. [Appeals to people's pity. Should age and loneliness, rather than income, determine a person's tax obligation?]

Sometimes writers ignore the question by appealing to readers' sense of what other people believe or do. One approach is **snob appeal,** inviting readers to accept an assertion in order to be identified with others they admire.

As any literate person knows, James Joyce is the best twentieth-century novelist. [But what qualities of Joyce's writing make him a superior novelist?]

A similar tactic invites readers to accept an assertion because everybody else does. This is the **bandwagon approach.**

As everyone knows, marijuana use leads to heroin addiction. [What is the evidence?]

Yet another diversion involves **flattery** of readers, in a way inviting them to join in a conspiracy.

We all understand campus problems well enough to see the disadvantages of such a backward policy. [What are the disadvantages of the policy?]

The **argument ad populum** ("argument to the people") asks readers to accept a conclusion based on shared values or even prejudices and nothing else.

Any truly patriotic American will support the President's action. [But why is the action worth taking?]

One final and very common kind of inappropriate emotional appeal addresses *not* the pros and cons of the issue itself but the real or imagined negative qualities of the people who hold the opposing view. This kind of argument is called **ad hominem,** Latin for "to the man."

One of the scientists has been treated for emotional problems, so his pessimism about nuclear waste merits no attention. [Do the scientist's previous emotional problems invalidate his current views?]

2 Recognizing oversimplifications

To **oversimplify** is to conceal or ignore complexities in a vain attempt to create a neater, more convincing argument than reality allows.

Hasty generalization

A **hasty generalization** is an assertion based on too little evidence or on evidence that is unrepresentative. (This fallacy is also called **jumping to a conclusion.**) For example:

> People who care about the environment recycle their trash. [Many people who care about the environment may not have the option of recycling.]

A variation of the hasty generalization is the **absolute statement** involving words such as *all, always, never,* and *no one* that allow no exceptions. Rarely can evidence support such terms. Moderate words such as *some, sometimes, rarely,* and *few* are more reasonable.

Another common hasty generalization is the **stereotype,** a conventional and oversimplified characterization of a group of people:

> People who live in cities are unfriendly.
> Californians are fad-crazy.
> Women are emotional.
> Men can't express their feelings.

(See also pp. 459–62 on sexist and other biased language.)

Reductive fallacy

The **reductive fallacy** oversimplifies (or reduces) the relation between causes and their effects. The fallacy (sometimes called **oversimplification**) often involves linking two events as if one caused the other directly, whereas the causes may be more complex or the relation may not exist at all. For example:

> Poverty causes crime. [If so, then why do people who are not poor commit crimes? And why aren't all poor people criminals?]
>
> The better a school's athletic facilities are, the worse its academic programs are. [The sentence assumes a direct cause-and-effect link between athletics and scholarship.]

Post hoc fallacy

Related to the reductive fallacy is the assumption that because *A* preceded *B,* then *A* must have caused *B.* This fallacy is called in Latin *post hoc, ergo propter hoc,* meaning "after this, therefore because of this," or the **post hoc fallacy** for short.

> In the two months since he took office, Mayor Holcomb has allowed crime in the city to increase 2 percent. [The increase in crime is probably attributable to conditions existing before Holcomb took office.]
>
> The town council erred in permitting the adult bookstore to open, for shortly afterward two women were assaulted. [It cannot be

assumed without evidence that the women's assailants visited or were influenced by the bookstore.]

Either/or fallacy

In the **either/or fallacy** (also called **false dilemma**), the writer assumes that a complicated question has only two answers, one good and one bad, both bad, or both good.

> City police officers are either brutal or corrupt. [Most city police officers are neither.]
>
> Either we permit mandatory drug testing in the workplace or productivity will continue to decline. [Productivity is not necessarily dependent on drug testing.]

False analogy

An **analogy** is a comparison between two essentially unlike things for the purpose of definition or illustration. (See also p. 112.) In arguing by analogy, a writer draws a likeness between things on the basis of a single shared feature and then extends the likeness to other features. For instance, the "war on drugs" equates a battle against a foe with a program to eradicate (or at least reduce) sales and use of illegal drugs. Both involve an enemy, a strategy of overpowering the enemy, a desired goal, officials in uniform, and other similarities.

Analogy can only illustrate a point, never prove it: just because things are similar in one respect, they are not *necessarily* alike in other respects. In the fallacy called **false analogy,** the writer assumes such a complete likeness. Here is the analogy of the war on drugs taken to its false extreme:

> To win the war on drugs, we must wage more of a military-style operation. Prisoners of war are locked up without the benefit of a trial by jury, and drug dealers should be, too. Soldiers shoot their enemy on sight, and officials who encounter big drug operations should, too. Military traitors may be executed, and corrupt law enforcers could be, too.

Exercise 2
Analyzing advertisements

Leaf through a magazine or watch television for half an hour, looking for advertisements that attempt to sell a product not on the basis of its worth but by snob appeal, flattery, or other inappropriate appeals to emotions. Be prepared to discuss the advertiser's techniques.

Exercise 3
Identifying and revising fallacies

Identify at least one fallacy illustrated by each of the following sentences. Then revise the sentence to make it more reasonable.

COLLABORATIVE LEARNING

Have students work in groups to list and analyze the fallacies found in Exercise 2. Ask each group to present the advertisement with the most blatant or surprising fallacy to the class.

ANSWERS: EXERCISE 2

Individual response.

ANSWERS: EXERCISE 3

Possible answers

1. Hasty generalization and begged question. *A revision:* A successful marriage demands a degree of maturity.

2. Hasty generalization and non sequitur.
   A revision: Students' persistent complaints about the unfairness of the grading system should be investigated.
3. Reductive fallacy.
   A revision: The United States got involved in World War II for many complex reasons. The bombing of Pearl Harbor was a triggering incident.
4. Either/or fallacy and hasty generalization.
   A revision: People watch television for many reasons, but some watch because they are too lazy to talk or read or because they want mindless escape from their lives.
5. Reductive fallacy and begged question.
   A revision: Racial tension may occur when people with different backgrounds live side by side.

COLLABORATIVE LEARNING

Ask students to work in groups on Exercise 4. After completing the exercise each group might go on to compose an advertisement in which the argument for the product contains each of these fallacies.

ANSWERS: EXERCISE 4

Possible answers

Though free of the most egregious appeals, the Sale essay and the Mobil advertisement do demonstrate several basic fallacies. Most notably:

Sale essay

Either/or: Either we achieve a *drastic overhaul of our civilization* or the environment will be destroyed (paragraph 3).

Begged question: The individualistic approach to environmental problems does not *challenge the belief in technofix or write-your-Congressperson solutions* [Do these not work?] or achieve an essential, fundamental change in thinking [Is the change essential?] (5).

False analogy: The analogy between recycling centers and hospitals (5) implies that a preventive approach (*ecological criteria* for packaging and production; preventive medicine) would eliminate the need for the institution. This isn't true of hospitals (people would still get sick), so how is it true of recycling centers?

1. A successful marriage demands a maturity that no one under twenty-five possesses.
2. Students' persistent complaints about the grading system prove that it is unfair.
3. The United States got involved in World War II because the Japanese bombed Pearl Harbor.
4. People watch television because they are too lazy to talk or read or because they want mindless escape from their lives.
5. Racial tension is bound to occur when people with different backgrounds are forced to live side by side.

Exercise 4
Identifying fallacies in arguments

Analyze the two arguments on pages 136–38 for fallacies. To what extent do any fallacies weaken either argument? Explain.

4c Developing an argument

In composing an argument, you try to illuminate an issue or solve a problem by finding the common ground between you and others who will read your work. Using critical thinking, you develop and test your own ideas. Using a variety of techniques, you engage readers in an attempt to narrow the distance between your views and theirs.

Sections 4c through 4g will be more helpful to you if you have already read Chapters 1 and 2 on the writing process.

1 Finding a topic and conceiving a thesis

An argument topic must be arguable—that is, reasonable people will disagree over it and be able to support their positions with evidence. This sentence implies the *do*'s and *don't*'s listed in the box opposite. If you feel uncertain about finding a topic for argument, try some of the techniques listed on page 37 for discovering ideas.

ESL The guidelines for an argument topic may make you uncomfortable if your native language is something other than English and you're not accustomed to the kinds of arguments discussed here. One way to find a topic for argument is to read a newspaper every day for at least a week, looking for issues that involve or interest you. Following the development of the issues in articles, editorials, and letters to the editor will give you a sense of how controversial they are, what the positions are, and what your position might be.

Once you have a topic, you may also have a thesis, or you may need to do some research and writing to find your angle. The **thesis** is the main idea of your paper (see pp. 47–51). In an argument the **thesis sentence** states the assertion that you want your readers to accept or act on. Here are two thesis sentences on the same subject:

Tests for an argument topic

A GOOD TOPIC:

- Concerns a matter of opinion—a conclusion drawn from evidence (see pp. 128–29).
- Can be disputed: others might take a different position.
- *Will* be disputed: it is controversial.
- Is something you care about and know about, or want to research.
- Is narrow enough to argue in the space and time available (see pp. 28–29).

A BAD TOPIC:

- Cannot be disputed because it concerns a fact, such as the distance to Saturn or the functions of the human liver.
- Cannot be disputed because it concerns a personal preference or belief, such as a liking for the color red or a moral commitment to vegetarianism.
- *Will not* be disputed because few if any disagree over it—the virtues of a secure home, for instance.

The new room fees are unjustified given the condition of the dormitories.

The administration should postpone the new room fees at least until conditions in the dormitories are improved.

Your thesis sentence must satisfy the same requirements as the topic (see the box above). But it must also specify the grounds of your argument, the general basis for your assertion. In the two thesis sentences above, the grounds for protesting the room fees are that the dormitories are in bad condition.

Note that the writer of either of these arguments must clarify the definition of *condition(s)* if the argument is to be clear and reasonable. Always take pains to define abstract and general terms that are central to your argument, preferably in or just after the thesis sentence. (See pp. 129–30.)

2 Analyzing your purpose and your audience

Your purpose in argument is, broadly, to engage readers in order to convince them of your position or persuade them to act. But arguments have more specific purposes as well, such as the following:

To strengthen the commitment of existing supporters
To win new supporters from the undecided
To get the opposition to reconsider

Mobil advertisement

Begged question: The fact is, oil industry offshore drilling operations cause less pollution than other sources of pollution (4). [But how much pollution *do* the drilling operations cause?]

Either/or: Either we move everyone to one place or we continue to use a disproportionate amount of the world's energy (7).

Either/or: Either we find more energy or the economy will not grow; either we find more energy or we will have to increase imports (2).

Begged question: Despite good conservation efforts, we still need petroleum exploration (12). [But why can't conservation be improved to eliminate the need for risky exploration?]

LISTING PRIORITIES AND VALUES

1. Ask groups of students first to list the five (or ten) issues they consider most worth arguing about and then to record their different opinions about the top two or three.
2. Ask students to prepare lists as in 1, above, but to restrict the list to a specific area, such as sports, the economy, or drugs. In so doing, you will create a situation in which students will need to go beyond obvious issues and opinions to complete their lists.

RESOURCES AND IDEAS

Kneupper, Charles W. "Teaching Argument: An Introduction to the Toulmin Model." *College Composition and Communication* 29 (1978): 237–41. Kneupper provides a brief review of Stephen Toulmin's simplified, practical logic, a system based primarily on three elements: data, claim, and warrant.

Lamb, Catherine E. "Beyond Argument in Feminist Composition." *College Composition and Communication* 42 (1991): 11–24. Lamb finds that the oral discourse modes of negotiation and mediation can be effectively used in conceiving the purpose and audience of a written argument. She says, "Argument still has a place, although now as a means, not an end. The end—a resolution of conflict that is fair to both sides—is possible even in the one-sidedness of written communication."

To inspire supporters to act
To deter the undecided from acting

It's no accident that each of these purposes characterizes the audience (*existing supporters, the undecided,* and so on). In argument even more than in other kinds of writing, achieving your purpose depends on the response of your readers, so you need a sense of who they are and where they stand. The "Questions About Audience" on page 33 can help you identify readers' knowledge, beliefs, and other pertinent background information. You also need to know their position on your topic—not only whether they agree or disagree generally, but also which specific assertions they will find more or less convincing.

Your purpose can help you fill in this information. If you decide to address supporters or opponents, you essentially select readers with certain inclinations and ignore other readers who may tune in. If you decide to win new supporters from those who are undecided on your topic, you'll have to imagine skeptical readers who will be convinced only by an argument that is detailed, logical, and fair. Like you when you read an argument critically, these skeptical readers seek to be reasoned with, not manipulated into a position or hammered over the head.

Exercise 5
Finding a topic; conceiving a thesis sentence

Analyze each topic in the following list to determine whether it is appropriate for argument. For each of the topics you deem arguable, draft a thesis sentence that specifies the grounds for an argument. If you prefer, choose five arguable topics of your own and draft a thesis sentence for each one. One thesis sentence should interest you enough to develop into a complete argument.

1. Granting of athletic scholarships
2. Care of automobile tires
3. History of the town park
4. Housing for the homeless
5. Billboards in urban residential areas or in rural areas
6. Animal testing for cosmetics research
7. Cats versus dogs as pets
8. [*Name*] for student-government president [or some other elected office]
9. Ten steps in recycling wastepaper
10. Benefits of being a parent

Exercise 6
Analyzing purpose and audience

Specify a purpose and likely audience for the thesis sentence you chose to develop in Exercise 5. What do purpose and audience suggest about the way you should develop the argument?

COLLABORATIVE LEARNING

AUDIENCE APPEALS

Have the class select two or three broad subjects; then, in small groups, have them decide what more focused purposes they could have in writing about such subjects and what evidence and appeals they would choose in writing for different audiences. If the topic is "censorship," for instance, you might have groups arguing for or against certain kinds of censorship for audiences ranging from the library trustees to the city council to the manager at a local videotape rental store.

ANSWERS: EXERCISE 5

Possible answers

Topics that are not appropriate for argument:

2. A matter of facts, and few people would disagree.
3. A matter of facts, and few people would disagree.
7. A matter of personal preference.
9. A matter of facts.
10. A matter of personal belief.

Possible thesis sentences for appropriate topics:

4d Using reason and evidence

As a reader of argument, you seek evidence for the writer's assertions and clear reasoning about the relationship of evidence to assertions. As a writer of argument, you seek to provide what the reader needs in a way that furthers your case.

 1 Reasoning inductively and deductively

The thesis of your argument is a conclusion you reach by reasoning about evidence. Two common processes of reasoning are induction and deduction—methods of thinking that you use all the time even if you don't know their names.

Induction

When you're about to buy a used car, you consult friends, relatives, and consumer guides before deciding what kind of car to buy. Using **inductive reasoning,** you make specific observations about cars (your evidence) and you induce, or infer, a **generalization** that Model X is the most reliable. Writing a paper on the effectiveness of print advertising, you might also use inductive reasoning:

First analyze statistics on advertising in print and in other media (evidence).
Then read comments by advertisers and publishers (more evidence).
Finally, form a conclusion that print is the most cost-effective advertising medium (generalization).

This reasoning uses the elements of an argument discussed earlier (p. 127): assertions requiring support, evidence supporting the assertions, and assumptions connecting evidence to assertions.

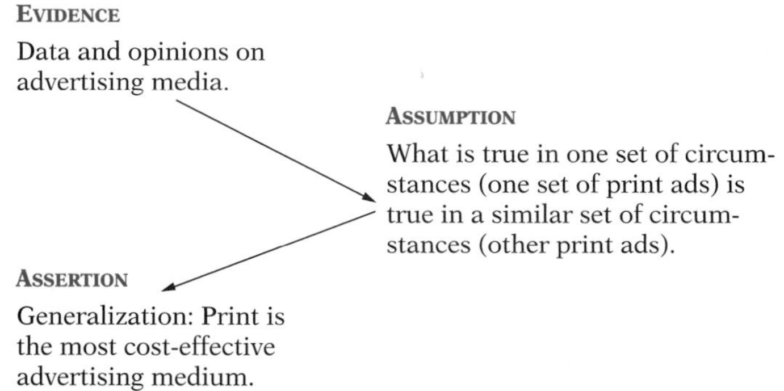

EVIDENCE
Data and opinions on advertising media.
ASSUMPTION
What is true in one set of circumstances (one set of print ads) is true in a similar set of circumstances (other print ads).
ASSERTION
Generalization: Print is the most cost-effective advertising medium.

With induction, you predict something about the unknown based on what you know: you create new knowledge out of old.

1. An athletic scholarship should be what the term implies: an award to one who is both a superior athlete and a superior scholar.
4. Until the city can construct private housing for the homeless, it must do more to make public shelters safe and clean.
5. Billboards help to destabilize urban neighborhoods by creating the impression that the neighborhoods are mere roadways.
6. Humane testing methods are adequate enough that cosmetics companies do not have to abuse animals in testing.
8. Goldberger has proved successful in representing both resident and commuter students to the administration.

arg 4d

COLLABORATIVE LEARNING

Exercises 5 and 6 work well as group projects. Encourage groups to come up with more than one possible thesis for each appropriate topic, then have each group present their most compelling thesis sentences along with their analyses of purpose and audience.

COMPUTER EXERCISE

If you are working in a networked classroom, you might post the list of potential topics in Exercise 5 and ask students to add thesis sentences with analyses of purpose and audience.

ANSWERS: EXERCISE 6

Individual response.

RESOURCES AND IDEAS

Gage, John T. "Teaching the Enthymeme: Invention and Arrangement." *Rhetoric Review* 2 (1983): 38–50. Gage argues that students can gain awareness and control over the context, logic, and structure of their arguments by stating their reasoning in enthymemic fashion, as a sentence containing an assertion and a because clause.

Porter, Jeffrey. "The Reasonable Reader: Knowledge and Inquiry in Freshman English." *College English* 49 (1987): 332–44. Porter argues that enthymemes organize readers' "participation in the text."

The more evidence you accumulate, the more probable it is that your generalization is true. Note, however, that absolute certainty is not possible. At some point you must *assume* that your evidence justifies your generalization, for yourself and your readers. Most errors in inductive reasoning involve oversimplifying either the evidence or the generalization. See pages 138–43 on fallacies.

Deduction

You use **deductive reasoning** when you proceed from your generalization that Model X is the most reliable used car to your own specific circumstances (you want to buy a used car) to the conclusion that you should buy a Model X car. Like induction, deduction uses the elements of argument—assertions, evidence, and assumptions—but differently. This diagram corresponds to the one on the previous page for induction, picking up the example of print advertising:

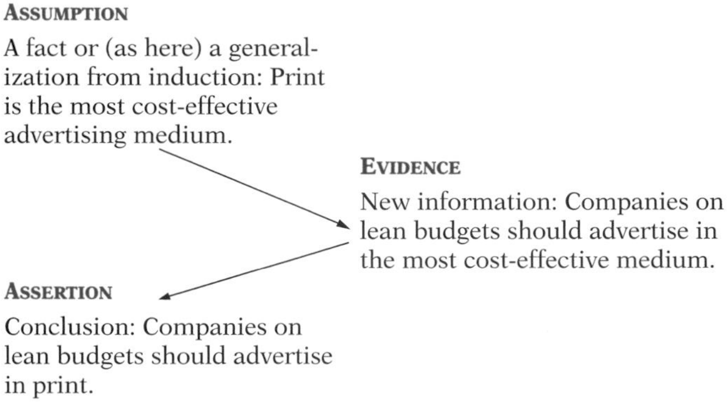

Assumption
A fact or (as here) a generalization from induction: Print is the most cost-effective advertising medium.

Evidence
New information: Companies on lean budgets should advertise in the most cost-effective medium.

Assertion
Conclusion: Companies on lean budgets should advertise in print.

With deduction, you apply old information to new.

The conventional way of displaying a deductive argument is in a **syllogism.** If you want the school administration to postpone new room fees for one dormitory, your deductive argument might be expressed in this syllogism:

> *Premise:* The administration should not raise fees on dorm rooms in bad condition. [A generalization, fact, or belief that you assume to be true.]
> *Premise:* The rooms in Polk Hall are in bad condition. [New information: a specific case of the first premise.]
> *Conclusion:* The administration should not raise fees on the rooms in Polk Hall.

As long as the premises of a syllogism are true, the conclusion derives logically and certainly from them.

The force of deductive reasoning depends on the reliability of the premises and the care taken to apply them in drawing conclu-

Tests for inductive and deductive reasoning

Induction

- Have you stated your evidence clearly?
- Is your evidence complete enough and good enough to justify your assertion? What is the assumption that connects evidence and assertion? Is it believable?
- Have you avoided fallacies? (See p. 138.)

Deduction

- What are the premises leading to your conclusion? Look especially for unstated premises.
- What does the first premise assume? Is the assumption believable?
- Does the first premise necessarily apply to the second premise?
- Is the second premise believable?
- Have you avoided fallacies? (See p. 138.)

sions. The reasoning process is **valid** if the premises lead logically to the conclusion. It is **true** if the premises are believable. Sometimes the reasoning is true but *not* valid:

> *Premise:* The administration should not raise fees on dorm rooms in bad condition.
> *Premise:* Tyler Hall is a dormitory.
> *Conclusion:* The administration should not raise fees on the rooms in Tyler Hall.

Both premises may be true, but the first does not *necessarily* apply to the second, so the conclusion is invalid.

Sometimes, too, the reasoning is valid but *not* true:

> *Premise:* All college administrations are indifferent to students' needs.
> *Premise:* The administration of Central State is a college administration.
> *Conclusion:* The administration of Central State is indifferent to students' needs.

This syllogism is valid but useless: the first premise is an untrue assumption, so the entire argument is untrue. Invalid and untrue syllogisms underlie many of the fallacies discussed on pages 138–43.

A particular hazard of deductive reasoning is the **unstated premise:** the basic assumption linking evidence and conclusion is not stated but implied. Here the unstated premise is believable and the argument is reasonable:

> Ms. Stein has worked with drug addicts for fifteen years, so she knows a great deal about their problems. [Unstated premise: Anyone who has worked fifteen years with drug addicts knows about their problems.]

But when the unstated premise is wrong or unfounded, the argument is false. For example:

> Since Jane Lightbow is a senator, she must receive money illegally from lobbyists. [Unstated premise: All senators receive money illegally from lobbyists.]

To avoid such false conclusions, you may be tempted to make your assertions sound more reasonable. But even a reasonable-sounding conclusion must be supportable. For instance, changing *must* to *might* modifies the unstated assumption about Senator Lightbow:

> Since Jane Lightbow is a senator, she might receive money illegally from lobbyists. [Unstated premise: *Some* senators receive money illegally from lobbyists.]

But it does not necessarily follow that Senator Lightbow is one of the "some." The sentence, though logical, is not truly reasonable unless evidence demonstrates that Senator Lightbow should be linked with illegal activities.

Using evidence

Whether your argument is reasonable or not depends heavily on the evidence you marshal to support it. The kinds of evidence and the criteria for evaluating evidence are discussed in detail on pages 130–33. How to find evidence is discussed under research writing on pages 522–58.

The kind and quantity of evidence you use should be determined by your purpose, your topic, and the needs of your audience. Some arguments, such as a plea for volunteer help in a soup kitchen, will rely most heavily on examples (including perhaps a narrative of your own experience) and on appeals to readers' beliefs. Other arguments, such as a proposal for mandatory side air bags in cars, will rely much more on statistics and expert opinions. Most arguments, including these, will mingle facts, examples, expert opinions, and appeals to readers' beliefs and needs (see also p. 152).

In using evidence for argument, you'll need to be especially wary of certain traps that carelessness or zeal can lure you into. These are listed in the following box:

Responsible use of evidence

- **Don't distort.** You mislead readers when you twist evidence to suit your argument—for instance, when you claim that crime in your city occurs five times more often than it did in 1955, without mentioning that the population is also seven times larger.

- **Don't stack the deck.** Ignoring damning evidence is like cheating at cards. You must deal forthrightly with the opposition (see p. 154).
- **Don't exaggerate.** Watch your language. Don't try to manipulate readers by characterizing your own evidence as *pure* and *rock-solid* and the opposition's as *ridiculous* and *half-baked*. Make the evidence speak for itself.
- **Don't oversimplify.** Avoid forcing the evidence to support more than it can. (See also p. 141.)
- **Don't misquote.** When you cite experts, quote them accurately and fairly.

Exercise 7
Reasoning inductively

Study the facts below and then evaluate each of the numbered conclusions following them. Which of the generalizations are reasonable given the evidence, and which are not? Why?

In 1990–91 each American household viewed an average of 48 hours and 32 minutes of television weekly.

Each individual viewed an average of 30 hours and 20 minutes per week.

Those viewing the most television per week (43 hours and 31 minutes) were women over age 55.

Those viewing the least television per week (21 hours and 10 minutes) were children ages 6 to 11.

Households earning under $30,000 a year watched an average of 52 hours and 57 minutes a week.

Households earning more than $60,000 a year watched an average of 47 hours and 13 minutes a week.

1. Households with incomes under $30,000 tend to watch more television than average.
2. Women watch more television than men.
3. Nonaffluent people watch less television than affluent people.
4. Women over age 55 tend to watch more television than average.
5. Children watch less television than critics generally assume.

Exercise 8
Reasoning deductively

Convert each of the following statements into a syllogism. (You may have to state unstated assumptions.) Use the syllogism to evaluate both the validity and the truth of the statement.

Example:

DiSantis is a banker, so he does not care about the poor.

Premise: Bankers do not care about the poor.
Premise: DiSantis is a banker.
Conclusion: DiSantis does not care about the poor.

The statement is untrue because the first premise is untrue.

COLLABORATIVE LEARNING

Students can work effectively together on Exercises 7 and 8. To foster a more active discussion of likely inferences and deductions, ask each group to note places where individuals disagree and to pose those cases to the class as a whole.

ANSWERS: EXERCISE 7

The unreasonable generalizations from the given evidence are statements 2 (can't be inferred from the facts), 3 (contradicted by the facts), and 5 (can't be inferred from the facts).

ANSWERS: EXERCISE 8

Possible answers

1. *Premise:* Anyone who has opposed pollution controls may continue to do so.
   Premise: The mayor has opposed pollution controls.
   Conclusion: The mayor may continue to do so.
   The statement is valid and true.
2. *Premise:* Government should not be left to the dishonest.
   Premise: Lawyers and professional politicians are dishonest.
   Conclusion: Government should not be left to lawyers and professional politicians.
   The statement is untrue because the second premise is untrue.
3. *Premise:* Many good artists trained at Parsons.
   Premise: Schroeder trained at Parsons.
   Conclusion: Schroeder is a good artist.
   The statement is invalid because the first premise does not necessarily apply to the second.

4. *Premise:* Those who use their resources to help others deserve our particular appreciation.
   Premise: Some wealthy athletes use their resources to help others.
   Conclusion: Some wealthy athletes deserve our particular appreciation.
   The statement is valid and, if the first premise is accepted, true.
5. *Premise:* Any employer who has hired only one woman is sexist.
   Premise: Jimson is an employer who has hired only one woman.
   Conclusion: Jimson is sexist.
   The statement is untrue because the first premise is not true: there may be other reasons besides sexism for hiring only one woman.

ANSWERS: EXERCISE 9

Individual response.

COLLABORATIVE LEARNING

After students have drafted an argument as suggested in Exercise 9, ask them to work in groups to help one another to test and to develop the structure and evidence for each argument further, and to identify inductive and deductive reasoning. Then ask each student to revise his or her argument using the group's comments.

COLLECTING APPEALS

Ask students to read, on their own, a relatively long and complex argumentative essay from a reader or a magazine of political or social opinion. In class, assign students to groups and ask each group (1) to identify purely logical appeals, purely emotional appeals, and mixed appeals in the essay and (2) to describe, if they can, the effect of each appeal on average readers (like the members of the group).

1. The mayor opposed pollution controls when he was president of a manufacturing company, so he may not support new controls or vigorously enforce existing ones.
2. Government demands so much honesty that we should not leave it to lawyers and professional politicians.
3. Schroeder is a good artist because she trained at Parsons, like many other good artists.
4. Wealthy athletes who use their resources to help others deserve our particular appreciation.
5. Jimson is sexist because she has hired only one woman.

Exercise 9
Using reason and evidence in your argument

Develop the structure and evidence for the argument you began in Exercises 5 and 6 (p. 146). (You may want to begin drafting at this stage.) Is your argument mainly inductive or mainly deductive? Use the box on page 149 to test the reasoning of the argument. Use the boxes on pages 133 and 150–51 to test your evidence.

4e Reaching your readers

To reach your readers in argument, you appeal directly to their reason and emotions, you account for views opposing yours, and you cast the argument in a clear, logical structure.

1 Appealing to readers

In forming convictions about arguable issues, we generally interpret the factual evidence through the filter of our values, beliefs, tastes, desires, and feelings. You may object to placing the new town dump in a particular wooded area because the facts suggest that the site is not large enough and that prevailing winds will blow odors back through the town. But you may also have fond memories of playing in the wooded area as a child, feelings that color your interpretation of the facts and strengthen your conviction that the dump should be placed elsewhere. Your conviction is partly rational, because it is based on evidence, and partly emotional, because it is also based on feelings.

In most arguments you will combine **rational appeals** to readers' capacities for reasoning logically from evidence to a conclusion with **emotional appeals** to readers' beliefs and feelings. The following passages, all arguing the same view on the same subject, illustrate how either a primarily rational or a primarily emotional appeal may be weaker than an approach that uses both.

Rational appeal

Advertising should show more physically challenged people. The millions of disabled Americans have considerable buying power, yet so far advertisers have made no attempt to tap that power. [Appeals to the logic of financial gain.]

EMOTIONAL APPEAL

Advertising should show more physically challenged people. By keeping the physically challenged out of the mainstream depicted in ads, advertisers encourage widespread prejudice against disability, prejudice that frightens and demeans those who hold it. [Appeals to the sense of fairness, open-mindedness.]

RATIONAL AND EMOTIONAL APPEALS

Advertising should show more physically challenged people. The millions of disabled Americans have considerable buying power, yet so far advertisers have made no attempt to tap that power. Further, by keeping the physically challenged out of the mainstream depicted in ads, advertisers encourage widespread prejudice against disability, prejudice that frightens and demeans those who hold it.

The third passage, in combining both kinds of appeal, gives readers both rational and emotional bases for agreeing with the writer.

For an emotional appeal to be successful, it must be appropriate for the audience and the argument:

- It must not misjudge readers' actual feelings.
- It must not raise emotional issues that are irrelevant to the assertions and the evidence. (See pp. 140–41 for a discussion of specific inappropriate appeals, such as bandwagon.)

A third kind of approach to readers, the **ethical appeal,** is the sense you give of being a competent, fair person who is worth heeding. A sound argument backed by ample evidence—a rational appeal—will convince readers of your knowledge and reasonableness. (So will your acknowledging the opposition. See the next section.) Appropriate emotional appeals will demonstrate that you share readers' beliefs and needs. In addition, a sincere and even tone will assure readers that you are a balanced person who wants to reason with them.

A sincere and even tone need not exclude language with emotional appeal—words such as *frightens* and *demeans* at the end of the third example above. But avoid certain forms of expression that will mark you as unfair:

- Insulting words such as *idiotic* or *fascist.*
- Biased language such as *fags* or *broads.* (See pp. 459–62.)
- Sarcasm—for instance, using the sentence *What a brilliant idea* to indicate contempt for the idea and its originator.
- Exclamation points! They'll make you sound shrill!

See also pages 33–35 on tone.

ANTICIPATING OPPOSITION

A good strategy for teaching students to anticipate opposition is to have them generate "yes, but" lists. Ask them to list all the strong points supporting their argument, then think of a counterargument for each point. (Sometimes they will be able to overcome these counterarguments; at other times they may have to concede the point.) For instance, if their thesis is "Raising the tuition at Golden College will reduce enrollment," they might produce a "yes, but" list like this:

Supporting point	"Yes, but" objection
Tuition rose 3 percent last year, and enrollment dropped by 2 percent.	Yes, but the recession and the lack of financial aid may also have contributed to lower enrollment.
There are cheaper schools in area.	Yes, but Golden College is rated in the top ten of small schools in the area.
Students can't afford higher tuition costs.	Yes, but they seem to afford all the clothes, cars, and CDs they want to buy. Where are their priorities?

COLLABORATIVE LEARNING

Group work is particularly useful in helping students to anticipate opposition to an argument. Ask the groups to play devil's advocate in order to test each writer's reasoning processes and use of evidence. To ensure that this is a supportive experience, remind groups to frame their questions about each writer's argument as a series of productive revision suggestions.

COMPUTER EXERCISE

CUT AND PASTE

Students who have access to computers can take particular advantage of their software's "cut and paste" or "block and move" capabilities to re-

2 Answering opposing views

A good test of your fairness in argument is how you handle possible objections. Assuming your thesis is indeed arguable, then others can marshal their own evidence to support a different view or views. You need to find out what these other views are and what the support is for them. Then, in your argument, you need to take these views on, refute those you can, grant the validity of others, and demonstrate why, despite their validity, the opposing views are less compelling than your own.

The student who wrote the following paragraph first stated an opposing view, then conceded its partial validity, and finally demonstrated its irrelevance.

> The athletic director argues against reducing university support for athletic programs on the grounds that they make money that goes toward academic programs. It is true that here at Springfield the surpluses from the football and basketball programs have gone into the general university fund, and some of that money may have made it into academic departments (the fund's accounting methods make it impossible to say for sure). But the athletic director misses the point. The problem is not that the athletic programs cost more than they take in but that they demand too much to begin with. For an institution that hopes to become first-rate academically, too many facilities, too much money, too much energy, and too many people are tied up in the effort to produce championship sports teams.

Before or while you draft your essay, list for yourself all the opposing views you can think of. You'll find them in your research, by talking to friends and classmates, and by critically thinking about your own ideas. (On a computer or on paper, you can annotate the assertions in your draft with opposing arguments for each one.)

To deal with opposing views, figure out which ones you can refute (do more research if necessary), and prepare to concede those views you can't refute. It's not a mark of weakness or failure to admit that the opposition has a point or two. Indeed, by showing yourself to be honest and fair, you strengthen your ethical appeal and thus your entire argument.

3 Organizing your argument

There are organizing schemes for arguments that relate directly to induction and deduction:

- An **inductive organization** moves from specific evidence to a generalization about the evidence.

- **A deductive organization** begins with a commonly held opinion or belief (the first premise of the syllogism), applies it to a new case (the second premise), and draws a conclusion.

In practice, your sense of purpose and audience may dictate that you vary these schemes—for example, stating your generalization (your thesis) first in an inductive argument to secure readers' attention. Further, your argument may be both inductive and deductive, so that you could not adhere strictly to either scheme.

Because of such variations in subject, purpose, audience, and form of reasoning, arguments can be effectively organized in many different ways. One trusty scheme appears in the box below:

Organization of an argument

Introduction

Statement of the significance of the argument; background on the issue; statement of thesis. (See pp. 117–19 on introductions, 47 and 145 on the thesis sentence.) The introduction may be one or more paragraphs, depending on the complexity of the issue, readers' knowledge of it, and the length of the whole paper.

Body

Assertions relating to the thesis, each developed in one or more paragraphs with the evidence for the assertion. If the argument consists of a string of supporting assertions, they are usually best arranged in order of increasing importance or persuasiveness. Sometimes the body of the argument will break into distinct sections, such as description of a problem, proposal for solving the problem, and advantages of the proposal. However arranged, the body is the meat of the argument and will run as long as needed.

Answering the opposition

Refutation of opposing views, with evidence; concession to views more valid than your own; demonstration of your argument's greater strength (see opposite). This material may come elsewhere in the argument, after the introduction or throughout the body. The choice depends mainly on whether you think readers need the opposition to be dealt with right away or can wait.

Conclusion

Restatement of the thesis; summary of the argument; last appeal to readers. (See pp. 120–21 on conclusions.) The conclusion may be one or more paragraphs, depending on the complexity and the length of your argument.

You may want to experiment with different arrangements of material in a given paper—such as where you put background information, how you order supporting assertions or their evidence,

arrange supporting claims and evidence until they find the best arrangement.

TRANSPARENCY MASTER 4.6

whether you answer the opposition near the beginning or near the end. You can do this experimentation on paper, of course, but it's easier on a computer. Try rearranging your outline as described on page 53. Or try rearranging your draft (work with a copy) by cutting and pasting parts of it for different emphases.

ANSWERS: EXERCISE 10

Possible answers

1. Primarily emotional appeal. Ethical appeal: fair, willing to sacrifice for others.
2. Primarily rational appeal. Ethical appeal: knowledgeable, reasonable.
3. Primarily rational appeal. Ethical appeal: knowledgeable, fair, willing to acknowledge opposing views.
4. Primarily emotional appeal. Ethical appeal: sympathetic toward animals (but perhaps unfair to *so-called scientists*).
5. Primarily rational appeal. Ethical appeal: knowledgeable, fair, willing to acknowledge opposing views.

COLLABORATIVE LEARNING

Ask students to work in small groups to identify the emotional, rational, and ethical appeals of the passages in Exercise 10 and then to identify similar grounds for appeal in their own arguments (as specified in Exercise 11).

ANSWERS: EXERCISE 11

Individual response.

Exercise 10
Identifying appeals

Identify each passage below as primarily a rational appeal or primarily an emotional appeal. Which passages make a strong ethical appeal as well?

1. Only complacency, indifference, or selfishness could allow us to ignore these people's hunger. We who have so much cannot in good conscience let others starve.
2. Thus the data collected by these researchers indicate that a mandatory sentence for illegal possession of handguns may lead to reduction in handgun purchases.
3. Most broadcasters worry that further government regulation of television programming could breed censorship—certainly, an undesirable outcome. Yet most broadcasters also accept that children's television is a fair target for regulation.
4. Anyone who cherishes life in all its diversity could not help being appalled by the mistreatment of laboratory animals. The so-called scientists who run the labs are misguided.
5. Many experts in constitutional law have warned that the rule violates the right to free speech. Yet other experts have viewed the rule, however regretfully, as necessary for the good of the community as a whole.

Exercise 11
Reaching your readers

Continuing your argument-in-progress from Exercise 9 (p. 152), analyze whether your assertions are rational or emotional and whether the mix is appropriate for your audience and argument. Analyze your ethical appeal, too, considering whether it can be strengthened. Then make a list of possible opposing views. Think freely at first, not stopping to censor views that seem far-fetched or irrational. When your list is complete, decide which views must be taken seriously and why, and develop a response to each one.

4f Revising your argument

When you revise your argument, do it in at least two stages—revising underlying meaning and structure, and editing more superficial elements. The checklists on pages 69 and 74–75 can be a guide. Supplement them with the following checklist, which encourages you to think critically about your own argument:

TRANSPARENCY MASTER 4.7

Checklist for revising an argument

- What is your thesis? In what ways is it an arguable assertion (p. 145)?
- Where have you provided the information readers need (p. 130)? Where have you considered their probable beliefs and values (p. 145)?
- Does your thesis derive from induction, deduction, or both (p. 147)? If induction, where have you related the evidence to your generalization? If deduction, is your syllogism both true and valid? Have you avoided fallacies in reasoning (p. 138)?
- Where, if at all, is your evidence not accurate, relevant, representative, and adequate (p. 132)? (Answer this question from the point of view of a neutral or even a skeptical reader.)
- Where do you make rational appeals or emotional appeals (p. 152)? Are both appropriate for your audience? What is your ethical appeal (p. 153)?
- Where have you answered opposing arguments (p. 154)? (Again, consider the neutral or skeptical reader.)
- How clear and effective is your organization (p. 155)?

4g Examining a sample argument

The following essay by Lee Morrison, a student, illustrates the principles discussed in this chapter. As you read the essay, notice especially the structure, the relation of assertions and supporting evidence, and the kinds of appeals Morrison makes.

Share the Ride

Introduction: identification of problem

Every year we encounter more bad news about the environment, and a good portion of it is due to the private automobile. Respected scientists warn that carbon dioxide emissions, such as those from cars, may produce disastrous global warming. Soot, sulfur, and other automobile emissions are contributing to reduced air quality almost everywhere. The oil that powers cars comes from rapidly depleting reserves, leading to an unhappy choice between imports of foreign oil and exploration, such as offshore drilling, that threatens the environment.

In its own way Beverly Community College contributes to the problem. Campus parking lots are filled with about 1800 cars every weekday, so that means 3600 trips a day are made to and from campus. If just a third of the solo drivers shared rides with one another, the total trips to and from campus would be reduced by at least 600. It is time for the BCC community to make a difficult move toward an organized car-pooling system that would achieve this modest goal.

Thesis sentence: proposal for a solution

The first step in getting car-pools going is to form a task force of administrators, faculty, and students to devise a workable system. School records would be used to connect people who live near each other and would be willing to car-pool. With administration backing, the task force would initiate a school-wide campaign of meetings, rallies, posters, and other public relations efforts to overcome resistance to car-pooling, answer questions, and win converts. The administration would assign staff to help with records and to keep the system current each term, since schedules and the student population change. As soon as administrators thought it was feasible, they could give a big boost to the system by creating monetary incentives to car-pool. Students who participate in car-pooling could receive a tuition rebate—say, $100 a term for full-time students. Faculty and staff could receive equivalent bonuses. In addition, parking fees could be instituted to discourage driving to school.

Explanation of the proposal

The most obvious advantage of this proposal is that it would reduce car trips and thus air pollution and needless use of oil. Burning a single gallon of gasoline produces 20 pounds of carbon dioxide. If the average length of a trip to or from BCC is 10 miles (a conservative number) and the average car gets 30 miles to the gallon (a generous number), then it takes only 3 trips to burn a gallon of gasoline. Saving just 600 trips a day would keep 4000 pounds of carbon dioxide out of the air. It would also keep 200 gallons of gasoline in the pumps.

Support for the proposal: first advantage

That unused gasoline would also save money for participants. If a full-time student drove half as often as now, the gasoline savings would be about $30 a term, plus the savings in wear and tear on the car. If the school instituted a $100 tuition rebate, the cash savings would rise to $130 a term. If the school instituted a parking fee of, say, $1 a day, the cash savings would rise to more than $160 a term. (All figures assume that car-pools consist of two people who share driving and expenses equally.)

Support for the proposal: second advantage

There are more abstract advantages, too. Individual freedom is a cherished right in our society, but it has no meaning outside the community. Like recycling and other environmental efforts, car-pooling would ask the individual to make a sacrifice on behalf of the community. Car-poolers would

Support for the proposal: third advantage

be actively participating in something larger than themselves, instead of just furthering their own self-interest.

Probable objection and response

Members of the BCC administration may point out that the proposed program asks for sacrifice from the school as well. They may object that rebates or bonuses and the costs of running the program are not feasible given the school's tight budget. True, $100 rebates or bonuses for an estimated 600 participants would cost $60,000 a term, and administrative time would also cost something. But considerable money could be raised by instituting a dollar parking fee, which could produce as much as $1500 a day, nearly $100,000 a term, in revenue. Furthermore, sponsoring a car-pooling system is no more than many corporations do that encourage their employees to take public transportation by contributing to their monthly passes. Businesses, schools, and other institutions that require their people to assemble in one place should help reduce the environmental cost of commuting.

Probable objection and response

Of course, it is the cost of commuters' convenience that will probably make or break the program. Students and faculty may have to arrive at school earlier than they want or leave later because of their car-pools. While considerable, this inconvenience could over time be turned to an advantage if car-poolers learned to use their extra on-campus time wisely to prepare for classes (work they would have to do at home anyway). In addition, this inconvenience might seem worthwhile in exchange for helping the environment and the concrete rewards of a rebate or bonus and savings on parking.

Probable objection

It is no small flaw in the proposal that not all commuters would be able to participate in the program, even if they wanted to. The fact is that many part-time faculty and students have schedules that are too complicated or erratic to permit car-pooling. Many teachers and students must make intermediate stops between their homes and BCC, such as for work. These commuters would not have access to the rebates or bonuses and still would be subject to the parking fee.

Response to probable objection and conclusion

This unfairness is regrettable but, for now, unavoidable; we have to start somewhere. A change away from single-passenger cars to car-pools is like all other significant changes we must make on behalf of the environment. The shift in consciousness and responsibility will be halting and prolonged, and the costs and benefits will not always be dis-

arg 4g

ANSWERS: EXERCISE 12

Possible answers

1. General assertions related to thesis sentence: the first sentences of paragraphs 4, 5, and 6; the first two sentences of 7; the first sentences of 8 and 9; and the conclusion. Supporting evidence: statistics (2, 4, 5, 7); other facts (1, 7, 8, 9); examples (4, 5); statements of belief (1, 6, 7, 10).
2. Appeals to reason: the explanation of the proposal (3); statistics (2, 4, 5, 11); detailed responses to probable objections (7–10). Appeals to emotion: *Respected scientists, unhappy choice* (1); the abstract advantages in 6; conclusion. The writer appeals mainly to readers' concern for the environment and their willingness to make sacrifices for good causes.
3. The ethical appeal is that of a concerned, fair-minded, reasonable citizen willing to make sacrifices.
4. The objections are raised and answered in 7–10: cost, inconvenience, unfairness. The first two are refuted. The third, the writer admits, cannot be refuted.
5. Answers will vary.
6. Individual response.

COLLABORATIVE LEARNING

Students can work effectively together to critique the essay in Exercise 12 and to use those same questions to critique each other's drafted arguments as specified by Exercise 13. If students have worked continuously with the same group throughout the process of developing their arguments (i.e., throughout Chapter 4) you might rearrange the groups for this final exercise so that each writer experiences a fresh set of responses to his or her argument.

ANSWERS: EXERCISE 13

Individual response.

tributed equally. One thing we can be sure of, however, is that the shift will not occur at all if we don't take the difficult first steps.

—Lee Morrison

Exercise 12
Critically reading an argument

Analyze the construction and effectiveness of the preceding essay by answering the following questions.

1. Where does Morrison make general assertions related to his thesis sentence, and where does he provide statistics or other evidence to support the assertions?
2. Where does Morrison appeal primarily to reason, and where does he appeal primarily to emotion? What specific beliefs, values, and desires of readers does he appeal to?
3. How would you characterize Morrison's ethical appeal?
4. What objections to his plan does Morrison anticipate? How does he respond to each one?
5. How effective do you find this argument? To what extent do you agree with Morrison about the problems identified in his introduction? To what extent does he convince you that his plan is desirable and workable and would address those problems? Does he fail to anticipate any major objections to his plan?
6. Write a critical evaluation of "Share the Ride." First summarize Morrison's views. Then respond to those views by answering the questions posed in item 5 above.

Exercise 13
Writing and revising your argument

Draft and revise the argument you have developed in Exercises 5 and 6 (p. 146), 9 (p. 152), and 11 (p. 156). Use the revision checklists on pages 69 and 157 to review your work.

Part II

Grammatical Sentences

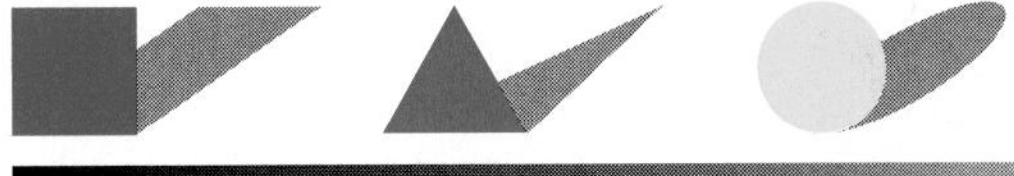

Chapter 5

Understanding Sentence Grammar

Grammar describes how language works. Following the rules of standard English grammar is what allows you to communicate with others across barriers of personality, region, class, or ethnic origin. If you are a native English speaker, you follow these rules mostly unconsciously. But when you're trying to improve your ability to communicate, it can help to make the rules conscious and learn the language used to describe them.

Grammar tells a lot about a sentence, even if you don't know the meanings of all the words.

The rumfrums prattly biggled the pooba.

You don't know what this sentence means, but you can infer that some things called *rumfrums* did something to a *pooba.* They *biggled* it, whatever that means, in a *prattly* way. Two grammatical cues, especially, tell you that this sentence is like *The students easily passed the test:*

- Word forms. The ending *-s* means more than one *rumfrum.* The ending *-ed* means that *biggled* is an action that happened in the past. The ending *-ly* means that *prattly* probably describes *how* the rumfrums biggled.
- Word order. *Rumfrums biggled pooba* resembles a common sequence in English: something (*rumfrums*) performed some action (*biggled*) to or on something else (*pooba*). Since *prattly* comes right before the action, it probably describes the action.

This chapter explains how such structures work and shows how practicing with them can help you communicate more effectively.

HIGHLIGHTS

In this chapter, students will encounter a brief descriptive grammar that can serve as a reference for explanations of basic grammatical terms and as a guide to how sentences are constructed and their major elements punctuated. The chapter builds cumulatively from the simplest sentence to increasingly complex expansions rather than compartmentalizing grammar into parts of speech and kinds of phrases, clauses, and sentences. Moreover, it treats punctuation in context, as part of the discussion of word groups and syntactic relationships that may require it.

Because of its whole sentence approach and because of the many sentence-combining and -modeling exercises it contains, this chapter can be useful for a wide range of students. Those whose writing displays fundamental problems with sentences will benefit from its clear treatment of sentence parts and structure and from the exercises that require manipulation of sentence elements. Those who have mastered basic sentence strategies will be able to develop many options for expression through sentence-combining exercises that introduce elements like verbal phrases, absolute phrases, and appositives. And all students will gain a greater understanding of punctuation when they see how it grows out of and communicates a sentence's structure and meaning.

This chapter uses almost entirely traditional terminology because such terminology, despite its weaknesses, is still the most widely used and most likely to be familiar to students and instructors. The overall description largely reflects a structural view of English grammar. It is as simple as possible while still including all the word classes and syntactic structures needed by the student to understand the twenty successive chapters on sentences and punctuation.

You may wish to emphasize or de-emphasize the chapter, depending in part on the preparation of your students and on how much you think an understanding of grammar can contribute to their writing. As may be obvious, this chapter of the handbook was prepared in the belief that a clear understanding of the essential structure of English sentences and of the uses of syntactic groups and compound structures can help many students not only to punctuate correctly but also to gain greater control of subordination and emphasis within their sentences. This process will take place only if students get a chance to put knowledge into action through exercises that ask

5a Understanding the basic sentence

The **sentence** is the basic unit of thought. Its grammar consists of words with specific forms and functions arranged in specific ways.

1 Identifying subjects and predicates

Most sentences make statements. First they name something; then they make an assertion about or describe an action involving that something. These two sentence parts are the **subject** and the **predicate.**

SUBJECT	PREDICATE
Art	can be controversial.
It	has caused disputes in Congress and in artists' studios.
Its meaning and value to society	are often the focus of debate.

ESL The subject of an English sentence may be a noun (*art*) or a pronoun that refers to a noun (*it*), but not both: Art [not Art it] *can be controversial.* See page 308.

2 Identifying the basic words: Nouns and verbs

The following five simple sentences consist almost entirely of two quite different kinds of words.

SUBJECT	PREDICATE
The earth	trembled.
The earthquake	destroyed the city.
The result	was chaos.
The government	sent the city aid.
The citizens	considered the earthquake a disaster.

The words in the subject position name things, such as *earth, earthquake,* and *government.* In contrast, the words in the predicate position express actions, such as *trembled, destroyed,* and *sent.*

These two groups of words work in different ways. *Citizen* can become *citizens,* but not *citizened. Destroyed* can become *destroys,* but not *destroyeds.* Grammar reflects such differences by identifying the **parts of speech** or **word classes** shown in the box on the next page. Except for *the* and *a,* which simply point to and help identify the words after them, the five sentences about the earthquake consist entirely of nouns and verbs.

them to manipulate and create sentences. In this regard, the sentence-combining exercises in the chapter can be coordinated with those in other chapters of the text to create a program of sentence combining designed to complement instruction in essay and paragraph writing.

gr 5a

RESOURCES AND IDEAS

Does grammar instruction help? The effectiveness of grammar instruction in improving writing and in helping students achieve correctness in their prose is still a hotly debated issue. The essays in *The Place of Grammar in Writing Instruction: Past, Present, Future,* edited by Susan Hunter and Ray Wallace, explore the various possibilities for integrating grammar into writing instruction, including Eric H. Hobson's "Taking Computer-Assisted Grammar Instruction to New Frontiers" (Portsmouth, NH: Boynton, 1995). A recent issue of *English Journal* (85: 7, Nov. 1996) is devoted to considerations surrounding the teaching of grammar. These essays range from historical overviews like Martha Kolln's "Rhetorical Grammar: A Modification Lesson" to the debates surrounding grammar instruction in Ed Vavra's "On Not Teaching Grammar" to specific discussions of how best to teach pronoun and verb usage.

Other useful works on grammar instruction include the following:

Enos, Teresa, ed. *A Sourcebook for Basic Writing Teachers.* New York: Random, 1987. This collection of essays explores the debates over the efficacy of grammar instruction for standard and for nonstandard dialect speakers. The collection includes Sarah D'Eloia's "The Uses—and Limits—of Grammar," which suggests ways to integrate instruction in writing and grammar, including dictation, paraphrase and conversion, imitation, follow-ups to writing assignments, and exercises that ask students to "discover" a rule from examples of it in operation (373–416).

Farr, Marcia, and Harvey Daniels. *Language Diversity and Writing Instruction.* New York: ERIC Clearinghouse on Urban Education, 1986. Though the issue is clearly far from resolved, the perspective offered in this work is promising. The authors look at standard and nonstandard dialects in the context of linguistic research and provide suggestions for shaping writing instruction as a whole (including instruction in formal grammar) in ways that

gr
5a

TRANSPARENCY MASTER 5.1

are likely to benefit speakers of nonstandard dialects.

Gorrell, Donna. "Controlled Composition for Basic Writers," *College Composition and Communication* 32 (1981): 308–16. Gorrell argues that students who learn to correct the grammar of their peers become more skilled in producing their own error-free sentences.

Newman, Michael. "Correctness and Its Conceptions: The Meaning of Language Form for Basic Writers." *Journal of Basic Writing* 15 (Summer 1996): 23–38. Newman discusses changing views on "correctness" and "error" since Mina Shaughnessy's pathbreaking *Errors and Expectations.*

Noguchi, Rei. R. *Grammar and the Teaching of Writing: Limits and Possibilities.* Urbana: NCTE, 1991. Noguchi has made an important contribution in helping teachers conceive of grammar instruction as a conceptual issue, and of student errors as an inseparable part of the larger concerns with meaning-making in writing instruction.

DICTATION

Read to your class the words in the list below (or in a similar one) and then go through the list again, giving students a minute or two to write sentences using the words in as many different roles (parts of speech) as they can. The word *good,* for example, can be an adjective or a noun.

well	post
set	bill
that	needle
while	bit
turn	

The parts of speech

Nouns name persons, places, things, ideas, or qualities: *Roosevelt, girl, Kip River, coastline, Koran, table, strife, happiness.* (See below.)

Pronouns usually substitute for nouns and function as nouns: *I, you, he, she, it, we, they, myself, this, that, who, which, everyone.* (See the next page.)

Verbs express actions, occurrences, or states of being: *run, bunt, inflate, become, be.* (See the next page.)

Adjectives describe or modify nouns or pronouns: *gentle, small, helpful.* (See p. 171.)

Adverbs describe or modify verbs, adjectives, other verbs, or whole groups of words: *gently, helpfully, almost, really, someday.* (See p. 171.)

Prepositions relate nouns or pronouns to other words in a sentence: *about, at, down, for, of, with.* (See p. 174.)

Conjunctions link words, phrases, and clauses. **Coordinating conjunctions** and **correlative conjunctions** link words, phrases, or clauses of equal importance: *and, but, or, nor; both . . . and, not only . . . but also, either . . . or.* (See p. 189.) **Subordinating conjunctions** introduce subordinate clauses and link them to main clauses: *although, because, if, whenever.* (See pp. 182–83.)

Interjections express feeling or command attention, either alone or in a sentence: *hey, oh, darn, wow.*

Nouns

Meaning

Nouns name. They may name a person (*Rosie O'Donnell, Jesse Jackson, astronaut*), a thing (*chair, book, Mt. Rainier*), a quality (*pain, mystery, simplicity*), a place (*city, Washington, ocean, Red Sea*), or an idea (*reality, peace, success*).

Form

Nouns change form to distinguish between singular (one) and plural (more than one). Most nouns add *-s* or *-es* for the plural: *earthquake, earthquakes; city, cities.* Some nouns have irregular plurals: *woman, women; child, children.*

ESL Some useful rules for forming noun plurals appear on pages 506–07. The irregular plurals must be memorized.

Most nouns also form the **possessive** to indicate ownership or source. Singular nouns usually add an apostrophe plus *-s* (*Auden's poems*); plural nouns usually add just an apostrophe (*citizens' rights*).

Nouns with *the, a,* and *an*

Nouns are often preceded by *the* or *a* (*an* before a vowel sound: *an apple*). These words are usually called **articles** or **determiners** and always indicate that a noun follows.

ESL See pages 259–61 for the rules governing the use of *the, a/an,* or no article at all before a noun.

Verbs

Meaning

Verbs express an action (*bring, change, grow*), an occurrence (*become, happen*), or a state of being (*be, seem*).

Form

Most verbs can be recognized by two changes in form:

- To indicate a difference between present and past time, most verbs add *-d* or *-ed* to the form listed in the dictionary: *They play today. They played yesterday.* Some verbs indicate past time irregularly: *eat, ate; begin, began* (see p. 209).
- When their subjects are singular nouns or some singular pronouns, all present-time verbs except *be* and *have* add *-s* or *-es* to the dictionary form: *The bear escapes. It runs. The woman begins. She sings.* The *-s* forms of *be* and *have* are *is* and *has.*

(See Chapter 7, pp. 207–09, for more on verb forms.)

Helping verbs

Certain forms of all verbs can combine with other words such as *do, have, can, might, will,* and *must.* These other words are called **helping verbs** or **auxiliary verbs.** In verb phrases such as *could run, will be running,* and *has escaped,* they help to convey time and other attributes. (See Chapter 7, pp. 214–18.)

A note on form and function

In different sentences an English word may serve different functions, take correspondingly different forms, and belong to different word classes. For example:

> The government sent the city *aid.* [*Aid* functions as a noun.]
> Governments *aid* citizens. [*Aid* functions as a verb.]

Because words can function in different ways, we must always determine how a particular word works in a sentence before we can identify what part of speech it is. **The *function* of a word in a sentence always determines its part of speech in that sentence.**

Pronouns

Most **pronouns** substitute for nouns and function in sentences as nouns do. In the following sentence all three pronouns—*who, they, their*—refer to *nurses.*

> Some nurses *who* have families prefer the night shift because *they* have more time with *their* children.

The most common pronouns are the **personal pronouns** (*I, you, he, she, it, we, they*) and the **relative pronouns** (*who, whoever, which, that*). Most of these change form to indicate their function in the sentence—for instance, *He called me. I called him back.* (See Chapter 6 for a discussion of these form changes.)

Exercise 1
Identifying subjects and predicates

Identify the subject and the predicate of each sentence below. Then use each sentence as a model to create a sentence of your own.

Example:

An important scientist spoke at commencement.

subject | predicate

An important scientist | spoke at commencement.
The hungry family ate at the diner.

1. The leaves fell.
2. October ends soon.
3. The orchard owners made apple cider.
4. They examined each apple carefully before using it.
5. Over a hundred people will buy cider at the roadside stand.

Exercise 2
Identifying nouns, verbs, and pronouns

In the following sentences identify all words functioning as nouns with *N,* all words functioning as verbs with *V,* and all pronouns with *P.*

Example:

We took the tour through the museum.

P V N N
We took the *tour* through the *museum.*

1. The trees died.
2. They caught a disease.
3. The disease was a fungus.
4. It ruined a grove that was treasured.
5. Our great-grandfather planted the grove in the last century.

Exercise 3
Using nouns and verbs

Identify each of the following words as a noun, as a verb, or as both. Then create sentences of your own, using each word in each possible function.

Example:

fly
Noun and verb.
The *fly* sat on the meat loaf. [Noun.] The planes *fly* low. [Verb.]

ANSWERS: EXERCISE 1

1. SUBJECT | PREDICATE: The leaves | fell.
   Sample imitation: The kite soared.
2. SUBJECT | PREDICATE: October | ends soon.
   Sample imitation: My class begins soon.
3. SUBJECT | PREDICATE: The orchard owners | made apple cider.
   Sample imitation: The couple grew summer squash.
4. SUBJECT | PREDICATE: They | examined each apple carefully before using it.
   Sample imitation: They dried each glass gingerly after washing it.
5. SUBJECT | PREDICATE: Over a hundred people | will buy cider at the roadside stand.
   Sample imitation: Few pool owners will swim at the public beach.

ANSWERS: EXERCISE 2

1. The trees (N) died (V).
2. They (P) caught (V) a disease (N).
3. The disease (N) was (V) a fungus (N).
4. It (P) ruined (V) a grove (N) that (P) was (V) treasured (V).
5. Our (P) great-grandfather (N) planted (V) the grove (N) in the last century (N).

ANSWERS: EXERCISE 3

Possible answers

1. Noun and verb.
   Blow out the candles and make a wish. [Noun.] The child wished for a new bicycle. [Verb.]

1. wish
2. tie
3. swing
4. mail
5. spend
6. label
7. door
8. company
9. whistle
10. glue

3 Forming sentence patterns with nouns and verbs

We build all our sentences, even the most complicated, on the five basic patterns shown in the box on the next page. As the diagrams indicate, the patterns differ in their predicates because the relation between the verb and the remaining words is different.

ESL The word order in English sentences may not correspond to word order in the sentences of your native language. English, for instance, strongly prefers subject first, then verb, then any other words, whereas some other languages prefer the verb first. The main exceptions to the word patterns discussed below appear on pages 193–95. See also pages 297–303 on positioning modifiers in sentences.

Pattern 1: The earth trembled.

In the simplest pattern the predicate consists only of the verb. Verbs in this pattern do not require following words to complete their meaning and thus are called **intransitive** (from Latin words meaning "not passing over").

Subject	Predicate
	Intransitive verb
The earth	trembled.
Mosquitoes	buzz.
The hospital	may close.

Pattern 2: The earthquake destroyed the city.

In pattern 2 the predicate consists of a verb followed by a noun that identifies who or what receives the action of the verb. This noun is a **direct object.** Verbs that require direct objects to complete their meaning are called **transitive** ("passing over"): the verb transfers the action from subject to object.

Subject	Predicate	
	Transitive verb	*Direct object*
The earthquake	destroyed	the city.
The people	wanted	peace.
Education	opens	doors.

ESL The distinction between transitive verbs and intransitive verbs like those in pattern 1 is important because only transitive

2. Noun and verb.
Many people purchase ties as Father's Day presents. [Noun.] Tie the rope into a square knot. [Verb.]
3. Noun and verb.
The swing hung from a large oak tree. [Noun.] Ted picked up his niece and swung her around and around. [Verb.]
4. Noun and verb.
The mail does not come on national holidays. [Noun.] Mail the package to her home address. [Verb.]
5. Verb.
He spends his free time doing volunteer work.
6. Noun and verb.
The label bore a poison warning. [Noun.] The companies must label their products. [Verb.]
7. Noun.
The door flew open by itself.
8. Noun.
My younger sister was good company.
9. Noun and verb.
The whistle released us from work. [Noun.] We whistle all the way home. [Verb.]
10. Noun and verb.
The glue stuck to my hands. [Noun.] We glue our models together. [Verb.]

RESOURCES AND IDEAS

Bushman, Donald, and Elizabeth Ervin. "Rhetorical Contexts of Grammar: Some Views from Writing Emphasis Instructors." *The Place of Grammar in Writing Instruction: Past, Present, Future.* Ed. Susan Hunter and Ray Wallace. Portsmouth, NH: Boynton, 1995. 136–58. This essay explains strategies for teaching grammar in cross-disciplinary rhetorical contexts.

Hashimoto, I. "Sentence Variety: Where Theory and Practice Meet and Lose." *Composition Studies: Freshman English News* 21 (Spring 1993): 66–77. Hashimoto explores the contradictions between the common injunctions to students about sentence variation and stylistic choices of professional writers.

gr 5a

TRANSPARENCY MASTER 5.2

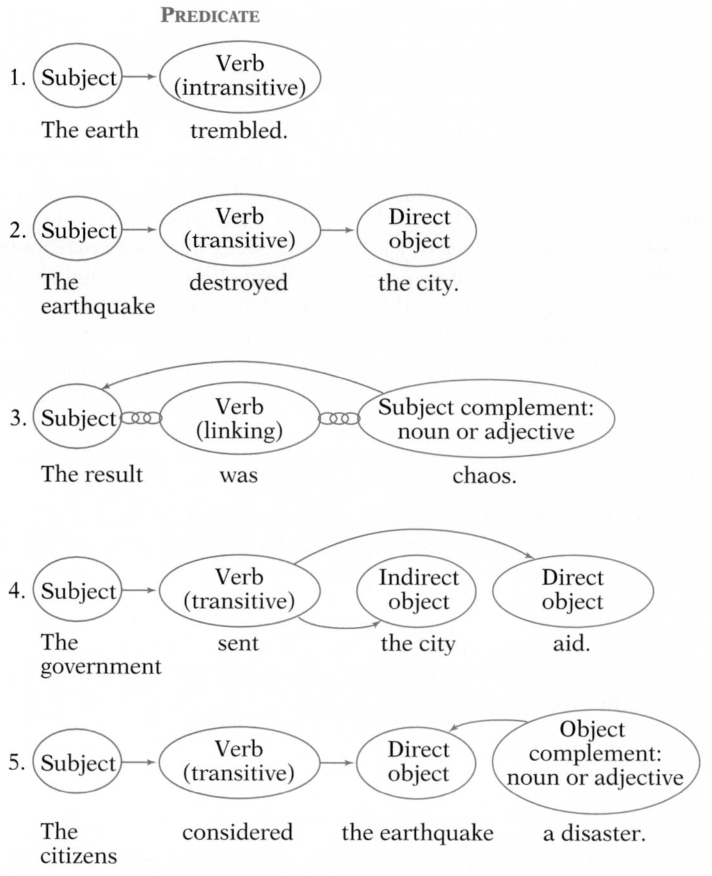

TRANSITIVE AND INTRANSITIVE VERBS (ESL)

Remind students that intransitive verbs *cannot* be followed by a direct object. Transitive verbs, in contrast, *must* have a direct object to complete the meaning of a sentence. Some transitive verbs can have both a direct object and an indirect object. For students who need additional practice with transitive and intransitive verbs and passive voice, Jocelyn Steer and Karen Carlisi include useful exercises in Chapters 5 and 11 of *The Advanced Grammar Book* (Boston: Heinle, 1991).

***TO BE* TEST (ESL)**

Advise students that one way to determine whether a sentence fits into pattern 5 is to insert the words *to be* between the first noun and the following noun or adjective: *The citizens considered the earthquake to be a disaster.*

verbs can be used in the passive voice (*The city was destroyed*). (See p. 230.) Your dictionary will indicate whether a verb is transitive or intransitive. For some verbs (*begin, learn, read, write,* and others), it will indicate both uses.

Pattern 3: The result was chaos.

In pattern 3 the predicate also consists of a verb followed by a single noun, but here the noun renames or describes the subject. We could write the sentence *The result = chaos.* The verb serving as an equal sign is a **linking verb** because it links the subject and the following description. The linking verbs include *be, seem, appear, become, grow, remain, stay, prove, feel, look, smell, sound,* and *taste.* The word that describes the subject is called a **subject complement** (it complements, or completes, the subject).

SUBJECT	PREDICATE	
	Linking verb	*Subject complement*
The result	was	chaos.
The trees	are	elms.
The man	became	an accountant.

Subject complements in this sentence pattern may also be adjectives, words such as *tall* and *hopeful* (see p. 171):

SUBJECT	PREDICATE	
	Linking verb	*Subject complement*
The result	was	chaotic.
Rents	are	high.
The apartments	seem	expensive.

Pattern 4: The government sent the city aid.

In pattern 4 the predicate consists of a verb followed by two nouns. The second noun is a direct object, identifying what was sent (see pattern 2). But t' e first noun, *city,* is different. This noun is an **indirect object,** identifying to or for whom the action of the verb is performed. The direct object and indirect object refer to different things, people, or places.

SUBJECT	PREDICATE		
	Transitive verb	*Indirect object*	*Direct object*
The government	sent	the city	aid.
Businesses	gave	the museum	money.
One company	offered	its employees	bonuses.

A number of verbs can take indirect objects, including those above and *allow, bring, buy, deny, find, get, leave, make, pay, read, sell, show, teach,* and *write.*

ESL With some verbs expressing action done to or for someone, the indirect object must be turned into a phrase beginning with *to* or *for.* These verbs include *admit, announce, demonstrate, explain, introduce, mention, prove, recommend, say,* and *suggest.* The *to* or *for* phrase then falls after the direct object.

FAULTY The manual explains workers the new procedure.

REVISED The manual explains the new procedure *to* workers.

gr 5a

gr 5a

Pattern 5: The citizens considered the earthquake a disaster.

In pattern 5 the predicate again consists of a verb followed by two nouns. But in this pattern the first noun is a direct object and the second noun renames or describes it. Here the second noun is an **object complement** (it complements, or completes, the object).

SUBJECT	PREDICATE		
	Transitive verb	*Direct object*	*Object complement*
The citizens	considered	the earthquake	a disaster.
The class	elected	Joan O'Day	president.
Reporters	declared	her	the winner.

Just as a subject complement (pattern 3) renames or describes a subject, so an object complement renames or describes a direct object. Like a subject complement, an object complement may be a noun or an adjective, as below.

SUBJECT	PREDICATE		
	Transitive verb	*Direct object*	*Object complement*
The citizens	considered	the earthquake	disastrous.
The results	proved	Sweeney	wrong.
Success	makes	some people	nervous.

Exercise 4
Identifying sentence patterns

In the following sentences, identify each verb as intransitive, transitive, or linking. Then identify each direct object (DO), indirect object (IO), subject complement (SC), and object complement (OC).

Example:
Children give their parents both headaches and pleasures.
Give is a transitive verb.
Children give their *parents* (IO) both *headaches* (DO) and *pleasures* (DO).

1. Many people find New Orleans exciting.
2. Tourists flock there each year.
3. Usually they visit the French Quarter first.
4. The Quarter's old buildings are magnificent.
5. In the Quarter, artists sell tourists their paintings.

Exercise 5
Creating sentences

Create sentences by using each of the following verbs in the pattern indicated. (For the meanings of the abbreviations, see the directions for Exercise 4.) You may want to change the form of the verb.

ANSWERS: EXERCISE 4

1. Find is transitive.
   Many people find New Orleans (DO) exciting (OC).
2. Flock is intransitive.
   No objects or complements.
3. Visit is transitive.
   Usually they visit the French Quarter (DO) first.
4. Are is linking.
   The Quarter's old buildings are magnificent (SC).
5. Sell is transitive.
   In the Quarter, artists sell tourists (IO) their paintings (DO).

ANSWERS: EXERCISE 5

Possible answers

1. The audience laughed.
2. The town elected Flynn mayor.
3. Pip stole the pie.
4. Josie caught the ball.

Example:
give (S-V-IO-DO)
Sam gave his brother a birthday card.

1. laugh (S-V)
2. elect (S-V-DO-OC)
3. steal (S-V-DO)
4. catch (S-V-DO)
5. bring (S-V-IO-DO)
6. seem (S-V-SC)
7. call (S-V-DO-OC)
8. become (S-V-SC)
9. buy (S-V-IO-DO)
10. study (S-V)

5b Expanding the basic sentence with single words

Most of the sentences we read, write, or speak are more complex and also more informative and interesting than those examined so far. Most sentences contain one or more of the following: (1) modifying words; (2) word groups, called phrases and clauses; and (3) combinations of two or more words or word groups of the same kind.

1 Using adjectives and adverbs

The simplest expansion of sentences occurs when we add modifying words to describe or limit the nouns and verbs. Modifying words add details.

Recently, the earth trembled.
The earthquake *nearly* destroyed the *old* city.
The *federal* government *soon* sent the city aid.
The grant was a *very generous* one but disappeared *too quickly.*

The italicized words represent two different parts of speech:

- **Adjectives** describe or modify nouns and pronouns. They specify which one, what quality, or how many.

old (adjective) city (noun) generous (adjective) one (pronoun) two (adjective) pears (noun)

- **Adverbs** describe or modify verbs, adjectives, other adverbs, and whole groups of words. They specify when, where, how, and to what extent.

nearly (adverb) destroyed (verb) too (adverb) quickly (adverb)
very (adverb) generous (adjective) Unfortunately, (adverb) taxes will rise. (word group)

An *-ly* ending often signals an adverb, but not always: *friendly* is an adjective; *never, not,* and *always* are adverbs. The only way to tell

5. My uncle brought me a cake.
6. Marilou seems unhappy.
7. One candidate called the other a crook.
8. We became reckless.
9. We bought ourselves a television set.
10. No one studied.

RESOURCES AND IDEAS

Herrington, Anne J. "Grammar Recharted: Sentence Analysis for Writing." In *Writing Exercises from "Exercise Exchange."* Ed. Charles R. Duke, vol. 2. Urbana: NCTE, 1984. 276–87. Herrington suggests using a five-column chart to analyze sentence patterns and help make students aware of syntax. The five columns in the chart—Preceding Subject, Subject, Between Subject and Verb, Verb, and Following Verb—allow the system to account for both relatively simple sentences and those to which considerable information has been added. The columns can be layered as well to account for compound sentences.

Herriman, Jennifer, and Aimo Seppänen. "What is an Indirect Object?" *English Studies* 77 (1996): 484–500. This essay contrasts the consensus on defining and teaching the "direct object" with the vaguer approaches to the indirect object.

whether a word is an adjective or an adverb is to determine what it modifies.

Adjectives and adverbs appear in three forms:

- The **positive** form is the basic form, the one listed in the dictionary: *good, green, angry; badly, quickly, angrily.*
- The **comparative** form indicates a greater degree of the quality named by the word: *better, greener, angrier; worse, more quickly, more angrily.*
- The **superlative** form indicates the greatest degree of the quality named: *best, greenest, angriest; worst, most quickly, most angrily.*

(For further discussion of these forms, see p. 255.)

 2 Using other words as modifiers

Nouns and special forms of verbs may sometimes serve as modifiers of other nouns. In combinations such as *office buildings, Thanksgiving prayer,* and *shock hazard,* the first noun modifies the second. In combinations such as *singing birds, corrected papers,* and *broken finger,* the first word is a verb form modifying the following noun. (These modifying verb forms are discussed in more detail on pp. 177–80.) Again, the part of speech to which we assign a word always depends on its function in a sentence.

ANSWERS: EXERCISE 6

1. The icy (ADJ) rain created glassy (ADJ) patches on the roads.
   Sample imitation: The blue bird turned graceful circles in the air.
2. Happily (ADV), children played in the slippery (ADJ) streets.
   Sample imitation: Quietly, we peeked into the silent cathedral.
3. Fortunately (ADV), no (ADJ) cars ventured out (ADV).
   Sample imitation: Impatiently, the old man gazed ahead.
4. Wise (ADJ) parents stayed indoors (ADV) where they could be warm (ADJ) and dry (ADJ).
   Sample imitation: Smart children go outdoors when they feel noisy and rambunctious.

Exercise 6
Identifying and using adjectives and adverbs

Identify the adjectives and adverbs in the following sentences. Then use each sentence as a model for creating a sentence of your own.

Example:

The red barn sat uncomfortably among modern buildings.

The *red* (adjective) barn sat *uncomfortably* (adverb) among *modern* (adjective) buildings.
The little girl complained loudly to her busy mother.

1. The icy rain created glassy patches on the roads.
2. Happily, children played in the slippery streets.
3. Fortunately, no cars ventured out.
4. Wise parents stayed indoors where they could be warm and dry.
5. The dogs slept soundly near the warm radiators.

Exercise 7
Using verb forms as modifiers

Use each of the following verb forms to modify a noun in a sentence of your own.

Example:

smoking
Only a *smoking cigar* remained.

1. scrambled
2. twitching
3. rambling
4. typed
5. painted
6. written
7. charging
8. ripened
9. known
10. driven

Exercise 8
Sentence combining: Single-word modifiers

To practice expanding the basic sentence patterns with single-word modifiers, combine each group of sentences below into one sentence. You will have to delete and rearrange words.

Example:

New Orleans offers tourists food. New Orleans offers food proudly. The food is delicious.

New Orleans *proudly* offers tourists *delicious* food.

1. The turn of the century ushered in technology and materials. The century was the twentieth. The technology was improved. The materials were new.
2. A skeleton made the construction of skyscrapers possible. The skeleton was sturdy. It was made of steel.
3. By 1913 the Woolworth Building, with its ornaments, stood 760 feet (55 stories). The building was towering. The ornaments were Gothic.
4. At 1450 feet the Sears Tower in Chicago doubles the height of the Woolworth Building. The doubling is now. The Woolworth height is puny. The puniness is relative.
5. Skyscrapers would not have been practical if Elisha Graves Otis had not built the elevator in 1857. It was the first elevator. The elevator was safe. It served passengers.

5c Expanding the basic sentence with word groups

Most sentences we read or write contain whole word groups that serve as nouns and modifiers. Such word groups enable us to combine several bits of information into one sentence and to make the relations among them clear, as in this sentence:

When the ice cracked, the skaters (subject), fearing an accident, sought (verb) safety (object) at the lake's edge.

Attached to *skaters sought safety,* the skeleton of this sentence, are three groups of words that add related information: *When the ice cracked, fearing an accident,* and *at the lake's edge.* These constructions are phrases and clauses.

5. The dogs slept soundly (ADV) near the warm (ADJ) radiators.
   Sample imitation: The babies lay quietly in their small cribs.

COLLABORATIVE LEARNING

Students can work effectively in pairs or small groups on Exercise 7. Encourage the groups to be imaginative about combining each sentence in more than one way, and to report back to the class on their most innovative combinations.

ANSWERS: EXERCISE 7

Possible answers

1. Jack woke up craving scrambled eggs.
2. The twitching limb relaxed when the sedative took effect.
3. The treasurer's rambling speech covered more topics than I can remember.
4. The typed manuscript contained many errors.
5. Painted birds decorate the window.
6. He wanted to know the origins of the written word.
7. The man escaped the charging animal.
8. We picked the ripened fruit.
9. All the known facts contradict his theory.
10. Driven people may have hypertension.

ANSWERS: EXERCISE 8

Possible answers

1. The turn of the twentieth century ushered in improved technology and new materials.
2. A sturdy steel skeleton made the construction of skyscrapers possible.
3. By 1913 the towering Woolworth Building, with its Gothic ornaments, stood 760 feet (55 stories).
4. At 1450 feet the Sears Tower in Chicago now doubles the relatively puny height of the Woolworth Building.
5. Skyscrapers would not have been practical if Elisha Graves Otis had not built the first safe passenger elevator in 1857.

- A **phrase** is a group of related words that lacks either a subject or a predicate or both: *fearing an accident, at the lake's edge.*
- A **clause** contains both a subject and a predicate: *When the ice cracked* and *the skaters sought safety* are both clauses, though only the second can stand alone as a sentence.

1 Using prepositional phrases

Prepositions are connecting words. Unlike nouns, verbs, and modifiers, which may change form, prepositions never change form. As the following box indicates, many prepositions signal relationships of time or space; others signal relationships such as addition, comparison or contrast, cause or effect, concession, condition, opposition, possession, and source. Notice that some prepositions consist of more than one word.

Common prepositions

Time or space (position or direction)		Other relationships (addition, comparison, etc.)
about	into	according to
above	near	as
across	next to	as for
after	off	aside from
against	on	because of
along	onto	concerning
along with	on top of	despite
among	out	due to
around	out of	except
at	outside	except for
before	over	excepting
behind	past	in addition to
below	since	in spite of
beneath	through	instead of
beside	throughout	like
between	till	of
beyond	to	on account of
by	toward	regarding
down	under	regardless of
during	underneath	unlike
for	until	with
from	up	without
in	upon	
inside	within	
inside of		

RESOURCES AND IDEAS

Dealing with error

Bartholomae, David. "The Study of Error." *College Composition and Communication* 31 (1980): 253–69. Bartholomae suggests that asking basic writers to read their papers aloud helps identify sources of error and can contribute to improvement in writing.

Horner, Bruce. "Discoursing Basic Writing." *College Composition and Communication* 47 (1996): 199–222. Horner discusses the larger trends in the basic writing movement since the 1970s, including changing approaches to error.

Shaughnessy, Mina P. *Errors and Expectations: A Guide for the Teacher of Basic Writing.* New York: Oxford UP, 1977. This valuable book focuses on basic writing but is also an important work for teachers of writing at all levels. It provides a detailed analysis of the causes of student errors as well as useful strategies for dealing with writing problems.

Viera, Carroll. "Helping Students to Help Themselves: An Approach to Grammar." *College Composition and Communication* 37 (1986): 94–96. Viera suggests having students analyze their own grammatical problems, do research in their handbooks, and present mini-lessons in small groups.

PREPOSITIONS AND DIALECTS

Regional and social dialects may contribute to prepositional confusion; for instance, students may become sick *in, on,* or *to* their stomachs. In parts of the Northeast, people stand *on,* not *in,* line. This issue is given full coverage in 31b.

RESOURCES AND IDEAS

Sentence combining: Background and suggestions

Many of the exercises in this chapter can be used as the basis for a sequence of sentence-combining activities. The appropriate exercises are 9, 11, 13, 14, 16, 17, 18, 22.

Exercises in other chapters that can be part of a sentence-combining sequence are listed in the discussion "A Sequence for Sentence Combining" in the essay "The Handbook in Composition Courses" beginning on p. IAE-23.

Note Some of the prepositions listed as signaling time or space also serve other functions and could be listed in the third column as well. *By,* for instance, may signal time (*by tomorrow*) and source (*by William Faulkner*).

A preposition connects a noun or pronoun to another word in the sentence: *Robins nest in trees.* The noun or pronoun so connected (*trees*) is the **object of the preposition.** The preposition plus its object and any modifiers is a **prepositional phrase.**

Preposition	Object
on	the surface
with	great satisfaction
upon	entering the room
from	where you are standing
except for	ten employees

Prepositions normally come before their objects. But in speech and informal writing the preposition sometimes comes after its object: *What do you want to see him about?*

Prepositional phrases function as adjectives (modifying nouns) or as adverbs (modifying verbs, adjectives, or other adverbs). As modifiers, they add details that make sentences clearer and more interesting for readers.

Life *on a raft* was an opportunity *for adventure.*
adjective phrase — adjective phrase

Huck Finn rode the raft *by choice.*
adverb phrase

ESL The meanings and idiomatic uses of English prepositions can be difficult to master; most must be memorized or looked up in a dictionary (a list of ESL dictionaries appears on p. 482). See pages 234–35 for the uses of prepositions in two-word verbs such as *look after* and pages 468–69 for the uses of prepositions in idioms.

Punctuating prepositional phrases

Since a prepositional phrase lacks a subject and a predicate, it should not be punctuated as a complete sentence. If it is, the result is a **sentence fragment** (Chapter 10):

Fragment Toward the sun.

The phrase must be attached to another group of words containing both a subject and a predicate:

Revised The plane turned *toward the sun.*

Much has been written about sentence combining over the past two decades. The twenty-three essays in *Sentence Combining: A Rhetorical Perspective,* ed. Donald A. Daiker, Andrew Kerek, and Max Morenberg (Carbondale: Southern Illinois UP, 1985) provide excellent perspectives on the strengths and weaknesses of sentence combining as a way of improving the quality of writing and of developing an understanding of language and style.

The following articles are also useful resources:

Daiker, Donald, Andrew Kerek, and Max Morenberg. "Sentence-Combining and Syntactic Maturity in Freshman English." *College Composition and Communication* 29 (1978): 36–41. The authors discuss the results of an experiment demonstrating the effectiveness of sentence combining over fifteen weeks of intensive instruction.

Johnson, Karen E. "Cognitive Strategies and Second Language Writers: A Re-evaluation of Sentence Combining." *Journal of Second Language Writing* 1 (1992): 61–75. This essay reviews debates over the effectiveness of sentence combining in the context of ESL writers.

PREPOSITION PROBLEMS (ESL)

Prepositions follow few specific rules, and, because of idiomatic usage, often cannot be translated directly into students' first languages. As a result, even advanced ESL students find prepositions difficult. Refer students who need additional practice to Unit 6 of Len Fox, *Focus on Editing: A Grammar Workbook for Advanced Writers* (White Plains: Longman, 1992), and Chapter 13 of Alan Meyers, *Writing with Confidence* (5th ed., New York: Longman, 1996).

gr
5c

A prepositional phrase that introduces a sentence is set off with punctuation, usually a comma, unless it is short (see p. 368).

> *According to the newspaper and other sources*, the governor has reluctantly decided to veto the bill.
>
> *In 1865* the Civil War finally ended.

A prepositional phrase that interrupts or concludes a sentence is *not* set off with punctuation when it restricts the meaning of the word or words it modifies (see p. 370).

> The announcement *of a tuition increase* surprised no one.
>
> Students expected new fees *for the coming year.*

When an interrupting or concluding prepositional phrase does *not* restrict meaning, but merely adds information to the sentence, then it *is* set off with punctuation, usually a comma or commas (see p. 370).

> The governor, *according to the newspaper and other sources*, has reluctantly decided to veto the bill.

As all the preceding examples illustrate, a preposition and its object are not separated by a comma.

Exercise 9
Identifying prepositional phrases

Identify the prepositional phrases in the following passage. Indicate whether each phrase functions as an adjective or as an adverb, and name the word that the phrase modifies.

> *Example:*
>
> After an hour I finally arrived at the home of my professor.
>
> *After an hour* [adverb] I finally arrived *at the home* [adverb] *of my professor* [adjective].

The woman in blue socks ran from the policeman on horseback. She darted down Bates Street and then into the bus depot. At the depot the policeman dismounted from his horse and searched for the woman. The entrance to the depot and the interior were filled with travelers, however, and in the crowd he lost sight of the woman. She, meanwhile, had boarded a bus on the other side of the depot and was riding across town.

ANSWERS: EXERCISE 9

The woman *in blue socks* [ADJ] ran *from the policeman* [ADV] *on horseback* [ADJ]. She darted *down Bates Street* [ADV] and then *into the bus depot* [ADV]. *At the depot* [ADV] the policeman dismounted *from his horse* [ADV] and searched *for the woman* [ADV]. The entrance *to the depot* [ADJ] and the interior were filled *with travelers* [ADV], however, and *in the crowd* [ADV] he lost sight *of the woman* [ADJ]. She, meanwhile, had boarded a bus *on the other side* [ADJ] *of the depot* [ADJ] and was riding *across town* [ADV].

Exercise 10
Sentence combining: Prepositional phrases

To practice writing sentences with prepositional phrases, combine each group of sentences below into one sentence that includes one or two prepositional phrases. You will have to add, delete, and rearrange words. Some items have more than one possible answer.

ANSWERS: EXERCISE 10

Possible answers

1. The slow loris of Southeast Asia protects itself well with a poisonous chemical.

Example:

I will start working. The new job will pay the minimum wage.
I will start working *at a new job for the minimum wage.*

1. The slow loris protects itself well. Its habitat is Southeast Asia. It possesses a poisonous chemical.
2. To frighten predators, the loris exudes the chemical. The chemical comes from a gland. The gland is on the loris's upper arm.
3. The loris's chemical is highly toxic. The chemical is not like a skunk's spray. Even small quantities of the chemical are toxic.
4. A tiny dose can affect a human. The dose would get in the mouth. The human would be sent into shock.
5. Predators probably can sense the toxin. They detect it at a distance. They use their nasal organs.

Using verbals and verbal phrases

Verbals are special verb forms such as *smoking* or *hidden* or *to win* that can function as nouns (*smoking is dangerous*) or as modifiers (*the hidden money, the urge to win*).

NOTE A verbal *cannot* stand alone as the complete verb in the predicate of a sentence. For example, *The man smoking* and *The money hidden* are not sentences but sentence fragments (see p. 266). Any verbal must combine with a helping verb to serve as the predicate of a sentence: *The man was smoking. The money is hidden.*

Because verbals cannot serve alone as sentence predicates, they are sometimes called **nonfinite verbs** (in essence, they are "unfinished"). **Finite verbs,** in contrast, can make an assertion or express a state of being without a helping verb (they are "finished"). Either of two tests can distinguish finite and nonfinite verbs.

Tests for finite and nonfinite verbs (verbals)

TEST 1 Does the word require a change in form when a third-person subject changes from singular to plural?

YES Finite verb: *It sings. They sing.*

NO Nonfinite verb (verbal): *bird singing, birds singing*

TEST 2 Does the word require a change in form to show the difference in present, past, and future?

YES Finite verb: *It sings. It sang. It will sing.*

NO Nonfinite verb (verbal): *The bird singing is/was/will be a robin.*

There are three kinds of verbals: participles, gerunds, and infinitives.

2. To frighten predators, the loris exudes the chemical from a gland on its upper arm.
3. Unlike a skunk's spray, the loris's chemical is highly toxic even in small quantities.
4. A tiny dose in the mouth can send a human into shock.
5. Predators probably can sense the toxin at a distance with their nasal organs.

gr 5c

USING READINGS

Students can analyze passages from an essay in a reader (or some other source), looking for verbal phrases, passive sentences, compound and complex sentences, or any other features that you feel contribute to the effect of the essay and should be part of the students' prose style.

COLLABORATIVE LEARNING

REDO THE READINGS

Using the passages from the activity above (or other passages), ask students to work together to transform each occurrence of a structure—verbal phrases or compound sentences, and so on—into alternate structures of their choice without changing the meaning of the passage. Then ask students to comment on how the changes affect the passage, if at all. This activity is particularly well suited for collaborative work.

TRANSPARENCY MASTER 5.3

GRAMMAR TERMS

Terminology like *gerund* is one reason many students are convinced they can't "do" grammar, despite the fact that they construct sophisticated sentences every day. You may want to use a synonym like *verbal noun* or *-ing noun* to help students become more comfortable with this term.

Participles

All verbs have two participle forms, a present and a past. The **present participle** consists of the dictionary form of the verb plus the ending *-ing: beginning, completing, hiding.* The **past participle** of most verbs consists of the dictionary form plus *-d* or *-ed: believed, completed.* Some common verbs have an irregular past participle: *begun, hidden.* (See pp. 209–11.)

Both present and past participles function as adjectives to modify nouns and pronouns.

> *Shopping* malls sometimes frustrate shoppers.
>
> Shoppers may feel *trapped.*

ESL For verbs expressing feeling, the present and past participles have different meanings: *It was a boring lecture. The bored students slept.* See page 258.

Gerunds

Gerund is the name given to the *-ing* form of the verb when it serves as a noun.

> subject
> *Strolling* through stores can exhaust the hardiest shopper.
>
> object
> Many children learn to hate *shopping.*

Present participles and gerunds can be distinguished *only* by their function in a sentence. If the *-ing* form functions as an adjective (*a teaching degree*), it is a present participle. If the *-ing* form functions as a noun (*Teaching is difficult*), it is a gerund.

ESL Always use a gerund rather than any other verb form as the object of a preposition: *Diners are prohibited from smoking.* See also the ESL note below.

Infinitives

The **infinitive** is the *to* form of the verb, the dictionary form preceded by the infinitive marker *to: to begin, to hide, to run.* Infinitives may function as nouns, adjectives, or adverbs.

> The question *to answer* is why shoppers endure mall fatigue.
> adjective
>
> The solution for mall fatigue is *to leave.*
> noun
>
> Still, shoppers find it difficult *to quit.*
> adverb

ESL Infinitives and gerunds may follow some verbs and not others and may differ in meaning after a verb: *The singer stopped to sing. The singer stopped singing.* (See pp. 232–34.)

Verbal phrases

Participles, gerunds, and infinitives—like other forms of verbs—may take subjects, objects, or complements, and they may be modified by adverbs. The verbal and all the words immediately related to it make up a **verbal phrase.** With verbal phrases, we can create concise sentences packed with information.

Like participles, **participial phrases** always serve as adjectives, modifying nouns or pronouns.

Buying things, most shoppers feel themselves in control.

They make selections *determined by personal taste.*

Gerund phrases, like gerunds, always serve as nouns.

subject
Shopping for clothing and other items satisfies personal needs.

object of preposition
Malls are good at *creating such needs.*

Infinitive phrases may serve as nouns, adverbs, or adjectives.

sentence subject — subject complement
To design a mall is *to create an artificial environment.*
noun phrase — noun phrase

Malls are designed *to make shoppers feel safe.*
adverb phrase

The environment supports the impulse *to shop for oneself.*
adjective phrase

Note When an infinitive or infinitive phrase serves as a noun after verbs such as *bear, let, help, make, see,* and *watch,* the infinitive marker *to* is omitted: *We all heard her tell* [not *to tell*] *the story.*

Punctuating verbals and verbal phrases

Verbal phrases punctuated as complete sentences are sentence fragments (Chapter 10). A complete sentence must contain a subject and a finite verb (p. 177).

Fragment *Treating* the patients kindly.
Revised *She treats* the patients kindly.

A verbal or verbal phrase serving as a modifier is almost always set off with a comma when it introduces a sentence (see p. 368).

To pay tuition, some students work at two jobs.

A modifying verbal or verbal phrase that interrupts or concludes a sentence is *not* set off with punctuation when it restricts the meaning of the word or words it modifies (see p. 370).

Jobs *paying well* are hard to find.

When an interrupting or concluding verbal modifier does *not* restrict meaning, but merely adds information to the sentence, it *is* set off with punctuation, usually a comma or commas (see p. 370).

> One good job**,** *paying twelve dollars an hour***,** was filled in fifteen minutes.

gr 5c

ANSWERS: EXERCISE 11

1. Written in 1850 by Nathaniel Hawthorne (ADJ), *The Scarlet Letter* tells the story of Hester Prynne.
2. Shunned by the community (ADJ), Hester endures her loneliness.
3. Hester is humble enough to withstand her Puritan neighbors' cutting remarks (ADV).
4. Despite the cruel treatment, the determined (ADJ) young woman refuses to leave her home (N).
5. By living a life of patience and unselfishness (N), Hester eventually becomes the community's angel.

COLLABORATIVE LEARNING

Students might work independently on Exercise 11, then compare answers in small groups and work together on Exercise 12. Encourage each group to create more than one combination for each pair of sentences in Exercise 12.

ANSWERS: EXERCISE 12

Possible answers

1. Air pollution is a health problem affecting millions of Americans.
2. Polluted mainly by industries and automobiles, the air contains toxic chemicals.
3. Environmentalists pressure politicians to pass stricter laws.
4. Wavering politicians are not necessarily against environmentalism.
5. The problems are too complex to be solved easily.

Exercise 11
Identifying verbals and verbal phrases

The following sentences contain participles, gerunds, and infinitives as well as participial, gerund, and infinitive phrases. First identify each verbal or verbal phrase. Then indicate whether it is used as an adjective, an adverb, or a noun.

> *Example:*
>
> Laughing, the talk-show host prodded her guest to talk.
>
> adjective adverb
> *Laughing,* the talk-show host prodded her guest *to talk.*

1. Written in 1850 by Nathaniel Hawthorne, *The Scarlet Letter* tells the story of Hester Prynne.
2. Shunned by the community, Hester endures her loneliness.
3. Hester is humble enough to withstand her Puritan neighbors' cutting remarks.
4. Despite the cruel treatment, the determined young woman refuses to leave her home.
5. By living a life of patience and unselfishness, Hester eventually becomes the community's angel.

Exercise 12
Sentence combining: Verbals and verbal phrases

To practice writing sentences with verbals and verbal phrases, combine each pair of sentences below into one sentence. You will have to add, delete, change, and rearrange words. Each item has more than one possible answer.

> *Example:*
>
> My father took pleasure in mean pranks. For instance, he hid the neighbor's cat.
>
> My father took pleasure in mean pranks such as *hiding the neighbor's cat.*

1. Air pollution is a health problem. It affects millions of Americans.
2. The air has been polluted mainly by industries and automobiles. It contains toxic chemicals.
3. Environmentalists pressure politicians. They think politicians should pass stricter laws.
4. Many politicians waver. They are not necessarily against environmentalism.
5. The problems are too complex. They cannot be solved easily.

3 Using absolute phrases

Absolute phrases consist of a noun or pronoun and a participle, plus any modifiers.

> Many ethnic groups, *their own place established* [absolute phrase], are making way for new arrivals.
>
> *Their native lands left behind* [absolute phrase], *an uncertain future looming* [absolute phrase], immigrants face many obstacles.

These phrases are called *absolute* (from a Latin word meaning "free") because they have no specific grammatical connection to a verb or any other word in the rest of the sentence. Instead, they modify the entire rest of the sentence, adding information or clarifying meaning.

Notice that absolute phrases, unlike participial phrases, always contain a subject. Compare the following:

> For many immigrants *learning English* [participial phrase], the language introduces American culture.
>
> *The immigrants having learned English* [absolute phrase], their opportunities widen.

We often omit the participle from an absolute phrase when it is some form of *be*, such as *being* or *having been*.

> *Two languages* [*being*] *at hand*, bilingual citizens in fact have many cultural and occupational advantages.

Punctuating absolute phrases

Absolute phrases are always set off from the rest of the sentence with punctuation, usually a comma or commas (see also p. 375).

> *Their future more secure*, these citizens will make room for new arrivals.
>
> These citizens, *their future more secure*, will make room for new arrivals.

Exercise 13
Sentence combining: Absolute phrases

To practice writing sentences with absolute phrases, combine each pair of sentences below into one sentence that contains an absolute phrase. You will have to add, delete, change, and rearrange words.

RESOURCES AND IDEAS

Solomon, Martha. "Teaching the Nominative Absolute." *College Composition and Communication* 26 (1975): 356–61. Solomon offers advice on analyzing and teaching the absolute.

EXPECTING PROBLEMS

As students begin practicing use of absolute phrases, you may find more comma splices and fragments in their essays. Warn students to expect these errors, so that they can proofread for such problems more carefully. Be understanding as you evaluate student papers in which the students are practicing these strategies for the first time. If you focus on grammar faults, they may lose the incentive to take further stylistic risks.

COLLABORATIVE LEARNING

Students can work productively in pairs or small groups to combine the sentences in Exercise 13. The collaborative effort and consequent discussion can be useful for students who are having difficulty with absolute phrases.

gr
5c

ANSWERS: EXERCISE 13

Possible answers

1. Her husband having died in office, Lindy Boggs was elected to his seat as a representative from Louisiana.
2. Representative Barbara Jordan spoke at the national Democratic convention, her voice thundering through the auditorium.
3. A vacancy having occurred, Sandra Day O'Connor was appointed the first female Supreme Court justice.
4. Her face beaming, Geraldine Ferraro enjoyed the crowd's cheers after her nomination for Vice President.
5. The election (having been) won, Susan Molinari was a US representative from New York.

RESOURCES AND IDEAS

Larsen, Richard B. "Sentence Patterning." *College Composition and Communication* 37 (1986): 103–04. Larsen describes a sequence in which students are introduced to a variety of sentence patterns and then asked to use the patterns in their writing, including paragraph-length compositions.

Example:

The flower's petals wilted. It looked pathetic.
Its petals wilted, the flower looked pathetic.

1. Her husband died in office. Lindy Boggs was elected to his seat as a representative from Louisiana.
2. Representative Barbara Jordan spoke at the national Democratic convention. Her voice thundered through the auditorium.
3. A vacancy had occurred. Sandra Day O'Connor was appointed the first female Supreme Court justice.
4. Geraldine Ferraro's face beamed. She enjoyed the crowd's cheers after her nomination for Vice President.
5. The election was won. Susan Molinari was a US representative from New York.

Using subordinate clauses

A **clause** is any group of words that contains both a subject and a predicate. There are two kinds of clauses, and the distinction between them is important.

- A **main** or **independent clause** makes a complete statement and can stand alone as a sentence: *The sky darkened.*
- A **subordinate** or **dependent clause** is just like a main clause *except* that it begins with a subordinating word: *when the sky darkened; whoever calls.* The subordinating word reduces the clause to a single part of speech: an adjective, an adverb, or a noun. Because it only modifies or names something, a subordinate clause cannot stand alone as a sentence (see the discussion of punctuation on p. 185). (The word *subordinate* means "secondary" or "controlled by another." It comes from the Latin *sub,* "under," and *ordo,* "order.")

The following examples show the differences between main and subordinate clauses:

main clause | main clause
The school teaches parents. It is unusual.

subordinate clause | main clause
Because the school teaches parents, it is unusual.

main clause | main clause
Some parents avoid their children's schools. They are often illiterate.

main clause
Parents *who are illiterate* often avoid their children's schools.
subordinate clause

Two kinds of subordinating words introduce subordinate clauses. **Subordinating conjunctions,** like prepositions, never change form in any way. In the following box they are arranged by the relationships they signal. (Some fit in more than one group.)

TRANSPARENCY MASTER 5.4

Common subordinating conjunctions

CAUSE OR EFFECT	CONDITION	COMPARISON OR CONTRAST	SPACE OR TIME
as	even if	as	after
because	if	as if	as long as
in order that	if only	as though	before
since	provided	rather than	now that
so that	since	than	once
	unless	whereas	since
CONCESSION	when	whether	till
although	whenever	while	until
as if	whether		when
even if		**PURPOSE**	whenever
even though		in order that	where
though		so that	wherever
		that	while

ESL Subordinating conjunctions convey their meaning without help from other function words, such as the coordinating conjunctions *and, but, for,* or *so* (p. 189).

FAULTY *Even though* the parents are illiterate, *but* their children may read well. [*Even though* and *but* have the same meaning, so both are not needed.]

REVISED *Even though* the parents are illiterate, their children may read well.

The second kind of subordinating word is the **relative pronoun.** Unlike subordinating conjunctions, relative pronouns usually act as subjects or objects in their own clauses, and two of them (*who* and *whoever*) change form accordingly (see p. 202).

Relative pronouns

which	what	who (whose, whom)
that	whatever	whoever (whomever)

Subordinate clauses function as adjectives, adverbs, or nouns.

Adjective clauses

Adjective clauses modify nouns and pronouns, providing necessary or helpful information about them. They usually begin with the relative pronoun *who, whom, whose, which,* or *that,* although a

gr
5c

few adjective clauses begin with *when* or *where* (standing for *in which, on which,* or *at which*). The pronoun is the subject or object of the clause it begins. The clause ordinarily falls immediately after the noun or pronoun it modifies.

> Parents *who are illiterate* often have bad memories of school.
>
> Schools *that involve parents* are more successful with children.
>
> One school, *which is open year-round,* helps parents learn to read.
>
> The school is in a city *where the illiteracy rate is high.*

Adverb clauses

Like adverbs, **adverb clauses** modify verbs, adjectives, other adverbs, and whole groups of words. They usually tell how, why, when, where, under what conditions, or with what result. They always begin with subordinating conjunctions.

> The school began teaching parents *when adult illiteracy gained national attention.*
>
> At first the program was not as successful *as its founders had hoped.*
>
> *Because it was directed at people who could not read,* advertising had to be inventive.

An adverb clause can often be moved around in a sentence with no loss of clarity. Compare the preceding example and this one:

> Advertising had to be inventive *because it was directed at people who could not read.*

Noun clauses

Noun clauses function as subjects, objects, and complements in sentences. They begin with *that, what, whatever, who, whom, whoever, whomever, when, where, whether, why,* or *how.* Unlike adjective and adverb clauses, noun clauses *replace* a word (a noun) within a clause; therefore, they can be difficult to identify.

> sentence subject
> *Whether the program would succeed* depended on door-to-door advertising.
>
> direct object
> Teachers explained in person *how the program would work.*
>
> sentence subject
> *Whoever seemed slightly interested* was invited to an open meeting.

object of preposition

A few parents were anxious about *what their children would think.*

Elliptical clauses

A subordinate clause that is grammatically incomplete but clear in meaning is an **elliptical clause** (*ellipsis* means "omission"). The meaning of the clause is clear because the missing element can be supplied from the context. Most often the elements omitted are the relative pronouns *that, which,* and *whom* from adjective clauses or the predicate from the second part of a comparison.

The parents knew their children could read better *than they* [*could read*].

Skepticism and fear were among the feelings [*that*] *the parents voiced.*

Though [*they were*] *often reluctant at first,* about a third of the parents attended the meeting.

CLAUSE CONNECTORS (ESL)

ESL students may try unsuccessfully to use ellipsis in writing. Remind students that generally, in formal writing, clause connectors such as *that* and the relative pronouns *that, which,* and *whom* are not omitted. Students *will not* go wrong if they keep the clause connectors in their writing, but they *may* be wrong if they omit them.

gr
5c

Punctuating subordinate clauses

Subordinate clauses punctuated as complete sentences are sentence fragments (Chapter 10). Though a subordinate clause contains a subject and a predicate and thus resembles a complete sentence, it also begins with a subordinating word that makes it into an adjective, adverb, or noun. A single part of speech cannot stand alone as a complete sentence.

FRAGMENT	Because a door was ajar.
REVISED	A door was ajar.
REVISED	The secret leaked *because a door was ajar.*

A subordinate clause serving as an adverb is almost always set off with a comma when it introduces a sentence (see p. 368).

Although the project was almost completed, it lost its funding.

A modifying subordinate clause that interrupts or concludes a main clause is *not* set off with punctuation when it restricts the meaning of the word or words it modifies (see p. 370).

The woman *who directed the project* lost her job.
The project lost its funding *because it was not completed on time.*

When an interrupting or concluding subordinate clause does *not* restrict meaning, but merely adds information to the sentence, it *is* set off with punctuation, usually a comma or commas (see p. 370).

The project lost its funding, *although it was almost completed.*
The director, *who holds a Ph.D.,* sought new funding.

ANSWERS: EXERCISE 14

1. Scientists who want to catch the slightest signals from space [ADJ] use extremely sensitive receivers.
2. Even though they have had to fight for funding [ADV], these scientists have persisted in their research.
3. The research is called SETI, which stands for Search for Extraterrestrial Intelligence [ADJ].
4. The theory is that intelligent beings in space are trying to get in touch with us [N (SUBJECT COMPLEMENT)].
5. The challenge is to guess what frequency these beings would use to send signals [N (DIRECT OBJECT)].

COLLABORATIVE LEARNING

Exercises 14 and 15 work well as collaborative projects. In particular, students with varying grammatical skills have the opportunity to discuss the parts of speech and their relative functions.

ANSWERS: EXERCISE 15

Possible answers

1. Moviegoers expect that movie sequels should be as exciting as the original films.
2. Although a few sequels are good films, most are poor imitations of the originals.
3. Whenever a sequel to a blockbuster film arrives in the theater, crowds quickly line up to see it.
4. Viewers pay to see the same villains and heroes whom they remember fondly.
5. Afterward, viewers often grumble about filmmakers who rehash tired plots and characters.

COLLABORATIVE LEARNING

CREATE YOUR OWN

Divide the class into groups. Ask each group to create its own set of sentence-combining exercises following the pattern of the exercises in the handbook. Then ask the groups to trade exercises, work on them, and return them to the authors with both positive comments and criticisms.

gr
5c

Exercise 14
Identifying subordinate clauses

Identify the subordinate clauses in the following sentences. Then indicate whether each is used as an adjective, an adverb, or a noun. If the clause is a noun, indicate what function it performs in the sentence.

Example:

The article explained how one could build an underground house.

The article explained *how one could build an underground house.* [noun] [Object of *explained.*]

1. Scientists who want to catch the slightest signals from space use extremely sensitive receivers.
2. Even though they have had to fight for funding, these scientists have persisted in their research.
3. The research is called SETI, which stands for Search for Extraterrestrial Intelligence.
4. The theory is that intelligent beings in space are trying to get in touch with us.
5. The challenge is to guess what frequency these beings would use to send signals.

Exercise 15
Sentence combining: Subordinate clauses

To practice writing sentences with subordinate clauses, combine each pair of main clauses below into one sentence. Use either subordinating conjunctions or relative pronouns as appropriate, referring to the lists on page 183 if necessary. You will have to add, delete, and rearrange words. Each item has more than one possible answer.

Example:

She did not have her tire irons with her. She could not change her bicycle tire.

Because she did not have her tire irons with her, she could not change her bicycle tire.

1. Moviegoers expect something. Movie sequels should be as exciting as the original films.
2. A few sequels are good films. Most are poor imitations of the originals.
3. A sequel to a blockbuster film arrives in the theater. Crowds quickly line up to see it.
4. Viewers pay to see the same villains and heroes. They remember these characters fondly.
5. Afterward, viewers often grumble about filmmakers. The filmmakers rehash tired plots and characters.

 Using appositives

An **appositive** is usually a noun that renames another noun nearby, usually just before it. (The word *appositive* derives from a Latin word that means "placed near to" or "applied to.") An appositive phrase includes modifiers as well.

> Bizen ware, *a dark stoneware,* has been produced in Japan since the fourteenth century.

> The name *Bizen* comes from the location of the kilns used to fire the pottery.

All appositives can replace the words they refer to: *A dark stoneware has been produced in Japan.*

Appositives are often introduced by words and phrases such as *or, that is, such as, for example,* and *in other words.*

> Bizen ware is used in the Japanese tea ceremony, *that is, the Zen Buddhist observance that links meditation and art.*

Appositives are economical alternatives to adjective clauses containing a form of *be.*

> Bizen ware, [*which is*] *a dark stoneware,* has been produced in Japan since the fourteenth century.

Although most appositives are nouns that rename other nouns, they may also be and rename other parts of speech.

> The pottery is thrown, or *formed on a potter's wheel.*

Punctuating appositives

Appositives punctuated as complete sentences are sentence fragments (see Chapter 10). To correct such fragments, you can usually connect the appositive to the main clause containing the word referred to.

> **Fragment** An exceedingly tall man with narrow shoulders.
>
> **Revised** He stood next to a basketball player, *an exceedingly tall man with narrow shoulders.*

An appositive is *not* set off with punctuation when it restricts the meaning of the word it refers to (see p. 370).

> The verb *howl* comes from the Old English verb *houlen.*

When an appositive does *not* restrict the meaning of the word it refers to, it *is* set off with punctuation, usually a comma or commas (see p. 370).

TEACHING TIP

As students begin using appositives, you may find more comma splices and fragments in their essays. Warn students to expect these errors, so that they will proofread more carefully. Be understanding as you evaluate student papers in which the students are practicing these strategies for the first time. If you focus on grammar faults, they may lose the incentive to take stylistic risks.

An aged elm, the tree was struck by lightning.
The tree, *an aged elm*, was struck by lightning.
Lightning struck the tree, *an aged elm*.

A nonrestrictive appositive is sometimes set off with a dash or dashes, especially when it contains commas (see p. 419).

Three people—*Will, Carolyn, and Tom*—object to the new procedure.

A concluding appositive is sometimes set off with a colon (see p. 417).

Two principles guide the judge's decisions: *justice and mercy*.

Exercise 16
Sentence combining: Appositives

To practice writing sentences with appositives, combine each pair of sentences into one sentence that contains an appositive. You will have to delete and rearrange words. Some items have more than one possible answer.

Example:

The largest land animal is the elephant. The elephant is also one of the most intelligent animals.

The largest land animal, *the elephant*, is also one of the most intelligent animals.

1. Some people perform amazing feats when they are very young. These people are geniuses from birth.
2. John Stuart Mill was a British philosopher. He had written a history of Rome by age seven.
3. Two great artists began their work at age four. They were Paul Klee and Gustav Mahler.
4. Mahler was a Bohemian composer of intensely emotional works. He was also the child of a brutal father.
5. Paul Klee was a Swiss painter. As a child he was frightened by his own drawings of devils.

ANSWERS: EXERCISE 16

Possible answers

1. Some people, geniuses from birth, perform amazing feats when they are very young.
2. John Stuart Mill, a British philosopher, had written a history of Rome by age seven.
3. Paul Klee and Gustav Mahler, two great artists, began their work at age four.
4. Mahler, a Bohemian composer of intensely emotional works, was also the child of a brutal father.
5. As a child the Swiss painter Paul Klee was frightened by his own drawings of devils.

RESOURCES AND IDEAS

Gorrell, Donna. "Controlled Composition for Basic Writers." *College Composition and Communication* 32 (1981): 308–16. Gorrell suggests having students manipulate and alter previously written material to develop basic skills.

5d Compounding words, phrases, and clauses

A **compound construction** combines words that are closely related and equally important. It makes writing clearer and more economical because it pulls together linked information.

Headaches can be controlled by biofeedback. Heart rate can be controlled by biofeedback.

compound subject
Headaches and heart rate can be controlled by biofeedback.

Without medication, biofeedback cures headaches. It steadies heart rate. It lowers blood pressure. It relaxes muscles.

compound predicate

Without medication, biofeedback *cures headaches, steadies heart rate, lowers blood pressure, and relaxes muscles.*

Using coordinating conjunctions and correlative conjunctions

Two kinds of words create compound constructions: coordinating and correlative conjunctions. **Coordinating conjunctions** are few and do not change form. In the following box the relationship that each conjunction signals appears in parentheses.

Coordinating conjunctions

and (*addition*)	nor (*alternative*)	for (*cause*)	yet (*contrast*)
but (*contrast*)	or (*alternative*)	so (*effect*)	

The coordinating conjunctions *and, but, nor,* and *or* always connect words or word groups of the same kind—that is, two or more nouns, verbs, adjectives, adverbs, phrases, subordinate clauses, or main clauses.

Biofeedback *or* simple relaxation can relieve headaches.
Biofeedback is effective *but* costly.
Relaxation also works well, *and* it is inexpensive.
Relaxation is effective *yet* inexpensive.

The conjunctions *for* and *so* connect only main clauses. *For* indicates cause; *so* indicates effect.

Biofeedback can be costly, *for* the training involves technical equipment and specialists.

Relaxation can be difficult to learn alone, *so* some people do seek help.

Some coordinating conjunctions pair up with other words to form **correlative conjunctions.** In the following box the relationship each conjunction signals appears in parentheses.

Common correlative conjunctions

both . . . and (*addition*)	neither . . . nor (*negation*)
not only . . . but also (*addition*)	whether . . . or (*alternative*)
not . . . but (*substitution*)	as . . . as (*comparison*)
either . . . or (*alternative*)	

Both biofeedback *and* relaxation can relieve headaches.

The techniques require *neither* psychotherapy *nor* medication.

The headache sufferer learns *not only* to recognize the causes of headaches *but also* to control those causes.

Punctuating compounded words, phrases, and clauses

Two words, phrases, or subordinate clauses that are connected by a coordinating conjunction are *not* separated by a comma (see p. 384).

The library needs *renovation and rebuilding.*

The work will begin *after the spring term ends but before the summer term begins.*

When two *main* clauses are joined into one sentence with a coordinating conjunction, a comma precedes the conjunction (see p. 365).

The project will be lengthy**,** *and* everyone will suffer some inconvenience.

When two main clauses are joined *without* a coordinating conjunction, they must be separated with a semicolon to avoid the error called a comma splice (see p. 390).

The work cannot be delayed**;** it's already overdue.

In a series of three or more items, commas separate the items, with *and* usually preceding the last item (see p. 376).

The renovated library will feature *new study carrels***,** *new shelving***,** *and a larger reference section.*

Semicolons sometimes separate the items in a series if they are long or contain commas (see p. 393).

A comma also separates two or more adjectives when they modify a noun equally and are not joined by a coordinating conjunction (see p. 377).

*Cracked***,** *crumbling* walls will be repaired.

The comma does *not* separate adjectives when the one nearer the noun is more closely related to it in meaning (see p. 377).

New reading lounges will replace the old ones.

 Using conjunctive adverbs

One other kind of connecting word, called a **conjunctive adverb**, relates only main clauses, not words, phrases, or subordinate

GRAMMAR TERMS

Terminology like *conjunctive adverb* is another reason that many students are convinced

clauses. In the following box the conjunctive adverbs are arranged by the relationships they signal.

Common conjunctive adverbs

Addition	Comparison or contrast	Cause or effect
also	however	accordingly
besides	in comparison	as a result
further	in contrast	consequently
furthermore	instead	hence
in addition	likewise	therefore
incidentally	nevertheless	thus
moreover	nonetheless	
Emphasis	otherwise	**Time**
certainly	similarly	finally
indeed		meanwhile
in fact		next
still		now
undoubtedly		then
		thereafter

It's important to distinguish between conjunctive adverbs and conjunctions (coordinating and subordinating) because they demand different punctuation (see the discussion on the next page). Conjunctive adverbs are *adverbs:* they describe the relation of ideas in two clauses, and, like most adverbs, they can move around in their clause:

> Relaxation techniques have improved; *however,* few people know them.
>
> Relaxation techniques have improved; few people know them, *however.*

In contrast, conjunctions bind two clauses into a single grammatical unit, and they cannot be moved:

> *Although* few people know them, relaxation techniques have improved. [The subordinating conjunction can't be moved: *Few people know them although, relaxation techniques have improved.*]
>
> Relaxation techniques have improved, *but* few people know them. [The coordinating conjunction can't be moved: *Relaxation techniques have improved, few people know them but.*]

Note Some connecting words have more than one use. *After, before, until,* and some other words may be either prepositions or subordinating conjunctions. Some prepositions, such as *behind, in,* and *outside,* can serve also as adverbs, as in *He trailed behind.* And some conjunctive adverbs, particularly *however,* may also serve

they can't "do" grammar, despite the fact that they construct sophisticated sentences every day. You may want to use a synonym like *movable adverb* or *floating adverb* to help students become more comfortable with this term.

COLLABORATIVE LEARNING

DECODING THE SENTENCE

Divide the class into small groups, and have each group write a set of nonsense sentences that conforms to English syntax and punctuation. Students should be sure to include nonsense prepositional phrases, verbals, appositives, absolutes, and subordinate and coordinate structures. Warn students to punctuate the sentences carefully. Students can use the nonsense sentences at the beginning of Chapter 5 as models.

Once the sentences are written, have groups exchange sentences or write them on the board and try to identify the part of speech for each nonsense word. If the creators of the sentences have made any errors in punctuation, the puzzle-solvers should be prepared to correct them. This exercise should help students see how grammar and punctuation work together to define a word's role in a sentence and to create different kinds of sentences.

gr
5d

simply as adverbs in sentences such as However *much it costs, we must have it.* Again, the part of speech of a word depends on its function in a sentence.

Punctuating sentences containing conjunctive adverbs

Because the two main clauses related by a conjunctive adverb remain independent units, they must be separated by a semicolon (see p. 388). If they are separated by a comma, the result is a comma splice (Chapter 11):

COMMA SPLICE	Interest rates rose, *therefore,* real estate prices declined.
REVISED	Interest rates rose**;** *therefore,* real estate prices declined.

A conjunctive adverb is almost always set off from its clause with a comma or commas (see p. 373).

The decline was small**;** *however***,** some investors were badly hurt.
The decline was small**;** some investors**,** *however***,** were badly hurt.

COLLABORATIVE LEARNING

Students can work effectively in groups on Exercise 17. Have each group try the effect of different conjunctive adverbs and coordinating and correlative conjunctions from the lists on pages 189–91 and discuss the effect that each change has on the meaning of the sentence.

ANSWERS: EXERCISE 17

Possible answers

1. All too often people assume that old age is not a productive time; however, many people in their nineties have made great achievements.
2. In his nineties the philosopher Bertrand Russell spoke vigorously for both international peace and nuclear disarmament.
3. Grandma Moses did not retire to an easy chair; instead, she began painting at age seventy-six and was still going at one hundred.
4. The British general George Higginson and the British archaeologist Margaret Murray published their memoirs after they were ninety.
5. The architect Frank Lloyd Wright designed his first building at age twenty and his last at age ninety.

Exercise 17
Sentence combining: Compound constructions

To practice compounding words, phrases, and clauses, combine each pair of sentences below into one sentence that is as short as possible without altering meaning. Use an appropriate connecting word of the type specified in parentheses, referring to the lists on pages 189 and 191 as necessary. You will have to add, delete, and rearrange words, and you may have to change or add punctuation.

Example:

The encyclopedia had some information. It was not detailed enough. (*Conjunctive adverb.*)

The encyclopedia had some information; *however,* it was not detailed enough.

1. All too often people assume that old age is not a productive time. Many people in their nineties have made great achievements. (*Conjunctive adverb.*)
2. In his nineties the philosopher Bertrand Russell spoke vigorously for international peace. He spoke for nuclear disarmament. (*Correlative conjunction.*)
3. Grandma Moses did not retire to an easy chair. She began painting at age seventy-six and was still going at one hundred. (*Conjunctive adverb.*)
4. The British general George Higginson published his memoirs after he was ninety. The British archaeologist Margaret Murray published her memoirs after she was ninety. (*Coordinating conjunction.*)

5. The architect Frank Lloyd Wright designed his first building at age twenty. He designed his last building at age ninety. (*Coordinating conjunction.*)

5e Changing the usual order of the sentence

So far, all the examples of basic sentence grammar have been similar: the subject of the sentence comes first, naming the performer of the predicate's action, and the predicate comes second. This arrangement of subject and predicate describes most sentences that occur in writing, but four other kinds of sentences alter the basic pattern.

Forming questions

The following are the most common ways of forming questions from statements. Remember to end a question with a question mark (p. 361).

- Move the verb or a part of it to the beginning of the question. The verb may be a form of *be.*

The rate *is* high.	*Is* the rate high?

  Or the verb may consist of a helping verb and a main verb. Then move the helping verb—or the first helping verb if there's more than one—to the front of the question.

Rates *can* rise.	*Can* rates rise?
Rates *have* been rising.	*Have* rates been rising?

  Questions formed this way can be answered *yes* or *no.*
- If the verb consists of only one word and is not a form of *be,* start the question with a form of *do* and use the plain form of the verb. (These questions can also be answered *yes* or *no*.)

Interest rates *rose.*	*Did* interest rates rise?

- Add a question word—*how, what, who, when, where, which, why*—to the beginning of a yes-or-no question. Such a question requires an explanatory answer.

Did rates rise today?	*Why* did rates rise today?
Is the rate high?	*Why* is the rate high?
Can rates rise?	*How* can rates rise?

- Add *who, what,* or *which* to the beginning of a question as the subject. Then the subject-verb order remains the same as in a statement.

Something is the answer.	*What* is the answer?
Someone can answer.	*Who* can answer?

2 Forming commands

We construct commands very simply: we merely delete the subject of the sentence, *you*.

Think of options.
Watch the news.

Eat your spinach.
Leave me alone.

THE PASSIVE VOICE

Students may have gathered from their high school educations that using the passive voice is somehow wrong. If that were true, of course, no one could say "I was born" without fear of correction. Instead, remind students that using the passive is a choice writers make for particular reasons; it's the unthinking, excessive, or inappropriate use of the passive voice that bothers many readers.

3 Writing passive sentences

When the subject of a sentence performs the action of the verb, the verb is in the **active voice.**

subject / active verb / object
Kyong wrote the paper.

We can change the form of the verb and make the object into the subject. The verb in this new sentence is in the **passive voice** because the subject *receives* the action.

subject / passive verb
The paper was written by Kyong.

Only transitive verbs (verbs that take objects) can be expressed in the passive voice. The passive verb consists of a form of *be* plus the past participle of the main verb (*paper was written, absences were excused*). The actual actor (the person performing the action of the verb) may be expressed in a prepositional phrase (as in the example above: *by Kyong*) or may be omitted entirely if it is unknown or unimportant: *The house was flooded.*

(For more on formation of the passive voice, see Chapter 7, p. 230. Also see p. 231 on overuse of the passive voice.)

EXPLETIVES (ESL)

Remind students that because English is a subject-verb-object language, something must fill the subject position when the subject is delayed. *There* and *it* fulfill this requirement by acting as dummy subjects.

4 Writing sentences with postponed subjects

The subject follows the predicate in two sentence patterns that are not questions, commands, or passive sentences. In one pattern the normal word order is reversed for emphasis:

Henry comes there. [Normal order.]
There comes Henry. [Reversed order.]

This pattern occurs most often when the normal order is subject–intransitive verb–adverb. Then the adverb moves to the front of the sentence while subject and predicate reverse order.

A second kind of sentence with a postponed subject begins with either *it* or *there*, as in the following:

verb / subject
There *will be* eighteen *people* attending the meeting.

verb / subject
It *was* surprising *that Marinetti was nominated.*

The words *there* and *it* in such sentences are **expletives.** Their only function is to postpone the sentence subject. Expletive sentences do have their uses (see pp. 478–79), but they can be unemphatic because they add words and delay the sentence subject. Usually, the normal subject-predicate order is more effective: *Eighteen people will attend the meeting. Marinetti's nomination was surprising.*

ESL Be careful not to omit *there* or *it* from an expletive construction. Only commands and some questions can begin with verbs (see pp. 193–94).

Faulty No one predicted the nomination. Were no polls showing Marinetti ahead.

Revised No one predicted the nomination. *There* were no polls showing Marinetti ahead.

Exercise 18
Forming questions and commands

Form a question and a command from the following noun and verb pairs.

Example:
wood, split
Did you *split* all this *wood?*
Split the *wood* for our fire.

1. water, boil
2. music, stop
3. table, set
4. dice, roll
5. telephone, use

ANSWERS: EXERCISE 18

Possible answers

1. Will the water boil?
   Boil the water, please.
2. Did the music stop?
   Stop the music.
3. Have you set the table?
   Set the table.
4. Have you rolled the dice yet?
   Roll the dice.
5. Who can use the telephone?
   Use the telephone.

Exercise 19
Rewriting passives and expletives

Rewrite each passive sentence below as active, and rewrite each expletive construction to restore normal subject-predicate order. (For additional exercises with the passive voice and with expletives, see pp. 232, 346, and 479.)

1. The screenplay for *Born on the Fourth of July* was cowritten by Ron Kovic.
2. The film was directed by Oliver Stone.
3. Tom Cruise was nominated for an Oscar by the Academy of Motion Picture Arts and Sciences.
4. It is possible that Tom Cruise will never have a better role.
5. There are few such roles that actors have available.

ANSWERS: EXERCISE 19

1. Ron Kovic cowrote the screenplay for *Born on the Fourth of July*.
2. Oliver Stone directed the film.
3. The Academy of Motion Picture Arts and Sciences nominated Tom Cruise for an Oscar.
4. That Tom Cruise will never have a better role is possible.
5. Actors have few such roles available.

5f Classifying sentences

We describe and classify sentences in two different ways: by function (statement, question, command, exclamation, and so forth) or by structure. Four basic sentence structures are possible: simple, compound, complex, and compound-complex.

A WRITER'S PERSPECTIVE

Prose is architecture, and the Baroque is over.
—Ernest Hemingway

gr 5f

RESOURCES AND IDEAS

Dawkins, John. "Teaching Punctuation as a Rhetorical Tool." *College Composition and Communication.* 46 (1995): 533–48. Dawkins makes a case for teaching the rhetorical thinking processes that accompany decisions about punctuation marks.

Herrington, Anne J. "Grammar Recharted: Sentence Analysis for Writing." *Writing Exercises from "Exercise Exchange."* Vol. 2. Urbana: NCTE, 1984. 276–87. Herrington offers a number of useful classroom activities.

1 Writing simple sentences

A **simple sentence** consists of a single main clause and no subordinate clause.

main clause
Last summer was unusually hot.

main clause
The summer made many farmers leave the area for good or reduced them to bare existence.

2 Writing compound sentences

A **compound sentence** consists of two or more main clauses and no subordinate clause. The clauses may be joined by a coordinating conjunction and a comma, by a semicolon alone, or by a conjunctive adverb and a semicolon.

main clause / main clause
Last July was hot, but August was even hotter.

main clause / main clause
The hot sun scorched the earth; the lack of rain killed many crops.

3 Writing complex sentences

A **complex sentence** contains one main clause and one or more subordinate clauses.

main clause / subordinate clause
Rain finally came, although many had left the area by then.

main clause / subordinate clause
Those who remained were able to start anew because the government came to their aid.
(subordinate clause: who remained)

Notice that length does not determine whether a sentence is complex or simple; both kinds can be short or long.

4 Writing compound-complex sentences

A **compound-complex sentence** has the characteristics of both the compound sentence (two or more main clauses) and the complex sentence (at least one subordinate clause).

subordinate clause / main clause
Even though government aid finally came, many people had already been reduced to poverty, and others had been forced to move.
(main clause: others had been forced to move)

ANSWERS: EXERCISE 20

MAIN
1. *Simple:* Joseph Pulitzer endowed the Pulitzer Prizes.

MAIN
2. *Simple:* Pulitzer, incidentally, was the publisher of the New York newspaper *The World.*

Exercise 20
Identifying sentence structures

Mark the main clauses and subordinate clauses in the following sentences. Identify each sentence as simple, compound, complex, or compound-complex.

Example:

The police began patrolling more often when crime in the neighborhood increased.

main clause / subordinate clause

Complex: The police began patrolling more often when crime in the neighborhood increased.

1. Joseph Pulitzer endowed the Pulitzer Prizes.
2. Pulitzer, incidentally, was the publisher of the New York newspaper *The World.*
3. Although the first prizes were for journalism and letters only, Pulitzers are now awarded in music and other areas.
4. For example, Berke Breathed won for his *Bloom County* comic strip, and Roger Reynolds won for his musical composition *Whispers out of Time.*
5. Although only one prize is usually awarded in each category, in 1989 Taylor Branch's *Parting the Waters* won a history prize, and it shared the honor with James M. McPherson's *Battle Cry of Freedom.*

3. *Complex:* Although the first prizes were for journalism and letters only, [SUBORDINATE] Pulitzers are now awarded in music and other areas. [MAIN]
4. *Compound:* For example, Berke Breathed won for his *Bloom County* comic strip, [MAIN] and Roger Reynolds won for his musical composition *Whispers out of Time.* [MAIN]
5. *Compound-Complex:* Although only one prize is usually awarded in each category, [SUBORDINATE] in 1989 Taylor Branch's *Parting the Waters* won a history prize, [MAIN] and it shared the honor with James M. McPherson's *Battle Cry of Freedom.* [MAIN]

gr 5f

Exercise 21
Sentence combining: Sentence structures

Combine each set of simple sentences below to produce the kind of sentence specified in parentheses. You will have to add, delete, change, and rearrange words.

Example:

The traffic passed the house. It never stopped. (*Complex.*)
The traffic that passed the house never stopped.

1. Recycling takes time. It reduces garbage in landfills. (*Compound.*)
2. People begin to recycle. They generate much less trash. (*Complex.*)
3. White tissues and paper towels biodegrade more easily than dyed ones. People still buy dyed papers. (*Complex.*)
4. The cans are aluminum. They bring recyclers good money. (*Simple.*)
5. Environmentalists have hope. Perhaps more communities will recycle newspaper and glass. Many citizens refuse to participate. (*Compound-complex.*)

COLLABORATIVE LEARNING

Exercises 20 and 21 work well as group projects. Students might begin by working individually on Exercise 20, then compare responses in small groups and work together on Exercise 21.

ANSWERS: EXERCISE 21

Possible answers

1. Recycling takes time, but it reduces garbage in landfills.
2. After people begin to recycle, they generate much less trash.
3. Although white tissues and paper towels biodegrade more easily than dyed ones, people still buy dyed papers.
4. Aluminum cans bring recyclers good money.
5. Environmentalists hope that more communities will recycle newspaper and glass, but many citizens refuse to participate.

gr

NOTE

Summary guides

The guides on this and the next five pages appear only in the *Instructor's Annotated Edition.* They are included here for use in conferences and labs. Each guide collects all the descriptions and conventions for a different element: nouns, pronouns, verbs and verbals, and modifiers. Thus the guides provide convenient indexes or texts for students having difficulty with, say, identifying and placing modifiers or distinguishing verbs and verbals. The listings under "Conventions" in each guide contain at least one example showing correct or preferred usage. For additional examples or detailed explanations, consult the sections or pages given in parentheses.

Guide to nouns

Summary and index of information in this book (consult sections or pages in parentheses).

Description of nouns

Nouns as sentence subjects (5a-1, 5a-2)
Nouns as direct and indirect objects (5a-3), object complements (5a-3), objects of prepositions (5c-1), appositives (5c-5), modifiers (9g)
Classes of nouns: proper, common, collective, count, mass, concrete, abstract (5a-2)
Forms of nouns: subjective and objective case (p. 199), possessive case (23a), and plural (34b-6)
Other structures serving as nouns: gerunds and gerund phrases (5c-2), infinitives and infinitive phrases (5c-2), subordinate clauses (5c-4)

Conventions regarding nouns

Forms of nouns

Possessive forms: *boy's* vs. *boys'; Park's* vs. *Parks's* vs. *Parkses'* (23a)
Possessives before gerunds: *Nguyen's writing is clear.* (6h)
Plurals of nouns and compound nouns: *dish, dishes; child, children; mother-in-law, mothers-in-law* (34b-6)

Nouns and other sentence parts

Agreement of subjects and verbs: *The towel was wet. The towels were wet.* (8a)
Agreement of antecedents and pronouns: *The children surrounded their father.* (8b)
Grammatical fit between subjects and predicates (avoiding mixed grammar): *In the supervision of others is the best preparation for a management career.* → *The supervision of others is the best preparation for a management career.* (15a)
Fit in meaning of subjects and predicates (avoiding faulty predication): *The use of the airwaves is the ideal medium for campaigning.* → *The airwaves are the ideal medium for campaigning.* (15b)

Clarity and effectiveness

Nouns as modifiers (avoiding overuse): *adult education grants workshop* → *workshop on grants for adult education* (9g)
Consistency in subjects and the voice of verbs: *Tony woke suddenly, but his eyes were kept shut.* → *Tony woke suddenly, but he kept his eyes shut.* (13c)

NOTE

This page does not appear in the students' edition.

gr

Guide to pronouns

Summary and index of information in this book (consult sections or pages in parentheses).

Description of pronouns

Pronouns as substitutes for nouns (5a-2, 8b)
Pronouns as subjects, objects, complements, appositives, modifiers (Chapter 6)
Case forms of pronouns: subjective, objective, possessive (Chapter 6)
Person, number, and gender of personal pronouns (5a-2, 8b)

Conventions regarding pronouns

Forms of pronouns

Subjective case for subjects and subject complements: *You and I can talk. It was she.* (6a)
Objective case for objects: *Ken gave me a dog. He gave her to me.* (6b)
We or *us* with nouns: *We drivers like highways. Many of us drivers like highways.* (6c)
Case in appositives: *Two drivers, she and Nell, won the award. The state rewarded two drivers, her and Nell.* (6d)
Case after *than* or *as: Nell likes Buddy more than* [*she likes*] *him. Nell likes Buddy more than he* [*likes Buddy*]. (6e)
Objective case for subjects and objects of infinitives: *We invited him to meet her.* (6f)
Who vs. *whom: Who can predict whom he will ask?* (6g)
Possesives before gerunds: *his working* (6h)
Possessive forms of personal pronouns: *hers* (not *her's*); *theirs* (not *their's*) (23b)
Possessive pronouns vs. contractions: *its* vs. *it's; your* vs. *you're; their* vs. *they're* (23c)

Pronouns and other sentence parts

Agreement of pronoun subjects and verbs: *Neither he nor they are late. Everybody is finished.* (8a)
Agreement of pronouns and antecedents: *Everybody finished his or her paper. Lisa or Maria left her notebook.* (8b)
Reference of pronouns to antecedents (avoiding unclear or remote reference): *The first act of the play seemed weak, but then it improved.* → *The first act of the play started weakly but then improved.* Or: *Though the first act was weak, the play then improved.* (12a–12f)

NOTE

This page does not appear in the students' edition.

gr

Guide to verbs and verbals

Summary and index of information in this book (consult sections or pages in parentheses).

Description of verbs and verbals

Verb as sentence predicate (5a-1, 5a-2, 5a-3)
Transitive, intransitive, and linking verbs (5a-3)
Forms of verbs: infinitive, past tense, past participle, present participle, -*s* form (pp. 207–218)
Regular vs. irregular verbs (7a)
Finite vs. nonfinite verbs (5c-2)
Helping (auxiliary) verbs (pp. 214–18)
Tense of verbs: present, past, future, etc. (pp. 219–26)
Mood of verbs: indicative, imperative, subjunctive (p. 227–29)
Voice of verbs: active and passive (pp. 230–31)
Verbals and verbal phrases: participles, gerunds, infinitives (5c-2)

Conventions regarding verbs and verbals

Forms and tenses of verbs

Principal parts of common irregular verbs: e.g., *begin, began, begun; run, ran, run* (7a)
Sit vs. *set, lie* vs. *lay,* and *rise* vs. *raise* (7b)
Needed -*s* and -*ed* endings: *He asks/asked too much.* (7c)
Needed helping verbs: *He is asking too much.* (7d)
Present tense (*runs*) and perfect tenses (*has/had/will have run*). (7e)
Sequence of tenses: e.g., *We would like to have gone* vs. *We would have liked to go.* (7f)
Subjunctive mood: *I wish I were there.* (7g)

Verbs and other sentence parts

Agreement of verbs and subjects: *The guests are here. Nobody is missing.* (8a)
Unseparated verb phrases and infinitives: *They had before long agreed to voluntarily surrender.* → *Before long they had agreed to surrender voluntarily.* (14e)
Grammatical fit between subjects and predicates (avoiding mixed grammar): *By saving is how they could buy a car.* → *By saving, they could buy a car.* (15a)
Fit in meaning of subjects and predicates (avoiding faulty predication): *The reason is because they were frugal.* → *The reason is that they were frugal.* (15b)

Problems with verbals

Verbs required in complete sentences (avoiding sentence fragments with verbals): *Rain falling silently.* → *Rain fell silently.* (10a, 10c)

Clear and logical modifiers (avoiding dangling modifiers): *Flying home, her thoughts remained behind.* → *As she flew home, her thoughts remained behind.* (14h)

PUNCTUATION WITH VERBALS

Commas after introductory verbal modifiers: *Struggling for air, the climbers reached the summit.* (21b)

Commas to set off nonrestrictive verbal modifiers: *The climbers, struggling for air, reached the summit.* (21c)

CLARITY AND EFFECTIVENESS

Active rather than passive voice: *Hands were raised by the students.* → *The students raised their hands.* (7h)

Consistency in voice: *Before you tighten the bolts, the car should be lowered to the ground.* → *Before you tighten the bolts, you should lower the car to the ground.* (13c)

Consistency in tense: *The hero escapes, but he was captured.* → *The hero escapes, but he is captured.* (13b)

Consistency in mood: *Unscrew the bolts, and then you remove the wheel.* → *Unscrew the bolts, and then remove the wheel.* (13b)

Strong rather than weak verbs (avoiding wordiness): *The book is a depiction of family strife.* → *The book depicts family strife.* (31c-3)

NOTE

This page does not appear in the students' edition.

gr

NOTE

This page does not appear in the students' edition.

gr

Guide to modifiers

Summary and index of information in this book (consult the sections or pages in parentheses).

Description of modifiers

Functions of adjectives: modifying nouns and pronouns (p. 250)
Functions of adverbs: modifying verbs, adjectives, other adverbs, phrases, and clauses (p. 250)
Forms of adjectives and adverbs: positive, comparative, superlative (9e)
Irregular adjectives and adverbs (9e-1)
Classes of adjectives: descriptive, limiting, proper, attributive, predicate (p. 813)
Classes of adverbs: modifiers of verbs, adjectives, and other adverbs (p. 250); transitional and parenthetical expressions (21b); conjunctive adverbs (5d-2)
Other structures serving as modifiers: nouns (9g); prepositional phrases (5c-1); participles and participial phrases (5c-2); infinitives and infinitive phrases (5c-2); subordinate clauses (5c-4)

Conventions regarding modifiers

Distinctions between adjectives and adverbs

Adverbs (not adjectives) to modify verbs, adjectives, adverbs: *Susan writes well* [not *good*]. (9a)
Adjectives after linking verbs, adverbs to modify other verbs: *I feel bad. She sings badly.* (9b)
Adjectives to modify objects, adverbs to modify verbs: *We believed him honest. We treated him honestly.* (9c)

Forms of adjectives and adverbs

Short vs. *-ly* forms of adverbs: *slow* vs. *slowly* (9d)
Comparatives and superlatives: *steady, steadier/more steady, steadiest/most steady; good/well, better, best* (9e-1); *most steadiest* → *most steady* (9e-2); *the bigger of two* and *the biggest of three* (9e-3); *most unique* → *unique* (9e-4)

Modifiers and other sentence parts

Clear placement of modifiers: *We waited for the rain to stop in a doorway.* → *We waited in a doorway for the rain to stop.* (14a–14e)
Clear and logical modifiers (avoiding dangling modifiers): *Watching the rain, our hands and feet froze.* → *As we watched the rain, our hands and feet froze.* (14h)

NOTE

This page does not appear in the students' edition.

Punctuation and mechanics with modifiers

Commas after most introductory modifiers: *Happily, we have friends.* (21b)
Commas to set off nonrestrictive modifiers: *Ellen, who is our best friend, checks in every day.* (21c)
Commas to set off absolute phrases: *Her workday finished, she calls us.* (21d)
Commas for coordinate adjectives: *She is a steady, reliable friend.* (21f-2)
Commas with conjunctive adverbs and transitional and parenthetical expressions: *Traffic was bad; we left, however, before it could get worse.* (21c-3, 22b)
Semicolons between clauses related by conjunctive adverbs: *We did not leave right away; instead, we waited for Ellen.* (11b, 22b)
Capital letters for proper adjectives: *Indian tea; Buddhist chant* (26d)
Figure vs. words for numbers: *327* vs. *twenty-three* (29a)
Hyphens in compound adjectives and numbers: *well-spoken words* vs. *words well spoken* (34d-1); *thirty-two minutes* (34d-2)

Clarity and effectiveness

Clear negation (avoiding double negatives): *They don't want no interruptions.* → *They don't want any interruptions.* Or: *They want no interruptions.* (9f)
Nouns as modifiers (avoiding overuse): *business managers spreadsheet analysis seminar* → *seminar in spreadsheet analysis for business managers* (9g)
Complete and logical comparisons: *The value of friendship is greater than money.* → *The value of friendship is greater than the value of* [or *that of*] *money.* (15d)

HIGHLIGHTS

The forms that nouns and pronouns take according to their role in a sentence are relatively few in English when compared with some other languages. Nonetheless, most students are likely to find compound subjects and objects or questions of *who* and *whom* occasionally troublesome. Others may need to review pronoun forms more extensively to gain control over this part of their writing.

This chapter opens with a review of the functions a pronoun can perform, functions that determine the form, or case, of the pronoun. In addition to the familiar list of forms of the personal pronouns, the chapter provides sentences illustrating the wide variety of uses for pronouns. Following this are brief discussions of the proper case for pronouns in contexts that usually cause difficulty for student writers, including compound subjects and objects, appositives, comparisons using *than* or *as,* possessive case with gerunds, and the different uses of *who* and *whom.*

The exercises ask students to select the appropriate forms of pronouns in the troublesome contexts treated in the discussion, to correct any case errors in a paragraph, and to combine sentences so as to use *who* or *whom* in relative clauses.

RESOURCES AND IDEAS

Redfern, Richard K. "Pronouns Are Highly Personal." *English Journal* 85 (1996): 80–1. Redfern presents further strategies for teaching pronoun usage.

BACK TO NOUNS

Distribute copies of a paragraph taken from a magazine article, an essay in a reader, or a student paper. Ask students to rewrite it, substituting the appropriate noun for each pronoun. This exercise will help students to understand the role of pronouns and see the relationship between the case of a pronoun and the function of the noun it stands for.

Chapter 6

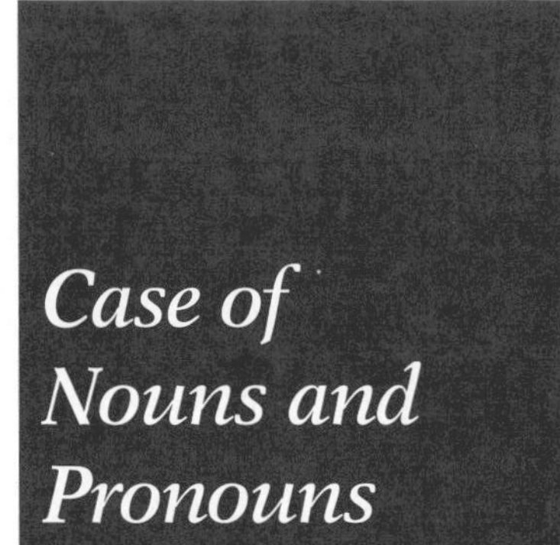

Case is the form of a noun or pronoun that shows the reader how it functions in a sentence—that is, whether it functions as a subject, as an object, or in some other way. As shown in the box on the facing page, only *I, we, he, she, they,* and *who* change form for each case. Thus these pronouns are the focus of this chapter.

The **subjective case** generally indicates that the word is a subject or a subject complement. (See pp. 163 and 169.)

subject
She and Novick discussed the proposal.
subject
The proposal ignores many *who* need help.
subject complement
The disgruntled planners were *she and Novick.*

The **objective case** generally indicates that the word is the object of a verb or preposition. (See pp. 167, 169, and 175.)

object of verb
The proposal disappointed *her and Novick.*
object of verb / object of verb
A colleague *whom* they respected let *them* down.
object of preposition
Their opinion of *him* suffered.

The **possessive case** generally indicates ownership or source:

Her counterproposal is in preparation.
Theirs is the more defensible position.
The problem is not *his.*

Case forms of nouns and pronouns

	SUBJECTIVE	OBJECTIVE	POSSESSIVE
NOUNS	boy	boy	boy's
	Jessie	Jessie	Jessie's
PERSONAL PRONOUNS			
Singular			
1st person	I	me	my, mine
2nd person	you	you	your, yours
3rd person	he	him	his
	she	her	her, hers
	it	it	its
Plural			
1st person	we	us	our, ours
2nd person	you	you	your, yours
3rd person	they	them	their, theirs
RELATIVE AND INTERROGATIVE PRONOUNS			
	who	whom	whose
	whoever	whomever	—
	which, that, what	which, that, what	—
INDEFINITE PRONOUNS			
	everybody	everybody	everybody's

NOTE Do not use an apostrophe to form the possessive of personal pronouns: *yours* (not *your's*); *theirs* (not *their's*). (See p. 400. See also p. 397 for the possessive forms of nouns, which do use apostrophes.)

6a Use the subjective case for compound subjects and for subject complements.

In compound subjects use the same pronoun form you would use if the pronoun stood alone as a subject.

> subject
> *She and Novick* will persist.

> subject
> The others may lend their support when *she and Novick* get a hearing.

If you are in doubt about the correct form, try the test in the box on the next page.

After a linking verb, such as a form of *be,* a pronoun renaming the subject (a subject complement) should be in the subjective case.

TRANSPARENCY MASTER 6.1

THE CHART

Students may be tempted to skip over this chart of the case forms of nouns and pronouns. Get them to pay attention by asking them to fill out the whole chart in class—without looking at the text. The act of remembering the forms or figuring them out will be more valuable than listening to an explanation. Students who have trouble completing the chart probably need to spend time reviewing the chapter.

ca
6b

A test for case forms in compound constructions

1. Identify a compound construction (one connected by *and, but, or, nor*).

   (*He, Him*) and (*I, me*) won the prize.
   The prize went to (*he, him*) and (*I, me*).

2. Write a separate sentence for each part of the compound.

   (*He, Him*) won the prize. (*I, Me*) won the prize.
   The prize went to (*he, him*). The prize went to (*I, me*).

3. Choose the pronouns that sound correct.

   He won the prize. *I* won the prize. [Subjective.]
   The prize went to *him.* The prize went to *me.* [Objective.]

4. Put the separate sentences back together.

   He and *I* won the prize.
   The prize went to *him* and *me.*

subject complement
The ones who care most are *she and Novick.*

subject complement
It was *they* whom the mayor appointed.

If this construction sounds stilted to you, use the more natural order: *She and Novick are the ones who care most. The mayor appointed them.*

6b Use the objective case for compound objects.

In compound objects use the same pronoun form you would use if the pronoun stood alone as an object.

direct object
The mayor nominated *Zhu and him.*

indirect object
The mayor gave *Zhu and him* awards.

object of preposition
Credit goes equally to *them and the mayor.*

If you are in doubt about the correct form, try the test in the box above.

ANSWERS: EXERCISE 1

1. I
2. she, I, we
3. her, me
4. she, I
5. I, we

Exercise 1
Choosing between subjective and objective pronouns
From the pairs in parentheses, select the appropriate subjective or objective pronoun(s) for each of the following sentences.

Example:

"Between you and (*I, me*)," the seller said, "this deal is a steal."
"Between you and *me,*" the seller said, "this deal is a steal."

1. Jody and (*I, me*) had been hunting for jobs.
2. The best employees at our old company were (*she, her*) and (*I, me*), so (*we, us*) expected to find jobs quickly.
3. Between (*she, her*) and (*I, me*) the job search had lasted two months, and still it had barely begun.
4. Slowly, (*she, her*) and (*I, me*) stopped sharing leads.
5. It was obvious that Jody and (*I, me*) could not be as friendly as (*we, us*) had been.

6c Use the appropriate case when the plural pronoun *we* or *us* occurs with a noun.

Whether to use *we* or *us* with a noun depends on the use of the noun.

Freezing weather is welcomed by *us* skaters. [*us* → object of preposition]

We skaters welcome freezing weather. [*We* → subject]

6d In appositives the case of a pronoun depends on the function of the word described or identified.

The class elected two representatives, DeShawn and *me.* [representatives: object of verb; DeShawn and *me*: appositive identifies object]

Two representatives, DeShawn and *I,* were elected. [representatives: subject; DeShawn and *I*: appositive identifies subject]

If you are in doubt about case in an appositive, try the sentence without the word the appositive identifies: *The class elected DeShawn and me; DeShawn and I were elected.*

Exercise 2
Choosing between subjective and objective pronouns

From the pairs in parentheses, select the appropriate subjective or objective pronoun for each of the following sentences.

Example:

Convincing (*we, us*) veterans to vote yes will be difficult.
Convincing *us* veterans to vote yes will be difficult.

1. Obtaining enough protein is important to (*we, us*) vegetarians.
2. Instead of obtaining protein from meat (*we, us*) vegetarians get our protein from other sources.

US THE PEOPLE

If students try out pronoun forms in sentences, they can often "hear" the contrast between correct and incorrect forms by relying on their implicit understanding of the language or by using familiar phrases as touchstones:

Us the people.
Us are the world.
Are you going with *we?*
Take *we* to the movies.

This approach will not work with students for whom standard English is a second language or a second dialect.

ANSWERS: EXERCISE 2

1. us
2. we
3. him
4. us
5. we, I

3. Jeff claims to know only two vegetarians, Helena and (*he, him*), who avoid all animal products, including milk.
4. Some of (*we, us*) vegetarians eat fish, which is a good source of protein.
5. (*We, Us*) vegetarians in my family, my parents and (*I, me*), drink milk and eat fish.

ca
6g

6e The case of a pronoun after *than* or *as* in a comparison depends on the meaning.

When a pronoun follows *than* or *as* in a comparison, the case of the pronoun indicates what words may have been omitted. When the pronoun is subjective, it must serve as the subject of an omitted verb.

subject
Some critics like Glass more than *he* [does].

When the pronoun is objective, it must serve as the object of an omitted verb.

object
Some critics like Glass more than [they like] *him*.

6f Use the objective case for pronouns that are subjects or objects of infinitives.

subject of infinitive
The school asked *him* to speak.

object of infinitive
Students chose to invite *him*.

6g The form of the pronoun *who* depends on its function in its clause.

To choose between *who* and *whom, whoever* and *whomever,* you need to figure out whether the word is a subject or an object.

At the beginning of questions use *who* for a subject and *whom* for an object.

subject
Who wrote the policy?

object
Whom does it affect?

To help find the correct case of *who* in a question, try the test in the following box:

MAKE UP YOUR OWN TEST

Give students time in class to write out five to ten sentences in quiz form. The easiest way for students to do this is to pattern their questions after the exercises and sample sentences in the handbook:

Most of (*we, us*) college students realize that finding a good job isn't easy.

There is a five-hundred-dollar reward for (*whomever, whoever*) finds the missing stock certificates.

Students can use the handbook in preparing the questions, and as long as they know that one of the possible answers they have provided must be right, they need not be sure which one it is.

When the tests are completed, students should exchange them and fill them out. Correcting the tests is best done in small groups so that students can help one another or turn to the instructor for any information necessary to provide answers to the toughest questions.

WHOM'S DOOM?

The distinction between *who* and *whom* is swiftly disappearing; in another half-century it may be gone in all but the most formal writing. Linguistically this change is understandable; ask students to compare the number of forms and inflections English nouns and pronouns have with the number of forms possible in French, German, or some other language. English has simplified its forms more than most other languages. The *who/whom* change is another example of this natural process occurring.

TRANSPARENCY MASTER 6.2

ca
6g

A test for *who* versus *whom* in questions

1. Pose the question.

   (*Who, Whom*) makes that decision?
   (*Who, Whom*) does one ask?

2. Answer the question, using a personal pronoun. Choose the pronoun that sounds correct, and note its case.

   (*She, Her*) makes that decision. *She* makes that decision. [Subjective.]

   One asks (*she, her*). One asks *her*. [Objective.]

3. Use the same case (*who* or *whom*) in the question.

   Who makes that decision? [Subjective.]
   Whom does one ask? [Objective.]

Note In speech the subjective case *who* is commonly used whenever it is the first word of a question, regardless of whether it is a subject or an object. But formal writing requires a distinction between the forms.

Spoken *Who* should we credit?

object
Written *Whom* should we credit?

In subordinate clauses use *who* and *whoever* for all subjects, *whom* and *whomever* for all objects.

The case of a pronoun in a subordinate clause depends on its function in the clause, regardless of whether the clause itself functions as a subject, an object, or a modifier.

subject
Credit *whoever* wrote the policy.

object
Research should reveal *whom* to credit.

If you have trouble determining which form to choose, try the test in the following box:

TRANSPARENCY MASTER 6.3

A test for *who* versus *whom* in subordinate clauses

1. Locate the subordinate clause.

   Few people know (*who, whom*) *they should ask*.
   They are unsure (*who, whom*) *makes the decision*.

(continued)

ca
6g

A test for *who* versus *whom* in subordinate clauses (*continued*)

2. Rewrite the subordinate clause as a separate sentence, substituting a personal pronoun for *who, whom.* Choose the pronoun that sounds correct, and note its case.

   They should ask (*she, her*). They should ask *her.* [Objective.]
   (*She, her*) makes the decision. *She* makes the decision. [Subjective.]

3. Use the same case (*who* or *whom*) in the subordinate clause.

   Few people know *whom* they should ask. [Objective.]
   They are unsure *who* makes the decision. [Subjective.]

Note Don't let expressions such as *I think* and *she says* confuse you when they come between the subject *who* and its verb.

subject →
He is the one *who* the polls say will win.

To choose between *who* and *whom* in such constructions, delete the interrupting phrase: *He is the one who will win.*

ANSWERS: EXERCISE 3

1. whom
2. who
3. whoever
4. Who
5. Whom

COLLABORATIVE LEARNING

Students might complete Exercise 3 independently, then compare answers and work on Exercise 4 in pairs or in small groups. Ask each group to create several sentences of their own using *who* and *whom,* and based on the models provided in Exercise 4. Each group might present some of their most inventive responses to the class by writing them on the chalkboard, on transparencies, or posting them on the network.

ANSWERS: EXERCISE 4

Possible answers

1. Some children who have undetected hearing problems may do poorly in school.

Exercise 3
Choosing between *who* and *whom*

From the pairs in parentheses, select the appropriate form of the pronoun in each of the following sentences.

Example:
My mother asked me (*who, whom*) I was going out with.
My mother asked me *whom* I was going out with.

1. The school administrators suspended Jurgen, (*who, whom*) they suspected of setting the fire.
2. Jurgen had been complaining to other custodians, (*who, whom*) reported him.
3. He constantly complained of unfair treatment from (*whoever, whomever*) happened to be passing in the halls, including pupils.
4. "(*Who, Whom*) here has heard Mr. Jurgen's complaints?" the police asked.
5. "(*Who, Whom*) did he complain most about?"

Exercise 4
Sentence combining: *Who* versus *whom*

Combine each pair of sentences below into one sentence that contains a clause beginning with *who* or *whom.* Be sure to use the appropriate case form. You will have to add, delete, and rearrange words. Each item may have more than one possible answer.

Example:

David is the candidate. We think David deserves to win.
David is the candidate *who* we think deserves to win.

1. Some children have undetected hearing problems. These children may do poorly in school.
2. They may not hear important instructions and information from teachers. Teachers may speak softly.
3. Classmates may not be audible. The teacher calls on those classmates.
4. Some hearing-impaired children may work harder to overcome their handicap. These children get a lot of encouragement at home.
5. Some hearing-impaired children may take refuge in fantasy friends. They can rely on these friends not to criticize or laugh.

2. They may not hear important instructions and information from teachers who speak softly.
3. Classmates whom the teacher calls on may not be audible.
4. Some hearing-impaired children who get a lot of encouragement at home may work harder to overcome their handicap.
5. Some hearing-impaired children may take refuge in fantasy friends whom they can rely on not to criticize or laugh.

6h Ordinarily, use a possessive pronoun or noun immediately before a gerund.

A **gerund** is the *-ing* form of a verb (*running, sleeping*) used as a noun (p. 178). Like nouns, gerunds are commonly preceded by possessive nouns and pronouns: *our vote* (noun), *our voting* (gerund).

The coach disapproved of *their* lifting weights.

The *coach's* disapproving was a surprise.

A noun or pronoun before an *-ing* verb form is not always possessive. Sometimes the *-ing* form will be a present participle modifying the preceding word.

Everyone had noticed *him* weightlifting. [Emphasis on *him.*]
objective pronoun — participle

Everyone had noticed *his* weightlifting. [Emphasis on the activity.]
possessive pronoun — gerund

Note that a gerund usually is not preceded by the possessive when the possessive would create an awkward construction.

Awkward A rumor spread about everybody's on the team wanting to quit.

Less awkward A rumor spread about everybody on the team wanting to quit.

Better A rumor spread that everybody on the team wanted to quit.

COLLABORATIVE LEARNING

CREATE A STORY

On the board, write a sentence or two that introduces as many people's names as possible. For example, you might write,

> Bob went to a party last night, and there he saw his first-grade teacher, Mrs. West; his neighbor George; his old girlfriend Sarah; and her children Susan and Jason. In the middle of the party, Bob's dog Bowser came racing into the living room.

Divide the class into small groups and ask each group to write a one-paragraph story that grows out of the sentences on the board. (In the example above, students would probably describe what happened after the dog's entrance.) In writing their story, students should try to use as many pronouns as possible without introducing any ambiguity into the tale.

Groups should then read their stories aloud or write them on the board so that other students can try to understand the stories and verify that all the pronoun cases are accurate.

ANSWERS: EXERCISE 5

Written four thousand years ago, *The Epic of Gilgamesh* tells of the friendship of Gilgamesh and Enkidu. Gilgamesh was a bored king who his people thought was too harsh. Then he met Enkidu, a wild man who had lived with the animals in the mountains. Immediately, he and Gilgamesh wrestled to see who was more powerful. After hours of struggle, Enkidu admitted that Gilgamesh was stronger than he. Now the friends needed adventures worthy of the two strongest men on earth. Gilgamesh said, "Between you and me, mighty deeds will be accomplished, and our fame will be everlasting." Among their acts, Enkidu and he defeated a giant bull, Humbaba, and cut down the bull's cedar forests. Their bringing back cedar logs to Gilgamesh's treeless land won great praise from the people. When Enkidu died, Gilgamesh mourned his death, realizing that no one had been a better friend than he. When Gilgamesh himself died many years later, his people raised a monument praising Enkidu and him for their friendship and their mighty deeds of courage.

Exercise 5
Revising: Case

Revise all inappropriate case forms in the following paragraph, and explain the function of each case form.

> Written four thousand years ago, *The Epic of Gilgamesh* tells of the friendship of Gilgamesh and Enkidu. Gilgamesh was a bored king who his people thought was too harsh. Then he met Enkidu, a wild man whom had lived with the animals in the mountains. Immediately, him and Gilgamesh wrestled to see whom was more powerful. After hours of struggle, Enkidu admitted that Gilgamesh was stronger than him. Now the friends needed adventures worthy of the two strongest men on earth. Gilgamesh said, "Between you and I, mighty deeds will be accomplished, and our fame will be everlasting." Among their acts, Enkidu and him defeated a giant bull, Humbaba, and cut down the bull's cedar forests. Them bringing back cedar logs to Gilgamesh's treeless land won great praise from the people. When Enkidu died, Gilgamesh mourned his death, realizing that no one had been a better friend than him. When Gilgamesh himself died many years later, his people raised a monument praising Enkidu and he for their friendship and their mighty deeds of courage.

Note See page 264 for an exercise involving case along with other aspects of grammar.

Chapter 7

The verb is the most complicated part of speech in English, changing form to express a wide range of information.

VERB FORMS

All verbs except *be* have five basic forms. The first three are the verb's **principal parts.**

- The **plain form** is the dictionary form of the verb. When the subject is a plural noun or the pronoun *I, we, you,* or *they,* the plain form indicates action that occurs in the present, occurs habitually, or is generally true.

  A few artists *live* in town today.
  They *hold* classes downtown.

- The **past-tense form** indicates that the action of the verb occurred before now. It usually adds *-d* or *-ed* to the plain form, although for some irregular verbs it forms in other ways (see p. 209).

  Many artists *lived* in town before this year.
  They *held* classes downtown. [Irregular verb.]

- The **past participle** is usually the same as the past-tense form, except in most irregular verbs. It combines with forms of *have* or *be* (*has climbed, was created*), or by itself it modifies nouns and pronouns (*the sliced apples*).

  Artists have *lived* in town for decades.
  They have *held* classes downtown. [Irregular verb.]

HIGHLIGHTS

Verbs can cause trouble for writers regardless of their level of skill. For some writers, choosing the correct tense or form of a verb can be a formidable challenge. In addition, certain regional and social dialects of English have different patterns for marking verb tenses and forms, which may add to the confusion. Even experienced writers may occasionally stumble over the choice between *sit* and *set* or struggle to maintain the correct sequence of tenses in a complex sentence.

For all these needs (and many others as well) this chapter can be useful, although it must be supplemented to provide the more sustained support and practice some students may require. Students whose first language is not English may benefit from the increased ESL coverage in this edition and the additional worksheets by Jocelyn Steer. If your campus is fortunate enough to have a writing center, your students may benefit from the extra support it can provide.

Students looking for help with verb *forms* will benefit from the chapter's thorough explanations, list of the principal parts of frequently used irregular verbs, discussion of the troublesome pairs *sit/set* and *lie/lay,* and treatment of two problems often associated with dialect interference: omitted *-s* and *-ed* endings and omitted helping verbs.

Students looking for help with verb *tense* can make use of the chapter's discussion of the major tenses and of appropriate sequences of tenses. Tense sequence becomes increasingly important as students begin to write ambitious narratives and expository or argumentative essays.

RESOURCES AND IDEAS

Yoder, Rhoda Byler. "Of Fake Verbs and Kid Words: Developing a Useful Grammar." *English Journal* 85 (1996): 82–7. Middle school teacher develops a simplified language for teaching students the functions of verbs and verbals.

- The **present participle** adds *-ing* to the verb's plain form. It combines with forms of *be* (*is buying*), modifies nouns and pronouns (*the boiling water*), or functions as a noun (*Running exhausts me*).

  A few artists are *living* in town today.
  They are *holding* classes downtown.

- The **-*s* form** ends in *-s* or *-es*. When the subject is a singular noun, a pronoun such as *everyone,* or the personal pronoun *he, she,* or *it,* the *-s* form indicates action that occurs in the present, occurs habitually, or is generally true.

  The artist *lives* in town today.
  She *holds* classes downtown.

The verb *be* has eight forms rather than the five forms of most other verbs.

PLAIN FORM	be		
PRESENT PARTICIPLE	being		
PAST PARTICIPLE	been		
	I	*he, she, it*	*we, you, they*
PRESENT TENSE	am	is	are
PAST TENSE	was	was	were

TRANSPARENCY MASTER 7.1

Terms used to describe verbs

FORM
The spelling of the verb that conveys time, mood, and other information. *Kick, kicked, kicking,* and *kicks* are forms of *kick.* (See p. 207.)

TENSE
The time of the verb's action—for instance, present (*kick*), past (*kicked*), future (*will kick*). (See p. 219.)

MOOD
The attitude of the verb's speaker or writer—the difference, for example, in *I kick the ball, Kick the ball,* and *I suggest that you kick the ball.* (See p. 227.)

VOICE
The distinction between the **active,** in which the subject performs the verb's action (*I kick the ball*), and the **passive,** in which the subject is acted upon (*The ball is kicked by me*). (See p. 230.)

PERSON
The verb form that reflects whether the subject is speaking (*I/we kick the ball*), spoken to (*You kick the ball*), or spoken about (*She kicks the ball*). (See p. 238.)

NUMBER
The verb form that reflects whether the subject is singular (*The girl kicks the ball*) or plural (*Girls kick the ball*). (See p. 238.)

Helping verbs

Helping verbs, also called **auxiliary verbs,** combine with some verb forms to indicate time and other kinds of meaning, as in *can run, was sleeping, had been eaten.* These combinations are **verb phrases.** Since the plain form, present participle, or past participle in any verb phrase always carries the principal meaning, it is sometimes called the **main verb.**

	Verb phrase	
	Helping	*Main*
Artists	*can*	*train* others to draw.
The techniques	*have*	*changed* little.

These are the most common helping verbs:

be able to	had better	must	used to
be supposed to	have to	ought to	will
can	may	shall	would
could	might	should	

Forms of *be:* be, am, is, are, was, were, been, being
Forms of *have:* have, has, had, having
Forms of *do:* do, does, did

See pages 214–18 for more on helping verbs.

7a Use the correct form of regular and irregular verbs.

Most verbs are **regular;** that is, they form their past tense and past participle by adding *-d* or *-ed* to the plain form.

Plain form	Past tense	Past participle
live	lived	lived
act	acted	acted

Since the past tense and past participle are created simply by adding to the plain form and since the two are identical, the forms of regular verbs do not often cause problems in speech and writing (but see p. 213).

About two hundred English verbs are **irregular;** that is, they form their past tense and past participle in some irregular way. For example:

Plain form	Past tense	Past participle
begin	began	begun
break	broke	broken
sleep	slept	slept

Check a dictionary under the plain form if you have any doubt about a verb's principal parts. If no other forms are listed, the verb is regular: both the past tense and the past participle add *-d* or *-ed* to the plain form. If the verb is irregular, the dictionary will list the plain form, the past tense, and the past participle in that order (*go, went, gone*). If the dictionary gives only two forms (as in *think, thought*), then the past tense and the past participle are the same.

The following list includes the most common irregular verbs. (When two forms are possible, as in *dived* and *dove,* both are included.)

Principal parts of common irregular verbs

Plain form	Past tense	Past participle
arise	arose	arisen
become	became	become
begin	began	begun
bid	bid	bid
bite	bit	bitten, bit
blow	blew	blown
break	broke	broken
bring	brought	brought
burst	burst	burst
buy	bought	bought
catch	caught	caught
choose	chose	chosen
come	came	come
cut	cut	cut
dive	dived, dove	dived
do	did	done
draw	drew	drawn
dream	dreamed, dreamt	dreamed, dreamt
drink	drank	drunk
drive	drove	driven
eat	ate	eaten
fall	fell	fallen
find	found	found
flee	fled	fled
fly	flew	flown
forget	forgot	forgotten, forgot
freeze	froze	frozen
get	got	got, gotten
give	gave	given
go	went	gone
grow	grew	grown
hang (suspend)	hung	hung
hang (execute)	hanged	hanged
hear	heard	heard
hide	hid	hidden

ONE-FORM PARAGRAPHS

Choose groups of three to five verbs, and have students create paragraphs using only one form of the verbs. Then have students rewrite the paragraphs using a different verb form. This exercise will reinforce consistent use of form and may make students more aware of the element of time in verb usage. Following are student-written examples that use the past-participle form of the verbs *break, bring, burst, buy,* and *catch.*

> *Because his bubble had burst and she had broken his heart, he had caught the next train home and had brought his mother some flowers.*
>
> —Jennifer Haas

> *We had brought the dishes out to the table to set it. When we looked we realized that we had broken some of them. We had burst out laughing, but it wasn't too funny when we realized that my mother had caught us.*
>
> —Nicole Hanna

> *He had broken the vase that she had brought. She had burst into tears. If only he had caught it.*
>
> —Jim Rosen

THE ORIGIN OF IRREGULAR VERBS

Irregular verbs are antiques reflecting the history of English well before the Norman Conquest of England in 1066. In the first few centuries AD, speakers of the Germanic languages that evolved into English used changes in the internal vowel structure of words to show tense. Thus, verbs like *drink, throw,* and especially *be* preserve a little of the linguistic history of our ancestors. A very readable account of this period is found in Joseph Williams, *Origins of the English Language* (New York: Free Press, 1975).

HYPOTHETICAL VERBS

A good game to play to show students how well they intuitively understand how irregular

Plain form	Past tense	Past participle
hold	held	held
keep	kept	kept
know	knew	known
lay	laid	laid
lead	led	led
leave	left	left
lend	lent	lent
let	let	let
lie	lay	lain
lose	lost	lost
pay	paid	paid
prove	proved	proved, proven
ride	rode	ridden
ring	rang	rung
rise	rose	risen
run	ran	run
say	said	said
see	saw	seen
set	set	set
shake	shook	shaken
shrink	shrank, shrunk	shrunk, shrunken
sing	sang, sung	sung
sink	sank, sunk	sunk
sit	sat	sat
slide	slid	slid
speak	spoke	spoken
spring	sprang, sprung	sprung
stand	stood	stood
steal	stole	stolen
swim	swam	swum
swing	swung	swung
take	took	taken
tear	tore	torn
throw	threw	thrown
wear	wore	worn
write	wrote	written

verbs are formed is to invent some (e.g., *flink*) and ask students to decide what their other forms would be (*flink, flank, flunk* or *flink, flought, flought*). A variation is to take a more regular verb and pretend it's irregular: *My engine won't crank in cold weather; My engine hadn't crunk.*

Exercise 1
Using irregular verbs

For each irregular verb in parentheses, give either the past tense or the past participle, as appropriate, and identify the form you used.

Example:

Though we had (*hide*) the cash box, it was (*steal*).

Though we had *hidden* the cash box, it was *stolen*. [Two past participles.]

ANSWERS: EXERCISE 1

1. The world population has grown by two-thirds of a billion people in less than a decade. (Past participle.)
2. Recently it broke the 6 billion mark. (Past tense.)
3. Experts have drawn pictures of a crowded future. (Past participle.)
4. They predict that the world population may have slid up to as much as 16 billion by 2100. (Past participle.)
5. Though the food supply rose in the last decade, the share to each person fell. (Both past tense.)

IRREGULAR VERBS AND THE DICTIONARY

The need to learn the uses of *sit* and *set, rise* and *raise,* and *lie* and *lay* makes a great excuse to introduce students to the wonders of the *Oxford English Dictionary,* either in its first or second edition. The entries for these words, among the longest in the *OED,* will show students the number of meanings words can have and the reasons all writers find these particular words so difficult.

1. The world population has (*grow*) by two-thirds of a billion people in less than a decade.
2. Recently it (*break*) the 6 billion mark.
3. Experts have (*draw*) pictures of a crowded future.
4. They predict that the world population may have (*slide*) up to as much as 16 billion by the year 2100.
5. Though the food supply (*rise*) in the last decade, the share to each person (*fall*).

7b Distinguish between *sit* and *set, lie* and *lay,* and *rise* and *raise.*

The forms of *sit* and *set, lie* and *lay,* and *rise* and *raise* are easy to confuse.

Plain form	Past tense	Past participle
sit	sat	sat
set	set	set
lie	lay	lain
lay	laid	laid
rise	rose	risen
raise	raised	raised

In each of these confusing pairs, one verb is **intransitive** (it does not take an object) and one is **transitive** (it does take an object). (See p. 167 for more on this distinction.)

Intransitive

The patients *lie* in their beds. [*Lie* means "recline" and takes no object.]

Visitors *sit* with them. [*Sit* means "be seated" or "be located" and takes no object.]

Patients' temperatures *rise.* [*Rise* means "increase" or "get up" and takes no object.]

Transitive

Orderlies *lay* the dinner trays on tables. [*Lay* means "place" and takes an object, here *trays.*]

Orderlies *set* the trays down. [*Set* means "place" and takes an object, here *trays.*]

Nursing aides *raise* the shades. [*Raise* means "lift" or "bring up" and takes an object, here *shades.*]

Exercise 2
Distinguishing *sit/set, lie/lay, rise/raise*

Choose the correct verb from the pair given in parentheses. Then supply the past tense or past participle, as appropriate.

Example:

After I washed all the windows, I (*lie, lay*) down the squeegee and then I (*sit, set*) the table.

After I washed all the windows, I *laid* down the squeegee and then I *set* the table.

1. Yesterday afternoon the child (*lie, lay*) down for a nap.
2. The child has been (*rise, raise*) by her grandparents.
3. Most days her grandfather has (*sit, set*) with her, reading her stories.
4. She has (*rise, raise*) at dawn most mornings.
5. Her toys were (*lie, lay*) out on the floor.

ANSWERS: EXERCISE 2

1. Yesterday afternoon the child lay down for a nap.
2. The child has been raised by her grandparents.
3. Most days her grandfather has sat with her, reading her stories.
4. She has risen at dawn most mornings.
5. Her toys were laid out on the floor.

vb 7c

7c Use the *-s* and *-ed* forms of the verb when they are required.

Speakers of some English dialects and nonnative speakers of English sometimes omit verb endings required by standard English. The *-s* form of a verb is required when *both* of these situations hold:

- The subject is a singular noun (*boy*), an indefinite pronoun (*everyone*), or *he, she,* or *it.*
- The verb's action occurs in the present.

The letter *asks* [not *ask*] for a quick response.
Delay *is* [not *be*] costly.

Watch especially for the *-s* forms *has, does,* and *doesn't* (for *does not*).

The company *has* [not *have*] delayed responding.
It *doesn't* [not *don't*] have the needed data.
The contract *does* [not *do*] depend on the response.

Another ending sometimes omitted is *-d* or *-ed,* as in *we bagged* or *used cars.* The ending is particularly easy to omit if it isn't pronounced clearly in speech, as in *asked, discussed, fixed, mixed, supposed, walked,* and *used.* Use the ending for a regular verb in *any* of these situations:

- The verb's action occurred in the past:

  The company *asked* [not *ask*] for more time.

- The verb form functions as a modifier:

  The data *concerned* [not *concern*] should be retrievable.

- The verb form combines with a form of *be* or *have:*

  The company is *supposed* [not *suppose*] to be the best.
  It has *developed* [not *develop*] an excellent reputation.

RESOURCES AND IDEAS

Speakers of Black English Vernacular may tend to use the verb forms of this dialect in their writing rather than those of standard written English, particularly by dropping *-s* and *-ed* endings. Becoming aware of the verb system of standard written English and the differences between it and the verb system of Black English Vernacular is an important step for students seeking control over their writing. But as Marcia Farr and Harvey Daniels point out in *Language Diversity and Writing Instruction* (New York: ERIC Clearing House on Urban Education and Urbana: NCTE, 1986), awareness of and practice in identifying and using the verb forms are useful only if they take place in a context that includes a wide range of reading and writing experiences; substantial practice in writing; collaborative activities; sentence combining or similar activities; and flexible, sensitive feedback from the instructor. Farr and Daniels also offer a detailed discussion of dialects and language variations, along with concrete suggestions for teaching.

ESL Some languages do not require endings equivalent to the *-s* or *-ed* in English. If English is not your native language and you find you omit one or both of these endings, you may need to edit your drafts just for them.

ANSWERS: EXERCISE 3

A teacher sometimes asks too much of a student. In high school I was once punished for being sick. I had missed some school, and I realized that I would fail a test unless I had a chance to make up the classwork. I discussed the problem with the teacher, but he said I was supposed to make up the work while I was sick. At that I walked out of the class. I received a failing grade then, but it did not change my attitude. Today I still balk when a teacher makes unreasonable demands or expects miracles.

Exercise 3
Using *-s* and *-ed* verb endings

Supply the correct form of each verb in parentheses. Be careful to include *-s* and *-ed* (or *-d*) endings where they are needed for standard English.

A teacher sometimes (*ask*) too much of a student. In high school I was once (*punish*) for being sick. I had (*miss*) some school, and I (*realize*) that I would fail a test unless I had a chance to make up the classwork. I (*discuss*) the problem with the teacher, but he said I was (*suppose*) to make up the work while I was sick. At that I (*walk*) out of the class. I (*receive*) a failing grade then, but it did not change my attitude. Today I still balk when a teacher (*make*) unreasonable demands or (*expect*) miracles.

7d Use helping verbs with main verbs appropriately.

Helping verbs combine with some verb forms to form verb phrases (see p. 209).

1 Use helping verbs when they are required.

Some English dialects omit helping verbs required by standard English. In the sentences below, the underlined helping verbs are essential:

> Archaeologists *are conducting* fieldwork all over the world. [Not *Archaeologists conducting*. . . .]
>
> Many *have been* fortunate in their discoveries. [Not *Many been*. . . .]
>
> Some *could be* real-life Indiana Joneses. [Not *Some be*. . . .]

In every example above, omitting the helping verb would create an incomplete sentence, or **sentence fragment** (see Chapter 10). In a complete sentence, some part of the verb (helping or main) must be capable of changing form to show changes in time: *I run, I ran; you are running, you were running* (see p. 267). But a present participle (*conducting*), an irregular past participle (*been*), and the infinitive *be* cannot change form in this way. They need helping verbs (which can change) to work as sentence verbs.

Combine helping verbs and main verbs appropriately for your meaning. ESL

Helping verbs and main verbs combine into verb phrases in specific ways.

Note The main verb in a verb phrase (the one carrying the main meaning) does not change to show a change in subject or time: *she has sung, you had sung*. Only the helping verb may change, as in these examples.

Form of *be* + present participle

The **progressive tenses** indicate action in progress (see p. 221). Create them with *be, am, is, are, was, were,* or *been* followed by the main verb's present participle.

She *is working* on a new book.

Be and *been* require additional helping verbs to form the progressive tenses.

can	might	should		have	
could	must	will	*be* working	has	*been* working
may	shall	would		had	

When forming the progressive tenses, be sure to use the *-ing* form of the main verb.

Faulty Her ideas are *grow* more complex. She is *developed* a new approach to ethics.

Revised Her ideas are *growing* more complex. She is *developing* a new approach to ethics.

Form of *be* + past participle

The **passive voice** of the verb indicates that the subject *receives* the action of the verb (see p. 230). Create the passive voice with *be, am, is, are, was, were, being,* or *been* followed by the main verb's past participle.

Her latest book *was completed* in four months.

Be, being, and *been* require additional helping verbs to form the passive voice.

have		am	was	
has	*been* completed	is	were	*being* completed
had		are		

will *be* completed

Be sure to use the main verb's past participle for the passive voice.

Faulty Her next book will be *publish* soon.
Revised Her next book will be *published* soon.

Note Use only transitive verbs to form the passive voice.

Faulty A philosophy conference *will be occurred* in the same week. [*Occur* is not a transitive verb.]
Revised A philosophy conference *will occur* in the same week.

See page 231 for advice on when to use and when to avoid the passive voice.

Forms of *have*

Four forms of *have* serve as helping verbs: *have, has, had, having.* One of these forms plus the main verb's past participle creates one of the **perfect tenses,** those expressing action completed before another specific time or action (see p. 221).

Some students *have complained* about the laboratory.
Others *had complained* before.

Will and other helping verbs sometimes accompany forms of *have* in the perfect tenses.

Several more students *will have complained* by the end of the week.

Forms of *do*

Do, does, and *did* have three uses as helping verbs, always with the plain form of the main verb:

- To pose a question: *How did the trial end?*
- To emphasize the main verb: *It did end eventually.*
- To negate the main verb, along with *not* or *never: The judge did not withdraw.*

Be sure to use the main verb's plain form with any form of *do.*

Faulty The judge did *remained* in court.
Revised The judge did *remain* in court.

Modals

The modal helping verbs include *can, could, may,* and *might,* along with several two- and three-word combinations, such as *have to* and *be able to.* (See p. 209 for a list of modals.)

Modals convey various meanings, with these being most common:

- **Ability:** *can, could, be able to*

The equipment *can detect* small vibrations. [Present.]

The equipment could *detect* small vibrations. [Past.]

The equipment is able to *detect small vibrations.* [Present. For past: *was able to.* For future: *will be able to.*]

- **Possibility:** *could, may, might, could/may/might have* + past participle

The equipment could *fail.* [Present.]
The equipment may *fail.* [Present or future.]
The equipment might *fail.* [Present or future.]
The equipment may have *failed.* [Past.]

- **Necessity or obligation:** *must, have to, be supposed to*

The lab must *purchase* a backup. [Present or future.]

The lab has to *purchase* a backup. [Present or future. Past: *had to.*]

The lab will have to *purchase* a backup. [Future.]

The lab is supposed to *purchase* a backup. [Present. Past: *was supposed to.*]

- **Permission:** *may, can, could*

The lab may *spend* the money. [Present or future.]

The lab can *spend* the money. [Present or future.]

The lab could *spend* the money. [Present or future, more tentative.]

The school then announced that the lab could *spend* the money. [Past.]

- **Intention:** *will, shall, would*

The lab will *spend* the money. [Future.]

Shall we *offer* advice? [Future. Use *shall* for questions requesting opinion or consent.]

We knew we would *offer* advice. [Past.]

- **Request:** *could, can, would*

Could [or can or would] you please *obtain* a bid? [Present or future.]

- **Advisability:** *should, had better, ought to, should have* + past participle

You should *obtain* three bids. [Present or future.]
You had better *obtain* three bids. [Present or future.]
You ought to *obtain* three bids. [Present or future.]
You should have *obtained* three bids. [Past.]

- **Past habit:** *would, used to*

In years past we would *obtain* five bids.
We used to *obtain* five bids.

The following conventions govern the combination of modals and main verbs shown in the examples:

- One-word modals do not change form to show a change in subject: *I could run, she could run.* Most two- and three-word modals do change form, like other helping verbs: *I have to run, she has to run.*
- Modals can sometimes indicate past, present, or future time, occasionally with a word change (*can* to *could,* for instance) or with a form change in a two- or three-word modal (such as *is/was able to*).
- For present or future time, modals are used with the plain form of the main verb: *he can go, I might drive, I will be able to drive.* For past time, some modals change spelling (especially *can* to *could*), and others add *have* before the past participle of the main verb: *might have driven.*
- Don't use *to* between a one-word modal and the main verb: *can drive,* not *can to drive.* (Most of the two- and three-word modals do include *to: ought to drive.*)
- Don't use two one-word modals together: *I will be able to drive,* not *I will can drive.*

ANSWERS: EXERCISE 4

1. Each year thousands of new readers have been discovering Agatha Christie's mysteries.
2. The books were written by a prim woman who had worked as a nurse during World War I.
3. Christie never expected that her play *The Mousetrap* would be performed for decades.
4. During her life Christie was always complaining about movie versions of her stories.
5. Readers of her stories have been delighted to be baffled by her.

ANSWERS: EXERCISE 5

1. A report from the Bureau of the Census has confirmed a widening gap between rich and poor.
2. As suspected, the percentage of people below the poverty level did increase over the last decade.
3. More than 17 percent of the population is making 5 percent of all the income.
4. About 1 percent of the population will be keeping (*or* will keep) an average of $500,0000 apiece after taxes.
5. Sentence correct.

Exercise 4
Using helping verbs

Add helping verbs in the following sentences where they are needed for standard English.

1. Each year thousands of new readers been discovering Agatha Christie's mysteries.
2. The books written by a prim woman who had worked as a nurse during World War I.
3. Christie never expected that her play *The Mousetrap* be performed for decades.
4. During her life Christie always complaining about movie versions of her stories.
5. Readers of her stories been delighted to be baffled by her.

Exercise 5
Revising: Helping verbs plus main verbs ESL

Revise the following sentences so that helping verbs and main verbs are used correctly. Circle the number of any sentence that is already correct.

Example:

The college testing service has test as many as 500 students at one time.

The college testing service has *tested* as many as 500 students at one time.

1. A report from the Bureau of the Census has confirm a widening gap between rich and poor.
2. As suspected, the percentage of people below the poverty level did increased over the last decade.
3. More than 17 percent of the population is make 5 percent of all the income.
4. About 1 percent of the population will keeping an average of $500,000 apiece after taxes.
5. The other 99 percent all together may retain about $300,000.
6. More than 80 percent of American families will may make less than $65,000 per family this year.
7. Fewer than 5 percent of families could to make more than $110,000 per family.
8. At the same time that the gap is widen, those in the 80 percent are work longer hours.
9. Many workers once might have change jobs to increase their pay.
10. Now these workers are remain with the jobs they have.

6. More than 80 percent of American families will make (*or* may make) less than $65,000 per family this year.
7. Fewer than 5 percent of families could make more than $110,000 per family.
8. At the same time that the gap is widening, those in the 80 percent are working longer hours.
9. Many workers once might have changed jobs to increase their pay.
10. Now these workers are remaining with the jobs they have.

t
7e

TENSE

Tense shows the time of a verb's action. The table on the next page defines and illustrates the tense forms for a regular verb in the active voice. (See pp. 209 and 230 on regular verbs and voice.)

7e Use the appropriate tense to express your meaning.

Many errors in verb tense are actually errors in verb form like those discussed earlier. Still, the present tense, the perfect tenses, and the progressive tenses can cause problems.

1 Observe the special uses of the present tense.

Most academic and business writing uses the past tense (*the rebellion occurred*), but the present tense has several distinctive uses.

Action occurring now
She *understands* the problem.
We *define* the problem differently.

Habitual or recurring action
Banks regularly *undergo* audits.
The audits *monitor* the banks' activities.

A general truth
The mills of the gods *grind* slowly.
The earth *is* round.

MEMORY AID

To help students remember special uses of the present tense, you might suggest that they use the acronym FACT as a memory aid:

Future time
Action recurring
Content of literature
Truth, general

TRANSPARENCY MASTER 7.2

t
7e

INVENTED VERBS

Concoct some plausible English verbs like *fliggle, displore,* or *frink.* Ask students to work out their forms and use them in all possible tenses. Students might then work in groups on the computer or on paper to concoct a story around their invented verb.

TIME LINES (ESL)

Tense use varies widely among languages; as a result, ESL students may have difficulty distinguishing tenses. Point out that the present perfect tense relates past events to present time and implies that an event may continue to occur in the future. Certain time words often accompany the present perfect, including *already, before, for, recently, (ever) since, so far,* and *ever* and *yet* (for questions and negative statements such as *Have you ever seen that dancer perform? No, I haven't seen her yet, but hope to*). Students often find time lines helpful in distinguishing the present perfect from the simple past tense:

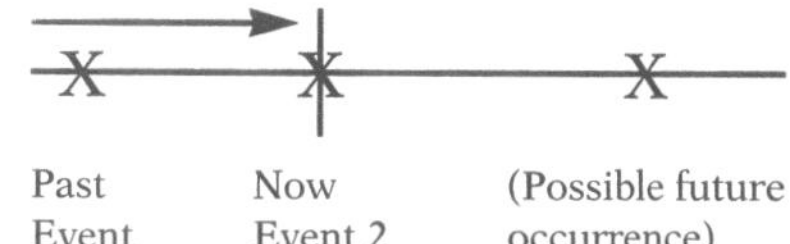

Past Event — Now Event 2 — (Possible future occurrence)

Past: The dancer performed here a year ago.

Present perfect: Critics have written about it ever since (and may continue to write about it).

In *The Advanced Grammar Book* (Boston: Heinle, 1991), Jocelyn Steer and Karen Carlisi include useful time lines for distinguishing tenses.

Tenses of a regular verb (active voice)

Present Action that is occurring now, occurs habitually, or is generally true

Simple present Plain form or *-s* form

I *walk.*
You/we/they *walk.*
He/she/it *walks.*

Present progressive *Am, is,* or *are* plus *-ing* form

I *am walking.*
You/we/they *are walking.*
He/she/it *is walking.*

Past Action that occurred before now

Simple past Past-tense form (*-d* or *-ed*)

I/he/she/it *walked.*
You/we/they *walked.*

Past progressive *Was* or *were* plus *-ing* form

I/he/she/it *was walking.*
You/we/they *were walking.*

Future Action that will occur in the future

Simple future Plain form plus *will*

I/you/he/she/it/we/they *will walk*

Future progressive *Will be* plus *-ing* form

I/you/he/she/it/we/they *will be walking.*

Present perfect Action that began in the past and is linked to the present

Present perfect *Have* or *has* plus past participle (*-d* or *-ed*)

I/you/we/they *have walked.*
He/she/it *has walked.*

Present perfect progressive *Have been* or *has been* plus *-ing* form

I/you/we/they *have been walking.*
He/she/it *has been walking.*

Past perfect Action that was completed before another past action

Past perfect *Had* plus past participle (*-d* or *-ed*)

I/you/he/she/it/we/they *had walked.*

Past perfect progressive *Had been* plus *-ing* form

I/you/he/she/it/we/they *had been walking.*

Future perfect Action that will be completed before another future action

Future perfect *Will have* plus past participle (*-d* or *-ed*)

I/you/he/she/it/we/they *will have walked.*

Future perfect progressive *Will have been* plus *-ing* form

I/you/he/she/it/we/they *will have been walking.*

Discussion of literature, film, and so on (see also p. 680)

Huckleberry Finn *has* adventures we all envy.
In that article the author *examines* several causes of crime.

Future time

Next week we *draft* a new budget.
Funding *ends* in less than a year.

(Time is really indicated here by *Next week* and *in less than a year.*)

2 Observe the uses of the perfect tenses.

The perfect tenses generally indicate action completed before another specific time or action. (The term *perfect* derives from the Latin *perfectus,* "completed.") The present perfect tense also indicates action begun in the past and continued into the present. The perfect tenses consist of a form of *have* plus the verb's past participle.

present perfect
The dancer *has performed* here only once. [The action is completed at the time of the statement.]

present perfect
Critics *have written* about the performance ever since. [The action began in the past and continues now.]

past perfect
The dancer *had trained* in Asia before his performance. [The action was completed before another past action.]

future perfect
He *will have performed* here again by next month. [The action begins now or in the future and will be completed by a specified time in the future.]

ESL With the present perfect tense, the words *since* and *for* are followed by different information. After *since,* give a specific point in time: *The United States has been a member of the United Nations since 1945.* After *for,* give a span of time: *The United States has been a member of the United Nations for half a century.*

3 Observe the uses of the progressive tenses. ESL

The progressive tenses indicate continuing (therefore progressive) action. They consist of a form of *be* plus the verb's *-ing* form (present participle). (The words *be* and *been* must be combined with other helping verbs. See p. 215.)

present progressive
The economy *is improving.*

past progressive
Last year the economy *was stagnating.*

future progressive
Economists *will be watching* for signs of growth.

THE USE OF PROGRESSIVE TENSES (ESL)

Some languages (for example, Arabic) use progressive tenses to express habitual activities, whereas English uses simple tenses. Explain to students that in English, the progressive tenses emphasize the *duration* or *continuous nature* of an action. Perfect progressive tenses are also used for ongoing action that is intersected by another action.

present perfect progressive
The government *has been expecting* an upturn.

past perfect progressive
Various indicators *had been suggesting* improvement.

future perfect progressive
By the end of this year, investors *will have been watching* the markets nervously for nearly a decade.

NOTE Verbs that express unchanging states (especially mental states) rather than physical actions do not usually appear in the progressive tenses. These verbs include *adore, appear, believe, belong, care, hate, have, hear, know, like, love, mean, need, own, prefer, remember, see, sound, taste, think, understand,* and *want.*

FAULTY She *is wanting* to study ethics.
REVISED She *wants* to study ethics.

t seq
7f

EXCEPTIONS (ESL)

As the text notes, verbs that express mental states or activities are generally not used in the progressive tenses. However, there are some exceptions:

see = *date* or *consult: Marsha isn't seeing John any more. Gina is seeing a doctor about her allergies.*
think = *consider: I'm thinking about taking a literature course next term.*
cumulative effects: *I'm understanding English better and better as I go through this course.*

COLLABORATIVE LEARNING

IMAGINARY REPORTING

A good activity is to ask students, either individually or in groups, to construct some imaginary event (an episode from a TV show, a football game, a newscast) and recount its chronology using the correct sequence of tenses. Students can work together to revise their reported events, and volunteer groups might read their responses to the class or post them on the network.

CREATING A STORY

Write on the board a sentence containing one or more characters and an action. Here are some examples:

As he rounded the corner, John heard a loud noise, somewhere between a crash and a bang.
As he came into the classroom, Jim noticed that Carolyn was already there reviewing her notes.

Ask students to form groups, and then require the groups to write paragraph-length (seven to eight sentences) stories. The stories

7f Use the appropriate sequence of verb tenses.

The term **sequence of tenses** refers to the relation between the verb tense in a main clause and the verb tense in a subordinate clause or phrase. The tenses need not be identical as long as they reflect changes in actual or relative time: in *He had left before I arrived,* the verbs are in clear sequence. The difficulties with tense sequence are discussed below. (For a discussion of tense shifts—changes *not* required by meaning—see pp. 292–93.)

1 Use the appropriate tense sequence with infinitives.

The tense of an infinitive is determined by the tense of the verb in the predicate. The **present infinitive** is the verb's plain form preceded by *to* (see p. 178). It indicates action *at the same time* as or *later* than that of the verb.

verb: present; infinitive: present
The researcher *expects to see* change.

verb: present perfect; infinitive: present
She *would have liked to see* [not *to have seen*] change before now.

The verb's **perfect infinitive** consists of *to have* followed by the past participle, as in *to have talked, to have won.* It indicates action *earlier* than that of the verb.

verb: present; infinitive: perfect
Other researchers *would like* [not *would have liked*] *to have seen* change as well.

verb: present — infinitive: perfect

They *judge* the data *to have been interpreted* correctly.

Use the appropriate tense sequence with participles.

The tense of a participle is determined by the tense of the verb in the predicate. The present participle shows action occurring *at the same time* as that of the verb.

participle: present — verb: past perfect

Testing a large group, the researcher *had posed* multiple-choice questions.

The past participle and the present perfect participle show action occurring *earlier* than that of the verb.

participle: past — verb: past

Prepared by earlier failures, she *knew* not to ask open questions.

participle: present perfect — verb: past

Having tested many people, she *understood* the process.

Use the appropriate tense sequence with the past or past perfect tense.

When the verb in the main clause is in the past or past perfect tense, the verb in the subordinate clause must also be past or past perfect.

main clause: past — subordinate clause: past

The researchers *discovered* that people *varied* widely in their knowledge of public events.

main clause: past — subordinate clause: past perfect

The variation *occurred* because respondents *had been born* in different decades.

main clause: past perfect — subordinate clause: past

None of them *had been born* when Warren G. Harding *was* President.

Exception Always use the present tense for a general truth, such as *The earth is round.*

main clause: past — subordinate clause: present

Most *understood* that popular Presidents *are* not necessarily good Presidents.

Use the appropriate tense sequence in conditional sentences. ESL

A **conditional sentence** states a factual relation between cause and effect, makes a prediction, or speculates about what might hap-

should begin with the sentence you have provided, and individual members of the group should add sentences to the narrative one by one until it is complete. The final story should maintain a correct sequence of tenses, contain proper verb forms, and use a variety of action verbs. Students may wish to use ideas or episodes from their journals in completing this exercise.

t seq

7f

COMPUTER EXERCISE

Both the "Creating a Story" and the "Discussion Story" exercises work well in a networked computer classroom. In each case, the teacher posts the opening prompt for the story on the network, then asks students to work in chatrooms or to work individually and e-mail their responses. Periodically, the teacher might post the entire story (or one group's version of the story) for the whole class to read and discuss. See Susan Lang's essay on "Using Computers to Teach Writing" beginning on page IAE-63 for related activities.

DISCUSSION STORY

Put a lead sentence (as in "Creating a Story"—above) on the board, and ask the class as a whole to decide on the events that follow it. Summarize the events briefly; then ask groups of students to write out the story as in the preceding activity, making it as vivid as they can. This entire exercise will provide both oral and written practice with verb tense and sequence.

pen. Such a sentence usually consists of a subordinate clause beginning with *if, when,* or *unless* along with a main clause stating the result. The three kinds of conditional sentences use distinctive verbs.

Factual relation

For statements that something always or usually happens whenever something else happens, use the present tense in both clauses.

subordinate clause: present — main clause: present

When a voter *casts* a ballot, he or she *has* complete privacy.

If the linked events occurred in the past, use the past tense in both clauses.

subordinate clause: past — main clause: past

When voters *registered* in some states, they *had* to pay a poll tax.

Prediction

For a prediction, generally use the present tense in the subordinate clause and the future tense in the main clause.

subordinate clause: present — main clause: future

Unless citizens *regain* faith in politics, they *will* not *vote.*

Sometimes the verb in the main clause consists of *may, can, should,* or *might* plus the verb's plain form: *If citizens regain faith, they may vote.*

Speculation

Speculations are mainly of two kinds, each with its own verb pattern. For events that are possible in the present, though unlikely, use the past tense in the subordinate clause and *would, could,* or *might* plus the verb's plain form in the main clause.

subordinate clause: past — main clause: *would* + verb

If voters *had* more confidence, they *would vote* more often.

Use *were* instead of *was* when the subject is *I, he, she, it,* or a singular noun. (See p. 228 for more on this distinctive verb form.)

subordinate clause: past — main clause: *would* + verb

If the voter *were* more confident, he or she *would vote* more often.

For events that are impossible in the present, that are contrary to fact, use the same forms as above (including the distinctive *were* when applicable).

subordinate clause: past — main clause: *might* + verb

If Lincoln *were* alive, he *might inspire* confidence.

For events that were impossible in the past, use the past perfect tense in the subordinate clause and *would, could,* or *might* plus the present perfect tense in the main clause.

subordinate clause: past perfect — main clause: *might* + present perfect

If Lincoln *had lived* past the Civil War, he *might have helped* stabilize the country.

Use the appropriate tense sequence with indirect quotations. ESL

An **indirect quotation** reports what someone said or wrote but not in the exact words and not in quotation marks: *Lincoln said that events had controlled him* (quotation: "Events have controlled me"). An indirect quotation generally appears in a subordinate clause (underlined above), with certain conventions governing verb tense in most cases.

When the verb in the main clause is in the present tense, the verb in the indirect quotation (subordinate clause) is in the same tense as the original quotation.

main clause: present — indirect quotation: present

Haworth *says* that Lincoln *is* our noblest national hero. [Quotation: "Lincoln *is* our noblest national hero."]

main clause: present — indirect quotation: past

He *says* that Lincoln *was* a complicated person. [Quotation: "Lincoln *was* a complicated person."]

When the verb in the main clause is in the past tense, the verb in the indirect quotation usually changes tense from the original quotation. Present tense changes to past tense.

main clause: past — indirect quotation: past

An assistant to Lincoln *said* that the President *was* always generous. [Quotation: "The President *is* always generous."]

Past tense and present tense change to past perfect tense. (Past perfect tense does not change.)

main clause: past — indirect quotation: past perfect

Lincoln *said* that events *had controlled* him. [Quotation: "Events *have controlled* me."]

When the direct quotation states a general truth or reports a situation that is still true, the verb in the indirect quotation remains in the present tense regardless of the verb in the main clause.

main clause: past — indirect quotation: present

Lincoln *said* that right *makes* might. [Quotation: "Right *makes* might."]

Note As several of these examples show, an indirect quotation differs in at least two additional ways from the original quotation: (1) the indirect quotation is usually preceded by *that,* and (2) the indirect quotation changes pronouns, especially from forms of *I* or *we* to forms of *he, she,* or *they.*

ANSWERS: EXERCISE 6

1. Diaries that Adolf Hitler was supposed to have written had surfaced in Germany.
2. Many people believed that the diaries were authentic because a well-known historian had declared them so.
3. However, the historian's evaluation was questioned by other authorities who called the diaries forgeries.
4. They claimed, among other things, that the paper was not old enough to have been used by Hitler.
5. Eventually, the doubters won the debate because they had the best evidence.

Exercise 6

Adjusting tense sequence: Past or past perfect tense

The tenses in each sentence below are in correct sequence. Change the tense of one verb as instructed. Then change the tense of infinitives, participles, and other verbs to restore correct sequence. Some items have more than one possible answer.

Example:

He will call when he reaches his destination. (*Change will call to called.*)

He *called* when he *reached* [or *had reached*] his destination.

1. Diaries that Adolf Hitler is supposed to have written have surfaced in Germany. (*Change have surfaced to had surfaced.*)
2. Many people believe that the diaries are authentic because a well-known historian has declared them so. (*Change believe to believed.*)
3. However, the historian's evaluation has been questioned by other authorities, who call the diaries forgeries. (*Change has been questioned to was questioned.*)
4. They claim, among other things, that the paper is not old enough to have been used by Hitler. (*Change claim to claimed.*)
5. Eventually, the doubters will win the debate because they have the best evidence. (*Change will win to won.*)

ANSWERS: EXERCISE 7

1. When an athlete turns professional, he or she commits to a grueling regimen of mental and physical training.
2. If athletes were less committed, they would disappoint teammates, fans, and themselves.
3. If professional athletes are very lucky, they may play until age forty.
4. Unless an athlete achieves celebrity status, he or she will have few employment choices after retirement.

Exercise 7

Revising: Tense sequence with conditional sentences ESL

Supply the appropriate tense for each verb in parentheses below.

Example:

If Babe Ruth or Jim Thorpe (*be*) athletes today, they (*remind*) us that even sports heroes must contend with a harsh reality.

If Babe Ruth or Jim Thorpe *were* athletes today, they *might* (or *could* or *would*) remind us that even sports heroes must contend with a harsh reality.

1. When an athlete (*turn*) professional, he or she commits to a grueling regimen of mental and physical training.

2. If athletes (*be*) less committed, they (*disappoint*) teammates, fans, and themselves.
3. If professional athletes (*be*) very lucky, they may play until age forty.
4. Unless an athlete achieves celebrity status, he or she (*have*) few employment choices after retirement.
5. If professional sports (*be*) less risky, athletes (*have*) longer careers and more choices after retirement.

Exercise 8
Using verb tenses in indirect quotations ESL

Each passage below comes from the British essayist Charles Lamb (1775–1834). Indirectly quote each passage in a sentence of your own, using the words given in parentheses.

Example:

"The greatest pleasure I know is to do a good action by stealth and to have it found out by accident." (*Charles Lamb said that. . . .*)

Charles Lamb said that the greatest pleasure he *knew was* to do a good action by stealth and to have it found out by accident.

1. "Coleridge holds that a man cannot have a pure mind who refuses apple-dumplings." (*Lamb cited Coleridge's observation that. . . .*)
2. "The human species, according to the best theory I can form of it, is composed of two distinct races, the men who borrow, and the men who lend." (*Lamb wrote that. . . .*)
3. "Nothing puzzles me more than time and space; and yet nothing troubles me less, as I never think about them." (*He muses that. . . .*)
4. "When I am not walking, I am reading; I cannot sit and think." (*He admitted that. . . .*)
5. "Sentimentally I am disposed to harmony. But organically I am incapable of a tune." (*He confesses that. . . .*)

MOOD

Mood in grammar is a verb form that indicates the writer's or speaker's attitude toward what he or she is saying. The **indicative mood** states a fact or opinion or asks a question.

The theater *needs* help. [Opinion.]
The ceiling is *falling* in. [Fact.]
Will you *contribute* to the theater? [Question.]

The **imperative mood** expresses a command or gives a direction. It omits the subject of the sentence, *you*.

Help the theater. [Command.]
Send contributions to the theater. [Direction.]

5. If professional sports were less risky, athletes would have longer careers and more choices after retirement.

vb 7

COLLABORATIVE LEARNING

Ask students to complete Exercise 8 individually and compare answers in pairs. Then have each pair create five additional examples, in which students take turns inventing direct quotes and then rephrasing them in indirect quotations. This exercise also works well in a computer classroom.

ANSWERS: EXERCISE 8

1. Lamb cited Coleridge's observation that a man could not have a pure mind who refused apple-dumplings.
2. Lamb wrote that the human species, according to the best theory he could form of it, was composed of two distinct races, the men who borrowed, and the men who lent.
3. He muses that nothing puzzles him more than time and space; and yet nothing troubles him less, as he never thinks about them.
4. He admitted that when he was not walking, he was reading; he could not sit and think.
5. He confesses that he is sentimentally disposed to harmony but organically incapable of a tune.

COLLABORATIVE LEARNING

Ask students to work together to scan their own work for examples of the indicative, imperative, and subjunctive moods. Have each group put one or two examples on the board, on transparencies, or on the network for the class.

vb
7g

The **subjunctive mood** expresses a suggestion, a requirement, or a desire, or it states a condition that is contrary to fact (that is, imaginary or hypothetical). The subjunctive mood uses distinctive verb forms.

- **Suggestion or requirement:** plain form with all subjects.

  The manager asked that he *donate* money. [Suggestion.]
  Rules require that every donation *be* mailed. [Requirement.]

- **Desire or present condition contrary to fact:** past tense; for *be,* the past tense *were.*

  We wish that the theater *had* more money. [Desire.]

  It would be in better shape if it *were* better funded. [Present condition contrary to fact.]

- **Past condition contrary to fact:** past perfect.

  The theater could have been better funded if it *had been* better managed.

With conditions contrary to fact, the verb in the main clause also expresses the imaginary or hypothetical with the helping verb *could* or *would,* as in the last two sample sentences above.

(For a discussion of keeping mood consistent within and among sentences, see p. 293.)

THE DISAPPEARING SUBJUNCTIVE

The blurring of the subjunctive mood is swiftly spreading; in another half-century it may be gone in all but the most formal writing. Linguistically this change is understandable; English has simplified its forms more than most other languages. The disappearance of the subjunctive is another example of this natural process occurring. A very readable book on this subject is Jean Aitchison's *Language Change: Progress or Decay?* (Suffolk: Fontana, 1981).

7g Use the subjunctive verb forms appropriately.

Contemporary English uses distinctive subjunctive verb forms in only a few constructions and idioms. (For the sequence of tenses in many subjunctive sentences, see pp. 223–25.)

Use the subjunctive in contrary-to-fact clauses beginning with *if* or expressing desire.

If the theater *were* saved, the town would benefit.
We all wish the theater *were* not so decrepit.
I wish I *were* able to donate money.

NOTE The indicative form *was* (*We all wish the theater was not so decrepit*) is common in speech and in some informal writing, but the subjunctive *were* is usual in formal English.

Not all clauses beginning with *if* express conditions contrary to fact. In the sentence *If Joe is out of town, he hasn't heard the news,* the verb *is* is correct because the clause refers to a condition presumed to exist.

Use *would* or *could* only in the main clause of a conditional statement.

The helping verb *would* or *could* appears in the main clause of a sentence expressing a condition contrary to fact. The helping verb does not appear in the subordinate clause beginning with *if.*

Not Many people would have helped if they *would have* known.
But Many people would have helped if they *had* known.

Use the subjunctive in *that* clauses following verbs that demand, request, or recommend.

Verbs such as *ask, demand, insist, mandate, require, recommend, request, require, suggest,* and *urge* indicate demand or suggestion. They often precede subordinate clauses beginning with *that* and containing the substance of the demand or suggestion. The verb in such a *that* clause should be in the subjunctive mood.

The board urged that everyone *contribute.*
The members insisted that they themselves *be* donors.
They suggested that each *donate* both time and money.

Note These constructions have widely used alternative forms that do not require the subjunctive, such as *The board urged everyone to contribute* or *The members insisted on donating.*

4 Use the subjunctive in some set phrases and idioms.

Several English expressions commonly use the subjunctive. For example:

Come rain or *come* shine.
Be that as it may.
The people *be* damned.

Exercise 9
Revising: Subjunctive mood

Revise the following sentences with appropriate subjunctive verb forms.

Example:
I would help the old man if I was able to reach him.
I would help the old man if I *were* able to reach him.

1. If John Hawkins would have known of the dangerous side effects of smoking tobacco, would he have introduced the dried plant to England in 1565?

COLLABORATIVE LEARNING

If students are struggling with the subjunctive mood, ask them to work in small groups on Exercise 9, then ask each group to compose three additional sentences in the subjunctive tense.

ANSWERS: EXERCISE 9

1. If John Hawkins had known of the dangerous side effects of smoking tobacco, would he have introduced the dried plant to England in 1565?

2. Hawkins noted that if a Florida Indian were to travel for several days, he would smoke tobacco to satisfy his hunger and thirst.
3. Early tobacco growers feared that their product would not gain acceptance unless it were perceived as healthful.
4. To prevent fires, in 1646 the General Court of Massachusetts passed a law requiring that a colonist smoke tobacco only if he were five miles from any town.
5. To prevent decadence, in 1647 Connecticut passed a law mandating that one's smoking of tobacco be limited to once a day in one's own home.

PASSIVE SENTENCES—COUNT THE WORDS

Write on the board a number of sentences in the active voice, the sentences ranging from simple to relatively complex. Ask students to change the sentences into the passive voice and then to count the number of words in each version. Finally, ask students to read some of the passive sentences aloud and comment on their effectiveness. This exercise will allow you to check students' understanding of the passive voice and at the same time demonstrate its wordiness.

PROBLEMS WITH THE PAST PARTICIPLE (ESL)

Not all languages include a passive voice. As a result, ESL students are not always certain about when passive voice is appropriate. Also, because ESL students do not always hear the past-participle *-ed* ending, particularly when *-ed* sounds like [t], they may omit *-ed* in writing passive voice. Encourage students to listen for the use of the passive voice *-ed* ending in political speeches or in news programs or documentaries. Unit 5 of Carroll Washington Pollock, *Communicate What You Mean: Grammar for High-Level ESL Students* (Englewood Cliffs: Prentice-Hall, 1982), and Chapter 11 of Jocelyn Steer and Karen Carlisi, *The Advanced Grammar Book* (Boston: Heinle, 1991), include useful exercises both in writing and in determining when to use passive voice.

2. Hawkins noted that if a Florida Indian was to travel for several days, he would have smoked tobacco to satisfy his hunger and thirst.
3. Early tobacco growers feared that their product would not gain acceptance unless it was perceived as healthful.
4. To prevent fires, in 1646 the General Court of Massachusetts passed a law requiring that a colonist smoked tobacco only if he was five miles from any town.
5. To prevent decadence, in 1647 Connecticut passed a law mandating that one's smoking of tobacco was limited to once a day in one's own home.

VOICE

The **voice** of a verb tells whether the subject of the sentence performs the action (**active voice**) or is acted upon (**passive voice**). See the illustrations in the box opposite. In the passive voice, the actual actor may be named in a prepositional phrase (such as *by the city*) or may be omitted.

ESL A passive verb always consists of a form of *be* plus the past participle of the main verb: *rents are controlled, people were inspired.* Other helping verbs must also be used with *be, being,* and *been: rents have been controlled, people would have been inspired.* Only a transitive verb (one that takes an object) may be used in the passive voice. (See pp. 215–16.)

Converting active to passive

To change a transitive verb from active to passive voice, convert either an indirect object or a direct object into the subject of the sentence, and use the passive verb form.

	subject	transitive verb	indirect object	direct object
ACTIVE	The city	gives	tenants	leases.
	new subject	passive verb	direct object	
PASSIVE	Tenants	are given	leases.	
	new subject	passive verb	indirect object	old subject
	Leases	are given	tenants	by the city.

Converting passive to active

To change a passive verb to active, name the verb's actor as subject, use an active verb form, and convert the old subject into an object.

	subject	passive verb	
PASSIVE	Tenants	are protected	by leases.
	new subject	active verb	old subject = object
ACTIVE	Leases	protect	tenants.

Active and passive voice

ACTIVE VOICE The subject acts.

The city controls rents.

PASSIVE VOICE The subject is acted upon.

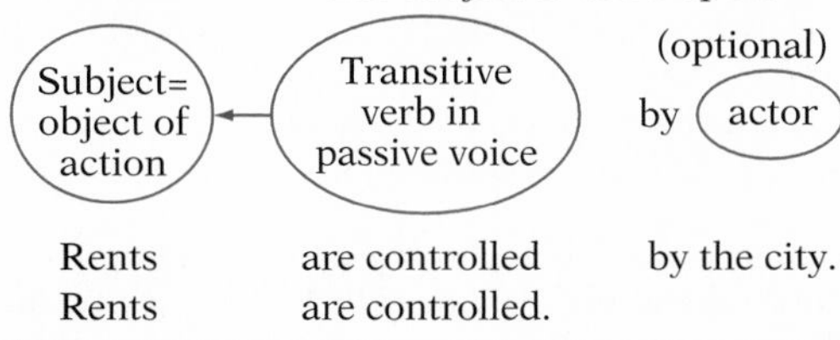

Rents are controlled by the city.
Rents are controlled.

TRANSPARENCY MASTER 7.3

7h Generally, prefer the active voice. Use the passive voice when the actor is unknown or unimportant.

Because the passive omits or de-emphasizes the actor (the performer of the verb's action), it can deprive writing of vigor and is often vague or confusing. The active voice is usually stronger, clearer, and more forthright.

WEAK PASSIVE The *Internet is used* for research by many scholars, and its *expansion* to the general public *has been criticized* by some.

STRONG ACTIVE Many *scholars use* the Internet for research, and *some have criticized* its expansion to the general public.

The passive voice is useful in two situations: when the actor is unknown and when the actor is unimportant or less important than the object of the action.

> The Internet *was established* in 1969 by the US Department of Defense. The network *has* now *been extended* internationally to governments, universities, foundations, corporations, and private individuals. [In the first sentence the writer wishes to stress the Internet rather than the Department of Defense. In the second sentence the actor is unknown or too complicated to name.]

> After the solution *had been cooled* to 10°C, the acid *was added.* [The person who cooled and added, perhaps the writer, is less important than the facts that the solution was cooled and acid was added. Passive sentences are common in scientific writing.]

Except in such situations, however, you should prefer the active voice in your writing.

COLLABORATIVE LEARNING

PASSIVE SENTENCES—FINDING PASSAGES

Have students, working in groups, locate passive sentences in an essay from a reader or a similar source. Ask them to decide if the passive voice provides emphasis appropriate for the essay or if the active voice would be better. Tell them to be ready to defend their choice of the passive or to offer a revision of the sentence in the active voice. Have each group present its most hotly debated case to the class.

SCIENTIFIC STYLE

Many editors of scientific journals now recommend that authors use first person pronouns and active verbs where possible instead of relying on the passive. They recommend that authors use the passive when the performer of the action is unknown or unimportant or when emphasis should be placed on the recipient of the action. Students writing in science courses should check with their instructors to see what stylistic guide they should follow; see also 40c and 40d.

COLLABORATIVE LEARNING

Ask students to work on Exercise 10 in small groups, then ask each group to compose additional examples of active- and passive-voiced sentences.

ANSWERS: EXERCISE 10

Possible answers

1. When engineers built the Eiffel Tower in 1889, the French thought it was ugly.
2. At that time industrial technology was still resisted by many people.
3. This technology was epitomized by the tower's naked steel construction.
4. People expected beautiful ornament to grace fine buildings.
5. Further, people could not even call the tower a building because it had no solid walls.

Exercise 10
Converting between active and passive voices

To practice using the two voices of the verb, convert the following sentences from active to passive or from passive to active. (In converting from passive to active, you may have to add a subject for the new sentence.) Which version of each sentence seems more effective, and why? (For additional exercises with the passive voice, see pp. 195, 342, and 479.)

Example:
The aspiring actor was discovered in a nightclub.
A *talent scout discovered* the aspiring actor in a nightclub.

1. When the Eiffel Tower was built in 1889, it was thought by the French to be ugly.
2. At that time many people still resisted industrial technology.
3. The tower's naked steel construction epitomized this technology.
4. Beautiful ornament was expected to grace fine buildings.
5. Further, the tower could not even be called a building because it had no solid walls.

CHOOSING BETWEEN GERUNDS AND INFINITIVES (ESL)

ESL students generally find gerunds more problematic than infinitives, perhaps because gerunds occur less frequently; as a result, students may use infinitives where gerunds are required. According to Marianne Celce-Murcia and Diane Larsen-Freeman in *The Grammar Book* (Boston: Heinle, 1983), gerunds tend to express "fulfilled action," whereas infinitives tend to express "unfulfilled action":

I *enjoyed meeting* your brother at the party. (The action, the meeting, was fulfilled.)
I *hoped to meet* your brother at the party. (The action, the hoped-for meeting, was unfulfilled.)
I'll always *remember calling* my son when he was overseas. (The action, calling, was fulfilled before the remembering.)
I *remembered to call* my son on his birthday. (The action, calling, was unfulfilled until after the remembering.)

Refer students who need additional practice distinguishing gerunds and infinitives to Unit 8 of

OTHER COMPLICATIONS

7i Use a gerund or an infinitive after a verb as appropriate. ESL

A **gerund** is the *-ing* form of a verb used as a noun (*opening*). An **infinitive** is the plain form of a verb preceded by *to* (*to open*). (See p. 178 for more on these forms.)

Gerunds and infinitives may follow certain verbs but not others. And sometimes the use of a gerund or infinitive with the same verb changes the meaning of the verb.

Either gerund or infinitive

A gerund or an infinitive may follow these verbs with no significant difference in meaning:

begin	hate	love
can't bear	hesitate	prefer
can't stand	intend	pretend
continue	like	start

The pump began *working*.
The pump began *to work*.

Meaning change with gerund or infinitive

With four verbs, a gerund has quite a different meaning from an infinitive:

forget	stop
remember	try

The engineer stopped *eating*. [He no longer ate.]
The engineer stopped *to eat*. [He stopped in order to eat.]

Gerund, not infinitive

Do not use an infinitive after these verbs:

admit	discuss	mind	recollect
adore	dislike	miss	resent
appreciate	enjoy	postpone	resist
avoid	escape	practice	risk
consider	finish	put off	suggest
deny	imagine	quit	tolerate
detest	keep	recall	understand

Faulty He finished *to eat* lunch.
Revised He finished *eating* lunch.

Infinitive, not gerund

Do not use a gerund after these verbs:

agree	decide	mean	refuse
ask	expect	offer	say
assent	have	plan	wait
beg	hope	pretend	want
claim	manage	promise	wish

Faulty He decided *checking* the pump.
Revised He decided *to check* the pump.

Noun or pronoun + infinitive

Some verbs may be followed by an infinitive alone or by a noun or pronoun and an infinitive. The presence of a noun or pronoun changes the meaning.

ask	dare	need	wish
beg	expect	promise	would like
choose	help	want	

He expected *to watch*.
He expected *his workers to watch*.

Carroll Washington Pollock, *Communicate What You Mean: Grammar for High-Level ESL Students* (Englewood Cliffs: Prentice-Hall, 1982), and Chapter 14 of Jocelyn Steer and Karen Carlisi, *The Advanced Grammar Book* (Boston: Heinle, 1991).

Some verbs *must* be followed by a noun or pronoun before an infinitive:

admonish	encourage	oblige	require
advise	forbid	order	teach
allow	force	permit	tell
cause	hire	persuade	train
challenge	instruct	remind	urge
command	invite	request	warn
convince			

He instructed *his workers to watch.*

Do not use *to* before the infinitive when it follows one of these verbs and a noun or pronoun:

feel	make ("force")
have	see
hear	watch
let	

He let his workers *learn* by observation.

ANSWERS: EXERCISE 11

1. A program called HELP Wanted tries to make citizens take action on behalf of American competitiveness.
2. Officials working on this program hope to improve education for work.
3. American businesses find that their workers need to learn to read.
4. In the next ten years the United States expects to face a shortage of 350,000 scientists.
5. Sentence correct.

Exercise 11
Revising: Verbs plus gerunds or infinitives ESL

Revise the following sentences so that gerunds or infinitives are used correctly with verbs. Circle the number preceding any sentence that is already correct.

Example:
A politician cannot avoid to alienate some voters.
A politician cannot avoid *alienating* some voters.

1. A program called HELP Wanted tries to make citizens to take action on behalf of American competitiveness.
2. Officials working on this program hope improving education for work.
3. American businesses find that their workers need learning to read.
4. In the next ten years the United States expects facing a shortage of 350,000 scientists.
5. HELP Wanted suggests creating a media campaign.

7j Use the appropriate particles with two-word verbs. ESL

Some verbs consist of two words: the verb itself and a **particle,** a preposition or adverb that affects the meaning of the verb. For example:

Look up the answer. [Research the answer.]
Look over the answer. [Examine the answer.]

The meanings of these two-word verbs are often quite different from the meanings of the individual words that make them up. (There are some three-word verbs, too, such as *put up with* and *run out of*.) A good ESL dictionary, such as those listed on page 482, will define two-word verbs for you. It will also tell you whether the verbs may be separated in a sentence, as explained below.

NOTE Many two-word verbs are more common in speech than in more formal academic or business writing. For formal writing, consider using *research* instead of *look up*, *examine* or *inspect* instead of *look over*.

Inseparable two-word verbs

Verbs and particles that may not be separated by any other words include the following:

break down	give up	play around	stay away
catch on	go out with	run across	stay up
come across	go over	run into	take care of
get along	grow up	run out of	turn out
get up	keep on	speak up	turn up at
give in	look into	speak with	work for

FAULTY Children *grow* quickly *up*.

REVISED Children *grow up* quickly.

Separable two-word verbs

Most two-word verbs that take direct objects may be separated by the object:

Parents *help out* their children.
Parents *help* their children *out*.

If the direct object is a pronoun, the pronoun *must* separate the verb from the particle:

FAULTY Parents *help out* them.

REVISED Parents *help* them *out*.

The separable two-word verbs include the following:

bring up	give back	make up	throw out
call off	hand in	point out	try on
call up	hand out	put away	try out
drop off	help out	put back	turn down
fill out	leave out	put off	turn on
fill up	look over	take out	turn up
give away	look up	take over	wrap up

ANSWERS: EXERCISE 12

1. American movies treat everything from going out (I) with someone to making up (S) an ethnic identity, but few people (a) look into their significance.
2. While some viewers stay away (I) from topical films, others (a) turn up at the theater simply because a movie has sparked debate.
3. Some movies aroused such strong responses that theaters were obliged to (c) throw out rowdy spectators *or* throw rowdy spectators out.
4. Filmmakers have always been eager to (c) point out their influence *or* point their influence out to the public.
5. Everyone agrees that filmmakers will (a) keep on creating controversy, if only because it can fill up (S) theaters.

Exercise 12
Revising: Verbs plus particles ESL

Identify any two- or three-word verbs in the sentences below, and indicate whether each is separable (S) or inseparable (I). Then fill the blank with the correct option for placing nouns or pronouns with verbs and particles. Consult an ESL dictionary if necessary.

Example:

Hollywood producers never seem to come up with entirely new plots, but they also never ____ to present the old ones.

a. run out of new ways
b. run new ways out of
c. Either a or b

Hollywood producers never seem to *come up with* (I) entirely new plots, but they also never (a) *run out of new ways* to present the old ones.

1. American movies treat everything from going out with someone to making up an ethnic identity, but few people ____.
   a. look into their significance
   b. look their significance into
   c. Either a or b
2. While some viewers stay away from topical films, others ____ simply because a movie has sparked debate.
   a. turn up at the theater
   b. turn at the theater up
   c. Either a or b
3. Some movies aroused such strong responses that theaters were obliged to ____.
   a. throw out rowdy spectators
   b. throw rowdy spectators out
   c. Either a or b
4. Filmmakers have always been eager to ____ to the public.
   a. point out their influence
   b. point their influence out
   c. Either a or b
5. Everyone agrees that filmmakers will ____, if only because it can fill up theaters.
   a. keep on creating controversy
   b. keep creating controversy on
   c. Either a or b

Exercise 13
Revising: Verb forms, tense, mood

Circle all the verbs and verbals in the following paragraph and correct their form, tense, or mood if necessary.

For centuries the natives of Melanesia, a group of islands laying northeast of Australia, have practice an unusual religion. It began in the eighteenth century when European explorers first have visited the islands. The natives were fascinated by the rich goods or "cargo" possessed by the explorers. They saw the wealth as treasures of the gods, and cargo cults eventually had arised among them. Over the centuries some Melanesians turned to Christianity in the belief that the white man's religion will bring them the white man's treasures. During World War II, American soldiers, having arrived by boat and airplane to have occupied some of the islands, introduced new and even more wonderful cargo. Even today some leaders of the cargo cults insist that the airplane is worship as a vehicle of the Melanesians' future salvation.

Note See page 264 for an exercise involving verbs along with other aspects of grammar.

ANSWERS: EXERCISE 13

For centuries the natives of Melanesia, a group of islands (lying) northeast of Australia, (have practiced) an unusual religion. It (began) in the eighteenth century when European explorers first (visited) the islands. The natives (were fascinated) by the rich goods or "cargo" (possessed) by the explorers. They (saw) the wealth as treasures of the gods, and cargo cults eventually (arose) among them. Over the centuries some Melanesians (turned) to Christianity in the belief that the white man's religion (would bring) them the white man's treasures. During World War II, American soldiers, (having arrived) by boat and airplane (to occupy) some of the islands, (introduced) new and even more wonderful cargo. Even today some leaders of the cargo cults (insist) that the airplane (be worshipped) as a vehicle of the Melanesians' future salvation.

COLLABORATIVE LEARNING

Ask students to compare their responses to Exercise 13 and then to circle and revise the verbs and verbals in one paragraph from each student's work. This kind of application of the skills learned in an exercise to examples from students' own work can be extremely beneficial.

HIGHLIGHTS

Some students may have difficulty with basic subject-verb agreement, particularly with the *-s* or *-es* endings that mark plural nouns and singular verbs in English. Almost all students encounter problems with subject-verb and pronoun-antecedent agreement when they begin writing complicated, information-filled sentences. This chapter addresses the needs of both groups of writers, paying special attention to sentence structures that make it difficult for student writers to determine the correct relationship in number between subjects and verbs or pronouns and antecedents.

Rather than treating agreement problems as errors resulting from ignorance, the chapter treats such problems as areas requiring special attention, even by experienced writers. Among the troublesome structures covered are compound subjects, collective nouns, relative and indefinite pronouns, phrases like "one of the," and widely separated subjects and verbs.

Recent changes in the language have given rise to some confusion over pronoun-antecedent agreement with indefinite pronouns. Moreover, in English, subjects that are singular in form, like *audience* or *the faculty,* may be plural in meaning. In speech, even educated speakers sometimes treat indefinite pronouns like *anybody* and *everybody* as plural: "Everybody ought to pay attention to their own business." This change in part reflects a desire to avoid the generic *he,* a form of usage many people regard as sexist. The discussions present alternatives designed to avoid sexist language, while at the same time making clear the need to treat *everybody, someone,* and the like as singular, at least in the more conservative written medium.

TRANSPARENCY MASTER 8.1

Chapter 8 Agreement

Agreement helps readers understand the relations between elements in a sentence. Subjects and verbs agree in number and person:

More *Japanese Americans* (subject) *live* (verb) in Hawaii and California than elsewhere.

Daniel Inouye (subject) *was* (verb) the first Japanese American in Congress.

Pronouns and their **antecedents**—the words they refer to—agree in person, number, and gender.

Inouye (antecedent) makes *his* (pronoun) home in Hawaii.

Hawaiians (antecedent) value his work for *them.* (pronoun)

Person and number in subject-verb agreement

Person	Number: *Singular*	Number: *Plural*
First	I eat.	We eat.
Second	You eat.	You eat.
Third	He/she/it eats.	They eat.
	The bird eats.	Birds eat.

8a Make subjects and verbs agree in number.

Most subject-verb agreement problems arise when endings are omitted from subjects or verbs or when the relation between sentence parts is uncertain.

 The *-s* and *-es* endings work differently for nouns and verbs.

An *-s* or *-es* ending does opposite things to nouns and verbs: it usually makes a noun *plural,* but it always makes a present-tense verb *singular.* Thus if the subject noun is plural, it will end in *-s* or *-es* and the verb will not. If the subject is singular, it will not end in *-s* and the verb will.

SINGULAR	PLURAL
The boy plays.	The boys play.
The bird soars.	The birds soar.

The only exceptions to these rules involve the nouns that form irregular plurals, such as *child/children, woman/women.* The irregular plural still requires a plural verb: The *children play.*

ESL Most noncount nouns—those that do not form plurals—take singular verbs: *That information is helpful.* (See p. 243 on collective nouns.)

Writers often omit *-s* and *-es* endings from nouns or verbs because they are not pronounced clearly in speech (as in *asks* and *lists*) or because they are not used regularly in some English dialects. However, the endings are required in standard English.

NONSTANDARD	The voter *resist* change.
STANDARD	The voter *resists* change.

Remember that the verb *be* is irregular.

PRESENT TENSE

he, she, it, singular nouns	*is*	all plurals	*are*

PAST TENSE

he, she, it, singular nouns	*was*	all plurals	*were*

NOTE In a verb phrase (main verb plus helping verb), the helping verb sometimes reflects the number of the subject and sometimes does not: *The car does run. The cars do run. The car/cars will run.* The main verb (*run*) does not change in any way.

THE RULE OF ONE -*S* (ESL)

Remind students that this is "the rule of one -*s*"—in the present tense, English sentences require one -*s* in the third person:

Singular noun + verb + *s*
Noun + *s* (plural noun) + verb

Refer students who need additional practice to Unit 3 of Len Fox, *Focus on Editing: A Grammar Workbook for Advanced Writers* (White Plains: Longman, 1992), and Chapter 5 of Alan Meyers, *Writing with Confidence* (5th ed., New York: Longman, 1996).

Summary of subject-verb agreement

- Basic subject-verb agreement (p. 239):

SINGULAR	PLURAL
The kite **flies.**	The kites **fly.**

- Words between subject and verb (below):

  The kite with two tails *flies* badly. The tails of the kite *compete.*
- Subjects joined by *and* (opposite):

  The kite and the bird *are* almost indistinguishable.
- Subjects joined by *or* or *nor* (opposite):

  The kite or the bird *dives.* Kites or birds *fill* the sky.
- Indefinite pronouns as subjects (p. 242):

  No one *knows.* All the spectators *wonder.*
- Collective nouns as subjects (p. 243):

  A flock *appears.* The flock *disperse.*
- Inverted word order (p. 243):

  Is the kite or the bird blue? *Are* the kite and the bird both blue?
- Linking verbs (p. 244):

  The kite *is* a flier and a dipper.
- *Who, which, that* as subjects (p. 244):

  The kite that *flies* longest wins. Kites that *fall* lose.
- Subjects with plural form and singular meaning (p. 244):

  Aeronautics *plays* a role in kite flying.
- Titles and words named as words (p. 245):

  Kite Dynamics *is* one title. Vectors *is* a key word.

WIDELY SEPARATED SUBJECTS AND VERBS

Ask students (working individually or in groups and using the handbook as a guide) to identify the sentence strategies that often result in widely separated subjects and verbs. Then ask them to write in their own words a description of these strategies (i.e., the grammatical rules governing them). Finally, ask students to write sentences using the strategies and containing proper subject-verb agreement. (This exercise can also be used with compound subjects, collective nouns, inverted word order, or other strategies that frequently lead to agreement problems.)

Subject and verb should agree even when other words come between them.

When the subject and verb are interrupted by other words, make sure the verb agrees with the subject.

> A catalog of courses and requirements often *baffles* [not *baffle*] students.

> The requirements stated in the catalog *are* [not *is*] unclear.

NOTE Phrases beginning with *as well as, together with, along with,* and *in addition to* do not change the number of the subject.

The president, as well as the deans, *has* [not *have*] agreed to revise the catalog.

If you really mean *and* in such a sentence, use it. Then the subject is compound, and the verb should be plural: *The president and the deans have agreed to revise the catalog.*

Subjects joined by *and* usually take plural verbs.

Two or more subjects joined by *and* usually take a plural verb, whether one or all of the subjects are singular.

Frost and Roethke *were* contemporaries.

Frost, Roethke, Stevens, and Pound *are* among the great American poets.

Exceptions When the parts of the subject form a single idea or refer to a single person or thing, they take a singular verb.

Avocado and bean sprouts *is* a California sandwich.

When a compound subject is preceded by the adjective *each* or *every,* the verb is usually singular.

Each man, woman, and child *has* a right to be heard.

But a compound subject *followed* by *each* takes a plural verb.

The man and the woman each *have* different problems.

When parts of a subject are joined by *or* or *nor,* the verb agrees with the nearer part.

When all parts of a subject joined by *or* or *nor* are singular, the verb is singular; when all parts are plural, the verb is plural.

Either the painter or the carpenter *knows* the cost.

The cabinets or the bookcases *are* too costly.

When one part of the subject is singular and the other plural, avoid awkwardness by placing the plural part closer to the verb so that the verb is plural.

Awkward Neither the owners nor the contractor *agrees.*

Revised Neither the contractor nor the owners *agree.*

TRUE COMPLEXITY

Sometimes the sample sentences we offer to students by way of illustrating a point of grammar or style seem a bit artificial or a bit too simple. Writers such as Charles Dickens and Henry James offer sentences with considerable variety and flair in structure that can be used either as models themselves or as patterns for sentences with a more contemporary content and cast. The following sentence, from James's preface to *The Princess Casamassima,* illustrates tight control of subject-verb and pronoun-antecedent agreement:

> The troubled life mostly at the center of our subject—whatever our subject, for the artistic hour, happens to be—embraces them [fools] and deals with them for its amusement and its anguish: they are apt largely indeed, on a near view, to be all the cause of its trouble.

Although students often produce grammatically complex sentences, particularly in response to readings, it can be fun and enlightening for them to practice different kinds of complexity. Copy a sentence like this one on the board, on a transparency, or on the network, and ask students to compose sentences that mimic, even parody, its complex structure.

When the subject consists of nouns and pronouns of different person requiring different verb forms, the verb agrees with the nearer part of the subject. Reword if this construction is awkward.

Awkward Either Juarez or I *am* responsible.

Revised Either Juarez *is* responsible, or I *am*.

5 With an indefinite pronoun, use a singular or plural verb as appropriate.

An **indefinite pronoun** is one that does not refer to a specific person or thing. Most indefinite pronouns take a singular verb, but some take a plural verb and some take a singular *or* a plural verb.

Common indefinite pronouns

Singular			Singular or plural	Plural
anybody	everyone	no one	all	both
anyone	everything	nothing	any	few
anything	much	one	more	many
each	neither	somebody	most	several
either	nobody	someone	some	
everybody	none	something		

The singular indefinite pronouns refer to a single unspecified person or thing, and they take a singular verb:

Something *smells*. Neither *is* right.

The plural indefinite pronouns refer to more than one unspecified thing, and they take a plural verb:

Both *are* correct. Several *were* invited.

The other indefinite pronouns take a singular or a plural verb depending on the meaning of the word they refer to. The word may be stated in the sentence:

All of the money *is* reserved for emergencies.

All of the funds *are* reserved for emergencies.

Or the word may be implied:

All *are* planning to attend. [*All* implies "all the people."]

ARE EVERYONE READY?

Though many students will not, at first, hear anything wrong with sentences like "Everyone ought to pay attention to their own business" (a pattern that has wide acceptance in speech), almost all will find sentences like these unacceptable: "Are everyone ready for lunch?" "Do everybody have enough money to buy tickets for the rides?" Anyone who finds the latter sentences acceptable is probably having trouble recognizing the singular and plural forms of verbs. Sample sentences can, therefore, help you identify the real source of a student's problems with agreement.

RESOURCES AND IDEAS

Kolln, Martha. "Everyone's Right to Their Own Language." *College Composition and Communication* 37 (1986): 100–02. The frequency with which students treat indefinite pronouns as plural suggests that the widely accepted rules of usage discussed in this section may in some ways conflict with practice. Kolln takes a radical stance, arguing that "dicta that designate all indefinite pronouns as singular have no basis either in actual usage or in the rules of logic" (102).

Sklar, Elizabeth S. "The Tribunal of Use: Agreement in the Indefinite Constructions." *College Composition and Communication* 39 (1988): 410–22. Sklar reviews historical and textbook treatments of agreement with indefinites and offers some pragmatic strategies for teachers to use.

All *is* lost. [*All* implies "everything."]

ESL See page 262 for the distinction between *few* ("not many") and *a few* ("some").

Collective nouns take singular or plural verbs depending on meaning.

A **collective noun** has singular form but names a group of individuals or things—for example, *army, audience, committee, crowd, family, group, team.* As a subject, a collective noun may take a singular or plural verb, depending on the context. When the group acts as one unit, use a singular verb.

The group *agrees* that action is necessary.

But when considering the group's members as individuals who act separately, use the plural form of the verb.

The old group *have* gone their separate ways.

The collective noun *number* may be singular or plural. Preceded by *a,* it is plural; preceded by *the,* it is singular.

A number of people *are* in debt.

The number of people in debt *is* very large.

ESL Some noncount nouns (nouns that don't form plurals) are collective nouns because they name groups: for instance, *furniture, clothing, mail.* These noncount nouns usually take singular verbs: *Mail arrives daily.* But some of these nouns take plural verbs, including *clergy, military, people, police,* and any collective noun that comes from an adjective, such as *the poor, the rich, the young, the elderly.* If you mean one representative of the group, use a singular noun such as *police officer* or *poor person.*

SEPARATED BY A COMMON LANGUAGE? (ESL)

In British usage, collective nouns are treated as plurals; students educated in British usage (such as those from former British dependencies) may use constructions like *The team were ready for the game.* Such constructions also appear in the works of British authors.

The verb agrees with the subject even when the normal word order is inverted.

Inverted subject-verb order occurs mainly in questions and in constructions beginning with *there* or *it* and a form of *be.*

Is voting a right or a privilege?

Are a right and a privilege the same thing?

There *are* differences between them.

agr
8a

In constructions beginning with *there,* you may use *is* before a compound subject when the first element in the subject is singular.

There *is* much work to do and little time to do it.

Word order may sometimes be inverted for emphasis. The verb still agrees with its subject.

From the mountains *comes* an eerie, shimmering light.

8 A linking verb agrees with its subject, not the subject complement.

A linking verb such as *is* or *are* should agree with its subject, usually the first element in the sentence, not with the noun or pronoun serving as a subject complement (see p. 169).

The child's sole support *is* her court-appointed guardians.

Her court-appointed guardians *are* the child's sole support.

A LITTLE INTERVENTION

Agreement problems with *who, which,* and *that* are often the result of a phrase separating the subject from the relative clause. Give students a few examples of such phrases:

is one of those people who
is the only one of the workers that
are often believed to be creatures that
are generally considered to be people who
is representative of those executives who

Then ask them to write sample sentences of their own employing these or similar phrases and avoiding problems of agreement.

9 *Who, which,* and *that* take verbs that agree with their antecedents.

When used as subjects, *who, which,* and *that* refer to another word in the sentence, called the **antecedent.** The verb agrees with the antecedent.

Mayor Garber ought to listen to the people who *work* for her.

Bardini is the only aide who *has* her ear.

Agreement problems often occur with relative pronouns when the sentence includes *one of the* or *the only one of the.*

Bardini is one of the aides who *work* unpaid. [Of the aides who work unpaid, Bardini is one.]

Bardini is the only one of the aides who *knows* the community. [Of the aides, only one, Bardini, knows the community.]

ESL In phrases like those above beginning with *one of the,* be sure the noun is plural: *Bardini is one of the* aides [not aide] *who work unpaid.*

REMINDER (ESL)

Remind students that phrases like *one of* also require *the* before the noun: *Bardini is one of the aides* (not *one of aides) who work unpaid.*

10 Nouns with plural form but singular meaning take singular verbs.

Some nouns with plural form (that is, ending in *-s*) are usually regarded as singular in meaning. They include *athletics, economics,* *linguistics, mathematics, measles, mumps, news, physics, politics,* and *statistics,* as well as place names such as *Athens, Wales,* and *United States.*

After so long a wait, the news *has* to be good.

Statistics *is* required of psychology majors.

A few of these words take plural verbs only when they describe individual items rather than whole bodies of activity or knowledge: *The statistics prove him wrong.*

Measurements and figures ending in *-s* may also be singular when the quantity they refer to is a unit.

Three years *is* a long time to wait.

Three-fourths of the library *consists* of reference books.

Titles and words named as words take singular verbs.

When your sentence subject is the title of a corporation or a work (such as a book) or a word you are defining or describing, the verb should be singular even if the title or the word is plural.

Hakada Associates *is* a new firm.

Dream Days *remains* a favorite book.

Folks *is* a down-home word for people.

Exercise 1
Revising: Subject-verb agreement

Revise the verbs in the following sentences as needed to make subjects and verbs agree in number. If the sentence is already correct as given, circle the number preceding it.

Example:
Each of the job applicants type sixty words per minute.
Each of the job applicants *types* sixty words per minute.

1. Weinstein & Associates are a consulting firm that try to make businesspeople laugh.
2. Statistics from recent research suggests that humor relieves stress.
3. Reduced stress in businesses in turn reduce illness and absenteeism.
4. Reduced stress can also reduce friction within an employee group, which then work together more productively.

COLLABORATIVE LEARNING

Ask students to work together on Exercise 1 and then to look for agreement problems in each other's journal writing, drafts, or completed work.

ANSWERS: EXERCISE 1

1. Weinstein & Associates is a consulting firm that tries to make businesspeople laugh.
2. Statistics from recent research suggest that humor relieves stress.
3. Reduced stress in businesses in turn reduces illness and absenteeism.
4. Reduced stress can also reduce friction within an employee group, which then works together more productively.

5. In special conferences held by one consultant, each of the participants practices making the others laugh.
6. One consultant to many companies suggests cultivating office humor with practical jokes such as a rubber fish in the water cooler.
7. When the manager or employees regularly post cartoons on the bulletin board, office spirit usually picks up.
8. Sentence correct.
9. In the face of levity, the former sourpuss becomes one of those who hide bad temper.
10. Every one of the consultants cautions, however, that humor has no place in life-affecting corporate situations such as employee layoffs.

COLLABORATIVE LEARNING

USING MAGAZINES OR A READER

Using essays from a reader or magazine articles, have students work in groups to find sentence structures often associated with agreement problems. Ask the groups to decide how important these structures are for expository prose and to write out what they consider to be the rules governing agreement within these structures.

5. In special conferences held by one consultant, each of the participants practice making the others laugh.
6. One consultant to many companies suggest cultivating office humor with practical jokes such as a rubber fish in the water cooler.
7. When employees or their manager regularly post cartoons on the bulletin board, office spirit usually picks up.
8. When someone who has seemed too easily distracted is entrusted with updating the cartoons, his or her concentration often improves.
9. In the face of levity, the former sourpuss becomes one of those who hides bad temper.
10. Every one of the consultants caution, however, that humor has no place in life-affecting corporate situations such as employee layoffs.

agr 8b

8b Make pronouns and their antecedents agree in person, number, and gender.

The **antecedent** of a pronoun is the noun or other pronoun it refers to.

Homeowners fret over *their* tax bills.
antecedent pronoun

Its constant increases make the tax *bill* a dreaded document.
pronoun antecedent

Since a pronoun derives its meaning from its antecedent, the two must agree in person, number, and gender.

Person, number, and gender in pronoun-antecedent agreement

	Number	
Person	***Singular***	***Plural***
First	*I*	*we*
Second	*you*	*you*
Third	*he, she, it* indefinite pronouns singular nouns	*they* plural nouns
Gender		
Masculine	*he,* nouns naming males	
Feminine	*she,* nouns naming females	
Neuter	*it,* all other nouns	

Summary of pronoun-antecedent agreement

- Basic pronoun-antecedent agreement:

  Old Faithful spews *its* columns of water, each of *them* over 115 feet high.
- Antecedents joined by *and* (below):

  Old Faithful and Giant are geysers known for *their* height.
- Antecedents joined by *or* or *nor* (p. 248):

  Either Giant or Giantess ejects *its* column the highest.
- Indefinite pronouns as antecedents (p. 248):

  Each of the geysers has *its* own personality. Anyone who visits has *his or her* memories.
- Collective nouns as antecedents (p. 249):

  A crowd amuses *itself* watching Old Faithful. The crowd go *their* separate ways.

ESL The gender of a pronoun should match its antecedent, not a noun that the pronoun may modify: *President Clinton appointed his* [not *her*] *wife to redesign health care.* Also, nouns in English have only neuter gender unless they specifically refer to males or females. Thus nouns such as *book, table, sun,* and *earth* take the pronoun *it.*

Antecedents joined by *and* usually take plural pronouns.

Two or more antecedents joined by *and* usually take a plural pronoun, whether one or all of the antecedents are singular.

Mr. Bartos and I cannot settle *our* dispute.

The dean and my adviser have offered *their* help.

Exceptions When the compound antecedent refers to a single idea, person, or thing, then the pronoun is singular.

My friend and adviser offered *her* help.

When the compound antecedent follows *each* or *every,* the pronoun is singular.

Every girl and woman took *her* seat.

When parts of an antecedent are joined by *or* or *nor*, the pronoun agrees with the nearer part.

When the parts of an antecedent are connected by *or* or *nor*, the pronoun should agree with the part closer to it.

Tenants or owners must present *their* grievances.

Either the tenant or the owner will have *her* way.

When one subject is plural and the other singular, the sentence will be awkward unless you put the plural one second.

AWKWARD Neither the tenants nor the owner has yet made *her* case.

REVISED Neither the owner nor the tenants have yet made *their* case.

CONFUSION OVER INDEFINITE PRONOUNS (ESL)

ESL students may be confused by the indefinite pronouns *everyone, everybody,* and *everything* because they mean *all* of a group but are grammatically singular. Explain to students that the *endings* to these words—*one, body,* and *thing*—cause them to be singular rather than plural.

With an indefinite pronoun as antecedent, use a singular or plural pronoun as appropriate.

Indefinite pronouns, such as *everybody* or *anyone,* refer to persons or things in general rather than to a specific person or thing: *Everybody agrees.* See page 242 for a list of indefinite pronouns.

Four indefinite pronouns are always plural in meaning: *both, few, many, several.* When these pronouns serve as antecedents to other pronouns, the other pronouns are plural:

Few realize how *their* athletic facilities have changed.

Five indefinite pronouns—*all, any, more, most, some*—may be singular or plural depending on the word they refer to:

Few women athletes had changing spaces, so most had to change in *their* rooms.

Most of the changing space was dismal, *its* color a drab olive green.

All other indefinite pronouns are singular and take singular pronouns:

Now everyone on the women's teams has *her* own locker.

Each of the men still has *his* own locker.

(Notice that the phrase *of the men,* with its plural, does not change the singular number of the pronoun *each*.)

In speech we commonly use a plural pronoun when the singular indefinite pronoun is intended to mean "many" or "all" rather than "one." In writing, however, you should revise sentences to avoid the misuse. (See also "The generic *he*," below.)

FAULTY Everyone deserves *their* privacy.

REVISED *All of the athletes* deserve *their* privacy.

The generic *he*

The meaning of an indefinite pronoun often includes both masculine and feminine genders, not one or the other. The same is true of other indefinite words such as *child, adult, individual,* and *person.* In such cases tradition has called for *he* (*him, his*) to refer to the antecedent. But this so-called **generic *he*** (or generalized *he*) appears to exclude females. To avoid it, try one of the techniques in the box below. (For more on avoiding bias, see pp. 459–62.)

TRANSPARENCY MASTER 8.2

Ways to avoid the generic *he*

GENERIC *HE* None of the students had the credits *he* needed.

- Substitute *he or she.*

REVISED None of the students had the credits *he or she* needed.

- To avoid awkwardness, don't use *he or she* more than once in several sentences.
- Recast the sentence using a plural antecedent and pronoun.

REVISED *All the students* in the class lacked the credits *they* needed.

- Rewrite the sentence to avoid the pronoun.

REVISED None of the students had the *needed credits.*

4 Collective noun antecedents take singular or plural pronouns depending on meaning.

Collective nouns such as *army, committee, family, group,* and *team* have singular form but may be referred to by singular or plural pronouns, depending on the meaning intended. When the group acts as a unit, the pronoun is singular.

The committee voted to disband *itself.*

When the members of the group act separately, the pronoun is plural.

The old group have gone *their* separate ways.

In the last example, note that the verb and pronoun are consistent in number (see also p. 243).

INCONSISTENT	The old group *has* gone *their* separate ways.
CONSISTENT	The old group *have* gone *their* separate ways.

ESL Collective nouns that are noncount nouns (they don't form plurals) usually take singular pronouns: *The mail sits in its own basket.* A few noncount nouns take plural pronouns, including *clergy, military, people, police, the rich,* and *the poor: The police support their unions.* (See also p. 243).

Exercise 2

Revising: Pronoun-antecedent agreement

Revise the following sentences so that pronouns and their antecedents agree in person and number. Some items have more than one possible answer. Try to avoid the generic *he* (see the previous page). If you change the subject of a sentence, be sure to change verbs as necessary for agreement. If the sentence is already correct as given, circle the number preceding it.

Example:

Each of the Boudreaus' children brought their laundry home at Thanksgiving.

Each of the Boudreaus' children brought *his or her* laundry home at Thanksgiving. *Or: All* of the Boudreaus' children brought *their* laundry home at Thanksgiving.

1. Each girl raised in a Mexican American family in the Rio Grande Valley of Texas hopes that one day they will be given a *quinceañera* party for their fifteenth birthday.
2. Such celebrations are very expensive because it entails a religious service followed by a huge party.
3. A girl's immediate family, unless they are wealthy, cannot afford the party by themselves.
4. Her parents will ask each close friend or relative if they can help with the preparations.
5. Surrounded by her family and attended by her friends and their escorts, the *quinceañera* is introduced as a young woman eligible for fashionable Mexican American society.

Exercise 3

Adjusting for agreement

In the sentences below, subjects agree with verbs and pronouns agree with antecedents. Make the change specified in parentheses after each sentence, and then revise the sentence as necessary to maintain agreement. Some items have more than one possible answer.

ANSWERS: EXERCISE 2

1. Each girl raised in a Mexican American family in the Rio Grande Valley of Texas hopes that one day she will be given a *quinceañera* party for her fifteenth birthday.
2. Such a celebration is very expensive because it entails a religious service followed by a huge party. *Or:* Such celebrations are very expensive because they entail a religious service followed by a huge party.
3. A girl's immediate family, unless it is wealthy, cannot afford the party by itself.
4. Her parents will ask each close friend or relative if he or she can help with the preparations. *Or:* Her parents will ask close friends or relatives if they can help with the preparations.
5. Sentence correct.

ANSWERS: EXERCISE 3

1. Biologists wish to introduce captive red wolves into the Smoky Mountains in order to increase the wild population of this endangered species.
2. When freed, the wolves naturally have no fear of humans and thus are in danger of being shot.
3. The first experiments to release the wolves were failures.
4. Now researchers pen the wolf puppies in the wooded area that will eventually be their territory.
5. The wolves have little contact with people, even their own keeper, during the year of their captivity.

Example:

The student attends weekly conferences with her teacher. (*Change* The student *to* Students.)

Students *attend* weekly conferences with *their* teacher.

1. A biologist wishes to introduce captive red wolves into the Smoky Mountains in order to increase the wild population of this endangered species. (*Change* A biologist *to* Biologists.)
2. When freed, the wolf naturally has no fear of humans and thus is in danger of being shot. (*Change* wolf *to* wolves.)
3. The first experiment to release the wolves was a failure. (*Change* experiment *to* experiments.)
4. Now researchers pen the wolf puppy in the wooded area that will eventually be its territory. (*Change* puppy *to* puppies.)
5. The wolf has little contact with people, even its own keeper, during the year of its captivity. (*Change* wolf *to* wolves.)

Exercise 4
Revising: Agreement

Revise the sentences in the following paragraphs to correct errors in agreement between subjects and verbs or between pronouns and their antecedents. Try to avoid the generic *he* (see p. 249).

The writers Richard Rodriguez and Maxine Hong Kingston, despite their differences, shares one characteristic: their parents was immigrants to California. A frequent theme of their writings are the difficulties of growing up with two languages and two cultures.

Children whose first language is not English is often ridiculed because he cannot communicate "properly." Rodriguez learned Spanish at home, but at school everyone expected him to use their language, English. He remembers his childish embarrassment because of his parents' poor English. College and graduate school, which usually expands one's knowledge, widened the gap between Rodriguez and his Hispanic culture. His essays suggests that he lost a part of himself, a loss that continue to bother him.

Kingston spoke Chinese at home and also learned her first English at school. She sometimes write of these experiences, but more often she write to recover and preserve her Chinese culture. *The Woman Warrior,* which offer a blend of autobiography, family history, and mythic tales, describe the struggle of Kingston's female relatives. *China Men* focus on Kingston's male ancestors; each one traveled to Hawaii or California to make money for their wife back in China. Kingston's work, like Rodriguez's essays, reflect the tension and confusion that the child of immigrants often feel when they try to blend two cultures.

Note See page 264 for an exercise involving agreement along with other aspects of grammar.

ANSWERS: EXERCISE 4

The writers Richard Rodriguez and Maxine Hong Kingston, despite their differences, share one characteristic: their parents were immigrants to California. A frequent theme of their writings is the difficulties of growing up with two languages and two cultures.

Children whose first language is not English are often ridiculed because they cannot communicate "properly." Rodriguez learned Spanish at home, but at school classmates and teachers expected him to use their language, English. He remembers his childish embarrassment because of his parents' poor English. College and graduate school, which usually expand one's knowledge, widened the gap between Rodriguez and his Hispanic culture. His essays suggest that he lost a part of himself, a loss that continues to bother him.

Kingston spoke Chinese at home and also learned her first English at school. She sometimes writes of these experiences, but more often she writes to recover and preserve her Chinese culture. *The Woman Warrior,* which offers a blend of autobiography, family history, and mythic tales, describes the struggle of Kingston's female relatives. *China Men* focuses on Kingston's male ancestors; each one traveled to Hawaii or California to make money for his wife back in China. Kingston's work, like Rodriguez's essays, reflects the tension and confusion that the child of immigrants often feels when he or she tries (*or:* that the children of immigrants often feel when they try) to blend two cultures.

COLLABORATIVE LEARNING

Ask students to work on Exercises 2, 3, and 4 in groups and then to read examples from their own work looking for subject-verb and pronoun-antecedent problems.

agr
8

HIGHLIGHTS

Many readers view misuse of adjectives and adverbs as a sign of ignorance or carelessness. You should alert students to the potential effect of errors, of course, and remind them that this text offers helpful advice.

Yet fear of failure can disrupt the writing process and cause students to drop effective phrases and sentences from an essay because they are uncertain about the correct form of a word. This chapter therefore takes a positive approach, showing students the correct way to use adjectives and adverbs rather than emphasizing the *don't's*. It also offers easily remembered advice to guide writers over trouble spots. The exercises in the chapter ask students not only to recognize errors but also to revise sentences to make sure adjectives and adverbs are used appropriately.

TRANSPARENCY MASTER 9.1

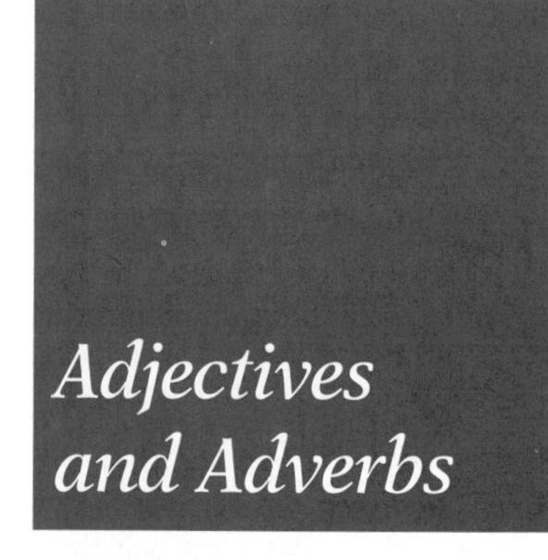

Chapter 9 Adjectives and Adverbs

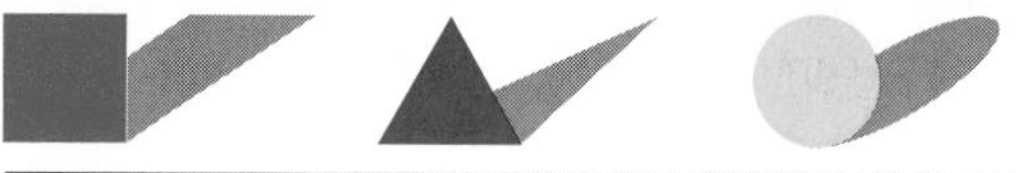

Adjectives and adverbs are modifiers that describe, restrict, or otherwise qualify the words to which they relate.

Functions of adjectives and adverbs

Adjectives modify nouns:	*serious* student
pronouns:	*ordinary* one
Adverbs modify verbs:	*warmly* greet
adjectives:	*only* three people
adverbs:	*quite* seriously
phrases:	*nearly* to the edge of the cliff
clauses:	*just* when we arrived
sentences:	*Fortunately,* she is employed.

Many of the most common adjectives are familiar one-syllable words such as *bad, strange, large,* and *wrong.* Many others are formed by adding endings such as *-al, -able, -ful, -less, -ish, -ive,* and *-y* to nouns or verbs: *optional, fashionable, beautiful, fruitless, selfish, expressive, dreamy.*

Most adverbs are formed by adding *-ly* to adjectives: *badly, strangely, largely, beautifully.* But note that we cannot depend on *-ly* to identify adverbs, since some adjectives also end in *-ly* (*fatherly, lonely*) and since some common adverbs do not end in *-ly* (*always, here, not, now, often, there*). Thus the only sure way to distinguish between adjectives and adverbs is to determine what they modify.

ESL In English an adjective does not change along with the noun it modifies to show plural number: *white* [not *whites*] *shoes*, *square* [not *squares*] *spaces*. Only nouns form plurals.

9a Use adjectives only to modify nouns and pronouns.

Adjectives modify only nouns and pronouns. Using adjectives instead of adverbs to modify verbs, adverbs, or other adjectives is nonstandard.

NONSTANDARD The groups view family values *different*.

STANDARD The groups view family values *differently*.

The adjectives *good* and *bad* often appear where standard English requires the adverbs *well* and *badly*.

NONSTANDARD Educating children *good* is everyone's focus.

STANDARD Educating children *well* is everyone's focus.

NONSTANDARD Some children suffer *bad*.

STANDARD Some children suffer *badly*.

ESL To negate a verb or an adjective, use the adverb *not*.

They are *not* learning. They are *not* stupid.

To negate a noun, use the adjective *no*.

No child should fail to read.

HOMEMADE QUIZZES

Ask students to follow the pattern of the sample sentences and exercises in the chapter and make up sentences containing common errors in the use of adjectives and adverbs. The uses of *well* and *good, bad* and *badly* are good starters. Collect the papers and distribute them as quizzes during the next class. Ask students to correct them in small groups.

9b Use an adjective after a linking verb to modify the subject. Use an adverb to modify a verb.

A **linking verb** is one that links, or connects, a subject and its complement: *They are golfers. He is lucky.* (See also pp. 168–69.) Linking verbs are forms of *be*, the verbs associated with our five senses (*look, sound, smell, feel, taste*), and a few others (*appear, seem, become, grow, turn, prove, remain, stay*).

Some of these verbs may or may not be linking, depending on their meaning in the sentence. When the word after the verb modifies the subject, the verb is linking and the word should be an adjective: *He feels strong.* When the word modifies the verb, however, it should be an adverb: *He feels strongly about that.*

Two word pairs are especially troublesome in this context. One is *bad* and *badly*.

The weather grew *bad*.
linking verb adjective

She felt *bad*.
linking verb adjective

Flowers grow *badly* in such soil.
verb adverb

The other pair is *good* and *well*. *Good* serves only as an adjective. *Well* may serve as an adverb with a host of meanings or as an adjective meaning only "fit" or "healthy."

Decker trained *well*.
verb adverb

She felt *well*.
linking verb adjective

Her health was *good*.
linking verb adjective

9c After a direct object, use an adjective to modify the object and an adverb to modify the verb.

After a direct object, an adjective modifies the object, whereas an adverb modifies the verb of the sentence. (See p. 167 for more on direct objects.)

Campus politics made Mungo *angry*.
adjective

Mungo repeated the words *angrily*.
adverb

You can test whether a modifier should be an adjective or an adverb by trying to separate it from the direct object. If you can separate it, it should be an adverb: *Mungo angrily repeated the words*. If you cannot separate it, it is probably an adjective.

The instructor considered the student's work *thorough*. [The adjective can be moved in front of *work* (*student's thorough work*), but it cannot be separated from *work*.]

The instructor considered the student's work *thoroughly*. [The adverb can be separated from *work*. Compare *The instructor thoroughly considered the student's work*.]

9d When an adverb has a short form and an *-ly* form, distinguish carefully between the forms.

Some adverbs have two forms, one with an *-ly* ending and one without. These include the following:

cheap, cheaply	loud, loudly	sharp, sharply
high, highly	near, nearly	slow, slowly
late, lately	quick, quickly	wrong, wrongly

With some of these pairs the choice of form is a matter of idiom, for the two forms have developed entirely separate meanings.

He went *late*. Winter is drawing *near*.
Lately he has been eating more. Winter is *nearly* here.

In other pairs the long and short forms have the same meaning. However, the short forms generally occur in informal speech and writing. The *-ly* forms are preferable in formal writing.

INFORMAL Drive *slow*.
FORMAL The funeral procession moved *slowly* through town.

Exercise 1
Revising: Adjectives and adverbs

Revise the following sentences so that adjectives and adverbs are used appropriately. If any sentence is already correct as given, circle the number preceding it.

Example:
The announcer warned that traffic was moving very slow.
The announcer warned that traffic was moving very *slowly*.

1. King George III of England declared Samuel Johnson suitably for a pension.
2. Johnson was taken serious as a critic and dictionary maker.
3. Thinking about his meeting with the king, Johnson felt proudly.
4. Johnson was relieved that he had not behaved badly in the king's presence.
5. After living cheap for over twenty years, Johnson finally had enough money from the pension to eat and dress good.

ANSWERS: EXERCISE 1

1. King George III of England declared Samuel Johnson suitable for a pension.
2. Johnson was taken seriously as a critic and dictionary maker.
3. Thinking about his meeting with the king, Johnson felt proud.
4. Sentence correct.
5. After living cheaply for over twenty years, Johnson finally had enough money from the pension to eat and dress well.

9e Use the comparative and superlative forms of adjectives and adverbs appropriately.

Adjectives and adverbs can show degrees of quality or amount with the endings *-er* and *-est* or with the words *more* and *most* or *less* and *least*. Most modifiers have three forms.

	ADJECTIVES	ADVERBS
POSITIVE The basic form listed in the dictionary	red awful	soon quickly
COMPARATIVE A greater or lesser degree of the quality named	redder more/less awful	sooner more/less quickly
SUPERLATIVE The greatest or least degree of the quality named	reddest most/least awful	soonest most/least quickly

If sound alone does not tell you whether to use *-er/-est* or *more/most,* consult a dictionary. If the endings can be used, the dictionary will list them. Otherwise, use *more* or *most.*

COLLABORATIVE LEARNING

SABOTAGING ESSAYS

Give each group a different short essay and have them introduce a number of errors into its adjective and adverb use. (They may want to use correction fluid for this task.) Then have students copy the essay so their corrections won't show and give it to a different group, which attempts to find all the changes the first group made. The first group comments on and critiques the "corrected" essay by comparing it to the original version. If students are working in a computer classroom, they can print out the error-ridden version of the essay for the other group.

Use the correct forms of irregular adjectives and adverbs.

The irregular modifiers change the spelling of their positive form to show comparative and superlative degrees.

Degrees of irregular adjectives and adverbs

Positive	Comparative	Superlative
Adjectives		
good	better	best
bad	worse	worst
little	littler, less	littlest, least
many, some, much	more	most
Adverbs		
well	better	best
badly	worse	worst

Use either *-er/-est* or *more/most,* not both.

A double comparative or double superlative combines the *-er* or *-est* ending with the word *more* or *most.* It is redundant.

Chang was the *wisest* [not *most wisest*] person in town.
He was *smarter* [not *more smarter*] than anyone else.

In general, use the comparative form for comparing two things and the superlative form for comparing three or more things.

It is the *shorter* of her two books. [Comparative.]
The Yearling is the *most popular* of the six books. [Superlative.]

In conversation the superlative form is often used to compare only two things: *When two people argue, the angriest one is usually wrong.* But the distinction between the forms should be observed in writing.

Use comparative or superlative forms only for modifiers that can logically be compared.

Some adjectives and adverbs cannot logically be compared—for instance, *perfect, unique, dead, impossible, infinite.* These absolute words can be preceded by adverbs like *nearly* and *almost* that mean "approaching," but they cannot logically be modified by *more* or *most* (as in *most perfect*). This distinction is sometimes ignored in speech, but it should always be made in writing.

NOT He was the *most unique* teacher we had.
BUT He was a *unique* teacher.

Exercise 2
Using comparatives and superlatives

Write the comparative and superlative forms of each adjective or adverb below. Then use all three forms in your own sentences.

Example:

heavy: heavier (comparative), heaviest (superlative)

The barbells were too *heavy* for me. The magician's trunk was *heavier* than I expected. Joe Clark was the *heaviest* person on the team.

1. badly
2. steady
3. good
4. well
5. understanding

Exercise 3
Revising: Comparatives and superlatives

Revise the sentences below so that the comparative and superlative forms of adjectives and adverbs are appropriate for formal usage.

Example:

Attending classes full-time and working at two jobs was the most impossible thing I ever did.

Attending classes full-time and working at two jobs was *impossible* [or *the hardest thing I ever did*].

1. Charlotte was the older of the three Brontë sisters, all of whom were novelists.
2. Some readers think Emily Brontë's *Wuthering Heights* is the most saddest novel they have ever read.
3. Of the other two sisters, Charlotte and Anne, Charlotte was probably the most talented.
4. Critics still argue about whether Charlotte or Emily wrote more better.
5. Certainly this family of women novelists was the most unique.

9f Avoid double negatives.

In a **double negative** two negative words such as *no, none, neither, barely, hardly,* or *scarcely* cancel each other out. For instance, *Jenny did not feel nothing* asserts that Jenny felt other than nothing, or something. For the opposite meaning, one of the negatives must be eliminated or changed to a positive: *She felt nothing* or *She did not feel anything.*

ANSWERS: EXERCISE 2

Possible answers

1. badly, worse, worst
   The favored horse performed badly in the race. He performed worse than all but one other horse. The horse that performed worst broke stride and left the race.
2. steady, steadier, steadiest
   The stool was not steady. It's steadier now that I've planed one leg. But it's still not the steadiest stool in the house.
3. good, better, best
   The fruit tasted good. The cheese tasted better. The chocolate pie tasted best.
4. well, better, best
   Julie did well on the test. Jack did better than Julie. Ellen did best of all.
5. understanding, more understanding, most understanding
   Professor Najarian was understanding about my late paper. She was more understanding than I had expected. She must be the most understanding professor in the department.

COLLABORATIVE LEARNING

Ask students to complete Exercise 2 independently, then revise their responses and the sentences in Exercise 3 in small groups.

ANSWERS: EXERCISE 3

1. Charlotte was the oldest of the three Brontë sisters, all of whom were novelists.
2. Some readers think Emily Brontë's *Wuthering Heights* is the saddest novel they have ever read.
3. Of the other two sisters, Charlotte and Anne, Charlotte was probably the more talented.
4. Critics still argue about whether Charlotte or Emily wrote better.
5. Certainly, this family of women novelists was unique.

FAULTY The IRS *cannot hardly* audit all tax returns. *None* of its audits *never* touch many cheaters.

REVISED The IRS *cannot* audit all tax returns. Its audits *never* touch many cheaters.

9g Use nouns sparingly as modifiers.

We often use one noun to modify another. For example:

child care flood control security guard

Such phrases can be both clear and concise, but overuse of noun modifiers can lead to flat, even senseless, writing. To avoid awkwardness or confusion, observe two principles. First, prefer possessives or adjectives as modifiers.

NOT A student takes the state medical *board* exams to become a *dentist* technician.

BUT A student takes the state medical *board's* exams to become a *dental* technician.

Second, use only short nouns as modifiers and use them only in two- or three-word sequences.

CONFUSING Minimex maintains a *plant employee relations improvement* program.

REVISED Minimex maintains a program *for improving* relations *among plant employees.*

PARTICIPLES (ESL)

Present participles generally describe inanimate or nonhuman nouns: The *storm was frightening.* Past participles generally describe animate nouns (since only animate beings experience feelings): The *horses were frightened.*

9h Distinguish between present and past participles as adjectives. ESL

Both present participles and past participles may serve as adjectives: *a burning building, a burned building.* As in the examples, the two participles usually differ in the time they indicate.

But some present and past participles—those derived from verbs expressing feeling—can have altogether different meanings. The present participle refers to something that causes the feeling: *That was a frightening storm.* The past participle refers to something that experiences the feeling: *They quieted the frightened horses.*

The following participles are among those likely to be confused:

amazing/amazed
amusing/amused
annoying/annoyed
astonishing/astonished
boring/bored
confusing/confused
depressing/depressed
embarrassing/embarrassed
exciting/excited
exhausting/exhausted
fascinating/fascinated
frightening/frightened
frustrating/frustrated
interesting/interested
pleasing/pleased
satisfying/satisfied

shocking/shocked tiring/tired
surprising/surprised worrying/worried

Exercise 4
Revising: Present and past participles ESL

Revise the adjectives in the following sentences as needed to distinguish between present and past participles. If the sentence is already correct as given, circle the number preceding it.

Example:
The subject was embarrassed to many people.
The subject was *embarrassing* to many people.

1. Several critics found Alice Walker's *The Color Purple* to be a fascinated book.
2. One confused critic wished that Walker had deleted the scenes set in Africa.
3. Another critic argued that although the book contained many depressed episodes, the overall impact was excited.
4. Since other readers found the book annoyed, this critic pointed out its many surprised qualities.
5. In the end most critics agreed that the book was a satisfied novel.

ANSWERS: EXERCISE 4

1. Several critics found Alice Walker's *The Color Purple* to be a fascinating book.
2. Sentence correct.
3. Another critic argued that although the book contained many depressing episodes, the overall impact was exciting.
4. Since other readers found the book annoying, this critic pointed out its many surprising qualities.
5. In the end most critics agreed that the book was a satisfying novel.

det 9i

9i Use *a, an, the,* and other determiners appropriately. ESL

Determiners are special kinds of adjectives that mark nouns because they always precede nouns. Some common determiners are *a, an,* and *the* (called **articles**) and *my, their, whose, this, these, those, one, some,* and *any.* They convey information to readers—for instance, by specifying who owns what, which one of two is meant, or whether a subject is familiar or unfamiliar.

Native speakers of English can rely on their intuition when using determiners, but nonnative speakers often have difficulty with them because many other languages use them quite differently or not at all. In English the use of determiners depends on the context they appear in and the kind of noun they precede:

- A **proper noun** names a particular person, place, or thing and begins with a capital letter: *February, Joe Allen, Red River.* Most proper nouns are not preceded by determiners.
- A **count noun** names something that is countable in English and can form a plural: *girl/girls, apple/apples, child/children.* A singular count noun is always preceded by a determiner; a plural count noun sometimes is.
- A **noncount noun** names something not usually considered countable in English, and so it does not form a plural. A noncount noun is sometimes preceded by a determiner. Here is a sample of noncount nouns, sorted into groups by meaning:

ARTICLE USE (ESL)

As the text notes, because other languages use articles differently from English or not at all, even advanced ESL students may find articles difficult; some students may never completely master article use. Refer students who need additional practice with article use to Unit 2 of Len Fox, *Focus on Editing: A Grammar Workbook for Advanced Writers* (White Plains: Longman, 1992), and Chapter 10 of Jocelyn Steer and Karen Carlisi, *The Advanced Grammar Book* (Boston: Heinle, 1991).

CATEGORIES OF NONCOUNT NOUNS (ESL)

Refer students who need additional practice with count and noncount nouns to Unit 2 of Len Fox, *Focus on Editing: A Grammar Workbook for Advanced Writers* (White Plains: Longman, 1992), and Chapter 1 of Jocelyn Steer and Karen Carlisi, *The Advanced Grammar Book* (Boston: Heinle, 1991).

Abstractions: confidence, democracy, education, equality, evidence, health, information, intelligence, knowledge, luxury, peace, pollution, research, success, supervision, truth, wealth, work

Food and drink: bread, candy, cereal, flour, meat, milk, salt, water, wine

Emotions: anger, courage, happiness, hate, joy, love, respect, satisfaction

Natural events and elements: air, blood, dirt, gasoline, gold, hair, heat, ice, oil, oxygen, rain, silver, smoke, weather, wood

Groups: clergy, clothing, equipment, furniture, garbage, jewelry, junk, legislation, machinery, mail, military, money, police, vocabulary

Fields of study: architecture, accounting, biology, business, chemistry, engineering, literature, psychology, science

An ESL dictionary will tell you whether a noun is a count noun, a noncount noun, or both. (See p. 482 for recommended dictionaries.)

NOTE Many nouns can be both count and noncount nouns.

The library has a *room* for readers. [*Room* is a count noun meaning "walled area."]

The library has *room* for reading. [*Room* is a noncount noun meaning "space."]

 Use *a, an,* and *the* where they are required.

With singular count nouns

A or *an* precedes a singular count noun when the reader does not already know its identity, usually because you have not mentioned it before.

A scientist in our chemistry department developed *a* process to strengthen metals. [*Scientist* and *process* are being introduced for the first time.]

The precedes a singular count noun that has a specific identity for the reader, usually because (1) you have mentioned it before, (2) you identify it immediately before or after you state it, (3) it is unique (the only one in existence), or (4) it refers to an institution or facility that is shared by a community.

A scientist in our chemistry department developed a process to strengthen metals. *The* scientist patented *the* process. [*Scientist* and *process* were identified in the preceding sentence.]

The most productive laboratory is *the* research center in the chemistry department. [*Most productive* identifies *laboratory,* and *in the chemistry department* identifies *research center.*]

The sun rises in *the* east. [*Sun* and *east* are unique.]

Many men and women aspire to *the* Presidency. [*Presidency* is a shared institution.]

The fax machine has changed business communication. [*Fax machine* is a shared facility.]

The is not used before a singular noun that names a general category.

Sherman said that *war* is hell. [*War* names a general category.]
The war in Croatia left many dead. [*War* names a specific war.]

With plural count nouns

A or *an* never precedes a plural noun. *The* does not precede a plural noun that names a general category. *The* does precede a plural noun that names specific representatives of a category.

Men and *women* are different. [*Men* and *women* name general categories.]

The women formed a team. [*Women* refers to specific people.]

With noncount nouns

A or *an* never precedes a noncount noun. *The* does precede a noncount noun that names specific representatives of a general category.

Vegetation suffers from drought. [*Vegetation* names a general category.]

The vegetation in the park withered or died. [*Vegetation* refers to specific plants.]

With proper nouns

A or *an* never precedes a proper noun. *The* generally does not precede a proper noun:

Garcia lives in *Boulder.*

There are exceptions, however. For instance, we generally use *the* before plural proper nouns (*the Murphys, the Boston Celtics*) and the names of groups and organizations (*the Department of Justice, the Sierra Club*), ships (*the Lusitania*), oceans (*the Pacific*), mountain ranges (*the Alps*), regions (*the Middle East*), rivers (*the Mississippi*), and some countries (*the United States, the Sudan*).

2 Use other determiners appropriately.

The uses of English determiners besides articles also depend on context and kind of noun. The following determiners may be used as indicated with singular count nouns, plural count nouns, or noncount nouns.

***A LOT OF* (ESL)**

ESL students tend to use *a lot of* in formal writing because they are unaware that it is an informal, conversational phrase. Give students formal substitutes for *a lot of,* such as *a large amount of* before noncount nouns and *many* before plural count nouns.

With any kind of noun (singular count, plural count, noncount)

my, our, your, his, her, its, their, possessive nouns (*boy's, boys'*)
whose, which(ever), what(ever)
some, any, the other
no

Their account is overdrawn. [Singular count.]
Their funds are low. [Plural count.]
Their money is running out. [Noncount.]

Only with singular nouns (count and noncount)

this, that

This account has some money. [Count.]
This information may help. [Noncount.]

Only with noncount nouns and plural count nouns

most, enough, other, such, all, all of the, a lot of

Most money is needed elsewhere. [Noncount.]
Most funds are committed. [Plural count.]

Only with singular count nouns

one, every, each, either, neither, another

One car must be sold. [Singular count.]

Only with plural count nouns

these, those
both, many, few, a few, fewer, fewest, several
two, three, and so forth

Two cars are unnecessary. [Plural count.]

NOTE *Few* means "not many" or "not enough." *A few* means "some" or "a small but sufficient quantity."

Few committee members came to the meeting.
A few members can keep the committee going.

Do not use *much* with a plural count noun.

Many [not *much*] members want to help.

Only with noncount nouns

much, more, little, a little, less, least, a large amount of

Less luxury is in order. [Noncount.]

NOTE *Little* means "not many" or "not enough." *A little* means "some" or "a small but sufficient quantity."

Little time remains before the conference.
The members need *a little* help from their colleagues.

Do not use *many* with a noncount noun:

Much [not *many*] work remains.

ANSWERS: EXERCISE 5

From the native American Indians who migrated from Asia 20,000 years ago to the new arrivals who now come by planes, the United States is a nation of foreigners. It is a country of immigrants who are all united under a single flag.

Back in the seventeenth and eighteenth centuries, at least 75 percent of the population came

Exercise 5
Revising: Articles ESL

For each blank below, indicate whether *a, an, the,* or no article should be inserted.

From ____ native American Indians who migrated from ____ Asia 20,000 years ago to ____ new arrivals who now come by ____ planes, ____ United States is ____ nation of foreigners. It is ____ country of immigrants who are all united under ____ single flag.

Back in ____ seventeenth and eighteenth centuries, at least 75 percent of the population came from ____ England. However, between 1820 and 1975 more than 38 million immigrants came to this country from elsewhere in ____ Europe. Many children of ____ immigrants were self-conscious and denied their heritage; many even refused to learn ____ native language of their parents and grandparents. They tried to "Americanize" themselves. The so-called Melting Pot theory of ____ social change stressed ____ importance of blending everyone together into ____ kind of stew. Each nationality would contribute its own flavor, but ____ final stew would be something called "American."

This Melting Pot theory was never completely successful. In the last half of this century, ____ ethnic revival has changed ____ metaphor. Many people now see ____ American society as ____ mosaic. Americans are once again proud of their heritage, and ____ ethnic differences make ____ mosaic colorful and interesting.

Exercise 6
Revising: Adjectives and adverbs

Revise the following paragraph so that it conforms to formal usage of adjectives and adverbs.

Americans often argue about which professional sport is better: basketball, football, or baseball. Basketball fans contend that their sport offers more action because the players are constant running and shooting. Because it is played indoors in relative small arenas, basketball allows fans to be more closer to the action than the other sports do. Fans point to how graceful the players fly through the air to the hoop. Football fanatics say they don't hardly stop yelling once the game begins. They cheer when their team executes a real complicated play good. They roar more louder when the defense stops the opponents in a goal-line stand. They yell loudest when a fullback crashes in for a score. In contrast, the supporters of baseball believe that it might be the most perfect sport played. It combines the one-on-one duel of pitcher and batter struggling valiant with the tight teamwork of double and triple plays. Because the game is played slow and careful, fans can analyze and discuss the manager's strategy. Besides, they don't never know when they might catch a foul ball as a souvenir. However, no matter what the sport, all fans feel happily only when their team wins!

Note See the next page for an exercise involving adjectives and adverbs along with other aspects of grammar.

from England. However, between 1820 and 1975 more than 38 million immigrants came to this country from elsewhere in Europe. Many children of the immigrants were self-conscious and denied their heritage; many even refused to learn the native language of their parents and grandparents. They tried to "Americanize" themselves. The so-called Melting Pot theory of social change stressed the importance of blending everyone together into a kind of stew. Each nationality would contribute its own flavor, but the final stew would be something called "American."

This Melting Pot theory was never completely successful. In the last half of this century, an ethnic revival has changed the metaphor. Many people now see American society as a mosaic. Americans are once again proud of their heritage, and ethnic differences make the mosaic colorful and interesting.

COLLABORATIVE LEARNING

Students can work in small groups to complete Exercises 5 and 6, then read each other's work to check article, adjective, and adverb usage.

ANSWERS: EXERCISE 6

Americans often argue about which professional sport is best: basketball, football, or baseball. Basketball fans contend that their sport offers more action because the players are constantly running and shooting. Because it is played indoors in relatively small arenas, basketball allows fans to be closer to the action than the other sports do. Fans point to how gracefully the players fly through the air to the hoop. Football fanatics say they hardly stop yelling once the game begins. They cheer when their team executes a really complicated play well. They roar more loudly when the defense stops the opponents in a goal-line stand. They yell most loudly when a fullback crashes in for a score. In contrast, the supporters of baseball believe that it might be the most nearly perfect sport played. It combines the one-on-one duel of pitcher and batter struggling valiantly with the tight teamwork of double and triple plays. Because the game is played slowly and carefully, fans can analyze and discuss the manager's strategy. Besides, they never know when they might catch a foul ball as a souvenir. However, no matter what the sport, all fans feel happy only when their team wins!

COLLABORATIVE LEARNING

Have students complete the exercise on page 264 individually, then ask them to discuss their responses in small groups.

ANSWERS: EXERCISE ON CHAPTERS 6–9

gr

Occasionally, musicians become "crossover artists" who can perform well in more than one field of music. For example, Wynton and Branford Marsalis were trained in jazz by their father, the great pianist Ellis Marsalis. Both of the sons have recently become successful classical artists. Branford's saxophone captures the richness of pieces by Ravel and Stravinsky. Wynton's albums of classical trumpet music from the Baroque period have brought him many awards. Still, if he were to choose which kind of music he likes better, Wynton would probably choose jazz. In contrast to the Marsalises, Yo-Yo Ma and Jean-Pierre Rampal grew up studying classical music. Then in the 1980s they were invited by Claude Bolling, a French pianist, to record Bolling's jazz compositions. In fact, Rampal's flute blended with Bolling's music so well that the two men have done three albums.

Such crossovers are often harder for vocalists. Each type of music has its own style and feel that are hard to learn. For example, Luciano Pavarotti and Kiri te Kanawa, two great opera performers, have sung popular music and folk songs in concerts and on albums. On each occasion, their technique was nearly perfect, yet each sounded as if he or she were simply trying to sing properly. It is even more difficult for pop or country vocalists to sing opera, as Linda Ronstadt and Gary Morris found when they appeared in *La Bohème*. Each of them has a clear, pure voice, but a few critics said that he and she lacked the vocal power necessary for opera. However, Bobby McFerrin has been successful singing both pop and classical pieces. He won a Grammy award for his song "Don't Worry, Be Happy." But he is equally able to sing classical pieces *a cappella* (without musical accompaniment). His voice's remarkable range and clarity allow him to imitate many musical instruments.

No matter how successful, all of these musicians have shown great courage by performing in a new field. They are willing to test and stretch their talents, and each of us music fans benefits.

Exercise on Chapters 6–9
Revising: Grammatical sentences

The paragraphs below contain errors in pronoun case, verb forms, subject-verb agreement, pronoun-antecedent agreement, and the forms of adjectives and adverbs. Revise the paragraphs to correct the errors.

Occasionally, musicians become "crossover artists" whom can perform good in more than one field of music. For example, Wynton and Branford Marsalis was train in jazz by their father, the great pianist Ellis Marsalis. Both of the sons has recent became successful classical artists. Branford's saxophone captures the richness of pieces by Ravel and Stravinsky. Wynton's albums of classical trumpet music from the Baroque period has brung him many awards. Still, if he was to choose which kind of music he likes best, Wynton would probable choose jazz. In contrast to the Marsalises, Yo-Yo Ma and Jean-Pierre Rampal growed up studying classical music. Then in the 1980s they was invited by Claude Bolling, a French pianist, to record Bolling's jazz compositions. In fact, Rampal's flute blended with Bolling's music so good that the two men have did three albums.

Such crossovers are often more harder for vocalists. Each type of music has their own style and feel that is hard to learn. For example, Luciano Pavarotti and Kiri te Kanawa, two great opera performers, have sang popular music and folk songs in concerts and on albums. On each occasion, their technique was the most perfect, yet each sounded as if he was simply trying to sing proper. It is even more difficulter for pop or country vocalists to sing opera, as Linda Ronstadt and Gary Morris founded when they appear in *La Bohème*. Each of them have a clear, pure voice, but a few critics said that him and her lacked the vocal power necessary for opera. However, Bobby McFerrin been successful singing both pop and classical pieces. He won a Grammy award for his song "Don't Worry, Be Happy." But he is equal able to sing classical pieces *a cappella* (without musical accompaniment). His voice's remarkable range and clarity allows him to imitate many musical instruments.

No matter how successful, all of these musicians has shown great courage by performing in a new field. They are willing to test and stretch their talents, and each of we music fans benefit.

Part III

Clear Sentences

HIGHLIGHTS

This chapter opens with a positive approach, showing students how to test sentences for completeness, revise any fragments, and punctuate revised fragments. Following the opening section are discussions of particular structures that are often mispunctuated as complete sentences: subordinate clauses; verbal and prepositional phrases; and other word groups such as appositives, parts of compound predicates, and nouns plus modifiers. The chapter concludes with a discussion of the acceptable uses of incomplete sentences.

Chapter 10 Sentence Fragments

A **sentence fragment** is part of a sentence that is set off as if it were a whole sentence by an initial capital letter and a final period or other end punctuation. Although writers occasionally use fragments deliberately and effectively (see p. 273), readers perceive most fragments as serious errors because, expecting complete sentences, they find partial sentences distracting or confusing. (Before reading further, you may find it helpful to review pp. 163–70 and 182–85 on sentences and clauses.)

TRANSPARENCY MASTER 10.1

Complete sentence versus sentence fragment

A **complete sentence** or **main clause**

- contains a subject and a verb (*The* <u>*wind blows*</u>)
- and is not a subordinate clause (beginning with a word such as *because* or *who*).

A **sentence fragment**

- lacks a verb (*The wind blowing*)
- or lacks a subject (*And blows*)
- or is a subordinate clause not attached to a complete sentence (*Because the wind blows*).

ESL In some languages other than English, the subject or the verb need not always be stated for a thought to be considered complete. However, English always requires you to state the subject and the verb. The only exception is a command (*Shut the door*), in which the subject *you* is understood.

10a Test your sentences for completeness, and revise any fragments.

The following three tests will help you determine whether a word group punctuated as a sentence is actually a complete sentence. If the word group does not pass *all three* tests, it is a fragment and needs to be revised.

Tests for sentence fragments

A sentence is complete only when it passes *all three* tests.

1. Find the verb.
2. Find the subject.
3. Make sure the clause is not subordinate.

Test 1: Find the verb.

Look for a verb in the group of words. If you do not have one, the word group is a fragment.

FRAGMENT Thousands of new sites on the World Wide Web. [Compare a complete sentence: *Thousands of new sites have appeared on the World Wide Web.*]

Any verb form you find must be a **finite verb,** one that changes form as indicated below. A verbal does not change; it cannot serve as a sentence verb without the aid of a helping verb.

	FINITE VERBS IN COMPLETE SENTENCES	VERBALS IN SENTENCE FRAGMENTS
SINGULAR	The network *grows.*	The network *growing.*
PLURAL	Networks *grow.*	Networks *growing.*
PRESENT	The network *grows.*	
PAST	The network *grew.*	The network *growing.*
FUTURE	The network *will grow.*	

ESL Some languages allow forms of *be* to be omitted as helping verbs or linking verbs. But English requires stating forms of *be.*

FRAGMENTS The network growing. It already larger than its developers anticipated. [Compare complete sentences: *The network is growing. It is already larger than its developers anticipated.*]

Test 2: Find the subject.

If you find a finite verb, look for its subject by asking who or what performs the action or makes the assertion of the verb. The subject of the sentence will usually come before the verb. If there is no subject, the word group is probably a fragment.

EXPLETIVES (ESL)

Remind students that because English is a subject-verb-object language, something must fill the subject position when the subject is delayed. *There* and *it* fulfill this requirement by acting as dummy subjects. (Refer students to p. 194 for more about *it* and *there.*)

TRANSPARENCY MASTER 10.2

RESOURCES AND IDEAS

Harris, Muriel. "Mending the Fragmented Free Modifier." *College Composition and Communication* 32 (1981): 175–82. Harris presents strategies for identifying kinds of fragments and correcting them.

Noguchi, Rei R. "Fragments and Beyond." Chapter 5 in *Grammar and the Teaching of Writing: Limits and Possibilities.* Urbana: NCTE, 1991. 84–112. Noguchi outlines a positive approach to teaching students how to recognize, revise, or make use of sentence fragments.

FRAGMENTS

Students have been bombarded with so many fragments in advertising and popular prose ("Less filling! Tastes great!") that they may in fact not realize that using subordinate clauses as complete sentences is usually unacceptable. Your first job may be to convince them that what is acceptable in speech and informal writing is not always desirable in formal writing.

NEWSCASTERS

The breathless style of radio and television newscasters often includes fragments. Ask students to write down examples from the evening news. Newspapers, especially tabloids, can be a good source, too.

FRAGMENT And has enormous popular appeal. [Compare a complete sentence: *And the Web has enormous popular appeal.*]

In one kind of complete sentence, a command, the subject *you* is understood: [*You*] *Experiment with the Web.*

SUBORDINATING-WORD CLUES (ESL)

Encourage students to look for subordinating words—that is, subordinating conjunctions or relative pronouns—as they read their papers. Remind students that a complete sentence with a subordinating word must include two subjects and verbs, one subject and verb in the subordinate clause and one subject and verb in the main clause. Reading papers backward, from last sentence to first, may help some students find sentence fragments.

frag 10a

Test 3: Make sure the clause is not subordinate.

A subordinate clause usually begins with a subordinating word.

SUBORDINATING CONJUNCTIONS			RELATIVE PRONOUNS	
after	once	until	that	who/whom
although	since	when	which	whoever/whomever
as	than	where		whose
because	that	whereas		
if	unless	while		

(See p. 183 for a longer list of subordinating conjunctions.)

Subordinate clauses serve as parts of sentences (nouns or modifiers), not as whole sentences.

FRAGMENT When the government devised the Internet. [Compare a complete sentence: *The government devised the Internet.* Or: *When the government devised the Internet, no expansive computer network existed.*]

FRAGMENT The reason that the government devised the Internet. [This fragment is a noun (*reason*) plus its modifier (*that . . . Internet*). Compare a complete sentence: *The reason that the government devised the Internet was to provide secure links among departments and defense contractors.*]

NOTE Questions beginning with *how, what, when, where, which, who, whom, whose,* and *why* are not sentence fragments: *Who was responsible? When did it happen?*

Revising sentence fragments

Almost all sentence fragments can be corrected in one of two ways, the choice depending on the importance of the information in the fragment.

 **Revision of sentence fragments**

- Rewrite the fragment as a complete sentence.
- Combine the fragment with the appropriate main clause.

Rewriting the fragment as a complete sentence gives the information in the fragment the same importance as that in other complete sentences.

FRAGMENT A recent addition to the Internet is the World Wide Web. *Which allows users to move easily between sites.*

REVISED A recent addition to the Internet is the World Wide Web. *It* allows users to move easily between sites.

Two main clauses may be separated by a semicolon instead of a period (see p. 388).

The second method of correcting a fragment, combining it with a main clause, subordinates the information in the fragment to the information in the main clause.

FRAGMENT The Web is easy to use. *Loaded with links and graphics.*

REVISED The Web**,** loaded with links and graphics**,** is easy to use.

In this example, commas separate the inserted phrase from the rest of the sentence because the phrase does not restrict the meaning of any word in the main clause but simply adds information (see p. 370). When a phrase or subordinate clause *does* restrict the meaning of a word in the main clause, a comma or commas do *not* separate the two elements.

FRAGMENT With the links, users can move to other Web sites. *That they want to consult.*

REVISED With the links, users can move to other Web sites that they want to consult.

Sometimes a fragment may be combined with the main clause using a colon or a dash (see pp. 416 and 419, respectively).

FRAGMENT The Web connects sites from all over the Internet. *Different databases, different software, different machines.*

REVISED The Web connects sites from all over the Internet**:** different databases, different software, different machines.

FRAGMENT The Internet and now the Web are a boon to researchers. *A vast and accessible library.*

REVISED The Internet and now the Web are a boon to researchers**—**a vast and accessible library.

Exercise 1
Identifying and revising sentence fragments

Apply the tests for completeness to each of the following word groups. If a word group is a complete sentence, circle the number preceding it. If it is a sentence fragment, revise it in two ways: by making it a complete sentence, and by combining it with a main clause written from the information given in other items.

Example:

And could not find his money.

The word group has a verb (*could . . . find*) but no subject.

ANSWERS: EXERCISE 1

Possible answers

1. Lacks a subject and a verb.
   Complete: An article about vandalism against works of art was interesting.
   Combined: In an interesting article about vandalism against works of art, the author says the vandals' motives vary widely.
2. Lacks a verb.
   Complete: The motives of the vandals vary widely.

Combined: The motives of the vandals varying widely, researchers can make few generalizations.
3. Complete sentence.
4. Lacks a subject and a verb.
Complete: But the vandal is not necessarily angry at the artist or the owner.
Combined: Whoever harms artwork is usually angry, but not necessarily at the artist or the owner.
5. Lacks a verb for the subject man.
Complete: For instance, a man hammered at Michelangelo's *Pietà*.
Combined: For instance, a man who hammered at Michelangelo's *Pietà* was angry at the Roman Catholic Church.
6. Lacks a subject.
Complete: And he knocked off the Virgin Mary's nose.
Combined: A man hammered at Michelangelo's *Pietà* and knocked off the Virgin Mary's nose.
7. Begins with subordinating conjunction.
Complete: He was angry at the Roman Catholic Church.
Combined: A man hammered at Michelangelo's *Pietà* because he was angry at the Roman Catholic Church.
8. Begins with *which* but is not a question.
Complete: The Church knew nothing of his grievance.
Combined: He was angry at the Roman Catholic Church, which knew nothing of his grievance.
9. Begins with subordinating conjunction.
Complete: Many damaged works can be repaired.
Combined: Although many damaged works can be repaired, even the most skillful repairs are forever visible.
10. Complete sentence.

COLLABORATIVE LEARNING

After students have completed Exercise 1 independently, have them compare responses in small groups and then read each other's work for examples of sentence fragments. For students who are struggling with the concept of sentence structure and of the sentence fragment, the move to recognize errors in their own work can be extremely helpful.

frag 10c

Revised into a complete sentence: And *he* could not find his money.

Combined with a new main clause: *He was lost* and could not find his money.

1. In an interesting article about vandalism against works of art.
2. The motives of the vandals varying widely.
3. Those who harm artwork are usually angry.
4. But not necessarily at the artist or the owner.
5. For instance, a man who hammered at Michelangelo's *Pietà*.
6. And knocked off the Virgin Mary's nose.
7. Because he was angry at the Roman Catholic Church.
8. Which knew nothing of his grievance.
9. Although many damaged works can be repaired.
10. Usually even the most skillful repairs are forever visible.

10b A subordinate clause is not a complete sentence.

Subordinate clauses contain both subjects and verbs, but they always begin with a subordinating conjunction (*although, if,* and so on) or a relative pronoun (*who, which, that*). (See p. 182.) Subordinate clauses serve as nouns or modifiers, but they cannot stand alone as complete sentences.

To correct a subordinate clause set off as a sentence, combine it with the main clause or remove or change the subordinating word to create a main clause.

FRAGMENT Many pine trees bear large cones. *Which appear in August.*

REVISED Many pine trees bear large cones, which appear in August.

REVISED Many pine trees bear large cones. *They* appear in August.

10c A verbal phrase or a prepositional phrase is not a complete sentence.

A **verbal phrase** consists of an infinitive (*to choose*), a past participle (*chosen*), or a present participle or gerund (*choosing*) together with any objects and modifiers it may have (see p. 179). A verbal phrase is a noun or modifier and cannot serve as the verb in a complete sentence.

FRAGMENT For many of the elderly, their house is their only asset. *Offering some security but no income.*

REVISED For many of the elderly, their house is their only asset, offering some security but no income.

Revised For many of the elderly, their house is their only asset. *It offers* some security but no income.

A **prepositional phrase** consists of a preposition (such as *in, on, to,* and *with*) together with its object and any modifiers (see p. 174). A prepositional phrase cannot stand alone as a complete sentence.

Fragment *In a squeeze between a valuable asset and little income.* Eventually many elderly people sell their homes.

Revised In a squeeze between a valuable asset and little income, eventually many elderly people sell their homes.

Revised *Many elderly people are* in a squeeze between a valuable asset and little income. Eventually they may sell their homes.

ESL Don't let prepositions of more than one word mislead you into writing sentence fragments.

Fragment In today's retirement communities, the elderly may have health care, housekeeping, and new friends. *As well as financial security.*

Revised In today's retirement communities, the elderly may have health care, housekeeping, and new friends, as well as financial security.

10d Any word group lacking a subject or a verb or both is not a complete sentence.

We often follow a noun with a modifier. No matter how long the noun and its modifier are, they cannot stand alone as a sentence.

Fragments *People waving flags and cheering. Lined the streets for the parade.*

Revised People waving flags and cheering lined the streets for the parade.

Fragment *Veterans who fought in Vietnam.* They are finally being honored.

Revised Veterans who fought in Vietnam are finally being honored.

Appositives are nouns, or nouns and their modifiers, that rename or describe other nouns (see p. 187). They cannot stand alone as sentences.

Fragment When I was a child, my favorite adult was an old uncle. *A retired sea captain who always told me long stories of wild adventures in faraway places.*

Revised When I was a child, my favorite adult was an old uncle, a retired sea captain who always told me long stories of wild adventures in faraway places.

CREATING PROBLEMS

If students have been assigned Chapter 11, "Comma Splices and Fused Sentences," along with this chapter, ask them to write sample sentences containing fused sentences, comma splices, and fragments. Then have them exchange papers and check to see if the errors have been executed properly. This exercise will help students recognize fused sentences, comma splices, and fragments. (It's much harder to create intentional errors, particularly sentence fragments, than most students will think.)

ANALYZING PATTERNS

If students are keeping an error log in their journals, ask them to analyze the pattern(s) that lead them to commit fragments. Most students will commit fragments with only one or two of the problem sentence patterns discussed in 10b–10d.

Compound predicates are predicates made up of two or more verbs and their objects, if any (see p. 188). A verb or its object cannot stand alone as a sentence.

FRAGMENT Uncle Marlon drew out his tales. *And embellished them.*
REVISED Uncle Marlon drew out his tales and embellished them.

FRAGMENT He described characters he had met. *And storms at sea.*
REVISED He described characters he had met and storms at sea.

NOTE Beginning a sentence with a coordinating conjunction such as *and* or *but* can lead to a sentence fragment. Check every sentence you begin with a coordinating conjunction to be sure it is complete.

frag 10d

ANSWERS: EXERCISE 2

Possible answers

1. Human beings who perfume themselves are not much different from other animals.
2. Animals as varied as insects and dogs release pheromones, chemicals that signal other animals.
3. Human beings have a diminished sense of smell and do not consciously detect most of their own species' pheromones.
4. The human substitute for pheromones may be perfumes, especially musk and other fragrances derived from animal oils.
5. Some sources say that humans began using perfume to cover up the smell of burning flesh during sacrifices to the gods.
6. No sentence fragment.
7. The earliest historical documents from the Middle East record the use of fragrances, not only in religious ceremonies but on the body.
8. In the nineteenth century chemists began synthesizing perfume oils, which previously could be made only from natural sources.
9. The most popular animal oil for perfume today is musk, although some people dislike its heavy, sweet odor.
10. Synthetic musk oil would preserve a certain species of deer whose gland is the source of musk.

Exercise 2
Revising sentence fragments

Correct any sentence fragment below either by combining it with a main clause or by making it a main clause. If an item contains no sentence fragment, circle the number preceding it.

Example:

Jujitsu is good for self-protection. Because it enables one to overcome an opponent without the use of weapons.

Jujitsu is good for self-protection because it enables one to overcome an opponent without the use of weapons.

1. Human beings who perfume themselves. They are not much different from other animals.
2. Animals as varied as insects and dogs release *pheromones*. Chemicals that signal other animals.
3. Human beings have a diminished sense of smell. And do not consciously detect most of their own species' pheromones.
4. The human substitute for pheromones may be perfumes. Especially musk and other fragrances derived from animal oils.
5. Some sources say that humans began using perfume to cover up the smell of burning flesh. During sacrifices to the gods.
6. Perfumes became religious offerings in their own right. Being expensive to make, they were highly prized.
7. The earliest historical documents from the Middle East record the use of fragrances. Not only in religious ceremonies but on the body.
8. In the nineteenth century chemists began synthesizing perfume oils. Which previously could be made only from natural sources.
9. The most popular animal oil for perfume today is musk. Although some people dislike its heavy, sweet odor.
10. Synthetic musk oil would help conserve a certain species of deer. Whose gland is the source of musk.

10e Be aware of the acceptable uses of incomplete sentences.

A few word groups lacking the usual subject-predicate combination are not sentence fragments because they conform to the expectations of most readers. They include exclamations (*Oh no!*); questions and answers (*Where next? To Kansas.*); and commands (*Move along. Shut the window.*). Another kind of incomplete sentence, occurring in special situations, is the transitional phrase (*So much for the causes, now for the results. One final point.*).

Experienced writers sometimes use sentence fragments when they want to achieve a special effect. Such fragments appear more in informal than in formal writing. Unless you are experienced and thoroughly secure in your own writing, you should avoid all fragments and concentrate on writing clear, well-formed sentences.

Exercise 3
Revising: Sentence fragments

Revise the following paragraph to eliminate sentence fragments by combining them with main clauses or rewriting them as main clauses.

Baby red-eared slider turtles are brightly colored. With bold patterns on their yellowish undershells. Which serve as a warning to predators. The bright colors of skunks and other animals. They signal that the animals will spray nasty chemicals. In contrast, the turtle's colors warn largemouth bass. That the baby turtle will actively defend itself. When a bass gulps down a turtle. The feisty baby claws and bites. Forcing the bass to spit it out. To avoid a similar painful experience. The bass will avoid other baby red-eared slider turtles. The turtle loses its bright colors as it grows too big. For a bass's afternoon snack.

NOTE See page 316 for an exercise involving sentence fragments along with comma splices, fused sentences, and other sentence errors.

frag 10e

COLLABORATIVE LEARNING

Students can work productively together on Exercises 2 and 3. Encourage each group to experiment with more than one response to each sentence.

ANSWERS: EXERCISE 3

Possible revision

Baby red-eared slider turtles are brightly colored. Bold patterns on their yellowish undershells serve as a warning to predators. The bright colors of skunks and other animals signal that the animals will spray nasty chemicals. In contrast, the turtle's colors warn largemouth bass that the baby turtle will actively defend itself. When a bass gulps down a turtle, the feisty baby claws and bites, forcing the bass to spit it out. To avoid a similar painful experience, the bass will avoid other baby red-eared slider turtles. The turtle loses its bright colors as it grows too big for a bass's afternoon snack.

Chapter 11

Comma Splices and Fused Sentences

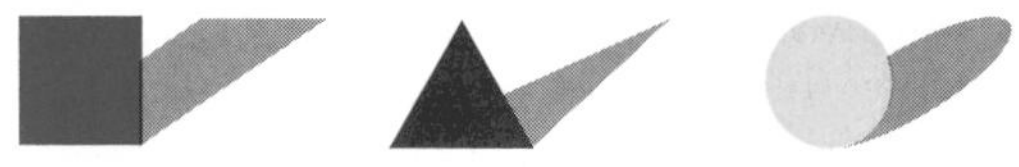

HIGHLIGHTS

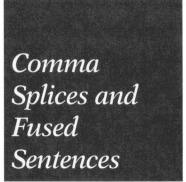

This chapter begins with a summary of the accepted methods for punctuating consecutive main clauses and follows with advice for recognizing and correcting comma splices and fused sentences. Correction of comma splices and fused sentences may involve strategies that students should employ more frequently in their sentences, particularly subordination and use of the semicolon. To encourage variety in sentence structure along with the avoidance of error, exercises for the chapter ask students to combine sentences following different strategies as well as to recognize and revise comma splices and fused sentences.

It's important to remember that students will naturally commit more of these errors as they struggle to master more complex syntactic patterns. Although you want to point out their mistakes, be careful not to focus too tightly on punctuation errors that occur as they strive for stylistic growth.

KNOWING YOUR ERRORS

Writers tend to produce repeated patterns of error (comma splices or sentence fragments, for example) and may struggle to recognize as well as to correct occurrences of those particular patterns of error in their work. It can be extremely helpful for students to learn which errors frequently occur in their work and to keep a list of corrected examples of those errors from previous work in order to look for those particular errors in future work.

RESOURCES AND IDEAS

Teachers and tutors who have little trouble punctuating sentences themselves may find it difficult to understand why some students have such difficulty with punctuation. In *The Practical Tutor* (New York: Oxford UP, 1987, 177–201), Emily Meyer and Louise Z. Smith offer detailed explanations of the causes of error and advice for diagnosing the roots of a student's punctuation difficulties. The teaching strategies they suggest include reading aloud, reading unpunctuated passages, asking probing questions (examples provided), and using simple diagrams. Rei R. Noguchi also offers innovative approaches to these errors in "Run-ons, Comma Splices, and Native-Speaker Abilities" in *Grammar and the Teaching of Writing: Limits and Possibilities* (Urbana: NCTE, 1991, 64–83).

A sentence or main clause contains at least a subject and a predicate, which together express a complete thought (see p. 163). We can separate two consecutive main clauses in one of four ways:

- With a period:

  The ship was huge**.** Its mast stood eighty feet high.

- With a semicolon:

  The ship was huge**;** its mast stood eighty feet high.

- With a comma preceding a coordinating conjunction that joins the clauses and specifies the relation between them:

  The ship was huge**,** *and* its mast stood eighty feet high.

- Occasionally with a colon when the second clause explains the first (see p. 416):

  The ship was huge**:** its mast stood eighty feet high.

The period, semicolon, or colon alone or the comma plus coordinating conjunction signals readers that one main clause (complete thought) is ending and another is beginning.

Two problems in punctuating main clauses deprive readers of this signal. One is the **comma splice,** in which the clauses are joined (or spliced) *only* with a comma.

COMMA SPLICE
The ship was huge, its mast stood eighty feet high.

The other problem is the **fused sentence,** in which no punctuation or coordinating conjunction appears between the clauses.

FUSED SENTENCE
The ship was huge its mast stood eighty feet high.

Comma splices and fused sentences are serious errors because they generally force the reader to reread for sense.

TRANSPARENCY MASTER 11.1

Situations that may produce comma splices and fused sentences

- The first clause is negative; the second, positive.

  SPLICE Petric is not a nurse, she is a doctor.
  REVISED Petric is not a nurse**;** she is a doctor.

- The second clause amplifies or illustrates the first.

  FUSED She did well in college her average was 3.9.
  REVISED She did well in college**:** her average was 3.9.

- The second clause contains a conjunctive adverb or other transitional expression, such as *however* or *for example* (see p. 277).

  SPLICE She had intended to become a biologist, *however,* medicine seemed more exciting.
  REVISED She had intended to become a biologist**;** *however,* medicine seemed more exciting.

- The subject of the second clause repeats or refers to the subject of the first clause.

  FUSED Petric is an internist *she* practices in Topeka.
  REVISED Petric is an internist**.** *She* practices in Topeka.

- Splicing or fusing is an attempt to link related ideas or to smooth choppy sentences.

  SPLICE She is very committed to her work, she devotes almost all her time to patient care.
  REVISED *Because* she is very committed to her work, she devotes almost all her time to patient care.
  REVISED She is *so* committed to her work *that* she devotes almost all her time to patient care.

- Words identifying the speaker divide a quotation between two complete sentences. (See p. 380 for the punctuation to use in this case.)

  SPLICE "Medicine is a human frontier," Petric says, "The boundaries are unknown."
  REVISED "Medicine is a human frontier," Petric says**.** "The boundaries are unknown."

cs/fs 11

EXCEPTION Experienced writers sometimes use commas between very brief main clauses that are grammatically parallel.

He's not a person, he's a monster.

However, many readers view such punctuation as incorrect. Unless you are certain that your readers will not object to the comma in a sentence like this one, separate the clauses with periods or semicolons, as described in this chapter.

COMMA SPLICES

11a Separate two main clauses with a comma *only* when they are joined by a coordinating conjunction.

A comma cannot separate main clauses unless they are linked by a coordinating conjunction (*and, but, or, nor, for, so, yet*). Readers expect the same main clause to continue after a comma alone. When they find themselves reading a second main clause before they realize they have finished the first, they may have to reread to understand your meaning.

If your readers point out comma splices in your writing, try one of the revision strategies below.

Making separate sentences

Revising a comma splice by making separate sentences from the main clauses will always be correct. The period is not only correct but preferable when the ideas expressed in the two main clauses are only loosely related.

COMMA SPLICE Chemistry has contributed much to our understanding of foods, many foods such as wheat and beans can be produced in the laboratory.

REVISED Chemistry has contributed much to our understanding of foods. Many foods such as wheat and beans can be produced in the laboratory.

ESL Making separate sentences may be the best option if you are used to writing very long sentences in your native language and often write comma splices in English.

Inserting a coordinating conjunction

When the ideas in the main clauses are closely related and equally important, you may correct a comma splice by inserting the appropriate coordinating conjunction immediately after the comma to join the clauses.

COMMA SPLICE Some laboratory-grown foods taste good, they are nutritious.

TEACHING TIP (ESL)

A mnemonic that helps students remember the coordinating conjunctions is *fanboys,* which is the first letter of each coordinating conjunction. Put the following chart on the board to illustrate:

	for	
	and	
	nor	
Sentence 1	*but*	Sentence 2
	or	
	yet	
	so	

Remind ESL students that after *nor,* English requires inverted word order.

Revision of comma splices and fused sentences

- Underline the main clauses in your draft.
- When two main clauses fall in the same sentence, check the connection between them.
- If nothing falls between the clauses or only a comma does, revise in one of the following ways, depending on the relation you want to establish between the clauses. (See the text discussion for examples.)

  Make the clauses into separate sentences.
  Insert a comma followed by *and, but,* or another coordinating conjunction. Or, if the comma is already present, insert just the coordinating conjunction.
  Insert a semicolon between clauses.
  Subordinate one clause to the other.

REVISED Some laboratory-grown foods taste good, *and* they are nutritious.

Using a semicolon

If the relation between the ideas expressed in the main clauses is very close and obvious without a conjunction, you can separate the clauses with a semicolon. (See also 11b.)

COMMA SPLICE Good taste is rare in laboratory-grown vegetables, they are usually bland.

REVISED Good taste is rare in laboratory-grown vegetables; they are usually bland.

Subordinating one clause

When the idea in one clause is more important than that in the other, you can express the less important idea in a phrase or a subordinate clause. (See p. 183 for a list of subordinating conjunctions.) Subordination is often more effective than forming separate sentences because it defines the relation between ideas more precisely.

COMMA SPLICE The vitamins are adequate, the flavor is deficient.

REVISED The vitamins are adequate. The flavor is deficient. [Both ideas receive equal weight.]

IMPROVED *Even though* the vitamins are adequate, the flavor is deficient. [Emphasis on the second idea.]

11b Separate main clauses related by *however, for example,* and so on.

Two kinds of words that are not conjunctions describe how one main clause relates to another:

CREATING PROBLEMS

If students have been assigned Chapter 10, "Sentence Fragments," along with this chapter, ask them to write sample sentences containing comma splices, fused sentences, and fragments. Then have them exchange papers and check to see if the errors have been executed properly. This exercise will help students recognize comma splices, fused sentences, and fragments. (It's much harder to create intentional errors, particularly fused sentences and sentence fragments, than most students will think.)

IN CONTEXT

Identifying sentence problems in the context of an essay can be more challenging and rewarding than working with single-sentence examples. The content and flow of an essay can draw attention away from punctuation and sentence structure, making it hard to identify errors but also providing an experience similar to that of proofreading. To supplement the paragraph exercise at the end of this chapter (or at the end of Chapter 10), revise part of a professional essay to introduce errors (or find an error-filled student essay), and then distribute the essay to the class, asking students to locate and revise the errors.

- **Conjunctive adverbs,** such as *consequently, finally, hence, however, indeed, therefore,* or *thus.* (See p. 191 for a longer list.)
- Other **transitional expressions,** such as *even so, for example, in fact, of course, to the right,* and *to this end.* (See pp. 100–01 for a longer list.)

When two clauses are related by a conjunctive adverb or a transitional expression, they must be separated by a period or by a semicolon. The adverb or expression is also generally set off by a comma or commas (see p. 373).

COMMA SPLICE	Most Americans refuse to give up unhealthful habits, consequently our medical costs are higher than those of many other countries.
REVISED	Most Americans refuse to give up unhealthful habits**.** Consequently**,** our medical costs are higher than those of many other countries.
REVISED	Most Americans refuse to give up unhealthful habits**;** consequently**,** our medical costs are higher than those of many other countries.

Conjunctive adverbs and transitional expressions are different from coordinating conjunctions (*and, but,* and so on) and subordinating conjunctions (*although, because,* and so on).

- Unlike conjunctions, conjunctive adverbs and transitional expressions do not join two clauses into a grammatical unit but merely describe the way two clauses relate in meaning.
- Thus, unlike conjunctions, conjunctive adverbs and transitional expressions can be moved from one place to another in a clause (see p. 191). No matter where in the clause an adverb or expression falls, though, the clause must be separated from another main clause by a period or semicolon.

COMMA SPLICE

The increased time devoted to watching television is not the only cause of the decline in reading ability, however, it is one of the important causes.

PERIOD

The increased time devoted to watching television is not the only cause of the decline in reading ability**.** *However***,** it is one of the important causes.

SEMICOLON

The increased time devoted to watching television is not the only cause of the decline in reading ability**;** *however***,** it is one of the important causes.

The increased time devoted to watching television is not the only cause of the decline in reading ability**;** it is**,** *however***,** one of the important causes.

Exercise 1

Identifying and revising comma splices

Correct each comma splice below in *two* of the ways described on pages 276–77. If an item contains no comma splice, circle the number preceding it.

Example:

Carolyn still had a headache, she could not get the child-proof cap off the aspirin bottle.

Carolyn still had a headache *because* she could not get the child-proof cap off the aspirin bottle. [Subordination.]

Carolyn still had a headache**,** *for* she could not get the child-proof cap off the aspirin bottle. [Coordinating conjunction.]

1. Money has a long history, it goes back at least as far as the earliest records.
2. Many of the earliest records concern financial transactions, indeed, early history must often be inferred from commercial activity.
3. Every known society has had a system of money, though the objects serving as money have varied widely.
4. Sometimes the objects have had real value, in modern times, however, their value has been more abstract.
5. Cattle, fermented beverages, and rare shells have served as money, each one had actual value for the society.

ANSWERS: EXERCISE 1

Possible answers

1. Money has a long history. It goes back at least as far as the earliest records.
   Money has a long history that goes back at least as far as the earliest records.
2. Many of the earliest records concern financial transactions; indeed, early history must often be inferred from commercial activity.
   Many of the earliest records concern financial transactions. Indeed, early history must often be inferred from commercial activity.
3. No comma splice.
4. Sometimes the objects have had real value. In modern times, however, their value has been more abstract.
   Sometimes the objects have had real value; in modern times, however, their value has been more abstract.
5. Cattle, fermented beverages, and rare shells have served as money, and each one had actual value for the society.
   Cattle, fermented beverages, and rare shells have served as money. Each one had actual value for the society.

fs
11c

FUSED SENTENCES

11c Combine two main clauses only with an appropriate conjunction or punctuation mark between them.

When two main clauses are joined without a word to connect them or a punctuation mark to separate them, the result is a **fused sentence.** Fused sentences can rarely be understood on first reading, and they are never acceptable in standard written English.

FUSED Our foreign policy is not well defined it confuses many countries.

Fused sentences may be corrected in the same ways as comma splices. See the box on page 277.

SEPARATE SENTENCES

Our foreign policy is not well defined**.** It confuses many countries.

COMMA AND COORDINATING CONJUNCTION

Our foreign policy is not well defined**,** *and* it confuses many countries.

SEMICOLON

Our foreign policy is not well defined**;** it confuses many countries.

SUBORDINATING CONJUNCTION

Because our foreign policy is not well defined, it confuses many countries.

ANSWERS: EXERCISE 2

Possible answers

1. Throughout history money and religion were closely linked because there was little distinction between government and religion.
   Throughout history money and religion were closely linked, for there was little distinction between government and religion.
2. The head of state and the religious leader were often the same person. All power rested in one ruler.
   The head of state and the religious leader were often the same person; all power rested in one ruler.
3. These powerful leaders decided what objects would serve as money, and their backing encouraged public faith in the money.
   These powerful leaders decided what objects would serve as money. Their backing encouraged public faith in the money.
4. When coins were minted of precious metals, the religious overtones of money were strengthened.
   Coins were minted of precious metals. The religious overtones of money were then strengthened.
5. People already believed the precious metals to be divine, so their use in money intensified its allure.
   People already believed the precious metals to be divine; their use in money intensified its allure.

COLLABORATIVE LEARNING

Ask students to complete Exercises 1 and 2 independently and compare their responses in small groups. Then ask each group to work together on Exercise 3 and 4. Finally, have the groups examine each other's work to find and revise examples of comma splices and fused sentences. For students who are having difficulty with these errors, the move from the handbook exercises to their own work can be extremely beneficial.

fs 11c

Exercise 2
Identifying and revising fused sentences

Revise each of the fused sentences below in *two* of the four ways shown above.

Example:

Tim was shy he usually refused invitations.
Tim was shy, *so* he usually refused invitations.
Tim was shy; he usually refused invitations.

1. Throughout history money and religion were closely linked there was little distinction between government and religion.
2. The head of state and the religious leader were often the same person all power rested in one ruler.
3. These powerful leaders decided what objects would serve as money their backing encouraged public faith in the money.
4. Coins were minted of precious metals the religious overtones of money were then strengthened.
5. People already believed the precious metals to be divine their use in money intensified its allure.

Exercise 3
Sentence combining: Comma splices and fused sentences

Combine each pair of sentences below into one sentence without creating a comma splice or fused sentence. Combine sentences by (1) supplying a comma and coordinating conjunction, (2) supplying a semicolon, or (3) subordinating one clause to the other. You will have to add, delete, or change words as well as punctuation.

Example:

The sun sank lower in the sky. The colors gradually faded.

As the sun sank lower in the sky, the colors gradually faded. [The first clause is subordinated to the second.]

1. The exact origin of paper money is unknown. It has not survived as coins, shells, and other durable objects have.
2. Perhaps goldsmiths were also bankers. Thus they held the gold of their wealthy customers.
3. The goldsmiths probably gave customers receipts for their gold. These receipts were then used in trade.
4. The goldsmiths were something like modern-day bankers. Their receipts were something like modern-day money.
5. The goldsmiths became even more like modern-day bankers. They began issuing receipts for more gold than they actually held in their vaults.

Exercise 4
Revising: Comma splices and fused sentences

Identify and revise the comma splices and fused sentences in the following paragraph.

All those parents who urged their children to eat broccoli were right, the vegetable really is healthful. Broccoli contains sulforaphane, moreover, this mustard oil can be found in kale and Brussels sprouts. Sulforaphane causes the body to make an enzyme that attacks carcinogens, these substances cause cancer. The enzyme speeds up the work of the kidneys then they can flush harmful chemicals out of the body. Other vegetables have similar benefits however, green, leafy vegetables like broccoli are the most efficient. Thus, wise people will eat their broccoli it could save their lives.

Note See page 316 for an exercise involving comma splices and fused sentences along with other sentence errors.

ANSWERS: EXERCISE 3

Possible answers

1. The exact origin of paper money is unknown because it has not survived as coins, shells, and other durable objects have.
2. Perhaps goldsmiths were also bankers; thus they held the gold of their wealthy customers.
3. The goldsmiths probably gave customers receipts for their gold, and these receipts were then used in trade.
4. The goldsmiths were something like modern-day bankers; their receipts were something like modern-day money.
5. The goldsmiths became even more like modern-day bankers when they began issuing receipts for more gold than they actually held in their vaults.

ANSWERS: EXERCISE 4

All those parents who urged their children to eat broccoli were right; the vegetable really is healthful. Broccoli contains sulforaphane; moreover, this mustard oil can be found in kale and Brussels sprouts. Sulforaphane causes the body to make an enzyme that attacks carcinogens, substances that cause cancer. The enzyme speeds up the work of the kidneys so that they can flush harmful chemicals out of the body. Other vegetables have similar benefits; however, green, leafy vegetables like broccoli are the most efficient. Thus, wise people will eat their broccoli; it could save their lives.

HIGHLIGHTS

Writers at all levels—advanced or struggling—will be likely to consult this chapter often, for problems with pronoun reference can arise in short, uncomplicated sentences as well as in papers that are ambitious in style and content. The discussion covers a number of particularly troublesome problems: unclear or ambiguous antecedents; broad reference with *this, that, which,* and *it;* indefinite use of *it* and *they;* and inappropriate use of *who, which,* and *that.* In each case, the discussion stresses the need for precision in reference as a way of ensuring that readers can follow the meaning of a passage. The examples and exercises mostly show reference problems within sentences as a way of keeping the discussion as simple and accessible as possible; however, the text points out that reference problems are just as likely to occur between sentences, and the paragraph exercise at the end of the chapter stresses this fact.

Because strings of pronouns are an important device for creating coherence over long stretches of discourse, reference problems between or among sentences can cause considerable misunderstanding. In this sense, pronoun reference errors can point to students' larger conceptual difficulties (such as defining or elaborating on key terms or thinking through a transition). This means that when students learn to recognize their pronoun reference errors, that recognition can provide the occasion for substantive revision and paragraph development.

RETRIEVING SENTENCES

Reverse the process of sentence combining by asking students to reconstruct (or retrieve) the shorter (kernel) sentences that lie behind a long sentence containing a reference error. You may wish to use sentences from the text as a basis for the exercise. This activity will help students spot ambiguity or vague reference in the long sentence. After they have found the shorter sentences, ask students to recombine, this time avoiding the reference problem.

Original sentence: After the van hit John's car, its engine stopped running and its radiator started leaking.

Chapter 12

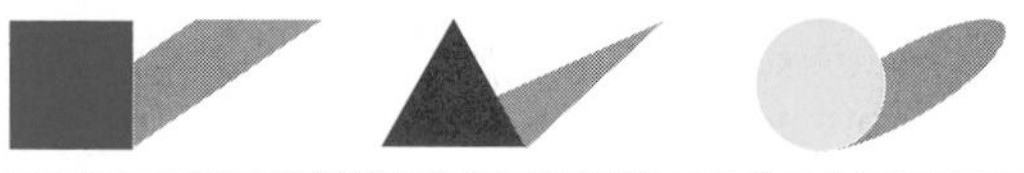

A **pronoun** such as *it* or *they* derives its meaning from its **antecedent,** the noun it substitutes for. Therefore, a pronoun must refer clearly and unmistakably to its antecedent in order for the meaning to be clear. A sentence such as *Jim told Mark he was not invited* is not clear because the reader does not know whether *he* refers to Jim or to Mark.

One way to make pronoun reference clear is to ensure that the pronoun and antecedent agree in person, number, and gender (see p. 246). The other way is to ensure that the pronoun refers unambiguously to a single, close, specific antecedent.

ESL A pronoun does need a clear antecedent nearby, but don't use both a pronoun and its antecedent as the subject of the same sentence or clause: *Jim* [not *Jim he*] *told Mark to go alone.* (See also p. 308.)

12a Make a pronoun refer clearly to one antecedent.

When either of two nouns can be a pronoun's antecedent, the reference will not be clear.

CONFUSING Emily Dickinson is sometimes compared with Jane Austen, but *she* was quite different.

Revise such a sentence in one of two ways:

Kernels: The van hit John's car. The van's engine stopped running. The van's radiator started leaking.

Recombined sentence: After the van hit John's car, the van's engine stopped running and its radiator started leaking.

Principal causes of unclear pronoun reference

- More than one possible antecedent (p. 282):

Confusing To keep birds from eating seeds, soak *them* in blue food coloring.

Clear To keep birds from eating seeds, soak *the seeds* in blue food coloring.

- Antecedent too far away (p. 284):

Confusing Employees should consult with their supervisor *who* require personal time.

Clear Employees *who* require personal time should consult with their supervisor.

- Antecedent only implied (p. 285):

Confusing Many children begin reading on their own by watching television, but *this* should be discounted in government policy.

Clear Many children begin reading on their own by watching television, but *such self-instruction* should be discounted in government policy.

See also pages 286–88.

- Replace the pronoun with the appropriate noun.

Clear Emily Dickinson is sometimes compared with Jane Austen, but *Dickinson* [or *Austen*] was quite different.

- Avoid repetition by rewriting the sentence. If you use the pronoun, make sure it has only one possible antecedent.

Clear Despite occasional comparison, Emily Dickinson and Jane Austen were quite different.

Clear Though sometimes compared with *her,* Emily Dickinson was quite different from Jane Austen.

Sentences that report what someone said, using verbs such as *said* or *told,* often require direct rather than indirect quotation.

Confusing Juliet Noble told Ann Torre that she was mistaken.

Clear Juliet Noble told Ann Torre, "I am mistaken."

Clear Juliet Noble told Ann Torre, "You are mistaken."

Note Avoid the awkward device of using a pronoun followed by the appropriate noun in parentheses, as in the following example:

ref 12a

Weak Noble should apologize to Torre, and *she (Noble)* should notify the press.

Improved Noble should apologize to Torre and notify the press.

12b Place a pronoun close enough to its antecedent to ensure clarity.

A clause beginning *who, which,* or *that* generally should fall immediately after the word it refers to.

Confusing Jody found a dress in the attic *that* her aunt had worn.

Clear In the attic Jody found a dress *that* her aunt had worn.

Even when only one word could possibly serve as the antecedent of a pronoun, the relationship between the two may still be unclear if they are widely separated.

Confusing Jane Austen had little formal education but was well educated at home. Far from living an isolated life in the English countryside, the Austens were a large family with a wide circle of friends who provided entertainment and cultural enrichment. They also provided material for *her* stories.

Clear Jane Austen had little formal education but was well educated at home. Far from living an isolated life in the English countryside, the Austens were a large family with a wide circle of friends who provided entertainment and cultural enrichment. They also provided material for *Jane Austen's* stories.

The confusing separation of pronoun and antecedent is most likely to occur in long sentences and, as illustrated above, in adjacent sentences within a paragraph.

ref
12b

Exercise 1

Revising: Ambiguous and remote pronoun reference

Rewrite the following sentences to eliminate unclear pronoun reference. If you use a pronoun in your revision, be sure that it refers to only one antecedent and that it falls close enough to its antecedent to ensure clarity.

Example:

Saul found an old gun in the rotting shed that was just as his grandfather had left it.

In the rotting shed Saul found an old *gun that* was just as his grandfather had left it.

ANSWERS: EXERCISE 1

Possible answers

1. There is a difference between the heroes of the twentieth century and the heroes of earlier times: twentieth-century heroes have flaws in their characters.
2. Sports fans still admire Pete Rose, Babe Ruth, and Joe Namath even though none of these heroes could be perfect.
3. Fans liked Rose for having his young son serve as batboy when Rose was in Cincinnati.

1. There is a difference between the heroes of the twentieth century and the heroes of earlier times: they have flaws in their characters.
2. Sports fans still admire Pete Rose, Babe Ruth, and Joe Namath even though they could not be perfect.
3. Fans liked Rose for having his young son serve as batboy when he was in Cincinnati.
4. Rose's reputation as a gambler and tax evader may overshadow his reputation as a ball player, but it will survive.
5. Rose amassed an unequaled record as a hitter, using his bat to do things no one else has ever done. It stands even though Rose has been banned from baseball.

4. Rose's reputation as a gambler and tax evader may overshadow his reputation as a ballplayer, but the latter will survive.
5. Rose amassed an unequaled record as a hitter, using his bat to do things no one else has ever done. The record stands even though Rose has been banned from baseball.

12c Make a pronoun refer to a specific antecedent, not an implied one.

ref 12c

A pronoun should refer to a specific noun or other pronoun. The reader can only guess at the meaning of a pronoun when its antecedent is implied by the context, not stated outright.

1 Use *this, that, which,* and *it* cautiously.

The most common kind of implied reference occurs when the pronoun *this, that, which,* or *it* refers to a whole idea or situation described in the preceding clause, sentence, or even paragraph. Such reference, often called **broad reference,** is acceptable only when the pronoun refers clearly to the entire preceding clause. In the following sentence, *which* could not possibly refer to anything but the whole preceding clause.

> I can be kind and civil to people, *which* is more than you can.
> —George Bernard Shaw

But if a pronoun might confuse a reader, you should avoid using it or provide an appropriate noun.

Confusing The faculty agreed on changing the requirements, but *it* took time.

Clear The faculty agreed on changing the requirements, but *the agreement* took time.

Clear The faculty agreed on changing the requirements, but *the change* took time.

Confusing The British knew little of the American countryside, and they had no experience with the colonists' guerrilla tactics. *This* gave the colonists an advantage.

RESOURCES AND IDEAS

Moskovit, Leonard. "When Is Broad Reference Clear?" *College Composition and Communication* 34 (1983): 454–69. The question of the acceptability of broad reference is a complicated one, as Moskovit points out, and anyone interested in looking at how broad reference operates in sophisticated prose will enjoy his essay.

Clear The British knew little of the American countryside, and they had no experience with the colonists' guerrilla tactics. This *ignorance and inexperience* gave the colonists an advantage.

2 Implied nouns are not clear antecedents.

A noun may be implied in some other word or phrase, such as an adjective (*happiness* implied in *happy*), a verb (*driver* implied in *drive*), or a possessive (*mother* implied in *mother's*). But a pronoun cannot refer clearly to an implied noun, only to a specific, stated one.

Confusing Cohen's report brought *her* a lawsuit.

Clear Cohen was sued over *her* report.

Confusing Her reports on psychological development are generally unnoticed outside *it.*

Clear Her reports on psychological development are generally unnoticed outside *the field.*

3 Titles of papers are not clear antecedents.

The title of a paper is entirely separate from the paper itself, so a pronoun should not be used in the opening sentence of a paper to refer to the title.

Title How to Row a Boat

Not *This* is not as easy as it looks.

But *Rowing a boat* is not as easy as it looks.

ref 12d

IT, WHICH,* AND *THEY

Distribute copies of a student paper that uses *it, which, they,* and other pronouns in sentences without supplying clear antecedents in preceding sentences. Ask students to work in groups to revise the reference problems. In each case ask the group to consider whether the revision simply involves correcting the error or whether it calls for the writer to clarify and develop his or her transition between sentences or paragraphs.

12d Use *it* and *they* to refer to definite antecedents. Use *you* only to mean "you, the reader."

In conversation we commonly use expressions such as *It says in the paper* or *In Texas they say*. But such indefinite use of *it* and *they* is inappropriate in writing. The constructions are not only unclear but wordy.

Confusing In Chapter 4 of this book, *it* describes the early flights of the Wright brothers.

Clear *Chapter 4* of this book describes the early flights of the Wright brothers.

CONFUSING	In the average television drama, *they* present a false picture of life.
CLEAR	The average television *drama* presents a false picture of life.

In all but very formal writing, *you* is acceptable when the meaning is clearly "you, the reader." But the context must be appropriate for such a meaning.

INAPPROPRIATE	In the fourteenth century *you* had to struggle simply to survive.
REVISED	In the fourteenth century *one* [or *a person*] had to struggle simply to survive.

12e Use the pronoun *it* only one way in a sentence.

We use *it* idiomatically in expressions such as *It is raining.* We use *it* to postpone the subject in sentences such as *It is true that more jobs are available to women today.* And we use *it* as a personal pronoun in sentences such as *Joan wanted the book, but she couldn't find it.* All these uses are standard, but two of them in the same passage can confuse the reader.

CONFUSING	*It* is true that the Constitution sets limits, but *it* is also flexible.
CLEAR	The Constitution does set limits, but *it* is also flexible.

12f Use *who, which,* and *that* for appropriate antecedents.

The relative pronouns *who, which,* and *that* commonly refer to persons, animals, or things. *Who* refers most often to persons but may also refer to animals that have names.

Dorothy is the girl *who* visits Oz.
Her dog, Toto, *who* accompanies her, gives her courage.

Which refers to animals and things.

The Orinoco River, *which* is 1,600 miles long, flows through Venezuela into the Atlantic Ocean.

That refers to animals and things and occasionally to persons when they are collective or anonymous.

CORRECTING A NARRATIVE

Find or write a brief narrative containing several events and more than one character. Introduce enough reference problems so that readers have difficulty unraveling the events. If you wish, include dialogue in the narrative in such a way that the reference problems make it hard to identify the speakers. (Using "He said" as a tag when there are two men in the narrative is one possibility.) Ask students to work in groups to untangle the problems in the narrative and to rewrite it, removing vague and ambiguous references.

USE OF *THAT* OR *WHICH*

Students are often confused about whether to use *which, who,* or *that* because they misunderstand restrictive and nonrestrictive elements. Students who suffer from this confusion should also consult Chapter 21 and *that/which* in the Glossary of Usage.

The rocket *that* failed cost millions.
Infants *that* walk need constant tending.

(See also p. 372 for the use of *which* and *that* in nonrestrictive and restrictive clauses.)

The possessive *whose* generally refers to people but may refer to animals and things to avoid awkward and wordy *of which* constructions.

The book *whose* binding broke was rare. [Compare *The book of which the binding broke was rare.*]

ref 12f

ANSWERS: EXERCISE 2

Possible answers

1. "Life begins at forty" is a cliché many people live by, and this saying may well be true.
2. When Pearl Buck was forty, her novel *The Good Earth* won the Pulitzer Prize.
3. Buck was a novelist who wrote primarily about China.
4. In *The Good Earth* the characters have to struggle, but fortitude is rewarded.
5. Buck received much critical praise and earned over $7 million, but she was very modest about her success (or the praise or the money).
6. Kenneth Kaunda was elected to the presidency of Zambia in 1964, at age forty.
7. When Catherine I became empress of Russia at age forty, the Russians feared more than loved her.
8. At forty, Paul Revere made his famous ride to warn American revolutionary leaders that the British were going to arrest them. His warning gave the colonists time to prepare for battle.
9. The members of the British House of Commons did not welcome forty-year-old Nancy Astor as the first female member when she entered in 1919.
10. In AD 610 Muhammad, age forty, began to have a series of visions that became the foundation of the Muslim faith. Since then, millions of people have become Muslims.

Exercise 2
Revising: Indefinite and inappropriate pronoun reference

Many of the pronouns in the following sentences do not refer to specific, appropriate antecedents. Revise the sentences as necessary to make them clear.

Example:

In Grand Teton National Park, they have moose, elk, and trumpeter swans.

Moose, elk, and trumpeter swans live in Grand Teton National Park.

1. "Life begins at forty" is a cliché many people live by, and this may well be true.
2. When she was forty, Pearl Buck's novel *The Good Earth* won the Pulitzer Prize.
3. Buck was a novelist which wrote primarily about China.
4. In *The Good Earth* you have to struggle, but fortitude is rewarded.
5. Buck received much critical praise and earned over $7 million, but she was very modest about it.
6. Kenneth Kaunda, past president of Zambia, was elected to it in 1964, at age forty.
7. When Catherine I became empress of Russia at age forty, they feared more than loved her.
8. At forty, Paul Revere made his famous ride to warn American revolutionary leaders that the British were going to arrest them. This gave the colonists time to prepare for battle.
9. In the British House of Commons they did not welcome forty-year-old Nancy Astor as the first female member when she entered in 1919.
10. In AD 610 Muhammad, age forty, began to have a series of visions that became the foundation of the Muslim faith. Since then, millions of people have become one.

Exercise 3
Revising: Pronoun reference

Revise the following paragraph so that each pronoun refers clearly to a single specific and appropriate antecedent.

In Charlotte Brontë's *Jane Eyre,* she is a shy young woman that takes a job as governess. Her employer is a rude, brooding man named Rochester. He lives in a mysterious mansion on the English moors, which contributes an eerie quality to Jane's experience. Eerier still are the fires, strange noises, and other unexplained happenings in the house; but Rochester refuses to discuss this. Eventually, they fall in love. On the day they are to be married, however, she learns that he has a wife hidden in the house. She is hopelessly insane and violent and must be guarded at all times, which explains his strange behavior. Heartbroken, Jane leaves the moors, and many years pass before they are reunited.

Note See page 316 for an exercise involving unclear pronoun reference along with sentence fragments, comma splices, and other sentence errors.

COLLABORATIVE LEARNING

Students can work productively together on Exercises 2 and 3. After they have completed both exercises, ask them to look for and revise instances of unclear pronoun references in other examples from each other's work. Each group might present one example of an unclear pronoun reference discovered in a student paper to the class.

ANSWERS: EXERCISE 3

Possible revision

In Charlotte Brontë's *Jane Eyre,* Jane is a shy young woman who takes a job as governess. Her employer is a rude, brooding man named Rochester. He lives in a mysterious mansion on the English moors, and both the mansion and the moors contribute an eerie quality to Jane's experience. Eerier still are the fires, strange noises, and other unexplained happenings in the house; but Rochester refuses to discuss them. Eventually, Jane and Rochester fall in love. On the day they are to be married, however, Jane learns that Rochester has a wife hidden in the house. The wife is hopelessly insane and violent and must be guarded at all times, circumstances that explain Rochester's strange behavior. Heartbroken, Jane leaves the moors, and many years pass before she and Rochester are reunited.

HIGHLIGHTS

Shifts in person and number, in tense and mood, in subject and voice, or between direct and indirect quotation can be irritating to readers and occasionally make it hard to follow the meaning of a passage. Often, however, students are not fully aware of the shifts or their effect on a reader. This chapter describes in detail and illustrates the various shifts so that students can learn to identify the problems in their own writing. The exercises ask students to revise sentences and a longer passage, much as they will need to in revising their own work.

Chapter 13 Shifts

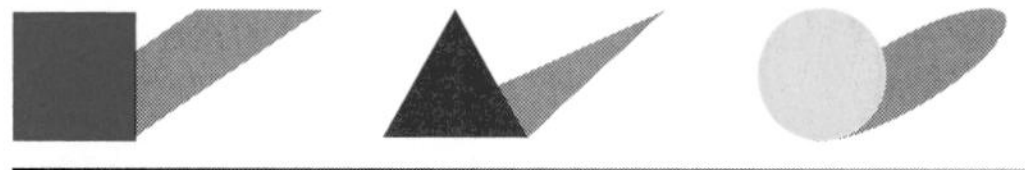

Inconsistencies in grammatical elements will confuse your readers and distort your meaning. In the following passage from a first draft, the italicized words highlight confusing inconsistencies in verbs and subjects.

First draft

A *bank* commonly *owes* more to its customers than *is held* in reserve. *They kept* enough assets to meet reasonable withdrawals, but panicked *customers* may demand all their deposits. Then demands *will exceed* supplies, and *banks failed.* These days, *a person's* losses are not likely to be great because the government insures *your* deposits.

Revised

A bank commonly owes more to its customers than *it holds* in reserve. *It keeps* enough assets to meet reasonable withdrawals, but panicked customers may demand all their deposits. Then demands will exceed supplies, and *the bank will fail.* These days, *customers'* losses are not likely to be great because the government insures *their* deposits.

Holds to match *owes*

Singular *It* and present tense *keeps* to match *bank . . . owes*

Singular *bank* to match *bank;* future tense to match *will exceed*

Plural *customers'* to match *customers*

Their to match *customers*

Shifts like those in the first draft are likely to occur while you are trying to piece together meaning during drafting. But you should straighten out your sentences during revision.

13a Keep a sentence or related sentences consistent in person and number.

Person in grammar refers to the distinction among the person talking (first person), the person spoken to (second person), and the person, object, or concept being talked about (third person). **Number** refers to the distinction between one (singular) and more than one (plural).

Shifts in person

Most shifts in person occur because we can refer to people in general, including our readers, either in the third person (*a person, one; people, they*) or in the second person (*you*).

People should not drive when *they* have been drinking.
One should not drive when *he or she* has been drinking.
You should not drive when *you* have been drinking.

Although any one of these possibilities is acceptable in an appropriate context, a mixture of them is inconsistent.

INCONSISTENT If a *person* works hard, *you* can accomplish a great deal.

REVISED If *you* work hard, *you* can accomplish a great deal.

REVISED If a *person* works hard, *he or she* can accomplish a great deal.

BETTER If *people* work hard, *they* can accomplish a great deal.

Shifts in number

Inconsistency in number occurs most often between a pronoun and its antecedent (see p. 246).

INCONSISTENT If a *student* does not understand a problem, *they* should consult the instructor.

REVISED If a *student* does not understand a problem, *he or she* should consult the instructor.

BETTER If *students* do not understand a problem, *they* should consult the instructor.

NOTE A singular noun or indefinite pronoun takes a singular pronoun with a definite gender: *he, she,* or *it.* When we use a noun like *student* or *person* or an indefinite pronoun like *everyone* or *each,* we often mean to include both males and females. To indicate this meaning, use *he or she* rather than *he* (as in the first revision above), rewrite in the plural (as in the second revision above), or rewrite to avoid the pronoun. See page 249 for more discussion and examples.

COMPUTER EXERCISE

HIGHLIGHTING AGREEMENT

Encourage students who compose on a word processor to use its highlighting or boldface capabilities to mark person and number, tense, or subject-verb agreement markers in a draft; this helps students see at a glance where they may need to revise.

COLLABORATIVE LEARNING

CHECK YOUR OWN

If shifts are a problem in the essays your class submits, go over the chapter in detail in class, and then ask students to go through their papers and circle each shift they find. This activity can be done on the day papers are to be handed in or with a set of graded papers on which you have not marked the shifts. The activity is also a good small-group exercise; students are often good at spotting shifts in someone else's writing.

Inconsistency in number can also occur between other words (usually nouns) that relate to each other in meaning.

Inconsistent All the *boys* have a good *reputation.*
Revised All the *boys* have good *reputations.*

The consistency in the revised sentence is called **logical agreement** because the nouns are consistent (the *boys* have *reputations,* not a single *reputation*).

ANSWERS: EXERCISE 1

1. When a taxpayer is waiting to receive a tax refund from the Internal Revenue Service, he or she begins to notice what time the mail carrier arrives. *Or:* When taxpayers are waiting to receive tax refunds . . . , they begin to notice what time the mail carrier arrives.
2. If the taxpayer does not receive a refund check within six weeks of filing a return, he or she may not have followed the rules of the IRS. *Or:* If taxpayers do not receive refund checks within six weeks of filing a return, they may not have followed the rules of the IRS.
3. If taxpayers do not include their Social Security numbers on returns, they will have to wait for refunds. *Or:* If a taxpayer does not include his or her Social Security number on a return, he or she will have to wait for a refund.
4. When taxpayers do not file their returns early, they will not get refunds quickly.
5. If one has made errors on the tax form, one might even be audited, thereby delaying a refund even longer. *Or:* If one has made errors on the tax form, he or she might even be audited, thereby delaying a refund even longer.

shift 13b

Exercise 1
Revising: Shifts in person and number

Revise the following sentences to make them consistent in person and number.

Example:

A plumber will fix burst pipes, but they won't repair waterlogged appliances.

Plumbers will fix burst pipes, but they won't repair waterlogged appliances.

1. When a taxpayer is waiting to receive a tax refund from the Internal Revenue Service, you begin to notice what time the mail carrier arrives.
2. If the taxpayer does not receive a refund check within six weeks of filing a return, they may not have followed the rules of the IRS.
3. If a taxpayer does not include the Social Security number on a return, you will have to wait for a refund.
4. When taxpayers do not file their return early, they will not get a refund quickly.
5. If one has made errors on the tax form, they might even be audited, thereby delaying a refund even longer.

13b Keep a sentence or related sentences consistent in tense and mood.

Shifts in tense

Within a sentence or from one sentence to another, certain changes in tense may be required to indicate changes in actual or relative time (see pp. 222–26). For example:

> Ramon *will graduate* from college twenty-three years after his father *arrived* in the United States.

But changes that are not required by meaning distract readers. Unnecessary shifts between past and present in passages narrating a series of events are particularly confusing.

Inconsistent Immediately after Booth *shot* Lincoln, Major Rathbone *threw* himself upon the assassin. But Booth *pulls* a knife and *plunges* it into the major's arm.

Revised Immediately after Booth *shot* Lincoln, Major Rathbone *threw* himself upon the assassin. But Booth *pulled* a knife and *plunged* it into the major's arm.

Use the present tense consistently to describe what an author has written, including the action in literature or a film.

Inconsistent The main character in the novel *suffers* psychologically because he *has* a clubfoot, but he eventually *triumphed* over his disability.

Revised The main character in the novel *suffers* psychologically because he *has* a clubfoot, but he eventually *triumphs* over his disability.

Shifts in mood

Shifts in the mood of verbs occur most frequently in directions when the writer moves between the imperative mood (*Unplug the appliance*) and the indicative mood (*You should unplug the appliance*). (See p. 227.) Directions are usually clearer and more concise in the imperative, as long as its use is consistent.

Inconsistent *Cook* the mixture slowly, and *you should stir* it until the sugar is dissolved.

Revised *Cook* the mixture slowly, and *stir* it until the sugar is dissolved.

Exercise 2
Revising: Shifts in tense and mood

Revise the following sentences to make them consistent in tense and mood.

Example:

Lynn ran to first, rounded the base, and keeps running until she slides into second.

Lynn ran to first, rounded the base, and *kept* running until she *slid* into second.

1. When your cholesterol count is too high, adjusting your diet and exercise level reduced it.
2. After you lowered your cholesterol rate, you decrease the chances of heart attack and stroke.
3. First eliminate saturated fats from your diet; then you should consume more whole grains and raw vegetables.
4. To avoid saturated fats, substitute turkey and chicken for beef, and you should use cholesterol-free margarine, salad dressing, and cooking oil.

ANSWERS: EXERCISE 2

1. When your cholesterol count is too high, adjusting your diet and exercise level reduces it.
2. After you lower your cholesterol rate, you decrease the chances of heart attack and stroke.
3. First eliminate saturated fats from your diet; then consume more whole grains and raw vegetables.
4. To avoid saturated fats, substitute turkey and chicken for beef, and use cholesterol-free margarine, salad dressing, and cooking oil.
5. A regular program of aerobic exercise, such as walking or swimming, improves your cholesterol rate and makes you feel much healthier.

CLASS READING

Use the passage below, or find or write another that contains several kinds of shifts. Distribute copies to the class and read through the passage with students, asking them to identify the problems. This exercise will help make students aware of the different kinds of shifts as they appear in the context of an essay.

> As soon as the avalanche was over, Jim pulls himself out of the snowbank and yells, "Where's everybody?" and were we still alive. As each of us in turn started digging out, you could see the damage the huge wall of snow had caused. The snow had destroyed the lodge and cars were swept away.

ANSWERS: EXERCISE 3

1. If students learn how to study efficiently, they will make much better grades on tests.
2. Conscientious students begin to prepare for tests immediately after they attend the first class.
3. Before each class the students complete all reading assignments and outline the material and answer any study questions.
4. In class they listen carefully and take good notes.
5. The students ask questions when they do not understand the professor.

5. A regular program of aerobic exercise, such as walking or swimming, improves your cholesterol rate and made you feel much healthier.

13c Keep a sentence or related sentences consistent in subject and voice.

When a verb is in the **active voice,** the subject names the actor: *Linda passed the peas.* When a verb is in the **passive voice,** the subject names the receiver of the action: *The peas were passed* [*by Linda*]. (See pp. 230–31.)

A shift in voice may sometimes help focus the reader's attention on a single subject, as in *The candidate campaigned vigorously and was nominated on the first ballot.* However, most shifts in voice also involve shifts in subject. They are unnecessary and confusing.

INCONSISTENT Internet *newsgroups cover* an enormous range of topics for discussion. *Forums* for meeting people with like interests *are provided* in these groups.

REVISED Internet *newsgroups cover* an enormous range of topics for discussion *and provide* forums for meeting people with like interests.

Exercise 3
Revising: Shifts in subject and voice

Make the following sentences consistent in subject and voice.

Example:

At the reunion they ate hot dogs and volleyball was played.
At the reunion they ate hot dogs and *played volleyball.*

1. If students learn how to study efficiently, much better grades will be made on tests.
2. Conscientious students begin to prepare for tests immediately after the first class is attended.
3. Before each class all reading assignments are completed, and the students outline the material and answer any study questions.
4. In class they listen carefully and good notes are taken.
5. Questions are asked by the students when they do not understand the professor.

13d Keep a quotation or a question consistently direct or indirect.

Direct quotations or questions report the exact words of a quotation or question.

"I am the greatest," bragged Muhammad Ali.
Was he right? In his day few people asked, *"Is he right?"*

Indirect quotations or questions report that someone said or asked something, but not in the exact words.

> Muhammad Ali bragged *that he was the greatest.*
> In his day few people asked *whether he was right.*

Shifts between direct and indirect quotations or questions are difficult to follow, especially when, as in the first example below, the direct quotation does not appear in quotation marks.

SHIFT IN QUOTATION	Kapek reported that the rats avoided the maze and as of this writing, none responds to conditioning.
REVISED (INDIRECT)	Kapek reported that the rats avoided the maze and *that as of his writing none responded to conditioning.*
REVISED (DIRECT)	Kapek reported, *"The rats avoid the maze.* As of this writing, none responds to conditioning."
SHIFT IN QUESTION	The reader wonders whether the experiment failed or did it perhaps succeed?
REVISED (INDIRECT)	The reader wonders whether the experiment failed or *whether it perhaps succeeded.*
REVISED (DIRECT)	*Did the experiment fail?* Or did it perhaps succeed?

For more on quotations, see pages 225–26 (tense and other changes in indirect quotations), 380 (commas with identifying words such as *she said*), 405–08 (quotation marks), and 591–95 (integrating quotations into your writing). For more on questions, see pages 360–62 (punctuation and word order).

Exercise 4
Revising: Shifts in direct and indirect quotations and questions

Revise each of the following sentences twice, once to make it consistently direct, once to make it consistently indirect. (You will have to guess at the exact wording of direct quotations and questions that are now stated indirectly.)

Example:

We all wonder what the new century will bring and will we thrive or not?

Direct: What will the new century bring? Will we thrive or not?

Indirect: We all wonder what the new century will bring and whether we will thrive or not.

1. One anthropologist says that the functions of marriage have changed and "nowhere more dramatically than in industrialized cultures."
2. The question even arises of whether siblings may marry and would the union be immoral?

shift
13d

COLLABORATIVE LEARNING

Students can create their own examples. of direct and indirect quotations and questions, using the models provided in Exercise 4. Ask students to work through Exercise 4 in small groups and then to create two or three additional examples.

Alternatively, you might ask students to compare their independent responses to Exercises 1–4, then work in small groups to revise the paragraph in Exercise 5. This gives students the opportunity to help each other recognize shifts and to discuss the effects of unnecessary shifts. You might have each group present their responses to one or two sentences of the paragraph in Exercise 5 and encourage the presenters to foreground the group's questions and comments.

ANSWERS: EXERCISE 4

1. *Direct:* One anthropologist says,"The functions of marriage have changed, nowhere more dramatically than in industrialized cultures."
   Indirect: One anthropologist says that the functions of marriage have changed, most dramatically in industrialized cultures.
2. *Direct:* May siblings marry? Would the union be immoral?
   Indirect: The question even arises of whether siblings may marry and whether the union would be immoral.
3. *Direct:* The author points out, "Sibling marriage is still illegal everywhere in the United States, and people are still prosecuted under the law."
   Indirect: The author points out that sibling marriage is still illegal everywhere in the

United States and that people are still prosecuted under the law.

4. *Direct:* She says, "Incest could be considered a universal taboo. The questions asked about the taboo vary widely."
   Indirect: She says that incest could be considered a universal taboo and that the questions asked about the taboo vary widely.
5. *Direct:* Is the taboo a way of protecting the family? Might it be instinctive?
   Indirect: Some ask whether the taboo is a way of protecting the family or whether it may be instinctive.

ANSWERS: EXERCISE 5

Possible revision

Driving in snow need not be dangerous if you practice a few simple rules. First, avoid fast starts, which prevent the wheels from gaining traction and may result in the car's getting stuck. Second, drive more slowly than usual, and pay attention to the feel of the car: if the steering seems unusually loose or the wheels do not seem to be grabbing the road, slow down. Third, avoid fast stops, which lead to skids. Be alert for other cars and intersections that may necessitate applying the brakes suddenly. If you need to slow down, reduce the car's momentum by downshifting as well as by applying the brakes. When braking, press the pedal to the floor only if you have antilock brakes; otherwise, pump the pedal in short bursts. If you feel the car skidding, release the brakes and turn the wheel into the direction of the skid, and then press or pump the brakes again. Repeating these motions will stop the skid and reduce the speed of the car.

3. The author points out, "Sibling marriage is still illegal everywhere in the United States" and that people are still prosecuted under the law.
4. She says that incest could be considered a universal taboo and "the questions asked about the taboo vary widely."
5. Some ask is the taboo a way of protecting the family or whether it may be instinctive.

Exercise 5
Revising: Shifts

Revise the following paragraph to eliminate unnecessary shifts in person, number, tense, mood, and voice.

Driving in snow need not be dangerous if you practice a few rules. First, one should avoid fast starts, which prevent the wheels from gaining traction and may result in the car's getting stuck. Second, drive more slowly than usual, and you should pay attention to the feel of the car: if the steering seemed unusually loose or the wheels did not seem to be grabbing the road, slow down. Third, avoid fast stops, which lead to skids. One should be alert for other cars and intersections that may necessitate that the brakes be applied suddenly. If you need to slow down, the car's momentum can be reduced by downshifting as well as by applying the brakes. When braking, press the pedal to the floor only if you have antilock brakes; otherwise, the pedal should be pumped in short bursts. If you feel the car skidding, the brakes should be released and the wheel should be turned into the direction of the skid, and then the brakes should be pressed or pumped again. If one repeated these motions, the skid would be stopped and the speed of the car would be reduced.

Note See page 316 for an exercise involving shifts along with sentence fragments, comma splices, and other sentence errors.

Chapter 14

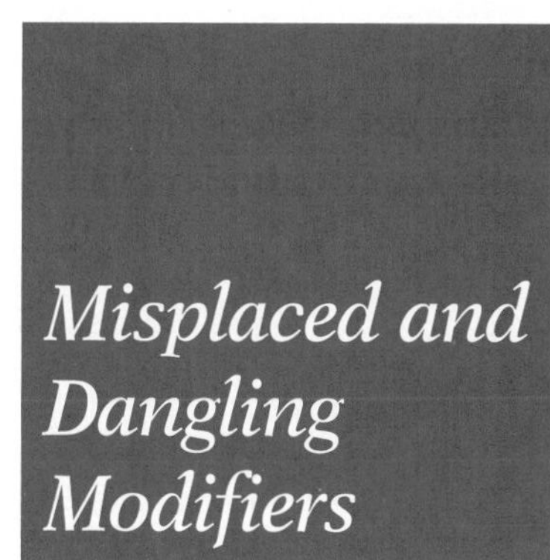

Misplaced and Dangling Modifiers

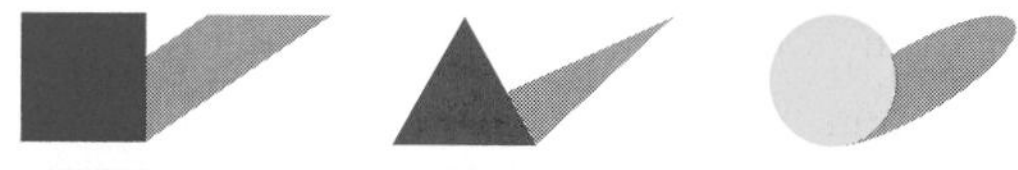

HIGHLIGHTS

Misplaced and dangling modifiers often interest students because the faulty constructions can be amusing. To tie together all the different problems discussed in the chapter, however, you may want to point out that they all illustrate the importance of position and arrangement in sentences. Split constructions (14d and 14e) conveniently emphasize the need to keep the parts of related syntactic groups clearly unified. Yet both standard speech and formal writing provide frequent examples of freely placed limiting modifiers and of split infinitives. Part of our difficulty in teaching composition is in giving students effective advice about when freedom is constructive and when it is confusing. As in all such matters, the advice of the handbook is largely conservative; you may therefore want to modify it somewhat.

In reading a sentence in English, we depend principally on the arrangement of the words to tell us how they are related. In writing, we may create confusion if we fail to connect modifiers to the words they modify.

MISPLACED MODIFIERS

A modifier is **misplaced** if readers can't easily connect it to the word it modifies. Misplaced modifiers may be awkward, confusing, or even unintentionally funny.

14a Place modifiers where they will clearly modify the words intended.

Readers tend to link a modifying word, phrase, or clause to the nearest word it could modify: *I saw a man in a green hat*. Thus the writer must place the phrase so that it clearly modifies the intended word and not some other.

CONFUSING He served steak to the men *on paper plates.*

REVISED He served the men steak *on paper plates.*

CONFUSING Many dogs are killed by automobiles and trucks *roaming unleashed.*

REVISED Many dogs *roaming unleashed* are killed by automobiles and trucks.

Confusing This is the only chocolate chip cookie in a bag that tastes like Mom's. [Actual advertisement.]

Revised This is the only *bagged* [or *packaged*] chocolate chip cookie that tastes like Mom's.

ANSWERS: EXERCISE 1

1. Women have contributed much of great value to American culture.
2. In 1821 Emma Willard founded the Troy Female Seminary, the first institution to provide a college-level education for women.
3. Sixteen years later Mary Lyon founded Mount Holyoke Female Seminary, the first true women's college with a campus and directors who would sustain the college even after Lyon's death.
4. *Una,* which was founded by Pauline Wright Davis in 1853, was the first American newspaper that was dedicated to gaining women's rights.
5. Mitchell's Comet, which was named for Maria Mitchell, was discovered in 1847.

mm 14b

Exercise 1
Revising: Misplaced clauses and phrases

Revise the following sentences so that prepositional phrases and subordinate clauses clearly modify the appropriate words.

Example:
I came to enjoy flying over time.
Over time I came to enjoy flying.

1. Women have contributed much to American culture of great value.
2. Emma Willard founded the Troy Female Seminary, the first institution to provide a college-level education for women in 1821.
3. Sixteen years later Mary Lyon founded Mount Holyoke Female Seminary, the first true women's college with directors and a campus who would sustain the college even after Lyon's death.
4. *Una* was the first American newspaper, which was founded by Pauline Wright Davis in 1853, that was dedicated to gaining women's rights.
5. Mitchell's Comet was discovered in 1847, which was named for Maria Mitchell.

MOVING *ONLY*

Ask students to create sentences whose meaning changes as a modifier like *only* moves from place to place:

Only students were asked to bring gym shorts and running shoes.
Students were *only* asked to bring gym shorts and running shoes.
Students were asked *only* to bring gym shorts and running shoes.
Students were asked to bring *only* gym shorts and running shoes.

14b Place limiting modifiers carefully.

Limiting modifiers include *almost, even, exactly, hardly, just, merely, nearly, only, scarcely,* and *simply.* They modify the expressions that immediately follow them. Compare the uses of *just* in the following three sentences:

Just the manuscript was discovered by an archaeologist.
The manuscript was *just* discovered by an archaeologist.
The manuscript was discovered *just* by an archaeologist.

In speech several of these modifiers frequently occur before the verb, regardless of the words they are intended to modify. In writing, however, these modifiers should fall immediately before the word or word group they modify to avoid any ambiguity.

Unclear He *only* discovered this manuscript on his last dig.

Revised He discovered *only* this manuscript on his last dig.

Revised He discovered this manuscript *only* on his last dig.

Exercise 2
Using limiting modifiers

Use each of the following limiting modifiers in two versions of the same sentence.

Example:

only
He is the *only* one I like.
He is the one *only* I like.

1. almost
2. even
3. hardly
4. simply
5. nearly

14c Make each modifier refer to only one grammatical element.

A modifier can modify only *one* element in a sentence—the subject, the verb, or some other element. A **squinting modifier** seems confusingly to refer to either of two words.

SQUINTING Snipers who fired on the soldiers *often* escaped capture.

CLEAR Snipers who *often* fired on the soldiers escaped capture.

CLEAR Snipers who fired on the soldiers escaped capture *often.*

When an adverb modifies an entire main clause, as in the last example, it can usually be moved to the beginning of the sentence: *Often, snipers who fired on the soldiers escaped capture.*

Exercise 3
Revising: Squinting modifiers

Revise each sentence twice so that the squinting modifier applies clearly first to one element and then to the other.

Example:

The work that he hoped would satisfy him completely frustrated him.

The work that he hoped would *completely* satisfy him frustrated him.

The work that he hoped would satisfy him frustrated him *completely.*

1. People who sunbathe often can damage their skin.
2. Sunbathers who apply a sunscreen frequently block some of the sun's harmful ultraviolet rays.
3. Men and women who lie out in the sun much of the time have leathery, dry skin.
4. Doctors tell sunbathers when they are older they risk skin cancer.
5. People who stay out of the sun usually will have better skin and fewer chances of skin cancer.

ANSWERS: EXERCISE 2

Possible answers

1. Almost everybody hates him.
   Everybody almost hates him.
2. Even now I remember the details of the event.
   Now I remember even the details of the event.
3. We hardly heard him call our names.
   We heard him hardly call our names.
4. Write simply.
   Simply write.
5. I nearly missed the performance that was booed off the stage.
   I missed the performance that was nearly booed off the stage.

mm
14c

COLLABORATIVE LEARNING

Students can work productively together (in pairs or small groups) on Exercises 2 and 3. This collaborative effort can be particularly useful when students are asked to create more than one possible revision.

ANSWERS: EXERCISE 3

1. People who often sunbathe can damage their skin. *Or:* People who sunbathe can often damage their skin.
2. Sunbathers who frequently apply a sunscreen avoid some of the sun's harmful rays. *Or:* Frequently, sunbathers who apply a sunscreen avoid some of the sun's harmful rays.
3. Men and women who often lie out in the sun have leathery, dry skin. *Or:* Often men and women who lie out in the sun have leathery, dry skin.
4. Doctors tell sunbathers they risk skin cancer when they are older. *Or:* Doctors tell older sunbathers they risk skin cancer.
5. People who usually stay out of the sun will have better skin and fewer chances of skin cancer. *Or:* People who stay out of the sun will usually have better skin and fewer chances of skin cancer.

THE MEDIA

Radio and television newscasts are rich sources of dangling and misplaced modifiers, perhaps because reporters have little time to pay attention to the structure of their sentences. Have students listen to newscasts and record errors: doing so will help them to understand the perspective of a reader who comes across similar errors in an essay. Newspaper headlines and public announcements are also rich sources; from time to time, magazine articles and paperback books appear with collections of particularly humorous errors. But students will be able to find many on their own by looking at the newspaper for headlines like *Young man slain with flowers.*

COLLABORATIVE LEARNING

HOME-GROWN STAR REPORTERS

Ask students to form groups in order to write their own newscasts filled with the kinds of errors they might spot through the activity above. The newscasts (and the errors) should be plausible in style and content, though the content will probably have to be the product of students' imaginations. Having heard many newscasts, however, students will probably have little trouble parodying them in form and matter.

14d Keep subjects, verbs, and objects together.

The movement from subject to verb to object is so familiar in English that modifiers between these elements can be awkward.

A subject and verb may be separated by an adjective that modifies the subject: *Kuwait, which has a population of 1.3 million, is a rich nation.* But an adverb of more than a word usually stops the flow of the sentence.

AWKWARD *Kuwait* [subject], after the Gulf War ended in 1991 [adverb], *began* [verb] returning to normal.

REVISED After the Gulf War ended in 1991 [adverb], *Kuwait* [subject] *began* [verb] returning to normal.

A modifier between a verb and its direct object is always awkward.

AWKWARD The war *had damaged* [verb] badly [adverb] *many* [object] of Kuwait's oil fields.

REVISED The war *had* badly [adverb] *damaged* [verb] *many* [object] of Kuwait's oil fields.

See below on inserting single-word adverbs between parts of a verb phrase, as in the revision above.

14e Keep parts of infinitives or verb phrases together.

An **infinitive** consists of the marker *to* plus the plain form of a verb: *to produce, to enjoy.* The two parts of the infinitive are widely regarded as a grammatical unit that should not be split.

AWKWARD The weather service expected temperatures *to* not *rise*. [infinitive]

REVISED The weather service expected temperatures not *to rise*. [infinitive]

A split infinitive may sometimes be natural and preferable, though it may still bother some readers.

Several US industries expect *to* more than *triple* [infinitive] their use of robots.

Here the split infinitive is more economical than the alternatives, such as *Several US industries expect to increase their use of robots by more than three times.*

A **verb phrase** consists of a helping verb plus a main verb, as in *will call, was going, had been writing* (see p. 209). We regularly insert single-word adverbs after the helping verb in a verb phrase (or the first helping verb if more than one): *Scientists have lately been* *using spacecraft to study the sun*. But when longer adverbs interrupt verb phrases, the result is almost always awkward.

AWKWARD The spacecraft *Ulysses will* [helping verb] after traveling near the sun [adverb] *report* [main verb] on the sun's energy fields.

REVISED After traveling near the sun, [adverb] the spacecraft *Ulysses will report* [verb phrase] on the sun's energy fields.

ESL In a question, place a one-word adverb after the first helping verb and the subject:

Will [helping verb] spacecraft [subject] ever [adverb] *be able to leave* [rest of verb phrase] the solar system?

Exercise 4

Revising: Separated sentence parts

Revise the following sentences to connect separated parts (subject-predicate, verb-object, verb phrase, infinitive).

Example:

Most children have by the time they are seven lost a tooth.
By the time they are seven, most children have lost a tooth.

1. Myra Bradwell founded in 1868 the *Chicago Legal News*.
2. Bradwell was later denied, although she had qualified, admission to the Illinois Bar Association.
3. In an attempt to finally gain admission to the bar, she carried the case to the Supreme Court, but the justices decided against her.
4. Bradwell was determined that no other woman would, if she were qualified, be denied entrance to a profession.
5. The Illinois legislature finally passed, in response to Bradwell's persuasion, a bill ensuring that no one on the basis of gender would be restricted from a profession.

ANSWERS: EXERCISE 4

1. In 1868 Myra Bradwell founded the *Chicago Legal News*.
2. Although she had qualified, Bradwell was later denied admission to the Illinois Bar Association.
3. In an attempt finally to gain admission to the bar, she carried the case to the Supreme Court, but the justices decided against her.
4. Bradwell was determined that no other woman would be denied entrance to a profession if she were qualified.
5. In response to Bradwell's persuasion, the Illinois legislature finally passed a bill ensuring that no one would be restricted from a profession on the basis of gender.

mm 14f

14f Position adverbs with care. ESL

Most adverbs may fall in several places in a sentence, as long as they clearly modify the intended word (14b, 14c) and do not separate sentence parts awkwardly (14d, 14e). A few adverbs are subject to additional conventions as well.

Adverbs of frequency

Adverbs of frequency include *always*, *never*, *often*, *rarely*, *seldom*, *sometimes*, and *usually*. They appear at the beginning of a sentence, before a one-word verb, or after the helping verb in a verb phrase.

Awkward Robots *have put* [verb phrase] sometimes [adverb] humans out of work.

Revised Robots *have* [helping verb] sometimes [adverb] *put* [main verb] humans out of work.

Revised Sometimes [adverb] robots *have put* [verb phrase] humans out of work.

Adverbs of frequency always follow the verb *be*.

Awkward Robots often [adverb] *are* [verb] helpful to workers.

Revised Robots *are* [verb] often [adverb] helpful to workers.

Adverbs of degree

Adverbs of degree include *absolutely, almost, certainly, completely, definitely, especially, extremely, hardly,* and *only*. They fall just before the word modified (an adjective, another adverb, sometimes a verb):

Awkward Robots have been *useful* [adjective] especially [adverb] in making cars.

Revised Robots have been especially [adverb] *useful* [adjective] in making cars.

Adverbs of manner

Adverbs of manner include *badly, beautifully, openly, sweetly, tightly, well,* and others that describe how something is done. They usually fall after the verb:

Awkward Robots smoothly [adverb] *work* [verb] on assembly lines.

Revised Robots *work* [verb] smoothly [adverb] on assembly lines.

Not

When the adverb *not* modifies a verb, place it after the helping verb (or the first helping verb if more than one):

Awkward Robots *do* [helping verb] *think* [main verb] not.

Revised Robots *do* [helping verb] not *think* [main verb].

Place *not* after a form of *be: Robots are not thinkers.*

When *not* modifies another adverb or an adjective, place it before the other modifier: *Robots are not sleek machines.*

mm 14g

14g Arrange adjectives appropriately. ESL

English follows distinctive rules for arranging two or three adjectives before a noun. (A string of more than three adjectives before a noun is rare.) The order depends on the meaning of the adjectives, as indicated in the following table:

DETERMINER	OPINION	SIZE OR SHAPE	AGE	COLOR	ORIGIN	MATERIAL	NOUN USED AS ADJECTIVE	NOUN
many			new				state	laws
	striking			green	Thai			birds
a	fine				German			camera
this		square				wooden		table
all			recent				business	reports
the				blue		litmus		paper

See page 377 for guidelines on punctuating two or more adjectives before a noun.

Exercise 5

Revising: Placement of adverbs and adjectives ESL

Revise the sentences below to correct the positions of adverbs or adjectives. If a sentence is already correct as given, circle the number preceding it.

Example:

Gasoline high prices affect usually car sales.
High gasoline prices *usually* affect car sales.

1. Some years ago Detroit cars often were praised.
2. Luxury large cars especially were prized.
3. Then a serious oil shortage led drivers to value small foreign cars that got good mileage.
4. Now with gas low prices, consumers are returning to American large cars.
5. However, the large cars not are luxury sedans but vans and wagons.

ANSWERS: EXERCISE 5

1. Some years ago Detroit cars were often praised.
2. Large luxury cars were especially prized.
3. Sentence correct.
4. Now with low gas prices, consumers are returning to large American cars.
5. However, the large cars are not luxury sedans but vans and wagons.

DANGLING MODIFIERS

14h Relate dangling modifiers to their sentences.

A **dangling modifier** does not sensibly modify anything in its sentence.

DANGLING *Passing the building,* the vandalism became visible. [The modifying phrase seems to describe *vandalism,* but vandalism does not pass buildings. Who was passing the building? Who saw the vandalism?]

RESOURCES AND IDEAS

Chaika, Elaine. "Grammars and Teaching." *College English* 39 (1978): 770–83. Chaika offers fresh explanations from a linguistic perspective for a number of standard errors, including dangling modifiers.

Pixton, William H. "The Dangling Gerund: A Working Definition." *College Composition and Communication* 24 (1973): 193–99. Pixton reviews discussions of dangling modifiers and, using a variety of sample sentences, formulates a definition of the dangling gerund.

Dangling modifiers usually introduce sentences, contain a verb form, and imply but do not name a subject: in the preceding example, the implied subject is the someone or something passing the building. Readers assume that this implied subject is the same as the subject of the sentence (*vandalism* in the example). When it is not, the modifier "dangles" unconnected to the rest of the sentence.

Certain modifiers are most likely to dangle:

- Participial phrases:

  Dangling *Passing the building,* the vandalism became visible. ?

  Revised *As we passed* the building, the vandalism became visible.

- Infinitive phrases:

  Dangling *To understand the causes,* vandalism has been extensively investigated. ?

  Revised To understand the causes, *researchers have* extensively *investigated* vandalism.

- Prepositional phrases in which the object of the preposition is a gerund:

  Dangling *After studying the problem,* vandals are now thought to share certain characteristics. ?

  Revised After studying the problem, *researchers think that* vandals share certain characteristics.

- Elliptical clauses in which the subject and perhaps the verb are omitted:

  Dangling *When destructive,* researchers have learned that vandals are more likely to be in groups. ?

  Revised When *vandals are* destructive, researchers have learned that *they* are more likely to be in groups.

Dangling modifiers are especially likely when the verb in the main clause is in the **passive voice** instead of the **active voice**—that is, when the verb expresses what is *done to* the subject instead of what the subject *does* (see p. 230). The passive voice appears in the second and third examples above: *vandalism has been investigated; vandals are thought.* The revisions recast the verbs and subjects as active: *researchers have investigated; researchers think.*

Note that a modifier may be dangling even when the sentence elsewhere contains a word the modifier might seem to describe, such as *vandals* below:

Dangling *When destructive,* researchers have learned that vandals are more likely to be in groups.

Identifying and revising dangling modifiers

- If the modifier lacks a subject of its own (e.g., *when in diapers*), identify what it describes.
- Verify that what the modifier describes is in fact the subject of the main clause. If it is not, the modifier is probably dangling.
- Revise a dangling modifier (*a*) by recasting it with a subject of its own or (*b*) by changing the subject of the main clause.

(modifier: *When in diapers*; subject: my mother)

Dangling *When in diapers,* my mother remarried.

Revision a When *I was* in diapers, my mother remarried.

Revision b When in diapers, *I attended my mother's second wedding.*

In addition, a dangling modifier may fall at the end of a sentence:

Dangling The vandalism was visible *passing the building.*

Revising dangling modifiers

Revise most dangling modifiers in one of two ways, depending on what you want to emphasize in the sentence.

- Change the subject of the main clause to a word the modifier properly describes.

Dangling *To express themselves,* graffiti decorate walls. (?)

Revised To express themselves, *some youths decorate* walls with graffiti.

- Rewrite the dangling modifier as a complete clause with its own stated subject and verb.

Revised *Because some youths need* to express themselves, graffiti decorate walls.

Exercise 6
Revising: Dangling modifiers

Revise the following sentences to eliminate any dangling modifiers. Each item has more than one possible answer.

Example:

Driving north, the vegetation became increasingly sparse.

Driving north, *we noticed that* the vegetation became increasingly sparse.

As we drove north, the vegetation became increasingly sparse.

1. After accomplishing many deeds of valor, Andrew Jackson's fame led to his election to the Presidency in 1828 and 1832.

TRANSPARENCY MASTER 14.1

dm 14h

COLLABORATIVE LEARNING

COLLECTING HOWLERS

An amusing exercise is to have students collect examples of misplaced and dangling modifiers to share; reward the team that collects the most examples with a prize like a day's extension on the next assignment. The "finds" may include some particularly funny ones like this: *Stitched on 14-count canvas, your daughter will enjoy learning to cross-stitch.*

ANSWERS: EXERCISE 6

Possible answers

1. After Andrew Jackson had accomplished many deeds of valor, his fame led to his election to the Presidency in 1828 and 1832.
2. By the time Jackson was fourteen, both of his parents had died.
3. To aid the American Revolution, Jackson chose service as a mounted courier.
4. Though not well educated, Jackson proved his ability in a successful career as a lawyer and judge.
5. Because Jackson won many military battles, the American public believed in his leadership.

COLLABORATIVE LEARNING

Have students work in small groups to discuss their responses to Exercises 6 and 7. Then ask each group to complete Exercise 8 together and present part of the revised paragraph to the class. As each group gives its presentation, encourage other groups to contribute their differing revisions of the same sentences. This helps students to become more aware of the numerous possibilities for revision.

ANSWERS: EXERCISE 7

Possible answers

1. As evening falls in the Central American rain forests, the tungara frogs begin their croaking chorus.
2. Croaking loudly at night, male tungara frogs sing "songs" designed to attract female frogs.
3. But predators, also hearing the croaking, gather to feast on the frogs.
4. Lured by their croaking dinners, the predators include bullfrogs, snakes, bats, and opossums.
5. Although the frogs hope to mate, their nightly chorus can result in death instead.

SENTENCE COMBINING

Exercise 7 requires students to combine pairs of sentences whose content and structure make them likely causes of misplaced or dangling modifiers. Extend this activity by having students create their own sentences that would be easy to miscombine. Choose the best pairs, copy them, and have the class do them for an exercise. This activity leads to considerable discussion and some imaginative and amusing results when the students work in groups.

ANSWERS: EXERCISE 8

Possible revision

Several nights a week, Central American tungara frogs silence their mating croaks. When not croaking, they reduce the chance that they will be eaten by predators. The frogs seem to believe fully in "safety in numbers." More than likely, they will croak along with a large group rather than by themselves. By forgoing croaking on some nights, the frogs prevent the species from "croaking."

2. By the age of fourteen, both of Jackson's parents had died.
3. To aid the American Revolution, service as a mounted courier was chosen by Jackson.
4. Though not well educated, a successful career as a lawyer and judge proved Jackson's ability.
5. Winning many military battles, the American public believed in Jackson's leadership.

Exercise 7
Sentence combining: Placing modifiers

Combine each pair of sentences below into a single sentence by rewriting one as a modifier. Make sure the modifier applies clearly to the appropriate word. You will have to add, delete, and rearrange words, and you may find that more than one answer is possible in each case.

Example:

Bob demanded a hearing from the faculty. Bob wanted to appeal the decision.

Wanting to appeal the decision, Bob demanded a hearing from the faculty.

1. Evening falls in the Central American rain forests. The tungara frogs begin their croaking chorus.
2. Male tungara frogs croak loudly at night. The "songs" they sing are designed to attract female frogs.
3. But predators also hear the croaking. They gather to feast on the frogs.
4. The predators are lured by their croaking dinners. The predators include bullfrogs, snakes, bats, and opossums.
5. The frogs hope to mate. Their nightly chorus can result in death instead.

Exercise 8
Revising: Misplaced and dangling modifiers

Revise the following paragraph to eliminate any misplaced or dangling modifiers.

Central American tungara frogs silence several nights a week their mating croaks. When not croaking, the chance that the frogs will be eaten by predators is reduced. The frogs seem to fully believe in "safety in numbers." They more than likely will croak along with a large group rather than by themselves. By forgoing croaking on some nights, the frogs' behavior prevents the species from "croaking."

NOTE See page 316 for an exercise involving misplaced and dangling modifiers along with other sentence errors.

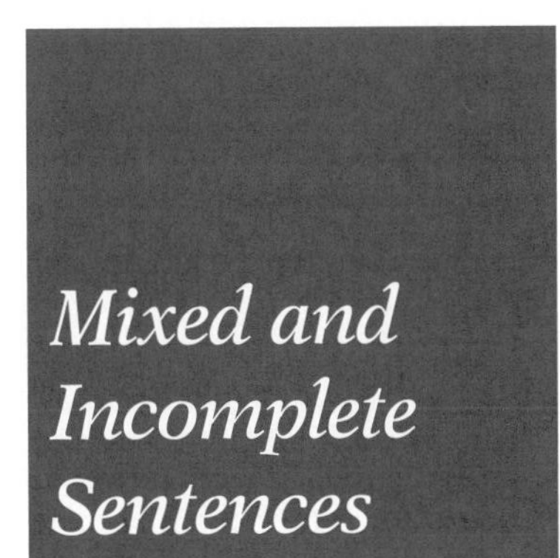

Chapter 15 Mixed and Incomplete Sentences

MIXED SENTENCES

A **mixed sentence** contains two or more parts that are incompatible—that is, the parts do not fit together. The misfit may be in grammar or in meaning.

15a Untangle sentences that are mixed in grammar.

Sentences mixed in grammar combine two or more incompatible grammatical structures.

Make sure subject and verb fit together grammatically.

A mixed sentence may occur when you start a sentence with one plan and end it with another.

[modifier (prepositional phrase): By paying more attention to impressions than facts] [verb: leads]

Mixed By paying more attention to impressions than facts leads us to misjudge others.

This mixed sentence makes a prepositional phrase work as the subject of *leads,* but prepositional phrases function as modifiers, not as nouns, and thus not as sentence subjects. (See p. 175.)

[modifier (prepositional phrase): By paying more attention to impressions than facts,] [subject + verb: we misjudge]

Revised By paying more attention to impressions than facts, *we misjudge* others.

HIGHLIGHTS

The first two sections of Chapter 15 treat sentences whose subjects and predicates are incompatible. The tangled sentences in some student writing have more complex causes than this brief discussion of mixed sentences can address. But the two most common problems do seem to be subjects and predicates that are incompatible in grammar and in meaning.

The third section deals with compound constructions that are grammatically or idiomatically incomplete. Ill-prepared students seem to encounter this problem less often than better-prepared students do, perhaps because only the latter use such constructions. On the other hand, incomplete comparisons (15d) are common, and you may wish to call particular attention to them.

The final section, covering omission of needed words, is designed primarily as an aid to grading papers. Instructors who notice words missing in a student essay can call attention to the problem by using the number-and-letter code to refer students to this section.

USING STUDENT WRITING

Because the mixed and incomplete sentences in student writing have complicated causes and because the problems in one student's essay are likely to differ widely from those in another student's paper, most instructors choose simply to discuss the chapter and use some of the exercises rather than elaborate with classroom activities and assignments. In working with individual students, however, most instructors are able to devise activities that suit individual needs. Instructors who wish to alert students to the problem of incomplete compound constructions, incomplete comparisons, and omission of needed words can draw from a student paper or write a passage containing these problems and then ask students to work with the passage, perhaps in small groups, proofreading it and correcting the errors. Student's journals and error logs are excellent sources of material as well as good places to practice revision strategies. Encourage students to keep a log of the patterns of error that tend to recur in their work, along with corrected examples. That log can provide a good resource for future revision and editing sessions.

subject (gerund phrase) — verb

Revised *Paying* more attention to impressions than facts *leads* us to misjudge others.

Mixed sentences are especially likely on a word processor when you connect parts of two sentences or rewrite half a sentence but not the other half. Mixed sentences may also occur when you don't focus your sentences on the subject and verb so that these elements carry the principal meaning. (See p. 477.) If you need help identifying the subject and verb, see pages 163 and 165. Otherwise, the cure for grammatically mixed sentences is careful editing and proofreading.

Here are two more examples of mixed grammar:

modifier (adverb clause) — verb

Mixed Although he was seen with a convicted thief does not make him a thief.

subject (noun clause) — verb

Revised *That* he was seen with a convicted thief does not make him a thief.

modifier (adverb clause) — subject + verb

Revised Although he was seen with a convicted thief, *he is* not necessarily a thief.

subject — modifier (adjective clause)

Mixed The fact that someone may be considered guilty just for associating with someone guilty.

subject verb

Revised The *fact is* that someone may be considered guilty just for associating with someone guilty.

subject — verb

Revised *Someone may be considered* guilty just for associating with someone guilty.

In some mixed sentences the grammar is so jumbled that the writer has little choice but to start over.

Mixed My long-range goal is through law school and government work I hope to help people deal with those problems we all deal with more effectively.

Possible My long-range goal is to go to law school and then work in government so that I can help people deal more effectively with problems we all face.

2 State parts of sentences, such as subjects, only once. ESL

In some languages other than English, certain parts of sentences may be repeated. These include the subject in any kind of clause or an object or adverb in an adjective clause. In English, however, these parts are stated only once in a clause.

Repetition of subject

You may be tempted to restate a subject as a pronoun before the verb. But the subject needs stating only once in its clause.

Faulty The *liquid it* reached a temperature of 180°F.
Revised The *liquid* reached a temperature of 180°F.

Faulty *Gases* in the liquid *they* escaped.
Revised *Gases* in the liquid escaped.

Repetition in an adjective clause

Adjective clauses begin with *who, whom, whose, which, that, where,* and *when.* The beginning word replaces another word: the subject (*He is the person who called*), an object of a verb or preposition (*He is the person whom I mentioned*), or a preposition and pronoun (*He knows the office where [in which] the conference will occur*).

Do not state the word being replaced in an adjective clause.

Faulty The technician *whom* the test depended on *her* was burned. [*Whom* should replace *her.*]
Revised The technician *whom* the test depended on was burned.

Adjective clauses beginning with *where* or *when* do not need an adverb such as *there* or *then.*

Faulty Gases escaped at a moment *when* the technician was unprepared *then.*
Revised Gases escaped at a moment *when* the technician was unprepared.

Note *Whom, which,* and similar words are sometimes omitted but are still understood by the reader. Thus the word being replaced should not be stated.

Faulty Accidents rarely happen to technicians the lab has trained *them.* [*Whom* is understood: *technicians whom the lab has trained.*]
Revised Accidents rarely happen to technicians the lab has trained.

15b Match subjects and predicates in meaning.

In a sentence with mixed meaning, the subject is said to be or do something it cannot logically be or do. Such a mixture is sometimes called **faulty predication** because the predicate conflicts with the subject.

mixed
15b

RESOURCES AND IDEAS

Krishna, Valerie. "The Syntax of Error." *Journal of Basic Writing* 1 (1975): 43–9. The author views problems like mixed constructions and shifts as the result of a weak sentence core, and she encourages teachers to pay attention to this underlying problem in helping students avoid such errors.

Shuman, R. Baird. "Grammar for Writers: How Much Is Enough." *The Place of Grammar in Writing Instruction: Past, Present, Future.* Ed. Susan Hunter and Ray Wallace. Portsmouth, NH: Boynton, 1995. 114–28. Shuman offers simplified strategies for presenting sentence structure as a meaningful concept in an effort to prevent some student errors.

Illogical equation with *be*

When a form of *be* connects a subject and a word that describes the subject (a complement), the subject and complement must be logically related.

Mixed A *compromise* between the city and the country would be the ideal *place* to live.

Revised A *community* that offered the best qualities of both city and country would be the ideal *place* to live.

Is when, is where

Definitions require nouns on both sides of *be*. Definition clauses beginning with *when* or *where* are common in speech but should be avoided in writing.

Mixed An *examination* is *when you are tested* on what you know.

Revised An *examination* is a *test* of what you know.

Reason is because

The commonly heard construction *The reason is because* . . . is redundant since *because* means "for the reason that."

Mixed The *reason* the temple requests donations *is because* the school needs expansion.

Revised The *reason* the temple requests donations *is that* the school needs expansion.

Revised The temple requests donations *because* the school needs expansion.

Other mixed meanings

Faulty predications are not confined to sentences with *be*.

Mixed The *use* of emission controls *was created* to reduce air pollution.

Revised Emission *controls were created* to reduce air pollution.

Mixed The *area* of financial mismanagement *poses* a threat to small businesses.

Revised Financial *mismanagement poses* a threat to small businesses.

Exercise 1
Revising: Sentences mixed in grammar or meaning

Revise the following sentences so that their parts fit together both in grammar and in meaning. Each item has more than one possible answer.

Example:

When they found out how expensive pianos are is why they were discouraged.

They were discouraged *because* they found out how expensive pianos are.

When they found out how expensive pianos are, *they* were discouraged.

1. A hurricane is when the winds in a tropical depression rotate counterclockwise at more than seventy-four miles per hour.
2. Because hurricanes can destroy so many lives and so much property is why people fear them.
3. Through high winds, storm surge, floods, and tornadoes is how a hurricane can kill thousands of people.
4. Among the hurricanes in history, they have become less deadly since 1950.
5. The reason for the lower death rates is because improved communication systems and weather satellites warn people early enough to escape the hurricane.

COLLABORATIVE LEARNING

Students can work together to create or to compare their responses to Exercise 1. Encourage each group to explore various possible answers.

ANSWERS: EXERCISE 1

Possible answers

1. A hurricane occurs when the winds in a tropical depression rotate counterclockwise at more than seventy-four miles per hour.
2. Because hurricanes can destroy so many lives and much property, people fear them.
3. Through high winds, storm surge, floods, and tornadoes, a hurricane can kill thousands of people.
4. Hurricanes have become less deadly since 1950.
5. The death rates are lower because improved communication systems and weather satellites warn people early enough to escape the hurricane.

mixed
15b

Exercise 2
Revising: Repeated sentence parts ESL

Revise the following sentences to eliminate any unnecessary repetition of sentence parts.

Example:

Over 79 percent of Americans they have heard of global warming.

Over 79 percent of *Americans have* heard of global warming.

1. Global warming it is caused by the gradual erosion of the ozone layer that protects the earth from the sun.
2. Scientists who study this problem they say that the primary causes of erosion are the use of fossil fuels and the reduction of forests.
3. Many nonscientists they mistakenly believe that aerosol spray cans are the primary cause of erosion.
4. One scientist whom others respect him argues that Americans have effectively reduced their use of aerosol sprays.
5. He argues that we will stop global warming only when the public learns the real causes then.

ANSWERS: EXERCISE 2

1. Global warming is caused by the gradual erosion of the ozone layer that protects the earth from the sun.
2. Scientists who study this problem say that the primary causes of erosion are the use of fossil fuels and the reduction of forests.
3. Many nonscientists mistakenly believe that aerosol spray cans are the primary cause of erosion.
4. One scientist whom others respect argues that Americans have effectively reduced their use of aerosol sprays.
5. He argues that we will stop global warming only when the public learns the real causes.

INCOMPLETE SENTENCES

The most serious kind of incomplete sentence is the fragment (see Chapter 10). But sentences are also incomplete when they omit one or more words needed for clarity.

15c Omissions from compound constructions should be consistent with grammar or idiom.

In both speech and writing, we commonly omit words not necessary for meaning, such as those in parentheses in the following examples. Notice that all the sentences contain compound constructions.

> By 2000 automobile-emission standards will be tougher, and by 2010 [automobile-emission standards will be] tougher still.
>
> Some cars will run on electricity; some [will run] on methane.
>
> Environmentalists have hopes for alternative fuels and [for] public transportation.

Such omissions are possible only when you omit words that are common to all the parts of a compound construction. When the parts differ in either grammar or idiom, all words must be included in all parts.

> One new car *gets* eighty miles per gallon; some old cars *get* as little as five miles per gallon. [One verb is singular, the other plural.]
>
> Environmentalists *were* invited to submit proposals and *were* eager to do so. [Each *were* has a different grammatical function: the first is a helping verb; the second is a linking verb.]
>
> They believe *in* and work *for* fuel conservation. [Idiom requires different prepositions with *believe* and *work*.]

Notice that in the sentence *My brother and friend moved to Dallas,* the omission of *my* before *friend* indicates that *brother* and *friend* are the same person. If two different persons are meant, the modifier or article must be repeated: *My brother and my friend moved to Dallas.*

(See p. 468 for a list of English idioms and pp. 331–34 for a discussion of grammatical parallelism.)

15d All comparisons should be complete and logical.

Comparisons make statements about the relation between two or more things, as in *Dogs are more intelligent than cats.*

1 State a comparison fully enough to ensure clarity.

A comparison must not omit words needed to clarify meaning.

Unclear Car makers worry about their industry more than environmentalists.

Clear Car makers worry about their industry more than environmentalists *do.*

Clear Car makers worry about their industry more than *they worry about* environmentalists.

The items being compared should in fact be comparable.

A comparison is logical only if it compares items that can sensibly be compared.

Illogical The cost of an electric car is greater than a gasoline-powered car. [Illogically compares a cost and a car.]

Revised The cost of an electric car is greater than *the cost of* [or *that of*] a gasoline-powered car.

Use *any* or *any other* appropriately in comparisons.

Comparing a person or thing with all others in the same group creates two units: (1) the individual person or thing and (2) all *other* persons or things in the group. The two units need to be distinguished.

Illogical Los Angeles is larger than *any* city in California. [Since Los Angeles is itself a city in California, the sentence seems to say that Los Angeles is larger than itself.]

Logical Los Angeles is larger than *any other* city in California.

Comparing a person or thing with the members of a *different* group assumes separate units to begin with. The two units do not need to be distinguished with *other.*

Illogical Los Angeles is larger than *any other* city in Canada. [The cities in Canada constitute a group to which Los Angeles does not belong.]

Logical Los Angeles is larger than *any* city in Canada.

Comparisons should state what is being compared.

Brand X gets clothes *whiter.* [Whiter than what?]
Brand Y is so much *better.* [Better than what?]

15e Include all needed articles, prepositions, and other words.

In haste or carelessness we sometimes omit small words such as articles and prepositions that are needed for clarity.

INCOMPLETE Regular payroll deductions are a type painless savings. You hardly notice missing amounts, and after period of years the contributions can add a large total.

REVISED Regular payroll deductions are a type *of* painless savings. You hardly notice *the* missing amounts, and after *a* period of years the contributions can add *up to* a large total.

ESL If your native language is not English, you may have difficulty knowing when to use the English articles *a, an,* and *the.* For guidelines on using articles, see pages 259–61.

Be careful not to omit *that* when the omission is confusing.

INCOMPLETE The personnel director expects many employees will benefit from the plan. [*Many employees* seems to be the object of *expects.*]

REVISED The personnel director expects *that* many employees will benefit from the plan.

Attentive proofreading is the best insurance against the kind of omissions described in this section. *Proofread all your papers carefully.* See page 77 for tips.

inc 15e

Exercise 3

Revising: Incomplete sentences

Revise the following sentences so that they are complete, logical, and clear. Some items have more than one possible answer.

Example:

Our house is closer to the courthouse than the subway stop.

Our house is closer to the courthouse than *it is* to the subway stop.

Our house is closer to the courthouse than the subway stop *is.*

1. The first ice cream, eaten in China in about 2000 BC, was more lumpy than the modern era.
2. The Chinese made their ice cream of milk, spices, and overcooked rice and packed in snow to solidify.
3. In the fourteenth century ice milk and fruit ices appeared in Italy and the tables of the wealthy.
4. At her wedding in 1533 to the king of France, Catherine de Médicis offered more flavors of fruit ices than any hostess offered.

ANSWERS: EXERCISE 3

Possible answers

1. The first ice cream, eaten in China in about 2000 BC, was more lumpy than ice cream in (or that in) the modern era.
2. The Chinese made their ice cream of milk, spices, and overcooked rice and packed it in snow to solidify.
3. In the fourteenth century ice milk and fruit ices appeared in Italy and on the tables of the wealthy.
4. At her wedding in 1533 to the King of France, Catherine de Médicis offered more flavors of fruit ices than any other hostess offered.
5. Modern sherbets resemble her ices; modern ice cream resembles her soft dessert of thick, sweetened cream.

5. Modern sherbets resemble her ices; modern ice cream her soft dessert of thick, sweetened cream.

Exercise 4
Revising: Mixed and incomplete sentences

Revise the following paragraph to eliminate mixed or incomplete constructions.

The Hancock Tower in Boston is thin mirror-glass slab that rises almost eight hundred feet. When it was being constructed in the early 1970s was when its windows began cracking, and some fell crashing to the ground. In order to minimize risks is why the architects and owners replaced over a third the huge windows with plywood until the problem could be found and solved. With its plywood sheath, the building was homelier than any skyscraper, the butt of many jokes. Eventually, however, it was discovered that the reason the windows cracked was because joint between the double panes of glass was too rigid. The solution of thicker single-pane windows was installed, and the silly plywood building crystallized into reflective jewel.

Note See the next page for an exercise involving mixed and incomplete sentences along with sentence fragments, comma splices, and other sentence errors.

COLLABORATIVE LEARNING

Exercises 3 and 4 work well as an extended group project. Encourage groups to experiment with alternate responses, and ask each group to present any problem points they encountered as well as their successful responses to one or more sections.

ANSWERS: EXERCISE 4

Possible revision

The Hancock Tower in Boston is a thin mirror-glass slab that rises almost eight hundred feet. When it was being constructed in the early 1970s, its windows began cracking, and some fell crashing to the ground. In order to minimize risks, the architects and owners replaced over a third of the huge windows with plywood until the problem could be found and solved. With its plywood sheath, the building was homelier than any other skyscraper, the butt of many jokes. Eventually, however, it was discovered that the windows cracked because the joint between the double panes of glass was too rigid. Thicker single-pane windows were installed, and the silly plywood building crystallized into a reflective jewel.

ANSWERS: EXERCISE ON CHAPTERS 10–15

Possible answers

Many people who are physically challenged have accomplished much, which proves that they are not "handicapped." Confined to wheelchairs, Bob Sampson and Stephen Hawking have forged successful careers. Despite his muscular dystrophy, Sampson has earned a law degree. He has also worked for United Airlines for more than thirty years. Stephen Hawking is most famous for his book *A Brief History of Time.* Hawking is unable to speak, but his voice synthesizer allows him to dictate his books, conduct public lectures, and teach mathematics classes at Cambridge University.

mng

Franklin D. Roosevelt, Ann Adams, and Itzhak Perlman all refused to let polio destroy their lives. Indeed, as President, Roosevelt led the United States during two of the worst periods of its history: the Great Depression and World War II. Roosevelt inspired hope and determination in the American public. Ann Adams, who was talented in art before polio paralyzed her, knew she had to continue to be an artist. Having retrained herself to draw with a pencil grasped in her teeth, she produced sketches of children and pets. These drawings were turned into greeting cards whose profits sustained her. Roosevelt and Adams were stricken with polio when they were adults; Itzhak Perlman was stricken when he was a child. He was unable to play sports; instead, he studied the violin. Now many think he is greater than any other violinist in the world.

Like Perlman, many physically challenged individuals turn to the arts. Perhaps they do so because (*or:* the reason is that) the joy of artistic achievement compensates for other pleasures they cannot experience. Ray Charles, Stevie Wonder, José Feliciano, and Ronnie Milsap all express their souls through their music. Although they are unable to see physically, their music reveals how well they truly see. Hearing impairment struck Ludwig van Beethoven and Marlee Matlin, but it did not stop them from developing their talents. Already a successful composer, Beethoven wrote many of his most powerful pieces after he became deaf. Similarly, Matlin has had excellent acting roles in movies, plays, and television programs; indeed, she won an Oscar for *Children of a Lesser God.* She encourages others to develop their abilities, and she has inspired many hearing-impaired actors.

Exercise on Chapters 10–15

Revising: Clear sentences

Clarify meaning in the following paragraphs by revising sentence fragments, comma splices, fused sentences, problems with pronoun reference, awkward shifts, misplaced and dangling modifiers, and mixed and incomplete sentences. Most errors can be corrected in more than one way.

Many people who are physically challenged. They have accomplished much. Which proves that they are not "handicapped." Confined to wheelchairs, successful careers have been forged by Bob Sampson and Stephen Hawking. Despite Sampson's muscular dystrophy, he has earned a law degree he has also worked for United Airlines for more than thirty years. Stephen Hawking most famous for his book *A Brief History of Time.* Unable to speak, Hawking's voice synthesizer allows him to dictate his books and conduct public lectures. And teach mathematics classes at Cambridge University.

Franklin D. Roosevelt, Ann Adams, and Itzhak Perlman all refused let polio destroy their lives. Indeed, Roosevelt led the United States during two of the worst periods of its history as President. The Great Depression and World War II. Reassured by his strong, firm voice, Roosevelt inspired hope and determination in the American public. Ann Adams, who was talented in art before polio paralyzed her, knew she had to continue to be one. Having retrained herself to draw with a pencil grasped in her teeth. She produces sketches of children and pets. That were turned into greeting cards. The profits from the cards sustained her. Roosevelt and Adams were stricken with polio when they were adults; Itzhak Perlman when a child. He was unable to play sports, instead he studied the violin, now many think he is greater than any violinist in the world.

Like Perlman, many physically challenged individuals turn to the arts. Perhaps the reason is because the joy of artistic achievement compensates for other pleasures they cannot experience. Ray Charles, Stevie Wonder, José Feliciano, and Ronnie Milsap all express, through their music, their souls. Although unable to see physically, their music reveals truly how well they see. Hearing impairment struck Ludwig van Beethoven and Marlee Matlin it did not stop them from developing their talents. Already a successful composer, many of Beethoven's most powerful pieces were written after he became deaf. Similarly, Matlin has had excellent acting roles in movies, plays, and television programs, indeed she won an Oscar for *Children of a Lesser God.* She encourages others to develop their ability, and many hearing-impaired actors have been inspired by her.

Part IV

Effective Sentences

HIGHLIGHTS

The discussion in this chapter emphasizes how writers can use coordination and subordination to relate ideas and distinguish central ideas from less important material. The opening section illustrates how coordination relates facts and ideas and then goes on to address the problems of excessive and faulty coordination. The second section follows a parallel pattern in discussing subordination, focusing on subordinate clauses. But since effective writing depends on a writer's ability to work with the whole range of subordinate structures, the uses of single words, appositives, and prepositional, verbal, and absolute phrases are also illustrated. The final section cautions briefly against the often unclear and misused connectors *like, while,* and *as.*

Included in this chapter are subsections on punctuating coordinated and subordinated elements, designed to help students not only punctuate correctly but also see punctuation as an instrument and extension of effective sentence structure. Coordination and subordination are strategies that can be enhanced by practicing sentence-combining techniques. Such practices work best if students are encouraged to work on them over the course of a semester, as this handbook recommends, rather than just in one unit or lesson. The exercises in this chapter ask students to revise sentences and longer passages and to combine sentences in ways that implement the range of strategies introduced in the chapter.

Good resources for sentence combining include the following:

Crowhurst, Marion. "Sentence Combining: Maintaining Realistic Expectations." *College Composition and Communication* 34 (1983): 62–72. Crowhurst offers pragmatic suggestions about what teachers should and shouldn't expect when introducing sentence combining into their classrooms.

Daiker, Donald, Andrew Kerek, and Max Morenberg. *Sentence Combining: A Rhetorical Perspective.* Carbondale: Southern Illinois UP, 1985.

O'Hare, Frank. *Sentence-Combining: Improving Student Writing without Formal Grammar Instruction.* Urbana: NCTE, 1973. O'Hare demonstrates the improvements that can be effected when students practice sentence combining.

Chapter 16 *Using Coordination and Subordination*

When clearly written, your sentences show the relations between ideas and stress the more important ideas over the lesser ones. Two techniques can help you achieve such clarity:

- **Coordination** shows that two or more elements in a sentence are equally important in meaning. You signal coordination with words such as *and, but,* and *or.*

  equally important
  Car and *health* insurance are modern necessities.

  equally important
  Car insurance is costly, but *health insurance seems a luxury.*

- **Subordination** shows that some elements in a sentence are less important than other elements for your meaning. Usually, the main idea appears in the main clause, and supporting information appears in single words, phrases, and subordinate clauses.

  less important (subordinate clause) — more important (main clause)
  Because accidents and thefts occur frequently, car insurance is costly.

  more important (main clause) — less important (phrase)
  The health-insurance industry is changing, *for better or worse.*

16a Coordinating to relate equal ideas

By linking equally important information, you can emphasize the relations for readers. Compare the passages on page 320.

Ways to coordinate and subordinate information in sentences

Use **coordination** to relate ideas of equal importance (p. 318).

- Link main clauses with a comma and a coordinating conjunction: *and, but, or, nor, for, so, yet* (p. 189).

  Independence Hall in Philadelphia is now restored, but fifty years ago it was in bad shape.

- Relate main clauses with a semicolon alone or a semicolon and a conjunctive adverb: *however, indeed, thus,* etc. (p. 191).

  The building was standing; however, it suffered from neglect.

- Within clauses, link words and phrases with a coordinating conjunction: *and, but, or, nor* (p. 189).

  The *people and officials* of the nation *were indifferent to Independence Hall or took it for granted.*

- Link main clauses or other structures (words and phrases) with a correlative conjunction: *both . . . and, not only . . . but also,* etc. (p. 189).

  People *not only took the building for granted but also neglected it.*

Use **subordination** to de-emphasize ideas (p. 323).

- Use a subordinate clause beginning with a subordinating conjunction: *although, because, if, whereas,* etc. (p. 183).

  Although some citizens had tried to rescue the building, they had not gained substantial public support.

- Use a subordinate clause beginning with a relative pronoun: *who, whoever, which, that* (p. 183).

  The first strong step was taken by the federal government, *which made the building a national monument.*

- Use a phrase (p. 174).

  Like most national monuments, Independence Hall is protected by the National Park Service. [Prepositional phrase.]

  Protecting many popular tourist sites, the service is a highly visible government agency. [Verbal phrase.]

- Use an appositive (p. 187).

  The National Park Service, *a branch of the Department of Interior,* also runs Yosemite and other wilderness parks.

- Use a modifying word.

  At the *red brick* Independence Hall, park rangers give *guided* tours and protect the *irreplaceable* building from vandalism.

TRANSPARENCY MASTER 16.1

Strong, William. "Creative Approaches to Sentence Combining." ERIC, 1986. ED 274 985. Strong offers a number of examples and classroom activities to help teach sentence-combining techniques.

Williams, James D. *Preparing to Teach Writing.* Mahwah, NJ: Lawrence Erlbaum Associates, 1996. See the section on "Style and Sentence Combining," which explores the connections between syntactic and developmental maturity in teaching sentence combining (124–130).

RESOURCES AND IDEAS

Melamed, Evelyn B., and Harvey Minkoff. "Transitions: A Key to Mature Reading and Writing." In *Teaching the Basics—Really!* Ed. Ouida Clapp. Urbana: NCTE, 1977. 17–21. The authors describe exercises to help students make logical links between sentences and parts of sentences with transitions.

String of simple sentences

We should not rely so heavily on oil. Coal and uranium are also overused. We have a substantial energy resource in the moving waters of our rivers. Smaller streams add to the total volume of water. The resource renews itself. Coal and oil are irreplaceable. Uranium is also irreplaceable. The cost of water does not increase much over time. The costs of coal, oil, and uranium rise dramatically.

Ideas coordinated

We should not rely so heavily on coal, oil, and uranium, for we have a substantial energy resource in the moving waters of our rivers and streams. Coal, oil, and uranium are irreplaceable and thus subject to dramatic cost increases; water, however, is self-renewing and more stable in cost.

The information in both passages is essentially the same, but the second is shorter and considerably easier to read and understand because it builds connections among coordinate ideas.

To link ideas, you can use coordinating conjunctions (*and, but, or, nor, for, so, yet*), correlative conjunctions (*both . . . and* and others), and conjunctive adverbs (*however, thus,* and others). These words signal certain relationships, such as addition (*and, both . . . and, moreover*) and contrast (*but, not . . . but, however*). See the full lists of these words on pages 189 and 191.

coord 16a

Punctuating coordinated words, phrases, and clauses

Most coordinated words, phrases, and subordinate clauses are not punctuated with commas (see p. 384). The exceptions are items in a series and coordinate adjectives.

We rely heavily on *coal*, *oil*, *and uranium.* [A series; see p. 376.]
Dirty, *unhealthy* air is one result. [Coordinate adjectives; see p. 377.]

In a sentence consisting of two main clauses, punctuation depends on whether a coordinating conjunction, a conjunctive adverb, or no connecting word links the clauses.

Oil is irreplaceable, *but* water is self-renewing. [See p. 365.]
Oil is irreplaceable; *however,* water is self-renewing. [See p. 390.]
Oil is irreplaceable; water is self-renewing. [See p. 388.]

1 Using coordination effectively

A string of coordinated elements—especially main clauses—creates the same effect as a string of simple sentences: it obscures the relative importance of ideas and details.

RESOURCES AND IDEAS

You may wish to remind students that section 5d of the handbook contains a detailed discussion of coordinating conjunctions. If students make a simple list of the conjunctions, they may find themselves becoming more aware of the words and their functions as they read and write:

and	or
but	for
nor	so
yet	

Excessive coordination The weeks leading up to the resignation of President Nixon were eventful, and the Supreme Court and the Congress closed in on him, and the Senate Judiciary Committee voted to begin impeachment proceedings, and finally the President resigned on August 9, 1974.

Such a passage needs editing to stress the important points (in italics below) and to de-emphasize the less important information:

Revised *The weeks leading up to the resignation of President Nixon were eventful,* as the Supreme Court and the Congress closed in on him and the Senate Judiciary Committee voted to begin impeachment proceedings. Finally, *the President resigned on August 9, 1974.*

Coordinating logically

Coordinated sentence elements should be logically equal and related, and the relation between them should be the one expressed by the connecting word. If either principle is violated, the result is **faulty coordination.**

Faulty John Stuart Mill was a nineteenth-century utilitarian, and he believed that actions should be judged by their usefulness or by the happiness they cause. [The two clauses are not separate and equal: the second expands on the first by explaining what a utilitarian such as Mill believed.]

Revised John Stuart Mill, *a nineteenth-century utilitarian,* believed that actions should be judged by their usefulness or by the happiness they cause.

Faulty Mill is recognized as a utilitarian, and he did not found the utilitarian school of philosophy. [The two clauses seem to contrast, requiring *but* or *yet* between them.]

Revised Mill is recognized as a utilitarian, *but* he did not found the utilitarian school of philosophy.

Sometimes faulty coordination occurs because the writer omits necessary information.

Faulty Jeremy Bentham founded the utilitarian school, and Mill was precocious. [The two clauses seem unrelated.]

Revised Jeremy Bentham founded the utilitarian school *before Mill was born,* and Mill *joined at the precocious age of twenty.*

RESOURCES AND IDEAS

You may wish to remind students that section 5d of the handbook contains a detailed discussion of conjunctive adverbs. You can help create awareness of conjunctive adverbs by asking students to make a list of the words. As they read and write later, students may pay greater attention to the conjunctive adverbs and their functions:

also	further
next	then
certainly	likewise
similarly	undoubtedly
however	anyway
therefore	now
meanwhile	finally
namely	still
besides	indeed
otherwise	thus

ANSWERS: EXERCISE 1

Possible revisions

1. Many chronic misspellers do not have the time or motivation to master spelling rules. They may rely on dictionaries to catch misspellings, but most dictionaries list words under their correct spellings. One kind of dictionary is designed for chronic misspellers. It lists each word under its common *mis*spellings and then provides the correct spelling and definition.
2. Henry Hudson was an English explorer, but he captained ships for the Dutch East India Company. On a voyage in 1610 he passed Greenland and sailed into a great bay in today's northern Canada. He thought he and his sailors could winter there, but the cold was terrible and food ran out. The sailors mutinied and cast Hudson and eight others adrift in a small boat. Hudson and his companions perished.

COLLABORATIVE LEARNING COMPUTER EXERCISE

Ask students to complete Exercises 1 and 2 individually and then to compare and revise their responses in small groups. You might ask each group to present a successful combination and to discuss why it seems more effective.

When students have completed these exercises, each group might create an additional exercise "paragraph" made up of short declarative sentences. (Students often enjoy the opportunity to create humorously short sentences on a topic of their choice.) Groups then trade exercises and revise them using the sentence-combining techniques suggested in Exercises 1 and 2. This exercise also works well in a computer classroom, where the additional exercise can be printed out and "assigned" to another group.

ANSWERS: EXERCISE 2

Possible answers

1. Because soldiers admired their commanding officers, they often gave them nicknames containing the word "old," even though not all of the commanders were old.

Exercise 1
Sentence combining: Coordination

Combine sentences in the following passages to coordinate related ideas in the way that seems most effective to you. You will have to supply coordinating conjunctions or conjunctive adverbs and the appropriate punctuation.

1. Many chronic misspellers do not have the time to master spelling rules. They may not have the motivation. They may rely on dictionaries to catch misspellings. Most dictionaries list words under their correct spellings. One kind of dictionary is designed for chronic misspellers. It lists each word under its common *mis*spellings. It then provides the correct spelling. It also provides the definition.
2. Henry Hudson was an English explorer. He captained ships for the Dutch East India Company. On a voyage in 1610 he passed by Greenland. He sailed into a great bay in today's northern Canada. He thought he and his sailors could winter there. The cold was terrible. Food ran out. The sailors mutinied. The sailors cast Hudson adrift in a small boat. Eight others were also in the boat. Hudson and his companions perished.

Exercise 2
Revising: Excessive or faulty coordination

Revise the following sentences to eliminate excessive or faulty coordination. Relate ideas effectively by adding or subordinating information or by forming more than one sentence. Each item has more than one possible answer.

Example:

My dog barks, and I have to move out of my apartment.

Because my dog's barking *disturbs my neighbors,* I have to move out of my apartment.

1. Often soldiers admired their commanding officers, and they gave them nicknames, and these names frequently contained the word "old," but not all of the commanders were old.
2. General Thomas "Stonewall" Jackson was also called "Old Jack," and he was not yet forty years old.
3. Another Southern general in the Civil War was called "Old Pete," and his full name was James Longstreet.
4. The Union general Henry W. Halleck had a reputation as a good military strategist, and he was an expert on the work of a French military authority, Henri Jomini, and Halleck was called "Old Brains."
5. General William Henry Harrison won the Battle of Tippecanoe, and he received the nickname "Old Tippecanoe," and he used the name in his Presidential campaign slogan "Tippecanoe and Tyler, Too," and he won the election in 1840, but he died of pneumonia a month after taking office.

16b Subordinating to distinguish main ideas

With **subordination** you use words or word groups to indicate that some elements in a sentence are less important than others. In the following sentence, it is difficult to tell what is most important:

Excessive coordination In recent years computer prices have dropped, and production costs have dropped more slowly, and computer manufacturers have had to contend with shrinking profits.

The following rewrite places the point of the sentence (shrinking profits) in the main clause and reduces the rest of the information to a subordinate clause:

Revised *Because* production costs have dropped more slowly than prices in recent years, computer manufacturers have had to contend with shrinking profits.

No rules can specify what information in a sentence you should make primary and what you should subordinate; the decision will depend on your meaning. But, in general, you should consider using subordinate structures for details of time, cause, condition, concession, purpose, and identification (size, location, and the like). You can subordinate information with the following structures:

- Subordinate clauses beginning with subordinating conjunctions (*because, when,* and others) or relative pronouns (mainly *who, which, that*). (See p. 183 for full lists of these words.) Because subordinate clauses are longer and grammatically more like main clauses than phrases or single words, they tend to place the greatest emphasis on subordinate information.
- Phrases, including appositives renaming nouns (*her son, a man named Carl*), prepositional phrases beginning with a preposition such as *in* or *on* (*in the book*), or verbal phrases beginning with a verb form such as *saving* or *to save*. (See pp. 187, 174, and 179, respectively, for more on these kinds of phrases.) Phrases give less weight than subordinate clauses but more than single words.
- Single words, such as adjectives and adverbs that modify other words. Single words give the least weight to subordinate information.

The following examples show how subordinate structures may convey various meanings with various weights. (Some appropriate subordinating conjunctions, relative pronouns, and prepositions for each meaning appear in parentheses.)

2. General Thomas "Stonewall" Jackson was also called "Old Jack," although he was not yet forty years old.
3. Another Southern general, whose full name was James Longstreet, was called "Old Pete."
4. The Union General Henry W. Halleck had a reputation as a good military strategist, and he was an expert on the work of a French military authority, Henri Jomini. Therefore, Halleck was called "Old Brains."
5. After General William Henry Harrison won a victory at the Battle of Tippecanoe, he received the nickname "Old Tippecanoe." He used the name in his Presidential campaign slogan "Tippecanoe and Tyler, Too." Although he won the election in 1840, he died of pneumonia a month after taking office.

COLLABORATIVE LEARNING

IDENTIFYING CONNECTORS

Have students, working in groups, identify the connectors (subordinating and coordinating conjunctions) in several essays: an essay from a reader, a news item in a newspaper, or a student essay. If the uses of subordination and coordination and the kinds of connectors differ in each kind of essay, ask students to try to account for the differences.

RESOURCES AND IDEAS:

Improving sentence style

Angell, David, and Brent Heslop. *The Elements of E-Mail Style.* Boston: Addison, 1994. This account of the particular conventions of E-mail style makes clear how the context and medium shape writers' stylistic choices and effects.

Lanham, Richard. *Analyzing Prose.* New York: Scribner's, 1983. Lanham offers extensive advice on revising for stylistic effect.

Williams, Joseph. *Style: Ten Lessons in Clarity and Grace.* 4th ed. New York: HarperCollins, 1994. Williams's how-to manual for improving style at the sentence and word level is especially strong in discussing coordination and subordination.

 **COLLABORATIVE LEARNING**

USING STUDENT WRITING

Ask students to share a paragraph or two from their drafts with the other members of their group. Group members should comment on the use of coordination and subordination and suggest places where more or less of either might aid the writer in achieving her or his purpose.

 **COLLABORATIVE LEARNING**

REDUCING

To help students practice subordination, create several groups, and give each group a different passage. Ask the groups to first reduce sentences to clauses and then to identify the subordinate clauses in each passage. At the end of the activity, the groups can exchange passages and repeat the process, comparing their work at the end with the work of the prior group.

GETTING A NEW LOOK AT YOUR WRITING

Give students a fresh look at their own writing by asking them to revise a portion of a graded essay following specific directions, such as "Add subordination" or "Use more imaginative subordinating words."

 **COLLABORATIVE LEARNING**

 **COMPUTER EXERCISE**

AVOIDING EXCESSIVE SUBORDINATION

Choose paragraphs from student essays that demonstrate overuse or faulty use of subordination, and distribute them to the class. Have students rewrite the paragraphs and then compare their versions to determine which are the most clear and effective revisions. This exercise may be used for small-group or individual work. It is also an effective exercise for the computer classroom.

SPACE OR TIME (*after, before, since, until, when, while; at, in, on, until*)

The mine explosion killed six workers. The owners adopted safety measures.

After the mine explosion killed six workers, the owners adopted safety measures. [Subordinate clause.]

After six deaths, the owners adopted safety measures. [Prepositional phrase.]

CAUSE OR EFFECT (*as, because, since, so that; because of, due to*)

Jones had been without work for six months. He was having trouble paying his bills.

Because Jones had been without work for six months, he was having trouble paying his bills. [Subordinate clause.]

Having been jobless for six months, Jones could not pay his bills. [Verbal phrase.]

CONDITION (*if, provided, since, unless, whenever; with, without*)

Forecasters predict a mild winter. Farmers hope for an early spring.

Whenever forecasters predict a mild winter, farmers hope for an early spring. [Subordinate clause.]

With forecasts for a mild winter, farmers hope for an early spring. [Prepositional phrase.]

CONCESSION (*although, as if, even though, though; despite, except for, in spite of*)

The horse looked gentle. It proved hard to manage.

Although the horse looked gentle, it proved hard to manage. [Subordinate clause.]

The horse, *a gentle-looking animal,* proved hard to manage. [Appositive.]

The *gentle-looking* horse proved hard to manage. [Single word.]

PURPOSE (*in order that, so that, that; for, toward*)

Congress passed new immigration laws. Many Vietnamese refugees could enter the United States.

Congress passed new immigration laws *so that many Vietnamese refugees could enter the United States.* [Subordinate clause.]

Congress passed new immigration laws, *permitting many Vietnamese refugees to enter the United States.* [Verbal phrase.]

IDENTIFICATION (*that, when, where, which, who; by, from, of*)

Old barns are common in New England. They are often painted red.

Old barns, *which are often painted red,* are common in New England. [Subordinate clause.]

Old barns, *often painted red,* are common in New England. [Verbal phrase.]

Old *red* barns are common in New England. [Single word.]

Punctuating subordinate constructions

A modifying word, phrase, or clause that introduces a sentence is usually set off from the rest of the sentence with a comma (see p. 368).

> *Unfortunately*, the bank failed.
> *In a little over six months*, the bank became insolvent.
> *When the bank failed*, many reporters investigated.

A modifier that interrupts or concludes a main clause is *not* set off with punctuation when it restricts the meaning of a word or words in the clause (see p. 370).

> One article *about the bank failure* won a prize.
>
> The article *that won the prize* appeared in the local newspaper.
>
> The reporter wrote the article *because the bank failure affected many residents of the town.*

When an interrupting or concluding modifier does *not* restrict meaning, but simply adds information to the sentence, it *is* set off with punctuation, usually a comma or commas (see p. 370).

> The bank, *over forty years old*, never reopened after its doors were closed.
>
> The bank managers, *who were cleared of any wrongdoing*, all found new jobs.
>
> Some customers of the bank never recovered all their money, *though most of them tried to do so.*

Like a modifier, an appositive is set off with punctuation (usually a comma or commas) only when it does *not* restrict the meaning of the word it refers to (see p. 372).

> The bank, *First City*, was the oldest in town.
>
> The newspaper the *Chronicle* was one of several reporting the story.

A dash or dashes may also be used to set off a nonrestrictive appositive, particularly when it contains commas (see p. 419). A concluding appositive is sometimes set off with a colon (see p. 417).

Subordinating logically

Use subordination only for the less important information in a sentence. **Faulty subordination** reverses the dependent relation the reader expects.

> **Faulty** Ms. Angelo was in her first year of teaching, although she was a better instructor than others with many years of

experience. [The sentence suggests that Angelo's inexperience is the main idea, whereas the writer intended to stress her skill *despite* her inexperience.]

Revised *Although Ms. Angelo was in her first year of teaching,* she was a better instructor than others with many years of experience.

Faulty Her class, which won a national achievement award, had twenty students. [Common sense says the important fact is the award.]

Revised Her class *of twenty students* won a national achievement award.

2 Using subordination effectively

Subordination can do much to organize and emphasize information. But it loses that power when you try to cram too much loosely related detail into one long sentence.

Overloaded The boats that were moored at the dock when the hurricane, which was one of the worst in three decades, struck were ripped from their moorings, because the owners had not been adequately prepared, since the weather service had predicted the storm would blow out to sea, which they do at this time of year.

Such sentences usually have more than one idea that deserves a main clause, so they are best revised by sorting their details into more than one sentence.

Revised Struck by one of the worst hurricanes in three decades, *the boats at the dock were ripped from their moorings. The owners were unprepared* because the weather service had said that hurricanes at this time of year blow out to sea.

A common form of excessive subordination occurs when a string of adjective clauses begin *which, who,* or *that,* as in the following:

Stringy The company opened a new plant outside Louisville, which is in Kentucky and which is on the Ohio River, which forms the border between Kentucky and Ohio.

To revise such sentences, recast some of the subordinate clauses as other kinds of modifying structures.

Revised The company opened a new plant outside Louisville, *Kentucky, a city across the Ohio River from Ohio.*

Exercise 3
Sentence combining: Subordination

Combine each of the following pairs of sentences twice, each time using one of the subordinate structures in parentheses to make a single sentence. You will have to add, delete, change, and rearrange words.

Example:

During the late eighteenth century, workers carried beverages in brightly colored bottles. The bottles had cork stoppers. (*Clause beginning that. Phrase beginning with.*)

During the late eighteenth century, workers carried beverages in brightly colored bottles *that had cork stoppers.*

During the late eighteenth century, workers carried beverages in brightly colored bottles *with cork stoppers.*

1. The bombardier beetle sees an enemy. It shoots out a jet of chemicals to protect itself. (*Clause beginning when. Phrase beginning seeing.*)
2. The beetle's spray is very potent. It consists of hot and irritating chemicals. (*Phrase beginning consisting. Phrase beginning of.*)
3. The spray's two chemicals are stored separately in the beetle's body and mixed in the spraying gland. The chemicals resemble a nerve-gas weapon. (*Phrase beginning stored. Clause beginning which.*)
4. The tip of the beetle's abdomen sprays the chemicals. The tip revolves like a turret on a World War II bomber. (*Phrase beginning revolving. Phrase beginning spraying.*)
5. The beetle defeats most of its enemies. It is still eaten by spiders and birds. (*Clause beginning although. Phrase beginning except.*)

Exercise 4
Revising: Subordination

Rewrite the following paragraph in the way you think most effective to subordinate the less important ideas to the more important ones. Use subordinate clauses, phrases, and single words as you think appropriate.

Many students today are no longer majoring in the liberal arts. I mean by "liberal arts" such subjects as history, English, and the social sciences. Students think a liberal arts degree will not help them get jobs. They are wrong. They may not get practical, job-related experience from the liberal arts, but they will get a broad education, and it will never again be available to them. Many employers look for more than a technical, professional education. They think such an education can make an employee's views too narrow. The employers want open-minded employees. They want employees to think about problems from many angles.

ANSWERS: EXERCISE 3

Possible answers

1. When the bombardier beetle sees an enemy, it shoots out a jet of chemicals to protect itself.
   Seeing an enemy, the bombardier beetle shoots out a jet of chemicals to protect itself.
2. Consisting of hot and irritating chemicals, the beetle's spray is very potent.
   The beetle's spray of hot and irritating chemicals is very potent.
3. Stored separately in the beetle's body and mixed in the spraying gland, the spray's two chemicals resemble a nerve-gas weapon.
   The spray's two chemicals, which are stored separately in the beetle's body and mixed in the spraying gland, resemble a nerve-gas weapon.
4. Revolving like a turret on a World War II bomber, the tip of the beetle's abdomen sprays the chemicals.
   Spraying the chemicals, the tip of the beetle's abdomen revolves like a turret on a World War II bomber.
5. Although the beetle defeats most of its enemies, it is still eaten by spiders and birds.
   The beetle defeats most of its enemies except spiders and birds.

COLLABORATIVE LEARNING

COMPUTER EXERCISE

Ask students to complete Exercise 3 individually and compare their responses in small groups. Then have each group create a response to Exercise 4 and present their resulting paragraph to the class. This assignment works well in a networked classroom where the resulting paragraphs in Exercise 4 can be posted so that the class as a whole can discuss the effectiveness of various subordinating strategies.

ANSWERS: EXERCISE 4

Possible revision

Many students today are no longer majoring in the liberal arts—that is, in such subjects as history, English, and the social sciences. Although students think a liberal arts degree will not help them get jobs, they are wrong. They may not get practical, job-related experience from the liberal arts, but they will get a broad education that will never again be available to them. Many employers look for more than a technical, professional education because they think such an education can make an employee's views too narrow. Instead, they want open-minded employees who can think about problems from many angles. Such flexibility—vital to the health of our society—is just what the liberal arts curriculum instills.

ANSWERS: EXERCISE 5

Possible answers

1. Because Genaro González is blessed with great writing talent, several of his stories and his novel *Rainbow's End* have been published.
2. Although he loves to write, he has also earned a doctorate in psychology.
3. His first story, which is entitled "Un Hijo del Sol," reflects his growing consciousness of his Aztec heritage and place in the world.
4. González writes equally well in English and Spanish. In 1990 he received a large fellowship enabling him to take a leave of absence from Pan American University, where he teaches psychology. During that year he could write without worrying about an income.
5. González wrote the first version of "Un Hijo del Sol" while he was a sophomore at Pan American. The university is in the Rio Grande valley of southern Texas, which González calls "el Valle" in the story.

REWRITING

Give students a passage from a student or professional essay, and ask them to rewrite it following a specified strategy: adding subordination, using different subordinators, or adding coordination. This exercise can be extended by having students rewrite the passage to change its emphasis.

sub 16c

The liberal arts curriculum instills such flexibility. The flexibility is vital to the health of our society.

Exercise 5
Revising: Faulty or excessive subordination

Revise the following sentences to eliminate faulty or excessive subordination. Correct faulty subordination by reversing main and subordinate structures. Correct excessive subordination by coordinating equal ideas or by making separate sentences.

Example:

Terrified to return home, he had driven his mother's car into a cornfield.

Having driven his mother's car into a cornfield, he was terrified to return home.

1. Genaro González is blessed with great writing talent, which means that several of his stories and his novel *Rainbow's End* have been published.
2. He loves to write, although he has also earned a doctorate in psychology.
3. His first story, which reflects his growing consciousness of his Aztec heritage and place in the world, is entitled "Un Hijo del Sol."
4. In 1990 González, who writes equally well in English and Spanish, received a large fellowship that enabled him to take a leave of absence from the Pan American University, where he teaches psychology, so that he could write without worrying about an income.
5. González wrote the first version of "Un Hijo del Sol" while he was a sophomore at Pan American, which is in the Rio Grande valley of southern Texas, which González calls "el Valle" in the story.

16c Choosing clear connectors

Most connecting words signal specific and unambiguous relations; for instance, the coordinating conjunction *but* clearly indicates contrast, and the subordinating conjunction *because* clearly indicates cause. A few connectors, however, require careful use, either because they are ambiguous in many contexts or because they are often misused.

1 Using *as* and *while* clearly

The subordinating conjunction *as* can indicate several relations, including comparison and time.

Comparison	Technicians work *as* rapidly as possible.
Time	One shift starts *as* the other stops.

Avoid using *as* to indicate cause. It is unclear.

Unclear	*As* the experiment was occurring, the laboratory was sealed. [Time or cause intended?]
Revised	*When* the experiment was occurring, the laboratory was sealed. [Time.]
Revised	*Because* the experiment was occurring, the laboratory was sealed. [Cause.]

The subordinating conjunction *while* can indicate either time or concession. Unless the context makes the meaning of *while* unmistakably clear, choose a more exact connector.

Unclear	*While* technicians work in the next room, they cannot hear the noise. [Time or concession intended?]
Revised	*When* technicians work in the next room, they cannot hear the noise. [Time.]
Revised	*Although* technicians work in the next room, they cannot hear the noise. [Concession.]

2 Using *as, like,* and *while* correctly

The use of *as* as a substitute for *whether* or *that* is considered nonstandard (it does not conform to spoken and written standard English).

Nonstandard	They are not sure *as* the study succeeded.
Revised	They are not sure *whether* [or *that*] the study succeeded.

Although the preposition *like* is often used as a conjunction in informal speech and in advertising (*Dirt-Away works like a soap should*), writing generally requires the conjunction *as, as if, as though,* or *that.*

Speech	It seemed *like* it did succeed.
Writing	It seemed *as if* [or *as though* or *that*] it did succeed.

The subordinating conjunction *while* is sometimes carelessly used in the sense of *and* or *but,* creating false subordination where coordination is intended.

Faulty	The institute will sponsor a new study *while* technicians take new precautions.
Revised	The institute will sponsor a new study, *and technicians will* take new precautions.

ANSWERS: EXERCISE 6

1. Many writers use *he* to denote both males and females, but others avoid the usage.
2. Some writers feel that substituting *he* for *a doctor* or *the engineer* insults female members of those professions.
3. Because women more frequently enter such fields now, writers can no longer safely use *he* to refer to a white-collar professional.
4. Nor can writers automatically use *she* to refer to a nurse or secretary, as if a man would not enter such a career.
5. Since they desire to be fair to both genders, many writers prefer plural nouns (for example, *doctors*) and *they*.

COLLABORATIVE LEARNING

Ask students to complete Exercise 6 individually and compare their responses in small groups. Then have each group create a response to Exercise 7. Encourage the groups to explore various possibilities for coordination and subordination and to discuss the effects those changes have on the meaning of the paragraph. This assignment also works well in a networked classroom where the resulting paragraphs in Exercise 7 can be posted for discussion.

ANSWERS: EXERCISE 7

Possible revision

Sir Walter Raleigh personified the Elizabethan Age, the period during which Elizabeth I ruled England, in the last half of the sixteenth century. Raleigh was a courtier, a poet, an explorer, and an entrepreneur. Supposedly, he gained Queen Elizabeth's favor by throwing his cloak beneath her feet at the right moment, just as she was about to step over a puddle. Although there is no evidence for this story, it illustrates Raleigh's dramatic and dynamic personality. His energy drew others to him, and he was one of Elizabeth's favorites. She supported him and dispensed favors to him. However, he lost his queen's good will when without her permission he seduced and eventually married one of her maids of honor. After Elizabeth died, her successor, James I, imprisoned Raleigh in the Tower of London on false charges of treason. Raleigh was released after thirteen years but arrested again two years later on the old treason charges. At the age of sixty-six he was beheaded.

sub 16c

Exercise 6
Revising: Clear connectors

Substitute a clear or correct connector in the following sentences where *as, while,* and *like* are unclear or misused.

Example:
He looked to me like he had slept in his clothes.
He looked to me *as if* he had slept in his clothes.

1. Many writers use *he* to denote both males and females, while others avoid the usage.
2. Some writers feel like substituting *he* for *a doctor* or *the engineer* insults female members of those professions.
3. As women more frequently enter such fields now, writers can no longer safely use *he* to refer to a white-collar professional.
4. Nor can writers automatically use *she* to refer to a nurse or secretary, like a man would not enter such a career.
5. As they desire to be fair to both genders, many writers prefer plural nouns (for example, *doctors*) and *they*.

Exercise 7
Revising: Coordination and subordination

The following paragraph consists entirely of simple sentences. Use coordination and subordination to combine sentences in the way you think most effective to emphasize main ideas.

Sir Walter Raleigh personified the Elizabethan Age. That was the period of Elizabeth I's rule of England. The period occurred in the last half of the sixteenth century. Raleigh was a courtier and poet. He was also an explorer and entrepreneur. Supposedly, he gained Queen Elizabeth's favor. He did this by throwing his cloak beneath her feet at the right moment. She was just about to step over a puddle. There is no evidence for this story. It does illustrate Raleigh's dramatic and dynamic personality. His energy drew others to him. He was one of Elizabeth's favorites. She supported him. She also dispensed favors to him. However, he lost his queen's good will. Without her permission he seduced one of her maids of honor. He eventually married the maid of honor. Elizabeth died. Then her successor imprisoned Raleigh in the Tower of London. Her successor was James I. Raleigh was charged falsely with treason. He was released after thirteen years. He was arrested again two years later on the old treason charges. At the age of sixty-six he was beheaded.

Note See page 356 for an exercise involving coordination and subordination along with parallelism and other techniques for effective sentences.

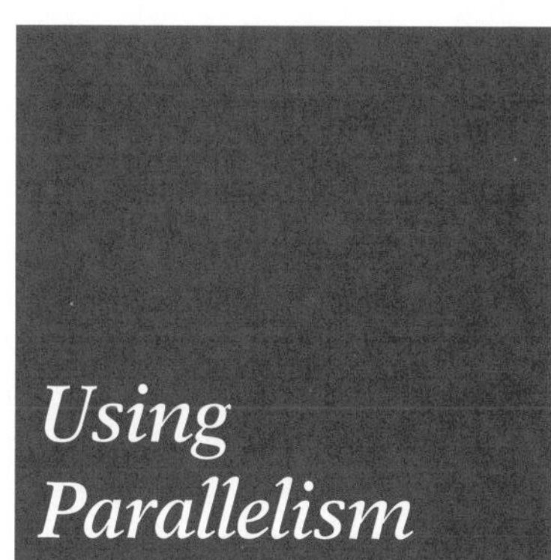

Chapter 17 Using Parallelism

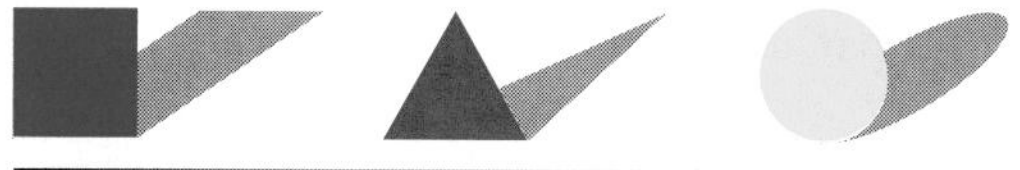

Parallelism is a similarity of grammatical form between two or more elements.

The air is dirtied by ‖ factories ‖ belching ‖ smoke
and ‖ cars ‖ spewing ‖ exhaust.

Parallel structure reinforces and highlights a close relation between compound sentence elements, whether words, phrases, or clauses.

The principle underlying parallelism is that form should reflect meaning: since the parts of compound constructions have the same function and importance, they should have the same grammatical form.

17a Using parallelism for coordinate elements

Use parallelism in all the situations illustrated in the box on the next page.

Note Parallel elements match each other in structure, as in the example above, but they do not always match word for word.

The pioneers passed ‖ *through the town*
and ‖ *into the vast, unpopulated desert.*

1 Using parallelism for elements linked by coordinating conjunctions

The coordinating conjunctions *and, but, or, nor,* and *yet* always signal a need for parallelism.

HIGHLIGHTS

This discussion of parallelism is divided into two sections, and moves from correctness to effective style. The opening section addresses the obligatory use of parallelism in coordinate constructions—those linked by coordinating conjunctions and correlative conjunctions; those in comparisons and contrasts; and those in lists, outlines, and the like. The second section examines how parallelism can be used within and among sentences to increase coherence, emphasize meaning, and heighten the effect. For some students you may wish to emphasize the items in the opening section. But students who have no trouble maintaining obligatory parallelism can often profit by working more creatively with parallelism to tighten and clarify their writing. Exercise 3, a sentence-combining exercise, is designed to give students a chance to explore the options for expression that parallelism provides. The exercise is likely to be most effective when students are given a chance to (1) discuss with one another the impact of various combinations or (2) work collaboratively in exploring various sentence-combining options.

RESOURCES AND IDEAS

Brooks, Phyllis. "Mimesis: Grammar and the Echoing Voice." *College English* 35 (1973): 161–68. Brooks suggests the writing of paragraphs that imitate the style of a writer but use different content. She indicates that the practice helps students learn to use a variety of structures, including parenthetical expressions, appositives and modifiers, and parallelism plus reference.

Graves, Richard L. "Symmetrical Form and the Rhetoric of the Sentence." *Rhetoric and Composition: A Sourcebook for Teachers.* Upper Montclair: Boynton/Cook, 1984. 119–27. Graves argues that since comparison is a natural way for humans to organize information, parallelism is an effective way of helping readers acquire and interpret information.

Walker, Robert L. "The Common Writer: A Case for Parallel Structure." *College Composition and Communication* 21 (1970): 373–79. Walker believes that students should be encouraged to use a variety of sentence structures and parallelism, which he considers important features of mature sentences.

TRANSPARENCY MASTER 17.1

Williams, Joseph M. "The Phenomenology of Error." *College Composition and Communication* 32 (1981): 152–68. Williams describes parallelism problems from the point of view of a writer's stylistic choices.

COLLABORATIVE LEARNING

PATTERNS FOR PARALLELISM

Working on their own, students might find it difficult to write many sentences containing correlative conjunctions, lists, and coordinate structures that require parallelism; but if you ask them to do this in groups, they can probably generate quite a few. As part of the assignment, ask students to vary the sentences as much as they can in content and in use of parallelism. Then ask the groups to judge each other's work for originality, clarity, and effectiveness.

SAMPLE ESSAYS

Journal entries and student drafts, along with essays from a reader or a similar source, provide a gold mine of material on which to practice. Ask students to look for parallelism in essays from a reader or a similar source. If the students are working in groups, ask them not only to reach consensus on which elements are parallel but also to decide what functions the parallelism performs.

Patterns of parallelism

Use parallel structures for all coordinated elements.

- For elements connected by coordinating conjunctions (*and, but, or,* etc.) or correlative conjunctions (*both . . . and, neither . . . nor,* etc.) (pp. 331–34):

  In 1988 a Greek cyclist, backed up by ‖ *engineers,*
  ‖ *physiologists,*
  and ‖ *athletes,*
  broke the world's record for human flight
  with neither ‖ *a boost*
  nor ‖ *a motor.*

- For elements being compared or contrasted (p. 334):

  ‖ *Pedal power*
  rather than ‖ *horse power*
  propelled the plane.

- For lists, outlines, or headings (p. 334):

  The four-hour flight was successful because
  ‖ (1) *the cyclist was very fit,*
  ‖ (2) *he flew a straight course over water,*
  and ‖ (3) *he kept the aircraft near the water's surface.*

The industrial base was *shifting* and *shrinking.*

Politicians rarely *acknowledged the problem* or *proposed alternatives.*

Industrial workers were understandably disturbed *that they were losing their jobs* and *that no one seemed to care.*

If sentence elements linked by coordinating conjunctions are not parallel in structure, the resulting sentence will be awkward and distracting.

NONPARALLEL Three reasons why steel companies kept losing money were that their plants were inefficient, high labor costs, and foreign competition was increasing.

REVISED Three reasons why steel companies kept losing money were *inefficient plants,* high labor costs, and *increasing foreign competition.*

All the words required by idiom or grammar must be stated in compound constructions (see also p. 312).

NONPARALLEL Given training, workers can acquire the skills and interest in other jobs. [*Skills* and *interest* require different prepositions, so both must be stated.]

Revised Given training, workers can acquire the skills *for* and interest in other jobs.

Often, the same word must be repeated to avoid confusion.

Confusing Thoreau stood up for his principles by not paying his taxes and spending a night in jail. [Did he spend a night in jail or not?]

Revised Thoreau stood up for his principles by not paying his taxes and *by* spending a night in jail.

Be sure that clauses beginning *who* or *which* are coordinated only with other *who* or *which* clauses.

Nonparallel Thoreau was the nineteenth-century essayist who retired to the woods and he wrote about nature.

Revised Thoreau was the nineteenth-century essayist who retired to the woods and *wrote* about nature.

Using parallelism for elements linked by correlative conjunctions

Correlative conjunctions are pairs of connectors. For example:

both . . . and	neither . . . nor	not only . . . but also
either . . . or	not . . . but	whether . . . or

They stress equality and balance and thus emphasize the relation between elements, even long phrases and clauses. The elements should be parallel to confirm their relation.

It is not *a tax bill* but *a tax relief bill,* providing relief not *for the needy* but *for the greedy.* —Franklin Delano Roosevelt

At the end of the novel, Huck Finn both *rejects society's values by turning down money and a home* and *affirms his own values by setting out for "the territory."*

Most errors in parallelism with correlative conjunctions occur when the element after the second connector does not match the element after the first connector.

Nonparallel Mark Twain refused either to ignore the moral blindness of his society or spare the reader's sensibilities. [*To* follows *either,* so it must also follow *or.*]

Revised Mark Twain refused either to ignore the moral blindness of his society or *to* spare the reader's sensibilities.

Nonparallel Huck Finn learns not only that human beings have an enormous capacity for folly but also enormous dignity. [The first element includes *that human beings have;* the second element does not.]

ADDING PARALLELISM

Take a loose-jointed student essay or a professional essay and distribute it to students (working individually or in groups), asking them to make the sentences denser by adding parallelism wherever possible. Ask them also to decide when the parallelism adds to the essay and when it detracts.

// 17a

REVISED Huck Finn learns *that human beings have* not only an enormous capacity for folly but also enormous dignity.

3 Using parallelism for elements being compared or contrasted

Elements being compared or contrasted should ordinarily be cast in the same grammatical form.

It is better *to live rich* than *to die rich.* —SAMUEL JOHNSON

WEAK The study found that most welfare recipients wanted to work rather than handouts.

REVISED The study found that most welfare recipients wanted *work* rather than handouts.

REVISED The study found that most welfare recipients wanted to work rather than *to accept* handouts.

4 Using parallelism for lists, outlines, or headings

The elements of a list or outline that divides a larger subject are coordinate and should be parallel in structure. Parallelism is essential in the headings that divide a paper into sections (see p. 766) and in a formal topic outline (see p. 55).

FAULTY	IMPROVED
Changes in Renaissance England	Changes in Renaissance England
1. Extension of trade routes	1. Extension of trade routes
2. Merchant class became more powerful	2. Increased power of the merchant class
3. The death of feudalism	3. Death of feudalism
4. Upsurging of the arts	4. Upsurge of the arts
5. The sciences were encouraged	5. Encouragement of the sciences
6. Religious quarrels began	6. Rise of religious quarrels

Exercise 1
Identifying parallel elements

Identify the parallel elements in the following sentences. How does parallelism contribute to the effectiveness of each sentence?

1. Eating an animal has not always been an automatic or an everyday affair; it has tended to be done on solemn occasions and for a special treat. —MARGARET VISSER
2. They [pioneer women] rolled out dough on the wagon seats, cooked with fires made out of buffalo chips, tended the sick,

// 17a

COLLABORATIVE LEARNING

Students can complete Exercise 1 individually or in groups and then compare responses. This gives students who are confused about the concept of parallelism the opportunity to practice identifying parallel structures in a nonintimidating environment. Ask each group to create one or two sentences that demonstrate parallelism, using the models provided by this exercise. Each group might then present their most creative response to the class as a whole.

ANSWERS: EXERCISE 1

1. The two sets of parallel phrases (*an automatic or an everyday affair; on solemn occasions and for a special treat*) and the parallel main clauses (*. . . has not been always . . . has tended to be*) emphasize the differences between then and now.
2. The parallel verbs (*rolled out . . . cooked . . . tended . . . marked*) stress the number and variety of the women's responsibilities.
3. Supporting *pleasantest* is a wealth of detail expressed in five parallel absolute phrases: *exhaustion . . . in; the sated mosquitoes . . . off; the room . . . garments; the vines . . . day;* and *the air conditioner . . . mosquitoes.* The phrases convey no action, emphasizing the stillness of the scene.
4. The limiting effects of aging are emphasized by the increasingly narrow parallel verbs—*paints, lies, imprisons*—and the parallel objects—*every action, every movement, and every thought.*

and marked the graves of their children, their husbands and each other. —Ellen Goodman

3. The mornings are the pleasantest times in the apartment, exhaustion having set in, the sated mosquitoes at rest on ceiling and walls, sleeping it off, the room a swirl of tortured bedclothes and abandoned garments, the vines in their full leafiness filtering the hard light of day, the air conditioner silent at last, like the mosquitoes. —E. B. White
4. Aging paints every action gray, lies heavy on every movement, imprisons every thought. —Sharon Curtin

Exercise 2
Revising: Parallelism

Revise the following sentences to make coordinate, compared, or listed elements parallel in structure. Add or delete words or rephrase as necessary.

Example:

After emptying her bag, searching the apartment, and she called the library, Jennifer realized she had lost the book.

After emptying her bag, searching the apartment, and *calling* the library, Jennifer realized she had lost the book.

1. The ancient Greeks celebrated four athletic contests: the Olympic Games at Olympia, the Isthmian Games were held near Corinth, at Delphi the Pythian Games, and the Nemean Games were sponsored by the people of Cleonae.
2. Each day of the games consisted of either athletic events or holding ceremonies and sacrifices to the gods.
3. In the years between the games, competitors were taught wrestling, javelin throwing, and how to box.
4. Competitors participated in running sprints, spectacular chariot and horse races, and running long distances while wearing full armor.
5. The purpose of such events was developing physical strength, demonstrating skill and endurance, and to sharpen the skills needed for war.
6. Events were held for both men and for boys.
7. At the Olympic Games the spectators cheered their favorites to victory, attended sacrifices to the gods, and they feasted on the meat not burned in offerings.
8. The athletes competed less to achieve great wealth than for gaining honor both for themselves and their cities.
9. Of course, exceptional athletes received financial support from patrons, poems and statues by admiring artists, and they even got lavish living quarters from their sponsoring cities.
10. With the medal counts and flag ceremonies, today's Olympians often seem not so much to be demonstrating individual talent as to prove their countries' superiority.

COLLABORATIVE LEARNING

Ask students to complete Exercise 2 individually and then to compare and revise their responses in small groups. Ask each group to present one or two of the most effective revisions to the class.

ANSWERS: EXERCISE 2

Possible answers

1. The ancient Greeks celebrated four athletic contests: the Olympic Games at Olympia, the Isthmian Games near Corinth, the Pythian Games at Delphi, and the Nemean Games at Cleonae.
2. Each day of the games consisted of either athletic events or ceremonies and sacrifices to the gods.
3. In the years between the games, competitors were taught wrestling, javelin throwing, and boxing.
4. Competitors ran sprints, participated in spectacular chariot and horse races, and ran long distances while wearing full armor.
5. The purpose of such events was developing physical strength, demonstrating skill and endurance, and sharpening the skills needed for war.
6. Events were held both for men and for boys.
7. At the Olympic Games the spectators cheered their favorites to victory, attended sacrifices to the gods, and feasted on the meat not burned in offerings.
8. The athletes competed less to achieve great wealth than to gain honor for both themselves and their cities.
9. Of course, exceptional athletes received financial support from patrons, poems and statues by admiring artists, and even lavish living quarters from their sponsoring cities.
10. With the medal counts and flag ceremonies, today's Olympians often seem not so much to be demonstrating individual talent as to be proving their countries' superiority.

17b Using parallelism to increase coherence

Parallelism makes sentences more coherent by clearly relating paired or opposed units. Consider this sentence:

> NONPARALLEL During the early weeks of the semester, the course reviews fundamentals, but little emphasis is placed on new material.

Here "the course" is doing two things—or doing one thing and not doing the other—and these are opposites. But the nonparallel construction of the sentence (*the course reviews . . . little emphasis is placed*) does not make the connection clear.

> REVISED During the early weeks of the semester, the course reviews fundamentals but *places little emphasis* on new material.

Effective parallelism will enable you to combine in a single, well-ordered sentence related ideas that you might have expressed in separate sentences. Compare the following three sentences with the original single sentence written by H. L. Mencken.

> Slang originates in the effort of ingenious individuals to make language more pungent and picturesque. They increase the store of terse and striking words or widen the boundaries of metaphor. Thus a vocabulary for new shades and differences in meaning is provided by slang.

> Slang originates in the effort of ingenious individuals *to make the language* more pungent and picturesque—*to increase the store* of terse and striking words, *to widen the boundaries* of metaphor, and *to provide a vocabulary* for new shades and differences in meaning.
> —H. L. MENCKEN

Parallel structure works as well to emphasize the connections among related sentences in a paragraph.

> *Lewis Mumford stands* high in the company of this century's sages. A scholar of cosmic cultural reach and conspicuous public conscience, a distinguished critic of life, arts, and letters, an unequaled observer of cities and civilizations, *he is* secure in the modern pantheon of great men. *He is* also an enigma and an anachronism. A legend of epic proportions in intellectual and academic circles, *he is* surprisingly little known to the public. —ADA LOUISE HUXTABLE

Here, Huxtable tightly binds her sentences with two layers of parallelism: the subject-verb patterns of all four sentences (italic and underlined) and the appositives of the second and fourth sentences (underlined). (See p. 97 for another illustration of parallelism among sentences.)

Exercise 3
Sentence combining: Parallelism

Combine each group of sentences below into one concise sentence in which parallel elements appear in parallel structures. You will have to add, delete, change, and rearrange words. Each item has more than one possible answer.

Example:

The new process works smoothly. It is efficient, too.
The new process works smoothly *and efficiently.*

1. People can develop Post-Traumatic Stress Disorder (PTSD). They develop it after experiencing a dangerous situation. They will also have felt fear for their survival.
2. The disorder can be triggered by a wide variety of events. Combat is a typical cause. Similarly, natural disasters can result in PTSD. Some people experience PTSD after a hostage situation.
3. PTSD can occur immediately after the stressful incident. Or it may not appear until many years later.
4. Sometimes people with PTSD will act irrationally. Moreover, they often become angry.
5. Other symptoms include dreaming that one is reliving the experience. They include hallucinating that one is back in the terrifying place. In another symptom one imagines that strangers are actually one's former torturers.

Exercise 4
Revising: Parallelism

Revise the following paragraph to create parallelism wherever it is required for grammar or for coherence.

The great white shark has an undeserved bad reputation. Many people consider the great white not only swift and powerful but also to be a cunning and cruel predator on humans. However, scientists claim that the great white attacks humans not by choice but as a result of chance. To a shark, our behavior in the water is similar to that of porpoises, seals, and sea lions—the shark's favorite foods. These sea mammals are both agile enough and can move fast enough to evade the shark. Thus the shark must attack with swiftness and noiselessly to surprise the prey and giving it little chance to escape. Humans become the shark's victims not because the shark has any preference or hatred of humans but because humans can neither outswim nor can they outmaneuver the shark. If the fish were truly a cruel human-eater, it would prolong the terror of its attacks, perhaps by circling or bumping into its intended victims before they were attacked.

Note See page 356 for an exercise involving parallelism along with other techniques for effective sentences.

ANSWERS: EXERCISE 3

Possible answers

1. People can develop Post-Traumatic Stress Disorder (PTSD) after experiencing a dangerous situation and fearing for their survival.
2. The disorder can be triggered by a wide variety of events, such as combat, natural disasters, or a hostage situation.
3. PTSD can occur immediately after the stressful incident or not until many years later.
4. Sometimes people with PTSD will act irrationally and angrily.
5. Other symptoms include dreaming that one is reliving the experience, hallucinating that one is back in the terrifying place, and imagining that strangers are actually one's former torturers.

COLLABORATIVE LEARNING

Ask students to complete Exercise 3 individually, and work together to compare and revise their responses. Then have each group create a response to Exercise 4 and present it to the class. In a networked classroom you might ask groups to post their revised paragraphs for the class to compare and discuss.

ANSWERS: EXERCISE 4

Possible revision

The great white shark has an undeserved bad reputation. Many people consider the great white not only swift and powerful but also a cunning and cruel predator on humans. However, scientists claim that the great white attacks humans not by choice but by chance. To a shark, our behavior in the water is similar to that of porpoises, seals, and sea lions—the shark's favorite foods. These sea mammals are both agile enough and fast enough to evade the shark. Thus the shark must attack swiftly and noiselessly to surprise the prey and give it little chance to escape. Humans become the shark's victims not because the shark has any preference for or hatred of humans but because humans can neither outswim nor outmaneuver the shark. If the fish were truly a cruel human-eater, it would prolong the terror of its attacks, perhaps by circling or bumping into its intended victims before attacking them.

HIGHLIGHTS

This chapter looks at two ways to achieve emphasis within sentences: by the distribution of information and by the choice of strategies to create a specific effect. Special features of the chapter are its treatment of cumulative and periodic sentences and discussion that stresses the rhetorical effect of each sentence pattern. The sentence-combining exercises that accompany the discussion are designed to help students feel comfortable using these patterns in their writing. The opening discussion also looks at the importance of sentence beginnings and endings and at the effective arrangement of items in a series. Most students benefit from some work with these basic ways of controlling emphasis as well as from discussion of using the active voice (18d) and of being concise (18e). Students who have problems with sentence structure, however, may have more difficulty with the effective uses of repetition (18b) and separation (18c) for emphasis.

RESOURCES AND IDEAS

An understanding of the roles of topics and comments and of the possible relationships of old and new information can be very useful for writers seeking greater clarity and more effective emphasis in their writing. To supplement the discussion in this section of the handbook you may wish to turn to three excellent texts:

Lanham, Richard. *Analyzing Prose.* New York: Scribner's, 1983. Lanham offers extensive advice on revising for stylistic effect.

Vande Koppel, William J. *Clear and Coherent Prose.* New York: HarperCollins, 1989.

Williams, Joseph M. *Style: Ten Lessons in Clarity and Grace.* 4th ed. New York: HarperCollins, 1994.

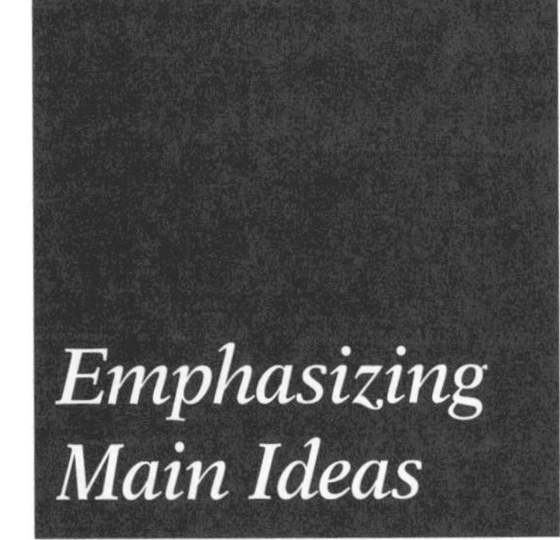

Chapter 18 Emphasizing Main Ideas

When you emphasize the main ideas in your sentences, you hold and channel readers' attention.

Ways to emphasize ideas

- Put important ideas in the beginnings or endings of sentences (opposite).
- Arrange series items in order of increasing importance (p. 340).
- Use an occasional balanced sentence (p. 341).
- Carefully repeat key words and phrases (p. 342).
- Set off important ideas with punctuation (p. 343).
- Use the active voice (p. 344).
- Write concisely (p. 345).

18a Arranging ideas effectively

To arrange ideas emphatically, keep the following two principles in mind:

- The beginning and ending of a sentence are the most emphatic positions, and the ending is generally more emphatic than the beginning.
- A parallel series of words, phrases, or clauses will be more emphatic if the elements are arranged in order of increasing importance.

Using sentence beginnings and endings

Readers automatically seek a writer's principal meaning in the main clause of a sentence—that is, in the subject that names a topic and the predicate that comments on the topic (see p. 163). Thus you can help readers understand your intended meaning by controlling the relation of the main clause and any modifiers attached to it.

The most effective way to call attention to information is to place it first or last in the sentence, reserving the middle for incidentals.

UNEMPHATIC Education remains the most important single means of economic advancement, in spite of its shortcomings. [Emphasizes shortcomings.]

REVISED In spite of its shortcomings, education remains the most important single means of economic advancement. [Emphasizes importance more than shortcomings.]

REVISED Education remains, in spite of its shortcomings, the most important single means of economic advancement. [De-emphasizes shortcomings.]

Many sentences begin with the subject and predicate plus their modifiers and then add more modifiers. Such sentences are called **cumulative** (because they accumulate information as they proceed) or **loose** (because they are not tightly structured).

CUMULATIVE Education has no equal in opening minds, instilling values, and creating opportunities.

CUMULATIVE Most of the Great American Desert is made up of bare rock, rugged cliffs, mesas, canyons, mountains, separated from one another by broad flat basins covered with sun-baked mud and alkali, supporting a sparse and measured growth of sagebrush or creosote or saltbush, depending on location and elevation. —EDWARD ABBEY

A cumulative sentence completes its main statement (topic and comment) and then explains, amplifies, or illustrates it. By thus accumulating information, the sentence parallels the way we naturally think.

The opposite kind of sentence, called **periodic,** saves the main clause until just before the end (the period) of the sentence. Everything before the main clause points toward it.

PERIODIC In opening minds, instilling values, and creating opportunities, education has no equal.

RESOURCES AND IDEAS

Christensen Francis. "A Generative Rhetoric of the Sentence." In *Notes Toward a New Rhetoric: Nine Essays for Teachers.* Ed. Francis Christensen and Bonniejean Christensen. 2nd ed. New York: HarperCollins, 1978. 23–44. Christensen demonstrates how to analyze the levels of generality in sentences and discusses and illustrates the structure of the cumulative sentence.

MEMORY AID

Thinking about cumulative and periodic sentences

The following examples may help students remember how to formulate and how to distinguish between cumulative and periodic sentences:

1. *Cumulative sentences:* A cumulative sentence is created much like a portrait, detail by detail. The diver (for example) paused at the end of the board, gazing down at the smooth, greenish-blue water meters below, his arms stretched out in front, his legs trembling slightly with anticipation and tension, drops of water falling from his fingertips into the swirling wind filled with murmurs from the crowd below and behind his solitary figure.
2. *Periodic sentences:* In a form that parallels the dramatic movement of a tragedy, the meaning of a periodic sentence is built from words and phrases preceding the main clause. In Shakespeare's play *Othello,* step by step, with slowly gathering force and filled with increasing tension and foreboding, the opening scenes create a situation that makes the tragic events inevitable.

Periodic With people from all over the world—Korean grocers, Jamaican cricket players, Vietnamese fishers, Haitian cabdrivers, Chinese doctors—the American mosaic is continually changing.

A variation of the periodic sentence names the subject at the beginning, follows it with a modifier, and then finishes with the predicate.

> Thirty-eight-year-old Dick Hayne, who works in jeans and loafers and likes to let a question cure in the air for a while before answering it, bears all the markings of what his generation used to call a laid-back kind of guy. —George Rush

The periodic sentence creates suspense for the reader by reserving important information for the end. But it requires careful planning so that the reader can remember all the information leading up to the main clause, and the effort should pay off. Most writers save periodic sentences for when their purpose demands climactic emphasis.

emph 18a

COLLABORATIVE LEARNING

MORE COMBINING

Give students a list of information about a topic, and ask them to combine the information to emphasize certain features or to achieve a particular rhetorical purpose. They can do the combining in groups or meet together to discuss and revise the results.

2 Arranging parallel elements effectively

Series

With parallelism, you use similar grammatical structures for ideas linked by *and, but,* and similar words (see Chapter 17). In addition, you should arrange the parallel ideas in order of their importance.

Unemphatic The storm ripped the roofs off several buildings, killed ten people, and knocked down many trees in town. [Buries the most serious damage—deaths—in the middle.]

Emphatic The storm knocked down many trees in town, ripped the roofs off several buildings, and killed ten people. [Arranges items in order of increasing importance.]

You may want to use an unexpected item at the end of a series for humor or for another special effect.

> Early to bed and early to rise makes a man healthy, wealthy, and dead. —James Thurber

But be careful not to use such a series carelessly. The following series seems thoughtlessly random rather than intentionally humorous.

Unemphatic The painting has subdued tone, intense feeling, and a length of about three feet.

Emphatic The painting, about three feet long, has subdued tone and intense feeling.

Balanced sentences

A sentence is **balanced** when its clauses are parallel—that is, matched in grammatical structure (pp. 331–33). Read the following examples aloud to hear their rhythm.

> The fickleness of the women I love is equalled only by the infernal constancy of the women who love me. —George Bernard Shaw

In a pure balanced sentence two main clauses are exactly parallel: they match item for item.

> Scratch a lover, and find a foe. —Dorothy Parker

But the term is commonly applied to sentences that are only approximately parallel or that have only some parallel parts.

> If thought corrupts language, language can also corrupt thought. —George Orwell

> As the traveler who has once been from home is wiser than he who has never left his own doorstep, so a knowledge of one other culture should sharpen our ability to scrutinize more steadily, to appreciate more lovingly, our own. —Margaret Mead

Balanced sentences are heavily emphatic but require thoughtful planning. When used carefully, they can be an especially effective way to alert readers to a strong contrast between two ideas.

Exercise 1
Sentence combining: Cumulative and periodic sentences

Combine each group of sentences below into a single cumulative sentence and then into a single periodic sentence. You will have to add, delete, change, and rearrange words. Each item has more than two possible answers. Does the cumulative or the periodic sentence seem more effective to you?

Example:

The woman refused any treatment. She felt that her life was completed. She wished to die.

Cumulative: The woman refused any treatment, feeling that her life was completed and wishing to die.

Periodic: Feeling that her life was completed and wishing to die, the woman refused any treatment.

1. Pat Taylor strode into the room. The room was packed. He greeted "Taylor's Kids." He nodded to their parents and teachers.
2. This was a wealthy Louisiana oilman. He had promised his "Kids" free college educations. He was determined to make higher education available to all qualified but disadvantaged students.

COLLABORATIVE LEARNING

Ask students to complete Exercise 1 individually and then to compare and revise their responses in groups. Have each group present one of their responses to the class, and encourage the other groups to call attention to places where they created an alternative response.

ANSWERS: EXERCISE 1

Possible answers

1. *Cumulative:* Pat Taylor strode into the packed room, greeting "Taylor's Kids" and nodding to their parents and teachers.
   Periodic: Greeting "Taylor's Kids" and nodding to their parents and teachers, Pat Taylor strode into the packed room.
2. *Cumulative:* This wealthy Louisiana oilman had promised his "Kids" free college educations because he was determined to make higher education available to all qualified but disadvantaged students.
   Periodic: Because he was determined to make higher education available to all qualified but disadvantaged students, this wealthy Louisiana oilman had promised his "Kids" free college educations.
3. *Cumulative:* The students welcomed Taylor, their voices singing, "You Are the Wind Beneath My Wings," their faces beaming with hope, their eyes flashing with self-confidence.

Periodic: Their voices joining in the song "The Wind Beneath My Wings," their faces beaming with hope, their eyes flashing with self-confidence, the students welcomed Taylor.

4. *Cumulative:* A college education had been beyond their dreams, seeming too costly and too demanding.
   Periodic: Seeming too costly and too demanding, a college education had been beyond their dreams.
5. *Cumulative:* Taylor created a bold plan for free college educations, rewarding good students, encouraging greater involvement of parents, and inspiring teachers to work more imaginatively.
   Periodic: Rewarding good students, encouraging greater involvement of parents, and inspiring teachers to work more imaginatively, Taylor created a bold plan for free college educations.

COLLABORATIVE LEARNING

Ask students to work in pairs or small groups on Exercise 2 and present their responses to the class. You might also ask each group to create two additional sentences, one with elements in a series and one with balanced elements.

ANSWERS: EXERCISE 2

Possible answers

1. Remembering her days as a "conductor" on the Underground Railroad made Harriet Tubman proud, but remembering her years as a slave made her angry.
2. Harriet wanted freedom regardless of personal danger, whereas her husband, John, wanted personal safety regardless of freedom.
3. Harriet proved her fearlessness in many ways: she disobeyed John's order not to run away, she was a spy for the North during the Civil War, and she led hundreds of other slaves to freedom.
4. To conduct slaves north to freedom, Harriet risked being caught by Southern patrollers, being returned to slavery, and being hanged for a huge reward.

3. The students welcomed Taylor. Their voices joined in singing. They sang "You Are the Wind Beneath My Wings." Their faces beamed with hope. Their eyes flashed with self-confidence.
4. A college education had been beyond their dreams. They had thought it seemed too costly. It had seemed too demanding.
5. Taylor created a bold plan for free college educations. He rewarded good students. He encouraged greater involvement of parents. He inspired teachers to work more imaginatively.

Exercise 2
Revising: Series and balanced elements

Revise the following sentences so that elements in a series or balanced elements are arranged to give maximum emphasis to main ideas.

Example:

The campers were stranded without matches, without food or water, and without a tent.

The campers were stranded without matches, without a tent, and without food or water.

1. Remembering her days as a "conductor" on the Underground Railroad made Harriet Tubman proud, but she got angry when she remembered her years as a slave.
2. Harriet wanted freedom regardless of personal danger, whereas for her husband, John, personal safety was more important than freedom.
3. Harriet proved her fearlessness in many ways: she led hundreds of other slaves to freedom, she was a spy for the North during the Civil War, and she disobeyed John's order not to run away.
4. To conduct slaves north to freedom, Harriet risked being returned to slavery, being hanged for a huge reward, and being caught by Southern patrollers.
5. After the war Harriet worked tirelessly for civil rights and women's suffrage; raising money for homes for needy former slaves was something else she did.

18b Repeating ideas

Careless repetition often clutters and weakens sentences (see p. 476). But planned repetition of key words and phrases can be an effective means of emphasis. Such repetition often combines with parallelism. It may occur in a series of sentences within a paragraph (see p. 98). Or it may occur in a series of words, phrases, or clauses within a sentence, as in the following examples:

> There is something uneasy in the Los Angeles air this afternoon, some unnatural stillness, some tension. —JOAN DIDION

We have the tools, all the tools—we are suffocating in tools—but we cannot find the actual wood to work or even the actual hand to work it. —ARCHIBALD MACLEISH

18c Separating ideas

When you save important information for the end of a sentence, you can emphasize it even more by setting it off from the rest of the sentence, as in the second example below:

Mothers and housewives are the only workers who do not have regular time off, so they are the great vacationless class.

Mothers and housewives are the only workers who do not have regular time off. They are the great vacationless class. —ANNE MORROW LINDBERGH

You can vary the degree of emphasis by varying the extent to which you separate one idea from the others. A semicolon provides more separation than a comma, and a period provides still more separation. Compare the following sentences:

Most of the reading which is praised for itself is neither literary nor intellectual**,** but narcotic.

Most of the reading which is praised for itself is neither literary nor intellectual**;** it is narcotic.

Most of the reading which is praised for itself is neither literary nor intellectual**.** It is narcotic. —DONALD HALL

Sometimes a dash or a pair of dashes will isolate and thus emphasize a part of a statement (see also pp. 419–20).

His schemes were always elaborate, ingenious, and exciting**—**and wholly impractical.

Athletics**—**that is, winning athletics**—**has become a profitable university operation.

Exercise 3
Emphasizing with repetition or separation

Emphasize the main idea in each sentence or group of sentences below by following the instructions in parentheses: either combine sentences so that parallelism and repetition stress the main idea, or place the main idea in a separate sentence. Each item has more than one possible answer.

Example:

I try to listen to other people's opinions. When my mind is closed, I find that other opinions open it. And they can change my mind when it is wrong. (*Parallelism and repetition.*)

5. After the war, Harriet worked tirelessly for civil rights and women's suffrage; she also raised money for homes for needy former slaves.

COLLABORATIVE LEARNING

REWRITE

Take a passage from a student essay or a professional essay and ask students to rewrite it, using different sentence patterns that give different emphasis to the content of the sentences. Split the class into groups and have them compare their versions with the original, trying to identify a new version that is in some ways clearer than the original and that contains more appropriate emphasis on the main ideas. Since students may well have decided to emphasize different ideas from those emphasized by the original writer, their analysis of the versions may involve matters of content as well as style.

COLLABORATIVE LEARNING

Have students work on Exercise 3 in pairs or small groups. Encourage each group to come up with more than one possible answer and ask them to present their most effective responses to the class.

ANSWERS: EXERCISE 3

Possible answers

1. One of the few worthwhile habits is daily reading: reading for information, reading for entertainment, reading for a broader view of the world.
2. Reading introduces new words and new styles of expression.
3. Students who read a great deal will write essays that are vivid, well structured, and grammatically correct. These students will have absorbed the style and sentence structures of other authors.
4. Reading gives knowledge about other cultures, knowledge about history and current events, and knowledge about human nature.
5. As a result of reading, writers have more resources and more flexibility. Thus reading creates better writers.

I try to listen to other people's opinions, for they can open my mind when it is closed and they can change my mind when it is wrong.

1. One of the few worthwhile habits is daily reading. One can read for information. One can read for entertainment. Reading can give one a broader view of the world. (*Parallelism and repetition.*)
2. Reading introduces new words. One encounters unfamiliar styles of expression through reading. (*Parallelism and repetition.*)
3. Students who read a great deal will write essays that are vivid, well structured, and grammatically correct, for these students will have absorbed the style and sentence structures of other authors. (*Separation.*)
4. Reading gives knowledge. One gets knowledge about other cultures. One will know about history and current events. One gains information about human nature. (*Parallelism and repetition.*)
5. As a result of reading, writers have more resources and more flexibility, and thus reading creates better writers. (*Separation.*)

USING THE PASSIVE

Students may have gathered from their high school educations that using the passive voice is somehow wrong. If that were true, of course, no one could say "I was born" without fear of correction. Instead, remind students that using the passive is a choice writers make for particular reasons; it's the unthinking, excessive, or inappropriate use of the passive voice that bothers many readers.

18d Preferring the active voice

In the **active voice** of the verb, the subject acts: *I peeled the onions.* In the **passive voice** the subject is acted upon: *The onions were peeled by me.* In the passive voice the actor is either relegated to a phrase (*by me*) or omitted entirely: *The onions were peeled.* (See pp. 230–31 for a more detailed explanation of voice.)

The passive voice is indirect because it obscures or removes the actor. The active voice is more direct, vigorous, and emphatic. Further, all sentences turn on their verbs, which give sentences their motion, pushing them along. And active verbs push harder than passive ones.

PASSIVE The new outpatient clinic was opened by the hospital administration and thus ensured that the costs of nonemergency medical care would be reduced.

ACTIVE The hospital *administration opened* the new outpatient clinic and *reduced* the costs of nonemergency medical care.

Sometimes the actor is unknown or unimportant, and many technical writers deliberately omit the actor in order to give impersonal emphasis to what is being acted upon. In these cases the passive voice can be useful.

Wellington was called the "Iron Duke."

Thousands of people are killed annually in highway accidents.
The mixture was then stirred.

Except in these situations, however, rely on the active voice. It is economical and creates movement.

18e Being concise

Conciseness—brevity of expression—aids emphasis no matter what the sentence structure. Unnecessary words detract from necessary words. They clutter sentences and obscure ideas.

Weak In my opinion the competition in the area of grades is distracting. It distracts many students from their goal, which is to obtain an education that is good. There seems to be a belief among a few students that grades are more important than what is measured by them.

Emphatic The competition for grades distracts many students from their goal of obtaining a good education. A few students seem to believe that grades are more important than what they measure.

Because conciseness comes mainly from deleting unneeded words, it receives detailed coverage in Chapter 31, on choosing and using words (see p. 473). The box below summarizes that discussion.

Ways to achieve conciseness

- Cut or shorten empty words or phrases (p. 473).

  Shorten filler phrases, such as *by virtue of the fact that.*
  Cut all-purpose words, such as *area, factor.*
  Cut unneeded qualifiers, such as *in my opinion, for the most part.*

- Cut unnecessary repetition (p. 476).
- Simplify word groups and sentences (p. 477).

  Make the subject and verb of each sentence identify its actor and action.
  Replace clauses with phrases and phrases with single words.
  Use strong verbs.
  Rewrite passive sentences as active.
  Avoid constructions beginning with *there is* or *it is.*
  Combine sentences.

- Cut or rewrite jargon (p. 480).

COLLABORATIVE LEARNING
COMPUTER EXERCISE

CLEAR THE CONFUSION

Choose a particularly confusing or unemphatic passage from a student essay, give it to student groups, and ask them to decide what devices covered in the chapter could be used to improve the passage. Ask them to make the changes as a group, and have a representative of each group write the revised passage on the board so that the class as a whole can compare the various revisions. This exercise works well in a networked classroom where responses can be posted for general discussion.

COLLABORATIVE LEARNING

Ask students to complete Exercise 4 (next page) in small groups and to present their most effective responses to the class.

ANSWERS: EXERCISE 4

Possible answers

1. Customers in restaurants must be wary of suggestive selling.
2. In suggestive selling, the waiter asks diners to buy additional menu selections besides what they ordered.
3. For each item on the menu, another food will naturally complement it.
4. For example, the waiter will ask customers if they want French fries with a sandwich or salad with a steak dinner.
5. Customers who give in to suggestive selling often find that their restaurant meals cost more than they had intended to pay.

COLLABORATIVE LEARNING

COMPUTER EXERCISE

Have students work in groups to revise the paragraph in Exercise 5. Encourage each group to discuss various possible responses and to make a case for the effectiveness of their revision. Then have each group present their revised paragraph to the class either by writing on the blackboard or by photocopying it for a subsequent class meeting. This exercise works well in a networked classroom where each group's response can be posted for general discussion.

emph 18e

ANSWERS: EXERCISE 5

Possible revision

Preparing pasta requires common sense and imagination rather than complicated recipes. The key to success is fresh ingredients for the sauce and perfectly cooked pasta. The sauce may contain just about any fresh fish, meat, cheese, herb, or vegetable. The pasta itself may be dried or fresh, although many experienced cooks find fresh pasta more delicate and flavorful. Dried pasta is fine with zesty sauces; fresh pasta is best with light oil and cream sauces. Dried pasta takes longer to cook than fresh pasta does. The cook should follow the package directions and should test the pasta before the cooking time is up. According to the Italians, who ought to know, the pasta is done when the texture is neither tough nor mushy but *al dente,* or "firm to the bite."

Exercise 4
Revising: Active voice; conciseness

Revise the following sentences to make them more emphatic by converting passive to active voice and by eliminating wordiness. (For additional exercises with the passive voice, see pp. 195, 232, and 479.)

Example:

The problem in this particular situation is that we owe more money than we can afford under present circumstances.

The *problem is* that we owe more money than we can afford.

1. As far as I am concerned, customers who are dining out in restaurants in our country must be wary of suggestive selling, so to speak.
2. In suggestive selling, diners are asked by the waiter to buy additional menu selections in addition to what was ordered by them.
3. For each item on the menu, there is another food that will naturally complement it.
4. For example, customers will be asked if they want French fries with a sandwich or salad with a steak dinner.
5. Due to the fact that customers often give in to suggestive selling, they often find that their restaurant meals are more costly than they had intended to pay.

Exercise 5
Revising: Emphasizing main ideas

Drawing on the advice in this chapter, rewrite the following paragraph to emphasize main ideas and to de-emphasize less important information.

In preparing pasta, there is a requirement for common sense and imagination rather than for complicated recipes. The key to success in this area is fresh ingredients for the sauce and perfectly cooked pasta. The sauce may be made with just about any fresh fish, meat, cheese, herb, or vegetable. As for the pasta itself, it may be dried or fresh, although fresh pasta is usually more delicate and flavorful, as many experienced cooks find. Dried pasta is fine with zesty sauces; with light oil and cream sauces fresh pasta is best used. There is a difference in the cooking time for dried and fresh pasta, with dried pasta taking longer. It is important that the package directions be followed by the cook and that the pasta be tested before the cooking time is up. The pasta is done when the texture is neither tough nor mushy but *al dente,* or "firm to the bite," according to the Italians, who ought to know.

Note See page 356 for an exercise involving emphasis along with parallelism and other techniques for effective sentences.

Chapter 19

Achieving Variety

In a paragraph or an essay, your sentences do not stand one by one. Rather, each stands in relation to those before and after it. To make sentences work together effectively, you need to vary their length, structure, and word order to reflect the importance and complexity of ideas. Variety sometimes takes care of itself, but you can practice established techniques for achieving varied sentences.

Ways to achieve variety among sentences

- Vary the length and structure of sentences so that important ideas stand out (p. 348).
- Vary the beginnings of sentences with modifiers, transitional words and expressions, and occasional expletive constructions (p. 351).
- Occasionally, invert the normal order of subject, predicate, and object or complement (p. 353).
- Use an occasional command, question, or exclamation (p. 354).

A series of similar sentences will prove monotonous and ineffective, as this passage illustrates:

> Ulysses S. Grant and Robert E. Lee met on April 9, 1865. Their meeting place was the parlor of a modest house at Appomattox Court House, Virginia. They met to work out the terms for the surrender of Lee's Army of Northern Virginia. One great chapter of

HIGHLIGHTS

This chapter asks students to think of sentences not as single units but as a sequence of ideas working together. Coordination, subordination, parallelism, and emphasis—topics covered in the preceding chapters—all come into play in the examples in this chapter. You will probably want to direct attention to the introduction to this chapter and to the first two sections, covering strategies for varying the length and structure of sentences and for varying sentence beginnings. You may have to decide, though, how much time to devote to the last two sections, which cover the occasional uses of inverted sentence order and of minor sentence types such as questions and commands.

RESOURCES AND IDEAS

Barrett, Edward. "Collaboration in the Electronic Classroom." *Technology Review* (February/March 1993): 51–55. This article suggests strategies for structuring group work using computers.

Lanham, Richard. *Analyzing Prose*. New York: Scribner's, 1983. Lanham offers extensive advice on revising for stylistic effect.

Rubin, Donald, and Kathryn Greene. "Gender-Typical Style in Written Language." *Research in the Teaching of English* 26 (1992): 7–40. The authors catalog stylistic and syntactic variations that fall along gender lines.

Walpole, Jane R. "The Vigorous Pursuit of Grace and Style." *The Writing Instructor* 1 (1982): 163–69. Walpole describes six ways students can manipulate a good but not great passage (improving their own prose in the process), along with an example to show how the procedure works.

COMPUTER EXERCISE

USING STYLE CHECKERS

Computerized style checkers are now widely available; however, the quality of the advice they offer varies considerably. These programs are based on standardized readability tests and are not particularly sensitive to writers' purposes or the levels of sophistication of their audiences. (For instance, try feeding the *Gettysburg Address* or *A Letter from Birmingham Jail* into such a program; the advice the style checkers provide for "improving" these essays will shock and amuse you.) If your students have access to such programs, you may want to discuss with them how to use the advice the computer might offer.

American life ended with their meeting, and another began. Grant and Lee were bringing the Civil War to its virtual finish. Other armies still had to surrender, and the fugitive Confederate government would struggle desperately and vainly. It would try to find some way to go on living with its chief support gone. Grant and Lee had signed the papers, however, and it was all over in effect.

These eight sentences are all between twelve and sixteen words long (counting initials and dates), they are about equally detailed, and they all begin with the subject. We get a sense of names, dates, and events but no sure sense of how they relate.

Now compare the preceding passage with the actual passage written by Bruce Catton. Here the four sentences range from eleven to fifty-five words, and only one sentence begins with its subject.

> When Ulysses S. Grant and Robert E. Lee met in the parlor of a modest house at Appomattox Court House, Virginia, on April 9, 1865, to work out the terms for the surrender of Lee's Army of Northern Virginia, a great chapter in American life came to a close, and a great new chapter began. [Suspenseful periodic sentence (p. 339) focuses attention on meeting. Details of place, time, and cause are in opening subordinate clause.]
>
> These men were bringing the Civil War to its virtual finish. [Short sentence sums up.] To be sure, other armies had yet to surrender, and for a few days the fugitive Confederate government would struggle desperately and vainly, trying to find some way to go on living now that its chief support was gone. [Cumulative sentence (p. 339) reflects lingering obstacles to peace.] But in effect it was all over when Grant and Lee signed the papers. [Short final sentence indicates futility of further struggle.]
>
> —BRUCE CATTON, "Grant and Lee"

The rest of this chapter suggests how you can vary your sentences for the kind of interest and clarity achieved by Catton.

var 19a

COLLABORATIVE LEARNING

SIMPLE SENTENCES

Take a professional or student essay, reduce it to simple sentences, and ask students to rewrite it, adding variety. Then ask them to work in groups to compare their versions with the original, analyze the differences, and decide as a group which versions are more effective and why.

VISUAL ANALYSIS

Students may wish to make bar charts showing sentence lengths to see the average lengths of sentences they use and to target the variations in length they might want to consider.

19a Varying sentence length and structure

The sentences of a stylistically effective essay will vary most obviously in their length and the arrangement of main clauses and modifiers. The variation in length and structure makes writing both readable and clear.

 1 Varying length

In most contemporary writing, sentences vary from about ten to about forty words, with an average of fifteen to twenty-five words.

If your sentences are all at one extreme or the other, your readers may have difficulty focusing on main ideas and seeing the relations among them.

- If most of your sentences contain thirty-five words or more, you probably need to break some up into shorter, simpler sentences.
- If most of your sentences contain fewer than ten or fifteen words, you probably need to add details to them or combine them through coordination (p. 318) and subordination (p. 323). Examine your writing particularly for a common problem: strings of main clauses, subjects first, in either simple or compound sentences.

 Rewriting strings of brief and simple sentences

A series of brief and simple sentences is both monotonous and hard to understand because it forces the reader to sort out relations among ideas. If you find that you depend on brief, simple sentences, work to increase variety by combining some of them into longer units that emphasize and link new and important ideas while de-emphasizing old or incidental information. (See pp. 318–26 and 338–41.)

The following examples show how a string of simple sentences can be revised into an effective piece of writing.

Monotonous The moon is now drifting away from the earth. It moves away at the rate of about one inch a year. Our days on earth are getting longer. They grow a thousandth of a second longer every century. A month will someday be forty-seven of our present days long. We might eventually lose the moon altogether. Such great planetary movement rightly concerns astronomers. It need not worry us. The movement will take 50 million years.

Revised The moon is now drifting away from the earth *at the rate of about one inch a year. At the rate of a thousandth of a second every century,* our days on earth are getting longer. A month will someday be forty-seven of our present days long, *if we don't eventually lose the moon altogether.* Such great planetary movement rightly concerns astronomers, *but* it need not worry us. It will take 50 million years.

In the revision italics indicate subordinate structures that were simple sentences in the original. With five sentences instead of the original nine, the revision emphasizes the moon's movement, our lengthening days, and the enormous span of time involved.

ADDITIONAL ACTIVITIES

Many of the student activities described in the annotations to Chapter 18 can be easily adapted for this chapter.

RESOURCES AND IDEAS

Lanham, Richard. *Analyzing Prose.* New York: Scribner's, 1983. Lanham offers extensive advice on revising for stylistic effect.

Walpole, Jane R. "The Vigorous Pursuit of Grace and Style." *The Writing Instructor* 1 (1982): 163–69. Walpole offers a number of exercises for developing students' "ear" for style, with particular emphasis on simple sentences.

Williams, Joseph. *Style: Ten Lessons in Clarity and Grace.* 4th ed. New York: HarperCollins, 1994. Williams provides an excellent how-to manual for improving style at the sentence and word level.

Rewriting strings of compound sentences

Because compound sentences are usually just simple sentences linked with conjunctions, a series of them will be as weak as a series of brief simple sentences, especially if the clauses of the compound sentences are all about the same length.

Monotonous Physical illness may involve more than the body, for the mind may also be affected. Disorientation is common among sick people, but they are often unaware of it. They may reason abnormally, or they may behave immaturely.

Revised Physical illness may involve the mind *as well as the body. Though often unaware of it,* sick people are commonly disoriented. They may reason abnormally *or behave immaturely.*

The first passage creates a seesaw effect. The revision, with some main clauses shortened or changed into modifiers (italics), is both clearer and more emphatic. (See p. 320 for more on avoiding excessive coordination.)

COLLABORATIVE LEARNING

COMPUTER EXERCISE

Have students work in groups to create responses to Exercise 1. Encourage each group to discuss various possible revisions and ask them to present their responses to the class. This exercise works well in a networked classroom where each group's responses can be posted for comparison and general discussion.

Exercise 1
Revising: Varied sentence structures

Rewrite the following paragraphs to increase variety so that important ideas receive greater emphasis than supporting information does. You will have to change some main clauses into modifiers and then combine and reposition the modifiers and the remaining main clauses.

1. Charlotte Perkins Gilman was a leading intellectual in the women's movement during the first decades of this century. She wrote *Women and Economics.* This book challenged Victorian assumptions about differences between the sexes. It explored the economic roots of women's oppression. Gilman wrote little about gaining the vote for women. Many feminists were then preoccupied with this issue. Historians have since focused their analyses on this issue. As a result, Gilman's contribution to today's women's movement has often been overlooked.

2. Nathaniel Hawthorne was one of America's first great writers, and he was descended from a judge. The judge had presided at some of the Salem witch trials, and he had condemned some men and women to death. Hawthorne could never forget this piece of family history, and he always felt guilty about it. He never wrote about his ancestor directly, but he did write about the darkness of the human heart. He wrote *The Scarlet Letter* and *The House of the Seven Gables,* and in those books he demonstrated his favorite theme of a secret sin.

ANSWERS: EXERCISE 1

Possible revisions

1. Charlotte Perkins Gilman was a leading intellectual in the women's movement during the first decades of this century. Her book *Women and Economics* challenged Victorian assumptions about the differences between the sexes and explored the economic roots of women's oppression. Gilman wrote little about gaining the vote for women, the issue that then preoccupied feminists and that historians have since focused their analyses on. As a result, Gilman's contribution to today's women's movement has often been overlooked.
2. Nathaniel Hawthorne was one of America's first great writers. He was descended from a judge who had presided at some of the Salem witch trials and had condemned some men and women to death. Hawthorne could never forget about this piece of family history, and he always felt guilty about it. Though he never wrote about his ancestor directly, he did write about the darkness of the human heart. In *The Scarlet Letter* and *The House of the Seven Gables,* he demonstrated his favorite theme: a secret sin.

19b Varying sentence beginnings

Most English sentences begin with their subjects.

> The defendant's lawyer relentlessly cross-examined the stubborn witness for two successive weeks.

However, an unbroken sequence of sentences beginning with the subject quickly becomes monotonous, as shown by the unvaried passage on Grant and Lee that opened this chapter (pp. 347–48). Your final arrangement of sentence elements should always depend on two concerns: the relation of a sentence to those preceding and following it and the emphasis required by your meaning. When you do choose to vary the subject-first pattern, you have several options.

Adverb modifiers

Adverbs modify verbs, adjectives, other adverbs, and whole clauses. They can often fall in a variety of spots in a sentence. Consider these different emphases:

> *For two successive weeks,* the defendant's lawyer *relentlessly* cross-examined the stubborn witness.
>
> *Relentlessly,* the defendant's lawyer cross-examined the stubborn witness *for two successive weeks.*
>
> *Relentlessly, for two successive weeks,* the defendant's lawyer cross-examined the stubborn witness.

Notice that the last sentence, with both modifiers at the beginning, is periodic and thus highly emphatic (see p. 339).

ESL Placing certain adverb modifiers at the beginning of a sentence requires you to change the normal subject-verb order as well. The most common of these modifiers are negatives, including *seldom, rarely, in no case, not since,* and *not until.*

(adverb: Not since 1992; subject: witness; verb phrase: has held)
Faulty Not since 1992 a *witness has held* the stand so long.

(adverb: Not since 1992; helping verb: has; subject: witness; main verb: held)
Revised Not since 1992 *has a witness held* the stand so long.

Adjective modifiers

Adjectives, modifying nouns and pronouns, may include participles and participial phrases, as in <u>*flying*</u> *geese* or *money* <u>*well spent*</u> (see p. 177). These modifiers may sometimes fall at the beginning of a sentence to postpone the subject.

RESOURCES AND IDEAS

Vande Kopple, William J. *Clear and Coherent Prose: A Functional Approach.* New York: HarperCollins, 1989. Vande Kopple offers detailed advice about creating clear and emphatic sentences, including helpful suggestions for sentence beginnings.

The witness was exhausted from his testimony, and he did not cooperate.

Exhausted from his testimony, the witness did not cooperate.

Coordinating conjunctions and transitional expressions

When the relation between two successive sentences demands, you may begin the second with a connecting word or phrase: a coordinating conjunction such as *and* or *but* (p. 189) or a transitional expression such as *first, for instance, however,* or *therefore* (p. 100).

The witness had expected to be dismissed after his first long day of cross-examination. He was not.

The witness had expected to be dismissed after his first long day of cross-examination. *But* he was not.

The price of clothes has risen astronomically in recent years. A cheap cotton shirt that once cost $6.00 now costs $25.00.

The price of clothes has risen astronomically in recent years. *For example,* a cheap cotton shirt that once cost $6.00 now costs $25.00.

Occasional expletive constructions

An expletive construction—*it* or *there* plus a form of *be*—may occasionally be useful to delay and thus emphasize the subject of the sentence.

His judgment seems questionable, not his desire.
It is his judgment that seems questionable, not his desire.

However, expletive constructions are more likely to flatten writing by adding extra words. You should use them rarely, only when you can justify doing so. (See also p. 478.)

COLLABORATIVE LEARNING

Have students complete Exercise 2 in small groups and present one or two of their responses to the class. During the group presentations, encourage a general discussion of the relative effectiveness of various responses. This may help students to focus on the connection between stylistic changes and sentence content.

ANSWERS: EXERCISE 2

Possible answers

1. Some people are champion procrastinators. Consequently, they seldom complete their work on time.

Exercise 2
Revising: Varied sentence beginnings

Follow the instructions in parentheses to revise each group of sentences below: either create a single sentence that begins with an adverb or adjective modifier, or make one sentence begin with an appropriate connector.

Example:

The *Seabird* took first place. It moved quickly in the wind. (*One sentence with adjective modifier beginning* moving.)

Moving quickly in the wind, the *Seabird* took first place.

1. Some people are champion procrastinators. They seldom complete their work on time. (*Two sentences with transitional expression.*)
2. Procrastinators may fear criticism. They may fear rejection.

They will delay completing an assignment. (*One sentence with adverb modifier beginning if.*)
3. Procrastinators often desire to please a boss or a teacher. They fear failure so much that they cannot do the work. (*Two sentences with coordinating conjunction.*)
4. Procrastination seems a hopeless habit. It is conquerable. (*One sentence with adverb modifier beginning although.*)
5. Teachers or employers can be helpful. They can encourage procrastinators. They can give procrastinators the confidence to do good work on time. (*One sentence with adjective modifier beginning helpfully.*)

Exercise 3
Revising: Varied sentence beginnings

Revise the following paragraph to vary sentence beginnings by using each of the following at least once: an adverb modifier, an adjective modifier, a coordinating conjunction, and a transitional expression.

Scientists in Egypt dug up 40-million-year-old fossil bones. They had evidence of primitive whales. The whale ancestors are called mesonychids. They were small, furry land mammals with four legs. These limbs were complete with kneecaps, ankles, and little toes. Gigantic modern whales have tiny hind legs inside their bodies and flippers instead of front legs. Scientists are certain that these two very different creatures share the same family tree.

19c Inverting the normal word order

The word order of subject, verb, and object or complement is strongly fixed in English (see pp. 167–70). Thus an inverted sentence can be emphatic.

> Voters once had some faith in politicians, and they were fond of incumbents. But now *all politicians,* especially incumbents, *voters seem to detest.*

Inverting the normal order of subject, verb, and complement can be useful in two successive sentences when the second expands on the first.

> Critics have not been kind to Presidents who have tried to apply the ways of private business to public affairs. Particularly *explicit was the curt verdict* of one critic of President Hoover: Mr. Hoover was never President of the United States; he was four years chairman of the board.
> —Adapted from EMMET JOHN HUGHES, "The Presidency vs. Jimmy Carter"

Inverted sentences used without need are artificial. Avoid de-

2. If procrastinators fear criticism or rejection, they will delay completing an assignment.
3. Procrastinators often desire to please a boss or a teacher. Yet they fear failure so much that they cannot do the work.
4. Although procrastination seems a hopeless habit, it is conquerable.
5. Helpfully encouraging procrastinators, teachers or employers can give them the confidence to do good work on time.

COLLABORATIVE LEARNING
COMPUTER EXERCISE

Have students work in pairs or in small groups to create responses to Exercise 3. This exercise works well in a networked classroom where groups can post their responses for general discussion.

var
19c

ANSWERS: EXERCISE 3

Possible revision

When scientists in Egypt dug up 40-million-year-old fossil bones, they had evidence of primitive whales. Called mesonychids, the whale ancestors were small, furry land-dwelling mammals with four legs. These limbs were complete with kneecaps, ankles, and little toes. In contrast, some gigantic modern whales have tiny hind legs inside their bodies, and they all have flippers instead of front legs. But scientists are certain that these two very different creatures share the same family tree.

USING FORMS

Tell students to write a paragraph making use of the strategies suggested in this chapter. Leave the content of the paragraph up to them; they will discover how form can help suggest content. Then have them work in groups to compare paragraphs written with these strategies in mind to paragraphs taken from previous papers. This kind of comparison can encourage students to become more aware of their stylistic strengths and weaknesses.

scriptive sentences such as *Up came Larry and down went Cindy's spirits.*

19d Mixing types of sentences

Most written sentences make statements. Occasionally, however, questions, commands, or exclamations may enhance variety.

Questions may set the direction of a paragraph, as in *What does a detective do?* or *How is the percentage of unemployed workers calculated?* More often, though, the questions used in exposition or argument do not require answers but simply emphasize ideas that readers can be expected to agree with. Such **rhetorical questions** are illustrated in the following passage:

> Another word that has ceased to have meaning due to overuse is *attractive. Attractive* has become verbal chaff. Who, by some stretch of language and imagination, cannot be described as attractive? And just what is it that attractive individuals are attracting?
>
> —Diane White

Commands occur frequently in an explanation of a process, particularly in directions, as this passage on freewriting illustrates:

> The idea is simply to write for ten minutes (later on, perhaps fifteen or twenty). Don't stop for anything. Go quickly, without rushing. Never stop to look back, to cross something out, to wonder how to spell something, to wonder what word or thought to use, or to think about what you are doing. —Peter Elbow

Notice that the authors of these examples use questions and commands to achieve some special purpose. Variety occurs because a particular sentence type is effective for the context, not because the writer set out to achieve variety for its own sake.

Exercise 4
Writing varied sentences

Imagine that you are writing an essay on a transportation problem at your school. Practice varying sentences by composing a sentence or passage to serve each purpose listed below.

1. Write a question that could open the essay.
2. Write a command that could open the essay.
3. Write an exclamation that could open the essay.
4. For the body of the essay, write an appropriately varied paragraph of at least five sentences, including at least one short and one long sentence beginning with the subject; at least one sentence beginning with an adverb modifier; at least one sentence beginning with a coordinating conjunction or transitional expression; and one rhetorical question or command.

COLLABORATIVE LEARNING
COMPUTER EXERCISE

Have students create individual responses to Exercise 4, then ask them to discuss their responses in small groups and create revisions. In a computer classroom, students might trade seats in order to read and comment on each other's work (in each case the commentator can add revision suggestions using a different font). Students can print out and share responses, or post them—in a networked classroom.

ANSWERS: EXERCISE 4

Possible answers

1. How many cars are registered on this campus?
2. Try to find a parking space on this campus any weekday morning after nine o'clock.
3. What an unexpected pleasure to find a parking space within two blocks of the library!
4. Can the frustration caused by the parking problem be healthy for students? They drive round and round the campus, the minutes of lost study or class time ticking away. Tension builds. As they pass filled row upon filled row in one lot after another, drivers begin to tremble, sweat, and swear. And the anger and panic, instead of abating when finally the car is safely stowed, stays with the students throughout the day.

COLLABORATIVE LEARNING

Have students complete Exercise 5 individually and then discuss their responses in small groups. Encourage students to debate the effects of sentence variety in the passage and to use detailed evidence from the passage to support their claims. You might follow up this group activity by leading a general discussion in which you invite groups to report back on the debates they have generated.

ANSWERS: EXERCISE 5

Possible answers

The shortest sentence is one word: *No.* The longest is sentence 5, *I pictured the man as....* The opening periodic sentence sets the scene before coming to the point. The longest sentence

Exercise 5
Analyzing variety

Examine the following paragraph for sentence variety. By analyzing your own response to each sentence, try to explain why the author wrote each short or long sentence, each cumulative or periodic sentence, each sentence beginning with its subject or beginning some other way, and each question.

That night in my rented room, while letting the hot water run over my can of pork and beans in the sink, I opened [H. L. Mencken's] *A Book of Prefaces* and began to read. I was jarred and shocked by the style, the clear, clean, sweeping sentences. Why did he write like that? And how did one write like that? I pictured the man as a raging demon, slashing with his pen, consumed with hate, denouncing everything American, extolling everything European or German, laughing at the weaknesses of people, mocking God, authority. What was this? I stood up, trying to realize what reality lay behind the meaning of the words. Yes, this man was fighting, fighting with words. He was using words as a weapon, using them as one would use a club. Could words be weapons? Well, yes, for here they were. Then, maybe, perhaps, I could use them as a weapon? No. It frightened me. I read on and what amazed me was not what he said, but how on earth anybody had the courage to say it. —RICHARD WRIGHT, *Black Boy*

Exercise 6
Revising: Variety

The following paragraph consists entirely of simple sentences that begin with their subjects. As appropriate, use the techniques discussed in this chapter to vary sentences. Your goal is to make the paragraph more readable and make its important ideas stand out clearly. You will have to delete, add, change, and rearrange words.

The Italian volcano Vesuvius had been dormant for many years. It then exploded on August 24 in the year AD 79. The ash, pumice, and mud from the volcano buried two busy towns. Herculaneum is one. The more famous is Pompeii. The ruins of both towns lay undiscovered for many centuries. Herculaneum and Pompeii were discovered in 1709 and 1748, respectively. The excavation of Pompeii was the more systematic. It was the occasion for initiating modern methods of conservation and restoration. Herculaneum was simply looted of its most valuable finds. It was then left to disintegrate. Pompeii appears much as it did before the eruption. A luxurious house opens onto a lush central garden. An election poster decorates a wall. A dining table is set for breakfast.

NOTE See the next page for an exercise involving variety along with parallelism and other techniques for effective sentences.

gains its length and power from the six modifying verbal phrases that convey Wright's first impression of Mencken. Wright relies on questions interspersed with tentative answers to show his own incremental awakening on discovering Mencken. Repetition—*fighting, fighting; using . . . using; maybe, perhaps*—also shows Wright wrestling with what he has found. The last question leads to the conclusion of the final three sentences, which gradually increase in length and complexity.

COLLABORATIVE LEARNING
COMPUTER EXERCISE

Ask students to complete Exercise 6 individually and then discuss their responses in groups in preparation for revising them. You might choose several of the revised responses to photocopy and hand out in order to generate discussion of the effects of variety. In a networked classroom, you might ask several student volunteers to post their revised responses in order to provide the basis for discussion.

ANSWERS: EXERCISE 6

Possible revision

After being dormant for many years, the Italian volcano Vesuvius exploded on August 24 in the year AD 79. The ash, pumice, and mud from the volcano buried two towns—Herculaneum and the more famous Pompeii—which lay undiscovered until 1709 and 1748, respectively. The excavation of Pompeii was the more systematic, the occasion for initiating modern methods of conservation and restoration. Whereas Herculaneum was simply looted of its most valuable finds and then left to disintegrate, Pompeii appears much as it did during the eruption. A luxurious house opens onto a lush central garden. An election poster decorates a wall. And a dining table is set for breakfast.

ANSWERS: EXERCISE ON CHAPTERS 16–19

Possible revision

Modern Americans owe many debts to Native Americans, including several pleasures. Native Americans originated two fine junk foods: popcorn and potato chips.

Native Americans introduced popcorn to the European settlers, Massasoit providing popcorn at the first Thanksgiving feast and the Aztecs offering popcorn to the Spanish explorer Hernando Cortés. The Aztecs and natives of the West Indies wore popcorn necklaces. Native Americans popped the corn in three ways. First, they roasted an ear skewered on a stick over the fire and ate the corn that fell outside the flames. Second, they scraped the corn off the cob, threw the kernels into a low fire, and ate the popped kernels that did not fall into the fire. Third and most sophisticated, they heated a shallow pottery vessel containing sand, stirred corn kernels into the hot sand, and ate what popped up to the surface.

A Native American chef named George Crum devised the crunchy potato chip. In 1853 Crum was cooking at Moon Lake Lodge in Saratoga Springs, New York. A customer complained that Crum's French-fried potatoes were too thick. Crum tried a thinner batch, but these were also unsuitable. Frustrated, Crum deliberately made the potatoes so thin and crisp that they could not be cut with a knife and fork. Crum's joke backfired, for the customer raved about the potato chips. Soon these Saratoga Chips appeared on the lodge's menu and throughout New England. Crum later opened his own restaurant, of course offering potato chips.

Now all Americans munch popcorn in movies, crunch potato chips at parties, and gorge on both when alone and bored. They can be grateful to Native Americans for these guilty pleasures.

eff

Exercise on Chapters 16–19
Revising: Effective sentences

Revise the paragraphs below to emphasize main ideas, de-emphasize supporting information, and achieve a pleasing, clear variety in sentences. As appropriate, use subordination, coordination, parallelism, and cumulative, periodic, and balanced sentences. Cut wordiness. Use the active voice. Edit the finished product for punctuation.

Modern Americans owe many debts to Native Americans. Several pleasures are among the debts. Native Americans originated two fine junk foods. They discovered popcorn. Potato chips were also one of their contributions.

Native Americans introduced popcorn to the European settlers. Massasoit provided popcorn at the first Thanksgiving feast. The Aztecs offered popcorn to the Spanish explorer Hernando Cortés. The Aztecs wore popcorn necklaces. So did the natives of the West Indies. There were three ways that the Native Americans popped the corn. First, they roasted an ear over the fire. The ear was skewered on a stick. They ate only some of the popcorn. They ate the corn that fell outside the flames. Second, they scraped the corn off the cob. The kernels would be thrown into the fire. Of course, the fire had to be low. Then the popped kernels that did not fall into the fire were eaten. The third method was the most sophisticated. It involved a shallow pottery vessel. It contained sand. The vessel was heated. The sand soon got hot. Corn kernels were stirred in. They popped to the surface of the sand and were eaten.

A Native American chef devised the crunchy potato chip. His name was George Crum. In 1853 Crum was cooking at Moon Lake Lodge. The lodge was in Saratoga Springs, New York. Complaints were sent in by a customer. The man thought Crum's French-fried potatoes were too thick. Crum tried a thinner batch. These were also unsuitable. Crum became frustrated. He deliberately made the potatoes thin and crisp. They could not be cut with a knife and fork. Crum's joke backfired. The customer raved about the potato chips. The chips were named Saratoga Chips. Soon they appeared on the lodge's menu. They also appeared throughout New England. Crum later opened his own restaurant. Of course, he offered potato chips.

Now all Americans munch popcorn in movies. They crunch potato chips at parties. They gorge on both when alone and bored. They can be grateful to Native Americans for these guilty pleasures.

Part V Punctuation

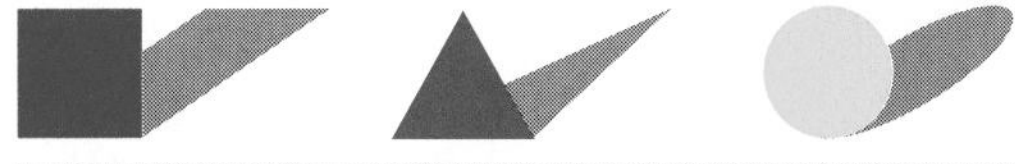

Commas, semicolons, colons, dashes, parentheses

(For explanations, consult the pages in parentheses.)

Sentences with two main clauses

The bus stopped, but no one got off. (p. 365)
The bus stopped; no one got off. (p. 388)
The bus stopped; *however,* no one got off. (p. 390)
The mechanic replaced the battery, the distributor cap, and the starter; *but* still the car would not start. (p. 392)
Her duty was clear: she had to locate the problem. (p. 416)

Introductory elements

MODIFIERS (p. 368)

After the argument was over, we laughed at ourselves.
Racing over the plain, the gazelle escaped the lion.
To dance in the contest, he had to tape his knee.
Suddenly, the door flew open.
With 125 passengers aboard, the plane was half full.
In 1983 he won the Nobel Prize.

ABSOLUTE PHRASES (p. 375)

Its wing broken, the bird hopped around on the ground.

p

Interrupting and concluding elements

NONRESTRICTIVE MODIFIERS (p. 370)

Jim's car, *which barely runs*, has been impounded.
We consulted the dean, *who had promised to help us.*
The boy, *like his sister*, wants to be a pilot.
They moved across the desert, *shielding their eyes from the sun.*
The men do not speak to each other, *although they share a car.*

NONRESTRICTIVE APPOSITIVES

Bergen's daughter, *Candice*, became an actress. (p. 372)
The residents of three counties—*Suffolk, Springfield, and Morrison*—were urged to evacuate. (p. 419)
Father demanded one promise: *that we not lie to him.* (p. 417)

RESTRICTIVE MODIFIERS (p. 384)

The car *that hit mine* was uninsured.
We consulted a teacher *who had promised to help us.*
The boy *in the black hat* is my cousin.
They were surprised to find the desert *teeming with life.*
The men do not speak to each other *because they are feuding.*

Restrictive appositives (p. 384)

Shaw's play *Saint Joan* was performed last year.
Their sons *Tony, William, and Steve* all chose military careers, leaving only Joe to run the family business.

Transitional or parenthetical expressions

We suspect**,** *however*, that he will not come. (p. 373)
Jan is respected by many people**—***including me.* (p. 420)
George Balanchine **(**1904–83**)** was a brilliant choreographer. (p. 421)

Absolute phrases (p. 375)

The bird**,** *its wing broken***,** hopped about on the ground.
The bird hopped about on the ground**,** *its wing broken.*

Phrases expressing contrast (p. 376)

The humidity**,** *not just the heat***,** gives me headaches.
My headaches are caused by the humidity**,** *not just the heat.*

Concluding summaries and explanations

The movie opened to bad notices**:** *the characters were judged shallow and unrealistic.* (p. 416)
We dined on gumbo and jambalaya**—***a Cajun feast.* (p. 420).

Items in a series

Three or more items

*Chimpanzees***,** *gorillas***,** *orangutans***,** *and gibbons* are all apes. (p. 376)
The cities singled out for praise were *Birmingham, Alabama***;** *Lincoln, Nebraska***;** *Austin, Texas***;** *and Troy, New York.* (p. 393)

Two or more adjectives before a noun (p. 377)

*Dingy***,** *smelly* clothes decorated their room.
The luncheon consisted of *one tiny watercress* sandwich.

Introductory series (p. 420)

*Appropriateness, accuracy, and necessity***—**these criteria should govern your selection of words.

Concluding series

Every word should be *appropriate, accurate, and necessary.* (p. 385)
Every word should meet three criteria**:** *appropriateness, accuracy, and necessity.* (p. 417)
Pay attention to your words**—***to their appropriateness, their accuracy, and their necessity.* (p. 420)

HIGHLIGHTS

This chapter discusses the three marks of punctuation used to end lines: periods, question marks, and exclamation points. Encourage students to see that these are not just physical boundaries but important parts of the meaning of sentences—and that they therefore deserve careful consideration.

RESOURCES AND IDEAS

Dawkins, John. "Teaching Punctuation as a Rhetorical Tool." *College Composition and Communication* 46 (1995): 533–48. Dawkins makes a case for teaching the rhetorical thinking processes that accompany decisions about punctuation marks.

POLITE DEMANDS

Students often question the punctuation of polite demands, such as "Would you please send me your catalog." These sentences are used frequently for requests that the writer expects to be granted. In business use they are punctuated with periods; however, it's never wrong to use a question mark if the writer is in doubt.

Chapter 20 End Punctuation

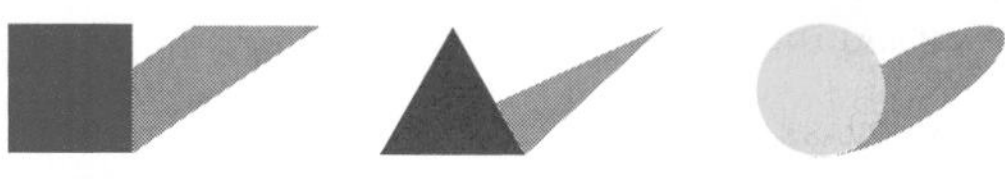

THE PERIOD

20a Use a period to end a statement, mild command, or indirect question.

STATEMENTS

These are exciting and trying times.
The airline went bankrupt.

MILD COMMANDS

Please do not smoke.
Think of the possibilities.

If you are unsure whether to use an exclamation point or a period after a command, use a period. The exclamation point should be used only rarely (see p. 363).

An **indirect question** reports what someone has asked but not in the form or exact words of the original.

INDIRECT QUESTIONS

Students sometimes wonder whether their teachers read the papers they write.

Abused children eventually stop asking why they are being punished.

ESL Unlike a direct question, an indirect question uses the wording and subject-verb order of a statement: *The reporter asked why the negotiations failed,* not *why did the negotiations fail.*

20b Use periods with many abbreviations.

Use periods with most abbreviations involving small letters.

p.	Mrs., Mr.	e.g.	Feb.
Ph.D.	Ms.	a.m., p.m.	ft.

Note that a period follows *Ms.,* even though it is not actually an abbreviation.

Many abbreviations of two or more words using all capital letters may be written with or without periods. Just be consistent.

BA or B.A.	US or U.S.	BC or B.C.	AM or A.M.

Omit periods from these abbreviations:

- The initials of a well-known person: *FDR, JFK.*
- The initials of an organization: *IBM, USMC.*
- A postal abbreviation: *NY, AVE.* (See also p. 750.)
- An **acronym,** a pronounceable word formed from initials: *UNESCO, VISTA.*

Note When an abbreviation falls at the end of a sentence, use only one period: *The school offers a Ph.D.*

See also pages 441–44 on uses of abbreviations in writing.

Exercise 1
Revising: Periods

Revise the following sentences so that periods are used correctly.

Example:
Several times I wrote to ask when my subscription ended?
Several times I wrote to ask when my subscription ended.

1. The instructor asked when Plato wrote *The Republic?*
2. Give the date within one century
3. The exact date is not known, but it is estimated at 370 B.C..
4. Dr Arn will lecture on Plato at 7:30 p.m..
5. The area of the lecture hall is only 1600 sq ft

ANSWERS: EXERCISE 1

1. The instructor asked when Plato wrote *The Republic*.
2. Give the date within one century.
3. The exact date is not known, but it is estimated at 370 BC.
4. Dr. Arn will lecture on Plato at 7:30 p.m.
5. The lecture hall is only 1600 sq. ft.

THE QUESTION MARK

20c Use a question mark after a direct question.

Direct questions

What is the difference between these two people?
Will economists ever really understand the economy?

After indirect questions, use a period: *The senator asked why the bill had passed*. (See p. 360.)

Questions in a series are each followed by a question mark.

> The officer asked how many times the suspect had been arrested. Three times**?** Four times**?** More than that**?**

The use of capital letters for questions in a series is optional (see p. 431).

Note Question marks are never combined with other question marks, exclamation points, periods, or commas.

> **Faulty** Readers ask, "What is the point?."
>
> **Revised** Readers ask, "What is the point**?**"

20d Use a question mark within parentheses to indicate doubt about the correctness of a number or date.

> The Greek philosopher Socrates was born in 470 (**?**) BC and died in 399 BC from drinking poison after having been condemned to death.

Note Don't use a question mark within parentheses to express sarcasm or irony. Express these attitudes through sentence structure and diction. (See Chapters 18 and 31.)

> **Faulty** Stern's friendliness (?) bothered Crane.
>
> **Revised** Stern's *insincerity* bothered Crane.

? 20d

Exercise 2
Revising: Question marks

Revise the following sentences so that question marks (along with other punctuation marks) are used correctly.

> *Example:*
> "When will it end?," cried the man dressed in rags.
> "When will it end**?**" cried the man dressed in rags.

1. In Homer's *Odyssey,* Odysseus took seven years to travel from Troy to Ithaca. Or was it eight years. Or more?
2. Odysseus must have wondered whether he would ever make it home?
3. "What man are you and whence?," asks Odysseus's wife, Penelope.
4. Why does Penelope ask, "Where is your city? Your family?"?
5. Penelope does not recognize Odysseus and asks who this stranger is?

ANSWERS: EXERCISE 2

1. In Homer's *Odyssey,* Odysseus took seven years to travel from Troy to Ithaca. Or was it eight years? Or more?
2. Odysseus must have wondered whether he would ever make it home.
3. "What man are you and whence?" asks Odysseus's wife, Penelope.
4. Why does Penelope ask, "Where is your city? Your family?"
5. Penelope does not recognize Odysseus and asks who this stranger is.

EXTRA HELP

The Little, Brown Workbook provides additional exercises for students who need more practice with the end marks of punctuation.

THE EXCLAMATION POINT

20e Use an exclamation point after an emphatic statement, interjection, or command.

No! We must not lose this election!
Come here immediately!

Follow mild interjections and commands with commas or periods, as appropriate.

No, the response was not terrific.
To prolong your car's life, change its oil regularly.

Note Exclamation points are never combined with other exclamation points, question marks, periods, or commas.

Faulty "This will not be endured!," he roared.
Revised "This will not be endured!" he roared.

COLLABORATIVE LEARNING

EXCLAMATION POINTS AND ADVERTISING

Have students scan advertisements in newspapers, magazines, and junk mail for exclamation points. Individually or in groups, ask them to decide whether the exclamation points are used effectively or overused. Encourage them to rewrite these advertising sentences to convey the emphasis without using exclamation points for spice.

20f Use exclamation points sparingly.

Don't express sarcasm, irony, or amazement with the exclamation point. Rely on sentence structure and diction to express these attitudes. (See Chapters 18 and 31.)

Faulty After traveling 4.4 billion miles through space, *Voyager 2* was off-target by 21 miles (!).

Revised After traveling 4.4 billion miles through space, *Voyager 2* was off-target by *a mere* 21 miles.

Relying on the exclamation point for emphasis is like crying wolf: the mark loses its power to impress the reader. Frequent exclamation points can also make writing sound overemotional. In the following passage, the writer could have conveyed ideas more effectively by punctuating sentences with periods.

> Our city government is a mess! After just six months in office, the mayor has had to fire four city officials! In the same period the city councilors have done nothing but argue! And city services decline with each passing day!

Exercise 3
Revising: Exclamation points

Revise the following sentences so that exclamation points (along with other punctuation marks) are used correctly. If a sentence is punctuated correctly as given, circle the number preceding it.

ANSWERS: EXERCISE 3

1. As the firefighters moved their equipment into place, the police shouted, "Move back!"
2. A child's cries could be heard from above: "Help me! Help!"
3. When the child was rescued, the crowd called, "Hooray!"
4. The rescue was the most exciting event of the day.
5. Sentence correct.

COLLABORATIVE LEARNING

Have students complete Exercise 4 individually and compare their responses in small groups. Then ask each group to review the punctuation of paragraphs from their own work and help each other to locate and revise punctuation errors. Ask each student to keep a list of the errors that commonly recur in his or her work (along with revised examples) and to use that list in future proofreading tasks.

ANSWERS: EXERCISE 4

When visitors first arrive in Hawaii, they often encounter an unexpected language barrier. Standard English is the language of business and government, but many of the people speak Pidgin English. Instead of an excited "Aloha!" the visitors may be greeted with an excited Pidgin "Howzit!" or asked if they know "how fo' find one good hotel." Many Hawaiians question whether Pidgin will hold children back because it prevents communication with the *haoles,* or Caucasians, who run businesses. Yet many others feel that Pidgin is a last defense of ethnic diversity on the islands. To those who want to make standard English the official language of the state, these Hawaiians may respond, "Just 'cause I speak Pidgin no mean I dumb." They may ask, "Why you no listen?" or, in standard English, "Why don't you listen?"

! 20f

Example:

"Well, now!," he said loudly.
"Well, now!" he said loudly.

1. As the firefighters moved their equipment into place, the police shouted, "Move back!".
2. A child's cries could be heard from above: "Help me. Help."
3. When the child was rescued, the crowd called "Hooray."
4. The rescue was the most exciting event of the day!
5. Let me tell you about it.

Exercise 4
Revising: End punctuation

Insert appropriate punctuation (periods, question marks, or exclamation points) where needed in the following paragraph.

When visitors first arrive in Hawaii, they often encounter an unexpected language barrier Standard English is the language of business and government, but many of the people speak Pidgin English Instead of an excited "Aloha" the visitors may be greeted with an excited Pidgin "Howzit" or asked if they know "how fo' find one good hotel" Many Hawaiians question whether Pidgin will hold children back because it prevents communication with the *haoles,* or Caucasians, who run businesses Yet many others feel that Pidgin is a last defense of ethnic diversity on the islands To those who want to make standard English the official language of the state, these Hawaiians may respond, "Just 'cause I speak Pidgin no mean I dumb" They may ask, "Why you no listen" or, in standard English, "Why don't you listen"

NOTE See page 428 for a punctuation exercise combining periods with other marks of punctuation.

Chapter 21 The Comma

Commas usually function within sentences to separate elements (see the box on the next page). Omitting needed commas or inserting needless ones can confuse the reader.

Comma needed	Though very tall Abraham Lincoln was not an overbearing man.
Revised	Though very tall**,** Abraham Lincoln was not an overbearing man.
Unneeded commas	The hectic pace of Beirut, broke suddenly into frightening chaos when the city became, the focus of civil war.
Revised	The hectic pace of Beirut broke suddenly into frightening chaos when the city became the focus of civil war.

21a Use a comma before *and, but,* or another coordinating conjunction linking main clauses.

The coordinating conjunctions are *and, but, or, nor, for, so,* and *yet.* When these link words or phrases, do not use a comma: *Dugain plays and sings Irish and English folk songs.* However, *do* use a comma when a coordinating conjunction joins main clauses. A **main clause** has a subject and a predicate (but no subordinating word at the beginning) and makes a complete statement (see p. 182).

Caffeine can keep coffee drinkers alert**,** *and* it may elevate their mood.

HIGHLIGHTS

The comma probably causes more anguish for apprentice writers than any other punctuation mark. There's no magic formula for accurate comma use. Most uses are conventional, but a few require judgment calls—and writers can develop the necessary judgment only through lots of reading and writing. For example, the problem of whether to use commas with restrictive and nonrestrictive modifiers is probably not a punctuation problem but a matter of understanding what these modifiers do. Commas, or their absence, are just a graphic way of reinforcing the meaning of the modifier. The text's discussion of how context determines a modifier's role in a sentence can help students see this point.

Forcing students to memorize these rules may not make them more accurate writers. Students need to learn how to take the generalizations conveyed by these rules and apply them to specific situations; that means helping them understand the rules, not just getting them to memorize.

RESOURCES AND IDEAS: COMMAS

The following are some good references for teaching about commas.

Meyer, Charles F. "Teaching Punctuation to Advanced Writers." *Journal of Advanced Composition* 6 (1985–86): 117–29. Meyer offers a number of strategies that can be used in any classroom.

Meyer, Emily, and Louise Z. Smith. *The Practical Tutor.* New York: Oxford UP, 1989. Chapter 9 offers a number of strategies for teaching punctuation.

Shaughnessy, Mina P. *Errors and Expectations: A Guide for the Teacher of Basic Writing.* New York: Oxford UP, 1977. 14–43. Shaughnessy explains teaching punctuation in the context of understanding students' hypotheses about their texts.

Thomas, Lewis. "Notes on Punctuation." *New England Journal of Medicine* 296 (1977): 1103–05. Reprinted in *The Medusa and the Snail: More Notes of a Biology Watcher.* New York: Viking, 1979. An experienced scientist and writer explores how punctuation use can affect the meaning of texts.

TRANSPARENCY MASTER 21.1

RESOURCES AND IDEAS

Though writing instructors often treat commas and other marks of punctuation as if they were primarily cues to grammatical structures, these marks also function legitimately as stylistic cues, as indicators of the writer's voice—or so argues Wallace Chafe in "What Good Is Punctuation?" (*The Quarterly of the National Writing Project and the Center for the Study of Writing* 10 [1988]: 8–11). Chafe supports his argument with examples from the work of Herman Melville and James Agee and concludes with some useful advice for teaching:

> Students, in addition to being sensitized to their inner voices, will benefit from knowing the range of punctuating options that are available, and from being shown, through examples, what is most appropriate to one style and another. They can learn from practice in writing advertising copy as well as the more academic kinds of exposition, and from experimenting with fiction that mimics the very different punctuation styles of, say, Melville and Agee. At the same time, developing writers need to know that there are certain specific rules for punctuating that violate the prosody of their inner voices and that simply have to be learned. These arbitrary rules are few in number and well defined, and to learn them need be no burden. . . . The bottom line is that punctuation contributes substantially to the effectiveness of a piece of writing, and that its successful use calls for an awareness of something that is, for this and other reasons, essential to good writing; a sensitivity to the sound of written language. (11)

"In Praise of the Humble Comma," a short amusing paean to the power of punctuation to affect meaning, might also be handed out to students as a useful reminder of the connections between grammar and content. (Pico Iyer, *Time*, June 13, 1988: 348).

RESOURCES AND IDEAS

Dawkins, John. "Teaching Punctuation as a Rhetorical Tool." *College Composition and Communication* 46 (1995): 533–48. Dawkins makes a case for teaching the rhetorical thinking processes that accompany decisions about punctuation marks.

Principal uses of the comma

- To separate main clauses linked by a coordinating conjunction (p. 365).

Main clause , { for and or / so but nor / yet } main clause .

The building is finished**,** *but* it has no tenants.

- To set off most introductory elements (p. 368).

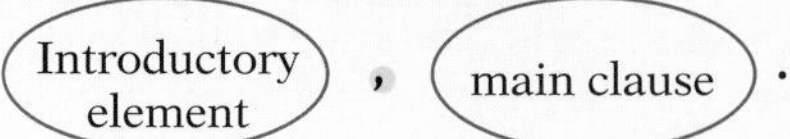

*Unfortunately***,** the only tenant pulled out.

- To set off nonrestrictive elements (p. 370).

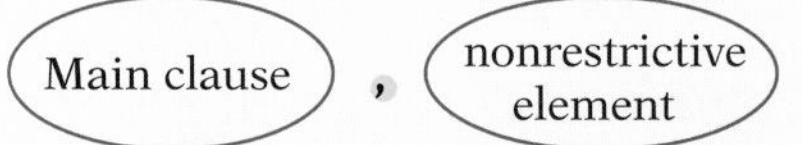

The empty building symbolizes a weak local economy**,** *which affects everyone.*

Beginning of main clause , nonrestrictive element , end of main clause .

The primary cause**,** *the decline of local industry***,** is not news.

- To separate items in a series (p. 376).

. . . item 1 , item 2 , { and / or } item 3 . . .

The city needs *healthier businesses***,** *new schools***,** *and improved housing.*

- To separate coordinate adjectives (p. 377).

. . . first adjective , second adjective word modified . . .

A *tall***,** *sleek* skyscraper is not needed.

Other uses of the comma:

To set off absolute phrases (p. 375).
To set off phrases expressing contrast (p. 376).
To separate parts of dates, addresses, long numbers (p. 378).
To separate quotations and identifying words (p. 380).
To prevent misreading (p. 382).

See also page 383 for when *not* to use the comma.

Caffeine was once thought to be safe, *but* now researchers warn of harmful effects.

Coffee drinkers may suffer sleeplessness, *for* the drug acts as a stimulant to the nervous system.

Note Do not add a comma *after* a coordinating conjunction between main clauses (see also p. 384).

Not Caffeine increases the heart rate, *and,* it constricts blood vessels.

But Caffeine increases the heart rate, *and* it constricts blood vessels.

Exceptions When the main clauses in a sentence are very long or grammatically complicated, or when they contain internal punctuation, a semicolon before the coordinating conjunction will clarify the division between clauses (see p. 392).

Caffeine may increase alertness, elevate mood, and provide energy; *but* it may also cause irritability, anxiety, stomach pains, and other ills.

When main clauses are very short and closely related in meaning, you may omit the comma between them as long as the resulting sentence is clear.

Caffeine helps but it also hurts.

If you are in doubt about whether to use a comma in such a sentence, use it. It will always be correct.

Exercise 1
Punctuating linked main clauses

Insert a comma before each coordinating conjunction that links main clauses in the following sentences.

Example:

I would have attended the concert and the reception but I had to baby-sit for my niece.

I would have attended the concert and the reception, but I had to baby-sit for my niece.

1. Parents once automatically gave their children the father's surname but some no longer do.
2. Instead, they bestow the mother's name for they believe that the mother's importance should be recognized.
3. The child's surname may be just the mother's or it may link the mother's and the father's with a hyphen.
4. Sometimes the first and third children will have the mother's surname and the second child will have the father's.
5. Occasionally the mother and father combine parts of their names and a new hybrid surname is born.

Meyer, Emily, and Louise Z. Smith, "Punctuation." In *The Practical Tutor.* New York: Oxford UP, 1987. The authors offer detailed advice for the often frustrating task of helping students develop effective punctuation skills.

^ 21a

ANSWERS: EXERCISE 1

1. Parents once automatically gave their children the father's surname, but some no longer do.
2. Instead, they bestow the mother's name, for they believe that the mother's importance should be recognized.
3. The child's surname may be just the mother's, or it may link the mother's and the father's with a hyphen.
4. Sometimes the first and third children will have the mother's surname, and the second child will have the father's.
5. Occasionally the mother and father combine parts of their names, and a new hybrid surname is born.

COLLABORATIVE LEARNING

Ask students to complete Exercise 2 individually and then discuss their responses in small groups. Have each group discuss the effect of alternative answers and then present one or two of the most successful responses.

ANSWERS: EXERCISE 2

Possible answers

1. Parents were once legally required to bestow the father's surname on their children, but these laws have been contested in court and found invalid.
2. Parents may now give their children any surname they choose, and the arguments for bestowing the mother's surname are often strong and convincing.
3. Critics sometimes question the effects of unusual surnames on children, or they wonder how confusing or fleeting the new surnames will be.
4. Children with surnames different from their parents' may suffer embarrassment or identity problems, for giving children their father's surname is still very much the norm.
5. Hyphenated names are awkward and difficult to pass on, so some observers think they will die out in the next generation or before.

^ , 21b

RESOURCES AND IDEAS

Collignon, Joseph. "Why Leroy Can't Write." *College English* 39 (1978): 852–59. Collignon suggests using oral reading to help students punctuate correctly and to provide them with models for writing.

COLLABORATIVE LEARNING

COURT REPORTER

To help students understand how commas affect understanding, have them play "court reporter." Ask one or two students to read a passage from their papers or some reading for the class while the other students try to write what they say. Then have the reporters prepare a transcript of what they heard, inserting punctuation where they think it is needed. Each group

Exercise 2
Sentence combining: Linked main clauses

Combine each group of sentences below into one sentence that contains only two main clauses connected by the coordinating conjunction in parentheses. Separate the main clauses with a comma. You will have to add, delete, and rearrange words.

Example:

The circus had come to town. The children wanted to see it. Their parents wanted to see it. (*and*)

The circus had come to town, *and* the children and their parents wanted to see it.

1. Parents were once legally required to bestow the father's surname on their children. These laws have been contested in court. They have been found invalid. (*but*)
2. Parents may now give their children any surname they choose. The arguments for bestowing the mother's surname are often strong. They are often convincing. (*and*)
3. Critics sometimes question the effects of unusual surnames on children. They wonder how confusing the new surnames will be. They wonder how fleeting the surnames will be. (*or*)
4. Children with surnames different from their parents' may suffer embarrassment. They may suffer identity problems. Giving children their father's surname is still very much the norm. (*for*)
5. Hyphenated names are awkward. They are also difficult to pass on. Some observers think they will die out in the next generation. Or they may die out before. (*so*)

21b Use a comma to set off most introductory elements.

An introductory element modifies a word or words in the main clause that follows. These elements are usually set off from the rest of the sentence with a comma.

Subordinate clause (p. 182)

Even when identical twins are raised apart, they grow up very like each other.

Because they are similar, such twins interest scientists.

Verbal or verbal phrase (p. 177)

Explaining the similarity, some researchers claim that one's genes are one's destiny.

Concerned, other researchers deny the claim.

Prepositional phrase (p. 174)

In a debate that has lasted centuries, scientists use identical twins to argue for or against genetic destiny.

Transitional or parenthetical expression (p. 373)
Of course, scientists can now look directly at the genes themselves.

The comma may be omitted after short introductory elements if its omission does not create confusion. (If you are in doubt, however, the comma is always correct.)

Clear *In a hundred years* genetics may no longer be a mystery.

Confusing Despite intensive research scientists still have more questions than answers.

Clear Despite intensive research, scientists still have more questions than answers.

Note Take care to distinguish *-ing* words used as modifiers from *-ing* words used as subjects. The former almost always take a comma; the latter never do.

modifier — subject — verb
Studying identical twins, geneticists learn about inheritance.

subject — verb
Studying identical twins helps geneticists learn about inheritance.

Exercise 3
Punctuating introductory elements

Insert commas where needed after introductory elements in the following sentences. If a sentence is punctuated correctly as given, circle the number preceding it.

Example:

After the new library opened the old one became a student union.

After the new library opened, the old one became a student union.

1. Moving in a fluid mass is typical of flocks of birds and schools of fish.
2. Because it is sudden and apparently well coordinated the movement of flocks and schools has seemed to be directed by a leader.
3. However new studies have discovered that flocks and schools are leaderless.
4. When each bird or fish senses a predator it follows individual rules for fleeing.
5. Multiplied over hundreds of individuals these responses look as if they have been choreographed.

Exercise 4
Sentence combining: Introductory elements

Combine each pair of sentences below into one sentence that begins with an introductory phrase or clause as specified in paren-

should compare the reporters' versions with the originals and solve any disputes over comma use by referring to the appropriate sections of this chapter.

COLLABORATIVE LEARNING

Have students complete Exercise 3 individually and then compare their responses in small groups. This allows students to debate different kinds of comma usage in a nonintimidating setting.

ANSWERS: EXERCISE 3

1. Sentence correct.
2. Because it is sudden and apparently well coordinated, the movement of flocks and schools has seemed to be directed by a leader.
3. However, new studies have discovered that flocks and schools are leaderless.
4. When each bird or fish senses a predator, it follows individual rules for fleeing.
5. Multiplied over hundreds of individuals, these responses look as if they have been choreographed.

COLLABORATIVE LEARNING

Ask students to complete Exercise 4 individually and then compare responses in small groups. You might then have each group create one or two sentences of their own involving introductory clauses set off by commas.

ANSWERS: EXERCISE 4

Possible answers

1. In an effort to explain the mysteries of flocks and schools, scientists have proposed bizarre magnetic fields and telepathy.
2. Since scientists developed computer models, they have abandoned earlier explanations.
3. Starting with each individual, the movement of a flock or school is rapidly and perhaps automatically coordinated among individuals.
4. Observing that human beings seek coherent patterns, one zoologist suggests that investigators saw purpose in the movement of flocks and schools where none existed.
5. To study the movement of flocks or schools, one must abandon a search for purpose or design.

theses. Follow the introductory element with a comma. You will have to add, delete, change, and rearrange words.

Example:

The girl was humming to herself. She walked upstairs. (*Phrase beginning Humming.*)

Humming to herself, the girl walked upstairs.

1. Scientists have made an effort to explain the mysteries of flocks and schools. They have proposed bizarre magnetic fields and telepathy. (*Phrase beginning In.*)
2. Scientists developed computer models. They have abandoned earlier explanations. (*Clause beginning Since.*)
3. The movement of a flock or school starts with each individual. It is rapidly and perhaps automatically coordinated among individuals. (*Phrase beginning Starting.*)
4. One zoologist observes that human beings seek coherent patterns. He suggests that investigators saw purpose in the movement of flocks and schools where none existed. (*Phrase beginning Observing.*)
5. One may want to study the movement of flocks or schools. Then one must abandon a search for purpose or design. (*Phrase beginning To.*)

UNDERSTANDING RESTRICTIVE AND NONRESTRICTIVE MODIFIERS

The difference between restrictive and nonrestrictive elements is one of the most difficult concepts for students to grasp. Try using these two examples as a way of illustrating the difference:

Bring me the books that are on the desk.
Bring me the books, which are on the desk.

In the first example, the restrictive modifier *that are on the desk* selects a specific group of books: only those that are on the desk, as opposed to others in the room. In the second sentence, the nonrestrictive modifier tells us that the location of the books is nonessential; the requester wants *all* the books, and they just happen to be on the desk. Ask students to make up other pairs of examples to show the difference between restrictive and nonrestrictive modifiers, and stress that only the nonrestrictive (nonselecting) modifier is set off by a comma.

^ 21c

21c Use a comma or commas to set off nonrestrictive elements.

Commas around part of a sentence often signal that the element is not essential to the meaning of the sentence. This **nonrestrictive element** may modify or rename the word it refers to, but it does not limit the word to a particular individual or group.

NONRESTRICTIVE ELEMENT

The company, *which is located in Oklahoma*, has a good reputation.

In contrast, a **restrictive element** *does* limit the word it refers to: the element cannot be omitted without leaving the meaning too general. Because it is essential, a restrictive element is *not* set off with commas.

RESTRICTIVE ELEMENT

The company rewards employees *who work hard.*

Nonrestrictive elements are *not* essential, but punctuation *is*. Restrictive elements *are* essential, but punctuation is *not*.

NOTE When a nonrestrictive element falls in the middle of a sentence, be sure to set if off with a pair of commas, one *before* and one *after* the element. Dashes or parentheses may also be used to set off nonrestrictive elements (see pp. 419 and 421).

A test for restrictive and nonrestrictive elements

1. Identify the element.

   Hai Nguyen *who emigrated from Vietnam* lives in Denver.
   Those *who emigrated with him* live elsewhere.

2. Remove the element. Does the fundamental meaning of the sentence change?

   Hai Nguyen lives in Denver. **No.**
   Those live elsewhere. **Yes.** [Who are *Those?*]

3. If **no**, the element is nonrestrictive and should be set off with punctuation.

   Hai Nguyen**,** who emigrated from Vietnam**,** lives in Denver.

   If **yes**, the element is *restrictive* and should *not* be set off with punctuation.

   Those who emigrated with him live elsewhere.

Meaning and context

The same element in the same sentence may be restrictive or nonrestrictive depending on your intended meaning and the context in which the sentence appears. For example, look at the second sentence in each passage below.

RESTRICTIVE
Not all the bands were equally well received, however. The band *playing old music* held the audience's attention. The other groups created much less excitement. [*Playing old music* identifies a particular band.]

NONRESTRICTIVE
A new band called Fats made its debut on Saturday night. The band**,** *playing old music***,** held the audience's attention. If this performance is typical, the group has a bright future. [*Playing old music* adds information about a band already named.]

Use a comma or commas to set off nonrestrictive clauses and phrases.

Clauses and phrases serving as adjectives and adverbs may be either nonrestrictive or restrictive. Only nonrestrictive clauses and phrases are set off with punctuation. In the following examples the italicized clauses and phrases could be omitted without changing the meaning of the words they modify.

TRANSPARENCY MASTER 21.2

RECOGNIZING NONRESTRICTIVE ELEMENTS

For students who are still uncertain about whether elements are nonrestrictive or restrictive, emphasize that nonrestrictive elements *require* punctuation and *follow* these types of items:

1. One of a kind (including proper nouns):
   Secretariat, a beautiful chestnut colt, won the Triple Crown in 1973.
2. All of a kind:
   United States senators, who serve six-year terms, face constant pressure to raise campaign funds.
3. Previously mentioned:
   Animal rights activists have been known to stage outrageous demonstrations. The activists, who seek media attention, are prepared to risk criticism to promote their cause.

21c

RESOURCES AND IDEAS

Christensen, Francis. "Restrictive and Nonrestrictive Modifiers Again." In *Notes Toward a New Rhetoric: Nine Essays for Teachers.* 2nd ed. Ed. Francis Christensen and Bonniejean Christensen. New York: HarperCollins, 1978. 117–32. Christensen discusses and illustrates uses of the comma with a variety of modifying elements.

WORD PUZZLES

Divide the class into small groups, and give them word puzzles like the following. Each of these puzzles can be solved only if the reader knows how restrictive and nonrestrictive phrases are punctuated.

1. You are a CIA agent whose job is to keep track of all the Russian spies in Melopolia. One day you receive this telegram from Washington: "All the Russian spies, formerly residing in the Russian embassy, have been sent home."

Is there anyone left for you to watch?

2. After a long and successful season the university basketball team played its cross-state rival for the conference championship. Pandemonium broke out when a long shot dropped in at the buzzer to give the university the victory. Parties were held all over campus.

When Professor Kean arrived at class the next morning, the students, who had celebrated long into the night, were fast asleep at their desks.

Can you tell what portion of the class was asleep?

3. A severe electrical storm swept through town just after noon. Lightning struck several buildings, including the computer center. Technicians repairing damage there found that the microcomputers which were not equipped with electrical surge protectors needed to have their circuit boards replaced.

Are any of the microcomputers still usable?

NONRESTRICTIVE

Elizabeth Blackwell was the first woman to graduate from an American medical school, *in 1849.*

She was a medical pioneer, *helping to found the first medical college for women.*

She taught at the school, *which was affiliated with the New York Infirmary.*

Blackwell, *who published books and papers on medicine,* practiced pediatrics and gynecology.

She moved to England in 1869, *when she was forty-eight.*

NOTE Most adverb clauses are restrictive because they describe conditions necessary to the main clause. They are set off by a comma only when they introduce sentences (see p. 368) and when they are truly nonrestrictive, adding incidental information (as in the last example above) or expressing a contrast beginning *although, even though, though, whereas,* and the like.

In the following sentences, the italicized elements restrict the meaning of the words they modify. Removing the elements would leave the meaning too general.

RESTRICTIVE

The history *of aspirin* began *with the ancient Greeks.*

Physicians *who sought to relieve their patients' pains* recommended chewing willow bark.

Willow bark contains a chemical *that is similar to aspirin.*

NOTE Whereas both nonrestrictive and restrictive clauses may begin with *which,* only restrictive clauses begin with *that.* Some writers prefer *that* exclusively for restrictive clauses and *which* exclusively for nonrestrictive clauses. See the Glossary of Usage, page 809, for advice on the use of *that* and *which.*

Use a comma or commas to set off nonrestrictive appositives.

An **appositive** is a noun or noun substitute that renames another noun just before it. (See p. 187.) Many appositives are nonrestrictive; thus they are set off, usually with commas.

NONRESTRICTIVE

Toni Morrison's fifth novel, *Beloved,* won the Pulitzer Prize in 1988.

Morrison, *a native of Ohio,* won the Nobel Prize in 1993.

Take care *not* to set off restrictive appositives; like other restrictive elements, they limit or define the word they refer to.

Restrictive

Morrison's novel *The Bluest Eye* is about an African American girl who longs for blue eyes.

The critic *Michiko Kakutani* says that Morrison's work "stands radiantly on its own as an American epic."

3 Use a comma or commas to set off transitional or parenthetical expressions.

Transitional expressions

Transitional expressions form links between ideas. They include conjunctive adverbs such as *however* and *moreover* as well as other words or phrases such as *for example* and *of course.* (See pp. 100–01 for a list of transitional words and phrases.) Transitional expressions are nonrestrictive, so set them off with a comma or commas.

American workers, *for example*, receive fewer holidays than European workers do.

When a transitional expression links main clauses, precede it with a semicolon and follow it with a comma. (See p. 390.)

European workers often have long paid vacations; *indeed*, they may receive a full month.

Note The conjunctions *and* and *but,* sometimes used as transitional expressions, are not followed by commas (see p. 384). Nor are commas required after some transitional expressions that we read without pauses, such as *also, hence, next, now,* and *thus.* A few transitional expressions, notably *therefore* and *instead,* do not need commas when they fall inside or at the ends of clauses.

American workers thus put in more work days. But the days themselves may be shorter.

Parenthetical expressions

Parenthetical expressions provide comments, explanations, digressions, or other supplementary information not essential to meaning—for example, *fortunately, unfortunately, all things considered, to be frank, in other words.* Set parenthetical expressions off with commas.

Few people would know, *or even guess*, the most celebrated holiday on earth.

That holiday is, *surprisingly*, New Year's Day.

(Dashes and parentheses may also set off parenthetical elements. See pp. 420 and 421, respectively.)

COMMAS AND PARENTHESES

Students who know math will appreciate that the commas around parenthetical expressions are like the parentheses in a mathematical equation; if you use one to open the expression, you must have one to close it, or it can't be "solved" properly.

Use a comma or commas to set off *yes* and *no*, tag questions, words of direct address, and mild interjections.

YES AND NO

Yes, the editorial did have a point.

No, that can never be.

TAG QUESTIONS

Jones should be allowed to vote, *should he not?*

They don't stop to consider others, *do they?*

DIRECT ADDRESS

Cody, please bring me the newspaper.

With all due respect, *sir,* I will not do that.

MILD INTERJECTIONS

Well, you will never know who did it.

Oh, they forgot all about the baby.

(You may want to use an exclamation point to set off a forceful interjection. See p. 363.)

COLLABORATIVE LEARNING

Have students complete Exercise 5 individually and then compare their responses in small groups. This allows students the opportunity to discuss the differences between restrictive and nonrestrictive elements in a supportive setting. You might then ask each group to present one or two of their corrected responses on the blackboard or on transparencies while explaining how they reached their conclusions.

ANSWERS: EXERCISE 5

1. Italians insist that Marco Polo, the thirteenth-century explorer, did not import pasta from China.
2. Pasta, which consists of flour and water and often egg, existed in Italy long before Marco Polo left for his travels.
3. Sentence correct.
4. Most Italians dispute this account, although their evidence is shaky.
5. Wherever it originated, the Italians are now the undisputed masters in making and cooking pasta.
6. Sentence correct.

Exercise 5
Punctuating restrictive and nonrestrictive elements

Insert commas in the following sentences to set off nonrestrictive elements, and delete any commas that incorrectly set off restrictive elements. If a sentence is correct as given, circle the number preceding it.

Example:

Our language has adopted the words, *garage* and *fanfare,* from the French.

Our language has adopted the words *garage* and *fanfare* from the French.

1. Italians insist that Marco Polo the thirteenth-century explorer did not import pasta from China.
2. Pasta which consists of flour and water and often egg existed in Italy long before Marco Polo left for his travels.
3. A historian who studied pasta places its origin in the Middle East in the fifth century.
4. Most Italians dispute this account although their evidence is shaky.
5. Wherever it originated, the Italians are now the undisputed masters, in making and cooking pasta.
6. Marcella Hazan, who has written several books on Italian cooking, insists that homemade and hand-rolled pasta is the best.

7. Most cooks must buy dried pasta lacking the time to make their own.
8. The finest pasta is made from semolina, a flour from hard durum wheat.
9. Pasta manufacturers choose hard durum wheat, because it makes firmer cooked pasta than common wheat does.
10. Pasta, made from common wheat, tends to get soggy in boiling water.

7. Most cooks must buy dried pasta, lacking the time to make their own.
8. Sentence correct.
9. Pasta manufacturers choose hard drum wheat because it makes firmer cooked pasta than common wheat does.
10. Pasta made from common wheat tends to get soggy in boiling water.

Exercise 6
Sentence combining: Restrictive and nonrestrictive elements
Combine each pair of sentences below into one sentence that uses the element described in parentheses. Insert commas as appropriate. You will have to add, delete, change, and rearrange words. Some items have more than one possible answer.

Example:

Mr. Ward's oldest sister helped keep him alive. She was a nurse in the hospital. (*Nonrestrictive clause beginning who.*)

Mr. Ward's oldest sister**,** *who was a nurse in the hospital***,** helped keep him alive.

1. American colonists first imported pasta from the English. The English had discovered it as tourists in Italy. (*Nonrestrictive clause beginning who.*)
2. The English returned from their grand tours of Italy. They were called *macaronis* because of their fancy airs. (*Restrictive phrase beginning returning.*)
3. A hair style was also called *macaroni.* It had elaborate curls. (*Restrictive phrase beginning with.*)
4. The song "Yankee Doodle" refers to this hairdo. It reports that Yankee Doodle "stuck a feather in his cap and called it macaroni." (*Restrictive clause beginning when.*)
5. The song was actually intended to poke fun at unrefined American colonists. It was a creation of the English. (*Nonrestrictive appositive.*)

COLLABORATIVE LEARNING

Ask students to complete Exercise 6 individually and then compare their responses in small groups. Encourage the groups to focus on the places where individuals reached alternative conclusions and to discuss the effects of those differences on the meaning of the sentence.

ANSWERS: EXERCISE 6

Possible answers

1. American colonists first imported pasta from the English, who discovered it as tourists in Italy.
2. The English returning from their grand tours of Italy were called *macaronis* because of their fancy airs.
3. A hair style with elaborate curls was also called *macaroni.*
4. The song "Yankee Doodle" refers to this hairdo when it reports that Yankee Doodle "stuck a feather in his cap and called it macaroni."
5. The song, a creation of the English, was actually intended to poke fun at unrefined American colonists.

21d Use a comma or commas to set off absolute phrases.

An **absolute phrase** modifies a whole main clause rather than any word in the clause, and it usually consists of at least a participle (such as *done* or *having torn*) and its subject (a noun or pronoun). (See p. 181.) Absolute phrases can occur at almost any point in the sentence, and they are always set off by a comma or commas.

*Domestic recycling having succeeded***,** the city now wants to extend the program to businesses.

Many businesses**,** *their profits already squeezed***,** resist recycling.

21e Use a comma or commas to set off phrases expressing contrast.

The essay needs less wit, *more pith.*
The substance, *not the style,* is important.
Substance, *unlike style,* cannot be faked.

Note Writers often omit commas around contrasting phrases beginning with *but: A full but hazy moon shone down.*

ANSWERS: EXERCISE 7

1. Prices having risen rapidly, the government debated a price freeze.
2. A price freeze, unlike a rise in interest rates, seemed a sure solution.
3. The President would have to persuade businesses to accept a price freeze, his methods depending on their recalcitrance.
4. No doubt the President, his advisers having urged it, would first try a patriotic appeal.
5. The President, not his advisers, insisted on negotiations with businesses.

Exercise 7
Punctuating absolute phrases and phrases of contrast

Insert commas in the following sentences to set off absolute phrases and phrases of contrast.

Example:

The recording contract was canceled the band having broken up.

The recording contract was canceled, the band having broken up.

1. Prices having risen rapidly the government debated a price freeze.
2. A price freeze unlike a rise in interest rates seemed a sure solution.
3. The President would have to persuade businesses to accept a price freeze his methods depending on their recalcitrance.
4. No doubt the President his advisers having urged it would first try a patriotic appeal.
5. The President not his advisers insisted on negotiations with businesses.

^ 21f

COLLABORATIVE LEARNING

WHEN HANDBOOKS DISAGREE

Often, the advice on using commas in a series varies from handbook to handbook and style guide to style guide. Ask students as teams to compare the comma rules given in this handbook with the advice in some other usage manual (for instance, *The AP Stylebook, The Elements of Style,* or the books available in the writing reference section of their library or bookstore) and report back to the class on where these guides agree and disagree. The rules in this handbook are based on the style of reference common to the humanities (see chapter 40); the advice in other handbooks may be based on styles appropriate to other disciplines.

21f Use commas between items in a series and between coordinate adjectives.

1 Use commas between words, phrases, or clauses forming a series.

Place commas between all elements of a **series**—that is, three or more items of equal importance.

Anna Spingle *married at the age of seventeen, had three children by twenty-one, and divorced at twenty-two.*

She worked as *a cook, a baby-sitter, and a crossing guard.*

Though some writers omit the comma before the coordinating conjunction in a series (*Breakfast consisted of coffee, eggs and kippers*), the final comma is never wrong and it always helps the reader see the last two items as separate.

CONFUSING Her new job involves typing, filing and answering correspondence.

CLEAR Her new job involves typing, filing**,** and answering correspondence.

EXCEPTION When items in a series are long and grammatically complicated, they may be separated by semicolons. When the items contain commas, they must be separated by semicolons. (See p. 393.)

Use commas between two or more adjectives that equally modify the same word.

When two or more adjectives modify the same word equally, they are said to be **coordinate.** The adjectives may be separated either by *and* or by a comma.

> Spingle's *scratched and dented* car is an eyesore, but it gets her to work.
>
> She has dreams of a *sleek***,** *shiny* car.

Adjectives are not coordinate—and should *not* be separated by commas—when the one nearer the noun is more closely related to the noun in meaning. In each of the next examples, the second

---

Punctuating two or more adjectives

1. Identify the adjectives.

   She was a *faithful sincere* friend.
   They are *dedicated medical* students.

2. Can the adjectives be reversed without changing meaning?

   She was a *sincere faithful* friend. **Yes.**
   They are *medical dedicated* students. **No.**

3. Can the word *and* be inserted between the adjectives without changing meaning?

   She was a *faithful and sincere* friend. **Yes.**
   They are *dedicated and medical* students. **No.**

4. If **yes** to both questions, the adjectives are coordinate and should be separated by a comma.

   She was a *faithful***,** *sincere* friend.

   If **no** to both questions, the adjectives are *not* coordinate and should *not* be separated by a comma.

   They are *dedicated medical* students.

TRANSPARENCY MASTER 21.3

^ 21f

adjective and the noun form a unit that is modified by the first adjective.

> Spingle's children work at *various odd* jobs.
> They all expect to go to a *nearby community* college.

See the box on the previous page for a test to use in punctuating adjectives.

Note Numbers are not coordinate with other adjectives.

Faulty Spingle has *three, teenaged* children.
Revised Spingle has *three teenaged* children.

Do not use a comma between the final adjective and the noun.

Faulty The children hope to avoid their mother's *hard, poor,* life.
Revised The children hope to avoid their mother's *hard, poor* life.

Exercise 8
Punctuating series and coordinate adjectives

Insert commas in the following sentences to separate coordinate adjectives or elements in series. Circle the number preceding each sentence whose punctuation is already correct.

Example:

Quiet by day, the club became a noisy smoky dive at night.

Quiet by day, the club became a noisy**,** smoky dive at night.

1. Shoes with high heels originated to protect feet from the mud garbage and animal waste in the streets.
2. The first known high heels worn strictly for fashion appeared in the sixteenth century.
3. The heels were worn by men and made of colorful silk brocades soft suedes or smooth leathers.
4. High-heeled shoes received a boost when the short powerful King Louis XIV of France began wearing them.
5. Eventually only wealthy fashionable French women wore high heels.

ANSWERS: EXERCISE 8

1. Shoes with high heels originated to protect feet from the mud, garbage, and animal waste in the streets.
2. Sentence correct.
3. The heels were worn by men and made of colorful silk brocades, soft suedes, or smooth leathers.
4. High-heeled shoes received a boost when the short, powerful King Louis XIV of France began wearing them.
5. Eventually only wealthy, fashionable French women wore high heels.

^, 21g

21g Use commas according to convention in dates, addresses, place names, and long numbers.

Use commas to separate most parts of dates, addresses, and place names: *June 20***,** *1950; 24 Fifth Avenue***,** *Suite 601; Cario***,** *Illinois*. Within a sentence, any element preceded by a comma should be followed by a comma as well, as in the examples below:

Dates

July 4**,** 1776**,** was the day the Declaration of Independence was signed.

US POSTAL REGULATIONS

In addresses on envelopes, the United States Postal Service now asks that the city name be written in block capitals with no comma, followed by the state abbreviation, one space, and the zip code, as in the following example: BERKELEY CA 94720. This format enables their automatic sorting devices to process mail more effectively.

Students using word-processing or mail-merge programs may find that the computer automatically puts addresses into this format.

The bombing of Pearl Harbor on Sunday, December 7, 1941, prompted American entry into World War II.

Do not use commas between the parts of a date in inverted order: *Their anniversary on 15 December 1991 was their fiftieth.* You need not use commas in dates consisting of a month or season and a year: *For the United States the war began in December 1941 and ended in August 1945.*

However, writers still use the format shown in these examples when writing town and state names in the body of their texts. (See 42a for a sample envelope that illustrates the format recommended by the Postal Service.)

Addresses and place names

Columbus, Ohio, is the capital of Ohio and the location of Ohio State University.

The population of Garden City, Long Island, New York, is 30,000.

Use the address 220 Cornell Road, Woodside, California 94062, for all correspondence.

As illustrated above, do not use a comma between a state and a zip code.

Long numbers

Use the comma to separate the figures in long numbers into groups of three, counting from the right. With numbers of four digits, the comma is optional.

A kilometer is 3,281 feet (*or* 3281 feet).

The new assembly plant cost $7,525,000 by the time it was completed.

ESL Usage in American English differs from that in some other languages, which use a period, not a comma, to separate the figures in long numbers.

^ ; 21g

Exercise 9
Punctuating dates, addresses, place names, numbers

Insert commas as needed in the following sentences.

Example:
The house cost $27000 fifteen years ago.
The house cost $27,000 fifteen years ago.

1. The festival will hold a benefit dinner and performance on March 10 1996 in Asheville.
2. The organizers hope to raise more than $100000 from donations and ticket sales.
3. Performers are expected from as far away as Milan Italy and Kyoto Japan.
4. All inquiries sent to Mozart Festival PO Box 725 Asheville North Carolina 28803 will receive a quick response.
5. The deadline for ordering tickets by mail is Monday February 10 1996.

ANSWERS: EXERCISE 9

1. The festival will hold a benefit dinner and performance on March 10, 1996, in Asheville.
2. The organizers hope to raise more than $100,000 from donations and ticket sales.
3. Performers are expected from as far away as Milan, Italy, and Kyoto, Japan.
4. All inquiries sent to Mozart Festival, PO Box 725, Asheville, North Carolina 28803, will receive a quick response.
5. The deadline for ordering tickets by mail is Monday, February 10, 1996.

AUDIENCE EXPECTATIONS

Discuss the notion of audience expectations when students say, "My biology teacher says to do this," and remind students that being consistent within a document and meeting the expectations of one's readers are the most important considerations in deciding how to use particular punctuation marks. Chapter 40 lists style guides for various disciplines, which offer students additional information in making the punctuation decisions expected by various communities of readers.

RESOURCES AND IDEAS

Benson, S. Kenneth. "Profitable Proofreading." In *Teaching the Basics—Really!* Ed. Ouida Clapp. Urbana: NCTE, 1977. 80–81. Benson describes exercises in proofreading and in getting students to pay attention to correction symbols.

A WRITER'S PERSPECTIVE

It is highly important to put [commas] in place as you go along. If you try to come back after doing a paragraph and stick them in the various spots that tempt you you will discover that they tend to swarm like minnows into all sorts of crevices whose existence you hadn't realized and before you know it the whole long sentence becomes immobilized and lashed up squirming in commas. Better to use them sparingly, and with affection, precisely when the need for one arises, nicely, by itself.

—Lewis Thomas, "Notes on Punctuation"

COMPUTER EXERCISE

GRAMMAR CHECKERS

If students are using computerized grammar checkers like *Grammatik* or *Right Writer,* they may find that the computer challenges punctuation that follows the rules in this book. (Commas in a series are particular targets.) Warn students that such programs may follow slightly different rules, and tell them which rules you want them to follow if such conflicts arise. As a useful case in point you might choose a paragraph of student work with errors and have students run it through various grammar checkers and then dis-

21h Use commas with quotations according to standard practice.

The words *he said, she replied,* and so on identify the source of a quotation. These identifying words may come before, after, or in the middle of the quotation. They must always be separated from the quotation by punctuation, usually a comma or commas. (See pp. 406–07 for a summary of this and other conventions regarding quotations.)

Ordinarily, use a comma with identifying words before or after a quotation.

> Eleanor Roosevelt said**,** "You must do the thing you think you cannot do."
>
> "Knowledge is power**,**" wrote Francis Bacon.

Exceptions Do not use a comma when identifying words follow a quotation ending in an exclamation point or a question mark.

> "Claude**!**" Mrs. Harrison called.
> "Why must I come home**?**" he asked.

Do not use commas with a quotation introduced by *that* or with a quotation that is integrated into your sentence structure.

> James Baldwin insists that "one must never, in one's life, accept . . . injustices as commonplace."
>
> Baldwin thought that the violence of a riot "had been devised as a corrective" to his own violence.

Use a colon instead of a comma to separate identifying words from a quotation when there is an emphatic break between them in meaning or in grammar or when the quotation is very formal or longer than a sentence. (See also p. 417.)

> The Bill of Rights is unambiguous**:** "Congress shall make no law respecting an establishment of religion, or prohibiting the free exercise thereof."

With an interrupted quotation, precede the identifying words with a comma and follow them with the punctuation required by the quotation.

Quotation

> "The shore has a dual nature, changing with the swing of the tides."

Identifying words

> "The shore had a dual nature**,**" observes Rachel Carson**,** "changing with the swing of the tides." [The identifying words interrupt the quotation at a comma and thus end with a comma.]

Quotation

"However mean your life is, meet it and live it; do not shun it and call it hard names."

Identifying words

"However mean your life is, meet it and live it**,**" Thoreau advises in *Walden***;** "do not shun it and call it hard names." [The identifying words interrupt the quotation at a semicolon and thus end with a semicolon.]

Quotation

"This is the faith with which I return to the South. With this new faith we will be able to hew out of the mountain of despair a stone of hope."

Identifying words

"This is the faith with which I return to the South**,**" Martin Luther King, Jr., proclaimed**.** "With this new faith we will be able to hew out of the mountain of despair a stone of hope." [The explanatory words interrupt the quotation at the end of a sentence and thus end with a period.]

Note Using a comma instead of a semicolon or a period in the last two examples would result in the error called a comma splice: two main clauses separated only by a comma. (See pp. 274–77.)

Place commas that follow quotations within quotation marks.

"Death is not the greatest loss in life**,"** claims Norman Cousins.

"The greatest loss**,"** Cousins says, "is what dies inside us while we live."

Exercise 10
Punctuating quotations

Insert commas or semicolons in the following sentences to correct punctuation with quotations. Circle the number preceding any sentence whose punctuation is already correct.

Example:
The shoplifter declared "I didn't steal anything."
The shoplifter declared**,** "I didn't steal anything."

1. The writer and writing teacher Peter Elbow suggests that an "open-ended writing process . . . can change you, not just your words."
2. "I think of the open-ended writing process as a voyage in two stages" Elbow says.
3. "The sea voyage is a process of divergence, branching, proliferation, and confusion" Elbow continues "the coming to land is a process of convergence, pruning, centralizing, and clarifying."

play the results for general discussion. While such a display of contradictory "rules" of grammar might seem unnecessarily confusing, it's important to keep in mind that students will be able to use punctuation more effectively when they understand the various reasons behind the rules.

ANSWERS: EXERCISE 10

1. Sentence correct.
2. "I think of the open-ended writing process as a voyage in two stages," Elbow says.
3. "The sea voyage is a process of divergence, branching, proliferation, and confusion," Elbow continues; "the coming to land is a process of convergence, pruning, centralizing, and clarifying."

4. "Keep up one session of writing long enough to get loosened up and tired," advises Elbow, "long enough in fact to make a bit of a voyage."
5. "In coming to new land," Elbow says, "you develop a new conception of what you are writing about."

COLLABORATIVE LEARNING

Ask students to complete Exercise 11 individually and then have them compare their responses in small groups. Encourage the groups to consider the effect of varied comma placement on the meaning of each sentence. As a follow-up exercise you might ask each student to bring in a sentence taken from a magazine or newspaper in which the removal or addition of a comma creates a noticeable change in meaning.

ANSWERS: EXERCISE 11

1. Though happy, people still have moments of self-doubt.
2. In research, subjects have reported themselves to be generally happy people.
3. Yet those who have, described sufferings as well as joys.
4. Of fifty, eight subjects reported bouts of serious depression.
5. For half, the preceding year had included at least one personal crisis.

4. "Keep up one session of writing long enough to get loosened up and tired" advises Elbow "long enough in fact to make a bit of a voyage."
5. "In coming to new land" Elbow says "you develop a new conception of what you are writing about."

21i Use commas to prevent misreading.

In some sentences words may run together in unintended and confusing ways unless a comma separates them.

CONFUSING Soon after the business closed its doors.
CLEAR Soon after, the business closed its doors.

Exercise 11
Punctuating to prevent misreading

Insert commas in the following sentences to prevent misreading.

Example:
To Laura Ann symbolized decadence.
To Laura, Ann symbolized decadence.

1. Though happy people still have moments of self-doubt.
2. In research subjects have reported themselves to be generally happy people.
3. Yet those who have described sufferings as well as joys.
4. Of fifty eight subjects reported bouts of serious depression.
5. For half the preceding year had included at least one personal crisis.

21j Use commas only where required.

Commas can make sentences choppy and even confusing if they are used more often than needed or in violation of rules 21a through 21h.

1 Delete any comma after a subject or a verb.

Commas interrupt the movement from subject to verb to object or complement (see pp. 167–69).

FAULTY The returning *soldiers, received* a warmer welcome than they expected. [Separation of subject and verb.]

REVISED The returning *soldiers received* a warmer welcome than they expected.

TRANSPARENCY MASTER 21.4

Principal misuses of the comma

- Don't use a comma after a subject or verb (facing page).

  FAULTY *Anyone* with breathing problems, *should not exercise* during smog alerts.

  REVISED Anyone with breathing problems should not exercise during smog alerts.

- Don't separate a pair of words, phrases, or subordinate clauses joined by *and, or,* or *nor* (p. 384).

  FAULTY Asthmatics are affected by *ozone, and sulfur oxides.*

  REVISED Asthmatics are affected by ozone and sulfur oxides.

- Don't use a comma after *and, but, although, because,* or another conjunction (p. 384).

  FAULTY Smog is dangerous and, sometimes even fatal.

  REVISED Smog is dangerous and sometimes even fatal.

- Don't set off restrictive elements (p. 384).

  FAULTY Even people, *who are healthy,* should be careful.

  REVISED Even people who are healthy should be careful.

- Don't set off a series (p. 385).

  FAULTY *Cars, factories, and even bakeries,* contribute to smog.

  REVISED Cars, factories, and even bakeries contribute to smog.

- Don't set off an indirect quotation or a single word that isn't a nonrestrictive appositive (p. 385).

  FAULTY Experts *say, that* the pollutant, *ozone,* is especially damaging.

  REVISED Experts say that the pollutant ozone is especially damaging.

FAULTY They had *chosen, to fight* for their country. [Separation of verb *chosen* and object *to fight.*]

REVISED They had chosen to fight for their country.

EXCEPTION Use commas between subject, verb, and object or complement only when other words between these elements require punctuation.

> Americans, who are preoccupied with other sports, have not developed a strong interest in professional soccer. [Commas set off a nonrestrictive clause.]

2 Delete any comma that separates a pair of words, phrases, or subordinate clauses joined by a coordinating conjunction.

When linking elements with *and, or,* or another coordinating conjunction, do not use a comma unless the elements are main clauses (see p. 365).

FAULTY Banks *could, and should* help older people manage their money. [Compound helping verb.]

REVISED Banks could and should help older people manage their money.

FAULTY Older people need special assistance *because they live* on fixed incomes, *and because they are not familiar* with new *accounts, and rates.* [Compound subordinate clauses *because . . . because* and compound object of preposition *with.*]

REVISED Older people need special assistance because they live on fixed incomes and because they are not familiar with new accounts and rates.

FAULTY *Banks, and community groups* can *help* the elderly, *and eliminate* the confusion they often feel. [Compound subject and compound predicate.]

REVISED Banks and community groups can help the elderly and eliminate the confusion they often feel.

3 Delete any comma after a conjunction.

The coordinating conjunctions (*and, but,* and so on) and the subordinating conjunctions (*although, because,* and so on) are not followed by commas.

FAULTY Parents of adolescents notice increased conflict at puberty, *and,* they complain of bickering.

REVISED Parents of adolescents notice increased conflict at puberty, and they complain of bickering.

FAULTY *Although,* other primates leave the family at adolescence, humans do not.

REVISED Although other primates leave the family at adolescence, humans do not.

4 Delete any commas that set off restrictive elements.

Commas do not set off a restrictive element, which limits the meaning of the word it refers to (see p. 370).

FAULTY Hawthorne's work, *The Scarlet Letter,* was the first major American novel. [The title of the novel is essential to distinguish the novel from the rest of Hawthorne's work.]

Revised Hawthorne's work *The Scarlet Letter* was the first major American novel.

Faulty The symbols, *that Hawthorne used,* influenced other novelists. [The clause identifies which symbols were influential.]

Revised The symbols that Hawthorne used influenced other novelists.

5 Delete any comma before or after a series unless a rule requires it.

Commas separate the items *within* a series (p. 376) but do not separate the series from the rest of the sentence.

Faulty The skills of, *hunting, herding, and agriculture,* sustained the Native Americans.

Revised The skills of hunting, herding, and agriculture sustained the Native Americans.

In the following sentence the commas before and after the series are appropriate because the series is a nonrestrictive appositive (see p. 372).

The four major television networks**,** *ABC, CBS, Fox, and NBC***,** face fierce competition from the cable networks.

However, many writers prefer to use dashes rather than commas to set off series functioning as appositives (see p. 419).

6 Delete any comma setting off an indirect quotation or a single word that isn't a nonrestrictive appositive.

Indirect quotation

Faulty The report *concluded, that* dieting could be more dangerous than overeating.

Revised The report concluded that dieting could be more dangerous than overeating.

Quoted or italicized word

A quoted or italicized word is a restrictive appositive when it limits the word it refers to (see p. 372). Do not use commas around a restrictive appositive.

Faulty James Joyce's story, "Araby," was assigned last year. [The commas imply wrongly that Joyce wrote only one story.]

Revised James Joyce's story "Araby" was assigned last year.

COLLABORATIVE LEARNING

REPUNCTUATING

Take an essay from a reader or a similar source, remove the punctuation you wish to emphasize, make copies of the essay, and ask students to work in groups in order to reach consensus about how it should be punctuated. Tell them not to look at the handbook but to decide on their own the best way to serve the reader's needs through punctuation. When the students have finished, they can compare their work with the original and, using the handbook as a reference, decide which punctuation they think best serves the needs of the essay and the reader. If they decide to disagree with the advice given in the handbook, ask them to write out their own punctuation rules.

Have students practice proofreading, first on articles taken from local newspapers or papers written by members of other classes, and then on their own papers. Discuss why it is more difficult to find mistakes in their own papers than in the writings of others; for many, the difficulty arises because they are looking for what they wanted to write, or thought they wrote, not what they actually put on the page. Advise students to wait several hours between writing and proofreading so that their short-term memories clear and they can see what they've actually written instead of what they wanted to write.

ANSWERS: EXERCISE 12

1. Nearly 32 million US residents speak a first language other than English.
2. After English the languages most commonly spoken in the United States are Spanish, French, and German.
3. Almost 75 percent of the people who speak foreign languages used the words "good" or "very good" when judging their proficiency in English.
4. Sentence correct.
5. The states with the highest proportion of foreign-language speakers are New Mexico and California.

Faulty The word, *open,* can be either a verb or an adjective.
Revised The word *open* can be either a verb or an adjective.

The following sentence requires commas because the quoted title is a nonrestrictive appositive:

Her only poem about death, "Mourning," was printed in *The New Yorker.*

Exercise 12
Revising: Needless or misused commas

Revise the following sentences to eliminate needless or misused commas. Circle the number preceding each sentence that is already punctuated correctly.

Example:

The portrait of the founder, that hung in the dining hall, was stolen by pranksters.

The portrait of the founder that hung in the dining hall was stolen by pranksters.

1. Nearly 32 million US residents, speak a first language other than English.
2. After English the languages most commonly spoken in the United States are, Spanish, French, and German.
3. Almost 75 percent of the people, who speak foreign languages, used the words, "good" or "very good," when judging their proficiency in English.
4. Recent immigrants, especially those speaking Spanish, Chinese, and Korean, tended to judge their English more harshly.
5. The states with the highest proportion of foreign language speakers, are New Mexico, and California.

Exercise 13
Revising: Commas

Insert commas in the following paragraphs wherever they are needed, and eliminate any misused or needless commas.

Ellis Island New York has reopened for business but now the customers are tourists not immigrants. This spot which lies in New York Harbor was the first American soil seen, or touched by many of the nation's immigrants. Though other places also served as ports of entry for foreigners none has the symbolic power of, Ellis Island. Between its opening in 1892 and its closing in 1954, over 20 million people about two-thirds of all immigrants were detained there before taking up their new lives in the United States. Ellis Island processed over 2000 newcomers a day when immigration was at its peak between 1900 and 1920.

As the end of a long voyage and the introduction to the New World Ellis Island must have left something to be desired. The "huddled masses" as the Statue of Liberty calls them indeed were huddled. New arrivals were herded about kept standing in lines for hours or days yelled at and abused. Assigned numbers they submitted their bodies to the pokings and proddings of the silent nurses and doctors, who were charged with ferreting out the slightest sign of sickness, disability or insanity. That test having been passed the immigrants faced interrogation by an official through an interpreter. Those, with names deemed inconveniently long or difficult to pronounce, often found themselves permanently labeled with abbreviations, of their names, or with the names, of their hometowns. But, millions survived the examination humiliation and confusion, to take the last short boat ride to New York City. For many of them and especially for their descendants Ellis Island eventually became not a nightmare but the place where life began.

Note See page 428 for a punctuation exercise combining commas with other marks of punctuation.

COLLABORATIVE LEARNING

Ask students to complete Exercise 12 individually and to compare their responses in small groups. Then have each group complete Exercise 13 as a collaborative project, encouraging each group to debate the placement and elimination of commas.

ANSWERS: EXERCISE 13

Ellis Island, New York, has reopened for business, but now the customers are tourists, not immigrants. This spot, which lies in New York Harbor, was the first American soil seen or touched by many of the nation's immigrants. Though other places also served as ports of entry for foreigners, none has the symbolic power of Ellis Island. Between its opening in 1892 and its closing in 1954, over 20 million people, about two-thirds of all immigrants, were detained there before taking up their new lives in the United States. Ellis Island processed over 2000 [*or* 2,000] newcomers a day when immigration was at its peak between 1900 and 1920.

As the end of a long voyage and the introduction to the New World, Ellis Island must have left something to be desired. The "huddled masses," as the Statue of Liberty calls them, indeed were huddled. New arrivals were herded about, kept standing in lines for hours or days, yelled at, and abused. Assigned numbers, they submitted their bodies to the pokings and proddings of the silent nurses and doctors who were charged with ferreting out the slightest sign of sickness, disability, or insanity. That test having been passed, the immigrants faced interrogation by an official through an interpreter. Those with names deemed inconveniently long or difficult to pronounce often found themselves permanently labeled with abbreviations of their names or with the names of their hometowns. But millions survived the examination, humiliation, and confusion to take the last short boat ride to New York City. For many of them, and especially for their descendants, Ellis Island eventually became, not a nightmare, but the place where life began.

HIGHLIGHTS

Many inexperienced writers are hesitant to use the semicolon. They may be unfamiliar with the purposes of the mark and therefore reluctant to use it. This chapter should help students understand the four main uses of the semicolon: to separate main clauses not joined by a coordinating conjunction; to separate main clauses joined by a conjunctive adverb; to separate main clauses if they are very long and complex, even when they are joined by a coordinating conjunction; and to separate items in a series if they are long or contain commas. The chapter also covers the places where the semicolon can be misused. When students take risks in using the semicolon, positive reinforcement from you will help encourage them to add this useful punctuation mark to their repertoire.

Chapter 22 The Semicolon

22a Use a semicolon between main clauses not joined by *and, but,* or another coordinating conjunction.

Main clauses contain a subject and a predicate and do not begin with a subordinating word (see p. 182). When you join two main clauses in a sentence, you have two primary options for separating them:

- Insert a comma and a coordinating conjunction: *and, but, or, nor, for, so, yet.* (See p. 365.)

  The drug does little to relieve symptoms**,** *and* it can have side effects.

- Insert a semicolon:

  The side effects are not minor**;** some leave the patient quite ill.

NOTE If you do not link main clauses with a coordinating conjunction and you separate them only with a comma or with no punctuation at all, you will produce a comma splice or a fused sentence. See Chapter 11.

The box on the next page distinguishes among the principal uses of three often-confused marks: semicolon, comma, and colon. Generally, use the semicolon in sentences like the one above: the first clause creates an expectation, and the second clause fulfills the expectation.

EXCEPTION Writers sometimes use a comma instead of a semicolon between very short and closely parallel main clauses.

TRANSPARENCY MASTER 22.1

Distinguishing the comma, the semicolon, and the colon

The **comma** chiefly separates both equal and unequal sentence elements.

- It separates main clauses when they are linked by a coordinating conjunction (p. 365).

  An airline once tried to boost sales by advertising the tense alertness of its crews**,** *but* nervous fliers did not want to hear about pilots' sweaty palms.

- It separates subordinate information that is part of or attached to a main clause, such as a nonrestrictive modifier or an introductory element (pp. 368, 370).

  Although the airline campaign failed**,** many advertising agencies**,** including some clever ones**,** copied its underlying message.

The **semicolon** chiefly separates equal and balanced sentence elements.

- It separates complementary main clauses that are *not* linked by a coordinating conjunction (facing page).

  The airline campaign had highlighted only half the story**;** the other half was buried in the copy.

- It separates complementary main clauses that are related by a conjunctive adverb or other transitional expression (p. 390).

  The campaign should not have stressed the pilots' insecurity**;** *instead,* the campaign should have stressed the improved performance resulting from that insecurity.

The **colon** chiefly separates unequal sentence elements.

- It separates a main clause from a following explanation or summary, which may or may not be a main clause (p. 416).

  Many successful advertising campaigns have used this message**:** the anxious seller is harder working and smarter than the competitor.

The poor live**,** the rich just exist.

But a semicolon is safer, and it is always correct.

Exercise 1
Punctuating between main clauses

Insert semicolons to separate main clauses in the following sentences.

; 22a

Example:

One man at the auction bid prudently another did not.
One man at the auction bid prudently**;** another did not.

1. More and more musicians are playing computerized instruments more and more listeners are worrying about the future of acoustic instruments.
2. The computer is not the first new technology in music the pipe organ and saxophone were also technological breakthroughs in their day.
3. Musicians have always experimented with new technology audiences have always resisted the experiments.
4. Most computer musicians are not merely following the latest fad they are discovering new sounds and new ways to manipulate sound.
5. Few musicians have abandoned acoustic instruments most value acoustic sounds as much as electronic sounds.

ANSWERS: EXERCISE 1

1. More and more musicians are playing computerized instruments; more and more listeners are worrying about the future of acoustic instruments.
2. The computer is not the first new technology in music; the pipe organ and saxophone were also technological breakthroughs in their day.
3. Musicians have always experimented with new technology; audiences have always resisted the experiments.
4. Most computer musicians are not merely following the latest fad; they are discovering new sounds and new ways to manipulate sound.
5. Few musicians have abandoned acoustic instruments; most value acoustic sounds as much as electronic sounds.

Exercise 2
Sentence combining: Related main clauses

Combine each set of three sentences below into one sentence containing only two main clauses, and insert a semicolon between the clauses. You will have to add, delete, change, and rearrange words. Most items have more than one possible answer.

Example:

The painter Andrew Wyeth is widely admired. He is not universally admired. Some critics view his work as sentimental.

The painter Andrew Wyeth is widely but not universally admired**;** some critics view his work as sentimental.

1. Electronic instruments are prevalent in jazz. They are also prevalent in rock music. They are less common in classical music.
2. Jazz and rock change rapidly. They nourish experimentation. They nourish improvisation.
3. Traditional classical music does not change. Its notes and instrumentation were established by a composer. The composer was writing decades or centuries ago.
4. Contemporary classical music not only can draw on tradition. It also can respond to innovations. These are innovations such as jazz rhythms and electronic sounds.
5. Much contemporary electronic music is more than just one type of music. It is more than just jazz, rock, or classical. It is a fusion of all three.

COLLABORATIVE LEARNING

Ask students to complete Exercise 2 individually and then to compare their responses in small groups. Encourage group members to discuss their varying responses and to consider the effects of those differences on the meaning of each sentence. Then have each group present one of their responses to the class and explain the reasons for their sentence-combining choices.

ANSWERS: EXERCISE 2

Possible answers

1. Electronic instruments are prevalent in jazz and rock music; they are less common in classical music.
2. Jazz and rock change rapidly; they nourish experimentation and improvisation.
3. Traditional classical music does not change; its notes and instrumentation were established by a composer writing decades or centuries ago.
4. Contemporary classical music not only can draw on tradition; it also can respond to innovations such as jazz rhythms and electronic sounds.
5. Much contemporary electronic music is more than just jazz, rock, or classical; it is a fusion of all three.

; 22b

22b Use a semicolon between main clauses related by *however, for example,* and so on.

Two kinds of words can relate main clauses: **conjunctive adverbs,** such as *consequently, hence, however, indeed,* and *thus* (see

p. 191), and other **transitional expressions,** such as *even so, for example,* and *of course* (see p. 100). When either of these connects two main clauses, the clauses should be separated by a semicolon.

> An American immigrant, Levi Strauss, invented blue jeans in the 1860s**;** *eventually,* his product clothed working men throughout the West.

The position of the semicolon between main clauses never changes, but the conjunctive adverb or transitional expression may move around within a clause. The adverb or expression is usually set off with a comma or commas.

> Blue jeans have become fashionable all over the world**;** *however***,** the American originators still wear more jeans than anyone else.
>
> Blue jeans have become fashionable all over the world**;** the American originators**,** *however***,** still wear more jeans than anyone else.

Its mobility distinguishes a conjunctive adverb or transitional expression from other connecting words, such as coordinating and subordinating conjunctions. See page 191 for more on this distinction.

NOTE If you use a comma or no punctuation at all between main clauses connected by a conjunctive adverb or transitional expression, you will produce a comma splice or a fused sentence. See Chapter 11.

Exercise 3
Punctuating main clauses related by conjunctive adverbs or transitional expressions

Insert a semicolon in each sentence below to separate main clauses related by a conjunctive adverb or transitional expression, and insert a comma or commas where needed to set off the adverb or expression.

Example:

He knew that tickets for the concert would be scarce therefore he arrived at the box office hours before it opened.

He knew that tickets for the concert would be scarce**;** therefore**,** he arrived at the box office hours before it opened.

1. Music is a form of communication like language the basic elements however are not letters but notes.
2. Computers can process any information that can be represented numerically as a result they can process musical information.
3. A computer's ability to process music depends on what software it can run it must moreover be connected to a system that converts electrical vibration into sound.
4. Computers and their sound systems can produce many different sounds indeed the number of possible sounds is infinite.

ANSWERS: EXERCISE 3

1. Music is a form of communication like language; the basic elements, however, are not letters but notes.
2. Computers can process any information that can be represented numerically; as a result, they can process musical information.
3. A computer's ability to process music depends on what software it can run; it must, moreover, be connected to a system that converts electrical vibration into sound.
4. Computers and their sound systems can produce many different sounds; indeed, the number of possible sounds is infinite.
5. The powerful music computers are very expensive; therefore, they are used only by professional musicians.

COLLABORATIVE LEARNING

Ask students to complete Exercise 3 individually and then to compare their responses in small groups. Have each group complete Exercise 4 as a collaborative project, and encourage group members to debate various possible answers to each question. Then have each group present one of their responses to the class and explain the reasons for their choices.

ANSWERS: EXERCISE 4

Possible answers

1. Most music computers are too expensive for the average consumer; however, digital keyboard instruments can be inexpensive and are widely available.
2. Inside the keyboard is a small computer that controls a sound synthesizer; consequently, the instrument can both process and produce music.
3. The person playing the keyboard presses keys or other controls; immediately, the computer and synthesizer convert these signals into vibrations and sounds.
4. The inexpensive keyboards can perform only a few functions; still, to the novice computer musician the range of drum rhythms and simulated instruments is exciting.
5. Would-be musicians can orchestrate whole songs from just the melody lines; thus (*or* thus,) they need never again play "Chopsticks."

COMPUTER EXERCISE

STYLE CHECKERS

Often, computerized style checkers like *Grammatik* or *Right Writer* may reject uses of semicolons like the ones shown here, since they are apparent exceptions to semicolon rules. When such conflicts arise, have students check to see that their sentences are well constructed and that the semicolons are needed. As a case in point, you might have students run a passage from a published writer (such as Thoreau or O'Connor) through their grammar checkers and present the results to the class. Encourage students to discuss the effects of semicolon placement on the meaning of each passage.

; 22c

5. The powerful music computers are very expensive therefore they are used only by professional musicians.

Exercise 4

Sentence combining: Main clauses related by conjunctive adverbs or transitional expressions

Combine each set of three sentences below into one sentence containing only two main clauses. Connect the clauses with the conjunctive adverb or transitional expression in parentheses, and separate them with a semicolon. (Be sure the adverbs and expressions are punctuated appropriately.) You will have to add, delete, change, and rearrange words. Each item has more than one possible answer.

> *Example:*
>
> The Albanians censored their news. We got little news from them. And what we got was unreliable. (*therefore*)
>
> The Albanians censored their news**;** *therefore***,** the little news we got from them was unreliable.

1. Most music computers are too expensive for the average consumer. Digital keyboard instruments can be inexpensive. They are widely available. (*however*)
2. Inside the keyboard is a small computer. The computer controls a sound synthesizer. The instrument can both process and produce music. (*consequently*)
3. The person playing the keyboard presses keys or manipulates other controls. The computer and synthesizer convert these signals. The signals are converted into vibrations and sounds. (*immediately*)
4. The inexpensive keyboards can perform only a few functions. To the novice computer musician, the range is exciting. The range includes drum rhythms and simulated instruments. (*still*)
5. Would-be musicians can orchestrate whole songs. They start from just the melody lines. They need never again play "Chopsticks." (*thus*)

22c Use a semicolon to separate main clauses if they are complicated or contain commas, even with a coordinating conjunction.

You would normally use a comma with a coordinating conjunction such as *and* or *but* between main clauses (see p. 365). But a semicolon makes a sentence easier to read if the main clauses contain commas or are grammatically complicated.

> By a conscious effort of the mind, we can stand aloof from actions and their consequences**;** *and* all things, good and bad, go by us like a torrent. —HENRY DAVID THOREAU

> I doubt if the texture of Southern life is any more grotesque than that of the rest of the nation, but it does seem evident that the Southern writer is particularly adept at recognizing the grotesque**;** and to recognize the grotesque, you have to have some notion of what is not grotesque and why. —FLANNERY O'CONNOR

22d Use semicolons to separate items in a series if they are long or contain commas.

You normally use commas to separate items in a series (see p. 376). But use semicolons instead when the items are long or internally punctuated. The semicolons help the reader identify the items.

> The custody case involved Amy Dalton, the child**;** Ellen and Mark Dalton, the parents**;** and Ruth and Hal Blum, the grandparents.

> One may even reasonably advance the claim that the sort of communication that really counts, and is therefore embodied into permanent records, is primarily written**;** that "words fly away, but written messages endure," as the Latin saying put it two thousand years ago**;** and that there is no basic significance to at least fifty per cent of the oral interchange that goes on among all sorts of persons, high and low. —MARIO PEI

Exercise 5
Punctuating long main clauses and series items

Substitute commas for semicolons in the following sentences to separate main clauses or series items that are long or contain commas.

Example:

After graduation he debated whether to settle in San Francisco, which was temperate but far from his parents, New York City, which was exciting but expensive, or Atlanta, which was close to home but already familiar.

After graduation he debated whether to settle in San Francisco, which was temperate but far from his parents**;** New York City, which was exciting but expensive**;** or Atlanta, which was close to home but already familiar.

1. The Indian subcontinent is separated from the rest of the world by clear barriers: the Bay of Bengal and the Arabian Sea to the east and west, respectively, the Indian Ocean to the south, and 1600 miles of mountain ranges to the north.
2. In the north of India are the world's highest mountains, the Himalayas, and farther south are fertile farmlands, unpopulated deserts, and rain forests.
3. India is a nation of ethnic and linguistic diversity, with numerous religions, including Hinduism, Islam, and Christianity,

ANSWERS: EXERCISE 5

1. The Indian subcontinent is separated from the rest of the world by clear barriers: the Bay of Bengal and the Arabian Sea to the east and west, respectively; the Indian Ocean to the south; and 1600 miles of mountain ranges to the north.
2. In the north of India are the world's highest mountains, the Himalayas; and farther south are fertile farmlands, unpopulated deserts, and rain forests.
3. India is a nation of ethnic and linguistic diversity, with numerous religions, including Hinduism, Islam, and Christianity; with distinct castes as well as Aryan, Dravidian, and Mongoloid ethnic groups; and with sixteen languages, including the official Hindi and the "associate official" English.
4. Between the seventeenth and nineteenth centuries, the British colonized most of India, taking control of government, the bureaucracy, and industry; and they assumed a social position above all Indians.
5. During British rule the Indians' own unresolved differences and their frustrations with the British erupted in violent incidents

with distinct castes as well as Aryan, Dravidian, and Mongoloid ethnic groups, and with sixteen languages, including the official Hindi and the "associate official" English.

4. Between the seventeenth and nineteenth centuries, the British colonized most of India, taking control of government, the bureaucracy, and industry, and they assumed a social position above all Indians.
5. During British rule the Indians' own unresolved differences and their frustrations with the British erupted in violent incidents such as the Sepoy Mutiny, which began on February 26, 1857, and lasted two years, the Amritsar Massacre on April 13, 1919, and violence between Hindus and Moslems during World War II that resulted in the separation of Pakistan from India.

such as the Sepoy Mutiny, which began on February 26, 1857, and lasted two years; the Amritsar Massacre on April 13, 1919; and violence between Hindus and Moslems during World War II that resulted in the separation of Pakistan from India.

MEMORY AID

Students may benefit from this brief list of ways *not* to use the semicolon.

Do not use a semicolon to separate a subordinate clause from a main clause.
Do not use a semicolon to introduce a series.
Do not overuse a semicolon.

; 22e

22e Use the semicolon only where required.

Semicolons do not separate unequal sentence elements and should not be overused.

Delete or replace any semicolon that separates a subordinate clause or a phrase from a main clause.

The semicolon does not separate subordinate clauses and main clauses, or phrases and main clauses.

FAULTY According to African authorities; only about 35,000 Pygmies exist today.

REVISED According to African authorities, only about 35,000 Pygmies exist today.

FAULTY They are in danger of extinction; because of encroaching development.

REVISED They are in danger of extinction because of encroaching development.

NOTE Many readers regard a phrase or subordinate clause set off with a semicolon as a kind of sentence fragment. See Chapter 10.

Delete or replace any semicolon that introduces a series or explanation.

Colons and dashes, not semicolons, introduce series, explanations, and so forth. (See pp. 416–21.)

FAULTY Teachers have heard all sorts of reasons why students do poorly; psychological problems, family illness, too much work, too little time.

Revised Teachers have heard all sorts of reasons why students do poorly**:** psychological problems, family illness, too much work, too little time.

Revised Teachers have heard all sorts of reasons why students do poorly**—**psychological problems, family illness, too much work, too little time.

3 Use the semicolon sparingly.

Use the semicolon only occasionally. Many semicolons in a passage, even when they are required by rule, often indicate repetitive sentence structure. To revise a passage with too many semicolons, you'll need to restructure your sentences, not just remove the semicolons. (See p. 347 for tips on varying sentences.)

Semicolon overused

The Make-a-Wish Foundation helps sick children; it grants the wishes of children who are terminally ill. The foundation learns of a child's wish; the information usually comes from parents, friends, or hospital staff; the wish may be for a special toy, perhaps, or a visit to Disneyland. The foundation grants some wishes with its own funds; for other wishes it appeals to those who have what the child desires.

Revised

The Make-a-Wish Foundation grants the wishes of children who are terminally ill. From parents, friends, or hospital staff, the foundation learns of a child's wish for a special toy, perhaps, or a visit to Disneyland. It grants some wishes with its own funds; for other wishes it appeals to those who have what the child desires.

; 22e

Exercise 6
Revising: Misused or overused semicolons

Revise the following sentences to eliminate misused or overused semicolons, substituting other punctuation as appropriate.

Example:

The doctor gave everyone the same advice; get exercise.
The doctor gave everyone the same advice**:** get exercise.

1. The main religion in India is Hinduism; a way of life as well as a theology and philosophy.
2. Unlike Christianity and Judaism; Hinduism is a polytheistic religion; with deities numbering in the hundreds.
3. Hinduism is unlike many other religions; it allows its creeds and practices to vary widely from place to place and person to person. Other religions have churches; Hinduism does not. Other religions have principal prophets and holy books; Hinduism does not. Other religions center on specially trained

ANSWERS: EXERCISE 6

1. The main religion in India is Hinduism, a way of life as well as a theology and philosophy.
2. Unlike Christianity and Judaism, Hinduism is a polytheistic religion, with deities numbering in the hundreds.
3. *Possible revision:* Unlike many other religions, Hinduism allows its creeds and practices to vary widely from place to place and person to person. Whereas other religions have churches and principal prophets and holy books, Hinduism does not. And whereas other religions center on specially trained priests or other leaders, Hinduism promotes the individual as his or her own priest.

4. In Hindu belief there are four types of people: reflective, emotional, active, and experimental.
5. Each type of person has a different technique for realizing the true, immortal self, which has infinite existence, infinite knowledge, and infinite joy.

COLLABORATIVE LEARNING

Ask students to complete Exercise 6 individually and to compare their responses in small groups. Then ask each group to work collaboratively on Exercise 7, encouraging them to debate the effectiveness of each change in punctuation.

ANSWERS: EXERCISE 7

The set, sounds, and actors in the movie captured the essence of horror films. The set was ideal: dark, deserted streets; trees dipping their branches over the sidewalks; mist hugging the ground and creeping up to meet the trees; looming shadows of unlighted, turreted houses. The sounds, too, were appropriate; especially terrifying was the hard, hollow sound of footsteps echoing throughout the film. But the best feature of the movie was its actors, all of them tall, pale, and thin to the point of emaciation. With one exception, they were dressed uniformly in gray and had gray hair. The exception was an actress who dressed only in black, as if to set off her pale yellow, nearly white, long hair, the only color in the film. The glinting black eyes of another actor stole almost every scene; indeed, they were the source of all the film's mischief.

; 22e

priests or other leaders; Hinduism promotes the individual as his or her own priest.

4. In Hindu belief there are four types of people; reflective, emotional, active, and experimental.
5. Each type of person has a different technique for realizing the true, immortal self; which has infinite existence, infinite knowledge, and infinite joy.

Exercise 7
Revising: Semicolons

Insert semicolons in the following paragraph wherever they are needed. Eliminate any misused or needless semicolons, substituting other punctuation as appropriate.

The set, sounds, and actors in the movie captured the essence of horror films. The set was ideal; dark, deserted streets, trees dipping their branches over the sidewalks, mist hugging the ground and creeping up to meet the trees, looming shadows of unlighted, turreted houses. The sounds, too, were appropriate, especially terrifying was the hard, hollow sound of footsteps echoing throughout the film. But the best feature of the movie was its actors; all of them tall, pale, and thin to the point of emaciation. With one exception, they were dressed uniformly in gray and had gray hair. The exception was an actress who dressed only in black; as if to set off her pale yellow, nearly white, long hair; the only color in the film. The glinting black eyes of another actor stole almost every scene, indeed, they were the source of all the film's mischief.

Note See page 428 for a punctuation exercise combining semicolons with other marks of punctuation.

Chapter 23

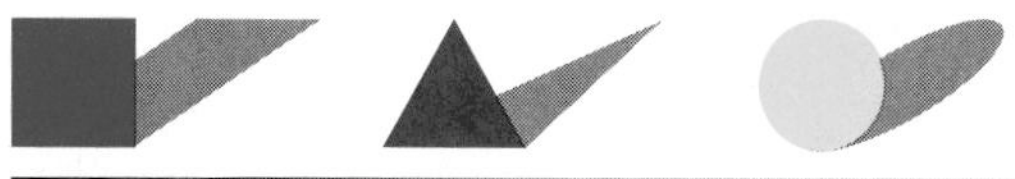

Unlike other punctuation marks, which separate words, the apostrophe (') appears as *part* of a word to indicate possession, the omission of one or more letters, or (in a few cases) plural number.

23a Use the apostrophe to indicate the possessive case for nouns and indefinite pronouns.

The **possessive case** shows ownership or possession of one person or thing by another. Possession may be shown with an *of* phrase (*the hair of the dog*); or it may be shown with the addition of an apostrophe and, usually, an *-s* (*the dog***'s** hair).

NOTE Apostrophes are easy to misuse. For safety's sake, check your drafts:

- Make sure that every word ending in *-s* neither omits a needed apostrophe nor adds an unneeded one.
- Remember that the apostrophe or apostrophe-plus-*s* is an *addition*. Before this addition, always spell the name of the owner or owners without dropping or adding letters: *girls* becomes *girls'*, not *girl's*.

You can use your computer to search for words ending in *-s* so that you can check their form. However, your computer cannot tell you that you've misused an apostrophe. A spelling checker can say only whether a word matches an entry in its dictionary, not whether that word is appropriate for the context in which you've used it. (See p. 499 for more on spelling checkers.)

HIGHLIGHTS

This chapter deals with the three reasons to use an apostrophe: to show possession; to indicate a contraction; or to form the plural of letters, numbers, and words named as words. It also explains when the apostrophe should not be used. The chapter focuses on the trouble spots writers are most likely to face and on the strategies they can use to avoid such problems.

RESOURCES AND IDEAS

Hashimoto, Irvin. "Pain and Suffering: Apostrophes and Academic Life." *Journal of Basic Writing* 7(2) (1988): 91–98. Hashimoto reviews, in often humorous fashion, some of the problems students have with apostrophe use.

Harvey S. Wiener. *The Writing Room: A Resource Book for Teachers of English*. New York: Oxford UP, 1981. 175–80. Wiener offers advice on explaining possession to students and describes several exercises designed to help them master the possessive forms of words.

COLLABORATIVE LEARNING

YELLOW PAGES

The apostrophe is a messy punctuation mark and is frequently misused. Help students see how popular use is changing the perception of apostrophes by asking students in groups to examine sections of the Yellow Pages or the advertisements in the local newspaper to find examples where expected apostrophes are missing (for instance, "Karins Kurtains" or "Farmers Market"). Encourage them to notice such misuses and bring them to the class's attention.

SPELLING CHECKERS

Computerized spelling checkers vary; some require both an apostrophe and an *s* after words ending in *s*, while others don't.

TRANSPARENCY MASTER 23.1

Uses and misuses of the apostrophe

USES

Possessives of nouns and indefinite pronouns (p. 397)

SINGULAR	PLURAL
Ms. Park**'s**	the Parks**'**
everyone**'s**	two weeks**'**
boy**'s**	boys**'**

Contractions (p. 401)

won**'**t	shouldn**'**t
they**'**re	it**'**s a girl

Optional: Plurals of letters, numbers, and words named as words (p. 403)

C**'**s or Cs	6**'**s or 6s
if**'**s or ifs	

MISUSES

Singular, not plural, possessives (p. 399)

NOT	BUT
the Kim's car	the Kim**s'** car
boy's fathers	boy**s'** fathers

Plurals of nouns (p. 400)

NOT	BUT
book's are	books are
candy's	candies

Third-person singulars of verbs (p. 400)

NOT	BUT
swim's	swims
go's	goes

Possessives of personal pronouns (p. 401)

NOT	BUT
it's toes	its toes
her's	hers

23a

Add *-'s* to singular nouns and indefinite pronouns.

Bill *Boughton'**s*** skillful card tricks amaze children.
*Anyone'**s*** eyes would widen. [Indefinite pronoun.]
Most tricks will pique an *adult'**s*** curiosity, too.

Add *-'s* as well to singular nouns that end in *-s*.

Henry *James'**s*** novels reward the patient reader.
Los *Angeles'**s*** weather is mostly warm.
The *business'**s*** customers filed suit.

EXCEPTION We typically do not pronounce the possessive *-s* of a few singular nouns ending in an *s* or *z* sound, especially names with more than one *s* sound (*Moses*), names that sound like plurals (*Rivers, Bridges*), and other nouns when they are followed by a word beginning in *s*. In these cases, many writers add only the apostrophe to indicate possession.

Moses' mother concealed him in the bulrushes.
Joan *Rivers'* jokes offend many people.
For *conscience'* sake she confessed her lie.

However, usage varies widely, and the final *-s* is not wrong with words like these (*Moses's*, *Rivers's*, *conscience's*).

Add *-'s* to plural nouns *not* ending in *-s*.

The bill establishes *children's* rights.
Publicity grabbed the *media's* attention.

Add only an apostrophe to plural nouns ending in *-s*.

Workers' incomes have not risen much over the past decade.
Many students benefit from several *years'* work after high school.
The *Jameses'* talents are extraordinary.

Note the difference in the possessives of singular and plural words ending in *-s*. The singular form usually takes *-'s*: *James's*. The plural takes only the apostrophe: *Jameses'*.

Add *-'s* only to the last word of compound words or word groups.

The *council president's* address was a bore.
The *brother-in-law's* business failed.
Taxes are always *somebody else's* fault.

With two or more words, add *-'s* to one or both depending on meaning.

INDIVIDUAL POSSESSION

Youngman's and *Mason's* comedy techniques are similar. [Each comedian has his own technique.]

JOINT POSSESSION

The child recovered despite her mother and father's neglect. [The mother and father were jointly neglectful.]

Exercise 1
Forming possessives

Form the possessive case of each word or word group in parentheses.

Example:

The (*men*) blood pressures were higher than the (*women*).
The *men's* blood pressures were higher than the women's.

ANSWERS: EXERCISE 1

1. In the myths of the ancient Greeks, the goddesses' roles vary widely.
2. Demeter's responsibility is the fruitfulness of the earth.
3. Athena's role is to guard the city of Athens.
4. Artemis's function is to care for wild animals and small children.
5. Athena and Artemis's father, Zeus, is the king of the gods.
6. Even a single goddess's responsibilities are often varied.
7. Over several centuries' time, Athena changes from a mariner's goddess to the patron of crafts.
8. Athena is also concerned with fertility and with children's well-being, since Athens's strength depended on a large and healthy population.
9. Athena often changes into birds' forms.
10. In Homer's *Odyssey* she assumes a sea eagle's form.
11. In ancient Athens the myths of Athena were part of everyone's knowledge and life.
12. A cherished myth tells how Athena fights to retain possession of her people's land when the god Poseidon wants it.
13. Athena's and Poseidon's skills are different, and each promises a special gift to the Athenians.
14. At the contest's conclusion, Poseidon has given water and Athena has given an olive tree, for sustenance.
15. The other gods decide that the Athenians' lives depend more on Athena than on Poseidon.

1. In the myths of the ancient Greeks, the (*goddesses*) roles vary widely.
2. (*Demeter*) responsibility is the fruitfulness of the earth.
3. (*Athena*) role is to guard the city of Athens.
4. (*Artemis*) function is to care for wild animals and small children.
5. (*Athena and Artemis*) father, Zeus, is the king of the gods.
6. Even a single (*goddess*) responsibilities are often varied.
7. Over several (*centuries*) time, Athena changes from a (*mariner*) goddess to the patron of crafts.
8. Athena is also concerned with fertility and with (*children*) well-being, since (*Athens*) strength depended on a large and healthy population.
9. Athena often changes into (*birds*) forms.
10. In (*Homer*) *Odyssey* she assumes a (*sea eagle*) form.
11. In ancient Athens the myths of Athena were part of (*everyone*) knowledge and life.
12. A cherished myth tells how Athena fights to retain possession of her (*people*) land when the god Poseidon wants it.
13. (*Athena and Poseidon*) skills are different, and each promises a special gift to the Athenians.
14. At the (*contest*) conclusion, Poseidon has given water and Athena has given an olive tree, for sustenance.
15. The other gods decide that the (*Athenians*) lives depend more on Athena than on Poseidon.

23b Delete or replace any apostrophe in a plural noun, a singular verb, or a possessive personal pronoun.

Not all words ending in *-s* take an apostrophe. Three kinds of words are especially likely to attract unneeded apostrophes.

Plural nouns

The plurals of nouns are generally formed by adding *-s* or *-es* (*boys, Smiths, families, Joneses*). Don't mistakenly add an apostrophe to form the plural.

FAULTY The unleashed *dog's* began traveling in a pack.
REVISED The unleashed *dogs* began traveling in a pack.

FAULTY The *Jones'* and *Bass'* were feuding.
REVISED The *Joneses* and *Basses* were feuding.

Singular verbs

Do not add an apostrophe to present-tense verbs used with *he, she, it,* and other third-person singular subjects. These verbs always end in *-s* but *never* with an apostrophe.

Faulty	The subway *break's* down less often now.
Revised	The subway *breaks* down less often now.

Possessives of personal pronouns

His, hers, its, ours, yours, theirs, and *whose* are possessive forms of the pronouns *he, she, it, we, you, they,* and *who.* They do not take apostrophes.

Faulty	The credit is *her's* not *their's.*
Revised	The credit is *hers,* not *theirs.*

The personal pronouns are often confused with contractions, such as *it's, you're,* and *who's.* See the next page.

Exercise 2
Distinguishing between plurals and possessives

Supply the appropriate form—possessive or plural—of each word given in parentheses. Some answers require apostrophes, and some do not.

Example:

A dozen Hawaiian (*shirt*), each with (*it*) own loud design, hung in the window.

A dozen Hawaiian *shirts,* each with *its* own loud design, hung in the window.

1. Demeter may be the oldest of the Greek (*god*), older than Zeus.
2. Many prehistoric (*culture*) had earth (*goddess*) like Demeter.
3. In myth she is the earth mother, which means that the responsibility for the fertility of both (*animal*) and (*plant*) is (*she*).
4. The (*goddess*) festival came at harvest time, with (*it*) celebration of bounty.
5. The (*people*) (*prayer*) to Demeter thanked her for grain and other (*gift*).

IT'S HUNTING

The most troublesome possessive is *its,* which many students confuse with the contraction *it's.* Ask students to keep a list in their journals of places where they see these words confused, including published work and other students' writing. *It's* hunting makes students learn the *its/it's* rule and become more aware of how they use these words in their own writing.

ANSWERS: EXERCISE 2

1. Demeter may be the oldest of the Greek gods, older than Zeus.
2. Many prehistoric cultures had earth goddesses like Demeter.
3. In myth she is the earth mother, which means that the responsibility for the fertility of both animals and plants is hers.
4. The goddess's festival came at harvest time, with its celebration of bounty.
5. The people's prayers to Demeter thanked her for grain and other gifts.

’ v 23c

23c Use an apostrophe to indicate the omission in a standard contraction.

it is	it's	let us	let's
he is	he's	does not	doesn't
she is	she's	were not	weren't
they are	they're	class of 1987	class of '87
you are	you're	of the clock	o'clock
who is	who's	madam	ma'am

Contractions are common in speech and in informal writing. They may also be used to relax style in more formal kinds of writing, as they are in this handbook. But be aware that many people disapprove of contractions in any kind of formal writing.

CONTRACTIONS

Some students may have been prohibited from using contractions in high school writing and remain unwilling to use such forms, for any audiences. Discuss with your classes the appropriate places for using contracted words.

NOTE Contractions are easily confused with the possessive personal pronouns.

CONTRACTION	POSSESSIVE PRONOUN
it's	its
they're	their
you're	your
who's	whose

FAULTY Legislators know *their* going to have to trim the budget to eliminate *it's* deficit.

REVISED Legislators know *they're* going to have to trim the budget to eliminate *its* deficit.

If you tend to confuse these forms, search for either spelling throughout your drafts (a word processor can help with this search). Then test for correctness:

- Do you intend the word to contain the sentence verb *is* or *are*, as in *It is a shame, They are to blame, You are right, Who is coming?* Then use an apostrophe: *it's, they're, you're, who's.*
- Do you intend the word to indicate possession, as in *Its tail was wagging, Their car broke down, Your eyes are blue, Whose book is that?* Then don't use an apostrophe.

Exercise 3
Forming contractions
Form contractions from each set of words below. Use each contraction in a complete sentence.

Example:
we are: we're
We're open to ideas.

1. she would
2. could not
3. they are
4. he is
5. do not
6. she will
7. hurricane of 1962
8. is not
9. it is
10. will not

Exercise 4
Revising: Contractions and personal pronouns
Revise the following sentences to correct mistakes in the use of contractions and personal pronouns. Circle the number preceding any sentence that is already correct.

Example:
The agencies give they're employees their birthdays off.
The agencies give *their* employees their birthdays off.

’ v 23c

ANSWERS: EXERCISE 3

Possible answers

1. She'd rather be dancing.
2. He couldn't see her in the crowd.
3. They're at the front door now.
4. He's my brother.
5. We don't like the beach.
6. She'll speak her mind.
7. The recent storm was nearly as bad as the hurricane of '62.
8. Isn't that your cousin?
9. It's a fact.
10. The door won't budge.

1. In Greek myth the goddess Demeter has a special fondness for Eleusis, near Athens, and it's people.
2. She finds rest among the people and is touched by their kindness.
3. Demeter rewards the Eleusians with the secret for making they're land fruitful.
4. The Eleusians begin a cult in honor of Demeter, whose worshiped in secret ceremonies.
5. Its unknown what happened in the ceremonies, for no participant ever revealed their rituals.

ANSWERS: EXERCISE 4

1. In Greek myth the goddess Demeter has a special fondness for Eleusis, near Athens, and its people.
2. Sentence correct.
3. Demeter rewards the Eleusians with the secret for making their land fruitful.
4. The Eleusians begin a cult in honor of Demeter, who's worshipped in secret ceremonies.
5. It's unknown what happened in the ceremonies, for no participant ever revealed their [correct] rituals.

23d An apostrophe is often optional in forming the plurals of abbreviations and dates and of letters, numbers, and words named as words.

Use the apostrophe with most plural abbreviations that contain periods. With unpunctuated abbreviations, you can omit the apostrophe. (See p. 361 on using periods with abbreviations.)

Ph.D.'s	CD-ROMs
B.A.'s	BAs

Plural abbreviations for measurements, however, do not take an apostrophe: *ins., gals., lbs.*

Add an *-s* to form the plural of a letter, number, or word that you are referring to as a word rather than using for its meaning. For most of these, you may also add an apostrophe, but the punctuation is optional. Just be consistent with your choice.

ts or t's 21s or 21's ifs or if's

The sentence has too many buts [or but's].

Two 3s [or 3's] and two &s [or &'s] appeared at the end of each chapter.

The apostrophe for years in a decade is also optional: 1990s or 1990's.

NOTE Letters, numbers, and words named as words are underlined (italicized), but the added *-s* and any apostrophe are not. (See p. 439 on this use of underlining or italics.) Dates are not underlined.

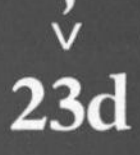

Exercise 5
Forming plurals of abbreviations, dates, letters, numbers, words

Form the plural of each item below by adding *-s*, by using or not using an apostrophe (as appropriate), and by underlining (italicizing) appropriately. Use the new plural in a complete sentence.

Example: x

Erase or white out typing mistakes. Do not use x's [or xs].

1. 7
2. q
3. if
4. and
5. SOS

Exercise 6
Revising: Apostrophes

In the following paragraph correct any mistakes in the use of the apostrophe or any confusion between contractions and possessive personal pronouns.

Landlocked Chad is among the worlds most troubled countries. The people's of Chad are poor: they're average per capita income equals $215 a year. Just over 15 percent of Chads population is literate, and every thousand people must share only two teacher's. The natural resources of the nation have never been plentiful, and now, as it's slowly being absorbed into the growing Sahara Desert, even water is scarce. Chads political conflicts go back beyond the turn of the century, when the French colonized the land by brutally subduing it's people. The rule of the French—who's inept government of the colony did nothing to ease tensions among racial, tribal, and religious group's—ended with independence in 1960. But since then the Chadians experience has been one of civil war and oppression, and now their threatened with invasions from they're neighbors.

NOTE See page 428 for a punctuation exercise involving apostrophes along with other marks of punctuation.

ANSWERS: EXERCISE 5

Possible answers

1. She drew 7's (*or* 7s) four times in a row.
2. She writes her g's (*or* gs) with flourishes.
3. That's too many if's (*or* ifs).
4. It's easy to use too many and's (*or* ands) in writing.
5. He sent repeated SOSs.

COLLABORATIVE LEARNING

Have students complete Exercise 6 individually and then compare their responses in groups. Then ask the groups to review paragraphs from each student's work in order to check apostrophe usage. It's important that students make the connection between the handbook exercises and correct apostrophe usage in their own work.

ANSWERS: EXERCISE 6

Landlocked Chad is among the world's most troubled countries. The peoples of Chad are poor: their average per capita income equals $215 a year. Just over 15 percent of Chad's population is literate, and every thousand people must share only two teachers. The natural resources of the nation have never been plentiful, and now, as it's [correct] slowly being absorbed into the growing Sahara Desert, even water is scarce. Chad's political conflicts go back beyond the turn of the century, when the French colonized the land by brutally subduing its people. The rule of the French—whose inept government of the colony did nothing to ease tensions among racial, tribal, and religious groups—ended with independence in 1960. But since then the Chadians' experience has been one of civil war and oppression, and now they're threatened with invasions from their neighbors.

Chapter 24

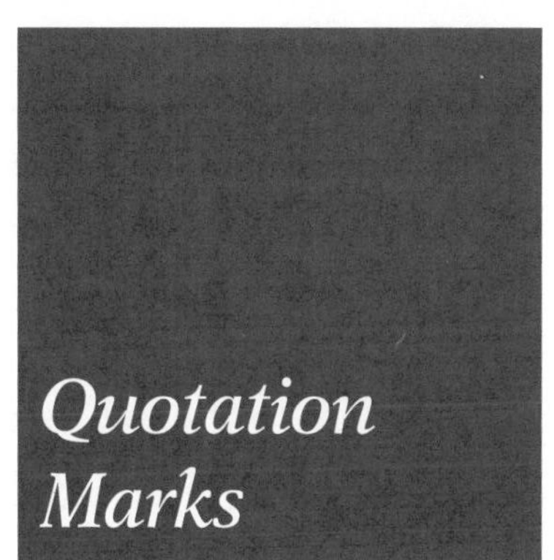

Quotation Marks

HIGHLIGHTS

The two most common problems students have with quotation marks are failing to close the quotation (see the special cautionary note before 24a) and misplacing other punctuation marks inside or outside quotation marks. Take time to review these rules and encourage students to double-check their use of quotation marks. Both practices may save you a great deal of time in marking papers, especially when the students are preparing papers that require the use of cited material.

Quotation marks—either double (" ") or single (' ')—mainly enclose direct quotations from speech and from writing. The chart on the next two pages summarizes this and other uses.

NOTE Always use quotation marks in pairs, one at the beginning of a quotation and one at the end.

24a Use double quotation marks to enclose direct quotations.

Direct quotations report what someone has said or written in the exact words of the original. Always enclose direct quotations in quotation marks.

> "Fortunately," said the psychoanalyst Karen Horney, "analysis is not the only way to resolve inner conflicts. Life itself still remains a very effective therapist."

Indirect quotations report what has been said or written, but not in the exact words of the person being quoted. Indirect quotations are *not* enclosed in quotation marks.

> The psychoanalyst Karen Horney remarked that analysis was not the only solution to inner conflicts, for life remained a good therapist.

Indirect quotation often involves a change in the tense of verbs, as in the example here. See pages 225–26.

(Text continues p. 408)

TRANSPARENCY MASTER 24.1

Handling quotations from speech or writing

(For explanations, consult the pages in parentheses.)

Direct and indirect quotation

Direct quotation (p. 405)

According to Lewis Thomas, **"**We are, perhaps uniquely among the earth's creatures, the worrying animal. We worry away our lives.**"**

Quotation within quotation (p. 408)

Quoting a phrase by Lewis Thomas, the author adds, **"**We are **'**the worrying animal.**'"**

Indirect quotation (p. 405)

Lewis Thomas says that human beings are unique among animals in their worrying.

Quotation marks with other punctuation marks

Commas and periods (p. 413)

Human beings are the "worrying animal**,"** says Thomas.
Thomas calls human beings "the worrying animal**."**

Semicolons and colons (p. 413)

Machiavelli said that "the majority of men live content"**;** in contrast, Thomas calls us "the worrying animal."

Thomas believes that we are "the worrying animal"**:** we spend our lives afraid and restless.

Question marks, exclamation points, dashes (p. 414)

When part of your own sentence

Who said that human beings are "the worrying animal**"?**
Imagine saying that we human beings "worry away our lives**"!**
Thomas's phrase**—"**the worrying animal**"—**seems too narrow.

When part of the original quotation

"Will you discuss this with me**?"** she asked.
"I demand that you discuss this with me**!"** she yelled.
"Please, won't you**—"** She paused.

Altering quotations

Brackets for additions (p. 423)

"We **[**human beings**]** worry away our lives," says Thomas.

“ ”
24a

Brackets for altered capitalization (p. 431)

"**[**T**]**he worrying animal" is what Thomas calls us. He says that "**[**w**]**e worry away our lives."

Ellipsis marks for omissions (p. 424)

"We are **. . .** the worrying animal," says Thomas.

Our worrying places us "uniquely among the earth's creatures**. . . .** We worry away our lives."

Punctuating identifying words with quotations

Introductory identifying words (p. 380)

He says**,** "We worry away our lives."

An answer is in these words by Lewis Thomas**:** "We are, perhaps uniquely among the earth's creatures, the worrying animal."

Thomas says that "the worrying animal" is afraid and restless.

Concluding identifying words (p. 380)

We are "the worrying animal**,"** says Thomas.
"Who says**?"** she demanded.
"I do**!"** he shouted.

Interrupting identifying words (p. 380)

"We are**,"** says Thomas**,** "perhaps uniquely among the earth's creatures, the worrying animal."

"I do not like the idea**,"** she said**;** "however, I agree with it."

"We are . . . the worrying animal**,"** says Thomas**.** "We worry away our lives."

See also:

Special kinds of quoted material

Dialogue (pp. 122, 408)
Poetry (p. 409)
Prose passages of more than four lines (p. 410)

Using quotations in your own text

Quotations versus paraphrases and summaries (p. 569)
Avoiding plagiarism when quoting (p. 578)
Introducing quotations in your text (p. 591)
Citing sources for quotations (Chapter 37)

NOTE

If you are using this chapter as part of a review of citation, it may be helpful to mention the ellipsis mark (25e) at this point as a means of omitting unnecessary material within a quotation. See Keith Grant-Davie's "Functional Redundancy: Ellipsis as Strategies in Reading and Writing" (*Journal of Advanced Composition* 15: 3 [1995]: 455–469). Grant-Davie looks at the differences between functional and needless redundancy in relation to the use of ellipses, particularly in the field of technical writing.

24b Use single quotation marks to enclose a quotation within a quotation.

When you quote a writer or speaker, use double quotation marks (see p. 405). When the material you quote contains yet another quotation, distinguish the two by enclosing the second quotation in single quotation marks.

> "In formulating any philosophy," Woody Allen writes, "the first consideration must always be: What can we know? . . . Descartes hinted at the problem when he wrote, **'**My mind can never know my body, although it has become quite friendly with my leg.**'"**

Notice that two different quotation marks appear at the end of the sentence—one single (to finish the interior quotation) and one double (to finish the main quotation).

Exercise 1

Using double and single quotation marks

Insert single and double quotation marks as needed in the following sentences. Circle the number preceding any sentence that is already correct.

Example:

The purpose of this book, explains the preface, is to examine the meaning of the expression Dance is poetry.

"The purpose of this book,**"** explains the preface, **"**is to examine the meaning of the expression **'**Dance is poetry.**'"**

1. Why, the lecturer asked, do we say Bless you! or something else when people sneeze but not acknowledge coughs, hiccups, and other eruptions?
2. She said that sneezes have always been regarded differently.
3. Sneezes feel more uncontrollable than some other eruptions, she said.
4. Unlike coughs and hiccups, she explained, sneezes feel as if they come from inside the head.
5. She concluded, People thus wish to recognize a sneeze, if only with a Gosh.

ANSWERS: EXERCISE 1

1. "Why," the lecturer asked, "do we say 'Bless you!' or something else when people sneeze but not acknowledge coughs, hiccups, and other eruptions?"
2. Sentence correct.
3. "Sneezes feel more uncontrollable than some other eruptions," she said.
4. "Unlike coughs and hiccups," she explained, "sneezes feel as if they come from inside the head."
5. She concluded, "People thus wish to recognize a sneeze, if only with a 'Gosh.' "

COLLABORATIVE LEARNING

Hand out a page from the class readings or from another printed source. Have students work in pairs to quote and respond to short passages from the reading. This exercise will help to remind students of the uses of quotation in their own work.

24c Set off quotations of dialogue, poetry, and long prose passages according to standard practice.

Dialogue

When quoting conversations, begin a new paragraph for each speaker.

> "What shall I call you? Your name?" Andrews whispered rapidly, as with a high squeak the latch of the door rose.
>
> "Elizabeth," she said. "Elizabeth."
>
> —GRAHAM GREENE, *The Man Within*

NOTE When you quote a single speaker for more than one paragraph, put quotation marks at the beginning of each paragraph but at the end of only the last paragraph. The absence of quotation marks at the end of each paragraph but the last tells readers that the speech is continuing.

Poetry

When you quote a single line from a poem, a song, or a verse play, run the line into your own text and enclose the line in quotation marks.

> Dylan Thomas remembered childhood as an idyllic time: "About the lilting house and happy as the grass was green" ("Fern Hill" line 2).

(The parenthetical information above and in the following examples provides source citations. See pp. 599–606 for an explanation.)

Poetry quotations of two or three lines may be placed in the text or displayed separately. If you place such a quotation in the text, enclose it in quotation marks and separate the lines with a slash surrounded by space.

> An example of Robert Frost's incisiveness is in two lines from "Death of the Hired Man": "Home is the place where, when you have to go there, / They have to take you in" (119-20).

Quotations of more than three lines of poetry should always be separated from the text with space and an indention. *Do not add quotation marks* where the yellow highlights fall in the example.

> Emily Dickinson stripped ideas to their essence, as in this description of "A narrow Fellow in the Grass," a snake:
>
> I more than once at Noon
> Have passed, I thought, a Whip lash
> Unbraiding in the Sun
> When stopping to secure it
> It wrinkled, and was gone – (12-16)

The *MLA Handbook for Writers of Research Papers,* the standard guide to manuscript format in English and some other humanities, recommends the following spacings for displayed poetry quotations:

INDENTED QUOTATIONS AND POETRY

Double-spacing indented quotes of poetry or prose is new to some students, who may have been taught to single-space such quotes in high school. If you are conducting draft-review workshops, ask students to check the spacing of such quotes in their drafts. If they are preparing papers on word processors, they may be able to take advantage of automatic indentation and spacing features to format such quotations.

- Double-space above and below the quotation.
- Indent the quotation one inch from the left margin.
- Double-space the quoted lines.

Unless your instructor specifies otherwise, follow these guidelines for your typewritten or handwritten papers.

NOTE Be careful when quoting poetry to reproduce faithfully all line indentions, space between lines, spelling, capitalization, and punctuation, such as the capitals and the closing dash in the Dickinson poem on the previous page.

TYPESETTING

Indented quotes in many printed texts are single-spaced because of typesetting requirements; it's expensive to leave extra white space between the lines. This single-spaced appearance may confuse students into thinking that their indented quotes should also be single-spaced; explain that all indented quotations must be double-spaced for ease of editing.

Long prose passages

Use an indention to set off long prose passages from body of your paper. The guidelines below are from the *MLA Handbook for Writers of Research Papers,* the style manual for English and some other humanities. Refer to Chapter 40 if you are writing in history, art history, or philosophy (p. 703); psychology or other social sciences (p. 720); or the natural or applied sciences (p. 733).

The *MLA Handbook* recommends setting off all prose quotations of more than four typed lines. Use space and an indention as described in the bulleted list above. *Do not add quotation marks* where the yellow highlights fall in the example:

> In his 1967 study of the lives of unemployed black men, Elliot Liebow observes that "unskilled" construction work requires more experience and skill than is generally assumed.
>
> > A healthy, sturdy, active man of good intelligence requires from two to four weeks to break in on a construction job. . . . It frequently happens that his foreman or the craftsman he services is not willing to wait that long for him to get into condition or to learn at a glance the difference in size between a rough 2 x 8 and a finished 2 x 10. (62)

(The parenthetical number at the end of the quotation is a source citation. See p. 599.)

Do not use a paragraph indention when quoting a single complete paragraph or a part of a paragraph. Use paragraph indentions only when quoting two or more complete paragraphs.

" "
24d

24d Put quotation marks around the titles of works that are parts of other works.

Use quotation marks to enclose the titles of short poems, articles in periodicals, short stories, essays, episodes of television and

Titles to be enclosed in quotation marks

Other titles should be underlined (italicized). See page 437.

Songs
"Lucy in the Sky with Diamonds"
"Mr. Bojangles"

Short poems
"Stopping by Woods on a Snowy Evening"
"Sunday Morning"

Articles in periodicals
"Comedy and Tragedy Transposed"
"Does 'Scaring' Work?"

Short stories
"The Battler"
"The Gift of the Magi"

Essays
"Politics and the English Language"
"Joey: A 'Mechanical Boy'"

Episodes of television and radio programs
"The Mexican Connection" (on 60 Minutes)
"Cooking with Clams" (on Eating In)

Subdivisions of books
"Voyage to the Houyhnhnms" (Part IV of Gulliver's Travels)
"The Mast Head" (Chapter 35 of Moby-Dick)

TRANSPARENCY MASTER 24.2

radio programs, the subdivisions of books, and other works that are published or released within larger works. Use quotation marks for song titles as well. Use underlining (italics) for all other titles, such as books, plays, periodicals, movies, television programs, and works of art. (See p. 437.)

Note Use single quotation marks for a quotation within a quoted title, as in the second article title and second essay title in the box above. And enclose all punctuation in the title within the quotation marks, as in the second article title.

See page 431 for guidelines on the use of capital letters in titles.

“ ”
24d

Exercise 2
Quoting titles

Insert quotation marks as needed for titles and words in the following sentences. If quotation marks should be used instead of underlining, insert them.

Example:

She published an article titled Marriage in Grace Paley's An Interest in Life.

She published an article titled "Marriage in Grace Paley's 'An Interest in Life.'"

1. In Chapter 8, titled How to Be Interesting, the author explains the art of conversation.

ANSWERS: EXERCISE 2

1. In Chapter 8, titled "How to Be Interesting," the author explains the art of conversation.
2. The Beatles' song "Let It Be" reminds him of his uncle.
3. The article that appeared in Mental Health [correct] was titled "Children of Divorce Ask, 'Why?' "
4. In the encyclopedia the discussion under "Modern Art" fills less than a column.
5. One prizewinning essay, "Cowgirls on Wall Street," first appeared in Entrepreneur [correct] magazine.

2. The Beatles' song Let It Be reminds him of his uncle.
3. The article that appeared in Mental Health was titled Children of Divorce Ask, "Why?"
4. In the encyclopedia the discussion under Modern Art fills less than a column.
5. One prizewinning essay, Cowgirls on Wall Street, first appeared in Entrepreneur magazine.

24e Quotation marks may be used to enclose words used in a special sense.

On movie sets movable "wild walls" make a one-walled room seem four-walled on film.

Writers often put quotation marks around a word they are using with irony—that is, with a different or even opposite meaning than usual.

With all the "compassion" it could muster, the agency turned away two-thirds of those seeking help. —Joan Simonson

Readers quickly tire of such irony, though, so use it sparingly.

Note For words you are defining, use underlining (italics). See page 439.

“ ” 24f

24f Use quotation marks only where they are required.

Don't use quotation marks in the titles of your papers unless they contain or are themselves direct quotations.

Not "The Death Wish in One Poem by Robert Frost"
But The Death Wish in One Poem by Robert Frost
Or The Death Wish in "Stopping by Woods on a Snowy Evening"

Don't use quotation marks to enclose common nicknames or technical terms that are not being defined.

Not As President, "Jimmy" Carter preferred to use his nickname.
But As President, Jimmy Carter preferred to use his nickname.

Not "Mitosis" in a cell is fascinating to watch.
But Mitosis in a cell is fascinating to watch.

Don't use quotation marks in an attempt to justify or apologize for slang and trite expressions that are inappropriate to your writing. If slang is appropriate, use it without quotation marks.

Not We should support the President in his "hour of need" rather than "wimp out" on him.

But We should give the President the support he needs rather than turn away like cowards.

(See pp. 456 and 472 for more discussion of slang and trite expressions.)

24g Place other marks of punctuation inside or outside quotation marks according to standard practice.

The position of another punctuation mark inside or outside a closing quotation mark depends on what the other mark is and whether it appears in the quotation.

1 Place commas and periods inside quotation marks.

Commas or periods fall *inside* closing quotation marks, even when (as in the third example) single and double quotation marks are combined.

Swift uses irony in his essay "A Modest Proposal."

Many first-time readers are shocked to see infants described as "delicious."

"'A Modest Proposal,'" wrote one critic, "is so outrageous that it cannot be believed."

(See pp. 380–81 for the use of commas, as in the last example above, to separate a quotation from words such as *she wrote* or *he said*.)

Exception When a parenthetical source citation immediately follows a quotation, place any period or comma *after* the citation.

One critic calls the essay "outrageous" (Olms 26).

Partly because of "the cool calculation of its delivery" (Olms 27), Swift's satire still chills a modern reader.

See page 605 for more on placing parenthetical citations.

2 Place colons and semicolons outside quotation marks.

A few years ago the slogan in elementary education was "learning by playing"; now educators are concerned with teaching basic skills.

We all know what is meant by "inflation": more money buys less.

NOTE

Students should note that this rule applies even when closing quotation marks are both single and double. Example: "The author of the article pointed out that the rock group The Police coined the word 'synchronicity.' "

FROM DISCIPLINE TO DISCIPLINE

This handbook's recommendations for using quotation marks conform to most disciplines' usage, but there may be variations in some style guides. When in doubt, students should consult their instructors or style guides in the appropriate disciplines. See Chapter 40 for lists of such guides.

Place dashes, question marks, and exclamation points inside quotation marks only if they belong to the quotation.

When a dash, question mark, or exclamation point is part of the quotation, put it *inside* quotation marks. Don't use any other punctuation such as a period or comma.

> "But must you**—"** Marcia hesitated, afraid of the answer.
>
> "Go away**!"** I yelled.
>
> Did you say, "Who is she**?"** [When both your sentence and the quotation would end in a question mark or exclamation point, use only the mark in the quotation.]

When a dash, question mark, or exclamation point applies only to the larger sentence, not to the quotation, place it *outside* quotation marks—again, with no other punctuation.

> One evocative line in English poetry**—"**After many a summer dies the swan**"—**was written by Alfred, Lord Tennyson.
>
> Who said, "Now cracks a noble heart**"?**
>
> The woman called me "stupid**"!**

ANSWERS: EXERCISE 3

1. In the title essay of her book "The Death of the Moth" and Other Essays, Virginia Woolf describes the last moments of a "frail and diminutive body." [Underlining correct for book title, but essay title within it is quoted.]
2. An insect's death may seem insignificant, but the moth is, in Woolf's words, "life, a pure bead."
3. The moth's struggle against death, "indifferent, impersonal," is heroic.
4. Where else but in such a bit of life could one see a protest so "superb"?
5. At the end Woolf sees the moth lying "most decently and uncomplainingly composed"; in death it finds dignity.

Exercise 3
Revising: Quotation marks

The underlined words in the following sentences are titles or direct quotations. Remove underlining where appropriate, and insert quotation marks. Be sure that other marks of punctuation are correctly placed inside or outside the quotation marks.

Example:

The award-winning essay is Science and Values.

The award-winning essay is **"**Science and Values.**"**

1. In the title essay of her book The Death of the Moth and Other Essays, Virginia Woolf describes the last moments of a frail and diminutive body.
2. An insect's death may seem insignificant, but the moth is, in Woolf's words, life, a pure bead.
3. The moth's struggle against death, indifferent, impersonal, is heroic.
4. Where else but in such a bit of life could one see a protest so superb?
5. At the end Woolf sees the moth lying most decently and uncomplainingly composed; in death it finds dignity.

COLLABORATIVE LEARNING

Ask students to complete Exercise 3 individually and to compare their responses in small groups. Then have the groups work through Exercise 4 as a collaborative project and present their conclusions to the class.

Exercise 4
Revising: Quotation marks

Insert quotation marks as needed in the following paragraph.

In one class we talked about a passage from I Have a Dream, the speech delivered by Martin Luther King, Jr., on the steps of the Lincoln Memorial on August 28, 1963:

> When the architects of our republic wrote the magnificent words of the Constitution and the Declaration of Independence, they were signing a promissory note to which every American was to fall heir. This note was a promise that all men would be guaranteed the unalienable rights of life, liberty, and the pursuit of happiness.

What did Dr. King mean by this statement? the teacher asked. Perhaps we should define promissory note first. Then she explained that a person who signs such a note agrees to pay a specific sum of money on a particular date or on demand by the holder of the note. One student suggested, Maybe Dr. King meant that those who wrote and signed the Constitution and Declaration had stated the country's promise that all people in America should have equal political rights and equal opportunity for the pursuit of happiness. He and over 200,000 people had gathered in Washington, DC, added another student. Maybe their purpose was to demand payment, to demand those rights for African Americans. The whole discussion was an eye opener for those of us (including me) who had never considered that those documents make promises that we should expect our country to fulfill.

Note See page 428 for a punctuation exercise involving quotation marks along with other marks of punctuation.

ANSWERS: EXERCISE 4

In one class we talked about a passage from "I Have a Dream," the speech delivered by Martin Luther King, Jr., on the steps of the Lincoln Memorial on August 28, 1963:

> When the architects of our republic wrote the magnificent words of the Constitution and the Declaration of Independence, they were signing a promissory note to which every American was to fall heir. This note was a promise that all men would be guaranteed the unalienable rights of life, liberty, and the pursuit of happiness.

"What did Dr. King mean by this statement?" the teacher asked. "Perhaps we should define 'promissory note' first." Then she explained that a person who signs such a note agrees to pay a specific sum of money on a particular date or on demand by the holder of the note. One student suggested, "Maybe Dr. King meant that those who wrote and signed the Constitution and Declaration had stated the country's promise that all people in America should have equal political rights and equal opportunity for the pursuit of happiness." "He and over 200,000 people had gathered in Washington, DC," added another student. "Maybe their purpose was to demand payment, to demand those rights for African Americans." The whole discussion was an eye opener for those of us (including me) who had never considered that those documents make promises that we should expect our country to fulfill.

HIGHLIGHTS

Chapter 25 covers the marks of punctuation not treated in the preceding chapters (20–24): the colon, the dash, parentheses, brackets, the ellipsis mark, and the slash. In addition to exercises for these marks of punctuation, an exercise at the end of the part (p. 428) asks students to practice using all the punctuation marks covered in Chapters 20–25.

Chapter 25 Other Punctuation Marks

COLONS WITH LISTS

In business and professional writing, colons often end phrases or subordinate clauses that precede lists formatted vertically:

The system requires:
386 MHz processor
8 Mbytes of RAM
DOS 3.0 or higher

THE COLON

25a Use the colon to introduce and to separate.

The colon is mainly a mark of introduction: it signals that the words following will explain or amplify. The colon also has several conventional uses, such as in expressions of time.

In its main use as an introducer, a colon is *always* preceded by a complete **main clause**—one containing a subject and a predicate and not starting with a subordinating word (see p. 182 for more on main clauses). A colon may or may not be followed by a main clause. This is one way the colon differs from the semicolon (see the box on the next page). The colon is often interchangeable with the dash, though the dash is more informal and more abrupt (see p. 419).

NOTE Don't use a colon more than once in a sentence. The sentence should end with the element introduced by the colon.

1 Use a colon to introduce a concluding explanation, series, appositive, or long or formal quotation.

EXPLANATION

Soul food is a varied cuisine**:** it includes spicy gumbos, black-eyed peas, and collard greens.

Soul food has a deceptively simple definition**:** the ethnic cooking of African Americans.

TRANSPARENCY MASTER 25.1

Distinguishing the colon and the semicolon

- The **colon** is a mark of introduction that separates elements of *unequal* importance, such as statements and explanations or introductions and quotations. The first element must be a complete main clause; the second element need not be. (See opposite.)

  The business school caters to working students**:** it offers special evening courses in business writing, finance, and management.

  The school has one goal**:** to train students to be responsible, competent businesspeople.

- The **semicolon** separates elements of *equal* importance, almost always complete main clauses. (See p. 388.)

  Few enrolling students know exactly what they want from the school**;** most hope generally for a managerial career.

Sometimes a concluding explanation is preceded by *the following* or *as follows* and a colon.

> A more precise definition might be *the following***:** ingredients, cooking methods, and dishes originating in Africa, brought to the New World by black slaves, and modified or supplemented in the Caribbean and the American South.

> SERIES (p. 376)
>
> At least three soul food dishes are familiar to most Americans**:** fried chicken, barbecued spareribs, and sweet potatoes.

> APPOSITIVE (p. 187)
>
> Soul food has one disadvantage**:** fat.

Certain expressions commonly introduce appositives, such as *namely* and *that is*. These expressions should *follow* the colon: *Soul food has one disadvantage***:** *namely, fat.*

> LONG OR FORMAL QUOTATION
>
> One soul food chef has a solution**:** "Soul food doesn't have to be greasy to taste good. . . . Instead of using ham hocks to flavor beans, I use smoked turkey wings. The soulful, smoky taste remains, but without all the fat of pork."

NOTE Depending on your preference, a complete sentence *after* the colon may begin with a capital letter or a small letter. Just be consistent throughout an essay.

2 Use a colon to separate titles and subtitles, the subdivisions of time, and the parts of biblical citations.

TITLES AND SUBTITLES

Charles Dickens: *An Introduction to His Novels*
Eros and Civilization: *A Philosophical Inquiry into Freud*

TIME	BIBLICAL CITATIONS
1:30 AM	Isaiah 28:1–6
12:26 PM	1 Corinthians 3:6–7

Use the colon only where required.

Use the colon only at the *end* of a main clause. Do not use it directly after a verb or preposition.

NOT Two entertaining movies directed by Steven Spielberg are: *E.T.* and *Raiders of the Lost Ark*.

BUT Two entertaining movies directed by Steven Spielberg are *E.T.* and *Raiders of the Lost Ark*.

NOT Shakespeare possessed the qualities of a Renaissance thinker, such as: humanism and a deep interest in classical Greek and Roman literature.

BUT Shakespeare possessed the qualities of a Renaissance thinker, such as humanism and a deep interest in classical Greek and Roman literature.

:
25a

ANSWERS: EXERCISE 1

1. In the remote parts of many Third World countries, simple signs mark human habitation: a dirt path, a few huts, smoke from a campfire.
2. In the built-up sections of industrialized countries, nature is all but obliterated by signs of human life, such as houses, factories, skyscrapers, and highways.
3. The spectacle makes many question the words of Ecclesiastes 1:4: "One generation passeth away, and another generation cometh; but the earth abideth forever."
4. Yet many scientists see the future differently: they hold that human beings have all the technology necessary to clean up the earth and restore the cycles of nature.
5. All that is needed is a change in the attitudes of those who use technology.

Exercise 1
Revising: Colons

Insert colons as needed in the following sentences, or delete colons that are misused.

Example:

Mix the ingredients as follows sift the flour and salt together, add the milk, and slowly beat in the egg yolk.

Mix the ingredients as follows: sift the flour and salt together, add the milk, and slowly beat in the egg yolk.

1. In the remote parts of many Third World countries, simple signs mark human habitation a dirt path, a few huts, smoke from a campfire.
2. In the built-up sections of industrialized countries, nature is all but obliterated by signs of human life, such as: houses, factories, skyscrapers, and highways.
3. The spectacle makes many question the words of Ecclesiastes 1:4 "One generation passeth away, and another cometh; but the earth abideth forever."

4. Yet many scientists see the future differently they hold that human beings have all the technology necessary to clean up the earth and restore the cycles of nature.
5. All that is needed is: a change in the attitudes of those who use technology.

THE DASH

25b Use a dash or dashes to indicate sudden changes in tone or thought and to set off some sentence elements.

The dash is mainly a mark of interruption: it signals an insertion or break.

Note In your papers, form a dash with two hyphens (--). Do not add extra space before, after, or between the hyphens.

1 Use a dash or dashes to indicate shifts and hesitations.

Shift in tone

The novel—if one can call it that—appeared in 1994.

Unfinished thought

If the book had a plot—but a plot would be conventional.

Hesitation in dialogue

"I was worried you might think I had stayed away because I was influenced by—" He stopped and lowered his eyes.

Astonished, Howe said, "Influenced by what?"

"Well, by—" Blackburn hesitated and for an answer pointed to the table. —Lionel Trilling

2 Use a dash or dashes to emphasize nonrestrictive elements.

Dashes may be used in place of commas or parentheses to set off and emphasize nonrestrictive elements. (See the box on the next page.) Dashes are especially useful when these elements are internally punctuated. Be sure to use a pair of dashes when the element interrupts a main clause.

Appositive (p. 187)

The qualities Monet painted—sunlight, rich shadows, deep colors—abounded near the rivers and gardens he used as subjects.

Modifier

Though they are close together—separated by only a few blocks—the two neighborhoods could be in different countries.

ADDING DASH

For many students, using dashes is a way of avoiding a decision about which punctuation mark to use. Dashes can be used this way in informal writing, but in more formal situations, students should use dashes only in the accepted ways discussed in the text.

TRANSPARENCY MASTER 25.2

Distinguishing dashes, commas, and parentheses

Dashes, commas, and parentheses may all set off nonessential information such as nonrestrictive elements.

- **Dashes** give the information the greatest emphasis (p. 419):

  Many students—including some employed by the college—disapprove of the new work rules.

- **Commas** are less emphatic (p. 370):

  Many students**,** including some employed by the college**,** disapprove of the new work rules.

- **Parentheses,** the least emphatic, signal that the information is just worth a mention (p. 421):

  Many students **(**including some employed by the college**)** disapprove of the new work rules.

PARENTHETICAL EXPRESSION (p. 421)

At any given time there exists an inventory of undiscovered embezzlement in—or more precisely not in—the country's businesses and banks. —JOHN KENNETH GALBRAITH

3 Use a dash to set off introductory series and concluding series and explanations.

INTRODUCTORY SERIES

Shortness of breath, skin discoloration or the sudden appearance of moles, persistent indigestion, the presence of small lumps—all these may signify cancer.

A dash sets off concluding series and explanations more informally and more abruptly than a colon does (see pp. 416–17).

CONCLUDING SERIES

The patient undergoes a battery of tests—CAT scan, bronchoscopy, perhaps even biopsy.

CONCLUDING EXPLANATION

Many patients are disturbed by the CAT scan—by the need to keep still for long periods in an exceedingly small space.

4 Use the dash only where needed.

Don't use the dash when commas, semicolons, and periods are more appropriate. And don't use too many dashes. They can create a jumpy or breathy quality in writing.

Not In all his life—eighty-seven years—my great-grandfather never allowed his picture to be taken—not even once. He claimed the "black box"—the camera—would rob him of his soul.

But In all his eighty-seven years my great-grandfather did not allow his picture to be taken even once. He claimed the "black box"—the camera—would rob him of his soul.

Exercise 2
Revising: Dashes

Insert dashes as needed in the following sentences.

Example:

What would we do if someone like Adolf Hitler that monster appeared among us?

What would we do if someone like Adolf Hitler**—**that monster **—**appeared among us?

1. The movie-theater business is undergoing dramatic changes changes that may affect what movies are made and shown.
2. The closing of independent theaters, the control of theaters by fewer and fewer owners, and the increasing ownership of theaters by movie studios and distributors these changes may reduce the availability of noncommercial films.
3. Yet at the same time the number of movie screens is increasing primarily in multiscreen complexes so that smaller films may find more outlets.
4. The number of active movie screens that is, screens showing films or booked to do so is higher now than at any time since World War II.
5. The biggest theater complexes seem to be something else as well art galleries, amusement arcades, restaurants, spectacles.

ANSWERS: EXERCISE 2

1. The movie-theater business is undergoing dramatic changes—changes that may affect what movies are made and shown.
2. The closing of independent theaters, the control of theaters by fewer and fewer owners, and the increasing ownership of theaters by movie studios and distributors—these changes may reduce the availability of noncommercial films.
3. Yet at the same time the number of movie screens is increasing—primarily in multiscreen complexes—so that smaller films may find more outlets.
4. The number of active movie screens—that is, screens showing films or booked to do so—is higher now than at any time since World War II.
5. The biggest theater complexes seem to be something else as well—art galleries, amusement arcades, restaurants, spectacles.

( ) 25c

PARENTHESES

25c Use parentheses to enclose nonessential elements within sentences.

Parentheses *always* come in pairs: one before and one after the punctuated material.

1 Use parentheses to enclose parenthetical expressions.

Parenthetical expressions include explanations, facts, digressions, and examples that may be helpful or interesting but are not essential to meaning. They are emphasized least when set off with a

PARENTHETICAL STYLE

Arthur L. Palacas in "Parenthetics and Personal Voice" (*Written Communication* 6 [1989]: 506–28) argues that the use of parenthetical expressions (including those punctuated by parentheses, commas, and dashes) is an important factor in developing a personal style.

ALTERNATE EXAMPLE

When you are enclosing a complete sentence within another complete sentence, you need not start the sentence in parentheses with a capital letter nor end it with a punctuation mark. For example:

> I spent the weekend buried in books (this is my usual practice) and emerged on Monday in time to go to the library.

pair of parentheses instead of commas or dashes. (See the box on p. 420.)

> The population of Philadelphia (now about 1.6 million) has declined since 1950.
>
> *Ariel* (published in 1965) contains Sylvia Plath's last poems.

NOTE Don't put a comma before a parenthetical expression enclosed in parentheses.

> NOT Philadelphia's population compares with Houston's, (just over 1.6 million).
>
> BUT Philadelphia's population compares with Houston's (just over 1.6 million).

A comma, semicolon, or period falling after a parenthetical expression should be placed *outside* the closing parenthesis.

> Philadelphia has a larger African American population (nearly 40 percent), while Houston has a larger Latino population (nearly 28 percent).

When it falls between other complete sentences, a complete sentence enclosed in parentheses has a capital letter and end punctuation.

> In general, coaches will tell you that scouts are just guys who can't coach. (But then, so are brain surgeons.) —ROY BLOUNT

Use parentheses to enclose letters and figures that label items in lists within sentences.

> Outside the Middle East, the countries with the largest oil reserves are (1) Venezuela (63 billion barrels), (2) Russia (57 billion barrels), and (3) Mexico (51 billion barrels).

When lists are set off from the text, the numbers or letters labeling them are usually not enclosed in parentheses.

Exercise 3

Revising: Parentheses

Insert parentheses as needed in the following sentences.

Example:

Students can find good-quality, inexpensive furniture for example, desks, tables, chairs, sofas, even beds in junk stores.

Students can find good-quality, inexpensive furniture (for example, desks, tables, chairs, sofas, even beds) in junk stores.

1. Many of those involved in the movie business agree that multiscreen complexes are good for two reasons: 1 they cut the costs of exhibitors, and 2 they offer more choices to audiences.

ANSWERS: EXERCISE 3

1. Many of those involved in the movie business agree that multiscreen complexes are good for two reasons: (1) they cut the costs of exhibitors: and (2) they offer more choices to audiences.
2. Those who produce and distribute films (and not just the big studios) argue that the multiscreen theaters give exhibitors too much power.
3. The major studios are buying movie theaters to gain control over important parts of the distribution process (what gets shown and for how much money).

2. Those who produce and distribute films and not just the big studios argue that the multiscreen theaters give exhibitors too much power.
3. The major studios are buying movie theaters to gain control over important parts of the distribution process what gets shown and for how much money.
4. For twelve years 1938–50 the federal government forced the studios to sell all their movie theaters.
5. But because they now have more competition television and videocassette recorders, the studios are permitted to own theaters.

BRACKETS

25d Use brackets within quotations to indicate your own comments or changes.

Brackets have specialized uses in mathematical equations, but their main use for all kinds of writing is to indicate that you have altered a quotation. If you need to explain, clarify, or correct the words of the writer you quote, place your additions in a pair of brackets.

> "That Texaco station [just outside Chicago] is one of the busiest in the nation," said a company spokesperson.

Also use brackets if you need to alter the capitalization of a quotation so that it will fit into your sentence. (See also p. 431.)

> "[O]ne of the busiest in the nation" is how a company spokesperson described the station.

You may also use a bracketed word or words to substitute for parts of the original quotation that would otherwise be unclear. In the sentence below, the bracketed word substitutes for *they* in the original.

> "Despite considerable achievements in other areas, [humans] still cannot control the weather and probably will never be able to do so."

The word *sic* (Latin for "in this manner") in brackets indicates that an error in the quotation appeared in the original and was not made by you.

> According to the newspaper report, "The car slammed thru [*sic*] the railing and into oncoming traffic."

But don't use *sic* to make fun of a writer or to note errors in a passage that is clearly nonstandard or illiterate.

4. For twelve years (1938–50) the federal government forced the studios to sell all their movie theaters.
5. But because they now have more competition (television and videocassette recorders), the studios are permitted to own theaters.

ADDITIONAL POINT

Brackets may also be used to supply missing letters to complete names that are given partly in initials in a quotation.

 TRANSPARENCY MASTER 25.3

RESOURCES AND IDEAS

Grant-Davie, Keith. "Functional Redundancy: Ellipsis as Strategies in Reading and Writing." *Journal of Advanced Composition* 15: 3 (1995): 455–69. Grant-Davie looks at the differences between functional and needless redundancy in relation to the use of ellipses, particularly in the field of technical writing.

THE ELLIPSIS MARK

25e Use the ellipsis mark to indicate omissions within quotations

The **ellipsis mark** consists of three spaced periods (. . .). It usually indicates an omission from a quotation, as illustrated in the following excerpts from this quotation about the Philippines:

ORIGINAL QUOTATION

"It was the Cuba of the future. It was going the way of Iran. It was another Nicaragua, another Cambodia, another Vietnam. But all these places, awesome in their histories, are so different from each other that one couldn't help thinking: this kind of talk was a shorthand for a confusion. All that was being said was that something was happening in the Philippines. Or more plausibly, a lot of different things were happening in the Philippines. And a lot of people were feeling obliged to speak out about it."

—JAMES FENTON, "The Philippine Election"

1. OMISSION OF THE MIDDLE OF A SENTENCE

"But all these places . . . are so different from each other that one couldn't help thinking: this kind of talk was a shorthand for a confusion."

2. OMISSION OF THE END OF A SENTENCE, WITHOUT SOURCE CITATION

"It was another Nicaragua. . . ." [The sentence period, closed up to the last word, precedes the ellipsis mark.]

3. OMISSION OF THE END OF A SENTENCE, WITH SOURCE CITATION

"It was another Nicaragua . . ." (25). [When the quotation is followed by a parenthetical source citation, as here, the sentence period follows the citation.]

4. OMISSION OF THE BEGINNING OF A SENTENCE

". . . [O]ne couldn't help thinking: this kind of talk was a shorthand for a confusion." [The brackets indicate a change in capitalization. See p. 431.]

5. OMISSION OF PARTS OF TWO SENTENCES

"All that was being said was that . . . a lot of different things were happening in the Philippines."

6. OMISSION OF ONE OR MORE SENTENCES

"It was the Cuba of the future. It was going the way of Iran. It was another Nicaragua, another Cambodia, another Vietnam. . . . All that was being said was that something was happening in the Philippines."

. . .
25e

7. **Use of partial sentence**

Fenton describes the "confusion" surrounding the Philippines. [No ellipsis mark needed.]

Note these features of the examples:

- Use an ellipsis mark when it is not otherwise clear that you have left out material from the source, as when the words you quote form a complete sentence that is different in the original (examples 1–5). You don't need an ellipsis mark at the beginning or end of a partial sentence because it will already be obvious that you omitted something (example 7).
- After a grammatically complete sentence, an ellipsis mark usually follows a sentence period and a space (examples 2 and 6). The exception occurs when a parenthetical source citation follows the quotation (example 3), in which case the sentence period falls after the citation.

If you omit one or more lines of poetry or paragraphs of prose from a quotation, use a separate line of ellipsis marks across the full width of the quotation to show the omission.

In "Song: Love Armed" from 1676, Aphra Behn contrasts two lovers' experiences of a romance:

> Love in fantastic triumph sate,
>   Whilst bleeding hearts around him flowed,
> . . . .
> But my poor heart alone is harmed,
>   Whilst thine the victor is, and free. (lines 1-2, 15-16)

(See p. 409 for the format of displayed quotations like this one. And see p. 604 on the source-citation form illustrated here.)

Note Pauses and unfinished statements in quoted speech may be indicated with an ellipsis mark instead of a dash (p. 419).

"I wish . . ." His voice trailed off.

Exercise 4
Using ellipsis marks

Use ellipsis marks and any other needed punctuation to follow the numbered instructions (next page) for quoting from the following paragraph.

Women in the sixteenth and seventeenth centuries were educated in the home and, in some cases, in boarding schools. Men were educated at home, in grammar schools, and at the universities. The universities were closed to female students. For women,

ANSWERS: EXERCISE 4

1. "To be able to read the Bible in the vernacular was a liberating experience. . . ."
2. "To be able to read the Bible in the vernacular . . . freed the reader from hearing only the set passages read in the church and interpreted by the church."
3. "Women in the sixteenth and seventeenth centuries were educated in the home and, in some cases, in boarding schools. . . . A Protestant woman was expected to read the scriptures daily, to meditate on them, and to memorize portions of them."

"learning the Bible," as Elizabeth Joceline puts it, was an impetus to learning to read. To be able to read the Bible in the vernacular was a liberating experience that freed the reader from hearing only the set passages read in the church and interpreted by the church. A Protestant woman was expected to read the scriptures daily, to meditate on them, and to memorize portions of them. In addition, a woman was expected to instruct her entire household in "learning the Bible" by holding instructional and devotional times each day for all household members, including the servants.

—CHARLOTTE F. OTTEN, *English Women's Voices, 1540–1700*

1. Quote the fifth sentence, but omit everything from *that freed the reader* to the end.
2. Quote the fifth sentence, but omit the words *was a liberating experience that.*
3. Quote the first and sixth sentences.

SLASHING

The rules governing when to put spaces around the slash confuse many students; it's worth a moment's time to review them. In addition, warn students that many word-processing programs that justify (align) the right margins of text may add or remove spaces around slashes.

/ 25f

THE SLASH

25f Use the slash between options and to separate lines of poetry that are run in to the text.

OPTION

I don't know why some teachers oppose pass/fail courses.

When used between options, the slash is not surrounded by extra space.

NOTE The options *and/or* and *he/she* should be avoided. (See the Glossary of Usage, pp. 795 and 801.)

POETRY

Many readers have sensed a reluctant turn away from death in Frost's lines "The woods are lovely, dark and deep, / But I have promises to keep."

When separating lines of poetry in this way, leave a space before and after the slash. (See p. 409 for more on quoting poetry.)

COLLABORATIVE LEARNING

Ask students to work individually or in pairs to complete Exercise 5, then have them work in small groups to compare and discuss their responses. In asking the groups to report on their findings, encourage students to debate the effect of each punctuation mark.

Exercise 5
Revising: Colons, dashes, parentheses, brackets, ellipsis marks, slashes

Insert colons, dashes, parentheses, brackets, ellipsis marks, or slashes as needed in the following paragraph. When different marks would be appropriate in the same place, be able to defend the choice you make.

"Let all the learned say what they can, 'Tis ready money makes the man." These two lines of poetry by the Englishman William

Somerville 1645–1742 may apply to a current American economic problem. Non-American investors with "ready money" pour some of it as much as $1.3 trillion in recent years into the United States. The investments of foreigners are varied stocks and bonds, savings deposits, service companies, factories, art works, even the campaigns of political candidates. Proponents of foreign investment argue that it revives industry, strengthens the economy, creates jobs more than 3 million, they say, and encourages free trade among nations. Opponents discuss the risks of heavy foreign investment it makes the American economy vulnerable to outsiders, sucks profits from the country, and gives foreigners an influence in governmental decision making. On both sides, it seems, "the learned say 'Tis ready money makes the man or country." The question is, whose money?

Note See the next page for a punctuation exercise combining colons, dashes, and parentheses with other marks of punctuation, such as commas and semicolons.

ANSWERS: EXERCISE 5

"Let all the learned say what they can, / 'Tis ready money makes the man." These two lines of poetry by the Englishman William Somerville (1645–1742) may apply to a current American economic problem. Non-American investors with "ready money" pour some of it—as much as $1.3 trillion in recent years—into the United States. The investments of foreigners are varied: stocks and bonds, savings deposits, service companies, factories, art works, even the campaigns of political candidates. Proponents of foreign investment argue that it revives industry, strengthens the economy, creates jobs (more than 3 million, they say), and encourages free trade among nations. Opponents discuss the risks of heavy foreign investment: it makes the American economy vulnerable to outsiders, sucks profits from the country, and gives foreigners an influence in governmental decision making. On both sides, it seems, "the learned say . . . / 'Tis ready money makes the man [or country]." The question is, whose money?

COLLABORATIVE LEARNING

Have students work in small groups to complete the following punctuation exercise. Encourage group members to debate the effect of each punctuation mark, and ask them to present some portion of the passage for class discussion.

ANSWERS: EXERCISE ON CHAPTERS 20–25

Brewed coffee is the most widely consumed beverage in the world. The trade in coffee beans alone amounts to well over $6,000,000,000 a year, and the total volume of beans traded exceeds 4,250,000 tons a year. It's believed that the beverage was introduced into Arabia in the fifteenth century AD [correct; *or* A.D.], probably by Ethiopians. By the middle or late sixteenth century, the Arabs had introduced the beverage to the Europeans, who at first resisted it because of its strong flavor and effect as a mild stimulant. The French, Italians, and other Europeans incorporated coffee into their diets by the seventeenth century; the English, however, preferred tea, which they were then importing from India. Since America was colonized primarily by the English, Americans also preferred tea. Only after the Boston Tea Party (1773) did Americans begin drinking coffee in large quantities. Now, though, the US [correct; *or* U.S.] is one of the top coffee-consuming countries, consumption having been spurred on by familiar advertising claims: "Good till the last drop"; "Rich, hearty aroma"; "Always rich, never bitter."

Produced from the fruit of an evergreen tree, coffee is grown primarily in Latin America, southern Asia, and Africa. Coffee trees require a hot climate, high humidity, rich soil with good drainage, and partial shade; consequently, they thrive on the east or west slopes of tropical volcanic mountains, where the soil is laced with potash and drains easily. The coffee beans—actually seeds—grow inside bright red berries. The berries are picked by hand, and the beans are extracted by machine, leaving a pulpy fruit residue that can be used for fertilizer. The beans are usually roasted in ovens, a chemical process that releases the beans' essential oil (caffeol), which gives coffee its distinctive aroma. Over a hundred different varieties of beans are produced in the world, each with a different flavor attributable to three factors: the species of plant (*Coffea arabica* and *Coffea robusta* are the most common) and the soil and climate where the variety was grown.

p

Exercise on Chapters 20–25
Revising: Punctuation

The following paragraphs are unpunctuated except for end-of-sentence periods. Insert periods, commas, semicolons, apostrophes, quotation marks, colons, dashes, or parentheses where they are required. When different marks would be appropriate in the same place, be able to defend the choice you make.

Brewed coffee is the most widely consumed beverage in the world. The trade in coffee beans alone amounts to well over $6000000000 a year and the total volume of beans traded exceeds 4250000 tons a year. Its believed that the beverage was introduced into Arabia in the fifteenth century AD probably by Ethiopians. By the middle or late sixteenth century the Arabs had introduced the beverage to the Europeans who at first resisted it because of its strong flavor and effect as a mild stimulant. The French Italians and other Europeans incorporated coffee into their diets by the seventeenth century the English however preferred tea which they were then importing from India. Since America was colonized primarily by the English Americans also preferred tea. Only after the Boston Tea Party 1773 did Americans begin drinking coffee in large quantities. Now though the US is one of the top coffee-consuming countries consumption having been spurred on by familiar advertising claims Good till the last drop Rich hearty aroma Always rich never bitter.

Produced from the fruit of an evergreen tree coffee is grown primarily in Latin America southern Asia and Africa. Coffee trees require a hot climate high humidity rich soil with good drainage and partial shade consequently they thrive on the east or west slopes of tropical volcanic mountains where the soil is laced with potash and drains easily. The coffee beans actually seeds grow inside bright red berries. The berries are picked by hand and the beans are extracted by machine leaving a pulpy fruit residue that can be used for fertilizer. The beans are usually roasted in ovens a chemical process that releases the beans essential oil caffeol which gives coffee its distinctive aroma. Over a hundred different varieties of beans are produced in the world each with a different flavor attributable to three factors the species of plant *Coffea arabica* and *Coffea robusta* are the most common and the soil and climate where the variety was grown.

Part VI Mechanics

HIGHLIGHTS

Capitalization at the beginning of sentences will probably not trouble most native speakers of English; however, capitalization within sentences, and in acronyms, can be a challenge for all writers. If your campus has a writing center, check to see if it has special instructional modules that students who have problems with capitalization can use for review.

RESOURCES AND IDEAS

Relatively little has been written about the teaching of capitalization, and most teachers probably assume that rules and drills are the only available instructional strategies. In *The Writing Room: A Resource Book for Teachers of English* (New York: Oxford UP, 1981, 172–74), however, Harvey S. Wiener looks at the sources of capitalization problems for many basic writers—particularly problems of misunderstanding the rules governing sentence boundaries, of confusion over the capitalization of *I* and other personal pronouns, and of difficulty with the sometimes inexact categories of words that are to be treated as proper nouns. Wiener suggests looking for patterns of error in a student's writing, creating groups of words illustrating a particular rule, and asking a student to prepare sentences that demonstrate his or her grasp of a particular convention. These strategies can be used for more skilled writers as well.

CAPITALIZATION PROBLEMS (ESL)

Nonnative students sometimes have trouble with the use of capitals; they need to become more familiar with English practice. Have such students review the rules in this chapter, then analyze the capitalization in some written document (for instance, a newsmagazine or textbook) to see how the rules are applied. ESL students may find that using the writing center's resources can also be very helpful.

Chapter 26 *Capitals*

The conventions for using capital letters change often, but the following pages and a recent dictionary can help you decide whether to capitalize a particular word.

NOTE The social, natural, and applied sciences require specialized capitalization for terminology, such as *Conditions A and B* or *Escherichia coli.* Consult one of the style guides listed on pages 707 (social sciences) and 729 (natural and applied sciences) for the requirements of the discipline you are writing in.

ESL Conventions of capitalization vary from language to language. English, for instance, is the only language to capitalize the first-person singular pronoun (*I*), and its practice of capitalizing proper nouns but not most common nouns also distinguishes it from some other languages.

26a Capitalize the first word of every sentence.

> Every writer should own a good dictionary.
> Will inflation be curbed?
> Watch out!

When quoting other writers, you must reproduce the capital letters beginning their sentences or indicate that you have altered the source. Whenever possible, integrate the quotation into your own sentence so that its capitalization coincides with yours.

> "Psychotherapists often overlook the benefits of self-deception," the author argues.

> The author argues that "the benefits of self-deception" are not always recognized by psychotherapists.

If you need to alter the capitalization in the source, indicate the change with brackets (see p. 423).

> "[T]he benefits of self-deception" are not always recognized by psychotherapists, the author argues.
>
> The author argues that "[p]sychotherapists often overlook the benefits of self-deception."

Note Capitalization of questions in a series is optional. Both examples below are correct.

> Is the population a hundred? Two hundred? More?
> Is the population a hundred? two hundred? more?

Also optional is capitalization of the first word in a complete sentence after a colon (see p. 417).

26b Capitalize most words in titles and subtitles of works.

Within your text, capitalize all the words in a title *except* the following: articles (*a, an, the*), *to* in infinitives, and connecting words (prepositions and coordinating and subordinating conjunctions) of fewer than five letters. Capitalize even these short words when they are the first or last word in a title or when they fall after a colon or semicolon.

The Sound and the Fury	*Management: A New Theory*
"Courtship Through the Ages"	"Once More to the Lake"
A Diamond Is Forever	*An End to Live For*
"Knowing Whom to Ask"	"Power: How to Get It"
Learning from Las Vegas	*File Under Architecture*
"The Truth About AIDS"	*Only when I Laugh*

Always capitalize the prefix or first word in a hyphenated word within a title. Capitalize the second word only if it is a noun or an adjective or is as important as the first word.

> "Applying Stage Make-up"
> *The Pre-Raphaelites*
> *Through the Looking-Glass*

Note Some academic disciplines require a different treatment of titles within source citations, such as capitalizing only the first words of some or all titles. See pages 710–19 (APA style for the social sciences) and 730–33 (CBE style for the natural and applied sciences).

COMPUTER EXERCISE

SPELLING CHECKERS

Sometimes computer spelling checkers will not distinguish between capitalized and noncapitalized words; as a result, students using these devices will not be alerted to misplaced or missing capitalizations. Have students check their capitalization visually as well as electronically to make sure they haven't made any mistakes.

 26c Always capitalize the pronoun *I* and the interjection *O*. Capitalize *oh* only when it begins a sentence.

I love to stay up at night, but, oh, I hate to get up in the morning.

He who thinks himself wise, O heavens, is a great fool. —VOLTAIRE

 26d Capitalize proper nouns, proper adjectives, and words used as essential parts of proper nouns.

Proper nouns name specific persons, places, and things: *Shakespeare, California, World War I.* **Proper adjectives** are formed from some proper nouns: *Shakespearean, Californian.*

1 Capitalize proper nouns and proper adjectives.

Capitalize all proper nouns and proper adjectives but not the articles (*a, an, the*) that precede them.

Proper nouns and adjectives to be capitalized

SPECIFIC PERSONS AND THINGS

Stephen King	the Leaning Tower of Pisa
Napoleon Bonaparte	Boulder Dam
Doris Lessing	the Empire State Building

SPECIFIC PLACES AND GEOGRAPHICAL REGIONS

New York City	the Mediterranean Sea
China	Lake Victoria
Europe	the Northeast, the South
North America	the Rocky Mountains

But: northeast of the city, going south

DAYS OF THE WEEK, MONTHS, HOLIDAYS

Monday	Yom Kippur
May	Christmas
Thanksgiving	Columbus Day

HISTORICAL EVENTS, DOCUMENTS, PERIODS, MOVEMENTS

World War II	the Middle Ages
the Vietnam War	the Age of Reason
the Boston Tea Party	the Renaissance
the Treaty of Ghent	the Great Depression
the Constitution	the Romantic Movement

GOVERNMENT OFFICES OR DEPARTMENTS AND INSTITUTIONS

House of Representatives	Polk Municipal Court
Department of Defense	Warren County Hospital
Appropriations Committee	Northeast High School

EXTRA EXAMPLES

Capitalizing compound words:

un-American
post-Victorian

PROPER NOUNS IN OTHER LANGUAGES (ESL)

Not all languages capitalize proper adjectives and proper nouns used as adjectives. Remind students that in English such words are always capitalized: *Swahili culture,* not *swahili culture.*

WHEN STYLES CONFLICT

Students may notice that newspapers and some magazines sometimes capitalize more words than the handbook advises them to capitalize. The trend is toward less rather than more capitalization, but popular periodicals often have their style guides and use capitals to reflect local interests, punch up their copy, or call attention to important distinctions (like Federal and State governments).

Political, social, athletic, and other organizations and associations and their members

Democratic Party, Democrats	Rotary Club, Rotarians
Sierra Club	League of Women Voters
Girl Scouts of America, Scout	Boston Celtics
B'nai B'rith	Chicago Symphony Orchestra

Races, nationalities, and their languages

Native American	Germans
African American, Negro	Swahili
Caucasian	Italian

But: blacks, whites

Religions and their followers

Christianity, Christians	Judaism, Orthodox Jew
Protestantism, Protestants	Hinduism, Hindu
Catholicism, Catholics	Islam, Muslims

Religious terms for the sacred

God	Buddha
Allah	the Bible (*but* biblical)
Christ	the Koran

Note Capitalization of pronouns referring to God is optional in most contexts, but it is often used in religious texts and should be used where necessary to avoid confusion.

Unclear Our minister spoke of God as though *he* loved every member of our congregation.

Revised Our minister spoke of God as though *He* loved every member of our congregation.

2 Capitalize common nouns used as essential parts of proper nouns.

Common nouns name general classes of persons, places, or things, and they generally are not capitalized. However, capitalize the common nouns *street, avenue, park, river, ocean, lake, company, college, county,* and *memorial* when they are part of proper nouns naming specific places or institutions.

Main Street	Lake Superior
Central Park	Ford Motor Company
Mississippi River	Madison College
Pacific Ocean	George Washington Memorial

NOTE

You may wish to point out that when a generic term occurs with a proper name, the generic term is capitalized (the Congo *River*), but when the generic term occurs with two or more proper names, it is usually capitalized when it precedes the proper names but lowercased when it succeeds them (*Lakes* Superior and Ontario; the Congo and Amazon *rivers*).

cap 26d

3 Capitalize trade names.

Trade names identify individual brands of certain products. When a trade name loses its association with a brand and comes to refer to a product in general, it is not capitalized. Refer to a dictionary for current usage when you are in doubt about a name.

Scotch tape	Xerox
Chevrolet	Bunsen burner

But: nylon, thermos

NOTE

You may wish to remind students not to capitalize *doctor, madame, sir,* or similar forms of address unless they occur directly before a name.

26e Capitalize most titles only when they precede proper names.

Professor Otto Osborne	Otto Osborne, a professor of English
Doctor Jane Covington	Jane Covington, a medical doctor
Governor Ella Moore	Ella Moore, the governor

NOT The Senator supported the bill.

BUT The *senator* supported the bill.

OR *Senator Carmine* supported the bill.

EXCEPTION Many writers capitalize a title denoting very high rank even when it follows a proper name or is used alone.

Lyndon Johnson, past President of the United States
the Chief Justice of the United States

26f Capitalize only when required.

cap 26f

In general, modern writers capitalize fewer words than earlier writers did. Capitalize only when a rule says you must, and especially avoid miscapitalizing in the following situations.

Use small letters for common nouns replacing proper nouns.

NOT I am determined to take an Economics course before I graduate from College.

BUT I am determined to take an economics course before I graduate from college.

OR I am determined to take Economics 101 before I graduate from Madison College.

Capitalize compass directions only when they refer to specific geographical areas.

The storm blew in from the northeast and then veered south along the coast. [Here *northeast* and *south* refer to general directions.]

Students from the South have trouble adjusting to the Northeast's bitter winters. [Here *South* and *Northeast* refer to specific regions.]

Use small letters for the names of seasons or the names of academic years or terms.

spring	autumn	senior year
summer	fall quarter	winter term

Capitalize the names of relationships only when they form part of or substitute for proper names.

my mother	the father of my friend
John's brother	

I remember how Father scolded us.

Aunt Annie, Uncle Jake, and Uncle Irvin died within two months of each other.

Exercise
Revising: Capitals

Capitalize words as necessary in the following sentences, or substitute small letters for unnecessary capitals. Consult a dictionary if you are in doubt. If the capitalization in a sentence is already correct, circle the number preceding the sentence.

Example:

The first book on the reading list is mark twain's *a connecticut yankee in king arthur's court.*

The first book on the reading list is Mark Twain's *A Connecticut Yankee in King Arthur's Court.*

1. San Antonio, texas, is a thriving city in the southwest.
2. The city has always offered much to tourists interested in the roots of spanish settlement of the new world.
3. The alamo is one of five Catholic Missions built by Priests to convert native americans and to maintain spain's claims in the area.
4. But the alamo is more famous for being the site of an 1836 battle that helped to create the republic of Texas.
5. Many of the nearby Streets, such as Crockett street, are named for men who gave their lives in that Battle.
6. The Hemisfair plaza and the San Antonio river link new tourist and convention facilities developed during mayor Cisneros's terms.
7. Restaurants, Hotels, and shops line the River. the haunting melodies of "Una paloma blanca" and "malagueña" lure passing tourists into Casa rio and other excellent mexican restaurants.

ANSWERS: EXERCISE

1. San Antonio, Texas, is a thriving city in the Southwest.
2. The city has always offered much to tourists interested in the roots of Spanish settlement of the New World.
3. The Alamo is one of five Catholic missions built by priests to convert the Native Americans and to maintain Spain's claims in the area.
4. But the Alamo is more famous for being the site of an 1836 battle that helped to create the Republic of Texas.
5. Many of the nearby streets, such as Crockett Street, are named for men who gave their lives in that battle.
6. The Hemisfair Plaza and the San Antonio River link new tourist and convention facilities developed during Mayor Cisneros's terms.
7. Restaurants, hotels, and shops line the river. The haunting melodies of "Una Paloma Blanca" and "Malagueña" lure passing tourists into Casa Rio and other excellent Mexican restaurants.
8. The University of Texas at San Antonio has expanded, and a medical center has been developed in the northwest part of the city.
9. Sentence correct.
10. The city has attracted high-tech industry, creating a corridor of economic growth between San Antonio and Austin and contributing to the Texas economy.

8. The university of Texas at San Antonio has expanded, and a Medical Center has been developed in the Northwest part of the city.
9. Sea World, on the west side of San Antonio, entertains grandparents, fathers and mothers, and children with the antics of dolphins and seals.
10. The City has attracted high-tech industry, creating a corridor of economic growth between san antonio and austin and contributing to the texas economy.

NOTE See page 452 for an exercise involving capitals along with underlining (italics) and other mechanics.

Chapter 27

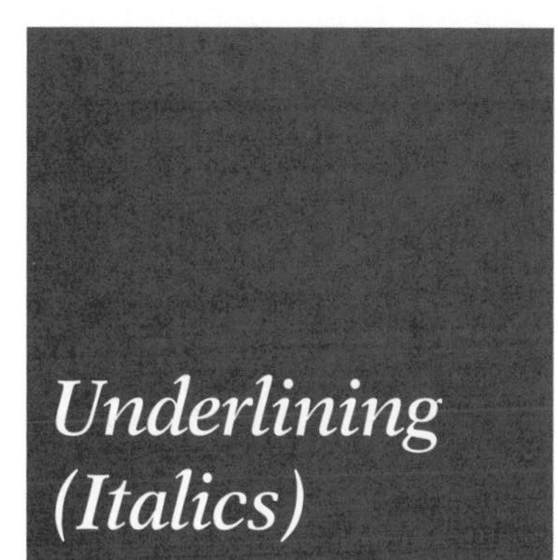

Underlining (Italics)

Underlining and *italic type* indicate the same thing: the word or words are being distinguished or emphasized. In business the almost universal use of computerized word processors makes both forms of highlighting possible, and italics may be preferred. In schools the use of italics is less common, and many disciplines continue to require underlining for works in source citations. Consult your instructor before you use italic type.

NOTE If you underline two or more words in a row, underline the space between the words, too: Criminal Statistics: Misuses of Numbers.

27a Underline the titles of works that appear independently.

Within your text, underline the titles of works, such as books and periodicals, that are published, released, or produced separately from other works (see the box on the next page). Use quotation marks for all other titles, such as short stories and articles in periodicals. (See p. 411.)

NOTE Underline marks of punctuation only when they are part of the title: *Did you read* Catch–22? (not Catch–22?). In titles of newspapers underline the name of the city only when it is part of the title.

New York Times   Manchester Guardian

When giving the title of a periodical in your text, you need not capitalize or underline the article *the,* even if it is part of the title.

She has the New York Times delivered to her in Alaska.

HIGHLIGHTS

Of all the chapters on mechanics, this chapter, on the uses of underlining or italics, most frequently needs to be reviewed, particularly by students writing essays or research papers that require incorporating material from outside the classroom. The chapter includes the rules for underlining titles; the names of various craft; foreign words and phrases that have not yet become part of the English language; and words, letters, numbers, and phrases named as words. It also gives the rules for underlining for emphasis.

A WRITER'S PERSPECTIVE

Her letters to Kitty, though rather longer, were much too full of lines under the words to be made public.

—JANE AUSTEN, *Pride and Prejudice*

COMPUTER EXERCISE

UNDERLINING THE SPACES

Students preparing papers on word processors have the option of underlining the spaces between words; make sure your students understand what option (to underline or not to underline) you recommend. This handbook, like most other style guides, shows spaces underlined, a style that is less distracting and also easier for students who aren't using word processors.

NOTE

When an apostrophe or an apostrophe plus an *s* is added to a title, the addition is not underlined.

Titles to be underlined (italicized)

Other titles should be placed in quotation marks. See page 411.

Books

War and Peace
And the Band Played On
Anatomy and Physiology: An Introduction

Plays

Hamlet
Summer and Smoke
The Phantom of the Opera

Pamphlets

The Truth About Alcoholism
On the Vindication of the Rights of Women

Long musical works

Tchaikovsky's *Swan Lake*
The Beatles' *Revolver*
But: Symphony in C

Television and radio programs

All Things Considered
Seinfeld
NBC Sports Hour

Long poems

Beowulf
The Song of Roland
Paradise Lost

Periodicals

Time
Philadelphia Inquirer
Mechanical Engineering
Yale Law Review

Published speeches

Lincoln's *Gettysburg Address*
Pericles's *Funeral Oration*

Movies and videotapes

Schindler's List
How to Relax
Beauty and the Beast

Works of visual art

Michelangelo's *David*
the *Mona Lisa*
Guernica

Exceptions Legal documents, the Bible, the Koran, and their parts are generally not underlined.

Not They registered their *deed*.
But They registered their deed.

Not We studied the *Book of Revelation* in the *Bible*.
But We studied the Book of Revelation in the Bible.

27b Underline the names of ships, aircraft, spacecraft, and trains.

Queen Elizabeth 2 | *Challenger* | *Orient Express*
Spirit of St. Louis | *Apollo XI* | *Montrealer*

27c Underline foreign words and phrases that have not been absorbed into English.

English has adopted many foreign words and phrases—such as the French expression "bon voyage"—and these need not be underlined. A foreign phrase should be underlined when it has not been absorbed into our language. A dictionary will say whether a phrase is still considered foreign to English.

> The scientific name for the brown trout is Salmo trutta. [The Latin scientific names for plants and animals are always underlined.]
>
> What a life he led! He was a true bon vivant.
>
> The Latin De gustibus non est disputandum translates roughly as "There's no accounting for taste."

27d Underline words, letters, numbers, and phrases named as words.

Use underlining to indicate that you are citing a character or word as a word rather than using it for its meaning.

> Some people say th, as in thought, with a faint s or f sound.
> Carved into the column, twenty feet up, was a mysterious 7.
> Try pronouncing unique New York ten times fast.

Use underlining also to highlight words you are defining.

> The word syzygy refers to a straight line formed by three celestial bodies, as in the alignment of the earth, sun, and moon.

27e Occasionally, underlining may be used for emphasis.

Underlining can stress an important word or phrase, especially in reporting how someone said something.

> "Why on earth would you do that?" she cried.

But use such emphasis very rarely. Excessive underlining will make your writing sound immature or hysterical.

> The settlers had no firewood and no food. Many of them starved or froze to death that first winter.

Consult Chapter 18 for other techniques to achieve emphasis.

Exercise
Revising: Underlining (italics)

Underline (italicize) words and phrases as needed in the following sentences, or circle any words or phrases that are underlined unnecessarily. Note that some underlining is correct as given.

Example:
Of Hitchcock's movies, Psycho is the scariest.
Of Hitchcock's movies, Psycho is the scariest.

NOTE

You may wish to remind students that when sounds (e.g., *kerplunk, oof*) are represented in writing, they are usually underlined.

COLLABORATIVE LEARNING

ADD THE MECHANICS

If you have assigned one or more of Chapters 26–30, this activity may be useful and interesting. Take an essay, either student or professional; remove capitals, italics, and the like; and ask students to work in groups reaching consensus on how to correct the mechanics in the "new" essay. Tell them not to look at the handbook but to decide on their own the best way to serve the readers' needs through mechanics. When the students have finished, they can compare their work with the original and, using the handbook as a reference, decide which choices in mechanics they think best serve the needs of the essay and the readers. If they decide to disagree with the advice given in the handbook, ask them to write out their own rules.

ANSWERS: EXERCISE

1. Of the many Vietnam veterans who are writers, Oliver Stone is perhaps the most famous for writing and directing the films Platoon and Born on the Fourth of July.
2. Tim O'Brien has written short stories for Esquire, GQ, and Massachusetts Review.
3. Going After Cacciato is O'Brien's dreamlike novel about the horrors of combat.

4. The word Vietnam is technically two words (Viet and Nam), but most American writers spell it as one word. [Viet and Nam were correctly underlined.]
5. American writers use words or phrases borrowed from the Vietnamese language, such as di di mau ("go quickly") or dinky dau ("crazy").
6. Philip Caputo's gripping account of his service in Vietnam appears in the book A Rumor of War.
7. Sentence correct.
8. David Rabe's plays—including The Basic Training of Pavlo Hummel, Streamers, and Sticks and Bones—depict the effects of the war not only on the soldiers but on their families.
9. Called "the poet laureate of the Vietnam war," Steve Mason has published two collections of poems: Johnny's Song and Warrior for Peace.
10. The Washington Post published rave reviews of Veteran's Day, an autobiography by Rod Kane.

1. Of the many Vietnam veterans who are writers, Oliver Stone is perhaps the most famous for writing and directing the films Platoon and Born on the Fourth of July.
2. Tim O'Brien has written short stories for Esquire, GQ, and Massachusetts Review.
3. Going After Cacciato is O'Brien's dreamlike novel about the horrors of combat.
4. The word Vietnam is technically two words (Viet and Nam), but most American writers spell it as one word.
5. American writers use words or phrases borrowed from the Vietnamese language, such as di di mau ("go quickly") or dinky dau ("crazy").
6. Philip Caputo's gripping account of his service in Vietnam appears in the book A Rumor of War.
7. Caputo's book was made into a television movie, also titled A Rumor of War.
8. David Rabe's plays—including The Basic Training of Pavlo Hummel, Streamers, and Sticks and Bones—depict the effects of the war not only on the soldiers but on their families.
9. Called the poet laureate of the Vietnam war, Steve Mason has published two collections of poems: Johnny's Song and Warrior for Peace.
10. The Washington Post published rave reviews of Veteran's Day, an autobiography by Rod Kane.

NOTE See page 452 for an exercise involving underlining (italics) along with capitals and other mechanics.

Chapter 28 Abbreviations

HIGHLIGHTS

The discussion in this chapter covers the rules for using abbreviations in general writing. The first four sections cover the use of standard abbreviations for titles, the appropriate use of familiar abbreviations and acronyms, the abbreviations that accompany dates and numbers to show time and amount, and the use of common Latin abbreviations. The last two sections deal with the misuse of abbreviations.

ADDITIONAL RULES

Civil and military titles are abbreviated only when used before a full name, not before the last name only.

Scholarly degrees are abbreviated when the degree follows a name. When a name is followed by an abbreviated title, no other title goes before the name.

The following guidelines on abbreviations pertain to the text of a nontechnical document. All academic disciplines use abbreviations in source citations, and much technical writing, such as in the sciences and engineering, uses many abbreviations in the document text. Consult one of the style guides listed on pages 696, 707, and 729 for the in-text requirements of the discipline you are writing in.

NOTE Usage varies, but writers increasingly omit periods from abbreviations of two or more words written in all-capital letters: *US, BA, USMC.* See page 361 on punctuating abbreviations.

28a Use standard abbreviations for titles immediately before and after proper names.

BEFORE THE NAME	AFTER THE NAME
Dr. James Hsu	James Hsu, MD
Mr., Mrs., Ms., Hon., St.,	DDS, DVM, Ph.D., Ed.D.,
Rev., Msgr., Gen.	OSB, SJ, Sr., Jr.

Use abbreviations such as *Rev., Hon., Prof., Rep., Sen., Dr.,* and *St.* (for *Saint*) only if they appear with a proper name. Spell them out in the absence of a proper name.

NOT We learned to trust the Dr.

BUT We learned to trust the *doctor.*

OR We learned to trust *Dr. Kaplan.*

The abbreviations for academic degrees—*Ph.D., MA, BA,* and the like—may be used without a proper name: *My brother took*

IBID. AND OP. CIT.

Many students are unsure about how to use scholarly abbreviations like *ibid.* ("in the same place") or *op. cit.* ("in the work cited"). These Latin abbreviations are no longer used in the citation styles of the Modern Language Association, American Psychological Association, or Council of Biology Editors. The *Chicago Manual of Style* still sanctions the use of *ibid.* in some circumstances; see 40b.

Abbreviations for nontechnical writing

- Titles before or after proper names: Dr. *Jorge Rodriguez; Jorge Rodriguez,* Ph.D. (p. 441).
- Familiar abbreviations and acronyms: *USA, AIDS* (below).
- *BC, AD, AM, PM, no.,* and *$* with dates and numbers (below).
- *I.e., e.g.,* and other Latin abbreviations within parentheses and in source citations (p. 443).
- *Inc., Bros., Co.,* and *&* with names of business firms (p. 443).

seven years to get his Ph.D. It will probably take me just as long to earn my BA.

COLLABORATIVE LEARNING

ABBREVIATIONS AND ARTICLES (ESL)

Abbreviations and acronyms can be particularly challenging for nonnative writers; for instance, when do we use words like *a, an,* or *the* (*the FBI* but *NATO*)? Encourage ESL students to build a word list of abbreviations and acronyms and sort them by the use (or nonuse) of such markers.

28b Familiar abbreviations and acronyms are acceptable in most writing.

An **acronym** is an abbreviation that spells a pronounceable word, such as WHO, NATO, and AIDS. These and other abbreviations using initials are acceptable in most writing as long as they are familiar. Abbreviations of two or more words written in all-capital letters may be written without periods (see p. 361).

INSTITUTIONS	LSU, UCLA, TCU
ORGANIZATIONS	CIA, FBI, YMCA, AFL-CIO
CORPORATIONS	IBM, CBS, ITT
PEOPLE	JFK, LBJ, FDR
COUNTRIES	USA

NOTE If a name or term (such as *operating room*) appears often in a piece of writing, then its abbreviation (*OR*) can cut down on extra words. Spell out the full term at its first appearance, give its abbreviation in parentheses, and use the abbreviation from then on.

ab 28c

28c Use *BC, AD, AM, PM, no.,* and *$* only with specific dates and numbers.

44 BC	8:05 PM (*or* p.m.)	no. 36 (*or* No. 36)
AD 1492	11:26 AM (*or* a.m.)	$7.41

NOT Hospital routine is easier to follow in the AM than in the PM.

BUT Hospital routine is easier to follow in the *morning* than in the *afternoon* or *evening*.

NOTE The abbreviation BC ("before Christ") always follows a date, whereas AD (*anno Domini,* Latin for "in the year of the Lord") precedes a date. Increasingly, these abbreviations are being replaced by BCE ("before the common era") and CE ("common era"), respectively. Both follow the date.

28d Generally, reserve Latin abbreviations for source citations and comments in parentheses.

i.e. *id est:* that is
cf. *confer:* compare
e.g. *exempli gratia:* for example
et al. *et alii:* and others
etc. *et cetera:* and so forth
NB *nota bene:* note well

He said he would be gone a fortnight (i.e., two weeks).
Bloom et al., editors, *Anthology of Light Verse*
Trees, too, are susceptible to disease (e.g., Dutch elm disease).

(Note that these abbreviations are generally not italicized or underlined.)

Some writers avoid these abbreviations in formal writing, even within parentheses.

INFORMAL The cabs of some modern farm machines (e.g., combines) look like airplane cockpits.

FORMAL The cabs of some modern farm machines (for example, combines) look like airplane cockpits.

28e Use *Inc., Bros., Co.,* or *&* (for *and*) only in official names of business firms.

NOT The Santini bros. operate a large moving firm in New York City.

BUT *The Santini brothers* operate a large moving firm in New York City.

OR *Santini Bros.* is a large moving firm in New York City.

NOT We read about the Hardy Boys & Nancy Drew.

BUT We read about the Hardy Boys *and* Nancy Drew.

ab 28f

28f Generally spell out units of measurement and names of places, calendar designations, people, and courses.

In most academic, general, and business writing, certain words should always be spelled out. (In source citations and technical writing, however, these words are more often abbreviated.)

WHEN TO ABBREVIATE

Many writers use abbreviations like *in.* or *yr.* in their drafts. However, in all but informal or technical writing situations, the audience expects such abbreviations to be spelled out. Writers who don't want to confuse their readers will make sure that their final drafts meet these expectations.

Units of measurement

The dog is thirty *inches* [not *in.*] high.
The building is 150 *feet* [not *ft.*] tall.

Exception Long phrases such as *miles per hour* (m.p.h.) or *cycles per second* (c.p.s.) are usually abbreviated, with or without periods: *The speed limit on that road was once 75 m.p.h.* (or *mph*).

Geographical names

The publisher is in *Massachusetts* [not *Mass.* or *MA*].
He came from Auckland, *New Zealand* [not *NZ*].
She lived on Morrissey *Boulevard* [not *Blvd.*].

Exceptions The United States is often referred to as the USA or the US. In writing of the US capital, we use the abbreviation DC for District of Columbia when it follows the city's name: Washington, DC.

Names of days, months, and holidays

The truce was signed on *Tuesday* [not *Tues.*], *April* [not *Apr.*] 16.
The *Christmas* [not *Xmas*] holidays are uneventful.

Names of people

James [not *Jas.*] Bennett ran for that seat.
Robert [not *Robt.*] Frost writes accessible poems.

Courses of instruction

I'm majoring in *political science* [not *poli. sci.*].
Economics [not *Econ.*] is a difficult course.

ab 28f

ANSWERS: EXERCISE

1. In the September 17, 1993, issue of *Science* magazine, Virgil L. Sharpton discusses a theory that could help explain the extinction of dinosaurs.
2. About 65 million years ago, a comet or asteroid crashed into the earth.
3. The result was a huge crater about 10 kilometers (6.2 miles) deep in the Gulf of Mexico.
4. Sharpton's new measurements suggest that the crater is 50 percent larger than scientists previously believed.
5. Indeed, 20-year-old drilling cores reveal that the crater is about 186 miles wide, roughly the size of Connecticut.
6. Sentence correct.
7. On impact, 200,000 cubic kilometers of rock and soil were vaporized or thrown into the air.

Exercise
Revising: Abbreviations

Revise the following sentences as needed to correct inappropriate use of abbreviations for nontechnical writing. Circle the number preceding any sentences in which the abbreviations are already appropriate as written.

Example:
One prof. lectured for five hrs.
One *professor* lectured for five *hours.*

1. In the Sept. 17, 1993, issue of *Science* magazine, Virgil L. Sharpton discusses a theory that could help explain the extinction of dinosaurs.
2. About 65 mill. yrs. ago, a comet or asteroid crashed into the earth.
3. The result was a huge crater about 10 km. (6.2 mi.) deep in the Gulf of Mex.
4. Sharpton's new measurements suggest that the crater is 50 pct. larger than scientists previously believed.

5. Indeed, 20-yr.-old drilling cores reveal that the crater is about 186 mi. wide, roughly the size of Conn.
6. The space object was traveling more than 100,000 m.p.h. and hit earth with the impact of 100 to 300 million megatons of TNT.
7. On impact, 200,000 cubic km. of rock and soil were vaporized or thrown into the air.
8. That's the equivalent of 2.34 bill. cubic ft. of matter.
9. The impact would have created 400-ft. tidal waves across the Atl. Ocean, temps. higher than 20,000 degs., and powerful earthquakes.
10. Sharpton theorizes that the dust, vapor, and smoke from this impact blocked the sun's rays for mos., cooled the earth, and thus resulted in the death of the dinosaurs.

Note See page 452 for an exercise involving abbreviations along with capitals and other mechanics.

8. That's the equivalent of 2.34 billion cubic feet of matter.
9. The impact would have created 400-foot tidal waves across the Atlantic Ocean, temperatures higher than 20,000 degrees, and powerful earthquakes.
10. Sharpton theorizes that the dust, vapor, and smoke from the impact blocked the sun's rays for months, cooled the earth, and thus resulted in the death of the dinosaurs.

HIGHLIGHTS

The representation of numbers in general writing is the subject of this chapter. The rules for when to use figures for numbers and when to write out numbers are few and easily memorized.

Chapter 29 Numbers

This chapter addresses the use of numbers (numerals versus words) in the text of a document. All disciplines use many more numerals in source citations.

USING NUMBERS

Audience expectations dictate whether or not numbers are spelled out. As the text notes, audiences that routinely use numerical data, like engineers or accountants, generally prefer figures. Other audiences, including other academic readers and general readers, follow the guidelines discussed here.

29a Use numerals according to standard practice in the field you are writing in.

Always use numerals for numbers that require more than two words to spell out.

> The leap year has *366* days.
> The population of Minot, North Dakota, is about *32,800.*

In nontechnical academic writing, spell out numbers of one or two words.

> *Twelve* nations signed the treaty.
>
> The ball game drew *forty-two thousand* people. [A hyphenated number may be considered one word.]

In much business writing, use numerals for all numbers over ten (*five reasons, 11 participants*). In technical academic and business writing, such as in science and engineering, use numerals for all numbers over ten, and use numerals for zero through nine when they refer to exact measurements (*2 liters, 1 hour*). (Technical usage does vary from discipline to discipline. Consult one of the style guides listed on pp. 707 and 729 for more details.)

Note Use a combination of numerals and words for round numbers over a million: *26 million, 2.45 billion.* And use either all numerals or all words when several numbers appear together in a passage, even if convention would require a mixture.

Inconsistent The satellite Galatea is about *twenty-six thousand* miles from Neptune. It is *110* miles in diameter and orbits Neptune in just over *ten* hours.

Revised The satellite Galatea is about *26,000* miles from Neptune. It is *110* miles in diameter and orbits Neptune in just over *10* hours.

ESL In American English a comma separates the numerals in long numbers (*26,000*), and a period functions as a decimal point (*2.06*).

29b Use numerals according to convention for dates, addresses, and other information.

Even when a number requires one or two words to spell out, we conventionally use numerals in the following situations:

Days and years

June 18, 1985 AD 12 456 BC 1999

Exception The day of a month may be expressed in words when it is not followed by a year (*June fifth; October first*).

Pages, chapters, volumes, acts, scenes, lines

Chapter 9, page 123
Isaiah 28:1 in the Bible
Hamlet, act 5, scene 3, lines 35–40

Decimals, percentages, and fractions

22.5
48% (*or* 48 percent)
3½

Addresses

RD 2
419 Stonewall Street
Washington, DC 20036

Scores and statistics

21 to 7
a mean of 26
a ratio of 8 to 1

Exact amounts of money

$4.50
$3.5 million (*or* $3,500,000)
$2,763 (or $2763)

The time of day

9:00 AM
3:45 AM
2:30 PM

Exceptions Round dollar or cent amounts of only a few words may be expressed in words: *seventeen dollars; fifteen hundred dollars; sixty cents.* When the word *o'clock* is used for the time of day, also express the number in words: *two o'clock* (not *2 o'clock*).

ADDITIONAL EXAMPLES

Biblical reference

II Kings 3.6

Measurements

55 miles per hour
2 liters
1 tablespoon
9 × 12-inch paper or 9″ × 12″ paper

DRAMATIC REFERENCES

The MLA recommends the numbers alone, separated by periods, for acts, scenes, and lines: *Hamlet* 5.1.35.

29c Always spell out numbers that begin sentences.

For clarity, spell out any number that begins a sentence. If the number requires more than two words, reword the sentence so that the number falls later and can be expressed as a numeral.

Not *3.3 billion* people live in Asia.
But The population of Asia is *3.3 billion.*

Exercise
Revising: Numbers

Revise the following sentences so that numbers are used appropriately for nontechnical writing. Circle the number preceding any sentence in which numbers are already used appropriately.

Example:
Carol paid two hundred five dollars for used scuba gear.
Carol paid $205 for used scuba gear.

1. The planet Saturn is nine hundred million miles, or nearly one billion five hundred million kilometers, from Earth.
2. Saturn revolves around the sun much more slowly than Earth does: a year on Saturn equals almost thirty of our years.
3. Thus, Saturn orbits the sun only two and four-tenths times during the average human life span.
4. It travels in its orbit at about twenty-one thousand six hundred miles per hour.
5. 15 to 20 times denser than Earth's core, Saturn's core measures 17,000 miles across.
6. The temperature at Saturn's cloud tops is minus one hundred seventy degrees Fahrenheit.
7. In nineteen hundred thirty-three, astronomers found on Saturn's surface a huge white spot 2 times the size of Earth and 7 times the size of Mercury.
8. Saturn's famous rings reflect almost seventy percent of the sunlight that approaches the planet.
9. The ring system is almost forty thousand miles wide, beginning 8,800 miles from the planet's visible surface and ending forty-seven thousand miles from that surface.
10. Saturn generates about one hundred thirty trillion kilowatts of electricity.

Note See page 452 for an exercise involving numbers along with abbreviations and other mechanics.

ANSWERS: EXERCISE

1. The planet Saturn is <u>900</u> million miles, or <u>1.5 billion</u> kilometers, from Earth.
2. Sentence correct.
3. Thus, Saturn orbits the sun only <u>2.4</u> times during the average human life span.
4. It travels in its orbit at about <u>21,600</u> miles per hour.
5. <u>Fifteen</u> to <u>twenty</u> times denser than Earth's core, Saturn's core measures <u>seventeen thousand</u> miles across.
6. The temperature at Saturn's cloud tops is <u>–170</u> degrees Fahrenheit.
7. In <u>1933</u>, astronomers found on Saturn's surface a huge white spot <u>two</u> times the size of Earth and <u>seven</u> times the size of Mercury.
8. Saturn's famous rings reflect almost <u>70</u> percent of the sunlight that approaches the planet.
9. The ring system is almost <u>40,000</u> miles wide, beginning 8,800 miles from the planet's visible surface and ending <u>47,000</u> miles from that surface.
10. Saturn generates about <u>130</u> trillion kilowatts of electricity.

Chapter 30

Word Division

HIGHLIGHTS

This chapter addresses one of the most frequent trouble spots in the mechanics of student writing—word division. Though errors in division are not more than misdemeanors, students can avoid the irritation and confusion that such errors afford readers by memorizing the few rules pertaining to word division.

As much as possible, avoid dividing words. If you must divide a word between the end of one line and the beginning of the next, follow these guidelines:

- Divide words only between syllables. (Consult a dictionary if necessary.)
- Put a hyphen at the end of the first line, never at the beginning of the second line.
- Try not to divide the last word on a page. In the act of turning the page, the reader may forget the beginning of the word.

Not all syllable breaks are appropriate for word division. Use the following rules to decide when and how to divide words.

NOTE Most word-processing programs will divide words automatically at appropriate breaks when you instruct them to do so.

COMPUTER EXERCISE

COMPUTER PUNCTUATION

Computer hyphenation programs may place hyphens in unacceptable positions, producing awkward or incorrect word divisions. Remind students to check their hyphens visually to avoid confusing their readers. *The Washington Post Deskbook on Style* by Robert A. Webb (New York: McGraw-Hill, 1978) has an especially useful section on hyphenation.

30a Leave at least two letters at the end of a line and at least three letters at the beginning of a line.

FAULTY A newspaper or television editorial for or *a-gainst* a candidate can sway an election.

REVISED A newspaper or television editorial for or *against* a candidate can sway an election.

FAULTY Counseling is required for every child *abus-er.*

REVISED Counseling is required for every child *abuser.*

30b One-syllable words should not be divided.

Since one-syllable words have no break in pronunciation, they should not be divided.

FAULTY	The shiny, spinning space capsule *drop-* *ped* suddenly from the clouds.
REVISED	The shiny, spinning space capsule *dropped* suddenly from the clouds.

30c Divide compound words only between the words that form them or at fixed hyphens.

Compound words are made up of two or more words (*draw-back, homecoming*). Their component words may be separated by a hyphen (*well-paying, cross-reference*), in which case the hyphen is called **fixed.** Compound words should be divided only between their component words and at fixed hyphens.

FAULTY	If you want to have friends, be *good-na-* *tured.*
REVISED	If you want to have friends, be *good-* *natured.*

(See pp. 512–14 for guidelines on when to use hyphens in spelling compound words.)

30d Make sure a word division will not confuse readers.

Some word divisions may momentarily confuse readers because the first or second part by itself forms a pronounceable (or unpronounceable) unit that does not fit with the whole—for example, *poi-gnant, read-dress, in-dict.* Avoid word divisions like these.

CONFUSING	Her walking out of class was an act of *her-* *oism.*
CLEAR	Her walking out of class was an act of *hero-* *ism.*

Exercise
Revising: Word division

Revise the following sentences to improve inappropriate word divisions. Consult a dictionary if necessary. Circle the number preceding any sentence in which word division is already appropriate.

Example:

I thought Harry's joke was sidesplit-
ting, but no one else even smiled.

I thought Harry's joke was *side-*
splitting, but no one else even smiled.

1. Samuel Johnson, British essayist and poet, compiled the first real dictionary of the English language.
2. He followed a method used by dictionary makers ever since.
3. First, he read books about a wide range of subjects.
4. As a result he was probably the most well-edu-
cated man in England.
5. When he saw a new use for a word, he marked the passage for his secretary to copy.
6. Since Johnson used a dark pencil to underline the passages, the books were damaged.
7. The books' owners were shocked when their well-thumb-
ed and smudged volumes were returned.
8. The words were arranged alphabetically in large ledger books, with e-
nough room between words for definitions.
9. For each word the definitions were organized with specialized uses last.
10. Finally, Johnson's secretaries recopi-
ed the entries onto clean paper for typesetting.

NOTE See the next page for an exercise involving word division along with capitals and other mechanics.

COLLABORATIVE LEARNING

Have students work in small groups to complete this exercise. You might ask each group to present one paragraph of the revised piece on the blackboard, to explain the changes they made, and to give their reasons for each change.

ANSWERS: EXERCISE

1. Sentence correct.
2. He followed a method used by dictionary makers
ever since.
3. Sentence correct.
4. As a result, he was probably the most well-
educated man in England.
5. When he saw a new use for a word, he
marked the passage for his secretary to copy.
6. Sentence correct.
7. The books' owners were shocked when their well-
thumbed and smudged volumes were returned.
8. The words were arranged alphabetically in large ledger books, with
enough room between words for definitions.
9. Sentence correct.
10. Finally, Johnson's secretaries recop-
ied the entries onto clean paper for typesetting.

ANSWERS: EXERCISE ON CHAPTERS 26–30

According to many sources—for example, the Cambridge Ancient History and Gardiner's Egypt of the Pharaohs—the ancient Egyptians devoted much attention to making life more convenient and pleasurable for themselves.

Our word pharaoh for the ancient Egyptian rulers comes from the Egyptian word pr`o, meaning "great house." Indeed, the Egyptians placed great emphasis on family residences, adding small bedrooms as early as 3500 BC. By 3000 BC, the Egyptians made ice through evaporation of water at night and then used it to cool their homes. About the same time they used fans made of palm fronds or papyrus to cool themselves in the day. To light their homes, the Egyptians abandoned the animal-fat lamps humans had used for fifty thousand years. Instead, around 1300 BC the people of Egypt devised the first oil lamps.

Egyptians found great pleasure in playing games. Around 4300 years ago they created one of the oldest board games known. The game involved racing ivory or stone pieces across a papyrus playing board. By 3000 BC, Egyptian children played marbles with semiprecious stones, some of which have been found in gravesites at Nagada, Egypt. Around 1300 BC, small children played with clay rattles covered (or cov-ered) in silk and shaped like animals.

To play the game of love, Egyptian men and women experimented with cosmetics applied to skin and eyelids. Kohl, history's first eyeliner, was used by both sexes to ward off evil. Five thousand years ago Egyptians wore wigs made of vegetable fibers or human hair. In 900 BC, Queen Isimkheb wore a wig so heavy that she needed assistance in walking. To adjust their make-up and wigs, Egyptians (or Egyp-tians) adapted the simple metal mirrors devised by the Sumerians in the Bronze Age, ornamenting them with carved handles of ivory, gold, or wood. Feeling that only those who smelled sweet could be attractive, the Egyptians made deodorants from perfumed oils, for example, cinnamon and citrus.

Exercise on Chapters 26–30
Revising: Mechanics

Revise the paragraphs below to correct any errors in the use of capital letters, underlining, abbreviations, numbers, and word division. (For abbreviations and numbers follow standard practice for nontechnical writing.) Consult a dictionary as needed.

According to many sources—e.g., the Cambridge Ancient History and Gardiner's Egypt of the Pharaohs—the
ancient egyptians devoted much attention to making Life
more convenient and pleasurable for themselves.

Our word pharaoh for the ancient egyptian rulers
comes from the egyptian word pr‘o, meaning "great house."
Indeed, the egyptians placed great emphasis on family res-
idences, adding small bedrms. as early as 3500 yrs. b.c.
By 3000 b.c., the egyptians made ice through evaporation
of water at night and then used it to cool their homes. A-
bout the same time they used fans made of palm fronds or
papyrus to cool themselves in the day. To light their
homes, the egyptians abandoned the animal-fat lamps Humans
had used for 50 thousand yrs. Instead, around 1300 b.c.
the people of Egt. devised the 1st oil lamps.

egyptians found great pleasure in playing games. Four
thousand three hundred yrs. ago or so they created one of
the oldest board games known. the game involved racing ivory
or stone pieces across a papyrus playing board. By three
thousand b.c., egyptian children played marbles with semiprecious stones, some of which have been found in gravesites at nagada, EG. Around one thousand three hundred
sixty b.c., small children played with clay rattles covered in silk and shaped like animals.

To play the game of love, egyptian men and women experimented with cosmetics applied to skin and eyelids.
kohl, history's first eyeliner, was used by both sexes
to ward off evil. 5000 yrs. ago egyptians wore wigs
made of vegetable fibers or human hair. In 9 hundred b.c.,
queen Isimkheb wore a wig so heavy that she needed assistance in walking. To adjust their make-up and wigs, e-
gyptians adapted the simple metal mirrors devised
by the sumerians in the bronze age, ornamenting them with
carved handles of ivory, gold, or wood. Feeling that only
those who smelled sweet could be attractive, the egyptians
made deodorants from perfumed oils, e.g., cinnamon and
citrus.

Part VII

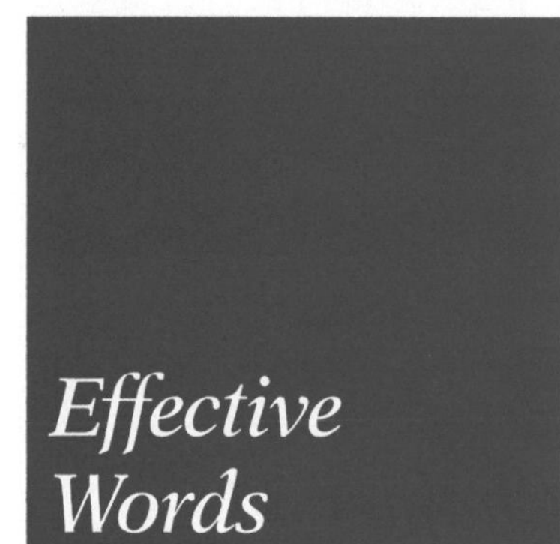

HIGHLIGHTS

There's no substitute for experience in helping students choose the right words, and students with limited experience in reading and writing, or whose first language is not English, may find diction a formidable hurdle. Time, encouragement, and careful explanations can help them gain confidence. Almost as difficult as choosing the right words is eliminating unnecessary ones. Students often revert to very simple sentence structures when they begin to cut flab from their sentences. You'll have to help them see that lean sentences can still be complex ones. If your campus has a writing center, check to see if it offers drills or instructional materials to help students improve their resources in language.

This edition of *The Little, Brown Handbook* includes much more material on biased language (31a-8): avoiding stereotypes of all kinds, avoiding sexist language, and using appropriate labels.

A WRITER'S PERSPECTIVE

Whenever we come upon one of those intensely right words . . . the resulting effect is physical as well as spiritual, and electrically prompt.

—MARK TWAIN, "William Dean Howells"

Chapter 31

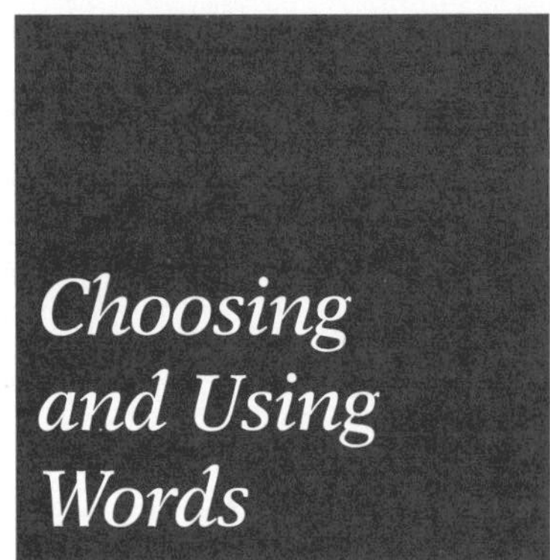

Expressing yourself clearly and effectively depends greatly on what words you choose and how you employ them in sentences. English offers an uncommonly rich and extensive vocabulary from which to select the words that precisely suit your meaning and your writing situation (31a and 31b). And the language is uncommonly flexible when it comes to pruning unneeded words that make writing weak or inexact (31c).

31a Choosing the appropriate word

Appropriate words suit your writing situation—your subject, purpose, and audience. Like everyone, you vary your words depending on the context in which you are speaking and writing. Look, for example, at the italicized words in these two sentences:

> Some patients decide to *bag* counseling because their *shrinks* seem *strung out.*
>
> Some patients decide to *abandon* counseling because their *therapists* seem *disturbed.*

The first sentence might be addressed to friends in casual conversation. The second sentence, in contrast, is more formal, more suitable for an academic audience.

The more formal diction of the second example is typical of what's called **standard English.** This is the written English normally expected and used in school, business, the professions, government, newspapers, and other sites where people of diverse backgrounds

Diction in academic and business writing

ALWAYS APPROPRIATE
Standard English (see facing page)

SOMETIMES APPROPRIATE
Regional words and expressions (p. 456)
Slang (p. 456)
Colloquial language (p. 457)
Neologisms (p. 458)
Technical language (p. 458)
Euphemisms (p. 458)

RARELY OR NEVER APPROPRIATE
Dialect (below)
Nonstandard language (below)
Archaic and obsolete words (p. 458)
Double talk (p. 459)
Pretentious writing (p. 459)
Biased language: sexist, racist, ethnocentric, etc. (p. 459)

must communicate with one another. It is "standard" not because it is better than other forms of English, but because it is accepted as the common language, much as dimes and quarters are accepted as the common currency.

The vocabulary of standard English is huge, allowing expression of an infinite range of ideas and feelings; but it does exclude words that only limited groups of people use, understand, or find inoffensive. Some of those more limited vocabularies should be avoided altogether; others should be used cautiously and in special situations, as when aiming for a special effect with an audience you know will appreciate it. Whenever you doubt a word's status, consult a dictionary (see pp. 486–87).

NOTE Many computerized style-checking programs will highlight and question nonstandard language, slang, colloquialisms, and other words whose appropriateness may be doubtful. When using such a program, you'll need to determine whether the flagged language is or is not appropriate for your writing situation, as explained below. (See p. 774 for more on style-checking programs.)

1 Revising dialect and nonstandard language

Like many countries, the United States consists of scores of regional, social, or ethnic groups with their own distinct **dialects,** or versions of English. Standard English is one of these dialects, and so is Black English, Appalachian English, Creole, and the English of coastal Maine. All the dialects of English share many features, but each also has its own vocabulary, pronunciation, and grammar.

If you speak a dialect of English besides standard English, you need to be careful about using your dialect in situations where

TRANSPARENCY MASTER 31.1

RESOURCES AND IDEAS

Students may have heard of popular usage commentators like William Safire, John Simon, or James Kilpatrick; ask students to review books or articles by these commentators in the library, see what diction issues they consider most important, and consider whether they agree. A good counterpoint to such commentators is Harvey A. Daniels's *Famous Last Words: The American Language Crisis Reconsidered* (Urbana: NCTE, 1983). See also, Bill Bryson's *Made in America: An Informal History of the English Language in the United States* (New York: Morrow, 1994) for an appealing historical overview of shifts in usage.

RESOURCES AND IDEAS

Simpson, Mary Scott. "Teaching Writing: Beginning with the Word." *College English* 39 (1978): 934–39. The author describes class activities and readings designed to develop sensitivity to words and build vocabulary.

HUCK FINN

You may wish to make the following examples the subject of class discussion. Students usually find them quite interesting.

In his explanatory note at the beginning of *The Adventures of Huckleberry Finn,* Mark Twain explains one of the difficulties with using nonstandard language:

> In this book a number of dialects are used, to wit: the Missouri negro dialect; the extremist form of the backwoods Southwestern dialect; the ordinary "Pike County" dialect; and four modified varieties of this last. The shadings have not been done in a haphazard fashion, or by guesswork; but painstakingly, and with the trustworthy guidance and support of personal familiarity with these several forms of speech. I make this explanation for the reason that without it many readers would suppose that all these characters were trying to talk alike and not succeeding.
>
> —THE AUTHOR

From the opening lines of *The Adventures of Huckleberry Finn:*

> You don't know about me without you have read a book by the name of *The Adventures of Tom Sawyer;* but that ain't no matter. That book was made by Mr. Mark Twain, and he told the truth, mainly. There was things which he stretched; but mainly he told the truth. That is nothing. I never seen anybody but lied one time or another, without it was Aunt Polly, or the widow, or maybe Mary. Aunt Polly—Tom's Aunt Polly, she is—and Mary, and the widow Douglas is all told about in that book, which is mostly a true book, with some stretchers, as I said before.

COLLABORATIVE LEARNING

STUDYING SLANG

Encourage students to collect examples of college slang and write about what they find. They can compare their research with the collections published in *College Slang 101* by Connie Eble (Georgetown: Spectacle Lane, 1989) or *Slang U* by Pamela Munro (New York: Harmony, 1989). Other topics for research reports might be the languages of rap or rock music, of some activity (skateboarding or football), or of some social group (fraternities, volunteer firefighters).

standard English is the norm, such as in academic or business writing. Otherwise, your readers may not understand your meaning, or they may perceive your usage as incorrect. (Dialects are not wrong in themselves, but forms imported from one dialect into another may still be perceived as wrong.)

Your participation in the community of standard English does not require you to abandon your own dialect. Of course, you will want to use it with others who speak it. You may want to quote it in an academic paper (as when analyzing or reporting conversation in dialect). And you may want to use it in writing you do for yourself, such as journals, notes, and drafts, which should be composed as freely as possible. But edit your drafts carefully to eliminate dialect expressions, especially those, like the ones below, that dictionaries label "nonstandard."

hisn, hern, hisself, theirselves
them books, them courses
this here school, that there building
knowed, throwed, hadn't ought, could of
didn't never, haven't no

 Using regionalisms only when appropriate

Regionalisms are expressions or pronunciations peculiar to a particular area. Southerners may say they *reckon,* meaning "think" or "suppose." People in Maine invite their Boston friends to come *down* rather than *up* (north) to visit. New Yorkers stand *on* rather than *in* line for a movie. Regional expressions are appropriate in writing addressed to local readers and may lend realism to regional description, but they should be avoided in writing intended for a general audience.

REGIONAL The Pentagon lies *down the road a piece* from Arlington National Cemetery.

REVISED The Pentagon lies *a short distance* from Arlington National Cemetery.

 Using slang only when appropriate

All groups of people—from musicians and computer scientists to vegetarians and golfers—create novel and colorful expressions called **slang.** The following quotation, for instance, is from an essay on the slang of "skaters" (skateboarders).

> Curtis slashed ultra-punk crunchers on his longboard, while the Rube-man flailed his usual Gumbyness on tweaked frontsides and lofty fakie ollies. —MILES ORKIN, "Mucho Slingage by the Pool"

"Slang," Orkin goes on to say, "is a convenient, creative, mildly poetic, cohesive agent in many subcultures." It reflects the experiences of a group and binds its members.

Some slang gives new meaning to old words, such as *bad* for "good." Some slang comes from other languages, such as *chow* (food) from the Chinese *chao,* "to stir or fry." The slang of a particular group may also spread to other groups, as *out to lunch, put on ice, funky,* and *dis* have spread beyond their African American origins.

Among those who understand it, slang may be vivid and forceful. It often occurs in dialogue, and an occasional slang expression can enliven an informal essay. Some slang, such as *dropout* (*She was a high school dropout*), has proved so useful that it has passed into the general vocabulary.

But most slang is too flippant and imprecise for effective communication, and it is generally inappropriate for college or business writing. Notice the gain in seriousness and precision achieved in the following revision.

Slang Many students start out *pretty together* but then *get weird.*

Revised Many students start out *with clear goals* but then *lose their direction.*

4 Using colloquial language only when appropriate

Colloquial language designates the words and expressions appropriate to everyday spoken language. Regardless of our backgrounds and how we live, we all try to *get along with* each other. We play with *kids, go crazy* about one thing, *crab* about something else, and in our worst moments try to *get back at* someone who has made us do the *dirty work.*

When you write informally, colloquial language may be appropriate to achieve the casual, relaxed effect of conversation. An occasional colloquial word dropped into otherwise more formal writing can also help you achieve a desired emphasis. But colloquial language does not provide the exactness needed in more formal college, business, and professional writing. In such writing you should generally avoid any words and expressions labeled "informal" or "colloquial" in your dictionary. Take special care to avoid **mixed diction,** a combination of standard and colloquial words.

Mixed diction According to a Native American myth, the Great Creator *had a dog hanging around with him* when he created the earth.

Revised According to a Native American myth, the Great Creator *was accompanied by a dog* when he created the earth.

Revising obsolete or archaic words and neologisms

Since our surroundings and our lives are constantly changing, some words pass out of use and others appear to fill new needs. **Obsolete** and **archaic** are dictionary labels for words or meanings of words that we never or rarely use but that appear in older documents and literature still read today. Obsolete words or meanings are no longer used at all—for example, *enwheel* ("to encircle") and *cote* ("to pass"). Archaic words or meanings occur now only in special contexts such as poetry—for example, *fast* ("near," as in *fast by the road*) and *belike* ("perhaps"). Both obsolete and archaic words are inappropriate in nonfiction writing for an academic audience.

Neologisms are words created (or coined) so recently that they have not come into established use. An example is *prequel* (made up of *pre-,* meaning "before," and the ending of *sequel*), a movie or book that takes the story of an existing movie or book back in time. Some neologisms do become accepted as part of our general vocabulary—*motel,* coined from *motor* and *hotel,* is an example. But most neologisms pass quickly from the language. Unless such words serve a special purpose in your writing and are sure to be understood by your readers, you should avoid them.

TECHNICAL JARGON

Using technical language is appropriate when both writers and readers understand the specialized body of knowledge to which the technical language refers. Have students practice translating between technical and nontechnical language to gain experience in deciding what level of language might be appropriate for particular situations. For a study of the sources of academic and newspaper jargon see Walter Nash's *Jargon: Its Uses and Abuses* (Oxford: Blackwell, 1993).

Using technical words with care

All disciplines and professions rely on special words or give common words special meanings. Chemists speak of *esters* and *phosphatides,* geographers and mapmakers refer to *isobars* and *isotherms,* and literary critics write about *motifs* and *subtexts.* Such technical language allows specialists to communicate precisely and economically with other specialists who share their vocabulary. But without explanation these words are meaningless to nonspecialists. When you are writing for nonspecialists, avoid unnecessary technical terms and carefully define terms you must use.

OVERBLOWN LANGUAGE

A good way to help students understand how pretentious language gets in the way of understanding is to give them "fancied-up" versions of common expressions and ask them to translate them. You might start with "Permit me to express my heartfelt felicitations on the celebration of your natal anniversary" for "Happy birthday" or "Scintillate, scintillate, asteroidal nimific" for "Twinkle, twinkle, little star," and work from there.

Revising indirect or pretentious writing

In most writing, small, plain, and direct words are preferable to big, showy, or evasive words. Avoid euphemisms, double talk, and pretentious writing.

A **euphemism** is a presumably inoffensive word that a writer or speaker substitutes for a word deemed potentially offensive or too blunt, such as *passed away* for *died.* Euphemisms appear whenever a writer or speaker wants to bury the truth, as when a governor mentions the *negative growth* (meaning decline) in her state. Use euphemisms only when you know that blunt, truthful words would needlessly hurt or offend members of your audience.

A kind of euphemism that deliberately evades the truth is **double talk** (also called **doublespeak** or **weasel words**): language intended to confuse or to be misunderstood. Today double talk is unfortunately common in politics and advertising—the *revenue enhancement* that is really a tax, the *biodegradable* bags that last decades. Double talk has no place in honest writing.

Euphemism and sometimes double talk seem to keep company with fancy writing. Any writing that is more elaborate than its subject requires will sound **pretentious**—that is, excessively showy. Choose your words for their exactness and economy. The big, ornate word may be tempting, but pass it up. Your readers will be grateful.

PRETENTIOUS To perpetuate our endeavor of providing funds for our elderly citizens as we do at the present moment, we will face the exigency of enhanced contributions from all our citizens.

REVISED We cannot continue to fund Social Security and Medicare for the elderly unless we raise taxes.

8 Revising sexist and other biased language

Even when we do not mean it to, our language can reflect and perpetuate hurtful prejudices toward groups of people, especially racial, ethnic, religious, age, and sexual groups. Such biased language can be obvious—words such as *nigger, honky, mick, kike, fag, dyke,* or *broad.* But it can also be subtle, generalizing about groups in ways that may be familiar but that are also inaccurate or unfair. For instance, people with physical disabilities are as varied a group as any other: the only thing they have in common is some form of impairment. To assume that people with disabilities share certain attitudes (shyness, helplessness, victimization, whatever) is to disregard the uniqueness of each person.

Biased language reflects poorly on the user, not on the person or persons whom it mischaracterizes or insults. Unbiased language does not submit to false generalizations. It treats people as individuals and labels groups as they wish to be labeled.

Avoiding stereotypes of race, ethnicity, religion, age, and other characteristics

A **stereotype** is a generalization based on poor evidence, a kind of formula for understanding and judging people simply because of their membership in a group.

Men are uncommunicative.
Women are emotional.
Liberals want to raise taxes.
Conservatives are affluent.

Alternatively, you might ask students to use their computer thesaurus programs to "translate" a professional or student-written paragraph into overly embellished language. This exercise can provide the basis for a useful discussion of appropriate uses of the thesaurus.

FILL IN THE BLANKS

Distribute copies of an essay with important words deleted, and ask students to fill in the blanks with the words they can find. Discuss the choices in class or in groups as a way of building students' vocabularies and of reaching consensus on questions of appropriateness and exactness.

A WRITER'S PERSPECTIVE

A good word is like a good tree whose roots are firmly fixed and whose top is in the sky.
—*The Koran* 14:24

RESOURCES AND IDEAS

Some excellent resources for discussing sexist and biased language are:

Goueffic, Louise. *Breaking the Patriarchal Code: The Linguistic Basis of Sexual Bias.* Manchester, CT: Knowledge, Ideas and Trends, 1996. Goueffic argues for the relationship between biased language and discriminatory social practices.

Maggio, Rosalie. *The Bias-Free Word Finder.* Boston: Beacon, 1992. Originally published as *The Dictionary of Bias-Free Usage: A Guide to Nondiscriminatory Language.* Phoenix: Oryx, 1991. Maggio provides a thesaurus of bias-free synonyms for gendered terms.

Miller, Casey, and Kate Swift. *The Handbook of Nonsexist Writing (For Writers, Editors, and Speakers).* 2nd ed. New York: HarperCollins, 1988. Miller and Swift's book is the standard handbook for people concerned with avoiding linguistic sexism.

Penelope, Julia. *Speaking Freely: Unlearning the Lies of the Fathers' Tongues.* New York: Pergamon, 1990. The author provides a scathing but illuminating critique of the effects of using biased language.

At best, stereotypes betray a noncritical writer, one who is not thinking beyond notions received from others. Worse, they betray a writer who does not mind hurting others, or even *wants* to hurt others.

In your writing, be alert for any general statements about people based on only one or a few characteristics. Be especially cautious about substituting such statements for the evidence you should be providing instead.

Stereotype Immigrants live off the taxes of citizens. [Asserts that all immigrants live on public assistance funded by taxes.]

Revised In 1991 immigrants received $50.8 billion in public assistance and paid $20.3 billion in taxes.

Stereotype Elderly drivers should have their licenses limited to daytime driving. [Asserts that all elderly people are poor night drivers.]

Revised Drivers with impaired night vision should have their licenses limited to daytime driving.

Some stereotypes have become part of the language, but they are still potentially offensive.

Stereotype The administrators are too blind to see the need for a new gymnasium.

Revised The administrators do not understand the need for a new gymnasium.

Avoiding sexist language

Among the most subtle and persistent biased language is that expressing narrow ideas about men's and women's roles, position, and value in society. This **sexist language** distinguishes needlessly between men and women in such matters as occupation, ability, behavior, temperament, and maturity. Like other stereotypes, it can wound or irritate readers, and it indicates the writer's thoughtlessness or unfairness. The following box suggests some ways of eliminating sexist language.

appr
31a

TRANSPARENCY MASTER 31.2

Eliminating sexist language

- Avoid demeaning and patronizing language.

Sexist Ladies are entering almost every occupation.

Revised *Women* are entering almost every occupation.

Sexist President Reagan came to Nancy's defense.

Revised President Reagan came to *Mrs. Reagan's* defense.

- Avoid occupational or social stereotypes.

  Sexist The considerate doctor commends a nurse when she provides his patients with good care.

  Revised The considerate doctor commends a nurse *who provides good care for patients.*

  Sexist The grocery shopper should save her coupons.

  Revised *Grocery shoppers* should save *their* coupons.

- Avoid referring needlessly to gender.

  Sexist Marie Curie, a woman chemist, discovered radium.

  Revised Marie Curie, *a chemist,* discovered radium.

  Sexist The patients were tended by a male nurse.

  Revised The patients were tended by *a nurse.*

- Avoid using *man* or words containing *man* to refer to all human beings.

  Sexist Man has not reached the limits of social justice.

  Revised *Humankind* [or *Humanity*] has not reached the limits of social justice.

  Sexist The furniture consists of manmade materials.

  Revised The furniture consists of *synthetic* materials.

- Avoid using *he* to refer to both genders. (See also p. 249.)

  Sexist The newborn child explores his world.

  Revised The newborn child explores *his or her* world. [Male and female pronouns.]

  Revised Newborn *children* explore *their* world. [Plural.]

  Revised The newborn child explores *the* world. [Pronoun avoided.]

Using appropriate labels

We often need to label groups: *swimmers, politicians, mothers, Christians, westerners, students.* But labels can be shorthand stereotypes when they generalize about groups of people on the basis of a single characteristic. They can also slight the person labeled and ignore the preferences of the group members themselves. Showing sensitivity when applying labels reveals you to be alert to readers' needs and concerns. Although sometimes dismissed as "political correctness," such sensitivity hurts no one and helps gain your readers' trust and respect.

Be careful to avoid labels that (intentionally or not) disparage the person or group you refer to. A person with emotional problems is not a *mental patient.* A person with cancer is not a *cancer victim.* A person using a wheelchair is not *wheelchair-bound.*

CORRECT LANGUAGE?

Some students may see the insistence on "bias-free" writing as an instance of "political correctness" and reject it; however, if you emphasize the need to win readers' good will, and help students see that offensive language usually diminishes that good will, you may be able to show them that avoiding biased language is normally to their advantage. In the end, if a writer deliberately uses nonstandard or biased language he or she should have considered its probable effect. Anne Matthews's satiric article "Brave, New 'Cruelty-Free' World" (*New York Times,* 7 July 1991. E11) might be a good model for students to discuss and imitate, since she offers many examples of "politically correct" terms for apparently innocuous phrases.

RESOURCES AND IDEAS

Ammirati, Theresa, and Ellen Strenski. "Using Astrology to Teach Connotation and Bias." *Exercise Exchange* 25 (1980): 9–11. The authors tell how to use the language in astrology books as a source of examples of connotation and bias.

Take care also that the name you use for a group reflects the preferences of the group's members, or at least many of them. Group labels change often, so the list below is tentative. To learn the current preferences of members of racial, ethnic, religious, and other groups, ask the members themselves, attend to usage in reputable newspapers and magazines, or check a recent dictionary. A helpful reference is Marilyn Schwartz's *Guidelines for Bias-Free Writing* (1995).

African American, black
Asian, Asian American, Japanese American, etc.
Latino/Latina (Spanish speaking), Mexican American, Puerto Rican, Central American, etc.
Native American, Indian
Muslim
deaf, hearing impaired
blind, visually impaired
disabled, physically challenged
gay, lesbian, homosexual, bisexual

COLLABORATIVE LEARNING

Ask students to complete Exercise 1 individually, with the aid of their own dictionaries. Then have students work in small groups to compare their responses and debate the appropriateness of each member's substitutions. This exercise can often provide the basis for a class-wide discussion on the correlation between word choice and context.

ANSWERS: EXERCISE 1

Possible answers

1. Acquired immune deficiency syndrome (AIDS) is a serious threat all over the world.
2. The disease is transmitted primarily by sexual intercourse, exchange of bodily fluids, shared needles, and blood transfusions.
3. Those who think the disease is limited to homosexuals and drug users are quite mistaken.
4. Statistics suggest that one in every five hundred college students carries the virus.
5. People with AIDS do not deserve others' exclusion or callousness. Instead, they need all the compassion, medical care, and financial assistance due the seriously ill.
6. A person with AIDS often sees a team of doctors or a single doctor with a specialized practice.

appr 31a

Exercise 1
Revising: Appropriate words

Rewrite the following sentences as needed for standard written English. Consult a dictionary to determine whether particular words are appropriate and to find suitable substitutes.

Example:

If negotiators get hyper during contract discussions, they may mess up chances for a settlement.

If negotiators *become excited or upset* during contract discussions, they may *harm* chances for a settlement.

1. Acquired Immune Deficiency Syndrome (AIDS) is a major deal all over the world.
2. The disease gets around primarily by sexual intercourse, exchange of bodily fluids, shared needles, and blood transfusions.
3. Those who think the disease is limited to homos and druggies are quite mistaken.
4. Stats suggest that one in every five hundred college kids carries the virus.
5. A person with AIDS does not deserve to be subjected to exclusionary behavior or callousness on the part of his fellow citizens. Instead, he has the necessity for all the compassion, medical care, and financial assistance due those who are in the extremity of illness.
6. An AIDS victim often sees a team of doctors or a single doctor with a specialized practice.
7. The doctor may help his patients by obtaining social services for them as well as by providing medical care.
8. The AIDS sufferer who loses his job may need public assistance.

9. For someone who is very ill, a full-time nurse may be necessary. She can administer medications and make the sick person as comfortable as possible.
10. Some people with AIDS have insurance, but others lack the bread for premiums.

7. The doctor may help patients by obtaining social services for them as well as providing medical care.
8. The person with AIDS who loses his or her job may need public assistance.
9. For someone who is very ill, a full-time nurse may be necessary. The nurse can administer medications and make the sick person as comfortable as possible.
10. Some people with AIDS have insurance, but others lack the money for premiums.

31b Choosing the exact word

To write clearly and effectively, you will want to find the words that fit your meaning exactly and convey your attitude precisely. If, like many people, you feel uncertain about words and their meanings, consult the next two chapters, on using a dictionary (32) and improving your vocabulary (33).

Don't worry too much about choosing exact words while you are drafting an essay. If the right word doesn't come to you, leave a blank. Revision (p. 67) or editing (p. 73) is the stage to consider tone, specificity, and precision.

1 Using the right word for your meaning

Precisely expressing your meaning requires understanding both the denotations and the connotations of words. A word's **denotation** is the thing or idea it refers to, the meaning listed in the dictionary without reference to the emotional associations it may arouse in a reader. Using words according to their established denotations is essential if readers are to grasp your meaning. Here are a few guidelines:

- Become acquainted with a dictionary. Consult it whenever you are unsure of a word's meaning.
- Distinguish between similar-sounding words that have widely different denotations.

  INEXACT Older people often suffer *infirmaries* [places for the sick].
  EXACT Older people often suffer *infirmities* [disabilities].

  Some words, called **homonyms** (from the Greek meaning "same name"), sound exactly alike but differ in meaning: for example, *principal/principle* or *rain/reign/rein*. (See pp. 500–01 for a list of commonly confused homonyms.)
- Distinguish between words with related but distinct denotations.

  INEXACT Television commercials *continuously* [unceasingly] interrupt programming.
  EXACT Television commercials *continually* [regularly] interrupt programming.

COLLABORATIVE LEARNING

SYNONYMY

To help students develop their sensitivity to denotation and connotation, give them a group of words and phrases like *overweight, out of money,* and *failing the class* and ask them to come up with as many different ways of expressing the term as possible. Then, either alone or in groups, have them decide what connotations each synonym has, and for what audiences and situations they might be appropriate. (Some synonyms for *overweight,* for instance, might be *plump* [neutral], *tubby* [probably negative], *porky* [negative], and so on.)

A WRITER'S PERSPECTIVE

Proper words in proper places make the true definition of a style.

—Jonathan Swift, "Letter to a Young Clergyman"

In addition to their emotion-free denotations, many words also carry associations with specific feelings. These **connotations** can shape readers' responses and are thus a powerful tool for writers. (At the same time they are a potential snare for readers. See p. 135.) Some connotations are personal: the word *dog,* for instance, may have negative connotations for the letter carrier who has been bitten three times. Usually, though, people agree about connotations. The following word pairs are just a few of many that have related denotations but very different connotations:

pride: sense of self-worth
vanity: excessive regard for oneself

firm: steady, unchanging, unyielding
stubborn: unreasonable, bullheaded

lasting: long-lived, enduring
endless: without limit, eternal

enthusiasm: excitement
mania: excessive interest or desire

daring: brave, bold
reckless: rash, careless

Understanding connotation is especially important in choosing among **synonyms,** words with approximately, but often not exactly, the same meanings. For instance, *cry* and *weep* both denote the shedding of tears, but *cry* more than *weep* connotes a sobbing sound accompanying the tears. *Sob* itself connotes broken, gasping crying, with tears, whereas *wail* connotes sustained sound, perhaps without tears.

Several resources can help you track down words with the exact connotations you want:

- A dictionary is essential. Many dictionaries list and distinguish among synonyms (see p. 498 for an example).
- A dictionary of synonyms lists and defines synonyms in groups (see p. 484 for a title).
- A thesaurus lists synonyms but does not distinguish among them (see p. 484 for a title).

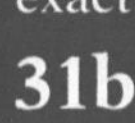

Note Because a thesaurus lacks definitions, it can only suggest possibilities. You will still need a dictionary to discover the words' exact denotations and connotations. Many computer programs offer thesauruses that make it easy to look up synonyms as you're writing and to insert the chosen word into your text. But with a computerized thesaurus, too, you must choose the word carefully to ensure that it expresses your meaning exactly. If you use such a resource without care, you could lose more in your reader's understanding and patience than you gain in efficiency. (See p. 775 for more on electronic thesauruses.)

Exercise 2
Revising: Denotation

Revise any underlined word below that is not used according to its established denotation. Circle any word used correctly. Consult a dictionary if you are uncertain of a word's precise meaning.

Example:

Sam and Dave are going to Bermuda and Hauppauge, respectfully, for spring vacation.

Sam and Dave are going to Bermuda and Hauppauge, *respectively,* for spring vacation.

1. Maxine Hong Kingston was rewarded many prizes for her first two books, *The Woman Warrior* and *China Men.*
2. Kingston sites her mother's tales about ancestors and ancient Chinese customs as the sources of these memoirs.
3. In her childhood Kingston was greatly effected by her mother's tale about a pregnant aunt who was ostracized by villagers.
4. The aunt gained avengeance by drowning herself in the village's water supply.
5. Kingston decided to make her nameless relative infamous by giving her immortality in *The Woman Warrior.*

Exercise 3
Considering the connotations of words

Fill the blank in each sentence below with the most appropriate word from the list in parentheses. Consult a dictionary to be sure of your choice.

Example:

Channel 5 _______ Oshu the winner before the polls closed. (*advertised, declared, broadcast, promulgated*)

Channel 5 *declared* Oshu the winner before the polls closed.

1. AIDS is a serious health _______. (*problem, worry, difficulty, plight*)
2. Once the virus has entered the blood system, it _______ T-cells. (*murders, destroys, slaughters, executes*)
3. The _______ of T-cells is to combat infections. (*ambition, function, aim, goal*)
4. Without enough T-cells, the body is nearly _______ against infections. (*defenseless, hopeless, desperate*)
5. To prevent exposure to the disease, one should be especially _______ in sexual relationships. (*chary, circumspect, cautious, calculating*)

2 Balancing the abstract and concrete, the general and specific

To understand a subject as you understand it, your readers need ample guidance from your words. When you describe a build-

ANSWERS: EXERCISE 2

1. Maxine Hong Kingston was awarded many prizes for her first two books, *The Woman Warrior* and *China Men.*
2. Kingston cites her mother's tales about ancestors and ancient Chinese customs as the sources of these memoirs.
3. In her childhood Kingston was greatly affected by her mother's tale about a pregnant aunt who was ostracized by villagers. [Ostracized correct.]
4. The aunt gained vengeance by drowning herself in the village's water supply.
5. Kingston decided to make her nameless relative famous by giving her immortality in *The Woman Warrior.* [Immortality correct.]

COLLABORATIVE LEARNING

When students have completed Exercises 2 and 3 individually, have them compare their answers in small groups. Encourage group members to discuss the connotation and denotation of each of the choices, and to consider the effect on the sentence when an inappropriate word is used.

ANSWERS: EXERCISE 3

1. AIDS is a serious health problem.
2. Once the virus has entered the blood system, it destroys T-cells.
3. The function of T-cells is to combat infections.
4. Without enough T-cells, the body is nearly defenseless against infections.
5. To prevent exposure to the disease, one should be especially cautious in sexual relationships.

FILLER WORDS

Asking students to come up with more descriptive synonyms for adjectives like *nice* or *good* in a draft is an easy way to begin discussion of the distinctions between abstract and concrete or general and specific words.

ing as beautiful and nothing more, you force readers to provide their own conceptions of the features that make a building beautiful. If readers bother (and they may not), they surely will not conjure up the image you had in mind. You'll be much more likely to achieve your purpose if you tell readers what you want them to know, that the beautiful building is *a sleek, silver skyscraper with blue-tinted windows,* for instance, or *a Victorian brick courthouse with tall, arched windows.*

Clear, exact writing balances abstract and general words, which outline ideas and objects, with concrete and specific words, which sharpen and solidify.

- **Abstract words** name qualities and ideas: *beauty, inflation, management, culture, liberal.* **Concrete words** name things we can know by our five senses of sight, hearing, touch, taste, and smell: *sleek, humming, brick, bitter, musty.*
- **General words** name classes or groups of things, such as *buildings, weather,* or *birds,* and include all the varieties of the class. **Specific words** limit a general class, such as *buildings,* by naming one of its varieties, such as *skyscraper, Victorian courthouse,* or *hut.*

Note that *general* and *specific* are relative terms: the same word may be more general than some words but more specific than others.

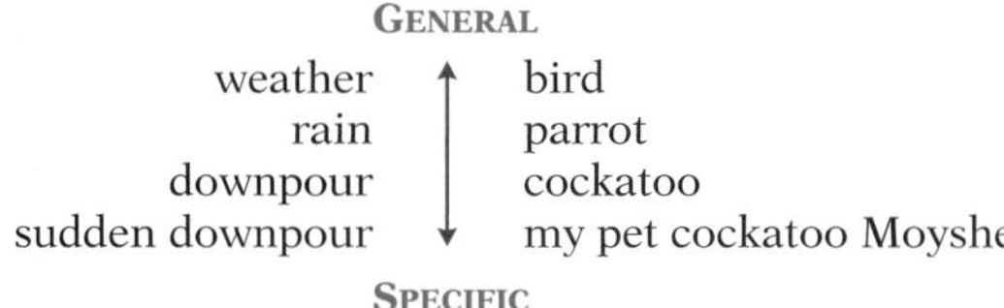

Abstract and general words are useful in the broad statements that set the course for your writing.

> The wild horse in America has a *romantic* history.
>
> We must be *free* from *government interference* in our *affairs.*
>
> *Relations* between the sexes today are only a *little* more *relaxed* than they were in the past.

But the sentences following these would have to develop the ideas with concrete and specific details. When your meaning calls for an abstract or general word, make sure you define it, explain it, and narrow it. Look at how concrete and specific information turns vague sentences into exact ones in the examples below:

> VAGUE The size of his hands made his smallness real. [How big were his hands? How small was he?]
>
> EXACT Not until I saw his white, doll-like hands did I realize that he stood a full head shorter than most other men.

VAGUE The long flood caused a lot of awful destruction in the town. [How long did the flood last? What destruction did it cause? Why was the destruction awful?]

EXACT The flood waters, which rose swiftly and then stayed stubbornly high for days, killed at least six townspeople and made life a misery for the hundreds who had to evacuate their ruined homes and stores.

NOTE If you write on a computer, you can use its search function to help you find and revise abstract and general words that you tend to overuse. Examples of such words include *nice, interesting, things, very, good, a lot, a little,* and *some.*

Exercise 4
Revising: Concrete and specific words

Make the following paragraph vivid by expanding the sentences with appropriate details of your own choosing. Substitute concrete and specific words for the abstract and general ones in italics.

I remember *clearly* how *awful* I felt the first time I *attended* Mrs. Murphy's second-grade class. I had *recently* moved from a *small* town in Missouri to a *crowded* suburb of Chicago. My new school looked *big* from the outside and seemed *dark* inside as I *walked* down the *long* corridor toward the classroom. The class was *noisy* as I neared the door; but when I *entered, everyone* became *quiet* and *looked* at me. I felt *uncomfortable* and *wanted* a place to hide. However, in a *loud* voice Mrs. Murphy *directed* me to the front of the room to introduce myself.

Exercise 5
Using concrete and specific words

For each abstract or general word below, give at least two other words or phrases that illustrate increasing specificity or concreteness. Consult a dictionary as needed. Use the most specific or concrete word from each group in a sentence of your own.

Example:

tired, *sleepy, droopy-eyed*

We stopped for the night when I became so *droopy-eyed* that the road blurred.

1. fabric
2. delicious
3. car
4. narrow-minded
5. reach (*verb*)
6. green
7. walk (*verb*)
8. flower
9. serious
10. pretty
11. teacher
12. nice
13. virtue
14. angry
15. crime

3 Using idioms

Idioms are expressions in any language whose meanings cannot be determined simply from the words in them or whose compo-

ANSWERS: EXERCISE 4

Possible revision

I remember as if it were last week how frightened I felt the first time I neared Mrs. Murphy's second-grade class. Just three days before, I had moved from a rural one-street town in Missouri to a suburb of Chicago where the houses and the people were jammed together. My new school looked monstrous from the outside and seemed forbiddingly dim inside as I walked haltingly down the endless corridor toward the classroom. The class was clamorous as I neared the door: but when I slipped inside, twenty faces became still and gawked at me. I felt terrified and longed for a place to hide. However, in a booming voice Mrs. Murphy ordered me to the front of the room to introduce myself.

COLLABORATIVE LEARNING

When students have completed Exercises 4 and 5 individually, have them discuss their responses in small groups. Encourage groups to discuss the impact of members' various concrete substitutions, and have each group present their most creative solutions to the class.

ANSWERS: EXERCISE 5

Possible answers

1. fabric, upholstery fabric, velvet
   She chose a wine-colored velvet for backing the pillow.
2. delicious, tart, lemony
   He made a meringue pie, lemony and delicately brown.
3. car, foreign car, Volvo station wagon
   He bought a 1973 Volvo station wagon.
4. narrow-minded, prejudiced, sexist
   My uncle's sexist attitudes cause many arguments in our family.
5. reach, stretch, lunge
   Each child lunged for the prize thrown by the clown.
6. green, dark green, bilious green
   The algae covered the surface with a bilious green scum.
7. walk, march, goose-step
   The soldiers goose-stepped menacingly.
8. flower, daisy, ox-eyed daisy
   Some people call the ox-eyed daisy a "brown-eyed Susan."

exact
31b

9. serious, solemn, grim
   His grim expression frightened us.
10. pretty; with small, regular features; with a button nose and a tiny, smiling mouth
    The infant, with a button nose and a tiny, smiling mouth, was a perfect model for baby products.
11. teacher, history teacher, American history teacher
    My American history teacher requires three research papers.

TRANSPARENCY MASTER 31.3

12. nice, considerate, sympathetic
    I need a sympathetic friend.
13. virtue, honesty, frankness
    His frankness was refreshing after I had heard so much flattery.
14. angry, furious, raging
    Raging uncontrollably, Andy insulted everyone around him.
15. crime, theft, armed robbery
    Drug addicts sometimes commit armed robbery to pay for their habits.

IDIOMS

Idioms are particularly challenging for nonnative speakers of English, but even native speakers may find some idioms impenetrable. Asking students to add to the lists in this chapter, or to examine dictionaries of idioms, may yield interesting discussions and paper topics.

nent words cannot be predicted by any rule of grammar; often, they violate conventional grammar. Examples of English idioms include *put up with, plug away at,* and *make off with.*

Idiomatic combinations of verbs or adjectives and prepositions can be confusing for both native and nonnative speakers of English. A number of these pairings are listed in the box below.

ESL If you are learning English as a second language, you are justified in stumbling over its prepositions because their meanings

Idioms with prepositions

abide *by* a rule
abide *in* a place or state

accords *with*
according *to*

accuse *of* a crime

adapt *from* a source
adapt *to* a situation

afraid *of*

agree *on* a plan
agree *to* a proposal
agree *with* a person

angry *with*

aware *of*

based *on*

capable *of*

certain *of*

charge *for* a purchase
charge *with* a crime

concur *in* an opinion
concur *with* a person

contend *for* a principle
contend *with* a person

dependent *on*

differ *about* or *over* a question
differ *from* in some quality
differ *with* a person

disappointed *by* or *in* a person
disappointed *in* or *with* a thing

familiar with

identical *with* or *to*

impatient *at* her conduct
impatient *of* restraint
impatient *for* a raise
impatient *with* a person

independent *of*

infer *from*

inferior *to*

involved *in* a task
involved *with* a person

oblivious *of* or *to* one's surroundings
oblivious *of* something forgotten

occupied *by* a person
occupied *in* study
occupied *with* a thing

opposed *to*

part *from* a person
part *with* a possession

prior *to*

proud *of*

related *to*

rewarded *by* the judge
rewarded *for* something done
rewarded *with* a gift

similar *to*

superior *to*

wait *at* a place
wait *for* a train, a person
wait *on* a customer

can shift depending on context and because they have so many idiomatic uses. In mastering English prepositions, you probably can't avoid memorization. But you can help yourself by memorizing related groups, such as those below:

- ***At/in/on* in expressions of time.** Use *at* before actual clock time: *at 8:30.* Use *in* before a month, year, century, or period: *in April, in 1985, in the twenty-first century, in the next month.* Use *on* before a day or date: *on Tuesday, on August 31, on my daughter's birthday.*
- ***At/in/on* in expressions of place.** Use *at* before a specific place or address: *at the school, at 511 Iris Street.* Use *in* before a place with limits or before a city, state, country, or continent: *in the house, in a box, in Oklahoma City, in China.* Use *on* to mean "supported by" or "touching the surface of": *on the table, on Iris Street, on page 150.*
- ***For/since* in expressions of time.** Use *for* before a period of time: *for an hour, for two years.* Use *since* before a specific point in time: *since 1995, since yesterday.*

A good ESL dictionary is the best source for the meanings of prepositions; see the recommendations on page 482. In addition, some references focus on prepositions. One is *Oxford Dictionary of Current Idiomatic English,* volume 1: *Verbs with Prepositions and Particles* (1985).

Exercise 6
Using prepositions in idioms

Insert the preposition that correctly completes each idiom in the following sentences. Consult the preceding list or a dictionary as needed.

Example:

I disagree _______ many feminists who say women should not be homemakers.

I disagree *with* many feminists who say women should not be homemakers.

1. As Mark and Lana waited _______ the justice of the peace, they seemed oblivious _______ the other people in the lobby.
2. But Mark inferred _______ Lana's glance at a handsome man that she was no longer occupied _______ him alone.
3. Angry _______ Lana, Mark charged her _______ not loving him enough to get married.
4. Impatient _______ Mark's childish behavior, Lana disagreed _______ his interpretation of her glance.
5. They decided that if they could differ so violently _______ a minor incident, they should part _______ each other.

PREPOSITIONS (ESL)

As the text notes, prepositions follow few specific rules, and, because of idiomatic usage, they often cannot be translated directly into students' first languages. As a result, even advanced ESL students find prepositions difficult.

In addition to consulting an ESL dictionary, as recommended in the text, students who need additional help with prepositions might refer to Unit 6 of Len Fox, *Focus on Editing: A Grammar Workbook for Advanced Writers* (White Plains: Longman, 1992), and Chapter 13 of Alan Meyers, *Writing with Confidence,* 5th ed. (New York: Longman, 1996).

ANSWERS: EXERCISE 6

1. As Mark and Lana waited for the justice of the peace, they seemed oblivious to (or of) the other people in the lobby.
2. But Mark inferred from Lana's glance at a handsome man that she was no longer occupied by him alone.
3. Angry with Lana, Mark charged her with not loving him enough to get married.
4. Impatient at Mark's childish behavior, Lana disagreed with his interpretation of her glance.
5. They decided that if they could differ so violently over a minor incident, they should part from each other.

RESOURCES AND IDEAS

Sossaman, Stephen. "Detroit Designers: A Game to Teach Metaphors." *Exercise Exchange* 21 (1976): 2–3. Sossaman points out that car names provide good examples of metaphoric language.

COLLABORATIVE LEARNING

BRAINSTORMING

Ask students to expand on Sossaman's ideas by brainstorming lists of car names and sorting them into categories (e.g., animals, natural forces, and so on). Students then can decide what kind of attributes each category of names suggests and speculate why car manufacturers might want to emphasize these attributes.

COLLABORATIVE LEARNING

FIGURATIVE CLICHES

Have students brainstorm commonplace figures of speech like those listed in the text (others might include "I was sick as a dog," "you lie like a rug," "he eats like a horse") and list them on the board. Ask students to work in small groups to identify the figurative connection implied in each saying, and then to substitute a fresher or more accurate image to convey a similar idea.

BLOCK THAT METAPHOR!

Sportswriting and broadcasting are productive sources of metaphor; encourage students to watch or read about games to identify apt, mixed, or misused metaphors and share them with the class.

4 Using figurative language

Figurative language (or a **figure of speech**) departs from the literal meanings (the denotations) of words, usually by comparing very different ideas or objects.

LITERAL As I try to write, I can think of nothing to say.
FIGURATIVE As I try to write, *my mind is a blank slab of black slate.*

Imaginatively and carefully used, figurative language can capture meaning more precisely and feelingly than literal language.

Figurative language is commonplace in speech. Having *slept like a log,* you may get up to find it *raining cats and dogs* and to discover that the Yankees *shelled* the Royals last night. But the rapid exchange of speech leaves little time for inventiveness, and most figures of daily conversation, like those above, are worn and hackneyed. Writing gives you time to reject the tired figure and to search out fresh, concrete words and phrases.

The two most common figures of speech are the **simile** and the **metaphor.** Both compare two things of different classes, often one abstract and the other concrete. A simile makes the comparison explicit and usually begins with *like* or *as.*

> Whenever we grow, we tend to feel it, *as* a young seed must feel the weight and inertia of the earth when it seeks to break out of its shell on its way to becoming a plant. —ALICE WALKER

> To hold America in one's thoughts is *like* holding a love letter in one's hand—it has so special a meaning. —E. B. WHITE

Instead of stating a comparison, the metaphor implies it, omitting such words as *like* or *as.*

> I cannot and will not cut my conscience to fit this year's fashions. —LILLIAN HELLMAN

> A school is a hopper into which children are heaved while they are young and tender; therein they are pressed into certain standard shapes and covered from head to heels with official rubber stamps. —H. L. MENCKEN

Two other figures of speech are **personification** and **hyperbole.** Personification treats ideas and objects as if they were human.

> The economy consumes my money and gives me little in return.

> I could hear the whisper of snowflakes, nudging each other as they fell.

Hyperbole deliberately exaggerates.

> She appeared in a mile of billowing chiffon, flashing a rhinestone as big as an ostrich egg.

I'm going to cut him up in small cubes and fry him in deep fat.

To be successful, figurative language must be fresh and unstrained, calling attention not to itself but to the writer's meaning. If readers reject your language as trite or overblown, they may reject your message. One kind of figurative language gone wrong is the **mixed metaphor,** in which the writer combines two or more incompatible figures. Since metaphors often generate visual images in the reader's mind, a mixed metaphor can be laughable.

MIXED Various thorny problems that we try to sweep under the rug continue to bob up all the same.

To revise a mixed metaphor, follow through consistently with just one image.

IMPROVED Various thorny problems that we try to weed out continue to thrive all the same.

Exercise 7
Analyzing figurative language

Identify each figure of speech in the following sentences as a simile or a metaphor, and analyze how it contributes to the writer's meaning.

1. A distant airplane, a delta wing out of nightmare, made a gliding shadow on the creek's bottom that looked like a stingray crossing upstream. —ANNIE DILLARD
2. Her roots ran deep into the earth, and from those roots she drew strength enough to hold still against all the forces of chance and disorder. —N. SCOTT MOMADAY
3. As a member of the winning team (the graduating class of 1940) I had outdistanced unpleasant sensations by miles. I was headed for the freedom of open fields. —MAYA ANGELOU
4. All artists quiver under the lash of adverse criticism. —CATHERINE DRINKER BOWEN
5. Every writer, in a roomful of writers, wants to be the best, and the judge, or umpire, or referee is soon overwhelmed and shouted down like a chickadee trying to take charge of a caucus of crows. —JAMES THURBER

Exercise 8
Using figurative language

Invent appropriate figurative language of your own (simile, metaphor, hyperbole, or personification) to describe each scene or quality below, and use the figure in a sentence.

Example:
The attraction of a lake on a hot day
The small waves *like fingers beckoned* us irresistibly.

1. The sound of a kindergarten classroom
2. People waiting in line to buy tickets to a rock concert

COLLABORATIVE LEARNING

Have students work in small groups to complete Exercise 7. Encourage groups to be imaginative in playing out the implications of each figure, and ask each group to report several of their responses to the class.

ANSWERS: EXERCISE 7

1. *A delta wing out of nightmare* is a metaphor. *Like a stingray cruising upstream* is a simile. Both convey the menace of an airplane and its shadow.
2. *Her roots ran deep into the earth* and *from those roots she draws strength* are both metaphors establishing the person's indomitability.
3. *Outdistanced unpleasant sensations* and *headed for the freedom of open fields* are both metaphors equating Angelou's sense of release with the runner's freedom.
4. *Lash of adverse criticism* is a metaphor that makes clear the words' power to hurt.
5. The judge is like a *chickadee* and the roomful of writers is like a *caucus of crows*—two similes that convey the judge's powerlessness in the face of the writers' bombast.

COLLABORATIVE LEARNING

When students have completed Exercise 8 individually, have them discuss their responses in small groups. Encourage groups to discuss the implications of various responses, and ask each group to present their most creative findings to the class.

ANSWERS: EXERCISE 8

Individual response.

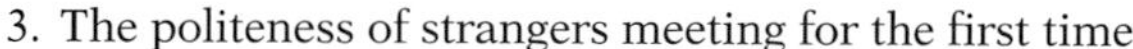

3. The politeness of strangers meeting for the first time
4. A streetlight seen through dense fog
5. The effect of watching television for ten hours straight

5 Using fresh expressions

Trite expressions, or **clichés,** are phrases so old and so often repeated that they have become stale. They include the following:

acid test	ladder of success
add insult to injury	moving experience
better late than never	needle in a haystack
beyond the shadow of a doubt	point with pride
brought back to reality	ripe old age
cool, calm, and collected	sadder but wiser
crushing blow	shoulder the burden
dyed in the wool	sneaking suspicion
easier said than done	sober as a judge
face the music	stand in awe
gentle as a lamb	strong as an ox
hard as a rock	thin as a rail
heavy as lead	tired but happy
hit the nail on the head	tried and true
hour of need	wise as an owl

Besides these old phrases, stale writing may also depend on fashionable words that are losing their effect: for instance, *lifestyle, enhance, excellent, fantastic,* and *caring.*

Many of these expressions were once fresh and forceful, but constant use has dulled them. They, in turn, will dull your writing by suggesting that you have not thought about what you are saying and have resorted to the easiest phrase.

Clichés may slide into your drafts while you are trying to express your meaning. In editing, then, be wary of any expression you have heard or used before. Substitute fresh words of your own or restate the idea in plain language.

TRITE A healthful *lifestyle enhances* your ability to *go for the gold,* allows you to *enjoy life to the fullest,* and helps you live *to a ripe old age.*

REVISED Living healthfully helps you perform well, enjoy life thoroughly, and live long.

NOTE Some computerized style-checking programs will flag trite expressions and ask if you want to revise them. The program can flag only what's listed in its dictionary, however, so it may ignore some clichés. Thus you have to rely on your own editing to make your writing fresh. (See pp. 774–75 for more on style-checking programs.)

TRANSPARENCY MASTER 31.4

COLLABORATIVE LEARNING

CLICHÉ HUNTING

Have students work in small groups to scan each other's drafts for trite expressions or clichés. (For this exercise, students might work in groups of three or four to scan each paper, circle possible clichés, then hand the paper to the next person in the group.) Each group should then consider the circled expressions and decide if they are appropriate to the context or could be replaced by fresher or more accurate expressions.

RESOURCES AND IDEAS

Nilsen, Don L. F. "Clichés, Trite Sayings, Dead Metaphors, and Stale Figures of Speech in Composition Instruction." *College Composition and Communication* 27 (1976): 278–82. Nilsen points out that reviving dead metaphors and clichés in class discussion can create an awareness of figurative language.

Exercise 9
Revising: Trite expressions

Revise the following sentences to eliminate trite expressions.

Example:

The basketball team had almost seized victory, but it faced the test of truth in the last quarter of the game.

The basketball team *seemed about to win*, but the *real test* came in the last quarter of the game.

1. The disastrous consequences of the war have shaken the small nation to its roots.
2. Prices for food have shot sky high, and citizens have sneaking suspicions that others are making a killing on the black market.
3. Medical supplies are so few and far between that even civilians who are as sick as dogs cannot get treatment.
4. With most men fighting or injured or killed, women have had to bite the bullet and bear the men's burden in farming and manufacturing.
5. Last but not least, the war's heavy drain on the nation's pocketbook has left the economy in a shambles.

COLLABORATIVE LEARNING

Have students complete Exercise 9 individually and then discuss their responses in small groups. Encourage groups to discuss the effects of the substitutions on the meaning of each sentence, and have them report their findings to the class. You might have each group follow up on this exercise by scanning samples of their own work for trite expressions in preparation for revision.

ANSWERS: EXERCISE 9

Possible answers

1. These disasters of the war have shaken the small nation severely.
2. Prices for food have risen markedly, and citizens suspect that others are profiting on the black market.
3. Medical supplies are so scarce that even very sick civilians cannot get treatment.
4. With most men fighting or injured or killed, the women have had to take the men's places in farming and manufacturing.
5. Finally, the war's high cost has destroyed the nation's economy.

CUTTING WORDS

Before your students hand in their essays, ask them to cut a specific number of words (ten to fifteen for a start) without harming the meaning. This approach can work with paragraphs as well and makes a good small-group activity.

31c Writing concisely

Writing concisely means cutting whatever adds nothing to your meaning or the freshness of your writing. It does not mean sacrificing necessary detail or original expression for mere brevity, however. Concise writing does not waste words but still includes the concrete and specific details that make meaning clear. In concise writing the length of an expression is appropriate to the thought.

You should not worry about conciseness while you are drafting. Focus on it during editing.

Note Any computerized style-checking program will identify at least some of the wordy structures discussed on the following pages, such as repeated words, weak verbs, passive voice, and *there is* and *it is* constructions. No program can identify all these structures, however, nor can it tell you whether the structure is appropriate for your ideas. In short, such programs can't substitute for your own careful reading and editing.

1 Cutting or shortening empty words and phrases

Empty words and phrases walk in place, gaining little or nothing in meaning. Shorten them to their essential meaning, or cut them entirely. Your writing will move faster and work harder.

TRANSPARENCY MASTER 31.5

THE LARD FACTOR

Richard Lanham in *Revising Prose* (3rd ed., New York: Macmillan, 1992) uses this equation to calculate the "lard factor" of unnecessary words in any piece of writing:

# of words cut from original ÷
# of words in original =
% of lard in original

Lanham argues that as much as 40 percent of any piece of writing may be lard; this estimate emphasizes the need to revise for unnecessary words. Ask students to revise sample passages of published writing or one another's work and calculate the lard factor to test this argument. Students working on computers can use the word count function of their software's spellchecker to estimate the "lard factor" in a longer piece.

Ways to achieve conciseness

WORDY (87 words)

The highly pressured nature of critical-care nursing is due to the fact that the patients have life-threatening illnesses. Critical-care nurses must have possession of steady nerves to care for patients who are critically ill and very sick. The nurses must also have possession of interpersonal skills. They must also have medical skills. It is considered by most health-care professionals that these nurses are essential if there is to be improvement of patients who are now in critical care from that status to the status of intermediate care.

- Cut or shorten empty words and phrases (p. 473), and focus on subject and verb (p. 477).
- Use strong verbs (p. 478).
- Cut unneeded repetition (p. 476).
- Combine sentences (p. 479).
- Rewrite passive sentences as active (p. 478).
- Eliminate *there is* constructions (p. 478).
- Cut unneeded repetition (p. 476), and reduce clauses and phrases (p. 477).

CONCISE (37 words)

Critical-care nursing is highly pressured because the patients have life-threatening illnesses. Critical-care nurses must possess steady nerves and interpersonal and medical skills. Most health-care professionals consider these nurses essential if patients are to improve to intermediate care.

Many empty phrases can be cut entirely:

all things considered	in a manner of speaking
as far as I'm concerned	in my opinion
for all intents and purposes	last but not least
for the most part	more or less

WORDY *As far as I am concerned,* discrimination against women continues to exist in medicine *for all intents and purposes.*

REVISED Discrimination against women continues in medicine.

Other empty words can be cut along with some of the words around them:

angle	character	kind	situation
area	element	manner	thing
aspect	factor	nature	type
case	field		

w 31c

Wordy The *type* of large expenditures on advertising that manufacturers must make is a very important *aspect* of the cost of detergents.

Concise Manufacturers' large advertising expenditures increase the cost of detergents.

Still other empty phrases can be reduced from several words to a single word:

For	Substitute
at all times	always
at the present time	now
at this point in time	now
in the nature of	like
for the purpose of	for
in order to	to
until such time as	until
for the reason that	because
due to the fact that	because
because of the fact that	because
by virtue of the fact that	because
in the event that	if
by means of	by
in the final analysis	finally

Wordy *At this point in time,* the software is expensive *due to the fact that* it has no competition.

Revised The software is expensive *now because* it has no competition.

Exercise 10
Revising: Empty words and phrases

Revise the following sentences to achieve conciseness by cutting or reducing empty words and phrases.

Example:

I came to college because of many factors, but most of all because of the fact that I want a career in medicine.

I came to college *mainly because* I want a career in medicine.

1. *Gerrymandering* refers to a situation in which the lines of a voting district are redrawn to benefit a particular party or ethnic group.
2. The name is explained by the fact that Elbridge Gerry, the governor of Massachusetts in 1812, redrew voting districts in Essex County.
3. On the map one new district looked in the nature of a salamander.
4. Upon seeing the map, a man who was for all intents and purposes a critic of Governor Gerry's administration cried out, "Gerrymander!"

COLLABORATIVE LEARNING

Have students complete Exercise 10 individually and then work in small groups to compare their responses. As a follow-up exercise, ask each group to create an overly wordy paragraph and then to exchange their invented paragraph with another group's as an additional exercise for revision.

ANSWERS: EXERCISE 10

Possible answers

1. *Gerrymandering* means redrawing the lines of a voting district to benefit a particular party or ethnic group.
2. The name refers to Elbridge Gerry, who as governor of Massachusetts in 1812 redrew voting districts in Essex County.
3. On the map one new district looked like a salamander.
4. Upon seeing the map, a critic of Governor Gerry's administration cried out, "Gerrymander!"
5. Now a political group may try to change a district's voting pattern by gerrymandering to exclude rival groups' supporters.

5. At the present time, a political group may try to change the character of a district's voting pattern by gerrymandering to exclude rival groups' supporters.

LEGAL TANGLES

Sometimes, particularly in legal language, phrases contain paired synonyms like *last will and testament.* These go back to the time immediately after the Norman Conquest of England in 1066, when English law proceedings were conducted in both French and English, and the words had to be clear to speakers of either language.

2 Cutting unnecessary repetition

Planned repetition and restatement can make writing more coherent (p. 98) or emphatic (p. 342). But unnecessary repetition weakens sentences.

Wordy Many unskilled workers *without training in a particular job* are unemployed *and do not have any work.*

Concise Many unskilled workers are unemployed.

The use of one word two different ways within a sentence is confusing.

Confusing Preschool instructors play a *role* in the child's understanding of male and female *roles.*

Clear Preschool instructors contribute to the child's understanding of male and female roles.

The simplest kind of useless repetition is the phrase that says the same thing twice. In the following examples, the unneeded words are italicized.

biography *of his life*	*habitual* custom
circle *around*	*important* (*basic*) essentials
consensus *of opinion*	large *in size*
continue *on*	puzzling *in nature*
cooperate *together*	repeat *again*
few *in number*	return *again*
final completion	revert *back*
frank and honest exchange	square (round) *in shape*
the future *to come*	*surrounding* circumstances

ESL Phrases like those above are redundant because the main word already implies the italicized word or words. The repetition is not emphatic but tedious. A dictionary will tell you what meanings a word implies. *Assassinate,* for instance, means "murder someone well known," so the following sentence is redundant: *Julius Caesar was assassinated and killed.*

W
31c

COLLABORATIVE LEARNING

When students have completed Exercise 11 individually, have them compare their responses and discuss the effects of their varying strategies.

Exercise 11
Revising: Unnecessary repetition

Revise the following sentences to achieve conciseness. Concentrate on eliminating repetition and redundancy.

Example:

Because the circumstances surrounding the cancellation of classes were murky and unclear, the editor of the student newspaper assigned a staff reporter to investigate and file a report on the circumstances.

Because the circumstances leading to the cancellation of classes were unclear, the editor of the student newspaper assigned a staffer to investigate and report the story.

1. Some Vietnam veterans coming back to the United States after their tours of duty in Vietnam had problems readjusting again to life in America.
2. Afflicted with post-traumatic stress disorder, a psychological disorder that sometimes arises after a trauma, some of the veterans had psychological problems that caused them to have trouble holding jobs and maintaining relationships.
3. Some who used to use drugs in Vietnam could not break their drug habits after they returned back to the United States.
4. The few veterans who committed crimes and violent acts gained so much notoriety and fame that many Americans thought all veterans were crazy, insane maniacs.
5. As a result of such stereotyping of Vietnam-era veterans, veterans are included into the same antidiscrimination laws that protect other victims of discrimination.

3 Simplifying word groups and sentences

Choose the simplest and most direct grammatical construction that fits your meaning. Focus on subjects and verbs, reduce clauses to phrases and phrases to single words, use strong verbs, use the active voice, eliminate *there is* and *it is,* and combine sentences.

Focusing on the subject and verb

The heart of every sentence is its subject, which names who or what the sentence is about, and its verb, which specifies what the subject does or is. When the subject and verb do not identify the key actor and action, the sentence is bound to be wordy. In the examples below, the subjects and verbs are italicized.

Wordy The *situation* that resulted in the building of the Channel Tunnel *was* a collaboration between the British and the French.

Revised The *Channel Tunnel resulted* from a collaboration between the British and the French.

Focusing on the subject and verb can help you with many of the editing techniques discussed below.

Reducing clauses to phrases, phrases to single words

Modifiers—subordinate clauses, phrases, and single words—can be expanded or contracted depending on the emphasis you want to achieve. (See pp. 173–85 on phrases and clauses and

ANSWERS: EXERCISE 11

Possible answers

1. After their tours of duty, some Vietnam veterans had problems readjusting to life in America.
2. Afflicted with post-traumatic stress disorder, some veterans had trouble holding jobs and maintaining relationships.
3. Some who used drugs in Vietnam could not break their habits after they returned to the United States.
4. The few veterans who committed crimes and violent acts gained so much notoriety that many Americans thought all veterans were crazy.
5. As a result of such stereotyping, Vietnam-era veterans are protected by antidiscrimination laws.

COLLABORATIVE LEARNING

DELIBERATE WORDINESS

To show students the effect of wordiness, give them a simple sentence like "I failed the test" and ask them to fatten it up. One student's final version read, "Due to mitigating circumstances involving the completion of specified educational objectives, the subject in question achieved a negative outcome in the completion of a standardized measuring instrument application."

COLLABORATIVE LEARNING

BUT IT SAYS IN THE CATALOG . . .

Members of educational institutions often resort to windy prose, especially when describing their goals and objectives or policies and procedures. Ask students to take a section from the college catalog or a similar document and rewrite it in "plain" English.

323–24 on working with modifiers.) When editing your sentences, consider whether any modifiers can be reduced without loss of emphasis or clarity.

Wordy The tunnel, *which was drilled for twenty-three miles,* runs *through a bed of solid chalk* under the English Channel.

Concise The *twenty-three-mile* tunnel runs *through solid chalk* under the English Channel.

Using strong verbs

Weak verbs such as *is, has,* and *make* stall sentences. Strong verbs such as *slice, bicker,* and *stroll* energize sentences, moving them along. Weak verbs usually carry extra baggage, too, such as unneeded prepositional phrases and long, abstract nouns or adjectives.

Wordy The drillers *made slow advancement,* and costs *were over* $5 million a day. The slow progress *was worrisome for* some backers.

Concise The drillers *advanced slowly,* and costs *topped* $5 million a day. The slow progress *worried* some backers.

Using the active voice

USING THE ACTIVE VOICE

Not all passives are undesirable; for instance, "I was born" is usually preferable to "My mother bore me." Encourage students to see that it's not the passive itself but its unnecessary use that weakens their writing.

When a verb is in the **active voice,** the subject of the sentence names the *performer* of the verb's action. When a verb is in the **passive voice,** the subject names the *receiver* of the action.

Active The *drillers used* huge rotary blades.

Passive Huge rotary *blades were used* by the drillers.

The passive voice is usually wordier than the active voice, simply because it requires a helping verb (*were*) and a prepositional phrase to name the actor (*by the drillers*). Further, passive constructions are indirect, burying the actor or sometimes omitting it entirely (*Huge rotary blades were used*).

Revise a passive construction by changing the verb to the active voice and positioning the actor as the subject. (If you need help with this change, see p. 230.)

Wordy passive As many as *fifteen feet* of chalk an hour *could be devoured* by the blades.

Concise active The *blades could devour* as many as fifteen feet of chalk an hour.

Eliminating *there is* and *it is* constructions

You can postpone the sentence subject with the words *there is* (*there are, there was, there were*) and *it is* (*it was*). (See p. 194.) These constructions can be useful to emphasize the subject (as when introducing it for the first time) or to indicate a change in direction. But often they just add words and create limp substitutes for more vigorous sentences.

Wordy *There were more than half a million shareholders who* had invested in the tunnel. *It was they and the banks that* expected to profit.

Concise *More than half a million shareholders* had invested in the tunnel. *They and the banks* expected to profit.

Combining sentences

Often the information in two or more sentences can be combined into one tight sentence.

Wordy Profits have not materialized. Even the banks have not profited. In 1996 the tunnel narrowly escaped bankruptcy. It restructured $1.56 billion of its debt.

Concise Profits have not materialized, even for the banks, and in 1996 the tunnel narrowly escaped bankruptcy by restructuring $1.56 billion of its debt.

A number of exercises in this handbook give you practice in sentence combining. For a list, see "Sentence combining" in the Index.

Exercise 12
Revising: Simplifying word groups and sentences

Rewrite each passage below into a single concise sentence. As necessary, focus on the subject and verb, reduce grammatical structures, replace weak verbs with strong ones, rewrite passive verbs as active, eliminate *there is* and *it is* constructions, and combine sentences.

Example:

He was taking some exercise in the park. Then several thugs were suddenly ahead in his path.

He was *exercising* (or *jogging* or *strolling*) in the park *when* several thugs suddenly *loomed* in his path.

1. Chewing gum was originally introduced to the United States by Antonio López de Santa Anna. He was the Mexican general.
2. After he had been defeated by the Texans in 1845, the general, who was exiled, made the choice to settle in New York.
3. A piece of chicle had been stashed by the general in his baggage. Chicle is the dried milky sap of the Mexican sapodilla tree.
4. There was more of this resin brought into the country by Santa Anna's friend Thomas Adams. Adams had a plan to make rubber.
5. The plan failed. Then the occasion arose for Adams to get a much more successful idea on the basis of the use to which the resin was put by General Santa Anna. That is, Adams decided to make a gum that could be chewed.

ANSWERS: EXERCISE 12

Possible answers

1. The Mexican general Antonio López de Santa Anna introduced chewing gum to the United States.
2. After defeat by the Texans in 1845, the exiled general chose to settle in New York.
3. In his baggage the general had stashed a piece of chicle, the dried milky sap of the Mexican sapodilla tree.
4. Santa Anna's friend Thomas Adams brought more of this resin into the country, planning to make rubber.
5. When the plan failed, Adams got a much more successful idea from the way General Santa Anna used the resin, as a gum for chewing.

REVISING STUDENT PARAGRAPHS

As a revision exercise, ask students to work in groups to identify paragraphs from their own work that seem jargon laden or that simply "don't sound right." You might display several of these sample paragraphs (using an overhead projector or networked computers and screen-sharing applications) to provide the basis for a class discussion on effective condensing strategies. Some teachers ask for paragraphs from student volunteers or only use examples from other classes because they fear that in-class attention to weaker paragraphs may discourage the students whose work is selected. However, if such discussions of student work are presented constructively, and if all students take a turn, students seems to benefit the most from working on their own texts.

COLLABORATIVE LEARNING

When students have completed Exercise 13 individually, have them discuss their responses in pairs, noting places where they used different strategies to achieve conciseness. As a follow-up to this exercise you might use several student revisions as the basis for a general discussion of the point at which a productive revision for conciseness might become reductive of the meaning of the passage.

ANSWERS: EXERCISE 13

Possible answers

After much thought, he concluded that carcinogens could be treated like automobiles. Rather than giving in to a fear of cancer, we should balance the benefits we receive from potential carcinogens (such as plastic and pesticides) against the damage they do. Similarly, rather than responding irrationally to the pollution caused by automobiles, we have decided to live with them and enjoy their benefits while simultaneously working to improve them.

Rewriting jargon

Jargon can refer to the special vocabulary of any discipline or profession (see p. 458). But it has also come to describe vague, inflated language that is overcomplicated, even incomprehensible. When it comes from government or business, we call it *bureaucratese.* It sounds almost as if the writer deliberately ignored every suggestion for clear, concise writing.

You may find yourself writing jargon when you are unsure of your subject or when your thoughts are tangled. It's fine, even necessary, to stumble and grope while drafting. But you should straighten out your ideas and eliminate jargon during revision and editing.

JARGON The necessity for individuals to become separate entities in their own right may impel children to engage in open rebelliousness against parental authority or against sibling influence, with resultant confusion of those being rebelled against.

TRANSLATION Children's natural desire to become themselves may make them rebel against bewildered parents or siblings.

JARGON The weekly social gatherings stimulate networking among members of management from various divisions, with the aim of developing contacts and maximizing the flow of creative information.

TRANSLATION The weekly parties give managers from different divisions a chance to meet and to share ideas.

Exercise 13
Revising: Conciseness

Make the following passage as concise as possible. Cut unneeded or repeated words, and simplify words and grammatical structures. Consult a dictionary as needed. Be merciless.

At the end of a lengthy line of reasoning, he came to the conclusion that the situation with carcinogens [cancer-causing substances] should be regarded as similar to the situation with the automobile. Rather than giving in to an irrational fear of cancer, we should consider all aspects of the problem in a balanced and dispassionate frame of mind, making a total of the benefits received from potential carcinogens (plastics, pesticides, and other similar products) and measuring said total against the damage done by such products. This is the nature of most discussions about the automobile. Rather than responding irrationally to the visual, aural, and air pollution caused by automobiles, we have decided to live with them (while simultaneously working to improve on them) for the benefits brought to society as a whole.

Chapter 32

A dictionary can answer most of the questions about words you may ask. This chapter will show you how to choose a dictionary that suits your purpose and how to read a dictionary without difficulty.

32a Choosing a dictionary

1 Abridged dictionaries

Abridged dictionaries are the most practical for everyday use. Often called desk dictionaries because of their convenient size, they usually list 150,000 to 200,000 words and concentrate on fairly common words and meanings. All of the following abridged dictionaries, listed alphabetically, are dependable.

Note Some of these dictionaries are available in both print and electronic form (on diskette and/or CD-ROM), and the others will soon be available electronically as well. With an electronic dictionary, you can look up words from your word-processing program to check spellings, meanings, synonyms, and other information. You may even be able to customize the dictionary with words and meanings it does not include. But you can use an electronic dictionary only with a computer, of course, and it is more expensive than its print equivalent.

The American Heritage College Dictionary, 3rd edition, available on diskette and CD-ROM as well as in print. This dictionary usually lists each word's most common meanings first. It is a more pre-

HIGHLIGHTS

Chapter 32 describes the information provided in a good dictionary, summarizes briefly the characteristics of several widely used desk dictionaries (in print and electronic form) and some unabridged and specialized dictionaries, and explains typical entries from two abridged dictionaries to help students find information. Although the unavoidable accumulation of detail in such a brief chapter makes dense reading in places, the chapter is organized for easy reference so that you and your students can single out the most useful sections. Throughout the handbook, students are urged to consult a dictionary for answers to particular questions—the right preposition to use in an idiom, the usage status of a word, the forms of an irregular verb, and the like. No other supplementary reference will serve students as well as a good desk dictionary, as long as they know how to use it and do so. Students should be required, whenever practicable, to purchase one of the standard desk dictionaries.

CHOOSING A DICTIONARY

To unify the answers that students give to the exercises in this chapter, select a dictionary suitable to your class's needs and make it a required text for your course. Some teachers allow students to bring in any one from a selected list of dictionaries, and then make their varied answers to exercises part of the ongoing class discussion.

A BRIEF HISTORY OF DICTIONARIES

1721—Nathaniel Bailey's *Universal Etymological Dictionary of the English Language*, the first dictionary to resemble the dictionaries we have at present.

1755—Samuel Johnson's two-volume *Dictionary*.

1828—Noah Webster's *American Dictionary of the English Language*.

1857–1928—The compilation of the most comprehensive dictionary, the twelve-volume (now sixteen-volume) *Oxford English Dictionary*.

scriptive dictionary than some of the others listed here, liberally applying usage labels (*slang, informal,* and so on) and appending usage notes to over four hundred entries. It contains an unusually large number of drawings and photographs.

Merriam-Webster's Collegiate Dictionary, 10th edition, available on diskette and CD-ROM as well as in print. This dictionary, based on the unabridged *Webster's Third New International* (see opposite), is more descriptive than prescriptive, emphasizing how the language is actually used. Thus it applies usage labels less frequently than do some other dictionaries. It also emphasizes word histories, arranging meanings in order of their appearance in the language.

The Random House Webster's College Dictionary. Based on the unabridged *Random House Dictionary* (see opposite), this dictionary also lists each word's most common meanings first. The dictionary avoids sexist language in definitions and explanations, and its usage notes indicate words or meanings considered offensive or disparaging to groups such as women and minorities. Appendixes include guidelines for avoiding sexist language.

Webster's New World Dictionary, 3rd college edition. This dictionary arranges meanings in order of their appearance in the language. Usage labels (*colloquial, slang,* and so on) are applied liberally, and words and phrases of American origin are starred.

ESL If English is not your first language, you probably should have a dictionary prepared especially for ESL students in addition to one of the dictionaries listed above. The dictionaries listed below give much more information on such matters as count versus noncount nouns, prepositions with verbs and adjectives, and other concerns of ESL students.

Longman Dictionary of Contemporary English. This dictionary includes 56,000 words and phrases along with usage and study notes. *Longman Dictionary of American English,* the American abridgment, is available on diskette as well as in print.

Oxford Advanced Learner's Dictionary. This dictionary includes 57,000 words and phrases along with usage notes and illustrations of plants, animals, and other common things. *Oxford ESL Dictionary* is the American edition.

 Unabridged dictionaries

Unabridged dictionaries are the most scholarly and comprehensive of all dictionaries, sometimes consisting of many volumes. They emphasize the history of words and the variety of their uses. An unabridged dictionary is useful when you are studying a word in depth, reading or writing about the literature of another century, or looking for a quotation containing a particular word. The following unabridged dictionaries are available at most libraries.

DICTIONARY VARIATION

Dictionaries come in many varieties, and students should be encouraged to examine the different kinds. For instance, the inexpensive dictionaries found in grocery store racks are probably less comprehensive than collegiate work demands. Dictionaries published more than a decade ago may lack up-to-date words or usage information.

USAGE EXPERTS

Some dictionary publishers ask panels of usage experts about the acceptability of certain terms. Though the recommendations are usually helpful, students should understand that these are still opinions, and they may not apply to the situations in the student's own writing. Some dictionaries also censor the terms they include, omitting vulgar words or other offensive terms.

ENGLISH AS A SECOND LANGUAGE (ESL)

For ESL students, the most difficult part of learning English is learning idiomatic usage. In addition to the dictionaries cited here, the following sourcebooks may be particularly helpful to these students:

Cowie, A. P., and R. Mackin. *The Oxford Dictionary of Current Idiomatic English.* 2 vols. London: Oxford UP, 1975.

Freeman, William. *A Concise Dictionary of English Idioms.* Boston: Writer, 1976.

Whitford, Harold C., and Robert J. Dixson. *Handbook of American Idioms and Idiomatic Usage.* New York: Regents, 1973.

The Oxford English Dictionary, 2nd edition, 20 volumes, available on CD-ROM as well as in print. This is the greatest dictionary of the English language, defining over half a million words. Its entries illustrate the changes in a word's spelling, pronunciation, and meaning with quotations from writers of every century. Some entries span pages. The dictionary focuses on British words and meanings but includes American words and meanings.

The Random House Dictionary of the English Language, 2nd edition, available on CD-ROM as well as in print. This dictionary is smaller (and less expensive) than many unabridged dictionaries. Its entries and definitions are especially up to date, and it includes hundreds of usage notes. Among its appendixes are short dictionaries of French, Spanish, Italian, and German.

Webster's Third New International Dictionary of the English Language. This dictionary attempts to record our language more as it *is* used than as it *should be* used. Therefore, usage labels (such as *slang*) are minimal. Definitions are given in order of their appearance in the language. Most acceptable spellings and pronunciations are provided. Plentiful illustrative quotations show variations in the uses of words.

Special dictionaries

Special dictionaries limit their attention to a single class of word (for example, slang, engineering terms, abbreviations), to a single kind of information (synonyms, usage, word origins), or to a specific subject (African American culture, biography, history). (See pp. 531–34 for lists of subject dictionaries.)

Special dictionaries on slang or word origins can help you locate uncommon information, and they make entertaining reading.

For information on slang

Partridge's Concise Dictionary of Slang and Unconventional English. Edited by Paul Beale.

Wentworth, Harold, and Stuart Berg Flexner. *Dictionary of American Slang*. 2nd supplemented edition.

For the origins of words

Oxford Dictionary of English Etymology. Edited by Charles T. Onions et al.

Partridge, Eric. *Origins: A Short Etymological Dictionary of Modern English*. 4th edition.

For guidance on English usage

Follett, Wilson. *Modern American Usage*. Edited by Jacques Barzun.

Morris, William, and Mary Morris. *Harper Dictionary of Contemporary Usage*. 2nd edition.

The New Fowler's Modern English Usage. 3rd edition. Edited by R. W. Burchfield.

ELECTRONIC SPELLING AIDS

Some students use electronic spelling aids to check their spelling. Because such machines have limited memories, they may not include all the words students use in their writing. Students need to understand the limits of such machines (and the need to keep extra batteries on hand). Since more and more students rely on spell-checking computer software, you might also remind students that spell-checkers are not context sensitive and are not usually case sensitive. However students can add words to customize and enlarge their electronic dictionaries.

For information about synonyms

Roget's International Thesaurus. 5th edition. Revised by Robert L. Chapman.
Webster's New Dictionary of Synonyms.

A thesaurus like *Roget's* provides extensive lists of words with related meanings. A dictionary of synonyms like *Webster's* contains discussions and illustrations of shades of meaning.

Note Many electronic dictionaries (see p. 481) include a thesaurus as well, and some thesauruses are available independently on diskette or CD-ROM. Use any thesaurus with care, ensuring that you know the meaning of a synonym before you use it. (See p. 464.)

32b Working with a dictionary's contents

An abridged dictionary is a quick and accessible reference for all kinds of information. Most dictionaries will tell you the atomic weight of oxygen, Napoleon's birth and death dates, the location of the Orinoco River, the population of Gambia, and similarly varied facts.

Of course, a dictionary is most useful on words. Dictionaries use abbreviations and symbols to squeeze a lot of information into a relatively small book. This system of condensed information may at first seem difficult to read. But all dictionaries include in their opening pages detailed information on the arrangement of entries, pronunciation symbols, and abbreviations. And the format is quite similar from one dictionary to another, so becoming familiar with the abbreviations and symbols in one dictionary makes reading any dictionary an easy routine.

Here is a fairly typical entry, from *Merriam-Webster's Collegiate Dictionary,* 10th edition. The labeled parts are discussed on the pages that follow.

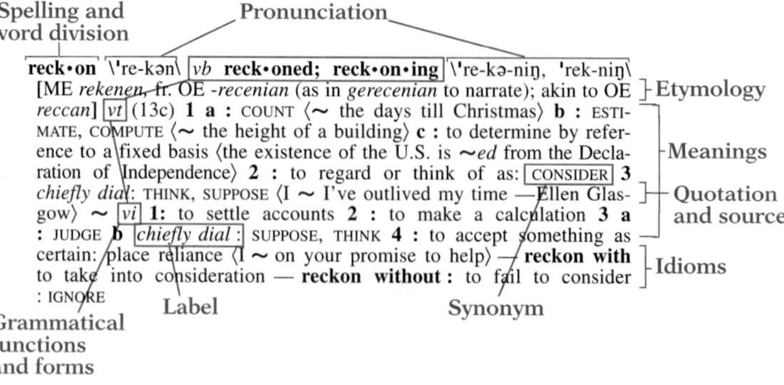

MISSPELLER'S DICTIONARY

Frequently, students complain that they cannot spell words correctly because they do not know how to find them in the dictionary without being able to spell them. Using a thesaurus is one solution to this problem. A second solution is to have students create a misspeller's dictionary based on the words incorrectly spelled in their papers. This dictionary would include all the variant spellings as well as the correct spellings for the misspelled words. The activity will use the efforts of both the good and the fair spellers and can be "published" for future use in classes that involve writing. The misspeller's dictionary can also be placed online so that students can add material to it each semester.

Spelling and word division

The small initial letters for *reckon* indicate that it is not normally capitalized. (In contrast, *Franklin stove* is capitalized in *Merriam-Webster's* because *Franklin* is a proper noun.)

The centered period in **reck•on** shows the division into syllables. If you are writing or typing a word of more than one syllable and need to break it at the end of a line, follow the dictionary's division of the word into syllables. (See also Chapter 30 for general rules about word division.) For a hyphenated compound word, such as *cross-question,* a dictionary shows the hyphen as part of the spelling: **cross-ques•tion.**

Dictionaries provide any variant spellings of a word at the beginning of an entry. For the word *dexterous, Merriam-Webster's* has "**dex•ter•ous** *or* **dex•trous,**" indicating that either spelling is acceptable.

Pronunciation

In *Merriam-Webster's* the pronunciation appears in reversed slashes (\\). The stressed syllable is preceded by an accent mark (ˈre-kən).

Dictionaries use symbols to indicate how to pronounce a word because the alphabet itself does not record all the sounds in the language. (Listen, for example, to the different sounds of *a* in only three words: *far, make,* and *answer.*) Most dictionaries provide a key to the pronunciation symbols at the foot of each page or every two facing pages. They also provide variant pronunciations, including regional differences.

Grammatical functions and forms

Dictionaries give helpful information about a word's functions and forms. The *Merriam-Webster's* entry for *reckon* shows the word to be a verb (*vb*), with the past tense and past participle *reckoned* and the present participle *reckoning,* and with both transitive (*vt*) and intransitive (*vi*) meanings. (For the definitions of these terms, see p. 167.)

Most dictionaries provide not only the principal forms of regular and irregular verbs but also the plural forms of irregular nouns and the *-er* and *-est* forms of adjectives and adverbs. An adjective or adverb without *-er* and *-est* forms in the dictionary requires the addition of *more* and *most* to show comparison (see p. 255).

Etymology

Dictionaries provide the **etymology** of a word (its history) to indicate its origin and the evolution of its meanings and forms. The

ADDITIONAL SAMPLE ENTRY

From Webster's *New Universal Unabridged Dictionary,* 1983.

reck'ŏn, v.t.; reckoned, pt., pp.; reckoning, ppr. (ME. *rekenen, reknen,* from AS, *gerecenian,* to explain. A derivative verb allied to AS, *gereccan,* to rule, direct, order, explain, tell; D. *rekenen:* Ice. *reikna,* to reckon.)

1. to count; to figure up; to compute; to calculate. I *reckoned* above two hundred and fifty on the outside of the church.
   —ADDISON
2. to consider as; to regard as being; to reute. He was *reckoned* among the transgressors.
   —LUKE XXII. 37
3. to make account or reckoning of. (Obs.) Faith was *reckoned* to Abraham for righteousness.
   —ROM. IV. 9
4. to judge; to consider; to estimate.
5. to suppose, think, or believe; as, *I reckon* it will rain. (Colloq. or Dial.)

reck'ŏn, v.i.,

1. to count up; to figure
2. to depend; to rely (with *on*)
3. to settle an account
4. to pay a penalty; to be answerable (Obs.)

If they fail in their bounden duty, they shall reckon for it one day.

—SANDERSON

to reckon for: to be answerable or responsible for.
to reckon with: (a) to balance accounts and make a settlement with; (b) to take into consideration.
to reckon without one's host: to ignore, in a transaction, one whose cooperation is essential; hence, to reckon without considering some important factor or factors.

READING THE WHOLE ENTRY

Remind students to read the entire entry, not just the spelling, when they look up a word. Many dictionaries include the word *alot,* for instance, defining it as "a common misspelling for *a lot.*" Students who see *alot* in the list of entries may assume it's correct if they don't actually read the definition.

dictionary can compress much information about a word into a small space through symbols, abbreviations, and different typefaces. An explanation of these systems appears in the dictionary's opening pages. *Merriam-Webster's* traces *reckon* back most recently to Middle English (ME) and then further back to Old English (OE). The notation "(13c)" before the first definition indicates that the first recorded use of *reckon* to mean "count" occurred in the thirteenth century. When seeking the etymology of a word, be sure to read the entire history, not just the most recent event.

Sometimes dictionaries do not give the etymology for a word. Their practices differ (and are explained in their opening pages), but in general they omit etymology when it is obvious, unknown, or available elsewhere in the dictionary.

Meanings

Dictionaries divide the general meaning of a word into particular meanings on the basis of how the word is or has been actually used. They arrange a word's meanings differently, however, explaining the basis of their arrangement in their opening pages. *Merriam-Webster's* and *Webster's New World* list meanings in order of their appearance in the language, earliest first. The *American Heritage* and abridged *Random House,* in contrast, usually place the word's most basic or common meaning first. Be sure you know the system of any dictionary you are consulting. Then read through the entire entry before settling on the meaning that fits the context of what you're reading or writing.

The *Merriam-Webster's* entry for *reckon* ends with two uses of the word in idiomatic expressions (*reckon with* and *reckon without*). These phrases are defined because, as with all idioms, their meanings cannot be inferred simply from the words they consist of (see p. 467).

Labels

Dictionaries apply labels to words or to particular meanings that have a special status or use. The labels are usually of four kinds: style, subject, region, and time.

Style labels restrict a word or one of its meanings to a particular level of usage:

- *Slang:* words or meanings inappropriate in writing except for a special effect, such as *crumb* for "a worthless or despicable person."
- *Informal* or *colloquial:* words or meanings appropriate for informal writing but not formal writing, such as *great* to mean "very good," as in a *great movie.*
- *Nonstandard* or *substandard:* words or meanings inappropriate for standard speech and writing, such as *ain't.*

ANALOGOUS FORMS

Students often invent new forms for words by analogy; thus, from *drink, drank, drunk* they create *think, thank, thunk.* Such irregular forms exist in a few verbs surviving from Anglo-Saxon times. However, since the time of the Norman Conquest of England in 1066, every new verb that has entered the English language has followed the regular verb pattern of *-d* or *-ed* ending for the past tense and the past participle.

REMINDER

For students: It is critical that you read the entire definition of a word before deciding its meaning for the context at hand. Careful reading of all the meanings of a word often reveals symbolism and intentions frequently missed by an assumed understanding of a word's usage.

ADDITIONAL EXAMPLES OF DICTIONARY LABELS

Slang—novel and colorful expressions that reflect a group's special experiences and set it off from others. Examples: *cool, into, funky, awesome.*

Colloquial—words and expressions appropriate to everyday spoken language and to informal writing. Example: Housework often takes a *bite* out of my weekend.

Regional—words and expressions used only in some geographical locations. For example, one kind of sandwich may be called a *hero,* a *hoagie,* a *submarine,* a *torpedo,* or a *grinder,* depending upon which region you are in.

Nonstandard—words and grammatical forms frequently used in speech but never acceptable in standard written English. Examples: *nowheres, hisself, throwed, could of,* and *hadn't ought.*

Obsolete or archaic—words or meanings of words that we never or rarely use but that appear in older documents and literature still read today. Examples: *enwheel* ("to encircle") and *belike* ("perhaps").

JUDGING STYLE

Some good references on these judgments are found in Harvey A. Daniels, *Famous Last Words: The American Language Crisis Reconsidered* (Ur-

- *Vulgar* or *vulgar slang:* words or meanings considered offensive in speech and writing, as in profanity.
- *Poetic* or *literary:* words or meanings used only in poetry or the most formal writing, such as *eve* for *evening* and *o'er* for *over.*

Subject labels tell us that a word or one of its meanings has a special use in a field of knowledge or a profession. In its entry for *relaxation,* for instance, the *American Heritage* dictionary presents specialized meanings with the subject labels *physiology, physics,* and *mathematics.*

Region labels indicate that a particular spelling, pronunciation, or meaning of a word is not national but limited to an area. A regional difference may be indicated by the label *dialect. Merriam-Webster's* labels as dialect (*dial*) the uses of *reckon* to mean "suppose" or "think" (as in *I reckon I'll do that*). More specific region labels may designate areas of the United States or other countries.

Time labels indicate words or their meanings that the language, in evolving, has discarded. *Obsolete* designates words or meanings that are no longer used; *archaic* designates words or meanings that are out of date but used occasionally.

See pages 454–62 for further discussion of levels of usage and their appropriateness in your writing.

Synonyms

Synonyms are words whose meanings are approximately the same, such as *small* and *little. Merriam-Webster's* defines *reckon* with some words in small capital letters (COUNT, ESTIMATE, CONSIDER, and so on). These are both synonyms and cross-references, in that each word may be looked up in its alphabetical place. Some dictionaries devote separate paragraphs to words with many synonyms. (See pp. 497–98 for a discussion of how to use the synonyms provided by a dictionary to increase your vocabulary.)

Illustrative quotations

Dictionaries are made by collecting quotations showing actual uses of words in all kinds of speech and writing. Some of these quotations, or others that the dictionary makers invent, may appear in the dictionary's entries as illustrations of how a word may be used. Five such quotations illustrate uses of *reckon* in the *Merriam-Webster's* entry (~ in these quotations stands for the word being illustrated).

Unabridged dictionaries usually provide many such quotations, not only to illustrate a word's current uses but also to show the changes in its meanings over time. Abridged dictionaries use quotations more selectively: to illustrate an unusual meaning of the word, to help distinguish between two closely related meanings of the same word, or to show the differences between synonyms.

bana: NCTE, 1983) and Dennis Baron, *Grammar and Good Taste* (New Haven: Yale UP, 1982). See also, Walter Nash's *An Uncommon Tongue: The Uses and Resources of English* (New York: Routledge, 1992) for a broader study of usage, including dictionaries, punctuation, paraphrase, and parody.

A WRITER'S PERSPECTIVE

The educated Southerner has no use for an r, *except at the beginning of a word.*

—MARK TWAIN, *Life on the Mississippi*

ADDITIONAL REFERENCE

For more synonyms and antonyms, students can consult Norman Lewis, *The New Roget's Thesaurus of the English Language in Dictionary Form* (New York: Putnam, 1978).

A DICTIONARY WITH PLENTY OF SYNONYMS

Of the many dictionaries that include synonyms with their definitions of words, the *Funk & Wagnall's New Standard College Dictionary* gives more extensive coverage than most. The *Funk & Wagnall's* includes paragraphs on synonyms that define the various shades of meaning.

A WRITER'S PERSPECTIVE

"When I use a word," Humpty Dumpty said, "it means just what I choose it to mean—neither more nor less."

"The question is," said Alice, "whether you can make words mean so many different things."

"The question is," said Humpty Dumpty, "which is to be master—that's all."

—LEWIS CARROLL, *Through the Looking-Glass*

ANSWERS: EXERCISE

The answers to the exercise in Chapter 32 will depend on the dictionary being consulted. The recommended desk dictionaries disagree, for instance, over many of the syllable divisions. Thus, no answers are provided.

Exercise
Using a dictionary

Consult your dictionary on five of the following words. First find out whether your dictionary lists the oldest or the most common meanings first in its entries. Then, for each word, write down (*a*) the division into syllables, (*b*) the pronunciation, (*c*) the grammatical functions and forms, (*d*) the etymology, (*e*) each meaning, and (*f*) any special uses indicated by labels. Finally, use the word in at least two sentences of your own.

1. depreciation	4. manifest	7. potlatch	10. toxic
2. secretary	5. assassin	8. plain (*adj.*)	11. steal
3. grammar	6. astrology	9. ceremony	12. obelisk

Chapter 33

HIGHLIGHTS

Most students can profit from systematic attention to improving their vocabulary; however, the course time available for such attention is often quite limited. Special workbooks are available, of course, for students with basic vocabulary problems. Chapter 33 provides a good introduction to vocabulary building for students who wish to enrich their vocabularies and suggests activities you may wish to assign. After glancing at the development of the English language and the variety of sources from which our rich vocabulary is drawn, the chapter looks at the roots, prefixes, and suffixes of words; it also looks at ways of learning new words from their context and the value of habitually consulting a dictionary—the best methods of gradually and continually expanding vocabulary while reading.

A precise and versatile vocabulary will help you communicate effectively in speech and writing. To a great extent, you can improve your vocabulary by frequent and inquisitive reading, by troubling to notice and learn the interesting or unfamiliar words used by other writers.

This chapter has a twofold purpose: to provide a sense of the potential of English by acquainting you with its history and range of words; and to help you increase the range, versatility, and precision of your own vocabulary.

33a Understanding the sources of English

English has over 500,000 words, probably more than any other language. This exceptional vocabulary and the power and range of expression that accompany it derive from its special mix of word sources. Unlike many other languages, English has borrowed a large number of words.

How English drew on its several sources and acquired its large vocabulary is the story of historical changes. The ancestor of English, Indo-European, was spoken (but not written) perhaps as far back as 5000 BC, and it eventually spread to cover the area from India west to the British isles. In what is now England, an Indo-European offshoot called Celtic was spoken extensively until the fifth century AD. But over the next few centuries, invaders from the European continent, speaking a dialect of Germanic, another Indo-

RESOURCES AND IDEAS

DiPardo, Anne. "Narrative Discourse in the Basic Writing Class: Meeting the Challenge of Cultural Pluralism." *Teaching English in the Two-Year College* 17 (1990): 45–53. DiPardo has found that student narratives are an excellent way for students to present their cultures, values, and linguistic styles.

Journal of Basic Writing 2 (1979). This special issue on vocabulary includes general articles and notes on specific strategies.

WATCHING THE HISTORY OF THE LANGUAGE

If your library has them, the videotapes from the Public Broadcasting System's series *The Story of English* are wonderfully accessible introductions to the history of the language; the companion book of the same title is by Robert McCrum, William Cran, and Robert MacNeil (New York: Viking, 1986).

HISTORY OF THE ENGLISH LANGUAGE

Prior to fifth century AD—Celtic-speaking peoples.
Fifth century—Anglo-Saxon invasion introduces Germanic dialects.
Eighth to twelfth century—In the Old English (OE) period the language combines Latin and Germanic dialects and contributes 183 of the 200 most frequently used words in Modern English. The Vikings arrive in AD 787 speaking Old Norse, which contributes hundreds of words to English.
AD 1066—The Normans invade and conquer England. Norman French, a dialect of Old French, replaces Old English as the official language of England, but English survives, continuing to evolve through the influence of French.
Twelfth century—English emerges in an altered form. Middle English (ME), which draws on both Old English and Norman French. Heavy borrowing of French words continues through the following centuries until the emergence of Modern English.
AD 1500 (approximately)—The language takes a form recognizable as Modern English.

European language, overran the native Britons. The Germanic dialect became the original source of English.

Old English, spoken from the eighth to the twelfth centuries, was a rugged, guttural language. It used a slightly different alphabet from ours (including the characters ð and þ for *th*), which has been transcribed in the sample below. The sample shows the opening lines of the Lord's Prayer: "Our Father, who art in heaven, hallowed be thy name. Thy kingdom come. Thy will be done on earth as it is in heaven."

> Fæder ure thu the eart on heofonum, si thin nama gehalgod. Tobecume thin rice. Gewurthe thin willa on eorthan swa swa on heofonum.

Many of our nouns, such as *stone, word, gift,* and *foot,* come from Old English. So do most of our pronouns, prepositions, and conjunctions, some (such as *he, under,* and *to*) without any change in spelling. Other Germanic tribes, using a similar dialect but settling on the European continent instead of in England, fostered two other languages, Dutch and German. As a result, Dutch, German, and English are related languages with some similar traits.

In 1066 the Normans, under William the Conqueror, invaded England. The Normans were originally Vikings who had settled in northern France and had forsaken Old Norse for their own dialect of Old French. They made Norman French the language of law, literature, and the ruling class in England. As a result, English acquired many French words, including many military and governmental words such as *authority, mayor, crime, army,* and *guard.* The common English people kept English alive during the Norman occupation, but they adopted many French words intact (*air, point, place, age*). Eventually, the French influence caused the language to shift from Old to Middle English, which lasted from the twelfth through the fifteenth centuries. During this time a great many Latin words also entered English, for Latin formed the background of Norman French and was the language of the Church and of scholars. English words that entered Middle English directly from Latin or from Latin through French include *language, luminous, memory, liberal,* and *sober.*

Middle English, as the following passage from Geoffrey Chaucer's *Canterbury Tales* shows, was much closer to our own language than to Old English.

> A clerk there was of Oxenford also,
> That unto logyk hadde longe ygo.
> As leene was his hors as is a rake,
> And he nas nat right fat, I undertake,
> But looked holwe, and therto sobrely.

Modern English evolved in the fourteenth and fifteenth centuries as the language's sound and spellings changed. This was the time of the Renaissance in Europe. Ancient Latin and Greek art, learning, and literature were revived, first in Italy and then throughout the continent. English vocabulary expanded rapidly, not only with more Latin and many Greek words (such as *democracy* and *physics*) but also with words from Italian and French. Advances in printing, beginning in the fifteenth century, made publications widely available to an increasingly literate audience. Modern American English is four centuries and an ocean removed from the Modern English of sixteenth-century England, but the two are fundamentally the same. The differences and the similarities are evident in this passage from the King James Bible, published in 1611:

> And the Lord God commanded the man, saying, Of euery tree of the garden thou mayest freely eate. But of the tree of the knowledge of good and euill, thou shalt not eate of it: for in the day that thou eatest thereof, thou shalt surely die.

33b Learning the composition of words

Words can often be divided into meaningful parts. A *handbook,* for instance, is a book you keep at hand (for reference). A *shepherd* herds sheep (or other animals). Knowing what the parts of a word mean by themselves, as you do here, can often help you infer approximately what they mean when combined.

The following explanations of roots, prefixes, and suffixes provide information that can open up the meanings of words whose parts may not be familiar or easy to see. For more information, refer to a dictionary's etymologies, which provide the histories of words (see pp. 485–86).

1 Learning roots

A **root** is the unchanging component of words related in origin and usually in meaning. Both *illiterate* ("unable to read and write") and *literal* ("sticking to the facts or to the first and most obvious meaning of an idea") share the root *liter,* derived from *littera,* a Latin word meaning "letter." A person who cannot understand the letters that make up writing is illiterate. A person who wants to understand the primary meaning of the letters (the words) in a contract is seeking the *literal* meaning of that contract.

At least half our words come from Latin and Greek. The list below includes some common Latin and Greek roots, their meanings, and examples of English words containing them.

IN TRANSLATION

If discussion of religious texts is accepted at your school, your students may enjoy looking at various versions of familiar religious texts like the nativity story or the Twenty-Third Psalm. You might want to try the Wycliffite Bible (fourteenth century), the King James version (early seventeenth century), the Bay Psalm Book (seventeenth century), and several modern versions to examine the effect changes of diction can have on familiar texts. Shirley Brice Heath's *Ways with Words* (New York: Cambridge UP, 1983) offers a chapter detailing other ways in which students can actively research language topics.

DICTIONARY TRIVIA

Currently, one of the longest words in English is *pneumonoultramicroscopicsilicovolcanoconiosis.* It's the name for a lung disease caused by breathing in the very tiny particles of dust thrown off by volcanic explosions. Broken down, it means

pneumono	the lungs
ultra	very
micro	small
scopic	seen
silico	dust from rocks
volcani	volcanic origins
coni	the conia, cells lining the lungs
osis	a disease involving inflammation

Students can look for (or construct) other long words made up of such strings of roots and affixes as they study word roots.

Root (source)	Meaning	English words
aster, astr (G)	star	astronomy, astrology
audi (L)	to hear	audible, audience
bene (L)	good, well	benefit, benevolent
bio (G)	life	biology, autobiography
dic, dict (L)	to speak	dictator, dictionary
fer (L)	to carry	transfer, referral
fix (L)	to fasten	fix, suffix, prefix
geo (G)	earth	geography, geology
graph (G)	to write	geography, photography
jur, jus (L)	law	jury, justice
log, logue (G)	word, thought, speech	astrology, biology, neologism
luc (L)	light	lucid, translucent
manu (L)	hand	manual, manuscript
meter, metr (G)	measure	metric, thermometer
op, oper (L)	work	operation, operator
path (G)	feeling	pathetic, sympathy
ped (G)	child	pediatrics
phil (G)	love	philosophy, Anglophile
phys (G)	body, nature	physical, physics
scrib, script (L)	to write	scribble, manuscript
tele (G)	far off	telephone, television
ter, terr (L)	earth	territory, extraterrestrial
vac (L)	empty	vacant, vacuum, evacuate
verb (L)	word	verbal, verbose
vid, vis (L)	to see	video, vision, television

Exercise 1
Learning roots

Define the following italicized words, using the list of roots above and any clues given by the rest of the sentence. Check the accuracy of your meanings in a dictionary.

1. After guiding me through college, my *benefactor* will help me start a career.
2. Always afraid of leading a *vacuous* life, the heiress immersed herself in volunteer work.
3. The posters *affixed* to the construction wall advertised a pornographic movie.
4. After his *auditory* nerve was damaged, he had trouble catching people's words.
5. The child *empathized* so completely with his mother that he felt pain when she broke her arm.

COLLABORATIVE LEARNING

Once students have completed Exercise 1 individually, have them compare their responses in small groups using their dictionaries as a reference. Encourage groups to discuss the inferences they have drawn from various root words and to consider their application in other words.

ANSWERS: EXERCISE 1

1. *Benefactor:* The root *bene* means "good," and so the benefactor is or does good. The rest of the sentence hints that the benefactor provides aid.
2. *Vacuous:* The root *vac* means "empty," which makes sense in the sentence. The heiress takes up volunteer work to avoid an empty life.
3. *Affixed:* The root *fix* means "to fasten," and so *affixed* means fastened.
4. *Auditory:* The root *audi* means "to hear." The *auditory nerve* is the nerve producing hearing.
5. *Empathized:* The root *path* means "feeling," and the context completes the meaning. The child felt as his mother did.

2 Learning prefixes

Prefixes are standard syllables fastened to the front of a word to modify its meaning. For example, the word *prehistory* is a combination of the word *history,* meaning "based on a written record explaining past events," and the prefix *pre-,* meaning "before." Together, prefix and word mean "before a written record explaining past events," or before events were recorded. Learning standard prefixes can help you improve vocabulary and spelling just as learning word roots can. The following lists group prefixes according to sense so that they are easier to remember. When two or more prefixes have very different spellings but the same meaning, they usually derive from different languages, most often Latin and Greek.

Prefixes showing quantity

Meaning	Prefixes in English words
half	*semi*annual; *hemi*sphere
one	*uni*cycle; *mon*arch, *mono*rail
two	*bi*nary, *bi*monthly; *di*lemma, *dicho*tomy
three	*tri*angle, *tri*logy
four	*quad*rangle, *quar*tet
five	*quin*tet; *penta*gon
six	*sex*tuplets; *hexa*meter
seven	*sept*uagenarian; *hept*archy
eight	*oct*ave, *octo*pus
nine	*nona*genarian
ten	*dec*ade, *deca*thlon
hundred	*cent*ury; *hecto*liter
thousand	*milli*meter; *kilo*cycle

Prefixes showing negation

Meaning	Prefixes in English words
without, no, not	*a*sexual; *il*legal, *im*moral, *in*valid, *ir*reverent; *un*skilled
not, absence of, opposing, against	*non*breakable; *ant*acid, *anti*pathy; *contra*dict
opposite to, complement to	*counter*clockwise, *counter*weight
do the opposite of, remove, reduce	*de*horn, *de*vitalize, *de*value
do the opposite of, deprive of	*dis*establish, *dis*arm
wrongly, bad	*mis*judge, *mis*deed

Prefixes showing time

Meaning	Prefixes in English words
before	*ante*cedent; *fore*cast; *pre*cede; *pro*logue
after	*post*war
again	*re*write

COLLABORATIVE LEARNING

When students have completed Exercise 2 individually, have them compare their responses in small groups using their dictionaries as a reference. Encourage groups to discuss the inferences they have drawn from the different prefixes and to brainstorm about other words in which those prefixes might be used.

ANSWERS: EXERCISE 2

1. *Quadricentennial* comes from *quadri*, meaning "four"; *cent*, meaning "hundred"; and *annus*, meaning "year." The cities will be celebrating their four-hundredth year.
2. *Octave* derives from *oct*, "eight"; *sestet* from *sex*, "six." The octave is eight lines; the sestet six.
3. The prefix *counter* means "opposite to"; a *countermeasure* is a measure opposed to another.
4. The prefix *fore* means "before"; in trying to *forestall* the squeeze, the representatives are, in effect, trying to stall it before it happens.
5. The prefix *circum* means "around"; to *circumnavigate* means to navigate around.

RESOURCES AND IDEAS

Stotsky, Sandra. "Teaching the Vocabulary of Academic Discourse. *Journal of Basic Writing* 2 (1979): 15–39. Stotsky examines the language of textbooks and suggests using reading, dictating, précis writing, and affix study to develop vocabulary for academic reading and writing.

SEXIST SUFFIXES

Some suffixes like *-ess* and *-ette* are considered demeaning when applied to people; consider the difference between *governor* and *governess* or *master* and *mistress*, for instance. Warn students to use such suffixes with care to maintain their readers' good will.

ANSWERS: EXERCISE 3

Possible answers

1. *magic*, noun and adjective
   adjective: *magical*

Prefixes showing direction or position

Meaning	Prefixes in English words
above, over	*super*vise
across, over	*trans*port
below, under	*infra*sonic; *sub*terranean; *hypo*dermic
in front of	*pro*ceed; *pre*fix
behind	*re*cede
out of	*e*rupt, *ex*plicit; *ec*stasy
into	*in*jection, *im*merse; *en*courage, *em*power
around	*circum*ference; *peri*meter
with	*co*exist, *col*loquial, *com*municate, *con*sequence, *cor*respond; *sym*pathy, *syn*chronize

Exercise 2
Learning prefixes

Provide meanings for the following italicized words, using the lists of prefixes and any clues given by the rest of the sentence. Check the accuracy of your meanings in a dictionary.

1. In the twenty-first century some of our oldest cities will celebrate their *quadricentennials*.
2. Most poems called sonnets consist of fourteen lines divided into an *octave* and a *sestet*.
3. When the Congress seemed ready to cut Social Security benefits again, some representatives proposed the *countermeasure* of increasing Medicare payments.
4. By increasing Medicare payments, the representatives hoped to *forestall* the inevitable financial squeeze on the elderly.
5. Ferdinand Magellan, a Portuguese sailor, commanded the first expedition to *circumnavigate* the globe.

3 Learning suffixes

Suffixes are standard syllables fastened to the end of a word to modify its meaning and usually its part of speech. The word *popular* is an adjective. With different suffixes, it becomes a different adjective, an adverb, two different verbs, and a noun.

Adjective	popular popul*ous*	Adverb	popul*arly*
Verb	popul*ate* popul*arize*	Noun	popul*ation*

Many words change suffixes in the same way. In fact, suffixes help us recognize what parts of speech many words are, as the following examples show.

Noun suffixes

mis*ery*	min*er*	intern*ship*	random*ness*
refer*ence*	base*ment*	presid*ency*	brother*hood*
relev*ance*	national*ist*	discus*sion*	king*dom*
operat*or*	national*ism*	agita*tion*	

Verb suffixes

hard*en*	pur*ify*
national*ize*	agit*ate*

Adjective suffixes

miser*able*	president*ial*	wonder*ful*	use*less*
ed*ible*	gigant*ic*	fibr*ous*	self*ish*
nation*al*	friend*ly*	adopt*ive*	flatul*ent*

The only suffix regularly applied to adverbs is *-ly: openly, selfishly, essentially.*

Note Inflectional endings—such as the plural *-s,* the possessive *-'s,* the past tense *-ed,* and the comparative *-er* or *-est*—appear at the ends of words but do not change a word's grammatical function.

Exercise 3
Learning suffixes

Identify the part of speech of each word below, and then change it to the part or parts of speech in parentheses by deleting, adding, or changing a suffix. Use the given word and each created word in a sentence. Check a dictionary, if necessary, to be sure suffixes and spellings are correct.

1. magic (*adjective*)
2. durable (*noun; adverb*)
3. refrigerator (*verb*)
4. self-critical (*noun*)
5. differ (*noun; adjective*)
6. equal (*noun; adverb*)
7. conversion (*verb; adjective*)
8. strictly (*adjective; noun*)
9. assist (*noun*)
10. qualification (*verb; adjective*)

33c Learning to use new words

You can learn a new word not only by understanding its composition but also by examining the context in which it appears and by looking it up in a dictionary—both ways to increase your vocabulary by multiplying and varying your experience with language.

His success must be the result of *magic.* She performed *magic* tricks. Drawing everyone into a *magical* world, the movie charmed the audience.

2. *durable,* adjective
noun: *durability:* adverb: *durably*
The *durable* chair withstood many years' wear. The *durability* of the old pitcher amazed the crowd. The pup tent was light but *durably* made.
3. *refrigerator,* noun
verb: *refrigerate*
Don't bother putting that in the *refrigerator.* I have already *refrigerated* it.
4. *self-critical,* adjective
noun: *self-criticism*
A *self-critical* stance is difficult to take. Her apparent *self-criticism* was really a plea for support.
5. *differ,* verb
noun: *difference;* adjective: *different*
We *differ* from each other. He was sure the campaign would not make any *difference.* The police found that she had committed a *different* crime.
6. *equal,* adjective
noun: *equality;* adverb: *equally*
Equal rights have not yet been achieved. *Equality* is the goal of a truly just society. The children were all punished, though all were not *equally* at fault.
7. *conversion,* noun
verb: *convert;* adjective: *convertible*
We expected her *conversion* to her new religion. To *convert* base metals into gold was the alchemists' dream. The *convertible* sofa comes in handy.
8. *strictly,* adverb
adjective: *strict:* noun: *strictness*
She was *strictly* raised. A *strict* parent need not be a tyrannical parent. The *strictness* of their morals makes the Victorians hard to understand today.
9. *assist,* verb
noun: *assistance*
Please *assist* us. Your *assistance* in this project will be greatly appreciated.
10. *qualification,* noun
verb: *qualify;* adjective: *qualitative*
The *qualification* he offered was important. To *qualify* for the Olympics, an athlete must be an amateur. The difference between the two tape decks is *qualitative.*

RESOURCES AND IDEAS

Hoover, Regina M. "In the Beginning: The Word." *Journal of Basic Writing* 2 (1979): 82–87. Copying sentences containing unfamiliar words can help build vocabulary and improve writing.

COLLABORATIVE LEARNING

BUILDING VOCABULARIES

Students can help one another build their vocabularies. For each class, ask two or three students to bring in three words new to them and explain to their classmates what the words mean and when they might be used. (Students might look to other courses and disciplines for some of these words.) All the students can add these new words to their vocabulary lists. Ask students to highlight these words when they use them in a paper, and reinforce this activity by giving extra credit for the appropriate use of these words.

1 Examining context

Often, you can guess the meaning of an unfamiliar word by looking at the familiar words around it. This technique is helpful when you don't want to interrupt your reading to look up every unfamiliar word. (When you've finished reading, though, check your guesses in your dictionary.)

Parallelism (Chapter 17) shows you which ideas line up or go together and can often suggest the meaning of a new word. Watch for parallel ideas in the following sentence.

> The kittens see their mother hunt and kill, and they in turn take up *predatory* behavior.

Context clues suggest the meaning of *predatory:* parallel construction (*kittens see . . . and they . . . take up*); the tip-off phrase *in turn;* and the suggested idea of imitation (kittens watching their mother and taking up her behavior). These clues lead to the correct conclusion that predatory behavior consists of hunting and killing.

The phrase *is called* or the word *is* often signals a definition.

> The point where the light rays come together is called the *focus* of the lens.

Sometimes definitions are enclosed in parentheses or set off by commas or dashes.

> In early childhood these tendencies lead to the development of *schemes* (organized patterns of behavior).

> Many Chinese practice *Tai Chi,* an ancient method of self-defense performed as exercise in slow, graceful motions.

> At *burnout*—the instant a rocket stops firing—the satellite's path is fixed.

Noticing examples can also help you infer the meaning of a word. The expressions *such as, for example, for instance, to illustrate,* and *including* often precede examples.

> Society often has difficulty understanding *nonconformists* such as criminals, inventors, artists, saints, and political protesters.

The examples of people who go beyond the average or beyond the rules suggest that *nonconformists* do not adapt themselves to the usual standards and customs of society.

Sometimes an example that reveals the meaning of an unfamiliar word is not announced by a phrase.

> During the first weeks of *rehabilitation,* Smith exercised as best he could, took his medicine daily, and thought constantly about the physical condition he once possessed.

Guessing the meaning of *rehabilitation* requires considering what occurred during it: (1) exercising "as best he could," as if Smith had some kind of limitation; (2) taking medicine, as if Smith were ill; and (3) thinking about his past physical condition, as if Smith were wishing for the good shape he used to be in. Putting these examples together suggests that *rehabilitation* is returning to a healthy condition, which is one of its meanings.

Exercise 4
Examining context

Use context to determine the meanings of the words italicized below (not including titles). Check the accuracy of your guess by consulting a dictionary.

1. Like America, Michael [Corleone, in *The Godfather*] began as a clean, brilliant young man endowed with incredible resources and believing in a humanistic idealism. Like America, Michael was an innocent who had tried to correct the ills and injustices of his *progenitors*. —Francis Ford Coppola
2. A photograph passes for *incontrovertible* proof that a given thing happened. The picture may distort; but there is always a presumption that something exists, or did exist, which is like what's in the picture. —Susan Sontag
3. It is not easy to describe or to account for our own culture's particular *predilection* for butter—a loyalty so fierce and so unreasoning that it is called, by those opposed to it, the "butter *mystique*." —Margaret Visser
4. "And this, too, shall pass away." How much [this sentence] expresses! How *chastening* in the hour of pride! How *consoling* in the depths of *affliction!* —Abraham Lincoln
5. In a community where public services have failed to keep *abreast* of private consumption, . . . in an atmosphere of private *opulence* and public *squalor*, the private goods have full sway. —John Kenneth Galbraith

COLLABORATIVE LEARNING

Have students complete Exercise 4 individually and then discuss their responses in small groups. Encourage groups to debate the meanings of words, using roots, prefixes, suffixes, and context as evidence for their cases, and using the dictionary to provide final arbitration. As a follow-up exercise, one group might choose an additional word from the dictionary, write it on the board in the context of an invented sentence, and challenge the other groups to define it. The group that "wins" chooses the next word . . . and so on.

ANSWERS: EXERCISE 4

Individual response.

2 Using the dictionary

The dictionary is a quick reference for the meanings of words (see p. 486). It can give the precise meaning of a word whose general meaning you have guessed by examining the word's context. It can also help you fix the word in your memory by showing its spelling, pronunciation, synonyms, and other features.

Although a dictionary of synonyms is the best source for the precise meanings of similar words (see p. 484), an abridged dictionary will supply much information about synonyms. Most abridged dictionaries list a word's common synonyms and either direct you to the entries for the synonyms or distinguish among them in one place. An example of the latter form is the paragraph below, which follows the main entry for the word *decrease* in *The American Heritage College Dictionary*. By drawing on this information as you edit, you can substitute a more precise word for *decrease* when your meaning calls for one.

> **Syns:** *decrease, lessen, reduce, dwindle, abate, diminish, subside*. These verbs mean to become or cause to become smaller or less. *Decrease* and *lessen* refer to steady or gradual diminution: *Lack of success decreases confidence. His appetite lessens as his illness progresses. Reduce* emphasizes bringing down in size, degree, or intensity: *The workers reduced their wage demands. Dwindle* suggests decreasing bit by bit to a vanishing point: *Their savings dwindled away. Abate* stresses a decrease in amount or intensity and suggests a reduction of excess: *Toward evening the fire began to abate. Diminish* implies taking away or removal: *The warden's authority diminished after the revolt. Subside* implies a falling away to a more normal level: *Our wild enthusiasm did not subside*.

ANSWERS: EXERCISE 5

Individual response.

Exercise 5
Using the dictionary

Consulting the dictionary entry above (and another dictionary if necessary), write five sentences that make precise use of *decrease* and four of its synonyms.

Chapter 34 Spelling

English spelling is difficult, even for some very experienced and competent writers. You can train yourself to spell better, and this chapter will help you. But you can also improve instantly by acquiring three habits:

- Carefully proofread your writing.
- Cultivate a healthy suspicion of your spellings.
- Compulsively check a dictionary whenever you doubt a spelling.

Note The spelling checkers for computerized word processors can help you find and track spelling errors in your papers. But their usefulness is limited, mainly because they can't spot the very common error of confusing words with similar spellings, such as *their/there/they're*. The following jingle has circulated widely as a warning about spelling checkers (we found it in the *Bulletin of the Missouri Council of Teachers of Mathematics*). The jingle contains thirteen misspellings that a spelling checker did not catch. Can you spot them?

I have a spelling checker,
It came with my PC;
It plainly marks four my revue
Mistakes I cannot sea.
I've run this poem threw it,
I'm sure your please too no.
Its letter perfect in it's weigh,
My checker tolled me sew.

A spelling checker cannot substitute for your own care.

HIGHLIGHTS

No quick formula exists for turning poor spellers into good ones. Students with serious spelling problems may need systematic instruction in spelling, which, like systematic instruction in vocabulary, is rarely allowed by course time. You may want to refer such students to a skills center on campus or, if there are no such services, to a good spelling workbook. There are, however, activities and assignments that can help. Most students can improve their spelling markedly by learning and actually applying the limited number of standard rules, by maintaining a record of words that repeatedly cause them trouble, and by faithfully practicing brief groups of words from a spelling list. Such advice, though uninspired and unoriginal, does produce real improvement if a student can be persuaded to follow it, perhaps with the added reminder that lack of confidence in spelling distracts the student from more important matters in writing.

A WRITER'S PERSPECTIVE

It's a poor imagination that can only think of one way to spell a word.

—Attributed to Mark Twain

A WRITER'S PERSPECTIVE

Everyone misspells occasionally, usually because of carelessness or simple failure to observe closely. Good spelling requires an eye for detail.

—William F. Irmscher

COMPUTER SPELLING CHECKERS

As this jingle makes clear, students should keep in mind the limitations of computerized spelling checkers. These programs can check only the spelling of the words in their memories (usually between 10,000 and 40,000 words), so some of the words students use won't be included. Most spelling checkers also can't distinguish between correctly spelled homonyms like *affect* and *effect*, for instance, or tell the difference between *red* and *read*. Students must check their papers visually as well as electronically to avoid making embarrassing mistakes.

CHAPTER REFERENCE LIST

The following is an outline of the chapter for quick reference.

TRANSPARENCY MASTER 34.1

34a

RESOURCES AND IDEAS

Some good references on teaching spelling are:

Brown, Alan S. "Encountering Misspellings and Spelling Performance: Why Wrong Isn't Right." *Journal of Educational Psychology* 80 (1988): 488–94. Brown analyzes the psychology of student misspellings.

Chomsky, Carol. "Reading, Writing, and Phonology." *Harvard Educational Review* 40 (1970): 287–309. Chomsky ties problems with spelling and word recognition to problems with hearing and distinguishing certain morphemes.

34a Recognizing typical spelling problems

Spelling well involves recognizing situations that commonly lead to misspelling: pronunciation can mislead you in several ways; different forms of the same word may have different spellings; and some words have more than one acceptable spelling.

1 Being wary of pronunciation

In English, unlike some languages, pronunciation of words is an unreliable guide to their spelling. The same letter or combination of letters may have different sounds in different words. (Say aloud these different ways of pronouncing the letters *ough: tough, dough, cough, through, bough.*) Another problem is that some words contain letters that are not pronounced clearly or at all, such as the *ed* in *asked,* the silent *e* in *swipe,* or the unpronounced *gh* in *tight.*

Pronunciation is a particularly unreliable guide in spelling **homonyms,** words pronounced the same though they have different spellings and meanings: *great/grate, to/too/two.* Some commonly confused homonyms and near-homonyms, such as *accept/except,* are listed below. (See p. 509 for tips on how to use spelling lists.)

Words commonly confused

accept (to receive)
except (other than)

affect (to have an influence on)
effect (result)

all ready (prepared)
already (by this time)

allude (to refer to indirectly)
elude (to avoid)

allusion (indirect reference)
illusion (erroneous belief or perception)

ascent (a movement up)
assent (agreement)

bare (unclothed)
bear (to carry, or an animal)

board (a plane of wood)
bored (uninterested)

born (brought into life)
borne (carried)

brake (stop)
break (smash)

buy (purchase)
by (next to)

capital (the seat of a government)
capitol (the building where a legislature meets)

cite (to quote an authority)
sight (the ability to see)
site (a place)

desert (to abandon)
dessert (after-dinner course)

discreet (reserved, respectful)
discrete (individual or distinct)

elicit (to bring out)
illicit (illegal)

fair (average, or lovely)
fare (a fee for transportation)

forth (forward)
fourth (after *third*)

gorilla (a large primate)
guerrilla (a kind of soldier)

hear (to perceive by ear)
here (in this place)

heard (past tense of *hear*)
herd (a group of animals)

hole (an opening)
whole (complete)

its (possessive of *it*)
it's (contraction of *it is*)

lead (heavy metal)
led (past tense of *lead*)

lessen (to make less)
lesson (something learned)

meat (flesh)
meet (encounter)

no (the opposite of *yes*)
know (to be certain)

passed (past tense of *pass*)
past (after, or a time gone by)

patience (forbearance)
patients (persons under medical care)

peace (the absence of war)
piece (a portion of something)

plain (clear)
plane (a carpenter's tool, or an airborne vehicle)

presence (the state of being at hand)
presents (gifts)

principal (most important, or the head of a school)
principle (a basic truth or law)

rain (precipitation)
reign (to rule)
rein (a strap for controlling an animal)

raise (to build up)
raze (to tear down)

right (correct)
rite (a religious ceremony)
write (to make letters)

road (a surface for driving)
rode (past tense of *ride*)

scene (where an action occurs)
seen (past participle of *see*)

seam (junction)
seem (appear)

stationary (unmoving)
stationery (writing paper)

straight (unbending)
strait (a water passageway)

their (possessive of *they*)
there (opposite of *here*)
they're (contraction of *they are*)

to (toward)
too (also)
two (following *one*)

waist (the middle of the body)
waste (discarded material)

weak (not strong)
week (Sunday through Saturday)

weather (climate)
whether (*if*, or introducing a choice)

which (one of a group)
witch (a sorcerer)

who's (contraction of *who is*)
whose (possessive of *who*)

your (possessive of *you*)
you're (contraction of *you are*)

2 Distinguishing between different forms of the same word

Spelling problems may occur when the noun form and the verb form of the same word are spelled differently. For example:

Clapp, Ouida, ed. *Teaching the Basics—Really!* Urbana: NCTE, 1977. The book includes several chapters on teaching spelling.

Clark, Roger, and I. Y. Hashimoto. "A Spelling Program for College Students." *Teaching English in the Two-Year College* 11 (1984): 34–38. The authors describe activities to help students improve spelling over the course of a semester.

Dobie, Ann R. "Orthographical Theory and Practice; or, How to Teach Spelling." *Journal of Basic Writing* 5 (1986): 41–48. Responses to this article appear in both the 1987 and 1988 volumes of this journal.

Irmscher, William F. *The Holt Guide to English.* 3rd ed. New York: Holt, 1981. Ch. 12. Irmscher offers concrete diagnostics and remedies for common spelling problems.

Sensenbaugh, Roger. "Spelling Instruction and the Use of Word Lists." *Composition Chronicle* 6.3 (April 1993): 8–9. The author describes techniques for helping students become better spellers.

Taylor, Karl, and Ede Kidder. "The Development of Spelling Skills from First Grade through Eighth Grade." *Written Communication* 5 (April 1988): 222–44. The authors tie spelling development to cognitive development and show instructors how to diagnose and help correct spelling problems.

COLLABORATIVE LEARNING

HOMONYM HOMEWORK

Sometimes the quickest way to learn distinctions in spelling between words that sound the same is to memorize the words and their definitions. The context in which the word is encountered can also become a kind of mnemonic (in addition to deliberately constructed mnemonics such as "the principal is a pal"). Divide this list of words among the class and have students work in groups to create exercise questions by posing one-sentence contexts for several of the words on this list, as for example: "(accept/except) I____the package from the UPS driver." The compiled exercise questions might be assigned as a quiz either in a subsequent class or on the network.

A WRITER'S PERSPECTIVE

The French don't care what they do, actually, so long as they pronounce it properly.

—ALAN JAY LERNER, *My Fair Lady*

RESOURCES AND IDEAS

Clark, Roger, and I. Y. Hashimoto. "A Spelling Program for College Students." *Teaching English in the Two-Year College* 11 (1984): 34–38. The authors present "a three-step program that emphasizes student participation in the diagnosis of spelling problems and practice in using an individualized reference dictionary created by students themselves from their own spelling errors."

EXTRA EXAMPLES

In addition to the words listed here, words that can be expressed by different forms, depending on the intended meaning, might also give students trouble. For example, *a while* is often written *awhile.* The two most frequently miswritten expressions, however, are *a lot* (commonly written "*alot*") and *all right* (commonly written "*alright*").

SPELLING PATRIOTICALLY

The confusion between British and American spellings can be blamed on American patriots at the time of the Revolutionary War. Led by Noah Webster, a group of linguistic patriots set out to make America linguistically independent of Britain and invented the American spellings of these common words.

LEARNING THE RULES

Most spelling rules have only a few exceptions, so it's often easier for students to memorize the short list of exceptions and assume that any other word follows the normal pattern. An excellent list of these deviations appears in the *National Labor Relations Board Style Manual* (Washington, DC: Government Printing Office, 1984).

VERB	NOUN	VERB	NOUN
advise	advice	enter	entrance
describe	description	marry	marriage
speak	speech	omit	omission

Sometimes the noun and the adjective forms of the same word differ.

NOUN	ADJECTIVE	NOUN	ADJECTIVE
comedy	comic	height	high
courtesy	courteous	Britain	British
generosity	generous		

The principal parts of irregular verbs are usually spelled differently.

begin, began, begun	know, knew, known
break, broke, broken	ring, rang, rung

Irregular nouns change spelling from singular to plural.

child, children	shelf, shelves
goose, geese	tooth, teeth
mouse, mice	woman, women

Notice, too, that the stem of a word may change its spelling in different forms.

four, forty   thief, theft

3 Using preferred spellings

Many words have variant spellings as well as preferred spellings. Often the variant spellings listed in an American dictionary are British spellings.

AMERICAN	BRITISH
color, humor	colour, humour
theater, center	theatre, centre
canceled, traveled	cancelled, travelled
judgment	judgement
realize	realise

sp
34b

34b Following spelling rules

Misspelling is often a matter of misspelling a syllable rather than the whole word. The following general rules focus on troublesome syllables, with notes for the occasional exceptions.

1 Distinguishing between *ie* and *ei*

Words like *believe* and *receive* sound alike in the second syllable, but the syllable is spelled differently. Use the familiar jingle to distinguish between *ie* and *ei:*

> *I* before *e,* except after *c,* or when pronounced "ay" as in *neighbor* and *weigh.*

i* BEFORE *e	believe grief chief	bier thief fiend	hygiene friend
ei* AFTER *c	ceiling receive	conceive deceit	perceive conceit
***ei* SOUNDED AS "AY"**	neighbor sleigh weight	freight eight vein	beige heinous

Exceptions In some words an *ei* combination neither follows *c* nor is pronounced "ay." These words include *either, neither, foreign, forfeit, height, leisure, weird, seize,* and *seizure.* This sentence might help you remember some of them: *The weird foreigner neither seizes leisure nor forfeits height.*

Exercise 1
Distinguishing between *ie* and *ei*

Insert *ie* or *ei* in the words below. Check doubtful spellings in a dictionary.

1. br__f	5. for__gn	9. l__surely	13. h__ght
2. dec__ve	6. pr__st	10. ach__ve	14. fr__ght
3. rec__pt	7. gr__vance	11. pat__nce	15. f__nt
4. s__ze	8. f__nd	12. p__rce	16. s__ve

ANSWERS: EXERCISE 1

1. brief	9. leisurely
2. deceive	10. achieve
3. receipt	11. patience
4. seize	12. pierce
5. foreign	13. height
6. priest	14. freight
7. grievance	15. feint
8. fiend	16. sieve

2 Keeping or dropping a final *e*

Many words end with an unpronounced or silent *e: move, brave, late, rinse.* Drop the final *e* when adding an ending that begins with a vowel.

advise + able = advisable	surprise + ing = surprising
force + ible = forcible	guide + ance = guidance

Keep the final, silent *e* if the ending begins with a consonant.

battle + ment = battlement	care + ful = careful
accurate + ly = accurately	like + ness = likeness

Exceptions The silent *e* is sometimes retained before an ending beginning with a vowel. It is kept when *dye* becomes *dyeing,* to avoid confusion with *dying*. It is kept to prevent mispronunciation of words like *shoeing* (not *shoing*) and *mileage* (not *milage*). And the final *e* is often retained after a soft *c* or *g*, to keep the sound of the consonant soft rather than hard.

courageous	changeable	noticeable
outrageous	manageable	embraceable

The silent *e* is also sometimes *dropped* before an ending beginning with a consonant, when the *e* is preceded by another vowel.

argue + ment = argument
due + ly = duly
true + ly = truly

ANSWERS: EXERCISE 2

1. malicious
2. lovable *or* loveable
3. serviceable
4. retirement
5. suing
6. virtuous
7. notable
8. battling
9. suspension

Exercise 2
Keeping or dropping a final *e*

Combine the following words and endings, keeping or dropping final *e*'s as necessary to make correctly spelled words. Check doubtful spellings in a dictionary.

1. malice + ious	4. retire + ment	7. note + able
2. love + able	5. sue + ing	8. battle + ing
3. service + able	6. virtue + ous	9. suspense + ion

3 Keeping or dropping a final *y*

Words ending in *y* often change their spelling when an ending is added to them. Change the final *y* to an *i* when it follows a consonant.

beauty, beauties	worry, worried	supply, supplies
folly, follies	merry, merrier	deputy, deputize

But keep the *y* when it follows a vowel, when the ending is *-ing*, or when it ends a proper name.

day, days	cry, crying	May, Mays
obey, obeyed	study, studying	Minsky, Minskys

ANSWERS: EXERCISE 3

1. implies
2. messier
3. applying
4. delaying
5. defiance
6. says
7. solidifies
8. Murphys
9. supplied

Exercise 3
Keeping or dropping a final *y*

Combine the following words and endings, changing or keeping final *y*'s as necessary to make correctly spelled words. Check doubtful spellings in a dictionary.

1. imply + s	4. delay + ing	7. solidify + s
2. messy + er	5. defy + ance	8. Murphy + s
3. apply + ing	6. say + s	9. supply + ed

Doubling consonants

Words ending in a consonant sometimes double the consonant when an ending is added. Whether to double the final consonant depends first on the number of syllables in the word.

In one-syllable words, double the final consonant when a single vowel precedes the final consonant.

slap, slapping	flat, flatter
tip, tipped	pit, pitted

However, *don't* double the final consonant when two vowels or a vowel and another consonant precede the final consonant.

pair, paired	park, parking
real, realize	rent, rented

In words of more than one syllable, double the final consonant when a single vowel precedes the final consonant and the stress falls on the last syllable of the stem once the ending is added.

submit, submitted	refer, referring
occur, occurred	begin, beginning

But *don't* double the final consonant when it is preceded by two vowels or by a vowel and another consonant, or when the stress falls on other than the stem's last syllable once the ending is added.

refer, reference	despair, despairing
relent, relented	beckon, beckoned

Exercise 4
Doubling consonants

Combine the following words and endings, doubling final consonants as necessary to make correctly spelled words. Check doubtful spellings in a dictionary.

1. repair + ing	4. shop + ed	7. drip + ing
2. admit + ance	5. conceal + ed	8. declaim + ed
3. benefit + ed	6. allot + ed	9. parallel + ing

ANSWERS: EXERCISE 4

1. repairing	6. allotted
2. admittance	7. dripping
3. benefited	8. declaimed
4. shopped	9. paralleling
5. concealed	

5 Attaching prefixes

Adding a prefix such as *dis-*, *mis-*, and *un-* does not change the spelling of a word. When adding a prefix, do not drop a letter from or add a letter to the original word.

uneasy	anti-intellectual	defuse	misstate
unnecessary	disappoint	de-emphasize	misspell
antifreeze	dissatisfied	misinform	

(See also p. 513 on when to use hyphens with prefixes: *prehistory* versus *ex-student.*)

IRREGULAR PLURALS

There are a few irregular plurals in English; most survive from Anglo-Saxon (for example, *child/children*) or are borrowed from other languages (*alumnus/alumni*). All native English nouns added since the Norman Conquest of England in 1066 have been regular, using the *-s* or *-es* suffixes to form the plural.

6 Forming plurals

Nouns

Most nouns form plurals by adding *-s* to the singular form.

boy, boys	table, tables
carnival, carnivals	Murphy, Murphys

ESL Noncount nouns do not form plurals and so do not add *-s.* Examples include *equipment, intelligence,* and *wealth.* See pages 260–61.

Some nouns ending in *f* or *fe* form the plural by changing the ending to *ve* before adding *-s.*

leaf, leaves	wife, wives
life, lives	yourself, yourselves

Singular nouns ending in *-s, -sh, -ch,* or *-x* form the plural by adding *-es.*

kiss, kisses	church, churches
wish, wishes	Jones, Joneses

(Notice that verbs ending in *-s, -sh, -ch,* or *-x* form the third-person singular in the same way. *Taxes* and *lurches* are examples.)

Nouns ending in *o* preceded by a vowel usually form the plural by adding *-s.*

ratio, ratios	zoo, zoos

Nouns ending in *o* preceded by a consonant usually form the plural by adding *-es.*

hero, heroes	tomato, tomatoes

EXCEPTIONS Some very common nouns form irregular plurals.

child, children	man, men
mouse, mice	woman, women

Some English nouns that were originally Italian, Greek, Latin, or French form the plural according to their original language:

analysis, analyses	datum, data
basis, bases	medium, media
beau, beaux	phenomenon, phenomena
crisis, crises	piano, pianos
criterion, criteria	thesis, theses

A few such nouns may form irregular or regular plurals: for instance, *index, indices, indexes; curriculum, curricula, curriculums.* The regular plural is more contemporary.

Compound nouns

Form plurals of compound nouns in one of two ways. Add *-s* to the last word when the component words are roughly equal in importance, whether or not they are hyphenated.

city-states　　breakthroughs
painter-sculptors　　bucket seats

Add *-s* to the noun when a noun is combined with other parts of speech.

fathers-in-law　　passersby

Note, however, that most modern dictionaries give the plural of *spoonful* as *spoonfuls.*

Exercise 5
Forming plurals
Make correct plurals of the following singular words. Check doubtful spellings in a dictionary.

1. pile	5. mile per hour	9. Bales	13. thief
2. donkey	6. box	10. cupful	14. goose
3. beach	7. switch	11. libretto	15. hiss
4. summary	8. sister-in-law	12. video	16. appendix

ANSWERS: EXERCISE 5

1. piles	9. Baleses
2. donkeys	10. cupfuls
3. beaches	11. librettos *or* libretti
4. summaries	12. videos
5. miles per hour	13. thieves
6. boxes	14. geese
7. switches	15. hisses
8. sisters-in-law	16. appendices *or* appendixes

34c Developing spelling skills

The essential steps in improving spelling skills were listed at the start of this chapter: proofread, be suspicious, and use a dictionary. These and a few additional aids are discussed below.

1 Editing and proofreading carefully

If spelling is a problem for you, give it high priority while editing your writing (p. 73) and again while proofreading, your last chance to catch misspelled words (p. 77). Reading a draft backward, word by word, can help you spot mistakes such as switched or omitted letters in words you know. Because the procedure forces you to consider each word in isolation, it can also highlight

CAREFUL PROOFREADING

Many of the errors made with spelling can be avoided through careful proofreading. Two proofreading techniques that force the writer to read more slowly and carefully are (1) reading the essay aloud and (2) reading the essay backward, from the last sentence to the first.

spellings you may be less sure of. A sense of uncertainty is crucial in spotting and correcting spelling errors, even for good spellers who make relatively few errors. Listen to your own uncertainty, and let it lead you to the dictionary.

COMPUTER EXERCISE

SPELLING LOGS

Most students benefit from keeping lists, or logbooks, of their spelling problems. After a few weeks of recording data, they may be able to see patterns of difficulty emerge. Students should add misspelled words found using a computer spelling checker to their spelling logs for those times when they are away from their machines or the computer is down. Some good examples of pattern recognition are found in Kristene F. Anderson, "Using a Spelling Survey to Develop Basic Writers' Linguistic Awareness," *Journal of Basic Writing* 6 (1987): 72–78.

MAKING WORDS YOUR OWN

One way to help students remember words they look up in a dictionary is to have them highlight the word, jot it down on an ongoing list, and then use it in a sentence of their own. At a later date, students should go back to their "dictionary list" and try to use each word in a one-sentence context. If students keep up this practice throughout a semester they will have added those words to their working vocabularies.

RESOURCES AND IDEAS

Harris, Muriel. "The Big Five: Individualizing Improvement in Spelling." In *Teaching the Basics—Really!* Ed. Ouida H. Clapp. Urbana: NCTE, 1977. 104–07. Harris suggests making students aware of their habitual problems deriving from homophones, pronunciation, doubled consonants, word roots, and the schwa.

2 Using a dictionary

How can you look up a word you can't spell? Start by guessing at the spelling and looking up your guess. If that doesn't work, pronounce the word aloud to come up with other possible spellings, and look them up. Unless the word is too specialized to be included in your dictionary, trial and error will eventually pay off.

If you're using a computerized spelling checker, it may do the guessing for you by providing several choices for misspelled words. But you may still need to check a dictionary to make your choice.

3 Pronouncing carefully

Careful pronunciation is not always a reliable guide to spelling (see p. 500), but it can keep you from misspelling words that are often mispronounced. For example:

athletics (*not* atheletics)
disastrous (*not* disasterous)
environment (*not* envirnment)
frustrate (*not* fustrate)
government (*not* goverment)
height (*not* heighth)
history (*not* histry)
irrelevant (*not* irrevelant)
laboratory (*not* labratory)
library (*not* libary)
lightning (*not* lightening)
mischievous (*not* mischievious)
nuclear (*not* nucular)
recognize (*not* reconize)
representative (*not* represenitive)
strictly (*not* stricly)

4 Tracking and analyzing your errors

Keep a list of the words marked "misspelled" or "spelling" or "sp" in your papers. This list will contain hints about your particular spelling problems, such as that you tend to confuse *affect* and *effect* or to form plurals incorrectly. (If you need help analyzing the list, consult your writing instructor.) The list will also provide a personalized study guide, a focus for your efforts to spell better.

5 Using mnemonics

Mnemonics (pronounced with an initial *n* sound) are techniques for assisting your memory. The *er* in *letter* and *paper* can remind you that *stationery* (meaning "writing paper") has an *er* near the end; *stationary* with an *a* means "standing in place." Or the word *dome* with its long *o* sound can remind you that the building in which the legislature meets is spelled *capitol,* with an *o*. The *capital* city is spelled with *al* like *Albany,* the capital of New York. If you identify the words you have trouble spelling, you can take a few minutes to think of your own mnemonics, which may work better for you than someone else's.

 6 Studying spelling lists

Learning to spell commonly misspelled words will reduce your spelling errors. For general improvement, work with the following list of commonly misspelled words. Study only six or seven words at a time. If you are unsure of the meaning of a word, look it up in a dictionary and try using it in a sentence. Pronounce the word out loud, syllable by syllable, and write the word out. (The list of similar-sounding words on pp. 500–01 should be considered an extension of the one below.)

absence
abundance
acceptable
accessible
accidentally
accommodate
accomplish
accumulate
accuracy
accustomed
achieve
acknowledge
acquire
across
actually
address
admission
adolescent
advice
advising
against
aggravate
aggressive
all right
all together
allegiance
almost
already
although

altogether
amateur
among
amount
analysis
analyze
angel
annual
answer
apology
apparent
appearance
appetite
appreciate
appropriate
approximately
arctic
argument
arrest
ascend
assassinate
assimilation
assistance
associate
atheist
athlete
attendance
audience
average

bargain
basically
because
beginning
belief
believe
beneficial
benefited
boundary
breath
Britain
bureaucracy
business

calculator
calendar
caricature
carrying
cede
ceiling
cello
cemetery
certain
changeable
changing
characteristic
chief
chocolate
choose

chose
climbed
coarse
column
coming
commercial
commitment
committed
committee
competent
competition
complement
compliment
conceive
concentrate
concert
condemn
conquer
conscience
conscious
consistency
consistent
continuous
controlled
controversial
convenience
convenient
coolly
course

MEMORY AID

Separating the *-sedes*

Students may learn to distinguish which *-sede* (*-ceed, -cede*) should be planted at the end of a word by memorizing the words *proceed, exceed, succeed,* and *supersede. Proceed, exceed,* and *succeed* are the only words ending in *-ceed. Supersede* is the only word ending in *-sede.* All the remaining *-cede* words end in *-cede.*

RESOURCES AND IDEAS

Gere, Anne Ruggles. "Alternatives to Tradition in Teaching Spelling." In *Teaching the Basics—Really!* Ed. Ouida H. Clapp. Urbana: NCTE, 1977. 100–03. Gere proposes the use of individualized word lists and classroom games and also the teaching of phoneme-grapheme correspondences and word division.

McClellan, Jane. "A Clinic for Misspellers." *College English* 40 (1978): 324–29. McClellan suggests using several kinds of word lists and frequent drills to bring about improvement.

courteous
criticism
criticize
crowd
cruelty
curiosity
curious
curriculum

deceive
deception
decide
decision
deductible
definitely
degree
dependent
descend
descendant
describe
description
desirable
despair
desperate
destroy
determine
develop
device
devise
dictionary
difference
dining
disagree
disappear
disappoint
disapprove
disastrous
discipline
discriminate
discussion
disease
disgusted
dissatisfied
distinction
divide
divine
division
doctor
drawer

easily
ecstasy
efficiency
efficient
eighth
either
eligible
embarrass
emphasize
empty
enemy
entirely
entrepreneur
environment
equipped
especially
essential
every
exaggerate
exceed
excellent
exercise
exhaust
exhilarate
existence
expense
experience
experiment
explanation
extremely

familiar
fascinate
favorite
February
fiery
finally
forcibly
foreign
foresee
forty
forward
friend
frightening
fulfill

gauge
generally
ghost
government
grammar
grief
guarantee
guard
guidance

happily
harass
height
heroes
hideous
humorous
hungry
hurriedly
hurrying
hypocrisy
hypocrite

ideally
illogical
imaginary
imagine
imitation
immediately
immigrant
incidentally
incredible
independence
independent
individually
inevitably
influential
initiate
innocuous
inoculate
insistent
integrate
intelligence
interest
interference
interpret
irrelevant
irresistible
irritable
island

jealousy
judgment

kindergarten
knowledge

laboratory
leisure
length
library
license
lieutenant
lightning
likelihood
literally
livelihood
loneliness
loose
lose
luxury
lying

magazine
maintenance
manageable
marriage
mathematics
meant
medicine
miniature
minor
minutes
mirror
mischievous
missile
misspelled
morale
morals
mortgage
mournful
muscle
mysterious

naturally
necessary
neighbor
neither
nickel
niece
ninety
ninth
noticeable

nuclear
nuisance
numerous

obstacle
occasion
occasionally
occur
occurrence
official
omission
omit
omitted
opinion
opponent
opportunity
opposite
ordinary
originally

paid
panicky
paralleled
parliament
particularly
peaceable
peculiar
pedal
perceive
perception
performance
permanent
permissible
persistence
personnel
perspiration
persuade
persuasion
physical
physiology
physique
pitiful
planning
playwright
pleasant
poison
politician
pollute
possession
possibly
practically
practice
prairie
precede
preference
preferred
prejudice
preparation
prevalent
primitive
privilege
probably
procedure
proceed
process
professor
prominent
pronunciation
psychology
purpose
pursue
pursuit

quandary
quantity
quarter
questionnaire
quiet
quizzes

realistically
realize
really
rebel
rebelled
recede
receipt
receive
recognize
recommend
reference
referred
relief
relieve
religious
remembrance
reminisce
renown
repetition
representative
resemblance
resistance
restaurant
rhyme
rhythm
ridiculous
roommate

sacrifice
sacrilegious
safety
satellite
scarcity
schedule
science
secretary
seize
separate
sergeant
several
sheriff
shining
shoulder
siege
significance
similar
sincerely
sophomore
source
speak
specimen
speech
sponsor
stopping
strategy
strength
strenuous
stretch
strict
studying
succeed
successful
sufficient
summary
superintendent
supersede
suppress
surely
surprise
suspicious

teammate
technical
technique
temperature
tendency
than
then
thorough
though
throughout
together
tomatoes
tomorrow
tragedy
transferred
truly
twelfth
tyranny

unanimous
unconscious
undoubtedly
unnecessary
until
usable
usually

vacuum
vegetable
vengeance
vicious
villain
visible

weather
Wednesday
weird
wherever
whether
wholly
woman
women
writing

yacht

34d Using the hyphen to form compound words

The hyphen (-) is a mark of punctuation used either to divide a word or to form a compound word. Always use a hyphen to divide a word at the end of a line and continue it on the next line, as explained in Chapter 30 on word division. Using a hyphen to form compound words is somewhat more complicated.

Compound words express a combination of ideas. They may be written as a single word, (*breakthrough*), as two words (*decision making*), or as a hyphenated word (*cave-in*). Sometimes compound words with the same element are spelled differently—for example, *cross-reference, cross section,* and *crosswalk*. Several generalizations can be made about using the hyphen for compound words. But if you doubt the spelling of a compound word, consult a dictionary.

THE A-B-C RULE

A useful rule for determining whether an adjective before a noun is compound and should be hyphenated is the *a-b-c rule.* For example, in the phrase *record-setting pace,* the first word, *record,* is term *a.* The second word, *setting,* is term *b,* and the noun being modified, *pace,* is term *c.* According to the *a-b-c rule,* if the writer can make the statement "The *c* was *a* and *b,*" no hyphen is needed. If that statement is impossible, *a* and *b* must be hyphenated. Since the writer can't say "The pace was record and setting," *record-setting pace* needs to be hyphenated. The test here is similar to the one for coordinate adjectives in 21f-2.

 1 Forming compound adjectives

When two or more words serve together as a single modifier before a noun, a hyphen or hyphens form the modifying words clearly into a unit.

> She is a *well-known* actor.
> The conclusions are based on *out-of-date* statistics.
> No *English-speaking* people were in the room.

When the same compound adjectives follow the noun, hyphens are unnecessary and are usually left out.

> The actor is *well known.*
> The statistics were *out of date.*
> Those people are *English speaking.*

Hyphens are also unnecessary in compound modifiers containing an *-ly* adverb, even when these fall before the noun: *clearly defined terms; swiftly moving train.*

When part of a compound adjective appears only once in two or more parallel compound adjectives, hyphens indicate which words the reader should mentally join with the missing part.

> School-age children should have eight- or nine-o'clock bedtimes.

 2 Writing fractions and compound numbers

Hyphens join the numerator and denominator of fractions.

three-fourths	one-half

The whole numbers twenty-one to ninety-nine are always hyphenated.

Eighteen girls and twenty-four boys took the bus.
The total is eighty-seven.

3 Forming coined compounds

Writers sometimes create (coin) temporary compounds and join the words with hyphens.

Muhammad Ali gave his opponent a classic come-and-get-me look.

4 Attaching some prefixes and suffixes

Prefixes are usually attached to word stems without hyphens: *predetermine, unnatural, disengage.* However, when the prefix precedes a capitalized word or when a capital letter is combined with a word, a hyphen usually separates the two: *un-American, non-European, A-frame.* And some prefixes, such as *self-, all-,* and *ex-* (meaning "formerly"), usually require hyphens no matter what follows: *self-control, all-inclusive, ex-student.* The only suffix that regularly requires a hyphen is *-elect,* as in *president-elect.*

A hyphen is sometimes necessary to prevent misreading, especially when a prefix and stem place the same two vowels together or when a stem and suffix place the same three consonants together.

deemphasize, de-emphasize
antiintellectual, anti-intellectual
trilllike, trill-like

Check a recent dictionary for the current form, particularly for words that join two *e*'s or *i*'s. If the word you seek does not appear in the dictionary, assume that it should be hyphenated.

5 Eliminating confusion

If you wrote the sentence *Doonesbury is a comic strip character,* the reader might stumble briefly over your meaning. Is Doonesbury a character in a comic strip or a comic (funny) character who strips? A hyphen would prevent any possible confusion: *Doonesbury is a comic-strip character.*

Adding prefixes to words can sometimes create ambiguity. *Recreation* (*creation* with the prefix *re-*) could mean either "a new creation" or "diverting, pleasurable activity." The use of a hyphen, *re-creation,* limits the word to the first meaning. Without a hyphen the word suggests the second meaning.

ANSWERS: EXERCISE 6

1. Correct
2. de-escalate
3. forty-odd soldiers
4. little-known bar
5. seven-eighths
6. seventy-eight
7. happy-go-lucky
8. pre-existing
9. senator-elect
10. Correct
11. two- and six-person cars
12. ex-songwriter
13. V-shaped
14. re-educate

Exercise 6
Using hyphens in compound words

Insert hyphens as needed in the following compounds. Circle all compounds that are correct as given. Consult a dictionary as needed.

1. reimburse
2. deescalate
3. forty odd soldiers
4. little known bar
5. seven eighths
6. seventy eight
7. happy go lucky
8. preexisting
9. senator elect
10. postwar
11. two and six person cars
12. ex songwriter
13. V shaped
14. reeducate

Part VIII

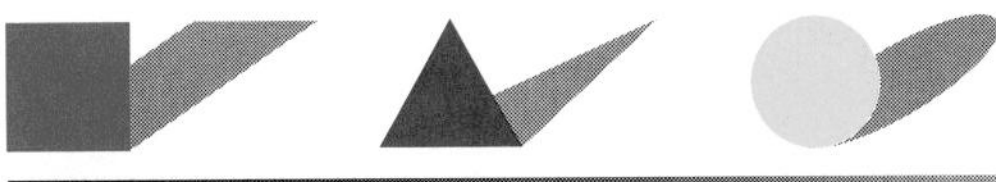

HIGHLIGHTS

Many students dislike or actively fear writing research papers—either because of misconceptions they have about the purpose of such assignments or because of previous unpleasant or purely mechanistic experiences with research writing. As a result, you may find that some students resist this type of writing. This chapter shows students not only how valuable and interesting research writing can be, but that it is an extension of the critical thinking, reading, and writing skills stressed in the handbook.

This section of the handbook offers a detailed overview of research writing, from finding information (using both electronic and print resources) to shaping it, documenting it, and presenting it according to a consistent set of standards. The material is illustrated throughout by student papers in progress, so that students can see how the strategies discussed in the text might be applied in actual first-year college writing projects. The section features a thorough discussion of computer-aided research and standard reference sources, a number of collaborative activities, and numerous examples to help students become more confident, successful researchers.

This chapter presents research gathering as a strategic task and offers a series of descriptions and suggestions to help students move through a research project effectively.

RESOURCES AND IDEAS

Nelson, Jennie. "The Research Paper: A 'Rhetoric of Doing' or a 'Rhetoric of the Finished Word'?" *Composition Studies* 22 (Fall 1994): 65–75. Nelson argues that the research paper does not serve any useful educational purpose unless students understand it as a learning process.

Wilson, Matthew. "Research, Expressivism and Silence." *Journal of Advanced Composition* 15 (1995): 241–60. A thought-provoking analysis of the challenges that teachers face in defining the research paper, and that students face in writing them.

Chapter 35 *Beginning a Research Project*

If you've ever watched a TV detective pursue a culprit, you know that research can be exciting. When an investigator has a goal in sight, the seemingly mundane work of digging through files, interviewing witnesses, and piecing together clues becomes a concentrated and enthusiastic search.

This same excitement can be yours as you conduct research in school. Honest and inquisitive research writing does demand close attention to details, but the work will not be tedious if you see the details as steadily contributing to discoveries about yourself and the world around you. As you consider what others have to say about your subject and build on that to create new knowledge, you will become an expert in your own right. You will have a significant, in-depth understanding of a subject you care about, and you will communicate that understanding to others.

Through research writing, you will also learn skills that will help you in school, in work, and in life:

- Using the library and the Internet for research
- Analyzing and evaluating others' work
- Drawing on others' work to form, support, and extend your own opinions
- Documenting your sources

Your investigation will be influenced by whether you are expected mainly to report, to interpret, or to analyze sources.

- In **reporting**, you survey, organize, and objectively present the available evidence about a topic.

- In **interpreting,** you examine a range of views on a topic in order to answer a question with your own conclusions.
- In **analyzing,** you attempt to solve a problem or answer a question through critical thinking about texts such as scholarly or literary works. (In this context, *analysis* stands for the entire process of critical reading and writing. See pp. 1–21.)

Reporting, interpreting, and analyzing are not exclusive: for instance, a paper analyzing a repeated image in a poet's work would also involve a survey of poems and an interpretation of their meaning. Because the three operations overlap, the research and writing process described in this and the next three chapters can generally serve any one of them.

Throughout these chapters at the notebook symbol opposite, we will follow the development of research papers by two students, Edward Begay and Vanessa Haley. Begay's work, emphasizing interpretation, receives somewhat more attention; Haley's work, emphasizing analysis, enters the discussion whenever her process differed significantly from Begay's.

35a Planning a research project

A thoughtful plan and systematic procedures will help you anticipate and follow through on the diverse and overlapping activities of research writing.

As soon as you receive an assignment for a research project, you can begin developing a strategy for completing it. The first step should be making a schedule that apportions the available time to the necessary work. A possible schedule appears on the next page. In it the research-writing process corresponds to the general writing process discussed in Chapters 1–2: planning or developing (steps 1–8), drafting (step 9), and revising and editing (step 10), plus the additional important stage of documenting the sources you use (steps 11–12). Like any other essay, a research paper evolves gradually, and the steps sometimes overlap and repeat. For instance, while you do research, your reading leads you to organize ideas; and while you organize ideas, you discover where you need to do more research.

Such shifts are inevitable, and allowing for them is one key to successful and rewarding research writing. While working on a project, carry index cards or a notebook with you at all times to use as a **research journal,** a place to record your activities and ideas. (See pp. 4 and 37 on journal keeping.) In the journal's dated entries, you can keep a record of sources you consult, the leads you want to pursue, any dead ends you reach, and, most important, your

RESOURCES AND IDEAS

Brent, Doug. *Reading as Rhetorical Invention: Knowledge, Persuasion, and the Teaching of Research-Based Writing.* Urbana: NCTE, 1992. Brent shows how students can use sources to generate researched essays including directed reading projects that help students to develop individualized topics.

Lutzker, Marilyn. *Research Projects for College Students: What to Write Across the Curriculum.* Westport: Greenwood, 1988. Lutzker provides a librarian's guide to intellectually challenging projects from all disciplines; she includes teaching tips and starter bibliographies.

Macrorie, Ken. *Searching Writing.* Upper Montclair: Boynton/Cook, 1986. Macrorie teaches students to conduct "I-search," personally motivated and inspired research using primary sources as well as library work.

Schwegler, Robert A., and Linda K. Shamoon. "The Aims and Processes of the Research Paper." *College English* 44 (1982): 812–24. The authors contend that all academic research begins with a review of the literature, followed by either examination of a theory, clarification or amplification of previous research, or contesting a hypothesis.

TRANSPARENCY MASTER 35.1

TEACHING TIP

Beginning college students need help in establishing a realistic schedule. Emphasize strongly that each of these four segments really will take about a quarter of the time. Share with them the schedule for a writing project you've recently completed, and point out the kinds of places where delays are likely to occur.

TEACHING TIP

If students have been assigned research projects in other courses, and the instructors of those other courses don't object, permit students to work on those papers in your class or to write a separate paper for you based on the same research materials. Such dual assignments help students transfer writing skills from your classroom to other courses, and your colleagues may appreciate your helping students to write better papers in their disciplines.

RESOURCES AND IDEAS

Pelham, Fran O'Byrne. "The Research Journal: Integrating Reading, Writing, and Research." *Composition Chronicle* 6.3 (April 1993): 4–5. O'Byrne recommends using a journal to supplement typical research activities and to allow students to "research, reflect, write, and then attend recursively to these events."

Randall, Sally N. "Information Charts: a Strategy for Organizing Student Research." *Journal of Adolescent and Adult Literacy* 39 (April 1996): 536–43. Randall suggests methods for helping students to organize information and plan further research strategies.

Strickland, James. "The Research Sequence: What to Do Before the Term Paper." *College Composition and Communication* 37 (1986): 233–36. Strickland presents a sequence moving students from opinion papers to documented research projects.

TEACHING TIP

Note cards or notebooks are fairly easy tools for inexperienced writers to use. However, some students just aren't comfortable with cards, and

Scheduling steps in research writing

(See the pages in parentheses for discussion of the steps.)

Complete by:

______ 1. Planning a research project (previous page)
______ 2. Finding and limiting a researchable topic (below)
______ 3. Becoming familiar with electronic searches (p. 522) and finding sources to refine your topic (p. 529)
______ 4. Making a working bibliography (p. 559)

______ 5. Evaluating and synthesizing sources (p. 563)
______ 6. Taking notes using summary, paraphrase, and direct quotation (p. 569) and avoiding plagiarism (p. 578)
______ 7. Developing a thesis sentence (p. 585)

______ 8. Creating a structure (p. 586)
______ 9. Drafting the paper (p. 589) and using and introducing summaries, paraphrases, and quotations (p. 590)

______ 10. Revising and editing the paper (p. 594)
______ 11. Citing sources in your text (p. 599)
______ 12. Preparing the list of works cited (p. 607)
______ 13. Preparing and proofreading the final manuscript (p. 597)
______ Final paper due

Each segment marked off by a horizontal line will occupy *roughly* one-fourth of the total time. The most unpredictable segments are the first two, so it's wise to get started early enough to accommodate the unexpected.

thoughts about sources, leads, dead ends, new directions, relationships, and anything else that strikes you. Notes on what your sources actually say should be taken and organized separately—for instance, in the computer files or on the note cards discussed on pages 571–72. The research journal is the place for tracking and developing your own ideas. You will probably find that the very act of writing in it opens your mind and clarifies your thinking, making your research increasingly productive and rewarding.

35b Finding a researchable topic and question

Before reading this section, you may want to review the suggestions given on pages 26–29 for finding and limiting an essay topic. Generally, the same procedure applies to writing any kind of research paper: take a subject assigned to you, or think of one that interests you, and narrow it to manageable dimensions by making it specific. However, selecting and limiting a topic for a research paper can present special opportunities and problems. If you have questions about your topic anywhere along the line, consult your instructor.

A topic for a research paper has four primary requirements, each with corresponding pitfalls:

1. Ample published sources of information are available on the topic. Other researchers should have had a chance to produce evidence on the topic, weigh the evidence, and publish their conclusions. And the sources should be accessible.

   Avoid (*a*) very recent topics, such as a new medical breakthrough, and (*b*) topics that are removed geographically, such as a minor event in Australian history.

2. The topic encourages research in the kinds and number of sources required by the assignment.

   Avoid (*a*) topics that depend entirely on personal opinion and experience, such as the virtues of your hobby; and (*b*) topics that require research in only one source, such as a straight factual biography or a how-to like "Making Lenses for Eyeglasses." (An exception to *b* is a paper in which you analyze a single work such as a novel or painting.)

3. The topic will lead you to an assessment of sources and to defensible conclusions. Even when a research paper is intended to persuade, the success of the argument will depend on the balanced presentation of all significant points of view.

   Avoid controversial topics that rest entirely on belief or prejudice, such as when human life begins or why women (or men) are superior. Though these topics may certainly be disputed, your own preconceptions could slant your research or conclusions. Further, your readers are unlikely to be swayed from their own beliefs.

Checklist for a good research topic

1. Published sources are ample: the topic is neither too recent nor too removed.
2. Sources are diverse: the topic is neither wholly personal nor wholly factual.
3. Sources can be assessed objectively: the topic is not solely a matter of belief, dogma, or prejudice.
4. Sources can be examined thoroughly in the assigned time and length: the topic is not too broad.

their research actually may suffer if they are forced to use them. If students have great trouble keeping cards, suggest that they keep their notes in their journal; the greater space may give them more freedom to compose effectively.

RESOURCES AND IDEAS

Capossela, Toni-Lee. "Students as Sociolinguists: Getting Real Research from Freshman Writers." *College Composition and Communication* 42 (1991): 75–79. Capossela uses students' command of their own language to engage in real-world issues and write research papers.

Dellinger, Dixie G. "Alternatives to Clip-and-Stitch: Real Research and Writing in the Classroom." *English Journal* 78 (1989): 31–38. Dellinger claims that engaging students in primary research helps them generate material and enthusiasm for writing.

Horning, Alice. "Advising Undecided Students Through Research Writing." *College Composition and Communication* 42 (1991): 80–84. Horning provides a sequence of assignments encouraging students to explore various career options, incorporating a number of research strategies.

Hult, Christine. "Expanded Roles for Computers in Writing Research Papers and Reports." *Teaching English in the Two-Year College* 17 (1990): 114–19. Hult describes how students can use the computer to find, organize, and store information as well as to compose, revise, and edit, thus illustrating that the computer can be well used throughout the process of writing the research paper.

TRANSPARENCY MASTER 35.2

TEACHING TIP

It's useful to work with the research librarians at your school throughout the process of planning and implementing a research course. In particular, you might consult with the librarians before students begin to generate topics for their research papers. The librarians can tell you which topics may have limited resources available, or describe new materials they've recently acquired. This will help you guide your students in selecting workable topics.

COLLABORATIVE LEARNING

Assign teams of students to interview researchers—professors in other departments, employees of local businesses, salespeople looking for new leads, and so on. Have them ask how these researchers go about looking for and limiting topics, what kinds of "tricks" or strategies they use, why they value research, and what rewards they get from it. In this way, students will see that research is a valued activity outside the writing classroom as well as in it. Each team should report its findings to the entire class.

RESOURCES AND IDEAS

Nelson, Jennie. "The Library Revisited: Exploring Students' Research Processes." In *Hearing Ourselves Think: Cognitive Research in the College Writing Classroom.* Ed. Ann M. Penrose and Barbara M. Sitko. New York: Oxford UP, 1993. 102–24. Includes case studies of students' composing processes throughout the research paper project, including assembling sources and developing topics.

Quantic, Diane. "Insights into the Research Process from Student Logs." *Journal of Teaching Writing* 6 (1986): 211–25. Quantic analyzes aspects of research projects that may cause writing anxiety or blocks and suggests ways to overcome these problems.

A WRITER'S PERSPECTIVE

Not the least part of discovery is asking the right questions.

—St. Augustine

4. The topic suits the length of paper assigned and the time given for research and writing.

   Avoid broad topics that have too many sources to survey adequately, such as a major event in history or the collected works of a poet.

The students Edward Begay and Vanessa Haley took slightly different approaches to finding and limiting topics. For a composition course, Begay's instructor assigned an interpretation with a persuasive purpose but left the selection of subject to the student. Begay had recently read several newspaper articles on a subject that intrigued him: what kind of future computers might bring. Taking this broad subject as his starting point, he used clustering (see p. 42) to pursue some implications. As the following cluster diagram shows, Begay found himself giving the most thought to the Internet. He posed questions until a cluster about access to the Internet led him to a question that seemed interesting and significant: "Will the poor be excluded from the Internet?"

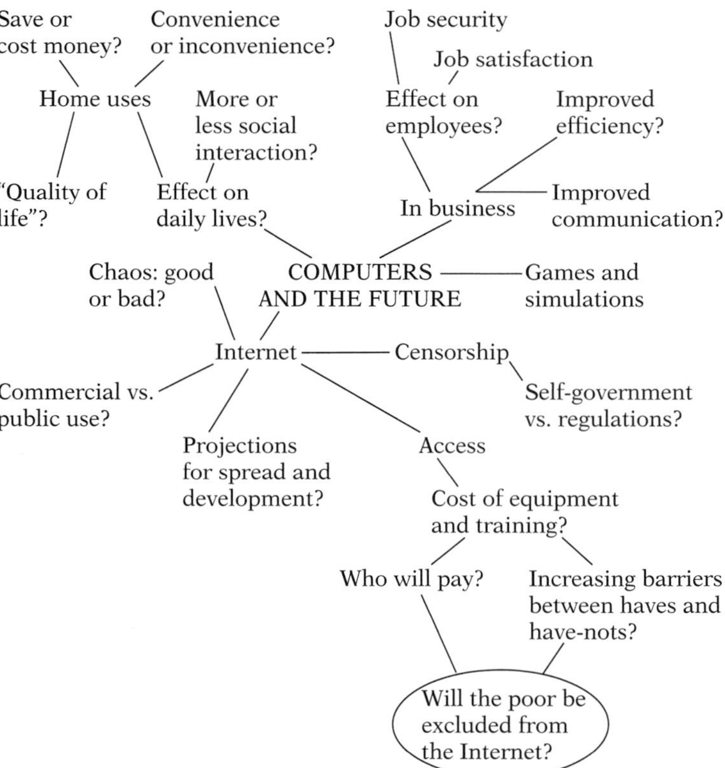

In developing a topic and question for an analysis paper assigned in a composition course, Vanessa Haley followed a somewhat different procedure. Instead of starting with a general subject, as Begay did, Haley began by looking for an unresolved question, interesting problem, or disagreement among the experts in some field of study. She had recently been reading an anthology of writings on the environment, and she had been disturbed by how many naturalists and environmentalists view human beings not as part of "nature" but as something separate from it, usually as its destroyer. In her journal, Haley wrote this entry:

> Many writers see nature as a place for humans to retreat to, or a wonderful thing that humans are ruining. Humans aren't considered natural themselves—human civilization isn't considered natural. Human civ. is "anti-natural." Isn't such a separation unrealistic and damaging? We *are* natural. We're here to stay, and we're not going back to the Stone Age, so we'd better focus on the connections between "us" and "it" (nature) rather than just the differences. Dillard seems to do this—seems to connect human and natural worlds. People are neither better nor worse than nature but just bound up in it. "Nature is as careless as it is bountiful, and . . . with that extravagance goes a crushing waste that will one day include our own cheap lives" ("Fecundity").

At the end of this entry, Haley refers to and quotes the writer Annie Dillard, one of the authors represented in the anthology. Haley decided to explore Dillard's views further by reading and analyzing more of her work. Haley's opening question for investigation, then, was "How does Annie Dillard see the place of humanity in nature?"

Exercise 1
Finding a topic and question

Choose three of the following subjects and narrow each one to at least one topic and question suitable for beginning work on a research paper. Or list and then limit three subjects of your own that you would enjoy investigating. (This exercise can be the first step in a research paper project that continues through Chapters 35–37.)

1. Bilingual education
2. Training of teachers
3. Dance in America
4. The history of women's suffrage
5. Food additives
6. Immigrants in the United States
7. Space exploration
8. Business espionage
9. The effect of television on professional sports
10. Child abuse
11. African Americans and civil rights
12. Recent developments in cancer research
13. Computer piracy
14. Homelessness
15. The European exploration of North America before Columbus
16. Hazardous substances in the workplace

COLLABORATIVE LEARNING

In Exercise 1 (as with all the exercises in this chapter) students should complete the assigned task individually in order to focus their research interests and develop their own projects. However, you can greatly enhance this process of individual learning by creating ongoing collaborative workshops in which students share their findings from each exercise and keep up on the progress of each other's research projects. When students have completed Exercise 1 for example, you might divide them into groups according to the topics they have chosen so that they have the opportunity to learn how other students narrowed particular topics in different directions. You might also invite students to propose other areas of interest which could be added to the list in Exercise 1 and then narrowed.

ANSWERS: EXERCISE 1

Individual response.

17. Television evangelism
18. Science fiction
19. Treatment or prevention of AIDS
20. Water pollution
21. Women writers
22. Campaign financing
23. Comic film actors
24. An unsolved crime
25. Genetic engineering
26. Male and female heroes in modern fiction
27. Computers and the privacy of the individual
28. Gothic or romance novels in the nineteenth and twentieth centuries
29. The social responsibility of business
30. Trends in popular music

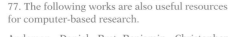

RESOURCES AND IDEAS

For more information on conducting electronic searches, see Susan Lang's article, "Using Computers to Teach Writing," pp. IAE-63–IAE-77. The following works are also useful resources for computer-based research.

Anderson, Daniel, Bret Benjamin, Christopher Busiel, and Bill Paredes-Holt. *Teaching Online: Internet Research, Conversation, and Composition*. New York: Longman, 1998. An extremely useful and practical guide to electronic research; in particular, see Chapter 5, "The Electronic Library."

Davis, Chris. "The I-Search Paper Goes Global: Using the Internet as a Research Tool," *English Journal* 84:6 (1995): 27–33. Davis shows how the Internet enhances students' abilities to develop and follow through on their own research interests.

Mark, Beth L., and Trudi E. Jacobson. "Teaching Anxious Students Skills for the Electronic Library." *College Teaching* 43.1 (Fall 1995): 28–31. Suggests *do*'s and *don't*'s when introducing students to electronic library databases, as for example, ERIC searches.

35c Conducting electronic searches

Computer technology has dramatically altered research methods. Today, most libraries' reference rooms are filled with computer terminals instead of drawers of cards. Electronic catalogs and indexes allow researchers to conduct sophisticated searches with only a few keystrokes, both in the library and from miles away over phone lines. The Internet—a vast network of computers—can bring information from around the world to your fingertips: for example, the catalogs of thousands of libraries, the developing ideas of experts, and the texts of newspapers, magazines, and scholarly journals.

These changes both aid and complicate the research process. You can now rapidly accumulate lists of sources, but they present you with the challenge of deciding which sources are most appropriate for your project.

This section explains how to find out what's available to you (below), offers guidelines for conducting an efficient and productive search (p. 525), and gives some ways of evaluating your search (p. 527).

1 Discovering what's available

Your search for electronic sources will be quicker and more productive if you take the time to find out what kinds of sources you have access to and how you can use them.

A tip for researchers

If you are unsure of how to locate or use your library's resources, ask a reference librarian. This person is very familiar with all the library's resources and with general and specialized research techniques, and it is his or her job to help you and others with research. Even very experienced researchers often consult reference librarians.

Kinds of electronic sources

Your school's library likely offers several kinds of electronic sources:

- The library's catalog of holdings is a database allowing you to search for books and other sources available in the library. You type a subject, an author's name, or a title into a computer terminal, and the screen displays a list of all items matching your request. The catalog may include not only your library's holdings but also those of other schools nearby or in your state. (See pp. 554–56 for more on searching electronic catalogs.)
- Databases on CD-ROM, or compact disk, include indexes, bibliographies, encyclopedias, and other references. You search such a database much as you search a catalog, by author, title, or subject. The CD-ROMs may be available at only certain computers in the library, but some schools distribute the databases over a network within the library or over the campus network. (For more on searching CD-ROMs, see pp. 525–26.)
- Online databases and text archives are stored on computers all over the world and are accessible over the Internet, either through your campus network, through a local Internet provider, or through a commercial service such as America Online. The online databases include many indexes, bibliographies, and other references. The text archives, containing the entire contents of sources, include the *New York Times* and other major newspapers, *Time* and other magazines, academic journals, proceedings of professional conferences, reports of government agencies, and files of discussion groups. (See pp. 535–46 for more on searching online sources.)

Your access to sources

Before beginning your research, you will need to find out what resources are available to you and how you can use them. For this, a library orientation is invaluable. Your instructor may arrange one, or the library itself may hold tours. (If so, ask if you must sign up in advance; such sessions can fill up rapidly.) If necessary, conduct your own orientation session: visit your library's reference area, examine any guides available for researchers, and ask questions.

Finding answers to the following sets of questions will give you a head start on your research and help smooth your way.

Computer access to library resources

Computers have changed research locations and times as well as research methods. Depending on your subject and your school's resources, you may even be able to conduct research from home in the middle of the night.

TEACHING TIP

Because libraries vary in the number of computerized resources they hold and the access they grant to them, you'll need to be flexible in guiding students' research strategies. And since these resources may vary from semester to semester, don't forget to check the library yourself to see what's available to your students. Also be aware that students with access to the Internet may be able to use a far wider array of sources than any one library can hold. Encourage your electronic explorers to share their discoveries with the rest of the class so that everyone can benefit from the information superhighway.

- Which, if any, library resources can be reached from computers elsewhere on campus or from home? If you don't have to be in the library to conduct a search or even to consult certain sources (such as encyclopedias or periodicals), you can budget your time accordingly.
- If you can reach the library from a remote computer, do you need special instructions or an account with a password? Can you gain access through the World Wide Web? (Some libraries have their own Web sites.)
- What software or hardware do you need to reach the library? Usually you'll need special communications software and a modem (a device that lets your computer talk to others over the telephone lines). Is the software provided? How do you install it?
- Whom do you ask for assistance in installing the software and connecting to the library?

Library resources and their formats

No library has all its holdings available in electronic form—books, for example, still occupy shelves and will continue to do so for the predictable future. Knowing what's available and in what form will help you plan and carry out your search.

- Which of the library's books are cataloged electronically? Some libraries list all their books electronically; others list only recent acquisitions—say, books less than ten years old. If your research topic requires you to consult both newer and older sources, you may need to search both the electronic catalog and a catalog bound in books or printed on film. (Few academic libraries still have a card catalog in drawers.)
- Which periodical indexes, bibliographies, and other reference works are available on CD-ROM or in other forms? Many older references have not yet been converted to electronic form, so you may need to consult a printed index for a newspaper dating back ten or so years. In addition, electronic indexes and other sources are expensive, so your library may purchase only some of them. What your library does not have may be available from another library nearby or over the Internet.
- Do certain collections within the library have their own catalogs, either printed or electronic? Some collections of rare or historical documents may not be included in the main catalog. If they might contain sources important to your topic, you will want to know how to reach them.

Recording information

You'll still need a pencil and paper to conduct research, but they aren't necessarily your only tools for recording information. The questions below will help you discover your options:

TEACHING TIP

Students are often confused when the library provides both an electronic catalog of its own books and access to online information services or CD-ROMs. They may think that every source they find on a CD-ROM is in the library, or that searching the library catalog is the same as searching the other databases. Make sure that students understand what kind of information is available from each source.

Also keep in mind that learning to use a new cataloging system (electronic or print) can be frustrating and slow and may involve a series of baffling dead ends. To help students through this process, you might implement a combination of the following:

plan frequent trips to the library (or allow for ongoing work with research databases in your own electronic classroom);

assign students to ongoing research teams, partnering students who are more skilled with computers in mentoring relationships with those who are tackling the electronic medium for the first time;

demonstrate (or ask your research librarian to demonstrate) common dead ends, such as key word searches that generate plentiful sources in one database and no sources in another;

frequently direct the class to bring their research journals to class and to report their progress and their setbacks, so that students understand that they are sharing a learning process; and

- Can you print search results in the library? Many libraries provide some printers so that users can print catalog items, periodical listings, and other references located on computer.
- Does the library restrict printing? Some libraries allow users to print only a certain number of references or pages at one session. Some libraries charge a fee for printing.
- Can you save search results on your own floppy disk? Many catalogs and most databases allow users to save copies of references with only a few keystrokes. (The instructions appear on screen or in a separate handbook.) You then have an electronic record of your search, usable outside the library (but see the next question). Later in your project you can rearrange and supplement source data for your working bibliography (see p. 559).
- What is required to "read" the search results you have downloaded on a floppy disk? Do you need certain hardware or software?

remind students to vary electronic information with material found in print sources (for example, the bibliography of one good article can often yield several more productive sources and start the student off on a new set of electronic searches).

RESOURCES AND IDEAS

Gavin, Christy. "Guiding Students Along the Information Highway: Librarians Collaborating with Composition Instructors." *Journal of Teaching Writing* 13:2 (1994): 225–35. Gavin explores the possibilities of cooperative instruction between reference librarians and writing teachers. Given the rapidly transforming nature of bibliographic instruction, this kind of collaborative work seems crucial.

2 Making your search efficient and productive

Once you determine what resources are available, you should plan your search. Careful planning is essential: a too-casual search can miss helpful sources while returning hundreds, even thousands, of irrelevant sources.

Probably the most important element in planning a search is to develop **keywords,** or **descriptors,** to describe your subject. Most electronic catalogs and databases, as well as many Internet search engines, operate by keywords: you type words that define your limited subject (see the box on the following page), and the computer searches for sources indexed by those words or using those words in titles and sometimes in summaries and texts. Edward Begay began with the keywords *Internet access,* which he thought would produce relevant sources and reject irrelevant ones.

To develop keywords, you need to understand what they do when you use them for a search. There are important differences between most databases and the search tools used on the Internet.

- In a database, sources are usually indexed by authors, titles, and publication years and also by keywords that describe the contents of sources. These keywords conform to the database's directory of terms. For the library's catalog, this directory is *Library of Congress Subject Headings* (*LCSH*), which is available in printed form in the library's reference room. Some other databases use *LCSH* as well, but many have their own directory in the form of a thesaurus (available either on the database or in printed form near the computer or at the reference desk). Using the database's own directory will speed your search. (See pp. 547–50 and 554–56 for more on searching databases.)

COMPUTER EXERCISE

Have students meet you in the library or the electronic classroom with individual lists of keywords generated from the *Library of Congress Subject Headings* in their areas of interest (students might start with a topic narrowed in Exercise 1, for example). Have students work in pairs to try their keywords in several databases, noting subheadings of interest and revising the keywords in places where the search engine works from a different system of subject headings. The goal of the exercise is not only to generate the variations on keywords that may be needed for different databases but also to narrow and define their topics further.

Ways to refine keywords

You can refine your keywords in ways now standard, with some variations, among most databases and search engines. When in doubt about whether or how to use any of the following devices, consult the "Help" section of the resource you are using.

- Use the word *not* or the symbol – ("minus") to narrow your search by excluding irrelevant words: for instance, the word *provider* often follows the phrase *Internet access* in discussions of and advertisements for commercial services. Using the keywords *(Internet access) not provider* omits such listings from the search.
- Use the word *and* or the symbol + to narrow your search by indicating that all the terms should appear in the source or its listing: for example, *Internet and access* or *Internet and education*.
- Use the word *or* to broaden your search: *(Internet and education) or (cyberspace issues)* would produce sources keyed by either phrase in parentheses. *Or* is especially helpful for words with similar meanings, or synonyms. For instance, *Internet or cyberspace or (information highway)* would produce sources containing any of the three terms.
- Use quotation marks or parentheses (as in some of the examples above) to indicate that you want to search for the entire phrase, not the separate words.
- Use the word *near* to indicate that the search words may be close to each other and on either side of each other: for example, *Internet near education*. Depending on the resource you're searching, *near* may specify that the words be directly next to each other or as many as a hundred words apart.
- To indicate that you will accept different versions of the same word, use a so-called wild card, such as *, in place of the optional letters: for example, *wom*n* includes both *woman* and *women; child** includes *child, children, childcare, childhood, childish, childlike,* and *childproof*. The example of *child** suggests that you have to consider all the variations allowed by your wild card and whether it will open up your search too much. If you seek only two or three from many variations, you will be better off using *or: child or children and (Internet use)*. (Note that some systems use ?, :, or + for a wild card instead of *.)
- Be sure to spell your keywords correctly. Some search tools will look for close matches or approximations, but correct spelling gives you the best chance of finding relevant sources.

35c

- The Internet itself has no directory like *LCSH* in which you can look up keywords to search with. Instead, there are so-called search engines that find all the Internet sources that use your keywords anywhere—author, title, summary, text—no matter how centrally or how often they are used. One search engine returned 400,000 listings for Edward Begay's preliminary keywords *Internet access* because these words appeared in that many sources. Begay found that he had to experiment with keywords to retrieve a narrower list of sources (see pp. 541–43 for more on his search).

Like Begay, you will probably have to use trial and error in developing your keywords. Because different databases have different directories and many search tools have no directory at all, you should count on occasionally running dry (turning up few or no sources) or hitting uncontrollable gushers (turning up hundreds or thousands of mostly irrelevant sources). But the process is not busywork—far from it. Besides leading you eventually to worthwhile sources, it can also teach you a great deal about your subject: how you can or should narrow it, how it is and is not described by others, what others consider interesting or debatable about it, what the major arguments are. For example, while Begay's *Internet access* turned up an unmanageable list of sources on the Internet, the same keywords produced practically nothing on a CD-ROM database, the *Social Sciences Index*. From misses like these, Begay learned, among other things, that *access* to the Internet did not have the same meaning for him as for most users of the word, and he resolved to explain his meaning if he used the word in his final paper.

3 Evaluating your search

Searching a variety of resources and experimenting with keywords can produce long lists of sources that are only partially relevant to your subject. You'll have to decide which ones to consult. Tempting as it may be, picking the first two or three items produced by each search is not an efficient approach: you'll end up with a good number of sources, perhaps, but not necessarily with the best sources for your purpose.

How many sources is "a good number"? For a paper of 1,800 to 2,500 words, try for ten to thirty promising titles as a start. To gauge whether the source is promising, use the information provided by the database or search engine: author, title, publication date, publisher, and description. (Sometimes a full summary, or abstract, and even the whole source will be available with a few keystrokes.) For most subjects, you seek a mix, as described below. (See also pp. 564–67 on evaluating individual sources when you examine them. The concerns are similar to those following, but more detailed.)

Primary and secondary sources

As much as possible, you should rely on **primary sources,** or firsthand accounts: historical documents (letters, speeches, and so

Have students bring several likely sources to class and work in pairs to review them, using the strategies for evaluating sources provided by the text.

As a follow-up exercise, you might have students present one of their sources verbally, identify it as primary or secondary, scholarly or popular, old or new, impartial or biased, describe useful features such as bibliographies and indexes, and suggest how its content might function in their research paper.

It is important for students to understand that this process of evaluating and synthesizing their sources will help them to generate a critical argument as well as the information for their paper. Discussing the different purposes and audiences for college writing will also help students who may have written successful research papers in high school using only an entry or two from a general encyclopedia.

RESOURCES AND IDEAS

Chappell, Virginia A., Randall Hensley, and Elizabeth Simmons-O'Neill. "Beyond Information Retrieval: Transforming Research Assignments into Genuine Inquiry." *Journal of Teaching Writing* 13:2 (1994): 209–24. Describes techniques for teaching students to evaluate sources, develop research questions, and analyze data within a range of disciplinary contexts.

on), eyewitness reports, works of literature, reports on experiments or surveys conducted by the writer, or your own interviews, experiments, observations, or correspondence. **Secondary sources** report and analyze information drawn from other sources (often primary ones): a reporter's summary of a controversial issue, a historian's account of a battle, a critic's reading of a poem, a physicist's evaluation of several studies. Secondary sources may contain helpful summaries and interpretations that direct, support, and extend your own thinking. However, most research-writing assignments expect your own ideas to go beyond those in such sources.

Scholarly and popular sources

The scholarship of acknowledged experts is essential for depth, authority, and specificity; the general-interest views and information of popular sources can help you apply more scholarly approaches to daily life.

- *Check the publisher.* Is it a scholarly journal (such as *Education Forum*) or a publisher of scholarly books (such as Harvard University Press), or is it a popular magazine (such as *Time* or *Newsweek*) or a publisher of popular books (such as Little, Brown)?
- *Check the author.* Have you seen the name elsewhere, which might suggest that the author is an expert?
- *Check the title.* Is it technical, or does it use a general vocabulary?
- *Check the electronic address.* Addresses for Internet sources often include an abbreviation that tells you something about the source: *edu* means the source comes from an educational institution, *gov* from a government body, *org* from a nonprofit organization, *com* from a commercial organization such as a corporation. (See p. 536 and 566 for more on interpreting electronic addresses.)

Older and newer sources

Check the publication date. For most subjects a combination of older, established sources (such as books) and current sources (such as newspaper articles or interviews) will provide both background and up-to-date information. Only historical subjects or very current subjects like Edward Begay's (the Internet) require an emphasis on one extreme or another.

Impartial and biased sources

Seek a range of viewpoints. Sources that attempt to be impartial can offer trustworthy facts and an overview of your subject. Sources with clear biases can offer a diversity of opinion. Of course, to discover bias, you may have to read the source carefully (see p. 565); but even a bibliographical listing can be informative.

- *Check the author.* You may have heard of the author before as a respected researcher (thus more likely to be objective) or as a leading proponent of a certain view (less likely to be objective).
- *Check the title.* It may reveal something about point of view. (Consider these contrasting titles uncovered by Edward Begay: "Computer Literacy and Ideology" versus "The Process of Introducing Internet-Based Classroom Projects and the Role of School Librarians.")

Sources with helpful features

Does the source have a bibliography (which might direct you to other sources) or an index (which could suggest additional keywords) or illustrations (which could clarify important concepts)?

35d Finding sources to refine your topic

Once you understand the basics of planning, conducting, and evaluating an electronic search, as explained in the previous section, you're ready to find sources. This section discusses the wide range of sources that may be available to you, both electronically and in print. (For a summary, see the box on the next page.)

Note If sources you need are not available from your library, you may be able to obtain them from another library, usually by mail, often by fax, sometimes electronically. Ask your librarian for help, and plan ahead: interlibrary loans can take a week or longer.

1 Using reference works

Reference works available in the library (often on CD-ROM or over the Internet) include encyclopedias, dictionaries, digests, bibliographies, indexes, atlases, almanacs, and handbooks. Your research *must* go beyond these sources, but they contribute early on:

- They can help you decide whether your topic really interests you and whether it meets the requirements for a research paper (pp. 519–20).
- They can direct you to more detailed sources on your topic.
- For an analysis paper, a specialized encyclopedia can identify the main debates in a field and the proponents of each side.
- Reference works can help you refine your keywords for computer searches by introducing you to the terminology of the field you're researching.

Edward Begay's use of reference works illustrates how helpful such sources can be as a starting point, even for a topic as current as

COLLABORATIVE LEARNING

Assign a small group of students to each category of reference works. Have the group find which of these sources their library holds and what kind(s) of information these works contain. Ask them to report to the class either orally or in writing. If students have begun to work on topics have them shape their reports around the usefulness of the resource for those particular topics.

Index to research sources

the Internet. Begay first consulted *Bibliographic Guide to the History of Computing, Computers, and the Information Processing Industry* (to get some background on computers and the Internet) and *Encyclopedia of Sociology* (to explore the concept of equality in education).

The following lists give the types of reference works. Once you have a topic, you can scan these lists for a reference work to start with. Or you can ask the reference librarian for a starting point. (The librarian can also advise you which sources are available on CD-ROM, over the Internet, or in print.)

General encyclopedias

General encyclopedias give brief overviews and bibliographies. Because they try to cover all fields, they are a convenient, but very limited, starting point. Be sure to consult the most recent edition.

Collier's Encyclopedia
The Columbia Encyclopedia
Encyclopedia Americana
Encyclopedia International
The New Encyclopaedia Britannica
Random House Encyclopedia

TEACHING TIP

Reference books are expensive, and few college libraries can afford to update all the references in their collections all the time. Remind students to check the edition and publication dates of the reference sources they use; the information in older works may need to be updated or supplemented.

Specialized encyclopedias, dictionaries, bibliographies

A specialized encyclopedia, dictionary, or bibliography generally covers a single field or subject. These works will give you more detailed and more technical information than a general reference work will, and many of them (especially bibliographies) will direct you to particular books and articles on your subject. Note that many of these references are available on CD-ROM or over the Internet as well as in print.

One general reference work providing information on sources in many fields is the *Essay and General Literature Index* (published since 1900 and now updated semiannually). It lists tens of thousands of articles and essays that appear in books (rather than periodicals) and that might not be listed elsewhere.

BUSINESS AND ECONOMICS
Accountant's Handbook
Dictionary of Business and Economics
Encyclopedia of Advertising
Encyclopedia of Banking and Finance
Encyclopedia of Business Information Sources
Encyclopedia of Management
Handbook of Modern Marketing
McGraw-Hill Encyclopedia of Economics
The MIT Dictionary of Modern Economics
The New Palgrave: A Dictionary of Economics

History

Afro-American Reference
Cambridge Ancient History
Cambridge History of China
Dictionary of American History
Dictionary of American Immigration History
Dictionary of the Middle Ages
Encyclopedia of Asian History
Encyclopedia of Latin-American History
Encyclopedia of World History
Guide to American Foreign Relations Since 1700
Guide to Research on North American Indians
Harvard Guide to American History
Modern Encyclopedia of Russian and Soviet History
New Cambridge Modern History
Oxford Classical Dictionary
The Study of the Middle East: Research and Scholarship in the Humanities and Social Sciences

Literature, theater, film, and television

Bibliographical Guide to the Study of the Literature of the U.S.A.
Cambridge Encyclopedia of Language
Cambridge Guide to Literature in English
CBS News Index
Film Research: A Critical Bibliography
Film Review Annual
Handbook to Literature
International Television and Video Almanac
Literary Criticism Index
McGraw-Hill Encyclopedia of World Drama
MLA International Bibliography of Books and Articles on the Modern Languages and Literatures
Modern Drama: A Checklist of Critical Literature on Twentieth Century Plays
New Cambridge Bibliography of English Literature
New Princeton Encyclopedia of Poetry and Poetics
Oxford Companion to American Literature
Oxford Companion to the Theatre
Reference Sources in English and American Literature: An Annotated Bibliography

Music and the visual arts

Architecture: From Prehistory to Post-Modernism
Crowell's Handbook of World Opera
Dance Encyclopedia
Encyclopedia of Pop, Rock, and Soul
Encyclopedia of World Art
New Harvard Dictionary of Music
International Cyclopedia of Music and Musicians
New Grove Dictionary of Music and Musicians
Oxford Companion to Twentieth-Century Art

Philosophy and religion

Catholic Encyclopedia
Concise Encyclopedia of Islam
Dictionary of the History of Ideas
Eastern Definitions: A Short Encyclopedia of Religions of the Orient
Encyclopedia Judaica
Encyclopedia of Ethics
Encyclopedia of Philosophy
Encyclopedia of Religion
Interpreter's Dictionary of the Bible
Library Research Guide to Religion and Theology
New Standard Jewish Encyclopedia
Oxford Dictionary of the Christian Church

Sciences, technology, and mathematics

American Medical Association Encyclopedia of Medicine
Bibliographic Guide to the History of Computing, Computers, and the Information Processing Industry
Dorland's Illustrated Medical Dictionary
Encyclopedia of Bioethics
Encyclopedia of Chemistry
Encyclopedia of Computer Science and Technology
Encyclopedia of Ecology
Encyclopedia of Electronics
Encyclopedia of Oceanography
Encyclopedia of Physics
Encyclopedic Dictionary of Mathematics
Information Sources in the Life Sciences
Introduction to the History of Science
Introduction to Reference Sources in Health Sciences
Larousse Encyclopedia of Animal Life
McGraw-Hill Encyclopedia of Engineering
McGraw-Hill Encyclopedia of the Geological Sciences
McGraw-Hill Encyclopedia of Science and Technology
Prentice-Hall Encyclopedia of Mathematics
Space Almanac
Van Nostrand's Scientific Encyclopedia
World Resources (environment)

Social sciences

Encyclopedia of Anthropology
Encyclopedia of Crime and Justice
Encyclopedia of Education
Encyclopedia of Educational Research
Encyclopedia of Psychology
Encyclopedia of Sociology
Funk and Wagnalls Standard Dictionary of Folklore, Mythology and Legend
Information Sources of Political Sciences
International Bibliography of the Social Sciences
International Encyclopedia of the Social Sciences

New Dictionary of the Social Sciences
Race and Ethnic Relations: A Bibliography
Sociology: A Guide to Reference Information Sources
Sources of Information in the Social Sciences: A Guide to the Literature

Unabridged dictionaries and special dictionaries on language

Unabridged dictionaries are more comprehensive than college or abridged dictionaries. Special dictionaries give authoritative information on individual aspects of language. (See Chapter 32 for more on the kinds of dictionaries and how to use them.)

UNABRIDGED DICTIONARIES

A Dictionary of American English on Historical Principles
The Oxford English Dictionary
The Random House Dictionary of the English Language
Webster's Third New International Dictionary of the English Language

SPECIAL DICTIONARIES

Cassidy, Frederic G., et al., eds. *Dictionary of American Regional English.*
Chapman, Robert L., ed. *Roget's International Thesaurus.* 5th ed.
Follett, Wilson. *Modern American Usage.* Ed. Jacques Barzun.
The New Fowler's Modern English Usage. 3rd ed. Ed. R. W. Burchfield.
Onions, Charles T., et al., eds. *The Oxford Dictionary of English Etymology.*
Partridge, Eric. *A Dictionary of Slang and Unconventional English.* 8th ed. Ed. Paul Beale.
Partridge, Eric. *Origins: A Short Etymological Dictionary of Modern English.*
Webster's New Dictionary of Synonyms
Wentworth, Harold, and Stuart Berg Flexner. *Dictionary of American Slang.*

Biographical reference works

If you want to learn about someone's life, achievements, credentials, or position, or if you want to learn the significance of a name you've come across, consult one of the reference works below. Note, in addition, that more specialized biographical sources are available in fields such as law, health care, and art.

American Men and Women of Science
Contemporary Authors
Current Biography
Dictionary of American Biography
Dictionary of American Negro Biography
Dictionary of Literary Biography
Dictionary of National Biography (British)
Dictionary of Scientific Biography

Two Thousand Notable American Women
Webster's New Biographical Dictionary
Who's Who in America
World Authors

Atlases and gazetteers

Atlases are bound collections of maps; gazetteers are geographical dictionaries.

Cosmopolitan World Atlas
Encyclopaedia Britannica World Atlas International
National Geographic Atlas of the World
Times Atlas of the World
Webster's New Geographical Dictionary

Almanacs and yearbooks

Both almanacs and yearbooks are annual compilations of facts. Yearbooks record information about the previous year in a country, field, or other subject. Almanacs give facts about a variety of fields.

Americana Annual
Britannica Book of the Year
Facts on File Yearbook
US Bureau of the Census. *Statistical Abstract of the United States.*
World Almanac and Book of Facts

2 Using the Internet

The Internet consists of millions of computers around the world that are connected by wires and satellites. Both for refining your topic and for gathering actual sources, the Internet has a number of distinct advantages:

- Since Internet publication is faster than print or even CD-ROM publication, you may find more current information on the Internet than in your library. For example, many government agencies post their data first online, then in print.
- Many scholarly journals are published online. Some are published *only* online, not in print.
- If your school's library has few resources on your subject, you can search catalogs at other libraries.
- If your library does not have some sources—such as government documents—located by your database searches, you can obtain the documents more quickly over the Internet than by interlibrary loan.
- You can get in touch with people who have an interest in your research topic by participating in a discussion group or conducting interviews online.

RESOURCES AND IDEAS

See Susan Lang's article, "Using Computers to Teach Writing," pp. IAE-63–IAE-77.

Crump, Eric, and Nick Carbone. *The English Student's Guide to the Internet.* New York: Houghten, 1996. A useful guide for narrowing the Internet's vast search capabilities toward directed areas.

Selfe, Cynthia L., and Richard J. Selfe, Jr. "The Politics of the Interface: Power and Its Exercise in Electronic Contact Zones." *College Composition and Communication* 45:4 (1994): 480–504. The authors probe some of the larger cultural issues surrounding technological innovations such as the Internet, including their political and ideological ramifications for education.

How do you use the Internet? The following pages introduce the main resources available: the World Wide Web, electronic mail, Listservs, Usenet groups, and synchronous communication such as MOOs and MUDs. Although the amount of material accessible through the Internet has skyrocketed in recent years, gaining access to this material has actually become easier through the document retrieval system known as the World Wide Web, which this chapter focuses on.

Note America Online, Prodigy, and other subscription services enable users to send electronic mail across the Internet, participate in discussion groups, read newspapers and magazines linked to the service, and browse the Web. The services are easy to use, but they do charge for the time spent online. If you plan to conduct much of your research on the Internet, you'll find it more economical to use your school's connection.

Understanding electronic addresses

To get the most from the Web, you need a software program called a **browser:** Netscape Navigator and Microsoft's Internet Explorer are the most popular, and one of them is probably already in use at your school. You also need to understand electronic addresses (called **Uniform Resource Locators,** or **URLs**), which specify a unique location for each online source. A URL has three parts and a fixed form: *protocol://domain/path.* Here is a translation of the address *http://www.nyu.edu/urban/leaders.html:*

- The **protocol** specifies what type of access you are requesting at a particular location. Most Web sites are accessed using *http* (hypertext transfer protocol). The protocol identifier is followed by a colon and two slashes.
- Immediately after the two slashes, the **domain** names the computer (called a **server**) that houses the document you seek. Each server has a unique name, usually referring to the organization that owns it—for instance, *www.nyu.edu* (*nyu* stands for New York University; *edu* indicates that it is an educational institution).
- The **path** specifies the location and name of the document you seek—for instance, */urban/leaders.html* identifies a file (*leaders.html*) within a directory (*urban*). (If you think the directory may contain other files that could be useful as well, you may be able to go there first by omitting the file name from the address—that is, stopping after *urban.*)

Note that an address must be typed exactly as you find it: same capitals and small letters, same punctuation, same spacing.

As you will see, you don't have to know a source's address to find the source: a search engine will find it for you, following your key-

Internet tools in addition to the World Wide Web

The World Wide Web now encompasses many of the older tools for finding and using Internet sources. You may use any of these tools through the Web, through an icon for the application, or through a so-called shell account at your school (activated by typing the application name at a prompt).

Gopher

Until recently, Gopher has been the preferred tool for locating and retrieving text documents over the Internet. It uses menus that are arranged in levels: they begin with general topics and become more specific as you proceed through a system. You can search for documents with the menus, or, using the search engine Veronica or Jughead, you can conduct a keyword search. Gopher remains popular and helpful, but many schools are now phasing it out in favor of the more interactive and flexible Web.

To visit a Gopher site from a shell account, type *gopher* at the shell prompt followed by a space and then the address of the Gopher server you wish to reach. To visit a Gopher site from a Web browser, type *gopher://* and the computer's address in the location window.

File Transfer Protocol (FTP)

FTP allows you to transfer files to and from another computer over a network. The files may be software, documents (from government statistics to the texts of whole books), or graphics, sound, or video. Generally, you transfer files via "anonymous FTP," which lets you copy specified public files without having an account at the remote computer. A search engine named Archie can help you find FTP files by a keyword search of file titles.

With a shell account, type *ftp* followed by a space and the address of the FTP server. When asked to log on to the server, use the name "anonymous" and provide a password, usually your e-mail address. Then use commands to view the files listed at the site and to download them. If you are not working from a shell account, look for an application called Fetch to transfer files. To reach an FTP site with a Web browser, type *ftp://* and the computer's address in the location window. Web browsers have automated access to many FTP sites so that a simple click on a file name will transfer it to your computer or account.

Telnet

Telnet allows you to use a computer at another site on the Internet. You can, for instance, reach government computers or use your school's network from across the country. Often, you must have an account on the remote computer, or *host,* to be able to log on to it, but some hosts, such as libraries, do not require accounts.

To connect to a remote computer with a shell account, type *telnet* followed by a space and the host's address. With a Web browser, type *telnet://* and the address in the location window.

words. But you will want to record the address once you have it so that you can return to the source without having to conduct another search. And you must have the address to document any Internet source you use in your final paper.

TEACHING TIP

Since sources found on the Web are sometimes difficult to evaluate, you might devote class time to helping students analyze sample sources. Begin by reviewing a sample item in class: What clues are there about whether the material is primary or secondary, scholarly or popular? Is it dated? Did the material come from an individual's homepage, an institutional archive? Is the author named? Has that author published additional work found in print? Is the material referenced in a scholarly bibliography? Does the author cite other sources; does the piece include a bibliography of its own sources? Then have each student bring in a printout of material gleaned from the Web along with a record of the search procedures he or she used to find it (in an electronic classroom you might have students work directly from the screen). Ask students to work in small groups to evaluate their sources and to report their findings on one source to the class.

The World Wide Web

The World Wide Web consists of millions of documents on millions of computers that you can reach easily with your browser. You can travel from document to document and even from computer to computer by clicking on highlighted words or images that provide **hypertext links,** instructions that tell the computer to find and load the new material specified. For instance, the government's White House Web page includes highlighted hypertext links to pictures and descriptions of the First Family, a description of the federal executive branch, a message from the President, and other material. Besides moving around easily and reading and retrieving text, Web users can also experience sound, images, video, and animation.

To find sources on the Internet, you use a **search engine** that conducts keyword searches (see p. 525) or that outlines content in a series of directories. There are over thirty search engines available, all of them accessible via your Web browser by clicking on "Net Search." The box on page 540 describes the most popular engines.

The screen shot below from the Excite search engine shows the features common to most of these tools.

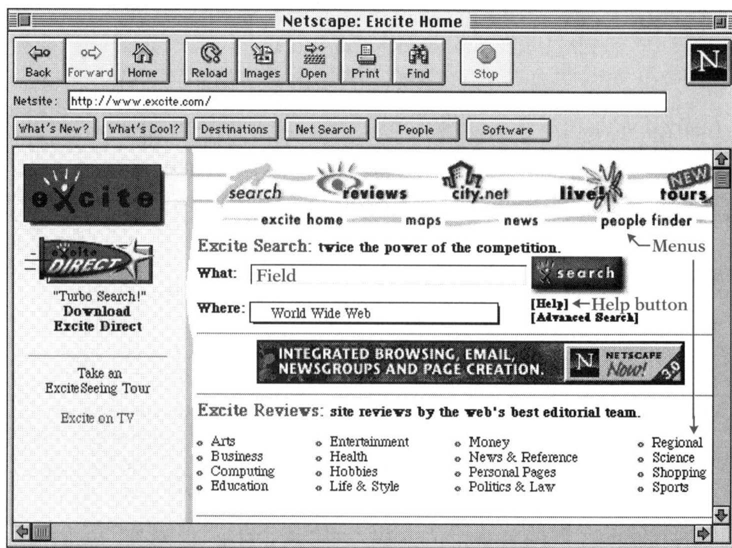

- The field is the place in which you type your keywords. (See pp. 525–27 on developing keywords.)
- Menus let you choose what and how to search—for instance, the entire Web, directories of Web sites, newsgroups, or some other set of directories that the search engine can reach.
- The "Help" button leads you to information on using the search engine:

  How to format keyword searches—for instance, whether you need to use *and, not, or,* and symbols such as + or –.

  How to link words to search for phrases using parentheses or quotation marks. A few search engines assume that two or more words in a row without any formatting constitute a phrase to search for.

  How to interpret the results of the search. When you perform a search using either keywords or a directory, the search engine generates a list of sites that match your search criteria. The matching sites, or **hits,** are listed in order of "relevance," which the search engine determines by a combination of the following: the number of times your search terms appear within a document; whether the terms appear at the beginning, middle, or end of a document; whether the terms appear in the title or the address of the document. If there are any special ways the search engine determines relevance, its "Help" information will specify them.

In addition, many search engines allow you to place an optional limit on the number of sources you want the search to return and an optional limit on the range of dates you're interested in. If you specify a date range, the search engine will return only sources posted on the Internet during that time.

When using a search engine, keep the following limitations and cautions in mind:

- No search engine can list every possible source for your keywords. The search engines cannot keep up with the daily additions to and deletions from the Internet.
- Because of constant change, you cannot be sure that the site you found on Monday will contain the same information on Friday. Some sites are designed and labeled as archives: they do not change except with additions. But other sites, such as those for newspapers and magazines, frequently replace old material with new. If you think you'll want to use something from such a site, you should consult it right away. If it seems useful, you should download it to your own computer or take notes from it (see pp. 569–77).
- Anyone with the right hardware and software can place information on the Internet, so your search could turn up sources

TRANSPARENCY MASTER 35.3

Web search engines

Here are six of the most popular search engines for the World Wide Web, with their main features. Click on "Help" whenever you need support from a search engine (see p. 539).

Alta Vista

Alta Vista lets you search the entire Web with two types of keyword searches. In a simple search, you enter only a keyword or keywords. In an advanced search, you use *and, or,* and other devices described on page 526 to refine the search. Alta Vista also allows you to specify the keywords that you think most important, so that sites containing those keywords will be listed first in the results. You may also specify starting and ending dates for sources.

Excite

Excite allows you to search a directory compiled by a team of people reviewing Internet sites. It also allows simple keyword searches but not advanced searches as on Alta Vista and some other engines. Excite updates addresses frequently and reviews more than sixty thousand Web sites.

Infoseek

Infoseek also allows you to search by directory or keyword. In addition, it lets you select the parts of the Internet that you want to search: the Web, Usenet newsgroups, corporate directories, recent news, or e-mail address directories.

Lycos

Lycos currently claims the largest catalog of Web sites. It can be searched by directory or by keyword. Additional services include travel maps and reviews of twenty thousand sites. Lycos also indexes sound, photographs, and other media, not just text documents.

Magellan

Magellan also allows you to search by directory or by keyword. You may search the entire Web, or you may limit your search to sites that have been reviewed and rated on the basis of their content, organization, and use of technology.

Yahoo

Yahoo is not actually a search engine but a directory of sites organized by subject. You may search the directory or conduct a keyword search, which is forwarded to and conducted by other search engines. Because you're searching seven or eight engines at once, you increase your chances of finding information; thus Yahoo is especially helpful with obscure topics.

with widely varying reliability: published articles, government documents, term papers written by high school students, the rantings of crackpots. With Internet sources, you need to be especially careful about evaluating your search (p. 527) and evaluating the individual sources you examine (p. 566).

- Most works on the Internet are copyrighted just as print sources are, and you must acknowledge them when you use them (see p. 578). Keep records of the sources that you find and use online. A list of elements to record appears on page 560.

For his initial search of the Web, Edward Begay started with the keywords *Internet access* on the search engine Alta Vista. But the search returned an overwhelming 400,000 hits, as Figure 1 shows. Clicking on Alta Vista's "Help" button to find out whether and how the sites were arranged, Begay discovered several criteria for ranking: (1) where keywords fall in the document (the closer to the beginning, the higher the rank); (2) whether the keywords fall near each other in the document; and (3) whether the keywords appear more than once in the document. However, none of the first twenty or so titles listed looked relevant to Begay's topic.

1. Alta Vista search using keywords *Internet access*

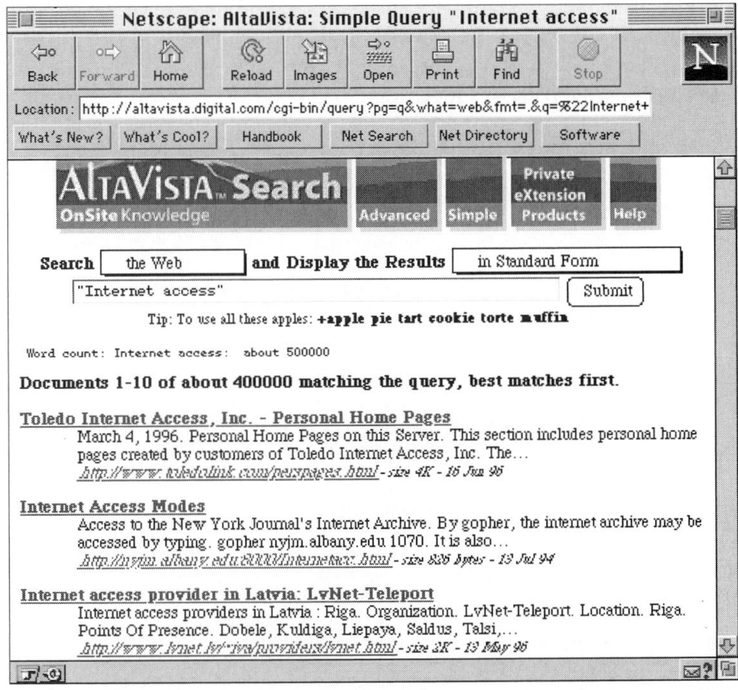

Since this was early in his research, Begay was not sure how to refine his keywords to narrow the search. Instead, he tried another search engine, Magellan, that allows directory searches. From the opening screen showing the directory categories, Begay chose the category *Internet;* then, from the next screen (Figure 2), he chose the category *Cyberspace Issues,* the one that seemed most promising for his subject. (*Access & Presence Providers,* Begay realized from his Alta Vista search, would direct him to sources on technical rather than economic access to the Internet.) With this search, Begay turned up at least one source that looked helpful, "Teaching with Electronic Technology" (Figure 3).

Using Magellan suggested ways for Begay to refine his keywords, so he returned to Alta Vista to try *cyberspace and (access issues).* (*And* limits the search to both terms; the parentheses specify a search for the exact phrase. See pp. 525–27 for more on these devices.) Begay also specified a 1996 beginning date for the search. This time Alta Vista returned only ninety-seven possibilities, a much more manageable list. From the list Begay chose several sources, including "Teaching, Learning & Technology" (Figure 4).

Begay continued to search Alta Vista, trying a variety of keywords such as *Internet and democracy* and *Internet and (economic access),* until he had ten solid sources. He decided to turn to periodical indexes next, to conduct a methodical search of scholarly journals. (See pp. 546–52.)

2. Magellan search using a directory

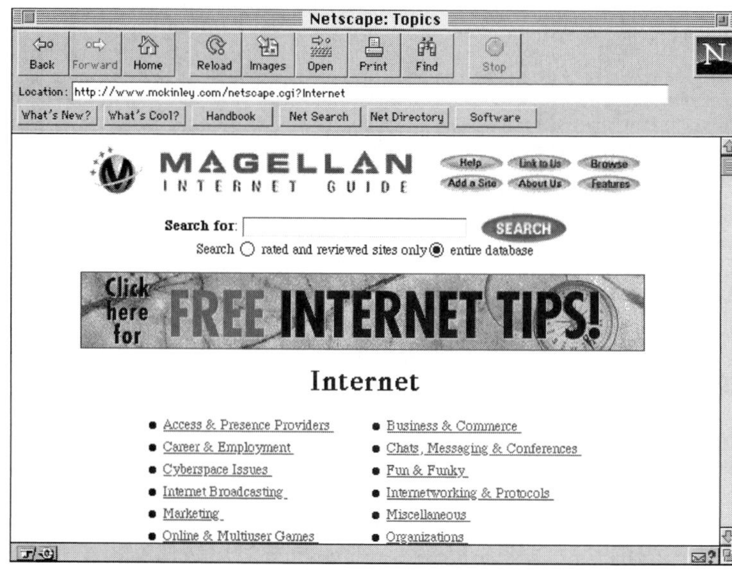

3. Magellan search results

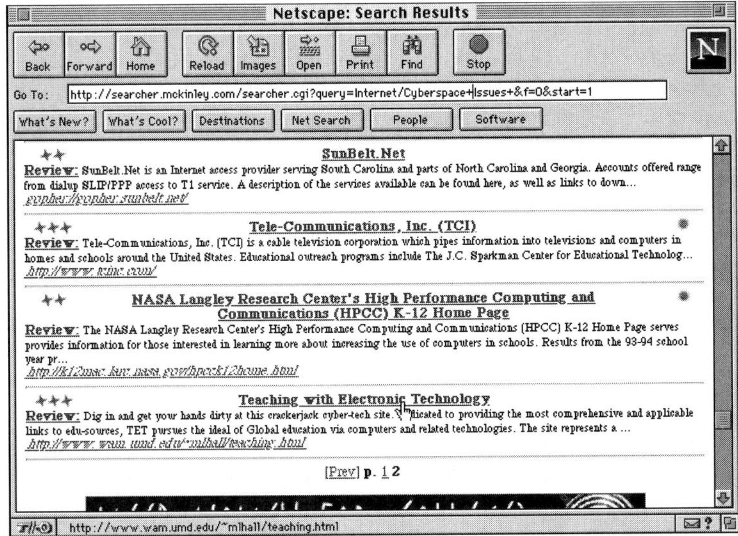

4. Alta Vista search results

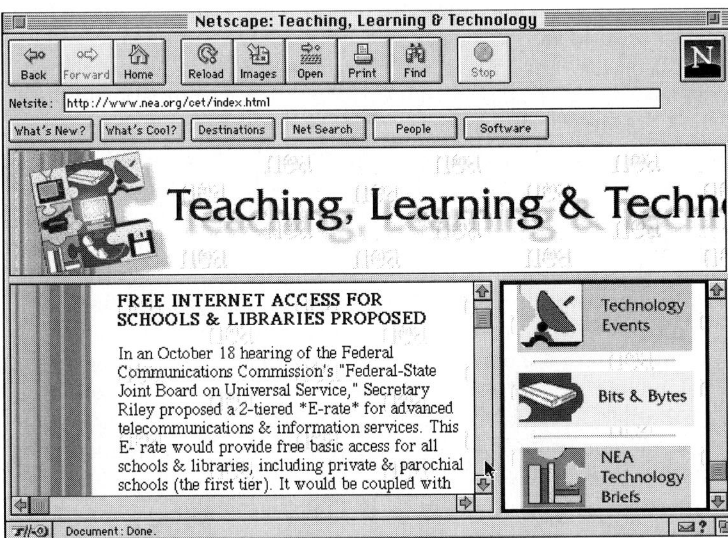

Electronic mail

With electronic mail (e-mail), you can send messages to and receive them from most people who use the Internet, as long as you know their addresses. (Some search engines provide the equivalent

35d

RESOURCES AND IDEAS

Anderson, Daniel, Bret Benjamin, Christopher Busiel, and Bill Paredes-Holt. *Teaching Online: Internet Research, Conversation, and Composition.* New York: Longman, 1998. An extremely useful and practical guide to electronic research; in particular, see Chapter 2, "Initiating Conversation: E-mail."

TEACHING TIP

E-mail can be an extremely productive forum, particularly in freeing students from the anxiety of formal writing. You can promote ongoing e-mail conversations by asking students to designate one or two e-mail partners in the class and encouraging them to write to each other once a week about their progress with the research project. You might occasionally assign an exercise that the e-mail partners should also "cc" to you, such as: "tell your e-mail partners exactly what you want to argue in your paper," or "describe one of the sources you've found to your e-mail partners in a way that makes them understand how interesting and important the source is to your project." You can also have students prepare for their revision groups by e-mailing and reading drafts before the class meeting.

of telephone books for e-mail accounts, but these are not complete.) If you have little computing experience, using e-mail may be a good way to get started because the terms are mostly familiar: you compose messages, address them to individuals or groups, and send them; your mail is stored in your mailbox; and you can sort, read, reply to, and discard e-mail as you do paper mail. See pages 757–58 for advice on e-mail format and etiquette.

As a research tool, e-mail allows you to communicate with others who are interested in your topic. You may, for instance, carry on an e-mail conversation with a teacher at your school or with other students. Or you may interview an expert in another state to follow up on a scholarly article he or she published. (See p. 557 on conducting interviews.)

Listservs

A **Listserv** (or **discussion group,** or just a **list**) is a group of individuals who discuss a common topic or topics. The Listserv software program acts as a specialized postal service: subscribers to a list send messages to its electronic address, and the software distributes the messages to all of the list's other subscribers via e-mail. Thousands of lists operate on the Internet, each with a particular purpose and audience. Through a Listserv, you may be able to discuss your subject with people the world over, representing diverse experiences and viewpoints.

To find lists that might be relevant to your research topic, use the keywords *list of listservs* (not *listserves*) to search the World Wide Web (p. 538). Your search will locate Web pages with information about subscribing to and using Listservs. When you find a list that interests you, see if it has a compilation of frequently asked questions (FAQs), which will list the topics covered (and *not* covered) by the group and will answer common questions. Spend a week or two reading the list's messages before sending any questions or comments of your own. By reading but not participating (called **lurking**), you can verify whether the list is relevant to your topic (and vice versa) and whether a particular person might be able to answer your questions. Most Listservs are archived, meaning that messages from past months and years are stored online and may be read and downloaded into your own files. Thus you may be able to find information on a topic even if it is not currently under discussion.

Another benefit of Listservs is that they make available subscribers' names and e-mail addresses. Although broad ranging and often very current, the information on Listservs is only as reliable as the subscriber who posts it. Having access to a subscriber list lets you find out who posted a message and communicate directly with that person. (See pp. 566–67 for advice on evaluating online sources.)

Usenet newsgroups

Like Listservs, **Usenet newsgroups** are forums in which people post messages on an enormous range of topics. However, newsgroups are not subscriber-based, and you do not receive postings automatically through your e-mail. Instead, you reach the groups via a Web browser such as Netscape Navigator or via special software. On a Web browser you can obtain a list of groups and other information by using the keywords *list of newsgroups*.

Newsgroups are roughly categorized by subject, indicated by the first letters of the address—for instance, *comp* for computers and computer science, *soc* for social issues, *biz* for business. This prefix will give you an idea of whether the group is relevant to your concerns. When you begin to examine a newsgroup, look for its frequently asked questions (FAQs): like those for Listservs, these documents explain the group's topics and answer common questions. As with Listservs, you should lurk a while before jumping into the discussion to be sure that the group is right for you and that your contributions are relevant.

Because newsgroups, unlike Listservs, are not subscriber-based, anyone can post messages on them, and you may not be able to find out who wrote a particular message. That makes it difficult to evaluate the reliability of a posting (see pp. 566–67 on evaluating sources). Unlike Listservs as well, newsgroups are not always archived, or they may be archived irregularly, so that you cannot read noncurrent postings.

Synchronous communication

With electronic mail, Listservs, and newsgroups, there's a delay between a message you send and any response you receive. But with **synchronous** (or simultaneous) **communication**, you and others can correspond in real time, as you might talk on the phone. As a research tool, synchronous communication can be especially useful for conducting interviews (see p. 557), and you can also participate in academic conferences and debates.

The following are three of the Internet's most popular synchronous programs:

- IRC (Internet Relay Chat) allows people anywhere in the world to talk with each other, either in groups or privately, over "channels." To use IRC, you need special software such as PowWow or IRCLe, which may be installed on your school's computers.
- MUDs and MOOs also provide environments where people can communicate "live." MUDs (multi-user domains or dungeons) started as online versions of role-playing games such as Dungeons and Dragons, but they have expanded well beyond game

playing to scholarly discussion and other uses. A MOO (MUD, object oriented) is a kind of MUD that enables users to create more complex virtual environments in which to play games or hold discussions. Some MUDs and MOOs may be reached via the Web, using the keywords *MUDs and MOOs*. Once you arrive at a site, you generally log on as a guest and receive directions for reaching the site's help files.

While IRC, MUDs, and MOOs can be useful tools, many schools have restricted their use because of their association with games. Check with your computer center to find out which programs are available to you.

A WRITER'S PERSPECTIVE

Magazines all too frequently lead to books.
—Fran Lebowitz

COLLABORATIVE LEARNING

Students can sometimes rely on books rather than periodical articles in an attempt to avoid the complications of periodical indexes. You can help them get started by planning a library visit in which students work in pairs to find and photocopy one periodical article each.

TEACHING TIP

If space and library regulations permit, consider holding office hours in the library while students are conducting their research. Your presence will encourage more consultation between you and your students. This practice is especially useful in conjunction with whatever library orientation programs your school offers first-year students.

3 Using periodicals

Periodicals—journals, magazines, and newspapers—are invaluable sources of information in research. The difference between journals and magazines lies primarily in their content, readership, frequency of issue, and page numbering.

- Magazines—such as *Psychology Today, Newsweek,* and *Esquire*—are nonspecialist publications intended for diverse readers. Most magazines appear weekly or monthly. In print, their pages are numbered anew with each issue. Online, their pages are often not numbered.
- Journals often appear quarterly or less frequently and contain scholarly, specialized information intended for readers in a particular field. Examples include *American Anthropologist, Journal of Black Studies,* and *Journal of Chemical Education.* Most journals, whether in print or online, number their pages. Some page each issue separately, like magazines. Others page issues sequentially for an entire annual volume, so that issue number 3 (the third issue of the year) may open on page 327. (The method of pagination determines how you cite a journal article in your list of works cited. See p. 617.)

Using indexes to periodicals

Several indexes provide information on the articles in journals, magazines, and newspapers. The contents, formats, and systems of abbreviation in these indexes vary widely, and they can be intimidating at first glance. But each one includes an introduction and explanation to aid the inexperienced user.

Many of the indexes listed on the following pages are available on CD-ROM and online over the Internet. Consult the library's list of databases to find the ones that seem most appropriate for your subject, or use an Internet search engine to find online indexes. Edward Begay, for instance, chose to avoid indexes of technical periodicals, such as *Applied Science and Technology Index* and *Computer Database,* because his subject was the social and economic effects of computers rather than the machines themselves. Instead, Begay chose databases such as *Sociofile,* for articles in sociology journals; *PsycLIT,* for articles in psychology journals; and *InfoTrac*'s *National Newspaper Index,* for recent newspaper articles.

Searching electronic periodical indexes is discussed under electronic searches on pages 525–26. To recap, you'll need keywords reflecting the index's own terms for categorizing articles—found either in *Library of Congress Subject Headings* or in the index's thesaurus. You enter these keywords in the space provided on the opening screen of the index; limit the publication dates to be searched, if appropriate; and click on "Search" or "Enter" to begin.

Here are the first two listings received by Edward Begay when he searched the *Social Sciences Index* using the keywords *Internet and education.* (The elements of the listings are labeled.)

```
1. EDUCATIONAL innovations--United States  ← Subject heading and subheading
A letter from Paul. By Van Horn, Royan  ← Article title and author
Presents updates on technological innovations affecting
the educational system in the United States as of Novem-
ber 1995. Includes a letter commending the contributions
of computers to education from Principal Paul Katnik;        [Summary]
Description of a teacher expert software program; Edu-
cation resources maximized by computers.
(Phi Delta Kappan, Nov95, Vol. 77 Issue 3, p261, 2p) (0031-7217)
 Journal title     Date  Volume and issue  Page number  Length
-----------------------------------------------------------------

2. HIGH technology & education--United States; COMPUTER-
   assisted instruction--United States
Networking the classroom. By Conte, Christopher
Questions whether computer technology will reform
education. Efforts to link schools to the computer
network; Question of whether computer networking
enhances learning; Issue of whether teachers are pre-
pared to take advantage of computer networking; Impact
of computer networking on gap between poor and affluent
Americans; High cost of networking; Government initia-
tives; Bibliography. INSET: Chronology.
(CQ Researcher, 10/20/95, Vol. 5 Issue 39, p921, 22p, 1
graph, 1 map, 1bw) (1056-2036)

** FullTEXT Available on CD-ROM **
```

If your first search of a periodical index returns a large number of sources (over fifty), you should try to narrow your search. Look among the first ten to twenty listings for titles that seem relevant to your subject and then for those titles' subject headings (such as

"HIGH technology & education" in the second listing on the previous page). Try your search again using one or more of those words or phrases. Experiment with a variety of keywords if necessary to find appropriate sources.

The *Social Sciences Index* is only one of many periodical indexes. Some are general indexes, meaning that their lists are not specialized. These include the following:

InfoTrac. Indexes more than fifteen hundred academic, business, technical, government, and popular publications, including five national newspapers.

NewsBank. Indexes more than five hundred newspapers.

The New York Times Index. Indexes the most complete US newspaper. The index can serve as a guide to national and international events and can indicate what issues of unindexed newspapers to consult for local reactions to such events.

Poole's Index to Periodical Literature. Indexes by subject British and American periodicals of the nineteenth century.

Popular Periodicals Index. Indexes about twenty-five contemporary popular periodicals not listed in major indexes.

ProQuest. Indexes periodicals in the humanities, education, and the social sciences.

Readers' Guide to Periodical Literature. Indexes articles published in more than a hundred popular magazines. For a current research project, consult several years' listings.

SilverPlatter. Indexes periodicals in psychology, sociology, and nursing.

Wall Street Journal Index. Indexes the leading business newspaper and *Barron's.*

Here, from Edward Begay's research, is a sample from a 1996 volume of the *Readers' Guide to Periodical Literature,* with its elements labeled.

INTERNET ← Subject heading

Cyberspace 101. il *Consumer Reports* v61 p12–13 My '96

Getting the message: the great e-mail shoot-out [AOL, CompuServe, MCI, the Microsoft Network, Prodigy, and the Internet] J. Heim. il *PC World* v14 p183–5+ F '96

The Net superstars. E. Ransdell. il *U.S. News & World Report* v120 p62–3+ My 27 '96

On the Net, fast and easy. M. K. Flynn. il *U.S. News & World Report* v120 p71–2 Ap 29 '96

Radio vs. the Internet. J. Garvey. il *Commonweal* v123 p7–8 My 3 '96

The spinal column of civilization. J. Holtzman. *Electronics Now* v67 p79–81 Ap '96

Article title → Taming the Internet. M. K. Flynn. il *U.S. News & World Report* v120 p60–1+ Ap 29 '96 ← Author; ← Magazine title

Volume and page numbers: v120 p60–1+ — Date of publication: Ap 29 '96

35d

For scholarly journals, most libraries have a variety of specialized indexes. Begay also consulted several of these, including the *Social Sciences Index* illustrated on page 547. Following are the most useful scholarly indexes, many of them available on CD-ROM and/or online over the Internet.

Humanities

America: History and Life
Art Index
Avery Index to Architectural Periodicals
Film Literature Index
Humanities Index
MLA International Bibliography of Books and Articles on the Modern Languages and Literatures
Musical Literature International
Music Index
Philosopher's Index
Religion Index

Law and social sciences

ABI/INFORM (business)
Business Periodicals Index
Criminal Justice Periodicals Index
Education Index
ERIC (Education Resources Information Center). *Current Index to Journals in Education.*
Index to Legal Periodicals
PsycINFO
PAIS (Public Affairs Information Service)
Social Sciences Index
Sociofile

Sciences, technology, and mathematics

ACM Guide to Computing Literature
Applied Science and Technology Index
Bibliography and Index of Geology
Biological and Agricultural Index
Computer Literature Index
Cumulative Index to Nursing and Allied Health Literature
Engineering Index
Environmental Index
General Science Index
Index Medicus
Mathfile

In addition to the general and specialized indexes listed above, your library may subscribe to online services such as Dialog (for many scholarly indexes as well as entire articles), Nexis (for newspapers, newsletters, corporate reports, and many other sources, as well as entire articles), and Lexis (for sources in law and litigation such as codes and cases). These services are essentially databases of databases: they gather indexes, periodicals, and other data into huge banks. The services cost money to subscribe to or to use, so your library may restrict access to them, charge for them, or encourage you to use CD-ROM databases instead.

Using abstracts and citation indexes

Article summaries—or **abstracts**—can tell you in advance whether you want to pursue a particular article further. Many periodical indexes include abstracts along with bibliographic information, as Edward Begay discovered in the *PsycLIT* index. One full entry is reproduced below:

```
  Media Type: 10   Journal Article
       Title: In defense of computer literacy.
   Author(s): Vasu, Michael L.; Vasu, Ellen S.
 Institution: North Carolina State U, US
      Source: Social Science Computer Review
              1989 Spr Vol 7(1) 27-35
        Year: 1989
        ISSN: 0894-4393
    Language: Engl
  Key Phrase: computer literacy programs in education &
              employment myths vs realities, UK, commen-
              tary
    Subjects: COMPUTER APPLICATIONS; COMPUTER ATTITUDES;
              EDUCATIONAL PROGRAMS; EMPLOYABILITY; PRO-
              FESSIONAL CRITICISM
Classification(s):
              35    Educational Psychology
              3530  Curriculum & Programs & Teaching
              Methods
    Abstract: Critiques K. Robins and F. Webster's (see
              PA, Vol 77:26855) discussion of computer
              literacy (CL). It is argued that they have
              drawn a limited definition of CL from some
              specific and minimal uses of computers in
              education and that education policy should
              be directed toward increasing CL instruc-
              tion to insure economic equity. (PsycLIT
              Database Copyright 1990 American Psycholog-
              ical Assn, all rights reserved)
    Doc Type: 10   Journal Article
 Entry Month: 9010
 Item Number: 77-26864
```

Abstracts are published in many academic disciplines and are also frequently available on CD-ROM or online via the Internet.

Abstracts in Anthropology
Abstracts of English Studies
America: History and Life (US and Canadian history)

Biological Abstracts
Chemical Abstracts
Communications Abstracts
Computer Abstracts
Criminal Justice and Police Science Abstracts
Dissertation Abstracts International (doctoral dissertations). Before 1969, the title was *Dissertation Abstracts.*
Ecology Abstracts
Environment Abstracts
Historical Abstracts (world history)
Human Resources Abstracts
International Political Science Abstracts
LLBA (*Linguistics and Language Behavior Abstracts*)
Mathematical Reviews
Physics Abstracts
Psychological Abstracts or *PsycLIT*
Religious and Theological Abstracts
Sociological Abstracts
Urban Affairs Abstracts
Wilson Business Abstracts

When you want to trace what has been written *about* an article or book you are consulting, use a **citation index.** This resource lists references to written works after they are published, as when one scientific article comments on an earlier article. The following is a partial list:

Arts and Humanities Citation Index
Science Citation Index
Social Sciences Citation Index

Finding and using periodicals

Every library lists its holdings of periodicals (usually called *serials*) either in the main catalog (see p. 554) or in a separate catalog. The listing for each periodical tells how far back the issues go and where and in what form the issues are stored.

These days many periodicals are available on CD-ROM, indicated both in the periodicals catalog and in periodical indexes listing the periodical. (See the sample from the *Social Sciences Index* on p. 547: one of the cited periodicals is available on CD-ROM.) If the periodical is not available electronically, its recent issues are probably held in the library's periodicals room. Back issues are usually stored elsewhere, in one of three forms: in bound volumes; on **microfilm,** a filmstrip showing pages side by side; or on **microfiche,** a sheet of film with pages arranged in rows and columns. Consulting periodicals stored on microfilm or microfiche requires using a special machine, or "reader," with which you locate the page and project it on a screen. (Some readers are also attached to coin-operated photocopiers.) Any member of the library's staff will show you how to operate the reader.

If the periodical you seek is not available in your library, you have at least two options:

- You may be able to obtain the article by interlibrary loan. The article may arrive by mail or by fax, and there may be a fee for the service. Even with fax transmissions, the process can sometimes take a week or more, so place your order early.
- You may be able to find the periodical online over the Internet. Your library may subscribe to a service such as Project MUSE, which carries over forty journals online. Or you may be able to locate the periodical on the Web using its title as your keywords. (Note that a periodical published both online and in print—especially a newspaper or popular magazine—may differ in its two versions: articles may appear in one form but not the other, or articles may be abridged in the online form. Thus an article you find listed in a periodical index may be shortened or omitted from the online version of the periodical.)

TEACHING TIP

Remind students to ask the reference librarians about the information kept in the library's vertical files. Each library has special collections of material that it keeps in response to the demands of its particular users. Often these "clip files" can yield vital information.

4 Using guides to pamphlets and government publications

Organizations such as social-service groups, professional societies, and all branches of government publish booklets, compilations of data, and other sources that usually cannot be retrieved through the library's book catalog or periodicals listings.

Pamphlets, bulletins, and other miscellaneous items are often stored in file drawers, called **vertical files.** To find out what is available in pamphlet form, consult the *Vertical File Index: A Subject and Title Index to Selected Pamphlet Materials.* If your library does not have the item you seek, the index tells you how to order it from its publisher. You'll need to allow extra time for such orders.

Government publications provide a vast array of data, public records, and other historical and contemporary information. For US government publications, by far the most numerous, consult the

Monthly Catalog of US Government Publications, available on computer. Many federal, state, and local government agencies post important publications—legislation, reports, press releases—on their own Web sites. You can find lists of sites for various federal agencies by using the keywords *United States federal government* with any search engine. Edward Begay took this approach to find statistics from the Department of Education on computer use in schools (see Figures 5 and 6).

Besides what's available online, your library will have a large collection of printed government publications only if it is a depository library (that is, designated to receive such documents). If yours is not a depository library, a librarian may be able to help you obtain a needed publication from another library.

5. Search of US Department of Education publications

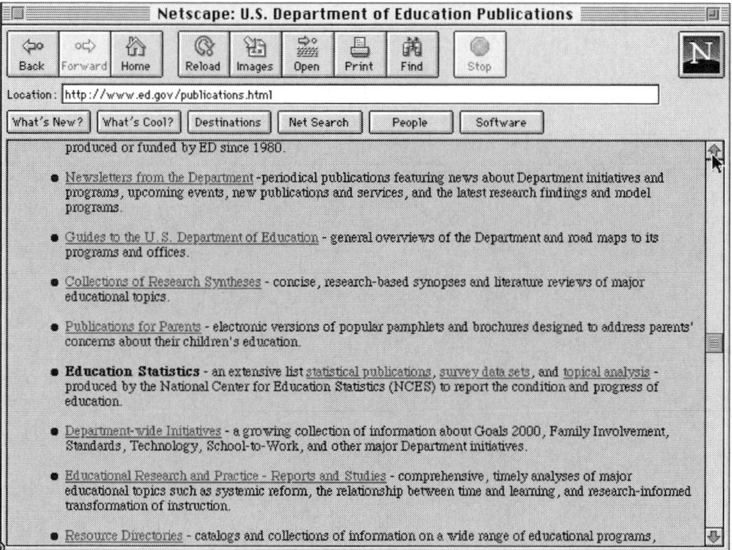

Netscape: U.S. Department of Education Publications

Location: http://www.ed.gov/publications.html

produced or funded by ED since 1980.

- Newsletters from the Department -periodical publications featuring news about Department initiatives and programs, upcoming events, new publications and services, and the latest research findings and model programs.
- Guides to the U.S. Department of Education - general overviews of the Department and road maps to its programs and offices.
- Collections of Research Syntheses - concise, research-based synopses and literature reviews of major educational topics.
- Publications for Parents - electronic versions of popular pamphlets and brochures designed to address parents' concerns about their children's education.
- **Education Statistics** - an extensive list statistical publications, survey data sets, and topical analysis - produced by the National Center for Education Statistics (NCES) to report the condition and progress of education.
- Department-wide Initiatives - a growing collection of information about Goals 2000, Family Involvement, Standards, Technology, School-to-Work, and other major Department initiatives.
- Educational Research and Practice - Reports and Studies - comprehensive, timely analyses of major educational topics such as systemic reform, the relationship between time and learning, and research-informed transformation of instruction.
- Resource Directories - catalogs and collections of information on a wide range of educational programs,

6. Department of Education statistics

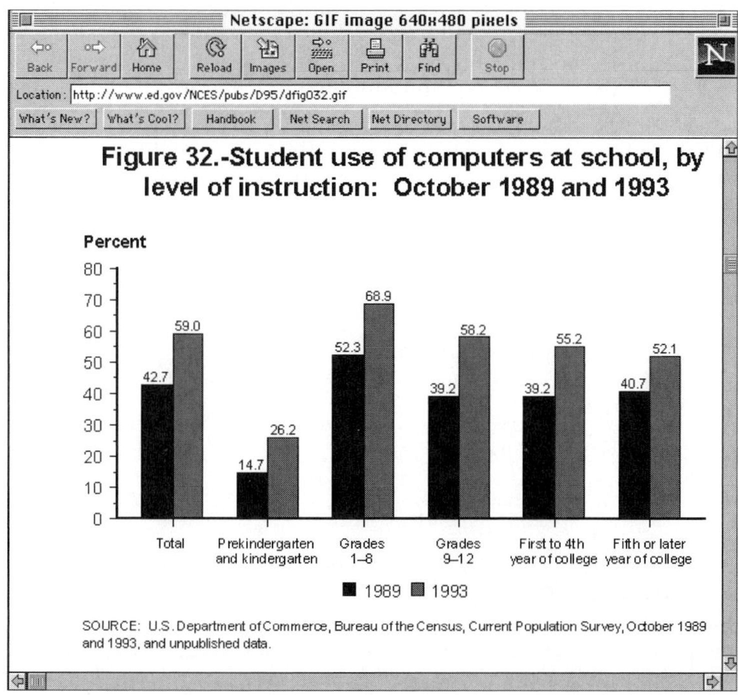

5 Using guides to books

The library catalog

The library's catalog lists books alphabetically by authors' names, titles of books, and subjects. If you are starting research on a subject you don't know very well, begin by looking under subject headings. If you know of an expert in the field and you want to find his or her books, look under the author's name. If you know the title of a relevant book but not the author's name, look for the title.

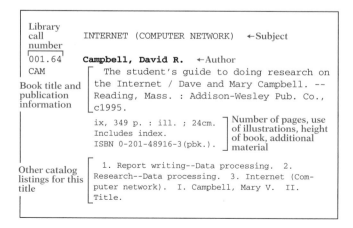

Most academic libraries store their book catalogs on computer; however, older volumes—say, those acquired more than ten years ago—may still be cataloged in bound volumes or on microfilm or microfiche (see p. 551). (Few academic libraries today use the once-familiar drawers of cards.) Before you search for books, you'll need to ask a librarian which books are cataloged on computer and which, if any, are not.

You may have access through a specialized computer network or other schools' Web sites to the book catalogs of other libraries in your area or state. You can search these catalogs as you do your own library's, and sometimes you can borrow books from another library in your area directly through the network or through a librarian. Ask your librarian for assistance with remote searches and loans. And allow time for the book to be sent after your request.

All book catalogs contain similar information, though it may be organized differently from one library to the other. By far the most widely used format derives from the Library of Congress card. A sample subject card appears below, with notes on its features.

TRANSPARENCY MASTER 35.4

Annotation	Card entry	Annotation
Library call number	INTERNET (COMPUTER NETWORK)	←Subject
	001.64 **Campbell, David R.**	←Author
Book title and publication information	CAM The student's guide to doing research on the Internet / Dave and Mary Campbell. -- Reading, Mass. : Addison-Wesley Pub. Co., c1995.	
	ix, 349 p. : ill. ; 24cm. Includes index. ISBN 0-201-48916-3(pbk.).	Number of pages, use of illustrations, height of book, additional material
Other catalog listings for this title	1. Report writing--Data processing. 2. Research--Data processing. 3. Internet (Computer network). I. Campbell, Mary V. II. Title.	

Search strategy

Unless you seek a specific author or title, your search in the library's catalog will be much more efficient and productive if you zero in on appropriate keywords to describe your subject.

In searching the library's book catalog, you can find such words in *Library of Congress Subject Headings* (*LCSH*). This multivolume work lists headings under which the Library of Congress catalogs books (subject headings but not proper names of people, places, and so on). Consulting this source and following its system of cross-references and headings at different levels of specificity, you will be able to discover the keywords most likely to lead to appropriate sources. Edward Begay used *LCSH* to eliminate the keyword *Internet,* which was much too broad for his needs. Instead, he combined *Internet* with some of its *LCSH* subheadings: *libraries and Internet* and *education and Internet.* (For more on selecting keywords for computer searches, see pp. 525–27.) Begay then used these keywords to search the library's computerized catalog, as illustrated below:

- Select the kind of search.

```
What type of search do you wish to do?
    1. TI - Title, journal title, series title, etc.
    2. AU - Author, illustrator, editor, organization, etc.
    3. SU - Subject heading assigned by library.
    4. NU - Call number, ISBN, ISSN, etc.
    5. KE - Words taken from a title, author or subject.
Enter number or code: 3    Then press SEND
```

- Enter your keywords.

```
Start at the beginning of the Library of Congress sub-
ject heading and enter as many words of the subject
heading as you know below. Choose the most specific
heading you can.
     Ex: Molecular biology (NOT biology)
     Ex: Bastille Day (NOT France--History)
Enter subject: LIBRARIES AND INTERNET    Then press SEND
```

- Select from the listings.

```
                    BRIEF RECORDS        Records 1-5 of 5
LIBRARIES AND INTERNET
No. Author          Title                         Date Format
1. Valauskas, Ed    The Internet initiative       1995 BOOK
2. Oleksy, Walte    Education and learning        1995 BOOK
3.                  The Internet unleashed        1994 BOOK
```

35d

```
4.                  Libraries and the Internet  1993 BOOK
5. Rittner, Don.  EcoLinking: everyone's gui  1992 BOOK
```

- View specific source information, including bibliographic data, library call number, and availability.

```
                       FULL RECORD
LIBRARIES AND INTERNET
Title:        The Internet initiative: libraries providing
              Internet services and how they plan, pay,
              and manage
Authorship:   edited by Edward J. Valauskas and Nancy R.
              John
Pubinfo:      Chicago: American Library Association, 1995
              xiv, 220 p. : ill. ; 28 cm.
Subject 1:    Internet (Computer network)
Subject 2:    Library information networks--United States
Addauth 1:    Valauskas, Edward J.
Addauth 2:    John, Nancy (Nancy R.)
OCLC:         ocm32859049

Location      Copy Call Number                 Status
SPRINGFIELD   Dir/Off/025.04/Inte/1995/Pb      Noncirc
OLD CAMPUS    Ref. 005.7 V                     Noncirc
```

References to books

Two types of references, both often available on CD-ROM, can help you identify general books that have information about your topic: publishing bibliographies and digests. Publishing bibliographies tell whether a book is still in print, whether a paperback edition is available, what books were published on a certain topic in a certain year, and so on.

Books in Print. Books indexed by author, title, and subject.
Cumulative Book Index
Paperbound Books in Print

You might, for example, want to know if the author of an encyclopedia article has published any relevant books since the date of the encyclopedia. You could look up the author's name in the latest *Books in Print* to find out.

If you want to evaluate a book's relevance to your topic before you search for it, a review index such as the following will direct you to published reviews of the book:

Book Review Digest. Summarizes and indexes reviews of books.
Book Review Index
Current Book Review Citations
Index to Book Reviews in the Humanities
Index to Book Reviews in the Social Sciences
Technical Book Review Index

6 Generating your own sources

Most of the sources you consult for a research project—and most of the resources of the library—are likely to be secondary sources whose authors draw their information from other authors. However, academic writing will also require you to consult primary sources and to conduct primary research for information of your own. In many papers this primary research will be the sole basis for your writing, as when you analyze a poem or report on an experiment you conducted. In other papers you will be expected to use your research to support, extend, or refute the ideas of others.

Chapters 39 and 40 discuss the textual analyses, surveys, experiments, and other primary sources you may use in writing for various academic disciplines. One primary source not covered there is the personal interview with an expert in the topic you are researching. Because of the give-and-take of an interview, you can obtain answers to questions precisely geared to your topic, and you can follow up on points of confusion and unexpected leads. In addition, quotations and paraphrases from an interview can give your paper immediacy and authority. Edward Begay used just such an interview in his paper on the Internet (see pp. 644–45).

You can conduct an interview in person, over the telephone, or online using electronic mail (see p. 543) or a form of synchronous communication such as Internet Relay Chat (see p. 545). A personal interview is probably preferable if you can arrange it, because you can see the person's expressions and gestures as well as hear his or her tone and words. But telephone and online interviews allow you to interview someone who resists a personal interview or who lives far away from you, while still retaining most advantages of interaction.

A few precautions will help you get the maximum information from an interview with the minimum disruption to the person you are interviewing.

- If you do not already know whom to consult for an interview, ask a teacher in the field or do some telephone or library research. Likely sources, depending on your topic, are those who have written about your topic or something closely related, officials in government, businesspeople, even a relative, if he or she is an expert in your topic because of experience, scholarship, or both.
- Call or write for an appointment. Tell the person exactly why you are calling, what you want to discuss, and how long you expect the interview to take. Be true to your word on all points.
- Prepare a list of open-ended questions to ask—perhaps ten or twelve for a one-hour interview. Plan on doing some research for these questions to discover background on the issues and your subject's published views on the issues.

RESOURCES AND IDEAS

Heath, Shirley Brice. *Ways with Words: Language, Life, and Work in Communities.* New York: Cambridge UP, 1983. Heath provides a thorough and accessible demonstration of how to conduct ethnographic research, illustrated by her study of the communities of Roadville and Trackton.

Tryzna, Thomas N. "Research Outside the Library: Learning a Field." *College Composition and Communication* 37 (1986): 217–23. Tryzna shows how to begin a research project outside the library and find valuable primary sources.

TEACHING TIP

Many instructors require students to begin their research projects with an interview so that they get a human perspective on their topic before they begin locating secondary sources.

TRANSPARENCY MASTER 35.5

- Give your subject time to consider your questions. Don't rush into silences with more questions.
- Pay attention to your subject's answers so that you can ask appropriate follow-up questions and pick up on unexpected but worthwhile points.
- Take care in interpreting answers, especially if you are online and thus can't depend on facial expressions, gestures, and tone of voice to convey the subject's attitudes. Ask for clarification when you need it.
- For in-person and telephone interviews, keep careful notes or, if you have the equipment and your subject agrees, tape-record the interview. For online interviews, save the discussion in a file of its own. (A synchronous discussion may require that you activate a "log" or "archive" function before you begin your interview in order to save it afterward.)
- Before you quote your subject in your paper, check with him or her to ensure that the quotations are accurate.
- Send a thank-you note immediately after the interview. Promise your subject a copy of your finished paper, and send the paper promptly.

ANSWERS: EXERCISE 2

Individual response.

Exercise 2
Using the library

To become familiar with the research sources available through your library, visit the library and find the answers to the following questions. (Ask a librarian for help whenever necessary.)

1. Which resources are available on computer? Can you print search results? Can you transfer data from the computers to your own disks? What restrictions are there on the use of library computers for research?
2. Where are reference books stored? How are they cataloged and arranged? Which ones are available on computer? Where and in what format(s) are (*a*) *Contemporary Authors,* (*b*) *Encyclopaedia Britannica,* and (*c*) *MLA International Bibliography of Books and Articles on the Modern Languages and Literatures?*
3. Where is the catalog of the library's periodicals? Where and in what format(s) are the following periodicals stored: (*a*) the *New York Times,* (*b*) *Harper's* magazine, and (*c*) *Journal of Social Psychology?*
4. Where are the library's periodical indexes? Which ones are available on computer? Where and in what format(s) are (*a*) the *New York Times Index,* (*b*) *InfoTrac,* and (*c*) *Social Sciences Index?*
5. What is the format or formats of the library's catalog of books? If any format is incomplete, what is not included? If the catalog (or part of it) is computerized, where are the terminals, and how are they operated?

6. What are the library call numbers of the following books: (*a*) *The Power Broker,* by Robert Caro; (*b*) *Heart of Darkness,* by Joseph Conrad; and (*c*) *The Hero with a Thousand Faces,* by Joseph Campbell?

Exercise 3
Finding sources

List at least five sources you can consult for further leads on each of the three topics you produced in Exercise 1 (p. 521) or for three other topics. Use the information provided in the preceding section and additional information at your library.

COLLABORATIVE LEARNING

Have students complete Exercise 3 individually and bring three of the sources to class. Then ask students to work in small groups to evaluate each source, using the categories provided under "Evaluating Your Search" (pp. 527–29).

ANSWERS: EXERCISE 3

Individual response.

35e Making a working bibliography

Trying to pursue every source lead as you came across it would prove inefficient and probably ineffective. Instead, you'll want to find out what is available before deciding which leads to follow, and that requires systematically keeping track of where information is and what it is. You can keep track of sources by making a **working bibliography,** a file of the books, articles, and other sources you believe will help you. When you have a substantial file, you can decide which sources seem most promising and look them up first or, if necessary, order them through interlibrary loan.

A working bibliography is your chance to record all the information you need to find your sources and, eventually, to acknowledge them in your paper. You can use whatever system you like to keep track of information. Some instructors require that the working bibliography be submitted on note cards (usually 3″ × 5″, with one source to a card), and this system has the advantage of allowing sources to be easily added, deleted, and rearranged. But many researchers have abandoned note cards because computers can print out pages of bibliographic information, sort sources by terms or by authors' last names, and transfer data to the user's own disk, where the data are available for use in final source citations. You can combine the two systems by cutting up computer-generated source listings and pasting or taping each source on a note card.

You should have a bibliographic reference for each source you think may be useful. Getting the necessary information about a source as soon as you decide to consult it will save you from having to retrace your steps later. Include all the information listed in the box on the following page. (If you keep your working bibliography on a computer, you can create a template from this box and fill in slots as you collect information.)

Two samples of source records from Edward Begay's working bibliography appear on page 559. The first, for a book, Begay hand-

TEACHING TIP

A student's research project can be ruined when unattended notes are lost or stolen in the library. Remind students to keep an eye on their materials while they're working.

TEACHING TIP

Students always ask, "How many sources do I need in my working bibliography?" A good rule of thumb is two sources per anticipated page of paper: if students are writing a five-page paper, they should try to find at least ten sources. This rule of thumb should give them ample material from which to choose while preventing them from becoming obsessed with finding sources rather than writing.

TRANSPARENCY MASTER 35.6

Information for a working bibliography

For books

Library call number
Name(s) of author(s), editor(s), translator(s), or others listed
Title and subtitle
Publication data:
 Place of publication
 Publisher's name
 Date of publication
Other important data, such as edition or volume number

For periodical articles

Name(s) of author(s)
Title and subtitle of article
Title of periodical
Publication data:
 Volume number and issue number (if any) in which article appears
 Date of issue
 Page numbers on which article appears

For electronic sources

Name(s) of author(s)
Title and subtitle
Publication data if source is also published in print
Electronic publication data:
 Date of release or online posting
 Name and vendor (or publisher) of a database or name of an online service or network (America Online, Internet, etc.)
 Medium (CD-ROM, online, etc.)
 Format of online source (e-mail, Listserv, Web page, etc.)
Date you consulted the source
Electronic address

For other sources

Name(s) of author(s) or others listed, such as a government department or a recording artist
Title of the work
Format, such as unpublished letter or live performance
Publication or production data:
 Publisher's or producer's name
 Date of publication, release, or production
 Identifying numbers (if any)

wrote on a note card. The second record, for a journal article available on CD-ROM, Begay transferred from a CD-ROM database to his own disk and rewrote in a standard format as discussed below. He then printed the record and pasted it on a note card.

When you turn in your paper, you will be expected to attach a list of the sources you have used. So that readers can check or follow up on your sources, your list must include all the information needed to find the sources, in a format readers can understand. Most academic disciplines have special formats used by their practitioners. Several such systems are discussed and illustrated in this handbook:

- Modern Language Association (MLA) style, used in English and some other humanities (pp. 599–627). This style is supplemented by additional formats for electronic sources endorsed by the Alliance for Computers and Writing (ACW).

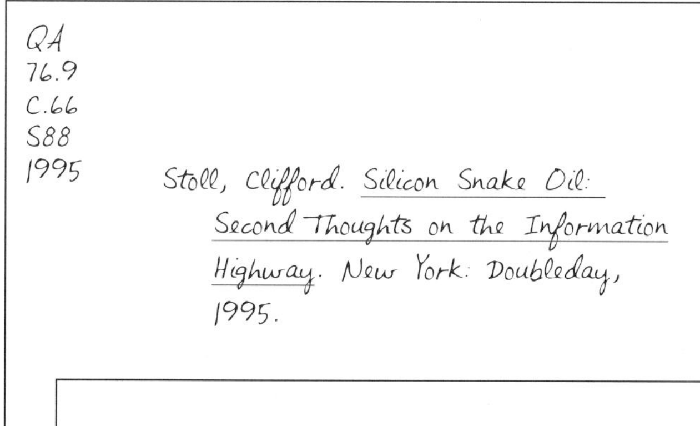

QA
76.9
C.66
S88
1995

Stoll, Clifford. Silicon Snake Oil: Second Thoughts on the Information Highway. New York: Doubleday, 1995.

Conte, Christopher. "Networking the Classroom." CQ Researcher 5 (1995): 921-43. Education on File. CD-ROM. SilverPlatter. June 1995.

- Chicago style, used in history and some other humanities (pp. 696–703).
- American Psychological Association (APA) style, used in psychology and other social sciences (pp. 707–20).
- Council of Biology Editors (CBE) style, used in the biological and other sciences (pp. 729–33).

Before compiling your working bibliography, ask your instructor what documentation style you should use. Then consult the relevant handbook section to determine what kind of information to include and how to arrange it. (Begay's cards above follow MLA style.)

Exercise 4
Compiling a working bibliography

Prepare a working bibliography of at least ten sources for a research paper on one of the following people or on someone of your own choosing. Begin by limiting the subject to a manageable size, focusing on a particular characteristic or achievement of the per-

 **COLLABORATIVE LEARNING**

Have students complete each of the following exercises individually, then ask them to work in small groups to review one another's bibliographies. Working together, students can often catch typos and misunderstandings of bibliographic form that they might miss individually.

ANSWERS: EXERCISE 4

Individual response.

son. Then consult reference books, periodical indexes, and the library's catalog of books. Record complete bibliographic information on note cards.

1. Bob Dylan, or another performer
2. Sandra Day O'Connor, or another Supreme Court justice
3. Emily Dickinson, or another writer
4. Magic Johnson, or another sports figure
5. Isamu Noguchi, or another artist

ANSWERS: EXERCISE 5

Individual response.

Exercise 5
Compiling a working bibliography

Using one of the topics and the possible references for it from Exercise 3 (p. 559), or starting with a different topic and references, prepare a working bibliography of at least ten sources for your developing research paper.

Chapter 36

Working with Sources and Writing the Paper

The previous chapter helped you lay the groundwork for a research project. This chapter takes you into the most personal, most intensive, and most rewarding parts of research writing: using the sources you've found, focusing and shaping your ideas, and drafting and revising the paper. In these stages you probe your topic deeply and make it your own. As before, the work of Edward Begay and Vanessa Haley will illustrate the activity and thought that go into research writing.

ESL Making a topic your own requires thinking critically about sources and developing independent ideas. These goals may at first be uncomfortable for you if your native culture emphasizes understanding and respecting established authority over questioning and enlarging it. This chapter offers guidance in evaluating, managing, and writing about sources so that you can become an expert in your own right and convincingly convey your expertise to others.

36a Evaluating and synthesizing sources

When should you shift gears from *seeking* sources to *using* them? The answer depends on the assigned length of the paper and on the complexity of your subject. You are probably ready to begin reading when your working bibliography suggests that you have explored most aspects of your topic and have found at least ten to twenty sources that deal directly with your central concern.

Once you have a satisfactory working bibliography, scan your list for the sources that are most likely to give you an overview of

HIGHLIGHTS

This chapter tackles one of the stickiest aspects of research writing: what students should do with the sources they have found. The process of critical thinking, reading, and writing outlined in the Introduction comes into play to help students shape their papers. The chapter focuses on helping students to evaluate, synthesize, and respond to their sources. It also provides exercises to help them understand and avoid plagiarism when they are incorporating their sources, with particular attention paid to note taking, summarizing, paraphrasing, and introducing quotes.

Examples from student papers also help students understand these crucial research skills. Edward Begay's and Vanessa Haley's papers-in-progress provide examples throughout the chapter, so that students can evaluate Begay's and Haley's work in progress by reading the final papers (presented in Chapter 38). Exercises provide practice in all aspects of handling sources, so that students' researched writing can be more effective.

RESOURCES AND IDEAS

Fulkerson, Richard. "Oh, What a Cite! A Teaching Tip to Help Students Document Researched Papers Accurately." *The Writing Instructor* 7 (1988): 167–72. Fulkerson suggests giving students a sample research paper with documentation removed to help them determine where and what kind(s) of citation must be used.

Higgens, Lorraine. "Reading to Argue: Helping Students Transform Source Texts." In *Hearing Ourselves Think: Cognitive Research in the College Writing Classroom.* Ed. Ann M. Penrose and Barbara M. Sitko. New York, Oxford: Oxford UP, 1993. 70–101. Higgens explores strategies through which students learn to use their sources, and debates between their sources, as the basis for developing their own arguments.

Kennedy, Mary Lynch. "The Composing Process of College Students Writing from Sources." *Written Communication* 2 (1985): 434–56. Kennedy's research shows that "fluent" readers and writers take more notes, do more planning, and reread more frequently than do less effective readers.

McGinley, William. "The Role of Reading and Writing while Composing from Sources."

Reading Research Quarterly 27 (1992): 227–48. McGinley demonstrates that students writing from sources use highly recursive nonlinear as well as linear reading, writing, and reasoning processes.

Pelham, Fran O'Byrne. "The Research Journal: Integrating Reading, Writing, and Research." *Composition Chronicle* 6.3 (April 1993): 4–5. O'Byrne advocates using a journal to supplement typical research activities and to allow students to "research, reflect, write, and then attend recursively to these events."

Spivey, Nancy Nelson. "The Shaping of Meaning: Options in Writing the Comparison." *Research in the Teaching of English* 25 (1991): 390–418. Spivey shows that the use of sources can affect students' processes of invention, arrangement, and style.

COLLABORATIVE LEARNING

TEACHING TIP

Because students are often unfamiliar with the clues provided by the publication context, bibliographic and indexing apparatus, and tone of a book or article, they can find the task of scanning sources difficult and confusing. Three kinds of classroom activities can help. For the first, you might photocopy the introductory material, first few pages, index, and bibliography of a book (or use a book or article that is already part of the class reading). Pose a sample paper topic that is related to the material found in the book and ask students to work in small groups (using the guidelines provided by the handbook) to evaluate the book for relevance and reliability. Then lead a general discussion in which you help students to identify the kinds of clues they used to help them decide whether the book was appropriate to the topic, whether it was too specialized or too simplistic, too out-of-date, or too biased.

As a follow-up exercise, ask students to bring one or two of their own possible sources to class and work with their groups to evaluate them, using the handbook's guidelines and the "clues" they discovered during the earlier exercise. Then ask each group to report their findings on one or

36a

your topic, and consult those sources first. Edward Begay, for instance, began investigating titles that indicated a focus on computer use in public schools and libraries. Vanessa Haley, in contrast, began by reading a book by Annie Dillard, the writer Haley had decided to focus on, and some journal articles that seemed to discuss Dillard's views of nature and humanity. For a paper like Haley's that seeks to analyze a writer's work, the work itself is always your starting point, but your own ideas may be supported and extended by those of critics and scholars.

1 Evaluating sources

When you first examine your sources, your purpose is to evaluate their usefulness and to develop your thinking, not to collect information. Scanning sources—gauging the kind and extent of ideas and information they offer—can help you determine whether your research is on track. For instance, if all your sources are very technical, assuming more background in the subject than you have, then you may need to search in more general-interest books and periodicals; or if all your sources discuss your subject at a very general level, you probably need to broaden your search—or even revise your topic—before proceeding. Scanning can also suggest the subdivisions of your topic, which will eventually help you structure your paper (p. 570).

When evaluating sources, you seek the kind of mix discussed on pages 527–29 under electronic searches: primary and secondary sources, scholarly and popular sources, older and newer sources, impartial and biased sources. This range reduces to two essential qualities: relevance and reliability.

Both relevance and reliability can be determined in part by consulting works *about* the source you are considering—that is, the works listed in citation indexes (p. 551) or book review indexes (p. 556). But unless you can dismiss the source on the basis of citations or reviews, you will also need to evaluate it yourself.

Relevance

To determine whether sources are relevant, scan the introductions to books and articles and the tables of contents of books. You're looking for opinions and facts that pertain directly to your topic. You're also ensuring that your sources are appropriate in level: you can understand them (if with some effort), and they also expand your knowledge. If you don't see what you need or the source is too high-level or too simple, you can drop it from your list.

Guidelines for evaluating sources

Determine **relevance:**

- Does the source devote some attention to your topic?
- Where in the source are you likely to find relevant information or ideas?
- Is the source appropriately specialized for your needs? Check the source's treatment of a topic you know something about, to ensure that it is neither too superficial nor too technical.
- How important is the source likely to be for your writing?

Judge **reliability:**

- How up to date is the source? Check the publication date.
- Is the author an expert in the field? Look for an author biography, look up the author in a biographical reference (p. 534), or try to trace the author over the Internet (p. 566).
- What is the author's bias? Check biographical information or the author's own preface or introduction. Consider what others have written about the author or the source.
- Whatever his or her bias, does the author reason soundly, provide adequate evidence, and consider opposing views? (See pp. 126–43.)

TRANSPARENCY MASTER 36.1

more of the sources, paying particular attention to their rationale for determining a source's relevance and reliability.

Finally, have each student prepare a short verbal presentation of one of their major sources, in which he or she makes a case for the source's relevance and reliability, and summarizes the author's main argument and approach.

Reliability

Reliability can be more difficult to judge than relevance. If you haven't already done so, study this book's Introduction and Chapter 4, especially pages 11–17 on analyzing and evaluating texts and pages 126–43 on reading an argument critically. When scanning potential sources, think critically, looking for assumptions, evidence, tone, fairness, and other features discussed on the pages cited. In addition, look for information about the author's background to satisfy yourself that the author has sufficient expertise in your subject. Then try to determine what his or her bias is. For instance, a book on parapsychology by someone identified as the president of the National Organization of Psychics may contain an authoritative explanation of psychic powers, but the author's view is likely to be biased. It should be balanced by research in other sources whose authors are more skeptical of psychic powers.

This balance or opposition is important. You probably will not find harmony among sources, for reasonable people often disagree in their opinions. Thus you must deal honestly with the gaps and conflicts in sources. Old sources, superficial ones, slanted ones—these should be offset in your research and your writing by sources that are more recent, more thorough, or more objective.

 **COMPUTER EXERCISE**

TEACHING TIP

Since electronic sources can pose additional problems, particularly for determining reliability, it will be helpful to conduct additional in-class evaluations of such sources. In a networked classroom, you might run through a short Internet search and then ask students to help you evaluate the reliability of the discovered source using the suggestions provided by the handbook. Then ask students to work in pairs to evaluate one or two of their own electronic sources and to report their findings to the class. In each case, encourage students to recount (and to keep journal records of) the methods they used to determine a source's reliability and relevance. Also, remind students about the electronic "Bookmark" function, a software feature that helps Internet users mark and return to specific web sites.

Evaluating electronic sources

Most books and periodical articles are reviewed before publication, so you can have some confidence in the information they contain. But many Internet sources are self-published by their authors with no preliminary review by others, so you must be the sole judge of reliability. To a great extent, the same critical reading that serves you with books and periodical articles will help you evaluate Internet sources (see the box on the previous page). But you should do some digging as well:

- *Check electronic addresses.* Look for an abbreviation that tells you where the source originates: *edu* (educational institution), *gov* (government body), *org* (nonprofit organization), or *com* (commercial organization). (Two-letter codes indicate origin outside the United States—for example, *uk* is United Kingdom.) Immediately before this abbreviation, the address will indicate the particular institution, government, or organization: for instance, *ed.gov* is the US Department of Education, *ca.gov* is the government of California, *greenpeace.org* is the environmental group Greenpeace, and *ibm.com* is the computer company IBM.
- *Check authorship.* Many sites list the author(s) or group(s) responsible for the site. You can research an author or group through a biographical dictionary, through a work such as the *National Directory of Addresses and Telephone Numbers,* or through a keyword search of the World Wide Web (see p. 538). A site on the Web may provide links to information about, or other work by, an author or group. The author or group may also show up in your other sources.
- *Communicate directly with the author.* For a posting on a Listserv or a Usenet newsgroup, try to reach the author directly to ask about publications and background or to seek further information about your subject. As discussed on page 544, Listservs usually publish subscribers' names and e-mail addresses, so it should be easy to reach an author. Newsgroups (p. 545) are generally more anonymous: you may have to address a posting to the author requesting his or her name and e-mail address. Drop the source from your list if you can't trace the author or the author fails to respond to your requests for information.
- *Check for references or links to reliable sources.* The source may offer as support the titles of sources that you can trace and evaluate—articles in periodicals, other Internet sources, and so on. A Web site may include links to these other sources.
- *Evaluate the source as a whole.* For Web sites, especially, consider the links to other sites. What is the purpose of the site in establishing and organizing links? Are the links worthwhile, or mere window dressing? Is the site trying to sell a particular

product, service, or idea? Do some links raise questions about the intentions of the source—because the links are frivolous, say, or indecent?

- *Back up Internet sources.* Always consider Internet sources in the context of other sources so that you can distinguish singular, untested views from more mainstream views that have been subjected to verification. As noted on page 565, only a range of sources will give you a broad and reliable picture of your topic.

2 Synthesizing sources

When you begin to locate the differences and similarities among sources, you move into the most significant part of research writing: forging relationships for your own purpose. This **synthesis,** an essential step in critical reading (pp. 15–16), continues through the drafting and revision of a research paper. As you infer connections—say, between one writer's ideas and another's or between two works by the same author—you create new knowledge.

All kinds of connections may occur to you as you work with sources. Edward Begay, researching the potential accessibility of the Internet to both the affluent and the poor, found data in one source to support another source's assertions about a technological gap between private and public schools. He also uncovered a central disagreement among sources over whether the Internet would prove a boon or an obstruction to education. Vanessa Haley, writing about Annie Dillard, sought and found similarities in Dillard's ideas about the place of humanity in nature, ideas expressed in varying contexts throughout Dillard's best-known book. Haley also discovered that her view of Dillard was partly supported by some of the critics she consulted but not supported by others. She knew she would have to take account of these diverging views in her paper.

Your synthesis of sources will grow more detailed and sophisticated as you proceed through the research-writing process. Unless, like Vanessa Haley, you are analyzing primary sources such as the works of a writer, at first read your sources quickly and selectively to obtain an overview of your topic and a sense of how the sources approach it. Don't get bogged down in taking detailed notes, but *do* record your ideas about sources in your research journal (p. 517):

- *Respond to sources.* Write down what your sources make you think. Do you agree or disagree with the author? Do you find his or her views narrow, or do they open up new approaches for you? Is there anything in the source that you need to research further before you can understand it? Does the source prompt questions that you should keep in mind while reading other sources?

RESOURCES AND IDEAS

Kantz, Margaret. "Helping Students Use Textual Sources Persuasively." *College English* 52 (1990): 74–91. Kantz suggests using analysis of the rhetorical situation and lists of questions to help students meet the demands of research essays.

TEACHING TIP

Assign students to review the material in the Introduction on synthesis, analysis, and evaluation as they work with their researched sources.

TEACHING TIP

Inexperienced researchers often have trouble keeping track of the sources they use at various points in their papers, especially as they move between notes and drafts. Remind students to collect full citation information for all their sources (keeping in mind that many databases provide that information in correct MLA or APA citation form). Also, reemphasize the need to indicate clearly when they are using source materials in their notes and drafts to avoid plagiarism problems later.

TEACHING TIP

Students often experience some difficulty in identifying connections and debates between their sources. Have students examine their principal sources to find (and follow up on) the additional sources cited approvingly or oppositionally by those authors. This helps students to develop a concrete sense of the debates surrounding their chosen topic, and of the major authors involved in those debates. As a follow-up exercise, you might have students work in groups to present verbally the connections and debates developed among three of their sources. You might also have students hand in a one-page analysis of the crucial connections among those three sources.

COLLABORATIVE LEARNING

Exercise 1 works well as a group project, particularly since the library may contain limited copies of Packard. You might consider putting this book on reserve so that each group can examine it for a limited amount of time. Have each group present their findings to the class, paying particular attention to the methods they used to evaluate the book. As the groups give their presentations, you might have students keep a running list of those methods on the blackboard, on the overhead, or on the computer network.

As a variation on Exercise 1 (or a follow-up to it) you might have one group work with Packard and other groups work with additional authors who have varying approaches to advertising (such as Michael Schudson, Mark Crispin Miller, or Stuart Ewen). This task will encourage students to identify differences in arguments and approaches.

ANSWERS: EXERCISE 1

Responses will vary. Packard's book is famously critical of advertising methods. Students should recognize Packard's bias while also valuing his expertise and evidence.

COLLABORATIVE LEARNING

As a preliminary activity to Exercise 2, have students work in groups to debate the similarities and differences among the three authors and their approaches. Encourage students to support

- *Connect sources.* When you notice a link between sources, jot it down. Do two sources differ in their theories or their interpretations of facts? Does one source illuminate another—perhaps commenting or clarifying or supplying additional data? Do two or more sources report studies that support a theory you've read about or an idea of your own?
- *Heed your own insights.* Apart from ideas prompted by your sources, you are sure to come up with independent thoughts: a conviction, a point of confusion that suddenly becomes clear, a question you haven't seen anyone else ask. These insights may occur at unexpected times—while you are showering, walking to class, drifting to sleep. Thus it's good practice to keep your research journal close at hand so that you can record and write about such flashes soon after they occur.

Exercise 1
Evaluating a source

Imagine that you are researching a paper on the advertising techniques that are designed to persuade consumers to buy products. You have listed the following book in your working bibliography:

Vance Packard, *The Hidden Persuaders,* revised edition, 1981.

On your own or with your classmates (as your instructor wishes), obtain this book from the library and evaluate it as a source for your paper. Use the guidelines on page 565.

Exercise 2
Synthesizing sources

The three passages below address the same issue, the legalization of drugs. What similarities do you see in the authors' ideas? What differences? Write a paragraph of your own in which you use these authors' views as a point of departure for your own view about drug legalization.

Perhaps the most unfortunate victims of drug prohibition laws have been the residents of America's ghettos. These laws have proved largely futile in deterring ghetto-dwellers from becoming drug abusers, but they do account for much of what ghetto residents identify as the drug problem. Aggressive, gun-toting drug dealers often upset law-abiding residents far more than do addicts nodding out in doorways. Meanwhile other residents perceive the drug dealers as heroes and successful role models. They're symbols of success to children who see no other options. At the same time the increasingly harsh criminal penalties imposed on adult drug dealers have led drug traffickers to recruit juveniles. Where once children started dealing drugs only after they had been using them for a few years, today the sequence is often reversed. Many children start using drugs only after working for older drug dealers for a while. . . . Legalization of drugs, like legalization of alcohol in the early 1930s, would drive the drug-dealing business off the streets and out of apartment buildings and into government-regulated, tax-paying stores. It also would force many of the gun-toting dealers out of the business and convert others into legitimate businessmen.

—ETHAN A. NADELMANN, "Shooting Up"

All studies show that those most likely to try drugs, get hooked, and die—as opposed to those who suffer from cirrhosis and lung cancer—are young people, who are susceptible to the lure of quick thrills and are terribly adaptable to messages provided by adult society. Under pressure of the current prohibition, the number of kids who use illegal drugs at least once a month has fallen from 39 percent in the late 1970s to 25 percent in 1987, according to the annual survey of high school seniors conducted by the University of Michigan. The same survey shows that attitudes toward drug use have turned sharply negative. But use of legal drugs is still strong. Thirty-eight percent of high school seniors reported getting drunk within the past two weeks, and 27 percent said they smoke cigarettes every day. Drug prohibition is working with kids; legalization would do them harm.

—MORTON M. KONDRACKE, "Don't Legalize Drugs"

I have to laugh at the debate over what to do about the drug problem. Everyone is running around offering solutions—from making drug use a more serious criminal offense to legalizing it. But there isn't a real solution. I know that. I used and abused drugs, and people, and society, for two decades. Nothing worked to get me to stop all that behavior except just plain being sick and tired. Nothing. Not threats, not ten-plus years in prison, not anything that was said to me. I used until I got through. Period. And that's when you'll win the war. When all the dope fiends are done. Not a minute before.

—MICHAEL W. POSEY, "I Did Drugs Until They Wore Me Out. Then I Stopped."

Exercise 3
Evaluating and synthesizing sources

Look up the sources in the working bibliography you made in Chapter 35, Exercise 5 (p. 562). Evaluate the sources for their relevance and reliability. If the sources seem unreliable or don't seem to give you what you need, expand your working bibliography and evaluate the new sources. In your research journal, write down your responses to sources, the connections you perceive among sources, and other original ideas that occur to you.

36b Taking notes using summary, paraphrase, and direct quotation

When you have decided which sources to pursue, you may be ready to gather information, or you may want to step back and get your bearings. Your choice will depend mainly on how familiar you are with the main issues of your topic and whether you have formed a central idea about it.

their views with evidence from the three passages. Then have each student create the paragraph specified by Exercise 2 and share it with their group. The collaborative approach will enrich students' interpretive responses to the passages, and will help make them aware that their own views on the topic are not self-evident, but must be argued on the basis of evidence.

ANSWERS: EXERCISE 2

The key similarities and differences are these:

Similarities: Nadelmann and Posey agree that crackdowns or penalties do not stop the drug trade. Nadelmann and Kondracke agree that the drug trade affects the young, who are most impressionable.

Differences: Nadelmann maintains that the illegal drug trade does more to entice youths to drugs than do the drugs themselves, whereas Kondracke maintains that the illegality discourages youths from using prohibited drugs. Posey, in contrast to Kondracke, claims that penalties do nothing to discourage drug abusers.

Students' paragraphs will depend on their views, but here is a sample response:

> Posey seems to invalidate the whole debate over drug legalization: nothing, he says from experience, will stop drug abuse. But such a futile view, whatever its truth, cannot stop the search for a solution. We have tried the prohibition favored by Kondracke. Even if, as he claims, students have increasingly negative attitudes toward illegal drugs, prohibition has not worked. It may be time to try the admittedly risky approach proposed by Nadelmann, legalizing drugs to "drive the drug-dealing business off the streets."

ANSWERS: EXERCISE 3

Individual response.

TEACHING TIP

Pick an essay or article to use in class, and practice taking notes from it with your students. If they all summarize, paraphrase, and quote from the same article and discuss their results in the classroom, they may gain confidence when moving on to their own research materials.

COMPUTER EXERCISE

Students can learn a great deal about the ethics of responsible summary, paraphrase, and quotation by practicing on each other. Have each student e-mail an abstract of his or her paper-in-progress to a partner in the class. Ask the partner to quote directly from the abstract, to paraphrase part of the abstract, and then to summarize the other person's project. Have each student check the accuracy of his or her partner's quote, paraphrase, and summary.

As an alternative kind of exercise you might ask each student's partner to deliberately misquote, or to paraphrase or summarize in a way that misrepresents the project. Then ask the student authors to identify the particular ways in which their work has been misrepresented.

- If you feel fairly confident that you know what you're looking for in sources, then you might proceed with reading and note taking, as discussed on the following pages.
- If you are attracted to several different main ideas, or you don't see how the various areas of the topic relate, then you might try drafting a thesis sentence to focus your thoughts and making an outline to discover relationships. These steps are discussed on pages 585–86 and 586–88, respectively.

1 Reading and note taking

The most efficient method of reading secondary sources during research is **skimming,** reading quickly to look for pertinent information. (Primary sources usually need to be read more carefully, especially when they are the focus of your paper.) When skimming:

- Read with a specific question in mind, not randomly in hopes of hitting something worthwhile.
- Consult the table of contents, index, or headings to find what you want.
- Concentrate on headings and main ideas, skipping material unrelated to the specific question you are researching.

When you find something relevant, read slowly and carefully to achieve a clear understanding of what the author is saying and to interpret and evaluate the material in the context of your own and others' opinions.

If it is effective, your final paper will show that you have understood and responded critically to your sources—work that can be performed most efficiently in note taking. Taking notes is not a mechanical process of copying from books and periodicals. Rather, as you read and take notes you analyze and organize the information in your sources. Thus your notes both prompt and preserve your thoughts.

Using a system for taking notes helps simplify the process and later makes writing the paper easier. Before you begin, decide on categories that your subject can be divided into. (If you have previously outlined your preliminary ideas, use outline headings for these categories.) Edward Begay, for instance, divided his general subject of Internet access into these categories:

History of the Internet
Traditional vs. innovative models of education
Business use of Internet
Differences between rich and poor schools
Training of Internet users
Costs of hooking up to the Internet
Internet and economic inequality

Role of librarians and teachers in Internet use
Role of businesses in Internet use

Headings for your categories will go at the top of each note to cue you about its content.

You can take notes either on note cards or on a computer. (You can also photocopy printed sources or download electronic sources. See p. 576.) Note cards are sometimes easier to rearrange; computer notes are easier to incorporate into your drafts.

Here are a few guidelines for note cards, illustrated by the sample cards beginning on the next page.

- Cards measuring 4″ × 6″ allow more room for notes than those measuring 3″ × 5″.
- Write only one fact or idea on a card so that you can easily rearrange information when you want to.
- If the same source gives you more than one idea or fact, make more than one card.
- Near the top of every card, write the author's last name and the page number(s) of the source so that you will always know where the note came from. (Write a short form of the title as well if you are using two or more sources by the same author.)
- Give the note a brief heading corresponding to one of your categories.

If you use a computer for taking notes from sources, follow these guidelines:

- Create one or more files for your notes with headings corresponding to your categories. You can then use a word processor's search function to find a particular category and the notes under it.
- Clearly separate consecutive notes with space and perhaps with a horizontal line. At the beginning of each note, record the source information: author's last name, title if the author is responsible for two or more sources, and page number(s).
- If a single source provides information relevant to two or more of your headings, sort the information among your categories accordingly.
- To search your notes individually as well as by category, use keywords with the computer's search function. You might, for instance, search by an author's last name or by a term such as *schools* or *libraries* or *businesses*.
- Print your notes at regular intervals. Then you'll have a paper copy if your instructor asks to see your notes and when you are away from your computer. (Since many computer monitors show less than a full page of text, printouts also allow you to scan your notes more quickly.)

Several computer programs are available that will create files and organize your notes automatically once you supply the appropriate commands.

You can use four kinds of notes: summary, paraphrase, direct quotation, and a combination of these methods.

RESOURCES AND IDEAS

Sherrard, Carol. "Summary Writing: A Topographical Study." *Written Communication* 3 (1986): 324–43. Sherrard discusses both common and effective summary-writing techniques of college students.

2 Summarizing

When you **summarize,** you condense an extended idea or argument into a sentence or more in your own words. A full discussion of summary appears on pages 10–11, and you should read that section if you have not already.

Summary is most useful when you want to record the gist of an author's idea without the background or supporting evidence. Edward Begay summarized the following quotation from one of his sources, Max Frankel, "The Moon, This Time Around," *New York Times Magazine,* page 42:

> A recent Rand study, with research supported by the Markle Foundation, concluded that in the foreseeable future the free market is likely to deliver e-mail to only half of America. Without a government-led drive toward universality, some e-mail systems may prove to be incompatible with others. And without induced subsidies, perhaps from Internet access fees, the computer industry may never produce the inexpensive technologies that would enable television sets, telephones and computer games to bring e-mail into the home. Interim subsidies and technologies would also be needed if less-affluent citizens are to get their e-mail outside the home, in apartment lobbies, libraries and schools.

Compare this passage with Begay's one-sentence summary, in which he picks out the kernel of Frankel's idea and expresses it in his own words:

> Internet and economic equality
>
> Frankel, p. 42
>
> Rand study says government direction and subsidy may be required to make e-mail technology universal and accessible to all.

36b

Paraphrasing

When you **paraphrase,** you follow much more closely the author's original presentation, but you still restate it in your own words. Paraphrase is most useful when you want to present or examine an author's line of reasoning but don't feel the original words merit direct quotation.

The following note card shows how Begay might have paraphrased the passage by Frankel given opposite.

> Internet and economic equality
>
> Frankel, p. 42
>
> If market forces prevail, according to Rand, e-mail may fail to reach many Americans. The government may have to direct an effort to make e-mail technology compatible and may have to underwrite the adaptation of household devices to e-mail, possibly by charging for use of the Internet. Similar measures will be required in the short term to make e-mail available to poorer people in public places.

Notice how the paraphrase differs from the Frankel passage in sentence structures and wording, except in the case of terms that lack synonyms such as *government* and *e-mail:*

Frankel's words	**Begay's paraphrase**
A recent Rand study, with research supported by the Markle Foundation, concluded that in the foreseeable future the free market is likely to deliver e-mail to only half of America.	If market forces prevail, according to Rand, e-mail may fail to reach many Americans.
Without a government-led drive toward universality, some e-mail systems may prove to be incompatible with others.	The government may have to direct an effort to make e-mail technology compatible . . .
And without induced subsidies, perhaps from Internet access fees, the computer industry may never produce the inexpensive technologies that would enable television sets, telephones and computer games to bring e-mail into the home.	. . . and may have to underwrite the adaptation of household devices to e-mail, possibly by charging for use of the Internet.

TEACHING TIP

A useful mnemonic that helps students remember how to paraphrase effectively is "New words and new word order." The emphasis on syntactic change in the mnemonic helps prevent simple synonym substitution.

TRANSPARENCY MASTER 36.2

36b

Frankel's words	**Begay's paraphrase**
Interim subsidies and technologies would also be needed if less-affluent citizens are to get their e-mail outside the home, in apartment lobbies, libraries and schools.	Similar measures will be required in the short term to make e-mail available to poorer people in public places.

Follow these guidelines when paraphrasing:

- Read the material several times to be sure you understand it.
- Restate the main ideas in your own words and sentence structures. You need not put down in new words the whole passage or all the details. Select what is pertinent and restate only that. If complete sentences seem too detailed or cumbersome, use phrases. Edward Begay might have written this more telegraphic paraphrase of the quotation by Frankel:

> Internet and economic inequality
>
> Frankel. p. 42
>
> From Rand: Mkt. forces may leave many Americans without e-mail. Thus govt. role: ensure compatible technology, underwrite adaptation of household devices, make e-mail available to poor in public places.

If you use such an abbreviated form of note taking, be sure to cast your notes as complete sentences in your draft.

- Be careful not to distort meaning. Don't change the source's emphasis or omit connecting words, qualifiers, and other material whose absence will confuse you later or cause you to misrepresent the source.

ESL If English is not your native language, you may have difficulty paraphrasing the ideas in sources because synonyms don't occur to you or you don't see how to restructure sentences. Before attempting a paraphrase, read the original passage several times. Then, instead of "translating" line by line, try to state the gist of the passage without looking at it. Check your effort against the original to be sure you have captured the source author's meaning and em-

COLLABORATIVE LEARNING

PRACTICE IN PARAPHRASING (ESL)

While ESL students may be comfortable using synonyms to express the content of a source, they may feel insecure about using other sentence structures. Emphasize to students that they must change the sentence structure as well as the vocabulary of the original in writing paraphrases. Collaborative work on paraphrasing helps students develop their vocabularies and find alternative ways to express ideas. In addition, more advanced ESL students (and native speakers) can reinforce their own writing skills by helping less advanced students.

phasis without using his or her words and sentence structures. If you need a synonym for a word, look it up in a dictionary.

4 Using direct quotation

Use direct quotation from secondary sources only when the exact words of the original are important. (See p. 592 for more on when to use quotations.) In a paper analyzing primary sources such as literary works, you will use direct quotation extensively to illustrate and support your analysis. (Vanessa Haley used many quotations from her primary source, a book by Annie Dillard; see her final paper on pp. 662–67.)

When recording a quotation from a source, take the following precautions to avoid plagiarism or misrepresentation of the source:

- Copy the material *carefully*. Take down the author's exact wording, spelling, capitalization, and punctuation.
- Proofread every direct quotation *at least twice*.
- Use big quotation marks around the quotation so that later you won't confuse it with a paraphrase or summary.
- If you want to add words for clarity or change the capitalization of letters, use brackets (see pp. 423, 431).
- If you want to omit irrelevant words or sentences, use ellipsis marks, usually three spaced periods (see p. 424).

The note card below shows how Edward Begay might have quoted part of the passage from Frankel on page 572, using ellipsis marks and brackets to make the quotation more concise and specific. (The brackets around the capital *W* in the second quoted sentence indicate that Begay replaced a small letter in the original.)

Internet and economic equality

Frankel, p. 42

"A recent Rand study . . . concluded that . . . the free market is likely to deliver e-mail to only [the more affluent] half of America. . . . [W]ithout induced subsidies, perhaps from Internet access fees, the computer industry may never produce the inexpensive technologies that would enable television sets, telephones and computer games to bring e-mail into the home. Interim subsidies . . . would also be needed if less-affluent citizens [who lack home computers] are to get their e-mail outside the home, in apartment lobbies, libraries and schools."

TEACHING TIP

Students often have trouble identifying the key passages or parts of passages that will become effective quotes. Remind students that the quote should represent the author's position fairly, and that it provides an occasion for the student to speak directly back to that author. It will also help to conduct workshops in which students practice choosing key quotes from a shared text and write one-paragraph responses to one of their chosen quotes.

 5 Combining quotation, summary, and paraphrase

Using quotation in combination with summary or paraphrase can help you shape the material to suit your purposes (although you must be careful not to distort the author's meaning). The card following shows how Edward Begay might have used a combination of quotation and paraphrase to record the statement by Frankel. Notice that the quotation marks are clearly visible and that the quotations are exact.

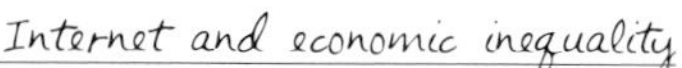
Internet and economic inequality

Frankel, p. 42

If market forces prevail, according to Rand, e-mail may fail to reach many Americans. The government may have to underwrite the adaptation of household devices "to bring e-mail into the home." Similar measures will be required in the short term "if less-affluent citizens [who lack home computers] are to get their e-mail outside the home, in apartment lobbies, libraries and schools."

Note If the material you are quoting, summarizing, or paraphrasing runs from one page to the next in the source, make a mark (such as a check mark) at the exact spot where one page ends and the next begins. When writing your paper, you may want to use only a part of the material (say, the first or second half). The mark will save you from having to go back to your source to find which page the material actually appeared on.

TEACHING TIP

Students working on popular topics or on topics for which little information is available might want to photocopy or download essential sources. Sources have a way of disappearing from the shelves, and students often aren't able to consult them again if they need to.

 6 Photocopying or downloading sources

Instead of taking notes, you may want to photocopy sources or download them from the Internet into your own computer or onto a floppy disk. Both photocopying and downloading have distinct advantages:

- They are convenient, particularly when material (such as journal articles) can't be removed from the library or requires too much time to examine closely online. You can also print a downloaded document if you prefer to read text on paper.

- Some researchers believe that photocopying or downloading is preferable to taking notes because it reduces the risk of distorting an author's ideas or introducing errors into quotations. With photocopying you need to write out a quotation only once, into your draft; with downloading you can move the quotation directly from source to draft.

But photocopying and downloading have some disadvantages, too:

- Unlike active note taking on cards or on a computer, photocopying or downloading sources may tempt you to glide through an essential stage of research writing: interpreting, analyzing, and synthesizing sources. Once you've run pages through a copier or clicked a mouse to download a file, your work with a source has just begun.
- Photocopying costs money. To economize, copy only sources you definitely want to use.
- Downloading is usually free as long as your Internet account does not charge for time online. However, you should check the source's copyright notice for any restrictions on downloading or requirements for acknowledging the source. (See also p. 582.)

When you photocopy or download a source, take the following additional steps:

- Make sure that you record complete bibliographical information from the source so that you don't have to retrace your steps for it. (Since online sources can change and disappear, retracing your steps may not even be possible.) Write bibliographic information directly on a photocopy, or add it to a downloaded file. See page 560 for a list of what information to record.
- Read the source as thoughtfully as you would any other. Annotate the relevant passages of a photocopy with underlining, circles, and marginal notes about their significance for your topic. You can accomplish the same work with a downloaded document by opening the downloaded file into your word-processing program and inserting highlights and comments at relevant passages.
- Do not import whole blocks of the source into your draft, especially with downloaded sources that you can excerpt electronically. The guidelines on page 592 for judicious use of quotations apply to sources you photocopy or download as well as to those you take notes from.
- To integrate notes on photocopied or downloaded sources into your other notes, make a cross-reference that briefly summarizes the photocopied or downloaded source—for example, "*Internet and economic equality* / Frankel, p. 42 / Disc. of measures needed for equal e-mail access / See photocopy."

Exercise 4
Summarizing and paraphrasing

Prepare two source notes, one containing a summary of the entire paragraph below and the other containing a paraphrase of the first four sentences (ending with the word *autonomy*). Use the format for a note card provided in the preceding section, omitting only the heading.

> Federal organization [of the United States] has made it possible for the different states to deal with the same problems in many different ways. One consequence of federalism, then, has been that people are treated differently, by law, from state to state. The great strength of this system is that differences from state to state in cultural preferences, moral standards, and levels of wealth can be accommodated. In contrast to a unitary system in which the central government makes all important decisions (as in France), federalism is a powerful arrangement for maximizing regional freedom and autonomy. The great weakness of our federal system, however, is that people in some states receive less than the best or the most advanced or the least expensive services and policies that government can offer. The federal dilemma does not invite easy solutions, for the costs and benefits of the arrangement have tended to balance out. —PETER K. EISINGER ET AL., *American Politics,* p. 44

Exercise 5
Combining summary, paraphrase, and direct quotation

Prepare a source note containing a combination of paraphrase or summary and direct quotation that states the major idea of the passage below. Use the format for a note card provided in the preceding section, omitting only the heading.

> Most speakers unconsciously duel even during seemingly casual conversations, as can often be observed at social gatherings where they show less concern for exchanging information with other guests than for asserting their own dominance. Their verbal dueling often employs very subtle weapons like mumbling, a hostile act which defeats the listener's desire to understand what the speaker claims he is trying to say (but is really not saying because he is mumbling!). Or the verbal dueler may keep talking after someone has passed out of hearing range—which is often an aggressive challenge to the listener to return and acknowledge the dominance of the speaker. —PETER K. FARB, *Word Play,* p. 107

36c Avoiding plagiarism

Plagiarism (from a Latin word for "kidnapper") is the presentation of someone else's ideas or words as your own. Whether deliberate or accidental, plagiarism is a serious and often punishable offense.

COLLABORATIVE LEARNING

Have students complete Exercise 4 individually and then discuss and revise their responses in small groups. Ask each group to report any strategies for condensing and organizing material that they discover in the process.

ANSWERS: EXERCISE 4

Possible summary

Eisinger et al., *American Politics,* p. 44

Federalism, unlike a unitary system, allows the states autonomy. Its strength and its weakness—which are in balance—lie in the regional differences it permits.

Possible paraphrase

Eisinger et al., *American Politics,* p. 44

Under federalism, each state can devise its own ways of handling problems and its own laws. The system's advantage is that a state can operate according to its people's culture, morals, and wealth. A unitary system like that in France does not permit such diversity.

COLLABORATIVE LEARNING

Have students complete Exercise 5 individually and then discuss and revise their responses in small groups. Students will learn a great deal by seeing the alternative strategies that other group members employed in completing the exercise. Encourage the groups to discuss the effectiveness of various strategies, and to consider how fairly Eisinger's views have been represented in each student's response.

ANSWERS: EXERCISE 5

Possible answer

Farb, *Word Play,* p. 107

Speakers at parties often "unconsciously duel" in conversations in order to assert "dominance" over others. A speaker may mumble, thus preventing a listener from understanding what is said. Or he or she may continue talking after the listener has moved away, a "challenge to the listener to return and acknowledge the dominance of the speaker."

- *Deliberate* plagiarism:

  Copying a phrase, a sentence, or a longer passage from a source and passing it off as your own.
  Summarizing or paraphrasing someone else's ideas without acknowledging your debt.
  Handing in as your own work a paper you have bought, had a friend write, or copied from another student.

- *Accidental* plagiarism:

  Forgetting to place quotation marks around another writer's words.
  Omitting a source citation for another's idea because you are unaware of the need to acknowledge the idea.
  Carelessly copying a source when you mean to paraphrase.

You do not plagiarize, however, when you draw on other writers' material and acknowledge your sources. That procedure is a crucial part of honest research writing, as we have seen. This section shows you how to avoid plagiarism by acknowledging sources when necessary and by using them accurately and fairly.

ESL More than in many other cultures, teachers in the United States value students' original thinking and writing. In some other cultures, for instance, students may be encouraged to copy the words of scholars without acknowledgment, to demonstrate their

Checklist for avoiding plagiarism

- What type of source are you using: your own independent material, common knowledge, or someone else's independent material? You must acknowledge someone else's material.
- If you are quoting someone else's material, is the quotation exact? Have you inserted quotation marks around quotations run into the text? Are graphs, statistics, and other borrowed data identical to the source? Have you shown omissions with ellipsis marks and additions with brackets?
- If you are paraphrasing or summarizing someone else's material, have you used your own words and sentence structures? Does your paraphrase or summary employ quotation marks when you resort to the author's exact language? Have you represented the author's meaning without distortion?
- If you are using someone else's material in your own online publication, have you obtained any needed permission for your use?
- Is each use of someone else's material acknowledged in your text? Are all your source citations complete and accurate? (See p. 599.)
- Does your list of works cited include all the sources you have drawn from in writing your paper? (See p. 607.)

OWNERSHIP OF INTELLECTUAL PROPERTY (ESL)

Ideas about ownership of intellectual property vary among cultures. In some cultures scholarly research consists of finding expert sources and copying information without attribution. ESL students who copy without attribution or too closely paraphrase sources may be following the procedures they have been taught. In their countries plagiarism may be considered less objectionable than in the United States or perhaps in their culture students are encouraged to use classic works in their own writing. (See p. IAE-82 for further discussion of ESL students' attitudes toward plagiarism.) Discuss the issue of intellectual ownership with your students, emphasizing that in the United States research and writing are valued for their originality. One way to encourage students to paraphrase and cite sources is to give a specific point value for each paraphrase and proper citation used in a research paper.

RESOURCES AND IDEAS

Kroll, Barry M. "How College Freshmen View Plagiarism." *Written Communication* 5 (1988): 203–21. A survey of 150 students shows the five most popular reasons they think plagiarism is wrong and discusses effective means to teach students the seriousness and possible consequences of plagiarism.

Whitaker, Elaine E. "A Pedagogy to Address Plagiarism." *College Composition and Communication* 44 (1993): 509–14. Whitaker describes classroom activities designed to help students understand and avoid plagiarism.

TRANSPARENCY MASTER 36.3

TEACHING TIP

Improved access to electronic communication means that students can obtain research papers by e-mail or fax. Guard against such plagiarism by requiring drafts and research reports and holding workshops to show work in progress. For more information see *College Composition and Communication*'s Intellectual Property Caucus Web site: http://tempest.english.purdue.edu/cccc-ip/

COLLABORATIVE LEARNING

TEACHING TIP

One way to teach students how not to plagiarize is to require deliberate plagiarism. Have students practice deliberately plagiarizing from a common article. Then have them exchange their plagiarized passages with fellow group members, who must locate and correct the plagiarism.

A WRITER'S PERSPECTIVE

If you copy from one author, it's plagiarism; if you copy from two, it's research.

—WILSON MIZNER

mastery of or respect for the scholars' work. But in the United States use of another's words or ideas without a source citation is plagiarism and is unacceptable. Always use quotation marks around a direct quotation and cite the source. Cite the source as well for any idea you borrow from someone else, even if you state the idea in your own words. When in doubt about the guidelines in this section, ask your instructor for advice.

1 Knowing what to acknowledge

When you write a research paper, you coordinate information from three kinds of sources: (1) your independent thoughts and experiences; (2) common knowledge, the basic knowledge people share; and (3) other people's independent thoughts and experiences. Of the three, you *must* acknowledge the third, the work of others.

Your independent material

You need not acknowledge your own independent material—your thoughts, compilations of facts, or experimental results, expressed in your words or format—to avoid plagiarism. Such material includes observations from your experience (for example, a conclusion you draw about crowd behavior by watching crowds at concerts) as well as diagrams you construct from information you gather yourself. Though you generally should describe the basis for your conclusions so that readers can evaluate your thinking, you need not cite sources for them. However, someone else's ideas and facts are not yours; even when you express them entirely in your words and sentence structures, they require acknowledgment.

Common knowledge

Common knowledge consists of the standard information of a field of study as well as folk literature and commonsense observations.

- Standard information includes the major facts of history, such as the dates of Charlemagne's rule as emperor of Rome (800–814). It does not include interpretations of facts, such as a historian's opinion that Charlemagne was sometimes needlessly cruel in extending his power.
- Folk literature, such as the fairy tale "Snow White," is popularly known and cannot be traced to a particular writer. Literature traceable to a writer is not folk literature, even if it is very familiar.
- A commonsense observation is something most people know, such as that inflation is most troublesome for people with low and fixed incomes. An economist's idea about the effects of inflation on Chinese immigrants is not a commonsense observation.

You may treat common knowledge as your own, even if you have to look it up in a reference book. You may not know, for example, the dates of the French Revolution or the standard definition of *photosynthesis,* although these are considered common knowledge. If you do not know a subject well enough to determine whether a piece of information is common knowledge, make a record of the source as you would for any other quotation, paraphrase, or summary. As you read more about the subject, the information may come up repeatedly without acknowledgment, in which case it is probably common knowledge. But if you are still in doubt when you finish your research, always acknowledge the source.

Someone else's independent material

You must always acknowledge other people's independent material—that is, any facts or ideas that are not common knowledge or your own. The source may be anything, including a book, an article, a movie, an interview, a microfilmed document, a computer program, or a newsgroup posting. You must acknowledge not only ideas or facts themselves but also the language and format in which the ideas or facts appear, if you use them. That is, the wording, sentence structures, arrangement of thoughts, and special graphic format (such as a table or diagram) created by another writer belong to that writer just as his or her ideas do.

The following example baldly plagiarizes the original quotation from Jessica Mitford's *Kind and Usual Punishment,* page 9.

Original The character and mentality of the keepers may be of more importance in understanding prisons than the character and mentality of the kept.

Plagiarism But the character of prison officials (the keepers) is more important in understanding prisons than the character of prisoners (the kept).

Though the writer has made some changes in Mitford's original and even altered the meaning slightly (by changing *may be* to *is*), she has plagiarized on several counts. She has copied key words (*character, keepers, kept*), duplicated the entire sentence structure, and lifted the idea—all without acknowledging the source. The next example is more subtle plagiarism, because it changes Mitford's sentence structure. But it still uses her words.

Plagiarism In understanding prisons, we should know more about the character and mentality of the keepers than of the kept.

You need to acknowledge another's material no matter how you use it, how much of it you use, or how often you use it. Whether you are quoting a single important word, paraphrasing a single sentence, or summarizing three paragraphs, and whether you are using the source only once or a dozen times, you must acknowledge the original author every time. See Chapter 37 for discussion and examples of how to acknowledge sources in your text.

If you read someone else's material during your research but do not include any of that material in your final draft, you need not acknowledge the source with a citation because you have not actually used the material. However, your instructor may ask you to include such sources in your list of works cited.

Acknowledgment of online sources

In general, you should acknowledge online sources when you would any other source: whenever you use someone else's independent material in any form. But online sources may present additional challenges as well:

- Keep in mind that online sources may change from one day to the next or even be removed entirely. Be sure to record complete source information as noted on page 560 each time you consult the source. Without the source information, you *may not* use the source.
- A World Wide Web site may include links to other sites that are copyrighted in their own right and require your acknowledgment. The fact that one person has used a second person's work does not release you from the responsibility to acknowledge the second work.
- If you want to use online material in something you publish online, such as your own site on the World Wide Web, then you may need to seek permission from the copyright holder in addition to citing the source (see pp. 782, 783).
- You may have to do additional research to discover the author of an online source such as a Listserv or newsgroup posting, whether for your citation or for reuse permission. See page 566 for advice on tracing online authors.

Quoting, summarizing, and paraphrasing honestly

When using direct quotation, be sure to copy the material from the source accurately and with clear quotation marks. Use the quotation marks in the running text of your paper even if you are quoting only a single word that the original author used in a special or central way. (See pp. 409–10 for the style to use with poetry and long quotations, which are set off from the text and not enclosed in quotation marks.) Acknowledge the source in the manner appropriate for the documentation style you are using. (See p. 599 for the MLA citation style, p. 696 for the Chicago style, p. 707 for the APA style, and p. 729 for the CBE style.)

To correct the plagiarism of Mitford's sentence on page 581, the writer could place Mitford's exact words in quotation marks and cite the source properly (in this case, in MLA style).

Quotation According to one critic of the penal system, "The character and mentality of the keepers may be of more importance in understanding prisons than the character and mentality of the kept" (Mitford 9).

Or the writer could paraphrase Mitford, using the writer's own words and sentence structure (with no quotation marks) and citing Mitford:

Paraphrase One critic of the penal system maintains that we may be able to learn more about prisons from the psychology of the prison officials than from that of the prisoners (Mitford 9).

If you adopt the source's sentence pattern and simply substitute synonyms for key words, or if you use the original words and merely change the sentence pattern, you are not paraphrasing but plagiarizing, even if you acknowledge the source, because both methods use someone else's expression without quotation marks. The inadequate paraphrase below plagiarizes the original source, Frederick C. Crews's *The Tragedy of Manners: Moral Drama in the Later Novels of Henry James,* page 8.

Original In each case I have tried to show that all the action in a "Jamesian novel" may be taken as a result of philosophical differences of opinion among the principal characters, and that these differences in turn are explainable by reference to the characters' differing social backgrounds.

Plagiarism According to Crews, the action in a "Jamesian novel" comes from philosophical differences of opinion between characters, differences that can be explained by examining the characters' differing social backgrounds (8).

Even though the writer acknowledges the author's work (by giving Crews's name and the parenthetical page number, 8), he plagiarizes because he does not also acknowledge Crews's exact words with quotation marks. The paraphrase below both conveys and acknowledges Crews's meaning, but it does not steal his manner of expression.

Paraphrase According to Crews, the characters in Henry James's novels live out philosophies acquired from their upbringing and their place in society (8).

In paraphrasing or summarizing you must not only devise your own form of expression (or place quotation marks around the author's expressions) but also represent the author's meaning exactly, without distorting it. In the following inaccurate summary the writer has not plagiarized but has stated a meaning exactly opposite that of the original. The original quotation, from the artist Henri Matisse, appears in Jack D. Flam, *Matisse on Art,* page 148.

ORIGINAL For the artist creation begins with vision. To see is itself a creative operation, requiring an effort. Everything that we see in our daily life is more or less distorted by acquired habits, and this is perhaps more evident in an age like ours when cinema posters and magazines present us every day with a flood of ready-made images which are to the eye what prejudices are to the mind.

INACCURATE SUMMARY Matisse said that the artist can learn how to see by looking at posters and magazines (qtd. in Flam 148).

The revision below combines summary and quotation to represent the author's meaning exactly.

IMPROVED SUMMARY Matisse said that the artist must overcome visual "habits" and "prejudices," particularly those developed in response to popular cultural images (qtd. in Flam 148).

To be sure you acknowledge sources fairly and do not plagiarize, review the checklist on page 579 both before beginning to write your paper and again after you have completed your first draft.

COLLABORATIVE LEARNING

Have students complete Exercise 6 individually and then discuss their responses in small groups. Encourage groups to debate the accuracy of each attempted quote or paraphrase, paying particular attention to items on which group members have differing responses. Students learn a great deal from the task of identifying the particular way in which a passage has been plagiarized or accurately represented.

ANSWERS: EXERCISE 6

1. Plagiarized: takes phrases directly from the original without quotation marks.
2. Acceptable.
3. Inaccurate and plagiarized: the passage uses phrases from the original without quotation marks and distorts its meaning.

Exercise 6
Recognizing plagiarism

The numbered items below show various attempts to quote or paraphrase the following passage. Carefully compare each attempt with the original passage. Which are plagiarized, inaccurate, or both, and which are acceptable? Why?

> I would agree with the sociologists that psychiatric labeling is dangerous. Society can inflict terrible wounds by discrimination, and by confusing health with disease and disease with badness.
>
> —GEORGE E. VAILLANT, *Adaptation to Life,* p. 361

1. According to George Vaillant, society often inflicts wounds by using psychiatric labeling, confusing health, disease, and badness (361).
2. According to George Vaillant, "psychiatric labeling [such as 'homosexual' or 'schizophrenic'] is dangerous. Society can inflict terrible wounds by . . . confusing health with disease and disease with badness" (361).
3. According to George Vaillant, when psychiatric labeling discriminates between health and disease or between disease and badness, it can inflict wounds on those labeled (361).

4. Psychiatric labels can badly hurt those labeled, says George Vaillant, because they fail to distinguish among health, illness, and immorality (361).
5. Labels such as "homosexual" and "schizophrenic" can be hurtful when they fail to distinguish among health, illness, and immorality.
6. "I would agree with the sociologists that society can inflict terrible wounds by discrimination, and by confusing health with disease and disease with badness" (Vaillant 361).

Exercise 7
Taking notes from sources

Continuing from Exercise 3 (p. 569), as the next step in preparing a research paper, make notes from sources you have not photocopied or downloaded. Use summary, paraphrase, direct quotation, or a combination as seems appropriate. Be careful to avoid plagiarism or inaccuracy. Mark each note with the author's name, title, and page number as well as with a heading summarizing its content. Mark this basic information on photocopied or downloaded sources as well, and annotate the sources to highlight and interpret what's significant for your topic.

4. Acceptable: puts the original into the author's own words and correctly conveys its meaning.
5. Inaccurate and plagiarized: fails to acknowledge the source and fails to convey accurately the concepts of "discrimination" and "confusing" outlined in the original.
6. Inaccurate: ellipses are needed to indicate that material was omitted, and brackets must be placed around lowercase *s* to indicate revision.

ANSWERS: EXERCISE 7

Individual response.

36d Developing a thesis sentence

Perhaps earlier in the research-writing process, but certainly once you have taken notes from your sources, you will want to express your central idea and perspective in a thesis sentence—or sentences, if you need more than one. (See p. 47 if you need guidance on developing a thesis sentence.) Drafting a thesis sentence will help you see the overall picture and organize your notes.

Edward Begay's and Vanessa Haley's work on their research papers illustrates how a thesis sentence evolves to become complete and specific. Before finishing his reading on access to the Internet, Begay wrote the following draft of a thesis sentence:

TENTATIVE THESIS SENTENCE

> Because of the cost of hooking up to the Internet and training people to use it, the nation faces the possibility of a widening gap between rich and poor in information, skills, and income.

This thesis sentence stated Begay's preliminary idea that the Internet poses a threat to equality. But with further reading Begay rethought this idea: many of his sources mentioned Internet access through public schools and libraries, and he began to focus on these institutions as a solution to the problem. The solution opened up new questions: how would schools and libraries have to change, and what would the change cost? With more reading Begay revised his thesis sentence:

TEACHING TIP

Have students complete this sentence in their journals or on a stick-on note they can post at their workplaces: "In this paper I intend to _[statement of purpose]_, so that my audience, _[describe intended readers]_, will _[desired result]_." This sentence reminds students to consider purpose, audience, and desired results as they write, and it should lead to clearer thesis statements.

COLLABORATIVE LEARNING

TEACHING TIP

Have students write their theses on large sheets of paper. Exchange thesis lists among groups, and have each group analyze and suggest revisions for the theses on their lists. The revising group should be prepared to explain its suggestions to the original writers.

In the later stages of their projects have students repeat this exercise as they read each other's drafts. In this case, groups should check to make sure that each student's thesis accurately represents the crucial project of his or her paper.

TEACHING TIP

Remind students that the thesis of a research paper can change. As they conduct their research and write their papers, they may find that their purpose, opinion, or conception of their audience has shifted. In such circumstances, revising the thesis may be not only desirable but necessary to compose an effective paper.

REVISED THESIS SENTENCE

To make Internet access universal, public libraries and schools face a double challenge: rethinking their purpose and mission in light of new technology and obtaining the necessary resources from government and business to go online.

For Vanessa Haley, framing a thesis sentence for her paper on Annie Dillard required drawing together (synthesizing) Dillard's ideas about humanity and nature into a single statement of Haley's own. The first draft merely conveyed Haley's interest in Dillard:

TENTATIVE THESIS SENTENCE

Unlike many other nature writers, Dillard does not reinforce the separation between humanity and nature.

Haley's revision stated her synthesis of Dillard's ideas:

REVISED THESIS SENTENCE

In her encounters with nature, Dillard probes a spiritual as well as a physical identity between human beings and nature that could help to heal the rift between them.

ANSWERS: EXERCISE 8

Individual response.

Exercise 8
Developing a thesis sentence

Draft and revise a thesis sentence for your research paper. Make sure the revised version specifically asserts your main idea. (If you need help, consult pp. 47–51.)

TEACHING TIP

Reassure students that they're not the only researchers who find interesting information that just doesn't fit in their final work. Historian Barbara Tuchman reports that while researching *The Guns of August*, she discovered that Emperor Franz Joseph gave his wife the same birthday present each year: a dozen hats, which he required her to wear. Tuchman says that she moved the note card from stack to stack, trying to fit it in her 500-plus-page book; however, she finally had to relegate it to the stack marked "unused." Tuchman told this story in an essay she wrote a decade after *The Guns of August*—it took that long for her to find a place to use it. You might also encourage students to use the endnote feature of their computer software programs to store information that doesn't seem immediately to fit into a draft in progress. When that draft gets printed out complete with endnotes, the student has another opportunity to review the material and decide whether it should become a formal footnote or endnote, whether it should be added in, or deleted.

36e

36e Creating a structure

Before starting to draft your research paper, organize your ideas and information so that you know the main divisions of your paper, the order you'll cover them in, and the important supporting ideas for each division. The goal is to create a structure that presents your ideas in a sensible and persuasive sequence and that supports ideas at each level with enough explanation and evidence. Consult the discussion of organization in Chapter 1 (pp. 52–61) if you need help distinguishing general and specific information, arranging groups of information, or using a computer effectively for developing a structure.

Creating a structure for a research paper involves almost constant synthesis, the forging of relationships among ideas (see p. 567). As you arrange and rearrange your notes, you find connections among ideas and determine which are most important, which are merely supportive, and which are not relevant at all.

To build a structure, follow these guidelines:

- Arrange your notes in groups of related ideas and information according to the subject headings you wrote on your note cards or computer files. Each of these groups should correspond to a main section of your paper: a key idea of your own that supports the thesis and the evidence for that idea.

- Review your research journal for connections between sources, opinions of sources, and other thoughts that can help you organize your paper.
- Look objectively at your groups of notes. If some groups are skimpy, with few notes, consider whether you should drop the category or conduct more research to fill it out. If most of your notes fall into one or two groups, consider whether the categories are too broad and should be divided. (Does any of this rethinking affect your thesis sentence? If so, revise it accordingly.)
- Within each group, distinguish between the main idea of the group (which should be your own) and the supporting ideas and evidence (which should come from your sources).

An outline can help you shape your research and also discover potential problems, such as inadequate support and overlapping or irrelevant ideas. For some research projects, you may find an **informal outline** sufficient: you list main points and supporting information in the order you expect to discuss them. Because of its informality, such an outline can help you try out different arrangements of material, even fairly early in the research process. Edward Begay experimented with an informal outline while examining his sources, in order to see how his developing ideas might fit together.

History of the Internet
Packet-switching networks—UK, France
ARPANET—linked US Defense Dept., contractors, universities
Network of networks—UNIX, NSFNET, and onward

Commercial vs. public use
1st users universities, libraries, govts.
Business sees commercial uses
PCs, modems increase home use

Access to Internet
Tech. skills needed
Problems for equality, democracy
Expense of going online
Imp. of Internet to democratic society
Libraries & schools: sites for widespread access
Libraries & schools need to adapt, find money to go online

This informal outline helped Begay decide not to continue researching the history of the Internet or the conflicts between commercial and public use (the first two sections) because they seemed likely to overwhelm his central concern, equal access to the Internet (last section). Note that Begay did include an endnote in his paper referring to the history of the Internet (p. 656).

COLLABORATIVE LEARNING

COMPUTER EXERCISE

The informal outline will probably be less intimidating than the formal one for students who find outlining paralyzing. As an alternative, reluctant outliners who are using word-processing programs may be able to use automatic outlining features to create effective formal outlines.

Some students will profit by using outlining as a revision strategy as well. Once students have written one or two successive drafts of their research paper have them work in pairs or small groups to outline their drafts, paying particular attention to connections between paragraphs and the presentation of major points.

RESOURCES AND IDEAS

Walvoord, B. E., V. J. Anderson, J. R. Breihan, L. P. McCarthy, S. M. Robinson, and A. K. Sherman. "Functions of Outlining Among College Students in Four Disciplines." *Research in the Teaching of English* 29 (1995): 390–421. This statistical study of the functions of outlining shows that students who produce successful papers tend to outline at several points in the drafting process.

Unlike an informal outline, a **formal outline** arranges ideas tightly and in considerable detail, with close attention to hierarchy and phrasing. The example below shows the formal outline's format and schematic content:

I. First main idea
   A. First subordinate idea
      1. First evidence for subordinate idea
         a. First detail of evidence
         b. Second detail of evidence
      2. Second evidence for subordinate idea
   B. Second subordinate idea
II. Second main idea

In this model main ideas are labeled with Roman numerals, the first sublevel with capital letters, the second with Arabic numerals, and the third with small letters. (A fourth sublevel, if needed, is labeled with Arabic numerals enclosed in parentheses.) Each level of the outline is indented farther than the one it supports.

A formal outline can help you decide not only what your main ideas are and how you will arrange them but also how you will support them. Some of this information may not emerge until you are drafting, however, so remain open to revising the outline as you proceed. And consider using a formal outline as a revision tool as well, creating a map of your completed first draft to check and improve the structure (see p. 68).

To be an effective organizer for your thoughts, or an effective revision tool, a formal outline should be detailed and should adhere to several principles of logical arrangement, clarity, balance, and completeness. These are discussed in detail and illustrated in Chapter 1, pages 56–58. Briefly:

- The outline should divide material into groups that indicate which ideas are primary and, under them, which are subordinate. A long, undivided list of parallel items probably needs to be subdivided.
- Parallel headings should represent ideas of equal importance and generality and should not overlap one another.
- Single sublevels should be avoided because they illogically imply that something is divided into only one part.

A formal outline is usually written either in phrases—a **topic outline**—or in sentences—a **sentence outline.** A complete topic outline is illustrated in Chapter 1, page 56. A complete sentence outline accompanies Edward Begay's research paper on pages 634–35. Either is suitable for a research paper, though a sentence outline, because it requires complete statements, conveys more information.

Exercise 9
Creating a structure

Continuing from Exercise 8 (p. 586), arrange your notes into a structure. As specified by your instructor, make an informal outline or a formal sentence or topic outline to guide the drafting of your paper.

ANSWERS: EXERCISE 9

Individual response.

36f Drafting the paper

Beginning a draft of what will be a relatively long and complicated paper can be difficult, so it may help to remember that you do not have to proceed methodically from beginning to end. Here are some ideas for writing a draft.

Tips for drafting a research paper

- To get your juices flowing and give yourself a sense of direction, write a quick two- or three-paragraph summary of what the paper will be about. (Pretend you're writing to a friend if that will help loosen you up.)
- Start with the section of the paper you feel most confident about. At first, skip any parts that scare you or give you undue trouble, even the introduction.
- Work in chunks, one unit or principal idea at a time. Fit the sections together only after you begin to see the draft take shape.
- Center each section on an idea of your own, using source material to back up the idea.
- Insert source information (author's name and page number) into the draft as you quote, paraphrase, or summarize.

1 Working section by section

In writing a first draft, remember that a primary reason for doing a research paper is learning how to interpret and evaluate the evidence in sources, draw your own conclusions from the evidence, and weave the two together in a way that establishes your expertise in your subject. The weaving will be easier if you view each principal idea in your outline as a unit. Depending on the importance of the idea to your scheme, on its complexity, and on the amount of evidence needed to support it, a unit may require a single paragraph or a block of several paragraphs.

Compose the units of your paper as if each will stand alone (though of course you will pull the units together before your draft is complete).

TEACHING TIP

A variation on the short summary suggested in the text is the five-minute overview. Students (perhaps in their journals) try, in five minutes, to give readers as full an overview of the paper they intend to write as they can. This five-minute overview might then serve as a road map for creating a draft of the paper itself.

To avoid the initial anxiety of beginning a draft, have students bring in their notes and outlines and write for a full class period. Then ask students to go home and rework this initial piece of writing into a typed rough draft that they can share with their revision groups.

TRANSPARENCY MASTER 36.4

- Begin each unit by stating the idea, which should be a conclusion you have drawn from reading and responding to your sources.
- Follow the statement with specific support from your notes: facts and examples; summaries, paraphrases, or quotations of secondary sources; quotations of passages from primary sources with your analysis.
- If your research focuses on or has uncovered a disagreement among experts, present the disagreement fairly and give the evidence that leads you to side with one expert or another.
- As much as possible, try to remain open to new interpretations or new arrangements of ideas that occur to you.

Proceeding in this way will help you avoid a common trap of research writing: allowing your sources to control you, rather than vice versa. Make sure each unit of your paper centers on an idea of your own, not someone else's, and that your paragraphs are pointed toward demonstrating that idea, not merely presenting sources.

2 Tracking source citations

As you draft your paper, insert the source of each summary, paraphrase, and quotation in parentheses in the text—for instance, "(Frankel 42)" referring to page 42 in a work by Frankel. If you are conscientious about inserting these notes and carrying them through successive drafts, you will be less likely to plagiarize accidentally and you will have little difficulty citing your sources in the final paper. (Citing sources is discussed in Chapter 37.)

3 Drafting on a computer

If you write on a word processor, the following suggestions could ease the transition from developing ideas and reading sources to drafting the paper:

- Copy your preliminary outline into your document file, and compose paragraphs directly under headings, deleting the remnants of the outline and adding transitions as you go along.
- If you have kept your source notes on a computer and your word processor can display separate files on the same screen, open both your document file and a copy of your notes file, one above the other. (Leave the original notes file intact in case you accidentally delete a note and need it later.) Then you can import your notes directly into your draft to support your ideas, using the word processor's editing functions to mesh source information into your own ideas and sentences.
- Instead of working with two files on the same screen, you can copy your notes file into your document file (again, leaving the

original notes file intact), arrange the notes under your outline headings, and write the parts of the draft that the notes support. Integrate the notes into your own text using the word processor's editing functions.

- If you do import your notes into your draft, you'll need to rewrite and edit the notes so that they work for your ideas and fit into your sentences. Avoid importing many long quotations from your sources. (See the box on the next page.)
- Be sure to include source information for every summary, paraphrase, and quotation, as described on pages 578–84.

36g Using and introducing summaries, paraphrases, and quotations

One of your challenges in writing a research paper will be deciding when, where, and how to introduce summaries, paraphrases, and quotations from your sources into your text.

1 Using borrowed material

The evidence of others' information and opinions should *back up* your conclusions. You don't want to let your evidence overwhelm your own point of view and voice. The point of research writing is to investigate and go beyond sources, to interpret them and use them to support your own independent ideas.

Most papers of ten or so pages should not need more than three to four quotations that are longer than a few lines each. Except when you are analyzing literature or other primary sources (see below), favor paraphrases and summaries over quotations. For quotations from secondary sources, use the tests on the next page.

In papers analyzing literature, historical documents, and other sources, quotations will often be both the target of your analysis and the chief support for your ideas. You may need to quote many brief passages, integrated into your sentences, and then comment on the quotations to clarify your analysis and win readers' agreement with it. Examples of such extensive quotation can be seen in Vanessa Haley's analysis of Annie Dillard's writing (pp. 662–67) and in the three literary analyses in Chapter 39 (pp. 680, 685, and 687).

Note If you need guidance in the mechanics of quotation, see the chart on pages 406–07, which summarizes all the conventions. For specific questions, see pages 380–81 (punctuating identifying words such as *he insists*), 409–10 (quoting poetry and long prose passages), 423 and 431 (using brackets for additions to quotations), and 424–25 (using ellipsis marks for deletions from quotations).

36g

TRANSPARENCY MASTER 36.5

Tests for direct quotations

The author's original satisfies one of these requirements:

- The language is unusually vivid, bold, or inventive.
- The quotation cannot be paraphrased without distortion or loss of meaning.
- The words themselves are at issue in your interpretation.
- The quotation represents and emphasizes a body of opinion or the view of an important expert.
- The quotation emphatically reinforces your own idea.
- The quotation is a graph, diagram, or table.

The quotation is as short as possible:

- It includes only material relevant to your point.
- It is edited to eliminate examples and other unneeded material. (For editing quotations, see the note on the previous page.)

COLLABORATIVE LEARNING

TEACHING TIP

Give each group a researched essay (student or professional). Ask students to highlight all of the introductory devices used to integrate quotations, and to discuss the effectiveness of each device.

2 Introducing borrowed material

When using summaries, paraphrases, and quotations, work to smooth the transition between your ideas and words and those of the source. At the same time, give the reader a context for interpreting the borrowed material.

NOTE The examples in this section use the MLA style of source documentation, discussed in Chapter 37. The source citations not only acknowledge that material is borrowed but also help to indicate where the borrowed material begins or ends. See page 605 for more on this topic.

Integrating borrowed material

Readers will be distracted from your point if borrowed material does not fit into your sentence. In the passage below, the writer has not meshed the structures of her own and her source's sentences:

> AWKWARD One editor disagrees with this view and "a good reporter does not fail to separate opinions from facts" (Lyman 52).

In the following revision the writer adds words to integrate the quotation into her sentence:

> REVISED One editor disagrees with this view, maintaining that "a good reporter does not fail to separate opinions from facts" (Lyman 52).

To mesh your own and your source's words, you may sometimes need to make a substitution or addition to the quotation, signaling your change with brackets:

Words added "The tabloids [of England] are a journalistic case study in bad reporting," claims Lyman (52).

Verb form changed A bad reporter, Lyman implies, is one who "[fails] to separate opinions from facts" (52). [The bracketed verb replaces *fail* in the original.]

Capitalization changed "[T]o separate opinions from facts" is the work of a good reporter (Lyman 52).

Noun supplied for pronoun The reliability of a news organization "depends on [reporters'] trustworthiness," says Lyman (52). [The bracketed noun replaces *their* in the original.]

Interpreting borrowed material

Even when it does not conflict with your own sentence structure, borrowed material will be ineffective if you merely dump it in readers' laps without explaining how you intend it to be understood.

Dumped Many news editors and reporters maintain that it is impossible to keep personal opinions from influencing the selection and presentation of facts. "True, news reporters, like everyone else, form impressions of what they see and hear. However, a good reporter does not fail to separate opinions from facts" (Lyman 52). [We must figure out for ourselves that the writer's sentence and the quotation state opposite points of view.]

Revised Many news editors and reporters maintain that it is impossible to keep personal opinions from influencing the selection and presentation of facts. Yet not all authorities agree with this view. One editor grants that "news reporters, like everyone else, form impressions of what they see and hear." But, he insists, "a good reporter does not fail to separate opinions from facts" (Lyman 52). [The writer's additions tell us what to expect in the quotation.]

A list of verbs for introducing borrowed material appears in the box on the following page.

Your interpretive words may precede the borrowed material, as above, or they may interrupt or follow it:

Addition interrupts "However," Lyman insists, "a good reporter does not fail to separate opinions from facts" (52).

Addition follows "[A] good reporter does not fail to separate opinions from facts," Lyman insists (52).

You can add information to a quotation to integrate it into your text and inform readers why you are using it. If your readers will recognize it, you can provide the author's name in the text:

TRANSPARENCY MASTER 36.6

Verbs for introducing summaries, paraphrases, and quotations

Introduce borrowed material with a verb that conveys information about the source author's attitude or approach to what he or she is saying. In the sentence *Smith ______ that the flood might have been disastrous,* filling the blank with *observes, finds,* or *insists* would create different meanings. (Note that all these verbs are in the present tense, the appropriate tense for discussions of others' writings.)

Author is neutral	Author infers or suggests	Author argues	Author is uneasy or disparaging
comments	analyzes	claims	belittles
describes	asks	contends	bemoans
explains	assesses	defends	complains
illustrates	concludes	disagrees	condemns
notes	finds	holds	deplores
observes	predicts	insists	deprecates
points out	proposes	maintains	derides
records	reveals	**Author agrees**	laments
relates	shows	admits	warns
reports	speculates	agrees	
says	suggests	concedes	
sees	supposes	concurs	
thinks		grants	
writes			

AUTHOR NAMED Harold Lyman grants that "news reporters, like everyone else, form impressions of what they see and hear." But, Lyman insists, "a good reporter does not fail to separate opinions from facts" (52).

If the source title contributes information about the author or the context of the quotation, you can provide it in the text:

TITLE GIVEN Harold Lyman, in his book *The Conscience of the Journalist,* grants that "news reporters, like everyone else, form impressions of what they see and hear." But, Lyman insists, "a good reporter does not fail to separate opinions from facts" (52).

Finally, if the quoted author's background and experience reinforce or clarify the quotation, you can provide these credentials in the text:

CREDENTIALS GIVEN Harold Lyman, a newspaper editor for more than forty years, grants that "news reporters, like everyone else, form impressions of what they see and hear." But, Lyman insists, "a good reporter does not fail to separate opinions from facts" (52).

36g

You need not always name the author, source, or credentials in your text. In fact, such introductions may get in the way when you are simply establishing facts or weaving together facts and opinions from varied sources. In the following passage from Edward Begay's paper, the information is more important than the sources, so the sources are mentioned only in a parenthetical acknowledgment:

> Several states have organized NetDay campaigns designed to bring educators, school boards, and community volunteers together to oversee installation of Internet capabilities in the public schools ("Louisiana NetDay96"; MacFarquhar B1).

Exercise 10
Using and introducing borrowed material

Drawing on the ideas in the following paragraph and using examples from your own observations and experiences, write a paragraph about anxiety. Integrate at least one direct quotation and one paraphrase from the following paragraph into your own sentences. In your paragraph identify the author by name and give his credentials: he is a professor of psychiatry and a practicing psychoanalyst.

> There are so many ways in which man is different from all the lower forms of animals, and almost all of them make us uniquely susceptible to feelings of anxiousness. Our imagination and reasoning powers facilitate anxiety; the anxious feeling is precipitated not by an absolute impending threat—such as the worry about an examination, a speech, travel—but rather by the symbolic and often unconscious representations. We do not have to be experiencing a potential danger. We can experience something related to it. We can recall, through our incredible memories, the original symbolic sense of vulnerability in childhood and suffer the feeling attached to that. We can even forget the original memory and still be stuck with the emotion—which is then compounded by its seemingly irrational quality at this time. It is not just the fear of death which pains us, but the anticipation of it; or the anniversary of a specific death; or a street, a hospital, a time of day, a color, a flower, a symbol associated with death.
>
> —Willard Gaylin, "Feeling Anxious," p. 23

36h Revising and editing the paper

When you have written a first draft, take a break for at least a day so that you can gain some objectivity about your work and read the draft critically when you begin to revise. Then evaluate your first draft according to the advice and revision checklist on pages 67–70. Deal with major revisions first, saving editing and formatting for later drafts. Be especially attentive to the following:

ANSWERS: EXERCISE 10

Sample paragraph

Why does a woman who is otherwise happy regularly suffer anxiety attacks at the first sign of spring? Why does a man who is otherwise a competent, relaxed driver feel panic whenever he approaches a traffic rotary? According to Willard Gaylin, a professor of psychiatry and a practicing psychoanalyst, such feelings of anxiety are attributable to the uniquely human capacities for remembering, imagining, and forming "symbolic and often unconscious representations" of experiences (23). The feeling of anxiety, Gaylin says, "is . . . compounded by its seemingly irrational quality": it may appear despite the absence of an immediate source of worry or pain (23). The anxious woman is not aware of it, but her father's death twenty years before in April has caused her to equate spring with death. Similarly, the man has forgotten that a terrible accident he witnessed as a child occurred at a rotary. For both people, the anxious feelings are not reduced but heightened because they seem to be unfounded.

COLLABORATIVE LEARNING

As a follow-up to Exercise 10, have students work in small groups to review every quotation in each other's drafts-in-progress. Is each quotation necessary and appropriate? Is the writer integrating the quote smoothly into the paper? Is the writer making effective use of the quotation, supplying an interpretation of it, and making it work towards some larger purpose in his or her own argument? This discussion can often help student writers rethink their uses of quotation and elaborate on their interpretive responses, thus helping them to create effective revisions of their drafts.

A WRITER'S PERSPECTIVE

> *Intelligent, even fastidious revision . . . is, or certainly should be, an art in itself.*
>
> —Joyce Carol Oates

TEACHING TIP

Students can panic when it becomes clear in the final revision stages that the paper still lacks a crucial source or a strong thesis. You can prepare students for these moments by helping them to understand that papers often develop beyond the scope or direction of writers' original research, outlines, and planned theses. Taking advantage of these developments by finding an additional source or writing a new thesis statement is often the key to a successful revision.

- Ensure that your thesis sentence accurately describes your topic and your perspective as they emerged during drafting, so that the paper is unified and coherent.
- Be alert for structural problems. (Outlining your draft as suggested on p. 68 can help you see your structure at a glance.)

  Illogical arrangements of ideas.
  Inadequate emphasis of important points and overemphasis of minor points.
  Imbalance between the views of others (support) and your own views (interpretation or analysis).
- Hunt out irrelevant ideas and facts that crept in just because you had notes on them.
- Look for places where supporting evidence is weak.
- Evaluate the reasonableness of your argument (see pp. 147–51).
- Consider where you need to define terms and clarify concepts that readers may be unfamiliar with.

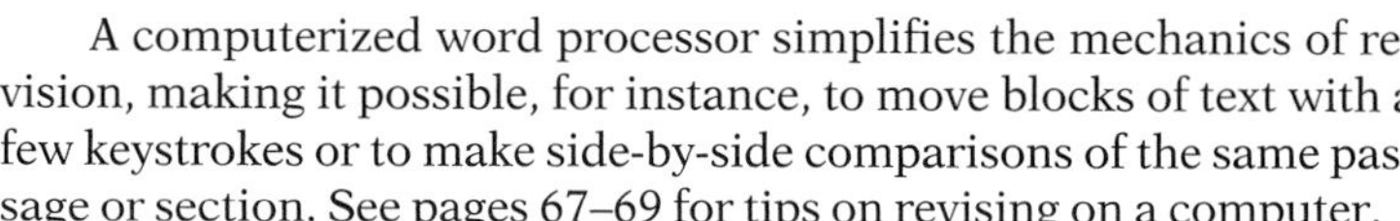

A computerized word processor simplifies the mechanics of revision, making it possible, for instance, to move blocks of text with a few keystrokes or to make side-by-side comparisons of the same passage or section. See pages 67–69 for tips on revising on a computer.

When you complete your revision—and only then—you are ready to edit. If you do not write on a computer, copy or retype the new draft if possible so that you have a clean copy to work on. If you write on a computer, you can edit directly on screen or print a clean copy. (Some writers find it easier to spot errors on paper than on screen.) For editing, consult the advice and checklist on pages 73–76. Try to read the paper from the point of view of someone who has not spent hours planning and researching but instead has come fresh to the paper. Look for lapses in sense, awkward passages, wordiness, poor transitions between ideas and evidence, unnecessary repetition, wrong or misspelled words, errors in grammar, punctuation, or mechanics—in short, anything that is likely to interfere with a reader's understanding of your meaning.

Note Before you prepare and proofread the final draft (next section), you must insert your source citations into the text and prepare your list of sources. See Chapter 37.

ANSWERS: EXERCISE 11

Individual response.

Exercise 11
Drafting and revising your paper

Draft the research paper you have been preparing throughout Chapters 35 and 36. Before beginning the first draft, study your research journal and your notes. While drafting, follow your notes, thesis sentence, and outline as closely as you need to, but stay open to new ideas, associations, and arrangements. Then revise and edit thoroughly and carefully, working to improve not only your presentation of ideas but also, if necessary, the ideas themselves.

36i Preparing and proofreading the final manuscript

Prepare the final draft of your paper when you have edited the text (previous page), added the source citations (p. 599), and written the list of works cited (p. 607). Most instructors expect research papers to be neatly typed with clear titling, double spacing, standard margins, and minimal handwritten corrections. Your instructor may have additional requirements, suggested by the discipline you are writing in. This book explains four such document formats:

- In English, foreign languages, and some other humanities, use the format of the *MLA Handbook for Writers of Research Papers.* See Appendix A (pp. 759–65) for a detailed description and the research papers of Edward Begay and Vanessa Haley (pp. 632–67) for illustrations.
- In history, art history, and some other humanities, use the Chicago format. See pages 697 and 703 for a description and illustrations.
- In psychology and other social sciences, use the format of the *Publication Manual of the American Psychological Association.* See pages 711 and 720–22 for a description and illustrations.
- In the life sciences, physical sciences, and mathematics, use the format of *Scientific Style and Format: The CBE Manual for Authors, Editors, and Publishers.* See pages 730 and 733 for a description and illustration.

In any discipline, you can use a computerized word processor to present your ideas effectively and attractively with readable typefaces, headings, illustrations, and other elements. See pages 765–72 for ideas and illustrations.

Before you submit your paper, proofread it carefully for typographical errors, misspellings, and other slight errors. (See p. 77 for proofreading tips.) Unless the errors are very numerous (more than several on a page), you can correct them by whiting out or crossing out (neatly) and inserting the correction (neatly) in ink. (See Appendix A, p. 764, for an example.) Don't let the pressure of a deadline prevent you from proofreading, for even minor errors can impair clarity or annoy readers and thus negate some of the hard work you have put into your project.

Exercise 12

Preparing and proofreading your final manuscript

After adding source citations and a list of works cited (Chapter 37), prepare the final draft of your research paper. Unless your instructor specifies otherwise, follow the manuscript format recommended in Appendix A. Proofread and correct the final paper before handing it in.

COLLABORATIVE LEARNING

It is very important to keep students working in collaborative groups throughout the research and revision process. Those groups can also be invaluable in the final stages described by Exercises 11 and 12 by editing and proofreading each other's drafts, reading drafts out loud to catch additional errors, helping to revise thesis statements, and honing the presentation of arguments.

ANSWERS: EXERCISE 12

Individual response.

HIGHLIGHTS

This chapter explains the procedure for documenting sources as stipulated by the Modern Language Association (MLA). It shows, with quick-reference indexes on pages 601 and 609, both how to document sources within the text using parenthetical citations and how to prepare a "Works Cited" list for the end of the paper. The chapter ends with a list of common abbreviations used in source citations.

RESOURCES AND IDEAS

Students who need to use a documentation style other than the four described in this text may wish to consult the general guide (Turabian) listed below.

TEACHING TIP

Students frequently ask why there are so many different styles for them to learn. Use the analogy of basketball: while some rules are the same in all games (regular field goals count as two points, free throws one), others differ depending on the court and players. For instance, the three-point line is farther from the basket in professional basketball than it is in college. These different rules are designed to suit the abilities and expectations of players at each level. Likewise, different documentation systems are designed for the needs of each audience. The social sciences value the timeliness of information, so the date of publication is included in text citations and emphasized in references. The humanities rely on descriptive titles, so titles are featured.

TEACHING TIP

MLA is not the only documentation style to require that only the first author's name be listed for works with more than three authors, using *et al.* to represent the other authors' names. A growing number of scholars now believe that this devalues the work of collaborators and overemphasizes the work of the first listed author. A number of disciplines are considering revising this requirement so that all authors' names are included in bibliographic citations, to represent fairly all their contributions.

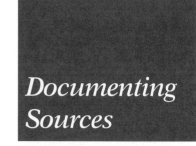

Chapter 37 Documenting Sources

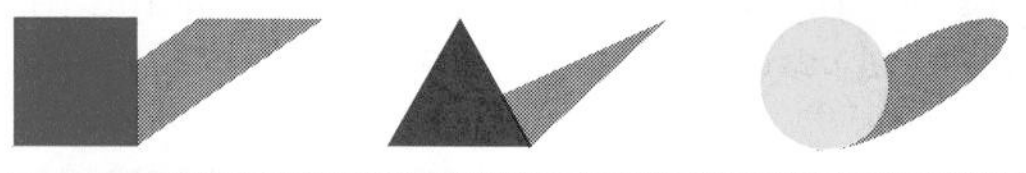

Every time you borrow the words, facts, or ideas of others, you must acknowledge the source to tell readers that you borrowed the material and where you borrowed it from. To cite sources is to **document** them, to supply references (documents) that legitimate your use of borrowed material and support your claims about its origins. Pages 578–82 discuss what kinds of information you must acknowledge.

As you draft your paper, you should note source information for every quotation, summary, and paraphrase. These notes and the information in your working bibliography (p. 559) should give you everything you need to write source citations.

37a Citing sources in academic writing

Editors and teachers in most academic disciplines require special documentation formats (or styles) in their scholarly journals and in students' papers. All the styles use a citation in the text that serves two purposes: it signals that material is borrowed, and it refers readers to detailed information about the source so that they can locate both the source and the place in the source where the borrowed material appears. The detailed source information appears either in footnotes or at the end of the paper.

Aside from these essential similarities, the disciplines' documentation styles differ markedly in citation form, arrangement of source information, and other particulars. Each discipline's style reflects the needs of its practitioners for certain kinds of information presented in certain ways. For instance, the currency of a source is important in the social sciences, where studies build on and correct each other, so in-text citations include a source's date of publication. In the humanities, however, currency is less important, so in-text citations do not include date of publication.

This book details four documentation styles:

- For English, foreign languages, and some other humanities, the style of the Modern Language Association (MLA) gives authors' names and page numbers for text citations and then a list of works cited, containing full bibliographic information, at the end of the paper. See below.
- For history, art, religion, and some other humanities, one style recommended by the *Chicago Manual of Style* gives raised numerals for text citations and correspondingly numbered footnotes (bottoms of pages) or endnotes (end of paper) containing full bibliographic information. The Chicago style also sometimes includes a separate list of works cited. See page 696.
- For psychology and most other social sciences, the style of the American Psychological Association (APA) gives authors' names, publication dates, and page numbers in the text citations and full bibliographic information in a list of references at the end of the paper. See page 707.
- For the life sciences, the physical sciences, and mathematics, one style recommended by the Council of Biology Editors (CBE) gives a list of numbered references (arranged in order of their citation in the text) at the end of the paper and uses corresponding numbers for text citations. See page 729.

Ask your instructor which style you should use. If your instructor does not require a particular documentation style, use the one above that's most appropriate for the discipline you're writing in. Do follow one system for citing sources—and one system only—so that you provide all the necessary information in a consistent format.

Note Various computer programs can help you format your source citations in the style of your choice. Such a program will prompt you for needed information (author's name, book title, date of publication, and so on) and will arrange, capitalize, underline, and punctuate the information as required by the style. The program will remove some tedium from documenting sources, but it can't substitute for your own care and attention in giving your sources accurate and complete acknowledgment.

37b Citing sources in your text: MLA style

The documentation system of the Modern Language Association is detailed in the *MLA Handbook for Writers of Research Papers,* 4th

COLLABORATIVE LEARNING

TEACHING TIP

Divide students into teams of three. Have the first student take five cards from the second student's working bibliography and make up correct citations for them. Ask the third student to check the first student's work. This activity allows students to confer on citations that puzzle them and to get help learning the fine points (such as where the periods and quotation marks go).

edition (1995). This style employs brief parenthetical citations within the text that direct readers to the list of works cited. For example:

> Only one article mentions this discrepancy (Wolfe 62).

The name Wolfe directs readers to the article by Wolfe in the list of works cited, and the page number 62 specifies the page in the article on which the cited material appears.

The following pages describe this documentation system: what must be included in a citation (below), where to place citations (p. 605), when to use footnotes or endnotes in addition to parenthetical citations (p. 607), and how to create the list of works cited (p. 607). Indexes opposite (parenthetical text citations) and on page 609 (works-cited entries) provide quick-reference guides to the models.

1 Writing parenthetical text citations

The in-text citations of sources have two requirements:

- They must include just enough information for the reader to locate the appropriate source in your list of works cited.
- They must include just enough information for the reader to locate the place in the source where the borrowed material appears.

Usually, you can meet both these requirements by providing the author's last name and the page(s) in the source on which the material appears. The reader can find the source in your list of works cited and find the borrowed material in the source itself. Refer to the index on the next page to find the form of reference for the kind of source and citation you are using.

TRANSPARENCY MASTER 37.1

1. Author not named in your text

When you have not already named the author in your sentence, provide the author's last name and the page number(s), with no punctuation between them, in parentheses.

> One researcher concludes that "women impose a distinctive construction on moral problems, seeing moral dilemmas in terms of conflicting responsibilities" (Gilligan 105).

See models 5 and 6 (p. 602) for the forms to use when the source numbers paragraphs instead of pages or does not provide numbers at all.

2. Author named in your text

If the author's name is already given in your text, you need not repeat it in the parenthetical citation. The citation gives just the page number(s).

Index to MLA parenthetical text citations

> One researcher, Carol Gilligan, concludes that "women impose a distinctive construction on moral problems, seeing moral dilemmas in terms of conflicting responsibilities" (105).

3. A work with two or three authors

If the source has two or three authors, give all their last names in the text or in the citation. Separate two authors' names with "and":

> As Frieden and Sagalyn observe, "The poor and the minorities were the leading victims of highway and renewal programs" (29).

> According to one study, "The poor and the minorities were the leading victims of highway and renewal programs" (Frieden and Sagalyn 29).

With three authors, add commas and also "and" before the final name:

> The text by Wilcox, Ault, and Agee discusses the "ethical dilemmas in public relations practice" (125).

> One text discusses the "ethical dilemmas in public relations practice" (Wilcox, Ault, and Agee 125).

4. A work with more than three authors

If the source has more than three authors, you may list all their last names or use only the first author's name followed by "et al." (the abbreviation for the Latin "and others"). The choice depends on what you do in your list of works cited (see p. 610).

> It took the combined forces of the Americans, Europeans, and Japanese to break the rebel siege of Beijing in 1900 (Lopez et al. 362).

> It took the combined forces of the Americans, Europeans, and Japanese to break the rebel siege of Beijing in 1900 (Lopez, Blum, Cameron, and Barnes 362).

5. A work with numbered paragraphs instead of pages

Some electronic sources number each paragraph instead of each page. In citing passages in these sources, give the paragraph number(s) and distinguish them from page numbers: after the author's name, put a comma, a space, and the abbreviation "par." (one paragraph) or "pars." (more than one paragraph).

> Twins reared apart report similar feelings (Palfrey, pars. 6-7).

6. An entire work or a work with no page or paragraph numbers

When you cite an entire work rather than a part of it, the citation will not include any page or paragraph number. Try to work the author's name into your text, in which case you will not need a parenthetical citation. But remember that the source must appear in the list of works cited.

> Boyd deals with the need to acknowledge and come to terms with our fear of nuclear technology.

Use the same format when you cite a specific passage from a work with no page or paragraph numbers, such as an online source. If the author's name does not appear in your text, put it in a parenthetical citation.

> Almost 20 percent of commercial banks have been audited for the practice (Friis).

7. A multivolume work

If you consulted only one volume of a multivolume work, your list of works cited will indicate as much (see p. 613), and you can treat the volume as any book. If you consulted more than one volume, give the appropriate volume in your text citation.

> After issuing the Emancipation Proclamation, Lincoln said, "What I did, I did after very full deliberations, and under a very heavy and solemn sense of responsibility" (5: 438).

The number 5 indicates the volume from which the quotation was taken; the number 438 indicates the page number in that volume. When the author's name appears in such a citation, place it before the volume number with no punctuation: (Lincoln 5: 438).

If you are referring generally to an entire volume of a multivolume work and are not citing specific page numbers, add the abbreviation "vol." before the volume number as in (vol. 5) or (Lincoln, vol. 5) (note the comma after the author's name). Then readers will not misinterpret the volume number as a page number.

8. A work by an author of two or more works

If your list of works cited includes two or more works by the same author, then your citation must tell the reader which of the author's works you are referring to. Give the title in the parenthetical citation: the full title if it is a word or two, or a shortened version of the title if it is longer.

> At about age seven, children begin to use appropriate gestures with their stories (Gardner, Arts 144-45).

The title *Arts* is shortened from Gardner's full title, *The Arts and Human Development* (see the works-cited entry for this book on p. 611). Often, as here, the first main word in the title is enough to direct the reader to the appropriate source.

9. An unsigned work

Refer to an anonymous source by a full or shortened version of the title, as explained above. In your list of works cited, you will alphabetize an anonymous work by the first main word of the title (see p. 612), so the first word of a shortened title should be the same.

> One article notes that a death-row inmate may demand his own execution to achieve a fleeting notoriety ("Right").

This citation refers to an unsigned article titled "The Right to Die." A page number is unnecessary because the article is no longer than a page (see the entry for the article on p. 618).

10. A government publication or a work with a corporate author

If the author of the work is listed as a government body or a corporation, cite the work by that organization's name. If the name is long, work it into the text to avoid an intrusive parenthetical citation.

> A 1996 report by the Hawaii Department of Education predicts an increase in enrollments (6).

11. An indirect source

When one of your sources quotes someone else and you want to use the quotation, try to find the original source and quote directly from it. (See p. 639). If you can't find the original source, then your citation must indicate that your quotation of it is indirect. In the following citation "qtd. in" ("quoted in") says that Davino was quoted by Boyd:

> George Davino maintains that "even small children have vivid ideas about nuclear energy" (qtd. in Boyd 22).

The list of works cited then includes only Boyd (the work consulted), not Davino.

12. A literary work

Novels, plays, and poems are often available in many editions, so your instructor may ask you to provide information that will help readers find the passage you cite no matter what edition they consult.

For novels, the page number comes first, followed by a semicolon and then information on the appropriate part or chapter of the work.

> Toward the end of James's novel, Maggie suddenly feels "the thick breath of the definite--which was the intimate, the immediate, the familiar, as she hadn't had them for so long" (535; pt. 6, ch. 41).

For poems that are not divided into parts, you can omit the page number and supply the line number(s) for the quotation. To prevent confusion with page numbers, precede the numbers with "line" or "lines" in the first citation; then just use the numbers.

> In Shakespeare's Sonnet 73 the speaker identifies with the trees of late autumn, "Bare ruined choirs, where late the sweet birds sang" (line 4). "In me," Shakespeare writes, "thou seest the glowing of such fire / That on the ashes of his youth doth lie" (9-10).

See pages 685–86 for a sample paper on a poem.

For verse plays and poems that are divided into parts, omit a page number and cite the appropriate part—act (and scene, if any), canto, book, and so on—plus the line number(s). Use Arabic numerals for parts, including acts and scenes (3.4), unless your instructor specifies Roman numerals (III.iv).

> Later in King Lear Shakespeare has the disguised Edgar say, "The prince of darkness is a gentleman" (3.4.147).

See pages 687–90 for a sample paper on a verse play.

For prose plays, provide the page number followed by the act and scene, if any. See the reference to *Death of a Salesman* on page 606.

13. The Bible

When you cite passages of the Bible in parentheses, abbreviate the title of any book longer than four letters—for instance, "Gen." (Genesis), "1 Sam." (1 Samuel), "Ps." (Psalms), "Matt." (Matthew), "Rom." (Romans). Then give the chapter and verse(s) in Arabic numerals.

> According to the Bible, at Babel God "did . . . confound the language of all the earth" (Gen. 11.9).

14. An electronic source

Cite an electronic source as you would any other source: usually by author's name or, if there is no author, by title.

> Business forecasts for the fourth quarter tended to be optimistic (White 4).

This example cites a source with page numbers. For a source with paragraph numbers or no numbering, see models 5 and 6 (p. 602).

15. More than one work

If you use a parenthetical citation to refer to more than a single work, separate the references with a semicolon.

> Two recent articles point out that a computer badly used can be less efficient than no computer at all (Gough and Hall 201; Richards 162).

Since long citations in the text can distract the reader, you may choose to cite several or more works in an endnote or footnote rather than in the text. See page 607.

2 Placing parenthetical citations

Position text citations to accomplish two goals:

- Make it clear exactly where your borrowing begins and ends.
- Keep the citation as unobtrusive as possible.

You can accomplish both goals by placing the parenthetical citation at the end of the sentence element containing the borrowed material. This sentence element may be a phrase or a clause, and it may begin, interrupt, or conclude the sentence. Usually, as in the examples below, the element ends with a punctuation mark.

> The inflation rate might climb as high as 30 percent (Kim 164), an increase that could threaten the small nation's stability.

> The inflation rate, which might climb as high as 30 percent (Kim 164), could threaten the small nation's stability.

> The small nation's stability could be threatened by its inflation rate, which, one source predicts, might climb as high as 30 percent (Kim 164).

In the last example the addition of "one source predicts" clarifies that Kim is responsible only for the inflation-rate prediction, not for the statement about stability.

For citations in your running text, generally place the parenthetical citation *before* any punctuation required by your sentence, as in the examples above. If the borrowed material is a quotation, place the citation *between* the closing quotation mark and the punctuation.

> Spelling argues that during the 1970s American automobile manufacturers met consumer needs "as well as could be expected" (26), but not everyone agrees with him.

The exception is a quotation ending in a question mark or exclamation point. Then use the appropriate punctuation inside the closing quotation mark, and follow the quotation with the text citation and a period:

> "Of what use is genius," Emerson asks, "if the organ . . . cannot find a focal distance within the actual horizon of human life?" ("Experience" 60). Mad genius is no genius.

When a citation appears after a quotation that ends in an ellipsis mark (. . .), place the citation between the closing quotation mark and the sentence period.

> One observer maintains that "American manufacturers must bear the blame for their poor sales . . ." (Rosenbaum 12).

When a citation appears at the end of a quotation set off from the text, place it one space *after* the punctuation ending the quotation. No additional punctuation is needed.

> In Arthur Miller's Death of a Salesman, the most poignant defense of Willie Loman comes from his wife, Linda:
>
> > He's not the finest character that ever lived. But he's a human being, and a terrible thing is happening to him. So attention must be paid. He's not to be allowed to fall into his grave like an old dog. Attention, attention must finally be paid to such a person. (56; act 1)

(This citation of a play includes the act number as well as the page number. See p. 604.)

See the two sample research papers starting on pages 632 and 662 for further examples of placing parenthetical references in relation to summaries, paraphrases, and quotations.

 Using footnotes or endnotes in special circumstances

Occasionally, you may want to use footnotes or endnotes in place of parenthetical citations. If you need to refer to several sources at once, listing them in a long parenthetical citation could be intrusive. In that case, signal the citation with a numeral raised above the appropriate line of text and write a note with the same numeral to cite the sources:

TEXT At least five studies have confirmed these results.[1]

NOTE [1] Abbott and Winger 266-68; Casner 27; Hoyenga 78-79; Marino 36; Tripp, Tripp, and Walk 179-83.

You may also use a footnote or endnote to comment on a source or provide information that does not fit easily in the text:

TEXT So far, no one has succeeded in confirming these results.[2]

NOTE [2] Manter reports spending a year trying to replicate the experiment, but he was never able to produce the high temperatures reported by the original experimenters (616).

In a note the raised numeral is indented five spaces and followed by a space. If the note appears as a footnote, place it at the bottom of the page on which the citation appears, set it off from the text with quadruple spacing, and single-space the note itself. If the note appears as an endnote, place it in numerical order with the other endnotes on a page between the text and the list of works cited; double-space all the endnotes. (See pp. 656–57 for examples of endnotes and the format to use in typing a page of endnotes.)

Exercise 1
Citing sources in your text

Using the preceding explanations and illustrations as a guide, prepare MLA-style text citations for your own research paper. (If you are instructed or given the option to do so, you may instead prepare citations in the style of the *Chicago Manual of Style,* p. 696; the American Psychological Association, p. 707; or the Council of Biology Editors, p. 729.)

ANSWERS: EXERCISE 1

Individual response.

37c Preparing the list of works cited: MLA style

In the documentation style of the *MLA Handbook,* your in-text parenthetical citations (discussed in 37b) refer the reader to complete information on your sources in a list you title "Works Cited" and place at the end of your paper. The list should include all the sources you quoted, paraphrased, or summarized in your paper. (If your instructor asks you to include sources you examined but did not cite, title the list "Works Consulted.")

Follow this format for the list of works cited:

- Arrange your sources in alphabetical order by the last name of the author. If an author is not given in the source, alphabetize the source by the first main word of the title (excluding *A, An,* or *The*).
- Type the entire list double-spaced (both within and between entries).
- Indent the second and subsequent lines of each entry one-half inch from the left.

For examples of the works-cited format, see the papers by Edward Begay (p. 658) and Vanessa Haley (p. 667).

The index on the facing page directs you to the MLA formats for specific kinds of sources you may use. The arrangement, spacing, and punctuation of information are precisely standardized to convey the most information in the least space.

Note You may have to combine formats for particular sources. For example, to list a work by four authors appearing in a monthly periodical, you will have to draw on model 3 ("A book with more than three authors") and model 25 ("A signed article in a monthly or bimonthly magazine"). Generally, arrange information in this order: author; title of part of book or periodical article; title of book or periodical; translator or editor; edition; volume(s) used; series title; publication information; page number(s).

Listing books

TRANSPARENCY MASTER 37.2

The basic format for a book includes the following elements:

① Gilligan, Carol. ② In a Different Voice: Psychological Theory and Women's Development. ③ Cambridge: Harvard UP, 1982.

ⓐ Cambridge ⓑ Harvard UP ⓒ 1982

1. *Author.* Use the author's full name: the last name first, followed by a comma, and then the first name and any middle name or initial. Omit any title or degree attached to the author's name on the source, such as Dr. or Ph.D. End the name with a period and one space.
2. *Title.* Give the full title, including any subtitle. Underline the title, capitalize all important words (see p. 431), separate the main title and the subtitle with a colon and one space, and end

MLA 37c

Index to MLA works-cited models

the title with a period and one space. When you cite an essay, story, or poem appearing in a book, give the title, in quotation marks, before the underlined book title (see model 19, p. 614).

3. *Publication information.* You can usually find this information on the book's title page or on the copyright page immediately following.

    a. The city of publication, followed by a colon and one space. Use only the first city if the source lists more than one.
    b. The name of the publisher, followed by a comma. Shorten most publishers' names—in many cases to a single word. For instance, use "Knopf" for Alfred A. Knopf and "Little" for Little, Brown. For university presses, use the abbreviations "U" and "P," as in the example. If the title page lists both an imprint and a publisher—for instance, Vintage Books and Random House—give both names with a hyphen between: "Vintage-Random."
    c. The date of publication, ending with a period.

When other information is required for a reference, it is generally placed either between the author's name and the title or between the title and the publication information, as specified in the models below.

1. A BOOK WITH ONE AUTHOR

Gilligan, Carol. In a Different Voice: Psychological Theory and Women's Development. Cambridge: Harvard UP, 1982.

2. A BOOK WITH TWO OR THREE AUTHORS

Frieden, Bernard J., and Lynne B. Sagalyn. Downtown, Inc.: How America Rebuilds Cities. Cambridge: MIT P, 1989.

Wilcox, Dennis L., Phillip H. Ault, and Warren K. Agee. Public Relations: Strategies and Tactics. 4th ed. New York: Harper, 1995.

Give the authors' names in the order provided on the title page. Reverse the first and last names of the first author *only*. Separate two authors' names with a comma and "and"; separate three authors' names with commas and with "and" before the third name.

3. A BOOK WITH MORE THAN THREE AUTHORS

Lopez, Robert S., et al. Civilizations: Western and World. Boston: Little, 1975.

You may, but need not, give all authors' names if the work has more than three authors. If you choose not to give all names, provide the name of the first author only, and follow the name with a comma and the abbreviation "et al." (for the Latin *et alii,* meaning "and others").

4. Two or more works by the same author(s)

Gardner, Howard. The Arts and Human Development. New York: Wiley, 1973.

---. The Quest for Mind: Piaget, Lévi-Strauss, and the Structuralist Movement. New York: Knopf, 1973.

Give the author's name only in the first entry. For the second and any subsequent works by the same author, substitute three hyphens for the author's name, followed by a period and one space. Within the set of entries for the author, list the sources alphabetically by the first main word of the title. Note that the three hyphens stand for *exactly* the same name or names. If the second source above were by Gardner and somebody else, both names would have to be given in full.

5. A book with an editor

Ruitenbeek, Hendrick, ed. Freud as We Knew Him. Detroit: Wayne State UP, 1973.

The abbreviation "ed.," separated from the name by a comma, identifies Ruitenbeek as the editor of the work.

6. A book with an author and an editor

Melville, Herman. The Confidence Man: His Masquerade. Ed. Hershel Parker. New York: Norton, 1971.

When citing the work of the author, give his or her name first, and give the editor's name after the title, preceded by "Ed." ("Edited by"). When citing the work of the editor, use the form above for a book with an editor, and give the author's name after the title preceded by "By": Parker, Hershel, ed. The Confidence Man: His Masquerade. By Herman Melville.

7. A translation

Alighieri, Dante. The Inferno. Trans. John Ciardi. New York: NAL, 1971.

When citing the work of the author, give his or her name first, and give the translator's name after the title, preceded by "Trans." ("Translated by"). When citing the work of the translator, give his or her name first, followed by a comma and "trans."; then follow the title with "By" and the author's name: Ciardi, John, trans. The Inferno. By Dante Alighieri.

When a book you cite by author has a translator *and* an editor, give the translator's and editor's names in the order used on the book's title page. For a translated selection from an edited book, see model 19, page 614.

8. A book with a corporate author

Lorenz, Inc. Research in Social Studies Teaching. Baltimore: Arrow, 1992.

List the name of the corporation, institution, or other body as author.

9. A government publication

Stiller, Ann. Historic Preservation and Tax Incentives. US Dept. of Interior. Washington: GPO, 1996.

Hawaii. Dept. of Education. Kauai District Schools, Profile 1996-97. Honolulu: Hawaii Dept. of Education, 1996.

United States. Cong. House. Committee on Ways and Means. Medicare Payment for Outpatient Occupational Therapy Services. 102nd Cong., 1st sess. Washington: GPO, 1991.

If an author is not listed for a government publication, give the appropriate agency as author. Provide information in the order illustrated, separating elements with a period and a space: the name of the government, the name of the agency (which may be abbreviated), and the title and publication information. For a congressional publication (last example), give the house and committee involved before the title, and give the number and session of Congress after the title. In the first and last examples, "GPO" stands for the US Government Printing Office.

10. An anonymous book

The Dorling Kindersley World Reference Atlas. London: Dorling, 1994.

List an anonymous book by its full title. Alphabetize the book by the title's first main word (here "Dorling"), omitting *A, An,* or *The.*

11. The Bible

The New English Bible. London: Oxford and Cambridge, 1970.

The Holy Bible. King James Version. Cleveland: World, n.d.

When citing the Bible, do not underline the title or the name of the version. The version may be included in the title (first example); if not, give it after the title (second example). The abbreviation "n.d."

at the end of the second example indicates that the source lists no date of publication.

12. A LATER EDITION

Bollinger, Dwight L. Aspects of Language. 2nd ed. New York: Harcourt, 1975.

For any edition after the first, place the edition number between the title and the publication information. Use the appropriate designation for editions that are named or dated rather than numbered—for instance, "Rev. ed." for "Revised edition."

13. A REPUBLISHED BOOK

James, Henry. The Golden Bowl. 1904. London: Penguin, 1966.

Place the original date of publication (but not the place of publication or the publisher's name) after the title, and then provide the full publication information for the source you are using.

14. A BOOK WITH A TITLE IN ITS TITLE

Eco, Umberto. Postscript to The Name of the Rose. Trans. William Weaver. New York: Harcourt, 1983.

When a book's title contains another book title (as here: The Name of the Rose), do not underline the shorter title. When a book's title contains a quotation or the title of a work normally placed in quotation marks, keep the quotation marks and underline both titles: Critical Response to Henry James's "Beast in the Jungle." (Note that the underlining extends under the closing quotation mark.)

15. A WORK IN MORE THAN ONE VOLUME

Lincoln, Abraham. The Collected Works of Abraham Lincoln. Ed. Roy P. Basler. 8 vols. New Brunswick: Rutgers UP, 1953.

Lincoln, Abraham. The Collected Works of Abraham Lincoln. Ed. Roy P. Basler. Vol. 5. New Brunswick: Rutgers UP, 1953. 8 vols.

If you use two or more volumes of a multivolume work, give the work's total number of volumes before the publication information ("8 vols." in the first example). Your text citation will indicate which volume you are citing (see p. 602). If you use only one volume, give that volume number before the publication information ("Vol. 5" in the second example). You may add the total number of volumes to the end of the entry ("8 vols." in the second example).

If you cite a multivolume work published over a period of years, give the inclusive years as the publication date: for instance, Cambridge: Harvard UP, 1978-90.

16. A work in a series

Bergman, Ingmar. The Seventh Seal. Mod. Film Scripts Ser. 12. New York: Simon, 1968.

Place the name of the series (no quotation marks or underlining) after the title, abbreviating common words such as *modern* and *series*. If the source has a series number, add it after the series title.

17. Published proceedings of a conference

Watching Our Language: A Conference Sponsored by the Program in Architecture and Design Criticism. 6-8 May 1996. New York: Parsons School of Design, 1996.

Whether in or after the title of the conference, supply information about who sponsored the conference, when it was held, and who published the proceedings. If you are citing a particular presentation at the conference, treat it as a selection from an anthology (model 19).

18. An anthology

Kennedy, X. J., and Dana Gioia, eds. Literature: An Introduction to Fiction, Poetry, and Drama. 6th ed. New York: Harper, 1995.

When citing an entire anthology, give the name of the editor or editors (followed by "ed." or "eds.") and then the title of the anthology.

19. A selection from an anthology

Kafka, Franz. "The Metamorphosis." Trans. Willa and Edwin Muir. Literature: An Introduction to Fiction, Poetry, and Drama. Ed. X. J. Kennedy and Dana Gioia. 6th ed. New York: Harper, 1995. 311-45.

The essentials of this listing are these: author of selection; title of selection (in quotation marks); title of anthology (underlined); editors' names preceded by "Ed." (meaning "Edited by"); publication information for the anthology; and inclusive page numbers for the selection (without the abbreviation "pp."). This source also requires a translator for the selection and an edition number for the anthology.

If the work you cite comes from a collection of works by one author and with no editor, use the following form:

Auden, W. H. "Family Ghosts." The Collected Poetry of W. H. Auden. New York: Random, 1945. 132-33.

If the work you cite is a scholarly article that was previously printed elsewhere, provide the complete information for the earlier publication of the piece, followed by "Rpt. in" ("Reprinted in") and the information for the source in which you found the piece:

Gibian, George. "Traditional Symbolism in Crime and Punishment." PMLA 70 (1955): 979-96. Rpt. in Crime and Punishment. By Feodor Dostoevsky. Ed. George Gibian. Norton Critical Editions. New York: Norton, 1964. 575-92.

20. Two or more selections from the same anthology

Chopin, Kate. "The Story of an Hour." Kennedy and Gioia 419-21.

Kennedy, X. J., and Dana Gioia, Literature: An Introduction to Fiction, Poetry, and Drama. 6th ed. New York: Harper, 1995.

Olsen, Tillie. "I Stand Here Ironing." Kennedy and Gioia 535-40.

When citing more than one selection from the same source, you may avoid repetition by giving the source in full (as in the Kennedy and Gioia entry) and then simply cross-referencing it in entries for the works you used. Thus, instead of full information for the Chopin and Olsen works, give Kennedy's and Gioia's names and the appropriate pages in their book. Note that each entry appears in its proper alphabetical place among other works cited.

21. An introduction, preface, foreword, or afterword

Donaldson, Norman. Introduction. The Claverings. By Anthony Trollope. New York: Dover, 1977. vii-xv.

An introduction, foreword, or afterword is often written by someone other than the book's author. When citing such a work, give its name without quotation marks or underlining. Follow the title of the book with its author's name preceded by "By." Give the inclusive page numbers of the part you cite. (In the example above, the small Roman numerals indicate that the cited work is in the front matter of the book, before page 1.)

When the author of a preface or introduction is the same as the author of the book, give only the last name after the title:

Gould, Stephen Jay. Prologue. The Flamingo's Smile: Reflections in Natural History. By Gould. New York: Norton, 1985. 13-20.

22. An article in a reference work

"Reckon." Merriam-Webster's Collegiate Dictionary. 10th ed. 1993.

Mark, Herman F. "Polymers." The New Encyclopaedia Britannica: Macropaedia. 15th ed. 1991.

List an article in a reference work by its title (first example) unless the article is signed (second example). For works with entries arranged alphabetically, you need not include volume or page numbers. For well-known works like those listed above, you may also omit the editors' names and all publication information except any edition number and the year of publication. For works that are not well known, give full publication information:

> "Hungarians in America." The Ethnic Almanac. Ed. Stephanie Bernardo. New York: Doubleday, 1981. 109-11.

2 Listing periodicals: Journals, magazines, and newspapers

TRANSPARENCY MASTER 37.3

The basic format for an article from a periodical includes the following information:

> ① Lever, Janet. ② "Sex Differences in the Games Children Play." ③ Social Problems 23 (1976): 478-87.
> ⓐ ⓑ ⓒ ⓓ

1. *Author.* Use the author's full name: last name first, followed by a comma, and then the first name and any middle name or initial. Omit any title or degree attached to the author's name on the source, such as Dr. or Ph.D. End the name with a period and one space.
2. *Title of the article.* Give the full title, including any subtitle. Place the title in quotation marks, capitalize all important words in the title (see p. 431), and end the title with a period (inside the final quotation mark) and one space.
3. *Publication information.*

   a. The title of the periodical, underlined, followed by a space. Omit any *A, An,* or *The* from the beginning of the title.
   b. The volume and/or issue number (in Arabic numerals), followed by a space. See the note following.
   c. The date of publication, followed by a colon and a space. See the note following.
   d. The inclusive page numbers of the article (without the abbreviation "pp."). For the second number in inclusive page numbers over 100, provide only as many digits as needed for clarity (usually two): 87–88, 100–01, 398–401, 1026–36, 1190–206.

Note The treatment of volume and issue numbers and publication dates varies depending on the kind of periodical being cited, as the models indicate. For the distinction between journals and magazines, see page 546.

23. A SIGNED ARTICLE IN A JOURNAL WITH CONTINUOUS PAGINATION THROUGHOUT THE ANNUAL VOLUME

Lever, Janet. "Sex Differences in the Games Children Play." Social Problems 23 (1976): 478-87.

Some journals number the pages of issues consecutively throughout a year, so that each issue after the first in a year begins numbering where the previous issue left off—say, at page 132 or 416. For this kind of journal, give the volume number after the title ("23" in the example above) and place the year of publication in parentheses. The page numbers will be enough to guide readers to the appropriate issue.

24. A SIGNED ARTICLE IN A JOURNAL THAT PAGES ISSUES SEPARATELY OR THAT NUMBERS ONLY ISSUES, NOT VOLUMES

Dacey, June. "Management Participation in Corporate Buy-Outs." Management Perspectives 7.4 (1994): 20-31.

Some journals page each issue separately (starting each issue at page 1). For these journals, give the volume number, a period, and the issue number (as in "7.4" in the Dacey entry above). Then readers know which issue of the periodical to consult. When citing an article in a journal that numbers only issues, not annual volumes, treat the issue number as if it were a volume number, as in model 23.

25. A SIGNED ARTICLE IN A MONTHLY OR BIMONTHLY MAGAZINE

Tilin, Andrew. "Selling the Dream." Worth Oct. 1996: 94-100.

Follow the magazine title with the month and the year of publication. (Abbreviate all months except May, June, and July.) Don't place the date in parentheses, and don't provide a volume or issue number.

26. A SIGNED ARTICLE IN A WEEKLY OR BIWEEKLY MAGAZINE

Stevens, Mark. "Low and Behold." New Republic 24 Dec. 1990: 27-33.

Follow the magazine title with the day, the month (abbreviated), and the year of publication. (Abbreviate all months except May, June, and July.) Don't place the date in parentheses, and don't provide a volume or issue number.

27. A SIGNED ARTICLE IN A DAILY NEWSPAPER

Ramirez, Anthony. "Computer Groups Plan Standards." New York Times 14 Dec. 1993, late ed.: D5.

Give the name of the newspaper as it appears on the first page (but without *A, An,* or *The*). If the name of the city is not in the title of a local newspaper, then add the city name in brackets after the title, without underlining: Gazette [Chicago]. Then follow model 26, with two differences: (1) If the newspaper lists an edition at the top of the first page, include that information after the date and a comma. (See "late ed." above.) (2) If the newspaper is divided into lettered or numbered sections, provide the section designation before the page number when the newspaper does the same (as in "D5" above); otherwise, provide the section designation before the colon (as in "sec. 1: 1+" below).

28. An unsigned article

"The Right to Die." Time 11 Oct. 1976: 101.

"Protests Greet Pope in Holland." Boston Sunday Globe 12 May 1985, late ed., sec. 1: 1+.

Begin the entry for an unsigned article with the title of the article. (Alphabetize it by the first main word of the title.) The page number "1+" indicates that the article does not run on consecutive pages but starts on page 1 and continues later in the issue.

29. An editorial or letter to the editor

"Bodily Intrusions." Editorial. New York Times 29 Aug. 1990, late ed.: A20.

Add the word "Editorial" or "Letter"—but without quotation marks—after the title if there is one or after the author's name, as follows:

Dowding, Michael. Letter. Economist 5-11 Jan. 1985: 4.

(The numbers "5-11" in this entry are the publication days of the periodical: the issue spans January 5 through 11.)

30. A review

Dunne, John Gregory. "The Secret of Danny Santiago." Rev. of Famous All over Town, by Danny Santiago. New York Review of Books 16 Aug. 1984: 17-27.

"Rev." is an abbreviation for "Review." The name of the author of the work being reviewed follows the title of the work, a comma, and "by." If the review has no title of its own, then "Rev. of . . ." (without quotation marks) immediately follows the name of the reviewer.

31. An abstract of a dissertation or article

Steciw, Steven K. "Alterations to the Pessac Project of Le Corbusier." Diss. U of Cambridge, England, 1986. DAI 46 (1986): 565C.

For an abstract appearing in *Dissertation Abstracts* (*DA*) or *Dissertation Abstracts International* (*DAI*), give the author's name and the title, "Diss." (for "Dissertation"), the institution granting the author's degree, the date of the dissertation, and the publication information.

For an abstract of an article, first provide the publication information for the article itself, followed by the information for the abstract. If the abstract publisher lists abstracts by item rather than page number, add "item" before the number.

> Lever, Janet. "Sex Differences in the Games Children Play." Social Problems 23 (1976): 478-87. Psychological Abstracts 63 (1976): item 1431.

3 Listing electronic sources

MLA formats for electronic sources vary according to the medium (for instance, CD-ROM or online) and whether the source is also published in print. The *MLA Handbook* does not include particular formats for some online sites that you may find useful, so this section supplements MLA style with models endorsed by the Alliance for Computers and Writing (pp. 622–24).

Note Try to locate all the information required in the following models, so that your readers can trace your sources with minimal difficulty. However, if you search for and still cannot find some information, then give what you can find.

32. Electronic mail or a public posting

> Millon, Michele. (1) E-mail to the author. (2) 4 May 1997. (3)

For e-mail, give the name of the writer (1); describe the transmission, including whom it was sent to (2); and provide the date of posting (3).

For an online posting on a bulletin board or discussion group, such as a Listserv or Usenet newsgroup, provide the author's name (1); the title (2); the date of posting (3); the words "Online posting" (4), without quotation marks or underlining; the name of the bulletin board or group (5); the name of the network (6); and the date of your access to the posting (7):

> Cramer, Sherry. (1) "Recent Investment Practices." (2) 26 Mar. 1997. (3) Online posting. (4) Newsgroup biz.investment.current. (5) Usenet. (6) 3 Apr. 1997. (7)

Note that you may have to correspond with the author directly to obtain his or her name. See page 566.

The following model includes (after "Available") the electronic address needed to reach a retrievable source. As discussed on page 622, the address is optional in MLA style: you may add it if your instructor requires it.

Tourville, Michael. "European Currency Reform." 6 Jan. 1997. Online posting. International Finance Discussion List. Bitnet. 23 Feb. 1997. Available infin@weg.isu.edu.

33. A source on CD-ROM

A periodical CD-ROM with information for a print version:

Ramirez, Anthony. "Computer Groups Plan Standards." New York Times 14 Dec. 1993, late ed.: D5. New York Times Ondisc. CD-ROM. UMI-ProQuest. June 1994.

If you are citing a source on CD-ROM that's issued periodically (like a journal or magazine), look for information about a print version of the same source. (The information is usually at the beginning of the source.) If there is such information, provide it as in the model above (1), referring to pages 616–18 as needed. Then provide the following information on the CD-ROM version, separating the elements with periods: the title of the CD-ROM (2), underlined; the medium, "CD-ROM" (3), without underlining or quotation marks; the name of the distributor (or vendor) of the CD-ROM (4); and the date of electronic publication (5).

For an abstract of an article or dissertation on CD-ROM, adapt model 31 (p. 618). Provide full information for the article or dissertation and then information for the CD-ROM abstract:

Steciw, Steven K. "Alterations to the Pessac Project of Le Corbusier." Diss. U. of Cambridge, England, 1986. DAI 46 (1986): 565C. Dissertation Abstracts Ondisc. CD-ROM. UMI-ProQuest. Oct. 1992.

A periodical CD-ROM without information for a print version:

"Vanguard Forecasts." Jan. 1997. Business Outlook. CD-ROM. Information Access. Mar. 1997.

If a source appears only on CD-ROM (not also in print), replace the print publication information with any date for the source (1), set off with periods. Then continue as in the Ramirez model above.

A nonperiodical CD-ROM:

Shelley, Mary Wollstonecraft. Frankenstein. Classic Library. CD-ROM. Alameda: Andromeda, 1993.

If you cite a single-issue CD-ROM, treat it as a book or a part of a book (pp. 608–15), with these exceptions: after the author (1) and source title (2), give the title of the CD-ROM (3), underlined, and the medium, "CD-ROM" (4), without quotation marks or underlining. Then continue as for a book with the CD-ROM's place of publication, publisher, and date of publication (5). Here is another example, this one without an author and with a reference to a part of the source (in quotation marks):

"Sugar." Concise Columbia Encyclopedia. 3rd ed. Microsoft Bookshelf. 1996-97 ed. CD-ROM. Redmond: Microsoft, 1996.

34. A source on diskette or magnetic tape

Project Scheduler 8000. Ver. 3.1. (1) Diskette. (2) Tacoma: Scitor, 1997.

Treat a source on diskette or magnetic tape as you would a book (pp. 608–15), except after the title add any version number (1), which corresponds to a book's edition number, and add the medium, either "Diskette" or "Magnetic tape" (2), without quotation marks or underlining.

35. An online source from a computer service

A source from a computer service with information for a print version:

Ramirez, Anthony. "Computer Groups Plan Standards." New York Times 14 Dec. 1993, late ed.: D5. (1) New York Times Online. (2) Online. (3) Nexis. (4) 16 July 1994. (5)

Sources available from computer services—such as Dialog, Nexis, and Lexis—are often also published in print. Look for information about a print version at the beginning of the source. If you find it, provide it first (1), following the models for books and articles on pages 608–19. Then provide the following information for the online version, separating the elements with periods: the title of the database you're using (2), underlined; the medium, "Online" (3), without quotation marks or underlining; the name of the service (4), not underlined; and the date you consulted the source (5).

A source from a computer service without information for a print version:

"Vanguard Forecasts." Jan. 1997. (1) Business Outlook. Online. America Online. 27 Mar. 1997.

If print publication information is not available for your source, substitute the date given for the source (1), set off with periods. Then continue as for an online source with print information, above.

MLA
37c

36. An online source from a computer network

An electronic text:

① Austen, Jane. Emma. Ed. Ronald Blythe. Harmondsworth: Penguin, 1972. ② Online. ③ Oxford Text Archive. ④ Internet. ⑤ 15 Dec. 1994. ⑥ Available ftp://black.ox.ac.uk.

For a text such as a novel or a historical document available over a computer network, provide the original source information (1) followed by these elements: the medium, "Online" (2), without quotation marks or underlining; the repository of the text (3); the name of the network (4); and the date you consulted the source (5). After the word "Available," you may also provide the electronic address for the source (6). MLA considers the address optional, depending on your instructor's wishes; but you will not be wrong to include it, and it can help readers trace your electronic sources.

Note If you include an electronic address and must break it from one line to the next, do not divide words or add any hyphen that is not part of the address. Break addresses *before* periods and *after* slashes, as in several of the examples on the next two pages.

An electronic journal or newsletter:

① Palfrey, Andrew. "Choice of Mates in Identical Twins." Modern Psychology 4.1 (1996): ② 12 pars. ③ Online. ④ Internet. ⑤ 25 Feb. 1996. ⑥ Available ftp://modpsy.liasu.edu/palfrey4(1).txt.

For an electronic journal or newsletter, use a model from pages 617–19 for a printed periodical article (1), up to the page numbers (2). For these, substitute the length given by the source in pages (for instance, "5 pp.") or in paragraphs (for instance, "12 pars.," as above)—or say "n. pag.," for "no pagination," if the length is not given. (See p. 602 for how to acknowledge such a source in your text.) After the length and a period, add the following: the medium, "Online" (3), without quotation marks or underlining; the network name (4); the date of your access to the source (5); and the electronic address (6) if you choose or are required to provide it.

37. ACW models for online sources

To supplement MLA models for online sources, Janice Walker of the University of South Florida prepared styles that have been endorsed by the Alliance for Computers and Writing (ACW). The ACW models are based on MLA style, with a few important differences:

- The medium (such as "Online") and the name of the network

(such as "Internet") are omitted. The access mode (such as "http") is evident from the electronic address.

- The electronic address always appears in the entry, but not preceded by the word "Available."
- The address includes only the punctuation needed to reach the source; for example, there's no final period if it's not part of the address. See opposite for how to break an address from one line to the next.
- The date on which you consulted the source falls at the end of the entry, in parentheses.

Note Ask your instructor whether you should use these ACW models or try to adapt the MLA models on pages 621–22 to your particular online sources.

A site on the World Wide Web:

Still, Lucia. "On the Battlefields of Business, Millions of Casualties." New York Times 3 Mar. 1996. http://www.nytimes.com/specials/downsize/03down1.html (17 Aug. 1996).

Give the author's name (1); the title (2), in quotation marks; the title of the periodical or other full source (3), underlined; the date of posting (4), if available; the electronic address (5); and the date you consulted the source (6), in parentheses.

An FTP (File Transfer Protocol) site:

Clarke, Kirsty. "A 'Near' Contract Experience." E Law--Murdoch Electronic Journal of Law. ftp://infolib.murdoch.edu.au/pub/subj/law/jnl/elaw/comment/clarke.txt (29 Feb. 1996).

Give the author's name (1); the source title (2), in quotation marks; the title of the periodical or other full source (3), underlined; the FTP address (4), including the path needed to obtain the file; and the date you consulted the source (5), in parentheses. Add the date of the source after the full title if it differs from the date of your access.

A Telnet site:

Johnson, Earl. "My House: Come On In." Houses of Cyberspace. 7 Aug. 1996. telnet://edwin.ohms.bookso.com 7777 @go #50827, press 10 (11 Aug. 1996).

Provide the author's name (1); the source title (2), if available, in quotation marks; the title of the periodical or other full source (3), underlined; the date of the source (4), if available; the Telnet address (5), including information needed to reach the document; and the date you consulted the source (6), in parentheses.

A Gopher site:

Goetsch, Sallie. "And What About Costume?" Didaskalia: Ancient Theater Today 2.2 (1995): n. pag. gopher://University of Warwick/Didaskalia/Didaskalia: Ancient Theater Today/ 03Features/Goetsch (17 Apr. 1996).

Give the author's name (1); the title of the source (2), in quotation marks; other publication information (3), such as periodical title, volume and issue numbers, date of publication, and pagination; the Gopher address (4), including the path needed to reach the document; and the date you consulted the source (5), in parentheses.

A synchronous communication (IRC, MUD, MOO):

Chartreuse_Guest. Tuesday cafe session. gopher://logos.daedalus .com:70/11/Alliance for Computers and Writing/NETORIC/ Tuesday Cafe log 13Feb. (7 Mar. 1996).

Chipault, Dorothy. Personal interview. telnet://hero.village .virginia.edu:7007 (1 July 1996).

Give the author's name (1); the nature of the communication (2); the address (3); and the date (4), in parentheses.

Listing other sources

38. A pamphlet

Medical Answers About AIDS. New York: Gay Men's Health Crisis, 1994.

Most pamphlets can be treated as books. In the example above, the pamphlet has no listed author, so the title comes first. If the pamphlet has an author, list his or her name first, followed by the title and publication information as given here.

39. An unpublished dissertation or thesis

Wilson, Stuart M. "John Stuart Mill as a Literary Critic." Diss. U of Michigan, 1970.

The title is quoted rather than underlined. "Diss." stands for "Dissertation." "U of Michigan" is the institution that granted the author's degree.

40. A MUSICAL COMPOSITION OR WORK OF ART

Fauré, Gabriel. Sonata for Violin and Piano no. 1 in A major, op. 15.

Don't underline musical compositions identified only by form, number, and key. Do underline titled operas, ballets, and compositions (Carmen, Sleeping Beauty).

For a work of art, underline the title and include the name and location of the owner. For a work you see only in a photograph, provide the complete publication information, too, as in the following model. Omit such information only if you examined the actual work.

Sargent, John Singer. Venetian Doorway. Metropolitan Museum of Art, New York. Sargent Watercolors. By Donelson F. Hoopes. New York: Watson, 1976. 31.

41. A FILM OR VIDEO RECORDING

Schindler's List. Dir. Steven Spielberg. Perf. Liam Neeson and Ben Kingsley. Universal, 1993.

Start with the title of the work you are citing, unless you are citing the contribution of a particular individual (see the next model). Give additional information (writer, lead performers, and so on) as seems appropriate. For a film, end with the film's distributor and date.

For a videocassette, filmstrip, or slide program, include the original release date (if any) and the medium (without underlining or quotation marks) before the distributor's name:

George Balanchine, chor. Serenade. Perf. San Francisco Ballet. Dir. Hilary Bean. 1981. Videocassette. PBS Video, 1987.

42. A TELEVISION OR RADIO PROGRAM

Kenyon, Jane, and Donald Hall. "A Life Together." Bill Moyers' Journal. PBS. WNET, New York. 17 Dec. 1993.

As in model 41, start with a title unless you are citing the work of a person or persons. The example above begins with the participants' names, then the episode title (in quotation marks), then the program title (underlined). Finish the entry with the name of the network, the local station and city, and the date.

43. A PERFORMANCE

The English Only Restaurant. By Silvio Martinez Palau. Dir. Susana Tubert. Puerto Rican Traveling Theater, New York. 27 July 1990.

Ozawa, Seiji, cond. Boston Symphony Orch. Concert. Symphony Hall, Boston. 25 Apr. 1997.

As with films and television programs, place the title first unless you are citing the work of an individual (second example). Provide additional information about participants after the title, as well as the theater, city, and date. Note that the orchestra concert in the second example is neither quoted nor underlined.

44. A recording

Siberry, Jane. "Caravan." Maria. Reprise, 1995.

Brahms, Johannes. Concerto no. 2 in B-flat, op. 83. Perf. Artur Rubinstein. Cond. Eugene Ormandy. Philadelphia Orch. LP. RCA, 1972.

Begin with the name of the individual whose work you are citing. If you're citing a song, give the title in quotation marks. Then provide the title of the recording, underlining the title (first example) unless it identifies a composition by form, number, and key (second example). After the title, provide the names of any artists not already listed, the medium if it is not a compact disk ("LP" in the second example), the manufacturer of the recording, and the date of release.

45. A letter

Buttolph, Mrs. Laura E. Letter to Rev. and Mrs. C. C. Jones. 20 June 1857. In The Children of Pride: A True Story of Georgia and the Civil War. Ed. Robert Manson Myers. New Haven: Yale UP, 1972. 334-35.

A published letter is listed under the writer's name. Specify that the source is a letter and to whom it was addressed, and give the date on which it was written. Treat the remaining information like that for a selection from an anthology (model 19, p. 614). (See also model 29, p. 618, for the format of a letter to the editor of a periodical. And see model 32, p. 619, for the format of e-mail and a public online posting.)

For a letter in the collection of a library or archive, specify the writer, recipient, and date, as above, and give the name and location of the archive as well:

James, Jonathan E. Letter to his sister. 16 Apr. 1970. Jonathan E. James Papers. South Dakota State Archive, Pierre.

For a letter you receive, give the name of the writer, note the fact that the letter was sent to you, and provide the date of the letter:

Packer, Ann E. Letter to the author. 15 June 1994.

Use the form above for personal electronic mail (e-mail) as well, substituting "E-mail" for "Letter": E-mail to the author (see p. 619).

MLA
37c

46. A lecture or address

Carlone, Dennis. "Architecture for the City of 2000." Tenth Symposium on Urban Issues. Cambridge City Hall, Cambridge. 22 Oct. 1996.

Give the speaker's name, the title (in quotation marks), the title of the meeting, the name of the sponsoring organization, the location of the lecture, and the date. If you do not know the title, replace it with "Lecture" or another description, but *not* in quotation marks.

Although the *MLA Handbook* does not provide a specific style for classroom lectures in your courses, you can adapt the preceding format for this purpose:

Ezzy, T. G. Class lectures on the realist novel. Dawson College. 22 Jan. 1996-13 May 1996.

A parenthetical text citation to a particular lecture would require a date: for example, (Ezzy, 12 Mar. 1996).

47. An interview

Graaf, Vera. Personal interview. 19 Dec. 1993.

Christopher, Warren. Interview. Frontline. PBS. WGBH, Boston. 13 Feb. 1996.

Begin with the name of the person interviewed. For an interview you conducted, specify "Personal interview," "Telephone interview," "E-mail interview," or "IRC interview," as appropriate—without quotation marks or underlining—and then give the date. For an interview you read, heard, or saw, provide the title if any or "Interview" if not, along with other bibliographic information and the date.

48. A map or other illustration

Women in the Armed Forces. Map. Women in the World: An International Atlas. By Joni Seager and Ann Olson. New York: Touchstone, 1992. 44-45.

List the illustration by its title (underlined). Provide a descriptive label ("Map," "Chart," "Table"), without underlining or quotation marks, and the publication information. If the creator of the illustration is credited in the source, put his or her name first in the entry, as with any author.

Exercise 2
Writing works-cited entries

Prepare works-cited entries from the following information. Follow the models of the *MLA Handbook* given in this chapter unless your instructor specifies a different style.

ANSWERS: EXERCISE 2

The citations below are in MLA style:

1. Kim, Jocelyn. "Credit and Consumer Confidence." Adaptation to Change 12.4 (1993): 101–06.
2. Clapham, Abraham, ed. Black Voices: An Anthology of Afro-American Literature. New York: New American [*or* NAL], 1968.
3. Downing, Jane, Bruce Newell, and Achibo Lauro. "The Meaning of The Funeral Elegy." Shakespeare 4.1 (1996): 37 pars. Online. Internet. 12 Mar. 1997. Available: http://www.shakespeare-cambridge.com/downing.html. [Address optional.]
4. Anderson, John Q. "The New Orleans Voodoo Ritual Dance and Its Twentieth-Century Survivals." Southern Folklore Quarterly 24 (1960): 135–43.
5. Chu, Susan. "1996 Election Returns May Widen Gender Gap." Politics and Values Jan. 1997: 21–26. Resource/One. CD-ROM. UMI-ProQuest. Mar. 1997.

COLLABORATIVE LEARNING

Have students work through Exercise 2 individually and then give them the opportunity to discuss and revise their entries in small groups. This process will allow students to develop specific questions about correct bibliographic form and then address them in a supportive setting.

As a follow-up to this exercise, have students work in groups to list their own sources in correct bibliographic form in preparation for Exercise 3. Ask groups to make note of entries that pose unusual classification or citation challenges and bring them to the attention of the class.

ANSWERS: EXERCISE 3

Individual response.

1. An article titled "Credit and Consumer Confidence" by Jocelyn Kim. The article appears in volume 12, issue 4, of *Adaptation to Change,* a journal that pages issues separately. Volume 12 is dated 1993. The article runs from page 101 to page 106.
2. A book called *Black Voices: An Anthology of Afro-American Literature,* published in 1968 by the New American Library in New York, edited by Abraham Clapham.
3. An article you consulted on March 12, 1997, over the Internet. The article is titled "The Meaning of *The Funeral Elegy*" and is by Jane Downing, Bruce Newell, and Achibo Lauro. It appears in the online journal *Shakespeare,* volume 4, issue 1, published in 1996. The article is thirty-seven paragraphs long. The address for the article is http://www.shakespeare-cambridge.com/downing.html.
4. An article in *Southern Folklore Quarterly,* volume 24, published in 1960. The article is "The New Orleans Voodoo Ritual Dance and Its Twentieth-Century Survivals," written by John Q. Anderson, on pages 135 through 143. The journal is paged continuously throughout the annual volume.
5. An article on CD-ROM that is also available in print. The author is Susan Chu. The title is "1996 Election Returns May Widen Gender Gap." The article appears in the January 1997 issue of *Politics and Values,* a monthly magazine, on pages 12 through 26. It also appears on the CD-ROM titled *Resource/One,* released in March 1997 by UMI-ProQuest.

Exercise 3
Preparing your list of works cited

Prepare the final list of works cited for your research paper. Unless your instructor specifies otherwise, follow MLA style, using the models on the preceding pages.

37d Understanding abbreviations

Most disciplines' documentation styles, including that of the MLA, use as few abbreviations as possible. However, they still use some, and you may encounter many more in your reading. The most common abbreviations found in source citations appear below.

anon.	anonymous
bk., bks.	book(s)
c., ca.	*circa* ("about"), used with approximate dates
ch., chs.	chapter(s)
col., cols.	column(s)
comp., comps.	compiled by, compiler(s)
diss.	dissertation
ed., eds.	edited by, edition(s), editor(s)
et al.	*et alii* ("and others")

ibid.	*ibidem* ("in the same place")
illus.	illustrated by, illustrator, illustration(s)
l., ll.	line(s)
loc. cit.	*loco citato* ("in the place cited")
ms., mss.	manuscript(s)
n., nn.	note(s), as in p. 24, n. 2
n.d.	no date (of publication)
no., nos.	number(s)
n.p.	no place (of publication), no publisher
n. pag.	no pagination
op. cit.	*opere citato* ("in the work cited")
P	Press (UP = University Press)
p., pp.	page(s)
q.v.	*quod vide* ("which see")
rev.	revised, revision, revised by, review
rpt.	reprint, reprinted
sec.	section
supp., supps.	supplement(s)
trans.	translator, translated by
univ., U	university (UP = University Press)
vol., vols.	volume(s)

HIGHLIGHTS

This chapter contains annotated versions of Edward Begay's and Vanessa Haley's research papers for students to examine and discuss. Both are presented as papers-in-progress throughout Chapters 35 and 36. We encourage you to discuss the papers carefully with students, so that they understand both the physical requirements and the rhetorical features of good research writing.

Chapter 38 *Two Sample Research Papers*

TEACHING TIP

Ask students to respond to these papers in their journals, and to discuss their responses in small groups. Since students have seen the papers develop in Chapters 35 and 36 they may have strong opinions about these final versions. What would they have done differently? What did Begay and Haley do that was surprising? As readers, what would they have liked to see Begay or Haley add, omit, or change in these papers?

The following pages show the research papers of Edward Begay and Vanessa Haley, whose work we followed in Chapters 35 and 36. (Begay's paper begins on p. 632, Haley's on p. 662.) Both students used the citation style recommended by the *MLA Handbook*, and both typed their papers following the advice on document format in Appendix A of this handbook. Accompanying both students' papers are comments on format, content, source citations, and other matters. The more extensive comments on Begay's paper are indexed below by text page number (*italic*) and comment number (**boldface**).

Mechanics of quotations

MLA text citations

MLA works-cited entries

Endnotes for supplementary information

The Information Superhighway: 1

Toll Road or Public Way?

By

Edward Begay

Ms. Derryfield

English 105

22 May 1997

1. **Title page format.** A title page is not required by MLA style but may be required by your instructor. If so, or if you are required to submit an outline with your paper, prepare a title page as shown opposite: the title of the paper about a third of the way down the page; your name (preceded by "By") about an inch below the title; and, starting about an inch below your name, your instructor's name, the course number, and the date. Center all lines in the width of the page and separate them from each other with at least one line of space. (If your instructor does not require a title page for your paper, follow MLA style: place your name, the identifying information, and the date on the first page of the paper. See Vanessa Haley's paper, p. 662, for this format.)

NEXT TWO PAGES

2. **Outline format.** If your instructor asks you to include your final outline, place it between the title page and the text, as Begay does on the following pages. Number the pages with small Roman numerals (i, ii), and place your last name just before the page numbers in case the pages of your paper become separated. Place the heading "Outline" an inch from the top of the first page, and double-space under the heading.
3. **Outline content.** Begay includes his final thesis sentence as part of his outline so that his instructor can see how the parts relate to the whole. Notice that each main division (numbered with Roman numerals) relates to the thesis sentence and that all the subdivisions relate to their main division.

   Begay casts his final outline in full sentences. Some instructors request topic outlines, in which ideas appear in phrases instead of in sentences and do not end with periods. (See p. 56 for this format.)

Begay i

Outline 2

Thesis sentence: To make Internet access universal, 3
public libraries and schools face a double challenge: rethinking their purpose in light of new technology and obtaining the necessary resources from government and business to go online.

I. Libraries will need to make internal changes and find external funding in order to serve the population.
    A. To preserve their historical role in maintaining an informed citizenry, libraries must go online.
    B. Technological advances necessitate changes in the way libraries operate.
        1. Connections will replace collections in the new library.
        2. Librarians' roles will change from maintaining materials to guiding electronic research.
    C. Commercialization of the Internet, although a possible threat to the Net's integrity, provides opportunities for funding public use of the Net.

II. Schools must investigate the role of the Internet in education as well as ways to fund school connections.
    A. Although some experts question the value of technology in the classroom, evidence suggests that computers enhance learning.
        1. Some critics say technology undermines education.
        2. Some teachers say that technology fits in well with recent theories of education.
        3. Students in schools across the country are using the Internet effectively.

Begay ii

B. Wealthy schools have far greater access to technology than poor ones.
   1. Wealthier school systems can fund Internet connections.
   2. Poorer systems lack funds for new technology.
   3. In poorer systems, outdated computers and lack of Internet access lead to "drill and skill" use of computers.

III. Libraries and schools must join with businesses and governments in seeking funds to go online and to train teachers and librarians to use technology.
   A. Local, state, and federal agencies must step up existing efforts to help put classrooms online and to train teachers.
   B. Businesses must also increase assistance to schools and libraries.
      1. High-technology companies can provide materials and training.
      2. Local businesses can form partnerships with schools.

Begay 1

The Information Superhighway: 4
Toll Road or Public Way?

The "information superhighway," referring to the 5
great communication potential of the Internet, has now
become a familiar term, even among those who are not
yet online. This mass of electronic connections has
grown dramatically in recent years,[1] accompanied by 6
constant predictions of how it will change our lives for
the better. But the superhighway has a serious problem
that receives less attention: its on-ramps--networked
computers and the knowledge to operate them--are not
accessible to everyone. Many observers see a real danger
that the Internet may widen the gap between rich and
poor in this country, creating, in the words of *New
York Times* columnist Max Frankel, a "technological
partition, a society of computer elites and illiterates
drifting apart and losing touch" (42). According to 7
Time magazine, "The stakes are high": Internet access 8
"may prove to be less a question of privilege or position
than one of *the basic ability to function in a democratic
society*" ("New Divide" 25; emphasis added). 9

How then can we make sure that computer technology helps us become a more equal society rather
than more unequal? Most analysts look to public
libraries and schools to provide widespread access to
the Internet because these institutions are open to all.
However, to make Internet access universal, public 10
libraries and schools face a double challenge: rethinking their purpose in light of new technology and obtaining the necessary resources from government and
business to go online.

4. **Title.** Begay's title plays on the image of the Internet as a highway to suggest his theme of accessibility. A more descriptive title, such as "Equality on the Internet," would also have been appropriate. **Paper format.** Because he provides a title page as requested by his instructor, Begay does not repeat his full name on the first page of text. For MLA style, which omits a title page, the following would appear in the upper left of this first page:

   Edward Begay

   Ms. Derryfield

   English 105

   22 May 1997

   (See the paper on p. 662 for this format.)

   Even with a title page, Begay centers his title an inch below the top edge of the first page, using no quotation marks or underlining. He provides his last name and the page number on the top right of every page, one-half inch below the top of the paper. The margins of the paper are one inch all around, and everything is double-spaced.
5. **Introduction.** Begay picks up the image of the superhighway from his title to lead into the problem of access. He delays presenting his thesis in order to establish some background about the risks of unequal access. The question at the beginning of the next paragraph sets up the thesis at the end of the page.
6. **Using an endnote for supplementary information.** Begay just mentions the growth of the Internet. For readers interested in more, he provides a source in a note at the end of the paper (p. 656). He signals the note with the raised numeral 1.
7. **Citation when the author is named in your text.** Because Begay uses Frankel's name in the text, he does not provide it along with the page number 42 in the parenthetical citation.
8. **Punctuation with quotations.** Begay adds a colon to connect the first and second parts of the *Time* quotation. Because the colon is not part of the original quotation, it falls outside the quotation marks.
9. **Adding emphasis to quotations.** Begay underlines important words in the quotation. He acknowledges this change inside the parenthetical citation with the words "emphasis added," separated by a semicolon from the page number. **Citation of an unsigned article.** Since Begay is citing an unsigned article, he uses a shortened form of the title for his citation. See the entry for this work in the list of works cited, page 660.
10. **Thesis sentence.** Begay's introduction has led up to this sentence, which states the idea that he will demonstrate in the paper.

Begay 2

Because libraries have long provided free access 11
to information, they are seen as an essential component
in our democratic society. According to the American
Library Association,

> At a time when only one of three American 12
> households owns a computer, our nation's
> . . . libraries are uniquely positioned to serve
> as the public's means of access to the infor-
> mation superhighway--a place where all
> people can tap into new technology with the
> expert assistance of a librarian. (Equity 5) 13

In the same publication, Betty J. Turock, 1995-96 presi- 14
dent of the American Library Association, emphasizes
that "[n]othing is more important to the future of our
democracy than ensuring public access to information.
That is why we need our nation's . . . libraries online"
(Equity 6).

But putting libraries online will probably change
the very nature of libraries themselves. According to
librarians Maurice Mitchell and Laverna Saunders of
the Nevada State University system, some librarians
envision a "virtual library" in the near future, "a 15
generic library that has no defined boundaries, no administration, no staff, and no budget" (par. 14). Borge 16
Sorensen, director of public libraries in Copenhagen,
Denmark, says, "The new library will not be judged by
its collections but by its potential for connecting users
with information" (qtd. in Grimes A21). Librarians' 17
jobs, too, will change. They will become "the guides and
gatekeepers, or perhaps the travel agents, on the information superhighway" (Grimes A21). 18

11. **Relation to outline.** This paragraph begins part I of Begay's outline (see p. 634). Part II begins on page 642 and part III on page 650.
12. **Format of long quotations.** This quotation exceeds four typed lines, so Begay sets it off from the text without quotation marks and with double spacing above and below. The quotation is double-spaced and is indented one inch from the left margin. **Editing quotations with ellipsis marks.** Begay uses an ellipsis mark to show that he has eliminated irrelevant material from the quotation (see p. 424). An ellipsis mark consists of three spaced periods with one space on either side.
13. **Citation with displayed quotation.** The parenthetical citation after the quotation falls *outside* the sentence period and is separated from the period by one space. **Citation of an unsigned source.** In the absence of an author's name, Begay uses the first main word of the title. (See p. 658.)
14. **Introducing quotations.** Here and elsewhere, Begay effectively introduces his quotations by integrating them into his own sentences and by establishing the source's credentials in an identifying phrase. (For more examples, see pp. 642 and 645. See pp. 591–95 for a discussion of introducing quotations.) **Altering capitalization in quotations.** In the source the word "nothing" began a sentence and was capitalized. To fit the quotation smoothly into his own sentence, Begay uses a small letter, and he inserts brackets to indicate that he altered the capitalization. (See pp. 423 and 431.)
15. **Omission of ellipsis marks.** Begay does not use ellipsis marks with the first two quotations in this paragraph because it is already clear that he has left material out of the original: the term "virtual library" and the phrase beginning "a generic library " are obviously not complete sentences. (See p. 424 for more on ellipsis marks.)
16. **Citation of a source using paragraph numbers.** Begay uses "par." ("paragraph") to indicate that the source numbers paragraphs rather than pages. He cites paragraph 14.
17. **Citation of indirect source.** With the use of "qtd. in" ("quoted in"), Begay indicates correctly that he obtained the quotation by Sorensen in the article by Grimes (Sorensen is an indirect source; Grimes is a direct source). **Indirect sources.** The use of an indirect source is appropriate only when the original material cannot be consulted, as in this case because Grimes interviewed Sorensen personally. (For a less appropriate case, see comment 35 on p. 649.)
18. **Citation when the author is not named in your text.** Because Begay has not used Grimes's name in the text, he provides it in the parenthetical citation along with the page number.

Begay 3

While librarians welcome these changes and are willing to accommodate technology, they worry about the commercialization of the Internet and about the costs of technology. Early users of the Internet were primarily public institutions. Now that business has arrived, the ground rules seem to have changed. As the Internet becomes more commercialized, market forces rather than public good have begun to dictate the nature of Internet services and their cost. For example, cable and telephone companies have already recognized the profit potential in offering various online services to private customers. This focus on profit may pose a threat to public users such as libraries and schools, altering the nature of the Internet environment. Mitchell and Saunders observe that until now the Internet has been

> a socialist/democratic environment in which
> all the participants simply "agree to agree" 19
> or not to participate. Now we see through the commercialism movement a shift to a capitalistic environment in which profit motive and economic advantage rule. (par. 15)

While concerned about the invasion of profit motive on the Internet, Mitchell and Saunders also report a potential benefit in business's interest: "Commercial interests present a new way to pay the costs of expanding
an infrastructure and resources" (par. 12). Max Frankel 20
suggests that fees be charged for "profitable private uses of the Internet . . . to subsidize the Net's penetration of every community" (42). In fact, many librarians believe that a business connection can help solve some of the financial problems associated with getting online, but as

19. **Quotation within a displayed quotation.** Begay uses double quotation marks for the quoted words inside this displayed quotation because a displayed quotation does not appear in quotation marks of its own. (He would use single quotation marks for the shorter quotation if the longer one did appear in quotation marks. See p. 408.)
20. **Selecting supporting evidence.** Begay uses two sources here to develop his point, mixing the views of professional librarians and a newspaper columnist who specializes in the communications media. The use of the authors' names to introduce the quotations clarifies who said what.

Mitchell and Saunders point out, the integrity of the library itself must be maintained, along with "funding to stay on the road and to establish a right-of-way for those who depend upon public transportation" (par. 22).

Of course, the first "public transportation" Ameri- 21
cans take in education is through the public school system. And it is in the schools that the most significant debates about access to the Internet take place. For the Internet to be truly democratic, the public schools must provide all students with access to it. But even more so in the classroom than in libraries, the questions raised by technology are complex.

Before considering how all students can have equal access to the Internet, it is necessary to look at the effect of technology on schools. A noted critic of computer technology, Clifford Stoll, calls networking "irrelevant to schooling" and states, "Only a teacher, live in the classroom, can bring about . . . inspiration. This can't happen over a speaker, a television or a computer screen" (96). Stoll argues that Internet projects "magnify the computing side, while making the learning experience seem trivial" and insists that "only human beings can
teach the connection between things" (108). In a New
York Times article on technology in the schools, Neil 22
MacFarquhar reports from interviews with a number of experts who share Stoll's doubts about whether technology enhances learning at all. In the naysayers' views,
Internet education is "a cut-and-paste style of learning," 23
one in which students "[parrot] trivial bites of information found on the computer screen" when they should be "developing the critical judgment and analysis engen-
dered by culling through books" (B4).[2] 24

21. **Relation to outline.** With this paragraph Begay begins part II of his outline (see p. 634). **Transitional paragraph.** Begay devotes a whole paragraph to his shift in direction, briefly reflecting the ideas in the introduction, summing up the preceding section, and introducing his next point.
22. **Introducing and citing a discussion of one work.** By mentioning MacFarquhar's name at the beginning of these two sentences, Begay indicates that what follows is from MacFarquhar's work. The page number at the end of the paragraph announces that the citation covers all the intervening material. If, instead, Begay had placed both parts of the citation together (the page number after the first sentence or MacFarquhar's name after the last sentence), readers might be unsure of how much material the citation covered. **Mixing summary, paraphrase, and quotation.** In this paragraph Begay summarizes, paraphrases, and quotes from MacFarquhar's article to give readers a good sense of the issue MacFarquhar raises.
23. **Punctuation with quotations.** A comma falls inside a closing quotation mark, as here. **Altering word forms in quotations.** To fit the quotation into his own sentence, Begay changed the word *parroting* in the original to *parrot*. The brackets around *parrot* indicate that the word is changed. (See p. 423.)
24. **Punctuating parenthetical citations.** The period ending a sentence containing a quotation comes after the citation.

Many educators, however, see the introduction of
technology as a welcome boost to newer education theories. Some theorists argue that the old “transmission” 25
model of education, in which teachers transmit knowledge to passive students, will not prepare students to
live and work in the next century (Conte 923-24). 26
Instead, these theorists favor a model closer to cognitive
psychology and constructivism, emphasizing active 27
learning and “dealing with complex, real-world problems”--a model well served by computer networking
(Conte 935-36).

In fact, many teachers see the Internet as the
most powerful resource in education. Mary E.
McArthur, a veteran teacher in Massachusetts, told me 28
in an online interview that the Internet presents new
possibilities for student learning:

> My students have a much better sense of the
> relevance of their education now that they're
> online. When we were studying ecology, for
> example, some students e-mailed a represen-
> tative of the EPA [Environmental Protection 29
> Agency] in Washington, asking questions
> and offering suggestions about a proposed
> local landfill, and received an immediate
> response. They took that response to the
> town's planning board when the landfill
> issue was discussed. 30

The Internet, according to McArthur, has made her students not only better learners but better citizens as well. And contrary to Stoll's vision of dehumanized classrooms, McArthur told me that since her students began using technology, “conversation is constant. Students

MLA 38

25. **Introducing borrowed material.** Begay here begins paraphrasing and quoting Conte as an expert, so he should have named Conte in the text and identified him with his credentials. (See pp. 593–94.) **Paraphrasing.** Begay paraphrases a quotation by Conte. His note card follows:

Traditional vs. innovative models of education

Conte, pp. 923-24

"[T]he traditional ✓classroom, with its strong central authority and its emphasis on training students to take orders and perform narrow tasks, may have prepared students for work in 20th-century factories. But it can't impart the skills they need in the workplace of the 21st century, where there's a premium on workers who are flexible, creative, self-directed and able to solve problems collaboratively."

Showing page breaks in notes. In this note card Begay inserted a check mark between "traditional" and "classroom" to indicate the location of a page break in the original source (see p. 576).

26. **Citation of a paraphrase.** Begay should have used Conte's name in the text, but because he did not he correctly gives Conte's name in the citation.
27. **Defining terms.** Begay uses two terms here, *cognitive psychology* and *constructivism,* that he picked up from Conte and other sources, but he does not make use of the terms by defining and applying them. Readers may be confused or may wonder whether Begay himself understands the terms. He should have omitted them or defined them.
28. **Primary source: personal interview.** Begay tested his ideas by conducting an e-mail interview of a teacher in a public school. He uses both paraphrase and quotation from the interview, with the subject's permission.
29. **Adding words to quotations.** Begay spells out the full name of the EPA for readers who may not recognize the abbreviation, and he encloses his addition in brackets. (See p. 423.)
30. **Omission of parenthetical citation.** Begay does not use a parenthetical citation at the end of the quotation because the source (an interview) has no page numbers and the necessary information (McArthur's name) appears in the text before the quotation.

are talking online, to each other, and to me--question-
ing, criticizing, analyzing what they're learning."

McArthur's and her students' experiences are not 31
unique: success stories about education on the Internet
are common in popular and scholarly sources.[3] But
many schools may not discover what they might accomplish with the Internet. The long-standing gap between
rich and poor in America has become a "digital divide"
in which some children "are being prepared for lives
and careers in the information age" while others "find
themselves held back" (Poole). 32

Statistics vary,[4] but all studies agree that a child's 33
chances of networking are significantly greater if he or
she lives in a middle-class or affluent area. A recent US
Department of Education study revealed that only "31
percent of [low-income] schools had Internet access,
compared with 62 percent for [high-income] schools"
(par. 14). A private study reports that only 12 percent
of actual classrooms--the vast majority of them in high-
income areas--are connected to the Internet (Quality
Education Data). According to the US General Account- 34
ing Office, one reason for this discrepancy is that "60
percent of schools in central cities . . . have insufficient
phone lines, electrical wiring or electrical power to
support communications technologies." The conclusion
drawn by the Department of Education is supported by
the other studies: "[M]inority and low-income students
are less likely to have classroom access to the Internet
than wealthier students" (par. 17).

Not only is Internet access impossible in many poorer schools, but the computer equipment these schools have is usually outdated and incapable of

31. **Transitional paragraph.** This paragraph within the section on schools shifts the emphasis from the educational value of technology to its cost. **Summary of sources.** Rather than belabor the Internet success stories, Begay wraps up with a summary. **Using an endnote for citation of several sources.** Begay avoids a lengthy and obtrusive parenthetical citation by referring readers to endnote 3, which lists several sources (see p. 656).
32. **Citation of one-page article.** Poole's article appears on only one page of the newspaper it is in, and Begay gives that page number in the list of works cited (see p. 660). Thus he does not need to repeat the page number in the parenthetical citation.
33. **Using an endnote for supplementary information.** Here Begay inserts a reference to a note at the end of the paper in which he explains the difficulty of interpreting statistics about computers in schools. **Revising a draft.** Begay had included the endnote information in his early drafts. He finally decided that while the material was relevant, it distracted readers from his main point. Here is Begay's edited draft of this passage:

   Statistics [vary,] ~~are difficult to interpret because they require comparing apples and oranges. For instance, one source discusses the number of classrooms with Internet access (Quality Education Data), while another discusses the number of schools with Internet access (US Department of Education), another discusses the number of students per computer terminal ("Study Finds"), and another discusses the number of computers per school library (McAvoy).~~ [but] ~~All~~ [all] studies agree~~, however,~~ that a child's chances of networking are significantly greater if he or she lives in a middle-class or affluent area. [Summarize apples-oranges problem in endnote.]

34. **Citation of a source with no page numbers.** Begay does not give page numbers for the Quality Education Data source cited here or for the US General Accounting Office source cited in the next sentence because neither of these electronic sources had numbered pages (or paragraphs). **Synthesis of a variety of sources.** Because no one government or private source provided comprehensive data on computers and Internet access in schools, Begay had to use and cite several sources to make his point.

Begay 7

supporting online services. An example is Anderson
Elementary School in a poor section of San Jose, California (Poole). Anderson is equipped with slow 1980s
computers with little processing power. Because of their
limitations, the computers cannot be connected to the
Internet. And without Internet access, students at Anderson and other poor schools are unable to match their
more affluent peers in communicating with experts or
with fellow students from other districts or countries.
Nor are they able to gain access to the many resources,
such as up-to-date specialized encyclopedias, that are
available online. Rather than interacting with others 35
through their computers, these students tend to use
computers for "drill and skill" work in reading and
arithmetic: they "learn to do what the computer tells
them," according to Delia Neuman of the University of
Maryland (qtd. in Conte 931).

Students who do not have access to the Internet may well find themselves left out of a society in which computer skills will earn a worker 15 percent more than another worker without such skills ("New Divide" 25). And society will suffer as well. According to Richard W. Riley, secretary of education under President Clinton,

> If the nation continues to ignore the educational needs of . . . low-income students . . . and continues to . . . link up their schools last, it will find itself in an economic bind of the first order. It will have a work force that does not know how to work. (51)

The problem for schools like Anderson Elemen- 36
tary is, of course, money. Leaders in poor school

35. **Combining paraphrase and quotation.** Begay had a long quotation from Neuman, but he did not want to devote quite so much space to the side issue of drill-and-skill teaching. Thus he paraphrased Neuman's idea and quoted only the most striking language. The entire quotation appears on the following note card:

> Difference between rich & poor schools
>
> Conte, p. 931
>
> From Delia Neuman, prof., U Maryland Coll. of Library & Information Services: "Economically disadvantaged students, who often use the computer for remediation and basic skills, learn to do what the computer tells them, while more affluent students, who use it to learn programming and tool application, learn to tell the computer what to do."

Indirect sources. Begay found Neuman's comments in the article by Conte and so uses "qtd. in" ("quoted in") in the source citation. But Conte gave full bibliographic information on Neuman's original article and even an Internet address for reaching Neuman. Instead of relying on the quotation in Conte, Begay should have gone directly to Neuman's article. Indirect sources (and "qtd. in") are appropriate only when the original material is not available for you to consult. (See also p. 639.)

36. **Drawing conclusions.** Rather than leaving it to his readers to figure out the significance of the preceding paragraphs, Begay here wraps up his discussion of schools with his own conclusions about the costs of and thus the limits on technological change in education.

Begay 8

districts are aware of the importance of technology, but they are also worried about leaking roofs, aging furniture, and overcrowded classrooms. The money to buy the equipment, make the connections, and train teachers to use and maintain the networks is not easily found even in middle-class school districts, much less in poorer districts.

If libraries and schools are to provide widespread 37
access to the Internet, they must find ways not only to integrate technology into their programs but also to pay the bills associated with going online. Adapting the work of libraries and schools to the technological age is the responsibility of the experts within those systems. But finding the money to finance technological advances involves a wider discussion in which more elements of society must take part. It will be necessary for government and business to play an active role in wiring libraries and schools and in training professionals to work with the technology.

Governments are already encouraging cooperation. For example, the President and members of his ad- 38
ministration have repeatedly urged telephone and cable
television companies to work with schools to achieve
rapid universal educational access. Several states have
organized NetDay campaigns designed to bring educators, school boards, and community volunteers together
to oversee installation of Internet capabilities in the public schools ("Louisiana NetDay96"; MacFarquhar B1). 39

It is clear, however, that governments need to offer more than mere encouragement. Just as federal and state governments have offered grants to schools in the past for constructing new buildings, they must now

37. **Relation to outline.** With this paragraph Begay begins part III of his outline (see p. 635). **Summary statement.** To introduce this final section of his paper, Begay begins this paragraph with a statement that ties together the two main ideas in his thesis, that schools and libraries must rethink their missions and that funding must be found to support going online.
38. **Common knowledge.** Begay knew of the White House's efforts to put schools online, and he discovered references to it in several sources. Thus he treats the information as common knowledge and does not cite a source for it. (See p. 580 for further discussion of common knowledge.)
39. **Parenthetical citation of more than one work.** Begay discovered information about NetDay campaigns in two sources, so he cites both in parentheses, separating the two with a semicolon (see p. 605).

offer grants to wire classrooms. They should also support teacher training. Richard Riley believes that the federal government "should provide every teacher in the United States with the opportunity to take advantage of first-class training in the latest and most up-to-date technologies available for the classroom" (52). Furthermore, since libraries seem to be the logical place for less-affluent citizens to access the Internet, local governments must increase library budgets to accommodate wiring, purchase of equipment, and training of staff. Openly espousing technology in the schools and libraries is not enough; governments must come through with funds if Internet access is to be truly democratic.

Business must also join in. Business has long recognized its responsibility to the larger community, for instance by supporting youth athletics and contributing to charities through the Chamber of Commerce. Now business needs to help put the community online. Some businesses are already working with schools to increase
Internet access. For a number of years IBM and Apple 40
have donated new and used computers to schools. And recently the 3COM Corporation of Santa Clara, California, provided not only a $100,000 grant to help local schools pay for computer technology but also full-time consultation to help educate teachers and students and "summer technology institutes" for students, teachers,
and administrators (Jordahl and Orwig 30). 41

For computer companies, cooperation with schools is obviously good business, paying off in free advertising, enhanced image, and potential sales. But almost every business has a vested interest in

40. **Common knowledge.** Begay already knew of IBM's and Apple's well-publicized programs to place computers in schools; in fact, he had used a donated IBM PC in high school. Thus he treats this information as common knowledge.
41. **Citation of a source with two authors.** Both authors' last names are given, separated by "and" and no punctuation.

Begay 10

widespread access to technology. As Richard Riley has noted, if today's students are not prepared for tomorrow's world, then businesses will suffer (51). That is one of the reasons why some noncomputer companies are working to help students become familiar with technology. In Fairfax, Virginia, for example, the Federal Home Loan Mortgage Corporation assigns employee mentors to public school students and provides funds for improving schools' networking capabilities (Jordahl and Orwig 31). And in South Carolina the Department of Education and the state Chamber of Commerce have created school-business networks in which businesspeople help schools with technical knowledge and fund raising (MacFarquhar B1). Such cooperative programs between schools and businesses are essential if students are to be prepared for citizenship in a technological age.

Internet access is or soon will be "access to the 42
central nervous system of our democracy," says Jeff Chester of the Center for Media Education (qtd. in "New Divide" 26). Providing this access through libraries and schools is perhaps the only way to ensure that both poor and rich have equal access to job opportunities and can participate equally in our democratic processes and institutions. But the schools and libraries cannot do the job alone. They need the strong support of business and government to help make the information superhighway a truly public way.

42. **Conclusion.** In his final paragraph Begay summarizes the main points of his paper to remind readers of both the need for universal Internet access and the ways it can be funded. By referring to the image of the information superhighway from his title and introduction, Begay comes full circle and leaves his readers with a vivid impression of his idea.

Begay 11

Notes 43

[1] For more information on the history of the Inter- 44
net, see Hardy.

[2] For additional criticism of computers in education, see Goodson et al. 45

[3] See, for example, MacFarquhar, Conte, and Jordahl and Orwig.

[4] It is difficult to compare and summarize statistics on this subject because they often measure different variables. For example, the Department of Education data provide the number of schools with Internet access, while Quality Education Data reports on the number of classrooms with Internet access. Still other studies provide the number of computers per student in a school or the number of school libraries with Internet access. Nonetheless, all of the numbers point to the inequities between wealthier and poorer schools.

43. **Format of notes.** The word "Notes" is centered one inch from the top of the page. (The heading would be singular—"Note"—if Begay had only one note.) The notes begin two lines (one double space) below the heading. The notes themselves are double-spaced. The first line of each is indented one-half inch and is preceded by a raised number corresponding to the number used in the text. A space separates the number and the note.
44. **Endnotes for additional relevant information.** Begay uses endnotes for sources and information that are somewhat relevant to his thesis but not essential and that don't fit easily into the text. Note 1 refers interested readers to an online article on the history of the Internet. Note 2 highlights a notable critique of computers in education. Note 3 cites several sources that would be obtrusive in a parenthetical text citation. And note 4 provides information on Begay's difficulties interpreting statistics. (See p. 607 for more on supplementary notes.)
45. **Citation for a source with more than three authors.** The Goodson citation indicates with "et al." ("and others") that Goodson was a co-author with at least two others. See the works-cited entry for this source on the next page.

Begay 12

Works Cited 46

Conte, Christopher. "Networking the Classroom." CQ Researcher 5 (1995): 923-43. 47

Equity on the Information Superhighway: Problems and Possibilities. Chicago: ALA, 1996. 48

Frankel, Max. "The Moon, This Time Around." New York Times Magazine 5 May 1996: 40+. New York Times Ondisc. CD-ROM. UMI-ProQuest. Nov. 1996. 49

Goodson, Ivor F., et al. "Computer Literacy as Ideology." British Journal of Sociology of Education 17 (1996): 65-80. 50

Grimes, William. "Libraries Ponder Role in the Digital Age." New York Times 29 Apr. 1996, late ed.: A21+. New York Times Ondisc. CD-ROM. UMI-ProQuest. Nov. 1996. 51

Hardy, Henry Edward. "A Short History of the Net." Ocean Home Page. 15 Oct. 1995. Online. Internet. 12 Mar. 1997. Available http://www.ocean.ic.net/doc/snethist.html. 52

Jordahl, Gregory, and Ann Orwig. "Getting Equipped and Staying Equipped, Part 2: Finding the Funds." Technology & Learning Apr. 1995: 28-37. 53

"Louisiana NetDay96: Issues for Consideration by School Districts." LA NetDay96. 15 May 1995. Online. Internet. 12 Mar. 1997. Available http://www.neill.net/netday/issues.html.

MacFarquhar, Neil. "The Internet Goes to School." New York Times 7 Mar. 1996, late ed.: B1+. New York Times Ondisc. CD-ROM. UMI-ProQuest. Oct. 1996.

46. **Format of list of works cited.** The heading "Works Cited" is centered one inch from the top of the page. The first entry is typed two lines (one double space) below the heading, and the entire list is double-spaced. The first line of each entry begins at the left margin; subsequent lines of the same entry are indented one-half inch. The entries are alphabetized by the last name of the first author or (for sources without authors) by the first main word of the title.
47. Entry for a **signed article in a journal with continuous pagination throughout an annual volume** (see p. 617).
48. Entry for a **pamphlet** (see p. 624). This entry also cites an **unsigned source** and so is listed and alphabetized by its title (see p. 612).
49. Entry for a **weekly magazine** (see p. 617) and a **source on CD-ROM that also appears in print** (see p. 620). The first date is the publication date of the article; the second is the publication date of the CD-ROM. This entry also illustrates an **article in which pagination is not consecutive.** The "+" indicates that the article does not continue on page 41 but farther back in the issue.
50. Entry for an **article with more than three authors.** A source with more than three authors may be listed with all authors' names or just with the first author's name followed by "et al." ("and others"). (See p. 610.) Begay had all the names in his working bibliography (see below), but he opted not to use them. His text reference is consistent with this decision (see p. 656).

Goodson, Ivor F., James Mangan, Christina Marshall, and Renee Van Horn. "Computer Literacy as Ideology." British Journal of Sociology of Education 17 (1996): 65-80.

51. Entry for an **article in a daily newspaper on CD-ROM.**
52. Entry for an **online source reached through a network** (see p. 622). Begay provides both the date the source was posted on the Internet (15 Oct. 1995) and the date he consulted the source (12 Mar. 1997). For all his online sources, Begay provides the electronic address after "Available," an option in MLA style.
53. Entry for a **signed article in a monthly magazine** (see p. 617) and for a **source with two authors** (see p. 610).

Begay 13

McArthur, Mary E. E-mail interview. 20 Mar. 1997. 54

Mitchell, Maurice, and Laverna Saunders. "The National 55
Information Infrastructure: Implications for
Libraries." Computers in Libraries 13.10 (Dec.
1993): 22 pars. Online. Internet. 21 Mar. 1997.
Available ftp://netlib.nevada.edu/pub/lib/3246.

"A New Divide Between Haves and Have-Nots?" Time 56
Special Issue: Welcome to Cyberspace Spring 1995:
25-26.

Poole, Gary Andrew. "A New Gulf in American Education, the Digital Divide." New York Times 29 Jan.
1996, late ed.: D3. New York Times Ondisc. CD-
ROM. UMI-ProQuest. June 1996.

Quality Education Data Inc. "12-Year Trend. Classrooms 57
per Computer: U.S. Public Schools." 22 Jan. 1997.
Online. Internet. 22 Mar. 1997. Available http://
www.qeddata.com/graphics/12year.jpg.

Riley, Richard W. "Connecting Classrooms, Computers,
and Communities." Issues in Science and Technology 12 (1996): 49-52.

Stoll, Clifford. Silicon Snake Oil: Second Thoughts on 58
the Information Highway. New York: Doubleday,
1995.

United States. Dept. of Education. "Equity Issues: Com- 59
puters in Schools." Jan. 1996: 18 pars. Online. Internet. 12 Mar. 1997. Available http://www.ed.gov/
statistics.html.

---. General Accounting Off. "Technology in Public 60
Schools." 18 Dec. 1995. Online. Internet. 22 Mar.
1997. Available http://www.gao.gov/technology
.html.

54. Entry for a **personal interview by e-mail** (see p. 627).
55. Entry for an **article from an online journal.** Online and print journals have similar citation formats (see p. 622). Like many online journals, this one numbers paragraphs rather than pages, so Begay provides the total number of paragraphs where he would otherwise give the total pages ("pars." is short for "paragraphs").
56. Entry for an **unsigned article in a periodical.** This source is listed by its title and alphabetized by the title's first main word. Entry for a **special issue of a periodical.** Begay had to improvise for this special issue of *Time* magazine because the MLA does not specify a format for such a source. In this case, Begay follows the cover of the magazine, where *Special Issue* was treated as part of the magazine's title and *Welcome to Cyberspace* was treated as a subtitle. He works this title into the MLA format for an unsigned magazine article.
57. Entry for a **source with a corporate author** (see p. 612).
58. Entry for a **book with one author** (see p. 610).
59. Entry for a **government publication located online.** In the source the paragraphs were numbered, so Begay gives this information ("18 pars.") in the reference.
60. Entry for the **second of two works by the same author**—in this case the US government. Since the previous entry also lists the United States as author, Begay replaces those words in this entry with three hyphens. (See p. 611.)

Haley 1

Vanessa Haley

Professor Moisan

English 101

24 March 1997

Format of heading and title when no title page is required

Annie Dillard's Healing Vision

Introduction of environmental theme

It is almost a commonplace these days that human arrogance is destroying the environment. Environmentalists, naturalists, and now the man or woman on the street seem to agree: the long-held belief that human beings are separate from nature, destined to rise above its laws and conquer it, has been ruinous.

Focus on issue to be resolved

Unfortunately, the defenders of nature tend to respond to this ruinous belief with harmful myths of their own: nature is pure and harmonious; humanity is corrupt and dangerous. Much writing about nature lacks a recognition that human beings and their civilization are as much a part of nature as trees and whales are, neither better nor worse. Yet without such a recognition, how can humans overcome the damaging sense of separation between themselves and the earth? How can humans develop realistic solutions to environmental problems that will work for humanity _and_ the rest of nature?

Introduction of Dillard to resolve issue

Thesis sentence

One nature writer who seems to recognize the naturalness of humanity is Annie Dillard. In her best-known work, the Pulitzer Prize-winning _Pilgrim at Tinker Creek_, she is a solitary person encountering the natural world, and some critics fault her for turning her back on society. But in those encounters with nature, Dillard probes a spiritual as well as a physical identity between human beings and nature that could help to heal the rift between them.

Haley 2

Dillard is not renowned for her sense of involvement with human society. Like Henry David Thoreau, with whom she is often compared, she retreats from rather than confronts human society. The critic Gary McIlroy points out that although Thoreau discusses society a great deal in Walden he makes no attempt "to find a middle ground between it and his experiment in the woods" (113). Dillard has been similarly criticized. For instance, the writer Eudora Welty comments that

Acknowledgment of opposing critical view

> Annie Dillard is the only person in her book, substantially the only one in her world; I recall no outside human speech coming to break the long soliloquy of the author. Speaking of the universe very often, she is yet self-surrounded and, beyond that, book-surrounded. Her own book might have taken in more of human life without losing a bit of the wonder she was after. (37)

It is true that Dillard seems detached from human society, but actually she was always close to it at Tinker Creek. In a later book, Teaching a Stone to Talk, she says of the neighborhood, "This is, mind you, suburbia. It is a five-minute walk in three directions to rows of houses. . . . There's a 55 mph highway at one end of the pond, and a nesting pair of wood ducks at the other" (qtd. in McIlroy 111).

First response to opposing view

Rather than hiding from humanity, Dillard seems to be trying to understand it through nature. In Pilgrim she reports buying a goldfish, which she names Ellery Channing. She recalls once seeing through a microscope "red blood cells whip, one by one, through the capillaries" of yet another goldfish (124). Now

Second response to opposing view

Haley 3

watching Ellery Channing, she sees the blood in his body as a bond between fish and human being: "Those red blood cells are coursing in Ellery's tail now, too, in just that way, and through his mouth and eyes as well, and through mine" (125). Gary McIlroy observes that this blood, "a symbol of the sanctity of life, is a common bond between Dillard and the fish, between animal and human life in general, and between Dillard and other people" (115).

Secondary source's analysis of Dillard

For Dillard, the terror and unpredictability of death unify all life. The most sinister image in Pilgrim--one that haunts Dillard--is that of the frog and the water bug. Dillard reports walking along an embankment scaring frogs into the water when one frog refused to budge. As Dillard leaned over to investigate, the frog "slowly crumpled and began to sag. The spirit vanished from his eyes as if snuffed. His skin emptied and dropped; his very skull seemed to collapse and settle like a kicked tent" (6). The frog was the victim of a water bug that injects poisons to "dissolve the victim's muscles and bones and organs" (6). Such events lead Dillard to wonder about a creator who would make all life "power and beauty, grace tangled in a rapture with violence" (8). Human beings no less than frogs and water bugs are implicated in this tangle.

Combination of quotation and Haley's own analysis (next four paragraphs): interprets and synthesizes Dillard's ideas

Mixture of summary and quotation: provides context and keeps quotations trim

Dillard is equally as disturbed by birth as by death. In a chapter of Pilgrim called "Fecundity," she focuses on the undeniable reproductive urge of entire species. Her attitude is far from sentimental:

Discussion of physical identity of all creatures: death and birth

> I don't know what it is about fecundity that so appalls. I suppose it is the teeming evidence that birth and growth, which we value,

Comment on quotation: advises reader what to look for

Haley 4

> are ubiquitous and blind, that life itself is so astonishingly cheap, that nature is as careless as it is bountiful, and that with extravagance goes a crushing waste that will one day include our own cheap lives. (160)

Long quotations, set off from the text: convey Dillard's voice as well as her ideas

The cheapness and brutality of life are problems Dillard wrestles with, wondering which is "amiss": the world, a "monster," or human beings, with their "excessive emotions" (177-78). No matter how hard she tries to leave human society, Dillard has no choice but to "bring human values to the creek" (179). The violent, seemingly pointless birth and death of all life are, spiritually,

Discussion of spiritual identity of all creatures

> two branches of the same creek, the creek that waters the world. . . . We could have planned things more mercifully, perhaps, but our plan would never get off the drawing board until we agreed to the very compromising terms that are the only ones that being offers. (180)

For Dillard, accepting the monstrousness as well as the beauty of "being" is the price all living things pay for freedom.

Haley's interpretation of Dillard's ideas

In "The Waters of Separation," the final chapter of Pilgrim, Dillard writes about a winged maple key, or seed. At this point in the book, the critic Sandra Humble Johnson notes, Dillard "has been humbled and emptied; she can no longer apply effort to her search for meaning in a parasitic world" (4). It is the winter solstice--the shortest day of the year. And then Dillard spies the maple key descending to earth and germination. "It rose, just before it would have touched a thistle, and

Resolution of Dillard's concerns

Haley 5

hovered pirouetting in one spot, then twirled on and finally came to rest" (267). The key moved, says Dillard, "like a creature muscled and vigorous, or a creature spread thin to that other wind, the wind of the spirit . . . a generous, unending breath" (268). Dillard vows to see the maple key in all of the earth and in herself. "If I am a maple key falling, at least I can twirl" (268).

According to the critic John Becker, "Annie Dillard does not walk out on ordinary life in order to bear witness against it"; instead, she uses the distance from other people "to make meaning out of the grotesque disjointedness of man and nature" (408). Gary McIlroy says, nonetheless, that Dillard "does not succeed in encompassing within her vision any but the most fragmentary consequences for society at large" (116). Possibly both are correct. In Pilgrim at Tinker Creek, Annie Dillard suggests a vision of identity among all living things that could inform modern humanity's efforts to thrive in harmony with its environment, but she does not make the leap to practicalities. Life, she says, "is a faint tracing on the surface of a mystery. . . . We must somehow take a wider view, look at the whole landscape, really see it, and describe what's going on here" (9). The description, and acting on it, may take generations. As we proceed, however, we may be guided by Dillard's efforts to mend the disjointedness, to see that human beings and maple keys alike twirl equally.

Conclusion: ties together divergent critical views, environmental theme, and Dillard's work

Haley 6

Works Cited

Becker, John E. "Science and the Sacred: From Walden to Tinker Creek." Thought: A Review of Culture and Idea 62 (1987): 400-13.

Dillard, Annie. Pilgrim at Tinker Creek. New York: Harper, 1974.

Johnson, Sandra Humble. The Space Between: Literary Epiphany in the Work of Annie Dillard. Kent: Kent State UP, 1992.

McIlroy, Gary. "Pilgrim at Tinker Creek and the Social Legacy of Walden." South Atlantic Quarterly 85.2 (1986): 111-16.

Welty, Eudora. Rev. of Pilgrim at Tinker Creek, by Annie Dillard. New York Times Book Review 24 Mar. 1974: 36-37.

By Sylvan Barnet

Chapter 39 Reading and Writing About Literature

HIGHLIGHTS

In classes in which literature is used, there's a temptation to spend more time talking about literature and less time writing about it, which can be counterproductive to the goals of a writing class. To keep students developing positively, this chapter stresses using the processes of critical reading, thinking, and writing skills as a way of analyzing imaginative writing. It also focuses on helping students to transfer the skills they have worked on throughout their writing course to other courses and purposes. The chapter covers writing about a variety of literary genres, offering students a wide range of possibilities for using their writing and reading skills to explore these texts.

RESOURCES AND IDEAS

Gould, Christopher. "Literature in the Basic Writing Course: A Bibliographic Survey." *College English* 49 (1987): 558–74. Gould provides a survey of "easily accessible materials that relate to the use of literature" in introductory courses.

Lindemann, Erika. "Freshman Composition: No Place for Literature." *College English* 55 (1993): 311–16. Lindemann warns that using literature in composition classes may lead to a deemphasis on student writing; she includes useful advice for class design.

Lynn, Steven. *Texts and Contexts: Writing About Literature with Critical Theory.* New York: HarperCollins, 1994. Lynn introduces a number of critical approaches from New Criticism through deconstruction to feminist studies, and he brings all methods to bear on a selected group of texts to demonstrate how they might "open up" texts for students.

Reilly, Jill M., et al. "The Effects of Prewriting on Literary Interpretation." ERIC, 1986. ED 276 058. Reilly shows how focused prewriting exercises can lead students to write more effectively about literature.

Tate, Gary. "A Place for Literature in Freshman Composition." *College English* 55 (1993): 317–21. Tate argues that using literature makes student writers more aware of the resources implicit in language.

Why read literature? Let's approach this question indirectly by asking why people *write* literature. A thousand years ago a Japanese writer, Lady Murasaki, offered an answer. Here is one of her characters talking about what motivates a writer:

> Again and again something in one's own life or in the life around one will seem so important that one cannot bear to let it pass into oblivion. There must never come a time, the writer feels, when people do not know about this.

When we read certain works—Murasaki's *The Tale of Genji* is one of them—we share this feeling; we are caught up in the writer's world, whether it is the Denmark of Shakespeare's *Hamlet* or the America of Toni Morrison's *Beloved.* In short, we read literature because it gives us an experience that seems important to us, usually an experience that is both new and familiar. A common way of putting this is to say that reading broadens us and helps us understand our own experience. A less lofty way of putting it is to say that reading gives us pleasure.

39a Reading and responding to literature

When we read nonliterary writings, it may be enough to get the gist of the argument; in fact, we may have to peer through a good deal of wordiness to find the heart of the matter—say, three claims on behalf of capital punishment. But when we read a story, a poem, or a play, we must pay extremely close attention to what might be called the feel of the words. For instance, the word *woods* in Robert Frost's "Stopping by Woods on a Snowy Evening" has a rural, folksy quality that *forest* doesn't have, and many such small distinctions contribute to the poem's effect.

Literary authors are concerned with presenting human experience concretely, with *showing* rather than *telling*. Consider the following proverb and an unmemorable paraphrase of it:

> A rolling stone gathers no moss.
>
> If a rock is always moving around, vegetation won't have a chance to grow on it.

The familiar original offers a small but complete world: hard (stone) and soft (moss), inorganic and organic, at rest and in motion. The original is also shapely: each noun (*stone, moss*) has one syllable, and each word of motion (*rolling, gathers*) has two syllables, with the accent on the first of the two. Such relationships unify the proverb into a whole that pleases us and stays in our minds.

 Reading a work of literature

Reading literature critically involves interacting with a text. The techniques complement those for critically reading any text, so if you haven't read this book's Introduction on such reading, you should do so. Responding critically is a matter not of making negative judgments but of analyzing the parts, interpreting their meanings, seeing how the parts relate, and evaluating significance or quality.

You can preview a literary text somewhat as you can preview any other text (p. 5). You may gauge the length of the text to determine if you can read it in one sitting, and you may read a biographical note to learn about the author. In a literary text, however, you won't find aids such as section headings or summaries that can make previewing other texts especially informative. You have to dive into the words themselves.

Do write while reading (pp. 4–5, 6–8). If you own the book you are reading, don't hesitate to underline or highlight passages that especially interest you for one reason or another. Don't hesitate to annotate the margins, indicating your pleasures, displeasures, and uncertainties with remarks such as *Nice detail* or *Do we need this long description?* or *Not believable.* If you don't own the book, make these notes on separate sheets or on your computer.

An effective way to interact with a text is to keep a **reading journal.** A journal is not a diary in which you record your doings but a place to develop and store your reflections on what you read, such as an answer to a question you may have posed in the margin of the text or a response to something said in class. You may, for instance, want to reflect on why your opinion is so different from that of another

TEACHING TIP

Students tend to have tunnel vision about literary interpretation, believing there's only one "right way" to read a work. In guiding their reading and response, encourage them to see the multiple possibilities implicit in literary works. You might ask them to compose point-counterpoint readings of texts or to use a text like Steven Lynn's *Texts and Contexts* (reference above) to construct a spectrum of responses to the literature they are reading. A consistent use of group workshops in which students discuss their varying responses to a literary text can also help students to recognize the multiplicity of possible responses.

A WRITER'S PERSPECTIVE

A poem is a perhaps.

—Ivor Williams

You can tear a poem apart to see what makes it technically tick, . . . but you come back to the mystery of having been moved by words.

—Dylan Thomas

LOOKING BACK

Remind students of the reasons they have been keeping journals throughout your course. You may want to encourage them to review 1e-1 as they begin keeping a reading journal.

student. You may even make an entry in the form of a letter to the author or from one character to another. You can keep a reading journal in a notebook or on your computer. Some readers prefer a two-column format like that illustrated on pages 7–8, with summaries, paraphrases, and quotations from the text on the left and with their own responses to these passages on the right. Or you may prefer a less structured format like that illustrated on pages 672–73.

Here is a very short story by Kate Chopin (1851–1904). (The last name is pronounced in the French way, something like "show pan.") Following the story are a student's annotations and journal entry on the story.

Kate Chopin

The Story of an Hour

Knowing that Mrs. Mallard was afflicted with a heart trouble, great care was taken to break to her as gently as possible the news of her husband's death.

It was her sister Josephine who told her, in broken sentences, veiled hints that revealed in half concealing. Her husband's friend Richards was there, too, near her. It was he who had been in the newspaper office when intelligence of the railroad disaster was received, with Brently Mallard's name leading the list of "killed." He had only taken the time to assure himself of its truth by a second telegram, and had hastened to forestall any less careful, less tender friend in bearing the sad message.

She did not hear the story as many women have heard the same, with a paralyzed inability to accept its significance. She wept at once with sudden, wild abandonment, in her sister's arms. When the storm of grief had spent itself she went away to her room alone. She would have no one follow her.

There stood, facing the open window, a comfortable, roomy armchair. Into this she sank, pressed down by a physical exhaustion that haunted her body and seemed to reach into her soul.

She could see in the open square before her house the tops of trees that were all aquiver with the new spring life. The delicious breath of rain was in the air. In the street below a peddler was crying his wares. The notes of a distant song which some one was singing reached her faintly, and countless sparrows were twittering in the eaves.

There were patches of blue sky showing here and there through the clouds that had met and piled one above the other in the west facing her window.

She sat with her head thrown back upon the cushion of the chair quite motionless, except when a sob came up into her throat and shook her, as a child who has cried itself to sleep continues to sob in its dreams.

She was young, with a fair, calm face, whose lines bespoke repression and even a certain strength. But now there was a dull stare in her eyes, whose gaze was fixed away off yonder on one of those patches of blue sky. It was not a glance of reflection, but rather indicated a suspension of intelligent thought.

There was something coming to her and she was waiting for it, fearfully. What was it? She did not know; it was too subtle and elusive to name. But she felt it creeping out of the sky, reaching toward her through the sounds, the scents, the color that filled the air.

Now her bosom rose and fell tumultuously. She was beginning to recognize this thing that was approaching to possess her, and she was striving to beat it back with her will—as powerless as her two white slender hands would have been.

When she abandoned herself a little whispered word escaped her slightly parted lips. She said it over and over under her breath: "Free, free, free!" The vacant stare and the look of terror that had followed it went from her eyes. They stayed keen and bright. Her pulses beat fast, and the coursing blood warmed and relaxed every inch of her body.

She did not stop to ask if it were not a monstrous joy that held her. A clear and exalted perception enabled her to dismiss the suggestion as trivial.

She knew that she would weep again when she saw the kind, tender hands folded in death; the face that had never looked save with love upon her, fixed and gray and dead. But she saw beyond that bitter moment a long procession of years to come that would belong to her absolutely. And she opened and spread her arms out to them in welcome.

There would be no one to live for her during those coming years; she would live for herself. There would be no powerful will bending her in the blind persistence with which men and women believe they have a right to impose a private will upon a fellow creature. A kind intention or a cruel intention made the act seem no less a crime as she looked upon it in that brief moment of illumination.

And yet she had loved him—sometimes. Often she had not. What did it matter! What could love, the unsolved mystery, count for in face of this possession of self-assertion which she suddenly recognized as the strongest impulse of her being.

"Free! Body and soul free!" she kept whispering.

Josephine was kneeling before the closed door with her lips to the keyhole, imploring for admission. "Louise, open the door! I beg; open the door—you will make yourself ill. What are you doing, Louise? For heaven's sake open the door."

"Go away. I am not making myself ill." No; she was drinking in the very elixir of life through that open window.

Her fancy was running riot along those days ahead of her. Spring days, and summer days, and all sorts of days that would be her own. She breathed a quick prayer that life might be long. It was only yesterday she had thought with a shudder that life might be long.

She arose at length and opened the door to her sister's importunities. There was a feverish triumph in her eyes, and she carried herself unwittingly like a goddess of Victory. She clasped her sister's waist and together they descended the stairs. Richards stood waiting for them at the bottom.

Some one was opening the front door with a latchkey. It was Brently Mallard who entered, a little travel-stained, composedly carrying his grip-sack and umbrella. He had been far from the scene of accident, and did not even know there had been one. He stood amazed at Josephine's piercing cry; at Richards' quick motion to screen him from the view of his wife.

But Richards was too late.

When the doctors came they said she had died of heart disease—of joy that kills.

A student, Janet Vong, made the following annotations on the first five paragraphs of Chopin's story.

> Knowing that Mrs. Mallard was afflicted with a heart trouble, great care was taken to break to her as gently as possible the news of her husband's death. *["heart disease" at end of story]*
>
> It was her sister Josephine who told her, in broken sentences, veiled hints that revealed in half concealing. Her husband's friend Richards was there, too, near her. It was he who had been in the newspaper office when intelligence of the railroad disaster was received, with Brently Mallard's name leading the list of "killed." He had only taken the time to assure himself of its truth by a second telegram, and had hastened to forestall any less careful, less tender friend in bearing the sad message. *[Too hasty, it turns out]*
>
> *[Would men have heard differently? Is au. sexist?]* She did not hear the story as many women have heard the same, with a paralyzed inability to accept its significance. She wept at once with sudden, wild abandonment, in her sister's arms. When the storm of grief had spent itself she went away to her room alone. She would have no one follow her. *[old-fashioned style]*
>
> There stood, facing the open window, a comfortable, roomy armchair. Into this she sank, pressed down by a physical exhaustion that haunted her body and seemed to reach into her soul.
>
> *[Notices spring: odd in a story of death]* She could see in the open square before her house the tops of trees that were all aquiver with the new spring life. The delicious breath of rain was in the air. In the street below a peddler was crying his wares. The notes of a distant song which some one was singing reached her faintly, and countless sparrows were twittering in the eaves.

Writing in her journal, Vong posed questions about the story—critical points, curiosities about characters, possible implications:

> Title nothing special. What might be a better title?
>
> Could a woman who loved her husband be so heartless? *Is* she heartless? *Did* she love him?

What are (were) Louise's feelings about her husband?
Did she want too much? *What* did she want?
Could this story happen today? Feminist interpretation?
Sister (Josephine)—a busybody?
Tricky ending—but maybe it could be true.
"And yet she had loved him—sometimes. Often she had not." Why does one love someone "sometimes"?
Irony: plot has reversal. Are characters ironic too?

Vong's journal entry illustrates brainstorming—the discovery technique of listing ideas (or questions) however they occur, without editing (see p. 41). Another productive journal technique is focused freewriting—concentrating on a single issue (such as one of Vong's questions) and writing nonstop for a set amount of time, again without editing (p. 40).

2 Analyzing a work of literature

Like any discipline, the study of literature involves particular frameworks of analysis—particular ways of seeing literary works that help determine what parts the critical reader identifies and how he or she interprets them (see pp. 12–13). Some of the critical frameworks you may encounter in studying literature are these:

- **Historical criticism** focuses on the context in which a literary work was created and how that context affected the work. The critic may examine the author's social, political, and intellectual surroundings or may concentrate on the author's own biography: his or her life experiences or psychological makeup.
- **Feminist criticism** focuses on the male domination of the literary canon—the body of work represented in the standard anthologies, discussed in the schools, and examined in the scholarly journals. Feminist critics are especially concerned with the writings of women and with the responses of women to the depiction of both sexes in literature.
- **Reader-response criticism** focuses on the reactions of an audience to a work of literature, asking why readers respond as they do to a text. In this view the meaning of the text lies not just on the page but in the interaction between the work and its reader.
- **Deconstructive criticism** regards a work of literature skeptically, resisting the obvious meanings and focusing on the ambiguities in the work, especially the internal contradictions. Perceiving that the relationship of words and their meanings is both arbitrary and forever changing—even within the same work—deconstructive critics emphasize multiple meanings and what a text does not say.

RESOURCES AND IDEAS

Biddle, Arthur W., and Toby Fulwiler, eds. *Reading, Writing, and the Study of Literature.* New York: McGraw, 1989. This collection of essays details many ways of introducing students to various methods of literary interpretation; the authors provide extensive bibliographies.

Lentricchia, Frank, and Thomas McLaughlin. *Critical Terms for Literary Study.* Chicago: U of Chicago P, 1989. The authors have compiled twenty-two cogent essays defining key terms in light of contemporary theory.

Rockas, Leo. *Ways In: Analyzing and Responding to Literature.* Upper Montclair: Boynton/Cook, 1984. Rockas offers students a number of ways of beginning the work of literary analysis, providing numerous examples and exercises.

- **Formalist criticism** (also called **New Criticism**) focuses primarily on a literary work as a constructed text, as an independent unity understood in itself rather than as an artifact of a particular context or reader response. Beginning with a personal response, the formalist critic tries to account for the response by examining the form of the work (hence *formalist*) and the relations among its elements.

This chapter emphasizes formalist criticism because it engages you immediately in the work of literature itself, without requiring extensive historical or cultural background, and because it introduces the conventional elements of literature that all critical approaches discuss, even though they view the elements differently. The box on the next two pages lists these elements—plot, characters, setting, and so on—and offers questions about each one that can help you think constructively and imaginatively about what you read.

One significant attribute of a literary work is its *meaning,* or what we can interpret to be its meaning. Readers may well disagree over the persuasiveness of someone's argument, but they will rarely disagree over its meaning. With literature, however, disagreements over meaning occur all the time because (as we have seen) literature *shows* rather than *tells:* it gives us concrete images of imagined human experiences, but it usually does not say how we ought to understand the images.

Further, readers bring to their reading not only different critical views, as noted above, but also different personal experiences. To take an extreme case, a woman who has recently lost her husband may interpret "The Story of an Hour" differently from most other readers. Or a story that bores a reader at age fifteen may deeply move her at twenty-five. The words on the page remain the same, but their meaning changes.

In writing about literature, then, we can offer only our *interpretation* of meaning rather than *the* meaning. Still, most people agree that there are limits to interpretation: it must be supported by evidence that a reasonable reader finds at least plausible if not totally convincing. For instance, the student who says that in "The Story of an Hour" Mrs. Mallard does not die but merely falls into a deathlike trance goes beyond the permissible limits because the story offers no evidence for such an interpretation.

TEACHING TIP

Most students will need to be convinced that critical thinking, reading, and writing skills (see Introduction) can be transferred to literature. Students sometimes acquire the attitude that literature is somehow "untouchable" from experiences that treated literature as "special," different from other works they read. Work through Janet Vong's critical strategies closely with your students to help them understand how the skills they've developed will enable them to read and write about literature.

39b Drafting and revising a literary analysis

The process for writing a literary analysis is similar to that for any other kind of essay: once you've done the reading and thought about it, you need to focus your ideas, gather evidence, draft, and revise.

TRANSPARENCY MASTER 39.1

Questions for a literary analysis

See later boxes for specific questions on fiction (p. 682), poetry (p. 684), and drama (p. 687).

- **Plot:** the relationships and patterns of events. (Even a poem has a plot—for instance, a change in mood from bitterness to resignation.)

  What actions happen?
  What conflicts occur?
  How do the events connect to each other and to the whole?

- **Characters:** the people the author creates (including the narrator of a story or the speaker of a poem).

  Who are the principal people in the work?
  How do they interact?
  What do their actions, words, and thoughts reveal about their personalities and the personalities of others?
  Do the characters stay the same, or do they change? Why?

- **Point of view:** the perspective or attitude of the speaker in a poem or the voice who tells a story. The point of view may be **first person** (a participant, using *I*) or **third person** (an outsider, using *he, she, it, they*). A first-person narrator may be a major or a minor character in the narrative, and may be **reliable** or **unreliable** (unable to report events wholly or accurately). A third-person narrator may be **omniscient** (knows what goes on in all characters' minds), **limited** (knows what goes on in the mind of only one or two characters), or **objective** (knows only what is external to the characters).

  Who is the narrator (or the speaker of a poem)?
  How does the narrator's point of view affect the narrative?

- **Tone:** the narrator's or speaker's attitude, perceived through the words (for instance, joyful, bitter, or confident).

  What tone (or tones) do you hear? If there is a change, how do you account for it?
  Is there an ironic contrast between the narrator's tone (for instance, confidence) and what you take to be the author's attitude (for instance, pity for human overconfidence)?

- **Imagery:** word pictures or visual details involving the senses (sight, sound, touch, smell, taste).

  What images does the writer use? What senses do they draw on?
  What patterns are evident in the images (for instance, religious or commercial images)?
  What is the significance of the imagery?

(continued)

COLLABORATIVE LEARNING

Have students work in small groups to analyze a key passage from Kate Chopin's "The Story of an Hour." Ask each group to consider the appropriate questions provided by the handbook: Does the passage reveal a significant move in the plot? Does it explore a key development for one of the characters? What evidence of point of view and tone are available in the passage? Does it contain imagery or symbolism? Then have each group give their analysis of the passage; where student readings differ markedly, encourage those groups to find additional evidence for their readings.

COLLABORATIVE LEARNING

TEACHING TIP

Divide the class into several groups, and have each group brainstorm about the many themes that occur in a particular work. Choose Kate Chopin's "The Story of an Hour" or another short work from an anthology. Have each group explain its three favorite themes to the rest of the class, supplying evidence for each theme with one or two explicated passages from the piece.

Questions for a literary analysis *(continued)*

- **Symbolism:** concrete things standing for larger and more abstract ideas (for instance, the American flag may symbolize freedom, a tweeting bird may symbolize happiness, or a dead flower may symbolize mortality).

  What symbols does the author use? What do they seem to signify?
  How does the symbolism relate to the other elements of the work, such as character or theme?

- **Setting:** the place where the action happens.

  What does the locale contribute to the work?
  Are scene shifts significant?

- **Form:** the shape or structure of the work.

  What *is* the form? (For example, a story might divide sharply in the middle, moving from happiness to sorrow.)
  What parts of the work does the form emphasize, and why?

- **Theme:** the central idea, a conception of human experience suggested by the work as a whole. Theme is neither plot (what happens) nor subject (such as mourning or marriage). Rather it is what the author says with that plot about that subject.

  Can you state the theme in a sentence? For instance, you might state the following about Kate Chopin's "The Story of an Hour": *Happiness depends partly on freedom.*
  Do certain words, passages of dialogue or description, or situations seem to represent the theme most clearly?
  How do the work's elements combine to develop the theme?

- **Appeal:** the degree to which the story pleases you.

  What do you especially like or dislike about the work?
  Do you think your responses are unique or common to most readers? Why?

1 Conceiving a thesis

After reading, rereading, and making notes, you probably will be able to formulate a tentative thesis sentence—a statement of your main point, your argument. (For more on thesis sentences, see pp. 47–51.) Clear the air by glancing over your notes and by jotting down a few especially promising ideas—brief statements of what you think your key points may be and their main support. The new notes will help you see the theme in your ideas.

At first Janet Vong considered the idea that the character of

Mrs. Mallard was unrealistic and thus unconvincing. But the more Vong examined the story, the more she believed that several reversals, or ironies, helped make Mrs. Mallard's own reversal from grief to joy believable. Vong explored this idea in her journal:

> title? "Ironies in an Hour" (?) "An Hour of Irony" (?) "Kate Chopin's Irony" (?)
> thesis: irony at end is prepared for
> chief irony: Mrs. M. dies just as she is beginning to enjoy life
> smaller ironies:
> 1. "sad message" brings her joy
> 2. Richards is "too late" at end
> 3. Richards is too early at start
> 4. "joy that kills"
> 5. death brings joy and life

From these notes Vong developed her thesis sentence:

> The irony of the ending is believable partly because it is consistent with earlier ironies in the story.

This thesis sentence states a specific idea that can be developed and convincingly argued with evidence from Chopin's story. A good thesis sentence will neither state a fact (*Mrs. Mallard dies soon after hearing that her husband has died*) nor overgeneralize (*The story is an insult to women*).

2 Gathering evidence

The evidence for a literary analysis always comes from at least one primary source (the work or works being discussed) and may come from secondary sources (critical and historical accounts about the primary sources). (See pp. 527–28 for more on primary and secondary sources.) For example, if you were writing about Chopin's "The Story of an Hour," the primary material would be the story itself, and the secondary material (if you used it) would be biographies and critical studies of Chopin.

The bulk of your evidence in writing about literature will usually be quotations from the work, although you will occasionally summarize or paraphrase as well (see pp. 572–75). When using quotations, keep in mind the criteria in the box on the next page.

Your instructor will probably tell you if you are expected to consult secondary sources for an assignment. (If so, see pp. 532 and 539 for lists of reference sources in literature.) Secondary sources can help you understand a writer's work, but your primary concern should always be the work itself, not what critics A, B, and C say about it. In general, then, quote or summarize secondary material sparingly. And always cite your sources. (See p. 599.)

COLLABORATIVE LEARNING

Ask each student to develop a thesis about Kate Chopin's "The Story of an Hour" or another short work from an anthology, and to compile evidence for that thesis. Then have students work in small groups to debate their various theses and the validity of the evidence.

TEACHING TIP

Students are often confused about how to incorporate source material into a literary analysis. Duplicate a short passage from a literary analysis, but remove the documentation. Have students decide where documentation is needed. You might also duplicate or contrive a passage with awkwardly long quotations and ask the class how to trim or paraphrase them to make the passage more effective.

Guidelines for using quotations in literary analysis

- Use quotations to support your assertions, not to pad the paper. Quote at length only when necessary to your argument.
- When you use a quotation, specify how it relates to your idea. Introduce the quotation—for example, *At the outset Chopin conveys the sort of person Richards is: "..."* Sometimes, comment after the quotation. (See pp. 591–95 for more on integrating quotations into your writing.)
- Reproduce spelling, punctuation, capitalization, and all other features exactly as they appear in the source. (See p. 423 for the use of brackets when you need to add something to a quotation, and see p. 424 for the use of an ellipsis mark when you need to omit something from a quotation.)
- Document your sources. (See p. 599.)

3 Writing a draft

Drafting your essay is your opportunity to develop your thesis or to discover it if you haven't already. (See pp. 63–65 for tips on drafting.) The draft below was actually Janet Vong's second: she deleted some digressions from her first draft and added more evidence for her points. The numbers in parentheses refer to the pages from which the quotations were drawn. Ask your instructor whether you should always give such citations, especially for a short poem or story like Chopin's. (See p. 599 for how to document a paper.)

Ironies in an Hour

After we know how the story turns out, if we reread it we find irony at the very start, as is true of many other stories. Mrs. Mallard's friends assume, mistakenly, that Mrs. Mallard was deeply in love with her husband, Brently Mallard. They take great care to tell her gently of his death. The friends mean well, and in fact they do well. They bring her an hour of life, an hour of freedom. They think their news is sad. Mrs. Mallard at first expresses grief when she hears the news, but soon she finds joy in it. So Richards's "sad message" (12), though sad in Richards's eyes, is in fact a happy message.

Among the ironic details is the statement that when Mallard entered the house, Richards tried to conceal him from Mrs. Mallard, but "Richards was too late" (13). This is ironic because earlier Richards "hastened" (12) to bring his sad message; if he had at the start been "too late" (13), Brently Mallard would have arrived at home first, and

Mrs. Mallard's life would not have ended an hour later but would simply have gone on as it had been. Yet another irony at the end of the story is the diagnosis of the doctors. The doctors say she died of "heart disease--of joy that kills" (13). In one sense the doctors are right: Mrs. Mallard has experienced a great joy. But of course the doctors totally misunderstand the joy that kills her.

The central irony resides not in the well-intentioned but ironic actions of Richards, or in the unconsciously ironic words of the doctors, but in her own life. In a way she has been dead. She "sometimes" (13) loved her husband, but in a way she has been dead. Now, his apparent death brings her new life. This new life comes to her at the season of the year when "the tops of trees . . . were all aquiver with the new spring life" (12). But, ironically, her new life will last only an hour. She looks forward to "summer days" (13), but she will not see even the end of this spring day. Her years of marriage were ironic. They brought her a sort of living death instead of joy. Her new life is ironic too. It grows out of her moment of grief for her supposedly dead husband, and her vision of a new life is cut short.

4 Revising and editing

As in other writing, use at least two drafts to revise and edit, so that you can attend separately to the big structural issues and the smaller surface problems. See pages 69 and 74–75, respectively, for general revision and editing checklists.

For a literary analysis, revise your paper against this checklist:

TRANSPARENCY MASTER 39.2

Checklist for revising a literary analysis

- Does the title of the essay do more than merely give the title of the work discussed? Your title should give the reader an idea of your topic.
- Does the introductory paragraph avoid openings such as "In this story . . ."? Name the author and the title so that the reader knows exactly what work you are discussing. Develop your thesis a bit so that readers know where they will be going.
- Is the organization effective? The essay should not dwindle or become anticlimactic; rather, it should build up.
- Do quotations provide evidence and let the reader hear the author's voice?

(continued)

Checklist for revising a literary analysis *(continued)*

- Is the essay chiefly devoted to analysis, not to summary? Do not summarize the plot in great detail. A couple of sentences may be helpful if your readers are not familiar with the work, but a summary is not an essay.
- Have you used the present tense of verbs to describe both the author's work and the action in the work (for example, *Chopin shows* or *Mrs. Mallard dies*)?
- If you have used the first-person *I* (for instance, *I find the ending highly plausible*), have you avoided using it so often that you sound egotistical?
- Is your evaluation of the work evident? It may be understood (as in Janet Vong's essay on "The Story of an Hour"), or it may be explicit. In either case, give the reasons for judging the work to be effective or not, worth reading or not. Remember that it is not enough to express your likes or dislikes; readers will be interested in an evaluation only if you support it with specific evidence from the work.
- Did you document your sources? (See p. 599.)

Janet Vong's final draft follows. The main changes are explained below and keyed by number to the draft.

1. Vong added a new introduction to set up the paper. It names the story's author and title, introduces the story's overall irony, very briefly summarizes the story, and states Vong's thesis.
2. At many points, Vong added details and quotations to clarify the ironies in the story by emphasizing the reversals.
3. Vong added a new page for her work cited. (See p. 608 for the format of such a page.)

An essay on fiction (no secondary sources)

Janet Vong

Mr. Romano

English 102

February 20, 1997

Ironies of Life in Kate Chopin's

"The Story of an Hour"

Kate Chopin's "The Story of an Hour"--which takes only a few minutes to read--has an ironic ending: Mrs. Mallard dies just when she is beginning to live. On first reading, the ending seems almost too

ironic for belief. On rereading the story, however, one sees that the
ending is believable partly because it is consistent with other ironies in
the story.

After we know how the story turns out, if we reread it we find
irony at the very start. Because Mrs. Mallard's friends and her sister assume, mistakenly, that she was deeply in love with her husband, Brently
Mallard, they take great care to tell her gently of his death. They mean
well, and in fact they do well, bringing her an hour of life, an hour of
joyous freedom, but it is ironic that they think their news is sad. True, 2
Mrs. Mallard at first expresses grief when she hears the news, but
soon (unknown to her friends) she finds joy. So Richards's "sad message" (12), though sad in Richards's eyes, is in fact a happy message.

Among the small but significant ironic details is the statement
near the end of the story that when Mallard entered the house,
Richards tried to conceal him from Mrs. Mallard, but "Richards was
too late" (13). This is ironic because almost at the start of the story, 2
in the second paragraph, Richards "hastened" (12) to bring his sad
message; if he had at the start been "too late" (13), Brently Mallard
would have arrived at home first, and Mrs. Mallard's life would not
have ended an hour later but would simply have gone on as it had
been. Yet another irony at the end of the story is the diagnosis of the
doctors. They say she died of "heart disease--of joy that kills" (13). In
one sense they are right: Mrs. Mallard has for the last hour experienced a great joy. But of course the doctors totally misunderstand the
joy that kills her. It is not joy at seeing her husband alive, but her re- 2
alization that the great joy she experienced during the last hour is
over.

All of these ironic details add richness to the story, but the central
irony resides not in the well-intentioned but ironic actions of Richards,
or in the unconsciously ironic words of the doctors, but in Mrs. Mallard's own life. She "sometimes" (13) loved her husband, but in a way she
has been dead, a body subjected to her husband's will. Now, his apparent 2
death brings her new life. Appropriately, this new life comes to her at
the season of the year when "the tops of trees . . . were all aquiver with
the new spring life" (12). But, ironically, her new life will last only an
hour. She is "Free, free, free" (12-13)--but only until her husband walks 2

through the doorway. She looks forward to "summer days" (13), but she will not see even the end of this spring day. If her years of marriage were ironic, bringing her a sort of living death instead of joy, her new life is ironic too, not only because it grows out of her moment of grief for her supposedly dead husband, but also because her vision of "a long pro- 2
cession of years" (13) is cut short within an hour on a spring day.

[New page.]

Work Cited 3

Chopin, Kate. "The Story of an Hour." Literature for Composition. Ed. Sylvan Barnet et al. 4th ed. New York: Harper, 1996. 12-13.

5 Preparing the final draft

Preparing the final draft involves several steps:

- Document your sources. Unless your instructor specifies otherwise, use the style of the Modern Language Association (MLA), detailed in Chapter 37. In this style, parenthetical citations in the text of the paper refer to a list of works cited at the end. Sample papers illustrating this style appear in Chapter 38 as well as in this chapter.
- Use MLA format for headings, margins, and other elements. See pages 759–65 for detailed instructions. See pages 662–67 for a full paper in this format. For the special formats of poetry and long prose quotations, see pages 409–10.
- Proofread. See page 77 for tips.

RESOURCES AND IDEAS

Rockas, Leo. *Ways In: Analyzing and Responding to Literature.* Upper Montclair: Boynton/Cook, 1984. Chapter 4 offers examples of and exercises for writing about fiction.

TRANSPARENCY MASTER 39.3

39c Writing about fiction

The "Questions for a literary analysis" on pages 675–76 will help you think about any work of literature, including a story or novel, and find a topic to write on. The box below provides additional questions for thinking about fiction. Not every question is relevant to every story. For an example of writing about fiction, see Janet Vong's essay on Kate Chopin's "The Story of an Hour," pages 680–82.

Questions for analyzing fiction

- What happens in the story? Summarize the plot (the gist of the happenings). Think about what your summary *leaves out.*
- Is the story told in chronological order, or are there flashbacks or

flashforwards? On rereading, what foreshadowing (hints of what is to come) do you detect?

- What conflicts does the work include?
- How does the writer reveal character—for instance, by explicit comment or by letting us see the character in action? With which character(s) do you sympathize? Are the characters plausible? What motivates them? What do minor characters contribute to the work?
- Who tells the story? Is the narrator a character, or does the narrator stand entirely outside the characters' world? What does the narrator's point of view contribute to the story's theme? (On narrative points of view, see p. 675.)
- What is the setting, the time and place of the action? What does it contribute to the work?
- Do certain characters or settings or actions seem to you to stand for something in addition to themselves—that is, are they symbolic?
- What is the theme—that is, what does the work add up to? Does the theme reinforce values that you hold, or does it challenge them?
- Is the title informative? Did its meaning change for you after you read the work?

39d Writing about poetry

Two types of essays on poetry are especially common. One is an analysis of some aspect of the poem in relation to the whole—for instance, the changes in the speaker's tone or the functions of meter and rhyme. The second is an **explication,** a line-by-line (sometimes almost word-by-word) reading that seeks to make explicit everything that is implicit in the poem. Thus an explication of the first line of Robert Frost's "Stopping by Woods on a Snowy Evening" (the line goes "Whose woods these are I think I know") might call attention to the tentativeness of the line ("I think I know") and to the fact that the words are not in the normal order ("I think I know whose woods these are"). These features might support the explanation that the poet is introducing—very quietly—a note of the *un*usual, in preparation for the experience that follows. Although one might conceivably explicate a long poem, the method is so detailed that in practice writers usually confine it to short poems or to short passages from long poems.

The "Questions for a literary analysis" on pages 675–76 will help you think about any work of literature, including a poem, and find a topic to write on. The box on the next page provides additional questions for thinking about poetry.

COLLABORATIVE LEARNING

TEACHING TIP

Students can learn a great deal about the choices a writer makes in creating a piece of fiction by writing fiction of their own. Ask each student to create a one-paragraph opening for a short story, then have students work in small groups to analyze their fictional paragraphs. What does that opening paragraph reveal about the kind of story being told—will it be comic, tragic, realistic, supernatural? What expectations does that opening set up about the characters and events that will follow? What questions does it raise?

As a follow-up to this exercise, ask each group to turn back to the Kate Chopin story and analyze its one-sentence opening with some of the same questions in mind. Having read the story, students may be surprised to find out how much they can deduce from that seemingly simple statement.

COMPUTER EXERCISE

Post the opening paragraph of a published short story on the network and ask students to create their own continuations of the story, keeping in mind the expectations about plot, character, setting, and tone that have been set up by that opening paragraph. Have students "publish" the resulting stories on the network, and lead a discussion about the different choices that various students made in their continuations, the elements in the original paragraph that they picked up on or discarded, and the extent to which the tone of the original was maintained or parodied. Encourage students to talk about the elements that they noticed in the original paragraph as they created their continuations.

RESOURCES AND IDEAS

Bizzaro, Patrick. *Responding to Student Poems: Applications of Critical Theory.* Urbana: NCTE, 1993. See Chapter 7 in particular for a discussion of having students read and produce poetry as complementary activities (159–91).

Hollander, John. *Rhyme's Reason: A Guide to English Verse.* New Haven: Yale UP, 1981. Hollander offers a brief guide to poetry analysis, with amusing examples and some innovative analysis strategies.

Rockas, Leo. *Ways In: Analyzing and Responding to Literature.* Upper Montclair: Boynton/Cook, 1984. Chapter 6 offers examples of and exercises for writing about poetry.

TRANSPARENCY MASTER 39.4

Questions for analyzing poetry

- What parts interest or puzzle you? What words seem especially striking or unusual?
- How would you describe the poem's **speaker** (sometimes called the **persona** or the **voice**)? (The speaker may be very different from the author.) What tone or emotion do you detect—for instance, anger, affection, sarcasm? Does the tone change during the poem?
- What is the structure of the poem? Are there stanzas (groups of lines separated by space)? If so, how is the thought related to the stanzas?
- What is the theme of the poem: what is it about? Is the theme stated or implied?
- What images do you find—evocations of sight, sound, taste, touch, or smell? Is there a surprising pattern of images—say, images of business in a poem about love? What does the poem suggest symbolically as well as literally? (Trust your responses. If you don't sense a symbolic overtone, move on. Don't hunt for symbols.)

The following sample paper on a short poem by Gwendolyn Brooks illustrates a literary analysis that draws not only on the poem itself but also on secondary sources—that is, critical works *about* the poem.

Notice that in the opening paragraph brief quotations from two secondary sources are used to establish the problem, the topic that the essayist will address. These quotations, like the two later quotations from secondary material, are used to make points, not to pad the essay.

An essay on poetry with secondary sources

Gwendolyn Brooks

The Bean Eaters

They eat beans mostly, this old yellow pair.
Dinner is a casual affair.
Plain chipware on a plain and creaking wood,
Tin flatware.

Two who are Mostly Good.
Two who have lived their day,
But keep on putting on their clothes
And putting things away.

And remembering . . .
Remembering, with tinklings and twinges,
As they lean over the beans in their rented back room that is
full of beads and receipts and dolls and cloths, tobacco
crumbs, vases and fringes.

Kenneth Scheff

Professor MacGregor

English 101A

February 7, 1997

Marking Time Versus Enduring in
Gwendolyn Brooks's "The Bean Eaters"

Gwendolyn Brooks's poem "The Bean Eaters" runs only eleven lines. It is written in plain language about very plain people. Yet its meaning is ambiguous. One critic, George E. Kent, says the old couple who eat beans "have had their day and exist now as time-markers" (141). However, another reader, D. H. Melhem, perceives not so much time marking as "endurance" in the old couple (123). Is this poem a despairing picture of old age or a more positive portrait?

"The Bean Eaters" describes an "old yellow pair" who "eat beans mostly" (line 1) off "Plain chipware" (3) with "Tin flatware" (4) in "their rented back room" (11). Clearly, they are poor. Their existence is accompanied not by friends or relatives--children or grandchildren are not mentioned--but by memories and a few possessions (9-11). They are "Mostly Good" (5), words Brooks capitalizes at the end of a line, perhaps to stress the old people's adherence to traditional values as well as their lack of saintliness. They are unexceptional, whatever message they have for readers.

The isolated routine of the couple's life is something Brooks draws attention to with a separate stanza:

> Two who are Mostly Good.
> Two who have lived their day,
> But keep on putting on their clothes
> And putting things away. (5-8)

Brooks emphasizes how isolated the couple is by repeating "Two who." Then she emphasizes how routine their life is by repeating "putting."

A pessimistic reading of this poem seems justified. The critic Harry B. Shaw reads the lines just quoted as perhaps despairing: "they are putting things away as if winding down an operation and readying for withdrawal from activity" (80). However, Shaw observes, the word <u>but</u> also indicates the couple's "determination to go on living, a refusal to give up and let things go" (80). This dual meaning is at the heart of

Brooks's poem: the old people live a meager existence, yes, but their will, their self-control, and their connection with another person--their essential humanity--are unharmed.

The truly positive nature of the poem is revealed in the last stanza. In Brooks's words, the old couple remember with some "twinges" perhaps, but also with "tinklings" (10), a cheerful image. As Melhem says, these people are "strong in mutual affection and shared memories" (123). And the final line, which is much longer than all the rest and which catalogs the evidence of the couple's long life together, is almost musically affirmative: "As they lean over the beans in their rented back room that is full of beads and receipts and dolls and cloths, tobacco crumbs, vases and fringes" (11).

What these people have is not much, but it is something.

[New page.]

Works Cited

Brooks, Gwendolyn. "The Bean Eaters." Literature: An Introduction to Fiction, Poetry, and Drama. Ed. X. J. Kennedy and Dana Gioia. 6th ed. New York: Harper, 1995. 655.

Kent, George E. A Life of Gwendolyn Brooks. Lexington: UP of Kentucky, 1990.

Melhem, D. H. Gwendolyn Brooks: Poetry and the Heroic Voice. Lexington: UP of Kentucky, 1987.

Shaw, Harry B. Gwendolyn Brooks. Twayne's United States Authors Ser. 395. Boston: Twayne, 1980.

39e Writing about drama

Because plays—even some one-act plays—are relatively long, analytic essays on drama usually focus on only one aspect of the play, such as the structure of the play, the function of a single scene, or a character's responsibility for his or her fate. The essay's introduction indicates what the topic is and why it is of some importance, and the introduction may also state the thesis. The conclusion often extends the analysis, showing how a study of the apparently small topic helps to illuminate the play as a whole.

The "Questions for a literary analysis" on pages 675–76 will help you think about any work of literature, including a play, and find a topic to write on. The box on the next page provides additional questions for thinking about drama.

TEACHING TIP

Many students have only read dramas in literature classes and have never seen them acted. If your campus or local library has videotapes of the dramas you are studying, arrange to show scenes (or even the entire work) to the class. Many students are genuinely shocked to see and hear how performers interpret (i.e., analyze) dramatic works, and their resulting papers often benefit from the insights they gain from watching performances.

COLLABORATIVE LEARNING

TEACHING TIP

Break the class into small groups and ask each group to perform a scene for their classmates. You can allow them to bring in props or encourage them to make their interpretations through voice and gesture. Then ask the rest of the class to analyze the group's interpretation. What aspects did the group emphasize, and why?

Questions for analyzing drama

- Does the plot (the sequence of happenings) seem plausible? If not, is the implausibility a fault? If there is more than one plot, are the plots parallel, or are they related by way of contrast?
- Are certain happenings recurrent? If so, how are they significant?
- What kinds of conflict are in the play—for instance, between two groups, two individuals, or two aspects of a single individual? How are the conflicts resolved? Is the resolution satisfying to you?
- How trustworthy are the characters when they describe themselves or others? Do some characters serve as **foils,** or contrasts, for other characters, thus helping to define the other characters? Do the characters change as the play proceeds? Are the characters' motivations convincing?
- What do the author's stage directions add to your understanding and appreciation of the play? If there are few stage directions, what do the speeches imply about the characters' manner, tone, and gestures?
- What do you make of the setting, or location? Does it help to reveal character or theme?
- Do certain costumes (dark suits, flowery shawls, stiff collars) or properties (books, pictures, candlesticks) strike you as symbolic?

TRANSPARENCY MASTER 39.5

RESOURCES AND IDEAS

Rockas, Leo. *Ways In: Analyzing and Responding to Literature.* Upper Montclair: Boynton/Cook, 1984. Chapter 5 contains examples of and exercises for writing about drama.

Suchet, David. "Caliban in *The Tempest.*" In *Players of Shakespeare.* Ed. Philip Brockbank. Cambridge: Cambridge UP, 1985. 167–79. Suchet, an experienced Shakespearean actor, shows how he reads and rereads a drama to find the clues that lead him to create a character.

An essay on drama (no secondary sources)

The following essay on William Shakespeare's *Macbeth* focuses on the title character, examining the extent to which he is and is not a tragic hero. Although the writer bases the essay on his personal response to the play, he does not simply state a preference, as if saying he likes vanilla more than chocolate; instead, he argues a case and offers evidence from the play to support his assertions.

The writer delays stating his thesis fully until the final paragraph: Macbeth is a hero even though he is a villain. But this thesis is nonetheless evident throughout the essay, from the title through the opening three paragraphs (which establish a context and the case the writer will oppose) through each of the five body paragraphs (which offer five kinds of evidence for the thesis).

Michael Spinter

Professor Nelson

English 211

May 6, 1996

Macbeth as Hero

When we think of a tragic hero, we probably think of a fundamentally sympathetic person who is entangled in terrifying circum-

39e

stances and who ultimately dies, leaving us with a sense that the world has suffered a loss. For instance, Hamlet must avenge his father's murder, and in doing so he performs certain actions that verge on the wrongful, such as behaving cruelly to his beloved Ophelia and his mother and killing Rosencrantz and Guildenstern; but we believe that Hamlet is fundamentally a decent man and that Denmark is the poorer for his death.

Macbeth, however, is different. He kills King Duncan and Duncan's grooms, kills Banquo, attempts to kill Banquo's son, and finally kills Lady Macduff and her children and her servants. True, the only people whom he kills with his own hands are Duncan and the grooms--the other victims are destroyed by hired murderers--but clearly Macbeth is responsible for all of the deaths. He could seem an utterly unscrupulous, sneaking crook rather than a tragic hero for whom a reader can feel sympathy.

Certainly most of the other characters in the play feel no sympathy for Macbeth. Macduff calls him a "hell-kite," or a hellish bird of prey (4.3.217), a "tyrant" (5.7.14), a "hell-hound" (5.8.3), and a "coward" (5.8.23). To Malcolm he is a "tyrant" (4.3.12), "devilish Macbeth" (4.3.117), and a "butcher" (5.8.69). Readers and spectators can hardly deny the truth of these characterizations. And yet Macbeth does not seem merely villainous. It would be going too far to say that we always sympathize with him, but we are deeply interested in him and do not dismiss him in disgust as an out-and-out monster. How can we account for his hold on our feelings? At least five factors play their parts.

First, Macbeth is an impressive military figure. In the first extended description of Macbeth, the Captain speaks of "brave Macbeth--well he deserves that name" (1.2.16). The Captain tells how Macbeth valiantly fought on behalf of his king, and King Duncan exclaims, "O valiant cousin! Worthy gentleman!" (1.2.2). True, Macbeth sometimes cringes, such as when he denies responsibility for Banquo's death: "Thou canst not say I did it" (3.4.51). But throughout most of the play, we see him as a bold and courageous soldier.

Of course, Macbeth's ability as a soldier is not enough by itself to explain his hold on us. A second reason is that he is in some degree a victim--a victim of his wife's ambition and a victim of the witches. Yes, he ought to see through his wife's schemes, and he ought to resist the witches, just as Banquo resists them, but surely Macbeth is partly tricked into crime. He is responsible, but we can imagine ourselves falling as he does, and his status as a victim arouses our sympathy.

A third source of his hold on us is that although Macbeth engages in terrible deeds, he almost always retains his conscience. For instance, after he murders Duncan he cannot sleep at night. When he tells Lady Macbeth that he has heard a voice saying, "Macbeth does murder sleep" (2.2.35), she ridicules him, but the voice is prophetic: he is doomed to sleepless nights. We in the audience are glad that Macbeth is tormented by his deed, since it shows that he knows he has done wrong and that he still has some decent human feelings.

A fourth reason why we retain some sympathy for Macbeth is that he eventually loses all of his allies, even his wife, and he stands before us a lonely, guilt-haunted figure. On this point, scene 2 of act 3 is especially significant. When Lady Macbeth asks Macbeth why he keeps to himself (line 8), he confides something of the mental stress that he is undergoing. But when she asks, "What's to be done?" (44), he cannot bring himself to tell her that he is plotting the deaths of Banquo and Fleance. Instead of further involving his wife, the only person with whom he might still have a human connection, Macbeth says, "Be innocent of the knowledge, dearest chuck . . ." (45). The word chuck, an affectionate form of chick, shows warmth and intimacy that are touching, but his refusal or his inability to confide in his wife and former partner in crime shows how fully isolated he is from all human contact. We cannot help feeling some sympathy for him.

Finally, Macbeth holds our interest, instead of disgusting us, because he speaks so wonderfully. The greatness of his language compels us to listen to him with rapt attention. Some speeches are very familiar, such as "My way of life / Is fall'n into the sear, the yellow leaf . . ." (5.3.23-24) and "Tomorrow and tomorrow and tomorrow / Creeps in this petty pace from day to day . . ." (5.5.19-20). But almost every speech Macbeth utters is equally memorable, from his first, "So foul and fair a day I have not seen" (1.3.38), to his last:

> Before my body
> I throw my warlike shield. Lay on, Macduff;
> And damned be him that first cries, "Hold, enough!"
> (5.8.32-34)

If we stand back and judge Macbeth only by what he does, we of course say that he is a foul murderer. But if we read the play attentively, or witness a performance, and give due weight to Macbeth's bravery, his role as a victim, his tormented conscience, his isolation, and especially his moving language, we do not simply judge him. Rather, we see that, villain though he is, he is not merely awful but also awesome.

[New page.]

Work Cited

Shakespeare, William. Macbeth. Ed. Sylvan Barnet. Rev. ed. New York: NAL, 1987.

Chapter 40

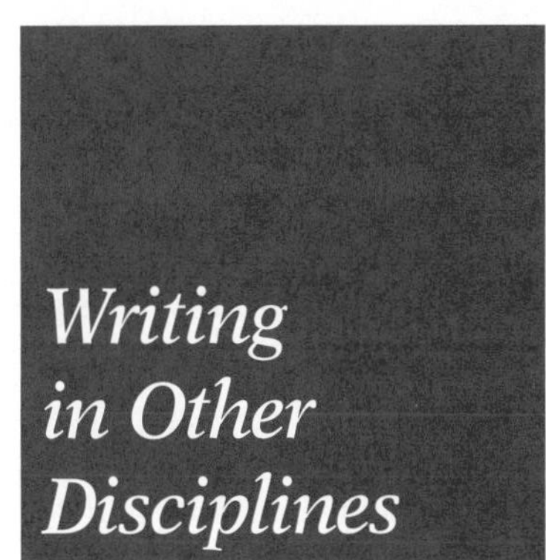

Writing in the academic disciplines you study in college does much more than simply demonstrate your competence. Writing is actually a way you learn concepts, focus ideas, analyze data, uncover assumptions, interpret patterns, and ask and answer questions.

This chapter builds on earlier material: the Introduction on critical thinking, Chapters 1–2 on the writing process, Chapter 4 on reading and writing arguments, and Chapters 35–38 on research writing. Study those chapters, if you have not already, because the skills discussed there are fundamental to academic writing.

In this chapter section 40a covers academic writing in general, section 40b covers the humanities besides literature (discussed in Chapter 39), section 40c covers the social sciences, and section 40d

Guidelines for academic writers

- For the discipline you are writing in, become familiar with the methodology and the kinds of evidence considered appropriate and valid.
- Analyze the special demands of the assignment—the kind of research and sources you need. The questions you set out to answer, the assertions you wish to support, will govern how you choose your sources and evidence.
- Become familiar with the specialized tools and language of the discipline.
- Use the style for source citations and document format customarily used by writers in the discipline.

HIGHLIGHTS

Students in their first semester of college are already learning that they will have to write in most of their classes, not just in their English classes. This new pressure can be overwhelming because students most likely will be required to use writing to show what they know to their professors. This chapter is designed to help students demonstrate their knowledge, but it also reminds students that writing can be a powerful tool for learning in all disciplines. While each discipline has its own conventions and expectations, students should see that the foundations of each one lie in critical thinking, reading, and writing and in the process of communicating what has been learned. This chapter offers students advice on finding and analyzing information in each discipline, and it covers three major documentation styles: the *Chicago Manual of Style* (CMS) footnote or endnote style for the humanities; the *American Psychological Association* (APA) name-date style for the social sciences; and the *Council of Biology Editors* (CBE) number style for the natural sciences and mathematics. Sample student papers illustrate how each style is used by writers in these disciplines.

A WRITER'S PERSPECTIVE

If no one knows what you have done, then you have done nothing.

—Attributed to Michel Montaigne

TRANSPARENCY MASTER 40.1

RESOURCES AND IDEAS

Bartholomae, David. "Inventing the University." *When a Writer Can't Write.* Ed. Mike Rose. New York: Guilford, 1985. 134–65. For Bartholomae, mastering the various specialized discourses of the academic community is an essential part of being a college student but is also a gradual process that is likely to pass through several stages, each more closely approximating the work of thinking and writing that characterizes a discipline.

Bazerman, Charles. *The Informed Writer: Using Sources in the Disciplines.* Boston: Houghton, 1985. Bazerman offers a number of examples and exercises to help students learn the discourse conventions of various academic disciplines.

College Composition and Communication 36 (1985). All four numbers of this volume are devoted to the role(s) writing plays in professional and academic disciplines; numbers 2 and 4 are particularly rich.

Fulwiler, Toby, and Art Young, eds. *Programs that Work: Models and Methods for Writing Across the Curriculum.* Upper Montclair: Boynton/Cook, 1990. Teachers describe how writing has been incorporated throughout the disciplines at their fourteen institutions nationwide.

Herrington, Anne, and Charles Moran, eds. *Writing, Teaching, and Learning in the Disciplines.* New York: MLA, 1992. The essays in this collection examine the "history, theory, practice, and prospects" of writing across the curriculum.

Kerr, Nancy H., and Madeleine Picciotto. "Linked Composition Courses: Effects on Student Performance." *Journal of Teaching Writing* 11.1 (1992): 105–28. The authors use a case study at Oglethorpe University to show the pros and cons of linking writing courses to introductory courses in the disciplines—a currently popular WAC approach.

McLeod, Susan H. "Writing Across the Curriculum: The Second Stage, and Beyond." *College Composition and Communication* 40 (1989): 337–43. The author surveys changes in writing-across-the-curriculum practices; she calls for continued emphasis on critical reading, writing, and thinking in all disciplines.

Morris, Barbara S. *Disciplinary Perspectives on Thinking and Writing.* Ann Arbor: U of Michigan English Curriculum Board, 1989. The essays in this collection demonstrate different modes of inquiry and writing strategies among the disciplines.

Walvoord, Barbara E. "The Future of WAC." *College English* 58.1 (1996): 58–79. Walvoord, a long-time WAC program administrator, examines the challenges facing this "movement," including its relationship to other programs and institutions and its role in assessment.

Young, Art, and Toby Fulwiler, eds. *Writing Across the Disciplines: Research into Practice.* Upper Montclair: Boynton/Cook, 1986. The essays in this collection describe and evaluate

covers the natural and applied sciences. For each field, the chapter introduces the basic information that will help you follow the guidelines on the preceding page.

40a Understanding the goals and requirements of the disciplines

Academic disciplines both resemble each other and differ in their methods and evidence, assignments, tools and language, and style for source citations and document format.

 Methods and evidence

The **methodology** of a discipline is the way its practitioners study their subjects—that is, how they proceed when investigating the answers to questions. Methodology relates to the way practitioners analyze evidence and ideas (see pp. 12–13). For instance, a literary critic and a social historian would probably approach Shakespeare's *Hamlet* quite differently: the literary critic might study the play for its poetic images; the historian might examine the play's relation to Shakespeare's context, England at the turn of the seventeenth century.

Whatever their approach, academic writers do not compose entirely out of their personal experience. Rather, they combine the evidence of their experience with that appropriate to the discipline, drawing well-supported conclusions about their subjects. The evidence of the discipline comes from research like that described in Chapters 35–36—from primary or secondary sources.

Primary sources are firsthand or original accounts, such as historical documents, works of art, and reports on experiments that the writer has conducted. When you use primary sources, you conduct original research, generating your own evidence. You might analyze a painting and then use examples as evidence for your interpretation of the painting. Or you might conduct a survey of fellow students and then use data from the survey to support your conclusions about students' attitudes. All the sample papers in this chapter and the preceding two chapters depend at least partly on primary sources.

Many primary sources can be found in the library. But more prevalent among a library's holdings are **secondary sources,** books and articles written *about* primary sources. Much academic writing requires that you use such sources to spark, extend, or support your own ideas, as when you review the published opinions on your subject before contributing conclusions from your original research.

 Assignments

For most academic writing, your primary purpose will be either to explain something to your readers or to persuade them to

accept your conclusions. To achieve your purpose, you will adapt your writing process to the writing situation, particularly to the kinds of evidence required by the assignment and to the kinds of thinking you are expected to do. Most assignments will contain key words that tell you what these expectations are—words such as *compare, define, analyze,* and *illustrate* that express customary ways of thinking about and organizing a vast range of subjects. Pages 106–14 and 740 explore these so-called patterns of development. You should be aware of them and alert to the wording in assignments that directs you to use them.

 3 Tools and language

When you write in an academic discipline, you use the scholarly tools of that discipline, including specialized references such as periodical indexes, abstracts, and computerized databases. (See pp. 529–35 and 549 for helpful lists of references.) In addition, you may use the aids developed by practitioners of the discipline for efficiently and effectively approaching research, conducting it, and recording the findings. Many of these aids, such as a system for recording evidence from sources, are discussed in Chapters 35 and 36 and can be adapted to any discipline. Other aids are discussed in later sections of this chapter.

Pay close attention to the texts assigned in a course and any materials given out in class, for these items may introduce you to valuable references and other research aids, and they will use the specialized language of the discipline. This specialized language allows practitioners to write to each other both efficiently and precisely. It also furthers certain concerns of the discipline, such as accuracy and objectivity. Scientists, for example, try to interpret their data objectively, so they avoid *undoubtedly, obviously,* and other words that slant conclusions. Some of the language conventions like this one are discussed in the following sections. As you gain experience in a particular discipline, keep alert for such conventions and train yourself to follow them.

 4 Source citations and document format

Most disciplines publish journals that require authors to use a certain style for source citations and a certain format for documents. In turn, most instructors in a discipline require the same of students writing papers for their courses.

When you cite your sources, you tell readers which ideas and information you borrowed and where they can find your sources. Thus source citations indicate how much knowledge you have and how broad and deep your research was. They also help you avoid **plagiarism,** the serious offense of presenting the words, ideas, and

a university-wide writing-across-the-curriculum program. Included are essays on writing in the social sciences, the humanities, and the natural and applied sciences.

COLLABORATIVE LEARNING

TEACHING TIP

Many students have trouble identifying the primary expectations of some assignments. It is important for students to learn to read assignments carefully, and to learn to ask teachers for more information when the assignment is unclear. Have students bring in paper assignments from previous and current courses. Choose a selection of assignments from various disciplines (5–10) and photocopy them for the class. Then ask students to work in small groups to highlight the primary expectations of each assignment, consider the goal implied by the assignment, and to make lists of additional questions that might help clarify each assignment further. As groups present their findings, you might also generate a discussion of the similarities and differences of expectations across the disciplines.

A WRITER'S PERSPECTIVE

Has not every one of us struggled for words, although the connection between "things" was already clear?

—Albert Einstein

RESOURCES AND IDEAS

Anderson, Worth, et al. "Cross-Curricular Underlife: A Collaborative Report on Ways with Academic Words." *College Composition and Communication* 41 (1990): 11–36. A research project by faculty and students revealed that the content of a typical first-year composition course had little in common with the type of writing expected in introductory courses within the disciplines.

Astin, Alexander. *What Matters in College?* San Francisco: Jossey-Bass, 1993. Astin argues that both the number of writing courses students take and the number of courses that require writing strongly affect students' general knowledge, skills, and success in college.

Burgar, Maria. "No Footnotes Necessary." *Bulletin of the Association for Business Communication* 52 (1989): 32–35. Burgar encourages English instructors to be familiar with and require the types of writing students may encounter in the core courses of their majors and in their professions. Burgar believes such a focus results in increased motivation and learning on the part of the students.

Griffin, C. W., ed. *New Directions for Teaching and Learning: Teaching Writing in All Disciplines.* San Francisco: Jossey-Bass, 1982. The essays in this collection look at ways to use writing as a tool for learning and at ways of helping students master the kinds of writing required by different disciplines.

Schlesinger, Mark A. "The Road to Teaching Thinking." *JGE: The Journal of General Education* 36 (1984): 182–96. Schlesinger surveys four contemporary approaches to teaching students to think, including those that address global skills like analysis and synthesis; those that focus on strategies for problem solving; those that rely on developmental models like those of Piaget and Perry; and those that stress generic thinking skills such as selective attention or identifying components. He points out the overlapping among these approaches and identifies both their strengths and weaknesses.

COLLABORATIVE LEARNING

TEACHING TIP

Divide students into groups according to their intended majors (humanities majors, business majors, and so on). Send them to the library to survey professional journals in their intended fields and discover what style(s) of documentation these journals require. (The style is often found in an "Instructions to Authors" section, usually located somewhere near the Contents pages.) Ask groups to report their discoveries to the class.

RESOURCES AND IDEAS

Beyer, Barry K. "Using Writing to Learn in History." *The History Teacher* 13 (1980): 167–78. Beyer suggests using writing not only to seek and report information but to help students understand the ways of thinking characteristic of historians.

data of others as if they were your own. (See pp. 578–84 on avoiding plagiarism.)

Document format includes such features as margins and the placement of the title. But it also extends to special elements of the manuscript, such as tables or an abstract, that may be required by the discipline.

The following sections direct you to the style guides published by different disciplines and outline the basic requirements of the ones used most often. If your instructor does not require a particular style, use that of the Modern Language Association, which is described and illustrated at length in Chapter 37 (source citations) and Appendix A (document format).

40b Writing in the humanities

The humanities include literature, the visual arts, music, film, history, philosophy, and religion. The preceding chapter discusses the particular requirements of reading and writing about literature. This section concentrates on history. The arts, religion, and other humanities have their own concerns, of course, but share many important goals and methods with literature and history.

1 Methods and evidence in the humanities

Writers in the humanities record and speculate about the growth, ideas, and emotions of human beings. Based on the evidence of written words, artworks, and other human traces and creations, humanities writers explain, interpret, analyze, and reconstruct the human experience.

The discipline of history focuses particularly on reconstructing the past. In Greek the word for history means "to inquire": historians inquire into the past to understand the events of the past. Then they report, explain, analyze, and evaluate those events in their context, asking such questions as what happened before or after the events or how the events were related to then existing political and social structures.

Historians' reconstructions of the past—their conclusions about what happened and why—are always supported with reference to the written record. The evidence of history is mainly primary sources, such as eyewitness accounts and contemporary documents, letters, commercial records, and the like. For history papers, you might also be asked to support your conclusions with those in secondary sources.

In reading historical sources, you need to weigh and evaluate their evidence. If, for example, you find conflicting accounts of the same event, you need to consider the possible biases of the authors. In general, the more a historian's conclusions are supported by public records such as deeds, marriage licenses, and newspaper accounts, the more reliable the conclusions are likely to be.

2 Assignments in the humanities

Papers in the humanities generally perform one or more of the following operations:

- Using **explanation,** you might show how a film director created a particular sequence or clarify a general's role in a battle.
- Using **analysis,** you might examine the elements of a story or painting or break down the causes of a historical event.
- Using **interpretation,** you might infer the meaning of a film from its images or the significance of a historical event from contemporary accounts of it.
- Using **synthesis,** you might find a pattern in a historical period or in a playwright's works.
- Using **evaluation,** you might judge the quality of an architect's design or a historian's conclusions.

Most likely, you will use these operations in combination—say, interpreting and explaining the meaning of a painting and then evaluating it. (These operations are discussed in more detail in the book's Introduction, pp. 11–17.)

3 Tools and language in the humanities

The tools of the humanities vary according to the discipline. In the arts, for instance, you may ask a series of questions to analyze and evaluate a work (a list of such questions for reading literature appears on pp. 675–76). In addition, a journal—a log of questions, reactions, and insights—can help you discover and record your thoughts.

In history the tools are those of any thorough and efficient researcher, as discussed in Chapters 35 and 36: a system for finding and tracking sources (pp. 516–61); a methodical examination of sources, including evaluating and synthesizing them (pp. 563–68); a system for taking notes from sources (pp. 569–72); and a separate system, such as a research journal, for tracking one's own evolving thoughts (pp. 517–18).

Historians strive for precision and logic. They do not guess about what happened or speculate about "what if." They avoid trying to influence readers' opinions with words having strongly negative or positive connotations, such as *stupid* or *brilliant* (see p. 464). Instead, historians show the evidence and draw conclusions from

Tuchman, Barbara. *Practicing History: Selected Essays.* New York: Knopf, 1981. Tuchman demonstrates and gives practical recommendations for analytic writing in history.

TEACHING TIP

If your students need more help in writing for the humanities, you might refer them to the following:

Barnet, Sylvan. *A Short Guide to Writing About Art.* 4th ed. New York: HarperCollins, 1995.

Corrigan, Timothy. *A Short Guide to Writing About Film.* 2nd ed. New York: HarperCollins, 1994.

Marius, Richard. *A Short Guide to Writing About History.* 2nd ed. New York: HarperCollins, 1995.

Steffens, Henry, and MaryJane Dickerson. *Writer's Guide: History.* Boston: Heath, 1987.

ASSIGNMENTS

COLLABORATIVE LEARNING

TEACHING TIP

Ask students to bring in examples of writing assignments from their other humanities courses and to classify them according to the list here. Which are most and least frequently used? Students might also interview professors from their other courses, individually or in teams, to learn which writing strategies are most important for success in those courses.

that. Generally, they avoid using *I* because it tends to draw attention away from the evidence and toward the writer.

Writing about history demands some attention to the tenses of verbs to maintain consistency. (See pp. 219–26 for explanations of verb tenses.) Generally, historians use the past tense to refer to events that occurred in the past. They reserve the present tense only for statements about the present or statements of general truths. For example:

> Franklin Delano Roosevelt *died* in 1945. Many of Roosevelt's economic reforms *persist* in programs such as Social Security, unemployment compensation, and farm subsidies.

Source citations and document format in the humanities

Writers in the humanities generally rely on one of the following guides for source-citation style and document format:

Chicago Manual of Style. 14th ed. 1993.
Gibaldi, Joseph. *MLA Handbook for Writers of Research Papers*. 4th ed. 1995.
Turabian, Kate L. *A Manual for Writers of Term Papers, Theses, and Dissertations*. 6th ed. Rev. John Grossman and Alice Bennett. 1996.

The recommendations of the *MLA Handbook* are discussed and illustrated in Chapter 37 and Appendix A. Unless your instructor specifies otherwise, use these recommendations for papers in English and foreign languages. You may also use MLA document format in other humanities as well. However, for source citations many humanities follow the footnote or endnote citation style of the *Chicago Manual of Style* and the student guide adapted from it, Turabian's *Manual for Writers of Term Papers, Theses, and Dissertations*. (These books also discuss another style using in-text parenthetical citations, which is like that of the American Psychological Association, widely used in the social sciences. See pp. 707–20.)

Chicago endnotes or footnotes

The *Chicago Manual* and *A Manual for Writers* detail a source-citation system of raised numerals in the text referring to footnotes (bottoms of pages) or endnotes (end of paper), along with an optional list of works cited at the end of the paper (see the note following).

Note The *Chicago Manual* does not require an alphabetical list of works cited if you provide complete source information in your notes. Alternatively, the guide allows you to shorten source information in notes and then provide full information in a list of works cited. *A Manual for Writers*, however, requires both full notes and a full list of works cited. Many instructors have the same requirement, so that the reader has a complete alphabetical list of sources and yet does not have to turn from notes to works-cited list for full information on a particular text citation. Ask your instructor what he or she requires. The following pages illustrate full notes and works-cited entries (699–702) as well as shortened notes (702–03).

Ask your instructor also whether you should provide footnotes or endnotes. Whichever you use, single-space the notes themselves and double-space between notes. With footnotes, separate the notes from the text with a short line, as shown in the following sample:

In 1901, Madras, Bengal, and Punjab were a few of the huge Indian provinces governed by the British viceroy.[6] British rule, observes Stuart Cary Welch, "seemed as permanent as Mount Everest."[7]

———— ← Line

5 spaces

6. Martin Gilbert, Atlas of British History (New York: Dorset Press, 1968), 96. — Single-space

← Double-space

7. Stuart Cary Welch, India: Art and Culture (New York: Metropolitan Museum of Art, 1985), 421. — Single-space

↕ 1"

With endnotes, use the format below for a list of works cited, substituting the heading "NOTES" and numbered entries as for footnotes.

For the list of sources at the end of the paper, use the format below. Arrange the sources alphabetically by the authors' last names.

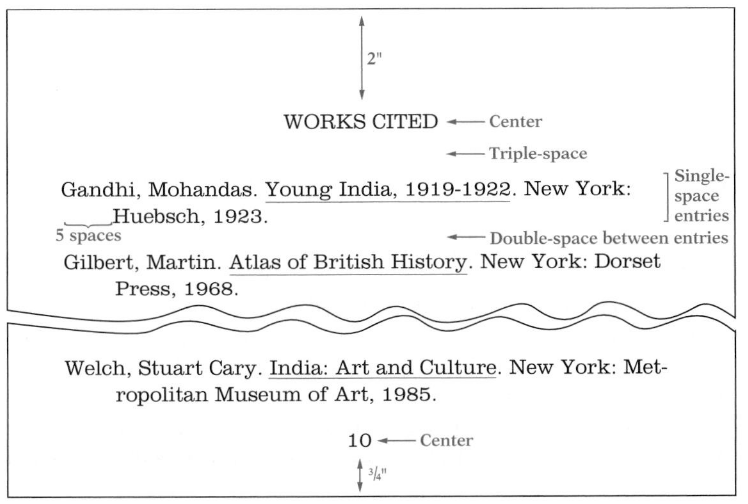
↕ 2"

WORKS CITED ← Center

← Triple-space

Gandhi, Mohandas. Young India, 1919-1922. New York: Huebsch, 1923. — Single-space entries

5 spaces

← Double-space between entries

Gilbert, Martin. Atlas of British History. New York: Dorset Press, 1968.

Welch, Stuart Cary. India: Art and Culture. New York: Metropolitan Museum of Art, 1985.

10 ← Center

↕ 3/4"

Chic 40b

The examples below illustrate the essentials of a note and a works-cited entry.

NOTE

6. Martin Gilbert, Atlas of British History (New York: Dorset Press, 1968), 96.

WORKS-CITED ENTRY

Gilbert, Martin. Atlas of British History. New York: Dorset Press, 1968.

Notes and works-cited entries share certain features:

- Underline or italicize the titles of books and periodicals (ask your instructor for his or her preference).
- Enclose in quotation marks the titles of parts of books or articles in periodicals.
- Do not abbreviate publishers' names, but omit "Inc.," "Co.," and similar abbreviations.
- Do not use "p." or "pp." before page numbers.

Notes and works-cited entries also differ in important ways:

NOTE	WORKS-CITED ENTRY
Start with a number (typed on the line and followed by a period) that corresponds to the note number in the text.	Do not begin with a number.
Indent the first line five spaces.	Indent the second and subsequent lines five spaces.
Give the author's name in normal order.	Begin with the author's last name.
Use commas between elements such as author's name and title.	Use periods between elements, followed by one space.
Enclose publication information in parentheses, with no preceding punctuation.	Precede the publication information with a period, and don't use parentheses.
Include the specific page number(s) you borrowed from, omitting "p." or "pp."	Omit page numbers except for parts of books or articles in periodicals.

Many computerized word-processing programs will automatically position footnotes at the bottoms of appropriate pages. Some will automatically number notes and even renumber them if you add or delete one or more.

In the following models for common sources, notes and works-cited entries appear together for easy reference. Be sure to use the

COMPUTER EXERCISE

TEACHING TIP

Students who use word processors will be able to number and format their notes on the page automatically. Remind these students that such word-processing programs usually have a Setup or Options menu that they can adjust to make the footnote or endnote print out with proper spacing, note numbers, and so forth.

Index to Chicago note and works-cited models

numbered note form for notes and the unnumbered works-cited form for works-cited entries.

1. A BOOK WITH ONE, TWO, OR THREE AUTHORS

1. Carol Gilligan, In a Different Voice: Psychological Theory and Women's Development (Cambridge: Harvard University Press, 1982), 27.

Gilligan, Carol. In a Different Voice: Psychological Theory and Women's Development. Cambridge: Harvard University Press, 1982.

1. Bernard J. Frieden and Lynne B. Sagalyn, Downtown, Inc: How America Rebuilds Cities (Cambridge: MIT Press, 1989), 16.

Frieden, Bernard J., and Lynne B. Sagalyn. Downtown, Inc.: How America Rebuilds Cities. Cambridge: MIT Press, 1989.

For a work with three authors, separate the authors' names with commas: Wilcox, Dennis L., Phillip H. Ault, and Warren K. Agee.

2. A BOOK WITH MORE THAN THREE AUTHORS

2. Joan Stryker and others, eds., Encyclopedia of American Life, 2d ed. (Boston: Winship, 1995), 126-28.

Stryker, Joan, William Hones, William Parker, and Sylvia Mannes, eds. Encyclopedia of American Life. 2d ed. Boston: Winship, 1995.

3. A book with an editor

3. Hendrick Ruitenbeek, ed., *Freud as We Knew Him* (Detroit: Wayne State University Press, 1973), 64.

Ruitenbeek, Hendrick, ed. *Freud as We Knew Him*. Detroit: Wayne State University Press, 1973.

4. An anonymous work

4. *Merriam-Webster's Collegiate Dictionary*, 10th ed. (Springfield, Mass.: Merriam-Webster, 1993).

Merriam-Webster's Collegiate Dictionary. 10th ed. Springfield, Mass.: Merriam-Webster, 1993.

5. A later edition

5. Dwight L. Bollinger, *Aspects of Language*, 2d ed. (New York: Harcourt Brace Jovanovich, 1975), 20.

Bollinger, Dwight L. *Aspects of Language*. 2d ed. New York: Harcourt Brace Jovanovich, 1975.

6. A work in more than one volume

6. Abraham Lincoln, *The Collected Works of Abraham Lincoln*, ed. Roy P. Basler (New Brunswick: Rutgers University Press, 1953), 5:426-28.

Lincoln, Abraham. *The Collected Works of Abraham Lincoln*. Ed. Roy P. Basler. Vol. 5. New Brunswick: Rutgers University Press, 1953.

7. A selection from an anthology

7. Rosetta Brooks, "Streetwise," in *The New Urban Landscape*, ed. Richard Martin (New York: Rizzoli, 1990), 38-39.

Brooks, Rosetta. "Streetwise." In *The New Urban Landscape*, ed. Richard Martin, 37-60. New York: Rizzoli, 1990.

8. An article in a journal with continuous pagination throughout the annual volume

8. Janet Lever, "Sex Differences in the Games Children Play," *Social Problems* 23 (1976): 482.

Lever, Janet. "Sex Differences in the Games Children Play." *Social Problems* 23 (1976): 478-87.

9. An article in a journal that pages issues separately

9. June Dacey, "Management Participation in Corporate Buy-Outs," *Management Perspectives* 7, no. 4 (1994): 22.

Dacey, June. "Management Participation in Corporate Buy-Outs." Management Perspectives 7, no. 4 (1994): 20-31.

10. An article in a popular magazine

10. Mark Stevens, "Low and Behold," New Republic, 24 December 1990, 28.

Stevens, Mark. "Low and Behold." New Republic, 24 December 1990, 27-33.

11. An article in a newspaper

11. Anthony Ramirez, "Computer Groups Plan Standards," New York Times, 14 December 1993, D5, late edition.

Ramirez, Anthony. "Computer Groups Plan Standards." New York Times, 14 December 1993, D5, late edition.

12. A government publication

12. House, Medicare Payment for Outpatient Physical and Occupational Therapy Services, 102d Cong., 1st sess., 1991, H. Doc. 409, 12-13.

US. House. Medicare Payment for Outpatient Physical and Occupational Therapy Services, 102d Cong., 1st sess., 1991. H. Doc. 409.

13. A work of art

13. John Singer Sargent, In Switzerland, watercolor, 1908, Metropolitan Museum of Art, New York.

Sargent, John Singer. In Switzerland, watercolor, 1908. Metropolitan Museum of Art, New York.

14. A source on CD-ROM or diskette

14. Anthony Ramirez, "Computer Groups Plan Standards," New York Times, 14 December 1993, D5, late edition, New York Times Ondisc [CD-ROM], UMI-ProQuest, June 1994.

Ramirez, Anthony. "Computer Groups Plan Standards." New York Times, 14 December 1993, D5, late edition. New York Times Ondisc [CD-ROM], UMI-ProQuest, June 1994.

When a source is also published in print, as above, give the print information first, followed by the electronic information.

15. An online source

15. Jane Austen, Emma [book online], ed. Ronald Blythe (Harmondsworth: Penguin, 1972), Oxford Text Archive, accessed 15 December 1995; available from ftp://black.ox.ac.uk.

Austen, Jane. Emma [book online]. Ed. Ronald Blythe. Harmondsworth: Penguin, 1972. Oxford Text Archive. Accessed 15 December 1995. Available from ftp://black.ox.ac.uk.

Give the date of your access to the source (after "accessed") as well as the electronic address (after "available from"). When a source is also published in print, give the print information first, as above.

15. Andrew Palfrey, "Choice of Mates in Identical Twins," Modern Psychology 4, no. 1 (1996): pars. 7-8 [journal online], accessed 25 February 1996; available from ftp://modpsy.liasu.edu/palfrey4(1).txt.

Palfrey, Andrew. "Choice of Mates in Identical Twins." Modern Psychology 4, no. 1 (1996) [journal online]. Accessed 25 February 1996. Available from ftp://modpsy.liasu.edu/palfrey4(1).txt.

16. Two or more citations of the same source

To minimize clutter in notes and to give readers a quick sense of how often you acknowledge a source, the Chicago style allows a shortened form for subsequent citations of a source you have already cited fully. The shortened form may also be acceptable for a first citation of a source if you provide full information in a list of works cited. (See the note on p. 696.)

You may use the Latin abbreviation "ibid." (meaning "in the same place") to refer to the same source cited in the preceding note:

8. Janet Lever, "Sex Differences in the Games Children Play," Social Problems 23 (1976): 482.

9. Ibid., 483.

For any source already cited in your notes, not just immediately before, you may use the author's name and (if the author is responsible for more than one cited source) a shortened form of the title.

1. Carol Gilligan, In a Different Voice: Psychological Theory and Women's Development (Cambridge: Harvard University Press, 1982), 27.

2. Carol Gilligan, "Moral Development in the College Years," The Modern American College, ed. A. Chickering (San Francisco: Jossey-Bass, 1981), 286.

3. Gilligan, In a Different Voice, 47.

Omit the title if you are using only one source by the cited author.

The Chicago style recommends in-text parenthetical citations when you cite one or more works repeatedly. This practice allows you to avoid many notes saying "ibid." or giving the same author's name. In the example following, the note number refers to the complete source information in an endnote; the numbers in parentheses are page numbers in the same source.

British rule, observes Stuart Cary Welch, "seemed as permanent as Mount Everest."[7] Most Indians submitted, willingly or not, to British influence in every facet of life (423-24).

Document format in the humanities

The illustrations on page 697 show several features of the document format recommended by Turabian's *Manual for Writers of Term Papers, Theses, and Dissertations.* The following list supplements those illustrations:

- Use a title page if your instructor requires one. Separate the title, your name, and the course identification and date as illustrated on page 632, but use all-capital letters.
- If your instructor does not require a title page, follow the style of the *MLA Handbook* for positioning your name, course identification, and date (see p. 761).
- Center your paper title two inches from the top of the first page, typed in all-capital letters. Treat section titles, such as "NOTES" or "WORKS CITED," the same way (see p. 697). Triple-space beneath the title or heading.
- Double-space everything except individual footnotes or endnotes and the individual entries in the list of works cited (single-space these as shown on p. 697).
- Number all pages except any preliminary pages (title page, outline) consecutively throughout the paper, including notes and the list of works cited. Place the number at the top of the page, either centered or at the right margin, with one exception: for pages with headings, such as "NOTES," center the page number at the foot of the page (as shown on p. 697).
- Set long quotations off from your text: poetry quotations of three or more lines and prose quotations of two or more sentences and eight or more lines. (You may display shorter prose quotations to emphasize them or to compare them.) Double-space above and below a displayed quotation, and single-space the quotation itself. Indent the quotation four spaces from the left margin. Do not use quotation marks for a displayed quotation.

40c Writing in the social sciences

The social sciences—including anthropology, economics, education, management, political science, psychology, and sociology—focus on the study of human behavior. As the name implies, the social sciences examine the way human beings relate to themselves, to their environment, and to each other.

RESOURCES AND IDEAS

Bazerman, Charles. *The Informed Writer: Using Sources in the Disciplines.* Boston: Houghton, 1985. Bazerman offers a number of examples and exercises to help students learn the discourse conventions of various academic disciplines.

College Composition and Communication 36 (1985). All four numbers of this volume are devoted to the role(s) writing plays in professional and academic disciplines; numbers 2 and 4 are particularly rich.

Daemmrich, Ingrid. "A Bridge to Academic Discourse: Social Science Research Strategies in the Freshman Composition Course." *College Composition and Communication* 40 (1989): 343–48. Daemmrich argues for use of social-science writing as a way to help students move from personal to academic writing.

Hemmeter, Thomas, and David Conners. "Research Papers in Economics: A Collaborative Approach." *Journal of Advanced Composition* 7 (1987): 81–91. The authors describe a course taught collaboratively by an economist and a writing specialist, focusing on activities leading to the term-ending research paper.

Shamoon, Linda K., and Robert A. Schwegler. "Sociologists Reading Student Texts: Expectations and Perceptions." *The Writing Instructor* 7 (1988): 71–81. The authors argue that the way sociologists perceive the features of a student paper differ considerably from the way composition instructors often perceive the features. Sociologists look first of all for a line of sociological reasoning carried throughout a paper, supported by evidence acceptable to sociologists and made clear by indicators such as topic sentences.

TRANSPARENCY MASTER 40.2

TEACHING TIP

If your students need more help in writing for the social sciences, you might refer them to some of the following:

Abrahamson, Mark. *Social Research Methods.* Englewood Cliffs: Prentice-Hall, 1983. Abrahamson provides a primer of research methods in the social sciences, including interviews and surveys.

Becker, Howard S., et al. *Writing for Social Scientists: How to Start and Finish Your Thesis, Book, or Article.* Chicago: U of Chicago P, 1986.

Bond, Lynne, and Anthony Magistrale. *Writer's Guide: Psychology.* Lexington: Heath, 1987.

Cuba, Lee. *A Short Guide to Writing About Social Science.* New York: HarperCollins, 1992.

40c

1 Methods and evidence in the social sciences

Researchers in the social sciences systematically pose a question, formulate a **hypothesis** (a generalization that can be tested), collect data, analyze those data, and draw conclusions to support or disprove their hypothesis. This is the scientific method developed in the natural sciences (see p. 726).

Social scientists gather data in several ways:

- They make firsthand observations of human behavior and record the observations in writing or on audio- or videotape.
- They interview subjects about their attitudes and behavior, recording responses in writing or on tape. (See pp. 557–58 for guidelines on conducting an interview.)
- They conduct broader surveys using questionnaires that ask people about their attitudes and behavior. (See the box at the bottom of the page.)
- They conduct controlled experiments, structuring an environment in which to encourage and measure a specific behavior.

In their writing, social scientists explain their own research or analyze and evaluate others' research.

Conducting a survey

- Decide what you want to find out—what your hypothesis is. The questions you ask should be dictated by your purpose.
- Define your population. Think about the kinds of people your hypothesis is about—for instance, college men, or five-year-old children. Plan to sample this population so that your findings will be representative.
- Write your questions. Surveys may contain closed questions that direct the respondent's answers (checklists and multiple-choice, true/false, or yes/no questions) or open-ended questions allowing brief, descriptive answers. Avoid loaded questions that reveal your own biases or make assumptions about subjects' answers, such as "Do you want the United States to support democracy in China?" or "How much more money does your father make than your mother?"
- Test your questions on a few respondents with whom you can discuss the answers. Eliminate or recast questions that respondents find unclear, discomforting, or unanswerable.
- Tally the results in actual numbers of answers, including any nonanswers.
- Seek patterns in the raw data that conform or conflict with your hypothesis. Revise the hypothesis or conduct additional research if necessary.

The research methods of social science generate two kinds of data:

- **Quantitative data** are numerical, such as statistical evidence based on surveys, polls, tests, and experiments. When public-opinion pollsters announce that 47 percent of Americans polled approve of the President's leadership, they are offering quantitative data gained from a survey. Social science writers present quantitative data in graphs, charts, and other illustrations that accompany their text.
- **Qualitative data** are not numerical but more subjective: they are based on interviews, firsthand observations, and inferences, taking into account the subjective nature of human experience. An example is the work of the anthropologist Margaret Mead, whose experiences among the people of Samoa led to an important description of how adolescent Samoans become aware of adult concerns and rituals. Mead's book *Coming of Age in Samoa* contains few numbers; the data are qualitative.

2 Assignments in the social sciences

Depending on what social science courses you take, you may be asked to complete a variety of assignments:

- **A summary or review of research** reports on the available research literature on a subject, such as infants' perception of color.
- **A case analysis** explains the components of a phenomenon, such as a factory closing.
- **A problem-solving analysis** explains the components of a problem, such as unreported child abuse, and suggests ways to solve it.
- **A research paper** interprets and sometimes analyzes and evaluates the writings of other social scientists about a subject, such as the effect of national appeals in advertising. An example appears in Chapter 38, page 632.
- **A research report** explains the author's own original research or the author's attempt to replicate someone else's research. A research report begins on page 722.

Many social science disciplines have special requirements for the content and organization of each kind of paper. The requirements appear in the style guides of the disciplines, such as the *Publication Manual of the American Psychological Association* (APA). (Guides for other disciplines are listed on p. 707.) The APA manual specifies the following outline for the text of a research report:

1. *Abstract:* a summary (about 100 words) of the subject, the research method, the findings, and the conclusions.

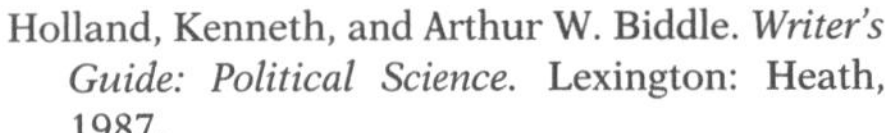

Holland, Kenneth, and Arthur W. Biddle. *Writer's Guide: Political Science.* Lexington: Heath, 1987.

McCloskey, Donald. *The Writing of Economics.* New York: Macmillan, 1987.

Richlin-Klonsky, Judith, and Ellen Strenski, eds. *A Guide to Writing Sociology Papers.* New York: St. Martin's, 1986.

COLLABORATIVE LEARNING

TEACHING TIP

Ask students to bring in examples of writing assignments from their social science courses and to classify them according to this list. Which are most and least frequently used? They might also interview professors from their other courses, individually or in teams, to learn which writing strategies are most important for success in those courses.

2. *Introduction:* a presentation of the problem researched, the research method used, the background (such as other relevant studies), the purpose of the research, and the hypothesis tested.
3. *Method:* a detailed discussion of how the research was conducted, including a description of the research subjects, any materials or tools used (such as questionnaires), and the procedure followed.
4. *Results:* a summary of the data collected and how they were statistically analyzed, along with a detailed presentation of the data, often in tables, graphs, or charts.
5. *Discussion:* an interpretation of the data and presentation of conclusions, related to the original hypothesis. (When the discussion is brief, it may be combined with the previous section under the heading "Results and Discussion.")

To this basic text are added a title page and a list of references (the latter described on pp. 710–20).

Because of the differences among disciplines and even among different kinds of papers in the same discipline, you should always ask your instructor what he or she requires for an assignment.

RESEARCH LOGS

Encourage any student considering a career in research to keep a research log. Almost every company that employs researchers will require those workers to document each day's activities in a log in order to record and protect potentially patentable research.

3 Tools and language in the social sciences

Although a **research journal** or **log** may not be required in your courses, such a notebook can be very helpful. Use it to pose preliminary questions as you begin formulating a hypothesis. Then in the field (that is, when conducting research), use the journal to react to the evidence you are collecting, to record changes in your perceptions and ideas, and to assess your progress. To avoid confusing your reflections on the evidence with the evidence itself, keep records of actual data—notes from interviews, observations, surveys, and experiments—separately from the field journal. (See pp. 4, 7–8, 37, and 517 for more on journals.)

Each social science discipline has specialized terminology for concepts basic to the discipline. In sociology, for example, the words *mechanism, identity,* and *deviance* have specific meanings different from those of everyday usage. And *identity* means something different in sociology, where it applies to groups of people, than in psychology, where it applies to the individual. Social scientists also use precise terms to describe or interpret research. For instance, they say *The subject expressed a feeling of* . . . rather than *The subject felt* . . . because human feelings are not knowable for certain; or they say *These studies indicate* . . . rather than *These studies prove* . . . because conclusions are only tentative.

Just as social scientists strive for objectivity in their research, so they strive to demonstrate their objectivity through language in their writing. They avoid expressions such as *I think* in order to focus attention on what the evidence shows rather than on the researcher's opinions. (However, many social scientists prefer *I* to the artificial *the researcher* when they refer to their own actions, as in *I then interviewed the subjects.* Ask your instructor for his or her preferences.) Social scientists also avoid direct or indirect expression of their personal biases or emotions, either in discussions of other researchers' work or in descriptions of research subjects. Thus one social scientist does not call another's work *sloppy* or *immaculate* and does not refer to his or her own subjects as *drunks* or *innocent victims.* Instead, the writer uses neutral language and ties conclusions strictly to the data.

4 Source citations and document format in the social sciences

As mentioned earlier, some of the social sciences publish style guides that advise practitioners how to organize, document, and type papers. The following is a partial list:

American Anthropological Association. "Style Guide and Information for Authors." *American Anthropologist* (1977): 774–79.
American Psychological Association. *Publication Manual of the American Psychological Association.* 4th ed. 1994.
American Sociological Association. "Editorial Guidelines." Inside front cover of each issue of *American Sociological Review.*
Linguistics Society of America. "LSA Style Sheet." Printed every December in *LSA Bulletin.*

Disciplines that do not have their own style guides may rely on one of those above or may recommend any of several guides. In business, for example, teachers and practitioners often use the *Publication Manual of the American Psychological Association* (APA), listed above; the *MLA Handbook for Writers of Research Papers* (p. 599); or the *Chicago Manual of Style* (p. 696).

Always ask your instructor in any discipline what style you should use. The APA style and manuscript format are explained and illustrated below because they are by far the most often used in the social sciences and are similar to the styles in sociology, economics, and other disciplines.

APA parenthetical text citations

The APA documentation style is like that of the Modern Language Association in that parenthetical citations within the text refer the reader to a list of sources at the end of the text. The APA style (like the MLA) thus uses footnotes or endnotes only for information that does not fit easily into the text.

TEACHING TIP

Remind students that since the social sciences prize the timeliness of research as much as the author's name, APA text citations combine name and date while references place the date just after the author's name. If students understand why a documentation system looks the way it does, they are more likely to learn how to use it correctly.

Index to APA parenthetical text citations

APA parenthetical citations contain the author's last name, the date of publication (a key difference from MLA style), and often the page number from which material is borrowed. See above for an index to the models for various kinds of sources.

TRANSPARENCY MASTER 40.3

1. Author not named in your text

> One critic of Milgram's experiments insisted that the subjects "should have been fully informed of the possible effects on them" (Baumrind, 1968, p. 34).

When you do not name the author in your text, place in parentheses the author's name, the date of the source, and the page number(s) preceded by "p." or "pp." Separate the elements with commas. Position the reference so that it is clear what material is being documented *and* so that the reference fits as smoothly as possible into your sentence structure. The following would also be correct:

> In the view of one critic of Milgram's experiments (Baumrind, 1968), the subjects "should have been fully informed of the possible effects on them" (p. 34).

2. Author named in your text

> Baumrind (1968) insisted that the subjects in Milgram's study "should have been fully informed of the possible effects on them" (p. 34).

When you use the author's name in the text, do not repeat it in the reference. Position the reference next to the author's name. If you cite the same source again in the paragraph, you need not repeat the reference as long as the page number (if any) is the same and it is clear that you are using the same source. Here is a later sentence from the paragraph containing the preceding example:

Baumrind also criticized the experimenters' rationale.

3. A WORK WITH TWO AUTHORS

Pepinsky and DeStefano (1987) demonstrate that a teacher's language often reveals hidden biases.

One study (Pepinsky & DeStefano, 1987) demonstrates the hidden biases often revealed in a teacher's language.

When given in the text, two authors' names are connected by "and." In a parenthetical citation, they are connected by an ampersand, "&."

4. A WORK WITH THREE TO FIVE AUTHORS

Pepinsky, Dunn, Rentl, and Corson (1983) further demonstrate the biases evident in gestures.

In the first citation of a work with three to five authors, name all the authors, as in the example above. In the second and subsequent references to a work with three to five authors, give only the first author's name, followed by "et al." (Latin for "and others"):

In the work of Pepinsky et al. (1983), the loaded gestures include head shakes and eye contact.

5. A WORK WITH SIX OR MORE AUTHORS

One study (Rutter et al., 1976) attempts to explain these geographical differences in adolescent experience.

For six or more authors, even in the first citation of the work, give only the first author's name, followed by "et al."

6. A WORK WITH A CORPORATE AUTHOR

An earlier prediction was even more somber (Lorenz, Inc., 1990).

For a work with a corporate or group author, treat the name of the corporation or group as if it were an individual's name.

7. AN ANONYMOUS WORK

One article ("Right to Die," 1976) noted that a death-row inmate may crave notoriety.

For an anonymous or unsigned work, use the first two or three words of the title in place of an author's name, excluding an initial *The, A,* or *An.* Underline book and journal titles. Place quotation marks around article titles. (In the list of references, however, do not use quotation marks for article titles. See pp. 715–16.) Capitalize the significant words in all titles cited in the text. (But in the reference list, treat only periodical titles this way. See pp. 715–16.)

8. One of two or more works by the same author(s)

At about age seven, most children begin to use appropriate gestures to reinforce their stories (Gardner, 1973a, pp. 144-145).

When you cite one of two or more works by the same author(s), the date will tell readers which source you mean—as long as your reference list includes only one source published by the author(s) in that year. If your reference list includes two or more works published by the same author(s) *in the same year,* the works should be lettered in the reference list (see p. 714). Then your parenthetical citation should include the appropriate letter, as in "1973a" above.

9. Two or more works by different authors

Two studies (Herskowitz, 1984; Marconi & Hamblen, 1990) found that periodic safety instruction can dramatically reduce employees' accidents.

List the sources in alphabetical order by the first author's name. Insert a semicolon between sources.

10. An indirect source

Supporting data appear in a study by Wong (cited in Marconi & Hamblen, 1990).

The phrase "cited in" indicates that the reference to Wong's study was found in Marconi and Hamblen. Only Marconi and Hamblen then appears in the list of references.

APA reference list

In APA style, the in-text parenthetical citations refer to the list of sources at the end of the text. This list, titled "References," includes full publication information on every source cited in the paper.

Caution The APA style is quite different from that of the *MLA Handbook* (p. 599). Don't confuse the two styles.

The following sample shows the format of the first page of the APA reference list:

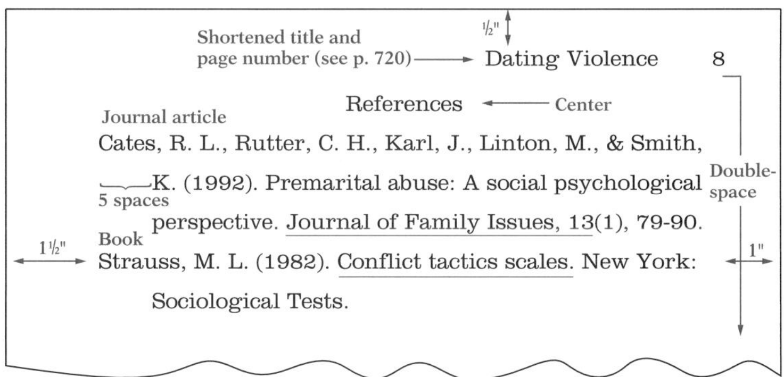

Shortened title and page number (see p. 720)
½"
Dating Violence 8
References
Center
Journal article
Cates, R. L., Rutter, C. H., Karl, J., Linton, M., & Smith,
K. (1992). Premarital abuse: A social psychological
5 spaces
Double-space
perspective. Journal of Family Issues, 13(1), 79-90.
1½"
Book
1"
Strauss, M. L. (1982). Conflict tactics scales. New York:
Sociological Tests.

Prepare APA "References" as follows:

- Arrange sources alphabetically by the author's last name or, if there is no author, by the first main word of the title.
- Double-space all entries.
- Use an appropriate indention for each entry. For papers that will be published, the APA recommends indenting the first line of each entry five to seven spaces, like so:

    Rodriguez, R. (1982). A hunger of memory: The education of Richard Rodriguez. Boston: Godine.

  When set into type for publication, the initial indentions are then converted into so-called hanging indentions, in which the first line is not indented while the others are. The hanging indention makes it easier for readers to spot authors' names, so the APA recognizes that students who are preparing final copy (not destined for publication) may wish to use the hanging indention for their references, like so:

  Rodriguez, R. (1982). A hunger of memory: The education of
      Richard Rodriguez. Boston: Godine.

  Because it is clearer for readers, the hanging indention is used in the sample page above and throughout the following models for references, with a five-space indention for the second and subsequent lines of each entry. Ask your instructor which format he or she prefers.
- List all authors last-name first, separating names and parts of names with commas. Use initials for first and middle names. Use an ampersand (&) before the last author's name.
- In titles of books and articles, capitalize only the first word of the title, the first word of the subtitle, and proper names; all

other words begin with small letters. In titles of journals, capitalize all significant words. Underline the titles of books and journals, along with any comma or period following. Do not underline or use quotation marks around the titles of articles.

- For sources that are not periodicals (such as books or government publications), give the city of publication. The following American cities do not require state names as well: Baltimore, Boston, Chicago, Los Angeles, New York, Philadelphia, and San Francisco. Follow their names with a colon. For all other cities, add a comma after the city name and give the two-letter postal abbreviation of the state (see p. 000 for a list). Then put a colon after the state.
- Also for nonperiodical sources, give the publisher's name after the place of publication and a colon. Use shortened names for many publishers (such as "Morrow" for William Morrow), and omit "Co.," "Inc.," and "Publishers." However, give full names for associations, corporations, and university presses (such as "Harvard University Press"), and do not omit "Books" or "Press" from a publisher's name.
- Use the abbreviation "p." or "pp." before page numbers in books and in newspapers, but *not* in other periodicals. For inclusive page numbers, include all figures: "667–668."
- Separate the parts of the reference (author, date, title, and publication information) with a period and one space.

Note You may have to combine models to provide the necessary information on a source—for instance, combining "A book with one author" (1) and "A book with an editor" (3) for a book with only one editor.

TRANSPARENCY MASTER 40.4

1. A book with one author

Rodriguez, R. (1982). A hunger of memory: The education of Richard Rodriguez. Boston: Godine.

The initial "R" appears instead of the author's first name, even though the author's full first name appears on the source. In the title, only the first words of title and subtitle and the proper name are capitalized.

2. A book with two or more authors

Nesselroade, J. R., & Baltes, P. B. (1979). Longitudinal research in the study of behavioral development. New York: Academic Press.

An ampersand (&) separates the authors' names.

Index to APA references

3. A BOOK WITH AN EDITOR

Dohrenwend, B. S., & Dohrenwend, B. P. (Eds.). (1974). Stressful life events: Their nature and effects. New York: Wiley.

List the editors' names as if they were authors, but follow the last name with "(Eds.)."—or "(Ed.)." with only one editor. Note the periods inside and outside the final parenthesis.

4. A BOOK WITH A TRANSLATOR

Trajan, P. D. (1927). Psychology of animals (H. Simone, Trans.). Washington, DC: Halperin.

The name of the translator appears in parentheses after the title, followed by a comma, "Trans.," a closing parenthesis, and a final period. Note also the absence of periods in "DC."

5. A BOOK WITH A CORPORATE AUTHOR

Lorenz, Inc. (1992). Research in social studies teaching. Baltimore: Arrow Books.

For a work with a corporate or group author, begin the entry with the corporate or group name. In the references list, alphabetize the

APA 40c

work as if the first main word (excluding *The, A,* and *An*) were an author's last name.

6. An anonymous book

Merriam-Webster's collegiate dictionary (10th ed.). (1993). Springfield, MA: Merriam-Webster.

When no author is named, list the work under its title, and alphabetize it by the first main word (excluding *The, A, An*).

7. Two or more works by the same author(s)

Gardner, H. (1973a). The arts and human development. New York: Wiley.

Gardner, H. (1973b). The quest for mind: Piaget, Lévi-Strauss, and the structuralist movement. New York: Knopf.

When citing two or more works by exactly the same author(s), arrange the sources in order of their publication dates, earliest first. When citing two or more works by exactly the same author(s), published in the same year—as in the examples above—arrange them alphabetically by the first main word of the title and distinguish the sources by adding a letter to the date. Both the date *and* the letter are used in citing the source in the text (see p. 710).

8. A later edition

Bollinger, D. L. (1975). Aspects of language (2nd ed.). New York: Harcourt Brace Jovanovich.

The edition number in parentheses follows the title and is followed by a period.

9. A work in more than one volume

Lincoln, A. (1953). The collected works of Abraham Lincoln (R. P. Basler, Ed.). (Vol. 5). New Brunswick, NJ: Rutgers University Press.

Lincoln, A. (1953). The collected works of Abraham Lincoln (R. P. Basler, Ed.). (Vols. 1-8). New Brunswick, NJ: Rutgers University Press.

The first entry cites a single volume (5) in the eight-volume set. The second cites all eight volumes. Use the abbreviation "Vol." or "Vols." in parentheses, and follow the closing parenthesis with a period. In the absence of an editor's name, the description of volumes would follow the title directly: The collected works of Abraham Lincoln (Vol. 5).

10. An article or chapter in an edited book

Paykel, E. S. (1974). Life stress and psychiatric disorder: Applications of the clinical approach. In B. S. Dohrenwend & B. P. Dohrenwend (Eds.), Stressful life events: Their nature and effects (pp. 239-264). New York: Wiley.

Give the publication date of the collection (1974 above) as the publication date of the article or chapter. After the article or chapter title and a period, say "In" and then provide the editors' names (in normal order), "(Eds.)" and a comma, the title of the collection, and the page numbers of the article in parentheses.

11. An article in a journal with continuous pagination throughout the annual volume

Emery, R. E. (1982). Marital turmoil: Interpersonal conflict and the children of discord and divorce. Psychological Bulletin, 92, 310-330.

See page 546 for an explanation of journal pagination. Note that you do not place the article title in quotation marks and that you capitalize only the first words of the title and subtitle. In contrast, you underline the journal title and capitalize all significant words. Separate the volume number from the title with a comma and underline the number. Do not add "pp." before the page numbers.

12. An article in a journal that pages issues separately

Dacey, J. (1994). Management participation in corporate buy-outs. Management Perspectives, 7(4), 20-31.

Again, consult page 546 for an explanation of journal pagination. In this case, place the issue number in parentheses after the volume number without intervening space. Do *not* underline the issue number.

13. An article in a magazine

Van Gelder, L. (1986, December). Countdown to motherhood: When should you have a baby? Ms., 37-39, 74.

If a magazine has volume and issue numbers, give them as in models 11 and 12. Also give the full date of the issue: year, followed by a comma, month, and day (if any). Give all page numbers even when the article appears on discontinuous pages, without "pp."

14. An article in a newspaper

Ramirez, A. (1993, December 14). Computer groups plan standards. The New York Times, p. D5.

Give month *and* day along with year of publication. Use The in the newspaper name if the paper itself does. For a newspaper (unlike a journal or magazine), precede the page number(s) with "p." or "pp."

15. An unsigned article

The right to die. (1976, October 11). Time, 121, 101.

List and alphabetize the article under its title, as you would an anonymous book (model 6, p. 714).

16. A review

Dinnage, R. (1987, November 29). Against the master and his men [Review of the book A mind of her own: The life of Karen Horney]. The New York Times Book Review, 10-11.

If the review is not titled, use the bracketed information as the title, keeping the brackets.

17. Computer software

Project scheduler 8000 [Computer software]. (1995). Orlando, FL: Scitor.

Generally, give the title first, not underlined. Follow it with the type of source in brackets and then the date in parentheses. For publication information, give the location and name of the producer of the software.

18. A source on CD-ROM

Ramirez, A. (1993, 14 December). Computer groups plan standards. The New York Times Ondisc [CD-ROM], p. D5. Available: UMI-ProQuest: New York Times Ondisc Item: 9340006210

Treat an article on CD-ROM as you would a print article from the same type of periodical—journal, newspaper, and so on—but add the medium in brackets after the title, and supply the source and item or file number after "Available:" at the end of the entry.

The following model illustrates citation of an abstract on CD-ROM:

Willard, B. L. (1992). Changes in occupational safety standards, 1970-1990 [CD-ROM]. Abstract from: ProQuest File: Dissertation Abstracts Item: 7770763

19. An online source

The online models given here are adapted from both the APA *Publication Manual* and *Electronic Style: A Guide to Citing Elec-*

tronic Information, by Xia Li and Nancy B. Crane (1993), which adapts APA style to a range of electronic sources and which the *Publication Manual* itself relies on.

NOTE For an online source that is not retrievable by others, the APA requires omitting the source from your list of references and citing it only in your text in parentheses: if the author is not already named, (G. M. Shay, personal communication, June 6, 1996); if the author is already named, (personal communication, June 6, 1996). Such nonretrievable sources generally include personal electronic mail and postings on electronic bulletin boards and discussion groups. However, some discussion groups archive their postings so that they are retrievable (see p. 544), and you may cite an archived posting in your reference list.

The following models illustrate several kinds of online sources. In general, give author and title as you would for a printed source. Between these elements, provide the date of posting given by the source or, if no date is given, provide the date of your access to the source. For an online journal article, add the length (if given) after the article title (see the Palfrey entry below). After the title of the full source, provide the medium in brackets. At the end of the entry, after "Available," provide the electronic address and any other information (such as directory or file name) needed to retrieve the source. Do not add any period that is not part of the electronic address, even at the end of the entry. See page 622 for suggestions on breaking an electronic address from one line to the next.

An article in an online periodical:

Palfrey, A. (1996, January). Choice of mates in identical twins [12 paragraphs]. Modern Psychology [Online serial], 4(1). Available: ftp://modpsy.liasu.edu/palfrey4(1).txt

Ramirez, A. (1993, 14 December). Computer groups plan standards. The New York Times Online [Online], p. D5. Available: Nexis File:NYT

A source on the World Wide Web:

Leppik, P. (1996, January 21). The two rules of Internet security [Online]. Available: http://www.thinck.com/insec.html

An FTP (File Transfer Protocol) site:

Clarke, K. (1996, January). A "near" contract experience. E-Law--Murdoch Electronic Journal of Law [Online serial], 3. Available: ftp://infolib.murdoch.edu.au/pub/subj/law/jnl/elaw/comment/clarke.txt

A Gopher site:

Goetsch, S. (1995). And what about costume? Didaskalia: Ancient Theater Today [Online serial], 2(2). Available: gopher:// University of Warwick/Didaskalia/Didaskalia: Ancient Theater Today/03Features/Goetsch

A Telnet site:

Johnson, E. (1996, August 11). My house: Come on in. Houses of Cyberspace [Online]. Available: telnet://edwin.ohms.bookso .com 7777 @go #50827, press 10

An archived discussion group:

Campion, D. (1997, January 23). Cincinnati halfway houses. Corrections Alternatives Discussion List [Online]. Available e-mail: coralts@wau.edu

Cite e-mail, discussion-group messages, and other personal communications only in your text unless they are retrievable by others (see p. 717). The Listserv cited above is archived and so may be cited in the list of references.

A synchronous communication (IRC, MUD, MOO):

Chartreuse_Guest. (1996, February 13). Tuesday cafe session [Online]. Available: telnet://logos.daedalus.com:70/11/Alliance for Computers and Writing/NETORIC/Tuesday Cafe log 13Feb.

20. An abstract of an article or dissertation

Emery, R. E. (1982). Marital turmoil: Interpersonal conflict and the children of discord and divorce. Psychological Bulletin, 92, 310-330. (From Psychological Abstracts, 69, Item 1320)

When you cite the abstract of an article, rather than the article itself, give full publication information for the article, followed, in parentheses, by the information for the collection of abstracts, including title, volume number, and either page number or other reference number ("Item 1320" above).

For an abstract of an unpublished doctoral dissertation, give the university and the year of the dissertation in parentheses after the title. Then give the source of the abstract, the volume number, and the page number.

Steciw, S. K. (1986). Alterations to the Pessac project of Le Corbusier (Doctoral dissertation, University of Cambridge, England, 1986). Dissertation Abstracts International, 46, 565C.

21. A report

Gerald, K. (1958). Medico-moral problems in obstetric care (Report No. NP-71). St. Louis, MO: Catholic Hospital Association.

Treat the report like a book, but provide any report number in parentheses immediately after the title, with no punctuation between them.

For a report from the Educational Resources Information Center (ERIC), provide the ERIC document number in parentheses at the end of the entry:

Jolson, M. K. (1981). Music education for preschoolers. (Report No. TC-622). New York: Teachers College, Columbia University. (ERIC Document Reproduction Service No. ED 264 488)

22. A government publication

U.S. Commission on Civil Rights. (1983). Greater Baltimore commitment. Washington, DC: Author.

If no individual is listed as author, list the publication under the name of the sponsoring agency. When the agency is both the author and the publisher, use "Author" in place of the publisher's name.

23. An interview

Brisick, W. C. (1988, July 1). [Interview with Ishmael Reed]. Publishers Weekly, 41-42.

List a published interview under the interviewer's name. Provide the publication information appropriate for the kind of source the interview appears in (here, a magazine). Immediately after the date, in brackets, specify that the piece is an interview and, if necessary, provide other identifying information. If the interview has its own title, insert it after the date, as with a review (model 16).

Note that interviews you conduct yourself are not included in the list of references. Instead, use an in-text parenthetical citation: if the subject is already named, (personal communication, July 7, 1996); if not, (L. Kogod, personal communication, July 7, 1996).

24. A videotape, recording, or other audiovisual source

Spielberg, S. (Director). (1993). Schindler's list [Videotape]. Los Angeles: Viacom.

Siberry, J. (1995). Caravan. On Maria [CD]. Burbank, CA: Reprise.

For audiovisual sources such as films, videotapes, television or radio programs, or recordings, begin with the name of the person whose work you are citing, followed by his or her function, if appropriate, in parentheses. Immediately after the title, give the medium in brackets. Then give the location and name of the distributor.

APA document format

In general, the guidelines of the APA for document format coincide with those of the MLA, explained in Appendix A of this book. There are, however, some important differences and additions. The APA *Publication Manual* distinguishes between documents intended for publication (which will be set in type) and those submitted by students (which are the final copy). The format illustrated on the facing page is appropriate for most undergraduate papers. Note these features:

- Use a 1½-inch margin on the left and 1-inch margins on the other sides. (The wider left margin allows for a binder.)
- Number pages consecutively, starting with the title page. Identify each page (including the title page) with a shortened version of the title as well as a page number, as illustrated opposite.
- Put the abstract (if there is one) on a page by itself immediately after the title page, with the centered heading "Abstract."
- Run into your text all quotations of fewer than forty words, and enclose them in quotation marks. For quotations of more than forty words, set them off from your text by indenting all lines five spaces, double-spacing above and below. For student papers, the APA allows single-spacing of displayed quotations, like so:

  Echoing the opinions of other Europeans at the time, Freud had a poor view of Americans:

  > The Americans are really too bad. . . . Competition is much more pungent with them, not succeeding means civil death to every one, and they have no private resources apart from their profession, no hobby, games, love or other interests of a cultured person. And success means money. (1961, p. 86)

  Do not use quotation marks around a quotation displayed in this way.
- Do not label the introduction with a heading. For other main sections of your paper, such as "Method" and "Results," type headings as follows:

  First-Level Heading

  <u>Second-Level Heading</u>

  <u>Third-level heading.</u> Run this heading into the paragraph of text.

  See page 723 for further examples of headings.

APA 40c

TITLE PAGE

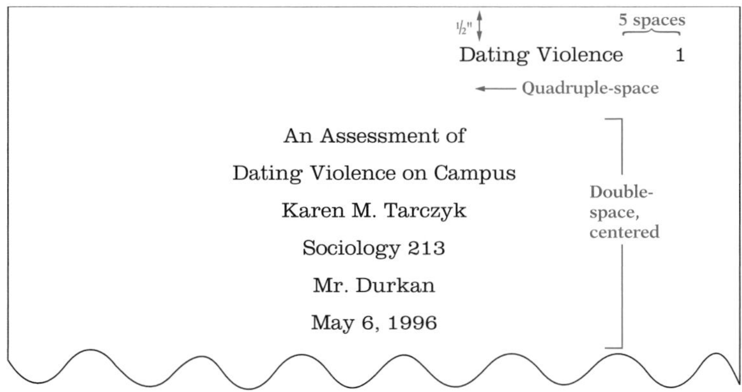

ABSTRACT (SUMMARY OF METHODS, FINDINGS, CONCLUSIONS)

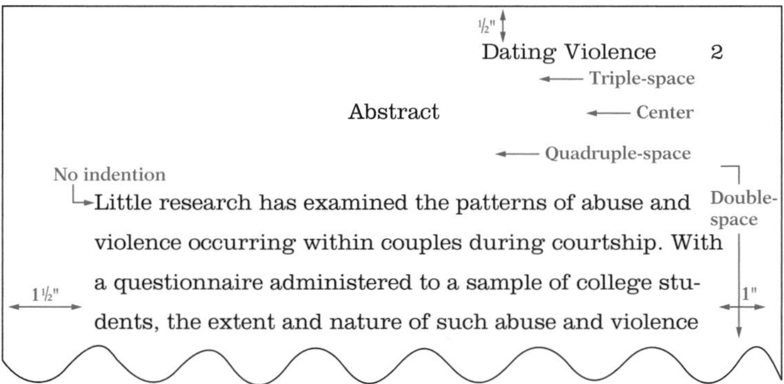

FIRST PAGE OF TEXT

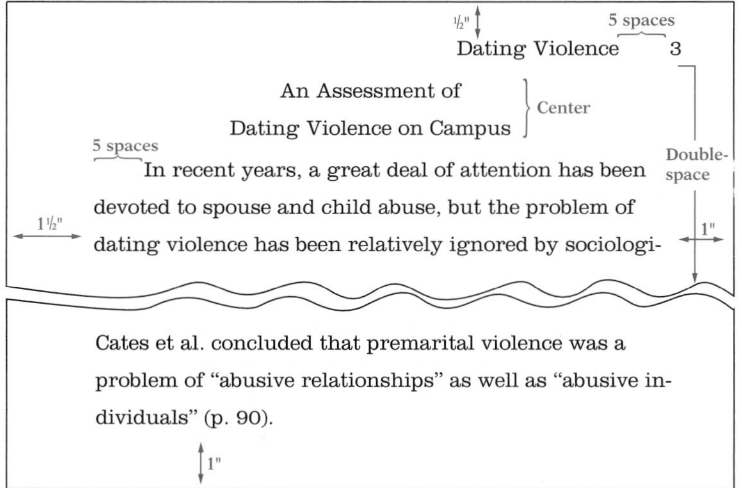

½"
5 spaces
Dating Violence 3
An Assessment of
Dating Violence on Campus
Center
5 spaces
In recent years, a great deal of attention has been devoted to spouse and child abuse, but the problem of dating violence has been relatively ignored by sociologi-
Double-space
1½"
1"
Cates et al. concluded that premarital violence was a problem of "abusive relationships" as well as "abusive individuals" (p. 90).
1"

- Present data in tables and figures (graphs or charts), as appropriate. (See the sample on p. 724 for a clear format to follow.) Begin each illustration on a separate page. Number each kind of illustration consecutively and separately from the other (Table 1, Table 2, etc., and Figure 1, Figure 2, etc.). Refer to all illustrations in your text—for instance, "(See Figure 3.)." Generally, place illustrations immediately after the text references to them. (See pp. 767–69 for more on illustrations.)
- Type the reference list as illustrated on page 711 and again with the sample paper on pages 725–26.

Because many departments and instructors have their own preferences for manuscript format, you should ask your instructor for his or her wishes before preparing your final draft.

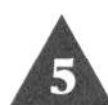 5 A sample social science paper

On the following pages are excerpts from a sociology paper. The student followed the organization described on pages 705–06 both in establishing the background for her study and in explaining her own research. She also followed the APA style of source citation and document format, although page borders and running heads are omitted here and only the required page breaks are indicated. See page 721 for spacing and other format details.

Excerpts from a research report (sociology)

[Title page.]

An Assessment of

Dating Violence on Campus

Karen M. Tarczyk

Sociology 213

Mr. Durkan

May 6, 1996

[New page.]

Abstract

Little research has examined the patterns of abuse and violence occurring within couples during courtship. With a questionnaire administered to a sample of 200 college students, the extent and nature of such abuse and violence were investigated. The results, some interpretations, and implications for further research are discussed.

[New page.]

An Assessment of
Dating Violence on Campus

In recent years, a great deal of attention has been devoted to spouse and child abuse, but the problem of dating violence has been relatively ignored by sociological research. It should be examined further since the premarital relationship is one context in which individuals learn and adopt behaviors that surface later in marriage.

The sociologist James Makepeace (1979) contends that courtship violence is a "potential mediating link" between violence in one's family of orientation and violence in one's later family of procreation (p. 103). Studying dating behaviors at Bemidji State University in Minnesota, Makepeace reported that one-fifth of the respondents had had at least one encounter with dating violence. He then extended these percentages to students nationwide, suggesting the existence of a major hidden social problem.

More recent research supports Makepeace's. Cates, Rutter, Karl, Linton, and Smith (1992) found that 22.3% of respondents at Oregon State University had been either the victim or the perpetrator of premarital violence. Another study (Cortes, 1996) found that so-called date rape, while much more publicized and discussed, was reported by many fewer woman respondents (2%) than was other violence during courtship (21%) (pars. 6-8).

[The introduction continues.]

All these studies indicate a problem that is being neglected. The present study's objective was to gather information on the extent and nature of premarital violence and to discuss some possible interpretations.

Method

Sample

I conducted a survey of 200 students (134 females, 66 males) at a large state university in the northeastern United States. The sample consisted of students enrolled in an introductory sociology course.

[The explanation of method continues.]

The Questionnaire

A questionnaire exploring the personal dynamics of relationships was distributed during regularly scheduled class. Questions were answered anonymously in a 30-minute time period. The survey consisted of three sections:

[The explanation of method continues.]

Section 3 required participants to provide information about their current dating relationships. Levels of stress and frustration, communication between partners, and patterns of decision making were examined. These variables were expected to influence the amount of violence in a relationship. The next part of the survey was adopted from Murray Strauss's Conflict Tactics Scales (1982). These scales contain 19 items designed to measure conflict and the means of conflict resolution, including reasoning, verbal aggression, and actual violence.

Results

The incidence of verbal aggression and threatened and actual dating violence was examined. A high number of students, 50% (62 of 123 subjects), reported that they had been the victim of verbal abuse. In addition, almost 14% (17 of 123) of respondents admitted being threatened with some type of violence, and more than 14% (18 of 123) reported being pushed, grabbed, or shoved. (See Table 1.)

[The explanation of results continues.]

[Table on a page by itself.]

Table 1

Incidence of Courtship Violence

Type of violence	Number of students reporting	Percentage of sample
Insulted or swore	62	50.4
Threatened to hit or throw something	17	13.8
Threw something	8	6.5
Pushed, grabbed, or shoved	18	14.6
Slapped	8	6.5
Kicked, bit, or hit with fist	7	5.7
Hit or tried to hit with something	2	1.6
Threatened with a knife or gun	1	0.8
Used a knife or gun	1	0.8

Discussion

Violence within premarital relationships has been relatively ignored. The results of the present study indicate that abuse and force do occur in dating relationships. Although the percentages are small, so was the sample. Extending them to the entire campus population would mean significant numbers. For example, if the nearly 6% incidence of being kicked, bitten, or hit with a fist is typical, then 300 students of a 5,000-member student body might have experienced this type of violence.

[The discussion continues.]

If the courtship period is characterized by abuse and violence, what accounts for it? The other sections of the survey examined some variables that appear to influence the relationship. Level of stress and frustration, both within the relationship and in the respondent's life, was one such variable. The communication level between partners, both the frequency of discussion and the frequency of agreement, was another.

[The discussion continues.]

The method of analyzing the data in this study, utilizing frequency distributions, provided a clear overview. However, more tests of significance and correlation and a closer look at the social and individual variables affecting the relationship are warranted. The courtship period may set the stage for patterns of married life. It merits more attention.

[New page.]

References

Cates, R. L., Rutter, C. H., Karl, J., Linton, M., & Smith, K. (1992). Premarital abuse: A social psychological perspective. Journal of Family Issues, 13(1), 79-90.

Cortes, Lana. (1996). Beyond date rape: Violence during courtship [20 paragraphs]. Electronic Journal of Intimate Violence [Online serial], 5(2). Available: www://acast.nova.edu/health/psy/file-disc/file50.html

Glaser, R., and Rutter, C. H. (Eds.). (1994). Familial violence [Special issue]. Family Relations, 43.

Makepeace, J. M. (1979). Courtship violence among college students. Family Relations, 28, 97-103.

Socko performance on campus. (1981, June 7). Time, 126, 66-67. Magazine Database [Online]. Available: Dialog Item 81-24327

Strauss, M. L. (1982). Conflict tactics scales. New York: Sociological Tests.

40d Writing in the natural and applied sciences

The natural and applied sciences include biology, chemistry, physics, mathematics, engineering, computer science, and their branches. Their purpose is to understand natural and technological phenomena. (A *phenomenon* is a fact or event that can be known by the senses.) Scientists conduct experiments and write to explain the step-by-step processes in their methods of inquiry and discovery.

1 Methods and evidence in the sciences

Scientists investigate phenomena by the **scientific method,** a process of continual testing and refinement. (See the box below.) Scientific evidence is almost always quantitative—that is, it consists of numerical data obtained from the measurement of phenomena. These data are called **empirical** (from a Greek word for "experience"): they result from observation and experience, generally in a controlled laboratory setting but also (as sometimes in astronomy or biology) in the natural world. Often the empirical evidence for scientific writing comes from library research into other people's reports of their investigations. Surveys of known data or existing literature are common in scientific writing.

The scientific method

- Observe carefully. Accurately note all details of the phenomenon being researched.
- Ask questions about the observations.
- Formulate a **hypothesis,** or preliminary generalization, that explains the observed facts.
- Test the hypothesis with additional observation or controlled experiments.
- If the hypothesis proves accurate, formulate a **theory,** or unified model, that explains *why.* If the hypothesis is disproved, revise it or start anew.

RESOURCES AND IDEAS

Greenway, William. "Imaginary Gardens with Real Toads: Nature Writing in the Curriculum." *Teaching English in the Two-Year College* 17 (1990): 189–92. Greenway demonstrates that nature writing, such as Annie Dillard's personal essays and Wordsworth's poetry, can help prepare students to write scientific research papers.

Hamilton, David. "Writing Science." *College English* 40 (1978): 32–40. Hamilton argues that instruction in science writing should emphasize writing not simply as a tool for scientists but as an essential and creative part of the scientific act.

Vargas, Marjorie Fink. "Writing Skills for Science Labs." *The Science Teacher* 53.8 (1986): 29–33. The author describes a fifty-minute class activity that helps students understand choices of person and voice dictated by the stylistic conventions of lab reports.

Winsor, Dorothy A. "Engineering Writing/Writing Engineering." *College Composition and Communication* 41 (1990): 58–70. Winsor uses "contemporary views about the textual shaping of knowledge" to examine engineers' writing and their "domain-specific" knowledge.

RESOURCES AND IDEAS

If your students need more help in writing about the sciences, you might refer them to these student texts:

Biddle, Arthur, and Daniel Bean. *Writer's Guide: Life Sciences.* Boston: Heath, 1987.

Day, Robert. *How to Write and Publish a Scientific Paper.* 4th ed. Phoenix: Oryx, 1994.

Pechenik, Jan. *A Short Guide to Writing About Biology.* 2nd ed. New York: HarperCollins, 1993.

2 Assignments in the sciences

No matter what your assignment, you will be expected to document and explain your evidence carefully so that anyone reading can check your sources and replicate your research. It is important for your reader to know the context of your research—both the previous experimentation and research on your particular subject (acknowledged in the survey of the literature) and the physical conditions and other variables surrounding your own work.

Assignments in the natural and applied sciences include the following:

- A **summary** distills a research article to its essence in brief, concise form. (Summary is discussed in detail on pp. 10–11.)
- A **critique** summarizes and critically evaluates a scientific report.
- A **laboratory report** explains the procedure and results of an experiment conducted by the writer. (An example begins on p. 733.)
- A **research report** reports on the experimental research of other scientists and the writer's own methods, findings, and conclusions.
- A **research proposal** reviews the relevant literature and explains a plan for further research.

A laboratory report has four or five major sections:

1. *Abstract:* a summary of the report. (See p. 734.)
2. *Introduction* or *Objective:* a review of why the study was undertaken, a summary of the background of the study, and a statement of the problem being studied.
3. *Method* or *Procedure:* a detailed explanation of how the study was conducted, including any statistical analysis.
4. *Results:* an explanation of the major findings (including unexpected results) and a summary of the data presented in graphs and tables.
5. *Discussion:* an interpretation of the results and an explanation of how they relate to the goals of the experiment. This section also describes new hypotheses that might be tested as a result of the experiment. If the section is brief, it may be combined with the previous section in a single section labeled *Conclusions.*

In addition, laboratory or research reports may include a list of references (if other sources were consulted). They almost always include tables and figures (graphs and charts) containing the data from the research (see p. 733).

COLLABORATIVE LEARNING

TEACHING TIP

Ask students to bring in examples of writing assignments from their science courses and to classify them according to this list. Which are most and least frequently used? They might also interview professors from their science courses, individually or in teams, to learn which writing strategies are most important for success in those courses.

RESOURCES AND IDEAS

Ambron, Joanna. "Writing to Improve Learning in Biology." *Journal of College Science Teaching* 16 (1987): 263–66. Ambron shows how using journal entries, freewriting, and short ungraded essays contribute to improved analytical skills.

Dodd, Janet S., et al. for the American Chemical Society. *ACS Style Guide: A Manual for Authors and Editors*. Washington: ACS, 1986.

Dorroh, John. "Reflections on Expressive Writing in the Science Class." *The Quarterly of the National Writing Project and the Center for the Study of Writing and Literacy* 15.3 (1993): 28–30. Dorroh describes use of an "expressive mode" notebook, portfolio grading, and writing-based instruction to improve student performance.

Goodman, W. Daniel, and John C. Bean. "A Chemistry Laboratory Project to Develop Thinking and Writing Skills." *Journal of Chemical Education* 60 (1983): 483–84. The authors outline "a method for conducting an undergraduate chemistry laboratory, in this case sophomore organic chemistry, that integrates a project laboratory with a writing task involving peer group interaction." The method requires "students to carry out an independent investigation of the synthesis of one or more aliphatic esters and to present their research in the form of professional papers."

Johnstone, Anne C., et al. *Uses for Journal-Keeping: An Ethnography of Writing in a University Science Class*. Norwood: Ablex, 1994. Johnstone offers an ethnographic study of the uses of different writing activities in learning science.

Killingsworth, M. Jimmie, and Michael K. Gilbertson. *Signs, Genres, and Communities in Technical Communication*. Amityville: Baywood, 1992. An examination of reports, manuals, and proposals characterizes them as "crystals of social action" within particular discourse communities.

Olmsted, John III. "Teaching Varied Technical Writing Styles in the Upper Division Laboratory." *Journal of Chemical Education* 61 (1984): 798–800. Olmsted describes a course that asks students to prepare reports in a variety of styles on experiments they have conducted. He describes in detail the twelve different kinds of reports students must submit during the course.

3 Tools and language in the sciences

Keeping a journal or notebook can help you reflect on and rethink your ideas for writing, pose and answer questions, or explore your changing attitudes about a subject. In the sciences, a **lab notebook** or **scientific journal** is almost indispensable for accurately recording the empirical data from observations and experiments. Use such a notebook or journal for these purposes:

- Record observations from reading, from class, or from the lab.
- Ask questions and refine hypotheses.
- Record procedures.
- Record results.
- Keep an ongoing record of ideas and findings and how they change as data accumulate.
- Sequence and organize your material as you compile your findings and write your report.

When writing in your notebook, try to observe as well the special conventions of language in the sciences. The main convention is the use of objective language that removes the writer as a character in the situation and events being explained, except as the impersonal agent of change, the experimenter. Although usage is changing, scientists still rarely use *I* in their reports and evaluations, and they often resort to the passive voice of verbs, as in *The mixture was then subjected to centrifugal force.* This conscious objectivity focuses attention (including the writer's) on the empirical data and what they show. It discourages the writer from, say, ascribing motives and will to animals and plants. For instance, instead of asserting that the sea tortoise *evolved* its hard shell *to protect* its body, a scientist would write only what could be observed: that the hard shell *covers and thus protects* the tortoise's body.

Science writers typically change verb tenses to distinguish between established information and their own research. For established information, such as that found in journals and other reliable sources, use the present tense (*Baroreceptors monitor blood pressure*). For your own research, use the past tense (*The bacteria died within three hours*).

As in the social sciences, each discipline in the natural and applied sciences has a specialized vocabulary that permits precise, accurate, and efficient communication. Some of these terms, such as *pressure* in physics, have different meanings in the common language and must be handled carefully in science writing. Others, such as *enthalpy* in chemistry, have no meanings in the common language and must simply be learned and used correctly.

Source citation and document format in the sciences

Within the natural and applied sciences, the practitioners of each discipline use a slightly different style of documentation and manuscript format. Following are some of the style guides most often consulted:

American Chemical Society. *ACS Style Guide: A Manual for Authors and Editors.* 2nd ed. 1997.

American Institute of Physics. *Style Manual for Guidance in the Preparation of Papers.* 4th ed. 1990.

American Mathematical Society. *A Manual for Authors of Mathematical Papers.* Rev. ed. 1990.

American Medical Association. *Manual of Style.* 8th ed. 1989.

Bates, Robert L., Rex Buchanan, and Marla Adkins-Heljeson, eds. *Geowriting: A Guide to Writing, Editing, and Printing in Earth Science.* 5th ed. 1992.

Council of Biology Editors. *Scientific Style and Format: The CBE Manual for Authors, Editors, and Publishers.* 6th ed. 1994.

Some documentation styles in the sciences closely resemble other styles discussed in this chapter: the Chicago system of in-text raised numerals referring to separate endnotes or footnotes (see p. 696) or the APA system of in-text parenthetical citations and a separate reference list (see p. 707). Ask your instructor what style you should use.

CBE numbered citations

A documentation style common in the health sciences, physics, mathematics, and other disciplines consists of in-text numbers that refer to a list of correspondingly numbered references. A version of this style, described here, appears in *Scientific Style and Format: The CBE Manual for Authors, Editors, and Publishers* (CBE is the Council of Biology Editors). For the text citations, follow the examples and instructions below.

Two standard encyclopedias[1,2] use this term.

These forms of immunity have been extensively researched.[3]

According to one report,[4] research into some forms of viral immunity is almost nonexistent.

Hepburn and Tatin[2] do not discuss this project.

- Within the text, use a raised number or numbers to refer to numbered sources in the reference list at the end of the text.

Wilkinson, A. M. "Jargon and the Passive Voice: Prescriptions and Proscriptions for Scientific Writing." *Journal of Technical Writing and Communication* 22 (1992): 319–25. The author reviews circumstances under which scientific writers should use the passive and warns against sweeping prohibitions of this strategy.

Young, Art, and Toby Fulwiler. *Writing Across the Disciplines: Research into Practice.* Upper Montclair: Boynton/Cook, 1986. This collection contains a number of essays demonstrating writing assignments in the sciences.

TEACHING TIP

Remind students that in mathematics and the natural and applied sciences, the hallmark of documentation is retrievability. Readers need to find references as easily as possible, since they may have to consider older work to interpret newer developments. The CBE's numerical system allows researchers to retrieve information quickly and easily. If students understand *why* the documentation works as it does, they will be better able to learn *how* to use it.

- The number for each source is based on the order in which you cite the source in the text: the first cited source is 1, the second is 2, and so on.
- When you cite a source you have already cited and numbered, use the original number again (see the last example on the previous page, which reuses the number 2 from the first example). This reuse is the key difference between the CBE numbered citations and numbered references to footnotes or endnotes (pp. 696–703). In the CBE style, each source has only one number, determined by the order in which the source is cited. With notes, in contrast, the numbering proceeds in sequence, so that sources have as many numbers as they have citations in the text.
- When you cite two or more sources at once, arrange their numbers in sequence and separate them with a comma and no space, as in the first example on the previous page.

NOTE Some versions of the numbered-citation style place citation numbers on the line of type (not raised) and between parentheses:

Two standard encyclopedias (1, 2) use this term.

CBE numbered references

The list of references for the numbered-citation style begins on a new page at the end of the text. Here is part of the first page:

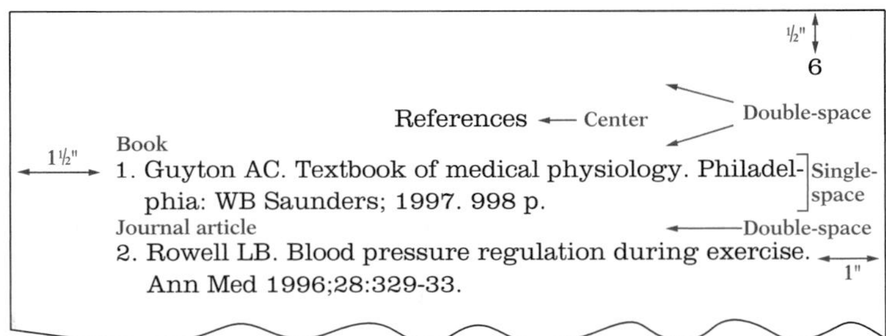

- Title the list of sources "References."
- Single-space each entry, and double-space between entries.
- Arrange the entries in numerical order—that is, in order of their citation in the text, *not* alphabetically.
- Begin each entry on a new line, and number it. Type the number on the line of type (not raised), and follow it with a period and a space. Indent subsequent lines of each entry directly under the first word of the first line.
- List authors' names with the last name first, followed by initials for first and middle names—for instance, Guyton AC in the

CBE
40d

Index to CBE references

first entry opposite. Do not use a comma after the last name or periods or space with initials.

- Separate authors' names with commas: Hepburn PX, Tatin JM.
- Do not underline or use quotation marks for any titles.
- For journal titles of more than one word, use abbreviations for main words of six or more letters (without periods) and omit most prepositions, articles, and conjunctions. Capitalize each word. For example, *Annals of Medicine* becomes Ann Med (see the second entry opposite), and *Journal of Chemical and Biochemical Studies* becomes J Chem Biochem Stud.
- For book and article titles, capitalize only the first word and any proper nouns (see both entries opposite).
- For books, separate the name of the publisher from the date of publication with a semicolon and a space: WB Saunders; 1997. End the reference with the total number of pages in the book: 998 p.
- For a journal article, put the date of publication after the abbreviated title of the journal, followed by the volume number and the inclusive page numbers for the article (with duplicated digits omitted): Ann Med 1996;28:329-33. For a journal that pages each issue separately, add the month (and day, if relevant) after the year, and add the issue number in unspaced parentheses after the volume number: 1993 3 Mar;16(8):16-7. For all journals, use no punctuation between title and date of publication. Put an unspaced semicolon between the date and volume number. Put an unspaced colon between the volume number (or parenthetical issue number) and the inclusive pages. (See models 6 and 7 following for more examples.)

1. A BOOK WITH ONE AUTHOR

1. Gould SJ. Time's arrow, time's cycle. Cambridge: Harvard Univ Pr; 1987. 222 p.

CBE
40d

2. A BOOK WITH MORE THAN ONE AUTHOR

2. Hepburn PX, Tatin JM. Human physiology. 3rd ed. New York: Columbia Univ Pr; 1995. 1026 p.

3. A BOOK WITH AN EDITOR

3. Jonson P, editor. Anatomy yearbook. Los Angeles: Anatco; 1997. 628 p.

4. A SELECTION FROM A BOOK

4. Krigel R, Laubenstein L, Muggia F. Kaposi's sarcoma. In: Ebbeson P, Biggar RS, Melbye M, editors. AIDS: a basic guide for clinicians. 2nd ed. Philadelphia: WB Saunders; 1997. p 100-26.

5. AN ANONYMOUS WORK

5. [Anonymous]. Health care for multiple sclerosis. New York: US Health Care; 1992. 86 p.

6. AN ARTICLE IN A JOURNAL WITH CONTINUOUS PAGINATION THROUGHOUT THE ANNUAL VOLUME

6. Ancino R, Carter KV, Elwin DJ. Factors contributing to viral immunity: a review of the research. Dev Biol 1993;40:156-9.

7. AN ARTICLE IN A JOURNAL THAT PAGES ISSUES SEPARATELY

7. Milbank Symposium. Medical decision making for the dying. Milbank Qtrly 1986 Feb;64(2):26-40.

8. AN ARTICLE IN A NEWSPAPER

8. Krauthammer C. Lifeboat ethics: the case of Baby Jesse. Washington Post 1986 June 13;Sect A:33(col 1).

9. AN ARTICLE IN A MAGAZINE

9. Van Gelder L. Countdown to motherhood: when should you have a baby? Ms. 1986 Dec:37-39.

10. A GOVERNMENT PUBLICATION

10. House (US). Medicare payment for outpatient occupational therapy services. 102nd Cong., 1st Sess. House Doc nr 409; 1991.

11. AN ELECTRONIC SOURCE

11. Project scheduler 8000 [computer program]. Version 3.1. Orlando (FL): Scitor; 1995. 1 computer disk: 3½ in. Accompanied by: 1 manual. System requirements: IBM PC or fully compatible computer; DOS 5.0 or higher; 320K RAM; hard disk with a minimum of 2 MB of free space.

12. Grady GF. The here and now of hepatitis B immunization. Today's Med [serial online] 1993 May 2;Doc nr 2:[2620 words]. Available from: Public Access Computer Systems Forum PACS-L via the Internet. Accessed 1996 Jan 21.

13. Reich WT, ed. Encyclopedia of bioethics [CD-ROM]. New York: Free Pr; 1978.

CBE document format

The CBE's *Scientific Style and Format* is not specific about margins, spacing for headings, and other elements of document format. Unless your instructor specifies otherwise, you can use the format of the APA (pp. 720–22). The CBE exception to this style is the list of references, which is described and illustrated on pages 730–31.

The most troublesome aspects of manuscript preparation in the sciences are equations or formulas and illustrations (tables and figures). When typing equations or formulas, be careful to reproduce alignments, indentions, underlining, and characters accurately. If your typewriter or word processor lacks special characters, write them in by hand. (Stationery and art-supply stores also have sheets of transfer type with special characters in different sizes that can be applied to your manuscript by rubbing.)

Because you will be expected to share your data with your readers, most of your writing for the sciences is likely to require illustrations to present the data in concise, readable form. Tables usually summarize raw data (see p. 735 for an example), whereas figures (mainly charts and graphs) recast the data to show noteworthy comparisons or changes. Follow the guidelines in Appendix A (pp. 767–69) for preparing tables and figures.

A sample science paper

The following biology paper illustrates many of the features described in the preceding pages. Some elements, such as page borders and identifiers, have been omitted. Except for the references list in CBE style, the format is APA style, for the reasons explained above.

A laboratory report (biology)

[Title page.]

Exercise and Blood Pressure

Liz Garson

Biology 161

Ms. Traversa

December 13, 1996

[New page.]

Abstract

The transient elevation of blood pressure following exercise was demonstrated by pressure measurements of twenty human subjects before and after exercise.

[New page.]

Exercise and Blood Pressure

Introduction

The purpose of this experiment was to verify the changes in blood pressure that accompany exercise, as commonly reported.[1,2] A certain blood pressure is necessary for the blood to supply nutrients to the body tissues. Baroreceptors near the heart monitor pressure by determining the degree to which blood stretches the wall of the blood vessel.

[The introduction continues.]

During exercise, the metabolic needs of the muscles override the influence of the baroreceptors and result in an increase in blood pressure. This increase in blood pressure is observed uniformly (irrespective of sex or race), although men demonstrate a higher absolute systolic pressure than do women.[3] During strenuous exercise, blood pressure can rise to 40 percent above baseline.[1]

Method

The subjects for this experiment were twenty volunteers from laboratory classes, ten men and ten women. All pressure measurements were performed using a standard sphygmomanometer, which was tested for accuracy. To ensure consistency, the same sphygmomanometer was used to take all readings. In addition, all measurements were taken by the same person to avoid discrepancies in method or interpretation.

The first pressure reading was taken prior to exercise as the subject sat in a chair. This pressure was considered the baseline for each subject. All subsequent readings were interpreted relative to this baseline.

In the experiment, the subjects ran up and down stairs for fifteen minutes. Immediately after exercising, the subjects returned to the laboratory to have their pressure measured. Thirty minutes later, the pressure was measured for the final time.

Results

Table 1 contains the blood pressure measurements for the male and female subjects. With the exception of subjects 3 and 14, all subjects demonstrated the expected post-exercise increase in blood pressure, with a decline to baseline or near baseline thirty minutes after exercise. The data for subjects 3 and 14 were invalid because the subjects did not perform the experiment as directed.

[Table on a page by itself.]

Table 1. Blood pressure measurements for all subjects (mmHg)

Subject	Baseline[a]	Post-exercise	30-minute reading
Male			
1	110/75	135/80	115/75
2	125/80	140/90	135/85
3	125/70	125/70	125/70
4	130/85	170/100	140/90
5	120/80	125/95	120/80
6	115/70	135/80	125/75
7	125/70	150/80	130/70
8	130/80	145/85	130/80
9	140/75	180/85	155/80
10	110/85	135/95	115/80
Female			
11	110/60	140/85	115/60
12	130/75	180/85	130/75
13	125/80	140/90	130/80
14	90/60	90/60	90/60
15	115/65	145/70	125/65
16	100/50	130/65	110/50
17	120/80	140/80	130/80
18	110/70	135/80	120/75
19	120/80	140/90	130/80
20	110/80	145/90	120/80

[a]Normal blood pressure at rest: males, 110-130/60-90; females, 110-120/50-80.

Discussion

As expected, most of the subjects demonstrated an increase in blood pressure immediately after exercise and a decline to near baseline levels thirty minutes after exercise. The usual pressure increase was 20-40 mmHg for the systolic pressure and 5-10 mmHg for the diastolic pressure.

In the two cases in which blood pressure did not elevate with exercise (subjects 3 and 14), the subjects simply left the laboratory and returned fifteen minutes later without having exercised. The experimental design was flawed in not assigning someone to observe the subjects as they exercised.

[New page.]

References

1. Guyton AC. Textbook of medical physiology. Philadelphia: WB Saunders; 1997. 998 p.

2. Rowell LB. Blood pressure regulation during exercise. Ann Med 1996;28:329-33.

3. Gleim GW, Stachenfeld NS. Gender differences in the systolic blood pressure response to exercise. Am Heart J 1991;121:524-30.

Part IX

Special Writing Situations

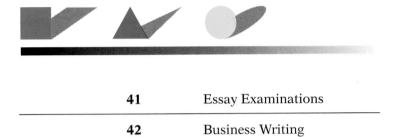

HIGHLIGHTS

Essay examinations in all courses force students to move swiftly through critical thinking, reading, and writing processes. At first, this may seem to violate the logic of the reflective writing process explained in this handbook. However, students need to learn how to use this process quickly when the situation and audience demand it. Essay exams are one way of making sure students understand their own writing processes as well as the content of a course; this chapter stresses the steps in the essay-writing process in order to help students become more aware of how they need to react under time pressure.

RESOURCES AND IDEAS

Berlin, James A. *Rhetoric and Reality: Writing Instruction in American Colleges, 1900–1985.* Carbondale: Southern Illinois UP, 1987. Berlin reviews in detail the spread of essay examinations throughout the curriculum.

Magistrale, Tony. "Examining the Essay Examination." In *Reading, Writing, and the Study of Literature.* Ed. Arthur W. Biddle and Toby Fulwiler. New York: McGraw, 1989. Magistrale discusses and summarizes bibliography on writing essay exams.

Ottens, Allen J. *Coping with Academic Anxiety.* New York: Rosen, 1984. Ottens provides a number of strategies for overcoming test anxiety.

A WRITER'S PERSPECTIVE

The papers they had written lay
in piles of blue and white;
But though they wrote it all by rote,
they did not write it right.

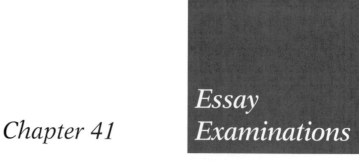

—ANONYMOUS

Chapter 41

In writing an essay for an examination, you summarize or analyze a topic, usually in several paragraphs or more and usually within a time limit. An essay question not only tests your knowledge of a subject (as short-answer and objective questions do) but also tests your ability to think critically about what you have learned. (If you have not already done so, read this book's Introduction on critical thinking, reading, and writing.)

41a Preparing for an essay examination

To do well on an essay exam, you will need to understand the course content, not only the facts but also the interpretation of them and the relations between them.

- Take careful lecture notes.
- Thoughtfully, critically read the assigned texts or articles. (See pp. 2–18.)
- Review regularly so the material has time to sink in and stimulate your thinking.
- Create summaries that recast others' ideas in your own words and extract the meaning from notes and texts. (See pp. 10–11 for instructions on summarizing.)
- Prepare notes or outlines that reorganize the course material around key topics or issues: in a business course, the advantages and disadvantages of several approaches to management; in a short-story course, a theme running through all the stories

you have read by a certain author or from a certain period; in a psychology course, various theorists' views of what causes a disorder such as schizophrenia. Any one of these is a likely topic for an essay question. Thinking of such categories can help you anticipate the kinds of questions you may be asked and increase your mastery of the material.

41b Planning your time and your answer

When you first receive an examination, take a few minutes to get your bearings and plan an approach. The time spent will not be wasted.

- Always read an exam all the way through at least once before you start answering any questions.
- As you scan the exam, determine which questions seem most important, which ones are going to be most difficult for you, and approximately how much time you'll need for each question. (Your instructor may help by assigning a point value to each question as a guide to its importance or by suggesting an amount of time for you to spend on each question.)

Planning continues when you turn to an individual essay question. Resist the temptation to rush right into an answer without some planning, for a few minutes can save you time later and help you produce a stronger essay.

- Read the question at least twice. You will be more likely to stick to the question and answer it fully.
- Examine the words in the question and consider their implications. Look especially for words such as *describe, define, explain, summarize, analyze, evaluate,* and *interpret,* each of which requires a different kind of response. Here, for example, is an essay question whose key term is *explain:*

  Question
  Given humans' natural and historical curiosity about themselves, why did a scientific discipline of anthropology not arise until the 20th century? Explain, citing specific details.

  See the box on the next page and consult earlier discussions of such terms on pages 44–45 and 106–14.
- After you are sure you understand the question, make a brief outline of the main ideas you want to include in your essay. Use the back of the exam sheet or booklet for scratch paper. In the following brief outline, a student planned her answer to the anthropology question above:

COLLABORATIVE LEARNING

TEACHING TIP

Divide students into groups according to their intended majors (humanities majors, education majors, and so on). Ask them to bring in examples of essay questions from examinations in their disciplines. (Some campus libraries or tutoring groups keep old copies of examinations on file for student use; these are prime sources of information.) Have each group determine the kinds of questions and key words used most often in their disciplines, then prepare a short report on the best strategies for writing successful essay answers for these questions.

A WRITER'S PERSPECTIVE

If a liberal education should teach students "how to think," not only in their own fields but in fields outside their own, . . . then bulling, even in its purest form, expresses an important part of what a pluralist university holds dear. . . . Good bull appears not as ignorance at all but as an aspect of knowledge. It is both relevant and "true." In a university setting, good bull is therefore of more value than "facts," which, without a frame of reference, are not even "true" at all.

—William G. Perry, Jr.

Sample instructions for essay examinations

Sample instructions	Key words	Strategies for answers	Examples of wrong answers
Define *dyslexia* and compare and contrast it with two other learning disabilities.	Define	Specify the meaning of *dyslexia*—distinctive characteristics, ways the impairment works, etc.	Feelings of children with dyslexia. Causes of dyslexia.
	Compare and contrast	Analyze similarities and differences (severity, causes, treatments, etc.).	Similarities without differences, or vice versa.
Analyze the role of Horatio in *Hamlet.*	Analyze	Break Horatio's role into its elements (speeches, relations with other characters, etc.).	Plot summary of *Hamlet.* Description of Horatio's personality.
Explain the effects of the drug Thorazine.	Explain	Set forth the facts and theories objectively.	Argument for or against Thorazine.
	Effects	Analyze the consequences.	Reasons for prescribing Thorazine.
Discuss term limits for elected officials.	Discuss	Explain and compare the main points of view on the issue.	Analysis of one view. Argument for or against one view.
Summarize the process that resulted in the Grand Canyon.	Summarize	Distill the subject to its main points, elements, or steps	Detailed description of the Grand Canyon.
How do you evaluate the Laffer curve as a predictor of economic growth?	Evaluate	Provide your opinion of significance or value, supported with evidence.	Explanation of the Laffer curve, without evaluation. Comparison of the Laffer curve and another predictor, without evaluation.

1. Unscientific motivations behind 19th-c anthro.

   Imperialist/colonialist govts.
   Practical goals
   Nonobjective and unscientific (Herodotus, Cushing)

2. 19th-c ethnocentricity (vs. cultural relativism)
3. 19th-c anthro. = object collecting

   20th-c shift from museum to univ.
   Anthro. becomes acad. disc. and professional (Boas, Malinowski)

- Write a brief thesis sentence for your essay that responds directly to the question and represents your view of the topic. (If you are unsure of how to write a thesis sentence, see pp. 47–51.) Include key phrases that you can expand with supporting evidence for your view. The thesis sentence of the student whose outline appears above concisely previews a three-part answer to the sample question:

  Anthropology did not emerge as a scientific discipline until the 20th century because of the practical and political motivations behind 19th-century ethnographic studies, the ethnocentric bias of Western researchers, and a strictly material conception of culture.

41c Starting the essay

An essay exam does not require a smooth and inviting opening. Instead, begin by stating your thesis immediately and giving an overview of the rest of your essay. Such a capsule version of your answer tells your reader (and grader) generally how much command you have and also how you plan to develop your answer. It also gets you off to a good start.

The opening statement should address the question directly and exactly, as it does in the successful essay answer beginning on the next page. In contrast, the opening of the unsuccessful essay (p. 743) restates the question but does not answer it, nor does the opening provide any sense of the writer's thesis.

41d Developing the essay

Develop your essay as you would develop any piece of sound academic writing:

- Observe the methods, terms, or other special requirements of the discipline you are writing in (see Chapters 39–40).
- Support your thesis sentence with solid generalizations (each one perhaps the topic sentence of a paragraph).

- Support each generalization with *specific, relevant* evidence (see pp. 130–33).

If you observe a few *don't*'s as well, your essay will have more substance:

- Avoid filling out the essay by repeating yourself.
- Avoid other kinds of wordiness that pad and confuse, whether intentionally or not. (See pp. 473–80.)
- Avoid substituting purely subjective feelings for real definition, analysis, or whatever is asked of you. (It may help to abolish the word *I* from the essay.)

The following essays illustrate a successful and an unsuccessful answer to the sample essay question on page 739 about anthropology. Both answers were written in the allotted time of forty minutes. Marginal comments on each essay highlight their effective and ineffective elements.

Successful essay answer

Anthropology did not emerge as a scientific discipline until the 20th century because of the practical and political motivations behind 19th-century ethnographic studies, the ethnocentric bias of Western researchers, and a strictly material conception of culture.

Gets right to the point with thesis statement.

Answers question directly and previews three-part response.

Before the 20th century, ethnographic studies were almost always used for practical goals. The study of human culture can be traced back at least as far as Herodotus's investigations of the Mediterranean peoples. Herodotus was like many pre-20th-century "anthropologists" in that he was employed by a government that needed information about its neighbors, just as the colonial nations in the 19th century needed information about their newly conquered subjects. The early politically motivated ethnographic studies the colonial nations sponsored tended to be isolated projects, and they aimed less to advance general knowledge than to solve a specific problem. Frank Hamilton Cushing, who was employed by the American government to study the Zuni tribe of New Mexico, and who is considered one of the pioneers of anthropology, didn't even publish his findings. The political and practical aims of anthropologists and the nature of their research prevented their work from being a scholarly discipline in its own right.

Point 1 of thesis: practical aims.

Example.

Example.

Anthropologists of the 19th century also fell short of the standards of objectivity needed for truly scientific study. This partly had to do with anthropologists' close connection to imperialist governments. But even independent researchers were hampered by the prevailing assumption that Western cultures were inherently superior. While the modern anthropologist believes that a culture must be studied in terms of its own values, early ethnographers were ethnocentric: they judged "primitive" cultures by their own "civilized" values. "Primitive" peoples were seen as uninteresting in their own right. The reasons to study them, ultimately, were to satisfy curiosity, to exploit them, or to prove their inferiority. There was even some debate as to whether so-called savage peoples were human.

Point 2 of thesis: ethnocentricity.

Finally, the 19th century tended to conceive of culture in narrow, material terms, often reducing it to a collection of artifacts. When not working for a government, early ethnographers usually worked for a museum. The enormous collections of exotica still found in many museums today are the legacy of this 19th-century object-oriented conception of anthropology, which ignored the myths, symbols, and rituals the objects related to. It was only when the museum tradition was broadened to include all aspects of a culture that anthropology could come into existence as a scientific discipline. When anthropologists like Franz Boas and Bronislaw Malinowski began to publish their findings for others to read and criticize and began to move from the museum to the university, the discipline gained stature and momentum.

Point 3 of thesis (with transition *Finally*): focus on objects.

Examples.

In brief, anthropology required a whole series of ideological shifts to become modern. Once it broke free of its purely practical bent, the cultural prejudices of its practitioners, and the narrow conception that limited it to a collection of objects, anthropology could grow into a science.

Conclusion restates thesis supported by essay.

Unsuccessful essay answer

The discipline of anthropology, the study of humans and their cultures, actually began in the early 20th century and was strength-

Introduction does not answer question.

ened by the Darwinian revolution, but the discipline did not begin to take shape until people like Franz Boas and Alfred Kroeber began doing scientific research among nonindustrialized cultures. (Boas, who was born in Germany but emigrated to the US, is the father of the idea of historical particularism.)

No thesis statement or sense of direction.

Irrelevant information.

Since the dawn of time, humans have always had a natural curiosity about themselves. Art and literature have always reflected this need to understand human emotions, thought, and behavior. Anthropology is yet another reflection of this need. Anthropologists have a different way of looking at human societies than artists or writers. Whereas the latter paint an individualistic, impressionistic portrait of the world they see, anthropologists study cultures systematically, scientifically. They are thus closer to biologists. They are *social scientists,* with the emphasis on both words.

Adds cliché to the language of the question without answering the question.

Wheel spinning by positioning contemporary anthropology as a scientific discipline.

Another reason why anthropology did not develop until the 20th century is that people in the past did not travel very much. The expansion of the automobile and the airplane has played a major role in the expansion of the discipline.

Not *Another reason* but the first reason given.

Assertion without support.

Cushing's important work among the Zuni Indians in New Mexico is a good example of the transition between 19th-century and 20th-century approaches to anthropology. Cushing was one of the first to develop the method of *participant observation.* Instead of merely coming in as an outsider, taking notes, and leaving, Cushing actually lived among the Zuni, dressing like them and following their customs. In this way, he was able to build a relationship of trust with his informants, learning much more than someone who would have been seen as an outsider.

Discussion of pioneers shows familiarity with their work but does not answer question.

Franz Boas, as mentioned earlier, was another anthropology pioneer. A German immigrant, Boas proposed the idea of *historical particularism* as a response to the prevailing theory of *cultural evolution.* Cultural evolution is the idea that cultures gradually evolve toward higher levels of efficiency and complexity. Historical particularism is the idea that every culture is unique and develops differently. Boas developed his theory to counter those who believed in cultural evolution. Working with the Kwakiutl Indians, he was also one of the first anthropologists to use a native assistant to help him gain access to the culture under study.

Repetition pads.

Information has unclear relevance to subject.

A third pioneer in anthropology was Malinowski, who developed a theory of *functionalism*—that culture responds to biological, psychological, and other needs. Malinowski's work is extremely important and still influential today.

Vague assertion without support.

Anthropologists have made great contributions to society over the course of the past century. One can only hope that they will continue the great strides they have made, building on the past to contribute to a bright new future.

Irrelevant and empty conclusion.

41e Rereading the essay

The time limit on an essay examination does not allow for the careful rethinking and revision you would give an essay or research paper. You need to write clearly and concisely the first time. But try to leave yourself a few minutes after finishing the entire exam for rereading the essay (or essays) and doing touch-ups.

- Correct illegible passages, misspellings, grammatical mistakes, and accidental omissions.
- Verify that your thesis is accurate—that it is, in fact, what you ended up writing about.
- Check to ensure that you have supported all your generalizations. Cross out irrelevant ideas and details, and add any information that now seems important. (Write on another page, if necessary, keying the addition to the page on which it belongs.)

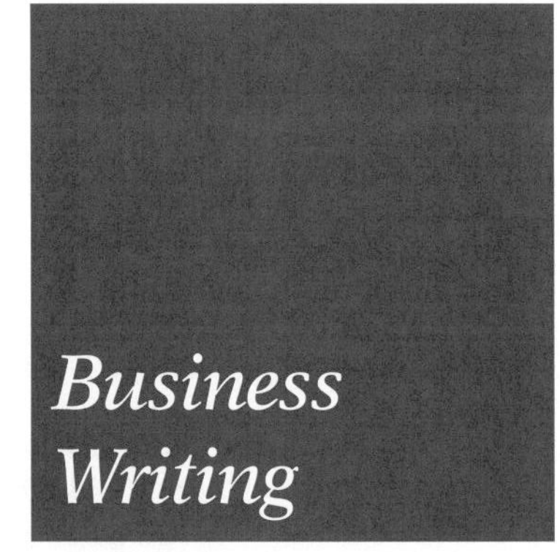

Chapter 42 Business Writing

HIGHLIGHTS

Business writing is likely to be popular with your students, for almost all of them can imagine a future in which it plays an important role. Although people in business generally write with less leisure than people in some other professions, they use the same critical thinking, reading, and writing skills presented throughout the handbook to analyze their audiences, plan their strategies, and compose their products. Because the writing businesspeople do represents their company or organization, they put an especially high value on correctness and clarity. This chapter emphasizes those virtues in both traditional and newer types of business writing, including letters, memos, job application documents, and electronic communications.

RESOURCES AND IDEAS

Drenk, Dean. "Teaching Finance Through Writing." *Teaching Writing in All Disciplines.* Ed. C. Williams Griffith. San Francisco: Jossey-Bass, 1982. 53–58. Drenk discusses the use of writing exercises to improve student handling of business discourse.

Hafer, Gary R. "Computer-Assisted Illustration and Instructional Documents in Technical Writing Classes." *Computers and Composition* 13 (1996): 49–56. Hafer argues for the advantages of teaching technical writing in the electronic classroom and offers practical advice on how to create instructional teams and design assignments.

Keene, Michael L. "Technical Information in the Information Economy." *Perspectives on Research and Scholarship in Composition.* Ed. Ben W. McClelland and Timothy R. Donovan. New York: MLA, 1985. Keene reviews research in technical and business communication.

Lanham, Richard. *Revising Business Prose.* 3rd ed. New York: Macmillan, 1991. Lanham offers strategies for recognizing and eliminating "businessese" from professional writing.

Mendelson, Michael. "Business Prose and the Nature of the Plain Style." *Journal of Business Communication* 24.2 (1987): 3–18. Mendelson demonstrates how various stylistic possibilities afford students different persuasive strategies.

Odell, Lee, and Dixie Goswami, eds. *Writing in Nonacademic Settings.* New York: Guilford,

When you write in business, you are addressing busy people who want to see quickly why you are writing and how they should respond to you. A wordy, incoherent letter or memo full of errors in grammar and spelling may prevent you from getting what you want, either because the reader cannot understand your wish or because you present yourself poorly. In business writing, follow these general guidelines:

- State your purpose right at the start.
- Be straightforward, clear, concise, objective, and courteous.
- Observe conventions of grammar and usage, which make your writing clear and impress your reader with your care.

ESL Business writing in your native culture may differ from American business writing. For instance, writers may be expected to begin with polite questions about the addressee or with compliments for the addressee's company. When writing to American businesspeople, get right to the point, even if at first your opening sounds abrupt or even impolite. See the examples on the following pages.

Writing in business demands efficiency, but efficiency does not mean haste. Developing, drafting, and revising—the three overlapping stages of the writing process discussed in Chapters 1 and 2—apply in business writing as much as in academic writing. Except for brief or routine letters and memos, plan what you want to say; work out your meaning freely, unself-consciously, without stopping to edit; and then revise and edit your draft so that it will achieve your purpose with your reader.

This chapter discusses business letters and job applications (below), business memos (p. 755), and the faxes and e-mail of the electronic office (p. 757). Additional information relevant to business communication appears in Appendix A on document design (pp. 765–72) and Appendix C on oral presentations (pp. 784–92).

42a Writing business letters and job applications

The formats of business letters and résumés are fairly standardized and are thus expected by your correspondents.

1 Using a standard form

Use either unlined white paper measuring 8½″ × 11″ or what is called letterhead stationery with your address printed at the top of the sheet. Type the letter single-spaced (with double space between elements) on only one side of a sheet. The two most common forms for business letters—the full block and the modified block—are illustrated and described on the following pages. (For long and complex letters, you may want to draw on some of the document-design techniques discussed on pp. 765–72.)

The letter

Unless you're using letterhead stationery, the **return-address heading** of the letter gives your address (but not your name) and the date. (See p. 750 for abbreviations of state names.) If you are using letterhead, you need add only the date. Place your heading at least an inch from the top of the page, or two lines below the letterhead if there is one. Align all lines of the heading on the left. In the block style, the return-address heading falls at the left margin (see the next page). In the modified block style, it falls to the right of the center of the paper (see p. 752).

The **inside address** shows the name, title, and complete address of the person you are writing to. (See p. 750 for abbreviations of state names.) Place the address at least two lines below the return-address heading. In both block and modified block styles, the address falls at the left margin of the page.

The **salutation** greets the addressee. In both styles it falls at the left margin, two lines below the inside address and two lines above the body of the letter. It is followed by a colon. If you are not addressing someone whose name you know, use a job title (*Dear Personnel Manager, Dear Customer Service Manager*) or use a general salutation (*Dear Smythe Shoes*). Use *Ms.* as the title for a woman when she has no other title, when you don't know how she prefers to be addressed, or when you know that she prefers to be addressed

1985. This essay collection encompasses the theory and practice of writing in the workplace, with heavy emphasis on ethnographic studies of "real" writers at work.

42a

TEACHING TIP

Encourage students to bring in copies of professional correspondence they have received (on the job, from the college or university, as junk mail) and discuss the different kinds of formats and rhetorical strategies they find. What similarities and differences do they discover? Can they relate these to the purpose and audience of each communication? Making students aware of such factors helps them realize that business communication employs the same writing strategies as other kinds of writing.

RESOURCES AND IDEAS

Mehaffy, Robert, and Constance Warloe. "Corporate Communications: Next Step for the Community Colleges?" *The Technical Writing Teacher* 16 (1989): 1–11. Mehaffy and Warloe show the curriculum design for a professional writing course taking into account adult learning styles, computer-assisted composition, reader-centered writing, interviewing for information, project management, and team design.

Business letter in block style

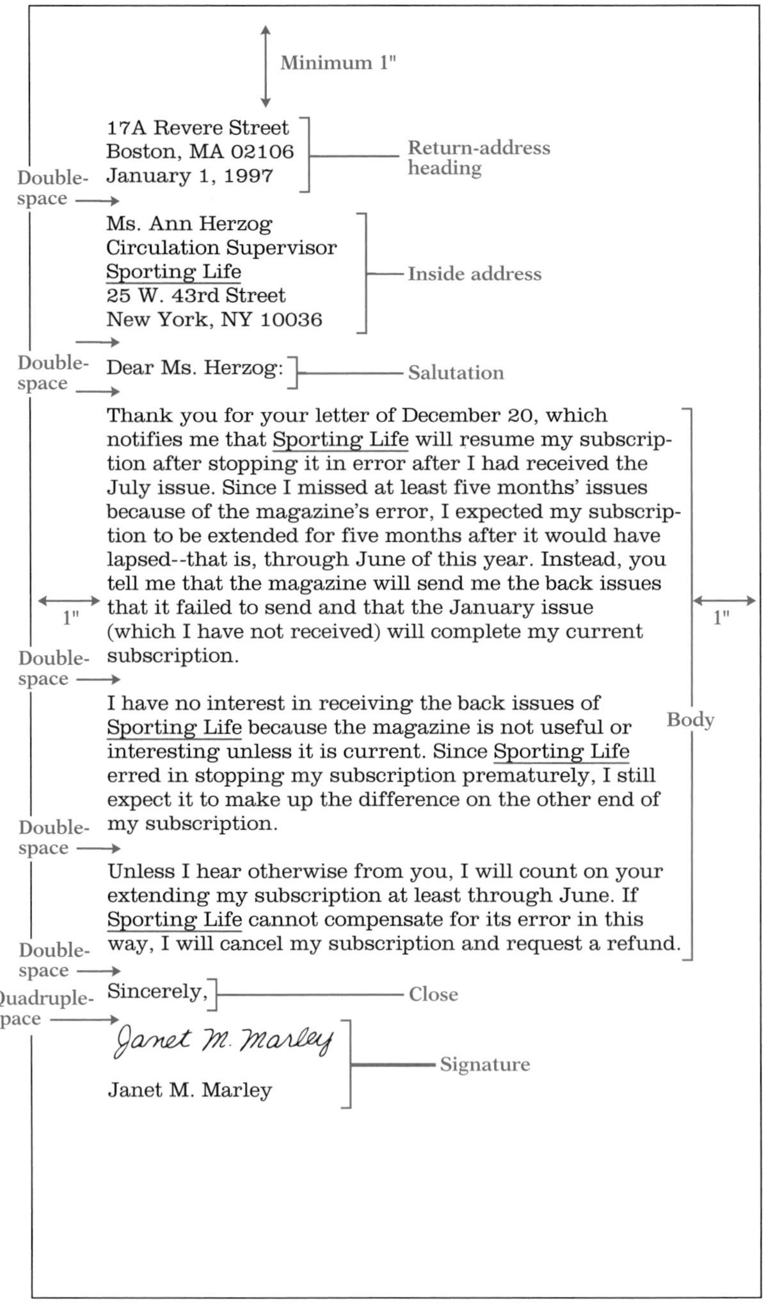
17A Revere Street
Boston, MA 02106
January 1, 1997

Ms. Ann Herzog
Circulation Supervisor
Sporting Life
25 W. 43rd Street
New York, NY 10036

Dear Ms. Herzog:

Thank you for your letter of December 20, which notifies me that Sporting Life will resume my subscription after stopping it in error after I had received the July issue. Since I missed at least five months' issues because of the magazine's error, I expected my subscription to be extended for five months after it would have lapsed--that is, through June of this year. Instead, you tell me that the magazine will send me the back issues that it failed to send and that the January issue (which I have not received) will complete my current subscription.

I have no interest in receiving the back issues of Sporting Life because the magazine is not useful or interesting unless it is current. Since Sporting Life erred in stopping my subscription prematurely, I still expect it to make up the difference on the other end of my subscription.

Unless I hear otherwise from you, I will count on your extending my subscription at least through June. If Sporting Life cannot compensate for its error in this way, I will cancel my subscription and request a refund.

Sincerely,

Janet M. Marley

Janet M. Marley

as *Ms.* If you know a woman prefers to be addressed as *Mrs.* or *Miss,* use the appropriate title.

The **body** of the letter, containing its substance, begins at the left margin in both letter styles. Instead of indenting the first line of each paragraph, place an extra line of space between paragraphs so that they are readily visible.

The letter's **close** begins two lines below the last line of the body and aligns with the return-address heading. That is, in the block style the close falls at the left margin (see the facing page), whereas in the modified block style it falls to the right of the center of the page (p. 752). The close should reflect the level of formality in the salutation. For formal letters, *Respectfully, Cordially, Yours truly,* and *Sincerely* are common closes. For less formal letters, you may choose to use *Warmest regards, Regards, Best wishes,* or the like. Only the first word of the close is capitalized, and the close is followed by a comma.

The **signature** of a business letter falls below the close and has two parts. One is your name typed on the fourth line below the close. The other is your handwritten signature, which fills the space between the close and your typed name. The signature should consist only of your name, as you sign checks and other documents.

Below the signature at the left margin, you may want to include additional information such as *Enc. 3* (indicating that there are three enclosures with the letter); *cc: Margaret Newton* (indicating that a copy is being sent to the person named); or *CHC/enp* (the initials of the author/the initials of the typist).

The envelope

The envelope of the letter (see below) should show your name and address in the upper-left corner and the addressee's name, title, and address in the center. Use an envelope that will adequately accommodate the letter once it is folded horizontally in thirds.

JANET M MARLEY
17A REVERE ST
BOSTON MA 02106

MS ANN HERZOG
CIRCULATION SUPERVISOR
SPORTING LIFE
25 W 43RD ST
NEW YORK NY 10036-7146

The United States Postal Service recommends a format for envelopes that makes them easy for machines to read. As illustrated on the previous page, use all capital letters and no punctuation (spaces separate the elements on a line).

The following are the common Postal Service abbreviations for addresses:

Street names

Avenue	AVE	Expressway	EXPY	Road	RD
Boulevard	BLVD	Freeway	FWY	Square	SQ
Circle	CIR	Lane	LN	Street	ST
Court	CT	Parkway	PKY	Turnpike	TPKE

Compass points

North	N	West	W	Southwest	SW
East	E	Northeast	NE	Northwest	NW

State names

Alabama	AL	Kentucky	KY	North Dakota	ND
Alaska	AK	Louisiana	LA	Ohio	OH
Arizona	AZ	Maine	ME	Oklahoma	OK
Arkansas	AR	Maryland	MD	Oregon	OR
California	CA	Massachusetts	MA	Pennsylvania	PA
Colorado	CO	Michigan	MI	Puerto Rico	PR
Connecticut	CT	Minnesota	MN	Rhode Island	RI
Delaware	DE	Mississippi	MS	South Carolina	SC
District of		Missouri	MO	South Dakota	SD
Columbia	DC	Montana	MT	Tennessee	TN
Florida	FL	Nebraska	NE	Texas	TX
Georgia	GA	Nevada	NV	Utah	UT
Hawaii	HI	New		Vermont	VT
Idaho	ID	Hampshire	NH	Virginia	VA
Illinois	IL	New Jersey	NJ	Washington	WA
Indiana	IN	New Mexico	NM	West Virginia	WV
Iowa	IA	New York	NY	Wisconsin	WI
Kansas	KS	North Carolina	NC	Wyoming	WY

COLLABORATIVE LEARNING

Invite students to write letters of complaint about issues (large or small) that have always bothered them, but that they have never taken the time to address. Then ask students to work in small groups to critique the letters from the vantage point of the community leaders, legislators, or businesspeople who might receive them. This exercise in role-playing may help students to understand the value of discretion and cogency, even in a complaint letter.

Writing requests and complaints

Letters requesting something—for instance, a pamphlet, information about a product, a T-shirt advertised in a magazine—must be specific and accurate about the item you are requesting. The letter should describe the item completely and, if applicable, include a copy or description of the advertisement or other source that prompted your request.

Letters complaining about a product or a service (such as a wrong billing from the telephone company) should be written in a reasonable but firm tone. (See the sample letter on p. 748.) Assume that the addressee is willing to resolve the problem when he or she has the relevant information. In the first sentence of the letter, say what you are writing about. Then provide as much background as needed, including any relevant details from past correspondence (as in the sample letter). Describe exactly what you see as the problem, sticking to facts and avoiding discourses on the company's social responsibility or your low opinion of its management. In the clearest and fewest possible words and sentences, proceed directly from one point to the next without repeating yourself. Always include your opinion of how the problem can be solved. Many companies are required by law to establish a specific procedure for complaints about products and services. If you know of such a procedure, be sure to follow it.

 Writing a job application and résumé

In applying for a job or requesting a job interview, send both a résumé and a letter. Both should be on high-quality 8½″ × 11″ paper. For the letter follow these guidelines, illustrated in the sample on the next page.

- Use the block or modified block style (pp. 748, 752).
- Think of the letter as an interpretation of your résumé for a particular job, not as a detailed account of the entire résumé. Instead of reciting your job history, highlight and reshape only the relevant parts.
- Announce at the outset what job you seek and how you heard about it.
- Include any special reason you have for applying, such as a specific career goal.
- Summarize your qualifications for this particular job, including relevant facts about education and employment and emphasizing notable accomplishments. Mention that additional information appears in an accompanying résumé.
- At the end of the letter, mention that you are available for an interview at the convenience of the addressee, or specify when you will be available (for instance, when your current job or classes leave you free).

The résumé that you enclose with your letter of application should follow these guidelines:

- Provide the following, in table form: your name and address, career objective, education, employment history, any special skills or awards, and information about how to obtain your references. (See the sample on p. 753.)

(Text continues p. 755)

 **COMPUTER EXERCISE**

TEACHING TIP

Students writing with a word processor may be able to take advantage of several commercially prepared résumé-formatting packages. Although these programs are useful, remind students that hiring officers at companies may see literally thousands of these cookie-cutter résumés each year. The time students spend individualizing their own résumés may result in documents that better catch and keep a reader's attention.

Whether they are using a typewriter or a computer printer, remind students to make sure that they use a new or nearly new ribbon or ink cartridge when printing out their résumés, in order to guarantee the clearest, sharpest copy possible. (This is especially important if the résumé will be photocopied or electronically scanned.)

COLLABORATIVE LEARNING

Have students work in groups to critique each other's résumés and job letters. Encourage the groups to ask each candidate about information that seems inconsistent or unclear as well as checking for proofreading errors.

Job-application letter in modified block style

3712 Swiss Avenue
Dallas, TX 75204
March 2, 1997

Personnel Manager
Dallas News
Communications Center
Dallas, TX 75222

Dear Personnel Manager:

In response to your posting in the English Department of Southern Methodist University, I am applying for the summer job of part-time editorial assistant for the Dallas News.

I am now enrolled at Southern Methodist University as a sophomore, with a dual major in English literature and journalism. My courses so far have included news reporting, copy editing, and electronic publishing. I worked a summer as a copy aide for my hometown newspaper, and for two years I have edited and written sports stories and features for the university newspaper. My feature articles cover subjects as diverse as campus elections, parking regulations, visiting professors, and speech codes.

As the enclosed résumé and writing samples indicate, my education and practical knowledge of newspaper work prepare me for the opening you have.

I am available for an interview at your convenience and would be happy to show more samples of my writing. Please call me at 744-3816 or e-mail me at ianirv@mail.smu.edu.

Sincerely,

Ian M. Irvine

Ian M. Irvine

Enc.

Résumé (traditional design)

Ian M. Irvine
3712 Swiss Avenue
Dallas, TX 75204
214-744-3816
E-mail: ianirv@mail.smu.edu

Position desired
Part-time editorial assistant.

Education
Southern Methodist University, 1995 to present.
Current standing: sophomore.
Major: English literature and journalism.
Journalism courses: news reporting, copy editing, electronic publishing, communications arts, broadcast journalism.

Abilene (Texas) Senior High School, 1991-1995.
Graduated with academic, college-preparatory degree.

Employment history
1995 to present. Reporter, Daily Campus, student newspaper of Southern Methodist University.
Write regular coverage of baseball, track, and soccer teams. Write feature stories on campus policies and events. Edit sports news, campus listings, features.

Summer 1996. Copy aide, Abilene Reporter-News.
Routed copy, ran errands, and assisted reporters with research.

Summer 1995. Painter, Longhorn Painters, Abilene.
Prepared and painted exteriors and interiors of houses.

Special skills
Fluent in Spanish.
Proficient in Internet research and word processing.

References
Available on request:

Placement Office
Southern Methodist University
Dallas, TX 75275

RÉSUMÉ (CONTEMPORARY DESIGN)

Ian M. Irvine

3712 Swiss Avenue
Dallas, TX 75204
214-744-3816
ianirv@mail.smu.edu

Position desired	Part-time editorial assistant.
Education	*Southern Methodist University,* 1995 to present. Current standing: sophomore. Major: English literature and journalism. Journalism courses: news reporting, copy editing, electronic publishing, communications arts, broadcast journalism. *Abilene (Texas) Senior High School*, 1991-1995. Graduated with academic, college-preparatory degree.
Employment history	1995 to present. Reporter, *Daily Campus*, student newspaper of Southern Methodist University. Write regular coverage of baseball, track, and soccer teams. Write feature stories on campus policies and events. Edit sports news, campus listings, features. Summer 1996. Copy aide, *Abilene Reporter-News.* Routed copy, ran errands, and assisted reporters with research. Summer 1995. Painter, Longhorn Painters, Abilene. Prepared and painted exteriors and interiors of houses.
Special skills	Fluent in Spanish. Proficient in Internet research and word processing.
References	Available on request: Placement Office Southern Methodist University Dallas, TX 75275

- Use headings to mark the various sections of the résumé, spacing around them and within sections so that important information stands out.
- Usage varies on capital letters in résumés. Keep in mind that passages with many capitals can be hard to read. Definitely use capitals for proper nouns (pp. 432–33), but consider dropping them for job titles, course names, department names, and the like. (See p. 434.)
- Limit your résumé to one page so that it can be quickly scanned. However, if your experience and education are extensive, a two-page résumé is preferable to a single cramped, unreadable page.

In preparing your résumé, you may wish to use some of the techniques of document design discussed on pages 765–72, such as variations in spacing and in type sizes and styles. The sample résumé appears opposite in a more contemporary format.

You may also wish to consult one of the many books devoted to application letters, résumés, and other elements of a job search. Two helpful guides are Richard N. Bolles, *What Color Is Your Parachute? A Practical Manual for Job-Hunters and Career Changers,* and Tom Jackson, *The Perfect Résumé.*

42b Writing business memos

Unlike business letters, which address people in other organizations, business memorandums (memos, for short) address people within the same organization. A memo can be quite long, but more often it reports briefly on a specific topic: an answer to a question, a progress report, an evaluation. The form and the structure of a memo are designed to get to the point and dispose of it quickly.

The memo has no return address, inside address, salutation, or close. Instead, as shown in the sample memo on the next page, the heading typically consists of the company's name, the addressee's name, the writer's name, the date, and a subject description or title. Type the body of the memo as you would the body of a business letter: single-spaced, double-spaced between paragraphs, and no paragraph indentions. Never sign a business memo, but do initial your name in the heading. If copies of the memo need to be sent to people not listed in the "To" line, list those people two spaces below the last line.

Immerse your reader in your subject at the very beginning of the memo. State your reason for writing in the first sentence, perhaps outlining a problem, making a request, referring to a request that prompted the memo, or briefly summarizing new findings. Do not,

COLLABORATIVE LEARNING

Encourage students to bring in memos from their current or previous places of business. Photocopy a set of five to ten memos and ask students to work in groups to identify indications of audience and tone, and to evaluate the clarity and effectiveness of each memo.

Bigelow Wax Company

TO: Aileen Rosen, Director of Sales
FROM: Patricia Phillips, Territory 12 PP
DATE: March 17, 1997
SUBJECT: 1996 sales of Quick Wax in Territory 12

Since it was introduced in January of 1996, Quick Wax has been unsuccessful in Territory 12 and has not affected the sales of our Easy Shine. Discussions with customers and my own analysis of Quick Wax suggest three reasons for its failure to compete with our product.

1. Quick Wax has not received the promotion necessary for a new product. Advertising--primarily on radio--has been sporadic and has not developed a clear, consistent image for the product. In addition, the Quick Wax sales representative in Territory 12 is new and inexperienced; he is not known to customers, and his sales pitch (which I once overheard) is weak. As far as I can tell, his efforts are not supported by phone calls or mailings from his home office.

2. When Quick Wax does make it to the store shelves, buyers do not choose it over our product. Though priced competitively with our product, Quick Wax is poorly packaged. The container seems smaller than ours, though in fact it holds the same eight ounces. The lettering on the Quick Wax package (red on blue) is difficult to read, in contrast to the white-on-green lettering on the Easy Shine package.

3. Our special purchase offers and my increased efforts to serve existing customers have had the intended effect of keeping customers satisfied with our product and reducing their inclination to stock something new.

Copies: L. Goldberger, Director of Marketing
L. MacGregor, Customer Service Manager

however, waste words with expressions like "The purpose of this memo is. . . ." Devote the first paragraph to a succinct presentation of your solution, recommendation, answer, or evaluation. The first paragraph should be short, and by its end your reader should know precisely what to expect from the rest of the memo: the details and reasoning that support your conclusion. Deliver that information in the body of the memo. The paragraphs may be numbered so that the main divisions of your message are easy to see.

A business memo can be more informal in tone than a business letter, particularly if you know the addressee; but it should not be wordy. Use technical terms if your reader will understand them, but otherwise keep language simple and use short sentences. Provide only the information that your reader needs to know.

See also pages 765–70 for techniques of document design (such as the numbered list in the sample memo) that can improve the readability of a business memo.

Note See page 771 for a sample of a business report, which is more formal in expression and format than a memo.

42c Communicating electronically

Communicating via electronic devices, especially facsimile (fax) machines and computerized electronic mail (e-mail), speeds up correspondence but also creates new challenges. For both fax transmissions and e-mail, the standards are the same as for other business correspondence: state your purpose at the outset and write straightforwardly, clearly, concisely, objectively, courteously, and correctly.

Faxes

For fax transmissions, follow the format of a letter (p. 747) or memo (p. 755), as appropriate.

- Provide a cover sheet containing the addressee's name, company, and fax number; the date, time, and subject; your own name and fax and telephone numbers (the telephone number is important in case something goes wrong with the transmission); and the total number of pages (including the cover sheet) in the fax.
- Because fax transmissions can go astray, it's often wise to advise your addressee to expect a fax. Such advice is essential if the fax is confidential, because the machine is often shared.
- Transmission by fax can imply that the correspondence is urgent. If yours isn't, consider using the mail. (Swamping your correspondents with needless faxes can make you the boy who cried wolf when you really have an urgent message to transmit.)

E-mail

Postings by electronic mail tend to be more offhand and informal than standard business letters on paper. E-mail can communicate very effectively with a little attention and structure:

RESOURCES AND IDEAS

Hawisher, Gail E., and Charles Moran, "Electronic Mail and the Writing Instructor." *College English* 55 (1993): 627–43. The authors discuss the use of e-mail in teaching, with extensive bibliography.

Spooner, Michael, and Kathleen Yancy. "Postings on a Genre of Email." *College Composition and Communication* 47:2 (1996): 252–78. The authors explore issues of collaboration and the nature of e-mail communication using print versions of actual e-mail dialogues.

- An e-mail posting announces itself in the reader's list of incoming mail, which may be extensive. Give your posting a title that accurately describes the contents, so that your reader knows what priority to assign it.
- Because an e-mail reader must scroll through a posting—and so cannot review two or more screens at once—your posting should be as short as possible. Take a few minutes to condense your draft message before sending it.
- Also because of scrolling, a posting will be more effective if it is tightly structured, with a clear forecast of its contents and a clear division into parts.
- Because many e-mail users cannot display a posting while they are responding to it, your postings should center on one or two points. Then the reader has a better chance of responding to your whole message.
- When you respond to someone else's posting, you can avoid restating it by excerpting relevant parts in your own message.
- Take the time to edit your posting. Errors in grammar, punctuation, and spelling will interfere with your message.
- E-mail usually does not allow underlining, italics, or boldface, so you can't emphasize or highlight words conventionally. E-mail writers have devised some substitutes, including asterisks before and after words to be emphasized (I *will not* be able to attend) or an underscore before and after a book title (Measurements coincide with those in _Joule's Handbook_). Don't use all-capital letters for emphasis: they yell too loudly.

Because it is sometimes anonymous as well as immediate, e-mail has been subject to abuses. Its users have developed some basic courtesies:

- The headings in an e-mail message are usually dictated by the network, but for business correspondence you can still address your reader(s) by name and sign off with your own name.
- Most e-mailers consider the medium more immediate than print mail and expect quick responses to their messages.
- E-mail, like faxes, may be broadcast to many recipients at once with a few keystrokes. Avoid flooding your correspondents with irrelevant postings: target your messages only to those who can actually use them.
- E-mail sometimes seems more free and impersonal than telephone conversations or print mail. But that's no justification for flaming, or attacking, correspondents. Address them respectfully and politely, as you would on paper.

Appendix A

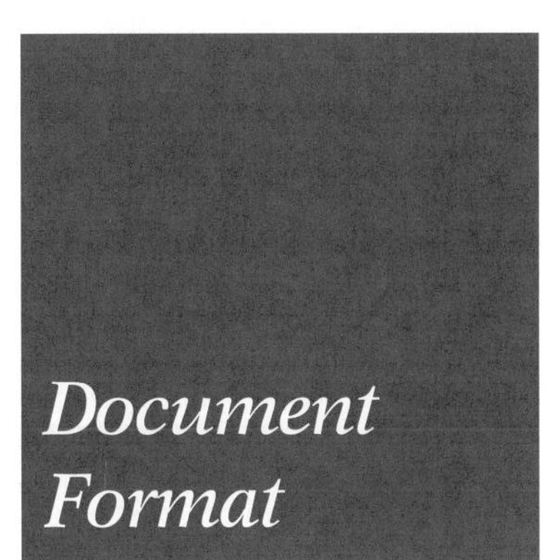

Document Format

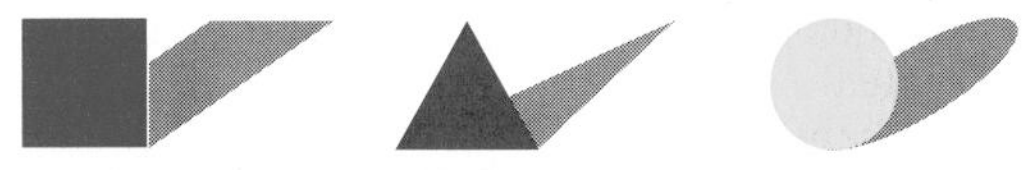

HIGHLIGHTS

Many students don't realize how important the final physical appearance of their text is and how a well-produced text can make the content more effective for readers. This appendix reemphasizes the presentation of a piece of writing as the fitting end to the writing process.

New material in section A2 offers tips for using a computer to design documents and includes full-page samples.

This appendix has two parts: it describes and illustrates a basic format for academic papers (below), and it describes and illustrates some ways you can use a computerized word processor or desktop publisher to present your documents attractively and effectively (pp. 765–72).

TEACHING TIP

Demonstrate to students the effect of different arrangements and presentations of the same text. Comparing formats in this way teaches them the importance of good manuscript presentation. You might handwrite, type, and print out a simple passage on several types of computer printers (with and without corrected errors), then display these on overhead transparencies for class discussion.

A1 Using a basic format for academic papers

A legible, consistent, and attractive document is a service to readers because it makes reading easier. The format recommended here is adapted from the *MLA Handbook for Writers of Research Papers,* the style guide for English, foreign languages, and some other disciplines. Most of these guidelines are standard, but your instructor may request that you follow different conventions in some matters or supplement these guidelines with those of other disciplines, as described elsewhere in this book:

- For history, art history, philosophy, and some other humanities, see page 703 on the Chicago format (*Chicago Manual of Style* and the student guide adapted from it, Kate L. Turabian's *Manual for Writers of Term Papers, Theses, and Dissertations*).
- For psychology and other social sciences, see pages 720–22 on the *Publication Manual of the American Psychological Association.*
- For the natural and applied sciences and mathematics, see page 733 on *Scientific Style and Format,* the guide of the Council of Biology Editors.

RESOURCES AND IDEAS

Connors, Robert J. "Actio: A Rhetoric of Manuscripts." *Rhetoric Review* 2 (1983): 64–73. Connors discusses the rhetorical effect of typefaces, paper, and format on readers.

Harris, Jeanette. "Proofreading: A Reading/Writing Skill." *College Composition and Communication* 38 (1987): 464–66. Harris discusses why students have proofreading problems and how they can improve their editing skills.

Madroso, Jan. "Proofreading: The Skill We've Neglected to Teach." *English Journal* 82.2 (1993): 32–41. Madroso suggests ways to make this activity more productive for students.

Checklist for preparing an academic paper

- Have you used sturdy white paper measuring 8½″ × 11″?
- Have you used only one side of each page?
- Is the type dark or the handwriting legible?
- Is everything double-spaced?
- Do your name, the instructor's name, the course title, and the date appear on the first page?
- Is your paper titled and the title centered?
- Are the margins at least one inch on all sides?
- Are all the pages numbered consecutively in the upper right, starting with page 1 for the first text page? Does your last name appear before each page number?
- If you have used sources, have you cited them in your text and attached a list of works cited?
- Have you proofread the paper and corrected all errors?
- Are the pages of your paper clipped, stapled, folded, or bound, as requested by your instructor?

NOTE For the special formats of source citations and a list of works cited or references, see pages 599–627 (MLA style), 696–703 (Chicago style), 707–20 (APA style), or 729–33 (CBE style).

a Paper and type

Whether you produce your papers on a word processor, on a typewriter, or in handwriting, your primary goals are legibility, durability, and the convenience of the reader.

Word-processed papers

Word processing offers various options for printers and paper.

- If you use a dot-matrix printer (which forms characters out of tiny dots), make sure the characters are legible and that the tails on letters such as *j, p,* and *y* descend below the line of type, as they do in the typeface used here.
- Be sure the printer's ribbon or cartridge produces a dark impression.
- Use standard-sized (8½″ × 11″ white bond paper of sixteen- or twenty-pound weight.
- If you use continuous paper folded like a fan at perforations, it will also come with a row of holes along each side for feeding the paper into the printer. Before submitting your paper, remove these strips of holes and separate the pages at the folds.

Typewritten papers

For papers you produce on a typewriter, use the following guidelines:

- Use 8½″ × 11″ white bond paper of sixteen- or twenty-pound weight, not onionskin sheets, paper torn from notebooks, or colored paper. Use the same type of paper throughout a project.
- Type on only one side of a sheet.
- Use a black typewriter ribbon that is fresh enough to make a dark impression, and make sure the keys of the typewriter are clean.
- To avoid smudging the page when correcting mistakes, use a liquid correction fluid or a correction tape. Don't use typed hyphens or *x*'s to cross out mistakes, and don't type corrections (strikeovers) on top of mistakes.

Handwritten papers

When your instructor accepts handwritten papers, follow these guidelines:

- Use regular white paper, 8½″ × 11″, with horizontal lines spaced between one-quarter and three-eighths of an inch apart. Don't use paper torn from a notebook, unlined paper, paper with narrow lines, colored paper, or paper other than 8½″ × 11″ (such as legal or stenographer's pads). Use the same type of paper throughout a project.
- Write on only one side of a sheet.
- Use black or dark blue ink, not pencil.
- If possible, use an ink eraser or eradicator to correct mistakes. If you must cross out material, draw a single line through it. Don't scribble over or black out a mistake, and don't write corrections on top of mistakes.

b Title and identification

The *MLA Handbook* does not require a title page for a paper. If your instructor asks you to supply a title page, see the illustration and instructions on pages 632–33. Otherwise, follow the sample on the next page, providing your name and the date, plus any other information requested by your instructor, on the first text page. Place this identification an inch from the top of the page, aligned with the left margin and double-spaced. Double-space again, and center the title. Don't underline the title or place quotation marks around it, and capitalize the words in the title according to guide-

TRANSPARENCY MASTER A.1

ms A1

FIRST PAGE OF PAPER WITH NO TITLE PAGE

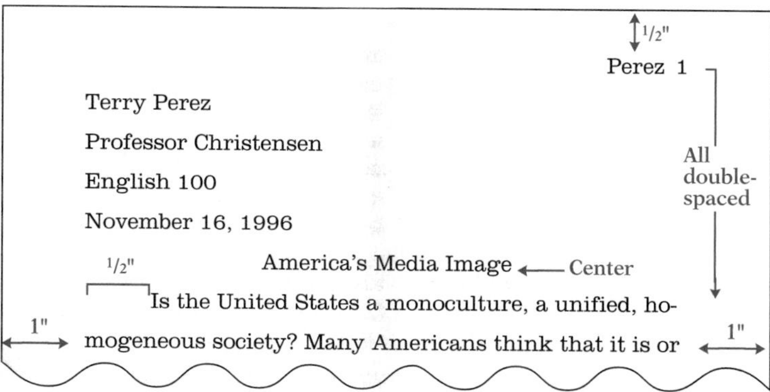

A LATER PAGE OF THE PAPER

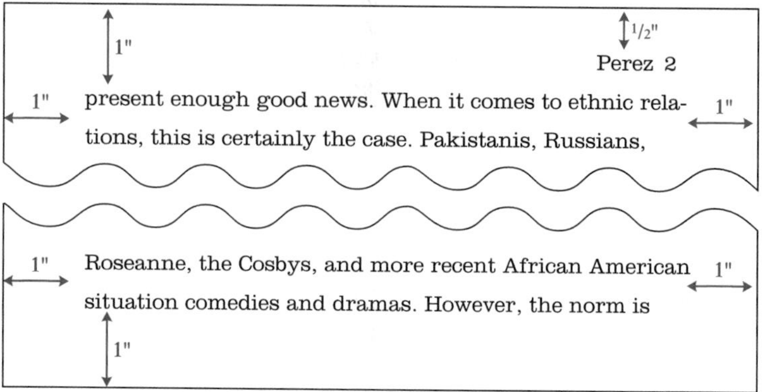

lines on page 431. Double-space between the title and the first line of text.

c Text

In text produced on a word processor or typewriter, follow the spacings in the samples above. In addition:

- Leave one space between words.
- Leave one space after all punctuation, with these exceptions:

Dash (two hyphens)	book--its
Hyphen	one-half
Apostrophe within a word	book's
Between two or more adjacent marks	book.")

Leave one space before the three dots of an ellipsis mark (see p. 424):

book . . . in   book. . . . The

- Don't start a line with a mark of punctuation other than a dash, an opening parenthesis, an opening quotation mark, an opening bracket, or an ellipsis mark.
- Don't end a line with an opening quotation mark, parenthesis, or bracket. Close these marks up to the word following.
- Don't break a two-hyphen dash or a three-dot ellipsis mark from one line to the next.
- If you must break a word at the end of a line, follow the guidelines in Chapter 30.
- Use handwriting to make any symbols that are not on your keyboard, leaving two or three spaces and then inserting the symbol in ink.
- Set off quotations of more than four lines of prose or three lines of poetry; two- or three-line poetry quotations may be set off or placed in the text. Indent all lines of a set-off quotation one inch from the left margin. Double-space above and below the quotation, and double-space the quotation itself. (See pp. 409–10 for samples.)
- For headings within the body of the text, follow the guidelines for document design on pages 766–67.

Most word processors offer a large variety of type styles, sizes, and weights. The section on document design (pp. 765–72) offers some tips for using these options effectively. However, many teachers consider a word processor's variations and embellishments to be a distraction from the work itself, for both reader and writer. Unless you know your instructor accepts alternatives, make your word-processed papers look like typewritten papers, with one size of type, <u>underlining</u> rather than *italics* for emphasis and source citations, and similar conventional elements.

Handwritten text should be reasonably uniform and clear. Be sure letters are easily distinguishable. Cross all *t*'s; dot all *i*'s with dots, not circles; form the loops of letters carefully. Make capital letters and small letters clearly different. Space consistently between words and between sentences. If your handwriting is difficult to read, submit a typed or word-processed paper if possible. If you don't have access to a typewriter and your handwriting is illegible or unusual in size, decoration, or slant, make it more legible or conventional when writing the final manuscript. Indent the first line of every paragraph about an inch. Write on every line or every other line as specified by your instructor. For displayed quotations, indent all lines an inch from the left margin.

ms
A1

d Margins

Use one-inch margins on all sides of each page. The top margin will contain the page numbers (see below). If the right margin is uneven, it should be no narrower than an inch. If you have a word processor or electronic typewriter that produces an even (or justified) right margin, use the feature only if it does not leave wide spaces between words and thus interfere with readability. When using a word processor, be sure to instruct the computer to set appropriate margins. Don't let the lines of type run across the perforations on continuous fanfold paper.

Paging

Begin numbering your paper on the first text page, and number consecutively through the end. Use Arabic numerals (1, 2, 3), and do not add periods, parentheses, hyphens, or the abbreviation "p." However, place your last name before the page number in case the pages become separated after you submit your paper (see the sample on p. 762). Align the page number with the right margin, and position it about half an inch from the top of the page, at least two lines above the first line of text.

A WRITER'S PERSPECTIVE

> *[After revising,] nothing should then remain that offends the eye.*
>
> —Robert Graves

Corrections

Proofread each page of your final work carefully, concentrating on spelling, punctuation, mechanics, and grammar. (See p. 77 for proofreading tips.) Business writing should be free of errors, but there's a little more latitude with most academic writing. If a page has several errors, produce a new, clean page by rewriting, retyping, or correcting on the word processor. If a page has one or two errors and you can't eradicate them, correct them in ink. Draw a single line through a word you want to delete. Don't try to correct a misspelled word without crossing out and rewriting the whole word. To replace a word, draw a line through the item, place a caret (^) underneath it, and write the new word or mark in the space above the old one. To add words or marks of punctuation, place a caret underneath the line at the point where you wish to insert the word or mark; then center the word or mark over the caret in the space above the line.

> An ecosystem is a community of ~~argapisms~~ ^organisms interacting with each other and with ^the environment.

If you have to add more words than will fit between the lines of text, produce a new, clean page.

When you submit your final paper, be sure the pages will stay together when the paper is shuffled in with others. Depending on the wishes of your instructor, you may fold the paper in half lengthwise, paper-clip or staple the pages in the upper left corner, or place the paper in a special binder.

A2 Designing documents

The preceding recommendations for document format will help you produce neat, legible papers, but sometimes your work may call for more. You may need headings to separate and label parts of the work, lists to highlight steps or conclusions, tables or graphs to organize data and show trends.

With computerized word processing, especially desktop publishing, it is possible to produce papers, reports, letters, and so on that look as if they have been professionally typeset and printed, like this book. But even if you work on a typewriter or a very basic word processor, many of the following guidelines can help you produce effective documents. The key elements are white space, type styles and sizes, lists, headings, tables and illustrations, and sometimes color.

NOTE Many word-processing and desktop-publishing programs include templates, or forms, for memos, reports, and other kinds of documents. You can select an appropriate template, and the computer will do the rest of the formatting for you.

RESOURCES AND IDEAS

Flammia, Madelyn. "Avoiding Desktop Disasters: Why Technical Communication Students Should Learn About Mechanical Paste Up Techniques." *Journal of Technical Writing and Communication* 23 (1993): 287–95. Flammia discusses a group of assignments intended to make students more aware of the principles of page design and layout.

a White space

The white space on a page eases crowding, highlights elements, and focuses readers' attention. On an otherwise full page, just the half-inch space of a paragraph indention gives readers a break and reassures them that you have divided ideas into manageable chunks. (See p. 115 on paragraph length.)

White space appears mainly in margins and around headings and lists. Use minimum one-inch margins on all sides of the page. Make headings stand out: in double-spaced copy, double- or triple-space above and double-space below; in single-spaced copy, double-space above and below.

b Type styles and sizes

Variations in the size of type and the style can affect the readability and the clarity of your work.

For your text, always choose a type size of 10 or 12 points.

Here are some samples:

12-point Courier	12-point Times Roman
10-point Courier	10-point Times Roman

For text use a typeface with **serifs**—the small lines finishing the letters in the samples above. **Sans serif** typefaces (*sans* means "without") include this one commonly found on word processors:

12-point Helvetica
10-point Helvetica

Though fine for headings, sans serif typefaces can be more difficult than serif faces to read in extended text.

Within the text you can use underlining or *italic* or **boldface** type to emphasize key words or sentences. For academic writing, instructors often prefer underlining to italics, especially for titles in source citations. Italics are more common in business writing. No matter what your writing situation, however, use such emphasis selectively to complement your meaning, not to decorate your work. Many readers consider type embellishments to be distracting.

 Lists

If your work contains a list of related items—for example, the steps in a process or the elements in a proposal—then consider indenting the items with numbers or bullets (centered dots or other devices). Bulleted lists appear throughout this handbook, as at the bottom of this page. A list is easier to read than a paragraph and adds white space to the page. Many word-processing programs can format a numbered or bulleted list automatically.

 Headings

In a research paper, business report, or similarly long and complex document, headings within the text can clarify organization and the relationships among parts. When you use headings, follow these guidelines:

- Create an outline of your document in order to plan where headings should go. Inconsistent, overlapping, or missing headings do more harm than good.
- Keep headings as short as possible while making them specific about the material that follows.
- Word headings consistently—for instance, all questions (*What Is the Scientific Method?*), all phrases with *-ing* words (*Under-*

standing the Scientific Method), or all phrases with nouns (*The Scientific Method*).
- Indicate the relative importance of headings with type size, positioning, and highlighting, such as capital letters and underlining.

FIRST-LEVEL HEADING

Second-Level Heading

Third-Level Heading

FIRST-LEVEL HEADING

Second-Level Heading

Third-Level Heading

- Keep the appearance simple: most reports or papers shouldn't need more than two type styles or two or three type sizes (including the body type). Except in promotional pieces, avoid extra-large letters and unusual styles of type (such as outline and shadow type).
- Don't break a page immediately after a heading. Push the heading to the next page.

NOTE Document format in psychology and some other social sciences requires a particular treatment of headings. See page 720.

e Tables and illustrations

Tables and illustrations (graphs, charts, diagrams, photographs) can often make a point for you more efficiently and effectively than words can. Tables and illustrations present data, make comparisons, explain processes, show changes, and represent what something looks like, among other uses. Whatever kind of table or illustration you plan, follow these guidelines:

- Focus on a purpose for the table or illustration—a single point you want it to make. Otherwise, it may be too complex and may confuse readers.
- Provide a title for the table or illustration so that the reader knows immediately what its purpose and content are. Generally, a table's title falls above the table, whereas an illustration's title falls below.
- Make the table or illustration legible and attractive.
- Provide clear labels for all parts, such as columns and rows in a table, bars in a graph, and parts of a machine in a drawing. In the interest of clarity, avoid abbreviations unless you know your readers will understand them.

RESOURCES AND IDEAS

Norton, Robert. "Commentary: Graphic Excellence for the Technical Communicator." *Journal of Technical Writing and Communication* 23 (1993): 1–6. Norton reminds students how good visuals can contribute to better understanding of difficult concepts.

- Provide a source note whenever the data or the entire table or illustration is someone else's independent material (see p. 581). Each discipline has a slightly different style for such source notes; those in the table below and the figures opposite reflect the style of the social sciences. See also Chapters 37 and 40.
- Number tables and figures separately (Table 1, Table 2, etc.; Figure 1, Figure 2, etc.).
- Refer to each table or figure (for instance, "See Figure 2") at the point(s) in the text where readers will benefit by consulting it.
- Unless your document includes many tables and/or illustrations, place each one on a page by itself immediately after the page that refers to it.

Many organizations and academic disciplines have preferred styles for tables and figures that may differ from those presented here. When in doubt about how to prepare and place tables and illustrations, ask your instructor or supervisor.

Tables

Tables usually summarize raw data, displaying the data concisely and clearly.

Table 1

Computers, Telephones, and Televisions per 1,000 People (1994)

Location	Computers	Telephones	Televisions
Worldwide	37	152	174
United States	365	965	900
Europe	93	508	419
Japan	105	645	625
Former Soviet republics	14	145	335

Note: From 8th Annual Computer Industry Almanac (p. 38), by K. P. Juliussen and E. Juliussen, 1995, Incline Village, NV: Computer Industry Almanac.

Illustrations

Illustrations often recast data into visual form. Pie charts, bar graphs, and line graphs are helpful for comparisons, such as changes and proportions.

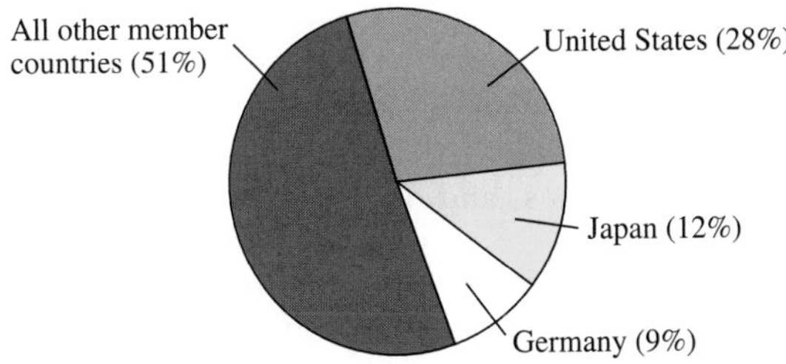

Figure 1. Member countries' assessments to United Nations budget of $1.1 billion in 1994. From "The U.N. at 50," by R. Mylan, 1995, October 18, *Newsweek,* p. 17.

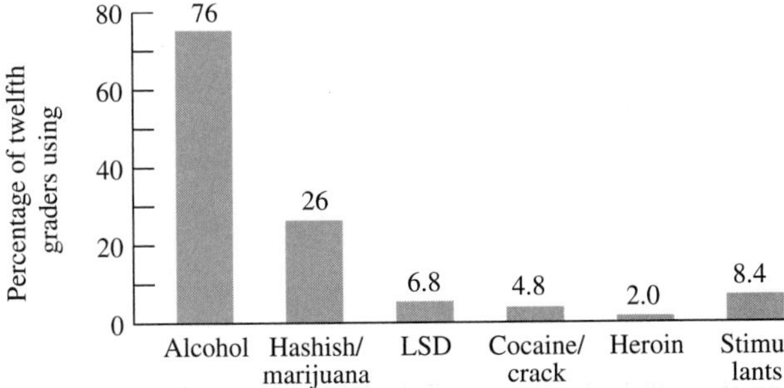

Figure 2. Use of alcohol, compared with other drugs, among twelfth graders (1993). Data from *Monitoring the Future Study,* 1994, Ann Arbor, MI: University of Michigan Press.

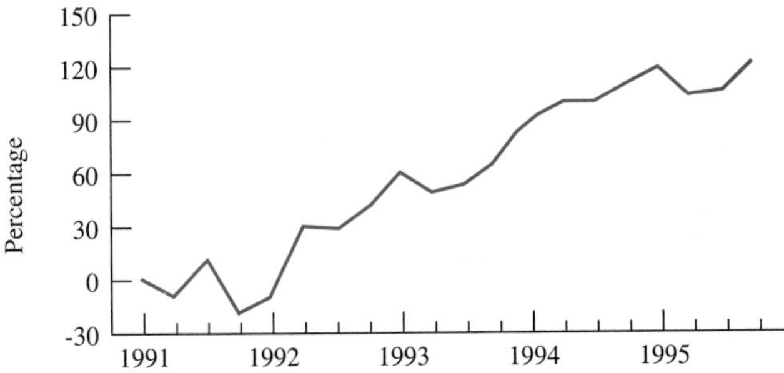

Figure 3. Five-year cumulative return for equities in Standard & Poor's 500 Index, 1991–1995.

ms
A2

 Color

With a color printer, many word processors and most desktop publishers can produce documents that use color for bullets, headings, box borders, illustrations, and other elements. Academic papers and business documents consisting only of text and headings may not need color. (Ask your instructor or supervisor for his or her preferences.) If you do use color, follow these guidelines:

- Employ color to clarify and highlight your content. Too much color or too many colors on a page will distract rather than focus readers' attention.
- Typefaces in color can be hard to read. Use color only for boldfaced or large headings, and choose colors that make the type easily readable. Stick to the same color for all headings at the same level (for instance, red for primary headings, black for secondary headings).
- For bullets, box borders, lines, and other nontext elements, color can be used more decoratively to enliven the page. Still, stick to only one or two colors to keep the page clean.
- For illustrations, use color to distinguish the segments of charts, the lines of graphs, and the parts of diagrams. (See the previous page for examples.) Use only as many colors as you need to make your illustration clear.

 Samples of document design

Two partial samples of documents designed on computers appear on the next two pages. The first is from a business report intended to outline a problem and propose a solution. It illustrates a restrained use of typefaces, suitable for a formal business-writing situation. The report's problem-solution organization is clearly represented in its design, with white space, headings, and similar elements.

The second example, from a newsletter distributed to about fifty people, is designed to engage, motivate, and inform volunteers who teach reading to veterans of the armed services. Because of its purpose, this newsletter is livelier in appearance than the business report, using extra-large type for title and headings, lines, borders, and color to catch the eye of readers and focus their attention on distinct elements. The borders, rules, and column format of this newsletter are available on many word processors and all desktop publishers.

Canada Geese at ABC Institute: An Environmental Problem

Summary

The flock of Canada geese on and around ABC Institute's grounds has grown dramatically in recent years. What was once a source of pleasure for institute employees and others using the grounds has become a nuisance and an environmental problem. This report reviews the problem, considers the options for reducing the flock, and proposes as a solution the cooperation of ABC Institute, the municipalities around Taylor Lake, and the US Fish and Wildlife Service to reduce the flock by humane means.

The Problem

Canada geese began living at Taylor Lake, adjacent to ABC Institute, when they were relocated there in 1970 by the state game department. As a nonmigratory flock, the geese are present year-round, with the highest population each year occurring in fall, winter, and early spring, after the young have fledged.

In recent years the flock of geese at Taylor Lake has grown dramatically. The Audubon Society's annual Christmas bird census shows a thirty-fold increase from the 37 geese counted in 1972 to the 1125 counted in 1996. The following chart illustrates the increase between 1985 and 1996:

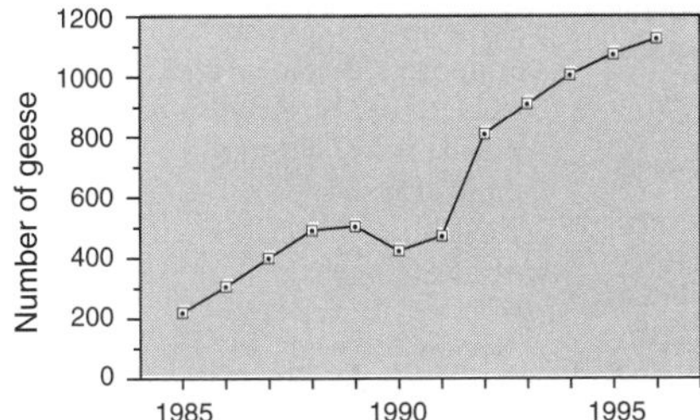

The principal environmental problem caused by the geese is pollution of grass and water by defecation. During high-population months, geese droppings cover the ABC Institute's grounds as well as the park's athletic fields and picnicking areas. The runoff from these droppings into Taylor Lake has substantially affected the quality of the lake's water, so that local authorities have twice (1995 and 1996) issued warnings against swimming.

The Solution

Several possible solutions to the goose overpopulation and resulting environmental problems are **not viable alternatives:**

- Harass the geese with dogs and audiovisual effects (light and noise) so that the geese choose to leave. This solution is inhumane to the geese and unpleasant for human neighbors.
- Feed the geese a chemical that will weaken the shells of their eggs and thus reduce growth of the flock. This solution is inhumane to the geese and also impractical, because geese are long-lived.
- Kill adult geese. This solution is, obviously, inhumane to the geese.

The most appropriate and humane solution is to thin the goose population by trapping and removing many geese (perhaps 600) to areas less populated by humans, such as wildlife preserves and wilderness areas. Though costly (see figures below), this solution would be efficient and harmless to the geese, provided that sizable netted enclosures are used for traps. [Discussion of solution continues, followed by "Recommendations."]

ms
A2

VA Literacy Volunteers

Springfield Veterans Administration Hospital **SPRING 1997**

From the director

Can you help us? With more and more learners in the VA's literacy program, we need more and more tutors. You may know people who would be interested in participating in the program, if only they knew about it.

Those of you who have been tutoring VA patients in reading and writing know both the great need you fulfill and the great benefits you bring to your students. New tutors need no special skills (we'll provide the training), only patience and an interest in helping others.

We've scheduled an orientation meeting for Friday, June 6, at 6:30 PM. Please come and bring a friend who is willing to contribute a couple of hours a week to our work.

Thanks,
Nancy Thomas

IN THIS ISSUE

AWARDS FOR STUDENTS AND TUTORS AT ANNUAL DINNER

The annual SVAH literacy dinner on February 25 was a great success. George Bello obtained food and beverage contributions from area restaurants and suppliers, and the students decorated the dining room on the theme of books and reading. In all, eighty-six people attended.

The highlight of the night was the awards ceremony. Ten students, recommended by their tutors, received certificates recognizing their efforts and special accomplishments in learning to read and write:

Ramon Berva
Edward Byar
David Dunbar
Tony Garnier
Chris Giugni
Akili Haynes
Pat Laird
Jim Livingston
Paul Obeid
B. J. Resnansky

In addition, ten tutors received certificates commemorating five years of service at SVAH:

Anita Crumpton
Felix Cruz-Rivera
Bette Eigen
Kelly Bortoluzzi
Amitav Ghosh
Harriotte Henderson
Andy Obiso
Carla Puente
Robert Smith
Sara Villante

Congratulations to all!

New Guidelines on PTSD

Most of us are working with veterans who have been diagnosed with post-traumatic stress disorder. Because this disorder is often complicated by alcoholism, depression, anxiety, and other problems, the National Center for PTSD has issued some guidelines for helping PTSD patients in a way that reduces their stress:

- The hospital must know your tutoring schedule, and you need to sign in and out before and after each tutoring session.
- Cancellations are stressful for patients. Stick to your schedule.
- To protect patients' privacy, meet them only in designated visiting and tutoring areas, never in their rooms.
- Treat patients with dignity and respect, even when (as sometimes happens) they grow frustrated and angry. Seek help from a nurse or orderly if you need it.

Appendix B

Writing with a Computer

HIGHLIGHTS

Increasing numbers of students are using computers and electronic technologies to research and write papers. Although learning a new software program can be challenging and at times frustrating, most students find these technologies exciting and liberating. This appendix suggests ways for both students and teachers to use computer technology throughout the writing process. See Susan Lang's essay on "Using Computers to Teach Writing" (pp. IAE-63–IAE-77) for further suggestions and bibliography. Exercises and activities that are particularly appropriate for use on the computer are marked throughout the handbook with the heading "Computer Exercise."

RESOURCES AND IDEAS

Anderson, Daniel, Bret Benjamin, Christopher Busiel, and Bill Paredes-Holt. *Teaching On-Line: Internet Research, Conversation and Composition.* New York: HarperCollins, 1996. An extremely useful and practical guide to computer technologies, including e-mail, the Internet, IRCs, MOOs, and electronic library databases.

Crafton, Robert E. "Promises, Promises: Computer-Assisted Revision and Basic Writers." *Computers and Composition* 13.3 (1996): 317–26. Crafton explores the difficulties that basic writers face in negotiating the seemingly contradictory goals of computer-based learning and traditional writing instruction.

Hawisher, Gail E., and Charles Moran. "Electronic Mail and the Writing Instructor." *College English* 55 (1993): 627–43. The authors discuss the use of e-mail in teaching, with extensive bibliography.

Hawisher, Gail E., and Cynthia L. Selfe, eds. *Evolving Perspectives on Computers and Composition Studies: Questions for the 1990s.* Urbana: NCTE, 1992. The essayists review the use of computers in writing instruction to date and provide an ambitious agenda for their use in the next decade.

Hawisher, Gail E., and Paul LeBlanc, eds. *Re-imagining Computers and Composition: Teaching and Research in the Virtual Age.* Portsmouth, NH: Boynton/Cook, 1992. This collection of essays explores the implications of using computers in the classroom, from electronic conferencing to hypermedia. Teachers who are new to computer technology

Computers have dramatically changed how we write and even what we write. At the symbol printed here in the margin, this handbook suggests specific ways to use or accommodate computers in reading, writing, and research. This appendix offers general advice for word processing (below), guidelines for writing collaboratively with computers (p. 775), and tips for creating a hypertext document such as a page on the World Wide Web (p. 778).

B1 Using a word processor

Writing with a word processor can save time and make writing easier. The advantage of word processing is that you can perform such operations as adding to notes, rearranging outlines, and rewriting first drafts without having to cut pages apart or retype entire pages. The machine will not think for you, but it may leave you more time for the important work of thinking, exploring ideas, focusing and organizing material, and improving content and clarity.

a Word-processing basics

Using a word processor does not require an understanding of computers or expert typing skills. All it takes is a little perseverance and a few hours of practice. When you begin, take some time to examine the materials that explain the system, such as a user's manual or tutorial. Study the keyboard, and make a list of the basic keystrokes you need to perform important commands, such as insert-

might benefit from Chapter 12, "What Are They Talking About? Computer Terms That English Teachers May Need to Know," by Richard J. Selfe (207–18).

Monroe, Rick. *Writing and Thinking with Computers: A Practical and Progressive Approach.* Urbana: NCTE, 1993. Monroe models hands-on practice in the computer classroom, including assignments and exercises such as "Electronic Read-Arounds" and "the business letter."

Myers, Linda, ed. *Approaches to Computer Writing Classrooms: Learning from Practical Experience.* Albany: State U of New York P, 1993. Essays by a number of experts examine a variety of practical and theoretical approaches to using computers in the writing classroom.

Selfe, Cynthia L., and Susan Hilligos. *Literacy and Computers: The Complications of Teaching and Learning with Technology.* New York: MLA, 1994. This collection of essays explores the uses of computer technology in literacy instruction and the larger context of changing definitions of computer-based literacy.

Turnan, Myron C., ed. *Literacy Online: The Promise (and Peril) of Reading and Writing with Computers.* Pittsburgh: U of Pittsburgh P, 1992. These essayists examine the relationship of computers and writing instruction to the new literacies of the 1990s.

Turnan, Myron C. *Word Perfect: Literacy in the Computer Age.* Pittsburgh: U of Pittsburgh P, 1992. Turnan examines why we expect so much more from computers than from typewriters and how using computers has affected our understanding of literacy.

A WRITER'S PERSPECTIVE

The word processor is God's gift, or at least science's gift, to the tinkerers and the refiners and the neatness freaks. . . . I began playing on page 1—editing, cutting, and revising—and have been on a rewriting high ever since.

—WILLIAM ZINSSER

B1

ing, deleting, pasting, saving, and printing text. Become familiar with the "Help" menus, usually accessible at the top of the screen. Be adventurous: experiment with commands, and learn by trial and error. Your play will not hurt the machine, and it will help you.

Computers do crash, but you can prevent permanent loss of your work by taking a few precautions:

- Save your work every fifteen minutes or so, either by instructing the computer to do so automatically or by manually saving the text you're working on.
- Label each project with its own file name for easy retrieval.
- Make a backup disk of your work at the end of each word-processing session as insurance against the loss or damage of your working disk.
- Keep your disks in dustproof containers, and store them safely away from heat, cold, or sources of magnetism such as the computer itself or a stereo or television.
- Regularly print paper copies of your work. They serve as second backup copies, and you may find it easier to work on them than on the screen when revising and editing (see pp. 67–76).

Specific suggestions for using a word processor during the writing process appear in Chapters 1 and 2.

b Optional programs

Many word processors either come with optional programs such as spelling checkers or are compatible with optional programs. The programs are often limited, for the reasons given below, but they can support and speed your efforts. The following are the kinds of programs you are most likely to see.

- *Invention or discovery programs* help you develop a topic by prompting you with a structured set of questions or by providing creative analogies that help you think imaginatively. These programs can help you get started, develop new insights, and conceive a purpose for your writing. One example, *The Writer's Workshop,* is available with this handbook.
- *Outlining programs* help you organize your work by providing automatic indentions, easy resequencing, and other features.
- *Documentation programs* help you format your source citations in just about any style (see p. 599 for more on these programs). The *Documentor* program that is available with this handbook is one example.
- *Style-checking programs* point out wordy and awkward phrases and incorrect grammar and punctuation. However, these programs can only call your attention to passages that *may* be faulty. They miss many errors because they are not yet capable

of analyzing the language in all its complexity (for instance, they can't accurately distinguish a word's part of speech when there are different possibilities, as *light* can be a noun, a verb, and an adjective). And the programs often question passages that don't need editing, such as an appropriate passive verb or an emphatic use of repetition. When you use a style-checking program, you must determine each time it questions something whether a change is needed at all and what change will be most effective. And you must read your text carefully on your own to find any errors the program may have missed.

- *Thesaurus programs* help with word choices by responding to your word with a display of several synonyms (words with similar meanings). A single keystroke allows you to replace your word with a displayed word. Thesaurus programs are limited because they display only some synonyms, not all, and because even a narrow list may contain words that do not suit your meaning. Like a printed thesaurus (see p. 464), an electronic thesaurus is no help if it leads you to misuse words whose meanings you don't know. Before you use a word suggested by a thesaurus, always check its meaning in a dictionary.
- *Spell-checking programs* help you find typographical errors and misspelled words, and they display correct spellings on the screen. They can be valuable proofreading aids. However, they are limited because they cannot store every possible word and thus may identify a word you use as misspelled even though it is correct. More important, they are unreliable because they cannot identify errors such as a confusion between *now* and *not, its* and *it's, your* and *you're,* or *there, their,* and *they're.* Maintain a file of your frequent misspellings and use the search command to check them yourself. (See p. 499 for more on spelling checkers.)

TEACHING TIP

If you are not working in a computer classroom and your campus computing facilities permit, you might hold a class meeting in the computer lab to familiarize students with the word-processing facilities available and to demonstrate some of the computer-assisted writing activities described in this chapter. You may also want to show them how to use any support programs like grammar reviews or spelling checkers that are available, and explain to them how to incorporate the advice from such programs into their revising and editing strategies.

B2 Collaborating using computers

Learning to write collaboratively will help you not only in school but also in work, because much business writing develops collaboratively. Computers, particularly networked computers, simplify some tasks of collaboration (such as making multiple copies of documents), and they open more phases of the writing process to collaboration.

 Possibilities for collaboration

If your classroom has only stand-alone computers (not connected to a network), you can still collaborate electronically by what's called keyboard sharing: all members of the group place their ideas or comments or changes on one computer that everyone has access to and works from individually, returning new drafts and comments to the shared computer.

If the classroom has a number of computers that are linked by a server (a central computer), you and your group will be able to share files. You may be able to retrieve another student's paper from the server, read it and make your comments online, and return the paper, along with your comments, to the server for the author to pick up later.

With a network that allows screen sharing, everyone can work simultaneously on the same material. From their own computers, group members can add text or comments that other members can see and respond to immediately. Revisions and comments can be copied and saved by all group members for later use.

A network also allows you to use personal e-mail or a discussion group for collaboration. Your instructor may create a Listserv—a subscriber-based discussion group (p. 544)—to distribute class assignments and announcements, to further class discussion, or to help students compose together. For example, you and your classmates could exchange experiences with various aspects of the writing process, talk about prospective paper topics, or post papers and evaluations for general class discussions. Listservs may also help you collaborate with students in other classes at your school or at other schools.

You may also have a chance to discuss papers or topics in "real time." Instead of waiting a few hours or days for classmates' responses, you and other members of your group can use a chat environment such as IRC or a MOO to meet and discuss topics as if you were in the same room—although you might be spread across campus or even across the country. (See pp. 545–46 for more on these environments.)

 Effective collaboration

Collaborating on computer requires many of the same outlooks and expectations as collaborating in person, so the guidelines on pages 80–81 can help you become an effective computer collaborator. But there are other considerations as well. For one thing, computer communication demands a certain etiquette:

- You wouldn't shout at a fellow student face-to-face, so don't shout by computer either. Temper your comments, and avoid using all-capital letters. (See p. 758 for more about online courtesy.)
- You may not be present to clarify your comments for your

readers when they receive them. If you mean a remark to be taken humorously, you may need to say so. Or use common *emoticons,* combinations of punctuation marks and other symbols that signal emotions: for instance, :-) read sideways shows a smile. You'll also want to avoid inside jokes that only a few group members will understand.

When you are collaborating by personal e-mail or a Listserv, keep these guidelines in mind:

- Discussions by e-mail or on a Listserv take longer than face-to-face discussions. Members of the group may not have the original message that prompted the discussion or may have forgotten important details. Take advantage of the common e-mail feature that allows you to extract portions of the message you are answering and copy them into your own message.
- If you are joining a discussion already in progress, take the time to read all messages so that you don't waste effort and exhaust the goodwill of your collaborators by asking questions or raising issues that have already been discussed. (If you don't know how to obtain past messages, ask your instructor or another group member.) To avoid cluttering everyone else's mailboxes, you may ask that answers to your questions be sent to you "off-list" (just to you, not to all the others on the list).
- If you are responding to another group member's request for information, send the reply off-list unless you think the entire list will benefit from your response.

Collaborating effectively in MOOs or other "live" discussions takes a bit of practice. The pace of these discussions can vary widely because comments appear on all participants' screens as soon as a speaker has composed them and pressed the "Return" or "Enter" key. The conversation may lag if people are spending a few minutes thinking or composing responses that are extended (six or seven sentences or more). Or your screen may fill rapidly with conversation if people are thinking and responding quickly, leaving you little time to read one comment before another appears. A few tips can help you make the most of the discussion:

- Always save a transcript of your MOO session for future reference. Check with your instructor or your computer center if you don't know how to create a transcript.
- Have a clear sense of what your group's goals are for a MOO or IRC session before beginning. If you sense at first that everyone is waiting for someone else to start, then do so by raising questions about the goals and plans for the session.
- If your group is meeting to comment on a paper, e-mail a copy of the paper to individual participants before the meeting time.

- If you find it impossible to read everyone's comments, pick a thread of conversation that seems most interesting or relevant to you and focus on the comments from the people involved. You can always go back and read the transcripts of other threads.
- Even if you can keep up with a fast-paced conversation, you may not see an opportunity to contribute to it. If you think that a conversation is about to leave you behind, ask the others to slow down for a minute so that you can catch up.
- Remember that you are participating in a conversation, not making a speech. You don't need to have a thought perfectly formed and worded in your mind before trying it out. Sometimes the smallest fragment of a thought may be just what the conversation needs.
- If you notice that some members of the group are not contributing, you may want to ask them what they are thinking to involve them in the conversation. Take the initiative, too, when you think the discussion is stuck or off-track.

B3 Creating hypertext documents

Computers make it possible to compose other types of documents besides the conventional word-processed essay. If you have browsed the World Wide Web, you have encountered **hypertext** documents that provide varied paths through the information they present. Clicking on highlighted links within the site, you may be taken to other spots in the same site (passages of text, video, sound, illustrations, compilations of statistics, and so on), or you may be taken to other sites on the Web. You choose your own path based on the information you want to find. You may also have a chance to interact with site's author(s) by answering questions, making suggestions, and even adding new information to the text. (For more on the World Wide Web, see pp. 538–43.)

You can create your own hypertext documents, either stored on your computer or posted on the World Wide Web. In some courses you may be asked to create electronic hypertext instead of a conventional printed essay. For example, you might develop a hypertext history project that shows text and images on the same screen and provides links to primary-source documents that are discussed in your main text. Or you might produce a hypertext chemistry project with links to three-dimensional or animated diagrams. Beyond your course work, you can create a hypertext document to share information about a hobby or other special interest or even about yourself. Many job seekers have created hypertext job applications that include a standard résumé (see pp. 751–55) as well as links to recommendations, personal statements, writing samples, and other supporting information.

 Technical requirements

If you are preparing a hypertext document for a course, your instructor may recommend specific software and may ask for the document on disk, to be viewed only by the instructor and perhaps other students in the course. The following introduction to creating hypertext documents assumes that you will use generally available software and will post your document on the World Wide Web. (Be aware, however, that some schools discourage students from posting Web pages because of the drain on limited computer facilities.)

- To compose the text of your document, you will need a simple text-editing application such as NotePad (for IBM compatibles) or SimpleText (for Macintoshes). The application should come with your computer. You may also use the word-processing software that you compose conventional essays with, but you will need to save documents as so-called plain text (or ASCII text) so that your Web browser can read them.
- To see what your Web page looks like, you'll need a web browser such as Netscape Navigator or Microsoft's Internet Explorer.
- To create attractive headings, links, and other features of a Web site, you will need a basic knowledge of HTML (HyperText Markup Language). HTML allows you to construct links within the document or with other Web documents and makes it possible to arrange text, images, sound, and video on a page. Using HTML, you code your document with tags, as illustrated in the following excerpt from a coded term project on the subject of electronic mail. The tags are between angle brackets (< >).

```
<html>
<head>
<title>Content Map</title>
</head>
<body>

<h2><center>The Computerized Post Office:<br>Sending and
Receiving Mail in the Late Age of Print</h2></center>
<center>Joyce R. Walker</center><br>
<IMG HEIGHT=5 WIDTH=100% SRC="bar2.jpg"><p>
<center><h3>Content Map</h3></center><p>
<a href= "EC1.html"><IMG Height=20 WIDTH=20 SRC="fire.gif"></a>
Electronic Communications Dynamics<p>
<a href="PP1.html"><IMG height=20 width=20 SRC="book.gif"></a>
Pedagogical Purposes<p>
<a href="DWG1.html"><IMG height=20 width=20 SRC="shakespere.gif">
```

```
</a> Dead White Guys and the History of Letter-Writing
Manuals<p>
<a href="EE1.html"><IMG height=20 width=20 SRC="smiley.gif"></a>
E-mail Etiquette: Online Guides to Playing Nice<p>

<pre> Some viewing suggestions:</pre>
<UL>
<li>For readers/viewers who feel the insatiable need for the
comfort of boundaries and content control, I've provided a
detailed map of the pages I've created which can be read to
supply the illusion of closure.
<li> When navigating through this essay using the hot buttons
above, a reader/viewer can keep track of the thread he/she
wishes to follow by taking note of the icons and page
backgrounds.
<li>For readers/viewers who wish to have a unique, nonlinear
viewing experience, the four small icons, which correspond to
particular threads, appear on every page of this essay. These
icons are also "hot buttons" which will link to other pages.

<TABLE BORDER=4>
<Center><TR><TD ROWSPAN=1> </TD><TH COLSPAN=3> </TR>
<TR><TD> <a href="linear.html">To View Linear Guide</a></TD>
<TD ALIGN=LEFT><a href="bib.html">To View Bibliography  </a>
</TD><TD ALIGN=CENTER> <a href="connotes1.html">To View
Construction Notes </a></TD></TR></Center>
</TABLE>

</body>
</html>
```

With a Web browser, the page coded above looks like this:

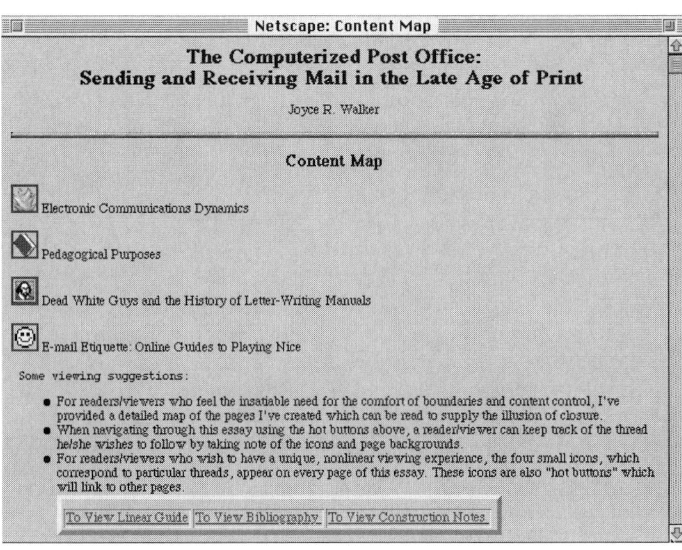

- You can obtain HTML instructions online, using the keywords *HTML and reference.* (See pp. 535–41 if you need help conducting an Internet search.) Bookstores also carry *HTML for Dummies, Teach Yourself HTML in 21 Days,* and other references, some of them packaged with a CD-ROM containing examples of HTML code that you can experiment with to create your own pages.

 Effective hypertext documents

To a great extent, creating an effective hypertext document requires the same considerations as creating an effective essay in print: a clear purpose and central idea, a sense of audience, a navigable structure. But its links, its integration of elements (text, image, audio, video), and its wide publication (for a Web page) demand other considerations as well.

Questions during planning

Because of its complexities, hypertext rewards careful planning. Consider the following questions:

- What is your purpose in creating this document? Your choice of links, images, and other features should be geared to this purpose.
- Who is your audience? If you are writing to a specific audience (your instructor, your classmates, prospective employers), you can use the questions on page 33 to analyze the audience's interests, biases, expectations, and so on. But if you're trying to create a site for a wide, unknown audience—anyone who might come across the site in an Internet search—then you need to think more broadly. For instance, you may want to avoid references to incidents or people known only on your campus.
- What do you want your pages to look like? Plan your pages on paper before coding them. Varied headings, text, photographs, video—all these may crowd together (especially on small computer screens) unless you arrange elements attractively, with plenty of space between them.
- What elements will best achieve your purpose? Add elements to your document to further your purpose, not simply for the sake of including them. A single image and a caption may help you illustrate a concept far more efficiently than a page of text alone. Sound or video clips may work as catalysts for discussion or as valuable evidence. But none of these elements should be used as distractions from an otherwise weak document.
- Will the reader be able to download the whole document? If you're posting your document online, consider whether your

readers will have access to all the elements you've included. Text can be downloaded fairly quickly; however, images, sound, and video take much longer, and the reader may choose not to wait for them. Furthermore, the reader's Web browser may not be able to decode complicated graphics, audio, or video. If you think that readers may miss some elements for either of these reasons, consider designing a "light" version of your document that fulfills your purpose without all the elements.

Questions about links

Aside from the technical requirements, probably the trickiest part of creating a hypertext document is making effective links within the document and to other documents. The following questions raise the key issues:

- How does each of your links further your purpose? Your instructor may suggest that your document have a minimum number of links, but don't use this suggestion as an excuse for creating irrelevant links. Each one should add some information that is vital to your central idea.
- Will readers understand the reason for each link? Sometimes your reason for creating a link will be obvious, and you need do no more than provide the highlighted words. Other times you'll need to be more explicit—for instance, "To learn more about the reign of Louis XIV, click here." And occasionally you'll need to explain your links carefully—for instance, giving the reasons for providing a whole text instead of just a relevant excerpt. The point is to think about what readers probably understand and to provide a variety of links geared to their understanding.
- Are the sources of your links clear? You have the same obligation to acknowledge sources in a hypertext document as you do in other academic writing. (See pp. 578–82 on what to acknowledge and pp. 598–99 on citing sources.)
- Have you sought permission for links to copyrighted material? If your hypertext document will be distributed privately (for instance, to your instructor and classmates), then it is enough to acknowledge the use of copyrighted material (see pp. 578–82). But if you are publishing your document on the World Wide Web, then you may be obliged to seek permission for using copyrighted material—just as print publishers do. Another reason for seeking permission is that the computer housing a linked source may not be capable of supporting many simultaneous users or may not be accessible around the clock.

Questions about nontext media

Images, backgrounds, icons, animation, video, and sound can add interest as well as substance to your hypertext document. When using such material, consider these questions:

- What does the element add to your document? A certain amount of window dressing may be appropriate, especially in the use of graphics. But an overloaded text will distract and even annoy readers. As mentioned earlier, nontext elements also increase the download time of your document and cannot always be decoded by Web browsers.
- Can you find the elements you need on the Web? A number of image libraries allow users (especially nonprofit users) to download visual and audio elements without formal permission and to reproduce the elements on the users' own pages. If you reproduce elements from such a source, always acknowledge the source (see pp. 598–99).
- Do you need to seek permission for use of nontext elements? You can download nontext materials from any site on the Web, not just image libraries. But unless the site explicitly allows copying without permission, you should seek permission to publish the material in your own Web document. (Text and nontext material are alike in this respect.) Of course, you must also acknowledge the source in your document (see pp. 598–99).

HIGHLIGHTS

Many educators, businesses, and institutions consider the ability to articulate ideas thoughtfully and effectively within a group or in larger public settings to be the most significant and most under-emphasized of educational goals. While writing classes often include an informal speech component, planned oral presentations can help students to develop their critical reading, writing, and *speaking* skills as part of a cohesive process. This appendix suggests ways to integrate a speechmaking component into the writing curriculum. In particular, it identifies ways in which the handbook's emphasis on critical thinking can be expanded to help students prepare and deliver oral presentation, including:

identifying the topic, purpose, and audience for the speech;
organizing and presenting the material in a way that effectively foregrounds the motivational or informational qualities of the speech;
becoming aware of various strategies for vocal and physical delivery, and of ways to cope with presentation anxiety.

The appendix also includes a "Checklist for an oral presentation" (facing page) which students can use in preparing for their speeches and in critiquing each other's presentations.

RESOURCES AND IDEAS

Two standard speech communication textbooks that can be used to integrate a speechmaking component onto the writing classroom are Stephen E. Lucas's *The Art of Public Speaking* (New York: Random, 1989), which can be combined with Lucas' videotaped collection, *Speeches for Analysis and Discussion* (New York: Random, 1989); and Bert E. Bradley's *Fundamentals of Speech Communication: The Credibility of Ideas* (Dubuque, Iowa: W. C. Braun, 1974).

Katherine E. Rowan's "A New Pedagogy for Explanatory Public Speaking: Why Arrangement Should Not Substitute for Invention" (*Communication Education* 44:3 [July 1995] 236–50) makes the case against current speech communication textbooks that focus on the organization of definitions, examples and visual aids without recognizing the process of critical thinking through which

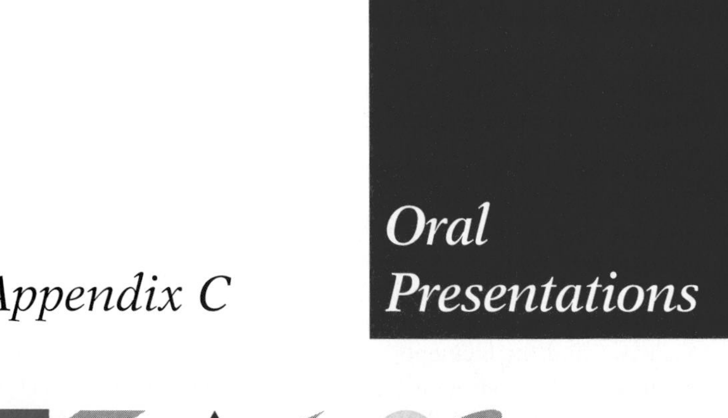

Appendix C Oral Presentations

At some point during your education or your work, you will probably be called upon to speak to a group. Oral presentation can be anxiety producing, even for those who are experienced at it. This appendix shows you how you can apply your experiences as a writer to public speaking, and it offers some techniques that are uniquely appropriate for effective oral presentations.

C1 Writing and speaking

Writing and speechmaking have much in common: both require careful consideration of your subject, purpose, and audience. Thus the mental and physical activities that go into the writing process can also help you prepare and present a successful oral presentation.

Despite many similarities, however, writing for readers is not the same as speaking to listeners. Whereas a reader can go back and reread a written message, a listener cannot stop a speech to rehear a section. Several studies have reported that immediately after hearing a short talk, most listeners cannot recall half of what was said.

Effective speakers adapt to their audience's listening ability by reinforcing their ideas through repetition and restatement. They use simple words, short sentences, personal pronouns, contractions, and colloquial expressions. In formal writing, these strategies might seem redundant and too informal; but in speaking, they improve listeners' comprehension.

Checklist for an oral presentation

- **Purpose:** What do you want your audience to know or do as a result of your presentation? How can your purpose be achieved by an oral presentation in the time and setting you've been given? (See below.)
- **Audience:** What do you know about the characteristics and opinions of your audience? How can this information help you adapt your presentation to your audience's interests, needs, and opinions? (See below.)
- **Organization and content:** How are your ideas arranged? Where might listeners have difficulty following you? What functions do your introduction and conclusion perform? How relevant and interesting is your supporting material for your topic and your audience? (See p. 786.)
- **Method of delivery:** What method of delivery do you plan: extemporaneous? reading from a text? memorized? a mixture? How does your method suit the purpose, setting, and occasion of your presentation? (See p. 788.)
- **Vocal and physical delivery:** In rehearsing your presentation, what do you perceive as your strengths and weaknesses? Is your voice suitably loud for the setting? Are you speaking clearly? Are you able to move your eyes around the room so that you'll be making eye contact during the presentation? Is your posture straight but not stiff? Do your gestures reinforce your ideas? Do you use visual aids appropriately? (See pp. 189–91.)
- **Confidence and credibility:** What techniques will you use to overcome the inevitable anxiety about speaking? How will you project your confidence and competence? (See p. 791.)

C2 Considering topic, purpose, and audience

The most important step in developing an oral presentation is to identify your purpose: what do you want your audience to know or do as a result of your speech? Topic and purpose are *not* the same thing. Asking "What am I talking about?" is not the same as asking "Why am I speaking?"

In school and work settings, oral presentations may include anything from a five-minute report before a few peers to an hour-long address before a hundred people. Whatever the situation, you're likely to be speaking for the same reasons that you write in school or at work: to explain something to listeners or to persuade listeners to accept your opinion or take an action. See page 30 for more on these purposes.

students develop the content of the speech in relation to effective modes of presentation. Tom Schachtman's *The Inarticulate Society: Eloquence and Culture in America* uses a historical overview of the changing value put on eloquence in American society to argue that there is a marked decline in public articulateness, a decline that is rapidly undermining the democratic system. Another possible resource is Ron Hoff's *I Can See You Naked,* a jocular approach to public speaking written for a popular audience, with sections on nervousness, boredom, understanding an audience, dealing with questions, and making use of criticism that could be excerpted for students.

The journal *The Speech Communication Teacher: Ideas and Strategies for Classrooms and Activities* is a compendium of speech-related teaching suggestions from contributors across the country and contains useful articles in every issue. For example, Gwendolyn F. Sullivan's "Improving Delivery Skills: The Practice Impromptu" (11:2 [Winter 1997] 5–6) describes group activities and preparatory exercises (like inviting a guest speaker) that help students learn to deliver impromptu speeches. Two articles on "CNEs" (Computerized Narrative Evaluations) identify the uses and limitations of programs that supply generic evaluations that can be tailored to individual student presentations: James R. Hallmark's "Using Your Computer to Evaluate Speeches" (9:3 [Spring 1995] 14–15); and Arnie Madson's follow-up piece, "Computer-Assisted Comments for Research Papers and Speeches" (9:3 [Spring 1995] 14–15). See also "Case Study in Business and Professional Speaking" (11:1 [Fall 1996] 1–2), which describes ways to make a speech class relevant to the actual demands of business by having students present researched case studies of particular businesses.

Have students refer to pages 24–46 of the handbook for additional information on discovering and limiting a topic, defining a purpose, and considering the audience. It's important for students to recognize the similarities between the critical thought that goes into an essay and the preparation for an oral presentation.

Adapting to your audience is a critical task in public speaking as well as in writing. You'll want to consider the questions about audience on page 33. But a listening audience requires additional considerations as well:

- Why is your audience assembled? Is it because these people want to hear you, because they are interested in your topic, because they have been required to attend, or because they always meet in this time and place? Listeners who are required to attend may be more difficult to interest and motivate than listeners who attend because they want to hear you and your ideas.
- How large is your audience? With a small group you can be informal. If you are speaking to a hundred or more people, you may need a public address system, a lectern, special lighting, and audiovisual equipment.
- Where will you speak? Your appearance should match the setting—more casual for a classroom, more formal for an auditorium. If the room is large and the audience small, you may ask the audience to fill in the front section of the room.
- How long are you scheduled to speak and when? A long speech early in the morning or late in the afternoon may find your audience too sleepy to listen well. And keep in mind that audiences lose patience with someone who speaks longer than the assigned time.

When speaking, unlike when writing, you can see and hear your audience's responses during your presentation. Thus you have the luxury and challenge of adapting your presentation to an audience as you speak. If you sense that an audience is bored, try to spice up your presentation. If an audience is restless, consult your watch to make sure you have not gone overtime. If you sense resistance, try to make midspeech adjustments to respond to that resistance.

C3 Organizing the presentation

An effective oral presentation, like an effective essay, has a recognizable shape. The arrangement of sections guides listeners through a presentation and helps them see how ideas and details are related to each other. The advice in Chapter 1 for organizing and outlining an essay serves the speechmaker as well as the writer (see p. 52). Here are additional considerations for the introduction, conclusion, and supporting material.

 The introduction

First impressions count. A strong beginning establishes an important relationship among three elements in an oral presentation: you, your topic, and your audience. More specifically, the beginning of an oral presentation should try to accomplish three goals:

- Gain the audience's attention and interest. When you begin to speak, your listeners may not be ready to pay attention: they may be talking to a neighbor or be preoccupied with other thoughts. To attract listeners' attention, begin with a question, an unusual example or statistic, or a short, relevant story.
- Put yourself in the speech by demonstrating your expertise, experience, or concern. Your audience will be more interested in what you say and more trusting of you.
- Introduce and preview your purpose and topic. By the time your introduction is over, listeners should know what your topic is and the direction in which you wish to take them as you develop your ideas. This information will give them expectations for your speech on which they can pin the specific points that follow.

In addition to these guidelines for beginning a speech, there are some important pitfalls to avoid:

- Don't try to cram too much into your introduction. Giving only a sneak preview of your speech can pique your audience's curiosity about what you have to say.
- Don't begin with an apology. A statement such as "I wish I'd been given more time to get ready for this presentation" will only undermine your listeners' confidence in you.
- Don't begin with "My speech is about. . . ." The statement is dull, and it does little to clarify purpose.

 Supporting material

Just as you do when writing, you can and should use facts, statistics, examples, and expert opinions to support spoken arguments (see pp. 130–31). In addition, as a speaker you can draw on other kinds of supporting material:

- Use vivid description to paint a mental image of a scene, a concept, an event, or a person.
- Use well-chosen quotations to add an emotional or humorous moment to your speech.
- Use true or fictional stories to rivet the audience's attention

and illustrate your point. Most listeners remember a good story long after they have forgotten other details from a speech.

- Use analogies—comparisons between essentially unlike things, such as a politician and a tightrope walker—to link concepts memorably. (For more on analogy, see p. 112.)

Use a variety of supporting material in your speech. A presentation that is nothing but statistics can bore an audience. Nonstop storytelling may interest listeners but fail to achieve your purpose.

C4

The conclusion

Last impressions count as much as first impressions. You may hope that listeners will remember every detail of your speech, but they are more likely to leave with a general impression and a few ideas about you and your message. You want your conclusion to be clear, of course, but you also want it to be memorable. Remind listeners of how your topic and main idea connect to their needs and interests. If your speech was motivational, tap an emotion that matches your message. If your speech was informational, give some tips on how to remember important details.

COLLABORATIVE LEARNING

Having students work in groups to prepare and practice their presentations can effectively reduce anxiety about public speaking and help students learn to articulate their ideas in smaller group settings. See also "Peer Support in Speech Preparation" by Don George, which describes exercises for cultivating a team approach to public speaking using debating club strategies (*The Speech Communication Teacher* 7:3 [Spring 1993] 4–5).

C4 Delivering the presentation

Writing and speaking differ most obviously in the form of delivery: the writer is represented in print; the speaker is represented in person. This section describes the methods and techniques of oral presentation (pp. 788–91) as well as some ways of coping with stage fright (pp. 791–92).

Methods of delivery

An oral presentation may be delivered impromptu, extemporaneously, from a text, or from memory. No one technique is best for all speeches; indeed, a single speech may include two or more forms or even all four—perhaps a memorized introduction, an extemporaneous body in which quotations are read from a text, and an impromptu response to audience questions during or after the speech.

- *Impromptu* means "without preparation": an impromptu presentation is one you deliver off-the-cuff, with no planning or practice. You may be called on in a class to express your opinion or to summarize something you've written. You may speak up at a neighborhood meeting. An audience member may ask you a question at the end of an oral presentation. The only way to prepare for such incidents is to be well prepared in general—to be caught up on course reading, for instance, or to know the facts in a debate.

- Extemporaneous speaking—that done with some preparation, but without reading from a text—is the most common form of presentation, typical of class lectures and business briefings. With extemporaneous speaking, you have time to prepare and practice in advance. Then, instead of following a script of every word, you speak from notes that guide you through the presentation. You can look and sound natural while still covering all the material you want to convey.
- Delivering a presentation from a text involves writing the text out in advance and then reading aloud from it. Unless you have considerable experience writing speeches and reading from a text, try to avoid this form of delivery for an entire presentation. If you do use it, write the text so that it sounds spoken (less formal) rather than written (more formal): for instance, the sentence *Although costs rose, profits remained steady* would sound fine in writing but stiff and awkward in speech because in conversation we rarely use such a structure. In addition, rehearse thoroughly so that you can read with expression and can look up frequently to make eye contact with listeners (see p. 790).
- A memorized presentation has a distinct advantage: complete freedom from notes or a text. However, while you can look at your audience every minute and can move away from a lectern and even into the audience, you risk forgetting your place or a whole passage. When you deliver a memorized presentation, always have some notes at hand to jog your memory.

b Vocal delivery

The sound of your voice will influence how your listeners receive you. When rehearsing, consider volume, speed, and articulation.

- Speak loudly. In a meeting with five other people, you can speak in a normal volume. As your audience grows in size, so should your volume. Most speakers can project to as many as a hundred people, but a larger audience may require a microphone. If you can rehearse in the room where you'll be speaking, ask a friend or colleague to sit at the back and tell you what volume is easy to hear. It may seem like shouting to you, but to your audience it will sound confident and clear.
- Speak slowly enough to be understandable. Most audiences prefer speech that's a little fast, around 150 words a minute;

but they have difficulty following too-rapid speech at, say, 190 words a minute.

- Speak clearly and correctly. To avoid mumbling or slurring words, practice articulating. Sometimes it helps to open your mouth a little wider than usual. And to avoid mispronouncing words and names, look up questionable ones or ask someone for the correct pronunciation.

 Physical delivery

You are more than your spoken words when you make an oral presentation. Your face and body also play a role in how your speech is received.

- Make eye contact with listeners. Looking directly in your listeners' eyes conveys your honesty, your confidence, and your control of your material. Don't look above the heads of the audience or at one friendly face. Instead, move your gaze around the entire room, settle on someone, and establish direct eye contact; then move on to someone else.
- Always stand for a presentation, unless it takes place in a small room where standing would be inappropriate. You can see more audience members if you stand, and they in turn can hear your voice and see your gestures more clearly.
- Stand straight, and move around. Turn your body toward one side of the room and the other, step out from behind any lectern or desk, and gesture appropriately, as you would in conversation. Let your gestures and movement support and draw attention to important words and ideas.

 Visual aids

Many speakers supplement their oral presentations with visual aids—from words on a chalkboard through posters and models and slides to computer-generated multimedia productions. Visual aids can emphasize key points, organize interrelated concepts, and illustrate complex procedures. They can gain listeners' attention and improve their understanding and memory.

The following guidelines can help you create effective and appropriate visual aids:

- Use visual aids to underscore your points. Short lists of key ideas, illustrations such as graphs or photographs, or objects such as models can make your presentation more interesting and memorable. But use visual aids judiciously: a battery of illustrations or objects will bury your message rather than amplify it.

- Match visual aids and setting. An audience of five people may be able to see a photograph and share a chart; an audience of a hundred will need projected images.
- Coordinate visual aids with your message. Time each visual aid to reinforce a point you're making. Tell listeners what they're looking at—what they should be getting from the aid. Give them enough viewing time so they don't mind turning their attention back to you.

Practice

Practicing an oral presentation is the speechmaker's equivalent of editing and proofreading a written text. Good speakers rehearse their presentations exactly as they intend to deliver them before an audience—even in the same room, if possible, certainly with the same audio equipment and visual aids. (Practicing an oral presentation silently in your head is not the same as practicing it aloud.) With conscientious practice, you can uncover words that are difficult to pronounce or concepts that are unclear. You can tell and retell stories until they sound natural. You can rehearse your introduction so that you can maintain constant eye contact with listeners.

Stage fright

Many people report that speaking in front of an audience is their number-one fear. Even many experienced and polished speakers have some anxiety about delivering an oral presentation, but they use this nervous energy to their advantage, letting it propel them into working hard on each presentation, preparing well in advance, and rehearsing until they're satisfied with their delivery. They know that once they begin speaking and concentrate on their ideas, enthusiasm will quell anxiety. They know, too, that the symptoms of anxiety are usually imperceptible to listeners, who cannot see or hear a racing heart, upset stomach, cold hands, and worried thoughts. Even speakers who describe themselves as nervous usually appear confident and calm to their audiences.

Several techniques can help you reduce your level of anxiety:

- Use simple relaxation exercises, such as deep breathing or tensing and relaxing your stomach muscles, to ease some of the physical symptoms of speech anxiety—stomachache, rapid heartbeat, and shaky hands, legs, and voice.

RESOURCES AND IDEAS

Menzel, Kent E., and Lori J. Carrell. "The Relationship Between Preparation and Performance in Public Speaking." *Communication Education* 43:1 (Jan. 1994):17–26. Explores the effects of factors like anxiety level, preparation time, and scholastic ability on the quality of oral presentations. The authors show, for example, that time spent on preparing visual aids adds to an effective delivery, partly because of the motivational and anxiety-reducing effects.

Whitworth, Randolph H., and Claudia Cochran. "Evaluation of Integrated Versus Unitary Treatment for Reducing Public Speaking Anxiety." *Communication Education* 45:4 (Oct. 1996): 306–21. A highly technical case study of the relative merits of using or combining skills training, visualization therapy and "communication orientation motivation therapy" in overcoming presentation anxiety. The results show the importance of combining skills training with other anxiety-reducing approaches.

- Think positively. Try to convert any negative and irrational thoughts about speaking into positive ones about yourself and your behavior. Instead of worrying about the mistakes you might make, concentrate on how well you've prepared and practiced your presentation and how significant your ideas are.
- Don't avoid chances to speak in public. Practice and experience build speaking skills and offer the best insurance for success.

Glossary of Usage

This glossary provides notes on words or phrases that often cause problems for writers. The recommendations for standard written English are based on current dictionaries and usage guides such as the ones listed on pp. 481–83. Items labeled **nonstandard** should be avoided in speech and especially in writing. Those labeled **colloquial** and **slang** occur in speech and in some informal writing but are best avoided in the more formal writing usually expected in college and business. (Words and phrases labeled *colloquial* include those labeled by many dictionaries with the equivalent term *informal.*) See Chapter 31, pp. 454–73, for further discussion of word choice and for exercises in usage. See pp. 484–87 for a description of dictionary labels. Also see pp. 500–01 for a list of commonly confused words that are pronounced the same or similarly. The words and definitions provided there supplement this glossary.

The glossary is necessarily brief. Keep a dictionary handy for all your writing, and make a habit of referring to it whenever you doubt the appropriateness of a word or phrase.

a, an Use *a* before words beginning with consonant sounds, including those spelled with an initial pronounced *h* and those spelled with vowels that are sounded as consonants: *a historian, a one-o'clock class, a university.* Use *an* before words that begin with vowel sounds, including those spelled with an initial silent *h: an orgy, an L, an honor.*

The article before an abbreviation depends on how the abbreviation is read: *She was once an AEC undersecretary* (*AEC* is read as three separate letters); *Many Americans opposed a SALT treaty* (*SALT* is read as one word, *salt*).

For the use of *a/an* versus *the,* see pp. 259–61.

accept, except *Accept* is a verb meaning "receive." *Except* is usually a preposition or conjunction meaning "but for" or "other than"; when it is used as a verb, it means "leave out." *I can accept all your suggestions except the last one. I'm sorry you excepted my last suggestion from your list.*

adverse, averse *Adverse* and *averse* both mean "opposed" or "hostile." But *averse* describes the subject's opposition to something, whereas *adverse* describes something opposed to the subject: *The President was averse to adverse criticism.*

advice, advise *Advice* is a noun, and *advise* is a verb: *Take my advice; do as I advise you.*

affect, effect Usually *affect* is a verb, meaning "to influence," and *effect* is a noun, meaning "result": *The drug did not affect his driving; in fact, it seemed to have no effect at all.* But *effect* occasionally is used as a verb meaning "to bring about": *Her efforts effected a change.* And *affect* is used in psychology as a noun meaning "feeling or emotion": *One can infer much about affect from behavior.*

aggravate *Aggravate* should not be used in its colloquial meaning of "irritate" or "exasperate" (for example, *We were aggravated by her constant arguing*). *Aggravate* means "make worse": *The President was irritated by the Senate's indecision because he feared any delay might aggravate the unrest in the Middle East.*

agree to, agree with *Agree to* means "consent to," and *agree with* means "be in accord with": *How can they agree to a treaty when they don't agree with each other about the terms?*

ain't Nonstandard for *am not, isn't,* or *aren't.*

all, all of Usually *all* is sufficient to modify a noun: *all my loving, all the things you are.* Before a pronoun or proper noun, *all of* is usually appropriate: *all of me, in all of France.*

all ready, already *All ready* means "completely prepared," and *already* means "by now" or "before now": *We were all ready to go to the movie, but it had already started.*

all right *All right* is always two words. *Alright* is a common misspelling.

all together, altogether *All together* means "in unison" or "gathered in one place." *Altogether* means "entirely." *It's not altogether true that our family never spends vacations all together.*

allusion, illusion An *allusion* is an indirect reference, and an *illusion* is a deceptive appearance: *Paul's constant allusions to Shakespeare created the illusion that he was an intellectual.*

almost, most *Almost* means "nearly"; *most* means "the greater number (or part) of." In formal writing, *most* should not be used as a substitute for *almost: We see each other almost* [not *most*] *every day.*

a lot *A lot* is always two words, used informally to mean "many." *Alot* is a common misspelling.

among, between In general, use *among* for relationships involving more than two people or things. Use *between* for relationships involving only two or for comparing one thing to a group to which it belongs. *The four of them agreed among themselves that the choice was between New York and Los Angeles.*

amongst Although common in British English, in American English *amongst* is an overrefined substitute for *among.*

amount, number Use *amount* with a singular noun that names something not countable (a noncount noun): *The amount of food varies.* Use *number* with a plural noun that names more than one of something countable (a plural count noun): *The number of calories must stay the same.*

an, and *An* is an article (see *a, an*). *And* is a coordinating conjunction. Do not accidentally omit the *d* from *and.*

and etc. *Et cetera* (*etc.*) means "and the rest"; *and etc.* therefore is redundant. See also *et al., etc.*

and/or *And/or* indicates three options: one or the other or both (*The decision is made by the mayor and/or the council*). If you mean all three options, *and/or* is appropriate. Otherwise, use *and* if you mean both, *or* if you mean either.

and which, and who *And which* or *and who* is correct only when used to introduce a second clause beginning with the same relative pronoun: *Jill is my cousin who goes to school here and who calls me constantly.* Otherwise, *and* is not needed: *WCAS is my favorite AM radio station, which* [not *and which*] *I listen to every morning.*

ante-, anti- The prefix *ante-* means "before" (*antedate, antebellum*); *anti-* means "against" (*antiwar, antinuclear*). Before a capital letter or *i*, *anti-* takes a hyphen: *anti-Freudian, anti-isolationist.*

anxious, eager *Anxious* means "nervous" or "worried" and is usually followed by *about. Eager* means "looking forward" and is usually followed by *to. I've been anxious about getting blisters. I'm eager* [not *anxious*] *to get new running shoes.*

anybody, any body; anyone, any one *Anybody* and *anyone* are indefinite pronouns; *any body* is a noun modified by *any; any one* is a pronoun or adjective modified by *any. How can anybody communicate with any body of government? Can anyone help Amy? She has more work than any one person can handle.*

any more, anymore *Any more* means "no more"; *anymore* means "now." Both are used in negative constructions: *He doesn't want any more. She doesn't live here anymore.*

anyplace Colloquial for *anywhere.*

anyways, anywheres Nonstandard for *anyway* and *anywhere.*

apt, liable, likely *Apt* and *likely* are interchangeable. Strictly speaking, though, *apt* means "having a tendency to": *Horace is apt to forget* *his lunch in the morning. Likely* means "probably going to": *Horace is leaving so early today that he's likely to catch the first bus.*

Liable normally means "in danger of" and should be confined to situations with undesirable consequences: *Horace is liable to trip over that hose.* Strictly, *liable* means "responsible" or "exposed to": *The owner will be liable for Horace's injuries.*

are, is Use *are* with a plural subject (*books are*), *is* with a singular subject (*book is*).

as Substituting for *because, since,* or *while, as* may be vague or ambiguous: *As we were stopping to rest, we decided to eat lunch.* (Does *as* mean "while" or "because"?) *As* should never be used as a substitute for *whether* or *who. I'm not sure whether* [not *as*] *we can make it. That's the man who* [not *as*] *gave me directions.*

Usage

as, like See *like, as.*

as, than In comparisons, *as* and *than* precede a subjective-case pronoun when the pronoun is a subject: *I love you more than he* [*loves you*]. *As* and *than* precede an objective-case pronoun when the pronoun is an object: *I love you as much as* [*I love*] *him.* (See also p. 202.)

assure, ensure, insure *Assure* means "to promise": *He assured us that we would miss the traffic. Ensure* and *insure* often are used interchangeably to mean "make certain," but some reserve *insure* for matters of legal and financial protection and use *ensure* for more general meanings: *We left early to ensure that we would miss the traffic. It's expensive to insure yourself against floods.*

as to A stuffy substitute for *about: The suspect was questioned about* [not *as to*] *her actions.*

at The use of *at* after *where* is wordy and should be avoided: *Where are you meeting him?* is preferable to *Where are you meeting him at?*

at this point in time Wordy for *now, at this point,* or *at this time.*

averse, adverse See *adverse, averse.*

awful, awfully Strictly speaking, *awful* means "awe-inspiring." As intensifiers meaning "very" or "extremely" (*He tried awfully hard*), *awful* and *awfully* should be avoided in formal speech or writing.

a while, awhile *Awhile* is an adverb; *a while* is an article and a noun. Thus *awhile* can modify a verb but cannot serve as the object of a preposition, and *a while* is just the opposite: *I will be gone awhile* [not *a while*]. *I will be gone for a while* [not *awhile*].

bad, badly In formal speech and writing, *bad* should be used only as an adjective; the adverb is *badly. He felt bad because his tooth ached badly.* In *He felt bad,* the verb *felt* is a linking verb and the adjective *bad* is a subject complement. (See also pp. 253–54.)

being as, being that Colloquial for *because,* the preferable word in formal speech or writing: *Because* [not *Being as*] *the world is round, Columbus never did fall off the edge.*

beside, besides *Beside* is a preposition meaning "next to." *Besides* is a preposition meaning "except" or "in addition to" as well as an adverb meaning "in addition." *Besides, several other people besides you want to sit beside Dr. Christensen.*

better, had better *Had better* (meaning "ought to") is a verb modified by an adverb. The verb is necessary and should not be omitted: *You had better* [not *better*] *go.*

between, among See *among, between.*

bring, take Use *bring* only for movement from a farther place to a nearer one and *take* for any other movement. *First, take these books to the library for renewal, then take them to Mr. Daniels. Bring them back to me when he's finished.*

bunch In formal speech and writing, *bunch* (as a noun) should be used only to refer to clusters of things growing or fastened together, such as bananas and grapes. Its use to mean a group of items or people is colloquial; *crowd* or *group* is preferable.

burst, bursted; bust, busted *Burst* is a standard verb form meaning "to fly apart suddenly" (principal parts *burst, burst, burst*). The past-tense form *bursted* is nonstandard. The verb *bust* (*busted*) is slang.

but, hardly, scarcely These words are negative in their own right; using *not* with any of them produces a double negative (see pp. 257–58). *We have but* [not *haven't got but*] *an hour before our plane leaves. I could hardly* [not *couldn't hardly*] *make out her face.*

but, however, yet Each of these words is adequate to express contrast. Don't combine them. *He said he had finished, yet* [not *but yet*] *he continued.*

but that, but what These wordy substitutes for *that* and *what* should be avoided: *I don't doubt that* [not *but that*] *you are right.*

calculate, figure, reckon As substitutes for *expect* or *imagine (I figure I'll go),* these words are colloquial.

can, may Strictly, *can* indicates capacity or ability, and *may* indicates permission: *If I may talk with you a moment, I believe I can solve your problem.*

can't help but This idiom is common but redundant. Either *I can't help wishing* or the more formal *I cannot but wish* is preferable to *I can't help but wish.*

case, instance, line Expressions such as *in the case of, in the instance of,* and *along the lines of* are usually unnecessary padding and should be avoided.

censor, censure To *censor* is to edit or remove from public view on moral or some other grounds; to *censure* is to give a formal scolding. *The lieutenant was censured by Major Taylor for censoring the letters her soldiers wrote home from boot camp.*

Usage

center around *Center on* is more logical than, and preferable to, *center around.*

climatic, climactic *Climatic* comes from *climate* and refers to weather: *Last winter's temperatures may indicate a climatic change. Climactic* comes from *climax* and refers to a dramatic high point: *During the climactic duel between Hamlet and Laertes, Gertrude drinks poisoned wine.*

complement, compliment To *complement* something is to add to, complete, or reinforce it: *Her yellow blouse complemented her black hair.* To *compliment* something is to make a flattering remark about it: *He complimented her on her hair. Complimentary* can also mean "free": *complimentary tickets.*

compose, comprise *Compose* means "to make up": *The parts compose the whole. Comprise* means "to consist of": *The whole comprises the parts.* Thus, *The band comprises* [not *is comprised of*] *twelve musicians. Twelve musicians compose* [not *comprise*] *the band.*

conscience, conscious *Conscience* is a noun meaning "a sense of right and wrong"; *conscious* is an adjective meaning "aware" or "awake." *Though I was barely conscious, my conscience nagged me.*

contact Often used imprecisely as a verb instead of a more exact word such as *consult, talk with, telephone,* or *write to.*

continual, continuous *Continual* means "constantly recurring": *Most movies on television are continually interrupted by commercials. Continuous* means "unceasing": *Some cable channels present movies continuously without commercials.*

convince, persuade In the strictest sense, to *convince* someone means to change his or her opinion; to *persuade* someone means to move him or her to action. *Convince* is thus properly followed by *of* or *that,* whereas *persuade* is followed by *to: Once he convinced Othello of Desdemona's infidelity, Iago easily persuaded him to kill her.*

could care less The expression is *could not* [*couldn't*] *care less. Could care less* indicates some care, the opposite of what is intended.

could of See *have, of.*

couple of Used colloquially to mean "a few" or "several."

credible, creditable, credulous *Credible* means "believable": *It's a strange story, but it seems credible to me. Creditable* means "deserving of credit" or "worthy": *Steve gave a creditable performance. Credulous* means "gullible": *The credulous Claire believed Tim's lies.* See also *incredible, incredulous.*

criteria The plural of *criterion* (meaning "standard for judgment"): *Our criteria are strict. The most important criterion is a sense of humor.*

data The plural of *datum* (meaning "fact"): *Out of all the data generated by these experiments, not one datum supports our hypothesis.* Usually, a more common term such as *fact, result,* or *figure* is preferred to *datum*. Though *data* is often used as a singular noun, most careful writers still treat it as plural: *The data fail* [not *fails*] *to support the hypothesis.*

device, devise *Device* is the noun, and *devise* is the verb: *Can you devise some device for getting his attention?*

different from, different than *Different from* is preferred: *His purpose is different from mine.* But *different than* is widely accepted when a construction using *from* would be wordy: *I'm a different person now than I used to be* is preferable to *I'm a different person now from the person I used to be.*

differ from, differ with To *differ from* is to be unlike: *The twins differ from each other only in their hair styles.* To *differ with* is to disagree with: *I have to differ with you on that point.*

discreet, discrete *Discreet* (noun form *discretion*) means "tactful": *What's a discreet way of telling Maud to be quiet? Discrete* (noun form *discreteness*) means "separate and distinct": *Within a computer's memory are millions of discrete bits of information.*

disinterested, uninterested *Disinterested* means "impartial": *We chose Pete, as a disinterested third party, to decide who was right. Uninterested* means "bored" or "lacking interest": *Unfortunately, Pete was completely uninterested in the question.*

don't *Don't* is the contraction for *do not,* not for *does not: I don't care, you don't care,* and *he doesn't* [not *don't*] *care.*

due to *Due* is an adjective or noun; thus *due to* is always acceptable as a subject complement: *His gray hairs were due to age.* Many object to *due to* as a preposition meaning "because of" (*Due to the holiday, class was canceled*). A rule of thumb is that *due to* is always correct after a form of the verb *be* but questionable otherwise.

due to the fact that Wordy for *because.*

each and every Wordy for *each* or *every*. Write *each one of us* or *every one of us,* not *each and every one of us.*

eager, anxious See *anxious, eager.*

effect See *affect, effect.*

elicit, illicit *Elicit* is a verb meaning "bring out" or "call forth." *Illicit* is an adjective meaning "unlawful." *The crime elicited an outcry against illicit drugs.*

emigrate, immigrate *Emigrate* means "to leave one place and move to another" (the Latin prefix *e-* means "out of": "migrate out of"): *The Chus emigrated from Korea. Immigrate* means "to move into a place where one was not born" (the Latin prefix *im-* means "into": "migrate into"): *They immigrated to the United States.*

ensure See *assure, ensure, insure.*

enthused Used colloquially as an adjective meaning "showing enthusiasm." The preferred adjective is *enthusiastic: The coach was enthusiastic* [not *enthused*] *about the team's victory.*

especially, specially *Especially* means "particularly" or "more than other things"; *specially* means "for a specific reason." *I especially treasure my boots. They were made specially for me.*

et al., etc. Use *et al.,* the Latin abbreviation for "and other people," only in source citations for works with more than three authors: *Jones et al.* (see pp. 601, 610–11). *Etc.,* the Latin abbreviation for "and other things," should be avoided in formal writing and should not be used to refer to people. When used, it should not substitute for precision, as in *The government provides health care, etc.* See also *and etc.*

everybody, every body; everyone, every one *Everybody* and *everyone* are indefinite pronouns: *Everybody* [or *Everyone*] *knows Tom steals. Every one* is a pronoun modified by *every,* and *every body* a noun modified by *every.* Both refer to each thing or person of a specific group and are typically followed by *of: The game commissioner has stocked every body of fresh water in the state with fish, and now every one of our rivers is a potential trout stream.*

everyday, every day *Everyday* is an adjective meaning "used daily" or "common"; *every day* is a noun modified by *every: Everyday problems tend to arise every day.*

everywheres Nonstandard for *everywhere.*

except See *accept, except.*

except for the fact that Wordy for *except that.*

explicit, implicit *Explicit* means "stated outright": *I left explicit instructions. The movie contains explicit sex. Implicit* means "implied, unstated": *We had an implicit understanding. I trust Marcia implicitly.*

farther, further *Farther* refers to additional distance (*How much farther is it to the beach?*), and *further* refers to additional time, amount, or other abstract matters (*I don't want to discuss this any further*).

feel Avoid this word in place of *think* or *believe: She thinks* [not *feels*] *that the law should be changed.*

fewer, less *Fewer* refers to individual countable items (a plural count noun), *less* to general amounts (a noncount noun, always singular): *Skim milk has fewer calories than whole milk. We have less milk left than I thought.*

field The phrase *the field of* is wordy and generally unnecessary: *Margaret plans to specialize in* [not *in the field of*] *family medicine.*

figure See *calculate, figure, reckon.*

fixing to Avoid this colloquial substitute for "intend to": *The school intends* [not *is fixing*] *to build a new library.*

flaunt, flout *Flaunt* means "show off": *If you have style, flaunt it.*

Flout means "scorn" or "defy": *Hester Prynne flouted convention and paid the price.*

flunk A colloquial substitute for *fail.*

former, latter *Former* refers to the first-named of two things, *latter* to the second-named: *I like both skiing and swimming, the former in the winter and the latter all year round.* To refer to the first- or last-named of three or more things, say *first* or *last: I like jogging, swimming, and hang gliding, but the last is inconvenient in the city.*

fun As an adjective, *fun* is colloquial and should be avoided in most writing: *It was a pleasurable* [not *fun*] *evening.*

further See *farther, further.*

get This common verb is used in many slang and colloquial expressions: *get lost, that really gets me, getting on. Get* is easy to overuse; watch out for it in expressions such as *it's getting better* (substitute *improving*) and *we got done* (substitute *finished*).

go As a substitute for *say* or *reply, go* is colloquial: *He says* [not *goes*], *"How do you do, madam?"*

good, well *Good* is an adjective, and *well* is nearly always an adverb: *Larry's a good dancer. He and Linda dance well together. Well* is properly used as an adjective only to refer to health: *You look well.* (*You look good,* in contrast, means "Your appearance is pleasing.")

good and Colloquial for "very": *I was very* [not *good and*] *tired.*

had better See *better, had better.*

had ought The *had* is unnecessary and should be omitted: *He ought* [not *had ought*] *to listen to his mother.*

half Either *half a* or *a half* is appropriate usage, but *a half a* is redundant: *Half a loaf* [not *A half a loaf*] *is better than none. I'd like a half-gallon* [not *a half a gallon*] *of mineral water, please.*

hanged, hung Though both are past-tense forms of *hang, hanged* is used to refer to executions and *hung* is used for all other meanings: *Tom Dooley was hanged* [not *hung*] *from a white oak tree. I hung* [not *hanged*] *the picture you gave me.*

hardly See *but, hardly, scarcely.*

have, of Use *have,* not *of,* after helping verbs such as *could, should, would, may,* and *might: You should have* [not *should of*] *told me.*

he, she; he/she Convention has allowed the use of *he* to mean "he or she": *After the infant learns to creep, he progresses to crawling.* However, many writers today consider this usage inaccurate and unfair because it excludes females. The construction *he/she,* one substitute for *he,* is awkward and objectionable to most readers. The better choice is to use *he or she,* to make the pronoun plural, or to rephrase. For instance: *After the infant learns to creep, he or she progresses to crawling. After* *infants learn to creep, they progress to crawling. After learning to creep, the infant progresses to crawling.* (See also pp. 249 and 461.)

herself, himself See *myself, herself, himself, yourself.*

hisself Nonstandard for *himself.*

hopefully *Hopefully* means "with hope": *Freddy waited hopefully for a glimpse of Eliza.* The use of *hopefully* to mean "it is to be hoped," "I hope," or "let's hope" is now very common; but since many readers continue to object strongly to the usage, you should avoid it. *I hope* [not *Hopefully*] *the law will pass.*

idea, ideal An *idea* is a thought or conception. An *ideal* (noun) is a model of perfection or a goal. *Ideal* should not be used in place of *idea: The idea* [not *ideal*] *of the play is that our ideals often sustain us.*

if, whether For clarity, use *whether* rather than *if* when you are expressing an alternative: *If I laugh hard, people can't tell whether I'm crying.*

illicit See *elicit, illicit.*

illusion See *allusion, illusion.*

immigrate, emigrate See *emigrate, immigrate.*

impact Both the noun and the verb *impact* connote forceful or even violent collision. Avoid the increasingly common diluted meanings of *impact:* "an effect" (noun) or "to have an effect on" (verb). The diluted verb (*The budget cuts impacted social science research*) is bureaucratic jargon.

implicit See *explicit, implicit.*

imply, infer Writers or speakers *imply,* meaning "suggest": *Jim's letter implies he's having a good time.* Readers or listeners *infer,* meaning "conclude": *From Jim's letter I infer he's having a good time.*

in, into *In* indicates location or condition: *He was in the garage. She was in a coma. Into* indicates movement or a change in condition: *He went into the garage. She fell into a coma. Into* is also slang for "interested in" or "involved in": *I am into Zen.*

in . . . A number of phrases beginning with *in* are unnecessarily wordy and should be avoided: *in the event that* (for *if*); *in the neighborhood of* (for *approximately* or *about*); *in this day and age* (for *now* or *nowadays*); *in spite of the fact that* (for *although* or *even though*); and *in view of the fact that* (for *because* or *considering that*). Certain other *in* phrases are nothing but padding and can be omitted entirely: *in nature, in number, in reality,* and *in a very real sense.* (See also pp. 473–75.)

incredible, incredulous *Incredible* means "unbelievable"; *incredulous* means "unbelieving": *When Nancy heard Dennis's incredible story, she was frankly incredulous.* See also *credible, creditable, credulous.*

individual, person, party *Individual* should refer to a single human being in contrast to a group or should stress uniqueness: *The US Constitution places strong emphasis on the rights of the individual.* For other meanings *person* is preferable: *What person* [not *individual*] *wouldn't want the security promised in that advertisement? Party* means "group" (*Can you seat a party of four for dinner?*) and should not be used to refer to an individual except in legal documents. See also *people, persons.*

infer See *imply, infer.*

in regards to Nonstandard for *in regard to, as regards,* or *regarding.* See also *regarding.*

inside of, outside of The *of* is unnecessary when *inside* and *outside* are used as prepositions: *Stay inside* [not *inside of*] *the house. The decision is outside* [not *outside of*] *my authority. Inside of* may refer colloquially to time, though in formal English *within* is preferred: *The law was passed within* [not *inside of*] *a year.*

instance See *case, instance, line.*

insure See *assure, ensure, insure.*

irregardless Nonstandard for *regardless.*

is, are See *are,* is.

is because See *reason is because.*

is when, is where These are faulty constructions in sentences that define: *Adolescence is a stage* [not *is when a person is*] *between childhood and adulthood. Socialism is a system in which* [not *is where*] *government owns the means of production.* (See also p. 310.)

its, it's *Its* is the pronoun *it* in the possessive case: *That plant is losing its leaves. It's* is a contraction for *it is: It's likely to die if you don't water it.* Many people confuse *it's* and *its* because possessives are most often formed with *-'s;* but the possessive *its,* like *his* and *hers,* never takes an apostrophe.

-ize, -wise The suffix *-ize* changes a noun or adjective into a verb: *revolutionize, immunize.* The suffix *-wise* changes a noun or adjective into an adverb: *clockwise, otherwise, likewise.* Avoid the two suffixes except in established words: *The two nations are ready to settle on* [not *finalize*] *an agreement. I'm highly sensitive* [not *sensitized*] *to that kind of criticism. Financially* [not *Moneywise*], *it's a good time to buy real estate.*

kind of, sort of, type of In formal speech and writing, avoid using *kind of* or *sort of* to mean "somewhat": *He was rather* [not *kind of*] *tall.*

Kind, sort, and *type* are singular and take singular modifiers and verbs: *This kind of dog is easily trained.* Agreement errors often occur when these singular nouns are combined with the plural adjectives *these* and *those: These kinds* [not *kind*] *of dogs are easily trained. Kind, sort,* and *type* should be followed by *of* but not by *a: I don't know what type of* [not *type* or *type of a*] *dog that is.*

Use *kind of, sort of,* or *type of* only when the word *kind, sort,* or *type* is important: *That was a strange* [not *strange sort of*] *statement.*

later, latter *Later* refers to time; *latter* refers to the second-named of two items. See also *former, latter.*

lay, lie *Lay* means "put" or "place" and takes a direct object: *We could lay the tablecloth in the sun.* Its main forms are *lay, laid, laid. Lie* means "recline" or "be situated" and does not take an object: *I lie awake at night. The town lies east of the river.* Its main forms are *lie, lay, lain.* (See also p. 212.)

leave, let *Leave* and *let* are interchangeable only when followed by *alone; leave me alone* is the same as *let me alone.* Otherwise, *leave* means "depart" and *let* means "allow": *Julia would not let Susan leave.*

less See *fewer, less.*

let See *leave, let.*

liable See *apt, liable, likely.*

lie, lay See *lay, lie.*

like, as In formal speech and writing, *like* should not introduce a full clause (with a subject and a verb) because it is a preposition. The preferred choice is *as* or *as if: The plan succeeded as* [not *like*] *we hoped. It seemed as if* [not *like*] *it might fail. Other plans like it have failed.*

When *as* serves as a preposition, the distinction between *as* and *like* depends on meaning. *As* suggested that the subject is equivalent or identical to the description: *She was hired as an engineer. Like* suggests resemblance but not identity: *People like her do well in such jobs.* See also *like, such as.*

like, such as Strictly, *such as* precedes an example that represents a larger subject, whereas *like* indicates that two subjects are comparable. *Steve has recordings of many great saxophonists such as Ben Webster and Lee Konitz. Steve wants to be a great jazz saxophonist like Ben Webster and Lee Konitz.*

Many writers prefer to keep *such* and *as* together: *Steve admires saxophonists such as* . . . rather than *Steve admires such saxophonists as.* . . .

likely See *apt, liable, likely.*

line See *case, instance, line.*

literally This word means "actually" or "just as the words say," and it should not be used to qualify or intensify expressions whose words are not to be taken at face value. The sentence *He was literally climbing the walls* describes a person behaving like an insect, not a person who is restless or anxious. For the latter meaning, *literally* should be omitted.

lose, loose *Lose* means "mislay": *Did you lose a brown glove? Loose* means "unrestrained" or "not tight": *Ann's canary got loose. Loose* also can function as a verb meaning "let loose": *They loose the dogs as soon as they spot the bear.*

lots, lots of Colloquial substitutes for *very many, a great many,* or *much.* Avoid *lots* and *lots of* in college or business writing. When you use either one informally, be careful to maintain subject-verb agreement: *There are* [not *is*] *lots of fish in the pond.*

may, can See *can, may.*

may be, maybe *May be* is a verb, and *maybe* is an adverb meaning "perhaps": *Tuesday may be a legal holiday. Maybe we won't have classes.*

may of See *have, of.*

media *Media* is the plural of *medium* and takes a plural verb: *All the news media are increasingly visual.* The singular verb is common, even in the media, but most careful writers still use the plural verb.

might of See *have, of.*

moral, morale As a noun, *moral* means "ethical conclusion" or "lesson": *The moral of the story escapes me. Morale* means "spirit" or "state of mind": *Victory improved the team's morale.*

most, almost See *almost, most.*

must of See *have, of.*

myself, herself, himself, yourself The *-self* pronouns refer to or intensify another word or words: *Paul helped himself; Jill herself said so.* The *-self* pronouns are often used colloquially in place of personal pronouns, but that use should be avoided in formal speech and writing: *No one except me* [not *myself*] *saw the accident. Our delegates will be Susan and you* [not *yourself*].

nohow Nonstandard for *in no way* or *in any way.*

nothing like, nowhere near These colloquial substitutes for *not nearly* are best avoided in formal speech and writing: *That program is not nearly* [not *nowhere near*] *as expensive.*

nowheres Nonstandard for *nowhere.*

number See *amount, number.*

of, have See *have, of.*

off of *Of* is unnecessary. Use *off* or *from* rather than *off of: He jumped off* [or *from,* not *off of*] *the roof.*

OK, O.K., okay All three spellings are acceptable, but avoid this colloquial term in formal speech and writing.

on, upon In modern English, *upon* is usually just a stuffy way of saying *on.* Unless you need a formal effect, use *on: We decided on* [not *upon*] *a location for our next meeting.*

on account of Wordy for *because of.*

Usage

on the other hand This transitional expression of contrast should be preceded by its mate, *on the one hand: On the one hand, we hoped for snow. On the other hand, we feared that it would harm the animals.* However, the two combined can be unwieldy, and a simple *but, however, yet,* or *in contrast* often suffices: *We hoped for snow. Yet we feared that it would harm the animals.*

outside of See *inside of, outside of.*

owing to the fact that Wordy for *because.*

party See *individual, person, party.*

people, persons In formal usage, *people* refers to a general group: *We the people of the United States. . . . Persons* refers to a collection of individuals: *Will the person or persons who saw the accident please notify. . . .* Except when emphasizing individuals, prefer *people* to *persons.* See also *individual, person, party.*

per Except in technical writing, an English equivalent is usually preferable to the Latin *per: $10 an* [not *per*] *hour; sent by* [not *per*] *parcel post; requested in* [not *per* or *as per*] *your letter.*

percent (per cent), percentage Both these terms refer to fractions of one hundred. *Percent* always follows a numeral (*40 percent of the voters*), and the word should be used instead of the symbol (%) in general writing. *Percentage* usually follows an adjective (*a high percentage*).

person See *individual, person, party.*

persons See *people, persons.*

persuade See *convince, persuade.*

phenomena The plural of *phenomenon* (meaning "perceivable fact" or "unusual occurrence"): *Many phenomena are not recorded. One phenomenon is attracting attention.*

plenty A colloquial substitute for *very: The reaction occurred very* [not *plenty*] *fast.*

plus *Plus* is standard as a preposition meaning *in addition to: His income plus mine is sufficient.* But *plus* is colloquial as a conjunctive adverb: *Our organization is larger than theirs; moreover* [not *plus*], *we have more money.*

practicable, practical *Practicable* means "capable of being put into practice"; *practical* means "useful" or "sensible": *We figured out a practical new design for our kitchen, but it was too expensive to be practicable.*

precede, proceed The verb *precede* means "come before": *My name precedes yours in the alphabet.* The verb *proceed* means "move on": *We were told to proceed to the waiting room.*

prejudice, prejudiced *Prejudice* is a noun; *prejudiced* is an adjective. Do not drop the *-d* from *prejudiced: I was fortunate that my parents were not prejudiced* [not *prejudice*].

pretty Overworked as an adverb meaning "rather" or "somewhat": *He was somewhat* [not *pretty*] *irked at the suggestion.*

previous to, prior to Wordy for *before.*

principal, principle *Principal* is an adjective meaning "foremost" or "major," a noun meaning "chief official," or, in finance, a noun meaning "capital sum." *Principle* is a noun only, meaning "rule" or "axiom." *Her principal reasons for confessing were her principles of right and wrong.*

proceed, precede See *precede, proceed.*

provided, providing *Provided* may serve as a subordinating conjunction meaning "on the condition (that)"; *providing* may not. *The grocer will begin providing food for the soup kitchen provided* [not *providing*] *we find a suitable space.*

question of whether, question as to whether Wordy substitutes for *whether.*

raise, rise *Raise* means "lift" or "bring up" and takes a direct object: *The Kirks raise cattle.* Its main forms are *raise, raised, raised. Rise* means "get up" and does not take an object: *They must rise at dawn.* Its main forms are *rise, rose, risen.* (See also p. 212.)

real, really In formal speech and writing, *real* should not be used as an adverb; *really* is the adverb and *real* an adjective. *Popular reaction to the announcement was really* [not *real*] *enthusiastic.*

reason is because Although colloquially common, this expression should be avoided in formal speech and writing. Use a *that* clause after *reason is: The reason he is absent is that* [not *is because*] *he is sick.* Or: *He is absent because he is sick.*

reckon See *calculate, figure, reckon.*

regarding, in regard to, with regard to, relating to, relative to, with respect to, respecting Stuffy substitutes for *on, about,* or *concerning: Mr. McGee spoke about* [not *with regard to*] *the plans for the merger.*

respectful, respective *Respectful* means "full of (or showing) respect": *Be respectful of other people. Respective* means "separate": *The French and the Germans occupied their respective trenches.*

rise, raise See *raise, rise.*

scarcely See *but, hardly, scarcely.*

sensual, sensuous *Sensual* suggests sexuality; *sensuous* means "pleasing to the senses." *Stirred by the sensuous scent of meadow grass and flowers, Cheryl and Paul found their thoughts growing increasingly sensual.*

set, sit *Set* means "put" or "place" and takes a direct object: *He sets the pitcher down.* Its main forms are *set, set, set. Sit* means "be seated" and does not take an object: *She sits on the sofa.* Its main forms are *sit, sat, sat.* (See also p. 212.)

Usage

shall, will *Will* is the future-tense helping verb for all persons: *I will go, you will go, they will go.* The main use of *shall* is for first-person questions requesting an opinion or consent: *Shall I order a pizza? Shall we dance?* (Questions that merely inquire about the future use *will: When will I see you again?*) *Shall* can also be used for the first person when a formal effect is desired (I *shall expect you around three*), and it is occasionally used with the second or third person to express the speaker's determination (*You shall do as I say*).

should, would *Should* expresses obligation: *I should fix dinner. You should set the table. Jack should wash the dishes. Would* expresses a wish or hypothetical condition: *I would do it. Wouldn't you?* When the context is formal, however, *should* is sometimes used instead of *would* in the first person: *We should be delighted to accept.*

should of See *have, of.*

since *Since* mainly relates to time: *I've been waiting since noon.* But *since* is also often used to mean "because": *Since you ask, I'll tell you.* Revise sentences in which the word could have either meaning, such as *Since you left, my life is empty.*

sit, set See *set, sit.*

situation Often unnecessary, as in *The situation is that we have to get some help* (revise to *We have to get some help*) or *The team was faced with a punting situation* (revise to *The team was faced with punting* or *The team had to punt*).

so Avoid using *so* alone as a vague intensifier: *He was so late. So* needs to be followed by *that* and a clause that states a result: *He was so late that I left without him.*

some *Some* is colloquial as an adverb meaning "somewhat" or "to some extent" and as an adjective meaning "remarkable": *We'll have to hurry somewhat* [not *some*] *to get there in time. Those are remarkable* [not *some*] *photographs.*

somebody, some body; someone, some one *Somebody* and *someone* are indefinite pronouns; *some body* is a noun modified by *some;* and *some one* is a pronoun or an adjective modified by *some. Somebody ought to invent a shampoo that will give hair some body. Someone told Janine she should choose some one plan and stick with it.*

someplace Informal for *somewhere.*

sometime, sometimes, some time *Sometime* means "at an indefinite time in the future": *Why don't you come up and see me sometime? Sometimes* means "now and then": *I still see my old friend Joe sometimes. Some time* means "a span of time": *I need some time to make the payments.*

somewheres Nonstandard for *somewhere.*

sort of, sort of a See *kind of, sort of, type of.*

specially See *especially, specially.*

such Avoid using *such* as a vague intensifier: *It was such a cold winter. Such* should be followed by *that* and a clause that states a result: *It was such a cold winter that Napoleon's troops had to turn back.*

such as See *like, such as.*

supposed to, used to In both these expressions, the *-d* is essential: *I used to* [not *use to*] *think so. He's supposed to* [not *suppose to*] *meet us.*

sure Colloquial when used as an adverb meaning *surely: James Madison sure was right about the need for the Bill of Rights.* If you merely want to be emphatic, use *certainly: Madison certainly was right.* If your goal is to convince a possibly reluctant reader, use *surely: Madison surely was right. Surely Madison was right.*

sure and, sure to; try and, try to *Sure to* and *try to* are the correct forms: *Be sure to* [not *sure and*] *vote. Try to* [not *Try and*] *vote early to avoid a line.*

take, bring See *bring, take.*

than, as See *as, than.*

than, then *Than* is a conjunction used in comparisons, *then* an adverb indicating time: *Holmes knew then that Moriarty was wilier than he had thought.*

that, which *That* always introduces restrictive clauses: *We should use the lettuce that Susan bought* (*that Susan bought* limits *lettuce* to a particular lettuce). *Which* can introduce both restrictive and nonrestrictive clauses, but many writers reserve *which* only for nonrestrictive clauses: *The leftover lettuce, which is in the refrigerator, would make a good salad* (*which is in the refrigerator* simply provides more information about the lettuce we already know of). Restrictive clauses (with *that* or *which*) are not set off by commas; nonrestrictive clauses (with *which*) are. (See also pp. 370–72.)

their, there, they're *Their* is the possessive form of *they: Give them their money. There* indicates place (*I saw her standing there*) or functions as an expletive (*There is a hole behind you*). *They're* is a contraction for *they are: They're going fast.*

theirselves Nonstandard for *themselves.*

then, than See *than, then.*

these kind, these sort, these type, those kind See *kind of, sort of, type of.*

this here, these here, that there, them there Nonstandard for *this, these, that,* or *those.*

thru A colloquial spelling of *through* that should be avoided in all academic and business writing.

thusly A mistaken form of *thus.*

till, until, 'til *Till* and *until* have the same meaning; both are acceptable. *'Til,* a contraction of *until,* is an old form that has been replaced by *till.*

time period Since a *period* is an interval of time, this expression is redundant: *They did not see each other for a long time* [not *time period*]. *Six accidents occurred in a three-week period* [not *time period*].

to, too, two *To* is a preposition; *too* is an adverb meaning "also" or "excessively"; and *two* is a number. *I too have been to Europe two times.*

too Avoid using *too* as an intensifier meaning "very": *Monkeys are too mean.* If you do use *too,* explain the consequences of the excessive quality: *Monkeys are too mean to make good pets.*

toward, towards Both are acceptable, though *toward* is preferred. Use one or the other consistently.

try and, try to See *sure and, sure to; try and, try to.*

type of See *kind of, sort of, type of.* Don't use *type* without *of: It was a family type of* [not *type*] *restaurant.* Or, better: *It was a family restaurant.*

uninterested See *disinterested, uninterested.*

unique *Unique* means "the only one of its kind" and so cannot sensibly be modified with words such as *very* or *most: That was a unique* [not *a very unique* or *the most unique*] *movie.*

until See *till, until, 'til.*

upon, on See *on, upon.*

usage, use *Usage* refers to conventions, most often those of a language: *Is "hadn't ought" proper usage? Usage* is often misused in place of the noun *use: Wise use* [not *usage*] *of insulation can save fuel.*

use, utilize Utilize can be used to mean "make good use of": *Many teachers utilize computers for instruction.* But for all other senses of "place in service" or "employ," prefer *use.*

used to See *supposed to, used to.*

wait for, wait on In formal speech and writing, *wait for* means "await" (*I'm waiting for Paul*), and *wait on* means "serve" (*The owner of the store herself waited on us*).

ways Colloquial as a substitute for way: *We have only a little way* [not *ways*] *to go.*

well See *good, well.*

whether, if See *if, whether.*

which See *that, which.*

which, who *Which* never refers to people. Use *who* or sometimes *that* for a person or persons and *which* or *that* for a thing or things: *The baby, who was left behind, opened the door, which we had closed.* (See also pp. 287–88.)

who, whom *Who* is the subject of a sentence or clause (*We don't know who will come*). *Whom* is the object of a verb or preposition (*We do not know whom we invited*). (See also p. 202.)

who's, whose *Who's* is the contraction of *who is: Who's at the door? Whose* is the possessive form of *who: Whose book is that?*

will, shall See *shall, will.*

-wise See *-ize, -wise.*

with regard to, with respect to See *regarding.*

would See *should, would.*

would have Avoid this construction in place of *had* in clauses that begin *if* and state a condition contrary to fact: *If the tree had* [not *would have*] *withstood the fire, it would have been the oldest in town.* (See also p. 229.)

would of See *have, of.*

you In all but very formal writing, *you* is generally appropriate as long as it means "you, the reader." In all writing, avoid indefinite uses of *you,* such as *In one ancient tribe your first loyalty was to your parents.* (See also pp. 286–87.)

your, you're *Your* is the possessive form of *you: Your dinner is ready. You're* is the contraction of *you are: You're bound to be late.*

yourself See *myself, herself, himself, yourself.*

Glossary of Terms

This glossary defines terms of grammar, rhetoric, literature, and Internet research. Page numbers in parentheses refer you to sections of the text where the term is explained more fully.

absolute phrase A phrase consisting of a noun or pronoun plus the *-ing* or *-ed* form of a verb (a participle): *Our accommodations arranged, we set out on our journey. They will hire a local person, other things being equal.* An absolute phrase modifies a whole clause or sentence (rather than a single word), and it is not joined to the rest of the sentence by a connector. (See p. 181.)

abstract and concrete Two kinds of language. **Abstract** words refer to ideas, qualities, attitudes, and conditions that can't be perceived with the senses: *beauty, guilty, victory.* **Concrete** words refer to objects, persons, places, or conditions that can be perceived with the senses: *Abilene, scratchy, toolbox.* See also *general and specific.* (See p. 466.)

acronym A pronounceable word formed from the initial letter or letters of each word in an organization's title: NATO (North Atlantic Treaty Organization).

active voice See *voice.*

adjectival A term sometimes used to describe any word or word group, other than an adjective, that is used to modify a noun. Common adjectivals include nouns (*wagon train, railroad ties*), phrases (*fool on the hill*), and clauses (*the man that I used to be*).

adjective A word used to modify a noun (*beautiful morning*) or a pronoun (*ordinary one*). (See Chapter 9.) Nouns, some verb forms, phrases, and clauses may also serve as adjectives: *book sale; a used book; sale of* *old books; the sale, which occurs annually.* (See *clauses, prepositional phrases,* and *verbals and verbal phrases.*)

Adjectives come in several classes:

- A **descriptive adjective** names some quality of the noun: *beautiful morning, dark horse.*
- A **limiting adjective** narrows the scope of a noun. It may be a **possessive** (*my, their*); a **demonstrative adjective** (*this train, these days*); an **interrogative adjective** (*what time? whose body?*); or a **number** (*two boys*).
- A **proper adjective** is derived from a proper noun: *French language, Machiavellian scheme.*

Adjectives also can be classified according to position:

- An **attributive adjective** appears next to the noun it modifies: *full moon.*
- A **predicate adjective** is connected to its noun by a linking verb: *The moon is full.* See also *complement.*

Terms

adjective clause See *adjective.*

adjective phrase See *adjective.*

adverb A word used to modify a verb (*warmly greet*), an adjective (*only three people*), another adverb (*quite seriously*), or a whole sentence (*Fortunately, she is employed*). (See Chapter 9.) Some verb forms, phrases, and clauses may also serve as adverbs: *easy to stop, drove by a farm, plowed the fields when the earth thawed.* (See *clause, prepositional phrase,* and *verbals and verbal phrases.*)

adverb clause See *adverb.*

adverbial A term sometimes used to describe any word or word group, other than an adverb, that is used to modify a verb, an adjective, another adverb, or a whole sentence. Common adverbials include nouns (*This little piggy stayed home*), phrases (*This little piggy went to market*), and clauses (*This little piggy went wherever he wanted*).

adverbial conjunction See *conjunctive adverb.*

adverb phrase See *adverb.*

agreement The correspondence of one word to another in person, number, or gender. A verb must agree with its subject (*The chef orders egg sandwiches*), a pronoun must agree with its antecedent (*The chef surveys her breakfast*), and a demonstrative adjective must agree with its noun (*She likes these kinds of sandwiches*). (See Chapter 8.)

Logical agreement requires consistency in number between other related words, usually nouns: *The students brought their books* (not *book*). (See p. 292.)

analogy A comparison between members of different classes, such as a nursery school and a barnyard or a molecule and a pair of dancers. Usually, the purpose is to explain something unfamiliar to readers through something familiar. (See p. 112.)

analysis The separation of a subject into its elements. Sometimes called **division,** analysis is fundamental to critical thinking, reading, and writing (pp. 12–13) and is a useful tool for developing essays (p. 44) and paragraphs (pp. 109–10).

antecedent The word to which a pronoun refers: *Jonah, who is not yet ten, has already chosen the college he will attend* (*Jonah* is the antecedent of the pronouns *who* and *he*). (See pp. 246–50.)

APA style The style of documentation recommended by the American Psychological Association and used in many of the social sciences. (For discussion and examples, see pp. 707–20.)

appeals Attempts to engage and persuade readers. An **emotional appeal** touches readers' feelings, beliefs, and values. An **ethical appeal** presents the writer as competent, sincere, and fair. A **rational appeal** engages readers' powers of reasoning. (See pp. 152–53.)

appositive A word or phrase appearing next to a noun or pronoun that renames or identifies it and is equivalent to it: *My brother Michael, the best horn player in town, won the state competition* (*Michael* identifies which brother is being referred to; *the best horn player in town* renames *Michael*). (See p. 187.)

argument Writing whose primary purpose is to convince readers of an idea or persuade them to act. (See Chapter 4.)

article The word *a, an,* or *the.* Articles are sometimes called **determiners** because they always signal that a noun follows. (See pp. 259–61 for when to use *a/an* versus *the.* See p. 793 for when to use *a* versus *an.*)

assertion A positive statement that requires support. Assertions are the backbone of any argument. (See p. 128.)

assumption A stated or unstated belief or opinion. Uncovering assumptions is part of critical thinking, reading, and writing (see pp. 13–15). In argument, assumptions connect assertions and evidence (see pp. 133–34).

audience The intended readers of a piece of writing. Knowledge of the audience's needs and expectations helps a writer shape writing so that it is clear, interesting, and convincing. (See pp. 31–35, 152–56.)

auxiliary verb See *helping verb.*

balanced sentence A sentence consisting of two clauses with parallel constructions: *Do as I say, not as I do. Befriend all animals; exploit none.* Their balance makes such sentences highly emphatic. (See p. 341.)

belief A conviction based on morality, values, or faith. Statements of belief often serve as assumptions and sometimes as evidence, but they are not arguable and so cannot serve as the thesis in an argument. (See p. 129.)

body In a piece of writing, the large central part where ideas supporting the thesis are presented and developed. See also *conclusion* and *introduction.*

brainstorming A technique for generating ideas about a topic: concentrating on the topic for a fixed time (say, fifteen minutes), you list every idea and detail that comes to mind. (See pp. 41–42.)

browser A computer program that makes it possible to search the World Wide Web. (See p. 536.)

cardinal number The type of number that shows amount: *two, sixty, ninety-seven*. Contrast *ordinal number* (such as *second, ninety-seventh*).

case The form of a noun or pronoun that indicates its function in the sentence. Most pronouns have three cases:

- The **subjective case** (*I, she*) for the subject of a verb or for a subject complement.
- The **objective case** (*me, her*) for the object of a verb, verbal, or preposition.
- The **possessive case** to indicate ownership, used either as an adjective (*my, her*) or as a noun (*mine, hers*).

(See p. 199 for a list of the forms of personal and relative pronouns.)

Nouns use the subjective form (*dog, America*) for all cases except the possessive (*dog's, America's*).

cause-and-effect analysis The determination of why something happened or what its consequences were or will be. (See pp. 45 and 112–13.)

CBE style A style of documenting sources recommended by the Council of Biology Editors and frequently used in the natural and applied sciences and in mathematics. (See pp. 729–33.)

characters The people in a literary work, including the narrator of a story or the speaker of a poem. (See p. 675.)

Chicago style A style of documentation recommended by *The Chicago Manual of Style* and used in history, art, and other humanities. (For discussion and examples, see pp. 696–703.)

chronological organization The arrangement of events as they occurred in time, usually from first to last. (See pp. 59, 94–95.)

citation In research writing, the way of acknowledging material borrowed from sources. Most systems of citation discussed in this handbook are basically similar: a number or brief parenthetical reference in the text indicates that particular material is borrowed and directs the reader to information on the source at the end of the work. The systems do differ, however. (See pp. 599–627 for MLA style, pp. 696–703 for Chicago style, pp. 707–20 for APA style, and pp. 729–33 for CBE style.)

classification The sorting of many elements into groups based on their similarities. (See pp. 44–45 and 110.)

clause A group of related words containing a subject and predicate. **A main (independent) clause** can stand by itself as a sentence. **A subordinate (dependent) clause** serves as a single part of speech and so cannot stand by itself as a sentence.

MAIN CLAUSE	*We can go to the movies.*
SUBORDINATE CLAUSE	We can go *if Julie gets back on time.*

A subordinate clause may function as an adjective (*The car that hit Fred was speeding*), an adverb (*The car hit Fred when it ran a red light*), or a noun (*Whoever was driving should be arrested*). (See pp. 182–85.)

clichés See *trite expressions.*

climactic organization The arrangement of material in order of increasing drama or interest, leading to a climax. (See pp. 60 and 96–97.)

clustering A technique for generating ideas about a topic: drawing and writing, you branch outward from a center point (the topic) to pursue the implications of ideas. (See pp. 42–43.)

coherence The quality of an effective essay or paragraph that helps readers see relations among ideas and move easily from one idea to the next. (See pp. 60 and 92.)

collaborative learning In a writing course, students working together in groups to help each other become better writers and readers. (See pp. 80–81, 775–78.)

collective noun See *noun.*

colloquial language The words and expressions of everyday speech. Colloquial language can enliven informal writing but is generally inappropriate in formal academic or business writing. See also *formal and informal.* (See p. 457.)

comma splice A sentence error in which two main clauses are separated by a comma with no coordinating conjunction. (See Chapter 11.)

COMMA SPLICE	The book was long, it contained useful information.
REVISED	The book was long; it contained useful information.
REVISED	The book was long, *and* it contained useful information.

common noun See *noun.*

comparative See *comparison.*

comparison The form of an adverb or adjective that shows its degree of quality or amount.

- The **positive degree** is the simple, uncompared form: *gross, clumsily.*
- The **comparative degree** compares the thing modified to at least one other thing: *grosser, more clumsily.*
- The **superlative degree** indicates that the thing modified exceeds all other things to which it is being compared: *grossest, most clumsily.*

The comparative and superlative degrees are formed either with the endings *-er* and *-est* or with the words *more* and *most, less* and *least.* (See pp. 255–57.)

comparison and contrast The identification of similarities (comparison) and differences (contrast) between two or more subjects. (See pp. 45 and 111–12.)

complement A word or word group that completes the sense of a subject, an object, or a verb. (See pp. 168–70.)

- A **subject complement** follows a linking verb and renames or describes the subject. It may be an adjective, noun, or pronoun. *I am a lion tamer, but I am not yet experienced* (the noun *lion tamer* and the adjective *experienced* complement the subject *I*). Adjective complements are also called **predicate adjectives.** Noun complements are also called **predicate nouns** or **predicate nominatives.**
- An **object complement** follows and modifies or refers to a direct object. The complement may be an adjective or a noun. *If you elect me president, I'll keep the students satisfied* (the noun *president* complements the direct object *me,* and the adjective *satisfied* complements the direct object *students*).
- A **verb complement** is a direct or indirect object of a verb. It may be a noun or pronoun. *Don't give the chimp that peanut* (*chimp* is the indirect object and *peanut* is the direct object of the verb *give;* both objects are verb complements).

complete predicate See *predicate.*

complete subject See *subject.*

complex sentence See *sentence.*

compound construction Two or more words or word groups serving the same function, such as a **compound subject** (*Harriet and Peter poled their barge down the river*), **compound predicate** (*The scout watched and waited*) or parts of a predicate (*She grew tired and hungry*), and **compound sentence** (*He smiled, and I laughed*). (See pp. 188–89.) **Compound words** include nouns (*featherbrain, make-up*) and adjectives (*two-year-old, downtrodden*).

compound-complex sentence See *sentence.*

compound predicate See *compound.*

compound sentence See *sentence.*

compound subject See *compound construction.*

conciseness Use of the fewest and freshest words to express meaning clearly and achieve the desired effect with readers. (See pp. 473–80.)

conclusion The closing of an essay, tying off the writer's thoughts and leaving readers with a sense of completion. (See pp. 120–21 for suggestions.)

A *conclusion* is also the result of deductive reasoning. See *deductive reasoning* and *syllogism.*

Terms

concrete See *abstract and concrete.*

conditional statement A statement expressing a condition contrary to fact and using the subjunctive mood of the verb: *If she were mayor, the unions would cooperate.* See also *mood.*

conjugation A list of the forms of a verb showing tense, voice, mood, person, and number. The conjugation of the verb *know* in present tense, active voice, indicative mood is *I know, you know, he/she/it knows, we know, you know, they know.* (See p. 220 for a fuller conjugation.)

conjunction A word that links and relates parts of a sentence.

- **Coordinating conjunctions** (*and, but, or, nor, for, so, yet*) connect words or word groups of equal grammatical rank: *The lights went out, but the doctors and nurses continued caring for their patients.* (See p. 189.)
- **Correlative conjunctions** or **correlatives** (such as *either . . . or, not only . . . but also*) are two or more connecting words that work together: *He was certain that either his parents or his brother would help him.* (See p. 189–90.)
- **Subordinating conjunctions** (*after, although, as if, because, if, when, while,* and so on) begin subordinate clauses and link them to main clauses: *The seven dwarfs whistle while they work.* (See pp. 182–83.)

conjunctive adverb (adverbial conjunction) An adverb (such as *besides, consequently, however, indeed,* and *therefore*) that relates two main clauses in a sentence: *We had hoped to own a house by now; however, housing costs have risen too fast.* (See pp. 190–92.) The error known as a comma splice results when two main clauses related by a conjunctive adverb are separated only by a comma. (See pp. 277–78.)

connector (connective) Any word or phrase that links words, phrases, clauses, or sentences. Common connectors include coordinating, correlative, and subordinating conjunctions; conjunctive adverbs; and prepositions.

connotation An association called up by a word, beyond its dictionary definition. Contrast *denotation.* (See p. 464.)

construction Any group of grammatically related words, such as a phrase, a clause, or a sentence.

contraction A condensation of an expression, with an apostrophe replacing the missing letters: for example, *doesn't* (for *does not*), *we'll* (for *we will*). (See p. 401.)

contrast See *comparison and contrast.*

coordinate adjectives Two or more adjectives that equally modify the same noun or pronoun: *The camera panned the vast, empty desert.* (See pp. 377–78.)

coordinating conjunction See *conjunction.*

coordination The linking of words, phrases, or clauses that are of equal importance, usually with a coordinating conjunction: *He and I laughed, but she was not amused.* Contrast *subordination.* (See pp. 318–21.)

correlative conjunction (correlative) See *conjunction.*

count noun See *noun.*

critical thinking, reading, and writing Looking beneath the surface of words and images to discern meaning and relationships and to build knowledge. (See pp. 1–21.)

cumulative (loose) sentence A sentence in which modifiers follow the subject and verb: *Ducks waddled by, their tails swaying and their quacks rising to heaven.* Contrast *periodic sentence.* (See p. 339.)

dangling modifier A modifier that does not sensibly describe anything in its sentence. (See pp. 303–05.)

> DANGLING *Having arrived late,* the concert had already begun.
>
> REVISED Having arrived late, *we found that* the concert had already begun.

database A collection and organization of information (data). A database may be printed, but the term is most often used for electronic sources.

declension A list of the forms of a noun or pronoun, showing inflections for person (for pronouns), number, and case. See p. 199 for a declension of the personal and relative pronouns.

deductive reasoning Applying a generalization to specific circumstances in order to reach a conclusion. See also *syllogism.* Contrast *inductive reasoning.* (See pp. 148–50.)

definition Specifying the characteristics of something to establish what it is and is not. (See pp. 44 and 108–09.)

degree See *comparison.*

demonstrative adjective See *adjective.*

demonstrative pronoun See *pronoun.*

denotation The main or dictionary definition of a word. Contrast *connotation.* (See p. 463.)

dependent clause See *clause.*

derivational suffix See *suffix.*

description Detailing the sensory qualities of a thing, person, place, or feeling. (See pp. 44 and 106–07.)

descriptive adjective See *adjective.*

descriptor See *keyword(s).*

determiner A word such as *a, an, the, my,* and *your* which indicates that a noun follows. See also *article.*

developing (planning) The stage of the writing process when one finds a topic, explores ideas, gathers information, focuses on a central theme, and organizes material. Compare *drafting* and *revising.* (See Chapter 1.)

dialect A variety of a language used by a specific group or in a specific region. A dialect may be distinguished by its pronunciation, vocabulary, and grammar. (See p. 455.)

diction The choice and use of words. (See Chapter 31.)

dictionary form See *plain form.*

direct address A construction in which a word or phrase indicates the person or group spoken to: *Have you finished, John? Farmers, unite.*

direct object See *object.*

direct question A sentence asking a question and concluding with a question mark: *Do they know we are watching?* Contrast *indirect question.*

direct quotation (direct discourse) See *quotation.*

division See *analysis.*

documentation In research writing, supplying citations that legitimate the use of borrowed material and support claims about its origins. Contrast *plagiarism.* (See Chapter 37.)

double negative A nonstandard form consisting of two negative words used in the same construction so that they effectively cancel each other: *I don't have no money.* Rephrase as *I have no money* or *I don't have any money.* (See p. 257.)

double possessive A possessive using both the ending *-'s* and the preposition *of: That is a favorite expression of Mark's.*

double talk (doublespeak) Language intended to confuse or to be misunderstood. (See p. 459.)

download To transfer data from another computer.

drafting The stage of the writing process when ideas are expressed in connected sentences and paragraphs. Compare *developing (planning)* and *revising.* (See pp. 63–66.)

editing A distinct step in revising a written work, focusing on clarity, tone, and correctness. Compare *revising.* (See pp. 73–76.)

ellipsis The omission of a word or words from a quotation, indicated by the three spaced periods of an **ellipsis mark:** *"that all . . . are created equal."* (See pp. 424–25.)

elliptical clause A clause omitting a word or words whose meaning is understood from the rest of the clause: *David likes Minneapolis better than [he likes] Chicago.* (See p. 185.)

emotional appeal See *appeals.*

emphasis The manipulation of words, sentences, and paragraphs to stress important ideas. (See Chapter 18.)

essay A nonfiction composition on a single subject and with a central idea or thesis.

ethical appeal See *appeals.*

etymology The history of a word's meanings and forms.

euphemism A presumably inoffensive word that a writer or speaker substitutes for a word deemed possibly offensive or too blunt—for example, *passed beyond* for "died." (See p. 458.)

evaluation A judgment of the quality, value, currency, bias, or other aspects of a work. (See pp. 16–17, 564–67.)

evidence The facts, examples, expert opinions, and other information that support assertions. (See pp. 130–33, 150–51.)

expletive A sentence that postpones the subject by beginning with *there* or *it* and a form of the verb *be: It is impossible to get a ticket. There should be more seats available.* (See pp. 194–95.)

exposition Writing whose primary purpose is to explain something about a topic.

fallacies Errors in reasoning. Some evade the issue of the argument; others oversimplify the argument. (See pp. 138–43.)

faulty predication A sentence error in which the meanings of subject and predicate conflict, so that the subject is said to be or do something illogical: *The installation of air bags takes up space in a car's steering wheel and dashboard.* (See pp. 309–10.)

figurative language (figures of speech) Expressions that suggest meanings different from their literal meanings in order to achieve special effects. (See pp. 470–71.) Some common figures:

- **Hyperbole,** deliberate exaggeration: *The bag weighed a ton.*
- **Metaphor,** an implied comparison between two unlike things: *The wind stabbed through our clothes.*
- **Personification,** the attribution of human qualities to a thing or idea: *The water beckoned seductively.*
- **Simile,** an explicit comparison, using *like* or *as,* between two unlike things: *The sky glowered like an angry parent.*

A **mixed metaphor** is a confusing or ludicrous combination of incompatible figures: *The wind stabbed through our clothes and shook our bones.*

finite verb Any verb that makes an assertion or expresses a state of being and can stand as the main verb of a sentence or clause: *The moose eats the leaves.* (See p. 177.) Contrast *verbal,* which is formed from a finite verb but is unable to stand alone as the main verb of a sentence: *I saw the moose eating the leaves.*

first person See *person.*

Terms

Terms

foil A character in a literary work who contrasts with another character and thus helps to define the other character. (See p. 687.)

formal and informal Levels of usage achieved through word choice and sentence structure. More informal writing, as in a letter to an acquaintance or a personal essay, resembles some speech in its colloquial language, contractions, and short, fairly simple sentences. More formal writing, as in academic papers and business reports, avoids these attributes of speech and tends to rely on longer and more complicated sentences.

format In a document such as an academic paper or a business letter, the arrangement and spacing of elements on the page. (See Chapter 42 and Appendix A.)

fragment See *sentence fragment.*

freewriting A technique for generating ideas: in a fixed amount of time (say, fifteen minutes), you write continuously without stopping to reread. (See pp. 39–41.)

function word A word, such as an article, conjunction, or preposition, that serves primarily to clarify the roles of and relations between other words in a sentence: *We chased the goat for an hour but finally caught it.* Contrast *lexical word.*

fused sentence (run-on sentence) A sentence error in which two main clauses are joined with no punctuation or connecting word between them. (See pp. 279–80.)

FUSED I heard his lecture it was dull.
REVISED I heard his lecture; it was dull.

future perfect tense See *tense.*

future tense See *tense.*

gender The classification of nouns or pronouns as masculine (*he, boy, handyman*), feminine (*she, woman, actress*), or neuter (*it, typewriter, dog*).

general and specific Terms designating the relative number of instances or objects included in a group signified by a word. The following list moves from most **general** (including the most objects) to most **specific** (including the fewest objects): *vehicle, four-wheeled vehicle, automobile, sedan, Ford Taurus, blue Ford Taurus, my sister's blue Ford Taurus named Hank.* See also *abstract and concrete.* (See p. 465.)

generalization An assertion inferred from evidence. See also *inductive reasoning.*

genitive case Another term for possessive case. See *case.*

gerund A verbal that ends in *-ing* and functions as a noun: *Working is all right for killing time* (*working* is the subject of the verb *is; killing* is the object of the preposition *for.*) See also *verbals and verbal phrases.* (See p. 178.)

gerund phrase A word group consisting of a gerund plus any modifiers or objects. See also *verbals and verbal phrases.*

grammar A description of how a language works.

helping verb (auxiliary verb) A verb used with another verb to convey time, obligation, and other meanings: *You should write a letter. You have written other letters.* The **modals** include *can, could, may, might, must, ought, shall, should, will, would.* The other helping verbs are forms of *be, have,* and *do.* (See pp. 209, 214–18.)

homonyms Words that are pronounced the same but have different spellings and meanings, such as *heard/herd* and *to/too/two.* (See pp. 500–01 for a list.)

HTML (HyperText Markup Language) A computer program for creating hypertext documents. (See p. 779.)

hyperbole See *figurative language.*

hypertext A system allowing computer users to move easily and variously among document through **links,** or cross-references. (See pp. 538 and 778.)

idiom An expression that is peculiar to a language and that may not make sense if taken literally: for example, *dark horse, bide your time,* and *by and large.* See p. 468 for a list of idioms involving prepositions, such as *agree with them* and *agree to the contract.*

illustration or support Supplying examples or reasons to develop an idea. (See pp. 44 and 107–08.)

imagery Pictures created by words that appeal to the sense of sight, hearing, touch, taste, or smell.

imperative See *mood.*

indefinite pronoun See *pronoun.*

independent clause See *clause.*

indicative See *mood.*

indirect object See *object.*

indirect question A sentence reporting a question, usually in a subordinate clause, and ending with a period: *Writers wonder whether their work must be lonely.* Contrast *direct question.*

indirect quotation (indirect discourse) See *quotation.*

inductive reasoning Inferring a generalization from specific evidence. Contrast *deductive reasoning.* (See pp. 147–48.)

infinitive A verbal formed from the plain form of the verb plus the **infinitive marker** *to: to swim, to write.* Infinitives and infinitive phrases may function as nouns, adjectives, or adverbs. See also *verbals and verbal phrases.* (See p. 178.)

infinitive marker See *infinitive.*

infinitive phrase A word group consisting of an infinitive plus any subject, objects, or modifiers. See also *verbals and verbal phrases.*

inflection The variation in the form of a word that indicates its function in a particular context. See *declension,* the inflection of nouns and pronouns; *conjugation,* the inflection of verbs; and *comparison,* the inflection of adjectives and adverbs.

inflectional suffix See *suffix.*

informal See *formal and informal.*

intensifier A modifier that adds emphasis to the word(s) it modifies: for example, *very slow, so angry.*

intensive pronoun See *pronoun.*

interjection A word standing by itself or inserted in a construction to exclaim or command attention: *Hey! Ouch! What the heck did you do that for?*

interpretation The determination of meaning or significance—for instance, in a work such as a poem or in the literature on some issue such as job discrimination. (See pp. 13–15, 517.)

interrogative Functioning as or involving a question.

interrogative adjective See *adjective.*

interrogative pronoun See *pronoun.*

intransitive verb A verb that does not take a direct object: *The woman laughed.* (See p. 167.)

introduction The opening of an essay, a transition for readers between their world and the writer's. The introduction often contains a statement of the writer's thesis. (See pp. 117–19 for suggestions.)

invention The discovery and exploration of ideas, usually occurring most intensively in the early stages of the writing process. (See pp. 36–46 for invention techniques.)

inversion A reversal of usual word order in a sentence, as when a verb precedes its subject or an object precedes its verb: *Down swooped the hawk. Our aims we stated clearly.*

IRC See *synchronous communication.*

irony The use of words to suggest a meaning different from what the words say literally: *What a happy face!* (said to someone scowling miserably); *With that kind of planning, prices are sure to go down* (written with the expectation that prices will rise).

irregular verb A verb that forms its past tense and past participle in some other way than by the addition of *-d* or *-ed* to the plain form: for example, *go, went, gone; give, gave, given.* Contrast *regular verb.* (See pp. 210–11 for a list of irregular verbs.)

jargon In one sense, the specialized language of any group, such as doctors or baseball players. In another sense, jargon is vague, pretentious, wordy, and ultimately unclear writing such as that found in some academic, business, and government publications. (See p. 480.)

journal A personal record of observations, reactions, ideas, and other thoughts. Besides providing a private place to think in writing, a journal is useful for making notes about reading (pp. 4, 517, 669), discovering ideas for essays (p. 37), and keeping track of research (pp. 517, 706).

journalist's questions A set of questions useful for probing a topic to discover ideas about it. (See p. 43.)

keyword(s) A word or words that define a subject, used for searching databases such as library catalogs and periodical indexes. (See p. 525.)

lexical word A word, such as a noun, verb, or modifier, that carries part of the meaning of language. Contrast *function word.*

linking verb A verb that relates a subject to its complement: *Julie is a Democrat. He looks harmless. The boy became a man.* Common linking verbs are the forms of *be*; the verbs relating to the senses, such as *look* and *smell;* and the verbs *become, appear,* and *seem.* (See pp. 168–69.)

Listserv An Internet discussion group consisting of subscribers who receive each other's postings through electronic mail. (See p. 544.)

logical agreement See *agreement.*

logical fallacies See *fallacies.*

main clause See *clause.*

main verb The part of a verb phrase that carries the principal meaning: *had been walking, could happen, was chilled.* See also *verb phrase.*

mass noun Another term for noncount noun. See *noun.*

mechanics The use of capital letters, underlining (italics), abbreviations, numbers, and divided words. (See Chapters 26–30.)

metaphor See *figurative language.*

misplaced modifier A modifier so far from the term it modifies or so close to another term it could modify that its relation to the rest of the sentence is unclear. (See Chapter 14.)

MISPLACED The boys played with firecrackers that they bought illegally *in the field.*

REVISED The boys played *in the field* with firecrackers that they bought illegally.

A **squinting modifier** could modify the words on either side of it: *The plan we considered seriously worries me.*

mixed construction A sentence containing two or more parts that do not fit together in grammar or in meaning. (See pp. 307–10.)

mixed metaphor See *figurative language.*

Terms

MLA style The style of documenting sources recommended by the Modern Language Association and used in many of the humanities, including English. (For explanation and examples, see Chapter 37.)

modal See *helping verb.*

modifier Any word or word group that limits or qualifies the meaning of another word or word group. Modifiers include adjectives and adverbs as well as words, phrases, and clauses that act as adjectives and adverbs.

MOO See *synchronous communication.*

mood The form of a verb that shows how the speaker or writer views the action. (See pp. 227–29.)

- The **indicative mood,** the most common, is used to make statements or ask questions: *The play will be performed Saturday. Did you get the tickets?*
- The **imperative mood** gives a command: *Please get good seats.*
- The **subjunctive mood** expresses a wish, a condition contrary to fact, a recommendation, or a request: *I wish George were coming with us. Did you suggest that he join us?*

MUD See *synchronous communication.*

narration Recounting a sequence of events, usually in the order of their occurrence. (See pp. 44 and 106.) Literary narration tells a story. (See Chapter 39.)

narrator The speaker in a poem or the voice who tells a story. (See p. 675.)

neologism A word coined recently and not in established use. (See p. 458.)

newsgroup An Internet discussion group with a common site where all postings are recorded. (See p. 545.)

nominal A noun, a pronoun, or a word or word group used as a noun: *Joan and I talked. The rich owe a debt to the poor* (adjectives acting as subject and object). *Baby-sitting can be exhausting* (gerund acting as subject). *I like to play with children* (infinitive phrase acting as object).

nominative Another term for subjective case. See *case.*

noncount noun See *noun.*

nonfinite verb See *verbals and verbal phrases.*

nonrestrictive element A word or word group that does not limit the term or construction it refers to and that is not essential to the meaning of the sentence's main clause. Nonrestrictive elements are usually set off by commas: *The new apartment building, in shades of tan and gray, will house fifty people* (nonrestrictive adjective phrase). *Sleep, which we all need, occupies a third of our lives* (nonrestrictive adjective clause). *His wife, Patricia, is a chemist* (nonrestrictive appositive). Contrast *restrictive element.* (See pp. 370–74.)

nonstandard Words and grammatical forms not conforming to standard English. (See p. 455.)

noun A word that names a person, place, thing, quality, or idea: *Maggie, Alabama, clarinet, satisfaction, socialism.* Nouns normally form the possessive case by adding *-'s* (*Maggie's*) and the plural by adding *-s* or *-es* (*clarinets, messes*), although there are exceptions (*men, women, children*). The forms of nouns depend partly on where they fit in certain overlapping groups:

- **Common nouns** name general classes and are not capitalized: *book, government, music.*
- **Proper nouns** name specific people, places, and things and are capitalized: *Susan, Athens, Candlestick Park.*
- **Count nouns** name things considered countable in English (they form plurals): *ounce/ounces, camera/cameras, person/people.*
- **Noncount nouns** name things not considered countable in English (they don't form plurals): *chaos, fortitude, silver, earth, information.*
- **Collective nouns** are singular in form but name groups: *team, class, family.*

noun clause A word group containing a subject and a verb and functioning as a subject, object, or complement: *Everyone wondered how the door opened. Whoever opened it had left.*

number The form of a noun, pronoun, demonstrative adjective, or verb that indicates whether it is singular or plural: *woman, women; I, we; this, these; runs, run.*

object A noun, pronoun, or word group that receives the action of or is influenced by a transitive verb, a verbal, or a preposition. (See pp. 167, 169, 175.)

- **A direct object** receives the action of a verb or verbal and frequently follows it in a sentence: *We sat watching the stars. Emily caught whatever it was you had.*
- **An indirect object** tells for or to whom something is done: *I lent Stan my car. Reiner bought us all champagne.*
- **An object of a preposition** usually follows a preposition and is linked by it to the rest of the sentence: *They are going to New Orleans for the jazz festival.*

object complement See *complement.*

objective See *case.*

opinion A conclusion based on facts; an arguable, potentially changeable assertion. Assertions of opinion form the backbone of any argument. (See p. 128.)

ordinal number The type of number that shows order: *first, eleventh, twenty-fifth.* Contrast *cardinal number* (such as *one, twenty-five*).

paragraph Generally, a group of sentences set off by a beginning indention and developing a single idea. That idea is often stated in a **topic sentence.** (See Chapter 3.)

Terms

parallelism Similarity of grammatical form between two or more coordinated elements: *Rising prices and declining incomes left many people in bad debt and worse despair.* (See Chapter 17.)

paraphrase The restatement of source material in one's own words and sentence structures, useful for borrowing the original author's line of reasoning but not his or her exact words. Paraphrases must always be acknowledged in source citations. (See pp. 573–75.)

parenthetical citation In the text of a paper, a brief reference, enclosed in parentheses, indicating that material is borrowed and directing the reader to the source of the material. See also *citation.*

parenthetical element A word or construction that interrupts a sentence and is not part of its main structure, called *parenthetical* because it could (or does) appear in parentheses: *Childe Hassam (1859–1935) was an American painter and etcher. The book, incidentally, is terrible.* (See p. 421.)

participial phrase A word group consisting of a participle plus any objects or modifiers. See also *verbals and verbal phrases.*

participle A verbal showing continuing or completed action, used as an adjective or part of a verb phrase but never as the main verb of a sentence or clause. (See p. 178.)

- A **present participle** ends in *-ing: My heart is breaking* (participle as part of verb phrase). *I like to watch the rolling waves* (participle as adjective).
- A **past participle** most commonly ends in *-d, -ed, -n,* or *-en* (*wished, shown, given*) but sometimes changes the spelling of the verb (*sung, done, slept*): *Jeff has broken his own record* (participle as part of verb phrase). *The meeting occurred behind a closed door* (participle as adjective).

See also *verbals and verbal phrases.*

particle A preposition or adverb in a two-word verb: *look up, catch on.* (See pp. 234–35.)

parts of speech The classes into which words are commonly grouped according to their form, function, and meaning: nouns, pronouns, verbs, adjectives, adverbs, conjunctions, prepositions, and interjections. See separate entries for each part of speech.

passive voice See *voice.*

past participle See *participle.*

past perfect tense See *tense.*

past tense See *tense.*

patterns of development Ways of thinking that can help develop and organize ideas in essays and paragraphs. (See pp. 44–45 and 106–15.)

perfect tenses See *tense.*

periodic sentence A suspenseful sentence in which modifiers precede the main clause, which falls at the end: *Postponing decisions about family while striving to establish themselves in careers, many young adults are falsely accused of shallowness or greed.* Contrast *cumulative sentence.* (See p. 339–40.)

person The form of a verb or pronoun that indicates whether the subject is speaking, spoken to, or spoken about. In English only personal pronouns and verbs change form to indicate difference in person. In the **first person,** the subject is speaking: *I am* [or *We are*] *planning a party.* In the **second person,** the subject is being spoken to: *Are you coming?* In the **third person,** the subject is being spoken about: *She was* [or *They were*] *going.*

personal pronoun See *pronoun.*

personification See *figurative language.*

phrase A group of related words that lacks a subject or a predicate or both and that acts as a single part of speech. See *absolute phrase, prepositional phrase, verbals and verbal phrases,* and *verb phrase.*

plagiarism The presentation of someone else's ideas or words as if they were one's own. Whether accidental or deliberate, plagiarism is a serious and often punishable offense. (See pp. 578–84.)

plain case Another term for the subjective case of nouns. See *case.*

plain form The dictionary form of a verb: *make, run, swivel.* See also *verb forms.*

planning See *developing (planning).*

plot The pattern of events in a work of literature. (See p. 675.)

plural More than one. See *number.*

point of view The perspective or attitude of the narrator or speaker in a work of literature. See also *person.* (See p. 675.)

positive degree See *comparison.*

possessive See *case.*

predicate The part of a sentence that makes an assertion about the subject. A predicate must contain a finite verb and may contain modifiers, objects of the verb, and complements. The **simple predicate** consists of the verb and its helping verbs: *A wiser person would have made a different decision.* The **complete predicate** includes the simple predicate and any modifiers, objects, and complements: *A wiser person would have made a different decision.* See also *intransitive verb, linking verb,* and *transitive verb.* (See p. 163.)

predicate adjective See *complement.*

predicate noun (predicate nominative) See *complement.*

prefix A letter or group of letters (such as *sub-, in-, dis-, pre-*) that can be added at the beginning of a root or word to create a new word:

sub- + *marine* = *submarine; dis-* + *grace* = *disgrace.* Contrast *suffix.* (See pp. 492–94.)

premise Generally, an assertion or assumption basic to an argument. In a deductive syllogism, one premise applied to another leads logically to a conclusion. See also *syllogism.* (See pp. 148–50.)

preposition A word that forms a noun or pronoun (plus any modifiers) into a prepositional phrase: *about love, down the steep stairs.* The common prepositions include these as well as *after, before, by, for, from, in, on, to,* and many others. (See p. 174.)

prepositional phrase A word group consisting of a preposition and its object, plus any modifiers. A prepositional phrase usually functions as an adjective (*The boy in green stood up*) or as an adverb (*He walked to the speaker's platform*). (See p. 175.)

present participle See *participle.*

present perfect tense See *tense.*

present tense See *tense.*

pretentious writing Writing that is more elaborate than the writing situation requires, usually full of fancy phrases and showy words. (See p. 459.)

primary source Firsthand information, such as an eyewitness account of events; a diary, speech, or other historical document; a work of literature or art; a report of a survey or experiment; and one's own interview, observation, or correspondence. Contrast *secondary source.* (See p. 527–28.)

principal clause A main or independent clause. See *clause.*

principal parts The plain form, past-tense form, and past participle of a verb. See *verb forms.* (See pp. 207–08.)

process analysis The explanation of how something works or how to do something. (See pp. 45 and 113–14.)

progressive tense See *tense.*

pronoun A word used in place of a noun. There are eight types of pronouns:

- **Personal pronouns** refer to a specific individual or to individuals: *I, you, he, she, it, we, they.* (See p. 199.)
- **Indefinite pronouns,** such as *everybody* and *some,* do not refer to specific nouns (*Everybody speaks*). (See p. 242.)
- **Relative pronouns**—*who, whoever, which, that*—relate groups of words to nouns or pronouns (*The book that won is a novel*). (See pp. 183, 199.)
- **Interrogative pronouns**—*who, which, what*—introduce questions (*Who will contribute?*).
- **Intensive pronouns**—personal pronouns plus *-self* or *-selves*—emphasize a noun or other pronoun (*He himself asked that question*).

- **Reflexive pronouns** have the same form as intensive pronouns. They indicate that the sentence subject also receives the action of the verb (*They injured themselves*).
- **Demonstrative pronouns** such as *this, that,* and *such* identify or point to nouns (*This is the problem*).
- **Reciprocal pronouns**—*each other* and *one another*—are used as objects of verbs when the subjects are plural (*They loved each other*).

proofreading Reading and correcting a final draft for misspellings, typographical errors, and other mistakes. (See p. 77.)

proper adjective See *adjective.*

proper noun See *noun.*

purpose For a writer, the chief reason for communicating something about a topic to a particular audience. (See pp. 30–31.)

quotation Repetition of what someone has written or spoken. In **direct quotation (direct discourse)**, the person's words are duplicated exactly and enclosed in quotation marks: *Polonius told his son, Laertes, "Neither a borrower nor a lender be."* An **indirect quotation (indirect discourse)** reports what someone said or wrote but not in the exact words and not in quotation marks: *Polonius advised his son, Laertes, not to borrow or lend.*

rational appeal See *appeals.*

reciprocal pronoun See *pronoun.*

reflexive pronoun See *pronoun.*

regional language Expressions common to the people in a particular geographical area. (See p. 456.)

regular verb A verb that forms its past tense and past participle by adding *-d* or *-ed* to the plain form: *love, loved, loved; open, opened, opened.* Contrast *irregular verb.* (See pp. 209–10.)

relative clause A subordinate clause beginning with a relative pronoun such as *who* or *that* and functioning as an adjective.

relative pronoun See *pronoun.*

restrictive element A word or word group that is essential to the meaning of a sentence because it limits the thing it refers to: removing it would leave the meaning unclear or too general. Restrictive elements are not set off by commas: *The keys to the car are on the table. That man who called about the apartment said he'd try again tonight.* Contrast *nonrestrictive element.* (See pp. 370–73.)

revising The stage of the writing process in which one considers and improves the meaning and underlying structure of a draft. Compare *developing (planning)* and *drafting.* (See pp. 67–73.)

rhetoric The principles for finding and arranging ideas and for using language in speech or writing to achieve the writer's purpose in addressing his or her audience.

Terms

rhetorical question A question asked for effect, with no answer expected. The person asking the question either intends to provide the answer or assumes it is obvious: *If we let one factory pollute the river, what does that say to other factories that want to dump wastes there?*

run-on sentence See *fused sentence.*

search engine A computer program that conducts Internet searches from keywords or directories. (See p. 538.)

secondary source A source reporting or analyzing information in other sources, such as a critic's view of a work of art or a sociologist's summary of others' studies. Contrast *primary source.* (See p. 528.)

second person See *person.*

sentence A complete unit of thought, consisting of at least a subject and a predicate that are not introduced by a subordinating word. Sentences can be classed on the basis of their structure in one of four ways. A **simple sentence** contains one main clause: *I'm leaving.* A **compound sentence** contains at least two main clauses: *I'd like to stay, but I'm leaving.* A **complex sentence** contains one main clause and at least one subordinate clause: *If you let me go now, you'll be sorry.* A **compound-complex sentence** contains at least two main clauses and at least one subordinate clause: *I'm leaving because you want me to, but I'd rather stay.* (See pp. 163, 195, 266.)

sentence fragment A sentence error in which a group of words is set off as a sentence even though it begins with a subordinating word or lacks a subject or a predicate or both. (See Chapter 10.)

Fragment	She lost the race. *Because she was injured.* [*Because,* a subordinating conjunction, makes the italicized clause subordinate.]
Revised	She lost the race because she was injured.
Fragment	He could not light a fire. *And thus could not warm the room.* [The italicized word group lacks a subject.]
Revised	He could not light a fire. Thus *he* could not warm the room.

sentence modifier An adverb or a word or word group acting as an adverb that modifies the idea of the whole sentence in which it appears rather than any specific word: *In fact, people will always complain.*

series A sequence of three or more items of equal importance: *The children are named John, Hallie, and Nancy.* The items in a series are separated with commas. (See pp. 376–77.)

server A computer that provides data to another computer. (See p. 536.)

setting The place where the action of a literary work happens. (See p. 676.)

sexist language Language expressing narrow ideas about men's and women's roles, positions, capabilities, or value. (See pp. 460–61.)

simile See *figurative language.*

simple predicate See *predicate.*

simple sentence See *sentence.*

simple subject See *subject.*

simple tense See *tense.*

singular One. See *number.*

slang Expressions used by the members of a group to create bonds and sometimes exclude others. Most slang is too vague, short-lived, and narrowly understood to be used in any but very informal writing. (See pp. 456–57.)

source A place where information or ideas may be found: book, article, Web site, work of art, television program, and so on.

spatial organization In a description of a person, place, or thing, the arrangement of details as they would be scanned by a viewer—for instance, from top to bottom or near to far. (See pp. 59 and 94.)

specific See *general and specific.*

split infinitive The often awkward interruption of an infinitive and its marker *to* by an adverb: *Management decided to immediately introduce the new product.* (See p. 300.)

squinting modifier See *misplaced modifier.*

standard English The English used and expected by educated writers and readers in colleges and universities, businesses, and professions. (See p. 454.)

subject In grammar, the part of a sentence that names something and about which an assertion is made in the predicate. The **simple subject** consists of the noun alone: *The quick brown fox jumps over the lazy dog.* The **complete subject** includes the simple subject and its modifiers: *The quick brown fox jumps over the lazy dog.* (See p. 163.)

subject complement See *complement.*

subjective See *case.*

subjunctive See *mood.*

subordinate clause See *clause.*

subordinating conjunction See *conjunction.*

subordination The use of grammatical constructions to de-emphasize one element in a sentence by making it dependent on rather than equal to another element: *Although I left six messages for him, the doctor failed to call.* Contrast *coordination.* (See pp. 323–26.)

substantive A word or word group used as a noun.

suffix A **derivational suffix** is a letter or group of letters that can be added to the end of a root word to make a new word, often a different part of speech: *child, childish; shrewd, shrewdly; visual, visualize.* (See p. 494.) **Inflectional suffixes** adapt words to different grammatical relations: *boy, boys; fast, faster; tack, tacked.*

summary A condensation and restatement of source material in one's own words and sentence structures, useful in reading for comprehending the material (see pp. 10–11) and in research writing for presenting the gist of the original author's idea (p. 572). Summaries appearing in a paper must always be acknowledged in source citations.

superlative See *comparison.*

syllogism A form of deductive reasoning in which two premises stating generalizations or assumptions together lead to a conclusion. *Premise:* Hot stoves can burn me. *Premise:* This stove is hot. *Conclusion:* This stove can burn me. See also *deductive reasoning.* (See pp. 148–50.)

symbolism The use of a concrete thing to suggest something larger and more abstract, as a red rose may symbolize passion or romance. (See p. 676.)

synchronous communication A system allowing simultaneous (synchronous) communication over the Internet, analogous to a conference call on a telephone. MOOs, MUDs, and Internet Relay Chat (IRC) are examples. (See pp. 545, 777.)

synonyms Words with approximately but not exactly the same meanings, such as *snicker, giggle,* and *chortle.* (See p. 464.)

syntax In sentences, the grammatical relations among words and the ways those relations are indicated.

synthesis Drawing connections among the elements within a work (such as the images in a poem) or among entire works (entire poems). Synthesis is an essential skill in critical thinking, reading, and writing (see pp. 15–16) and in research writing (pp. 567–68.)

tag question A question attached to the end of a statement and consisting of a pronoun, a helping verb, and sometimes the word *not: It isn't raining, is it? It is sunny, isn't it?*

tense The form of a verb that expresses the time of its action, usually indicated by the verb's inflection and by helping verbs.

- The **simple tenses** are the **present** (*I race, you go*), the **past** (*I raced, you went*), and the **future,** formed with the helping verb *will* (*I will race, you will go*).
- The **perfect tenses,** formed with the helping verbs *have* and *had,* indicate completed action. They are the **present perfect** (*I have raced, you have gone*), the **past perfect** (*I had raced, you had gone*), and the **future perfect** (*I will have raced, you will have gone*).
- The **progressive tenses,** formed with the helping verb *be* plus the present participle, indicate continuing action. They include the **present progressive** (*I am racing, you are going*), the **past progressive** (*I was racing, you were going*), and the **future progressive** (*I will be racing, you will be going*).

(See p. 220 for a complete list of tenses with examples.)

theme The main idea of a work of literature. (See p. 676.)

thesis The central, controlling idea of an essay, to which all assertions and details relate. (See p. 47.)

thesis sentence A sentence that asserts the central, controlling idea of an essay and perhaps previews the essay's organization. (See pp. 48–51.)

third person See *person.*

tone The sense of a writer's attitudes toward self, subject, and readers revealed by words and sentence structures as well as by content. (See pp. 33–35, 134–35, 153.)

topic The subject of an essay, narrowed so that it is appropriately specific for the prescribed purpose, length, and deadline. (See pp. 28–29.)

topic sentence See *paragraph.*

transitional expression A word or phrase, such as *thus* or *for example,* that links sentences and shows the relations between them. (See pp. 100–01 for a list.) The error known as a comma splice occurs when two main clauses related by a transitional expression are separated only by a comma. (See pp. 277–78.)

transitive verb A verb that requires a direct object to complete its meaning. (See p. 167.)

trite expressions (clichés) Stale expressions that dull writing and suggest that the writer is careless or lazy. (See p. 472.)

two-word verb A verb plus a preposition or adverb that affects the meaning of the verb: *jump off, put away, help out.* (See pp. 234–35.)

Uniform Resources Locator (URL) An address for a source on the Internet, specifying **protocol** (the type of access requested), **domain** (the location of the computer housing the source), and **path** (the location and name of the source). (See p. 536.)

unity The quality of an effective essay or paragraph in which all parts relate to the central idea and to each other. (See pp. 60 and 87.)

Usenet newsgroup See *newsgroup.*

variety Among connected sentences, changes in length, structure, and word order that help readers see the importance and complexity of ideas. (See Chapter 19.)

verb A word or group of words indicating the action or state of being of a subject. The inflection of a verb and the use of helping verbs with it indicate its tense, mood, voice, number, and sometimes person. See separate listings for each aspect and *predicate.* (See Chapter 7.)

verbals and verbal phrases **Verbals** are verb forms used as adjectives (*swimming children*), adverbs (*designed to succeed*), or nouns (*addicted to running*). The verbals in the preceding examples are a participle, an infinitive, and a gerund, respectively. (See separate entries for each type.) Verbal phrases consist of verbals plus objects or modifiers: *Swimming fast, the children reached the raft. Willem tried to unlatch the gate. Running in the park is his only recreation.* (See p. 179.)

A verbal is a **nonfinite verb:** it cannot serve as the only verb in the predicate of a sentence. For that, it requires a helping verb. (See p. 177.)

verb forms Verbs have five distinctive forms. The first three are the verb's **principal parts:**

- The **plain form** is the dictionary form: *live, swim.*
- The **past-tense form** adds *-d* or *-ed* to the plain form if the verb is regular: *live, lived.* If the verb is irregular, the plain form changes in some other way, such as *swim, swam.*
- The **past participle** is the same as the past-tense form for regular verbs. For irregular verbs, the past participle may differ (*swum*).
- The **present participle** adds *-ing* to the plain form: *living, swimming.*
- The **-*s* form** adds *-s* or *-es* to the plain form: *lives, swims.*

verb phrase A verb consisting of a helping verb and a main verb: *has started, will have been invited.* A verb phrase can serve as the predicate of a clause: *The movie has started.*

voice The form of a verb that tells whether the sentence subject performs the action or is acted upon. In the **active voice** the subject acts: *We made the decision.* In the **passive voice** the subject is acted upon: *The decision was made by us.* (See pp. 230–31.)

word order The arrangement of the words in a sentence, which plays a large part in determining the grammatical relation among words in English.

writing process The mental and physical activities that go into producing a finished piece of writing. The overlapping stages of the process—developing or planning, drafting, and revising—differ for different writers and even for the same writer in different writing situations. (See Chapters 1–2.)

writing situation The unique combination of writer, subject, and audience that defines an assignment and helps direct the writer's choices. (See pp. 24–25.)

Terms

Credits

AltaVista Web page "Internet access." AltaVista, the AltaVista logo and the Digital logo are trademarks of Digital Equipment Corporation. Reprinted with the permission of Digital Equipment Corporation

The American Heritage College Dictionary. Synonyms for "decrease." Copyright © 1993 by Houghton Mifflin Company. Reproduced by permission from *The American Heritage College Dictionary,* Third Edition.

Bogdanovich, Peter. Excerpted from "Bogie in Excelsis" in *Pieces of Time*. © 1973 by Peter Bogdanovich. Used by permission of Arbor House Publishing Company and the author.

Britt, Suzanne. Excerpt from "That Lean and Hungry Look," *Newsweek*, 9 October 1978. Copyright © 1978, 1988 by Suzanne Britt. Reprinted by permission.

Brooks, Gwendolyn. "The Bean Eaters" from *Blacks* by Gwendolyn Brooks. Copyright © 1991 by Gwendolyn Brooks. Published by Third World Press, Chicago.

Catton, Bruce. From "Grant and Lee: A Study in Contrasts." Copyright © 1956 United States Capitol Historical Society. All rights reserved. Reprinted with permission.

Dickinson, Emily. Poem #986, "A Narrow Fellow in the Grass," from *The Poems of Emily Dickinson.* Copyright 1951, ©1955, 1979, 1983 by the President and Fellows of Harvard College. Reprinted by permission of the publishers and Trustees of Amherst College from *The Poems of Emily Dickinson,* Thomas H. Johnson, ed., Cambridge, Mass.: The Belknap Press of Harvard University Press.

Dillard, Annie. Excerpt from "Sojourner" from *Teaching a Stone to Talk* by Annie Dillard. Copyright © 1982 by Annie Dillard. Reprinted by permission of HarperCollins Publishers, Inc.

Drucker, Peter F. From "How Best to Protect the Environment," *Harper's* Magazine, January 1972. Copyright © 1971 by Minneapolis Star and Tribune Co., Inc. Reprinted by permission of the author.

Dyson, Freeman J. Excerpt from *Disturbing the Universe* by Freeman J. Dyson. Copyright © 1979 by Freeman J. Dyson. Reprinted by permission of HarperCollins Publishers, Inc.

Eisinger, Peter, et al. From *American Politics: The People and the Polity*. Copyright © 1978 by Little, Brown and Company. Reprinted by permission.

Excite Web page, "Excite home." Excite, Excite Search, Excite Reviews, Excite City.Net, City.Net, Excite Direct, ExciteSeeing Tours, Excite Direct and the Excite Logo are trademarks of Excite, Inc. and may be registered in various jurisdictions. Excite screen displays copyright © 1996 Excite, Inc. Reprinted by permission of Excite, Inc.

Farb, Peter. From *Word Play: What Happens When People Talk*. Copyright © 1973 by Peter Farb. Reprinted by permission of Alfred A. Knopf, Inc., and Brandt & Brandt.

Fenton, James. From "The Philippine Election" in *Granta*, 18, 1986. Copyright © 1986 by James Fenton. Reprinted by permission of Sterling Lord Literistic, Inc.

Frost, Robert. Two lines from "The Death of the Hired Hand." Copyright © 1930, 1939, © 1969 by Henry Holt and Company, Inc. Copyright © 1958 by Robert Frost. Copyright © 1967 by Lesley Frost Ballentine. Reprinted by permission of Henry Holt and Company.

Frost, Robert. From "Stopping By Woods on a Snowy Evening" from *The Poetry of Robert Frost*, edited by Edward Connery Lathem. Copyright 1951 by Robert Frost. Copyright 1923, © Henry Holt and Company, Inc.

Gates, Henry Louis, Jr. From "Two Nations . . . Both Black" by Henry Louis Gates, Jr. First appeared in *Forbes* Magazine, September 14, 1992. Copyright © 1992 by Henry Louis Gates, Jr. Reprinted by permission of Brandt & Brandt Literary Agents, Inc.

Gaylin, Willard. Excerpt from *Feelings: Our Vital Signs* by Willard Gaylin. Copyright © 1979 by Willard Gaylin. Reprinted by permission of HarperCollins Publishers, Inc.

Goreau, Angeline. From "Worthy Women Revisited" by Angeline Goreau, *The New York Times*, December 11, 1986. Copyright © 1986 by The New York Times. Reprinted by permission.

Hughes, Emmet John. From "The Presidency vs. Jimmy Carter," *Fortune*, 4 December 1978. Reprinted by permission.

Huxtable, Ada Louise. "The Sage of the Skyline." *The New York Times Book Review,* November 26, 1989, p. 3.

Ik, Kim Yong. From "A Book-Writing Venture" by Kim Yong Ik. Originally published in *The Writer*, October 1965. Copyright © Kim Yong Ik. Reprinted by permission of the author.

"In defense of computer literacy" from PsycLIT Index. All rights reserved. Reprinted by permission of the American Psychological Association, publisher of *Psychological Abstracts* and the PsycLIT Database.

"Internet" from *Readers' Guide to Periodical Literature*, July 1996. Reprinted by permission of H. W. Wilson Company.

Jeffery, Mac. From "Does Rx Spell Rip-Off?" by Mac Jeffery, *The New York Times*, August 7, 1978. Copyright © 1978 by The New York Times. Reprinted by permission.

Kondracke, Morton M. From "Don't Legalize Drugs" in *The New Republic*, June 27, 1988. Reprinted by permission of *The New Republic*, © 1988, The New Republic, Inc.

Kuralt, Charles. From *Dateline America*. Text copyright © 1979 by CBS, Inc. Reprinted by permission of Harcourt Brace Jovanovich, Inc.

Levine, John R., and Carol Baroudi. Condensed from three paragraphs in *The Internet for Dummies*, San Mateo, CA: IDG Books, 1993, p. 229.

Magellan Web pages, "Netscape: Topics" and "Netscape: Search Results." Magellan Internet Guide and the Magellan logo are trademarks of the McKinley Group, Inc. and may be registered in various jurisdictions. Magellan screen displays copyright © 1996 The McKinley Group, Inc. Reprinted by permission of Excite, Inc.

Mayer, Lawrence A. From "The Confounding Enemy of Sleep." *Fortune*, June 1974. Reprinted by permission.

Merriam-Webster's Collegiate® Dictionary, Tenth Edition. Entry for "reckon" by permission from *Merriam-Webster's Collegiate® Dictionary*, Tenth Edition © 1993 by Merriam-Webster Inc., publisher of the Merriam-Webster ® dictionaries.

Mobil Oil Corporation. "Myths We Wouldn't Miss" by Mobil Oil Corporation in *The New York Times*, April 11, 1991. Copyright © 1991 Mobil Corporation. Reprinted by permission.

Nadelman, Ethan A. From "Shooting Up" by Ethan A. Nadelman in *The New Republic*, June 1988. Reprinted by permission of *The New Republic*, © 1988, The New Republic, Inc.

Naylor, Gloria. From "Sexual Equality in a TV Fantasy" in *The New York Times*, January 30, 1986. Copyright © 1986 by Gloria Naylor. Reprinted with permission of Sterling Lord Literistic, Inc.

NEA. Internet Web page "Teaching, Learning & Technology" by NEA. Reprinted by permission of the National Education Association.

Ornstein, Robert. Excerpt from "A Letter from the Director," *Human Nature*, August 1978. Copyright © 1978 by Human Nature, Inc. Reprinted with permission of the publisher.

Otten, Charlotte F. From Otten, ed., *English Women's Voices*. Gainesville: University Press of Florida, 1992, p. 4. Reprinted with permission.

Ouchi, William G. From *Theory Z: How American Business Can Meet the Japanese Challenge*, Copyright © by Addison-Wesley Publishing Company, Inc.

Posey, Michael W. From "I Did Drugs Until They Wore Me Out. Then I Stopped" by Michael W. Posey in *The New York Times*, December 15, 1989. Copyright © 1989 by The New York Times Company. Reprinted by permission.

Rose, Phyllis. Excerpt from "On Shopping." From *Never Say Goodbye* by Phyllis Rose. Copyright © 1991 by Phyllis Rose. Reprinted by permission of Doubleday, a division of Bantam Doubleday Dell Publishing Group, Inc.

Rosen, Ruth, "Search for Yesterday." Todd Gitlin, editor, *Watching Television*. New York: Pantheon Books, 1986.

Sale, Kirkpatrick, "The Environmental Crisis Is Not Our Fault" by Kirkpatrick Sale from *The Nation* Magazine, April 30, 1990. Copyright © 1990 The Nation Company, Inc. Reprinted by permission.

Social Sciences Index. Listings for Christopher Conte, "Networking in the Classroom," and Royan Van Horn, "A Letter from Paul," from *Social Sciences Index*. Reprinted by permission of H. W. Wilson Company.

Sowell, Thomas. "Student Loans" from *Is Reality Optional?* by Thomas Sowell. Copyright © 1993 by Thomas Sowell. Reprinted by permission of the author.

Staples, Brent. From "Black Men and Public Space" by Brent Staples, as appeared in *Harper's*, December 1986. Copyright © 1986 Brent Staples. Reprinted by permission of the author.

Tan, Amy. From "The Language of Discretion" in *State of Language*, 1990 Edition, edited by Christopher Ricks and Leonard Michaels. Copyright © 1989 The Regents of the University of California. Reprinted by permission.

Tuchman, Barbara. From "The Decline of Quality" by Barbara Tuchman, *The New York Times*, November 2, 1980. Copyright © 1980 by The New York Times Company. Reprinted by permission.

Walker, Joyce R. "The Computerized Post Office: Sending and Receiving Mail in the Late Age of Print" (hypertext page). Reprinted by permission of the author.

Wax, Judith. From *Starting in the Middle*. Copyright © 1979 by Judith Wax. Reprinted by permission of Henry Holt and Company.

White, Diane. From "At Large" column in *The Boston Globe*, January 27, 1979. Reprinted courtesy of The Boston Globe.

Wright, Richard. Excerpt from *Black Boy* by Richard Wright. Copyright © 1937, 1942, 1944, 1945 by Richard Wright. Copyright renewed 1973 by Ellen Wright. Reprinted by permission of HarperCollins Publishers, Inc.

Zinsser, William. From *The Lunacy Boom* by William Zinsser. Copyright © 1966, 1968, 1969, 1970 by William Zinsser. Reprinted by permission of Carol Brissie.

Index

IAE Index

The marginal index covers material found only in this Instructor's Annotated Edition: the six introductory chapters headed "Designing and Teaching Composition Courses" and the authors of resources listed next to the students' text.

Index

Index

Index

Y

Z

G

Index

O

Index

P

Index

Index

Index

Index

Index

Index

Index